Birds of India

Richard Grimmett dedicates this book to Francis ('Frank') Grimmett – a wonderful father and inspiration to the family.

Carol and Tim are grateful to their mothers, Joyce Robinson and Francesca Inskipp, for their constant support and encouragement.

In memory also of Carl d'Silva in appreciation of his fine illustrations which grace this volume.

PRINCETON FIELD GUIDES

Birds of India

Pakistan, Nepal, Bangladesh, Bhutan, Sri Lanka, and the Maldives

THIRD EDITION

Richard Grimmett, Carol Inskipp, and Tim Inskipp

Illustrated by
Richard Allen, Adam Bowley, Clive Byers, Daniel Cole, John Cox, Carl d'Silva, Gerald Driessens, Martin Elliott, Kim Franklin, John Gale, Alan Harris, Ren Hathway, Peter Hayman, Dave Nurney, Craig Robson, Chris Rose, Brian Small, Jan Wilczur, Martin Woodcock and Tim Worfolk

Princeton University Press
Princeton and Oxford

Published in the United States, Canada, and the Philippines in 2026
by Princeton University Press
41 William Street, Princeton, New Jersey 08540
press.princeton.edu

First published in the United Kingdom by Helm/Bloomsbury Publishing Plc in 2011.
This third edition published in 2026.

Library of Congress Control Number 2025933347
ISBN 978-0-691-26982-5
Ebook ISBN 978-0-691-27897-1

Design and maps by Julie Dando

Front cover image: Pied Thrush (Tim Worfolk)
Back cover images: Layard's Parakeet (Carl d'Silva), Fire-tailed Sunbird (Richard Allen), Lesser Florican (Gerald Driessens)

Printed and bound in Dubai

1 3 5 7 9 10 8 6 4 2

CONTENTS

ACKNOWLEDGEMENTS

Numerous people generously provided assistance to Richard Grimmett in the preparation of the identification texts in our original book, *Birds of the Indian Subcontinent* (Grimmett *et al.* 1998), and these people are acknowledged in that work. We would like to again extend our thanks to all those acknowledged in this work - we feel the fruits of this monumental effort have stood the test of time. Richard would like to acknowledge yet again the important reference collection of bird skins held by the Natural History Museum, Tring, UK, with thanks to Mark Adams who arranged and hosted his most recent visits.

We are also grateful to the many people who helped with the preparation of this current guide. Richard would like to thank Helen, George and Ella, for being so supportive of this long-running venture. Ella helped with the original arrangement of the species texts. Carol and Tim would like to thank their mothers for their constant support and encouragement.

Special thanks go to the artists whose work illustrates this book, including those who have painted the plates for this new edition: Richard Allen, Adam Bowley, Clive Byers, Daniel Cole, John Cox, Gerald Driessens, the late Carl d'Silva, Martin Elliott, Kim Franklin, John Gale, Alan Harris, Ren Hathway, Peter Hayman, Dave Nurney, Craig Robson, Chris Rose, Brian Small, Jan Wilczur, Tim Worfolk and the late Martin Woodcock. Much of the great work first published in 1998 has also stood the test of time and remains among the best illustrations available of the subcontinent's birds. We extend particular thanks to Martin Elliot who has repainted the 'large white-headed gulls' and for his great help with the identification text for this group.

Preparing maps, especially given the major advances in knowledge mentioned in the Introduction, is a huge undertaking and we are especially grateful to Praveen J for providing data for some of the species maps, drawing on the ever-expanding datasets held by eBird. The eBird data sets have been invaluable in preparing many of the other maps. We are grateful also to Deepal Warakagoda for the use of maps from his forthcoming update to his book on the birds of Sri Lanka.

As always, we have greatly benefitted from the continued strong interest in ornithological publishing by Bloomsbury and we are very grateful to Jim Martin and Amy Hodkin who have overseen the commissioning, editorial and production processes. We thank Julie Dando for the excellent design and layout and for very skillfully making digital adjustments to some illustrations.

We acknowledge, with great appreciation, the Macaulay Library at the Cornell Lab of Ornithology for the hugely valuable online library of images (www.macaulaylibrary.org), and prior to this the Oriental Bird Club's Oriental Birding Images, and the many photographers who have provided their photographs and videos. We also acknowledge the online database of sound recordings made available by the Xeno-canto Foundation (www.xeno-canto.org) and the many recordists who have deposited their material there. We have frequently referred to Cornell's online *Birds of the World* and in order to provide standardisation have taken in most cases the species lengths from this work, as well as details of some vocalisations.

This map is not an authority on internal or international borders

Map of the Indian Subcontinent

INTRODUCTION

This is a fully revised edition of the field guide *Birds of the Indian Subcontinent* (2011). There are 246 colour plates, 20 more than in the first edition. Species texts have been significantly increased for almost all species.

There have been huge advances in information and knowledge since the last edition in 2011. In particular, there has continued to be a rapid uptake of birding in the region, and with that now widespread use of citizen science tools such as eBird, and initiatives such as Bird Count India and the online journal *Indian Birds*. The book has drawn extensively from the literature, and published material up to early 2024 has been reviewed.

The guide continues to provide the most essential information for identification, in a volume that is portable in the field. The guide should help observers identify all of the bird species recorded in the subcontinent, and it is hoped that, once basic identification skills have been acquired, birders will record their observations and use them to expand what is known about the distribution of the region's birds, to further the conservation of threatened species, and to learn more about birds and the environment in which they live.

The whole of the region is covered, comprising the countries of India, Pakistan, Bangladesh, Sri Lanka, Nepal, Bhutan and the Maldives. The classic *Handbook of the Birds of India and Pakistan* by Salim Ali and S. Dillon Ripley, which also covers the entire subcontinent and was first published in ten volumes (1968–75), listed about 1,200 species. In recent years many additional species have been recorded in the region with a total of 1,429 species covered in this edition.

Future fieldwork will certainly lead to major advances on this work, and existing published or unpublished material will undoubtedly have been missed or given insufficient attention. The authors (c/o the publishers, Bloomsbury) would be very grateful to receive, for use in future editions, any information which corrects or updates that presented herein.

Borders depicted in the maps in this book do not in any way imply an expression of opinion on the part of the authors as to the location of international or internal boundaries.

HOW TO USE THIS BOOK

SPECIES INCLUDED

All species that are known to have been reliably recorded in the subcontinent up to the end of 2023 have been included. Those species considered to be regularly occurring are covered by species accounts and maps (see below) with adjacent illustrations. Brief descriptions and illustrations of vagrants are given in the appendix at the end of the book.

TAXONOMY AND NOMENCLATURE

Taxonomy, nomenclature and English names follow eBird taxonomy v2023 (https://www.birds.cornell.edu/clementschecklist/wpcontent/uploads/2023/10/ebird_taxonomy_v2023.xlsx), except in three instances: House Swift *Apus nipalensis* is not recognised as a separate species from Little Swift *A. affinis* because the two taxa are virtually indistinguishable morphologically and their supposed sympatry in Nepal was based on an incorrect interpretation of the data. Bank Swallow is an American name for *Riparia riparia* adopted by eBird, but the other species in the genus are all known as martins, and so the more appropriate name used here is Sand Martin. The eBird name for *Fulvetta ludlowi* is Brown-throated Fulvetta but this species has a white throat with brown streaks, similar to the *chumbiensis* subspecies of White-browed Fulvetta *F. vinipectus*. The more distinctive name of Ludlow's Fulvetta is used here to avoid this confusion.

The shifting sands of taxonomy and nomenclature can be very challenging even for experts and we have decided to follow eBird because of its very wide and increasing use by birders in the subcontinent, and we hope that this guide will help further its application. Users of eBird and Cornell's *Birds of the World* will be able to track further changes online as they are adopted.

SPECIES ACCOUNTS

On the colour plates distinctive sexual and racial variations are illustrated, as well as immature plumages whenever possible. While the guide has aimed to be as comprehensive as possible, some plumages recognisable in the field have not been illustrated owing to space limitations. Distribution maps and species texts are on the page facing the species illustration(s) on the relevant plate. The text comprises identification features (**ID**), including **Voice** for most species, as well as approximate body length, including bill and tail, in centimetres. Length is expressed as a range when there is marked variation within the species (e.g. as a result of sexual dimorphism or racial differences). Habitat and Habits (**HH**) that are useful for identification are also included where space allows. A taxonomic note (**TN**) and alternative name (**AN**) are given where nomenclature differs from *Birds of the Indian Subcontinent* (2011). We have followed the eBird sequence as far as possible although we have kept together some species with the same common family names even though they are now separated by recent taxonomic studies, both for ease of reference and use in the field (e.g. laughingthrushes, fulvettas and rosefinches).

Key to the maps

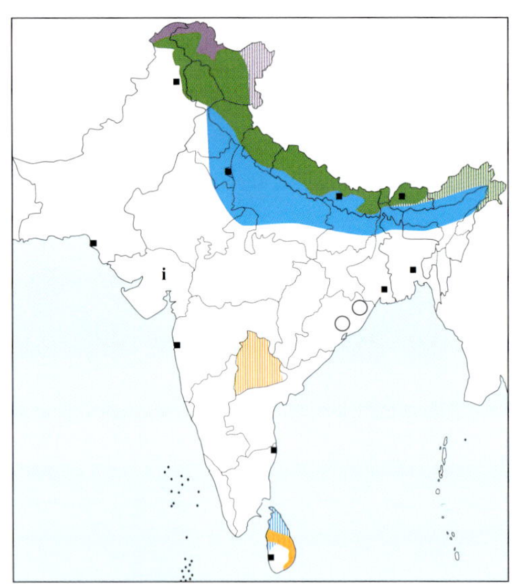

PLUMAGE TERMINOLOGY

The figures below illustrate the main plumage tracts and bare-part features, and are based on Grant & Mullarney (1988–89). This terminology for bird topography has been used in the species texts. Other terms have been used and are defined in the glossary. Juvenile plumage is the first plumage on fledging and, in many species, it is looser and fluffier than subsequent plumages. In some families, juvenile plumage is retained only briefly after leaving the nest (e.g. pigeons), or hardly differs from adult plumage (e.g. many babblers), while in other groups it may be retained for the duration of long migrations or for many months (e.g. many waders). In some species (e.g. *Aquila* eagles), it may be several years before all juvenile feathers are finally moulted. The relevance of the juvenile plumage to field identification therefore varies considerably. Some species reach adult plumage after their first post-juvenile moult (e.g. larks), whereas others go through a series of immature plumages. The term 'immature' has been employed more generally to denote plumages other than adult, and is used either where a more exact terminology has not been possible or where more precision would give rise to unnecessary complexity. Terms such as 'first-winter' (resulting from a partial moult from juvenile plumage) or 'first-summer' (plumage acquired prior to the breeding season of the year after hatching) have, however, been used where it was felt that this would be useful.

Many species assume a more colourful breeding plumage, which is often more striking in the male compared to the female. This either can be realised through a partial (or in some species complete) body moult (e.g. waders) or results from the wearing-off of pale or dark feather fringes (e.g. redstarts and buntings).

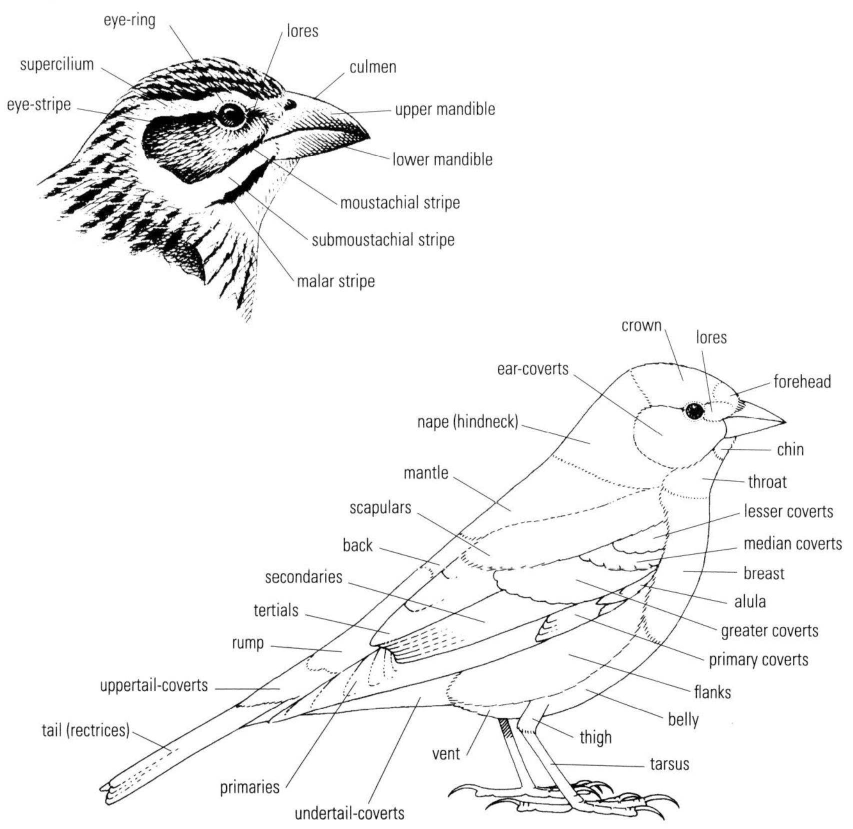

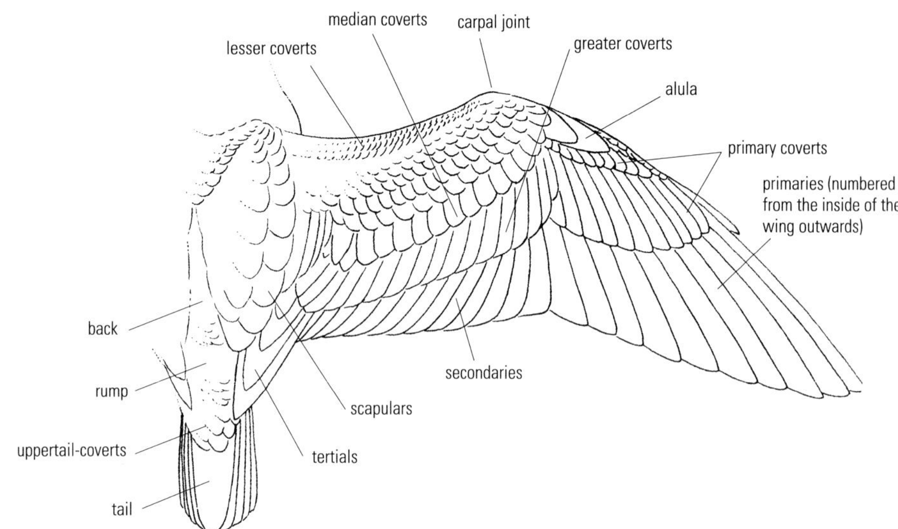

GLOSSARY

See also figures on p. 13 and above, which cover bird topography.

Allopatric: where species are geographically separated (thus confusion in the field is unlikely).

Altitudinal migrant: a species which breeds at high elevations (in mountains) and moves to lower levels and valleys in the non-breeding season.

Arboreal: tree-dwelling.

Axillaries: the feathers in the armpit at the base of the underwing.

Biotope: a particular area which is substantially uniform in its environmental conditions and its flora and fauna.

Cap: a well-defined patch of colour or bare skin on the top of the head.

Carpal: the bend of the wing, or carpal joint.

Carpal patch: a well-defined patch of colour on the underwing in the vicinity of the carpal joint.

Casque: an enlargement on the upper surface of the bill, in front of the head, as on hornbills.

Cere: a fleshy (often brightly coloured) structure at the base of the bill and containing the nostrils.

Collar: a well-defined band of colour that encircles or partly encircles the neck.

Culmen: the ridge of the upper mandible.

Eclipse plumage: a female-like plumage acquired by males of some species (e.g. ducks or some sunbirds) during or after breeding.

Edgings or edges: outer feather margins, which can frequently result in distinct paler or darker panels of colour on wings or tail.

Filoplume: a thin, hair-like feather.

Flight feathers: the primaries, secondaries and tail feathers (although not infrequently used to denote the primaries and secondaries alone).

Fringes: complete feather margins, which can frequently result in a scaly appearance to body feathers or wing-coverts.

Gape: the mouth and fleshy corner of the bill, which can extend back below the eye.

Gonys: a bulge in the lower mandible, usually distinct on gulls and terns.

Graduated tail: a tail in which the longest feathers are the central pair and the shortest the outermost, with those in between intermediate in length.

Gregarious: living in flocks or communities.

Gular pouch: a loose and pronounced area of skin extending from the throat (e.g. in hornbills).

Gular stripe: a usually very narrow (and often dark) stripe running down the centre of the throat.

Hackles: long and pointed neck feathers which can extend across the mantle and wing-coverts (e.g. on junglefowls).

Hand: the outer part of the wing, from the carpal joint to the tip of the wing.

Hepatic: used with reference to the rufous-brown morph of some (female) cuckoos.

Iris (plural irides): the coloured membrane which surrounds the pupil of the eye and which can be brightly coloured.

Lappet: a wattle, particularly one at the gape.

Leading edge: the front edge of the forewing.

Local: occurring or common within a small or restricted area.

Mandible: the lower or upper half of the bill.

Mask: a dark area of plumage surrounding the eye and often covering the ear-coverts.

Morph: a distinct plumage type which occurs alongside one or more other distinct plumage types exhibited by the same species.

Nomenclature: the scientific naming of species and subspecies, and of the genera, families and other categories in which species may be classified.

Nominate: the first-named race of a species, which has its scientific racial name the same as the specific name.

Nuchal: relating to the hindneck, used with reference to a patch or collar.

Ocelli: eye-like spots of iridescent colour; a distinctive feature in the plumage of peafowls.

Orbital ring: a narrow circular ring of feathering or bare skin surrounding the eye.

Pelagic: of the open sea.

Plantation: a group of trees (usually exotic or non-native species) planted in close proximity to each other, used for timber or as a crop.

Primary projection: the extension of the primaries beyond the longest tertial on a closed wing; this can be of critical importance in identification (e.g. of larks or *Acrocephalus* warblers).

Race (subspecies): a geographical population whose members all show constant differences (e.g. in plumage or size) from those of other populations of the same species.

Rectrices (singular rectrix): the tail feathers.

Remiges (singular remex): the primaries and secondaries.

Rictal bristles: bristles, often prominent, at the base of the bill.

Shaft streak: a fine line of pale or dark colour in the plumage, produced by the feather shaft.

Shola: a patch of montane evergreen wet temperate forest, usually in a sheltered hill valley among rolling grassy hills from about 1,500m upwards, found in southern India and Sri Lanka.

Speculum: the often-glossy panel across the secondaries of, especially, dabbling ducks, often bordered by pale tips to these feathers and a greater covert wing-bar.

Subspecies: see Race.

Subterminal band: a dark or pale band, usually broad, situated inside the outer part of a feather or feather tract (used particularly in reference to the tail).

Sympatric: where different species occur alongside each other (thus confusion in the field is possible).

Taxonomy: the science of classification of species, subspecies, genera, families and other categories in which species may be classified.

Terai: the undulating alluvial, often marshy, strip of land 25–45 km wide lying north of the Gangetic plain, extending from Uttarakhand through Nepal and northern West Bengal to Assam, naturally supports tall Elephant Grass interspersed with dense forest, but large areas have been drained and converted to cultivation.

Terminal band: a dark or pale band, usually broad, at the tip of a feather or feather tract (especially the tail); cf. Subterminal band.

Terrestrial: living or occurring mainly on the ground.

Trailing edge: the rear edge of the wing, often darker or paler than the rest of the wing; cf. Leading edge.

Vent: the area around the cloaca (anal opening), just behind the legs (should not be confused with the undertail-coverts).

Vermiculated: marked with narrow wavy lines, usually visible only at close range.

Wattle: a lobe of bare, often brightly coloured skin attached to the head (frequently at the bill-base), as on mynas or wattled lapwings.

Wing-linings: the entire underwing-coverts.

Wing-panel: a pale or dark band across the upperwing (often formed by pale edges to the remiges or coverts), broader and generally more diffuse than a wing-bar.

Wing-bar: generally, a narrow and well-defined dark or pale bar across the upperwing, and often referring to a band formed by pale tips to the greater or median coverts (or both, as in 'double wing-bar').

THE INDIAN SUBCONTINENT

CLIMATE

There are great contrasts in climate within the subcontinent. The extremes range from the almost rainless Great Indian or Thar desert to the wet evergreen forests of the Khasi Hills, Meghalaya, where an annual rainfall of 1,300cm has been recorded at Cherrapunji (one of the wettest places on Earth), and to the arctic conditions of the Himalayan peaks, where only alpine flowers and cushion plants flourish at over 4,900m. There are similar contrasts in temperature ranges. In the Thar desert, summer temperatures soar as high as 50°C while winter temperatures drop to 0°C. On the Kerala coast, the annual and daily ranges of temperature and humidity are small; the average temperature is about 27°C and the average relative humidity is 60–80%.

Despite these variations, one feature dominates the subcontinent's climate, and that is the monsoons. Most of the rain in the region falls between June and September, during the south-west monsoon season. Typically, the monsoon begins in Kerala and the far north-east in late May or early June and moves north and west to extend over the rest of the region by the end of June, although it starts rather earlier in Sri Lanka and the Andaman Islands. In the Himalayas, the monsoon rains reach the east first and leave this area last. The monsoon begins to retreat from the north-west at the beginning of September, and usually withdraws completely by mid-October.

Rain continues, however, in the southern peninsula, and in the south-east around half the annual rain falls between October and mid-December. This is brought by winds coming from the north-east during the north-east monsoon. In contrast, in much of the northern part of the subcontinent there is generally clear, dry weather in October, November and early December. Low-pressure systems from the west during this season do, however, bring some light to moderate precipitation to Pakistan and northern India.

According to a 2023 Intergovernmental Panel on Climate Change report, human-induced climate change is causing dangerous and widespread disruption in nature. Ecosystems least able to cope are being hardest hit. The IPCC identified South Asia as one of the regions most likely to be impacted. Impacts of climate change are already occurring. Unusual and unprecedented spells of hot weather are occurring far more frequently and cover much larger areas. There has been a decline in monsoon rainfall since the 1950s, whereas the frequency of heavy rainfall events has also increased. Parts of South Asia have become drier since the 1970s with an increase in the number of droughts. Most Himalayan glaciers – where a substantial part of the moisture is supplied by the summer monsoon – have been retreating over the past century (IPCC 2023).

MAIN HABITATS AND BIRD SPECIES

The bird habitats of the Indian subcontinent can be roughly divided into forest, scrub, wetlands (inland and littoral), marine, grassland, desert, and agricultural land. There is some overlap between habitats: for example, mangrove forest can also be considered as wetland, as can seasonally flooded grassland. Many bird species require mixed habitat types.

Forests

There is a great variety of forest types in the region. Tropical forest ranges from coastal mangroves to wet, dense evergreen forest, dry deciduous forest and open-desert thorn forest. In the Himalayas, temperate forest includes habitats of mixed broadleaf, moist oak and rhododendron, and dry coniferous forest of pines and firs; higher up, subalpine forest of birch, rhododendron and juniper occurs.

The forest areas of the region are vitally important for many of its birds. Over 40% of the bird species in the subcontinent identified by BirdLife International as globally threatened and around two-thirds of the region's endemic birds are dependent on forest.

Primary tropical and subtropical broadleaved evergreen forest supports the greatest diversity of bird species. Significant areas of these forest habitats still remain in the eastern Himalayas and adjacent hills of north-east India, in the Western Ghats, on the Andaman and Nicobar Islands, and in Sri Lanka. They also contain a higher number of endemic and globally threatened species than any other habitat in the region.

Tropical deciduous forest, including moist and dry sal and teak forest, riverine forest and dry thorn forest, once covered much of the plains and lower hills of the subcontinent. Several widespread endemic species are chiefly confined to these habitats, including Plum-headed Parakeet *Psittacula cyanocephala*.

Temperate and subalpine forest grows in the Himalayas. These forest types support a relatively high proportion of species with restricted distributions, notably White-throated Tit *Aegithalos niveogularis*.

Scrub

Scrub has developed in the region where trees are unable to grow, either because soils are poor and thin, or because they are too wet, as at the edges of wetlands or in seasonally inundated floodplains. Scrub also grows naturally in extreme climatic conditions, as in semi-desert or at high elevations in the Himalayas. In addition, there are now large areas of scrubland in the region where forest has been overexploited for fodder and fuel collection or grazing.

Relatively few birds in the subcontinent are characteristic of scrub habitats alone, but many are found in scrub mixed with grassland, in wetlands or at forest edges.

Wetlands

Wetlands are abundant in the region and support a rich array of waterfowl. As well as providing habitats for breeding resident species, they include major staging and wintering grounds for waterfowl breeding in Central and northern Asia. The region possesses a wide range of wetland types, distributed almost throughout, including mountain glacial lakes, freshwater and brackish marshes, large water-storage reservoirs, village tanks, saline flats and coastal mangroves and mudflats. A total of 26 of the subcontinent's wetland bird species is globally threatened.

The subcontinent's most important wetland sites include Chilika Lake, a brackish lagoon in Odisha on the east Indian coast; wetlands in the Indus Valley in Pakistan; the Sundarbans in the Ganges/Brahmaputra delta in Bangladesh and India; the extensive seasonally flooded man-made lagoons of Keoladeo Ghana National Park; the vast saline flats of the Ranns of Kutch in north-west India; wetlands in the moist tropical and subtropical forest of Assam and Arunachal Pradesh; the marshes, jheels and terai swamps of the Gangetic plain; Point Calimere and Pulicat Lake on India's east coast; the Haor basin of Sylhet and east Mymensingh in north-east Bangladesh; and the Brahmaputra floodplain in the Assam lowlands. Small water-storage reservoirs or tanks are a distinctive feature in India and provide important feeding and nesting areas for a wide range of waterbirds in some places, for example on the Deccan plateau.

Grasslands

The most important grasslands for birds in the subcontinent are the seasonally flooded areas occurring in the Himalayan foothills and in the floodplains of the Indus and Brahmaputra Rivers, the arid grassland of the Thar desert, and grasslands in peninsular India, especially those in Madhya Pradesh, Maharashtra and Karnataka. These lowland grasslands support distinctive bird communities, with a number of specialist endemic species. Most of the region's endemic grassland birds are seriously at risk including Lesser Florican *Sypheotides indicus*, Great Indian Bustard *Ardeotis nigriceps*, Bristled Grassbird *Schoenicola striata* and Finn's Weaver *Ploceus megarhynchus*.

Desert

The Thar desert is the largest desert in the region, covering an area of 200,000km^2 in north-west India and Pakistan. There are other extensive arid areas in Pakistan: the hot deserts of the Chagai, a vast plain west of the main mountain ranges of Baluchistan, and the Thal, Cholistan and Sibi deserts in central and eastern Pakistan. The far northern mountain regions, which the monsoon winds do not penetrate, experience a cold-desert climate. One bird species, White-browed Bushchat *Saxicola macrorhynchus*, is endemic to the region.

Seas

As a result of increased watching by dedicated observers, several seabirds have been added to the region's avifauna since the publication of the first edition of this guide: Light-mantled Albatross *Phoebetria palpebrata*, Matsudaira's Storm-petrel *Hydrobates matsudairae*, Leach's Storm-petrel *H. leucorhous* and Cory's Shearwater *Calonectris borealis*. Seabird breeding colonies in the subcontinent are concentrated chiefly in the Maldives and Lakshadweep.

IMPORTANCE FOR BIRDS

Up to the time of finalising the text for this publication (February 2024), a total of 1,429 species had been confirmed in the Indian subcontinent. As many as 13% of the world's birds have been recorded in the region. These include 221 endemic species, a total comprising more than 15% of the region's avifauna.

Globally threatened species

A total of 119 globally threatened species has been recorded in the subcontinent; these are annotated at the end of each relevant species account. The globally threatened species comprise: 19 Critically Endangered, 25 Endangered, 74 Vulnerable and one Data Deficient species.

New species

No new species have been described from the subcontinent since the Bugun Liocichla in 2006. However, two potential new species are awaiting formal description: Great Nicobar Crake *Rallina* sp., known only from a single individual photographed in November 2011 (Rajeshkumar *et al.* 2012), and Lisu Wren Babbler *Spelaeornis* sp., described and photographed in 2022 from south-east Arunachal Pradesh (Praveen *et al.* 2022). Some apparently resident species have been newly recorded in the region since the first edition (2011): Grey-eyed Bulbul *Iole propinqua*, Yunnan Nuthatch *Sitta yunnanensis*, Black-headed Greenfinch *Chloris ambigua* and Godlewski's Bunting *Emberiza godlewskii*.

Extinct species

Two species from the subcontinent may now be globally extinct. These are Pink-headed Duck *Rhodonessa caryophyllacea* and Himalayan Quail *Ophrysia superciliosa*, although some ornithologists consider that they could still survive.

Recent rediscoveries

Two species endemic to India have been rediscovered quite recently. Jerdon's Courser *Rhinoptilus bitorquatus* was re-found in 1986, having last been recorded in 1900, although there are concerns once again that it is extinct given that there have been no recent sightings. Forest Owlet *Athene blewitti* was located in 1997; the previous reliable record was as long ago as the 19th century.

Reasons for species-richness

The Indian subcontinent is rich in species. This is partly because of its wide elevational range, extending from sea level up to the summit of the Himalayas, the world's highest mountains. Another reason is the region's highly varied climate and associated diversity of vegetation. The other major factor contributing to the subcontinent's species-richness is its geographical position in a region of overlap between three biogeographical provinces: the Indomalayan (South and South-east Asia), Palearctic (Europe and northern Asia), and Afrotropical (Africa) realms. As a result, species typical of all three realms occur. Most species are Indomalayan, typified by the ioras and minivets; some are Palearctic, including the accentors; and a small number, for instance Spotted Creeper *Salpornis spilonota*, originate in Africa.

Restricted-range species and Endemic Bird Areas

BirdLife International has analysed the distribution patterns of birds with restricted ranges, that is landbird species which have, throughout historical times (i.e. post-1800), had a total global breeding range smaller than 50,000 km^2 (about the size of Sri Lanka) (Stattersfield *et al.* 1998). At the time of publication a total of 99 restricted-range species were recognised as breeding in the subcontinent, with another four non-breeding visitors from areas outside the region (Stattersfield *et al.* 1998). Major taxonomic changes since then mean that more species will now be in these categories. BirdLife's analysis showed that restricted-range species tend to occur in places that are often islands or isolated patches of a particular habitat. These are known as centres of endemism, and are often called Endemic Bird Areas. BirdLife has identified eight centres of endemism in the Indian subcontinent.

The wet lowland and montane rainforest zones of the eastern Himalayas in India, Nepal and Bhutan (also extending into Myanmar and south-west China) form an important Endemic Bird Area. Further isolated endemic-rich areas of rainforest are on the coastal flanks of the Western Ghats and in south-western Sri Lanka. The other Endemic Bird Areas are the western Himalayas in India, Nepal and Pakistan; the central Himalayas; the Assam plains, which lie in the floodplain of the Brahmaputra in Bangladesh and India; and the Andaman and Nicobar Islands in the Bay of Bengal. Seven of the subcontinent's eight Endemic Bird Areas are largely forest areas.

More widespread species

The subcontinent still supports very large populations of some large waterbirds and birds of prey, such as the Painted Stork *Mycteria leucocephala*, which is now extirpated or rare in South-East Asia.

Migration

The large majority (>1,000) of the species recorded in the region are resident, although the numbers of some of these are augmented by winter visitors breeding farther north. Some residents are sedentary year-round, while others undertake irregular movements, either locally or more widely within the region, depending on water conditions or food supply. Many Himalayan residents are altitudinal migrants, the level to which they descend in winter frequently depending on weather conditions; for instance, the Grandala *Grandala coelicolor* summers at up to 5,500m and winters chiefly down to 3,000m, but it has been recorded as low as 1,950m in bad weather. A number of other residents in the subcontinent breed in the Himalayas and winter farther south in the region, one example being the endemic Pied Thrush *Geokichla wardii*, which spends the winter in Sri Lanka.

Thirty species are summer visitors to the region, several of which are possibly resident and a few other species are also passage migrants. Most summer visitors, such as Lesser Cuckoo *Cuculus poliocephalus*, winter in Africa. Several species breed chiefly to the north and west of the subcontinent and extend just into Pakistan and north-west India, for instance European Bee-eater *Merops apiaster*. Some species move south-eastwards, perhaps as far as Malaysia and Indonesia, for example some cuckoos and White-throated Needletail *Hirundapus caudacutus*.

The subcontinent attracts more than 200 winter visitors, some of which are also passage migrants and residents. The subcontinent is the main wintering range for many of them including Greenish Warbler *Phylloscopus trochiloides* and Black-headed *Emberiza melanocephala* and Red-headed Buntings *E. bruniceps*. In addition, there is a small number of species (nine) which are known only as passage migrants. The winter visitors originate mostly in northern and Central Asia.

Information on migration routes in the region is still patchy, but it is believed that many of the subcontinent's winter visitors come through Pakistan, mainly en route to India and Sri Lanka. Ringing recoveries have shown that many winter visitors enter the subcontinent via the Indus plains. There is less information about migration routes in the north-east of the region, but the Brahmaputra River and its tributaries are thought to form a flyway for birds from north-east Asia. Increasing evidence suggests that some birds breeding in the Palearctic, mainly non-passerines, migrate directly across the Himalayas to winter in the subcontinent. Other birds follow the main valleys, such as those of the Kali Gandaki, Dudh Kosi and Arun in Nepal. Birds of prey, especially *Aquila* eagles, have also been found to use the Himalayas as an east–west pathway in autumn, presumably migrating onwards to the Middle East and Africa. Spot-winged Starling *Saroglossa spilopterus* also undertakes east–west movements along the Himalayas, and it is possible that other species perform similar migrations.

A number of pelagic and coastal passage migrants and wintering species travel by oceanic or coastal routes. One identified coastal flyway lies on India's east coast, linking Point Calimere in Tamil Nadu with Chilika and Pulicat Lakes. Migration patterns of seabirds are particularly poorly understood, but there is now evidence that some species occur more regularly than previously thought, especially around the time of the south-west monsoon. A few species that breed outside the region and winter in East Africa migrate through Pakistan and north-west India, for example Rufous-tailed Rock-Thrush *Monticola saxatilis*. As they occur mainly on autumn passage, they presumably use a different route in spring.

In addition to the subcontinent's residents, summer and winter visitors and passage migrants, 137 vagrant species have been recorded.

THREATS AND CONSERVATION

RELIGIOUS ATTITUDES AND TRADITIONAL PROTECTION

The enlightened and benevolent attitudes of Hinduism and Buddhism towards wildlife have undoubtedly helped to conserve the rich natural heritage of the Indian subcontinent that still remains today. India has a tradition of protection of all forms of animals dating from as early as 3,000 years ago, when the Rig Veda mentioned the right of animals to live. Communities across the region protect living creatures in daily life. Sacred groves, village tanks and temples where the hunting and killing of all forms of life are prohibited can be found throughout the subcontinent.

CURRENT THREATS

Birds in the region are currently confronted by many threats, the most important of which are habitat loss and degradation. The root causes of loss of and damage to habitats are complex, interlinked and often controversial. Overpopulation is often blamed for the region's environmental ills; India for example was projected to overtake China as the world's most populous nation in 2023, with about 1.425 billion people (up from 558 million in 1970) (UN 2023). Other factors are, however, important including poverty, social insecurity, agricultural intensification, continued reliance on wood for fuel, inequitable land distribution and tenure, and weak or misguided policies and government practices. Climate change is likely to significantly exacerbate and add to these factors.

Threats to forests

Forest cover has declined historically throughout much of the region, although according to the UN Food and Agricultural Organisation (FAO) the area of naturally regenerating forest was stable between 1990 and 2020. According to the FAO's Global Forest Resources Assessment (FAO 2020), India's natural forest cover was 19.8% of the country's land area. Natural forest coverage in Nepal and Sri Lanka was higher (40% and 29.7% respectively) and Bangladesh and Pakistan lower (13.2% and 4.5% respectively). However, there is much debate about these statistics, particularly that they overstate the situation, and little doubt that the remaining forests in these countries are continuing to be degraded. The World Bank estimates 41% of India's forest cover to be in a degraded state, with c.250 million people still dependent on forests for sustenance, firewood and their livelihoods (Mundial 2006). Bhutan still retains much of its forest relatively intact, with 70.9% of its land area under natural forest (FAO 2020), and the country possesses some of the best forest habitats left in the Himalayas.

The major threats to natural forest are overexploitation for fuelwood, timber and livestock fodder, overgrazing which prevents forest regeneration, and the conversion of forest to other land uses: agriculture, notably shifting cultivation, tree plantations, urbanisation, and reservoirs through dam construction. Forest conversion is continuing rapidly in some sectors. For example, the area under oil palm plantations expanded 30-fold in India from 1991 to 2015, with most of this expansion taking place in the tropical rainforest biome (Srinivasan *et al.* 2021).

Threats to wetlands

Wetland destruction and degradation in the region is reducing the diversity of wetlands and the populations of many bird species. Major threats include overexploitation of wetland resources, as local demands often exceed their regenerative capacity. Increasing hydroelectric developments are altering the characteristics and dynamics of entire river ecosystems. Drainage and siltation of wetlands and intensive prawn cultivation in coastal regions are other major threats. Many wetlands are becoming polluted by sewage, industrial effluents and agricultural fertilisers and pesticides. Other significant threats include overgrazing of shorelines and marshes, and widespread mining of gravel from coastal and riverine ecosystems. Mangrove areas have also been severely damaged in many parts of India and completely eradicated in some areas.

While many of the region's natural wetlands have disappeared, new wetlands have been created. These include lakes and marshes upstream of dams and barrages on some rivers, which can now provide habitat for waterbirds. Other wetlands have developed as a result of faulty drainage systems and overspill from irrigation canals. Rice production has also created large areas of seasonally useful habitat for some waterbirds, although natural wetlands are being converted for such purposes, notably in Bangladesh. The over-use of fertilisers has led to nutrient enrichment in water, and eutrophication, which is harmful to all freshwater life, including birds. In Nepal use of some wetlands for recreation is causing much disturbance to waterbirds, for instance hire of boats at Barju.

Threats to grasslands and deserts

Grassland has been greatly reduced, fragmented and degraded by large-scale expansion of agriculture, conversion to other kinds of land use (including plantation forestry), drainage, and overgrazing. The practice of setting aside land for fodder production as a communal reserve in times of drought has declined. Apart from grasslands located within protected areas, practically every grass-growing tract in the region is grazed by domestic livestock. Encroachment by graziers is also increasing in protected areas. Large increases in livestock as well as recovering wild herbivore populations have led to widespread overgrazing, and this problem has been exacerbated as more grazing lands have been converted to other land uses.

The spread of irrigation has significantly reduced the habitat of desert birds. Between 1950 and 1990, the area under irrigation increased by 70% in Pakistan and by as much as 118% in India. As with grasslands, high stocking levels and overgrazing have degraded desert regions.

Grasslands and deserts are increasingly impacted by the rapid roll-out of renewable energy infrastructure such as wind turbines and solar farms and their associated energy transmission lines (Uddin *et al.* 2021). Some species such as bustards and cranes are highly vulnerable to collision with energy infrastructure, whilst eagles, buzzards and vultures are frequently electrocuted.

Agricultural practices

Agricultural practices have significantly intensified in recent years, leading to increased yields but with damaging impacts on bird populations. Bird populations in Europe declined by a quarter between 1980 and 2016, particularly of once common agricultural species, mainly due to farmland practices (Rigal *et al.* 2023). There is increasing circumstantial evidence that the same is happening in the Indian subcontinent with previously common birds in the agricultural landscape, such as shrikes, bee-eaters and Indian Roller, no longer so.

Current agricultural practices in Nepal have been shown to be unsustainable, resulting in degradation of farmlands, forests and wetlands. Together with high pesticide and fertiliser use and a major switch to cash crops, agricultural methods are now having a highly damaging impact on Nepal's birds (Inskipp & Baral 2011).

Poisoning by diclofenac, a drug used to treat livestock ailments, and other nonsteroidal anti-inflammatory drugs (NSAIDs), has been identified as responsible for the now highly threatened status of vultures in the region with declines of more than 90% in a number of species (Prakash *et al.* 2005, 2019). Steps are being taken to stop this practice, as well as the establishment of Vulture Safe Zones, and there are now some signs that vulture populations have stabilised. Another threat is the deliberate poisoning of carcasses, intended to kill dogs and other carnivores, but which puts vultures and other scavengers such as Steppe Eagle *Aquila nipalensis* at additional risk.

Pesticide use has increased, including the use of persistent chemicals organochlorines, which do not readily break down in the environment. India has banned the use of many pesticides and encourages the use of biopesticides, but illegal use of banned pesticides continues and new pesticides are being promoted and used (Deccan Herald 2023).

Hunting and trade

Hunting is a major threat to some species in Pakistan (notably cranes and bustards), in Bangladesh (particularly migratory waterfowl and waders), and in north-east India (where a wide variety and large number of birds are hunted and sold in markets). Fishermen collect eggs of seabirds where they nest colonially in Pakistan and the Maldives. Similar predation is also reported on Black-bellied Tern *Sterna acuticauda*, River Tern *S. aurantia* and Indian Skimmer *Rynchops albicollis* along some rivers in the subcontinent and have contributed to the decline in these species. In parts of India and Nepal, hunting is on the increase as traditional values wane, and is now significant for many species, notably threatened bustards, pheasants and waterbirds.

Until recently there was a large domestic and international bird trade in India but, since 1991, all bird trade has been banned. Undercover operations have, however, revealed that thousands of birds are still regularly caught and traded, both within India and for export, although in much-reduced numbers compared to those previously traded. Caged birds are popular in Pakistan. Two recent studies revealed that the illegal wild bird trade is widespread there (Ilyas 2018, Hussain & Khan 2021). A TRAFFIC investigation of the owl trade in India recorded 16 of India's 36 owl species in the live owl trade. Owls in India are victims of superstitious beliefs and rituals often promoted amongst the unsuspecting public by local mystic practitioners (Badola 2021).

Alien invasive species

Serious threats are posed by some invasive alien plants in the region. Water Hyacinth *Eichhornia crassipes* can quickly cover wetlands, thereby changing the habitat for many waterbirds. Recently, the introduced Bittervine *Mikania micrantha,* which can smother all other plants including tall forest trees, at an alarming rate, has become a major problem in India, Nepal and Bangladesh. Of concern in the Western Ghats of India is the spread of Wattle *Acacia melanoxylon* which is impacting high-altitude grasslands, whilst in arid regions the spread of the highly invasive Mesquite *Prosopis juliflora* has rendered vast areas unsuitable for open-country birds (SoIB 2023), as well as potentially replacing indigenous *Acacia* savanna habitats favoured by migrant passerines.

In addition, invasive and non-native mammals, reptiles and amphibians, fish and crustacea, as well as feral dogs and cats, are of increasing concern, and this is especially true in relation to island ecosystems – great care including preventative measures is needed in areas of high endemism such as the Andaman and Nicobar Islands.

Diseases

The region has recently suffered major outbreaks of Highly Pathogenic Avian Influenza (H5N1) ('bird flu'). Originating from poultry farming, this has spread aggressively through wild bird populations. With climate change, there is concern that avian malaria will reach higher into the Himalayas impacting on species lacking in immunity (Mozaffer *et al.* 2022).

Climate change

The impacts of climate change on the subcontinent's birds are likely to be significant but remain poorly understood. Ecological conditions within protected areas and some habitats are likely to change beyond limits conducive for some of the species currently found there. Species with specific habitat requirements will be unable to move if suitable habitat does not exist outside protected areas, for example the Critically Endangered Bengal Florican *Houbaropsis bengalensis*, a grassland specialist. Some habitats, such as forests, are highly fragmented in the subcontinent. While habitat generalists can migrate through fragmented landscapes, many habitat specialists are unable to do so (Inskipp & Baral 2019).

A 2012 report by the government of Sikkim found an upward extension or shift in altitudinal ranges among many Himalayan bird species as climate change is rendering their current locations less favourable. This is resulting in range reductions as the birds move upslope, for example Blood Pheasant *Ithaginis cruentus*. High-altitude species, such as snowcocks are especially at risk (Acharya & Chettri 2012).

Changes in phenology are also having important impacts on bird populations. Some species are breeding earlier, leading to a mismatch between the timing of breeding and available food sources for young birds (Dunn & Moller 2014). In contrast, studies on birds in Sikkim found that many species are breeding later because of unexpected weather events, such as drought or storms, often resulting in reproductive failure (Acharya & Chettri 2012).

It is often difficult to separate the impacts of climate change from other threats to bird species. For example, the globally Vulnerable Sarus Crane *Antigone antigone* is threatened by the drying out of wetlands resulting from climate change. However, it is also at risk from a wide range of other significant factors, including habitat loss through urbanisation, pesticides reducing its food supply, water pollution, and collisions with overhead wires (Katuwal 2016).

SoIB (2023) points out there is an acute scarcity of information on climate change impacts on birds in the subcontinent and this should be an urgent research priority.

Conservation measures

Loss and deterioration of habitats and other threats have resulted in widespread declines in bird populations, but we can only speculate on the changes that are occurring for most species. However, the annual waterfowl counts organised by Wetlands International, and the blossoming of citizen sciences schemes such as eBird and the work described in the SoIB (2023) mean the gap in knowledge is now being quickly addressed. BirdLife International's annual Red List assessments mean that there is a regular update for the region on those species most in need of conservation measures from a global perspective.

Seminal works such as BirdLife's *Threatened Birds of Asia* (Collar *et al.* 2001) and *Saving Asia's Threatened Birds: a guide for government and civil society* (BirdLife International 2003), although a little dated, set out priorities for the conservation of birds and habitats in the region. SoIB (2023) provides a more recent pointer towards the conservation needs of India's birds.

Traditional protection, religious beliefs, legal measures and the efforts of conservation organisations have all helped to counter, albeit only partially, the threats confronting birds in the subcontinent. There is a concerted effort, often led by local citizens and groups, to prevent species extinctions (e.g. for White-winged Duck *Asarcornis scutulata*, Bengal and Lesser Floricans, Great Indian Bustard, Indian Skimmer, and many others). Without them, the region's extinct and threatened bird species would be much greater in number, and we salute these efforts.

Essential in any conservation agenda is the identification and protection of the most important places for nature. There is reasonable protected-area coverage in many parts of the region, particularly given the high human population densities. According to IUCN's Protected Planet (https://www.protectedplanet.net): Pakistan has 178 protected areas, covering 98,285km^2 or 12.31% of the country; India has 41 protected areas, covering 230,168km^2 or 7.52% of the country; Nepal has 49 protected areas covering 34,898km^2 or 23.63% of the country; Bhutan has 22 protected areas covering 19,835km^2 or 46.67% of the country; Bangladesh has 52 protected areas covering 6,468km^2 or 4.61% of the country, and Sri Lanka has 660 protected areas covering 19.897km^2 or 4.61% of the country. However, as stated in SoIB (2023), the protected area estate in India does not provide adequate protection for some ecologically important habitats such as grasslands, inland riverine ecosystems, coastal habitats such as mudflats, and seasonally flooded wetlands.

An important reference point for directing site management and expanding the protected areas network is the work led by BirdLife International in the identification of Important Bird and Biodiversity Areas (IBAs). These are sites that have been identified as being globally important for the conservation of birds and other biodiversity on the basis of internationally agreed criteria relating to populations of globally threatened, restricted-range, biome-restricted and congregatory bird species. More than 13,000 sites have been identified and documented worldwide in terrestrial, freshwater and marine ecosystems including: 55 sites in Pakistan covering 46,701km² (6% of the country); 554 in India covering 194,316km² (6% of the country); 42 in Nepal covering 26,516km² (28% of the country); 23 in Bhutan covering 12,133km² (32% of the country); 20 in Bangladesh covering 5,444km² (4% of the country), and 70 in Sri Lanka covering 3,947km² (6% of the country) (https://datazone.birdlife.org.; see also Rahmani *et al.* 2016, Grimmett *et al.* 2019, 2021, and BCN *et al.* 2023).

The subcontinent's birds will not be adequately conserved by targeted action for particular species and site-based measures alone. Direct threats such as hunting and trade and the pervasive impacts of land use intensification and change, and climate change, can only be addressed by a seismic shift in societal and governmental attitudes, policies and land-use practices, and funding, which put planetary sustainability centre stage. Whether this needs to come before or after economic development and poverty alleviation is the subject of much political debate but given that the planet is facing a climate and biodiversity crisis, and there is no 'planet B', there is surely no time to lose.

Commitments have been made to take urgent action. The United Nations Convention on Biological Diversity (UNCBD) has been ratified by all countries in the region. This commits countries to conserve the variety of animals and plants within their jurisdiction and to aim to ensure that the use of biological resources is sustainable, with each country putting in place national biodiversity strategies and action plans (NBSAPs). In 2022, governments signed up to the Kunming-Montreal Global Biodiversity Framework, which includes 23 global targets for urgent action which need to be initiated immediately and completed by 2030. These include ensuring that at least 30% of areas of degraded terrestrial, inland water, and marine and coastal ecosystems are under effective restoration (Target 2); that by 2030 at least 30% of terrestrial and inland water areas, and of marine and coastal areas, especially areas of particular importance for biodiversity and ecosystem functions and services, are effectively conserved and managed (Target 3), and that urgent management actions are taken to halt human-induced extinction of threatened species and for the recovery and conservation of species, in particular threatened species, to significantly reduce extinction risk (Target 4) (CBD 2022). We live in hope that governments, the private sector, and civil society will rise to this challenge.

FAMILY SUMMARIES

ORDER: Anseriformes

WHISTLING DUCKS, SWANS, GEESE AND DUCKS Anatidae (43 species)

Stocky with short legs and webbed feet. Bill is short, flattened and rounded at tip. Aquatic and highly gregarious, typically migrating, feeding, roosting and resting together, often in mixed flocks. Most species are chiefly vegetarian when adult, feeding on seeds, algae, plants and roots, often supplemented by aquatic invertebrates. Their main foraging methods are diving, surface-feeding or dabbling, and grazing. They also upend, wade, filter and sieve water and debris for food and probe with the bill. They have a direct flight with sustained fast wingbeats, and characteristically they often fly in V-formation.

ORDER: Galliformes

MEGAPODES Megapodiidae (1 species)

Stocky, medium-large chicken-like, terrestrial birds with small heads and large feet. They are also known as incubator birds or mound-builders as they build massive nest-mounds of decaying vegetation, which the male attends, adding or removing litter to regulate the internal heat while the eggs hatch. Megapodes are super-precocial, hatching from their eggs in the most mature condition of any birds. Their diet includes leaves, seeds, berries, buds, and a wide variety of invertebrates (insects, worms, snails, centipedes, etc.), and even small lizards.

PARTRIDGES, PHEASANTS AND ALLIES Phasianidae (45 species)

Stout-bodied with short, stout bill and short rounded wings. They nest on the ground, but many species roost in trees at night. They are good runners, often preferring to escape on foot rather than taking to the air. Their flight is powerful and fast but, except in the case of the migratory quail, it cannot be sustained for long periods. Typically, they forage by scratching the ground with strong feet to expose food hidden among dead leaves or in the soil. They eat mainly seeds, fruit, buds, roots and leaves, complemented by invertebrates.

ORDER: Phoenicopteriformes

FLAMINGOS Phoenicopteridae (2 species)

Large wading birds with long neck, very long legs, webbed feet and pink plumage. The angled bill is highly specialised for filter-feeding. Flamingos often occur in huge numbers and are found mainly on salt lakes and lagoons. The only two species in the subcontinent are the Greater Flamingo *Phoenicopterus roseus* and Lesser Flamingo *P. minor*.

ORDER: Podicipediformes

GREBES Podicipedidae (5 species)

Aquatic birds adapted for diving from the surface and swimming underwater to catch fish and aquatic invertebrates. Their strong legs are placed near the rear of their almost tailless body, and their feet are lobed. In flight grebes have an elongated appearance, with the neck extended, and feet hanging lower than the humped back. They usually feed singly, but may form loose congregations in the non-breeding season.

ORDER: Columbiformes

PIGEONS AND DOVES Columbidae (35 species)

Pigeons and doves have stout, compact bodies, rather short necks, and small heads and bills. Their flight is swift and direct, with fast wingbeats. Most species are gregarious outside the breeding season. Seeds, fruits, buds and leaves form their main diet, but many species also eat small invertebrates. They have soft plaintive cooing or booming voices that are often monotonously repeated.

ORDER: Pterocliformes

SANDGROUSE Pteroclidae (9 species)

Sandgrouse are dove-like in shape and live in arid, treeless habitats, eating chiefly seeds. They forage in flocks and congregate at water sources in the early morning or at the end of the day. The birds nest far from water, but the males especially have belly feathers adapted to hold water that can be flown back to their chicks.

ORDER: Otidiformes

BUSTARDS Otididae (6 species)

Medium-sized to large terrestrial birds of extensive grasslands. They have fairly long legs, stout bodies, long necks, crests and neck plumes, which are exhibited in display. The wings are broad and long, and in flight the neck is outstretched. Their flight is powerful and can be very fast. When feeding, bustards have a steady deliberate gait. They are more or less omnivorous, and feed opportunistically on large insects, such as grasshoppers and locusts, young birds, shoots, leaves, seeds and fruits. Males perform elaborate and spectacular displays in the breeding season.

ORDER: Cuculiformes

CUCKOOS, MALKOHAS AND COUCALS Cuculidae (26 species)

Cuckoos have elongated bodies with fairly long necks, tails varying from medium length to long and graduated and quite long, decurved bills. Almost all cuckoos are arboreal. Cuckoos eat hairy caterpillars. Male cuckoos of most species are very noisy in the breeding season, calling frequently during the day, especially if cloudy, and often into the night. When not breeding, they are silent and unobtrusive, and as a result their status and distribution at this season are very poorly known. Cuckoos are notorious for their nest parasitism.

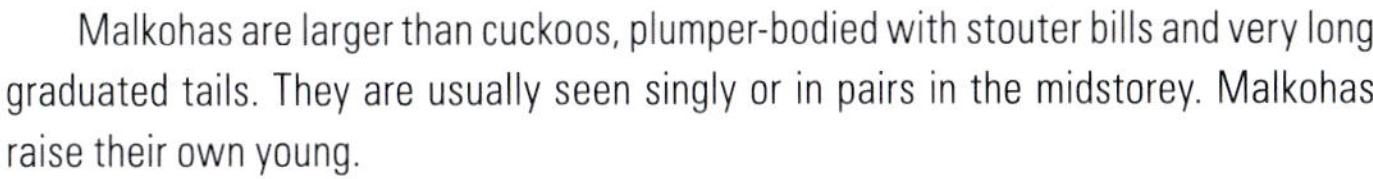

Malkohas are larger than cuckoos, plumper-bodied with stouter bills and very long graduated tails. They are usually seen singly or in pairs in the midstorey. Malkohas raise their own young.

Coucals are large, skulking birds with long graduated tails and weak flight. They are terrestrial, frequenting dense undergrowth, bamboo, tall grassland or scrub jungle. Coucals eat small animals and invertebrates.

ORDER: Caprimulgiformes

FROGMOUTHS Podargidae (2 species)

Frogmouths have the same cryptic colouring, soft plumage, wide gape and nocturnal habits as nightjars, but differ in some of their habitats. They are more arboreal than nightjars, nesting and roosting in trees and hunting from them at night by pouncing on prey. Hodgson's *Batrachostomus hodgsoni* and Sri Lanka Frogmouths *B. moniliger* are the only two species from this family recorded in the region.

NIGHTJARS Caprimulgidae (11 species)

Small to medium-sized birds with long, pointed wings, and gaping mouths with long bristles that help to catch insects in flight. Nightjars are crepuscular and nocturnal in habit, with soft owl-like, cryptically patterned plumage. By day they perch on the ground or lengthwise on a branch and are difficult to detect. They eat flying insects that are caught on the wing. Typically, they fly erratically to and fro over and among vegetation occasionally wheeling, gliding and hovering to pick insects from foliage. Most easily located by their calls.

SWIFTS Apodidae (15 species)

Swifts have long pointed wings, compact bodies, short bills with a wide gape and very short legs. They spend most of the day swooping and wheeling in the sky with great agility and grace. Typical swift flight is a series of rapid shallow wingbeats interspersed with short glides. They feed entirely in the air, drink and bathe while swooping low over the water, and regularly pass the night in the air. Swifts eat mainly tiny insects, caught by flying back and forth among aerial concentrations of these with their large mouths open; they also pursue individual insects.

TREESWIFTS Hemiprocnidae (1 species)

Long wings and forked tails. Unlike 'true' swifts, will perch on exposed branches. Like 'true' swifts, have short bills with a wide gape and very short legs. They spend much time on the wing, catching flying insects. Crested Treeswift *Hemiprocne coronata* is the only member of the family recorded in the region.

ORDER: Gruiformes

RAILS, CRAKES AND COOTS Rallidae (20 species)

Small to medium-sized birds, with moderate to long legs for wading and short rounded wings. With the exception of Eurasian Moorhen *Gallinula chloropus* and Eurasian Coot *Fulica atra*, which spend much time swimming in the open, rails are mainly terrestrial. Many occur in marshes. They fly reluctantly and feebly, with legs dangling, for a short distance and then drop into cover again. However, some species such as Eurasian Coot are long-distance migrants. Most are heard more often than seen, and are generally voluble at dusk and at night. Their calls consist of strident or raucous repeated notes. They eat insects, crustaceans, amphibians, fish and vegetable matter.

FINFOOTS Heliornithidae (1 species)

Medium-sized aquatic birds with a comparatively long and thick neck, the bill is thick and tapering, the toes have wide lobes and the tail is relatively long and stiff. They swim, dive and run well, but rarely fly. There is only one species in the region, Masked Finfoot *Heliopais personatus*.

CRANES Gruidae (6 species)

Stately long-necked, long-legged birds with tapering bodies and long inner secondaries which drape over the tail. Their flight is powerful, with head and neck extended forwards and feet stretched out behind. Flocks of cranes often fly in V-formation, and they sometimes soar at considerable heights. Most cranes are gregarious outside the breeding season, and flocks are often very noisy. Cranes have a characteristic resonant and far-reaching musical trumpet-like call. A wide variety of plant and animal food is taken. The bill is used to probe and dig for plant roots and to graze and glean vegetable material above the ground. Both sexes have a spectacular and beautiful dance that takes place throughout the year.

ORDER: Charadriiformes

THICK-KNEES Burhinidae (4 species)

Medium-sized to large waders, with long legs, and short stout bills. Mainly crepuscular or nocturnal, with cryptically patterned plumage. They eat invertebrates and small animals.

STILTS AND AVOCETS Recurvirostridae (2 species)

Stilts and avocets are waders with characteristic long bills, and longer legs in proportion to their body than other birds except flamingos. They inhabit marshes, lakes and pools. Black-winged Stilt *Himantopus himantopus* is the only stilt and Pied Avocet *Recurvirostra avosetta* is the only avocet recorded in the subcontinent.

IBISBILL Ibidorhynchidae (1 species)

Ibisbill *Ibidorhyncha struthersii* is the only species in this family. In the region it frequents Himalayan streams, some birds wandering south to lower elevations in winter. They use their downcurved bill to probe for food around large cobbles in streambeds.

OYSTERCATCHERS Haematopodidae (1 species)

Oystercatchers are waders that usually inhabit the seashore. They have all-black or black-and-white plumage. The bill is long, stout, orange-red and adapted for opening shells of bivalve molluscs. Eurasian Oystercatcher *Haematopus ostralegus* is the only family member recorded in the region.

PLOVERS AND LAPWINGS Charadriidae (20 species)

Plovers and lapwings are small to medium-sized waders with rounded heads, short necks and short bills. Typically, they forage by running in short spurts, pausing and standing erect, then stooping to pick up invertebrate prey. Their flight is swift and direct.

PAINTED-SNIPES Rostratulidae (1 species)

Waders that frequent marshes and superficially resemble snipes but have spectacular plumages. Bill long, and wings short and broad. The female is more brightly coloured than the male as the male takes care of the nest. Greater Painted-snipe *Rostratula benghalensis* is the only species in the family recorded in the region.

JACANAS Jacanidae (2 species)

Jacanas characteristically have very long toes, which enable them to walk over floating vegetation. They inhabit freshwater lakes, ponds and marshes. Like painted-snipes after laying the eggs females leave parenting duties to the males.

SNIPES, CURLEWS, SANDPIPERS AND STINTS Scolopacidae (42 species)

Woodcocks and snipes are small to medium-sized waders with very long bills, fairly long legs and cryptically patterned plumages. If approached, they usually crouch at first on the ground and 'freeze', preferring to rely on their protective plumage pattern to escape detection. They generally inhabit marshy ground. Godwits and curlews are

wading birds with quite long to very long legs and a long bill. Sandpipers and stints are small to medium-sized, rather plump waders, with short, medium or longish bills and short (stints) or medium-long legs. All species feed mainly by probing with their bills in soft substrates and also by picking from the surface. Their diet consists mostly of small invertebrates.

BUTTONQUAILS Turnicidae (3 species)

These small, plump terrestrial birds are now placed in Charadriiformes having previously been regarded as a family in the order Gruiformes. They are found in a wide variety of habitats having a dry, often sandy substrate and low ground cover under which they can readily run or walk. Buttonquails are very secretive and fly with great reluctance, with weak whirring beats low over the ground, dropping quickly into cover. They feed on grass and weed seeds, grain, greenery and small insects, picking food from the ground surface or scratching with the feet.

CRAB-PLOVER Dromadidae (1 species)

A mainly white wader, the distinctively shaped thick black bill is adapted for preying on crabs and other crustaceans, which it hunts chiefly on coastal mudflats and reefs. Usually found singly, in pairs and in small parties, but hundreds occur at traditional roost sites. Mainly crepuscular.

COURSERS AND PRATINCOLES Glareolidae (6 species)

Coursers are waders with an upright posture, small head, long legs, and short toes, which are perfectly adapted for running through the sparsely vegetated habitats they frequent. Pratincoles have arched and pointed bills, wide gapes and long, pointed wings. Most are short-legged and catch most of their prey in the air, although they also feed on the ground. All live near water.

JAEGERS AND SKUAS Stercorariidae (5 species)

Aerial seabirds, with a strong, hooked bill, long, pointed wings, short legs, and webbed feet. Jaegers feed by chasing other seabirds, especially terns, until they drop or disgorge their food. They are usually found in marine waters, some distance from land, but are occasionally found inshore and may occur inland after monsoon storms.

GULLS, TERNS, NODDIES AND SKIMMERS Laridae (38 species)

Gulls are medium-sized to large birds with relatively long, narrow wings, usually a stout bill, moderately long legs and webbed feet. Immatures are brownish and cryptically patterned. In flight, gulls are graceful and soar easily in updraughts. All species swim buoyantly and well. They are highly adaptable, and most species are opportunistic feeders with a varied diet including invertebrates. Most species are gregarious.

Terns are small to medium-sized aerial birds with gull-like bodies but are generally more delicately built. The wings are long and pointed, typically narrower than in gulls, and their flight is buoyant and graceful. Terns are highly vocal, and most species are gregarious. *Sterna* terns generally have deeply forked tails. They mainly eat small fish and crabs caught by hovering and then plunge-diving from the air, often submerging completely, but they also pick prey from the water surface.

Skimmers are distinguished by their long, strong scissor-like bills with elongated lower mandibles. They feed by skimming the water surface with the bill open and lower mandible partly immersed to snap up fish. Indian Skimmer *Rynchops albicollis* is the only skimmer species occurring in the region.

ORDER: PHAETHONTIFORMES

TROPICBIRDS Phaethontidae (3 species)

Aerial seabirds with long wings and elongated central tail feathers. They range over tropical and subtropical waters, and nest mainly on oceanic and offshore islands. Graceful and pigeon-like flight with flapping and circling, alternating with long glides. Usually solitary but may congregate with flocks of feeding terns. They feed by first hovering to locate prey (mainly fish and squid) and then plunge-diving on half-closed wings. All three species currently recognised have been recorded in the subcontinent: Red-billed *Phaethon aethereus*, Red-tailed *P. rubricauda* and White-tailed Tropicbirds *P. lepturus*.

ORDER: GAVIIFORMES

LOONS Gaviidae (2 species)

Fish-eating birds of cold northern waters, which are vagrants to the Indian subcontinent. These sleek foot-propelled divers have torpedo-shaped bodies, feet with webs, but flattened for a knife-like upstroke and placed far back on the body to generate a powerful downstroke. Loons are so adapted to their aquatic lifestyle that they cannot really walk on land.

ORDER: PROCELLARIIFORMES

ALBATROSSES Diomedeidae (1 species)

Albatrosses have the longest and narrowest wings of any bird, which equip them for flying for very long periods, with hardly any effort in sufficient wind. They are pelagic and typically are found over colder ocean waters where upwelling makes food more abundant. The only family member recorded in the subcontinent, Light-mantled Albatross *Phoebetria palpebrata*, is a vagrant.

SOUTHERN STORM-PETRELS Oceanitidae (3 species)

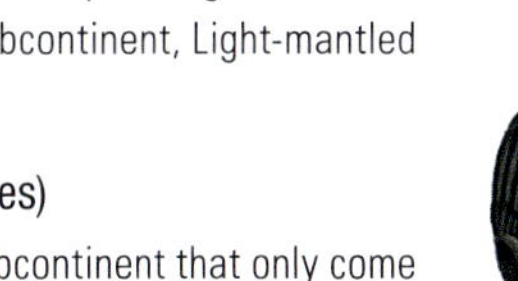

Southern Storm-petrels are non-breeding visitors to the subcontinent that only come ashore to breed. They are swallow-like inhabitants of the open sea, and can often be seen following ships or cetaceans. When foraging, they tend to flutter their wings above their backs, pattering their feet on the water surface.

NORTHERN STORM-PETRELS Hydrobatidae (4 species)

Northern Storm-petrels are similar to Southern Storm-petrels but have shorter legs and skulls and longer wings. They are also non-breeding visitors to the subcontinent, only coming ashore to breed. They flutter low over the water and pluck zooplankton, small fish, squid, and small crustaceans from the water's surface with their bills. Though they sometimes sit on the water in rafts, they do essentially all their foraging on the wing.

SHEARWATERS AND PETRELS Procellariidae (12 species)

Long-winged, marine species that are mainly non-breeding visitors to the subcontinent. They come ashore only to breed, and feed on zooplankton, squid, fish and offal, seized on or below the water surface. Gregarious, often gathering in flocks at food concentrations. Typically, they fly by a combination of rapid, rather stiff wingbeats, interspersed with long glides (gliding or 'shearing' being more pronounced in strong winds). Have 'tubenoses' through which they are able to exude salt.

ORDER: Ciconiiformes

STORKS Ciconiidae (8 species)

Large or very large birds with long bills, necks and legs, long and broad wings and short tails. In flight, the legs are extended and the neck is outstretched. They have a powerful, slow-flapping flight and frequently soar for long periods, often at great heights. They capture fish, frogs, snakes, lizards, large insects, crustaceans and molluscs while walking slowly in marshes, at the edge of lakes and rivers, and in grasslands.

ORDER: Suliformes

FRIGATEBIRDS Fregatidae (3 species)

Large aerial seabirds that rarely land on water, and roost and nest in trees and bushes. Agile in the air, and can soar for long periods. Noted for chasing other seabirds, especially boobies, until they drop or disgorge their food, but also capture their own prey by diving to the water surface. They are chiefly storm-driven visitors to the coast, typically during monsoons. Three members from this family have been recorded in the subcontinent's marine waters: Great *Fregata minor*, Lesser *F. ariel* and Christmas Frigatebirds *F. andrewsi*.

BOOBIES Sulidae (4 species)

Large seabirds. They forage on the wing, scanning the sea, and on sighting fish or squid they plunge-dive at an angle. Flight is direct with alternating periods of flapping and gliding. Masked *Sula dactylatra*, Brown *S. leucogaster* and Red-footed Boobies *S. sula* have been recorded in the region's marine waters.

DARTERS Anhingidae (1 species)

Large aquatic birds adapted for hunting fish underwater. Darters have long slender necks and heads, long wings and very long tails. Only one species in the family has been recorded in the region: Oriental Darter *Anhinga melanogaster*.

CORMORANTS Phalacrocoracidae (4 species)

Medium-sized to large aquatic birds. They are long-necked, with hook-tipped bills of moderate length and long, stiff tails. Cormorants swim with the body low in the water, the neck straight and the head and bill pointing slightly upwards. They eat mainly fish, which are caught by underwater pursuit. In flight, the neck is extended and the head is held slightly above the horizontal. Typically they often perch for long periods in upright posture with spread wings and tail on trees, posts or rocks.

ORDER: Pelecaniformes

PELICANS Pelecanidae (3 species)

Large aquatic, gregarious fish-eating birds. The wings are long and broad, and the tail is short and rounded. They have characteristic long, straight, flattened bills, hooked at the tip, and a large expandable pouch suspended on the lower mandible. Many pelicans often fish cooperatively by swimming forward in a semi-circular formation, driving fish into shallow water, each bird then scoops up fish from the water into its pouch before swallowing the food. Pelicans fly together in V-formation or in lines, and often soar for considerable periods in thermals. They are powerful fliers, proceeding by steady flaps with the head drawn back between the shoulders. When swimming the closed wings are typically held above the back. Three species occur in the subcontinent: Great White *Pelecanus onocrotalus*, Spot-billed *P. philippensis* and Dalmatian Pelicans *P. crispus*.

HERONS AND BITTERNS Ardeidae (24 species)

Medium-sized to large birds, with long legs for wading. The diurnal herons (including egrets) have slender bodies and a long head and neck; night herons are squatter, with a shorter neck and legs. All fly with leisurely flaps, with the legs outstretched and projecting beyond the tail, and nearly always with neck and head drawn back. They frequent marshes and the shores of lakes and rivers. Typically, herons feed by standing motionless at the water's edge waiting for prey to swim within reach, or by slow stalking in shallow water or on land.

Bitterns usually skulk in reed swamps, although occasionally one may forage in the open, and they can clamber about tangled stems with agility. Normally they are solitary and crepuscular, and are most often seen flying low over tall swamp thickets with slow wingbeats, soon dropping into cover again. When in danger, bitterns freeze, pointing the head and neck upward and compressing their feathers so that the whole body appears elongated. The bitterns are characterised by their booming territorial calls. Herons and bitterns feed on a wide variety of aquatic prey.

IBISES AND SPOONBILLS Threskiornithidae (4 species)

Large birds with long necks and legs, partly webbed feet and long broad wings. Ibises have long, decurved bills and forage by probing in shallow water, mud and grass. Spoonbills have long spatulate bills and catch floating prey in shallow water. Only one spoonbill species occurs in the region: Eurasian Spoonbill *Platalea leucorodia*.

ORDER: ACCIPITRIFORMES

OSPREY Pandionidae (1 species)

A specialised raptor similar to other hawks. Adapted to feed on fish with a reversible outer toe and spiny foot-pads to help grasp prey. Hovers over open water and then plunge-dives feet first to catch fish. Wings long and narrow and tail is short. Female is larger than the male and sexes are similar in appearance.

HAWKS, EAGLES, HARRIERS AND VULTURES etc. Accipitridae (61 species)

A large and varied family of raptors, ranging in size from the Besra *Accipiter virgatus* to the huge Himalayan Griffon *Gyps himalayensis*. In most species, the vultures being an exception, the female is larger than the male, and is often duller and brownish. The Accipitridae feed on mammals, birds, reptiles, amphibians, fish, crabs, molluscs and insects – dead or alive. All have hooked, sharp-tipped bills and very acute sight, and all except the vultures have powerful feet with long curved claws. They frequent all habitat types, ranging from dense forests, deserts and mountains to fresh waters.

ORDER: Strigiformes

BARN OWLS Tytonidae (5 species)

Large-headed with a heart-shaped facial disc, long legs and strong feet. Habits similar to those of the typical owls.

TYPICAL OWLS Strigidae (34 species)

Owls have large and rounded heads, big forward-facing eyes surrounded by a broad facial disc, and short tails. Most are nocturnal and cryptically coloured and patterned, making them inconspicuous when resting during the day. When hunting, owls either quarter the ground or scan and listen for prey from a perch. Their diet consists of small animals and invertebrates. Owls are usually located by their distinctive and often weird calls, which are diagnostic of the species and advertise their presence and territories.

ORDER: Trogoniformes

TROGONS Trogonidae (3 species)

Brightly coloured, short-necked, medium-sized birds with long tails, short rounded wings and rather short, broad bills. They are usually found singly or in widely separated pairs. Characteristically, they perch almost motionless in an upright posture for long periods in the middle or lower storey of dense forests. Trogons are insectivorous but also eat leaves and berries. They capture flying insects on the wing when moving from one vantage point to another, twisting with the agility of a flycatcher. Three species in this family occur in the subcontinent: Red-headed *Harpactes erythrocephalus*, Malabar *H. fasciatus* and Ward's Trogons *H. wardi*.

ORDER: Bucerotiformes

HOOPOES Upupidae (1 species)

Hoopoes have a distinctive appearance with long decurved bills, short legs and rounded wings. They are insectivorous and forage by pecking and probing the ground. Flight is undulating, slow and butterfly-like. Common Hoopoe *Upupa epops* is the only species in the family occurring in the region.

HORNBILLS Bucerotidae (10 species)

Medium-sized to large birds with massive bills and a variable-sized casque. Mainly arboreal, feeding chiefly on wild figs *Ficus*, berries and drupes, supplemented by small animals and insects. Flight is powerful and slow, and for most species consists of a few wingbeats followed by a sailing glide with the wingtips upturned. In all but the smaller species, the wingbeats make a distinctive loud puffing sound audible over some distance. Hornbills often fly one after another in a follow-my-leader fashion. Usually found in pairs or small parties, sometimes in flocks of up to 30 or more where food is abundant.

ORDER: Coraciiformes

KINGFISHERS Alcedinidae (13 species)

Small to medium-sized birds, with large heads, long strong bills and short legs. Most kingfishers spend long periods perched alone or in well-separated pairs, watching intently before plunging swiftly downwards to seize prey with the bill; they usually return to the same perch. They eat mainly fish, tadpoles and invertebrates; larger species also eat frogs, snakes, crabs, lizards and rodents. Their flight is direct and strong, with rapid wingbeats and often close to the water surface.

BEE-EATERS Meropidae (7 species)

Brightly coloured birds with long decurved bills, pointed wings and very short legs. They catch large flying insects on the wing, by making short swift sallies like a flycatcher from an exposed perch such as a treetop, branch, post or telegraph wire; insects are pursued in a lively chase with a swift and agile flight. Some species also hawk insects in flight like swallows. Most species are sociable. Their flight is graceful and undulating, a few rapid wingbeats followed by a glide.

ROLLERS Coraciidae (4 species)

Stoutly built, medium-sized birds with large heads and short necks, which mainly eat large insects. Typically, they keep singly or in widely spaced pairs. Flight is buoyant, with rather rapid deliberate wingbeats.

ORDER: PICIFORMES

ASIAN BARBETS Megalaimidae (11 species)

Stocky, short-tailed birds with stout bills. Arboreal, and usually found in the treetops. Despite their bright coloration, they can be very difficult to see, especially when silent, their plumage blending remarkably well with tree foliage. They often perch motionless for long periods. Barbets call persistently and monotonously in the breeding season, sometimes throughout the day; in the non-breeding season they are usually silent. They are chiefly frugivorous, many species favouring figs *Ficus*. Their flight is strong and direct, with deep woodpecker-like undulations.

HONEYGUIDES Indicatoridae (1 species)

Small, inconspicuous birds that inhabit forest or forest edge. A peculiarity of the family is that they also eat wax, usually from bee combs. Spend long periods perched upright and motionless. Feed by clinging to bee combs, often upside-down, and by aerial sallies. Yellow-rumped Honeyguide *Indicator xanthonotus* is the only family member in the region.

WRYNECKS, PICULETS AND WOODPECKERS Picidae (37 species)

Chiefly arboreal, and usually seen clinging to, or climbing up, vertical trunks and lateral branches. Typically, they work up trunks and along branches in jerky spurts, directly or in spirals. Some species feed regularly on the ground, searching mainly for termites and ants. Most species have powerful bills, for boring into wood to extract insects and for excavating nest holes. Woodpeckers feed chiefly on ants, termites, and grubs, and pupae of wood-boring beetles. Most woodpeckers also hammer rapidly against tree trunks with their bill, producing a loud rattle, known as 'drumming', which is used to advertise and defend their territories. Their flight is strong and direct, with marked undulations. Many species can be located by their characteristic loud calls. Piculets are tiny woodpeckers with similar habits. Eurasian Wryneck *Jynx torquilla* is unusual as it behaves more like a passerine, but often twists its neck to look over its back.

ORDER: Falconiformes

FALCONS Falconidae (14 species)

Small to medium-sized birds of prey which resemble the Accipitridae in having hooked bills, sharp curved talons, and remarkable powers of sight and flight. Like other raptors they are mainly diurnal, although a few are crepuscular. Some falcons kill flying birds in a surprise attack, often by stooping at great speed (e.g. Peregrine *Falco peregrinus*); others hover then swoop on prey on the ground (e.g. Common Kestrel *F. tinnunculus*) and several species hawk insects in flight (e.g. Amur Falcon *F. amurensis*).

ORDER: Psittaciformes

PARROTS AND PARAKEETS Psittacidae (14 species)

Parrots have short necks and short, stout hooked bills with the upper mandible strongly curved and overlapping the lower mandible. Most parrots are noisy and highly gregarious. They associate in family parties and small flocks and gather in large numbers at concentrations of food, such as paddyfields. Their diet is almost entirely vegetarian: fruit, seeds, buds, nectar and pollen. Their flight is swift, powerful and direct. Hanging parrots are small with short tails lacking streamers. They habitually sleep upside-down.

ORDER: Passeriformes

TYPICAL BROADBILLS Eurylaimidae (2 species)

Small to medium-sized plump birds with rounded wings and short legs, most species having a distinctively broad bill. Typically, they inhabit the midstorey of forest and feed mainly on invertebrates gleaned from leaves and branches. Broadbills are active when foraging but are often unobtrusive and lethargic at other times.

PITTAS Pittidae (6 species)

Brilliantly coloured, terrestrial forest passerines of medium size, stocky and long-legged, with short square tails, stout bills and an erect carriage. Most of their time is spent foraging for invertebrates on the forest floor, flicking leaves and other vegetation, and probing with their strong bill into leaf litter and damp earth. Pittas usually progress on the ground by long hopping bounds. Typically, they are skulking and are often most easily located by their high-pitched whistling calls or songs. They sing in trees or bushes.

CUCKOOSHRIKES, MINIVETS AND ALLIES Campcphagidae (15 species)

Cuckooshrikes are arboreal, insectivorous birds that usually keep high in the trees. They are of medium size, with long pointed wings, moderately long rounded tails and an upright carriage when perched.

Minivets are small to medium-sized, mostly brightly coloured passerines with moderately long tails and an upright stance when perched. They are arboreal, and feed on insects by flitting about in the foliage to glean prey from leaves, buds and bark, sometimes hovering in front of a sprig or making short aerial sallies. They usually keep in pairs in the breeding season, and in small parties when not breeding. When feeding and in flight they continually utter contact calls.

VIREOS AND ALLIES Vireonidae (6 species)

Small, big-billed, arboreal birds of woodland and forest. Genetic studies have shown that White-bellied Erpornis *Erpornis zantholeuca* (previously regarded as a yuhina but now in its own monospecific genus) and the *Pteruthius* shrike-babblers are best treated in this family.

WHISTLERS Pachycephalidae (1 species)

Whistlers are reminiscent of chats and flycatchers but more strongly built with a thick rounded head, short thick neck and short heavy bill. They pick insects from branches and foliage but also fly-catch. Mangrove Whistler *Pachycephala cinerea* is the only family member recorded in the region.

OLD WORLD ORIOLES Oriolidae (6 species)

Medium-sized colourful passerines with short, stout bills. Arboreal and usually keep hidden in the leafy canopy. Orioles have beautiful, fluty, whistling songs and harsh grating calls. They are usually seen singly, in pairs or in family parties. Their flight is powerful and undulating, with fast wingbeats. They feed mainly on insects and fruit.

WOODSWALLOWS Artamidae (2 species)

Plump birds with long pointed wings, short tail and legs, and wide gapes. They feed on insects, usually captured in flight, and spend prolonged periods on the wing. They are sociable and perch close together on a bare branch or wire, and often waggle their tail from side to side. Ashy *Artamus fuscus* and White-breasted Woodswallows *A. leucorynchus* are the only two members of the family in the subcontinent.

VANGAS AND ALLIES Vangidae (5 species)

Mainly a Malagasy and African family which also includes the flycatcher-shrikes *Hemipus* and woodshrikes *Tephrodornis.* Flycatcher-shrikes are small, pied birds with arboreal flycatching habits and an upright stance, when perched. Bar-winged Flycatcher-shrike is the only species of this genus recorded in the region. Woodshrikes are medium-sized, arboreal, insectivorous passerines. The bill is stout and hooked, the wings are rounded, and the tail is short.

IORAS Aegithinidae (2 species)

Ioras are a small, lively group of passerines that feed in trees, mainly on insects and especially on caterpillars. The only species of this family recorded in the region are Common *Aegithina tiphia* and White-tailed Ioras *A. nigrolutea.*

FANTAILS Rhipiduridae (3 species)

Small, confiding, arboreal birds, perpetually on the move in search of insects. Characteristically they erect and spread their tails like fans, and droop their wings, while pirouetting and turning from side to side with jerky, restless movements. When foraging, they flit from branch to branch, making frequent aerial sallies after winged insects. They call continually. Fantails arc usually found singly or in pairs, and often join mixed hunting parties with other insectivorous birds.

DRONGOS Dicruridae (10 species)

Medium-sized passerines with characteristic black and often glossy plumage, long often deeply forked tails, and a very upright stance when perched. They are arboreal and insectivorous, catching larger-winged insects by aerial sallies from a perch. Usually found singly or in pairs. Their direct flight is swift, strong and undulating. Drongos are rather noisy and have a varied repertoire of harsh calls and pleasant whistles; some species are good mimics.

MONARCHS Monarchidae (4 species)

Most species are small to medium-sized, with a medium-length or long tail. They feed mainly on insects. Black-naped Monarch *Hypothymis azurea* and three species that were once treated as subspecies of Asian Paradise-flycatcher *Terpsiphone paradisi* are the representatives of this family found in the region. Male paradise-flycatchers are notable for their very elongated central tail feathers.

SHRIKES Laniidae (13 species)

Medium-sized, predatory passerines with strong stout bills, hooked at the tip of the upper mandible, strong legs and feet, large heads, and long tails with graduated tips. Shrikes search for prey from a vantage point, such as the top of a bush or small tree or post. They swoop down to catch invertebrates or small animals from the ground or in flight. Over long distances their flight is typically undulating. Their calls are harsh, but most have quite musical songs and are good mimics. Shrikes typically inhabit open country with scattered bushes or light scrub.

CROWS, MAGPIES AND JAYS Corvidae (26 species)

These are robust perching birds which differ considerably from each other in appearance, but which have a number of features in common: a fairly long straight bill, very strong feet and legs, and a tuft of nasal bristles extending over the base of the upper mandible. The sexes are alike or almost alike in plumage. They are strong fliers. Most are gregarious, especially when feeding or roosting. Typically, they are noisy birds, uttering loud, discordant squawks, croaks or screeches. Most crows are highly inquisitive and adaptable.

FAIRY FLYCATCHERS AND ALLIES Stenostiridae (2 species)

Small-bodied insectivores of wooded areas, with small bills and long tails. They forage actively by flitting rapidly to and fro, sallying out to catch a flying insect, or darting to grab prey on nearby vegetation. There are two members of this family in the region: Yellow-bellied Fantail-Flycatcher *Chelidorhynx hypoxanthus* and Grey-headed Canary-flycatcher *Culicicapa ceylonensis*.

TITS Paridae (15 species)

Tits are small, active, highly acrobatic passerines with short bills and strong feet. Their flight over long distances is undulating. They are mainly insectivorous, although many species also depend on seeds, particularly from trees in winter, and some also eat fruit. They probe bark crevices, search branches and leaves, and frequently hang upside-down from twigs. Tits are chiefly arboreal, but also descend to the ground to feed, hopping about and flicking aside leaves and other debris. In the non-breeding season, most species join roving flocks of other insectivorous birds.

PENDULINE-TITS Remizidae (1 species)

Behave like parids, actively foraging near the tips of branches, often hanging upside-down. They also hold onto large prey items with one foot as they tear them apart, but, unlike parids, they often use their sharp bills to probe into a gall or stem and then open the bill to access prey hidden inside. They feed primarily on insects and arthropods. One species in this family occurs in the region: White-crowned Penduline-Tit *Remiz coronatus*.

LARKS Alaudidae (23 species)

Terrestrial cryptically coloured passerines, generally small-sized, which usually walk and run on the ground, and often have a very elongated hindclaw. Their flight is strong and undulating. Larks take a wide variety of food, including insects, molluscs, arthropods, seeds, flowers, buds and leaves. Many species have a melodious song, which is often delivered in a distinctive, steeply climbing or circling aerial display, and also from a conspicuous low perch. They live in a wide range of open habitats, including grassland and cultivation.

BEARDED REEDLING Panuridae (1 species)

Bearded Reedling *Panurus biarmicus* is the only species in this family. It is a small, long-tailed inhabitant of dense reedbeds, more often heard than seen. It lives in groups, eating insects in the spring and summer and reed seeds in the winter.

CISTICOLAS AND ALLIES Cisticolidae (17 species)

Includes the cisticolas *Cisticola*, prinias *Prinia* and tailorbirds *Orthotomus*.

Cisticolas are a group of tiny, short-tailed, insectivorous passerines. The tail is longer in winter than in summer. They are found in grassy habitats, and many have aerial displays.

Prinias have long, graduated tails, longer in winter than in summer. Most inhabit grassland, marsh vegetation or scrub. They forage by gleaning insects and spiders from vegetation, and some species also feed on the ground. When perched, the tail is often held cocked and slightly fanned. Their flight is weak and jerky.

Tailorbirds have long, decurved bills, short wings and graduated tails, the latter held characteristically cocked. They sew together leaves to make a nest, hence their name.

REED WARBLERS Acrocephalidae (14 species)

Genetic work has established this grouping as a separate family including *Acrocephalus*, *Iduna* and *Hippolais* warblers as well as Thick-billed Warbler *Arundinax aedon*.

Acrocephalus warblers are medium-sized to large warblers with prominent bills and rounded tails. They usually occur singly. Many species are skulking, typically keeping low down in dense vegetation. Most frequent marshy habitats, and can clamber about readily in reeds and vertical stems of other marsh plants. Their songs are harsh and often monotonous.

Iduna and *Hippolais* warblers are medium-sized warblers, with large bills, square-ended tails and a distinctive domed head shape with a rather sloping forehead and peaked crown. Their songs are harsh and varied. They clamber about vegetation with a rather clumsy action.

GRASSHOPPER WARBLERS AND GRASSBIRDS Locustellidae (14 species)

Includes the *Locustella* warblers and grassbirds. Now included in *Locustella*, based on recent genetic studies, are several species previously regarded as *Bradypterus* bush warblers.

Locustella warblers are very skulking, medium-sized warblers with rounded wings, usually found singly. Characteristically, they keep low down or on the ground among dense wetland vegetation, walking furtively and scurrying off when startled.

They fly at low level, flitting between plants, or rather jerkily over longer distances, ending in a sudden dive into cover.

Grassbirds are brownish warblers with longish tails. They inhabit damp tall grassland. Males perform song flights in the breeding season.

CUPWINGS Pnoepygidae (3 species)

Small, rotund and almost tailless, with proportionately large bills, legs and feet. Named for the cup-like shape of their short, rounded wings. Forage in forests and forest edges on the ground and low down in the undergrowth. Previously known as wren-babblers. Three species occur in the region: Pygmy *Pnoepyga pusilla*, Nepal *P. immaculata* and Scaly-breasted Cupwings *P. albiventer.*

MARTINS AND SWALLOWS Hirundinidae (17 species)

Gregarious, rather small passerines with a distinctive slender, streamlined body, long pointed wings and small bills. The long-tailed species are often called swallows, and the shorter-tailed species termed martins. All hawk day-flying insects in swift, agile sustained flight, sometimes high in the air. Many species have a deeply forked tail, which affords greater manoeuvrability. Hirundines catch most of their food while flying in the open. They readily perch on exposed branches and wires.

BULBULS Pycnonotidae (25 species)

Medium-sized passerines with soft, fluffy plumage, rather short and rounded wings, medium-long to long tails, slender bills and short, weak legs. Bulbuls feed on berries and other fruits, often supplemented by insects, and sometimes also nectar and buds of trees and shrubs. Many species are noisy, especially when feeding. Typically, bulbuls have a variety of cheerful, loud, chattering, babbling and whistling calls. Most species are gregarious in the non-breeding season.

LEAF WARBLERS Phylloscopidae (37 species)

Now included in *Phylloscopus,* based on recent genetic studies, are several species previously regarded as being in a separate genus *Seicercus.* Leaf warblers are rather small, slim and short-billed warblers. Useful identification features are voice, strength of the supercilium, colour of underparts, rump, bill and legs, and presence or absence of wing-bars, of coronal bands or of white on the tail. The coloration of upperparts and underparts and the presence or prominence of wing-bars are affected by wear. Leaf warblers are fast-moving and restless, hopping and creeping about actively and often flicking their wings. They mostly glean small insects and spiders from foliage, twigs and branches, often first disturbing prey by hovering and fluttering; they also make short flycatching sallies.

BUSH WARBLERS Scotocercidae (18 species)

Genetic studies have separated out a number of disparate taxa and grouped them as bush warblers, including the *Cettia* and *Horornis* bush warblers, tesias, *Abroscopus* warblers, and Mountain Tailorbird *Phyllergates cucullatus.* Bush warblers are medium-sized warblers with rounded wings and tail that inhabit marshes, grassland and forest undergrowth. They are usually found singly. Bush warblers call frequently and are usually heard more often than seen. *Cettia* species have surprisingly loud voices, and some can be identified by their distinctive melodious songs. *Tesia* species are almost tailless and largely terrestrial. When excited, these birds flick their wings and tail.

LONG-TAILED TITS Aegithalidae (7 species)

Very small birds, with relatively long tails and large heads. They use their short conical bills to extract insects from small crevices in buds and bark. Foraging in groups, they are constantly on the move through forest and woodland vegetation, keeping in touch through a series of high-pitched calls.

SYLVIA WARBLERS Sylviidae (15 species)

A much-reduced family (previously including the Acrocephalidae, Locustellidae and Phylloscopidae warblers for example), but now including only the *Sylvia* (and the recently separated *Curruca*) warblers, *Fulvetta* fulvettas, *Chrysomma* and Fire-tailed Myzornis *Myzornis pyrrhoura*. The *Sylvia* and *Curruca* warblers are small to medium-sized passerines with fine bills. Typically, they inhabit bushes and scrub and feed chiefly by gleaning insects from foliage and twigs; they sometimes also consume berries in autumn and winter.

PARROTBILLS Paradoxornithidae (10 species)

The parrotbills have stout bills, strong legs and feet, and long tails. They frequent stands of bamboo and tall grasses, including in evergreen forest.

WHITE-EYES AND YUHINAS Zosteropidae (9 species)

Taxonomic studies have now grouped the yuhinas (previously included in the Timaliidae) with the white-eyes. Yuhinas are crested passerines with fine, pointed bills. Restless, often in flocks and at times tit-like in their feeding behaviour. White-eyes are small or very small insectivorous passerines with slightly decurved and pointed bills, brush-tipped tongues, and a white ring around each eye. White-eyes frequent forest edge, and bushes in gardens.

SCIMITAR BABBLERS AND ALLIES Timaliidae (35 species)

Previously this family comprised a much larger group of babblers, but recent taxonomic work has separated off the Pnoepygidae (cupwings), Pellorneidae (ground babblers) and Leiotrichidae (laughingthrushes and allies). They are small to medium-sized passerines, with soft, loose plumage, short or fairly short wings, and strong legs and feet. The sexes are alike. The scimitar babblers have longish, downcurved bills.

GROUND BABBLERS Pellorneidae (12 species)

Comprises some species previously included in the Timaliidae (e.g. the *Pellorneum* babblers) but also incorporating Rufous-vented *Laticilla burnesii* and Swamp Grass Babblers *L. cinerascens* (previously considered to be prinias) and Indian Grass-babbler *Graminicola bengalensis* (previously included in the Cisticolidae). Varied morphologically and in habits and habitat, but most species are skulking and favour undergrowth or dense tall grasses.

LAUGHINGTHRUSHES AND ALLIES Leiothrichidae (62 species)

Another family split off from the Timaliidae but still comprising a large number of genera including the *Turdoides* and related babblers, *Alcippe* fulvettas, laughingthrushes, babax, sibias, mesia, leiothrix, minlas, liocichlas and barwings. Laughingthrushes are medium-sized, long-tailed babblers that are gregarious even in the breeding season. They often feed on the ground and their flight is short and clumsy.

KINGLETS Regulidae (1 species)

Tiny, energetic passerines that glean insects from bark crevices, twigs and leaf clusters, often hovering at overhanging vegetation to snatch a prey item they have spotted from below. They often forage in flocks of their own or other species, giving high-pitched calls. Only one species in the region, Goldcrest *Regulus regulus*.

WALLCREEPER AND SPOTTED CREEPERS Tichodromidae (2 species)

Wallcreeper *Tichodroma muraria* breeds in rocky alpine areas and moves to similar habitat lower down in winter. It blends into grey rock faces as it forages for invertebrates, but becomes conspicuous when flying, as it flashes its bright red and pink flight feathers. Indian Spotted Creeper *Salpornis spilonota* is resident in India and probably sedentary. It has a very distinctive appearance with spotted and barred plumage, and a long, slender, decurved bill which it uses to glean invertebrates from bark crevices. Its slightly rounded tail is not used for support while climbing trees, unlike treecreepers.

NUTHATCHES Sittidae (10 species)

Nuthatches are small, energetic, compact passerines with short tails, large strong feet and long bills. They are agile tree climbers and can move with ease upwards, downwards, sideways and upside-down over trunks or branches, progressing by a series of jerky hops, and do not use the tail as a prop. Their flight is direct over short distances and undulating over longer ones. Nuthatches capture insects, spiders, seeds and nuts. They are often found singly or in pairs; outside the breeding season, they often join foraging flocks of other insectivorous birds.

TREECREEPERS Certhiidae (5 species)

Small, quiet, arboreal passerines with slender, decurved bills and stiff tails that they use as a prop when climbing, like that of the woodpeckers. Treecreepers forage by creeping up vertical trunks and along the underside of branches, spiralling upwards in a series of jerks in search of insects and spiders; on reaching the top of a tree, they fly to the base of the next one. Their flight is undulating and weak, and is usually only over short distances. Treecreepers are non-gregarious, but outside the nesting season they usually join hunting parties of other insectivorous birds.

WRENS Troglodytidae (1 species)

Very small birds, often with their characteristically short tails cocked over their backs. They have an energetic nature and loud assertive songs, out of proportion to their body size. Eurasian Wren *Troglodytes troglodytes* is the only species occurring in the region.

SPOTTED ELACHURA Elachuridae (1 species)

Spotted Elachura *Elachura formosa* is the only member of this family and closely resembles the wren-babblers in appearance and habitat. It frequents dense undergrowth in broadleaved evergreen temperate and semi-tropical forests, where it prefers densely vegetated, steep-sided gullies.

DIPPERS Cinclidae (2 species)

Aquatic passerines that spend all their lives along fast-flowing streams. Unique among songbirds, dippers dive underwater and walk along the submerged streambed with long, strong legs and feet in search of aquatic invertebrates that cling to rocks. Adaptations for their aquatic lives include thick, uniform feathering and a large oil gland for waterproofing. Two species occur in the region: White-throated *Cinclus cinclus* and Brown Dippers *C. pallasii.*

STARLINGS AND MYNAS Sturnidae (24 species)

Robust, medium-sized passerines with strong legs and bills, moderately long wings and square tails. The flight is direct, strong and fast in the more pointed-wing species (*Sturnus*) and rather slower with more deliberate flapping in the more rounded-winged ones. Most species walk with upright stance in a characteristic, purposeful, jaunty fashion, broken by occasional short runs and hops. Their calls are often loud, harsh and grating, and the song of many species is a variety of whistles; mimicry is common. Most are highly gregarious at times. Some starlings are mainly arboreal and feed on fruits and insects; others are chiefly ground-feeders and are omnivorous. Many are closely associated with human cultivation and habitation.

THRUSHES Turdidae (38 species)

Includes *Turdus, Zoothera* and *Geokichla* thrushes, these are medium-sized passerines with rather long, strong legs, slender bills and fairly long wings. On the ground they progress by hopping. All are insectivorous, but many eat fruit as well. Some are chiefly terrestrial and others arboreal. Most thrushes have loud and varied songs, which are used to proclaim and defend their territories when breeding. Many species gather in flocks outside the breeding season. Also includes the cochoas, which are fairly large, robust, colourful birds with fairly broad bills. Shy, unobtrusive, arboreal and frugivorous. Taxonomic work has now assigned some genera to Muscicapidae.

CHATS AND OLD WORLD FLYCATCHERS Muscicapidae (108 species)

Chats are a diverse group of small/medium-sized passerines that includes the chats, blue robins, magpie robins, redstarts, forktails, wheatears and rock thrushes. Most are terrestrial or partly terrestrial, some are arboreal, and some are closely associated with water. Their main diet is insects, but they also consume fruits, especially berries. They forage mainly by hopping about on the ground in search of prey, or by perching on a low vantage point and then dropping to the ground onto insects or making short sallies to catch them in the air. Found singly or in pairs.

Flycatchers are small insectivorous birds with small, flattened bills, and bristles at the gape that help capture flying insects. They normally have a very upright stance when perched. Many species frequently flick the tail and hold the wings slightly drooped. Generally, flycatchers frequent trees and bushes. Some species regularly perch on a vantage point, from which they catch insects in mid-air in short aerial sallies or by dropping to the ground, often returning to the same perch. Other species capture insects while flitting among the branches or by picking them from foliage. Flycatchers are usually found singly or in pairs; a few join mixed hunting parties of other insectivorous birds.

WAXWINGS Bombycillidae (1 species)

Only one species occurs in the region, Bohemian Waxwing *Bombycilla garrulus*, which is a vagrant. A medium-sized passerine with a prominent crest and short tail. Feeds on fruit year-round.

HYPOCOLIUS Hypocoliidae (1 species)

Hypocolius *Hypocolius ampelinus* is the only member of this family. It is a slim, long-tailed bird with strong and direct flight. Frugivorous all year, it forages chiefly by hopping and clambering about in trees and bushes. Quiet and shy.

FLOWERPECKERS Dicaeidae (11 species)

Flowerpeckers are very small passerines with short bills and tails, and tongues adapted for nectar-feeding. They usually frequent the tree canopy and feed mainly on soft fruits, berries and nectar; also on small insects and spiders. Flowerpeckers are very active, continually flying about restlessly. Normally they live singly or in pairs; some species form small parties in the non-breeding season.

SUNBIRDS AND SPIDERHUNTERS Nectariniidae (15 species)

Sunbirds have bills and tongues adapted to feed on nectar; they also eat small insects and spiders. The bill is long, thin and curved for probing the corollas of flowers. The tongue is very long, tubular and extensible far beyond the bill, and is used to draw out nectar. Sunbirds feed mainly at the blossoms of flowering trees and shrubs. They flit and dart actively from flower to flower, clambering over the blossoms, often hovering momentarily in front of them, and clinging acrobatically to twigs. Sunbirds usually keep singly or in pairs, although several may congregate in flowering trees, and some species join mixed foraging flocks. They have sharp, metallic calls and high-pitched trilling and twittering songs.

Spiderhunters are small, robust arboreal forest birds with very long decurved bills. Very active with fast dashing flight. Usually found singly or in pairs. They feed on nectar and small invertebrates.

FAIRY BLUEBIRDS Irenidae (1 species)

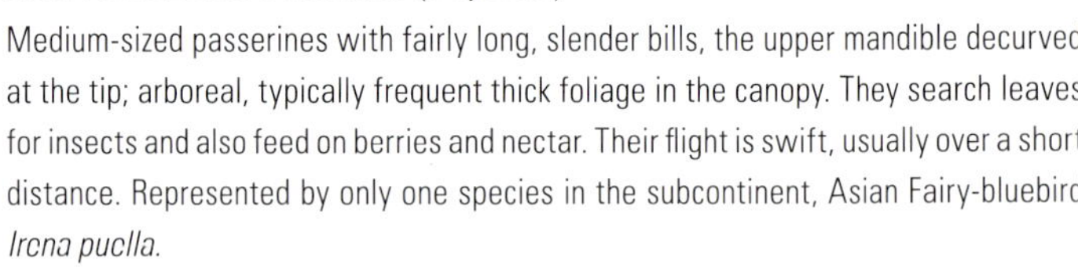

Medium-sized passerines with fairly long, slender bills, the upper mandible decurved at the tip; arboreal, typically frequent thick foliage in the canopy. They search leaves for insects and also feed on berries and nectar. Their flight is swift, usually over a short distance. Represented by only one species in the subcontinent, Asian Fairy-bluebird *Irena puella*.

LEAFBIRDS Chloropseidae (4 species)

Medium-sized green-and-yellow birds with slender downcurved bills. They are arboreal and feed on nectar from flowering trees, fruit, and invertebrates.

WEAVERS Ploceidae (4 species)

Small, rather plump, passerines with large conical bills. Adults feed chiefly on seeds and grain, supplemented by invertebrates. Weavers inhabit grassland, marshes, cultivation and very open woodland. They are highly gregarious, roosting and nesting communally, and are noted for weaving their elaborate roofed nests from grasses.

MUNIAS Estrildidae (10 species)

Small, slim passerines with short, stout conical bills. They feed chiefly on small seeds which they pick from the ground or gather by clinging to stems and pulling the seeds directly from seed heads. Outside the breeding season all species are gregarious. Flight is fast and undulating.

ACCENTORS Prunellidae (8 species)

Small, compact birds resembling *Passer* sparrows in appearance, but with slenderer and more pointed bills. Accentors forage quietly and unobtrusively on the ground, moving by hopping or a shuffling walk; some species also run. In summer accentors are chiefly insectivorous, and in winter they feed mainly on seeds. Their flight is usually low over the ground and sustained over only short distances.

OLD WORLD SPARROWS Passeridae (13 species)

Small passerines with thick, conical bills. This family includes *Passer*, the true sparrows, some of which are closely associated with human habitation. Most species feed on seeds taken on or near the ground. *Passer* sparrows are rather noisy, using a variety of harsh, chirping notes.

PIPITS AND WAGTAILS Motacillidae (21 species)

Small, slender, terrestrial birds with long legs, relatively long toes and thin, pointed bills. Some wagtails exhibit wide geographical plumage variation. All walk with a deliberate gait and run rapidly. The flight is undulating and strong. Most wagtails wag their long tail up and down, as so do some pipits. They feed mainly by picking insects from the ground as they walk along, or by making short rapid runs to capture insects they have flushed; they also catch prey in mid-air. Occur in scattered flocks in autumn and winter.

FINCHES Fringillidae (49 species)

Small to medium-sized passerines with strong, conical bills used for eating insects. They forage on the ground, some species also feed on seedheads of tall herbs, and blossoms and berries of bushes and trees. Finches are highly gregarious outside the breeding season. Their flight is fast and undulating.

LONGSPURS Calcariidae (1 species)

Longspurs are small passerines of open country that move south from their northern breeding areas in winter. The only family member recorded in the subcontinent, Lapland Longspur *Calcarius lapponicus*, is a vagrant. It is a stocky, long-winged small bird, with a stout yellowish bill.

BUNTINGS Emberizidae (21 species)

Small to medium-sized, terrestrial passerines with strong, conical bills designed for shelling seeds, usually of grasses. They forage by hopping or creeping on the ground. Their flight is undulating. Buntings are usually gregarious outside the breeding season, feeding and roosting in flocks and occur in a wide variety of open habitats.

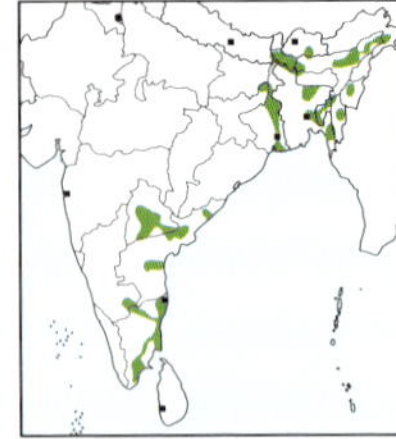

Fulvous Whistling Duck *Dendrocygna bicolor* 45–53cm

Resident. Mainly NE, SE India and Bangladesh. Vagrant: Pakistan, Nepal, Bhutan. **ID** Larger than Lesser Whistling Duck, with bigger, squarer head and larger bill. Adult from adult Lesser by warmer rufous-orange head and neck, dark blackish line down hindneck, dark striations on neck, more prominent white striping on flanks, indistinct chestnut-brown patch on forewing, and white band across uppertail-coverts. Often associates with Lesser. **Voice** Very noisy in flight and at rest; a repeated whistle *k-weeoo.* **HH** Keeps in small flocks, often with Lesser. Feeds chiefly at night by upending and dabbling. Roosts during day on undisturbed ground or waterbodies near its feeding grounds. Freshwater marshes, flooded paddyfields, and shallow lakes and ponds with emergent vegetation and partly submerged trees.

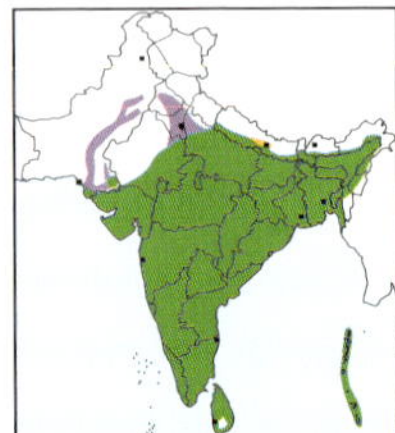

Lesser Whistling Duck *Dendrocygna javanica* 38–42cm

Widespread resident except most of NW. **ID** Smaller and more neatly proportioned than Fulvous. Like Fulvous, has weak, deep-flapping flight, appears very dark on the upperwing and underwing, and is very noisy with repeated whistling. From Fulvous by greyish-buff head and neck, dark brown crown, lack of or less prominent dark line down hindneck, indistinct or no white striping on flanks, bright chestnut patch on forewing, and chestnut uppertail-coverts. **Voice** Incessant wittering call in flight; at rest, a clear whistled *whi-whee,* also, a subdued quacking. **HH** Similar to Fulvous but more gregarious. Flooded grassland and paddyfields, freshwater marshes and shallow ponds and lakes, prefers those with emergent vegetation and partly submerged trees.

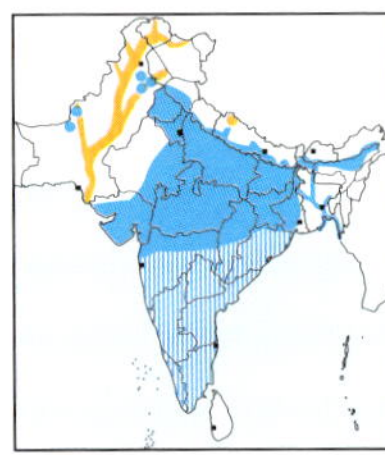

Greylag Goose *Anser anser* 76–89cm

Winter visitor. Mainly N subcontinent. Vagrant: Bhutan, Sri Lanka. **ID** Large, grey goose, with stout pink bill and pink legs and feet. Head and neck similar in coloration to rest of body. In flight shows pale grey forewing and underwing-coverts (wings above and below more uniformly dark in similar species). Juvenile is like adult, but has less prominent pale fringes to upperparts, flanks and belly. See Vagrants for differences from Tundra and Taiga Bean Goose. **Voice** Loud cackling and honking, deeper than in other 'grey' geese with repeated deep *aahng-ahng-ung.* **HH** Feeds mainly at night, chiefly by grazing in wet grassland and crops, also, by upending in shallow water. Spends daytime on large lakes or rivers or loafing on spits or in open fields. Continuously gabbles in flight and as it feeds.

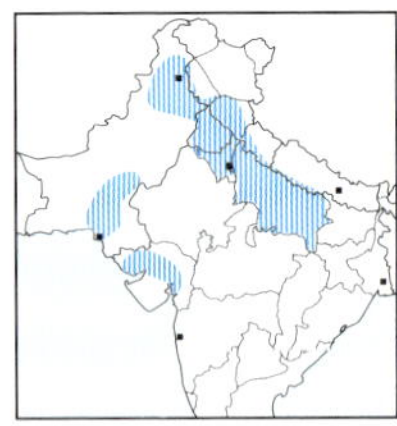

Greater White-fronted Goose *Anser albifrons* 66–86cm

Winter visitor. Pakistan and mainly N and NW India. Vagrant: Nepal, Bhutan, Bangladesh. **ID** Adult best told from Greylag by broad white band at front of head, browner coloration, black barring on belly, and orange legs and feet. Has more uniform upperwing and underwing in flight, darker back and rump and darker base to tail than Greylag. Juvenile lacks white frontal band and barring on belly; is more like Greylag, but best told by smaller size and less stocky build, browner coloration, darker feathering at base of bill, dark tip (nail) to bill, and orange legs and feet. **Voice** Cackling and honking flight call is higher pitched than Taiga and Tundra Bean Goose (see Appendix) and contains distinctive musical *lyo-lyok* phrase. **HH** Habits like Greylag's. Large rivers and lakes.

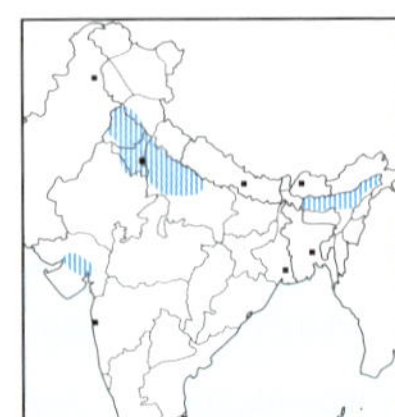

Lesser White-fronted Goose *Anser erythropus* 53–66cm

Winter visitor. NW India and Assam. Vagrant: Pakistan, Bangladesh. **ID** Adult from Greater by white frontal band on head extending as point at front of crown, and yellow eye-ring. Has slightly darker head and neck, and less extensive black barring on belly. Also, 'squarer' head, with more steeply rising forehead, and is smaller and more compact, with stout triangular bill. Juvenile lacks white frontal band and black barring on belly, and is best distinguished from juvenile Greater by yellow eye-ring, slightly darker head and neck, white nail to bill, and structural differences described above. **Voice** Call is like Greater but higher pitched; includes repeated *kyu-yu-yu* phrase. **HH** Similar to Greylag's. Globally threatened.

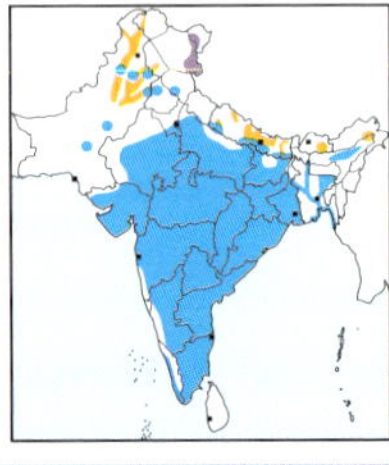

Bar-headed Goose *Anser indicus* 71–76cm

Breeds in Ladakh; widespread winter visitor. **ID** Yellowish legs and black-tipped yellow bill. Adult has white head, variably stained yellow, with black banding across crown, and white line down grey neck. Juvenile has white face and dark grey crown and hindneck. Plumage paler steel-grey, with more uniform pale grey forewing, and stronger contrast with black flight feathers, compared to Greylag. **Voice** Honking flight call but notes more nasal and more slowly uttered compared to Greylag. **HH** Feeds mainly at night in cultivation or grassland on riverbanks; roosts by day on sandbanks of large rivers. Breeds on swampy ground by high-altitude lakes; winters near large rivers, lakes and reservoirs; also, coastal islands in the Sundarbans, Bangladesh.

ad
juv
Fulvous
Whistling Duck
ad
juv
Lesser
Whistling Duck
ad
juv
Greylag Goose
ad
ad
juv
Greater
White-fronted Goose
ad
ad
juv
Lesser
White-fronted Goose
ad
juv
ad
Bar-headed
Goose

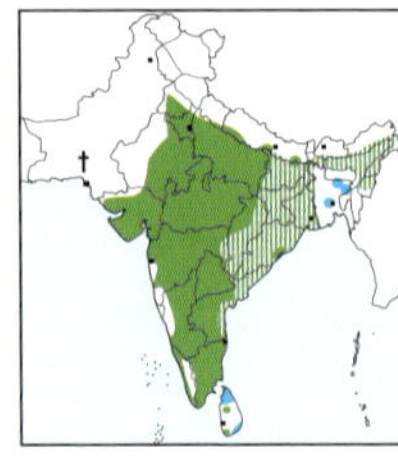

Knob-billed Duck *Sarkidiornis melanotos* 64–79cm

Resident. Widespread in India, also, Nepal lowlands and Bangladesh. **ID** Whitish head speckled with black, and whitish underparts with incomplete narrow breast-band. Upperwing and underwing blackish. Male has blackish upperparts glossed bronze, blue and green, with fleshy 'comb' at base of bill and yellowish-buff wash to sides of head and neck in summer; comb much reduced in winter. Female much smaller with duller upperparts and no comb. Juvenile has pale supercilium contrasting with dark crown and eye-stripe, buff scaling on upperparts, and rufous-buff underparts with dark scaling on sides of breast. **Voice** Generally silent, though sometimes gives low croak when flushed. **HH** Grazes in marshes and wet grassland, also, wades and dabbles in shallows. Lowland pools and lakes in well-wooded country.

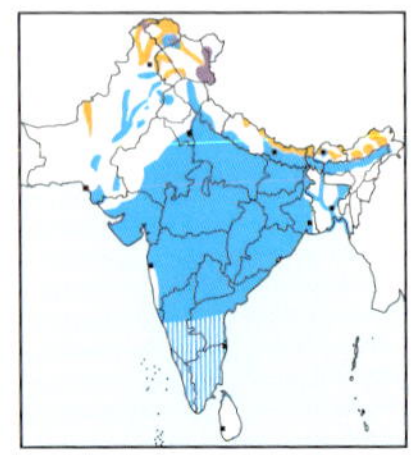

Ruddy Shelduck *Tadorna ferruginea* 50–67cm

Breeds in Himalayas; widespread winter visitor. Vagrant: Sri Lanka. **ID** Rusty-orange, with buff to orange head; white upperwing- and underwing-coverts contrast with black remiges in flight. Breeding male has black neck-collar, which is less distinct or absent in non-breeding plumage. Female very similar to male, but lacks neck-collar and often has diffuse whitish face patch. Juvenile as female, but has browner and duller upperparts and underparts, and greyish tone to head. **Voice** A honking *aakh* and trumpeted *pok-pok-pok-pok* when taking off. **HH** Usually feeds by grazing on banks of rivers and lakes; also, by wading in shallows, dabbling and upending. Breeds around high-altitude lakes and swamps; winters by large open lakes and rivers, especially with sandbanks and sandy islets.

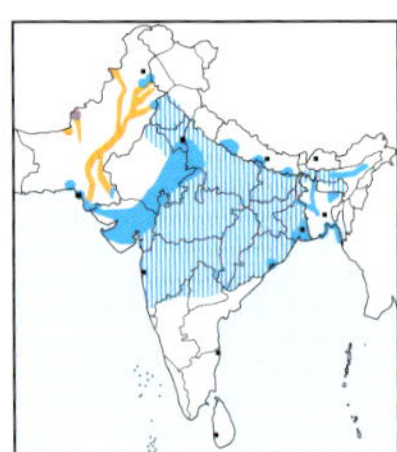

Common Shelduck *Tadorna tadorna* 58–67cm

Has bred Balochistan; widespread winter visitor and passage migrant. **ID** Adult has greenish-black head and neck, and largely white body with chestnut breast-band and black scapular stripe. White upperwing- and underwing-coverts contrast with black remiges in flight. Female slightly smaller than male, has narrower chestnut breast-band and lacks knob on bill. Adult eclipse duller and greyer, with less distinct breast-band. Juvenile lacks breast-band and has sooty-brown crown, hindneck and upperparts, and white forehead, cheeks, foreneck and underparts; legs greyish rather than pink. Flight pattern similar to adult (though less contrasting), but shows white trailing edge to secondaries. **Voice** Relatively silent. **HH** Feeds by walking on mud and dabbling at surface and wading in shallows and upending. Open freshwater lakes and rivers; also, coasts and salt lakes in Pakistan.

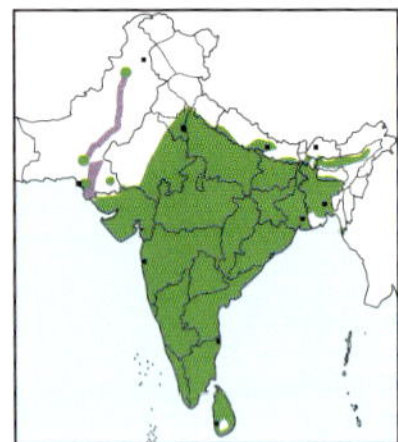

Cotton Pygmy Goose *Nettapus coromandelianus* 30–37cm

Widespread resident except the NW. Small size. **ID** Male has broad white band across wing, and female has white trailing edge to wing. Male has white head and neck, black cap, greenish-black upperparts, and black breast-band. Eclipse male, female and juvenile are duller and have dark stripe through eye. **Voice** Male utters sharp staccato cackle, *car-car-carawak* or *quack-quack-quacky-duck*. Female gives weak *quack*. **HH** Forages by dabbling and grazing among floating vegetation; picks food from surface and dips head and neck underwater. Vegetation-covered pools, irrigation tanks, channels and shallow lagoons.

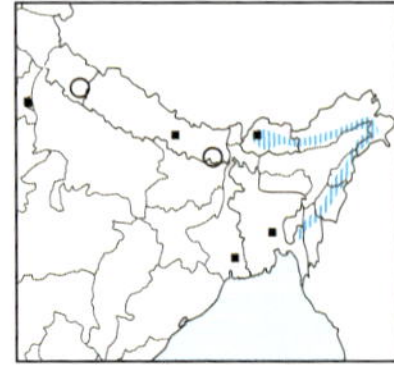

Mandarin Duck *Aix galericulata* 41–51cm

Very local winter visitor Bhutan and NE India. Vagrant: Nepal and Bangladesh Male is spectacular. Most striking features are reddish bill, orange 'mane' and 'sails', white stripe behind eye, and black-and-white stripes on side of breast. Female and eclipse male are mainly greyish with white 'spectacles' and white spotting on breast and flanks. In flight, shows dark upperwing and underwing, with narrow white trailing edge, and white belly. **Voice** Silent except during display. **HH** Forages by dabbling and head-dipping in shallow water. Perches readily in trees. Large rivers.

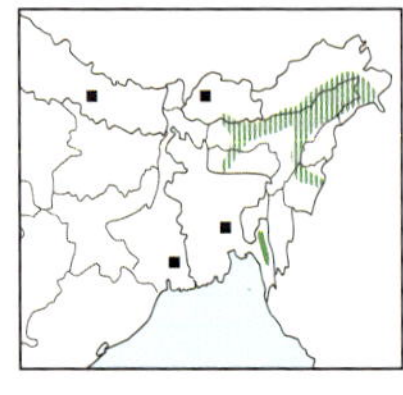

White-winged Duck *Asarcornis scutulata* 66–81cm

Resident. Bhutan, NE India and Bangladesh. **ID** Large size. White upperwing -coverts, and white head and neck variably speckled with black. Bill orange variably marked with black (can be mainly black). Eye strikingly orange. Sexes similar, but female duller with more heavily speckled head, and underparts more extensively rufous-brown. Juvenile like female, although duller and browner, with brownish head. **Voice** A prolonged, vibrant wailing honk in flight. **HH** Flies to feeding grounds at dawn; roosts in forest trees at night. Small stagnant and slow-flowing freshwater wetlands, often with dead trees, in tropical forest. Globally threatened.

♂
Ruddy Shelduck
♂
♂
♂
♀
♀
Knob-billed Duck
juv
juv
♂
Common Shelduck
♂
juv
♀
♀
♂
juv
♂ eclipse
♂
♀
Cotton
Pygmy Goose
♂
♀
♂
♂
White-winged
Duck
Mandarin Duck

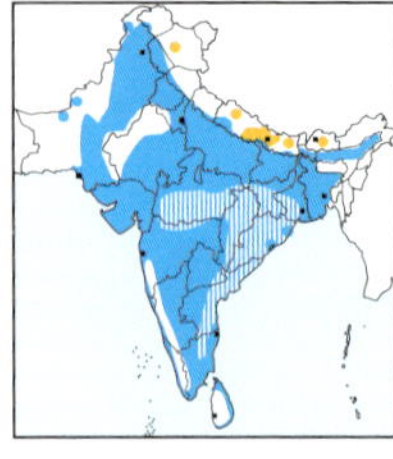

Green-winged Teal *Anas crecca* 34–38cm

Widespread winter visitor. **ID** Male has chestnut head with green band behind eye, white stripe along scapulars, and yellowish patch on undertail-coverts. Female has rather uniform head, lacking pale loral spot and dark cheek-bar of female Garganey, and has less prominent supercilium; further, bill often shows orange at base, and has prominent white streak at sides of undertail-coverts. Eclipse male much as female. In flight, both sexes have broad white band on greater coverts, and green speculum with narrow white trailing edge; forewing brown. **Voice** Male has distinctive soft, throaty whistle, *preep preep*. Female utters a sharp *quack* when flushed. **HH** During the day feeds by dabbling, head-dipping, upending and grazing on marshes, and forages in fields at night. Shallow inland freshwater and brackish wetlands. **AN** Common Teal.

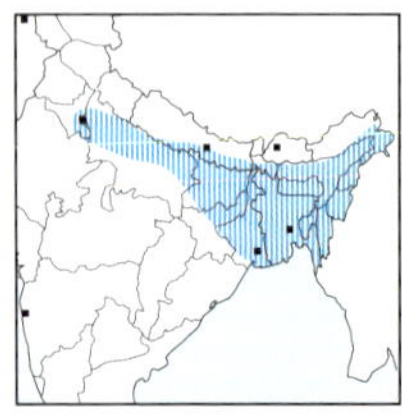

Baikal Teal *Sibirionetta formosa* 39–43cm

Winter visitor. N subcontinent. Vagrant: Pakistan, Nepal, Bhutan, Bangladesh. **ID** Male has white supercilium, striking dark green and yellow pattern to face, white vertical stripe on sides of breast, black undertail-coverts, and chestnut-edged scapulars. Female has complex (albeit variable) head pattern: typical birds show dark-bordered white loral spot, buff supercilium broken above eye by dark crown, and white throat which curves up to form half-moon-shaped cheek-stripe. Both sexes have grey forewing, narrow chestnut greater covert wing-bar, and broad white trailing edge to wing in flight (recalling Northern Pintail). Eclipse male is like female but more rufous and with less well-defined loral spot. **Voice** Chuckling *wot-wot-wot* by male. **HH** Large rivers and lakes. **TN** Formerly placed in *Anas*.

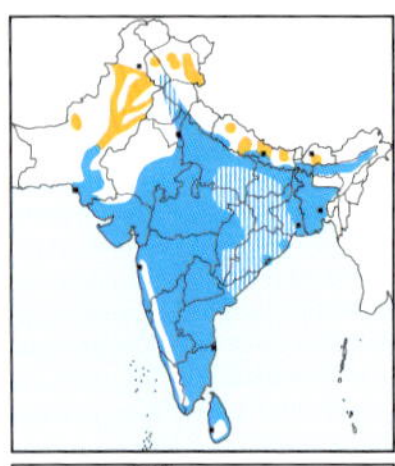

Garganey *Spatula querquedula* 37–41cm

Widespread winter visitor. **ID** Male has white stripe behind eye, and brown breast contrasting with grey flanks; shows blue-grey forewing in flight. Female has more patterned head than female Green-winged Teal, with pale supercilium, whitish loral spot, pale line below dark eye-stripe, dark cheek-bar, and whiter throat; in flight shows prominent white belly, grey forewing and broad white trailing edge to wing. Eclipse male is like female but has upperwing pattern of breeding male. **Voice** Male has dry cackling call if alarmed; female has Green-winged Teal-like quack. **HH** Usually keeps among emergent vegetation. Freshwater wetlands; also, coastal lagoons. **TN** Formerly placed in *Anas*.

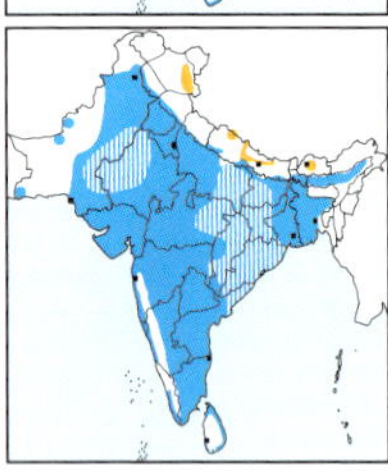

Northern Shoveler *Spatula clypeata* 44–52cm

Widespread winter visitor. **ID** Long spatulate bill and bluish forewing. Male has dark green head, white breast, chestnut flanks and blue forewing. Female recalls female Mallard in plumage, but has greyish-blue forewing and lacks white trailing edge. Eclipse male recalls female, but is more rufous-brown, especially on flanks and belly, and has upperwing pattern of breeding male. Immature male resembles breeding male, but has black scaling on breast and flanks and whitish facial crescent between bill and eye. **Voice** Usually silent. **HH** Often feeds by sweeping the bill from side to side while swimming. All types of shallow fresh waters. **TN** Formerly placed in *Anas*

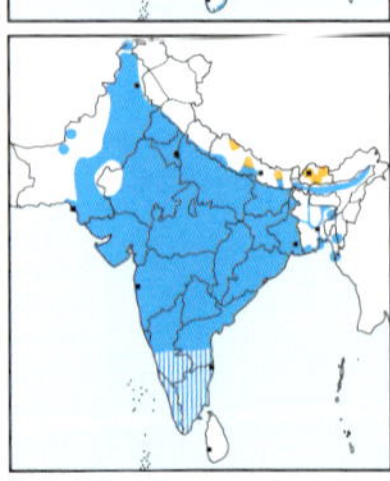

Gadwall *Mareca strepera* 46–58cm

Widespread winter visitor. Vagrant: Sri Lanka. **ID** White patch on inner secondaries in all plumages (can be indistinct in female); lacking metallic speculum shown by Mallard. Male is mainly grey, with white belly and black rear end; bill is dark grey. Female like female Mallard; orange sides to dark bill, clear-cut white belly and white inner secondaries are best features. Eclipse male is similar to female but has more uniform grey upperparts and upperwing pattern of breeding male. **Voice** Usually silent. **HH** Feeds mainly by dipping head into shallow water; sometimes also by upending. Keeps close to emergent vegetation. Freshwater marshes and lakes with extensive aquatic and emergent vegetation. **TN** Formerly placed in *Anas*.

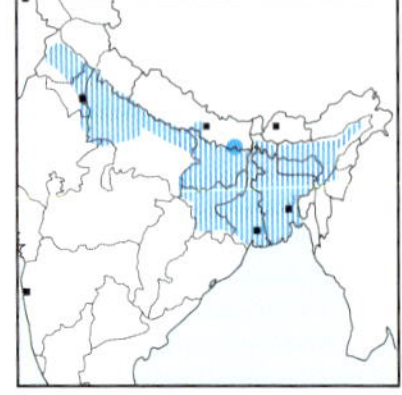

Falcated Duck *Mareca falcata* 46–54cm

Winter visitor. N subcontinent. Vagrant: Pakistan, Bhutan. **ID** Male has bottle-green head with maned hindneck, white throat, elongated black-and-grey tertials, and black-bordered yellow patch at sides of vent; shows pale grey forewing in flight. Female has rather plain greyish head (with maned appearance), a dark bill, and variable greyish-white fringes to tertials; shows greyish forewing and white greater covert bar in flight (a useful feature when visible at rest); does not show white secondary patch and whitish belly of Gadwall. Eclipse male is like female, but has darker upperparts and paler grey forewing. **Voice** Distinctive loud, piercing whistle in flight; utters a chuckling note like that of male Mallard while swimming. **HH** Feeds mainly by dabbling and upending; usually keeps close to emergent vegetation. Lakes and large rivers. **TN** Formerly placed in *Anas*.

♀
♂
Green-winged Teal
♂
♀
♂
♀
♀
Baikal Teal
♀
♂
♂
♀
♂
♀
♂
♀
♂
Northern Shoveler
♀
Garganey
♀
♀
♂
♂
♂
♀
Gadwall
♂
♀
♀
Falcated Duck

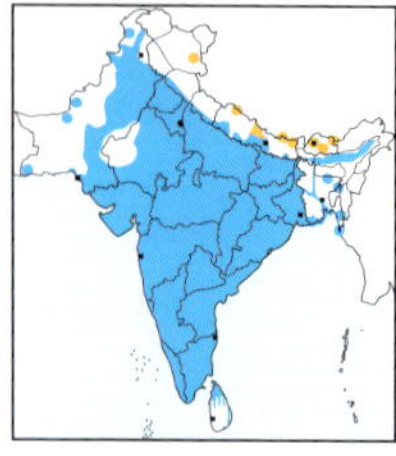

Eurasian Wigeon ***Mareca penelope*** 45–51cm

Widespread winter visitor. **ID** Male has yellow forehead and forecrown, chestnut head, and pinkish breast; shows white forewing in flight. Female has rather uniform brownish head, breast and flanks. In all plumages, shows white belly and rather pointed tail in flight. Eclipse male is like female, but is more rufous on head and breast, and has white forewing. **Voice** Male has distinctive whistled *wheeooo* call and female a low growled *krrr.* **HH** Highly gregarious. Feeds chiefly by grazing on waterside grasslands and in wet paddyfields, grazes more than other ducks; also, feeds by dabbling at surface and by upending. Open lakes, reservoirs, rivers, pools, marshes, tidal creeks and saltmarshes. **TN** Formerly placed in *Anas.*

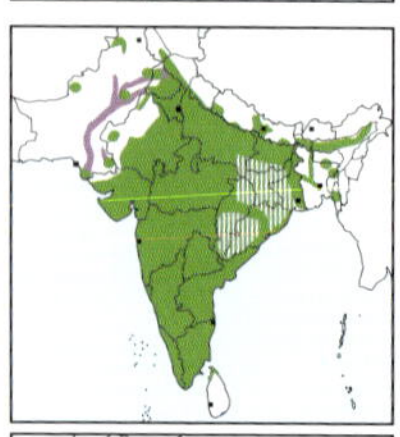

Indian Spot-billed Duck ***Anas poecilorhyncha*** 58–63cm

Widespread resident. Vagrant: Bhutan. **ID** Has yellow-tipped black bill, greyish-white head and neck with black crown and eye-stripe, blackish spotting on breast, white scalloping on flanks, and largely white tertials. In flight, wings appear dark except for white on tertials and white underwing-coverts. Male has prominent red loral spot and is more strongly marked than female and juvenile (the red loral spot is less conspicuous on female and lacking on juvenile). **Voice** As Mallard. **HH** Feeds by dabbling, head-dipping, upending, and walking among marsh vegetation. Freshwater marshes, lakes, irrigation tanks, and pools with extensive emergent vegetation.

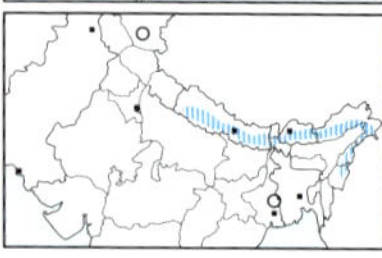

Eastern Spot-billed Duck ***Anas zonorhyncha*** 58–63cm

Visitor to N India, Bhutan and Nepal. Has yellow tip to bill like Indian Spot-billed. From Indian by lack of red loral spot, diffusely marked breast, more uniform sooty-black upperparts and flanks, blue (rather than green) speculum, dark grey tertials (with whitish fringes), and dusky bar across cheeks. Sexes similar. **Voice** At least some calls like Mallard's. **HH** Similar to Indian Spot-billed's.

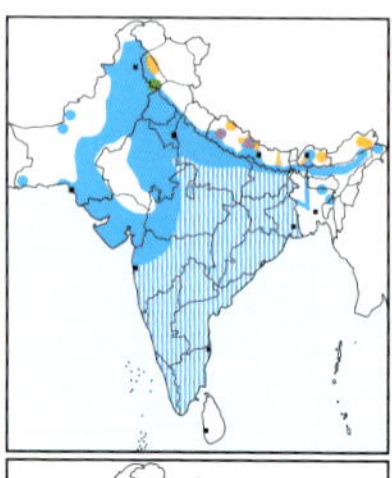

Mallard ***Anas platyrhynchos*** 50–65cm

Breeds in Himalayas; widespread winter visitor. In all plumages, has white-bordered purplish speculum. Male has yellow bill, dark green head and purplish-chestnut breast, mainly grey body, and black rear end. Female is pale brown and boldly patterned with dark brown. Bill variable, patterned mainly in dull orange and dark brown. Eclipse male is like female, but with (less heavily marked) rusty-brown breast, blackish (glossed green) crown and eye-stripe, and uniform olive-yellow bill. **Voice** Male has soft, rasping *kreep*, and female a distinctive, laughing *quack-quack-quack-quack*. **HH** Feeds by dabbling, head-dipping, grazing and upending. Freshwater marshes, reed-edged lakes.

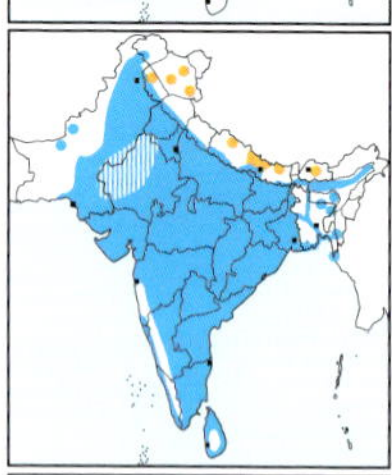

Northern Pintail ***Anas acuta*** 50–56cm

Widespread winter visitor. **ID** Long neck and pointed tail. Male has chocolate-brown head, with white stripe down sides of neck. Female has comparatively uniform buffish head, slender grey bill, and (as male) shows white trailing edge to secondaries and greyish underwing in flight. Eclipse male resembles female, but has grey tertials, and bill pattern and upperwing pattern as breeding male. **Voice** Male gives a mellow *prop prop*; female a descending series of weak quacks and a low croak when flushed. **HH** Forages at night in marshes and flooded paddyfields; roost by day on open waters with aquatic vegetation, freshwater marshes, brackish lagoons, and estuaries.

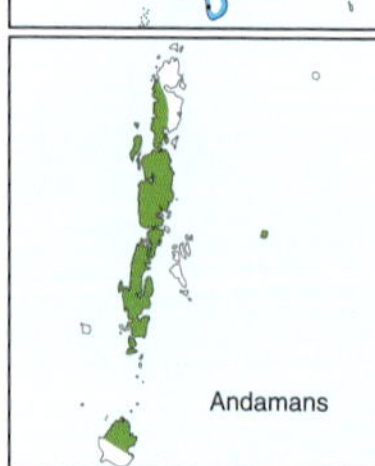

Andaman Teal ***Anas albogularis*** 37–47cm

Resident. Andaman and Nicobar Islands. **ID** Compared with other teal species, has comparatively large head and slim neck; male has pronounced forehead. Brown, with variable white markings on head, and spotted underparts. Bill bluish. Typically has white throat and eye-patch, but occasionally head and neck are largely white, and juvenile has more uniform head, with whitish eye-ring and only slightly paler throat. In flight, shows white axillaries and broad white band across greater coverts. **Voice** Calls poorly known. Said to include a low soft whistle and low quacking. **HH** Freshwater pools and marshes; tidal creeks and paddyfields. **TN** Previously considered conspecific with Sunda Teal *Anas gibberifrons.*

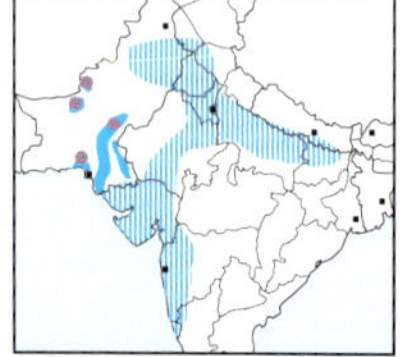

Marbled Duck ***Marmaronetta angustirostris*** 39–45.6cm

Breeds in Pakistan; winter visitor to N and NW India. **ID** Adult is pale sandy-brown with shaggy hood, dusky grey mask through eye, and diffuse buffish spotting on upperparts and underparts. In flight, has whitish underwing, rather uniform upperwing with pale brown coverts and greyish flight feathers, and pale leading edge to carpal. Juvenile similar to adult, but is more diffusely spotted and lacks shaggy hood. **Voice** Silent except during display. **HH** Feeds mainly by dabbling in shallow water; shy and secretive. Shallow freshwater lakes and ponds with extensive emergent vegetation. **AN** Marbled Teal.

♀
♂
Eurasian Wigeon
♀
♂
♂
Indian
Spot-billed Duck
♂
♀
♂
♂
Eastern
Spot-billed Duck
♂
♀
Mallard
♂
♀
Andaman Teal
♀
♂
♂
♀
♂
Northern Pintail
♂
♀
ad
Marbled Duck

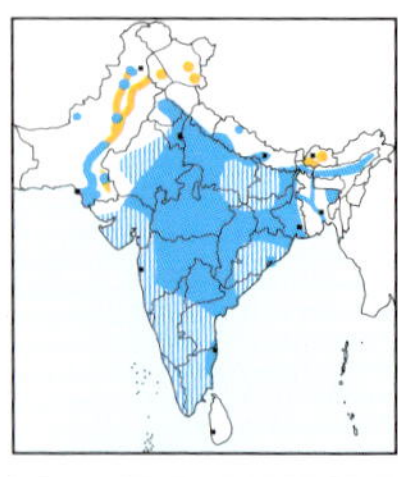

Red-crested Pochard *Netta rufina* 53–57cm

Widespread winter visitor; unrecorded in Sri Lanka. **ID** Large, with square-shaped head. Shape at rest and in flight more like a dabbling duck. Male has red bill, rusty-orange head, and white flanks which contrast with black breast and ventral region. Female has pale cheeks contrasting with brown cap, and dark bill with pink towards tip. Both sexes have largely white flight feathers on upperwing, and whitish underwing. Eclipse male very similar to female, but with reddish iris and bill. **Voice** Silent away from breeding grounds. **HH** Feeds chiefly by diving; occasionally by upending and head-dipping. Large lakes with fairly deep open water and plentiful submerged and fringing vegetation; occasionally rivers.

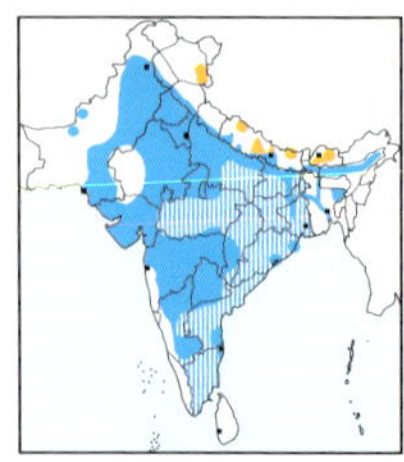

Common Pochard *Aythya ferina* 42–49cm

Widespread winter visitor; unrecorded in Sri Lanka. **ID** Large, with domed head. Pale grey flight feathers and grey forewing result in different upperwing pattern from other *Aythya* ducks. Male has chestnut head, black breast, and grey upperparts and flanks. Female has brownish head and breast contrasting with paler brownish-grey upperparts and flanks; usually shows indistinct pale patch on lores, and pale throat and streak behind eye. Eye of female is dark and bill has grey central band. Does not show white undertail-coverts of Ferruginous Duck. Eclipse male and immature male recall breeding male but are duller with browner breast. **Voice** Silent away from breeding grounds. **HH** Highly gregarious. Feeds chiefly by diving in open water. Lakes, jheels and reservoirs with large areas of open water; occasionally rivers. Globally threatened.

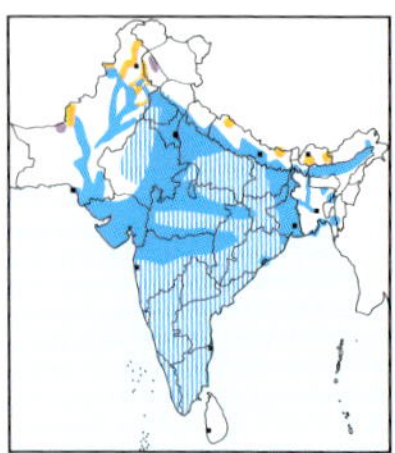

Ferruginous Duck *Aythya nyroca* 38–42cm

Breeds in Balochistan, Kashmir and Ladakh; widespread winter visitor. Smallest *Aythya* duck, with dome-shaped head. Breeding male is unmistakable, with rich chestnut head, neck and breast and white iris. Female is chestnut-brown on head, neck, breast and flanks, and has dark iris. Eclipse male resembles female, but is brighter on head and breast and has white iris. In flight, shows extensive white wing-bar extending further onto outer primaries than on other *Aythya* species; and striking white belly (less pronounced in female). **Voice** Silent away from breeding areas. **HH** Feeds chiefly by diving. Seeks refuge beyond the surf in coastal areas. Freshwater pools and irrigation tanks with extensive marginal and submerged vegetation; also, coastal lagoons. .

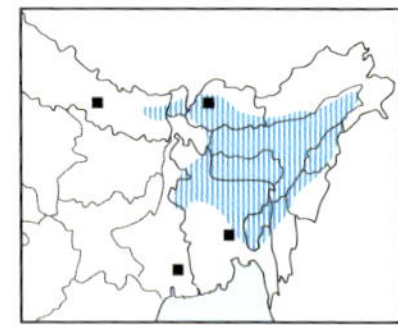

Baer's Pochard *Aythya baeri* 41–47cm

Winter visitor. Mainly NE India and Bangladesh. Vagrant: Pakistan, Bhutan. **ID** Greenish cast to dark head and neck, which contrast with chestnut-brown breast. White patch on fore flanks visible above water, and white undertail-coverts. Male has white iris. Female and immature male have duller head and breast than adult male. Female has dark iris and pale and diffuse chestnut-brown loral spot. **Voice** Silent away from breeding areas. **HH** Feeds mainly by diving. Shy, usually found in pairs or small parties. Large rivers and lakes. Globally threatened.

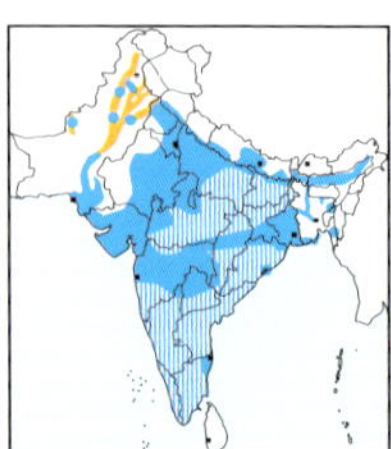

Tufted Duck *Aythya fuligula* 40–47cm

Widespread winter visitor. Vagrant: Sri Lanka. **ID** Breeding male is glossy black, with prominent crest and white flanks. Eclipse/immature males duller, with greyish flanks, and less pronounced crest. Female is dusky brown, with paler flanks; some may show scaup-like white face patch, but they usually also show tufted nape and squarer head. Female has yellow iris; dark in female Common and Baer's Pochards and Ferruginous Duck. **Voice** Silent way from breeding grounds. **HH** Gregarious. Feeds in the day mainly by diving; also, upends, dips head or picks items from surface. Lakes and reservoirs with large open areas and deep enough to permit diving.

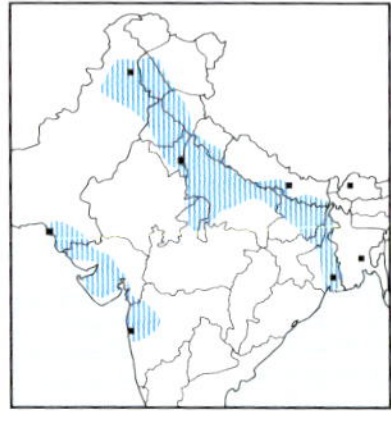

Greater Scaup *Aythya marila* 40–51cm

Winter visitor. N and NW subcontinent. Vagrant: Pakistan, Nepal, Bangladesh. **ID** Larger and stockier than Tufted Duck, with more rounded head and lacks any sign of crest. Bill is larger and wider, and has smaller black nail at tip than Tufted. Male has grey upperparts contrasting with black rear end and green gloss to blackish head. Female has broad white face patch, which is less extensive on juvenile/immature. Female usually has greyish-white vermiculations ('frosting') on upperparts and flanks. Eclipse/immature male has brownish-black head, neck and breast, and variable patch of grey on upperparts. **Voice** Silent except during display. **HH** Feeds mainly by diving, loafs in open water when not feeding. Large lakes and rivers.

♂
♀
♀
♂
Red-crested
Pochard
Common
Pochard
♂
♂
♂ imm
♀
♀
♂
♂
♂
♂ imm
♂
♀
Ferruginous Duck
♀
Baer's Pochard
♂
♀
♀
♂
Tufted Duck
Greater Scaup
♀
♀ imm
♀
♀
♂
♂
♂ imm
♂ imm

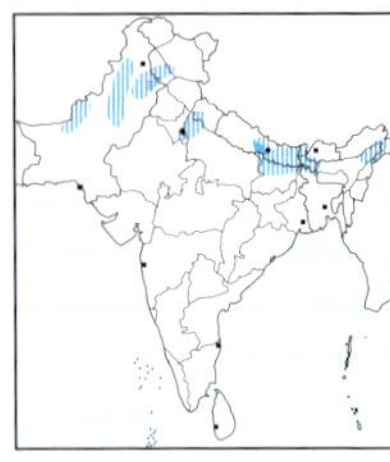

Common Goldeneye *Bucephala clangula* 40–51cm

Winter visitor. N subcontinent. Vagrant: Bangladesh, Bhutan. **ID** Stocky, with bulbous head. Male has dark green head, with large white patch on lores, and black-and-white patterned upperparts. Female has brown head, indistinct whitish collar, and grey body, with white wing patch usually visible at rest. Immature male resembles female but shows pale loral spot and has some white in scapulars. Eclipse male resembles female, but wing pattern as breeding male. In flight, both sexes show distinctive white pattern on wing. **Voice** Silent except during display. **HH** Swims with body flattened, and partially spreads wings when diving. Feeds mainly by diving in daytime, group members often submerging simultaneously; occasionally dabbles and upends. Open-water areas in freshwater lakes and large rivers.

Smew *Mergellus albellus* 35–44cm

Winter visitor. N subcontinent. Vagrant: Nepal, Bangladesh. **ID** A small, stocky 'sawbill' with square-shaped head. In flight, both sexes show dark upperwing with white wing-covert patch. Male is mainly white, with black face, crest-stripe, breast stripes and back. Flanks are grey. Female, and first-winter and eclipse male, have chestnut cap and white cheeks, and mainly dark grey body. **Voice** Generally silent. **HH** Feeds diurnally, mainly by diving; members of a flock typically submerge in unison or in quick succession. Freshwater lakes, rivers and Himalayan streams.

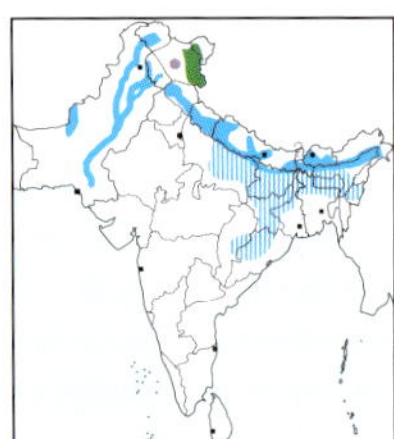

Common Merganser *Mergus merganser* 54–71cm

Breeds in Ladakh, Nepal? Winters mainly in N subcontinent. Vagrant: Bangladesh. **ID** Male has dark green head and whitish breast and flanks (with variable pink wash). Shows extensive white patch on wing-coverts and secondaries in flight. Female and eclipse/immature male have chestnut head and upper neck with shaggy crest, which contrasts with white throat and greyish neck, and show white secondaries in flight. Eclipse male has upperwing pattern like breeding male. **Voice** Silent except during display. **HH** Usually in small parties. Forages in daytime, often fishing cooperatively. Feeds mainly by diving, usually after scanning with head submerged. An expert swimmer and diver. Flight usually follows the watercourse. Lakes, rivers and streams; occasionally coastal waters in Pakistan. **AN** Goosander.

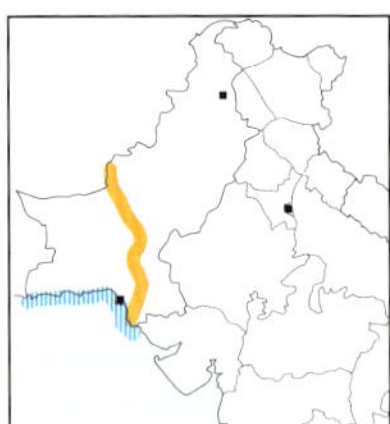

Red-breasted Merganser *Mergus serrator* 51–64cm

Winter visitor. Mainly Pakistan. Vagrant: India, Nepal, Bangladesh. **ID** Male has spiky crest, white collar, ginger breast, and grey flanks. Female and eclipse/immature male more closely resemble respective plumages of Common and are best told by slimmer appearance, with slimmer bill, and narrower head with weaker and more ragged crest. Chestnut of head and upper neck is duller and contrasts less with grey lower neck and breast, throat is only slightly paler, and has browner body. In flight, white wing patch is broken by black bar, unlike on Common. **Voice** Silent, except during display. **HH** Habits like Common Merganser's. Coastal waters in Pakistan; large rivers and lakes.

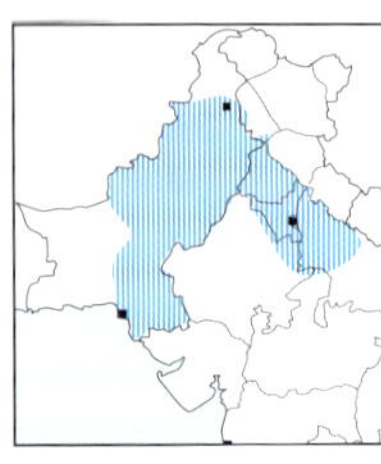

White-headed Duck *Oxyura leucocephala* 43–48cm

Winter visitor. Pakistan and N India. **ID** Swollen base to bill and pointed tail, which is often held erect. Breeding male has white head with black cap, and bright blue bill. Eclipse male has duller, less rufous body, grey bill, and black of cap more extensive and less clearly defined. Female and juvenile have grey bill, and striped head pattern (with dark cap, pale stripe below eye and dark stripe across cheeks). Immature male can have much black on head, which can even be all black. **Voice** Silent except during display. **HH** Very reluctant to fly; prefers to escape by diving or by swimming away while partially submerged. Large fresh waters, lakes and brackish lagoons with extensive submerged aquatic vegetation. Globally threatened.

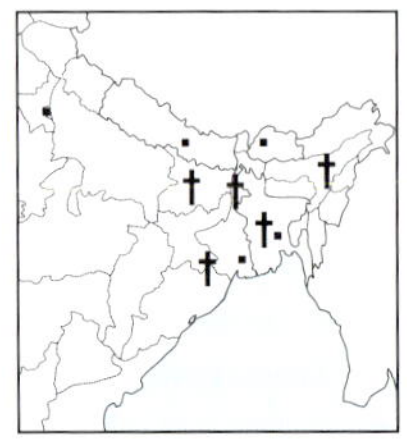

Pink-headed Duck *Rhodonessa caryophyllacea* 60cm

May be extinct. Mainly NE India. Nepal: one on passage collected in 19th century. Bangladesh: former rare resident. **ID** Long neck and body and triangular head. Male has combination of pink head and hindneck, and dark brown foreneck and body; bill pink. Female similar, but with paler, dull brown body, greyish-pink head, and brownish crown and hindneck. In flight, pale fawn secondaries, contrasting dark forewing, and pale pink underwing with dark body. **Voice** Male has a low weak whistle and female a low quack. **HH** Shy and secretive. Fed by dabbling on the water surface but could also dive; occasionally perched in trees. Secluded pools and marshes in elephant-grass jungle. Globally threatened.

♂
♀
♀
♂
Common Goldeneye
♂
♀
Smew
♂
♀
♂
♂
♀
♀
Red-breasted
Merganser
♂
Common
Merganser
♂
♀
♀
♀
♂
♂
Pink-headed Duck
♀
White-headed Duck

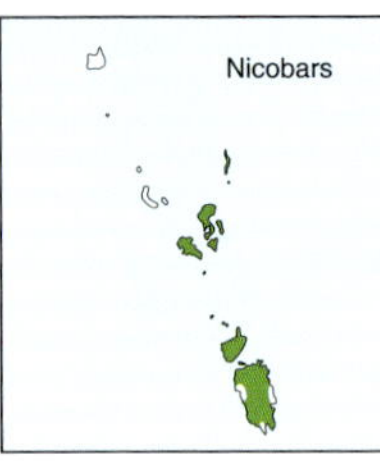

Nicobar Megapode *Megapodius nicobariensis* 37–43cm

Resident. Nicobars. **ID** Robust with very large legs and feet, and crested appearance. Chestnut-brown upperparts, cinnamon-brown to brownish-grey underparts, and bare red facial skin. Immature has bare facial skin restricted to lores and around eye. **Voice** Male's territorial call is *kyouououou-kyou-kou-koukoukoukoukou*, rising in pitch on the first note and gradually decreasing over the staccato series; contact call a cackling *kuk-a-kuk-kuk*. **HH** Partly nocturnal. Forages by scratching in leaf litter. Often run about calling noisily to each other. Forest undergrowth by sandy beaches. Globally threatened.

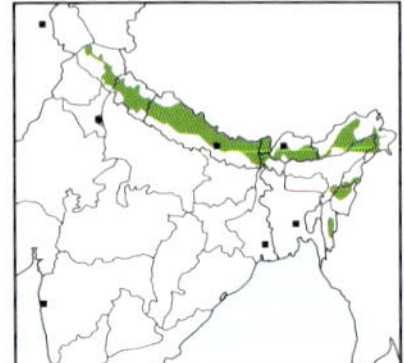

Hill Partridge *Arborophila torqueola* 28–30cm

Resident. Himalayas and NE India. **ID** Male from Rufous-throated Partridge by orange to chestnut crown and orange ear-coverts, black eye-patch and eye-stripe, white neck-sides heavily streaked with black, and white collar. Female has grey-brown crown and ear-coverts, lacks white collar of male and is easily confusable with Rufous-throated. From this species by buff supercilium (although it can be greyish-white and more like Rufous-throated), black barring on mantle (best definitive feature), and lacks black border between duller rufous-orange foreneck and grey breast. Legs and feet are duller orangish or pinkish-brown (more strikingly pink or reddish in Rufous-throated). **Voice** Smoothly rising and mournful *whoop* repeated. **HH** Keeps in thick cover. Digs for food among leaves and humus on the forest floor. Ravines and slopes in damp, dense broadleaved, evergreen forest.

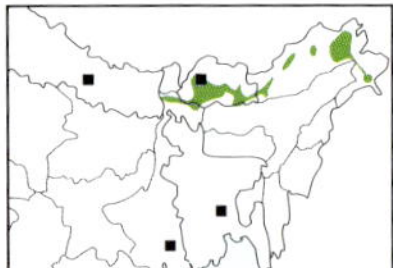

Chestnut-breasted Partridge *Arborophila mandellii* 28–30cm

Resident. Very local in E Himalayas. **ID** From other *Arborophila* by combination of greyish supercilium, white collar bordered below with black, black-spotted orange throat and sides of neck, and chestnut crown and breast. Sexes are similar. **Voice** Includes a series of fluty, long-drawn melancholy whistles ascending to a climax. **HH** Habits like White-cheeked. Dense undergrowth with bamboo in broadleaved evergreen forest.

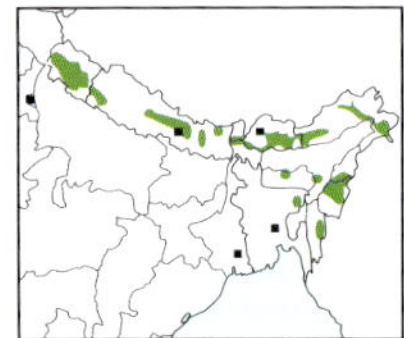

Rufous-throated Partridge *Arborophila rufogularis* 26–29cm

Resident. Himalayas, NE India and Bangladesh. **ID** Sexes similar unlike Hill Partridge, both with rufous-orange throat and neck with black streaking. Broad greyish-white supercilium and grey-brown crown, lack of orange cheek-patch, and lack of white collar, means separation from male Hill is straightforward. Best told from female Hill by broad greyish-white supercilium, diffuse white moustachial stripe, unbarred mantle, variable black border between rufous-orange foreneck and grey breast, and brighter pink or reddish legs and feet. *A. r. intermedia*, east and south of Brahmaputra River, has brighter orange foreneck, black throat, and lacks black border to breast. **Voice** Several well-spaced plaintive, drawn-out whistles leading into a varying series of repeated double notes, gradually increasing in pitch and volume, *whuu... whuu...whu-hu..whu-hu whu-hu..whu-hu*. **HH** Habits similar to Hill's. Dense understorey of moist broadleaved evergreen forest and second growth.

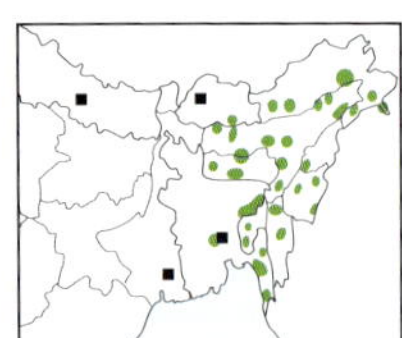

White-cheeked Partridge *Arborophila atrogularis* 25–28cm

Resident. E Himalayas, NE India, and Bangladesh. **ID** White supercilium and cheeks, black mask and throat, barred upperparts, black-streaked orange-yellow hindneck, and absence of rufous streaking on flanks. Sexes similar. **Voice** Accelerating and ascending series of 12–18 far-carrying, throaty *whew* notes, ending abruptly. **HH** Feeds in scattered groups. Flushes suddenly from almost underfoot. Bamboo thickets and undergrowth in less dense broadleaved forests than those inhabited by Hill and Rufous-throated.

ad
Nicobar Megapode
♂
♀
Hill Partridge
ad
Chestnut-breasted
Partridge
♀
♂ rufogularis
♂ intermedia
Rufous-throated
Partridge
ad
White-cheeked
Partridge

PLATE 8: PEAFOWLS AND SPURFOWLS

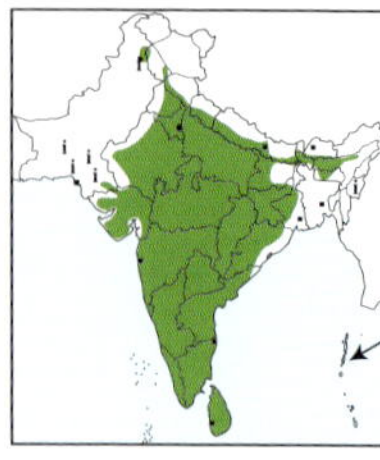

Indian Peafowl *Pavo cristatus* M 185–225cm, F 95cm

Resident. India, SE Pakistan, Nepal and Bhutan. **ID** Male has blue neck and breast, and spectacular glossy green train of elongated uppertail-covert feathers with numerous ocelli. Female lacks train; has whitish face and throat, bronze-green neck, brown upperparts and white belly. Primaries of female are brown (chestnut in male). First-year male is like female, but head and neck are usually blue, and primaries are chestnut with dark brown mottling. Second-year male has a short train, which lacks ocelli and is barred with green and brown. Length of train increases until fifth or sixth year. **Voice** Trumpeting, far-carrying and mournful *kee-ow, kee-ow, kee-ow*. Also, series of short, gasping screams, *ka-an... ka-an... ka-an*, repeated 6–8 times, and *kok-kok* and *cain-kok* when alarmed. **HH** Gregarious. Roosts in tall trees. Emerges from dense thickets in early mornings and afternoons to feed in forest clearings and fields at forest edges. Protected in parts of India for religious or cultural reasons where it has become very tame; quite shy and secretive where hunted. In the wild state inhabits dense riverine vegetation and undergrowth in sal forest, often near streams; where semi-feral found in villages and cultivation.

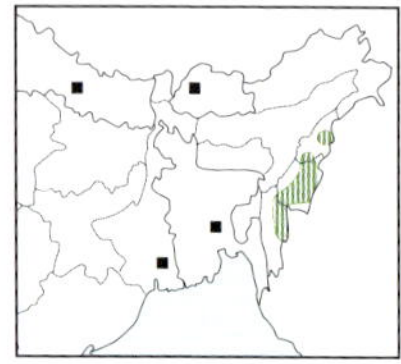

Green Peafowl *Pavo muticus* M 180–300cm, F 100–110cm

Former resident? NE India and Bangladesh. **ID** Male has erect tufted crest, and is mainly green, with long green train of elongated uppertail-covert feathers with numerous ocelli. Female lacks long train, otherwise like male, but upperparts are browner. Immature male resembles female; has long train, lacking ocelli, by second year **Voice** Male gives far-carrying, repeated *ki-wao* from roost site, less harsh and piercing than Indian's similar call. Female gives loud *aow-aa* with emphasis on first syllable, often repeated after short interval. **HH** Habits like Indian's, but extremely shy everywhere and generally does not emerge into forest clearings and edges. Dense forest near streams and clearings. Globally threatened.

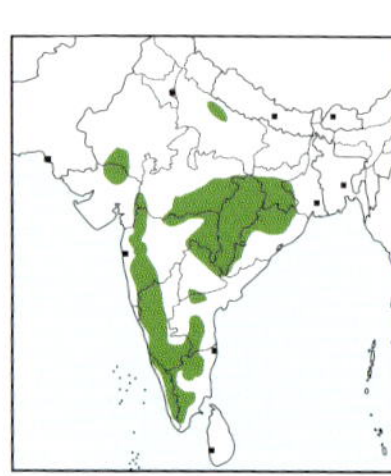

Red Spurfowl *Galloperdix spadicea* 35.5–38cm

Resident. India. **ID** Red facial skin and legs/feet. Male of nominate has brownish-grey head and neck and darker brown crown, rufous upperparts and underparts scaled with grey and buff, and brownish-black unbarred tail. Female of nominate has browner head and neck, buffish-brown upperparts with bold blackish markings, rufous underparts with irregular blackish barring, and buff barring on tail. Male *stewarti* of Kerala is deeper chestnut-red than nominate. Male *caurina* of Rajasthan and parts of Gujarat is paler and less rufous than nominate; female has paler, more rufous-brown upperparts, which lack bold black mottling of female nominate. **Voice** Male gives a crowing *k-r-r-r-kwek, kr-kr-kwek, kr-kr-kwek* repeated rapidly. Harsh, cackling *kuk-kuk-kuk-kukaak* in alarm. **HH** Very skulking and rarely flushed. When startled runs off rapidly, dashing from one thicket to another. Dense scrub, bamboo thickets and second growth.

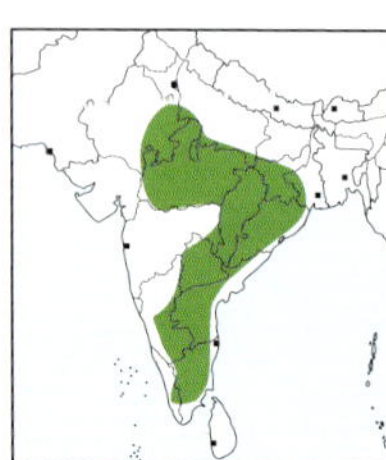

Painted Spurfowl *Galloperdix lunulata* 27–34cm

Resident. India. **ID** Dark bill and legs/feet. Male has greenish-black head and neck barred with white, chestnut-red upperparts and yellowish-buff underparts with spotting and barring. Female from female Red Spurfowl by dark olive-brown upperparts and breast (becoming paler brownish-buff on lower breast and belly); buff throat and malar stripe; chestnut forehead, supercilium and ear-coverts; absence of red facial skin, and dark legs and feet. **Voice** Fowl-like cackling; also a loud, rapidly repeated *chur, chur, chur.* **HH** If disturbed, sprints away clucking as it goes. If hard pressed will fly a few metres, then run again or hide among rocks. Very secretive. Dry stony foothills with dense thorn scrub or bamboo thickets.

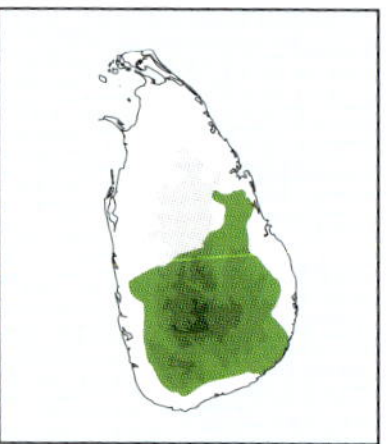

Sri Lanka Spurfowl *Galloperdix bicalcarata* 30–35.5cm

Resident. Sri Lanka. **ID** Red facial skin and legs/feet. Male is boldly streaked and spotted with white; back and rump are chestnut and tail black. Female has chestnut upperparts with blackish vermiculations, rufous underparts, dark brown crown and whitish chin and throat. **Voice** Song is a duet, male uttering a shrill *kik-kik-kik-kikeeyu* repeated about five times, followed by a repeated, very loud musical *yuhuhu-yuyu-yuyu...*, female interposing a softer, sharp, whistling *ki-ki-ki-ki-ki*, each series rising in pitch and volume, both sexes ending with yet another similar series, and replied to by other pairs in the neighbourhood. **HH** Very shy and secretive. Tall, undisturbed, dense forest.

Indian Peafowl
♀
♂
♂
♀
Green Peafowl
♂ spadicea
Red Spurfowl
♀ spadicea
♂ stewarti
♀
♂
♂
♀
Painted Spurfowl
Sri Lanka Spurfowl

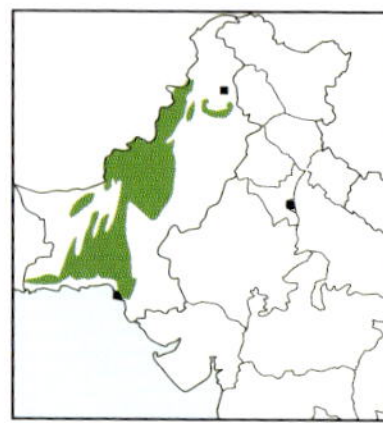

See-see Partridge ***Ammoperdix griseogularis*** 22–25cm

Resident. Pakistan. **ID** Lacks black throat gorget of Chukar. Bill orange and legs/feet yellowish. Shows rufous tail in flight. Male has white eye-stripe, black supercilium and chestnut-and-black flank stripes. Female rather plain with cream supercilium and throat, grey flecking on neck, diffuse flank striping, and pinkish-buff and grey vermiculations on mantle and breast. **Voice** Male gives far-carrying and repeated *wheet-div* or *hoe-it* from an exposed position, the first syllable possessing a whiplash quality. **HH** Active in early morning and at dusk. Very confiding where not hunted. Reluctant to fly when disturbed, escapes by rapid running and agile climbing. Dry rocky foothills with light scrub, sand dunes and edges of cultivation in narrow valleys.

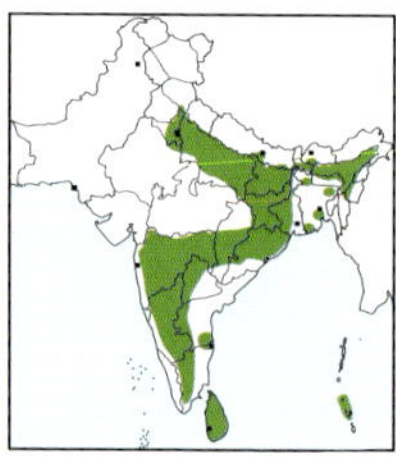

Blue-breasted Quail ***Synoicus chinensis*** 12–15cm

Widespread resident; unrecorded in north-west. **ID** Small size. Male has black-and-white patterned throat, slaty-blue flanks, and chestnut belly. Overall appearance is very dark with white on throat. Female like *Coturnix* quails but noticeably smaller, with rufous-buff forehead and supercilium, barred breast and flanks, and more uniform upperparts. **Voice** Typical call is a high-pitched series of two or three descending piping notes, *ti-yu* or *quee-kee-kew*. **HH** Habits like Common. Keeps in pairs or small family parties. Wet grassland, marshes, paddyfield edges and scrub. **AN** King Quail. **TN** Formerly placed in *Coturnix*.

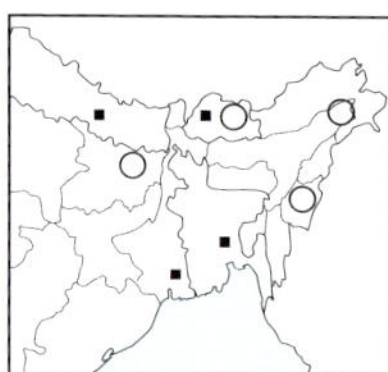

Japanese Quail ***Coturnix japonica*** 17–19cm

Winter visitor, probably breeds. Assam and Bhutan. **ID** Breeding male has rufous face and throat, with suggestion of dark anchor mark in some; pattern of throat in non-breeding male and female much as Common and probably indistinguishable in the field. In non-breeding plumage both sexes have pointed and elongated throat feathers, forming short 'beard'. **Voice** Best told from Common Quail by very different song: explosive, rasping, unmusical and often loud, barked *churck-chur-rr* repeated at c.10-second intervals. **HH** Habits like those of Common Quail. Crops and grassland.

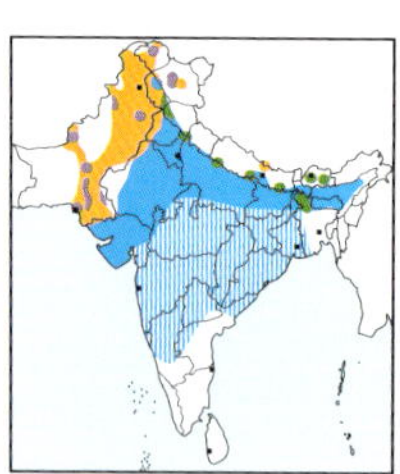

Common Quail ***Coturnix coturnix*** 16–20cm

Widespread but erratic winter visitor and passage migrant, mainly in north. **ID** Male has black 'anchor' mark on throat and buff gorget, although head pattern is variable and black anchor lacking in some. Some males have rufous face and throat, with or without black anchor (and are thus very similar to Japanese Quail). Female has less striking head pattern and lacks black anchor; probably indistinguishable from female Japanese. **Voice** Song is a far-carrying *whit, whit-tit* repeated in quick succession. **HH** Secretive. Usually occurs singly or in pairs. If flushed rises rapidly with whirring wingbeats and brief glides on down-turned wings, plunging into cover again. In breeding areas males sing persistently in early morning, evening, and sometimes during the day. Crops, paddy stubbles and grassland.

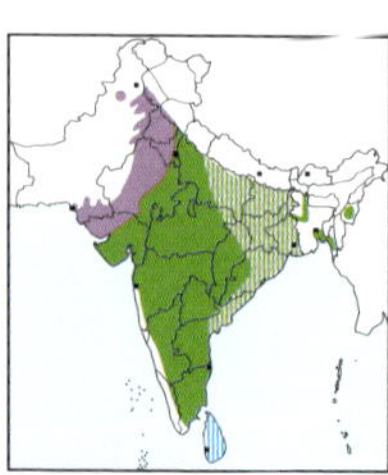

Rain Quail ***Coturnix coromandelica*** 16–18cm

Widespread resident, with some nomadic movement. Vagrant: Nepal, Bangladesh. **ID** Male similar in appearance to male Common, but has more strongly marked head pattern, variable black breast-patch and streaking on flanks, and cinnamon sides to neck and breast. Female smaller than female Japanese and Common; with unbarred primaries. **Voice** Utters a loud, metallic and high-pitched *whit-whit* repeated in runs of 3–5 calls. **HH** Habits like Common Quail. Sometimes in parties up to six birds. During breeding season in the monsoon can be heard frequently throughout the day. Crops, grassland, paddy stubbles, grass and scrub jungle.

♀
See-see Partridge
♂
♀
♂
Blue-breasted Quail
♀
♂
Japanese Quail
♀
♂
♀
Common Quail
♂
Rain Quail

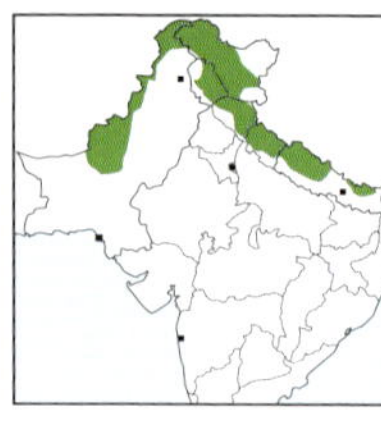

Chukar *Alectoris chukar* 34–38cm

Resident. Pakistan hills and Himalayas. **ID** A stocky, medium-sized partridge. Has black stripe through eye which extends to form black gorget, encircling creamy-white throat; broad chestnut and black rib-like bars on flanks, and bright red bill and legs. Displays rufous corners to tail in flight. Sexes similar, female lacking leg spurs. **Voice** Utters a rapidly repeated *chuck, chuck-aa*; when flushed, an anxious 'rolled together' *chuck, chuck, chuck*. **HH** If flushed the covey disperses, flying very fast and strongly, and in hilly regions flies downhill hugging the contours. Open, arid rocky hills, barren hillsides with scattered scrub, grassy slopes, dry terraced cultivation, and stony ravines near a water source. **AN** Chukar Partridge.

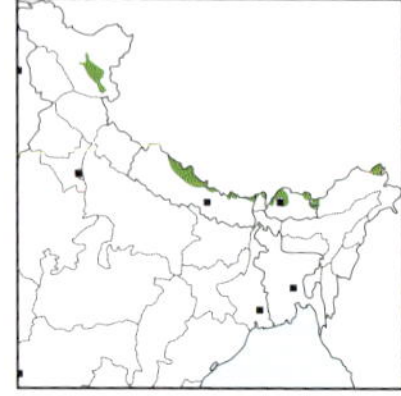

Tibetan Snowcock *Tetraogallus tibetanus* 50–56cm

Resident. Himalayas. **ID** From Himalayan Snowcock by prominent white patch on ear-coverts offset against grey of head and neck, double band of grey across upper breast (absent, or just a single band, on some birds), white underparts with broad black flank stripes, and more pronounced whitish fringes to coverts and scapulars. Bill strikingly pinkish or orange with variable patch of red facial skin behind eye. In flight, wing pattern is very different, Tibetan showing only a small amount of white in primaries but extensive white in secondaries. Also has chestnut coloration on rump and uppertail-coverts. **Voice** Similar to Himalayan's: a subdued chuckling becoming louder and reaching a climax, a whistle and a call reminiscent of Eurasian Curlew. **HH** Habits like Himalayan's. Alpine rocky slopes and ridges and alpine meadows.

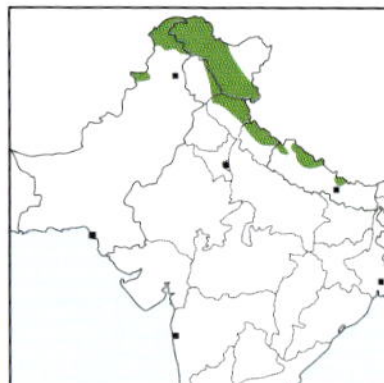

Himalayan Snowcock *Tetraogallus himalayensis* 55–74cm

Resident. Himalayas. **ID** Distinguished from Tibetan by dark chestnut stripes down sides of largely white neck which join to form band across upper breast, greyish-white breast (variably barred with black) contrasting with dark grey underparts; strong contrast between pale grey hindneck/upper-mantle and dark grey rest of upperparts. Bill grey with variable patch of yellowish facial skin around eye. In flight, Himalayan shows extensive white in primaries but little or none in secondaries, and greyish coloration on rump and uppertail-coverts. **Voice** Makes a far-carrying inflected whistle ending on two shorter, rising whistled notes, *cour-lee-whi-whi* repeated at intervals and reminiscent of Eurasian Curlew; also, a *chok, chok, chok* which often accelerates into a rapid chatter. **HH** Escapes by running uphill or, if pressed, by flying a long distance very fast downhill before settling. Alpine pastures near the snowline, bare stony ridges, and steep slopes.

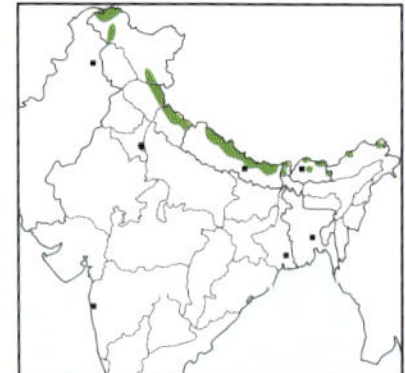

Snow Partridge *Lerwa lerwa* 30–40cm

Resident. Himalayas. **ID** Has head, neck, upper breast and upperparts finely vermiculated dark brown and white, with a chestnut wash. Underparts are heavily streaked with chestnut. Bill, legs and feet are red. Sexes are similar. Shows a narrow white trailing edge to wings in flight, blackish primaries and finely barred tail. **Voice** Male gives repeated whistle *jijiu, jijiu, jijiu* that increases in speed and pitch. **HH** Very tame where not hunted. When disturbed, plunges downhill with much wing clattering. Close to the snowline on steep rocky or grassy slopes interspersed with dwarf scrub.

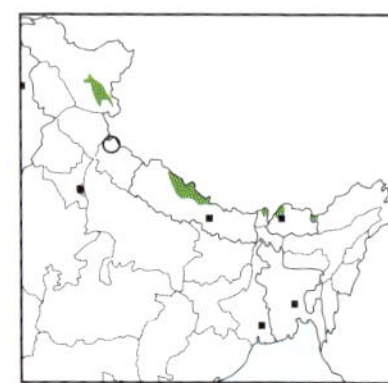

Tibetan Partridge *Perdix hodgsoniae* 28–31cm

Resident. N Himalayas. **ID** Has white supercilium, black patch on white face, rufous hindneck, and black-and-rufous barring on underparts (with variable black patch on belly). Shows rufous tail in flight. *P. h. caraganae* of the NW Himalayas has paler rufous-orange collar and is paler overall compared to the nominate subspecies. **Voice** Male gives rattling and repeated *scherrrrreck-scherrrrreck* from a large rock; when flushed a shrill *chee, chee, chee, chee*. **HH** When disturbed runs fast uphill, calling loudly, if pressed scatters in different directions and dives downhill. Trans-Himalayan semi-desert and rocky slopes with scattered dwarf scrub.

Chukar
Tibetan Snowcock
Himalayan Snowcock
Snow Partridge
Tibetan Partridge

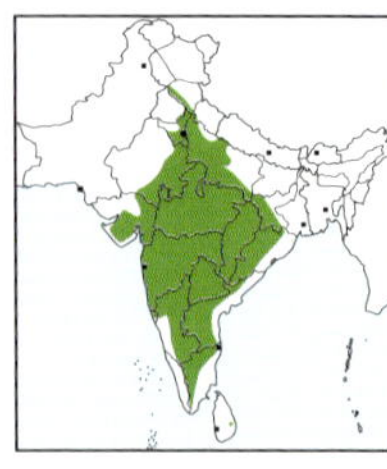

Jungle Bush Quail *Perdicula asiatica* 15–18cm

Widespread resident; unrecorded in NW and NE subcontinent. **ID** Male has strongly barred underparts, rufous-orange throat and supercilium (latter edged broadly above and narrowly below with white), variable white moustachial stripe (some with rufous-orange centre), well-defined brown ear-coverts, and orange-buff vent. Female has unbarred vinaceous-buff underparts, with head pattern like male. **Voice** A harsh grating *chee-chee-chuck, chee-chee-chuck*; also, soft musical whistling *whi-whi-whi-whi-whi-whi* after covey has scattered. **HH** Found in coveys of up to 20 birds outside the breeding season. Uses a network of runs through the grass to move in single file between feeding grounds. When approached, birds in a covey bunch up and squat low before suddenly bursting into flight in all directions with a loud whirring of wings. Soon reassemble by making rallying calls to each other. Dry grass and scrub and deciduous forest; chiefly on dry and stony ground.

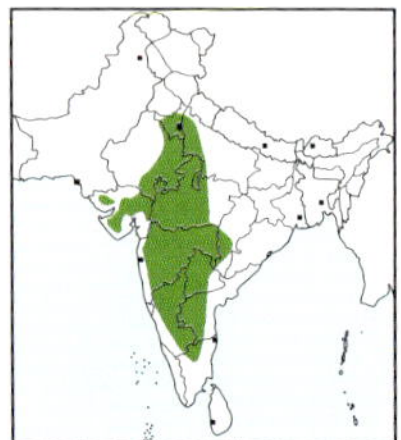

Rock Bush Quail *Perdicula argoondah* 15–18cm

Resident. Mainly C and W India. **ID** Male has strongly barred underparts and rufous-orange throat, and is superficially similar to Jungle Bush Quail. Head pattern is subtly different; has a pronounced whitish supercilium but sides to crown are rufous-orange. In Jungle, the supercilium is rufous-orange and is strikingly edged above with white. Upperparts of Rock are more uniform and generally lack the bold black blotching on the scapulars of Jungle, and the vent is concolorous with the underparts. Female has vinaceous-buff underparts, including throat and ear-coverts, and whitish supercilium. Head pattern of female much plainer, and upperparts more uniform, than in female Jungle. **Voice** Song a long piping series starting as a rapid trill, rising in volume and slightly in pitch, becoming more strident, then changing into disyllabic, more scratchy notes. The trill is like Jungle's but slower and less uniform. **HH** Habits like Jungle's. Dry rocky and sandy areas thinly vegetated with thorn scrub in plains and foothills. Found in less well vegetated and stonier country than Jungle.

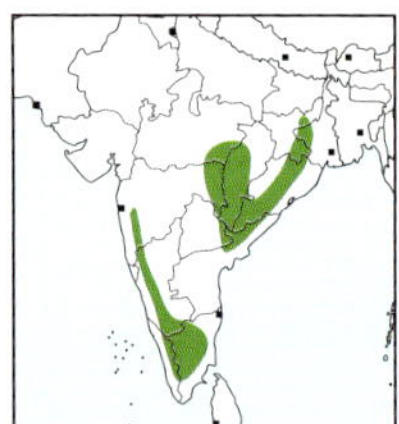

Painted Bush Quail *Perdicula erythrorhyncha* 16–18cm

Resident. Mainly Western and Eastern Ghats. **ID** Black spotting on upperparts and flanks, and red bill and legs. Male has white supercilium and throat, and black chin and mask. Female has rufous supercilium, ear-coverts and throat. **Voice** Male's breeding call is a pleasant *kirikee, kirikee*. Contact calls involve very soft whistles, rising, then falling again. **HH** Habits similar to those of Jungle Bush Quail. In coveys of up to 15 birds for most of the year. Forages in more open areas in mornings and evenings. Often dust-bathes at edges of tracks. Thin scrub and scrub at forest edges, often interspersed with cultivation in plains and foothills.

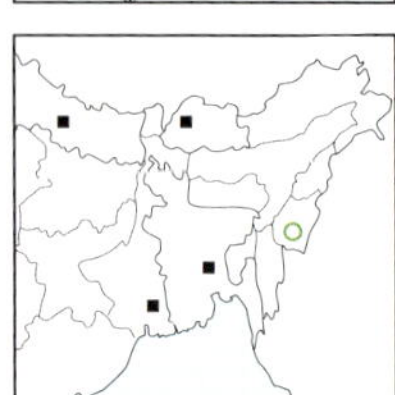

Manipur Bush Quail *Perdicula manipurensis* 19–20cm

Very rare and local resident. NE India. No recent accepted records. **ID** White eye-patch, dark olive-grey upperparts, and golden-buff underparts with black cross-shaped markings. Male has chestnut forehead and throat, which are brownish-grey on female. *P. m. inglisi* (north of Brahmaputra River) is paler, greyer and less boldly marked with black than nominate. **Voice** A clear, softly whistled *whit-it-it-it-t-t*, with each successive note slightly higher in tone. **HH** Keeps in parties of 6–8 birds. Very secretive and mainly stays in dense cover; may move into shorter grass at dawn. Most easily located by its distinctive call. Tall moist grassland and scrub in foothills; also swamps. Globally threatened.

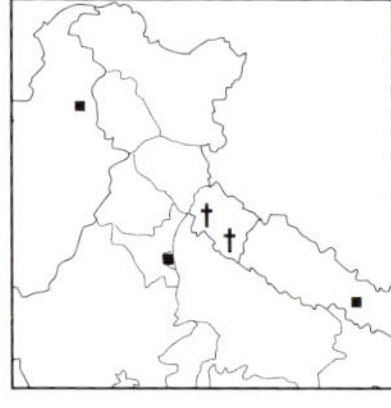

Himalayan Quail *Ophrysia superciliosa* 25cm

Uttaranchal, W Himalayas in India. No records since 1876 but considered probably still extant by BirdLife International because of difficulty of detection. **ID** Red bill and legs/feet. Both sexes with white marks in front of and behind eye. Male with black-and-white patterned head, including white supercilium and patch on ear-coverts. Body brownish-slate, streaked with black, with white-barred undertail-coverts. Female with greyish-cinnamon supercilium, ear-coverts and throat, broken by brown eye-stripe. Body cinnamon-brown, marked with black. Tail long, broad and rounded. **Voice** A shrill whistle when disturbed. Contact call when feeding low, short and quail-like. **HH** In coveys of 6–12 birds. Rarely left thick cover and very reluctant to take flight, preferring to run in and out between grass stalks. If flushed, birds flew slowly and heavily, soon dropped into vegetation and reunited by using shrill whistles. Long grass and brushwood on steep slopes. Globally threatened.

♀
Jungle Bush Quail
♂
♀
♂
Rock Bush Quail
♂
♀
Painted
Bush Quail
♂
manipurensis
♀
manipurensis
Manipur Bush Quail
♀
♂
Himalayan Quail

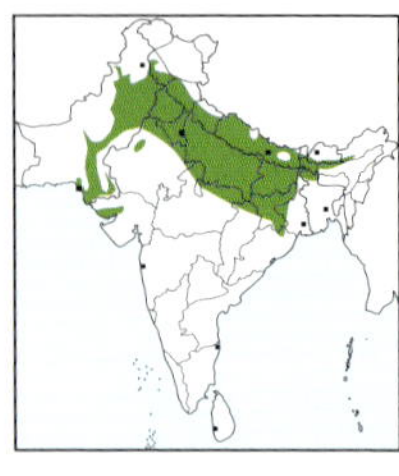

Black Francolin *Francolinus francolinus* 31–36cm

Resident. N subcontinent. **ID** Male has black face with white ear-covert patch, rufous collar, and black underparts with white spotting on flanks. Female from female Painted Francolin by rufous hindneck, dark stripe behind eye, streaked (rather than spotted) appearance to mantle, and dark-barred rather than white-spotted appearance to underparts (although underparts can be like Painted). Shows blackish tail in flight. **Voice** Loud, penetrating, frequently repeated, harsh *kar-kar, kee, ke-kee.* **HH** Active early mornings and late afternoons, returning into cover in heat of day. If much disturbed, escapes by running away swiftly, or flies off strongly and at great speed. Requires good ground cover and water close by. Cultivation, tea estates, tall grass and scrub in plains and hills.

Painted Francolin *Francolinus pictus* 31–32cm

Resident. Peninsular India and Sri Lanka. **ID** Sexes similar, with plain, rufous-orange face (and often throat), and bold white spotting on upperparts and underparts. Vent rufous (pale in Grey Francolin). Shows blackish tail in flight. **Voice** Gives a *click... cheek-cheek-keray*, almost indistinguishable from Black. **HH** Very skulking and if disturbed will squat in cover. Leaves cover to forage in early morning and late afternoon. Males call throughout day in breeding season. Tall thick grassland and cultivation with scattered trees and bushes; open forest; partial to thick cover.

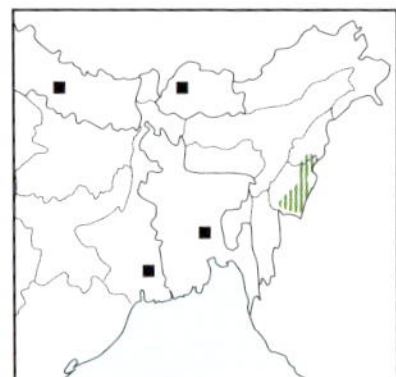

Chinese Francolin *Francolinus pintadeanus* 31–34cm

Very local resident. Manipur. **ID** Male striking with orange-buff sides of crown, black eye-stripe, white ear-coverts and throat divided by black moustachial stripe, chestnut scapulars, and extensive white spotting on underparts. Female similar, but less strikingly marked and upperparts browner and heavily barred. Shows blackish tail in flight. **Voice** From prominent post or stump male gives a series of 5–6 loud, harsh, metallic notes, *kak-kak-kuich, ka-ka* or *wi-ta-tak-takaa.* **HH** Very skulking and remains under cover. Very noisy in breeding season. Dry open dipterocarp forest and oak scrub in hills.

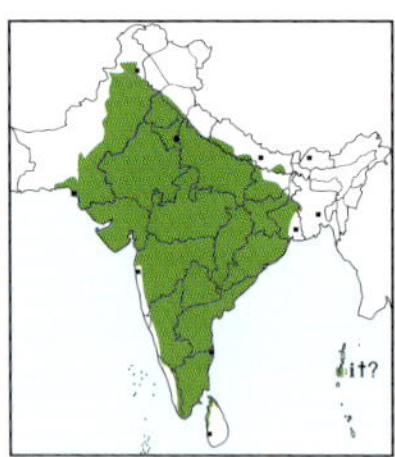

Grey Francolin *Ortygornis pondicerianus* 30–35cm

Widespread resident in lowlands and low hills; unrecorded in north-east. **ID** Plain buffish face, and buffish-white throat with fine necklace of dark spotting. Finely barred upperparts and underparts. Shows rufous tail in flight. The nominate subspecies of S peninsular India and Sri Lanka has a buffish-orange coloration to face and throat, and has darker, more chestnut upperparts and breast, compared to northern *F. p. interpositus* and *F. p. mecranensis* (which are paler and greyer, and have a whiter throat). **Voice** Makes a rapidly repeated *khateeja-khateeja-khateeja*; also, softer, more whistling *kila-kila-kila*, and a high, whirring *khirr-khirr.* **HH** Keeps in pairs or small groups which roost together in scrub. Usually escapes by running, seldom flies. Dry open grass plains and thorn scrub, often near dry cultivation, and stony semi-desert. **TN** Formerly placed in *Francolinus.*

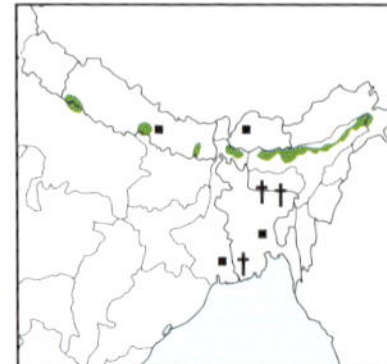

Swamp Francolin *Ortygornis gularis* 36–38cm

Very local resident in lowland strip south of Himalayas from Nepal and N Uttar Pradesh east to Assam. **ID** Rufous-orange throat, buff supercilium and cheek-stripe (separated by dark eye-stripe), finely barred upperparts, and bold white streaking on underparts. Sexes similar, male with large leg spur. Shows rufous primaries and tail in flight. **Voice** A loud *kew-care* when alarmed, occasional *qua, qua, qua* ascending in tone, and a harsh *chukeroo, chukeroo, chukeroo* preceded by several chuckles and croaks. May sound like Grey Francolin but louder. **HH** In marshes often wades through shallow water or mud and climbs up onto reeds in deep water. Reluctant to fly, but if flushed, it rises clumsily and noisily with loud chuckling and whirring of wings. Roosts in thorny trees and on broken reeds in swamps. Tall wet grassland and swamps. **TN** Formerly placed in *Francolinus.*

♀
Black Francolin
♂
♀
♂
Painted Francolin
♀
♂
Grey Francolin
Chinese Francolin
Swamp Francolin

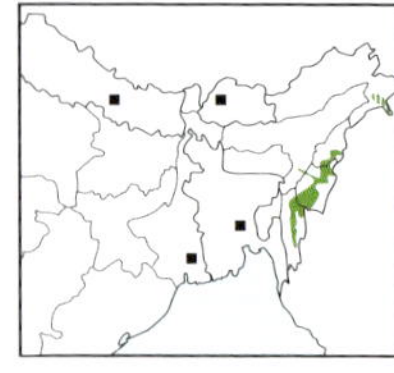

Mountain Bamboo Partridge ***Bambusicola fytchii*** 32–37cm

Resident. NE India and Bangladesh. **ID** Long tail, orange throat, chestnut spotting on breast and upperparts, blackish spotting on flanks, and buffish supercilium. Male has prominent blackish eye-stripe which extends to nape; it is rufous and less pronounced in female. Shows rufous in primaries and sides of tail in flight. **Voice** Similar call to Black Francolin but less shrill and high-pitched: resonant *che-chirree-che-chirree, chirree, chirree, chirree.* Males are very noisy in spring, calling from a mound or tree stump. **HH** Keeps in parties of up to five or six birds outside the breeding season. Shy, coming into the open to feed only in early mornings and evenings. Difficult to flush, flies rapidly a short distance before landing again in dense grass or trees. Thick grass; scrub in foothills.

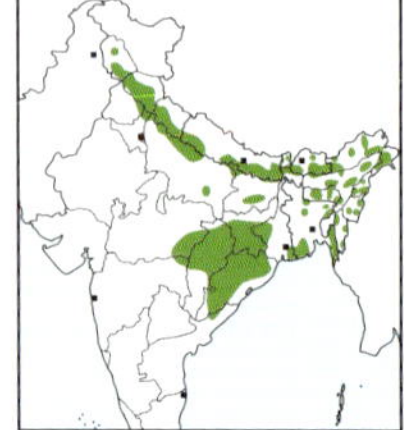

Red Junglefowl ***Gallus gallus*** M 65–78cm, F 41–46cm

Resident. Himalayas, NE and E India, and Bangladesh. **ID** Male has rufous-orange hackles, blackish-brown underparts, rufous wing-panel, white tail-base, and long greenish-black, sickle-shaped tail. There is an eclipse plumage, after the summer moult, when the hackles are replaced by short, dark brown feathers, and the central tail feathers are lacking. Female has 'shawl' of elongated (edged golden-buff, black-centred) feathers, rufous head, and naked reddish face. Immature male much duller than adult male; hackles less developed (with black centres); lacks elongated central tail feathers. **Voice** Male's loud *cock-a-doodle-doo* is very similar to a crowing domestic cockerel; both sexes make cackling and clucking notes. **HH** Frequently wary and very secretive, though confiding where not hunted. If flushed, rises cackling with a clatter of wings. In early mornings and late afternoons, forages on forest tracks, firebreaks and fields at forest edges. Inhabits well-watered areas, undergrowth in moist mixed forest, and scrub jungle interspersed with cultivation.

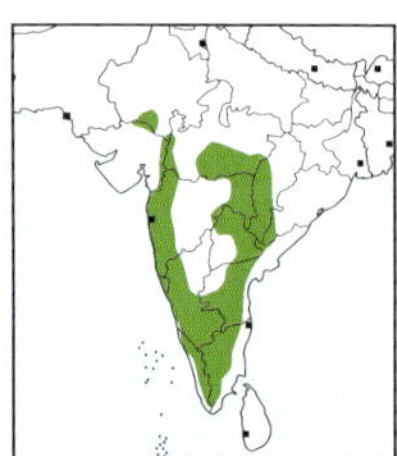

Grey Junglefowl ***Gallus sonneratii*** M 70–80cm, F 38cm

Resident. Peninsular India. **ID** Male has 'shawl' of white and pale golden-yellow spotting; band of golden spotting on scapulars, grey underparts, and long sickle-shaped, purplish-black tail. Eclipse male has shorter, brownish-black neck hackles, and shorter tail. Female is like Red Junglefowl, but has buffish face, bold white streaking on underparts, and yellowish (rather than greyish) legs. Immature male resembles adult male, but has much-reduced 'shawl' of yellowish-white spotting, smaller comb and wattles, and has shorter tail. **Voice** Male's distinctive crowing call is a repeated, loud, staccato *kuk-ka-kurruk-ka.* **HH** Similar to Red Junglefowl's. Normally very shy, never venturing far from cover, but tame where not hunted. Undergrowth in broadleaved evergreen and deciduous forests, second growth and bamboo thickets.

Sri Lanka Junglefowl ***Gallus lafayettii*** M 66–72.5cm, F 35cm

Resident. Sri Lanka. **ID** Only junglefowl occurring naturally in Sri Lanka (although beware domestic chickens). Male has orange-red breast and belly, yellow centre to oblong-shaped comb, and purplish-black wings and elongated sickle-shaped tail. Legs are pinkish or yellowish, and iris is bright yellow. There is no distinct eclipse plumage. Female like female Red Junglefowl, but has black scaling on white underparts, prominent dark brown and buff barring in wings, and yellowish legs. Immature male has rufous-orange head and neck, deep rufous coloration to body, poorly developed comb and wattles, and shorter tail. **Voice** Cock's crow is a staccato, musical ringing *chiok, chaw-choyik*, the terminal *ik* higher on the scale; hen's cackle is a high-pitched metallic *kwikkuk kwikkukkuk.* **HH** Similar to Red Junglefowl's. Non-breeding males often feed in large groups. Confined to large forest areas.

Mountain Bamboo Partridge

Red Junglefowl

Grey Junglefowl

Sri Lanka Junglefowl

PLATE 14: PEACOCK PHEASANT, BLOOD PHEASANT AND MONALS

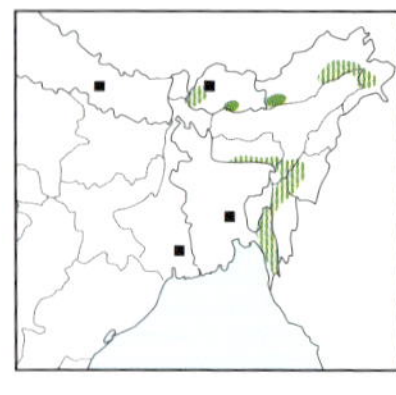

Grey Peacock Pheasant *Polyplectron bicalcaratum* M 56–76cm, F 48–55cm

Resident. E Himalayas and Bangladesh. **ID** Greyish with white throat and long, broad tail. Male has prominent purple and green ocelli, particularly on wing-coverts and tail; and has short tufted crest. Female and immature male are smaller and browner, with shorter tail and smaller and duller ocelli. **Voice** Makes a deep guttural *hoo*, rapidly repeated about seven times, and soft chuckling notes; also, an *ok-kok-kok-kok*. **HH** Singly, in pairs or family groups. Extremely secretive and skulks in dense vegetation at the least disturbance. Rarely seen and most easily detected by its call; may be heard sporadically at any time of day in breeding season. Dense undergrowth in tropical and subtropical moist, broadleaved evergreen and semi-evergreen forest.

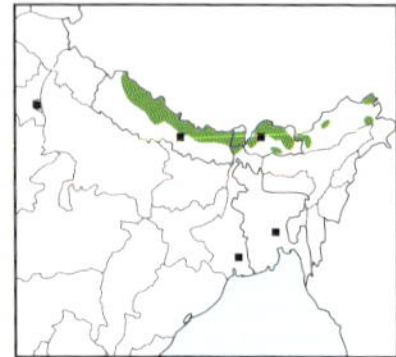

Blood Pheasant *Ithaginis cruentus* M 44–48cm, F 39.5–42cm

Resident. Himalayas. **ID** Crested head, and red orbital skin and legs/feet. Male has blood-red throat, grey upperparts streaked with white, greenish underparts, and plumage is splashed with red. Female has grey crest and nape, rufous-orange face, dark brown upperparts, and rufous-brown underparts. Subspecies variation is marked; males vary in pattern of red and black on head, and in extent of red on underparts, with *kuseri* of E Arunachal having the most extensive red on underparts. **Voice** Repeated *chuck*, and loud, grating *kzeeuk-cheeu-cheeu-chee*. **HH** In coveys of up to 30 or more. Tame and confiding. Rarely flies except to go to roost. Forages actively throughout day, scratching the ground like a domestic fowl, and turning over leaves and grasses with its feet. Can dig through snow. High-altitude shrubberies and forest.

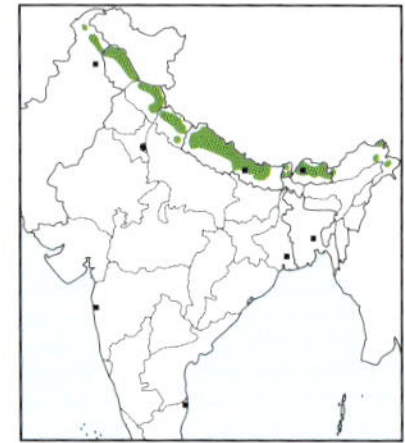

Himalayan Monal *Lophophorus impejanus* M 70–72cm, F 63–64cm

Resident. Himalayas. **ID** Male is iridescent green, copper and purple above, with small white patch on back and cinnamon-brown tail; underparts are velvety black. Has spatulate-tipped crest. Female has pale streaking on underparts, prominent white throat, short crest, and bright blue orbital skin. In flight, shows whitish 'horseshoe' on uppertail-coverts and narrow white tip to tail. **Voice** A series of upward-inflected whistles, *kur-leiu* or *kleeh-vick*, alternated with a higher-pitched *kleeh*; reminiscent of snowcocks and Eurasian Curlew. In alarm *kleeh-wick-kleeh-wick*, alternating with *kwick-kwick*. **HH** Loosely gregarious even in breeding season. Feeds mainly by digging with its strong bill and can dig deep in snow. Although cautious, less shy than other Himalayan pheasants. Summers on steep rocky and grass-covered slopes above treeline; winters in broadleaved and coniferous forests; forest edges and clearings, and fields.

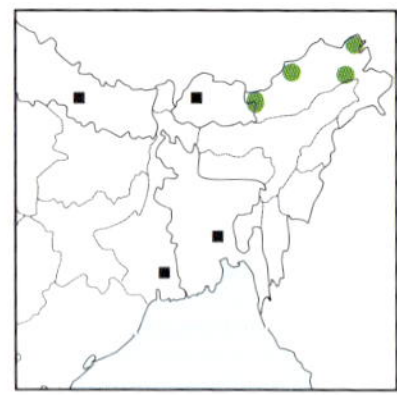

Sclater's Monal *Lophophorus sclateri* 63–68cm

Resident. E Himalayas in Arunachal Pradesh. **ID** Male from Himalayan Monal by tufted crest, extensive bare patch of blue around eye, larger area of white on lower back and rump/uppertail-coverts, and white-tipped or all-white tail. Female is like female Himalayan, but lacks crest, has pale lower back and rump, broader white terminal band to tail, darker underparts lacking bold splashes of greyish-white, yellowish bill, and indistinct whitish throat. Nominate male (E Arunachal) has cinnamon tail with broad white tip; *arunachalensis* (W Arunachal) has white tail; intermediates occur. **Voice** Territorial call is a far-carrying, plaintive, howling scream, with a distinctive rise in pitch at the end, *waaaaaaahee*. A repeated shrill, harsh, plaintive cry in alarm; also, a wild ringing whistle. **HH** In summer keeps in flocks among scrub and cliffs above treeline. Fairly gregarious, even when breeding. Forages in early morning and late evenings. Inhabits dense rhododendron undergrowth in fir forest.

♀
♂
Grey Peacock Pheasant
♀
cruentus
♂
cruentus
♂
cruentus
Blood Pheasant
♂
kuseri
♂
tibetanus
♀
♂
Himalayan Monal
♂
sclateri
♀
sclateri
Sclater's Monal

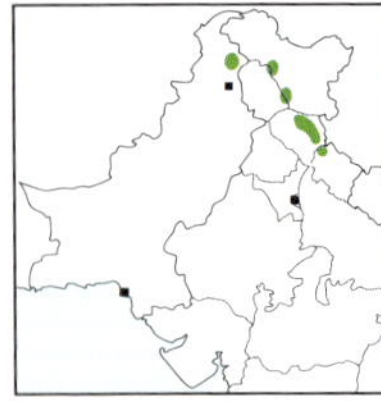

Western Tragopan ***Tragopan melanocephalus*** **M 68–73cm, F 60cm**

Resident. W Himalayas. **ID** Male has flame-orange foreneck, red hindneck, white-spotted blackish underparts, and white-spotted grey upperparts with large white spots on uppertail-coverts. Facial skin is red. Female from female Satyr Tragopan by dark grey-brown (rather than rufous) coloration to underparts. Immature male has dull brownish-red hindneck, and more uniformly grey upperparts and underparts with fewer and smaller white spots. White-spotted grey underparts help separate from immature Satyr. **Voice** Nasal, wailing repeated *khuwaah* usually uttered at dawn and dusk; when alarmed, an anxious *waa waa waa*. **HH** Usually found singly or in pairs. Normally extremely wary and skulking, but sometimes forages in forest glades or on open slopes. Feeds on the ground, mainly in early morning and from late afternoon to dusk. Roosts in trees. Territorial in breeding season. Dense undergrowth in temperate and subalpine forest. Globally threatened.

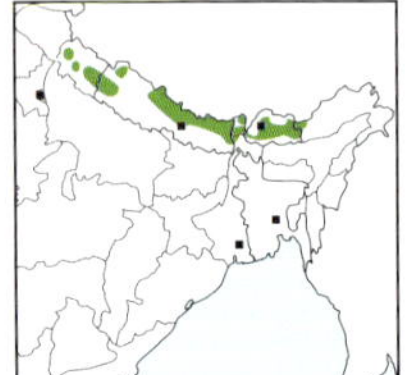

Satyr Tragopan ***Tragopan satyra*** **M 67–72cm, F 57.5cm**

Resident. Himalayas. **ID** Male has red underparts with black-bordered white spots, and olive-brown coloration to upperparts including rump and uppertail-coverts which are also covered in black-bordered white spots. Facial skin is blue. Female varies from rufous-brown to ochraceous-brown in coloration; wings, tail and underparts are generally brighter and more rufescent than on other female tragopans. Immature male is more like female, but with black on head, and red on neck, upper mantle and breast. **Voice** Repeated deep, wailing drawn-out call *wah, waah! oo-ah! oo-aaaaa!* rising in volume and becoming more protracted; also, *wah, wah*. **HH** Habits like Western. Generally wary, but tame where not hunted, such as in parts of Bhutan. Dense undergrowth in temperate and subalpine forest.

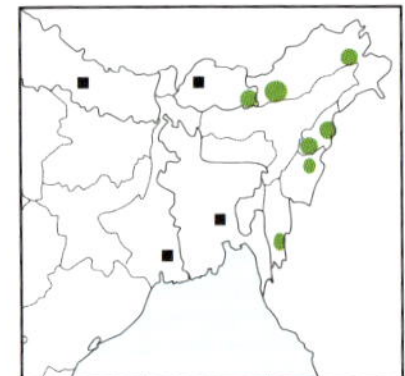

Blyth's Tragopan ***Tragopan blythii*** **M 65–70cm, F 58cm**

Resident. E Himalayas and NE India. **ID** Male has orange facial skin, and red neck and upper breast clearly defined from sandy-grey breast and belly. Upperpart coloration is similar to Satyr but has striking band of pinkish-white uppertail-covert feathers. Female from female Satyr by paler underparts lacking strong rufous tone, and from female Temminck's by paler underparts with less distinct white spotting. Immature male like immature male Satyr but has yellowish facial skin, pinkish uppertail-coverts, and uniform brownish-grey underparts (lacking white spots). *T. b. molesworthi* (NE Himalayas) differs from *T. b. blythii* (NE India, south of Brahmaputra River) in having a narrower band of red across breast and being paler, with more uniform sandy-grey underparts. **Voice** A deep *mao, mao* in early morning and evening. **HH** Habits like Western. Often in parties of four or five. Thick undergrowth in broadleaved forest. Globally threatened.

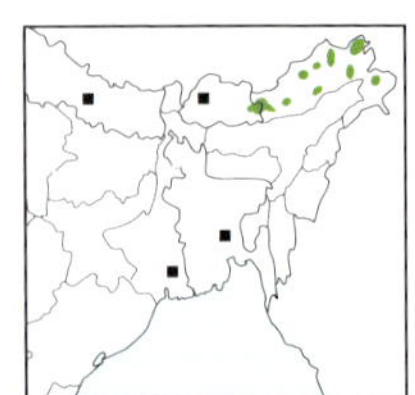

Temminck's Tragopan ***Tragopan temminckii*** **M 64cm, F 58cm**

Resident. E Himalayas in Bhutan and Arunachal Pradesh. **ID** Male from male Satyr by larger, greyish-white spotting (without black borders) on red underparts, brighter orange-red neck, mainly red upperparts with black-bordered greyish-white spotting, and brighter and more strikingly blue facial skin. Female more conspicuously spotted with white on underparts than other female tragopans, and lacks the strong rufous tones of female Satyr. Immature male is very similar to immature male Satyr, but has more prominent wedge-shaped white spotting on underparts. **Voice** Series of moaning notes, gradually increasing in length and volume, terminated by a nasal grumbling note: *woh... woah... woah... waah... waah... waah... waah... griiiik*. **HH** Habits like Western, but very arboreal. Dense undergrowth in temperate and subalpine forest.

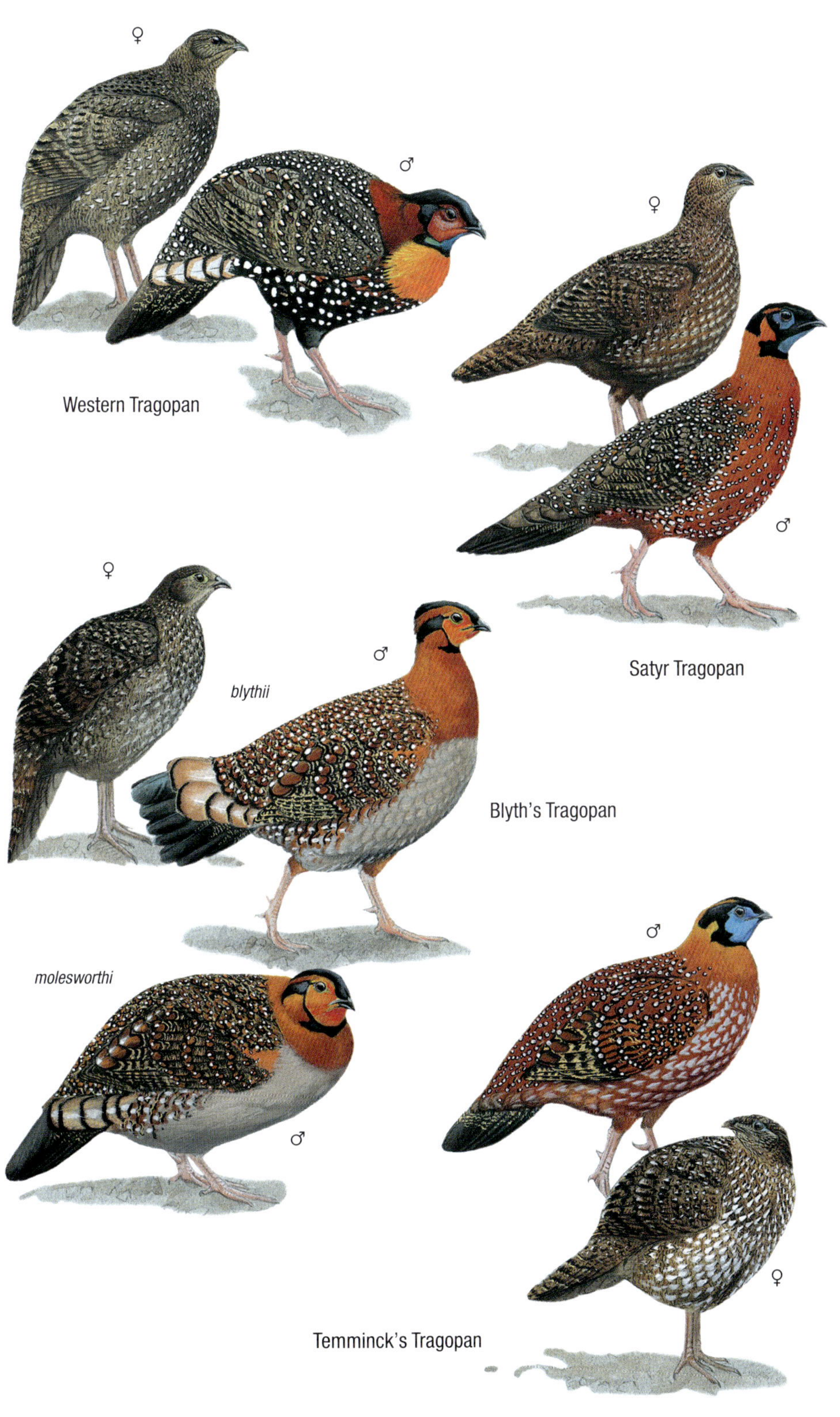
♀
♂
Western Tragopan
♀
♂
Satyr Tragopan
♀
♂
blythii
Blyth's Tragopan
moleswort hi
♂
♂
♀
Temminck's Tragopan

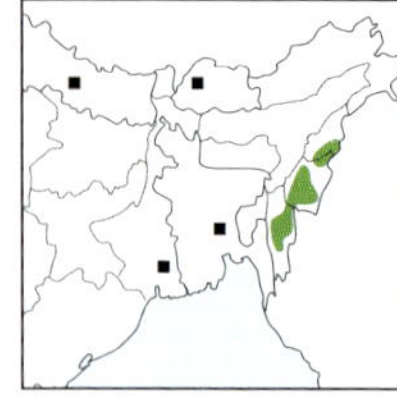

Mrs Hume's Pheasant *Syrmaticus humiae* M 90cm, F 60cm

Resident. NE India. **ID** Male is chestnut and blue-black, with white banding along scapulars and across wings, and has greyish rump and long greyish tail banded with chestnut and black. Female is mainly grey-brown (marked with black) on upperparts, and pale rufous-brown (barred with buff) on underparts. Has suggestion of greyish band on scapulars, and narrow whitish wing-bars. Tail is shorter than male's; tail feathers are tipped with white and outer tail feathers are mainly chestnut. **Voice** Very distinctive crowing *cher-a-per, cher-a-per, cher-cher-cheria-cherja*. Also repeated cackling *waaak* notes; a sharp *tuk tuk* and loud screech in alarm. **HH** Habits like Cheer. When foraging, keeps close to, or within, dense grasses and bushes at forest edges. Steep rocky slopes with open oak and pine forest, and long grass and bushes.

Cheer Pheasant *Catreus wallichii* M 90–118cm, F 61–76cm

Resident. W Himalayas. **ID** Long, broadly barred tail, pronounced crest, and red facial skin. Male is more cleanly and strongly marked than female, with pronounced barring on mantle, unmarked neck, rufous rump, and broader barring on tail. Female is browner above, more heavily barred on breast, and has grey-brown rump. **Voice** Far-carrying, loud *chir-a-pir, chir-a-pir, chir, chir chirwa, chirwa*. Dusk and pre-dawn high piercing whistles, *chewewoo*, interspersed with short *chut* calls and short staccato notes. **HH** Extremely wary and skulking. When disturbed, prefers to run off rapidly or crouch in thick undergrowth rather than fly. If flushed, rises noisily and dives downhill. Tends to feed in the same area day after day. Birds often roost together in trees. Steep hillsides with scrub and stunted trees and wooded ravines or with some scrub and grass cover; second growth. Globally threatened.

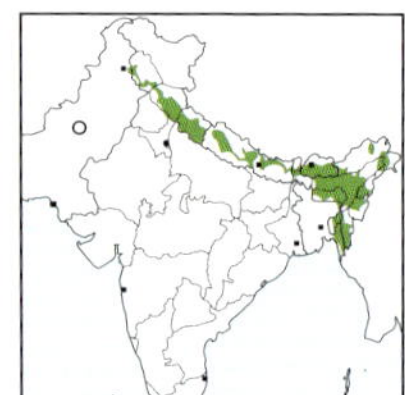

Kalij Pheasant *Lophura leucomelanos* M 63–74cm, F 50–60cm

Resident. Himalayas, NE India and Bangladesh. **ID** Both sexes have red facial skin and downcurved tail. Male has blue-black upperparts, and variable amounts of white on rump and underparts. Female varies from dull brown to reddish-brown, with greyish-buff fringes producing scaly appearance. Marked subspecies variation with males varying in colour of crest and underparts and extent of pale barring to upperparts, with *hamiltonii* in W Himalayas having most white in plumage, and *lathami* in NE being darkest. **Voice** Loud, whistling chuckle or *chirrup*; guinea-pig-like squeaks and chuckles when flushed. **HH** Habits like Red Junglefowl. Spends much time digging and scratching for food. Emerges into open to forage at forest edges and on tracks in early mornings and late afternoons. All forest types with dense undergrowth.

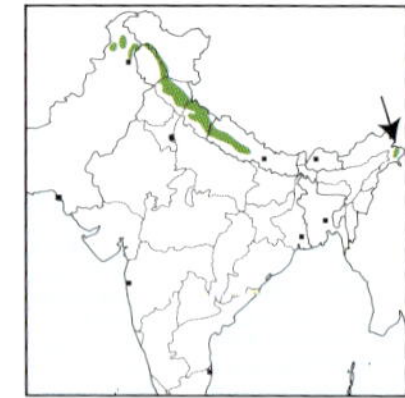

Koklass Pheasant *Pucrasia macrolopha* M 58–64cm, F 52.5–56cm

Resident. W Himalayas and E Arunachal Pradesh. **ID** Male has bottle-green head and ear-tufts, chestnut on breast, and streaked appearance to body. Female has white throat, short buff ear-tufts, and streaked body. Both sexes have wedge-shaped tail. Males of *P. m. castanea* and *biddulphi* (W Himalayas) have dark chestnut on hindneck and upper mantle, are mainly dark chestnut on breast and belly, and have blackish flanks (streaked with white). Males of *P. m. macrolopha* and *nipalensis* (C Himalayas) have less chestnut in plumage (restricted to centre of breast and belly); mantle and sides of breast are buffish-grey (streaked black) in *macrolopha* and black (streaked buff) in *nipalensis*. Racial identity of birds in NE Arunachal not known but assumed to be *P. m. meyeri* which has golden hindneck, narrow stripe of chestnut on breast, and mainly rufous tail. **Voice** Far-carrying and loud *kok, kark, kuk... kukuk*. **HH** Very secretive and wary. When disturbed, runs away quickly through undergrowth or bursts upwards, giving a noisy alarm, before hurtling downslope twisting between trees at great speed. Dense undergrowth in temperate and subalpine forest.

♂
♀
Mrs Hume's
Pheasant
♂
♀
♂
Cheer Pheasant
♂
♂
♀
♂
leucomelanos
♀
♂
melanota
♂
hamiltonii
♂
lathami
Kalij Pheasant
♀
♂
macrolopha
♀
meyeri
♂
nipalensis
Koklass Pheasant
♂
meyeri

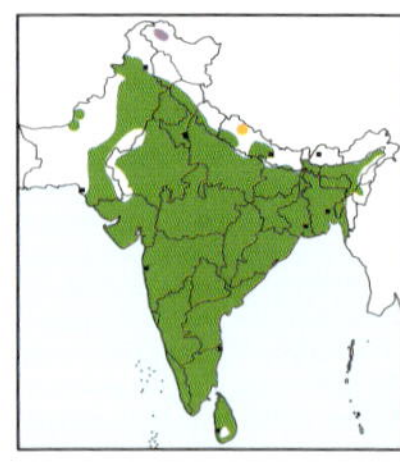

Little Grebe ***Tachybaptus ruficollis*** 25–29cm

Widespread resident; unrecorded in parts of NW subcontinent. **ID** Small size, often with puffed-up rear end. Shows whitish secondaries in flight. In breeding plumage, has rufous cheeks and neck-sides and yellow patch at base of bill. In non-breeding plumage, has buff cheeks, foreneck and flanks. Juvenile is like non-breeder but has brown stripes on cheeks. **Voice** Utters a drawn-out whinnying trill in breeding season, and a sharp *wit wit* in alarm. **HH** Often singly or in pairs among aquatic vegetation when breeding; in non-breeding season keeps in small loose flocks in open water. Lakes, ponds, village tanks, reservoirs, ditches, and slow-moving rivers; rarely on coastal waters.

Horned Grebe ***Podiceps auritus*** 31–38cm

Winter visitor. Pakistan and NW India. **ID** Bill is stouter and does not appear upturned, unlike Eared Grebe. Has two white patches on upperwing, with white patch on wing-coverts usually lacking on Eared. Triangular-shaped head, with crown peaking at rear. White cheeks contrasting with black crown and white foreneck in non-breeding plumage. Yellow ear-tufts and rufous neck and breast in breeding plumage. Juvenile as non-breeder but may show faint dark stripes on cheeks and rufous on neck. Usually swims with neck erect, in contrast to Eared. **Voice** Silent outside breeding season. **HH** Lakes and coastal waters. **AN** Slavonian Grebe.

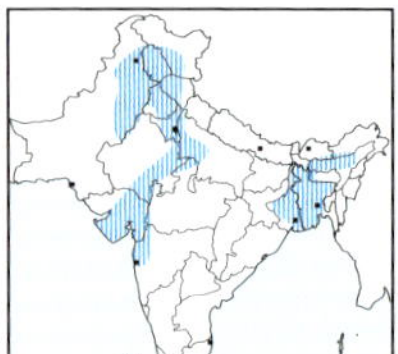

Red-necked Grebe ***Podiceps grisegena*** 40–50cm

Winter visitor. NW and NE subcontinent. Vagrant: Pakistan, Bangladesh. **ID** Slightly smaller than Great Crested Grebe with stouter neck, squarer head, and stockier body which is often puffed up at rear end. Black-tipped yellow bill. Unlike Great Crested, Red-necked often leaps clear of water when diving. Black crown extends to eye (including lores), and has dusky cheeks and foreneck in non-breeding plumage. Whitish cheeks and reddish foreneck in breeding plumage. Juvenile is like non-breeder but has brown striping on cheeks and rufous foreneck. **Voice** Silent away from breeding grounds. **HH** Habits like Great Crested Grebe. Lakes.

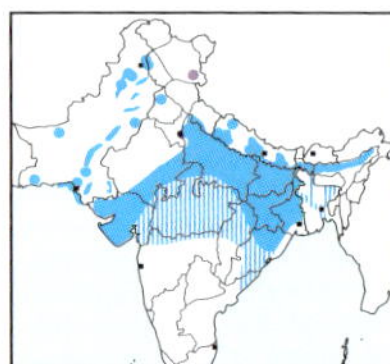

Great Crested Grebe ***Podiceps cristatus*** 46–61cm

Breeds in NW subcontinent; winter visitor to N subcontinent. **ID** Large and slender-necked with pinkish bill. Black crown does not extend to eye, and has white cheeks and foreneck in non-breeding plumage. Rufous-orange ear-tufts and white cheeks and foreneck in breeding plumage. Juvenile is similar to non-breeder, but has brown striping on cheeks. **Voice** On breeding grounds, a harsh rolling *aooorrr* and chattering *kek-kek*. **HH** A typical grebe. Swims with body low in water and neck held erect. Both sexes perform striking, ritualised courtship displays. Favours open water: lakes, jheels and reservoirs; also, coastal waters and saltpans.

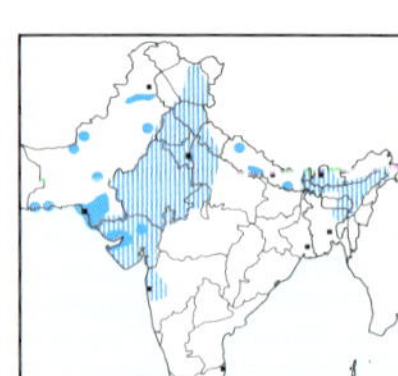

Eared Grebe ***Podiceps nigricollis*** 28–35cm

Breeds locally in Pakistan; winters mainly in Pakistan, NW India and Nepal. Vagrant: Bhutan, Bangladesh. Steep forehead, with crown typically peaking at front or centre. Compared with Horned Grebe, black of crown extends below eye, ear-coverts are dusky grey, and white throat curves up behind ear-coverts in non-breeding plumage. Yellow ear-tufts, black neck and breast and rufous flanks in breeding plumage. Juvenile as non-breeder but may show buff wash to cheeks and foreneck and more closely resembles Little. **Voice** Short whistles and trills at nest site. **HH** Habits like Little Grebe. Typically swims with curved neck, in contrast to Horned Grebe. Reed-edged lakes with emergent vegetation; also, coastal waters in winter. **AN** Black-necked Grebe.

non-br
br
Little Grebe
non-br
br
Horned Grebe
br
non-br
Red-necked Grebe
non-br
br
Great Crested Grebe
br
non-br
Eared Grebe

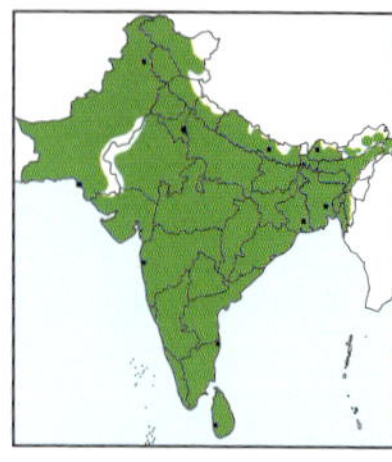

Rock Pigeon *Columba livia* 29–36cm

Widespread resident. **ID** Grey tail with blackish terminal band, and broad black bars on greater coverts and tertials/secondaries. Darker grey and lacks whitish tail-band of Hill Pigeon. Northern subspecies *neglecta* has pale grey to whitish back, and is slightly paler grey on underparts than *intermedia* of peninsular India and Sri Lanka. Feral populations differ considerably in coloration and patterning. **Voice** Gives a deep, repeated *gootr-goo, gootr-goo.* **HH** Wild birds roost on cliff ledges and fissures in cliffs and ruins. Lives in colonies all year. Feeds chiefly in cultivation, mainly on seeds, also eats green shoots. Feral birds live in villages and towns; wild birds frequent cliffs, gorges and ruins. **AN** Common Pigeon.

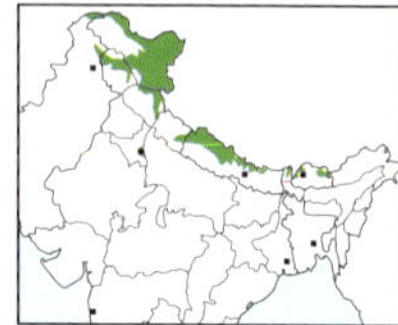

Hill Pigeon *Columba rupestris* 31–35cm

Resident. Himalayas. **ID** Similar to Rock Pigeon , but paler grey, with white back and white band across tail contrasting with blackish terminal band. Juvenile is browner and lacks iridescence on neck; feathers of neck and breast are fringed with rusty-buff, and coverts are fringed with creamy-buff. **Voice** A quickly repeated, gurgling *gut-gut-gut-gut* higher-pitched and more halting than Rock Pigeon. **HH** Similar to those of wild Rock. Often very tame. Feeds on grain in cultivation and along mule tracks. High-altitude villages and cliffs, mainly trans-Himalayas.

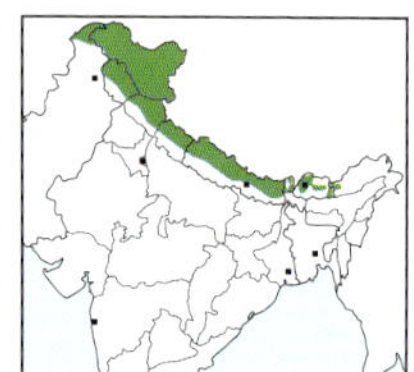

Snow Pigeon *Columba leuconota* 31–34cm

Resident. Himalayas. **ID** Adult has slate-grey head, creamy-white collar and underparts, fawn-brown mantle contrasting with pale grey wing-coverts, white back contrasting with blackish rump and uppertail-coverts, and white band on blackish tail. Upperwing has three diffuse dark bars. Juvenile has greyish-buff wash to neck, breast and underparts, and fine whitish fringes to coverts and scapulars. **Voice** Commonest call a short series of staccato *kuk* or *ki-kup* notes (somewhat squirrel-like). Also, a quiet, hollow and ventriloquial song. **HH** In pairs and small parties in summer, large flocks in winter. Forages on grass and rocky slopes and cultivation; in summer also, at edge of melting snow-fields. Cliffs and gorges in mountains with plentiful rainfall; absent in dry steppe regions.

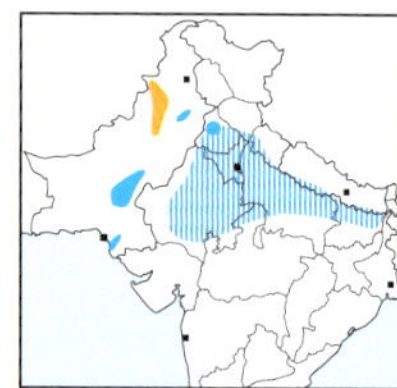

Yellow-eyed Pigeon *Columba eversmanni* 25–31cm

Winter visitor and passage migrant. Pakistan and N India. **ID** Smaller than Rock Pigeon, with narrower and shorter black wing-bars. Iris and orbital skin yellowish, and tip of bill can be distinctly yellowish. Has variable brownish cast and scaly appearance to upperparts, purplish cast to grey crown and nape, and greyish-white back and upper rump. Also, slight differences in tail pattern from Rock Pigeon: dark terminal band is less clear cut and shows diffuse paler grey subterminal band. Juvenile is like adult (e.g. with yellow orbital skin), but iris is tinged brown, and lacks green-and-purple gloss to neck, mantle and breast. **Voice** Usually silent but gives quiet *oo-oo-oo* in breeding season. **HH** Similar to Rock but roosts in groves. Forages in small parties or flocks in nearby fields, often with Rock. Plains cultivation. Globally threatened.

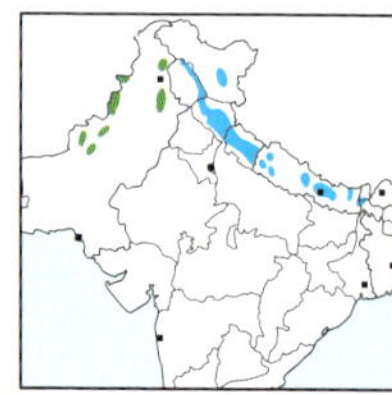

Common Wood Pigeon *Columba palumbus* 41–45cm

Resident. Balochistan and Himalayas east to Kashmir, winters sporadically east to West Bengal. **ID** Much larger than Rock Pigeon. Has white wing patch and dark tail-band, buff neck patch, and deep vinous underparts. In flight, from below, shows greyish-white band across tail and grey undertail-coverts are concolorous with base of tail. Juvenile is duller and browner, and lacks green gloss and buff patch on neck. **Voice** A deep and throaty *kookooo-koo....kookoo* repeated three or four times. **HH** Usually in small parties, sometimes in larger flocks in the non-breeding season. Clambers among foliage when feeding; may hang upside-down to reach food items. Scrub-covered and wooded hillsides, valleys and nullahs, with oaks, junipers and firs, also, cultivation.

ad
neglecta
ad
intermedia
Rock Pigeon
ad
Hill Pigeon
ad
Snow Pigeon
ad
Yellow-eyed Pigeon
ad
Common Wood Pigeon

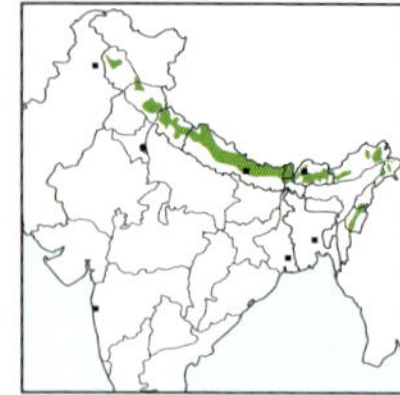

Speckled Wood Pigeon *Columba hodgsonii* 32–36cm

Resident. Himalayas and NE Indian hills. **ID** From Ashy Wood Pigeon by lack of buff patch on neck, white spotting on wing-coverts, 'speckled' underparts, and dark grey vent and undertail-coverts which are concolorous with undertail. Like Ashy, shows very dark underwing and blackish uppertail and undertail in flight. Bill dark grey (pale in Ashy). Male has maroon mantle and maroon on underparts, replaced by grey on female. Juvenile is like female, but neck pattern is less distinct, has finer white tips to coverts, and underparts are more diffusely patterned. **Voice** Low-pitched *whock-whrooo-whrooo*, the last note longest and more rolling. **HH** Mainly frugivorous and arboreal; sometimes feeds on grain in crop stubbles. Clambers about trees when feeding like Common Wood Pigeon. Mainly oak-rhododendron forest; sometimes open country.

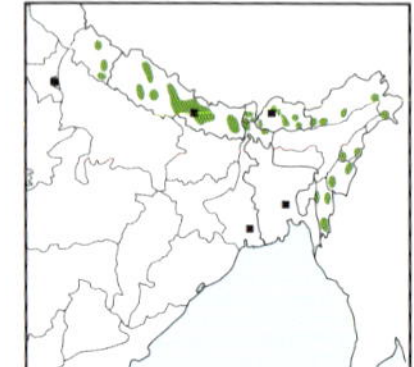

Ashy Wood Pigeon *Columba pulchricollis* 31–36cm

Resident. Himalayas and NE Indian hills. **ID** From Speckled by combination of buff collar contrasting strongly with uniform dark slate-grey breast without 'speckling', no white spotting on wing-coverts, and creamy-buff belly and undertail-coverts which contrast with dark undertail. Buff collar is formed by rufous-buff tips to neck feathers contrasting with dark bases, creating checkerboard pattern, and has metallic green-and-purple sheen to lower neck and back. Juvenile has browner upperparts, with less distinct pattern on neck, and has rufous fringes to feathers of breast and belly. **Voice** Advertising call: a repeated single, emphatic, low-pitched hoot, *whooh....whooh....whooh.* **HH** Chiefly arboreal and frugivorous; wanders in search of fruiting trees. Typically perches very quietly, concealed amongst foliage in the canopy. Dense broadleaved subtropical and temperate forest.

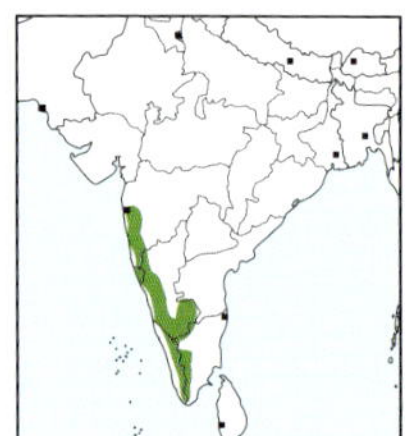

Nilgiri Wood Pigeon *Columba elphinstonii* 36–42cm

Resident. Western Ghats. **ID** Smaller than Mountain Imperial Pigeon, with darker maroon-brown upperparts, darker underwing, and uniform slate-grey tail (banded on Mountain Imperial). Adult has black-and-white chequered pattern on hindneck, and purple-and-green gloss on mantle, foreneck and breast. Male has paler grey crown and more extensive maroon-brown on upperparts than female. Juvenile has less distinct chequered hindneck, almost lacks purple-and-green iridescence, and has chestnut fringes to mantle and coverts. **Voice** Advertising call: long drawn-out low-pitched hoots combined with multisyllabic hooting notes, e.g. *whoooh....whu-hu-hu-hoo....whoooh...whu-hu-hu.* **HH** Similar to Ashy. Sometimes feeds on forest floor. Moist broadleaved evergreen forest; cardamom sholas with tall shade trees in Kerala.

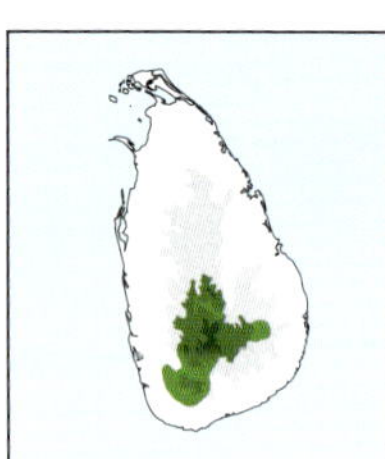

Sri Lanka Wood Pigeon *Columba torringtoniae* 33–36cm

Resident. Sri Lanka. **ID** A medium-sized, dark pigeon. Adult has dark slate-grey upperparts, including wings and tail, and lilac-grey head, neck and underparts. Has black-and-white chequered pattern on hindneck, and strong purplish (and weaker green) gloss on mantle, neck and breast. Juvenile is duller with diffuse chestnut fringes to grey underparts, and feathers of hindneck are broadly tipped with grey. **Voice** Mainly silent. Single low-pitched hoots given at intervals, *whooh...whooh...* and more quavering hoots, *whu-hu-hoo.* **HH** Very shy. Feeds in the forest canopy on fruits and berries, especially wild cinnamon. Forest; sometimes fruiting trees in gardens and around villages.

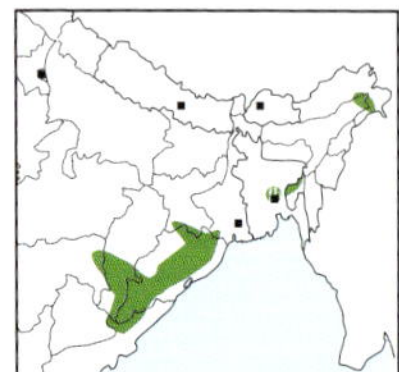

Pale-capped Pigeon *Columba punicea* 36–41cm

Resident. Eastern Ghats and NE India. Vagrant: Bangladesh, Sri Lanka. **ID** Pale cap, vinous-chestnut underparts, and maroon-brown mantle and wing-coverts with green-and-purple gloss. Sexes are similar, but female is darker with darker grey crown. Juvenile initially lacks cap; upperparts browner, with chestnut fringes, and underparts mixed grey and rufous-buff. **Voice** Almost unknown. In groups, individuals give very faint contact calls: *rhuhuhuhu.* **HH** Feeds in trees on fruits and wild figs, on seeding bamboo and on grain in fields. Perches inconspicuously amongst foliage. Tropical and subtropical forest, second growth and cultivation. Globally threatened.

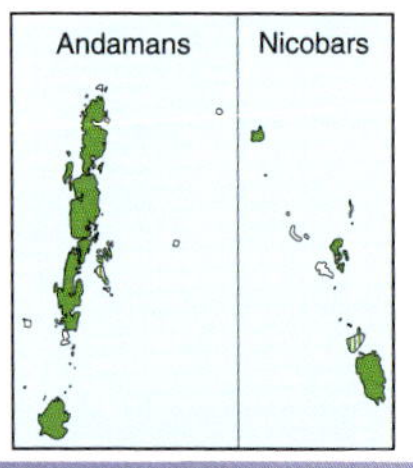

Andaman Wood Pigeon *Columba palumboides* 36–41cm

Resident. Andamans and Nicobars. **ID** Dark slate-grey upperparts and grey underparts, including undertail-coverts, with paler head and neck, latter with indistinct checkerboard pattern. Reddish cere, base of yellow bill and eye-patch. Upper mantle and breast have metallic green sheen, and feathers of rest of upperparts are variably fringed with metallic purple. Underwing and undertail appear almost blackish in flight. Female is darker than male. Juvenile lacks metallic green and purple sheens and is darker and browner. **Voice** Advertising call: a repeated single mellow hoot, *whooo.* **HH** Wanders from one island to another in search of fruiting trees. Dense broadleaved evergreen forest.

♂
♀
Speckled Wood Pigeon
ad
Ashy Wood Pigeon
ad
Nilgiri Wood Pigeon
ad
Sri Lanka Wood Pigeon
ad
juv
Pale-capped Pigeon
ad
Andaman Wood Pigeon

PLATE 20: DOVES AND NICOBAR PIGEON

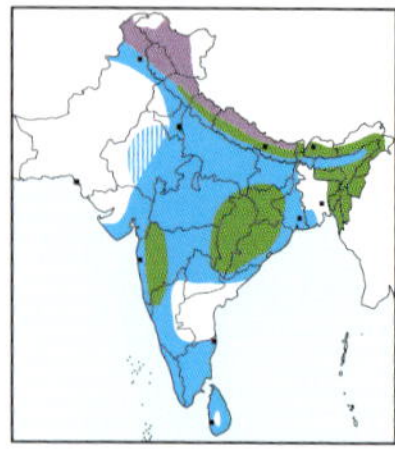

Oriental Turtle Dove *Streptopelia orientalis* 33–35cm

Resident and winter visitor. Himalayas, NE India and Bangladesh south to S peninsular India and Sri Lanka. Not in arid north-west. **ID** Rufous-scaled scapulars and wing-coverts, dusky underparts, and barring on neck. In flight, has dusky-grey underwing and, in all but one Indian subspecies, grey sides and tip to the tail. Juvenile lacks neck-barring, and has buffish-grey head and underparts, and pale buff fringes to dark-centred feathers of upperparts. Subspecies *S. o. meena* (W Himalayas) has white rather than grey sides and tip to tail, white not grey undertail-coverts, and paler underparts. *S. o. agricola* (E Himalayas and NE subcontinent) has deeper vinaceous-pink tinge to head, neck and underparts. *S. o. erythrocephala* (Peninsula) has a reddish-brown head, neck and mantle. See Vagrants for differences from European Turtle Dove. **Voice** A hoarse, mournful repeated *goor... gur-grugroo.* **HH** Singly or in pairs when breeding; in small parties in winter, may form flocks. A ground-feeder seeking grain. Open forest, mainly broadleaved, sometimes coniferous, often near cultivation and orchards. **AN** Rufous Turtle Dove.

Eurasian Collared Dove *Streptopelia decaocto* 30–31cm

Widespread resident; unrecorded in W Pakistan, N Himalayas, SW India and Sri Lanka. **ID** Sandy-brown with black half-collar, white sides to tail, and white underwing-coverts. Juvenile lacks neck-collar, and feathers of upperparts are fringed with buff. **Voice** A repeated cooing *kukkoo... kook.* **HH** Habits like Oriental Turtle Dove. Open dry country with cultivation and groves; also, desert areas in Pakistan.

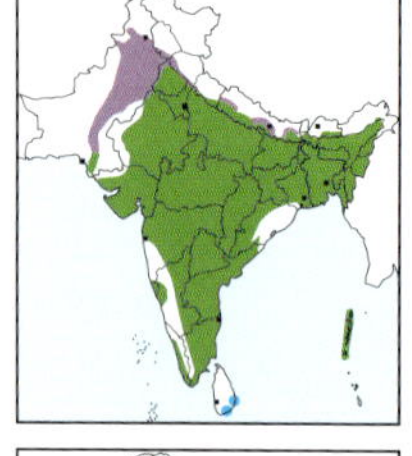

Red Collared Dove *Streptopelia tranquebarica* 20.5–23cm

Widespread resident; unrecorded in N Himalayas and SW India. Vagrant: Sri Lanka. **ID** Male has blue-grey head with black half-collar, pinkish-maroon upperparts, and pink underparts. Compared to Eurasian Collared, female has darker buffish-grey underparts, darker fawn-brown upperparts, greyer underwing-coverts, white (rather than grey) vent, and is smaller with shorter tail. Juvenile lacks neck-collar, and feathers of upperparts and breast are fringed with buff. **Voice** A harsh, rolling, repeated *groo-gurr-goo.* **HH** Habits like Oriental Turtle Dove, but less associated with habitation. Light woodland and trees in open country; in Pakistan prefers more wooded areas such as canal or roadside plantations.

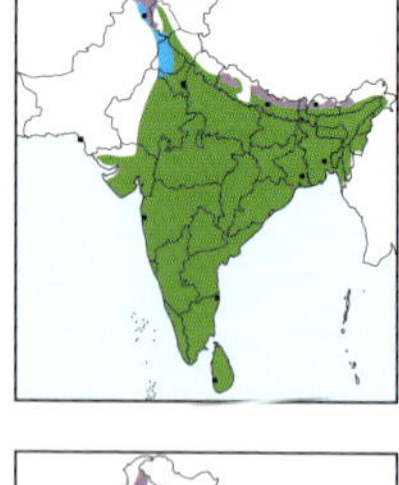

Spotted Dove *Spilopelia chinensis* 30cm

Common and widespread resident except the north-west. **ID** Upperparts are broadly spotted with pinkish-buff. Has extensive black-and-white chequered patches on sides of neck, vinaceous-pink tinged neck and breast, and dark grey-brown rump and tail with blackish base to outer tail feathers. Juvenile is paler and browner, lacks chequered patch on sides of neck, and has faintly barred mantle and scapulars and narrow rufous fringes to wing-coverts. In NE India and Bangladesh race *tigrina* ('Eastern Spotted Dove') has duller upperparts narrowly fringed buff (thus appearing dark rather than pale-spotted), and yellow to orange iris and greyish eye-ring (verses iris and eye-ring reddish). **Voice** A soft, mournful *krookruk-krukroo... kroo-kroo-kroo.* **HH** Habits like Oriental Turtle Dove. Cultivation, habitation and open woodland. **TN** Formerly placed in *Streptopelia.*

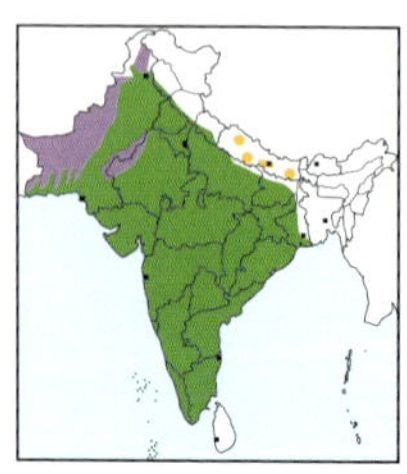

Laughing Dove *Spilopelia senegalensis* 27cm

Widespread resident; unrecorded in most of Himalayas, the north-east and Sri Lanka. Vagrant: Bhutan, Bangladesh. **ID** Slim, small, with long tail. Brownish-pink head and underparts, uniform upperparts, and black stippling on upper breast. Lacks black collar or chequered patches on hindneck. Juvenile duller, lacks black stippling, and has whitish fringes to scapulars and coverts. **Voice** A soft *coo-rooroo-rooroo* or *cru-do-do-do-do.* **HH** Habits similar to Oriental Turtle Dove. Cultivation around villages, and stony and scrub-covered hills in dry country. **TN** Formerly placed in *Streptopelia.*

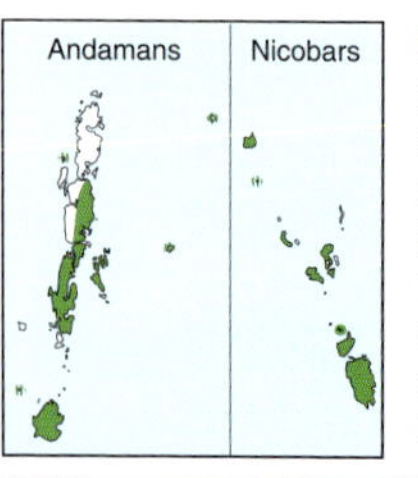

Nicobar Pigeon *Caloenas nicobarica* 32–38cm

Resident. Nicobars (all groups) and Andamans (some smaller islands). **ID** A stocky, broad-winged, short-tailed pigeon. At rest, adult has long blue-black, metallic green and copper neck hackles which extend across mantle, metallic green-and-bronze back and wing-coverts, and white tail. Bill has small 'horn' at base. Juvenile is duller, lacks neck hackles, and has a blackish tail. **Voice** Typically silent, although has harsh guttural croak, short deep cooing and pig-like grunting when threatening others. **HH** Forages actively on forest floor, often crepuscular. Very shy; when disturbed it flies up swiftly with a noisy flutter into thick foliage in the treetops. Readily flies long distances from island to island in search of food. Dense broadleaved, evergreen forest.

ad
meena
ad
agricola
Oriental Turtle Dove
ad
erythrocephala
juv
agricola
Eurasian
Collared
Dove
ad
♀
♂
Red Collared Dove
ad
suratensis
Spotted Dove
ad
tigrina
Nicobar Pigeon
ad
Laughing
Dove
ad

PLATE 21: CUCKOO DOVES AND OTHER PIGEONS

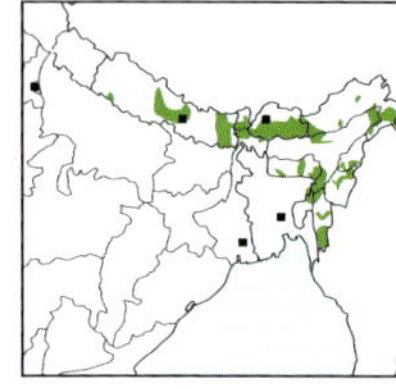

Barred Cuckoo Dove *Macropygia unchall* 37–41cm

Resident. Himalayas and NE Indian hills. Vagrant: Bangladesh. **ID** Long, graduated tail, slim body and small head. Face, belly and vent pale. Upperparts and tail rufous, barred with dark brown. Male has unbarred head and neck with extensive purple-and-green gloss. Female is heavily barred on head, neck and underparts, with gloss restricted to nape and sides of neck. Juvenile is more uniformly dark and heavily barred. **Voice** Repeated hoot, preceded by a soft introductory syllable audible only at close range *hu-whoOOow*. **HH** Feeds in forest trees, clambering about and sometimes hanging upside-down to reach food. Also gleans seeds from cultivation in forest clearings. Dense broadleaved evergreen and secondary forest in tropical, subtropical and temperate zones.

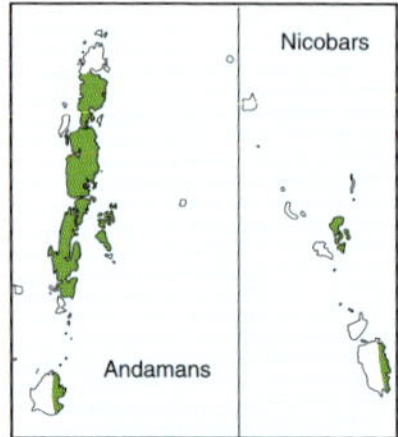

Andaman Cuckoo Dove *Macropygia rufipennis* 39–40cm

Resident. Andamans and Nicobars; only cuckoo dove in these islands. **ID** Long, graduated tail, slim body and small head. Rufous head and underparts, rufous-brown upperparts and unbarred tail. In flight, shows rufous flash across (inner webs of) primaries and rufous underwing-coverts. Male has brown barring on breast and belly, and unmarked rufous head. Female is more rufous with black mottling on crown and nape, and unbarred underparts. **Voice** Repeated two-note phrase, *whaw-whup..whaw-wup...*, somewhat like a Common Cuckoo. **HH** Habits like Barred. Dense broadleaved evergreen and secondary forest.

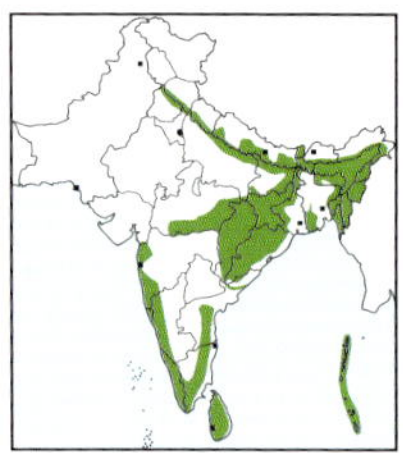

Asian Emerald Dove *Chalcophaps indica* 23–27cm

Resident. Himalayas, NE, SW and E India, and Sri Lanka. **ID** Stocky, broad-winged, short-tailed pigeon with emerald-green upperparts and black-and-white banding on back. Male has grey crown, white forehead and supercilium, and deep vinaceous-pink head-sides and underparts; white shoulder patch. Female is warm brown on crown, neck and underparts, has forehead and supercilium suffused with grey, and shoulder patch is generally warm brown. Juvenile resembles female, but has dark grey barring on buffy-white forehead, narrow buff fringes (and some dark subterminal bars) to neck and underparts, dark brown tertials with chestnut tips, brown primaries with chestnut edges and tips, rufous-brown rump, and brownish bill. Male *C. i. robinsoni* of Sri Lanka has grey of crown extending as broad line on sides of neck to upper mantle. **Voice** Repeated, low-pitched, mournful hoot, preceded by a soft hiccup, *ti-whoooo*. **HH** Feeds on the ground, often on forest tracks. Frequently seen flying away rapidly and directly through the forest and dense second growth. Moist tropical and subtropical broadleaved forest. **AN** Emerald Dove.

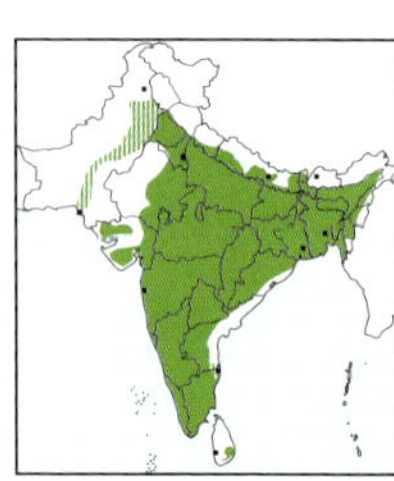

Yellow-footed Green Pigeon *Treron phoenicopterus* 33cm

Widespread resident; unrecorded in most of north-west. **ID** Large size, grey cap, broad olive-yellow collar, pale greyish-green upperparts, mauve shoulder patch, variable yellowish band at base of tail, chestnut-and-white undertail-coverts, and yellow legs and feet. Sexes are similar, although female is duller. *T. p. chlorigaster* and *T. p. phillipsi* of peninsular India and Sri Lanka have greenish-yellow belly and flanks almost concolorous with yellow of breast. Belly and flanks are grey in the northern subspecies (*T. p. phoenicopterus*) and clearly demarcated from breast. Intermediates occur. **Voice** Modulated mellow whistles; often a short rising whistle followed by a longer falling one. **HH** Habits like Orange-breasted. Deciduous forest, groves, fruiting trees around villages and cultivation in tropical and subtropical zones.

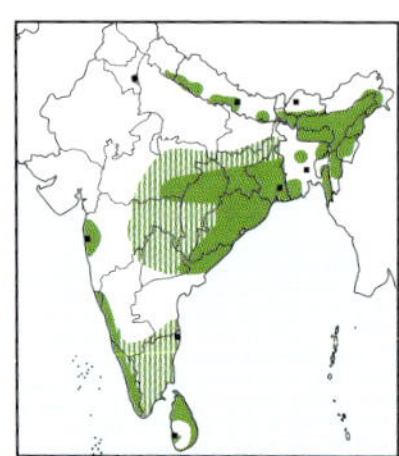

Orange-breasted Green Pigeon *Treron bicinctus* 29cm

Resident. Himalayas, hills of India, Bangladesh and Sri Lanka. Vagrant: Pakistan. **ID** Has green forehead and forecrown and grey central tail feathers in both sexes (at rest, tail appears grey rather than green). Male from other green pigeons by orange breast bordered above by lilac band and yellowish-green forehead merging into pale blue-grey hindcrown and nape. Mantle uniformly green. Female has yellow cast to breast and belly, and grey hindcrown and nape. In Sri Lanka, lacks pronounced yellow forehead and throat of female *T. pompadora*. **Voice** Rapid sequence of gurgling notes preceded by a rising, nasal whistle. **HH** Normally in small flocks, which unite into large ones where food is plentiful. Often in mixed feeding parties with other frugivorous birds such as other green pigeons, barbets and hornbills. Usually at tops of tall trees, coming to the ground to drink. Clambers about branches with great agility to reach fruit. Keeps well concealed in foliage, when approached 'freezes' and can be hard to see. Moist broadleaved evergreen and moist deciduous forest and well-wooded country in subtropical zone.

Barred
Cuckoo Dove
♀
♂
♂
♀
Andaman
Cuckoo Dove
Asian
Emerald Dove
♀
♂
ad
chlorigaster
ad
phoenicopterus
ad
chlorigaster
Yellow-footed
Green Pigeon
♂
♀
Orange-breasted
Green Pigeon

Sri Lanka Green Pigeon *Treron pompadora* 27–28cm

Resident. Sri Lanka. **ID** In Sri Lanka, only similar species is Orange-breasted. Has green central tail feathers (at rest tail appears green, versus grey in Orange-breasted). Male from Orange-breasted by maroon mantle (green in Orange-breasted), uniform green breast, yellow forehead and throat, and whitish undertail-coverts (rufous in Orange-breasted). Female has green mantle and is best told from female Orange-breasted by yellow forehead and throat, and green-streaked whitish undertail-coverts (uniform cinnamon in female Orange-breasted). **Voice** Song a long, fluctuating, mellow, human-like whistle; slower, lower-pitched and more drawn out than song of Ashy-headed, Grey-fronted and Andaman Green Pigeons. **HH** Habits like Orange-breasted. Wet and dry zone forests, open areas with tall trees and wooded cultivation. **TN** This and the following three green pigeons previously treated as conspecific, using the name Pompadour Green Pigeon for the complex.

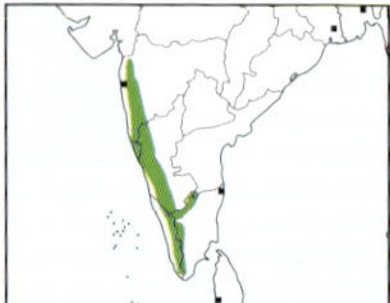

Grey-fronted Green Pigeon *Treron affinis* 27cm

Resident. Western Ghats. **ID** In W peninsular India, only similar species is Orange-breasted. Male from that species by maroon mantle, uniform green breast, pale blue-grey cap, yellowish face and throat, and darker chestnut undertail-coverts. Female has green mantle, and is best told from female Orange-breasted by yellowish face and throat, pale blue-grey cap and green scaling on whitish undertail-coverts. **Voice** Song a mellow series of fluty, rich, meandering whistles, with the initial note starting lowest. **HH** Habits like Orange-breasted. Foothill broadleaved evergreen and moist-deciduous forests.

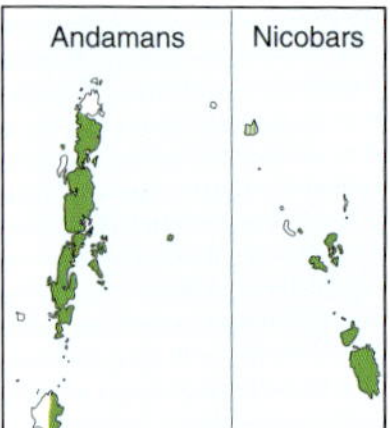

Andaman Green Pigeon *Treron chloropterus* 27cm

Resident. Andamans (North, South and associated islets) and Nicobars (all main islands). The only green pigeon on the Andaman and Nicobar Islands. **ID** Compared to other green pigeons in the 'Pompadour group' is much larger with heavier bill, maroon mantle of male is less extensive and pronounced (not extending to inner wing-coverts, which are green), has bright lime-green rump, and undertail-coverts are yellowish with dark green markings. Mantle of female is green. **Voice** Song like Ashy-headed, but overall has a much more nasal quality. **HH** Habits like Orange-breasted. Broadleaved evergreen forest and forest edge.

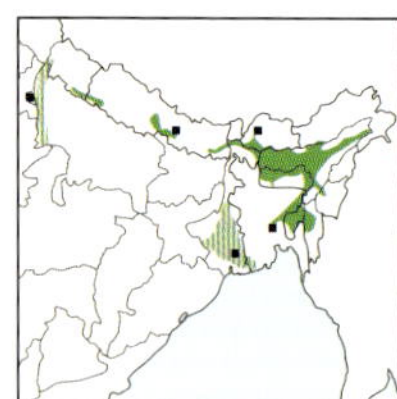

Ashy-headed Green Pigeon *Treron phayrei* 27cm

Resident. Himalayan foothills and NE India. **ID** Both sexes from Thick-billed Green Pigeon by thin blue-grey bill (without prominent red base) and lack of prominent greenish orbital skin. Male has maroon mantle; further differences from male Thick-billed are diffuse orange patch on breast, greenish-yellow throat, and uniform dark chestnut undertail-coverts. Female lacks maroon mantle. Green central tail feathers, greyish cap, yellowish throat and white undertail-coverts help separate from female Orange-breasted. Tail shape and paler green coloration help separate from female Wedge-tailed. **Voice** Song like, but much lower-pitched than, Grey-fronted. **HH** Habits like Orange-breasted. Foothill broadleaved evergreen and moist-deciduous forests.

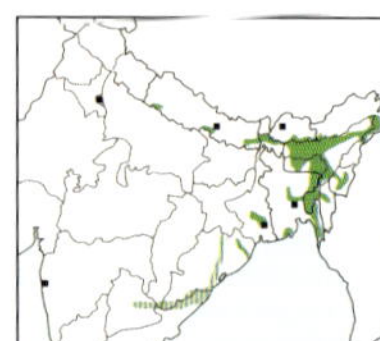

Thick-billed Green Pigeon *Treron curvirostra* 22.5–31cm

Resident. C and E Himalayas, NE India and Bangladesh. **ID** Both sexes from Ashy-headed by thick bill with red base, prominent greenish orbital skin and pronounced whitish scaling on greenish vent. Male has maroon mantle and green breast without orange wash. **Voice** A sequence of drawn-out, melodious, dove-like whistles with a sudden frequency shift up and down in the middle of the whistle. **HH** Habits like Orange-breasted. Dense broadleaved evergreen and mixed broadleaved forests in the tropical and subtropical zones.

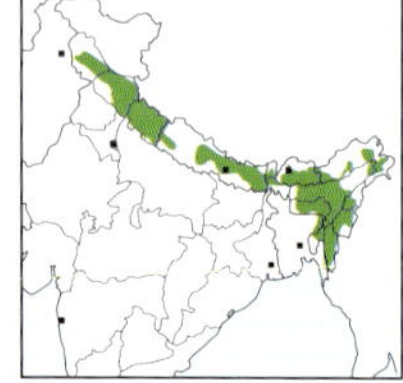

Wedge-tailed Green Pigeon *Treron sphenurus* 30–33cm

Resident. Himalayas, NE India and Bangladesh. **ID** Male from male Ashy-headed by larger size, long and wedge-shaped tail, less extensive maroon patch on upperparts, darker olive-green back and rump, and only indistinct, fine yellow edges to greater coverts and tertials. In flight, more uniform tail, lacking pale grey terminal band of Ashy-headed. Orange wash to crown, and very long pale cinnamon undertail-coverts are further differences. Female is mainly green, lacking orange coloration to crown and breast and maroon on upperparts of male. Undertail-coverts yellowish-white with grey-green centres. From female Ashy-headed by differences in tail shape and colour, lack of prominent yellow in wing and uniform green head (lacking grey crown). **Voice** Three melodious whistles, followed by a series of accelerating short notes, and ending with three drawn-out whistles *whooo...whoooo...whoo...whu-whu-wuwuwuwu.. whoou..uwhoo..whohoohoo.* **HH** Habits like Orange-breasted, but less gregarious. Subtropical and temperate broadleaved forest.

♀
♂
Sri Lanka
Green Pigeon
♀
♂
Grey-fronted
Green Pigeon
♀
♂
Andaman
Green Pigeon
♀
♂
Ashy-headed
Green Pigeon
♀
♂
♀
♂
Thick-billed
Green Pigeon
Wedge-tailed
Green Pigeon

PLATE 23: PIN-TAILED GREEN PIGEON AND IMPERIAL PIGEONS

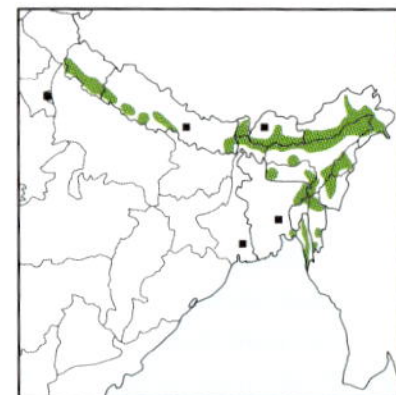

Pin-tailed Green Pigeon *Treron apicauda* 28–36cm

Resident. Himalayas, NE India and Bangladesh. **ID** Large green pigeon with extended and pointed central tail feathers. Grey tail (with greenish tip to central feathers), contrasting with lime-green rump and uppertail-coverts, are additional features from female Wedge-tailed. Green crown, wing-coverts and mantle are additional differences from male Wedge-tailed. Has blue cere and bill base and naked blue lores (lores feathered on Wedge-tailed). Male has longer central tail feathers, pale orange wash to breast, and more pronounced grey cast to upper mantle compared with female. **Voice** Distinctive, deep, tuneful short melody: *oou. . .ou-ruu...oo-ru...ou-rooou*. Much richer, less meandering and more tuneful than Wedge-tailed. **HH** Habits like Orange-breasted. Tall broadleaved forests especially evergreen in tropical and subtropical zones.

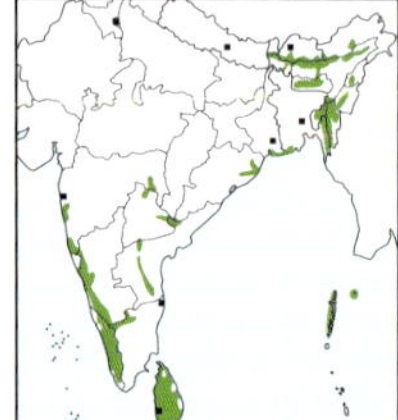

Green Imperial Pigeon *Ducula aenea* 34–39cm

Resident. Mainly Western Ghats, the north-east, Bangladesh, Sri Lanka and Andamans. Vagrant: Nepal. **ID** From Mountain and Malabar Imperial by dark metallic bronze-and-green upperparts, uniform dark green tail (distinctly banded on Mountain and Malabar), and maroon undertail-coverts, contrasting with, and appearing darker than, grey breast and belly. **Voice** Low-pitched, growling or purring, bisyllabic *rhu-rrhuuu* with emphasis on final syllable and typically preceded (or followed) by a shorter and softer note. **HH** Gathers in small flocks at fruiting trees, often with other frugivorous birds. Swift and powerful flight well above treetops when moving between feeding grounds. Other habits are like green pigeons', see Orange-breasted. Tropical broadleaved evergreen, moist deciduous and secondary forests.

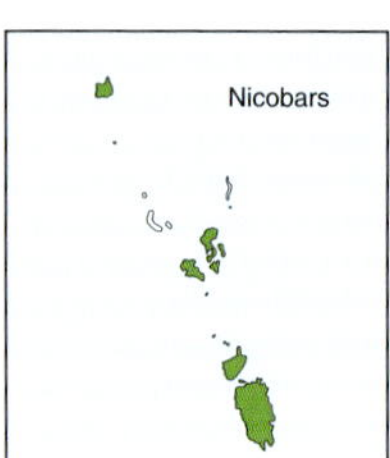

Nicobar Imperial Pigeon *Ducula nicobarica* 35.5–39.5cm

Resident. Nicobars. **ID** Compared to allopatric Green Imperial Pigeon, has darker (less metallic) and more bluish or purplish upperparts; underparts are purer grey, lacking lilac wash, and undertail-coverts are brown or grey. **Voice** Includes pleasant, mellow, short burbling *bullullul(lu)* repeated once or twice per second; also, a mellow, steeply rising then falling *uhwhuuuuu* (both not given by Green) and a deep growling *ghoom*, the latter more like Green. **HH** Frugivorous. Often found singly, in pairs or small groups, usually feeding in the upper canopy. Evergreen forests.

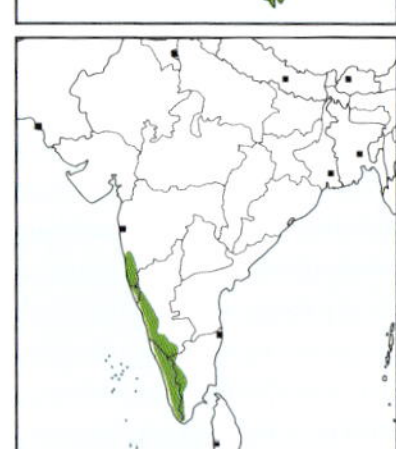

Malabar Imperial Pigeon *Ducula cuprea* 36–39cm

Resident. Western Ghats. **ID** From Green Imperial Pigeon, which also occurs in the Western Ghats, by browner upperparts, whitish throat, grey terminal band to tail, and buff (rather than much darker maroon) undertail-coverts. Care needed as upperparts of Malabar can look quite greenish. Lacks white eye-ring and feathering at base of bill of Green, and bill appears darker (purplish with darker tip). Compared to allopatric Mountain Imperial Pigeon, has more prominent pale throat and deeper purplish-grey (verses paler pinkish-grey) underparts with ochre vent. Crown, nape and upper mantle are purplish-grey (versus pinkish-grey), and lower mantle is greenish-brown (verses purplish-brown). Eye is dark (striking pale iris in Mountain). **Voice** Advertisement call structurally similar to Mountain, but noticeably less hurried with longer interval between second and third hoots resulting in a longer total phrase. **HH** Usually forages in canopy and just below in small flocks. Evergreen forest and dense deciduous forest, mainly in hills. **TN** Previously considered conspecific with Mountain Imperial Pigeon.

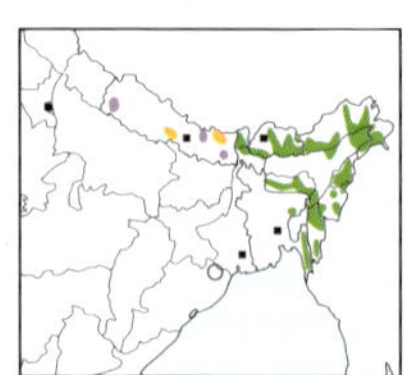

Mountain Imperial Pigeon *Ducula badia* 43–51cm

Resident. Himalayas, NE Indian hills. **ID** From Green Imperial by brownish upperparts, creamy-white chin and throat, pale terminal band to tail, and pale buff undertail-coverts, which are paler (not darker) than belly and vent. Juvenile has rufous fringes to mantle and wing-coverts, with chestnut leading edge to wing, and tail pattern is less well defined. **Voice** Repeated low-pitched sequence of three resonant hoots *hu-huuu...huu*. **HH** Habits like Green Imperial. Seen mostly when flying high above forest from one feeding ground to another, or in breeding season when regularly makes late afternoon flights in wide circles high over the trees. Tall broadleaved evergreen forest in tropical, subtropical and temperate zones.

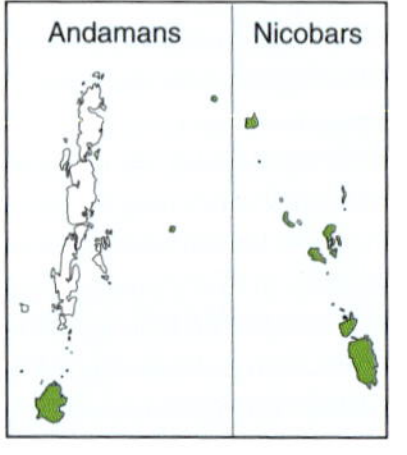

Pied Imperial Pigeon *Ducula bicolor* 35–42cm

Resident on Nicobars; possibly only seasonal visitor to Andamans. **ID** Creamy-white, with black flight feathers and black terminal band to tail. Has blue-grey bill and dark eye contrasting with white head. Juvenile has diffuse ginger-buff tips to feathers of head, upperparts and underparts. **Voice** Advertising call: series of five descending notes *whoo whoo whoo hoo hoo*. Several other calls including a loud, deep, groaning *wuum wuum*. **HH** Frugivorous and arboreal. Usually in small parties in treetops but may gather in large flocks and wander island to island wherever food is plentiful. Evergreen broadleaved forest, favours mangroves.

Pin-tailed
Green Pigeon
♂
♀
ad
Green
Imperial Pigeon
ad
Nicobar
Imperial Pigeon
ad
Malabar
Imperial Pigeon
ad
Mountain
Imperial Pigeon
ad
Pied
Imperial Pigeon

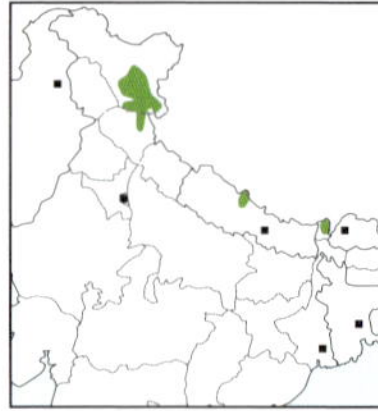

Tibetan Sandgrouse *Syrrhaptes tibetanus* 40cm

Resident. NW Nepal and NW India (from Ladakh to N Himachal), and N Sikkim, 4,200–5,540m (–3,800m in winter). **ID** Large and pin-tailed. In flight, black flight feathers contrast with sandy coverts on upperwing, and underwing is mainly black except white lesser coverts and trailing edge to primaries. Both sexes are distinctive, with pale orange face and throat, fine black barring on crown and breast, sandy upperparts with bold black spotting on scapulars, and white lower breast and belly. Male has unbarred sandy mantle and wing-coverts, and fawn wash across lower breast. Female is like male, but has fine black barring on mantle, coverts and tertials, and more extensive black barring on breast. Immature is similar to female, but has only faint traces of pale orange on throat and lacks pin-tail. **Voice** Calls include deep, disyllabic *guk-guk* or *caga-caga* notes; in alarm a jerky, coarse *uvva, uvva, av-va*. **HH** Drinks irregularly, unlike most sandgrouse. Usually tame. High-altitude, barren, stony semi-desert.

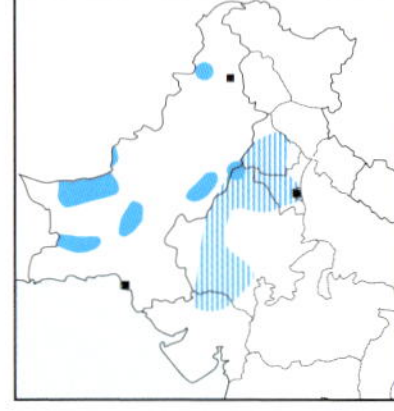

Pin-tailed Sandgrouse *Pterocles alchata* 31–39cm

Occasionally breeds in W Pakistan; winter visitor to Pakistan and NW India. **ID** Has pin-tail. Black eye-stripe, white belly, with two (male) or three (female) narrow black bands across neck and breast. White underwing-coverts with black wingtips and trailing edge; pale grey upperside to primaries. Male in breeding plumage has greenish upperparts with yellowish spotting, and black throat. In non-breeding plumage, male has buff upperparts barred with black, and has white throat. Female breeding has upperparts, including crown and hindneck, barred with golden-buff, grey and black. Has black bar across lower throat, in addition to the two across breast. In non-breeding plumage, female lacks grey barring on upperparts; throat is spotted with black, but lacks clear black band across lower throat. Juvenile is similar to respective non-breeding adult, but pattern less well defined, and lacks pin-tail. **Voice** A loud *catar-catar* in flight, a nasal *ga-ga-ga* and more guttural *gang gang*. **HH** Highly gregarious in winter and on migration. Flies to water in huge flocks in early mornings and late afternoons; also, at midday in very hot weather. Very difficult to approach. Arid, sandy desert, scrub desert and fallow land in partly cultivated semi-desert.

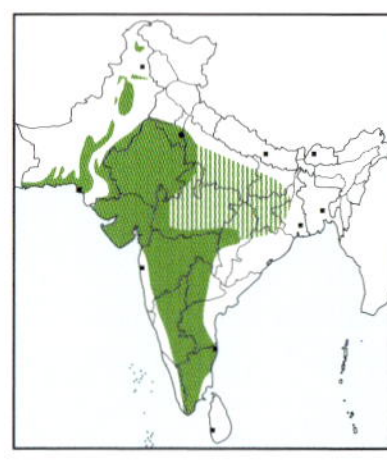

Chestnut-bellied Sandgrouse *Pterocles exustus* 31–33cm

Widespread resident; unrecorded in Himalayas, the north-east, Sri Lanka and parts of E India and the north-west. Subject to erratic local movements depending on food supply and rainfall. **ID** Pin-tailed, with dark underwing, dark belly and black breast line. Male is dusky buff, with yellowish wash to face; has black-fringed yellowish spots on wing-coverts, and diffuse blackish-chestnut belly. Female is heavily spotted with black on breast and barred black on upperparts, and belly patch is dark brown indistinctly barred with rufous. Buff banding across upperwing-coverts and lack of black gorget across throat are useful distinctions from female Black-bellied. Juvenile is like female, but is duller, has less heavily barred upperparts, lacks breast-band, and has shorter tail. **Voice** Flight call a three-note phrase *whit!-kt-arrr*, first note a staccato whistle, the second and third are lower-pitched, goose-like and guttural. In flocks, a constant nasal duck-like squabbling. **HH** Usually keeps in flocks of up to 30 outside breeding season or when flying to drink. Flies to drinking places in early to mid-morning. Birds usually land some distance from water before flying or walking to the water's edge. Sandy deserts, barren plains, sparse thorn scrub and fallow fields and stubbles at the desert edge.

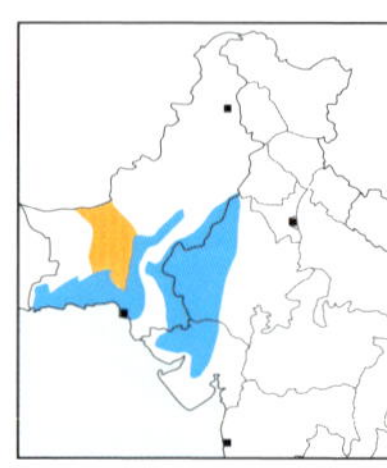

Spotted Sandgrouse *Pterocles senegallus* 30–35cm

Breeds in S Pakistan; winters in Pakistan and NW India. **ID** Pin-tailed (noticeably so compared to Crowned). Rather pale upperwing with dark trailing edge, and whitish belly with black line down centre. Underwing lacks strong contrast between black remiges and whitish coverts of Crowned. Male is sandy olive-brown above, with buff spotting on wing-coverts, and has greyish supercilium and unmarked breast. Main plumage differences from male Crowned are lack of black-and-white head pattern and presence of black centre to belly. Female is boldly spotted with black on upperparts and breast; from female Crowned by warmer orange-buff coloration, sparser but more prominent spotting on upperparts and breast, unbarred lower breast and belly, and black centre to belly and vent. Juvenile is similar to female, but lacks orange throat and is more finely barred. Unbarred belly, with black line down centre, helps separate it from juvenile Crowned. **Voice** Flight call a loud repeated double-noted *whik!-kaaw*. In flocks, a constant, nasal, nervous yapping sound. **HH** Usually in flocks of 100 or more outside the breeding season or in flights to drinking places. Regularly flies to water about two hours after sunrise; also in evening in hot weather; birds fly directly to the water's edge or may even land on the water. Barren, sandy desert and arid stony foothills.

♀
♂
♂
Tibetan Sandgrouse
♀
♂
♀
♂
Pin-tailed Sandgrouse
♂
♀
♀
♂
Chestnut-bellied Sandgrouse
♂
♂
♀
Spotted Sandgrouse

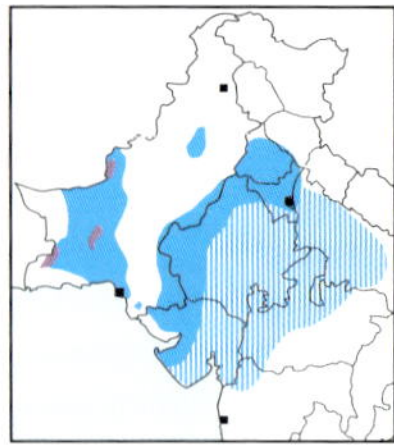

Black-bellied Sandgrouse *Pterocles orientalis* 33–39cm

Breeds in Balochistan, Pakistan; winters in Pakistan and NW India. **ID** Large, stocky sandgrouse, lacking pin tail; both sexes have black belly, buff breast-band and narrow black gorget across breast. Most like Chestnut-bellied, but stockier, with broader-based wings, lacks elongated central tail feathers, and has white underwing-coverts, which contrast strongly with black flight feathers. Male has greyish head, neck and upper breast, black-and-chestnut throat, and yellowish spotting to upperparts. Female is heavily marked with black on upper breast and upperparts. Additional features from female Chestnut-bellied are black throat-collar and lacks buff banding on wing of that species. Juvenile is like female, but very soon resembles dull version of respective adult. **Voice** Flight call distinctive, a far-carrying liquid bubbling trill slowing towards the end, *chorrrrerereh*; also, a soft, gurgling *tchowrrr rerr-rerr.* **HH** Makes daily flights to water two hours or so after sunrise, and less regularly in the late afternoon. Very wary; flocks may circle over drinking places before landing. Thorn scrub in semi-desert and fallow cultivation at the desert edge.

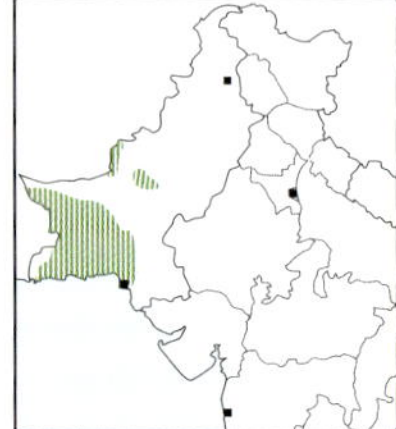

Crowned Sandgrouse *Pterocles coronatus* 27–30cm

Resident. Mainly Pakistan. **ID** Small, compact and short-tailed. Blackish flight feathers contrast with coverts on both surfaces of wing. Male is sandy-brown, with prominent buff spotting on scapulars and coverts. From male Spotted by black-and-white pattern to head, darker rufous crown, and more prominent buff spotting on upperparts. Female is sandy-buff all over, heavily spotted and barred with black. From female Spotted by colder coloration, less prominent spotting, barred lower breast and belly, and lack of black centre to belly and vent. Possibly confusable with female Lichtenstein's, but has orange-buff throat. Juvenile is similar to female, but has whiter throat and is more finely barred. Immature resembles respective adult, but head pattern of young male is indistinct (and more closely resembles male Spotted). **Voice** Gives soft *kla kla kla* or staccato but far-carrying *cha-chagarra*, with a soft bisyllabic *hu hu* in alarm. **HH** Typically flies to drink in the early morning in flocks of up to 30 birds, settles a few hundred metres from the water until a large party gathers, then cautiously walks to drinking place. Very barren and arid desert regions.

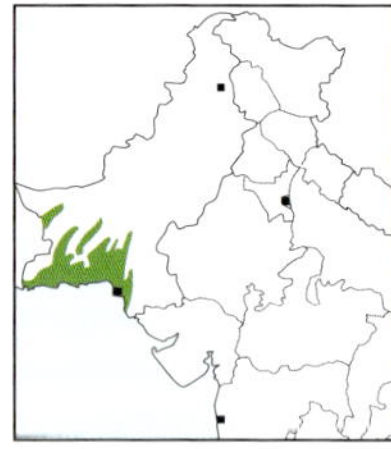

Lichtenstein's Sandgrouse *Pterocles lichtensteinii* 22–26cm

Resident. SW Pakistan. **ID** Small, stocky, and heavily barred. Underwing dark grey. Male has orange bill, white forehead and forecrown crossed by two black bands, golden-buff banding across closed wing, and yellowish-buff and black banding on breast. Female has dark bill, is heavily barred all over, and lacks pattern on head and bands across breast of male. Juvenile is like female, but more finely barred. Immature as adult, but male may lack black-and-white pattern on head, and breast-bands may be poorly defined. **Voice** Gives repeated, liquid *wheet-wheet-wheet* or *quitoo* in flight. Flocks in chorus sound wheezy and tinkly. **HH** Habits are very similar to Painted. Low stony hills with scattered scrub in desert and dry rocky nullahs.

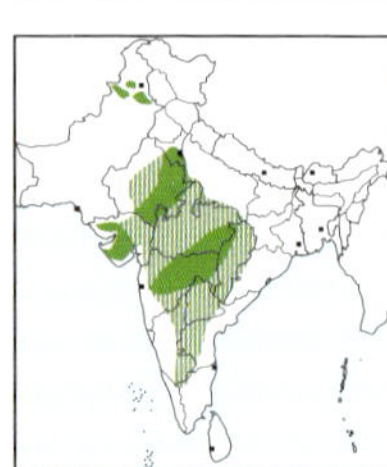

Painted Sandgrouse *Pterocles indicus* 28cm

Resident, subject to local movements. N Pakistan and India. **ID** Small, stocky, and heavily barred. Underwing dark grey. Both sexes have orange bill. Male has white forehead divided by black cross-band, and strongly banded breast. More richly coloured and strongly marked than Lichtenstein's (no overlap in range), and has unbarred buffish-orange neck, breast and inner wing-coverts. Female is heavily barred all over, and lacks male's pattern on head and breast. Is like female Lichtenstein's, but has unspotted creamy face and throat, more broadly and coarsely barred upperparts with warmer buff and rufous tones, and darker, more densely barred belly; outer greater coverts are unbarred and show as distinct buff area in wing. Immature similar to female but is more closely barred. **Voice** Flight call a rapid sequence of 2–4 staccato gravelly notes, with emphasis on the last one *dji-dji-chik!* or *wi-chik!* repeated at intervals. **HH** Less gregarious than other species, except Lichtenstein's; usually keeping in twos, threes or small groups of up to ten. Drinks only after dusk, usually settling some distance from water before moving in to drink. Low hills with scattered thorn scrub or open rocky and grassy areas; firebreaks in deciduous forest and shallow rocky ravines.

♂
♂
Black-bellied Sandgrouse
♀
♂
♂
Crowned Sandgrouse
♀
♂
♂
♀
Lichtenstein's Sandgrouse
♂
♀
♂
Painted Sandgrouse

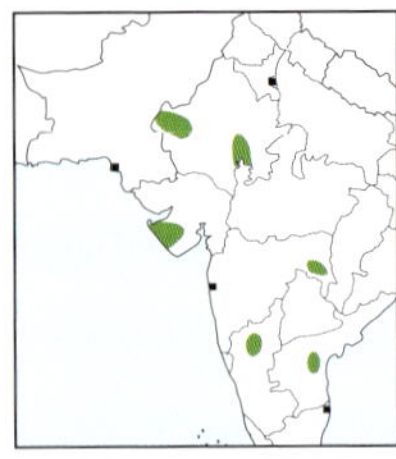

Great Indian Bustard *Ardeotis nigriceps* 76–122cm

Resident. Now mainly only in Rajasthan India. **ID** Very large. Flight action is stiff, with wingbeats slow and heavy; upperwing mainly dark with whitish tips to blackish coverts. Male has black breast-band and almost white neck. Female smaller; with greyer neck, whitish supercilium, and breast-band is broken or absent. **Voice** A bark or bellow in alarm; in display, has a deep booming moan. **HH** Normally in small parties. Feeds chiefly in early mornings and late afternoons. Flight is steady, quite close to ground and can be sustained over long distances. Males gather at traditional sites to perform their displays; the throat sac is greatly distended, and the bird emits a deep boom and struts with cocked tail and drooping wings. Arid and semi-arid grasslands with good cover of bushes; also, adjacent open dry deciduous forest. Globally threatened.

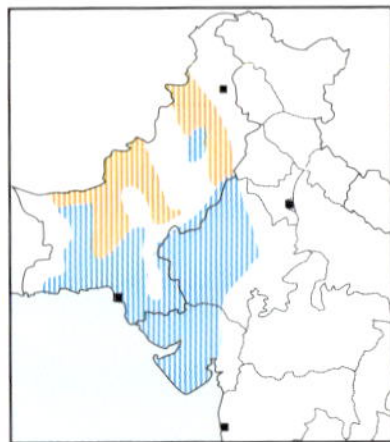

Macqueen's Bustard *Chlamydotis macqueenii* 55–75cm

Mainly winter visitor to Pakistan and NW India; a few breed in W Pakistan. **ID** Medium-sized, short-legged bustard with long tail. Appears crested and has a dark vertical stripe on neck. Upperparts are sandy, with distinct dark bars. In flight, shows extensive white patch on outer primaries and pale panel across greater coverts. Sexes similar, but female is smaller, crest and dark neck stripe are less pronounced, with less distinct pale panel across greater coverts. **Voice** Silent. **HH** Chiefly nocturnal in Pakistan where disturbance is high. Extremely shy and wary. Semi-desert with sand dunes and sparsely scattered shrubs, sandy grasslands; also, mustard fields in winter. Globally threatened.

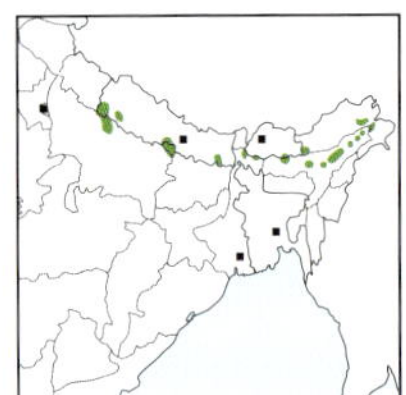

Bengal Florican *Houbaropsis bengalensis* 64–68cm

Resident. Fragmented populations in lowlands of N India, Assam and S Nepal. **ID** Larger and stockier than Lesser Florican, with broader head and thicker neck. Breeding male has black head, neck and underparts, and white patch on wing-coverts visible at rest. In flight wings are entirely white except black tips on upperwing and black underwing-coverts. Non-breeding male is like female but has largely white wings and retains some black on belly. Female is larger than male and has buffish neck and underparts, and pale buff coverts with dark flight feathers. Immature is like female but has banding on flight feathers and wing-coverts are more heavily marked. **Voice** Normally silent, but a shrill, metallic *chik-chik-chik* when disturbed. **HH** Usually solitary, although small groups of males gather briefly in breeding season. Forages in short grass areas in early mornings and late afternoons, then retires into tall grass cover. Most easily seen in breeding season when males perform striking displays, leaping above grassland in early mornings and evenings. Tall grassland with scattered bushes and interspersed with short-grass areas. Globally threatened.

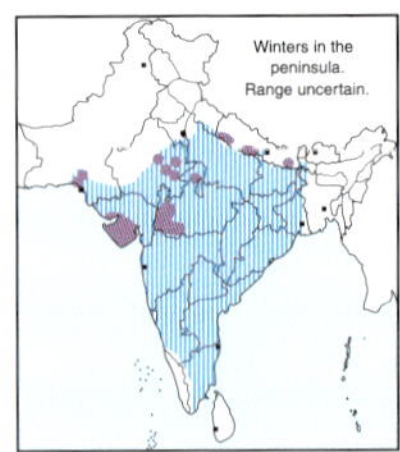

Lesser Florican *Sypheotides indicus* 46–51cm

Resident. Breeds NW India; winters south to SE India. Now very rare visitor to Nepal. **ID** Smaller and slimmer than Bengal, with smaller head, slimmer neck and more rapid wingbeats. Male breeding has black head/neck and underparts, and white patch on wing-coverts visible at rest. Differs by white throat, spatulate-tipped head plumes, and white 'hind collar'; also, white of wing is less extensive, and has rufous banding on dark flight feathers. Non-breeding male similar to female, but has whiter wing-coverts and black underwing-coverts. Female and immature from Bengal by dark crescent below eye, dark stripes on foreneck, and rufous-barred primaries. **Voice** Frog-like croak during display; short whistle when disturbed. **HH** Less shy than other bustards. Males are conspicuous in breeding season when they repeatedly perform a spectacular display flight. Dry grassland with scattered bushes and cotton and millet crops. Globally threatened.

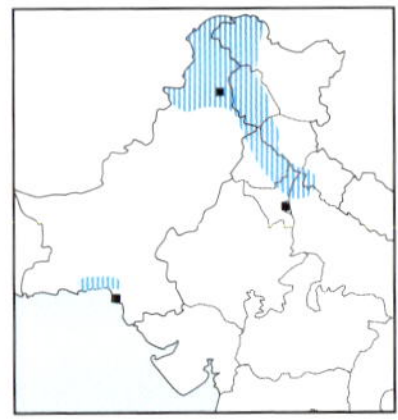

Little Bustard *Tetrax tetrax* 40–45cm

Winter visitor. Pakistan and N India. **ID** Small, stocky bustard, which shows extensive white panel across secondaries and inner primaries in flight. Has distinctive rapid 'winnowing' flight action on stiff, noticeably bowed wings, interspersed with short glides. Breeding male has grey face, and black-and-white pattern on neck and breast. Non-breeding male is similar to female but is less heavily marked on upperparts and whiter on underparts, and shows more white in wing. Female is warm buff-brown, with extensive black streaking on head and neck; has coarse blackish markings on upperparts, and black barring and chevrons on breast and flanks. **Voice** A hoarse grunt when flushed. **HH** Usually in small parties. Flight is swift and direct, with occasional erratic turns. Male produces whistling sound in flight, produced by an emarginated primary feather. Open grassland and short crops.

♂
♂
Great
Indian Bustard
♀
♂
♀
♂
Macqueen's
Bustard
imm
♀
♂
♂
♀
♂ br
♂ non-br
Bengal
Florican
♂ br
♂ non-br
Lesser
Florican
♀
♀
♂ br
♂ br
Little Bustard

Green-billed Coucal *Centropus chlororhynchos* 43–46cm

Resident. Sri Lanka. **ID** From Greater Coucal, which also occurs in Sri Lanka, by greenish or ivory rather than black bill and in distinctive call. Head and underparts duller and browner in coloration compared with Greater. Wings are maroon-brown and contrast less with head and body. Eyes are usually dark (but can be red as in Greater). Juvenile has duller bill and eyes and dark barring on coverts. **Voice** Similar to Greater but usually only two or three syllables and is deeper with a sonorous mournful quality: *hooo-pooop* or *hooo-poo-pooop*. **HH** Habits similar to Greater but very secretive. Tall damp forest with dense undergrowth of bamboo and cane brakes. Globally threatened.

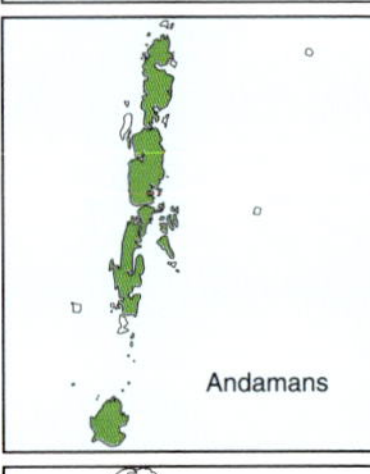

Andaman Coucal *Centropus andamanensis* 45–48cm

Resident. Andamans. **ID** The only coucal in the Andamans. Like Greater, with striking chestnut wings, but head and body are sooty-brown to fawn-brown, with brown rump and tail. Some have paler, dirty buff head and underparts, and greyish-buff tail which is distinctly darker towards tip. Juvenile is indistinctly and diffusely barred with brown on head, mantle and entire underparts. **Voice** A deep *boom, boom, boom.* **HH** Habits like Greater. Forest edges, gardens and cultivation and mangroves. **AN** Brown Coucal.

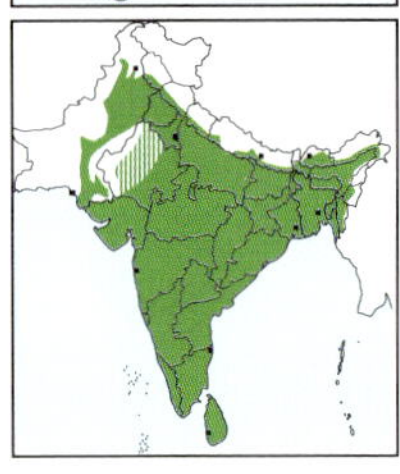

Greater Coucal *Centropus sinensis* 47–56cm

Resident. Pakistan east through base of Himalayas and N Gangetic plain to Bangladesh, peninsular India and Sri Lanka. **ID** Adult from adult breeding Lesser Coucal by much larger size, black underwing-coverts, and brighter and more uniform chestnut wings. Juvenile has brownish-black head and body, with chestnut spotting on crown and nape (becoming barred on mantle), and diffuse whitish barring on entire underparts; chestnut-brown coverts and flight feathers are barred dark brown, and tail is narrowly barred buff or greyish-white. Immature resembles adult, although head and body are duller black and has barred (juvenile) flight feathers and tail. In peninsular India and Sri Lanka *C. s. parroti* ('Southern Coucal') is smaller; head and body have a blue-green rather than purplish gloss, shows less rufous on mantle and has brownish forehead and throat. Most notably, juvenile *parroti* is similar in plumage to adult with head and body dull blackish and lacking prominent barring; chestnut wings are duller, and coverts and tertials are marked with black. In Sri Lanka it thus more closely resembles Green-billed. **Voice** Deep, resonant and primate-like *hoop-hoop-hoop-hoop-hoop-hoop*, descending slightly at first then rising towards the end. **HH** Walks sedately with tail held horizontal, or skulks in dense vegetation. Slow, weak and clumsy flight. Tall grassland, bamboo or scrub jungle, shrubbery in cultivation and gardens and thick cover adjacent to wetlands.

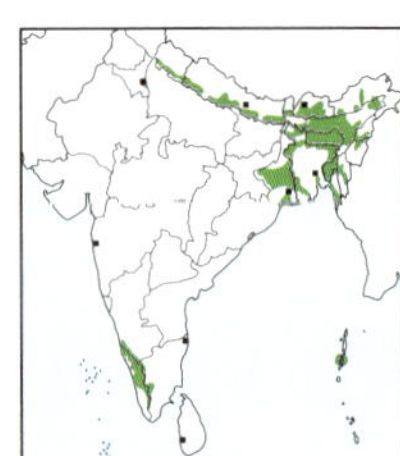

Lesser Coucal *Centropus bengalensis* 31–34cm

Resident. Himalayas, NE, E and SW India, and Bangladesh. **ID** Smaller than Greater, with stouter bill, duller chestnut mantle and wings (including browner tertials and primary tips), and chestnut underwing-coverts. Note Greater and Lesser can be much closer in size in SW India. Eyes are dark (red in Greater). Often shows buff streaking on some scapulars and wing-coverts (unlike Greater). Adult non-breeding has dark brown head and mantle with prominent buff shaft streaks, and dark brown and rufous barring on rump and very long uppertail-coverts. Wings and tail are like adult breeding. Juvenile is similar to adult non-breeding, but has dark barring on crown, mantle and back, dark brown barring on wings, and narrow rufous barring on tail. Immature has head and body as adult non-breeding, but wings and tail are barred as in juvenile. **Voice** Series of deep resonant *pwoop-pwoop-pwoop* notes, very similar to Greater, but usually slightly faster and more interrogative, initially ascending, then descending and decelerating. **HH** Habits like Greater. Tall grassland, reedbeds and dense shrubbery; in Nepal also in grass with scattered trees and bushes.

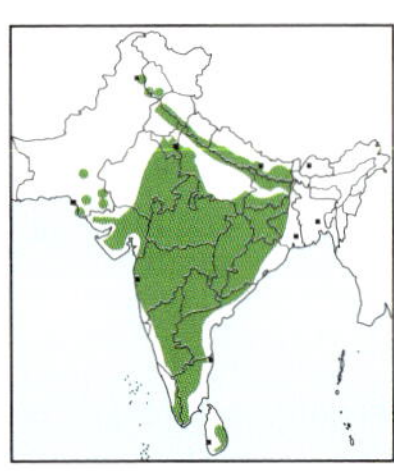

Sirkeer Malkoha *Taccocua leschenaultii* 43cm

Widespread resident; unrecorded in NE and parts of N and NW subcontinent. Vagrant: Bangladesh. **ID** Adult mainly sandy grey-brown, with yellow-tipped red bill and whitish-edged dark facial skin giving masked appearance. Black shaft streaking on crown, mantle and breast, throat buff, belly rufous-buff. Has long, graduated, white-tipped tail. Immature very similar, but has indistinct buff fringes to wing-coverts, scapulars and tertials. Juvenile has broad dark brown streaking on head, mantle, throat and breast, and buff fringes to mantle, wing-coverts and tertials; bill is dull greyish-pink. **Voice** Normally silent; occasional shriek, *kek-kek-kek-kerek-kerek*. **HH** Largely terrestrial. Sometimes clambers among shrubs and small trees. Thorn scrub and acacia bushes in stony places; also, semi-desert. **TN** Formerly placed in *Phaenicophaeus*.

ad
Andaman Coucal
ad
uv
Green-billed
Coucal
juv
ad
parroti
ad
sinensis
imm
Greater Coucal
juv
br
non-br
Sirkeer Malkoha
ad
Lesser Coucal

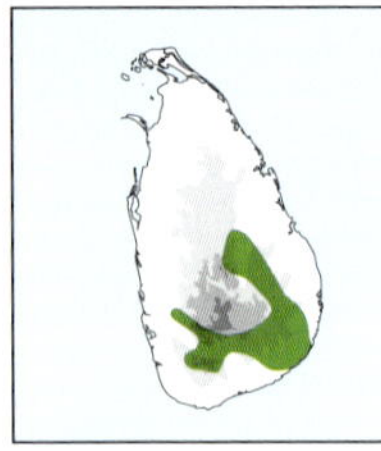

Red-faced Malkoha *Phaenicophaeus pyrrhocephalus* 40–47cm

Resident. Sri Lanka. **ID** A very large, dark-green malkoha. Adult has stout apple-green bill, large red face patch, whitish chin and malar stripe contrasting with black throat and breast, white flecking on crown and nape, striking white belly, and very broad white tips to tail feathers. Eyes are dark in male and white in female. Juvenile has smaller red face patch, brown streaking on crown and nape, and extensive greyish-white streaking on throat, neck-sides and breast. **Voice** Usually silent; sometimes a *grrr-GRRRRR-GRRRRR* and short single yelping whistles. **HH** Habits like Green-billed but frequents the tree canopy. Typically threads its way through foliage, creepers and branches. Frequently associates with mixed feeding flocks of other species. Dense, tall, broadleaved mainly evergreen forest. Globally threatened.

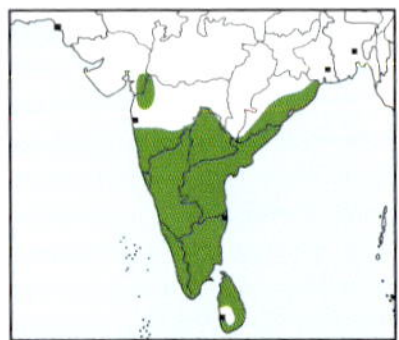

Blue-faced Malkoha *Phaenicophaeus viridirostris* 39cm

Resident. Peninsular India and Sri Lanka. **ID** From the larger Green-billed Malkoha (which it replaces in S India and Sri Lanka) in having blue rather than red eye-patch, darker green coloration to head and nape (lacking pale-streaked supercilium), darker grey throat and breast with buffish streaking, distinctly buffish lower belly and vent, and broader white tips to tail feathers. **Voice** A low croaking *kra*. **HH** Habits like Green-billed. Bushes, thorn scrub and open second growth. **TN** Formerly placed in *Rhopodytes*.

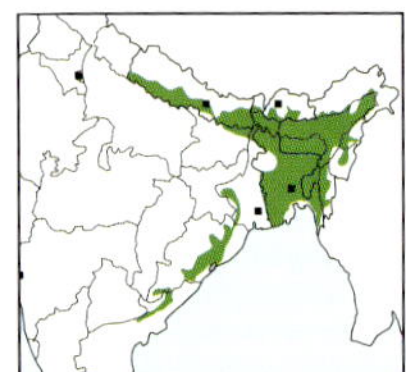

Green-billed Malkoha *Phaenicophaeus tristis* 50–60cm

Resident. Himalayas, NE and E India and Bangladesh. **ID** Large and very long-tailed. Greyish-green in coloration, with lime-green bill, red eye-patch, white-streaked supercilium, and broad white tips to tail feathers. Underparts pale, with dark shaft streaks on throat, becoming darker towards vent. **Voice** Low croaking *ko... ko... ko*, and a chuckle when flushed. **HH** Shy; usually keeps out of sight. Creeps and clambers unobtrusively through branches low down in thick vegetation. A weak flier, usually makes short laboured flights from one thicket to another. Dense broadleaved evergreen and moist deciduous thickets. **TN** Formerly placed in *Rhopodytes*.

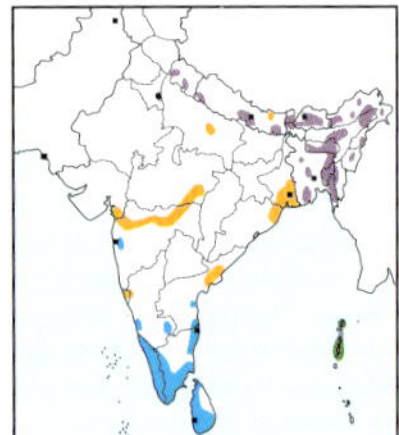

Chestnut-winged Cuckoo *Clamator coromandus* 38–46cm

Breeds in Himalayas, NE India and Bangladesh; winter visitor to S India and Sri Lanka. **ID** Prominent crest, whitish collar, chestnut wings, and orange wash to throat and breast. Long black tail has narrow greyish-white feather tips. Lacks white in wing. Juvenile has shorter crest, rufous fringes to upperparts, buff collar, whitish throat and breast, broad buff tips to rectrices, and paler bill. Immature is like adult, but retains some buff tips to scapulars, coverts and tail feathers. **Voice** A series of double metallic whistles, *breep breep*; also, a harsh grating scream. **HH** Arboreal and retiring, favours the canopy and usually inconspicuous when perched among foliage. Often descends to lower storey of bushes to feed. Broadleaved evergreen and moist deciduous forest and scrub jungle.

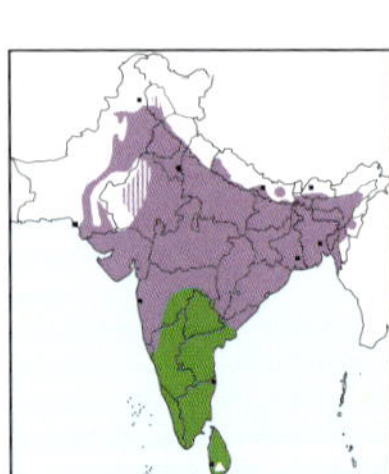

Pied Cuckoo *Clamator jacobinus* 31–34cm

Widespread resident and partial migrant. **ID** Black and white with crest. Has white patch at base of primaries, and prominent white tips to tail feathers. Juvenile has browner upperparts, grey wash to throat and upper breast, and buffish wash to rest of underparts. Has smaller crest than adult, with smaller white wing patch, and paler bill. **Voice** Loud metallic *piu... piu... pee-pee piu, pee-pee piu*. **HH** Conspicuous, often perching in the open. Chiefly arboreal, but often searches for food in low bushes and sometimes hops on ground. Forest, well-wooded areas including in gardens and cultivation, bushes in semi-desert, and irrigated forest plantations in Pakistan. **AN** Jacobin Cuckoo.

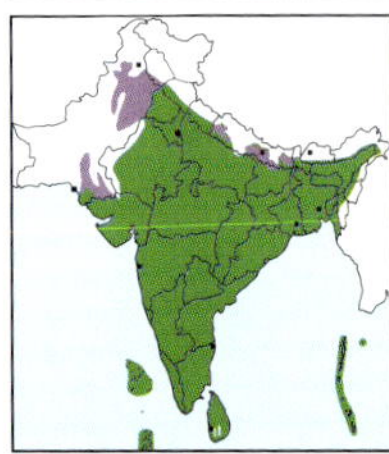

Asian Koel *Eudynamys scolopaceus* 39–46cm

Mainly resident. NE and SE Pakistan, widespread elsewhere in subcontinent. **ID** Large, with long and broad tail. Male is glossy black (with green iridescence), with a dull lime-green bill and brilliant red eye. Female is brown above (with faint green gloss), spotted and barred white and buff, and white below, strongly barred dark brown. Also, has striking red eye. Juvenile blackish, with white or buff tips to wing-coverts and tertials, and variable white barring on underparts; tail black, although shows pronounced rufous barring in some. Eye dull. **Voice** Loud, rising and increasingly anxious repeated *ko-el...ko-el...ko-el* and a bubbling more rapidly repeated *koel... koel*. **HH** Typically concealed in dense foliage when not feeding, although may sun itself from a treetop in early morning. Usually seen when it flies hurriedly from one tree to another. Open woodland, gardens, groves around cultivation, parks in towns and cities; irrigated plantations in Pakistan.

ad
Blue-faced
Malkoha
♂
♀
Red-faced
Malkoha
juv
ad
Green-billed
Malkoha
juv
ad
Pied Cuckoo
juv
Chestnut-winged
Cuckoo
♂
juv
Asian Koel
♀
juv

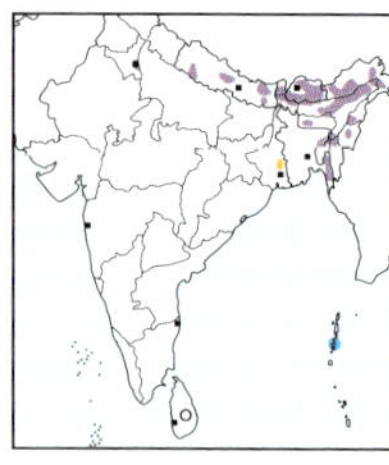

Asian Emerald Cuckoo *Chrysococcyx maculatus* 17–18cm

Summer visitor to C and E Himalayas, NE India and Bangladesh; winter visitor to Andamans and Nicobars. Vagrant: Nepal and Sri Lanka. **ID** Male has emerald-green head, breast and upperparts, and bold dark green barring on white underparts (much of head, throat and breast barred as rest of underparts in immature male). Female has rufous-orange crown and nape and unbarred bronze-green mantle and wings. Yellow bill with dark tip. Juvenile has rufous fringes to upperparts and rufous-orange wash to barred throat and breast. **Voice** Loud descending *kee-kee-kee-kee*, loud whistled twitters and a sharp *chweek* in flight. **HH** Usually keeps to leafy canopy of tall trees, but on arrival in spring often flies about conspicuously. Very active, moving rapidly from branch to branch and making sallies to capture flying insects. Has a habit of perching along a branch, rather than across it. Flight is fast and direct. Evergreen broadleaved forest.

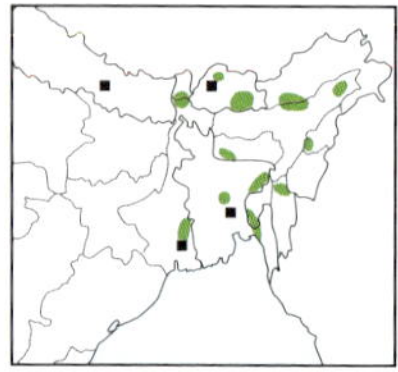

Violet Cuckoo *Chrysococcyx xanthorhynchus* 16cm

Resident or summer visitor to E Himalayas and NE Indian hills. Vagrant: Nepal. **ID** Male has purple upperparts. Female has uniform bronze-brown upperparts, with variable greenish tinge, and white underparts with brownish-green barring. Male has orange bill (immature with dark tip); orangish with darker tip in female. Juvenile like juvenile Asian Emerald, but upperparts rufous with dark greenish spotting and barring (mantle and wings appear greenish, boldly barred rufous in some), and lacks rufous-orange wash to face and throat. **Voice** A *che-wick*, often in flight; also, a shrill descending trill preceded by a triple note *seer-se-seer, seeseeseesee*. **HH** Habits very poorly known; presumably similar to Asian Emerald. Tree clumps in secondary evergreen forest and orchards.

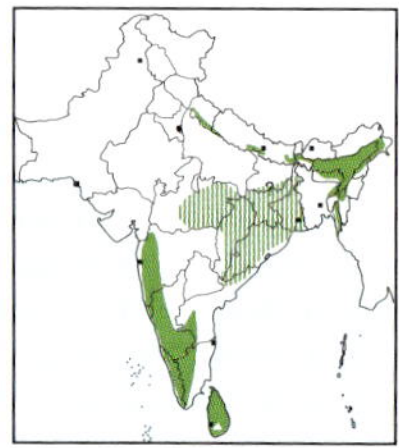

Banded Bay Cuckoo *Cacomantis sonneratii* 22–24cm

Resident, Sri Lanka, SW, E and NE India, and S Himalayas. **ID** White supercilium (finely barred with black, and encircles brown ear-coverts), finely barred white underparts, and fine and regular dark barring on rufous upperparts. Juvenile has broader (and more diffuse) barring on underparts, and crown and nape have some buff barring. In Sri Lanka (*C. s. waiti*) is almost uniform dark bronze-brown above, and more strongly barred below. **Voice** A shrill, whistled *pi-pi-pew-pew*, the first two notes on the same pitch, the last two descending. **HH** Favours the bare branches of treetops, from which it calls, usually holding the tail depressed, wings drooping and rump feathers fluffed out. Dense broadleaved forest in Nepal, lightly wooded country in India; forest edges, patches of shifting cultivation and open forest in Sri Lanka.

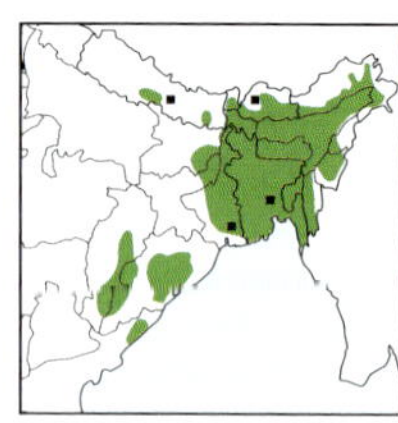

Plaintive Cuckoo *Cacomantis merulinus* 18–23.5cm

Resident. Resident, E and NE India, C and E Himalayas, and Bangladesh. **ID** Adult has brownish-grey head and upperparts and orange underparts. On hepatic female, compared to Grey-bellied, base colour of underparts is pale rufous, upperparts are duller rufous-brown with more regular dark barring, and tail is strongly barred. Juvenile has bold streaking on rufous-orange head and breast, and is distinct from hepatic and juvenile Grey-bellied. **Voice** A mournful whistle *tay... ta... tee*, the second note lower and the third note higher than the first; also, *tay... ta... ta... tay* repeated with increasing speed and ascending in pitch. **HH** Habits and habitat like Grey-bellied.

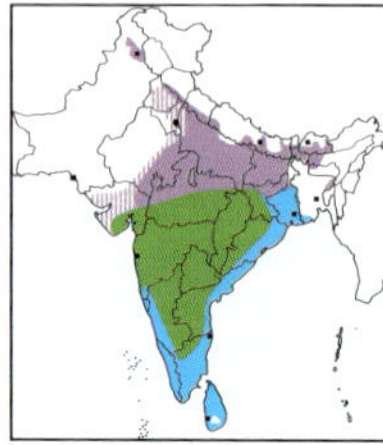

Grey-bellied Cuckoo *Cacomantis passerinus* 18–22cm

Summers in Himalayas; widespread resident or winter visitor further south; unrecorded in north-west. **ID** Grey adult is grey with white vent and undertail-coverts. On hepatic female, which is most frequent, base colour of underparts is mainly white, upperparts are bright rufous with crown and nape only sparsely barred, and tail is unbarred (compare Banded Bay and Plaintive Cuckoos). Juvenile varies. Some have uniform brownish-black upperparts (without distinct barring), dusky-grey underparts with indistinct and diffuse buffish-grey barring mainly on belly and flanks (some are more heavily barred on underparts), and tail dark grey-brown with each feather finely notched with greyish-white. Others are barred rufous on upperparts, and underparts are like hepatic female; tail is dark brown, barred rufous (pattern similar to tail of Plaintive). Intermediates occur, e.g. with uniform grey upperparts and strong rufous barring on tail. **Voice** A clear interrogative *pee-pipee-pee... pipee-pee* ascending in scale and higher-pitched with each repetition; also, a plaintive single whistle *piteer* frequently repeated at short intervals. **HH** Keeps mainly to leafy tops of trees and bushes; sometimes descends briefly to ground to pick up caterpillars, or sallies after insects. Repeatedly flies rapidly to different vantage points and calls. When calling holds wings loosely, tail depressed and rump feathers fluffed out. All types of lightly wooded country: open forest, groves, wooded gardens and shade trees in plantations.

Asian Emerald Cuckoo
♂
♀
♂ imm
juv
Violet Cuckoo
♂
♀
juv
Banded Bay Cuckoo
ad
juv
juv
ad
Plaintive Cuckoo
♀ hepatic
ad
♀ hepatic
Grey-bellied Cuckoo
grey juv
rufous juv

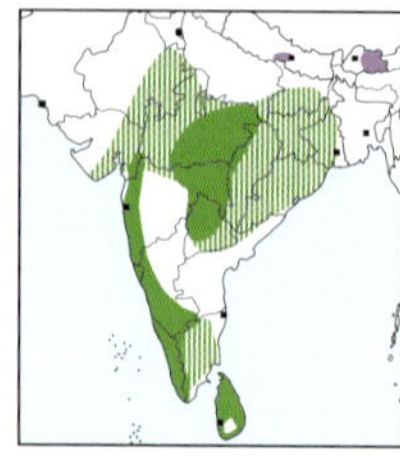

Fork-tailed Drongo Cuckoo *Surniculus dicruroides* 22–26cm

Resident. Hills of C and SW India and Sri Lanka; also, summer visitor Himalayan foothills and NE India. However, distribution uncertain because of confusion in separating this species from Square-tailed. Fork-tailed was described from Nepal in 19th century. **ID** Adult is glossy black, except fine white barring on very long undertail-coverts, white thighs, and tiny white patch on nape (difficult to see in field). Tail noticeably forked compared with Square-tailed, but this character is not always reliable as the tail can appear squarish from some angles or if individuals are moulting tail feathers. Best told from a drongo by fine, downcurved black bill and white-barred undertail-coverts. Juvenile similar, but dull black, spotted with white. **Voice** Song a piercing series of rich whistles evenly ascending the scale, with second note higher than first. Frequency lower than Square-tailed but difficult to separate in the field, though easily told apart on sonograms. **HH** Resembles a drongo, but is less active and hawks flying insects with direct flight. Perches on a bare branch when calling, but otherwise usually keeps in canopy. Forest edges and clearings, open secondary forest and well-wooded areas.

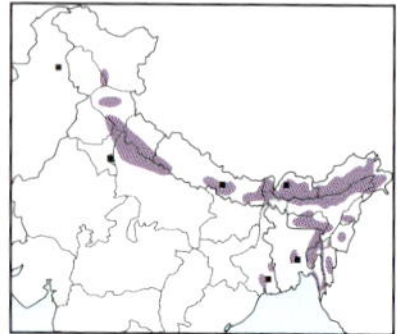

Square-tailed Drongo Cuckoo *Surniculus lugubris* 24–25cm

Resident. Summer visitor. Himalayas from Kashmir to NE Indian hills and Bangladesh. Presumably winters outside the subcontinent. **ID** Adult and juvenile much as Fork-tailed Drongo Cuckoo but tail lacks noticeable fork (square-ended or with slight indent). **Voice** High-pitched, piercing series of sharp whistles ascending the scale. Like Fork-tailed but much higher-pitched, shriller, faster, the second note lower than the first. **HH** Open forest and shade trees in tea plantations. Very similar to Fork-tailed.

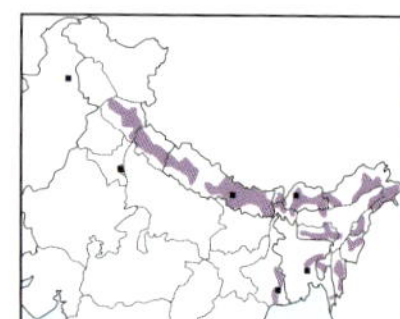

Large Hawk Cuckoo *Hierococcyx sparverioides* 38–40cm

Breeds in Himalayas and NE India; scattered winter records in subcontinent. Vagrant: Pakistan. **ID** Larger than Common Hawk Cuckoo, with browner mantle (contrasting with slate-grey head), blackish chin, grey streaking on throat and breast, irregular rufous breast-band, broad dark brown barring on underparts, and broader and stronger dark tail bands. Underwing-coverts white, barred dark brown. Juvenile has strongly barred rather than spotted underparts, and broader tail-bands. Immature has darker slate-grey head than immature Common, with blackish chin and grey throat streaking. **Voice** A shrill *pee-pee-ah... pee-pee-ah*, which is repeated and rises in pitch to a hysterical crescendo. **HH** Usually keeps well hidden among foliage of forest canopy, even when calling. *Accipiter*-like in flight; flies low with a few fast wingbeats followed by a glide, then rises abruptly to land in a tree. Often calls throughout the night. Usually broadleaved forest; sometimes mixed broadleaved/coniferous forest and groves.

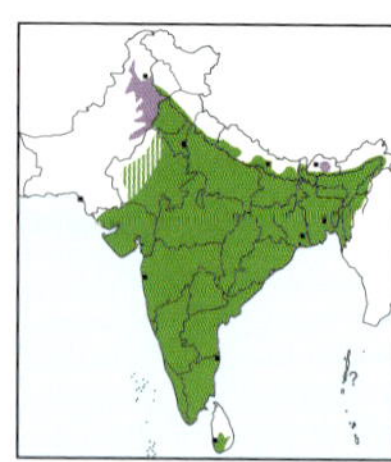

Common Hawk Cuckoo *Hierococcyx varius* 33cm

Widespread resident and partial migrant except the north-west. **ID** Smaller than Large, with whitish or greyish chin and throat, uniform grey upperparts, more rufous on underparts, indistinct barring on belly and flanks, and narrower tail bands. Underwing-coverts rufous and only faintly barred. In juvenile, flanks typically less heavily marked than in Large, with spots or chevrons rather than bars (some very similar), while rufous tail-bands and tail tip are typically brighter and more clearly defined. *H. v. ciceliae* of Sri Lanka is darker grey on upperparts, with stronger streaking on throat and dark barring on underparts (and is very like Large, although tail-bands narrower). **Voice** Call as Large, but shriller and more manic. **HH** Habits similar to Large, but more often seen because it frequents less thickly wooded habitat. Well-wooded country, favours mangroves, orchards, gardens; irrigated plantations in Pakistan and tea estates in Sri Lanka.

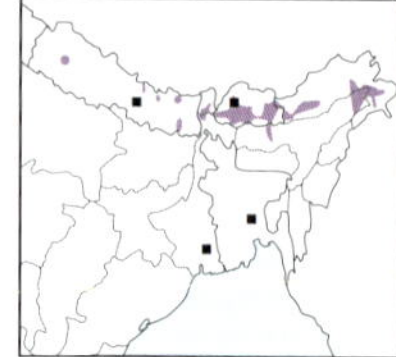

Hodgson's Hawk Cuckoo *Hierococcyx nisicolor* 28–30cm

Resident or summer visitor. Mainly E Himalayas and NE Indian hills. Vagrant: Bangladesh. **ID** Smaller than Common, with stouter (yellow-based) bill. Upperparts are a darker slate-grey, with slate-grey chin, more extensive rufous on underparts, and unbarred white belly and flanks. Throat and breast may show grey streaking. Tail lacks narrow whitish bands of Common and has more pronounced rufous tip. Frequently shows a single pale inner tertial (on both wings in some) (not present on Common). Juvenile has darker brown and more uniform upperparts than juvenile Common, and broader (squarer) spots on underparts. Immature has dark grey chin, ear-coverts and crown, rufous barring to upperparts, and strongly streaked underparts with arrow-shaped marks on lower flanks. **Voice** A shrill, thin *gee-whiz* repeated up to 20 times, becoming more frantic and high-pitched. **HH** Usually keeps to low trees or bushes but moves higher in trees when calling. Broadleaved evergreen and moist deciduous forest. **TN** Formerly placed in *H. fugax*.

Fork-tailed Drongo Cuckoo
juv
ad
Square-tailed Drongo Cuckoo
juv
ad
imm
Large Hawk Cuckoo
juv
ad
ad
Common Hawk Cuckoo
imm
juv
ad
Hodgson's Hawk Cuckoo
imm
juv

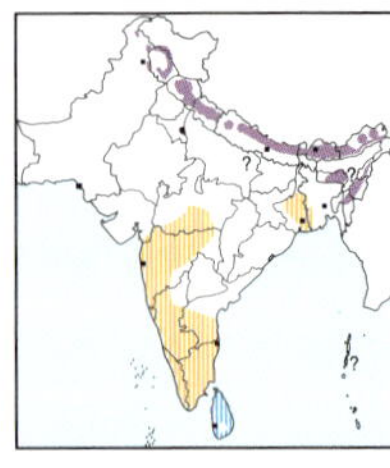

Lesser Cuckoo *Cuculus poliocephalus* 22–27cm

Breeds in Himalayas and NE India; passage migrant in peninsula, winters in Sri Lanka. Vagrant: Bangladesh. **ID** Smaller than Himalayan (although Himalayan can be similar-sized) with finer bill. Plumage almost identical, but has darker rump and uppertail-coverts, contrasting less with tail. Hepatic morph of female prevails and is typically more rufous than hepatic Himalayan (some with almost unmarked rufous crown, nape, rump and uppertail-coverts). Juvenile like juvenile Himalayan but with dark grey-brown upperparts and whiter (broadly barred) underparts. **Voice** A strong, cheerful *pretty-peel-lay-ka-beet*, often one of the first birds to sing at dawn. **HH** Habits like Indian. Frequently calls noisily in flight, often above the canopy as well as when perched. Forest and well-wooded country.

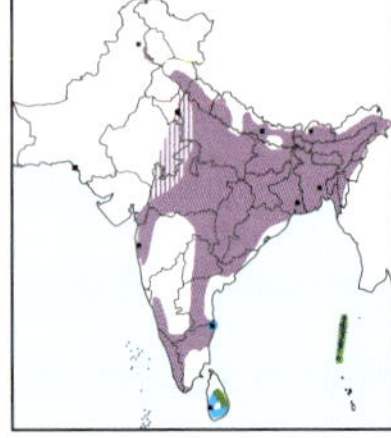

Indian Cuckoo *Cuculus micropterus* 32–33cm

Breeding in widespread areas. Absent from the northwest and much of SW and SE India. **ID** From Common and Himalayan Cuckoos by browner mantle, and broader, more widely spaced black barring on underparts. Tail has broader (diffuse) dark subterminal band, broader white barring on outer tail feathers and larger white spots on central feathers. Eyes brown or reddish-brown (yellow in Common; yellow or brown in Himalayan). Female has rufous-buff wash to base of grey breast, and rufous suffusion to whitish barring of lower breast. There is no hepatic female morph. Juvenile distinctive with broad and irregular white tips to feathers of crown, nape, scapulars and wing-coverts; throat and breast are creamy-white with irregular brown markings, and barring on rest of underparts is broader and more irregular than in Common and Himalayan. **Voice** A descending four-noted whistle, *kwer-kwah... kwah-kurh*. **HH** Frequents the tops of forest trees and foliage of the canopy; sometimes flies hawk-like above the forest. Often calls at night during the breeding season. Forest, groves and well-wooded country.

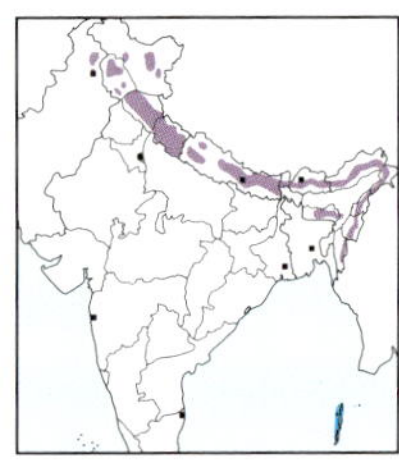

Himalayan Cuckoo *Cuculus saturatus* 32–33cm

Breeds in Himalayas and NE India; winter visitor to Andamans and Nicobars. Vagrant: Bangladesh. **ID** Extremely like Common. Has broader black barring on buffish-white (rather than pure white) underparts, and darker grey upperparts, sometimes showing contrast with paler head, and can be distinctly smaller. Female and juvenile, like Common, occur as grey and rufous morphs, and have broader black barring, especially on breast, back, rump and tail than in Common. **Voice** A resonant *ho... ho... ho... ho*, which can be confused with call of Common Hoopoe, although has at least four notes rather than two or three of Common Hoopoe. **HH** Habits like Indian, but usually keeps hidden among foliage and is less noisy at night. Forest, well-wooded country and orchards. **TN** Formerly considered conspecific with Oriental Cuckoo *C. optatus*.

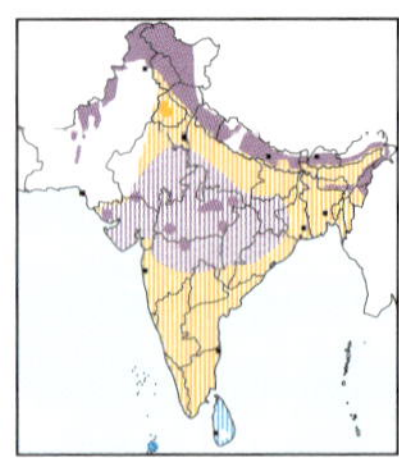

Common Cuckoo *Cuculus canorus* 32–34cm

Breeds in hills of Pakistan, Himalayas, and N, NE and C India; scattered winter records. **ID** Almost identical to Himalayan and best distinguished by song; for subtle differences, see that species. Non-hepatic female has rufous wash to lower border of grey breast. Hepatic female is rufous-brown above and whitish below, strongly barred all over with dark brown. Juvenile is very variable, some superficially resembling grey adult, others hepatic female, with whitish fringes to upperparts and white nape patch. **Voice** Male has a loud, pleasant, repetitive *cuck-oo... cuck-oo*; both sexes have a bubbling call. **HH** Habits similar to Indian, but less vocal at night. Sometimes also feeds close to or on the ground as well as in treetops. Often perches conspicuously in the open when calling in the breeding season. Forest, well-wooded country, second growth, montane dwarf shrubbery and alpine meadows. **AN** Eurasian Cuckoo.

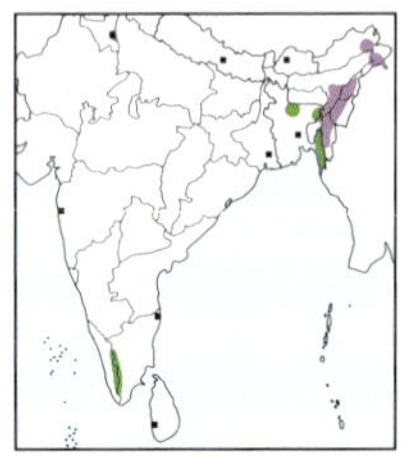

Great Eared Nightjar *Lyncornis macrotis* 31–40cm

Resident. Mainly NE India, Bangladesh and Western Ghats. Vagrant: Sri Lanka. **ID** A very large, richly coloured nightjar. At rest, shows prominent ear-tufts, and is generally more richly marked with golden-buff and rufous than other nightjars. Has black ear-coverts and throat (with fine rufous barring), prominent white collar, blackish breast, buff underparts boldly barred with dark brown, and tail broadly banded with golden-buff and dark brown. In flight appears large, with slow and buoyant action (often feeding high in the air), and lacks white or buff spots on wings or tail. **Voice** A whistled *put, wee-oo* or *put, weeow-oo*. **HH** Emerges at dusk to circle high over forest and clearings, descending lower as darkness gathers. Tropical and subtropical broadleaved evergreen and moist deciduous forest and second growth. **TN** Formerly placed in *Eurostopodus*.

♂
♀
♂
♀
♀
hepatic
Lesser Cuckoo
juv
juv
Indian Cuckoo
♂
♂
♀
hepatic
♀
hepatic
Himalayan Cuckoo
Common Cuckoo
Great Eared Nightjar
ad

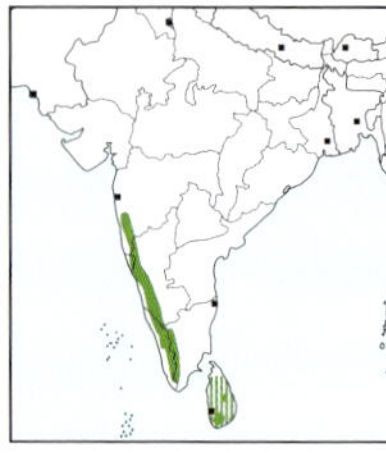

Sri Lanka Frogmouth *Batrachostomus moniliger* 23cm

Resident. Western Ghats and Sri Lanka. **ID** Smaller and shorter-tailed than Hodgson's Frogmouth, with bigger-looking head and bill. Male is brownish-grey, with irregular black-and-white markings and vermiculations. White markings typically form narrow 'collar' on upper mantle and irregular line of spotting on breast, and are usually prominent on scapulars, wing-coverts and belly/flanks. Female is more uniform, and rufous to rufous-brown, with odd whitish spots on scapulars and coverts, belly/flanks, and often forming an irregular hind 'collar'. **Voice** Series of rapid, rolling chuckles, plaintive whistles, slow screeches and hissing sounds. **HH** Roosts by day in forest undergrowth. Bamboo and cane forest; dense tropical and subtropical evergreen forest.

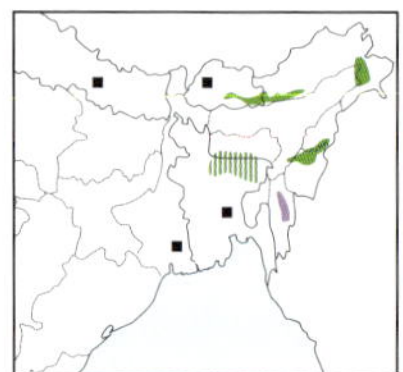

Hodgson's Frogmouth *Batrachostomus hodgsoni* 22–27cm

Resident. E Himalayas, NE India and Bangladesh. **ID** Male is rufous-brown. Upperparts are heavily marked with black, especially on head, with irregular bold whitish markings particularly on scapulars and upper mantle (forming 'collar' on some birds). Underparts are heavily and irregularly marked with black, white and rufous. Female is more uniformly rufous, with irregular black-tipped white spots on upper mantle, scapulars and underparts. **Voice** Female gives single long whistle, rising, then falling to initial pitch; male call a series of up to ten short, soft rising whistles. **HH** Subtropical broadleaved evergreen forest.

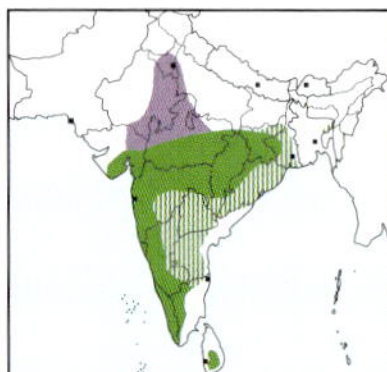

Jungle Nightjar *Caprimulgus indicus* 21.5–24cm

Resident and summer visitor from E Rajasthan to Bihar and Odisha, and south through W peninsula to Sri Lanka. **ID** Smaller, paler and less heavily marked than Grey, with buff edges to scapulars giving rise to more patterned appearance to upperparts, and greyish-white or buffish (rather than rufous-buff) spotting on wing-coverts. Dark tail-bands are narrower. Male has white patches on throat and in primaries and tail. Female has buff throat patch and primary patches, and lacks any white patches in tail. **Voice** Slow, evenly spaced, prolonged series of sweet-toned, clearly bisyllabic notes. **HH** Forest clearings and scrub-covered slopes.

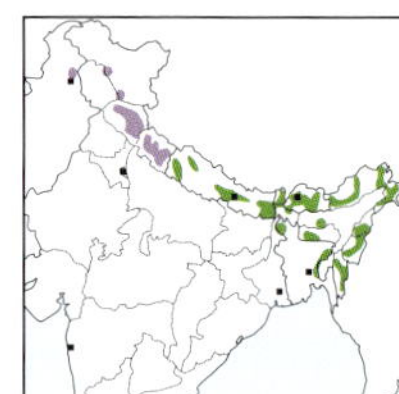

Grey Nightjar *Caprimulgus jotaka* 24–27cm

Summer visitor to NE Pakistan and Himalayas from Himachal through Uttaranchal; resident Nepal through Arunachal, S Assam and SE Bangladesh. **ID** Dark grey-brown and heavily marked with black. More cold-coloured and less strongly patterned than Large-tailed Nightjar, with greyer upperparts and lacks diffuse warm rufous-brown nuchal collar. Breast is dark grey-brown, lacking warm buff or brown tones. Further, has bold, irregular black markings on scapulars, usually lacking prominent pale edges, variable but rather poorly defined rufous-buff spotting on coverts, and broader dark bands on tail (with less white at tip than Large-tailed). Male has white patches on throat and in primaries and tail. Female has buff throat patch and primary patches, and lacks any white patches in tail. **Voice** Loud, evenly spaced, rapid, downturned, musical, monosyllabic and whiplash-like notes; more rapidly given and less resonant than Large-tailed. **HH** Like other nightjars crepuscular and nocturnal. Catches all its food on the wing in erratic flight. Forest clearings and open forest. **TN** Previously treated as conspecific with Jungle Nightjar.

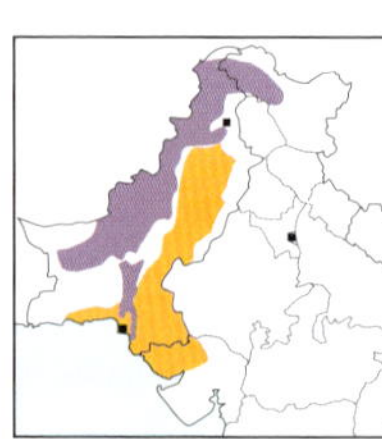

Eurasian Nightjar *Caprimulgus europaeus* 25cm

Mainly summer visitor and passage migrant. Pakistan and NW Gujarat. **ID** Bold streaking on crown, nape and scapulars (lacking on Savanna). More cleanly and regularly streaked than Grey, underparts are more neatly barred and generally paler grey. Buffish outer edges to scapulars form prominent line, and line of whitish or buff spotting on wing-coverts is usually clearly defined. Can be pale sandy-grey or pale grey in coloration, when more similar in appearance to Sykes's and Egyptian. Longer wings and tail, boldly streaked crown and scapulars, buff scapular line, and prominent buffish-white spots on coverts separate from Sykes's; see Egyptian for differences. Male has white patches on throat and in primaries and white tail corners, lacking in female. **Voice** Song a continuous churring, very similar to Sykes's but louder and varying in pitch; soft *quoit quoit* in flight. **HH** Rocky slopes with scattered bushes. **AN** European Nightjar.

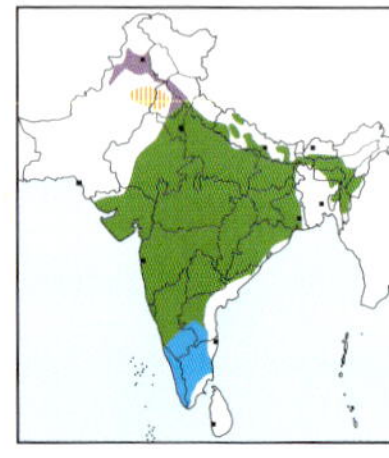

Savanna Nightjar *Caprimulgus affinis* 20–26cm

Widespread resident; unrecorded in Sri Lanka, most of Pakistan and parts of NW India.. **ID** A medium-sized, dark brownish-grey nightjar. Less strikingly marked than other nightjars; crown and mantle are finely vermiculated, and lack bold dark streaking; has more uniform coverts with fine dark vermiculations and irregular rufous-buff markings, and scapulars are usually edged rufous-buff. Male has largely white outer tail feathers. **Voice** Call is a loud, repetitive *chwip* or *chweep* given mainly in flight. **HH** Habits like Grey. Open forest and stony areas with scrub.

♀
♂
Sri Lanka Frogmouth
♀
♂
Hodgson's Frogmouth
♂
♀
♂
Jungle Nightjar
♂
♂
♀
Grey Nightjar
♂
Eurasian Nightjar
♂
♀
♂
Savanna Nightjar

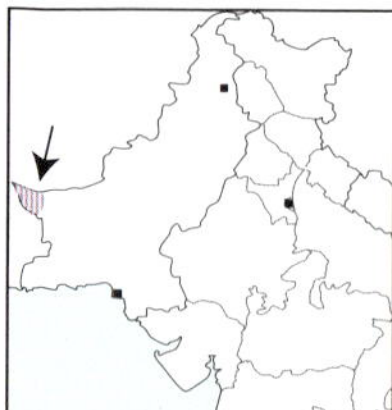

Egyptian Nightjar *Caprimulgus aegyptius* 24–26cm

Summer visitor. SW Pakistan. **ID** Larger than Sykes's Nightjar, with longer wings and tail. Similar in plumage to some Sykes's, although crown and nape are relatively unmarked, with only fine dark streaking (Sykes's generally shows more pronounced small dark arrowhead-shaped markings on crown, and irregular buff spotting on nape forms indistinct collar), and lacks white/buffish patches in wings or tail. Some Eurasian can be similarly coloured, but Egyptian has finely streaked crown, relatively unmarked scapulars with buff mottling and black marks, and coverts have prominent irregular buff mottling. **Voice** Song is a long series of purring *kowrr* notes; sings from ground, mainly at dusk and dawn. **HH** Semi-desert.

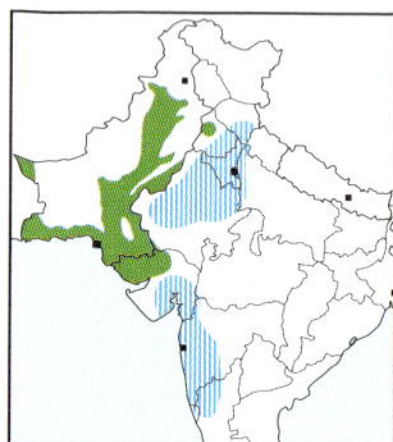

Sykes's Nightjar *Caprimulgus mahrattensis* 22–24cm

Resident. Breeds in Pakistan and parts of NW India; winters south to C India. Vagrant: Nepal. **ID** Small, grey nightjar. Has finely streaked crown, black marks on scapulars, large white patch on sides of throat, and irregular buff spotting on nape forming indistinct collar. Compared to Indian Nightjar, which is similarly proportioned, crown is much less heavily marked, lacks well-defined rufous-buff nuchal collar, scapulars are relatively unmarked, and central tail feathers are more strongly barred. Male has large white patches in primaries and at tip of tail, buffish in female. **Voice** Continuous churring song, like Eurasian, but softer; low, soft *chuck-chuck* in flight. **HH** Habits like Grey. Roosts on the ground, often in shade of a bush. Breeds in semi-desert; wide variety of habitats in winter.

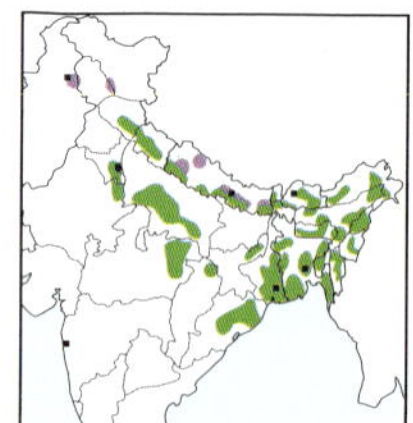

Large-tailed Nightjar *Caprimulgus macrurus* 25–29cm

Resident. Himalayas, NC, E and NE India and Bangladesh. **ID** Larger, longer-tailed and more warmly coloured and strongly patterned than Grey, with pale rufous-brown nuchal collar, complete white throat, well-defined buff edges and bold wedge-shaped black centres to scapulars, broad buff tips to coverts forming triple wing-bars, and more extensive white or buff in outer tail feathers. Male has large white patches in primaries and at tip of tail, buffish in female. **Voice** Series of loud, resonant calls: *chaunk-chaunk-chaunk*, repeated at rate of c.100 per minute. **HH** Habits like Grey. Often squats on forest paths and roads at night. Forest edges.

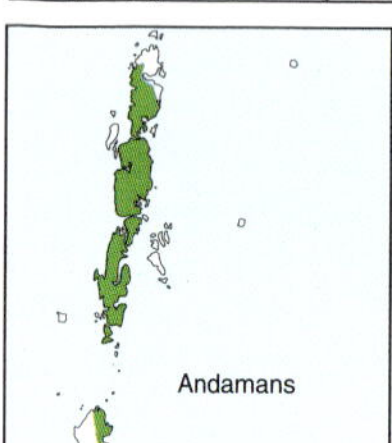

Andaman Nightjar *Caprimulgus andamanicus* 22–23cm

Resident. Andamans. **ID** Medium-sized, dark-coloured nightjar. Compared with Large-tailed, smaller and darker, scapulars have less pronounced pale edgings, coverts are comparatively uniform with irregular buff spots, and lacks prominent nuchal collar. More similar to migrant Grey Nightjar which has occurred on the islands and is larger, greyer with more varied and extensive marbling on upperparts. **Voice** Song is a quickly repeated and long series of relatively weak, short *tyuk* notes. **HH** Roosts among leaves on forest floor. Open teak forest and open country with scattered trees.

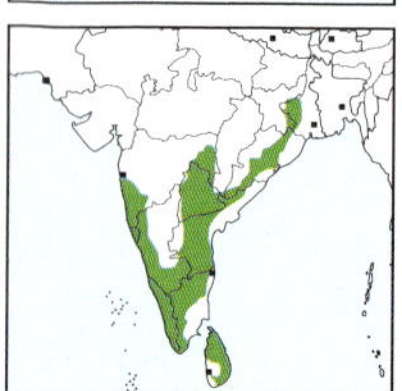

Jerdon's Nightjar *Caprimulgus atripennis* 25.5–27cm

Resident. C, E and S peninsular India and Sri Lanka. **ID** More warmly coloured and strongly patterned than Jungle. Has all-white throat, well-defined buff edges to scapulars, and broad, buff tips to black-centred coverts forming triple wing-bars. Tail shorter than in Large-tailed Nightjar, lacking rufous nuchal collar, with unbarred brown breast. Male has large white patches in primaries and at tip of tail, buffish in female. **Voice** Song of male is a repetitive, liquid *ow-r-r-r-r*, often preceded by low *grog* sounds. **HH** Habits like Grey. Clearings and edges of secondary jungle in evergreen and moist deciduous broadleaved forest.

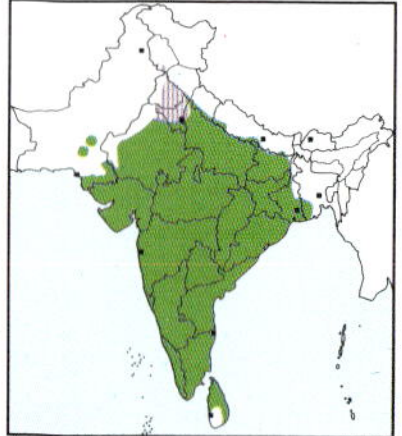

Indian Nightjar *Caprimulgus asiaticus* 23–24cm

Widespread resident; unrecorded in north-west and most of north-east. **ID** Grey, sandy-grey to brownish-grey in coloration. Best told by combination of small size and relatively short wings and tail, boldly streaked crown, rufous-buff markings on nape forming distinct collar, bold black centres and broad buff edges to scapulars, prominent buff or rufous-buff spotting on wing-coverts, and pale, relatively unmarked central tail feathers. Similar in appearance to Large-tailed, but much smaller, with shorter tail; note broken patches of white on sides of throat and more uniform tail. Male has extensive white tips to tail, less extensive and more buffish in female. **Voice** Song is a far-carrying *chuk-chuk-chuk-chuk-tukaroo* likened to a ping-pong ball bouncing; short sharp *qwit-qwit* in flight. **HH** Habits like Grey. Open wooded country in plains and foothills.

Egyptian Nightjar
♂
♂
♀
Sykes's Nightjar
♂
Large-tailed Nightjar
♂
♀
♂
Andaman Nightjar
♂
Jerdon's Nightjar
♂
Indian Nightjar
♂

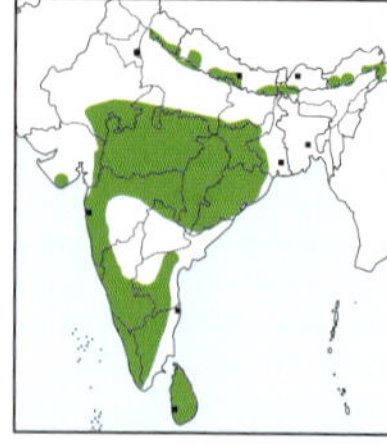

Crested Treeswift *Hemiprocne coronata* 23–25cm

Widespread resident; unrecorded in Pakistan, parts of NW, N, NE and C India. Vagrant: Bangladesh. **ID** Large size with sickle-shaped wings and long, deeply forked tail, which is usually held closed and pointed in flight. Typically, flies above tree canopy with mixture of rapid and rather heavy fluttering and periods of banking and gliding. In flight, appears mainly blue-grey with darker upperwing and tail, and whitish abdomen and undertail-coverts. At rest, both sexes show prominent dark green-blue crest, and wing-coverts are glossed with blue. Male has dull orange ear-coverts. Female has dark grey ear-coverts, forming dark mask, bordered below by whitish moustachial stripe. Juvenile has extensive white fringes to upperparts (especially noticeable on lower back and rump), and feathers of underparts are fringed with white and have grey-brown subterminal bands. **Voice** A harsh *whit-tucck... whit-tuck* in flight. **HH** In loose parties and hawks insects; does not wander far when foraging. Unlike other swifts, perches readily in trees. Forages over well-wooded areas and forest, usually deciduous.

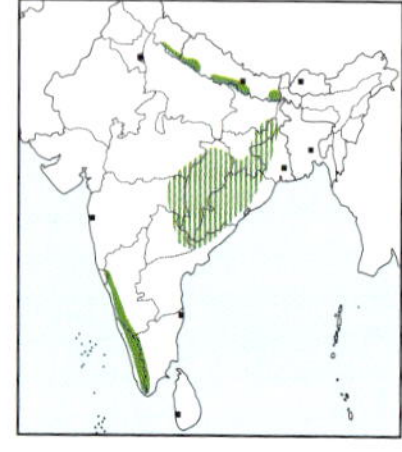

White-rumped Spinetail *Zoonavena sylvatica* 11cm

Resident. Himalayas, E and SW India. Vagrant: Bangladesh. **ID** Small and stocky, with broad wings, pinched in at base and pointed at tip. Flight is fast with rapid wingbeats, banking from side to side, interspersed with short glides on slightly bowed wings. Upperparts mainly blue-black with contrasting white rump; throat and breast are grey-brown, merging into whitish lower belly and undertail-coverts. Long white undertail-coverts contrast with black of sides and tip of undertail. 'Spines' at tip of tail visible at close range. Wing shape and flight action different from House Swift and lacks white throat. **Voice** Twittering *chick-chick* in flight. **HH** In flocks of up to 50 birds. Hawks over forest with great manoeuvrability. Broadleaved evergreen and moist deciduous forest.

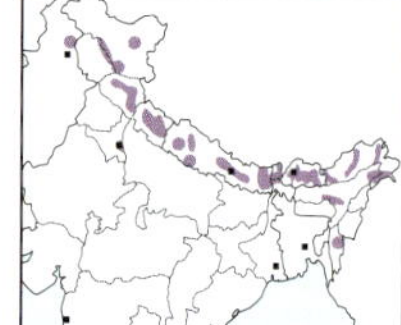

White-throated Needletail *Hirundapus caudacutus* 19–21cm

Summer visitor. Himalayas and NE India. **ID** Like other needletails, a magnificent flier combining very strong flapping with swooping, gliding and soaring, often at very high speeds. Like other species has pale 'saddle' on upperparts, and striking white 'horseshoe' crescent at rear end. Best told from Silver-backed and Brown-backed Needletails by clearly demarcated white throat, and white inner webs to tertials (showing as white patch, although may be obscured). Additional differences from Brown-backed include smaller size, dark lores, and more contrasting pale 'saddle'. Also, has shorter, square-ended tail projection beyond white undertail-coverts, and tail 'spines' are less distinct. Juvenile has less clear-cut white throat (and is much more like Silver-backed); has black streaking and spotting on white of rear flanks, and dark fringes to white undertail-coverts. **Voice** Feeble, rapid metallic chittering, audible only at close range. **HH** Usually occurs singly or in loose parties. Roosts colonially on cliffs and trees. Skims low over mountain ridges and forest, and dashes around crags with amazing adroitness. Covers huge distances in a day's foraging. Over ridges, cliffs, forest, upland grassland and river valleys.

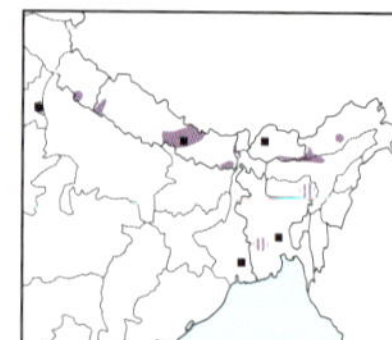

Silver-backed Needletail *Hirundapus cochinchinensis* 20–22cm

Resident. Himalayas and hills of NE India, Vagrant: Bhutan, Bangladesh. **ID** Throat pale brown or grey and can appear distinctly pale greyish-white, but never pure white and sharply divided from breast as in White-throated. Tertials have a pale grey inner web which may be visible in the field (strikingly white in White-throated). Care needed to avoid confusion with juvenile White-throated but latter has more uniform upperparts and dark scaling on undertail-coverts. Noticeably smaller than Brown-backed, usually shows paler throat and dark lores, and has more contrasting pale 'saddle'. Also, tends to show shorter, square-ended tail projection beyond white undertail-coverts, and tail 'spines' are less distinct. Juvenile has dark fringes to white undertail-coverts. **Voice** A soft rippling *trp-trp-trp-trp-trp*. **HH** Habits like White-throated. Mainly hawks over forest and forested hills.

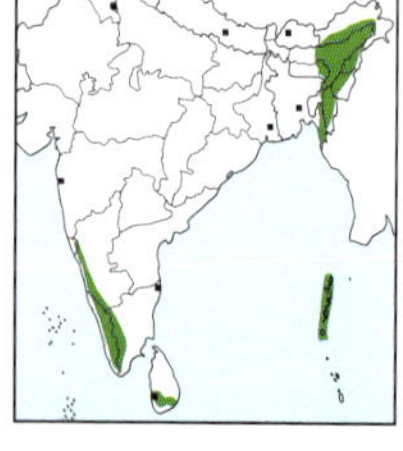

Brown-backed Needletail *Hirundapus giganteus* 21–26.5cm

Resident. Hills of NE India and Bangladesh, Western Ghats, Sri Lanka and Andaman Islands. **ID** Largest and most powerful of the needletails; 'needles' of tail larger and longer than on other species and often easy to see in the field. Compared to Silver-backed has white lores, brown throat concolorous with rest of underparts, and less contrasting pale 'saddle' (uniformly pale brown, lacking silvery-white centre), with longer and rounded or point-ended tail. Juvenile has dark fringes to white undertail-coverts. **Voice** As Silver-backed and White-throated. **HH** Habits like White-throated. Roosts communally in old tree hollows. Hawks over broadleaved evergreen and moist deciduous forest and clearings.

♀
♀
♂
juv
♂
Crested Treeswift
ad
White-rumped
Spinetail
ad
ad
ad
White-throated
Needletail
Silver-backed
Needletail
Brown-backed
Needletail

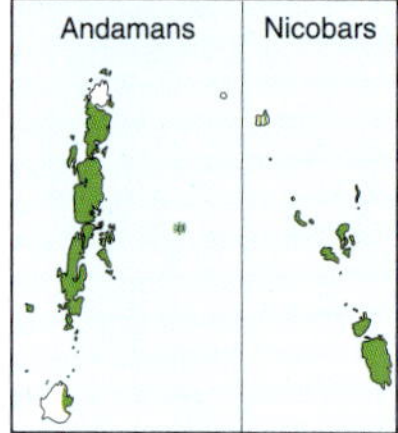

Plume-toed Swiftlet *Collocalia affinis* 9–10cm

Resident. Andamans and Nicobars (all major islands). **ID** From White-nest Swiftlet by smaller size, glossy blue-black upperparts, square-ended tail (with only slight indentation), white belly contrasting with dark grey throat and breast, and dark undertail-coverts and undertail. Shows pale fringing and dark blotching on lower breast, and extent of white on underparts varies. **Voice** Erratic short bursts of squeaky twittering, going up and down the scale. **HH** Flight is very fluttering and erratic. Breeds in large colonies in buildings. **TN** Usually treated as conspecific with Glossy Swiftlet *Collocalia esculenta*.

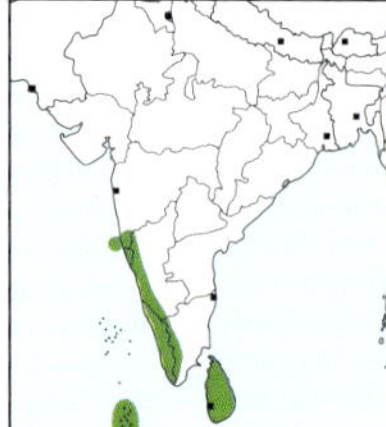

Indian Swiftlet *Aerodramus unicolor* 12cm

Resident. Western Ghats, islets on Malabar coast, Sri Lanka (only swiftlet in this range). **ID** Small brownish swiftlet with slight gloss to upperparts, and paler greyish-brown underparts. Has uniform upperparts (occasionally with very indistinctly paler rump), and only slight indentation to tail. Like other swiftlets, has bat-like flight with rapid flapping broken by banking and gliding. **Voice** Shrill clicking calls when roosting in caves enables them to navigate by echolocation. **HH** Roosts clustered together in caves, clinging like small bats to vertical rock faces or to old nests, sometimes in huge numbers. Leaves the roost with a noisy rush of wings before dawn, returning at dusk. Breeds in large colonies in caves in rocky islands and cliffs in the hills. **TN** Often placed in *Collocalia*.

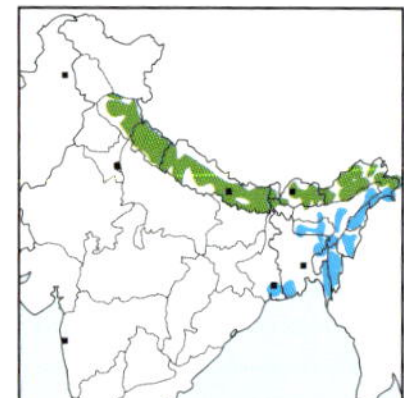

Himalayan Swiftlet *Aerodramus brevirostris* 13–14cm

Resident. Himalayas and NE India. Winters in NE India and Bangladesh. **ID** A stocky brown swiftlet with slight gloss to upperparts, and pronounced indentation to tail. Has paler grey-brown underparts than upperparts, and distinct pale grey rump band. Only swiftlet over much of range, although does occur as a migrant in Andamans (confusable with White-nest) and could occur in range of Indian. From White-nest by larger size, greater tail indentation, browner upperparts with less gloss (and less contrast between upperparts and underparts), and broader, less clearly defined rump band. From Indian by larger size, more pronounced tail indentation, and pale rump band. **Voice** Low, rattling call and twittering *chit-chit* at roost. **HH** Habits like Indian. Roosts in caves; often forages over forest. Breeds in colonies, with nests close together, either at random, or in rows, but not in clusters. **TN** Often placed in *Collocalia*.

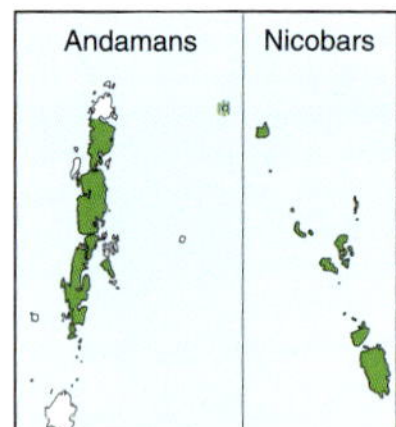

White-nest Swiftlet *Aerodramus fuciphagus* 11.5–12.5cm

Resident. Andamans and Nicobars. **ID** From Plume-toed by larger size, noticeable indentation to tail, dusky-black upperparts, uniform greyish-brown underparts, and narrow greyish (although sometimes very indistinct) rump band. For differences from Himalayan Swiftlet, see that species. **Voice** A loud metallic *zwing*. **HH** Breeds communally in caves. Nests are made entirely of saliva and are collected commercially to make birds' nest soup. Inhabits the coast and areas around habitation. Hawks around mangrove swamps and habitation in the day; roosts in caves and cliff fissures at night. **TN** Often placed in *Collocalia*. **AN** Edible-nest Swiftlet.

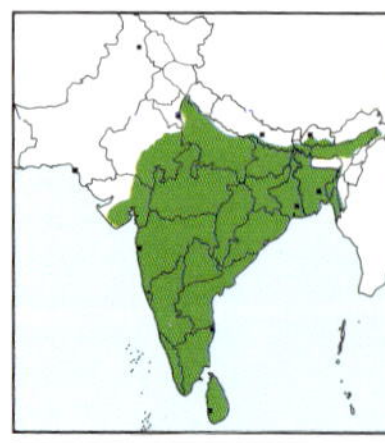

Asian Palm Swift *Cypsiurus balasiensis* 11–13cm

Resident. Widespread; unrecorded in Pakistan and parts of NW India. **ID** Small and very slim with fine scythe-shaped wings and deeply forked tail (usually held closed). Rapid fluttering wingbeats are interspersed with short glides. Throat is slightly paler than rest of underparts, and may also show a slightly paler rump. Much smaller than Crested Treeswift, with weaker, more fluttering flight, and is browner in coloration (does not show whiter belly and undertail-coverts). In S Assam (*C. b. infumatus*) is darker with narrower tail fork. **Voice** Trilling *te-he-he-he-he*. **HH** Usually hawks insects around palms. Roosts clinging to a palmyra leaf, also in eaves of thatched roofs of village houses in NE India. Breeds solitarily. Open country and cultivation; strongly associated with palms, especially palmyra and sometimes betelnut palm; also, forest clearings in NE India.

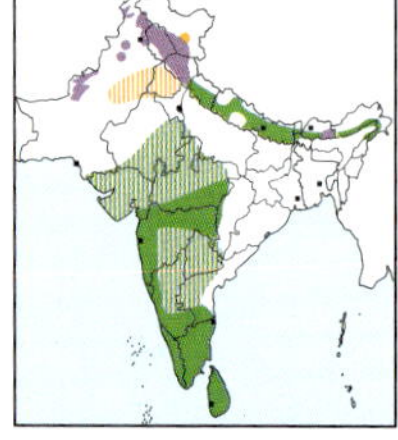

Alpine Swift *Tachymarptis melba* 20–22cm

Resident (?) locally in subcontinent. Vagrant: Bhutan. **ID** A large and powerful swift, with deeper and slower wingbeats. Best told by white throat with brown breast-band, and white breast and belly contrasting with brown underwing, flanks and vent. Birds breeding in the Himalayas have mid-brown upperparts and wings, paler brown than Common Swift. Birds in Western Ghats and Sri Lanka are smaller and darker with broader breast-band. **Voice** High-pitched trilling *tri-hi-hi-hi-hi*. **HH** Usually in scattered flocks. Roosts and nests in clefts in rock faces. Skims over hills and mountains; may occur briefly over any habitat.

ad
Plume-toed Swiftlet
ad
Indian Swiftlet
Himalayan Swiftlet
ad
ad
White-nest Swiftlet
ad
ad
Asian Palm Swift
Alpine Swift

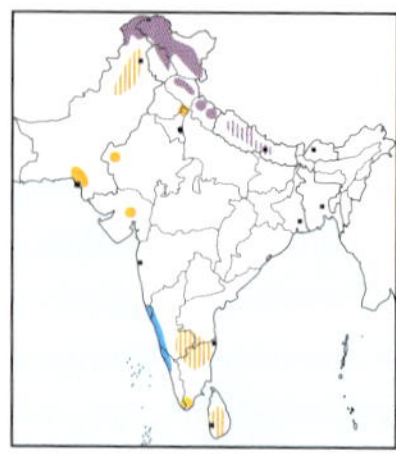

Common Swift *Apus apus* 16–18cm

Mainly summer visitor. Balochistan and W Himalayas. **ID** From Blyth's Swift by uniform brown upperparts (lacking white rump). For differences from the very similar Pallid and Dark-rumped Swifts, see those species. Juvenile is blacker than adult (and Pallid); has whiter forehead and more extensive white throat, and more pronounced pale scaling on underparts. **Voice** High-pitched screaming *screee... screee... screee.* **HH** Habits like Alpine. Chiefly mountains but can occur over any habitat. Breeds colonially in cracks in cliffs in Pakistan.

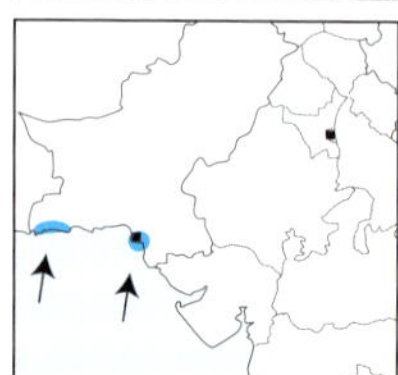

Pallid Swift *Apus pallidus* 16cm

Winter visitor. Pakistan. **ID** Paler grey-brown than Common, with more extensive pale throat and forehead, which contrasts with darker eye-patch. Has dark outer primaries and leading edge to wing, contrasting on both upperside and underside with pale rest of wing (especially with pale greater primary coverts on upperwing). Underparts more distinctly scaled than in Common, and shows greater contrast between head and mantle and between mantle and wings (often giving rise to dark-saddled, pale-headed appearance). Also, Pallid is slightly bulkier and broader-winged, and has blunter tips to wings and slightly shallower fork to tail. **Voice** Disyllabic *cheeu-eet* or *churr-ic.* **HH** Habits like Alpine. Coastal areas.

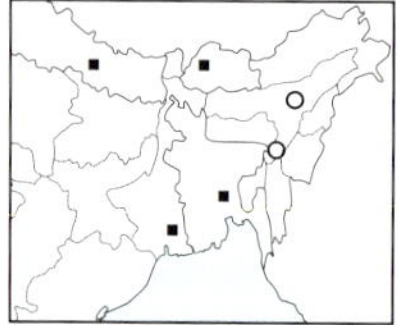

Pacific Swift *Apus pacificus* 17–19.5cm

Status uncertain; possible winter visitor NE India (Assam, Nagaland and Manipur). Larger than Blyth's Swift with whitish fringes to feathers of underparts (giving rise to greyish cast on breast and belly at a distance), more prominent white throat (lacking dark shaft streaks) and broader white rump band. **Voice** Said to be largely silent in non-breeding season, but sometimes heard on migration; differences from Blyth's not described. **HH** As Blyth's. **AN** Fork-tailed Swift.

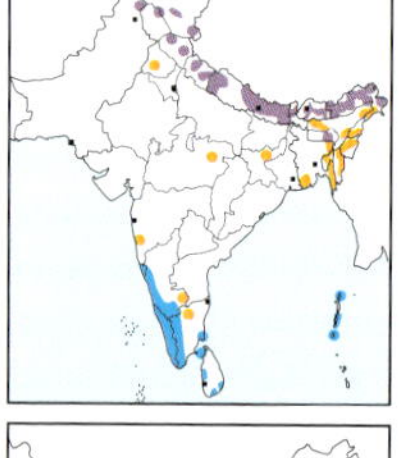

Blyth's Swift *Apus leuconyx* 14–15cm

Breeds in Himalayas and NE India; winters in W Ghats; scattered winter records in peninsula. Vagrant: Sri Lanka. **ID** Dark swift with prominent white rump and deeply forked tail. Best told from Little Swift by narrower white rump band, less well-defined whitish throat (which has dark shaft streaks), longer, deeply forked tail, and slimmer-bodied and longer-winged appearance. **Voice** Call is less wheezy and softer than Common, a *sreee.* **HH** Builds nests in small colonies inside fissures in cliff faces. Favours hawking over open ridges or hilltops. **TN** Previously treated as conspecific with Pacific Swift *A. pacificus.*

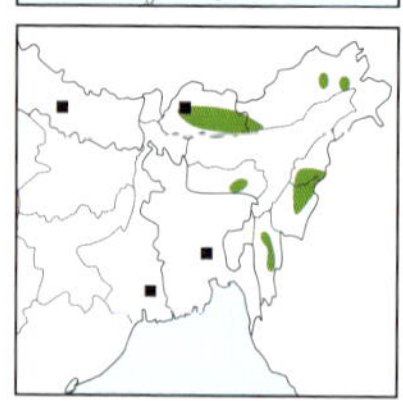

Dark-rumped Swift *Apus acuticauda* 16–17cm

Resident. Meghalaya, Bhutan, Arunachal Pradesh, Nagaland, Manipur and Mizoram. **ID** An all-dark swift recalling Blyth's, but separated by all-dark rump and lack of clearly defined white throat. Throat is greyish-white, with dark streaking, and merges with rest of underparts (which are broadly fringed with white). Does not appear as slim and long-winged as Blyth's, and tail fork is sharper, with narrower and more pointed outer tail feathers. Very similar to Common; look for heavily marked throat, bold scaling on underparts (belly often appears pale grey in strong light) and darker vent. **Voice** Very high-pitched call around breeding cliffs. **HH** Stays close to nesting cliffs when breeding; nests in clefts in cliff faces. Rocky cliffs and gorges. Globally threatened.

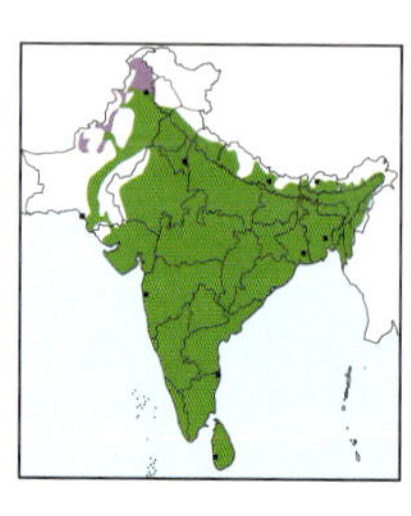

Little Swift *Apus affinis* 12cm

Widespread resident; unrecorded in parts of north-west. **ID** A small, stocky swift with prominent white throat and rump band. From Blyth's Swift by smaller size, shorter and broader wings, stout body and rather big head, and little or no tail fork. Flight is weaker than Blyth's, consisting of a few rapid wing strokes followed by long swooping glides and many twists and turns. Widespread nominate is stouter and paler than *A. a. nipalensis* in Himalayas and NE India ('House Swift') with broader white rump band and more prominent white on forehead. Nominate has square-ended tail – more rounded when open; NE Indian birds have shallow tail fork. **Voice** Rapid and shrill *sik-sik-sik-sik... sik-sik-sik-sik-sik-sik.* **HH** Usually in large scattered flocks and within wide vicinity of nesting areas when breeding. Nests colonially with nests built one upon another, under eaves. Flight weaker than Blyth's, consisting of a few rapid wing strokes followed by long swooping glides with many twists and turns. Villages, towns, cities, cliffs, bridges, verandas and ruins. **TN** 'House Swift' is sometimes erroneously treated as a separate species *A. nipalensis.*

Common Swift
juv
ad
Pallid Swift
ad
ad
ad
Pacific Swift
Blyth's Swift
ad
Dark-rumped Swift
ad
affinis
ad
nipalensis
Little Swift

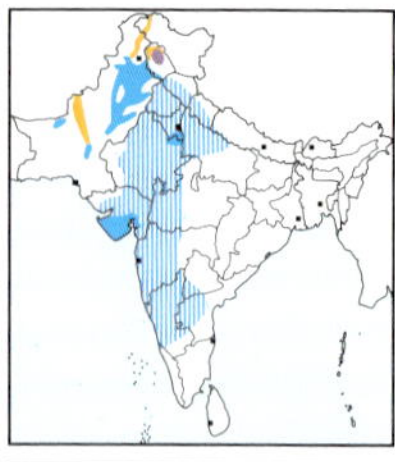

Water Rail *Rallus aquaticus* 25–28cm

Breeds in Kashmir; winter visitor, mainly to N subcontinent. Vagrant: Nepal. **ID** Longish and slightly downcurved bill with red at base. Legs pinkish. Adult has dark-streaked olive-brown upperparts, grey face and underparts, black-and-white barring on flanks, and white undertail-coverts. Juvenile has upperparts like adult, but underparts are buff with extensive dark brown mottling, flank barring is brown and buff, and undertail-coverts are rufous-buff. **Voice** Squeals and grunts including a call like a squealing pig that rises in pitch then dies away. **HH** Skulking, usually crepuscular, though sometimes emerges from cover during the day. Flies reluctantly for a short distance with legs dangling, then drops into cover again. More often heard than seen, most voluble in evening and at night. Reedy marshes with muddy edges.

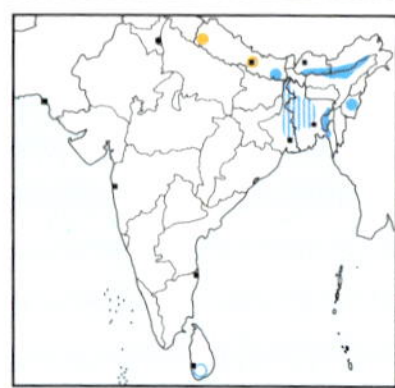

Brown-cheeked Rail *Rallus indicus* 23–29cm

Winter visitor. C and E Himalayas, NE India and Bangladesh. Vagrant: Nepal, Sri Lanka. **ID** Similar to Water Rail but has more pronounced supercilium (due to darker eye-stripe), browner wash on breast, and barred undertail-coverts. Juvenile like juvenile Water Rail but has barred undertail-coverts. **Voice** Very different from Water Rail; a metallic, strident *skrink, skrink* beginning explosively and repeated after a few seconds. **HH** Habits are poorly known. Shy and skulking. Marshes. **TN** Formerly treated as conspecific with Water Rail *R. aquaticus*.

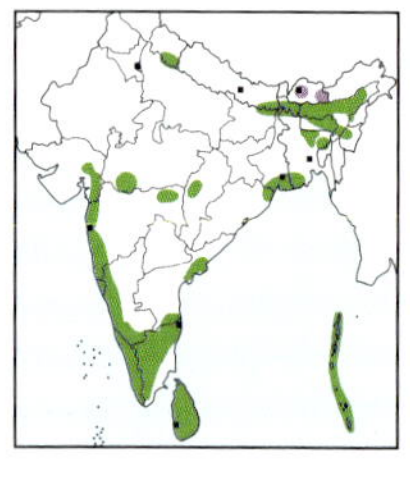

Slaty-breasted Rail *Lewinia striata* 25–30cm

Mainly resident. Far W, W and S peninsular India, the north-east, Bangladesh and Sri Lanka; unrecorded in north-west. Rare and very local, possibly resident in Nepal. **ID** Longish bill with red at base (stouter and straighter than in Water Rail). Legs olive-grey. Adult has chestnut crown and nape, slate-grey foreneck and breast, white barring and spotting on the upperparts, and white barring on the dark grey belly, flanks and undertail-coverts. Female duller than male, with browner breast. Juvenile duller, with crown and nape being dark-streaked olive-brown (some with rufous tinge), upperparts paler olive-brown and more sparsely marked with white, and underparts browner with less pronounced barring on flanks. *L. s. obscurior* of Andamans darker, including darker slate on sides of head, foreneck and breast; the juvenile is almost blackish with whitish barring on the wing-coverts and flanks. **Voice** Calls infrequently; a sharp whistle, repeated sharp *kerrek*, and noisy *ka-ka-ka*. **HH** Typical rail, see Water Rail. Reedy marshes, mangroves, village irrigation tanks and paddyfields. **TN** Formerly placed in *Gallirallus*.

Spotted Crake *Porzana porzana* 22–24cm

Fairly widespread winter visitor. Vagrant: Nepal, Bangladesh. **ID** Profuse white spotting on head, neck and breast. Stout bill, irregularly barred flanks, and unmarked buff undertail-coverts. Adult has yellowish bill with red at base, and grey head and breast. Sexes similar, but female has less grey on head, neck and breast, and is more profusely spotted with white. Juvenile like female but with buffish-brown head and breast, and bill is browner. **Voice** Usually silent away from breeding areas, although song may be heard on migration: a swishing *h-wet... hwet*, resembling a whiplash. **HH** See Ruddy-breasted Crake. Reedy marshes and reed-edged jheels, reservoirs and canals.

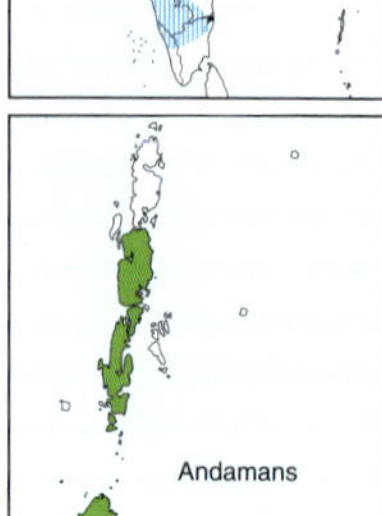

Andaman Crake *Rallina canningi* 34cm

Resident. Andamans. **ID** Deep maroon-chestnut upperparts with bold black-and-white barring on underparts and conical yellowish to greenish-yellowish bill. Larger size, deeper chestnut coloration, unbarred chestnut undertail-coverts, and bill size/coloration are best features from Slaty-legged Crake. Juvenile has duller chestnut head, breast and upperparts, and barring on underparts is less pronounced (dark brown and greyish-white). **Voice** A deep throaty croak, *kroop... kroop*; a sharp *chick, chick* when alarmed. **HH** Poorly known, presumably like other rails, see Water Rail. Marshes in forest and large, open areas of marshland.

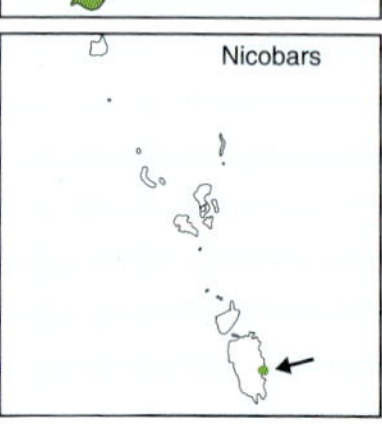

Great Nicobar Crake *Rallina* [undescribed species]

Great Nicobars. **ID** Superficially like Andaman Crake but has stocky orange-red legs and feet (greenish in Andaman). Also conical yellowish to greenish-yellowish bill, prominent orange-red eye-ring, is more orange-brown on head and breast and rufescent brown on upperparts (more uniform chestnut in Andaman), wing-coverts are barred, and black barring on underparts is broader. Structurally is stockier with shorter tail. Green bill is best feature from much smaller Red-legged Crake (see Vagrants); legs are longer and heavier and has broader black barring on underparts. **Voice** Undescribed. **HH** Undescribed.

ad
juv
ad
Water Rail
Brown-cheeked Rail
♂
juv
ad
Slaty-breasted Rail
juv
ad
Spotted Crake
juv
ad
Great Nicobar Crake
Andaman Crake

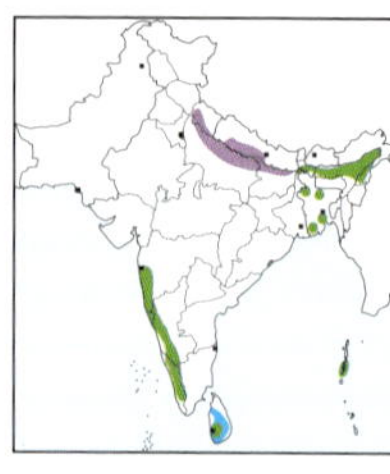

Slaty-legged Crake *Rallina eurizonoides* 21–28cm

Resident. Mainly SW, S, E and NE India, Bangladesh and Sri Lanka. Very local in Nepal and Uttarakhand. **ID** Leg colour and extensive black-and-white barring on underparts are best features from Ruddy-breasted. Adult from similar Red-legged Crake (see Vagrants) by greenish or grey legs, lack of prominent white-and-black barring on wings, olive-brown mantle contrasting with rufous neck and breast, narrower and more numerous white bars on underparts, prominent white throat, and dull greyish-pink orbital ring. Juvenile from juvenile Red-legged by leg colour, darker olive-brown upperparts, and lack of prominent barring on wings. **Voice** Repeated *kek-kek* or nasal *ow-ow*, often given persistently by night; a loud drumming croak, a subdued *kok*, and a *krrrr* alarm call. **HH** Typical rail, see Water Rail, though partly nocturnal. Marshes in forests and well-wooded country.

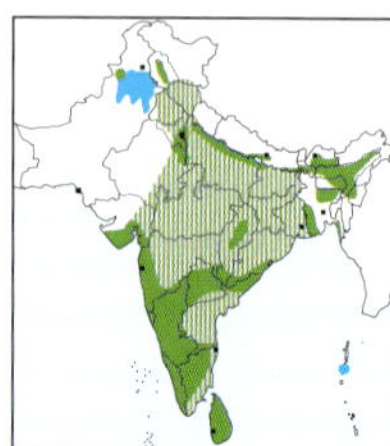

Ruddy-breasted Crake *Zapornia fusca* 21–23cm

Widespread resident except in the north-west. **ID** From other crakes by combination of dull chestnut underparts, unmarked dark olive-brown upperparts, indistinct dark brown-and-white barring on rear flanks and undertail-coverts (much more restricted than in Slaty-legged and Andaman Crakes) and red legs. Juvenile dark olive-brown, with white-barred undertail-coverts and fine greyish-white mottling/barring on rest of underparts. Legs duller and iris brown (rather than red as in adult). **Voice** A single soft *crake* at considerable intervals; a loud metallic *twek* repeated at 2–3-second intervals, often followed by a squeaky trill recalling Little Grebe, and a short *chuck* when feeding. **HH** Typical rail. Very skulking, emerging from thick cover early morning and at dusk. Walks with rhythmic movements of head and neck, and jerks tail. Reedy marshes, edges of flooded paddyfields and canals with emergent vegetation. **TN** Formerly placed in *Porzana*.

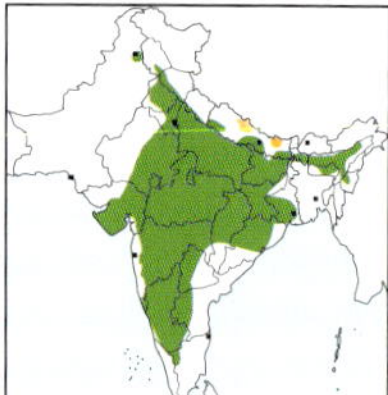

Brown Crake *Zapornia akool* 26–28cm

Widespread resident, except most of NW, NE, S and SE India. **ID** Olive-brown upperparts, grey face and breast, and olive-brown flanks and undertail-coverts; underparts lack barring. Has red iris, greenish bill and pinkish-brown to purple legs. Juvenile similar to adult, but has dull iris and paler grey underparts. **Voice** Calls include a shrill rattle, a long, drawn-out vibrating whistle and a short plaintive note. **HH** Typical crake, see Ruddy-breasted. Reedy marshes and vegetation bordering watercourses. **TN** Formerly placed in *Amaurornis*.

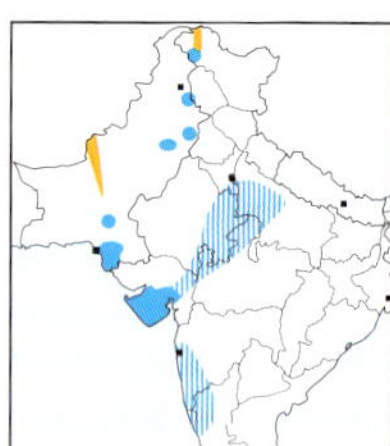

Little Crake *Zapornia parva* 18–20cm

Winter visitor and passage migrant. Pakistan and NW India. **ID** Longer wings and tail than Baillon's (primaries extending noticeably beyond tertials at rest), with less extensive barring on underparts, and pronounced pale edges to scapulars and tertials (in all plumages). Adult also has red at base of bill. Male is blue-grey below. Female has blue-grey on supercilium and cheeks, but underparts are buff. Juvenile is like female, but has whiter face and breast, and more extensive barring on flanks (but less than on Baillon's). **Voice** Usually silent away from breeding areas though song may be heard on migration: a repeated loud, nasal *quek... quek... quek*, sometimes accelerating then falling in pitch to end with *ak-uk-u-u-u*; also, a *quek* contact call and a *tyiick* alarm. **HH** See Ruddy-breasted Crake. Marshes with dense reed cover. **TN** Formerly placed in *Porzana*.

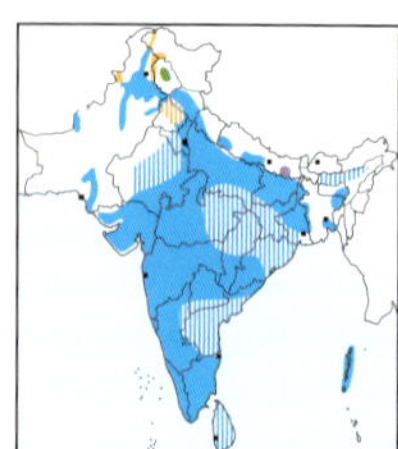

Baillon's Crake *Zapornia pusilla* 17–19cm

Breeds in Indian Himalayas, has bred in Nepal Himalayas; widespread winter visitor and passage migrant except in north-west. **ID** Adult has rufous-brown upperparts (brighter than in male Little) extensively marked with white; barring on flanks extends further forward than on Little, and bill is all green. Sexes similar (unlike Little). Juvenile has buff underparts; compared to Little, wings are shorter, barring on underparts more extensive, has more extensive white flecking on warmer brown upperparts, and lacks pronounced pale fringes to tertials and scapulars. **Voice** Song heard in breeding areas and sometimes on migration: a rattling rasp, *trrrrr-trrrrr*, sounding like a fingernail being drawn across a comb, also, a *tyiuk* alarm call. **HH** See Ruddy-breasted. Reedy marshes, edges of lakes and pools with emergent vegetation, and flooded paddyfields. **TN** Formerly placed in *Porzana*.

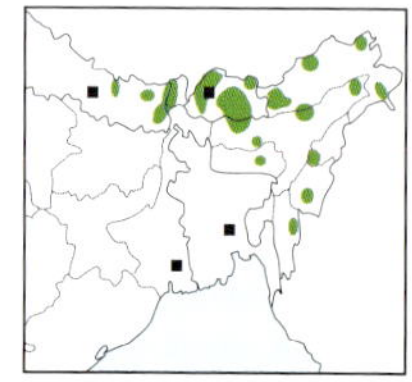

Black-tailed Crake *Zapornia bicolor* 20–22cm

Resident. E Himalayas and NE India. **ID** Red legs, iris and eye-ring. Bill greenish with variable red at base. Sooty-grey head and underparts, rufous-brown upperparts, and sooty-black tail and undertail-coverts. Juvenile is dark brown on upperparts and brownish-olive on underparts, with some white mottling on breast and belly; iris is brown, and bill and legs are duller/browner. **Voice** Quite harsh rasping notes, often followed by a prolonged trill which is more obviously descending than that of Ruddy-breasted Crake. **HH** See Ruddy-breasted. Forest pools and marshes, dense undergrowth at paddyfield edges. **TN** Formerly placed in *Porzana*.

ad
juv
Slaty-legged
Crake
ad
Ruddy-breasted
Crake
juv
ad
Brown Crake
♀
♂
juv
Little Crake
ad
Baillon's Crake
juv
ad
juv
Black-tailed Crake

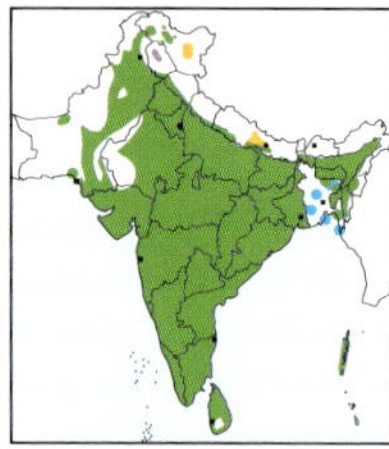

Eurasian Moorhen *Gallinula chloropus* 30–38cm

Widespread resident and winter visitor. Throughout most of subcontinent, except parts of north-west, north-east and Himalayas. Vagrant: Bhutan. **ID** White lateral undertail-coverts, with black central stripe, and usually shows white line on flanks. Breeding adult has blackish head and neck, slate-grey underparts, and dark olive-brown upperparts; red bill with yellow tip and red frontal shield. Non-breeding adult has duller bill and legs. Juvenile has dull green bill, and is mainly brown with whitish throat, grey wash to breast and flanks, and variable whitish patch on belly. **Voice** A *cuk cuk cuk* and *kekuk* in alarm; also, a loud explosive *kurr-ik* and *kark*; and soft muttering *kook… kook*. **HH** Diurnal. Usually forages swimming in open, also on land. Lakes, jheels, marshes, ditches and irrigation tanks with emergent vegetation. **AN** Common Moorhen.

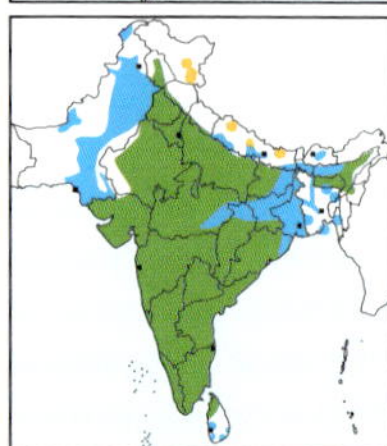

Eurasian Coot *Fulica atra* 36–39cm

Widespread resident and winter visitor. Throughout most of subcontinent, except parts of north-west, north-east and Himalayas. **ID** Blackish, with white bill and frontal shield. Shows paler trailing edge to secondaries in flight. Juvenile grey-brown, with whitish throat and breast; bill dull and lacks white frontal shield. **Voice** Calls include a high-pitched *pyee* and a series of long, soft *dp… dp* notes. **HH** Standing fresh waters with large areas of open water and marginal emergent vegetation.

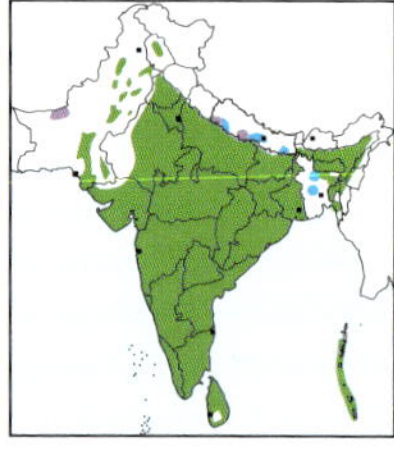

Grey-headed Swamphen *Porphyrio poliocephalus* 38–50cm

Widespread resident. Throughout most of the subcontinent except parts of north-west, north-east and Himalayas. Vagrant: Bhutan. **ID** Large size, purplish-blue coloration with variable greyish head, and huge red bill and frontal shield. Female smaller than male. Juvenile is duller than adult, with greyer neck and underparts, more olive-brown above, duller red bill (blackish at first), and duller legs and feet. **Voice** Very variable: explosive, nasal, rising *cooah* in alarm; song is a long series of powerful nasal rattles *quinquinkrrkrr* etc.; also, a soft *chuck-chuck*. **HH** Diurnal. Forages mainly in reedbeds. Large marshes and extensive reedbeds bordering wetlands; also, paddyfields locally in Nepal, causing crop damage. **TN** Formerly treated as conspecific with Purple Swamphen *P. porphyrio*.

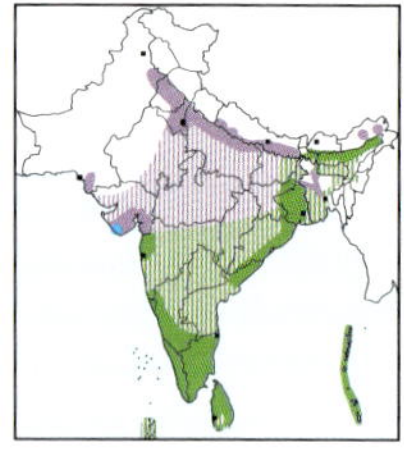

Watercock *Gallicrex cinerea* M 42–43cm, F 34.5–36cm

Resident in well-watered areas, summer visitor elsewhere. Widespread, but mainly in north-east, south India and Sri Lanka. Vagrant: Bhutan. **ID** Breeding male is mainly greyish-black, with yellow-tipped red bill and red shield and horn. Upperparts fringed grey and buff. Legs bright red. First-summer male has broad rufous-buff fringes to plumage. Non-breeding male and female have buff underparts with fine barring, and buff fringes to dark brown upperparts. Legs greenish. Juvenile has uniform rufous-buff underparts, and rufous-buff fringes to upperparts. Male is much larger than female with heavier bill. **Voice** A series of 10–12 *kok-kok-kok* notes followed by a deep, hollow *utumb-utumb-utumb* repeated 10–12 times, and then by five or six *kluck-kluck-kluck* notes. **HH** Very similar to other rails, see Ruddy-breasted Crake. Reedy marshes, flooded fields, and canals, ponds and ditches with emergent vegetation.

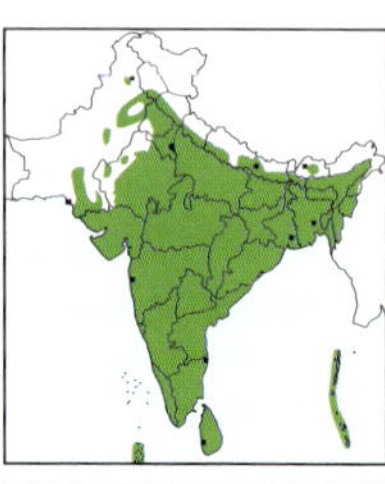

White-breasted Waterhen *Amaurornis phoenicurus* 28–33cm

Widespread resident except most of north-west and Himalayas. **ID** Adult has grey upperparts and white face, foreneck and breast; undertail-coverts rufous-cinnamon. Bill and legs greenish or yellowish, with swollen reddish base to upper mandible. Juvenile has greyish face, foreneck and breast, and olive-brown upperparts; bill and legs duller. In Car Nicobars *A. p. leucocephala* can have an all-white head. **Voice** Mainly vocal when breeding; calls include a metallic *krr-kwaak-kwaak* and a *kook... kook... kook* often preceded by loud roars, croaks and chuckles. **HH** Less shy than other rails, often feeds in open, sometimes diurnally and on dry land. Fresh waters edged by thick cover.

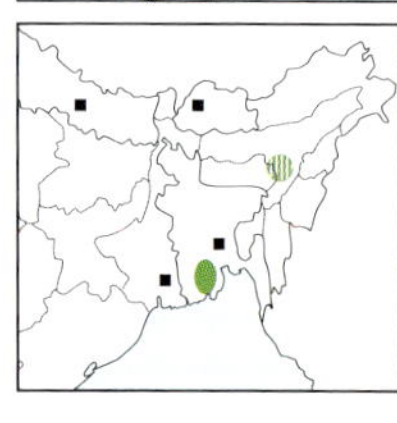

Masked Finfoot *Heliopais personatus* 43–55cm

Resident. Bangladesh and formerly Assam. **ID** A large, grebe-like bird with huge yellow bill, green legs and feet and long pointed tail. Male has black forehead, throat and foreneck, white stripe extending down sides of neck, and small yellow horn at base of bill (in breeding condition). Female has white throat and foreneck. Immature is like female but has duller head pattern and bill. **Voice** Deep bubbling notes, followed by an accelerating series of clucking sounds. **HH** Shy and retiring, typically keeping close to marginal vegetation. Swims well and if alarmed will sink until only head and neck are visible. Perennial pools in dense forest and mangrove creeks. Globally threatened.

Eurasian Coot
ad
juv
juv
ad
Eurasian Moorhen
ad
Grey-headed
Swamphen
juv
♂ br
Watercock
♀
♀ juv
♂ non-br
(transitional ad)
ad
juv
Masked Finfoot
♀
♂
White-breasted
Waterhen

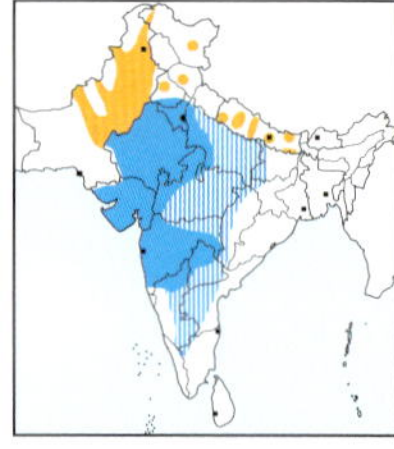

Demoiselle Crane *Anthropoides virgo* 90–100cm

Winter visitor mainly to W India. Passage migrant: Pakistan and Nepal. Vagrant: Bhutan, Bangladesh. **ID** Small crane, with short, fine bill. Adult has black head and neck with white tuft behind eye and grey crown; black neck feathers extend as a point beyond breast, and elongated tertials project in shallow arc beyond body, affording distinctive shape. Immature is initially almost all grey, with slate-grey foreneck, and shorter all-grey tertials. By first winter (on arrival in subcontinent) is like adult, but head and neck dark grey and less contrasting, tuft behind eye is grey and less prominent, has brown cast to upperparts, and elongated foreneck and tertial feathers are shorter. In flight, black breast helps separate from Common Crane at a distance; also, legs and neck appear relatively shorter, and wings shorter and broader-based. **Voice** Flight call a *garrooo*, higher pitched than Common. **HH** Very gregarious, sometimes with Common. Feeds in morning and late afternoon in winter crops and stubble fields, retires for rest of day to river sandbanks and jheels. Cultivation, large rivers with sandbanks and reservoirs. In Pakistan rests in remote desert areas on migration. **TN** Formerly placed in *Grus*.

Siberian Crane *Leucogeranus leucogeranus* 140cm

(Not mapped) Former winter visitor, mainly to Keoladeo Ghana Bird Sanctuary; former passage migrant Pakistan. **ID** Adult is white, with bare red face and bill base, pinkish-red legs, and noticeably downcurved reddish bill; long, downcurved white tertials conceal black primaries at rest. Immature has brownish bill and fully feathered head at first, strongly marked with cinnamon-brown on head, neck, mantle and wings, with some white body feathers by first winter; by third winter, red mask is apparent and body feathers are mainly white. In flight, both adult and immature show black primaries, which contrast with rest of wing. **Voice** Usually heard only before going to roost; a musical *ahooya* in flight, and a subdued *krroum* or *turr* in alarm. **HH** Feeds by probing for aquatic plants while wading. Freshwater marshes. Globally threatened. **TN** Formerly placed in *Grus*.

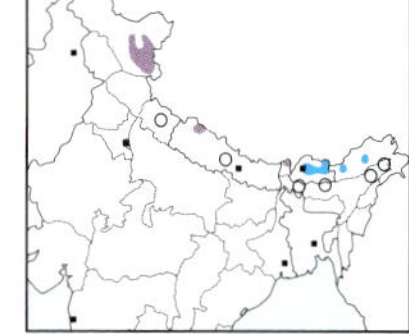

Black-necked Crane *Grus nigricollis* 115cm

Breeds in Ladakh, recorded NW Nepal in summer; winters mainly in Bhutan. **ID** Large, stocky crane, with comparatively short neck and legs. Adult is pale grey with contrasting black head, upper neck and bunched tertials; shows more contrast between black flight feathers and pale grey coverts than Common and has black tail-band. Immature has buff or brownish head, neck, mantle and mottling to wing-coverts. As adult by second winter. **Voice** Variety of calls, most slightly higher pitched than Common, but difficult to distinguish. **HH** Typical crane. Gregarious in winter. Summers by high-altitude lakes; winters in fallow cultivation and marshes.

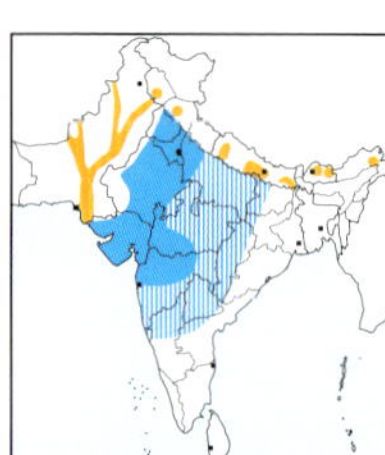

Common Crane *Grus grus* 95–120cm

Winter visitor, now mainly NW India, also, Nepal and Bhutan. Vagrant: Bangladesh. **ID** Adult has mainly black head and foreneck, with white stripe behind eye extending down side of neck; red patch on crown is visible at close range. Immature has brown markings on upperparts with buff or grey head and neck; adult head pattern apparent on some by first winter and as adult by second winter. In flight, adult and immature show black primaries and secondaries which contrast with grey wing-coverts. **Voice** Flight call a loud, trumpeting *krrooah*; on ground utters similar bugling calls including typical *kroo-krii-kroo-krii* duet. **HH** Habits like Demoiselle. Winter crops, rivers with sandbanks, lakes, jheels, and reservoirs.

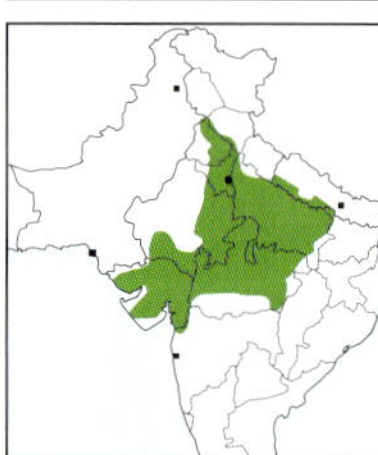

Sarus Crane *Antigone antigone* 152–176cm

Resident. Mainly NW and NC India and W Nepal. **ID** A huge, pale grey crane with reddish legs and very large bill. Adult is grey, with bare red head and upper neck, and bare ashy-green crown. In flight, black primaries contrast with rest of wing. Immature has rusty-buff head and neck feathering, and upperparts marked with brown; older immatures are like adult but have dull red head and upper neck, and lack greenish crown of adult. *A. a. sharpii*, recorded in NE subcontinent, is darker grey than nominate, with uniform grey neck (whiter on lower neck in nominate), and elongated tertials concolorous with rest of upperparts (contrastingly white in nominate). **Voice** Very loud trumpeting, usually a duet by pairs at rest or in flight. **HH** Tame where undisturbed. Usually makes regular daily flights to and from roosting sites. Cultivation in well-watered country; also, marshes, jheels, lakes and large rivers. Globally threatened. **TN** Formerly placed in *Grus*.

Demoiselle Crane
juv
ad
ad
ad
Siberian Crane
juv
ad
juv
Black-necked Crane
ad
ad
juv
Common Crane
ad
ad
Sarus Crane
ad antigone
juv
ad sharpii
ad antigone

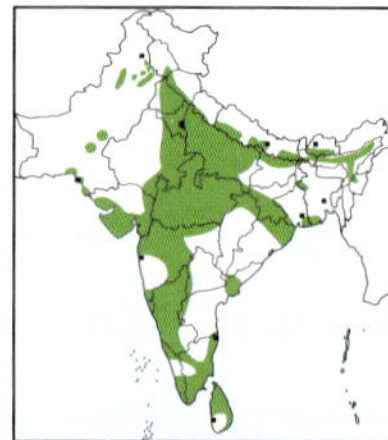

Great Thick-knee *Esacus recurvirostris* 41.5–54cm

Widespread resident, except most of north-west, north-east and E India. **ID** Has large, slightly upturned black-and-yellow bill and yellow eye. At rest, most striking features are white forehead and 'spectacles' contrasting with black ear-coverts, and blackish and whitish bands on wing-coverts. In flight, has grey panel on wings and white patches on primaries. Sexes similar. Juvenile as adult and only distinguishable at close range by buffish fringes to upperparts. **Voice** Rising, wailing whistle of two or more syllables; a loud, harsh *see-eek* alarm call. **HH** Usually solitary. Mainly nocturnal, though often seen by day. If disturbed, relies on camouflage or runs off. Stony banks of larger rivers and lakes; coastal wetlands.

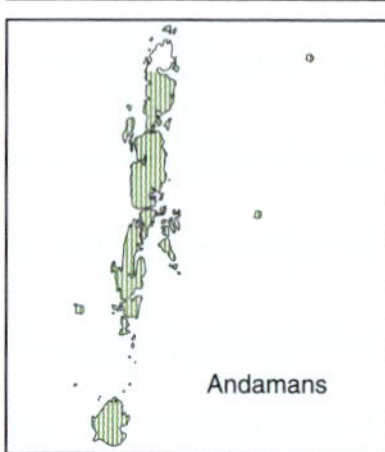

Beach Thick-knee *Esacus magnirostris* 51–57cm

Resident. Andamans. **ID** Stouter and straighter bill than Great Thick-knee. Has different head pattern, with mainly black forehead and lores, and more black on sides of crown and ear-coverts (enclosing white supercilium). In flight, has different wing pattern from Great, with grey (rather than mainly black) secondaries and white inner primaries lacking black subterminal bar. Sexes similar. Juvenile as adult and only distinguishable at close range by pale fringes to upperparts. **Voice** Harsh, wailing *wee-loo*; a *quip* or *peep* alarm call. **HH** Mainly nocturnal. Habits like Great though often hides during day. Sandy and muddy shores and coral reefs. **AN** *Esacus neglectus*.

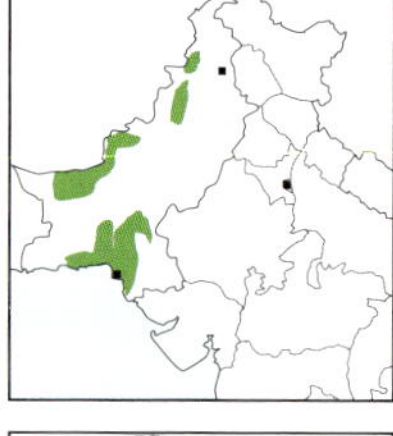

Eurasian Thick-knee *Burhinus oedicnemus* 40–44cm

Probably resident. W and S Pakistan and Balochistan. **ID** Large, sandy-brown and streaked, with short yellow-and-black bill, striking yellow eye, and long yellow legs. Has comparatively smaller bill, longer tail and shorter tarsi than Indian Thick-knee. Feet do not extend noticeably beyond tail in flight. Bill is more extensively yellow, with yellow prominent on lower mandible (extending two-thirds of bill length). Sandier brown in coloration and less heavily streaked, dark and pale bars on wing-coverts are less prominent, with more white in primaries, but differences are subtle, variable and difficult to apply in the field. **Voice** Mainly vocal at night. Slurred whistles building in pitch and volume to a series of clear, loud *cur-lee* calls, then dying away; also, variants of *cur-lee*. **HH** Habits like Indian's. Open stony or scrubby desert and semi-desert, and riverine scrub.

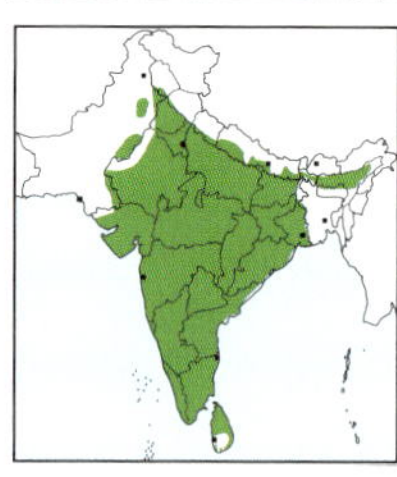

Indian Thick-knee *Burhinus indicus* 40–44cm

Widespread resident except parts of the north-west and north-east. **ID** Large, brown and heavily streaked, with short yellow-and-black bill, striking yellow eye, and very long yellow legs. From Great Thick-knee by much smaller bill, very different head pattern, and heavily streaked upperparts. Very similar to Eurasian Thick-knee, but larger bill, shorter tail, and longer tarsi. Feet extend noticeably beyond tail in flight. Bill is two-thirds black (with well-defined yellow wedge at base of upper mandible and yellow often barely apparent on lower mandible). See Eurasian for further differences. **Voice** Piercing calls recalling Great Thick-knee as much or more than Eurasian. **HH** Very wary; if suspicious, runs off with head low, and squats on ground. When foraging, makes short runs, stopping to swiftly snatch prey. Gregarious in non-breeding season. Dry scrub, stony dry riverbeds with scrub.

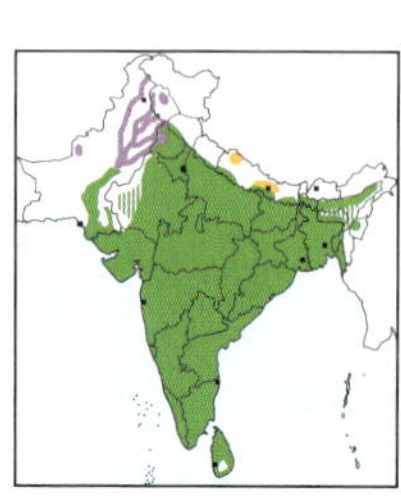

Pheasant-tailed Jacana *Hydrophasianus chirurgus* 31–58cm

Widespread resident except most of the north-west. Vagrant: Bhutan. **ID** Extensive white on upperwing, and white underwing. Yellowish patch on sides of neck. Adult breeding has mainly white head with striking black eye, yellow hindneck, brown underparts and long, curved dark tail. Adult non-breeding and juvenile lack elongated tail and have white underparts; a dark eye-stripe continues down sides of neck and connects to a dark breast-band. The area of yellow on neck is paler and reduced in extent. Upperwing-coverts have a broad brown wing-bar. Juvenile has prominent barring to wing-coverts, and breast-band is initially indistinct. **Voice** Distinctive *me-e-ou* or *me-oup* in breeding season, and a nasal *tewu*. **HH** Walks or rests on floating vegetation. Swims well. Low, flapping flight, with legs dangling. Freshwater wetlands well vegetated with floating plants.

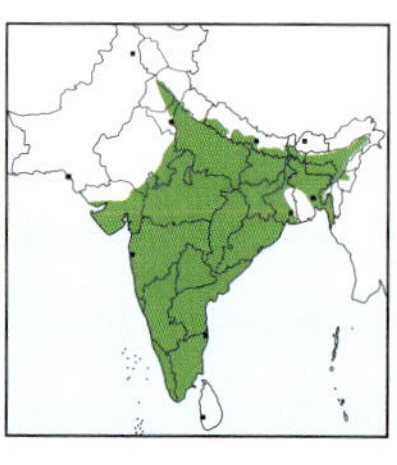

Bronze-winged Jacana *Metopidius indicus* 28–31cm

Widespread resident; largely absent from Pakistan, NW India and Sri Lanka. Vagrant: Bhutan. **ID** Dark upperwing and underwing. Bill is stouter and yellow compared to Pheasant-tailed Jacana. Adult has white stripe behind eye, bronze-green upperparts, blackish underparts, and chestnut rump and tail. At close range has blue-grey shield on forehead and top of upper mandible, with red patch at base. Juvenile has orange-buff neck and breast, rufous crown and narrow white supercilium, and broad whitish cheek-stripe. Lacks the dark neckline and breast-band of Pheasant-tailed, and yellowish bill further aids identification. **Voice** Short, harsh grunt and a wheezy, piping *seek-seek-seek*. **HH** Similar to Pheasant-tailed.

Great Thick-knee
ad
Beach Thick-knee
ad
ad
ad
Eurasian Thick-knee
ad
juv
Indian Thick-knee
Pheasant-tailed
Jacana
Bronze-winged
Jacana
ad
non-br
br
imm

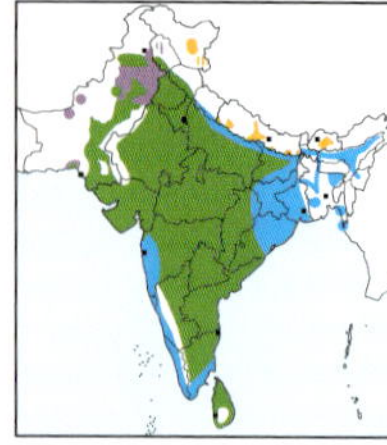

Black-winged Stilt *Himantopus himantopus* 35–40cm

Widespread. Winter visitor to W Ghats and parts of NE and E India; passage migrant in Himalayas, and mainly resident elsewhere. **ID** Slender appearance, with long pinkish legs, and a fine straight bill. Black upperwing strongly contrasts with white back V in flight. Adult at rest shows mainly white head, neck and underparts, contrasting with upperparts, and reddish-pink legs. Both sexes can show variable amounts of black and/or dusky grey on the crown and hindneck. Juvenile has browner upperparts with buff fringes. In Sri Lanka, two distinct variations occur, mainly in males, which resemble other species: those with black hindneck and head markings resemble Australian *H. leucocephalus*, and some that show black on both head and hindneck superficially resemble American *H. mexicanus*; some intermediates also occur. **Voice** A noisy wader, readily agitated; calls include *kek... kek* and a rather anxious *kikikikiki*. **HH** Gregarious throughout the year; sometimes breeds in colonies. A graceful wader that walks slowly and deliberately. Forages on dry mud and by wading, sometimes in water up to the belly and in deeper water than other waders; also, by free-floating in deep saltpans. Sometimes immerses head and neck in water. Freshwater wetlands, brackish marshes, irrigation tanks and saltpans.

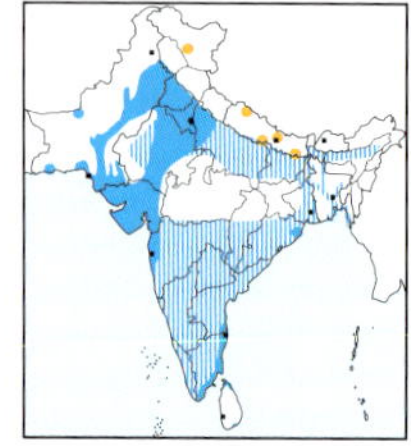

Pied Avocet *Recurvirostra avosetta* 42–45cm

Breeds in parts of Pakistan and NW India; widespread winter visitor and passage migrant. Vagrant: Bhutan. **ID** Upward kink to black bill and long bluish-grey legs. Distinctive black-and-white pattern, including black cap, black scapular line and bar across coverts, and black wingtips. Juvenile is similar in appearance although black markings are browner and has brown-and-buff mottling on mantle and scapulars. **Voice** A throaty *quib... quib*. Noisy at breeding colonies. **HH** Gregarious most of the year; usually breeds in colonies. Characteristically feeds by sweeping bill and head from side to side in shallow water; also, often swims and upends like a dabbling duck, and picks from the surface of water or mud. Eats small crustaceans, molluscs and insects. Favours shallow alkaline and brackish pools; also, coastal wetlands.

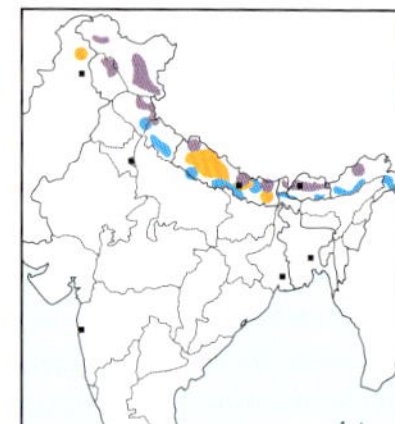

Ibisbill *Ibidorhyncha struthersii* 39–41cm

Resident. Himalayas. **ID** Adult has black face with narrow white border, downcurved dark red bill, and black and white breast-bands. In flight, shows white patch at base of inner primaries and blackish tail-band. Juvenile has brownish upperparts with buff fringes, faint breast-band, and dull legs and bill. **Voice** A ringing *klew-klew* and rapid *tee-tee-tee-tee*. **HH** Singles, pairs or small groups forage inconspicuously and quietly in mountain rivers and streams. Usually quite wary; if alarmed nervously bobs its head and wags its tail. Seeks aquatic invertebrates by walking slowly through water, using its long decurved bill to probe around and under stones; frequently wades belly-deep. Fast-flowing mountain streams and rivers with shingle beds.

Eurasian Oystercatcher *Haematopus ostralegus* 40–47.5cm

Winter visitor mainly to coasts. Vagrant: Nepal. **ID** Black and white, with broad white wing-bar. Bill and eye reddish, and legs pinkish. White collar in non-breeding plumage. Shows broad white wing-bar in flight. Juvenile and first-winter have browner upperparts and darker tip to bill; legs and feet are initially greyish. **Voice** A piping *pi... peep... peep... peep* and *pi-peep*. **HH** Feeds and roost on seashore, often with other waders. Flight is strong and direct with shallow wingbeats. Runs about on intertidal wet sand, probing for food and dislodges molluscs from rocks. Sandy and rocky coasts.

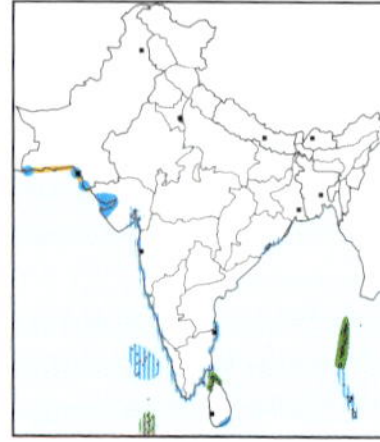

Crab-plover *Dromas ardeola* 38–41cm

Winter visitor to coasts and Maldives; breeds in Sri Lanka. Vagrant: Bangladesh. **ID** Black-and-white plumage, with stout black bill and very long blue-grey legs. In flight shows black mantle and flight feathers contrasting with white wing-coverts. Juvenile like washed-out version of adult with black streaking on nape and grey rather (than black) mantle. **Voice** Nasal, yappy *kirruc* flight call recalls tern; also, *kwerk-kwerk-kwerk-kwerk*. **HH** Found singly, in pairs or in small parties, but hundreds recorded at traditional sites. Mainly crepuscular and often wary, taking flight at a distance. Feeds chiefly on crabs which it hunts in typical plover-like manner, either on mudflats or in shallow water. Flies with neck and legs extended. Feeds on intertidal mudflats and coral reefs; roosts on reefs, sand spits and shores, and coastal rocks.

juv
juv
Pied Avocet
ad
ad
Black-winged
Stilt
Ibisbill
ad
Eurasian
Oystercatcher
br
juv
non-br
ad
juv
Crab-plover

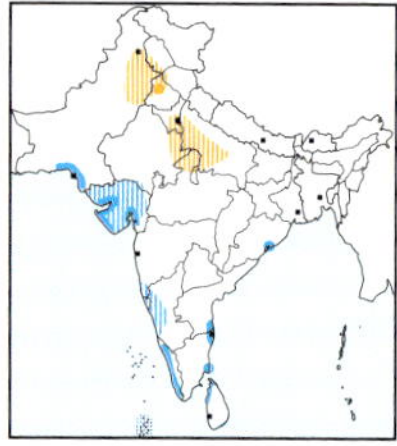

Common Ringed Plover *Charadrius hiaticula* 18–20cm

Winter visitor, mainly to W coasts and Gujarat. Vagrant: Bhutan. **ID** Prominent breast-band and white hind collar. Larger and stockier than Little Ringed, with prominent wing-bar in flight. Adult breeding has orange legs and bill base (legs duller in non-breeder, more olive-yellow in juvenile; bill mainly dark). Non-breeding and juvenile have duller head pattern, and less distinct breast-band which can appear broken in centre; whitish supercilium and forehead more prominent compared with Little Ringed. **Voice** Soft *too-li* in flight; *tooee*; *too weep* when alarmed. **HH** Habits like Little Ringed. Mud banks of freshwater and coastal wetlands.

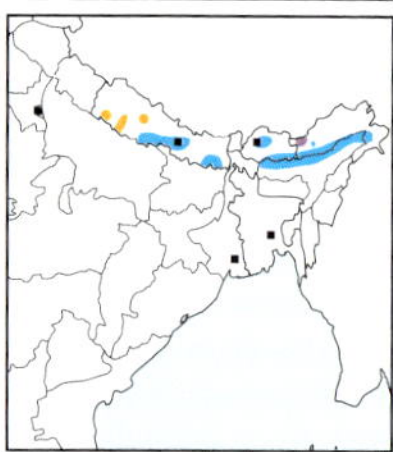

Long-billed Plover *Charadrius placidus* 18–21cm

Winter visitor, mainly to N subcontinent; unrecorded in Pakistan. Vagrant: Bangladesh. **ID** Like a large Little Ringed, but has longer bill, longer tail with clearer dark subterminal bar, and more prominent white wing-bar. Adult breeding has black band on forecrown, ear-coverts are usually brown (never cleanly black), and has less distinct eye-ring than Little Ringed. Black breast-band is narrow, extending as a fine line across upper mantle, and is bordered with paler brown on sides of breast. In non-breeding plumage pattern of head and breast duller but usually still apparent. Juvenile has brown crown and ear-coverts, buffish supercilium and narrow buff fringes to upperparts; pale forehead and supercilium usually more prominent compared with Little Ringed. **Voice** Clear, penetrating *piwee* in flight. **HH** Habits like Little Ringed, but usually solitary. Shingle banks of large rivers.

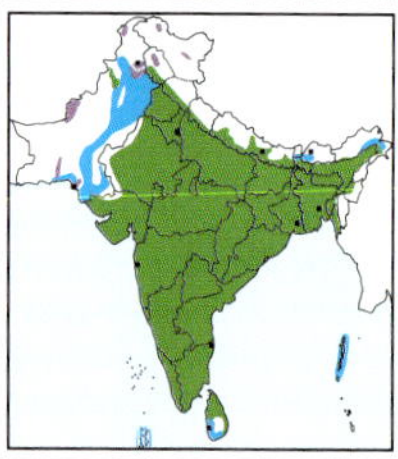

Little Ringed Plover *Charadrius dubius* 14–17cm

Widespread resident and winter visitor except parts of Pakistan. **ID** Small, elongated and small-headed appearance, and uniform upperwing with only a very narrow wing-bar. Bill small and mainly dark. Legs yellowish or pinkish. Adult breeding has striking yellow eye-ring. Adult non-breeding and juvenile have more uniform head pattern than Common Ringed with buff forehead and supercilium. **Voice** Clear, descending *pee-oo* or shorter *peeu* in flight. **HH** In pairs or small flocks. Typical plover feeding behaviour, makes short runs, then pauses, often rapidly vibrates one foot probably to attract prey to the surface. Freshwater and coastal wetlands.

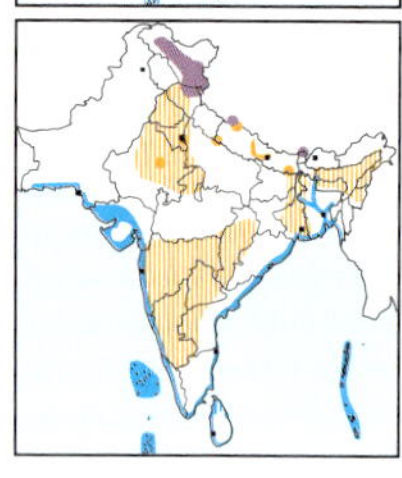

Tibetan Sand Plover *Anarhynchus atrifrons* 18–21cm

Breeds in N Himalayas, India and NW Nepal; winters on coasts of subcontinent. Vagrant: Bhutan. **ID** Larger and longer-legged than Kentish, lacking white hind collar. From extremely similar Greater Sand Plover by smaller and stouter bill (equal to or shorter than distance between bill base and rear of eye, with blunt tip), more rounded head, and shorter dark grey or dark greenish legs. In flight, white wing-bar is more even in width and narrower across primaries. Breeding male typically shows full black mask and forehead and more extensive rufous on breast compared to Greater (although there is variation). **Voice** Hard *chitik*, *chi-chi-chi*, and *kruit-kruit* in flight. **HH** Gait and feeding behaviour, see Little Ringed. Breeds on Tibetan Plateau; winters at coastal wetlands. **TN** Formerly placed in *Charadrius* and treated as Lesser Sand Plover *C. mongolus*.

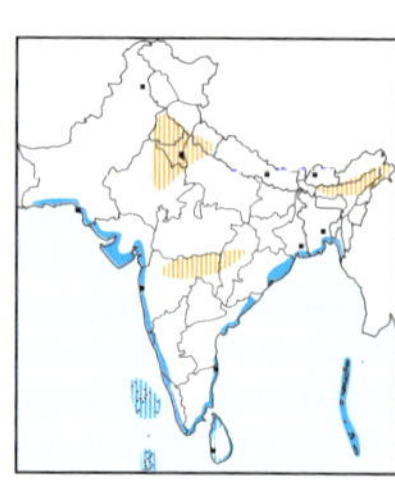

Greater Sand Plover *Anarhynchus leschenaultii* 20–25cm

Winter visitor to coasts. Vagrant: Nepal, Bhutan. **ID** Very challenging to distinguish from Tibetan Sand Plover; is larger and lankier, with longer and larger bill, usually with pronounced gonys and more pointed tip (longer than distance between bill base and rear of eye). Longer legs (owing to proportionately longer tibia) are paler, with distinct yellowish or greenish tinge. In flight, feet project more noticeably beyond tail, has more pronounced dark subterminal band to tail, and has broader white wing-bar on primaries. In breeding plumage, male typically has white forehead and black mask; rufous on breast is less extensive than in Tibetan. **Voice** In flight a trilling *prrrirt* or *kyrrrr... trrr*, softer and longer than Tibetan. **HH** Gait and feeding behaviour typical of plovers, see Little Ringed. Coastal wetlands. **TN** Formerly placed in *Charadrius*.

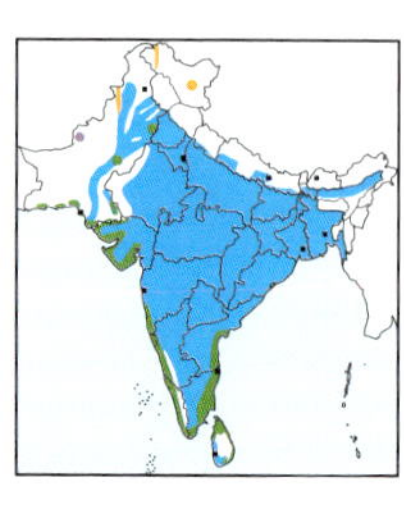

Kentish Plover *Anarhynchus alexandrinus* 15–17.5cm

Breeds locally in Pakistan, India and Sri Lanka; widespread winter visitor. Vagrant: Bhutan. **ID** Small size and stocky appearance. White hind collar and usually small, well-defined patches on sides of breast. Upperparts paler, more sandy, than Common Ringed. Legs usually appear blackish; may be brownish or olive. Male of widespread nominate has rufous cap and black eye-stripe and forecrown; male *seebohmi*, of Sri Lanka and S India, has brown rather than rufous cap. **Voice** Flight call a soft *pi... pi... pi*, or rattling trill *prrr* or *prrtut* (harsher than Tibetan Sand); and a plaintive *whoheet*. **HH** See Little Ringed, but runs about more rapidly. Sandy shores, banks of freshwater wetlands and saltpans. **TN** Formerly placed in *Charadrius*.

br
non-br
Common Ringed Plover
non-br
br
Long-billed Plover
br
non-br
non-br
non-br
Little Ringed Plover
non-br
♀ br
non-br
♂ br
non-br
♂ br
Tibetan Sand Plover
♀ br
Greater Sand Plover
non-br
br
seebohmi
non-br
♂ br
Kentish Plover

Caspian Plover *Anarhynchus asiaticus* 18–20cm

Winter visitor: India and Sri Lanka coasts. Vagrant: Maldives. **ID** Slim bill, slender appearance and complete breast-band. Supercilium more striking than in sand plovers. Narrow white wing-bar, whiter underwing-coverts, and shorter greenish or brownish legs best distinctions from Oriental Plover (see Vagrants). Breeding male has chestnut breast-band with a black lower border. Juvenile has rufous-and-buff fringes to upperparts. **Voice** Gives a loud, sharp *tyup*, a long rattling *tptptptptp*, a soft piping *tik*, and a shrill *kwhitt*. **HH** Gait and feeding behaviour of plovers, see Pacific Golden. Dry grassland, dry mud near fresh water or (rarely) on intertidal mud. **TN** Formerly placed in *Charadrius*.

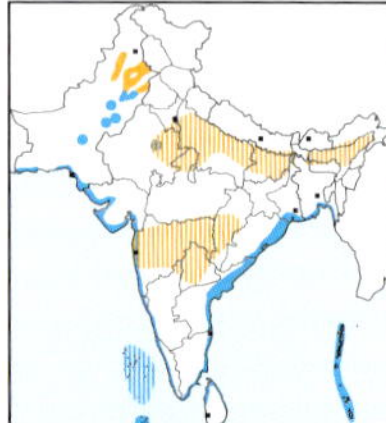

Black-bellied Plover *Pluvialis squatarola* 27–31cm

Winter visitor, mainly to coasts. Vagrant: Nepal. **ID** Stockier, with stouter bill and shorter legs, than Pacific Golden. White underwing and black axillaries, whitish rump and prominent white wing-bar are further differences. Adult breeding has black on face, foreneck and underparts, with striking white sides to neck and breast. Upperparts have extensive white spangling; upperparts mainly grey in non-breeder (in all plumages lacks golden spangling of Pacific Golden). **Voice** A mournful *chee-woo-ee*. **HH** Habits similar to Pacific Golden, but usually less gregarious, often in pairs or small groups with other wader species. Sandy shores, mudflats, tidal and mangrove creeks. **AN** Grey Plover.

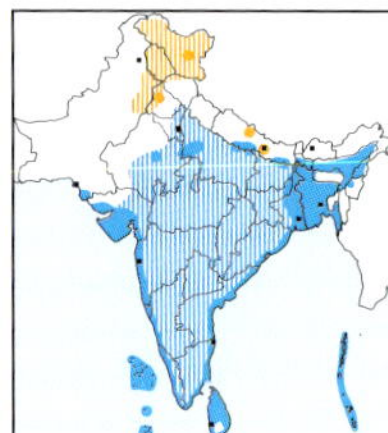

Pacific Golden Plover *Pluvialis fulva* 23–26cm

Widespread winter visitor except the north-west. **ID** In all plumages, from Black-bellied Plover by golden-yellow markings on upperparts, dusky-grey underwing-coverts and axillaries, dark rump, and finer white wing-bar. Also, slimmer-bodied, with longer neck and small bulbous head, and bill is finer. Legs appear longer (owing to proportionately longer tibia). Adult breeding has black on face, foreneck, breast and belly, strikingly bordered by white. Adult non-breeding and juvenile have yellowish-buff wash to supercilium, cheeks and neck; usually show pronounced supercilium which often curves down as diffuse crescent behind ear-coverts, and a dark patch on rear ear-coverts. **Voice** An abrupt disyllabic *chi-vit* and a plaintive *tu-weep*. **HH** Associates in flocks which scatter when feeding. Very wary and if disturbed groups rise almost simultaneously in a compact flock, twisting and turning rapidly in unison. Typical plover feeding behaviour: runs in short spurts and mincing steps, pausing to dip down without bending legs and pick up food. Muddy banks of rivers, lakes and pools, ploughed fields and grassland.

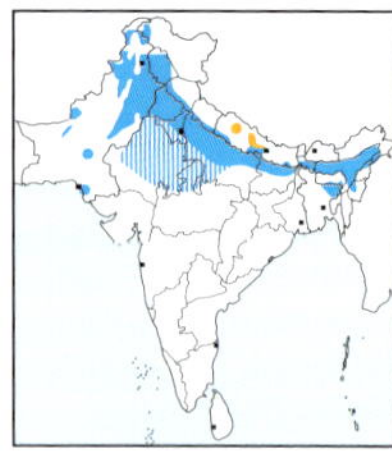

Northern Lapwing *Vanellus vanellus* 28–31cm

Winter visitor to N subcontinent. **ID** Stocky with comparatively short, pinkish legs. Black crest, white (or buff) and black face pattern, black breast-band, and dark green upperparts. Juvenile has prominent buff fringes to mantle, scapulars and wing-coverts. Has very broad, rounded wingtips. Shows whitish rump and blackish tail-band in flight. **Voice** A mournful *eu-whit* but usually silent in winter. **HH** Gregarious and often in flocks. Feeding behaviour is like Red-wattled. Agile in flight, capable of sharp dives, rolls and zigzags. Wet grassland, marshes, lake margins, shingle riverbanks; sometimes fallow fields and dry stubbles.

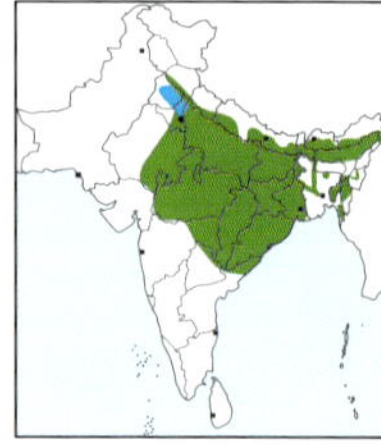

River Lapwing *Vanellus duvaucelii* 29.5–31.5cm

Resident. N subcontinent; unrecorded in Pakistan. **ID** Black crest, face and throat, grey sides to neck, and black bill and legs. Small black patch on belly. In flight, shows broad white greater covert wing-bar contrasting with black flight feathers, black crescent at carpal, and black tail. Juvenile is similar to adult, but black of head is partly obscured by white tips, and has buff fringes and dark subterminal marks to feathers of upperparts. **Voice** A sharp insistent, high pitched *did, did, did*, sometimes ending with *did-did-do-weet*. **HH** Usually occurs singly, in pairs or in small groups. Feeding behaviour and flight like Red-wattled. Often has a hunched posture with head drawn in. Well camouflaged in its riverine habitat. Noisy in breeding season. Mainly sandbanks and shingle banks of rivers, also, estuaries in Bangladesh.

♂ br
non-br
Caspian Plover
non-br
Black-bellied Plover
br
br
non-br
non-br
Pacific Golden Plover
♂ br
non-br
ad
Northern Lapwing
non-br
River Lapwing

Yellow-wattled Lapwing *Vanellus malabaricus* 24–28cm

Resident. Mainly India except most of the north-west and north-east. Vagrant: Bhutan. **ID** Yellow wattles and legs. White eye-stripes join at nape, dark cap, brown breast with narrow blackish breast-band. In flight, shows white greater covert wing-bar contrasting with black flight feathers, and white tail with black subterminal band. Juvenile has small and dull yellow wattles, white chin, brown cap, and prominent buff fringes and dark subterminal bars to feathers of upperparts. **Voice** A strident *chee-eet* and a hard *tit-tit-tit*. **HH** In pairs, and sometimes in small flocks in non-breeding season. Foraging behaviour like Red-wattled. Much less noisy than that species. Flight is buoyant with rather slow wingbeats. Dry stubbles, fallow fields, stony ground and open dry country.

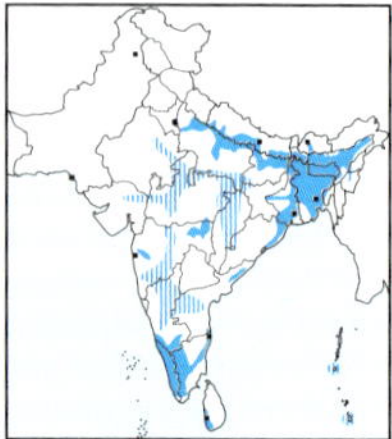

Grey-headed Lapwing *Vanellus cinereus* 34–37cm

Winter visitor. Mainly Nepal, NE India, and Bangladesh. Vagrant: Bhutan, Sri Lanka. **ID** Yellow bill with black tip, and yellow legs. Grey head, neck and breast, latter with diffuse black border, and black tail-band. Secondaries white. Juvenile has brownish head and neck, lacks dark breast-band, and has prominent buff fringes to feathers of upperparts. **Voice** A plaintive *chee-it, chee-it* but normally quiet in winter. **HH** Usually found in small parties or flocks of up to 50 birds. Feeding behaviour and flight like Red-wattled, with which it often feeds. Riverbanks, marshes and wet fields.

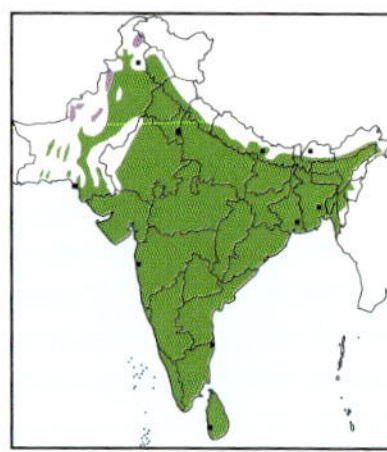

Red-wattled Lapwing *Vanellus indicus* 32–35cm

Widespread resident except parts of the north-west. **ID** Black cap and breast, red bill with black tip, bare red lores, and yellow legs. In flight, shows white greater covert wing-bar and black tail-band. Juvenile is duller than adult, with whitish throat and pale fringes to upperparts. *V. i. atronuchalis*, of E India, has black head, neck and breast, with white patch on ear-coverts and white collar. **Voice** An agitated and penetrating *did he do it, did he do it* and a less intrusive *did did did*. **HH** In pairs or small flocks of up to about 12 birds. A vigilant and noisy bird; when alarmed calls loudly and frantically while circling overhead. Forages by walking or running in short spurts, then stops and probes, with body tilted forward and legs unflexed; also, vibrates its foot rapidly on surface to flush invertebrates. Feeds mainly at night and in early mornings and evenings. Usually flies slowly with deep flaps though capable of great speed when chasing an intruder. Open flat ground near water.

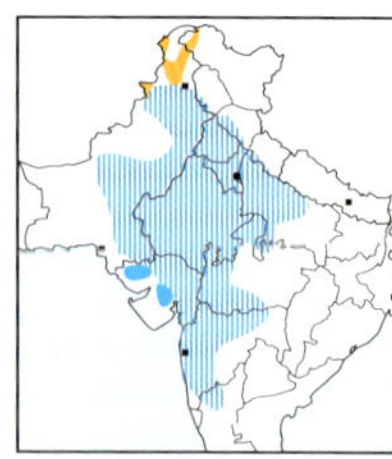

Sociable Lapwing *Vanellus gregarius* 27–30cm

Winter visitor, now mainly to Pakistan and N and NW India. Vagrant: Maldives, Sri Lanka. **ID** Dark cap, with white supercilia which join at nape. Black bill and legs. In flight, white secondaries contrast with black primaries and sandy-brown upperwing-coverts, and has black tail band. Adult breeding has yellow wash to sides of head, and black-and-maroon patch on belly. Non-breeding and juvenile have duller head pattern, white belly and streaked breast. Juvenile additionally has prominent buff fringes and dark subterminal crescents to scapulars and coverts. **Voice** Calls include a harsh, abrupt note, though mainly quiet in winter. **HH** Feeding behaviour and flight are like Red-wattled. Dry fallow fields, stubbles and scrub desert. Globally threatened.

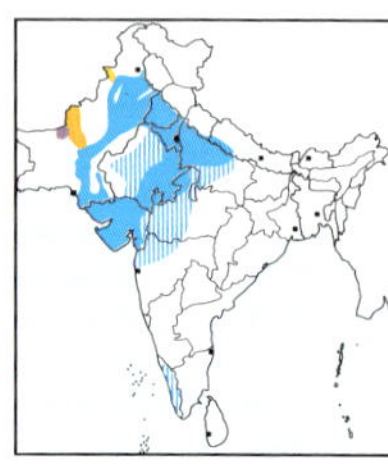

White-tailed Lapwing *Vanellus leucurus* 26–29cm

Breeds in Balochistan; winters in N subcontinent. Vagrant: Bangladesh. **ID** Blackish bill, large dark eyes and very long yellow legs. Plain head. Tail all white, lacking black band of other *Vanellus* lapwings. Juvenile has dark subterminal marks and pale fringes to feathers of upperparts, and paler neck and breast than adult; crown is mottled with dark brown. **Voice** Calls include a *pet-oo-wit* and *pee-wick* recalling Northern Lapwing. **HH** Often in small parties in winter. Habits like those of other lapwings, see Red-wattled, but frequently wades and feeds in water. Freshwater marshes, marshy lake edges, and grassland.

ad
ad
juv
Yellow-wattled Lapwing
non-br
non-br
juv
Grey-headed Lapwing
ad
atronuchalis
ad
indicus
juv
indicus
Red-wattled Lapwing
br
ad
juv
ciable Lapwing
non-br
ad
White-tailed
Lapwing

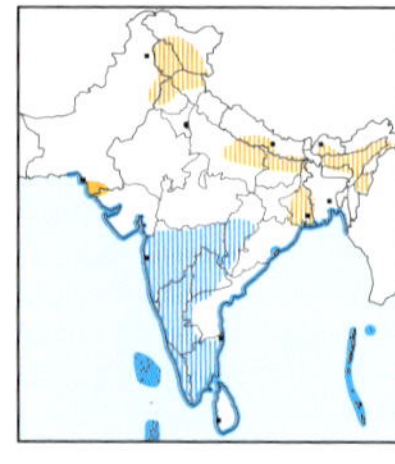

Whimbrel *Numenius phaeopus* 40–46cm

Widespread winter visitor, mainly to coasts. Rare visitor: Nepal. Vagrant: Bhutan. **ID** Smaller than Eurasian Curlew, with shorter bill, often with more marked downward kink. Has prominent whitish supercilium and crown-stripe, contrasting with blackish eye-stripe and sides to crown, resulting in more striking head pattern. Juvenile as adult. Eastern *variegatus* (possibly winters in north-east) has back and rump, as well as underwing, marked heavily with brown (nominate has white back V and whiter underwing) and shows much less white on belly. **Voice** Almost invariably calls in flight, a distinctive, *he-he-he-he-he-he-he*, flat-toned and laughter-like. **HH** Walks on mud and feeds chiefly by picking from surface, also, by probing. Mainly estuaries, tidal creeks and mangroves, occasionally on inland waters on passage; on all coasts in Sri Lanka.

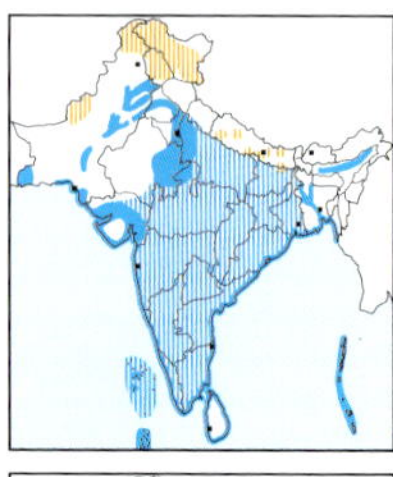

Eurasian Curlew *Numenius arquata* 50–60cm

Widespread winter visitor, mainly to coasts. Vagrant: Bhutan. **ID** From Whimbrel by larger size, much longer bill, more uniform head pattern. Juvenile has shorter bill. See Vagrants for differences from Eastern Curlew. **Voice** Has distinctive mournful rising *cur-lew* call and an anxious *were-up* in alarm, both of which are often heard in winter and on passage. Calls may be mixed with short bursts of its distinctive song: a sequence of bubbling phrases, accelerating and rising in pitch. **HH** Gregarious. Feeds by walking on mud and probing deeply, also, by picking from the surface. Generally wary and difficult to approach. Mainly estuaries, tidal creeks and mangroves; uncommonly on large rivers and inland lakes.

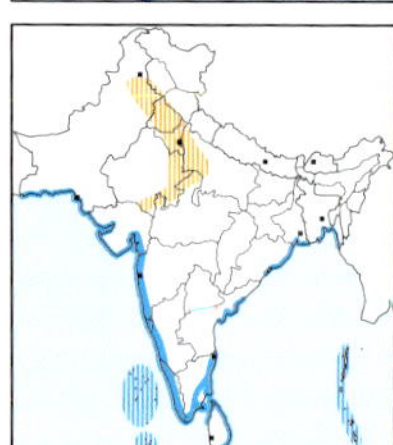

Bar-tailed Godwit *Limosa lapponica* 37–39cm

Widespread winter visitor, mainly to coasts. **ID** Lacks wing-bar, has barred tail and white V on back. At rest, stockier than Black-tailed, with shorter legs, and shorter, more upturned bill. Breeding male has chestnut-red head, neck and underparts; underparts are unbarred and mantle and scapulars are more uniformly streaked than Black-tailed. Breeding female has pale chestnut underparts, although many as non-breeding. Non-breeding has dark streaking on breast and streaked appearance to upperparts. Juvenile like non-breeding, but with buff wash to underparts, buff edges to mantle/scapulars, and buff notching to tertials. **Voice** A barking *kak-kak* and deep *kirruc*. **HH** Habits like Black-tailed but often feeds in shallower water. Estuaries, lagoons and saltpans, rarely on inland waters.

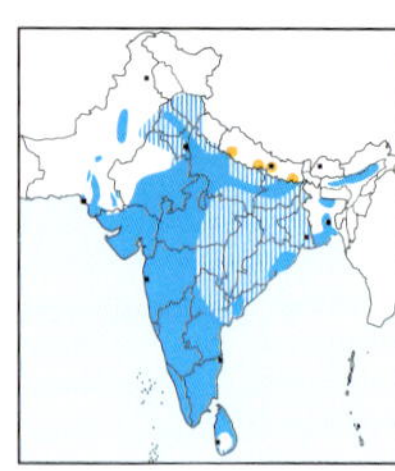

Black-tailed Godwit *Limosa limosa* 36–44cm

Widespread winter visitor except parts of the north-west and north-east. **ID** White wing-bar and white rump with black tail-band. At rest, appears lankier with longer neck, legs and bill compared to Bar-tailed Godwit. Long straight bill is mainly pinkish with darker tip, and has long dark legs. In breeding plumage, male has rufous-orange neck and breast, with blackish barring on underparts and white belly; mantle and scapulars more unevenly patterned than Bar-tailed; breeding female larger and duller than male. In non-breeding plumage, uniform grey on neck, upperparts and breast. Juvenile has cinnamon underparts and cinnamon fringes to dark-centred upperparts. *L. l. melanuroides* ('Eastern Black-tailed Godwit') occurs and is more similar in shape to Bar-tailed Godwit and shows narrower wing-bar in flight; male breeding has deeper and more extensive red on underparts, and in non-breeding plumage is darker grey on upperparts and breast, compared to nominate. **Voice** A yapping *kek-kek* in flight. **HH** Feeds mainly by walking slowly and probing in open mud or shallows. Mainly shallows and mud banks of fresh waters.

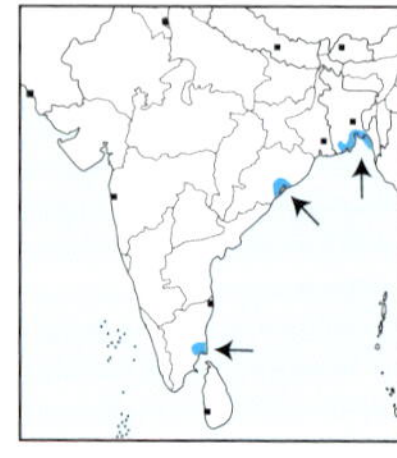

Asian Dowitcher *Limnodromus semipalmatus* 33–36cm

Winter visitor to coasts of India and Bangladesh. Vagrant: Sri Lanka. **ID** From Bar-tailed Godwit by straight, broad-based all-black bill, with swollen tip; also, by smaller size and stouter appearance, and square-shaped head with steeply rising forehead. Eye appears set back and high in head. Has distinctive 'sewing-machine' feeding action. In flight, diffuse pale band on secondaries, greyish (finely barred) tail, and dark markings on lower back and rump (lacking clean white V of Bar-tailed). Underparts brick-red in breeding plumage, with chestnut fringes to dark feathers of mantle and scapulars. Upperparts and underparts heavily streaked in non-breeding plumage. Juvenile has buff fringes to upperparts and wash to breast; tertials neatly fringed with buff rather than prominently notched as in Bar-tailed. See Vagrants for differences from Long-billed Dowitcher. **Voice** A yelping *chep-chep* or *chowp* and a soft moaning *kiaow*. **HH** Often feeds and flies in tight flocks. Mixes with godwits and other waders at roost. Flight powerful and often aerobatic. Intertidal mudflats and mud banks of large tidal rivers.

ad
phaeopus
Whimbrel
ad
phaeopus
ad
variegatus
Eurasian Curlew
ad
ad
♂ br
♂ br
♀ br
non-br
non-br
Bar-tailed Godwit
juv
non-br
limosa
♂ br
limosa
♂ br
melanuroides
non-br
melanuroides
juv
♂ br
Black-tailed Godwit
br
juv
non-br
Asian Dowitcher

Solitary Snipe *Gallinago solitaria* 29–31cm

Resident and winter visitor. Balochistan, Himalayas and NE India. **ID** Large, dull-coloured snipe with long bill. Compared to Wood Snipe is colder-coloured and less boldly marked, with less striking head pattern and narrower white mantle and scapular stripes. Further, has gingery-brown breast finely spotted and barred with white, and rufous barring on mantle and scapulars. Wings longer and narrower than in Wood. Legs yellowish. **Voice** If flushed gives a harsh *kensh*, deeper than Common. In aerial display utters a deep *chok-achock-a* call, combined with a mechanical bleating produced by outer tail feathers. **HH** If flushed, zigzags away more heavily and slowly than Common and soon settles again. Male has an aerial 'drumming' display in breeding season. High-altitude bogs, marshy edges and beds of mountain streams; lower levels in winter.

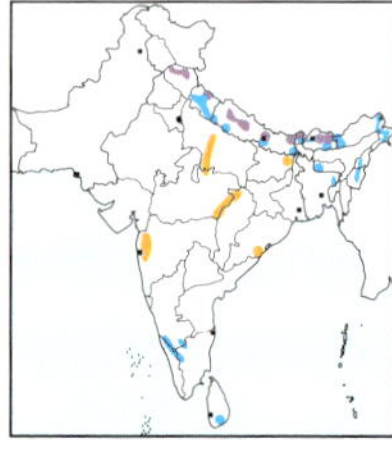

Wood Snipe *Gallinago nemoricola* 28–32cm

Breeds in Himalayas and NE India; winters in Himalayas and S Indian hills. Vagrant: Bangladesh, Sri Lanka? **ID** Large, with heavy and direct flight on broad wings. Bill relatively short and broad-based. More boldly marked than Solitary, with buff and blackish head stripes, broad buff stripes on blackish mantle and scapulars (white in juvenile), and warm buff neck and breast with brown streaking. Legs greenish. **Voice** A long series of nasal notes from ground, *check-check-check* on breeding area. In display flight a nasal *che-dep, che-dep, che-dep, ip-ip-ip, ock ock*; and a *che-dep, che-dep* when flushed. **HH** Slow, heavy, wavering flight; soon settles after being flushed. Aerial display in breeding season. Breeds in alpine meadows and dwarf scrub; winters in forest marshes. Globally threatened.

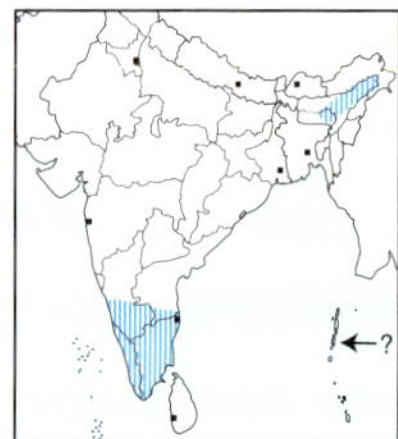

Swinhoe's Snipe *Gallinago megala* 27–29cm

Winter visitor. Mainly NE subcontinent and S India. Vagrant: Bangladesh, Maldives, Sri Lanka? **ID** From Common Snipe by same features as differentiate Common from Pin-tailed Snipe. Not safely separable in the field from Pin-tailed, with no consistent plumage or structural differences. Thus, safely identified only in the hand by the shape of the outer tail feathers (narrow 'pins' in Pin-tailed; only the outermost tail feather is pin-like in Swinhoe's, the rest broadening towards the centre). A number of structural differences are indicative, with Swinhoe's being, on average, heavier, with longer bill, wings and tail but there is much overlap. **Voice** Call thought to be lower pitched, flatter and throatier than Pin-tailed; less frequently vocal on being flushed. **HH** Habits and habitat like Pin-tailed.

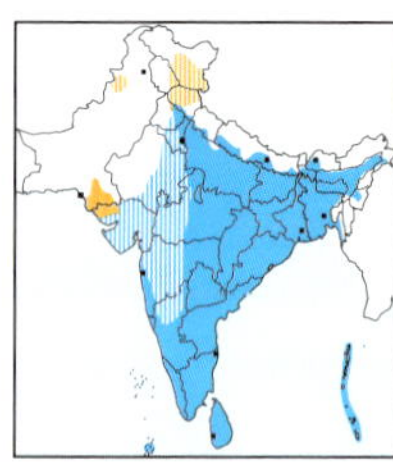

Pin-tailed Snipe *Gallinago stenura* 25–27cm

Widespread winter visitor except most of the north-west. **ID** Compared with Common, has shorter bill, more rounded wings, and slower and more direct flight. Lacks well-defined white trailing edge to secondaries, and has densely barred underwing-coverts and pale upperwing-covert panel. Feet project beyond tail in flight. At rest, shows little or no tail projection beyond wings. Usually shows bulging supercilium in front of eye, with little contrast between buff supercilium and cheeks, and eye-stripe often narrow in front of eye and poorly defined behind it. Width and colour of edges to lower large scapulars similar on inner and outer webs, creating scalloped appearance. **Voice** Short, rasping *tetch*, deeper than Common if flushed. **HH** Flushes with little or no zigzagging; usually drops into cover more quickly than Common. Marshy pool edges, damp paddyfields; sometimes dry ground, also, coasts in Bangladesh.

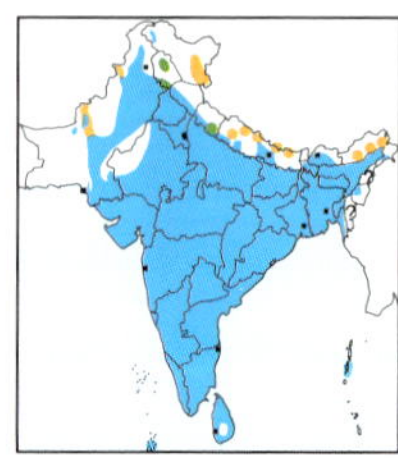

Common Snipe *Gallinago gallinago* 25–27cm

Breeds in NW Himalayas; widespread winter visitor. **ID** Compared with Pin-tailed, wings more pointed, faster and more erratic flight. In flight, shows prominent white trailing edge to wing, white banding on underwing-coverts, and more extensive white belly patch. At rest, noticeable projection of tail beyond wings, poorly defined median covert panel, buff supercilium contrasts with white cheek-stripe, and broad buff edges to outer webs of lower scapulars contrast with narrower, browner inner webs. **Voice** Anxious, rising, grating *scaaap* if flushed. **HH** When flushed, rises steeply with rapid zigzagging, while uttering a hoarse cry, circles high and lands some distance away. Drumming display in breeding season. Marshes and wet paddy stubbles.

Solitary Snipe
ad
Wood Snipe
ad
ad
tail
flight
juv
Swinhoe's Snipe
ad
juv
flight
tail
Pin-tailed Snipe
tail
ad
juv
flight
Common Snipe

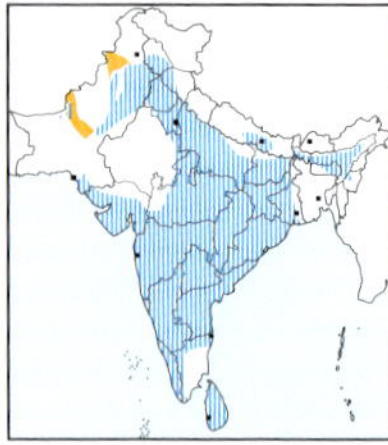

Jack Snipe *Lymnocryptes minimus* 17–19cm

Widespread winter visitor except most of the north-west. Vagrant: Bhutan, Bangladesh. **ID** Small, with short bill. Flight weaker and slower than that of Common Snipe, with rounded wingtips. Has divided supercilium but lacks pale crown-stripe. Mantle and scapular stripes very prominent. **Voice** Invariably silent when flushed. **HH** When feeding, bobs body constantly. If flushed flies off more slowly than Common, without zigzagging and soon drops into cover. Marshes and wet paddy stubbles.

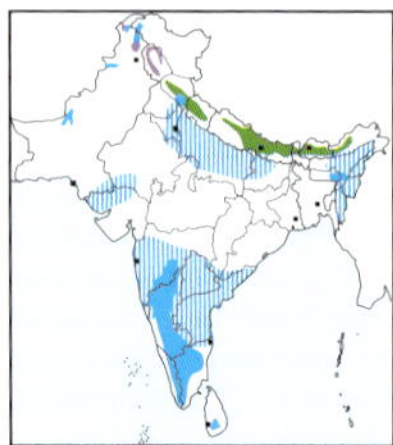

Eurasian Woodcock *Scolopax rusticola* 33–35cm

Breeds in Pakistan hills and Himalayas; winters in Himalayas, Indian hills and Sri Lanka. Vagrant: Bangladesh. **ID** Bulky with broad, rounded wings. Has black-and-buff banded crown and nape, black loral stripe, and large rearward-set eye. Upperparts are intricately barred and mottled with rufous, black and buff; lacks sharply defined mantle and scapular stripes. **Voice** Usually silent when flushed. A sharp repeated *chiwich* in roding display. **HH** Solitary, nocturnal, passing the day in thick cover. Silent when flushed; zigzags and quickly drops into cover. Most easily located by the male's characteristic roding display flight in breeding season; at dawn and dusk makes a regular circuit low over the treetops with slow, deliberate wingbeats. Dense forest, also plantations in S India.

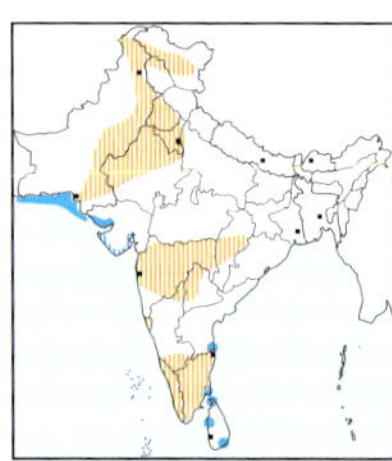

Red-necked Phalarope *Phalaropus lobatus* 18–20cm

Mainly winter visitor to Pakistan and NW India coasts. Vagrant: Nepal, Bhutan, Bangladesh. **ID** Typically seen swimming. More delicately built than Red Phalarope (see Appendix), with finer bill. Adult breeding has white throat and red stripe down side of grey neck; female much more strikingly patterned. Adult non-breeding has prominent black mask and cap, with dark line running down hindneck; has darker grey upperparts than Red, with white edges to mantle and scapular feathers forming fairly distinct lines. Juvenile also has dark cap and mask, but has dark grey upperparts with orange-buff mantle and scapular lines. **Voice** Single *twick*, lower-pitched than Red (vagrant). **HH** Swims buoyantly, spins around, darts erratically here and there. Winters at sea; on migration also on saltpans and shallow pools and lakes inland.

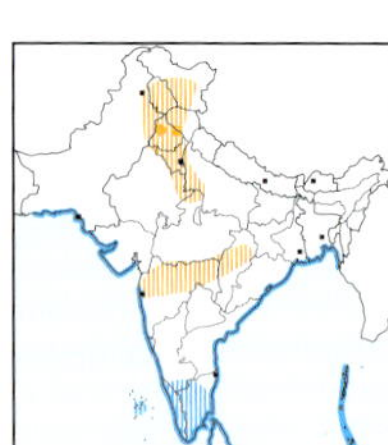

Terek Sandpiper *Xenus cinereus* 22–25cm

Widespread winter visitor, mainly to coasts, also inland. Vagrant: Nepal. **ID** Longish, upturned bill and short yellowish legs. In flight, shows prominent white trailing edge to secondaries and grey rump and tail. Adult breeding has blackish scapular lines, upperparts uniform grey in non-breeding. Juvenile is like adult but has buff fringes and dark subterminal marks to feathers of upperparts. **Voice** Flight call a soft pleasant whistle *hu-hu-hu* and a sharper *twit-wit-wit-wit* recalling Common. **HH** Runs here and there erratically to chase prey; also, probes deeply and feeds in shallow water. Mainly coastal wetlands.

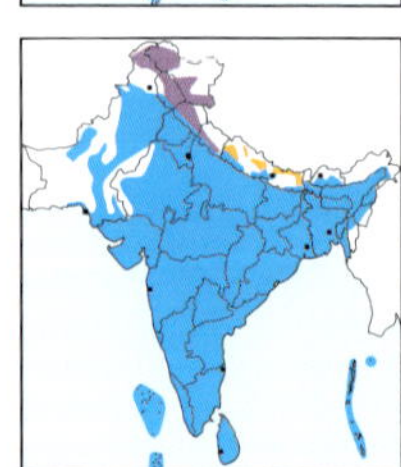

Common Sandpiper *Actitis hypoleucos* 19–21cm

Breeds in NW Himalayas; widespread winter visitor except most of W Pakistan. **ID** Horizontal stance, long tail projecting well beyond closed wings and constant bobbing action. White wing-bar and brown rump and centre of tail in flight, with distinctive rapid shallow wingbeats and bowed-wing glides. In breeding plumage, has irregular dark streaking and barring on upperparts, lacking in non-breeding. Juvenile has buff fringes and dark subterminal crescents to upperparts. **Voice** Call an anxious *wee-wee-wee* when flushed or alarmed. **HH** Characteristically rocks rear end of body and bobs head constantly when feeding. Flies low over the water, with rapid, shallow wingbeats alternating with brief glides on stiff downcurved wings. Breeds by mountain streams and rivers; winters on fresh water and coastal wetlands.

ad
ad
Jack Snipe
Eurasian Woodcock
ad
non-br
juv
br
non-br
Red-necked Phalarope
br
non-br
br
non-br
Terek Sandpiper
juv
br
juv
juv
Common Sandpiper

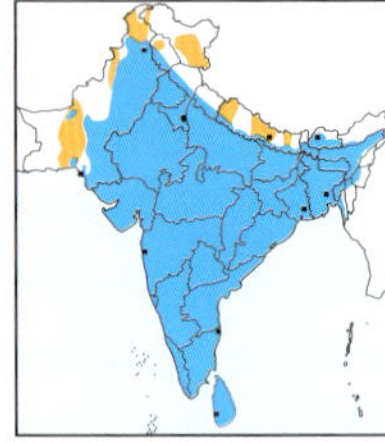

Green Sandpiper *Tringa ochropus* 21–24cm

Widespread winter visitor and passage migrant. Vagrant: Maldives. **ID** From Wood Sandpiper by shorter greenish legs and stockier appearance, darker and less heavily spotted upperparts, more pronounced breast line, and supercilium indistinct or absent behind eye. In flight, shows very dark underwing, strongly contrasting with white belly and vent, and striking white rump is distinctive. Adult breeding has white streaking on crown and neck, heavily streaked breast, and prominent whitish spotting on upperparts. Adult non-breeding is more uniform on head and breast and is less distinctly spotted on upperparts. Juvenile has browner upperparts with buff spotting. **Voice** Ringing *tluee-tueet* and *tuee-weet-weet* calls. **HH** Usually solitary when feeding, may gather in small flocks on migration. Shy and bobs rear body when nervous. Flies off readily, giving its distinctive call. Forages in marginal vegetation and shallows, picking prey from the water or mud. Mainly freshwater wetlands.

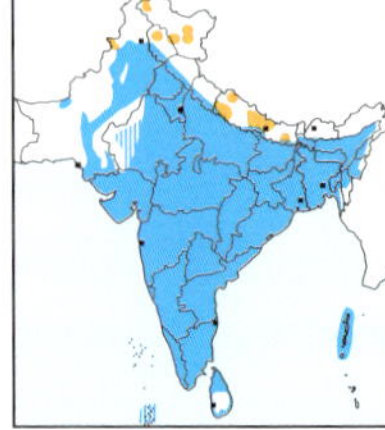

Wood Sandpiper *Tringa glareola* 19–23cm

Widespread winter visitor except W Pakistan; passage migrant in Himalayas. Vagrant: Bhutan. **ID** From Green by longer, yellowish legs and slimmer appearance, heavily speckled upperparts, and prominent supercilium behind eye; in flight by call, slimmer body and narrower wings, toes projecting clearly beyond tail, paler underwing contrasting less with white underparts, and paler brown upperparts contrasting less with smaller white rump. Adult breeding has heavily streaked breast and barred flanks; upperparts barred and spotted pale grey-brown and white. Adult non-breeding has more uniform grey-brown upperparts, spotted whitish, and breast brownish and lightly streaked. Juvenile has warm brown upperparts speckled warm buff, and lightly streaked buff breast. **Voice** Soft *chiff-if* or *chiff-if-if* flight call. **HH** Often forages in scattered parties and frequently occurs in flocks on migration. Feeds in shallow water and on mud by probing, picking from the surface, and sweeping its bill from side to side in water. Usually towers if flushed, giving its characteristic call. Freshwater and coastal wetlands.

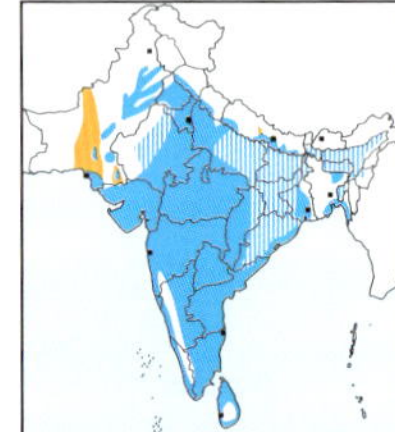

Marsh Sandpiper *Tringa stagnatilis* 22–26cm

Widespread winter visitor except parts of the north-west and north-east. **ID** Smaller and daintier than Common Greenshank, with proportionately longer legs and finer bill. Legs greenish or yellowish. Upperparts grey and foreneck and underparts white in non-breeding plumage, when the pale lores, forehead and chin create a pale-faced appearance. In breeding plumage, foreneck and breast streaked, and upperparts blotched and barred. Juvenile upperparts appear streaked blackish, with feathers notched and fringed with buff, and head-sides, hindneck and upper mantle streaked dark grey and white. **Voice** An abrupt, dull *yup* flight call; also, rapid, excitable series of *kiu-kiu-kiu* notes. **HH** A particularly graceful wader, often with other waders, dabbling ducks or egrets. Forages actively, often in water or at water's edge, also on mud; picks delicately from the surface, making frequent rapid darts to seize prey; probes occasionally. Mainly freshwater wetlands.

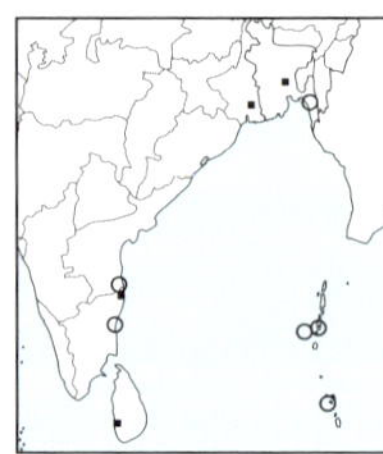

Grey-tailed Tattler *Tringa brevipes* 23–27cm

Rare passage migrant. India and Bangladesh. In all plumages, shows prominent white supercilium contrasting with dark eye-stripe, uniform grey wings lacking prominent wing-bar, grey rump and tail, and grey underwing contrasting with white belly. Adult breeding has barring on breast and flanks. Adult non-breeding uniform grey on upperparts and breast. Juvenile has indistinct white spotting on upperparts. **Voice** Typical call is *tu-weet, tu-weet*, recalling Common Ringed Plover; *tuu-tuu-tuu* in alarm. **HH** Often quite tame. Frequently bobs head and rear body up and down. Flies fast and low and raises wings vertically on alighting. Mudflats, mangrove creeks and rocky shores on coast.

br
non-br
non-br
Green Sandpiper
br
non-br
juv
non-br
Wood Sandpiper
br
non-br
non-br
Marsh Sandpiper
br
non-br
Grey-tailed Tattler
non-br
juv

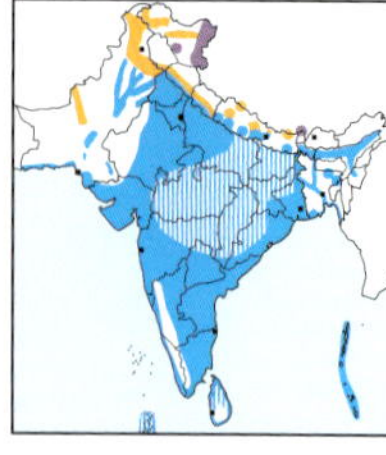

Common Redshank *Tringa totanus* 27–29cm

Breeds in NW Himalayas; widespread winter visitor except parts of the north-west and north-east. **ID** Orange-red at base of bill, orange-red legs, and broad white trailing edge to wing. Non-breeding plumage is grey-brown above, with grey breast. Neck and underparts heavily streaked in breeding plumage, upperparts with variable dark brown and cinnamon markings. Juvenile quite different from juvenile Spotted, with brown upperparts entirely fringed and spotted with buff, underparts heavily streaked with dark brown, and dull orange legs and base to bill. **Voice** Very noisy. An anxious *teu-hu-hu* flight call and a mournful *tyuuu* on the ground. Typically wary, often giving its alarm call. **HH** Singly or in small groups, often with other waders. Feeds by walking briskly and picking from the surface; also, probes and wades in shallow water. Fresh and coastal waters.

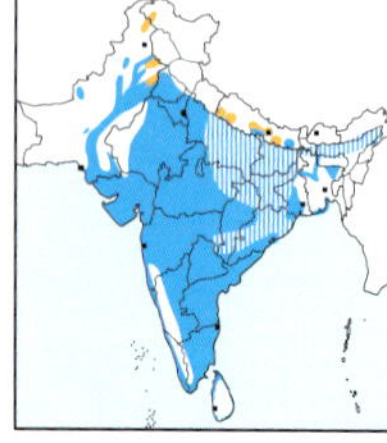

Spotted Redshank *Tringa erythropus* 29–32cm

Widespread winter visitor except parts of the north-west and north-east. Vagrant: Bhutan, Maldives, Sri Lanka. **ID** Red at base of bill and red legs. Longer bill and legs than Common Redshank, lacking broad white trailing edge to wing. Non-breeding plumage is paler grey above and whiter below than Common with more prominent white supercilium. Underparts black in breeding plumage. In first-summer plumage has dark barring on underparts and dark-mottled upperparts; legs can be black. Juvenile like non-breeding adult, but has darker grey upperparts more heavily spotted with white, and underparts are finely barred with grey. **Voice** A distinctive *tu-ick* in flight and a shorter *chip* alarm call. **HH** Solitary or in small flocks, often with other waders. Feeds by picking from the surface, often after a short dash. Frequently also forages in water, often in compact flocks. Swims readily and upends like a surface-feeding duck. Mainly fresh waters, muddy banks and shallows of rivers and lakes; also, tidal estuaries and creeks.

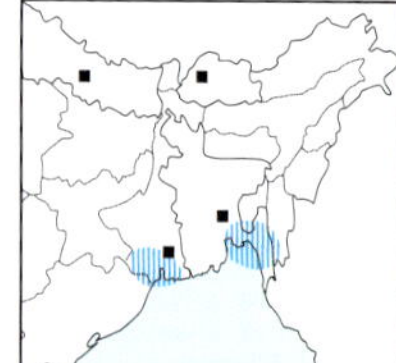

Nordmann's Greenshank *Tringa guttifer* 29–32cm

Rare passage migrant. India and Bangladesh. **ID** Stockier than Common Greenshank, with shorter, yellowish legs, and deeper bill with blunt tip. Breeding adult has black spotting on breast and prominent white notching on scapulars and tertials. Non-breeding has paler and more uniform upperparts than Common. Juvenile has rather uniform upperparts, with paler fringes to wing-coverts, and strongly bicoloured bill. **Voice** Usually silent. Flight call is *kwork* or *gwaak*, very different from Common Greenshank. **HH** Wary. Has a horizontal stance, unlike Common Greenshank. Feeding behaviour is like Terek Sandpiper's: makes rapid runs after prey with bill held low; often feeds belly-deep in water. Freshwater and coastal wetlands. Globally threatened.

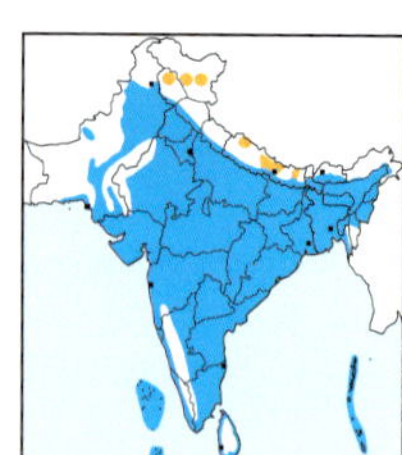

Common Greenshank *Tringa nebularia* 30–35cm

Widespread winter visitor except parts of the north-west; mainly passage migrant in Himalayas. **ID** Stocky, with long, stout (and slightly upturned) bill and long, stout greenish legs. Upperparts grey and foreneck and underparts white in non-breeding plumage. In breeding plumage, foreneck and breast streaked, upperparts untidily streaked. Juvenile has neat, dark-streaked upperparts with fine buff or whitish fringes and notching to tertials. See similar Nordmann's Greenshank. **Voice** Loud, ringing *tu-tu-tu* flight call and if flushed; sometimes a throatier *kyoup-kyoup-kyoup*. **HH** Usually forages singly, may gather in small parties to roost. Generally wary and when alarmed bobs head and body nervously. Feeds actively, chiefly in shallow water or at water's edge. Detects prey mainly by sight and makes frequent rapid runs to seize fast-moving prey. Flies strongly and erratically. Wide range of fresh and saltwater wetlands.

br
non-br
non-br
juv
Common Redshank
br
juv
non-br
non-br
Spotted Redshank
br
non-br
juv
non-br
Nordmann's Greenshank
br
non-br
non-br
Common Greenshank

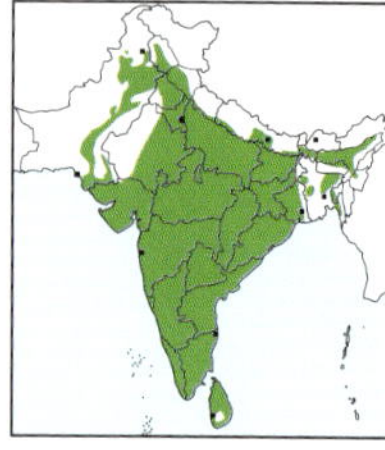

Greater Painted-snipe *Rostratula benghalensis* 23–28cm

Widespread resident except parts of the north-west. Vagrant: Bhutan. **ID** Rail-like wader, with broad, rounded wings and longish, downcurved bill. Long legs and feet project noticeably beyond tail in flight. White or buff 'spectacles' and 'braces'. Adult female has maroon head and neck and dark greenish wing-coverts. Adult male and juvenile duller, with buff spotting on wing-coverts; juvenile lacks dark breast-band and throat and breast are finely streaked. **Voice** Occasionally an explosive *kek* when flushed; female has a soft *koh koh* in display. **HH** Chiefly crepuscular or nocturnal. Skulking, and reluctant to fly if approached; rises heavily with legs trailing and lands in cover again a short distance away. Bobs rear body when feeding. Has roding display flight like Eurasian Woodcock. Freshwater marshes, vegetated pools; also, mangroves in Bangladesh.

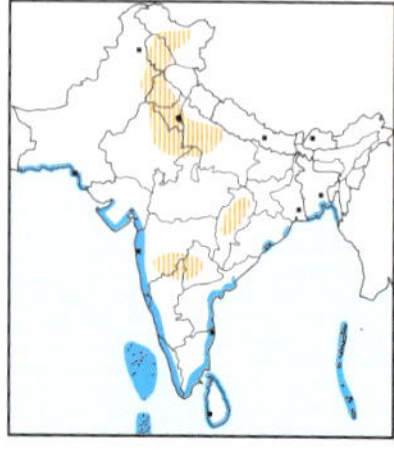

Ruddy Turnstone *Arenaria interpres* 21–26cm

Widespread winter visitor to coasts, occasional on passage inland. Vagrant: Nepal. **ID** Stocky with short bill and orange legs. In flight, shows white stripes on wings and back and black tail-band. In breeding plumage, has complex black-and-white neck and breast pattern and much chestnut-orange on upperparts; duller and less strikingly patterned in non-breeding plumage, but continues to show dark breast pattern. Juvenile like adult non-breeding with buff fringes to upperparts. **Voice** A rolled *trik-tuk-tuk-tuk* or *tuk-er-tuk*; a sharp *chick-ik* or *kuu* when flushed. **HH** Runs actively, turning over pebbles and shells to catch small invertebrate prey sheltering below; also, probes into soft sand and pokes into rock crevices and among detritus. Rocky coasts; also occurs on tidal mudflats and sandy shores in Pakistan and Gulf of Kutch.

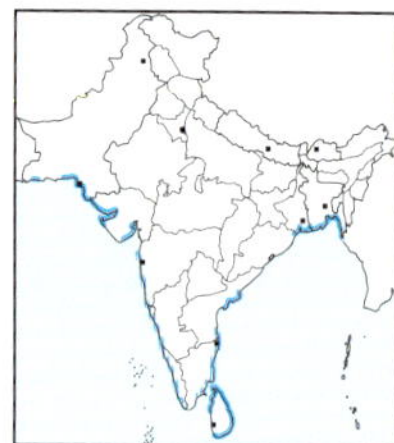

Great Knot *Calidris tenuirostris* 26–28cm

Winter visitor to coasts, very occasional records inland. **ID** Larger than Red Knot, with longer, slightly down-curved bill; less neatly proportioned, with head looking smaller and neck and body longer, at times recalling Ruff. At rest, closed wings extend beyond tail, while in flight shows more clearly defined white rump contrasting with grey tail. Adult breeding heavily marked with black on breast and flanks, and chestnut pattern on scapulars. Adult non-breeding typically more heavily streaked on upperparts and breast than Red Knot. Juvenile has darker centres and white fringes to upperparts, and more heavily marked breast and flanks, compared to juvenile Red Knot. **Voice** A low disyllabic *nyut nyut*. **HH** Feeds slowly, chiefly by probing deeply into mud or sand. Intertidal flats and tidal creeks. Globally threatened.

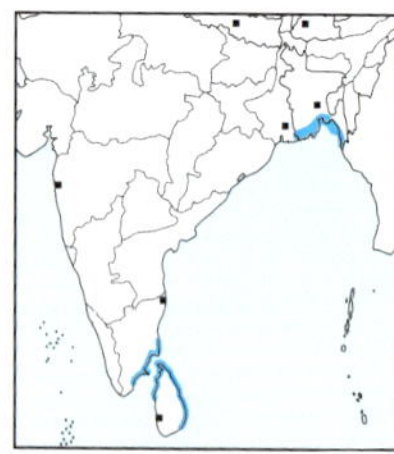

Red Knot *Calidris canutus* 23–25cm

Winter visitor to coasts. Vagrant: Nepal, Pakistan. **ID** Stocky, with short, straight bill. Adult breeding is brick-red on underparts; upperparts boldly marked with chestnut, becoming almost blackish with wear. Adult non-breeding whitish on underparts and uniform grey on upperparts. In flight, shows a narrow white wing-bar but rump appears grey and is not strikingly differentiated from rest of upperparts. Juvenile has buff fringes and dark subterminal crescents to upperparts and buff wash on breast and flanks. **Voice** A low short *knutt… knutt*; often silent. **HH** Feeds chiefly by probing in soft mud and picking from surface. Mainly intertidal mudflats.

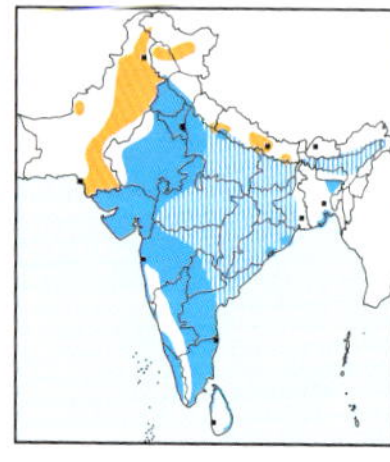

Ruff *Calidris pugnax* M 26–32cm, F 20–25cm

Widespread winter visitor and passage migrant except parts of the north-west. Vagrant: Bhutan. **ID** Distinctive shape, with long neck, small head, short and slightly downcurved bill, and long yellowish or orangey legs. In all plumages, lacks prominent supercilium and, in flight, shows narrow white wing-bar and prominent white sides to uppertail-coverts. Male is considerably larger than female. Non-breeding and juvenile have neatly fringed upperparts, juvenile with buff underparts. Breeders typically have black and chestnut markings on upperparts, male with striking ruff of various colours. **Voice** Generally silent. **HH** Freshwater lakes, pools and marshes, flooded fields, grassland and intertidal mudflats. **TN** Formerly placed in *Philomachus*.

♀
Greater Painted-snipe
juv
♂
non-br
non-br
Ruddy Turnstone
br
non-br
juv
non-br
br
Great Knot
juv
non-br
br
juv
Red Knot
non-br
non-br
♂ br
♂ br
Ruff
♂ non-br
♂ br
♀ br
♂ juv
♀ juv
♀ juv

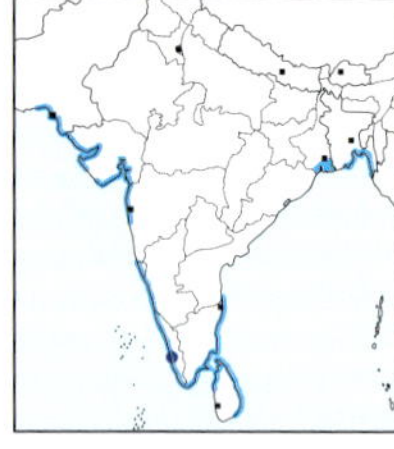

Broad-billed Sandpiper *Calidris falcinellus* 16–18cm

Winter visitor to coasts, very occasional inland. **ID** Distinctive shape: stockier than Dunlin with legs set well back and downward-kinked bill. In all plumages, has more prominent supercilium than Dunlin, with 'split' before eye, and contrasting dark eye-stripe (although differences very subtle in non-breeding plumage). Adult breeding has bold streaking on neck and breast contrasting with white belly, and rufous-fringed mantle and scapular feathers with narrow whitish mantle and scapular lines. Birds in worn breeding plumage can appear uniformly very dark on upperparts. Non-breeding has dark patch at bend of wing (sometimes obscured by breast feathers); dark inner wing-coverts show as dark leading edge to wing in flight; crown, upperparts and breast more distinctly streaked than in non-breeding Dunlin. Juvenile has buff mantle/scapular lines and streaked breast; lacks black markings on belly of juvenile Dunlin. **Voice** Flight call a buzzing *chrrreet* and a shorter *tzit* or *trr*. **HH** Feeds in similar way to Dunlin by pecking and probing. Usually found singly in winter and in small flocks on passage. Mud banks of creeks, intertidal mudflats and brackish lagoons. **TN** Formerly placed in *Limicola*.

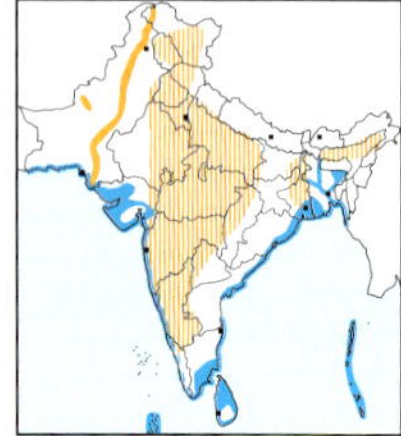

Curlew Sandpiper *Calidris ferruginea* 18–23cm

Winter visitor, mainly to coasts, also inland. Vagrant: Nepal, Bhutan. **ID** White rump. More elegant than Dunlin, with longer, more downcurved bill, and longer legs. Adult breeding has chestnut-red head and underparts. Adult non-breeding paler grey than Dunlin, with more distinct supercilium. Juvenile has strong supercilium, buff wash to breast, unmarked belly, and buff fringes and dark subterminal marks to feathers of upperparts. **Voice** Flight call a low, purring *prrriit*. **HH** Feeds in wet sand in similar way to Dunlin, also, by wading in deeper water than used by other *Calidris*, immersing head and bill below the surface. In flocks, often with other waders. Mainly coastal: intertidal mudflats, seashore, saltpans; rare inland by rivers and lakes.

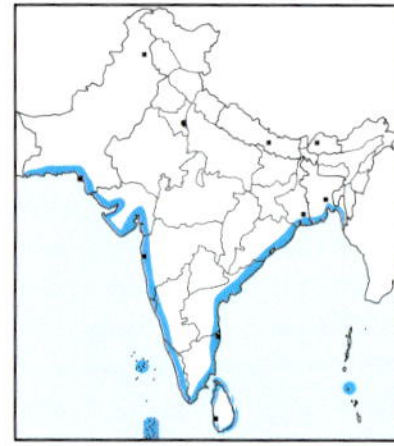

Sanderling *Calidris alba* 18–20cm

Winter visitor, mainly to coasts. Vagrant: Nepal. **ID** Stocky, with short bill. Very broad white wing-bar. Adult breeding variable in appearance; initially mottled grey and black, head and breast become more rufous with wear. Rufous birds possibly confusable with Little and Red-necked Stints, but Sanderling is considerably larger, with broader wing-bar, has patterned tertials, and lacks hind toe. Sides of head distinctly streaked compared to Red-necked. Non-breeding is pale grey above and very white below. Has blackish lesser wing-coverts, which are especially noticeable in flight but also show at rest as black patch at bend of wing (unless concealed by breast feathers). Juvenile chequered black and white above and buff wash to streaked sides of breast. **Voice** Call a liquid *plit*. **HH** Extremely active; runs swiftly after retreating waves, stopping suddenly to catch tiny prey or probe in sands. Forages in small parties on shoreline of sandy beaches.

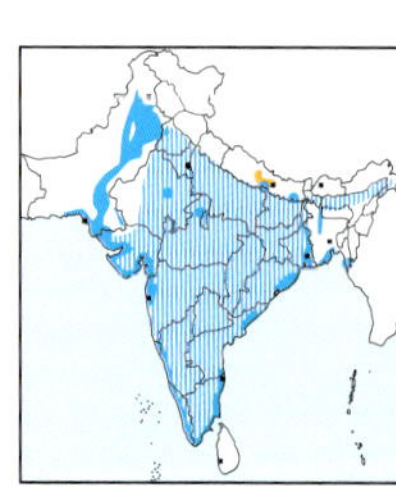

Dunlin *Calidris alpina* 16–22cm

Winter visitor, to coasts, also inland. Vagrant: Sri Lanka. **ID** Shorter legs and bill compared with Curlew Sandpiper, and dark centre to rump. Adult breeding has black belly. Adult non-breeding darker grey-brown than Curlew Sandpiper, with less distinct supercilium. Juvenile has streaked belly, rufous fringes to mantle and scapulars, and buff mantle V. **Voice** Flight call a distinctive slurred *screet*. **HH** Usually in flocks, often with other waders. Typically has a hunched posture when foraging; makes short runs over wet mud and wades near the water's edge. Pecks or probes, often making a series of vigorous, rapid jabs into mud. Flies swiftly in close packs, with erratic changes of direction performed in unison. Intertidal mudflats, seashore, tidal creeks, riverbanks, sand bars and flooded fields.

br
juv
non-br
br
non-br
juv
Broad-billed Sandpiper
juv
br
br
non-br
juv
non-br
Curlew Sandpiper
non-br
juv
non-br
non-br
br
br
Sanderling
br
non-br
non-br
br
juv
Dunlin

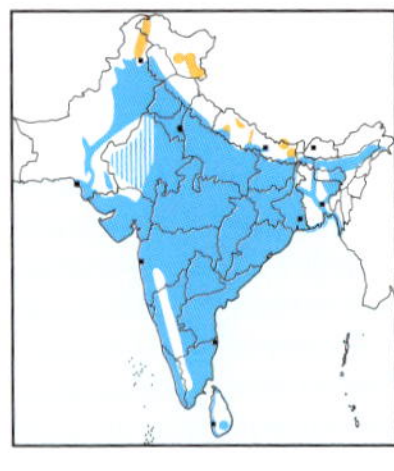

Temminck's Stint *Calidris temminckii* 13–15cm

Widespread winter visitor except parts of the north-west. **ID** More elongated than Little, with more horizontal stance, and tail extends beyond closed wings at rest. In flight, shows white sides to tail. Legs yellowish. In all plumages, lacks mantle V and is usually rather uniform, with complete breast-band and indistinct supercilium. Adult breeding has irregular dark markings on upperparts and juvenile has regular buff fringes (pattern very different from Little). **Voice** A trilling, cicada-like *trrrrrit*. **HH** Unobtrusive. Forages more among vegetation at wetland edges than other stints. Feeds more slowly than Little, runs less and methodically searches for food. If flushed typically towers jerkily upwards and flies off swiftly. Favours vegetated freshwater habitats; also, brackish marshes, mudflats and tidal lagoons.

Long-toed Stint *Calidris subminuta* 13–16cm

Winter visitor. Mainly E subcontinent. Vagrant: Nepal. **ID** Long yellowish legs, longish neck, and upright stance recall miniature Wood Sandpiper. In all plumages, has prominent supercilium and heavily streaked foreneck and breast. Adult breeding and juvenile have prominent rufous fringes to upperparts, and rufous-tinged crown; juvenile has very striking mantle V. In winter, upperparts more heavily marked than Little. **Voice** Call a soft *prit* or *chirrup*, like but less purring than that of Curlew Sandpiper. **HH** Often feeds with other stints; runs about energetically to pick up tiny invertebrates. Towers like Temminck's if flushed. Freshwater and brackish marshes, lakes, riverbanks and intertidal mudflats.

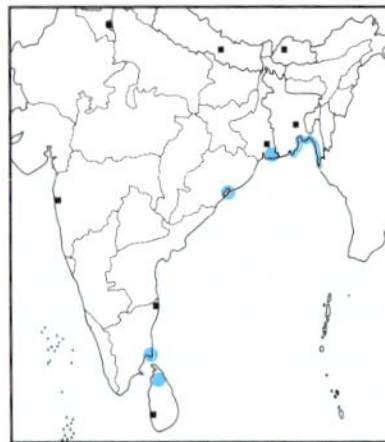

Spoon-billed Sandpiper *Calidris pygmaea* 14–16cm

Winter visitor. India and Bangladesh. Vagrant: Sri Lanka. **ID** Stint-sized. Spatulate tip to bill (although bill shape can be difficult to see side-on). Adult non-breeding has paler grey upperparts than Little Stint, with more pronounced white supercilium, forehead and cheeks; underparts appear cleaner and whiter. Adult breeding more uniform rufous-orange on face and breast compared to Little (recalling Red-necked). Juvenile very similar to Little Stint, but shows more white on face and darker eye-stripe and ear-coverts (masked appearance). **Voice** Flight call is a quiet, rolled *preep*, or a shrill *wheet*. **HH** Feeds mostly by sweeping bill from side to side in shallow water, while walking; also, picks at food items from water and mud surface and uses drill-like action with bill tip in mud. Intertidal mudflats. Globally threatened. **TN** Formerly placed in monotypic genus *Eurynorhynchus*.

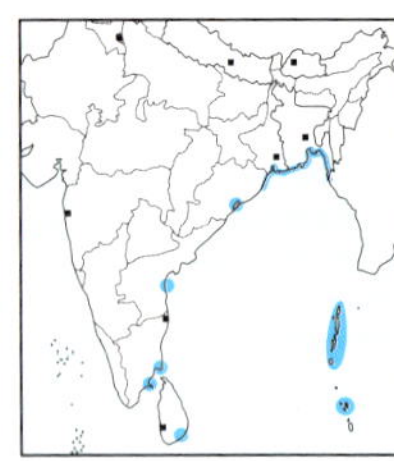

Red-necked Stint *Calidris ruficollis* 13–16cm

Winter visitor. India and Bangladesh. Vagrant: Sri Lanka. **ID** Very similar to Little Stint; very subtle structural differences include stouter, deeper-tipped bill, shorter legs, and longer wings which give rise to more elongated appearance. Adult non-breeding is almost identical to Little, but is cleaner and paler grey above, with clearer and less extensive dark centres to mantle and scapulars, and markings on sides of breast are more clearly defined. Adult breeding typically has unstreaked rufous-orange throat, foreneck and upper breast, white sides of lower breast streaked dark, and greyish-centred tertials and wing-coverts (with greyish-white fringes). Juvenile lacks or has indistinct mantle V; has different coloration and pattern to lower scapulars (grey with dark subterminal marks and whitish or buffish fringes; typically blackish with rufous fringes in Little), and grey-centred, whitish- or buffish-edged tertials (usually blackish with rufous edges in Little); supercilium not usually split in front of eye. **Voice** Call a high-pitched rasping *chriit*. **HH** Habits very similar to Little. Coastal.

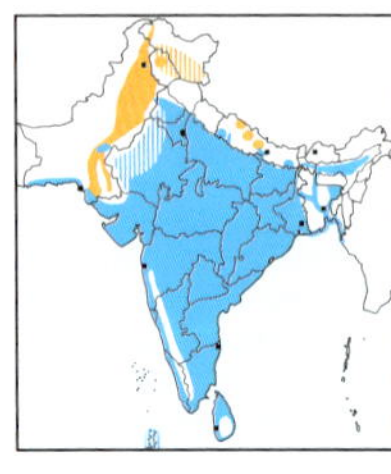

Little Stint *Calidris minuta* 12–14cm

Widespread winter visitor except parts of the north-west. **ID** More rotund and upright than Temminck's, with dark legs. In flight, shows grey sides to tail. Adult breeding has pale mantle V, rufous wash to face, neck-sides and breast, and rufous fringes to upperpart feathers. Non-breeding has untidy, mottled/streaked appearance (Temminck's more uniform), with grey breast-sides. Juvenile has whitish mantle V, greyish nape, prominent white supercilium which typically splits above eye (not shown in Plate), and rufous fringes to upperparts. **Voice** Flight call a weak *pi, pi, pi*. **HH** Gregarious; often gathers in flocks mixed with other small waders. An active wader, rapidly picks at the surface, and frequently darts about to catch very tiny prey items; probes occasionally. Flies in tight flocks when disturbed, birds twisting and turning in unison. Mudflats, coastal lagoons, tidal creeks, marshes, paddyfields and lakes.

non-br
br
br
non-br
juv
juv
Temminck's Stint
br
non-br
br
juv
non-br
Long-toed Stint
non-br
br
juv
non-br
Spoon-billed Sandpiper
juv
dull variant
non-br
br fresh
non-br
juv
juv
br worn
Red-necked Stint
br fresh
non-br
non-br
juv
juv
br worn
Little Stint
juv
dull variant

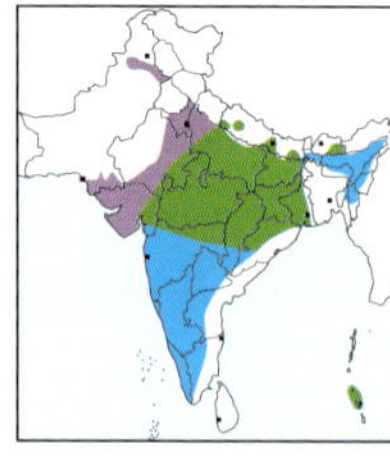

Yellow-legged Buttonquail *Turnix tanki* 15–18cm

Partly resident; summer visitor to north-west; winter visitor to most of peninsula and the north-east. Widespread, chiefly in lowlands. Yellow legs and bill (with variable dark culmen and tip). Bold black spotting to buff coverts and upper flanks. Upperparts more uniform than Small, varying from grey and finely dotted, to more heavily marked with black and diffusely with rufous (with buff edges to some feathers, although not as prominent on Small). Some (breeding?) females distinctive, with almost unmarked greyish upperparts, rufous nape and upper mantle, rufous-orange throat, sides of neck and breast, and black-speckled crown. Other females less striking with buff crown-stripe, indistinct rufous collar, and orange-buff breast. Rufous collar lacking in male. **Voice** Low-pitched hoot, repeated with increasing strength. **HH** Habits like Small. Scrub and grassland.

Barred Buttonquail *Turnix suscitator* 13.5–17.5cm

Resident. Widespread except the north-west, mainly in lowlands. **ID** Grey bill and legs, and bold black barring on sides of neck, breast and wing-coverts. Orange-rufous to orange-buff flanks and belly clearly demarcated from barred breast. Most show buff crown-stripe, and speckled supercilium is often apparent. Female generally, but not always, has black throat and centre of breast. Male usually has greyish- or buffish-white throat. Males of some races can have black throat. Four races on subcontinent, varying mainly in extent of black and rufous markings on upperparts and in depth of coloration of belly and flanks. **Voice** Calls include a rattling *drr-r-r-r-r-r* and a booming *hoon-hoon-hoon-hoon*. **HH** Habits like Little. Scrub and grassland.

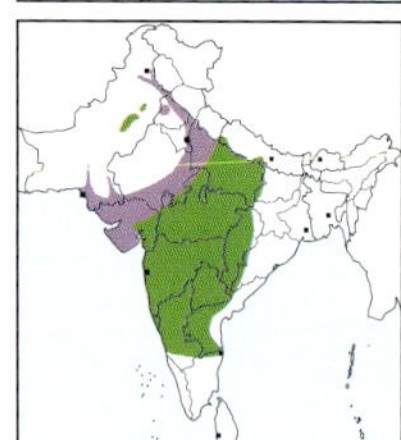

Small Buttonquail *Turnix sylvaticus* 13–16cm

Widespread except the north-west; summer visitor to north-west India. Vagrant: Sri Lanka. **ID** Very small with pointed tail. Bill greyish, and legs pinkish to greyish. More heavily marked above than Yellow-legged Buttonquail; buff edges to scapulars and tertials form prominent lines. Has variable rufous hindneck and mantle fringed with buff. Buff-fringed, dark-centred coverts result in spotted appearance, but less prominently so than in Yellow-legged. Underparts are like many Yellow-legged, with orange-buff lower throat and breast, and bold black spotting on sides of breast (becoming chestnut spotting on flanks). Female has brighter and more extensive rufous on neck than male, and face is greyish-white, speckled with black (recalling Barred). **Voice** Repetitive booming call. **HH** Very secretive, prefers to escape by walking away. Scrub and grass at cultivation edges, also grassland.

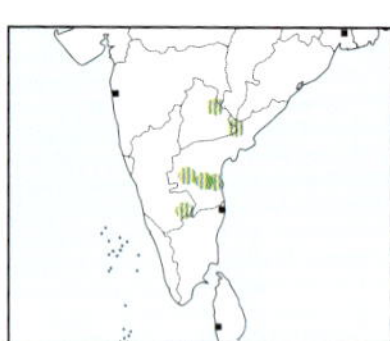

Jerdon's Courser *Rhinoptilus bitorquatus* 27cm

Very local and very rare resident; no recent records. Andhra Pradesh. **ID** Adult has broad buffish supercilium and narrow crown-stripe, orange throat patch, and white and brown bands across breast. Huge eye, with prominent pale eye-ring, short yellow bill with black tip, and long yellow legs. In flight, shows broad black tail-band and white patch at tip of black primaries. Juvenile undescribed. **Voice** Poorly described, a plaintive cry. **HH** Nocturnal. Prefers to walk, although it can fly well. Bare patches of open ground among thin scrub forest in rocky foothills. Globally threatened.

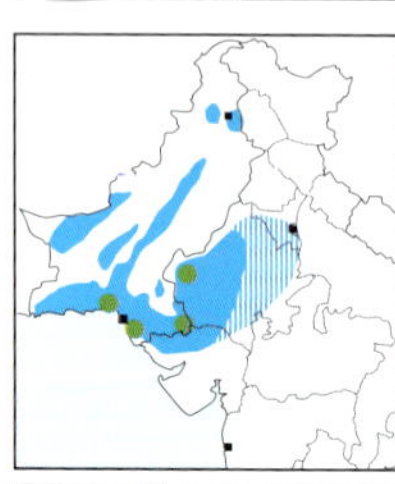

Cream-coloured Courser *Cursorius cursor* 19–24cm

Resident and winter visitor. Pakistan and NW India. **ID** Pale sandy upperparts and underparts. Like Indian Courser, has striking white supercilium, bordered below by black eye-stripe, which curves down and joins at nape. Adult has sandy-rufous forehead, grey nape and pale lores. In flight shows dark underwing (as does Indian Courser). Juvenile has buffish crown, less distinct head pattern, fine dark scaling on upperparts, and streaked breast. **Voice** Most common call a sharp, piping whistle; also, penetrating *praak-praak* in flight. **HH** Diurnal. Prefers to run off, rather than fly. When alert has very erect posture. Runs rapidly in short bursts and pauses to bend down and pick up or dig for prey. Open arid desert country, sand dunes and stony desert.

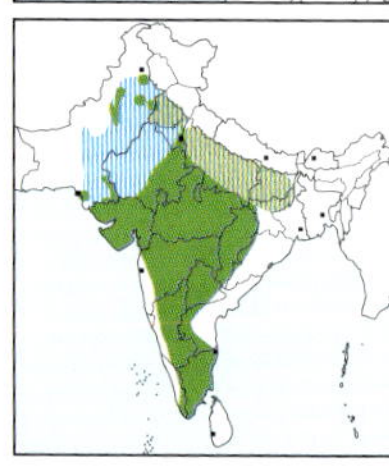

Indian Courser *Cursorius coromandelicus* 23–26cm

Widespread resident in plains. **ID** Has striking white supercilium, bordered below by black eye-stripe, which curves down and joins at nape. Adult from Cream-coloured by rich orange underparts contrasting with grey-brown upperparts, and by blackish centre of belly, chestnut crown, and black lores. In flight, shows white band across uppertail-coverts and, like Cream-coloured, very dark underwing. Juvenile has dark brown crown, pale lores, strong brown-and-cream barring and blotching on upperparts, and brown markings on pale chestnut-brown underparts. Initially lacks dark patch on belly. **Voice** Usually silent. A low *gwut* or *wut*. **HH** Habits like Cream-coloured. Dry fallow fields, stony plains and dry river beds; favours less arid habitats than those preferred by Cream-coloured.

♂
♀
Yellow-legged Buttonquail
Barred Buttonquail
♂
♀
ad
Small Buttonquail
ad
Jerdon's Courser
ad
Cream-coloured Courser
juv
ad
Indian Courser

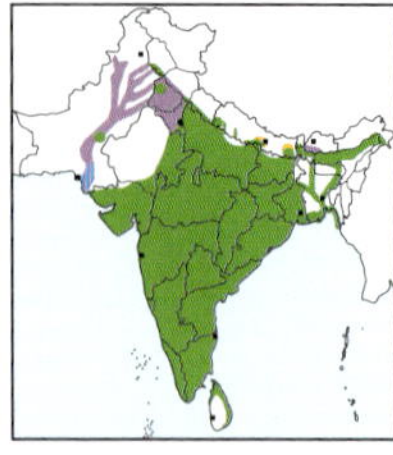

Small Pratincole *Glareola lactea* 15.5–19cm

Widespread resident except parts of the north-west. **ID** Small size, with sandy-grey coloration and square-ended tail (or with shallow fork). White panel across secondaries, blackish underwing-coverts and black tail-band in flight. Adult breeding has black lores and buff wash to throat; non-breeder lacks these features and has streaked throat. Juvenile has indistinct buff fringes and brown subterminal marks to upperparts. **Voice** High-pitched, rattling *tiririt*. **HH** Habits like Collared but often hawks insects later in the evening. Chiefly large rivers with sand or shingle banks; also lakes.

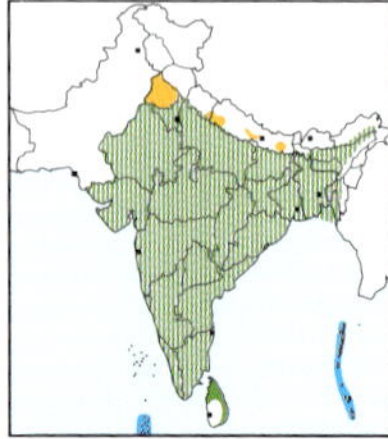

Oriental Pratincole *Glareola maldivarum* 23–25cm

Widespread resident; Maldives: visitor. Vagrant: Pakistan, Bhutan. **ID** Lacks white trailing edge to secondaries. Only shallow tail fork, tail tip falling well short of wingtip at rest. Often has strong peach-orange wash on underparts in breeding plumage. Adult breeding has cream throat bordered by black gorget; with gorget of faint streaking in non-breeding plumage (features also shown by Collared). Juvenile has upperpart feathers fringed buff with dark subterminal marks (as Collared). **Voice** Sharp *kyik, chik-chik* or *chet* calls; a loud *cherr* and rising *tooeet*. **HH** Habits like Collared. Dried-out bare flats by larger rivers and marshes; also, low-lying pastures and fields, often near water.

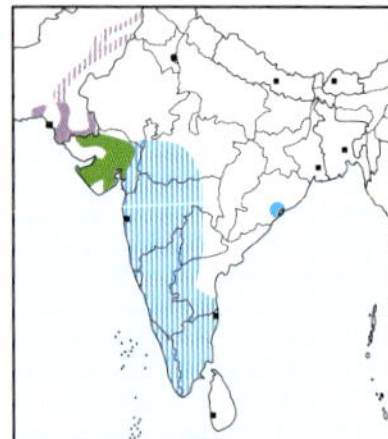

Collared Pratincole *Glareola pratincola* 22–25cm

Breeds in Pakistan; winter visitor: India. Vagrant: Maldives and Sri Lanka. **ID** White trailing edge to secondaries (can be difficult to see). Pronounced fork to tail, with tail tip reaching tips of closed wings on adult at rest. Adult breeding has cream throat bordered by black gorget, and red base to bill; throat is buffish and has a gorget of faint streaking in non-breeding plumage. Juvenile similar to adult non-breeding but has shorter outer tail feathers, and upperpart feathers are fringed buff with dark subterminal marks; white trailing edge is best feature from juvenile Oriental. **Voice** A *kirik... kirik... kirik* and a rolled-together *pirrit... pirrit... pirrit*. **HH** Gregarious all year. Usually crepuscular, also active when overcast. Rests during heat of day, squatting on ground. Hawks insects with mouth wide open in powerful swallow-like flight. Also, feeds on ground like a plover, making short dashes to capture prey. Open, dry bare ground around seasonal lakes, swamps and tidal creeks.

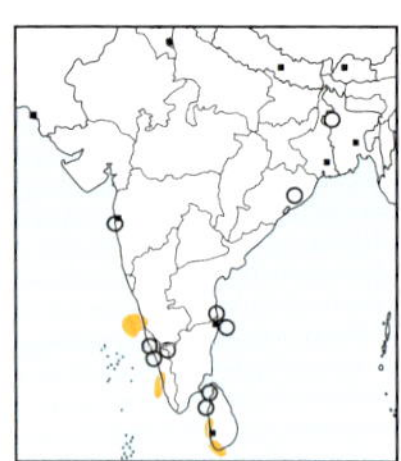

Long-tailed Jaeger *Stercorarius longicaudus* 48–53cm (inc. tail-streamers)

SW India, Maldives and Sri Lanka. **ID** More lightly built than Parasitic, with slimmer body, narrower wings, longer-looking rear end, and light almost tern-like flight. Adult breeding, non-breeding and juvenile plumages very similar to Parasitic, but show contrast above between dark remiges and paler brown-grey wing-coverts, lacks prominent white flashes on underside of primaries, lacks clear-cut white belly, and has longer tail-streamers. There is no dark-morph adult. Non-breeding lacks dark cap and best told from non-breeding Parasitic by structural differences. Juvenile as variable as in Parasitic, but many are greyer with whiter nape/head and boldly barred upper- and undertail-coverts; bill short with pale base and has blunt tail tip. **Voice** Higher pitched than other jaegers, repeated *kew* and *kriep*. **HH** Pelagic. **AN** Long-tailed Skua.

br
Small Pratincole
br
non-br
non-br
br
br
Oriental Pratincole
juv
br
br
non-br
juv
Collared Pratincole
juv
dark
non-br
juv
pale
Long-tailed Jaeger
br
juv
intermediate

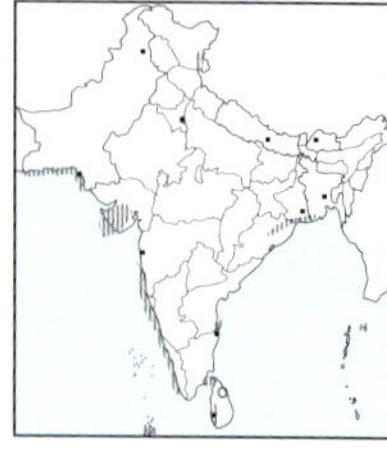

Parasitic Jaeger ***Stercorarius parasiticus*** 45cm

Visitor to coasts, mainly Pakistan and western India; vagrant elsewhere including Bangladesh and Sri Lanka. **ID** Smaller and more lightly built than Pomarine, with slimmer bill and narrower-based wings. Adult breeding has pointed tip to elongated central tail feathers. Both pale and dark morphs. Adult non-breeding as Pomarine but has more pointed tail tip. Juvenile more variable than juvenile Pomarine, ranging from grey and buff with heavy barring to completely blackish-brown, and many have rusty-orange to cinnamon-brown cast to head and nape (not found on Pomarine); except all-dark juveniles, further distinctions are dark streaking on head and neck and pale tips to primaries. **Voice** Many calls including low-pitched nasal mewing calls rising in pitch towards the end, *nyeeAh- nyeeAh- nyeeAh- nyeeAh*. **HH** Commonly associates with terns and gulls which it parasitises like other jaegers and skuas. Normal flight is buoyant, with jerky wingbeats alternating with glides; swift, dashing and falcon-like when harrying other seabirds for their food. Coastal waters, often near mouths of major creeks, rivers and lagoons with roosting and feeding gulls and terns. **AN** Arctic Skua.

Pomarine Jaeger ***Stercorarius pomarinus*** 46–51cm (incl. central tail-streamers)

Visitor. Pakistan, India, Maldives, Sri Lanka. **ID** Larger and stockier than Parasitic, with heavier bill (and more pronounced dark tip) and broader-based wings. In flight, appears slower and heavier, with deeper chest. Adult breeding from Parasitic by long, broad central tail feathers twisted at end to form swollen tip (although tips can be broken off). Both pale and dark morphs. Prominent pink base to bill, black cap extends below gape, brighter yellow neck, more prominent breast-band, and dark flank barring are additional features from pale-morph Parasitic. Adult non-breeding (pale morph) has indistinct cap, and barring to breast and upper- and undertail-coverts; as in Parasitic uniform dark underwing-coverts distinguish it from first- and second-winter plumages. Broader round-tipped central tail feathers best distinction from Parasitic. Juvenile variable, typically dark brown with broad pale barring on uppertail- and undertail-coverts and underwing-coverts. Combination of strongly barred uppertail-coverts and dark uniform head diagnostic of Pomarine, and head, neck and underparts never appear rufous-coloured as on some juvenile Parasitic. Other juvenile plumages appear virtually identical to Parasitic; additional finer features are the second pale crescent at base of primary coverts on underwing, diffuse vermiculations (never streaking) on nape and neck, lack of (or very indistinct) pale tips to primaries, and blunt-tipped or almost non-existent projection of central tail feathers (more prominent and pointed in juvenile Parasitic). Dark-morph not distinguishable from dark-morph Parasitic on plumage. **Voice** Feeding birds at sea utter sharp *which-yew, which-yew* followed by repeated *week, week, week*. **HH** Like other jaegers and skuas parasitises gulls and terns for food and often associates with feeding flocks of terns. When not hunting, flight is direct and powerful, with steadily flapping wingbeats. Coastal waters, often near mouths of creeks and promontories with feeding terns; also, often well offshore. **AN** Pomarine Skua.

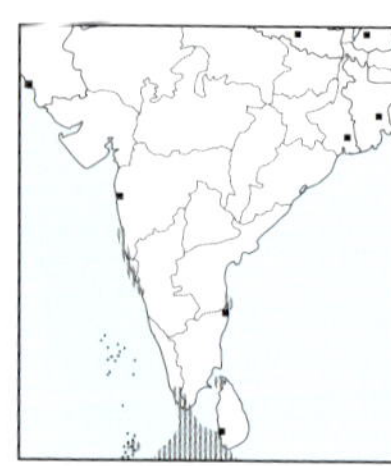

Brown Skua ***Stercorarius antarcticus*** 52–64cm

Visitor: Maldives. Vagrant: W India coast, Sri Lanka. **ID** Large and broad-winged with white patches at base of primaries. Larger and more powerful than South Polar Skua (see Vagrants), with broader-based wings and larger bill. Adult from dark-morph South Polar by warmer brown coloration to upperparts and underparts, and pale streaking and rufous-brown mottling on mantle and scapulars, which can show as large white blotches (upperparts more uniformly dark on dark-morph South Polar). Some can be paler brown on upperparts and underparts, but lack contrast between head, underparts and mantle shown by intermediate-morph South Polar. Juvenile is warmer brown on upperparts and underparts, some with rufous-brown coloration below. **Voice** Mainly vocal on breeding grounds. **HH** Normal flight is purposeful and direct, with steady shallow wingbeats, but is swift, dashing and hawk-like in pursuit of gulls and terns. Coastal waters.

juv
dark
br
pale morph
non-br
pale morph
juv
intermediate
juv
pale
Parasitic Jaeger
br
dark morph
juv
intermediate
br
pale morph
juv
dark
br
dark morph
Pomarine Jaeger
non-br
pale morph
ad
juv
Pomarine
South Polar Skua
for comparison
Brown Skua

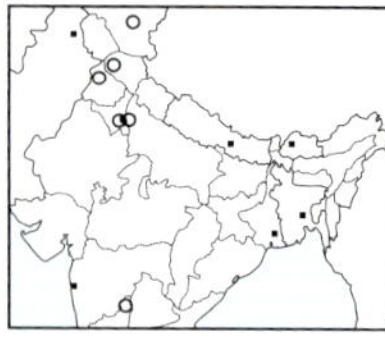

Little Gull *Hydrocoloeus minutus* 25–30cm

Visitor to N India. **ID** Smaller than Black-headed, with short legs and blackish bill. Adult has dark grey underwing and white upperwing. Has blackish head, red legs and pinkish flush to underparts in breeding plumage. Adult non-breeding has blackish rear crown and spot behind eye, and duller pinkish legs. First-winter has distinctive black M-mark on upperwing. **Voice** A dry, short *kek* or *kik*. **HH** A dainty gull which flies lightly and swims buoyantly. Feeds on insects from the water surface or by hawking. Coastal and inland waters.

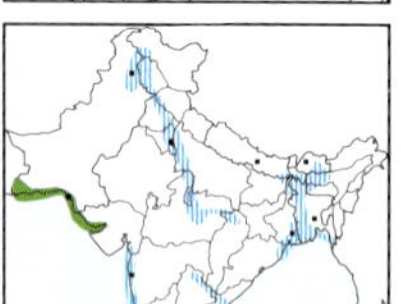

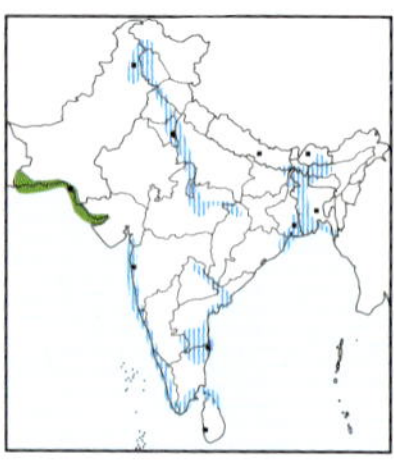

Slender-billed Gull *Chroicocephalus genei* 42–44cm

Resident in Pakistan and NW India; winter visitor to India and Sri Lanka. Vagrant: Bhutan and Nepal. **ID** Gently sloping forehead, longish neck, and longer bill than Black-headed; in flight, neck and tail appear longer. Adult always has white head (may show grey ear-covert spot in winter), deep red bill (often looking blackish), pale iris (dark in Black-headed), and variable pink flush on underparts. First-winter/first-summer from Black-headed by paler and less distinct darker ear spot (sometimes completely lacking), pale iris, paler orange bill (with dark tip smaller or absent), and paler legs. Juvenile has grey-brown upperparts with pale fringes (paler and lacking ginger-brown coloration of juvenile Black-headed). **Voice** Slightly deeper than that of Black-headed. **HH** Feeds in shallow waters by dipping to the surface; fishes cooperatively in small groups, probes on intertidal mud, aerially forages for insects, rarely scavenges. Coastal wetlands, offshore, and inland salt lakes.

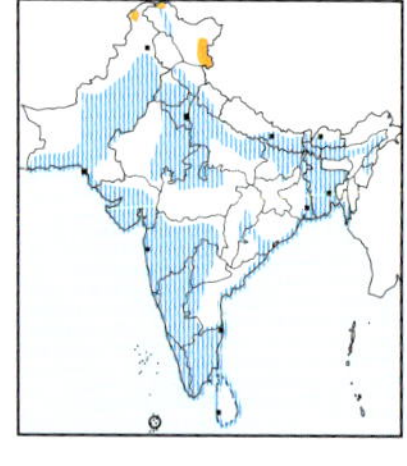

Black-headed Gull *Chroicocephalus ridibundus* 37–43cm

Widespread winter visitor and passage migrant. Vagrant: Bhutan, Maldives, Sri Lanka. **ID** Smaller than Brown-headed, with finer bill and narrower and more pointed wings. In all plumages, has distinctive white 'flash' on primaries of upperwing, and black on wingtips and upperwing is much less extensive than in Brown-headed. Bill blackish-red and hood uniform dark brown in breeding plumage. In non-breeding and first-winter plumages, bill tipped black and head largely white with dark ear-covert patch; can have more similar wing pattern to Brown-headed but has longer 'fingers' of grey extending into black primary tips. **Voice** A nasal *kyaaar*, short *keck* and deeper *kuk*. **HH** Gregarious. Scavenges rubbish, follows ships, forages on short grassland and crops. Coasts, harbours, fishing villages, estuaries, large rivers and inland lakes.

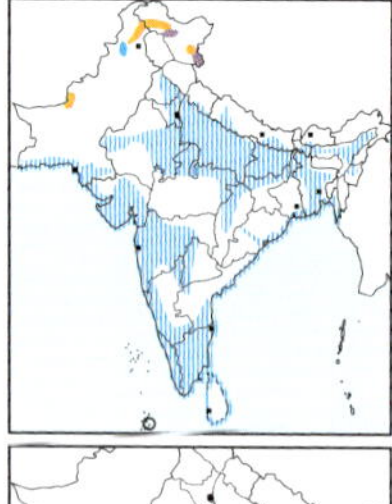

Brown-headed Gull *Chroicocephalus brunnicephalus* 41–45cm

Breeds in Ladakh; widespread winter visitor and passage migrant. Vagrant: Maldives. **ID** Slightly larger than Black-headed, with more rounded wingtips, and broader bill. Adult has broad black wingtips (broken by white 'mirrors') and white patch on outer primaries and primary coverts; underside to primaries largely black; iris pale yellow (brown in Black-headed). In breeding plumage, hood paler brown than Black-headed. Juvenile and first-winter have broad black wingtips contrasting with white patch at base of primaries. **Voice** As Black-headed but deeper and gruffer. **HH** Breeds on high-altitude lakes on Tibetan Plateau. Winters on coasts, tidal creeks and large inland lakes and rivers.

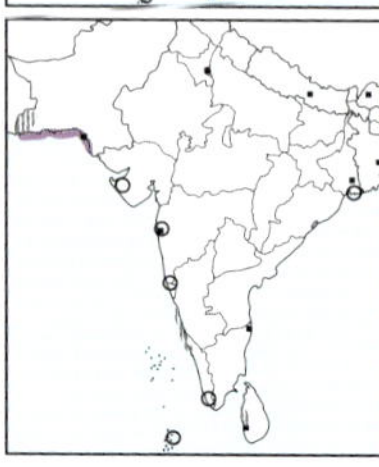

Sooty Gull *Ichthyaetus hemprichii* 43–48cm

Breeds in Pakistan; visitor to India's coasts, Vagrant: Maldives, Sri Lanka. **ID** In all plumages has heavy, two-toned bill, broad white trailing edge to secondaries, and very dark underwing. Adult has dark brown hood, whitish collar, brown breast-band, and greyish-brown upperparts; bill yellowish with black-and-red tip. Juvenile, first- and second-winter have rather uniform brownish head and breast, brown mantle and wing-coverts (with pale fringes in juvenile), and dark tail-band; bill greyish with black tip. See Vagrants for differences from White-eyed Gull. **Voice** Loud mewing *kaarr*, or *keee-aaar*; also, high-pitched *kee-kee-kee*. **HH** Gregarious. Widely commensal with humans and commonly associates with fishermen, following boats and frequenting harbours and ports. Coasts, very rare inland.

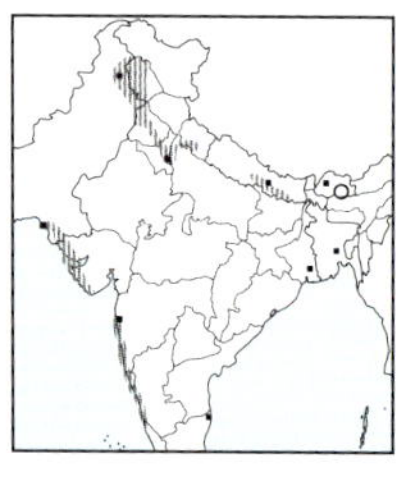

Common Gull *Larus canus* 41–46cm

Visitor. NE, S and W Pakistan, NW India. Vagrant: Nepal, Bhutan. **ID** Smaller and daintier than Caspian, with finer bill; in flight, wings are proportionately longer and slimmer. Bill yellowish-green, with dark subterminal band in non-breeding plumage. Head and hindneck heavily marked in non-breeding (unlike adult non-breeding Caspian). First-winter/first-summer have grey mantle; unbarred greyish greater coverts forming mid-wing-panel, narrow black subterminal tail-band, and well-defined dark tip to greyish/pinkish bill, which are differences from grey-mantled second-year Caspian. Second-winter has black on primary coverts but is otherwise like adult. **Voice** Calls include a nasal *keow* and a drawn-out shrill *glieeoo*. **HH** Recorded on lakes and large rivers in the region, also coasts in its normal range. **AN** Mew Gull.

1st-winter
non-br
non-br
Slender-billed
Gull
2nd-winter
br
br
br
1st-winter
Little Gull
Black-headed
Gull
br
st-winter
non-br
br
non-br
br
t-winter
br
br
juv
non-br
Brown-headed
Gull
non-br
2nd-winter
br
inter
br
Sooty Gull
1st-winter
1st-winter
mmer
non-br
non-br
2nd-winter
Common Gull

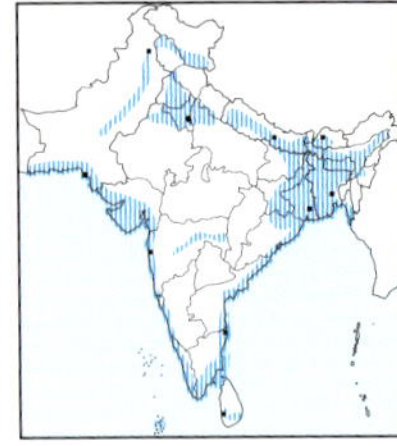

Pallas's Gull *Ichthyaetus ichthyaetus* 60–72cm

Widespread winter visitor. Vagrant: Maldives. **ID** Larger than 'Heuglin's', 'Steppe' and most Caspian and Mongolian Gulls. Head is more angular, with gently sloping forehead, and crown peaks behind eye; bill is longer and strikingly dark-tipped (except in juvenile), with pronounced gonys. Eyes always dark. Adult breeding has black hood with bold white eye-crescents, and yellow bill with red tip and black subterminal band. White tips to primaries contrast with black subterminal marks, and white wedge-shaped patch on outer wing contrasts with pale grey coverts. Adult non-breeding has largely white head with variable black mask (and white eye-crescents). Juvenile has brown mantle and scapulars with pale fringes, resulting in scaly pattern. From juvenile Caspian by combination of structural features, more pronounced dark mottling on hindneck and sides of breast contrasting with whitish underparts, paler bar on greater coverts, and more clearly defined black tail-band; dark mask is pronounced. First-winter/first-summer has grey mantle and scapulars (unlike in Caspian). From second-winter Caspian by dark mask and streaking across hindcrown (as adult non-breeding), more pronounced brown mottling on hindneck and sides of breast on otherwise cleaner underparts and clear-cut dark tail-band. May acquire partial hood as first-summer. Second-winter has largely grey upperwing, with variable dark markings in lesser coverts, dark tail band, but adult-like grey secondaries, and extensive black on primaries and primary coverts. Third-winter as adult non-breeding, but has more black on primaries. **Voice** A corvid-like *kra-ah*. **HH** Coasts and fishing boats at sea, rarely in harbours, also, lakes and large rivers.

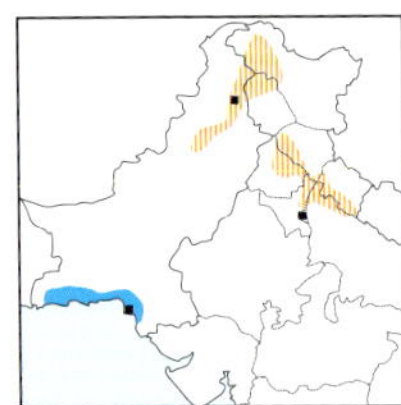

Caspian Gull *Larus cachinnans* 58–68cm

Uncertain status. **ID** Head appears elongated due to longer bill and nasal feathering and a sloping crown peaking behind eye. Eyes appear small and set higher on head. Adult has paler grey upperparts than 'Heuglin's', 'Steppe' and Mongolian, and birds approaching 'Steppe' may be intergrades. Head whiter in non-breeding plumage especially around eye but may show faint streaking on hindneck. Eyes usually appear dark, although can be yellow. Adult typically shows more white on longest primaries than 'Heuglin's' (typically with complete white tip to 10th primary and large white mirror to 9th primary), with less black at wingtips also due to grey inner webs of 7th–10th primaries being more extensive. 'Steppe' is more similar but averages more black on mid primaries and inner webs of outer primaries. Juvenile and first-winter similar to 'Heuglin's' and 'Steppe' but dark areas are paler, with paler 'window' on inner primaries, whiter underwing-coverts (with less extensive brown barring), usually narrower tail band with sparsely marked upper and under tail-coverts, and whiter head and underparts; paler tips to wing-coverts create diffuse pale bands. Earlier fledging and paler plumage mean Caspian are often much paler and more worn/bleached than 'Heuglin's' in their first-winter. Second-year has paler grey mantle than second-year 'Heuglin's' and often retains more immature feathers in wing-coverts. By second year, bill has extensive pink base and can recall immature Pallas's Gull (which see). Note third-year Caspian (and all other large gulls) have more black in inner and mid primaries, and reduced – or even absent – mirrors in the outer primaries (especially 9th primary) and thus show primary patterns closer to adult 'Steppe' or Mongolian. However, third-years in all taxa show at least some black in their outer primary coverts (some have dark marks in tail, inner-wing coverts, and on average duller bare-parts). 'Large-white headed gull' identification in the Subcontinent is extremely challenging, and there is a strong possibility that many birds wintering in the region are from a large overlap zone in the extralimital breeding grounds between Caspian and either 'Steppe' or 'Heuglin's'. Caspian-like birds occur that are closer to or intermediate with 'Steppe' and are either regarded as 'Eastern' Caspian or intergrades with 'Steppe'. Compared to typical Caspian they are more compact; adult upperparts are slightly darker, bare-parts brighter in winter, wing-pattern closer to 'Steppe' with smaller 'mirrors' and less extensive pale inner webs to outer primaries. See also account for Mongolian Gull below. **Voice** Call a loud, rapid *haaa-haaa-haa-ha-ha-ha-ha-ha-ha-ha-ha*, with a characteristic nasal, laughing quality. **HH** Habits like Lesser Black-backed. Coasts and inland waters.

Pallas's Gull
2nd-winter
br
1st-winter
non-br
br
1st-winter
'Eastern'
Caspian
non-br
Caspian Gull
1st-winter
2nd-win
non-br
♀ br
♂ non-br
1st-winter
(Feb)
1st-winter
(Nov)

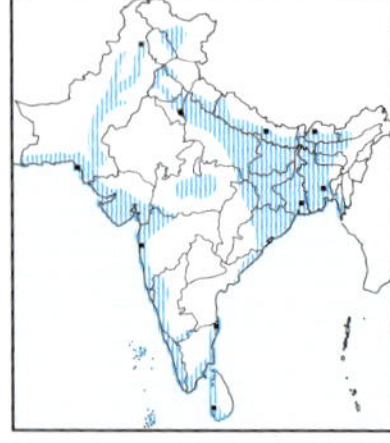

Lesser Black-backed Gull *Larus fuscus* 51–61cm

Winter visitor, mainly to coasts. **ID** Darkest large gull in region. Two forms occur, *L. f. heuglini* ('Heuglin's Gull') and *L. f. barabensis* ('Steppe Gull'). '**Heuglin's Gull**' is generally stockier and squarer-headed than Caspian and 'Steppe'. Adult has darker grey upperparts than Caspian and 'Steppe', and head more heavily streaked in non-breeding plumage. Eyes usually yellow (appear small and usually dark in Caspian). Adult shows more black on wingtips than Caspian, typically with large white 'mirror' at tip of 10th primary (rather than complete white tip) and often no mirror on 9th primary. Adult 'Heuglin's' is also in active primary moult in early winter (when completed in similar taxa) and are often still growing 9th and 10th primaries as late as February, and consequently white primary tips are fresher and neater. Juvenile and first-winter from Caspian by darker inner primaries, greater coverts and underwing-coverts, and broad tail-band and more heavily-marked upper/under tail-coverts. Retains neat pale-fringed juvenile mantle feathers later into year than Caspian (to December) due to later fledging and arrival in the region, and replaced feathers are fresher and greyer than in corresponding second-generation feathers of Caspian and 'Steppe' which were replaced two to three months earlier and are thus more worn and bleached. Adult of the form '*taimyrensis*', which may occur, has slightly paler upperparts, and often has pink legs. '**Steppe Gull**' averages smaller than Caspian, with shorter and blunter bill and shorter legs. Upperparts are darker grey than Caspian, closer to 'Heuglin's' with fuller black wingtips. Most are dark-eyed. Adult breeding has deeper yellow bill, and more extensive red gonys spot than Caspian (extending onto upper mandible and variably mixed with black); legs can be brighter orange-yellow. Bill paler in winter with dark subterminal marks and pale tip. Like Caspian moults juvenile mantle feathers by autumn (thus one to two months earlier than 'Heuglin's'), otherwise very similar in juvenile plumage to 'Heuglin's but in direct comparison 'Steppe' will be more worn and bleached and in early winter show more advanced moult. See also account for Mongolian Gull below. **Voice** Braying *ka-yaow-owowow-ow-ow ow.* **HH** Wide variety of coastal and inland waters. **TN** Much change and confusing. Heuglin's Gull *Larus heuglini* (including recognition of subspecies *L. h. taimyrensis*) and Steppe Gull *L. barabensis* are regarded as separate species by some authorities; 'Steppe' is also included with Caspian as *L. c. barabensis* or may be intergrades between *heuglini* and Caspian. '*Taimyrensis*' is regarded as either paler *heuglini* from the eastern end of their range or hybrids with Vega Gull *L. vegae*.

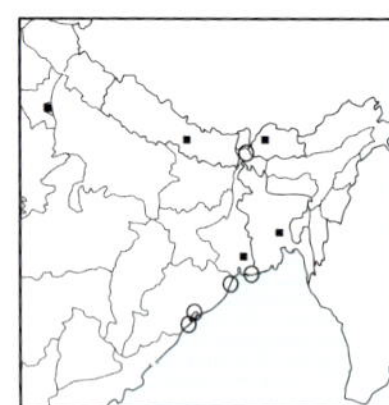

Mongolian Gull *Larus mongolicus* 56–68cm

Visitor to E India. **ID** A large, long-winged gull, with stout legs. Adult has grey mantle and wings which are slightly darker than Caspian (and paler than 'Heuglin's' and 'Steppe') with broader white tertial tips and trailing edge to secondaries and more extensive black wingtips. Black marks often start from 3rd and 4th primary, and outer primaries are blacker than Caspian due to more extensive black inner webs, and complete white tip to the 10th primary are rare. Legs can be pink or yellow. First-winter is a distinctive large 'white-headed gull'; wing coverts are sparsely and boldly barred with white equal to or more extensive than black as are replaced scapulars. From mid-winter at least head and body are very white so any juvenile tertials and primaries are the only dark areas on a standing bird. Tail pattern is almost diagnostic – a clean, narrow black tail band, with clean white base and very sparsely barred/spotted upper and under tail-coverts and rump. Inner primary 'window' is similar to Caspian, but due to pale-barred inner wing does not show Caspian's greater and median covert bars. Many replace coverts and tertials with even more sparsely barred feathers. Bill often has extensive pale base with dark outer third but is variable. Second-winter is equally clean and pale on head and body, with streaks confined to hind-neck and breast sides; upperparts and variable numbers of wing-coverts clean grey, older coverts usually very bleached. This plumage is arguably closest to first-winter and second-winter Pallas's but lacks dark mask and white eye-crescents, and with more prominent pale 'window' in inner primaries, paler and more coarsely marked wing-coverts, and narrower/broken dark tail-band. **HH** coastal and inland habitats including islands, beaches, mudflats, fields, beside lakes and rivers, in grassy areas of airports, and rubbish dumps. **TN** Treated as subspecies of Caspian Gull *L. cachinnans mongolicus*, or as a subspecies of Herring Gull *L. argentatus mongolicus*, or most closely related to Vega Gull *L. vegae*, by various authorities.

1st-winter
2nd-winter
non-br
1st-winter
(late)
♂
non-br
'Heuglin's Gull'
juv
♀ br
2nd-winter
non-br
1st-winter
Lesser Black-backed Gull
juv
'Steppe Gull'
♀ br
1st-winter
(late)
♂
non-br
2nd-winter
non-br
1st-winter
♂
non-br
1st-winter
Mongolian Gull

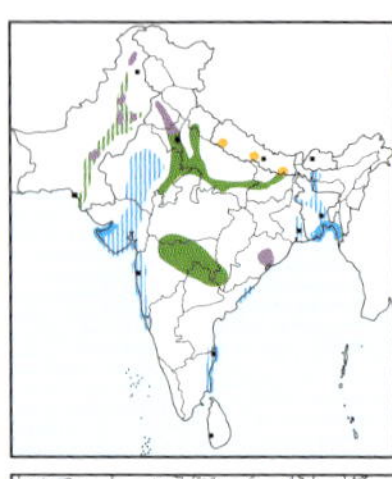

Indian Skimmer *Rynchops albicollis* 38–43cm

Resident. Mainly N and C subcontinent. **ID** Adult has large, drooping orange-red bill with yellowish tip (and lower mandible projects noticeably beyond upper), black cap, and black mantle and wings contrasting with white underparts. In flight, shows broad white trailing edge to upperwing, white underwing with blackish primaries, and white rump and tail with black central tail feathers. In non-breeding plumage, cap and upperparts are browner. Juvenile has whitish fringes to browner mantle and upperwing-coverts, diffuse cap, and dull orange bill with black tip. **Voice** Nasal *kap kap*. **HH** Crepuscular. Flies close to the surface with tip of its much longer lower mandible in the water and bill held open. Mainly larger rivers with sandbanks. Globally threatened.

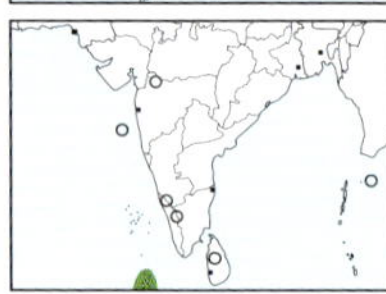

White Tern *Gygis alba* 23–33cm

Breeds on Maldives. Vagrant: India and Andamans. **ID** Adult all white except dark primary shafts, beady black 'eye' and black upturned bill. Flight feathers are translucent; shallow fork to tail. Juvenile has variable buff-and-brown barring on upperparts. Very short legs are bluish. **Voice** Calls include *grrich-grrich-grrich* or *eenk-eenk-eenk*. **HH** Erratic and fluttering flight. Pelagic, except when breeding.

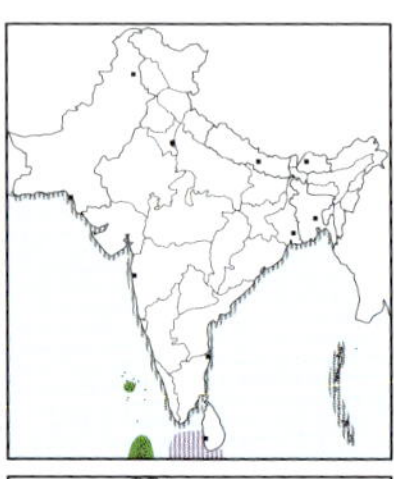

Brown Noddy *Anous stolidus* 40–45cm

Breeds in Lakshadweep. Widespread, has bred in Maldives; also recorded off other coasts. **ID** Adult is dark chocolate-brown with pale grey forehead and crown. In flight, shows paler upperwing-coverts than flight feathers and tail is a slightly darker brownish-black than upperparts. Underwing-coverts paler than remiges. Bill stouter, proportionately shorter and noticeably downcurved compared with Black (see Vagrants) and Lesser Noddies. Juvenile has browner forehead and crown, and indistinct pale fringes to upperparts. **Voice** Nesting calls include harsh crow-like *caw* and varied guttural barks. **HH** Swift flight with rapid wingbeats. Pelagic, except when breeding.

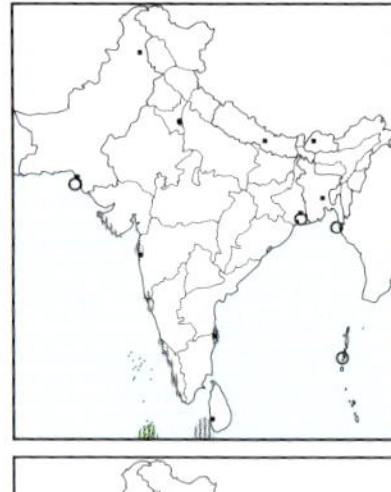

Lesser Noddy *Anous tenuirostris* 30–34cm

Widespread mainly on coast of W India; has bred in Maldives; rare migrant to Sri Lanka. **ID** Smaller and slimmer than Brown, with longer and slimmer bill, and darker grey-brown appearance. Pale greyish lores, concolorous with forehead, contrast with black patch in front of eye, and has variable greyish neck. Otherwise upper- and underwing-coverts more concolorous with remiges than in Brown. Juvenile has pale fringes to mantle and scapulars; pale cap is more sharply demarcated from nape. See Vagrants for differences from Black Noddy. **Voice** Nesting birds repeat grating *arrrk arrrk*; also, lower pitched *ugugug*. **HH** Like Brown, but flight is faster and more fluttery. Pelagic, except when breeding.

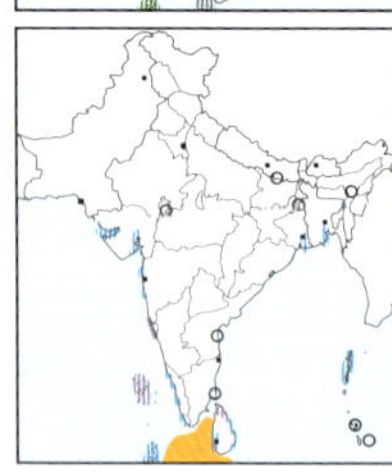

Sooty Tern *Onychoprion fuscatus* 36–45cm

Breeds Vengurla Rocks off S Maharashtra coast, Lakshadweep and NW Sri Lanka. Mainly in non-breeding season in adjacent seas and Maldives, where has bred. Vagrant: Nepal. **ID** Larger and more powerful than Bridled, with blackish upperparts (concolorous with cap), more extensive blackish underside to primaries (contrasting with white underwing-coverts), black tail with white outer tail feathers, and broader white forehead patch not extending over eye (with narrower black loral stripe). Adult non-breeding may show white spotting on crown and white fringes to upperparts; upperparts may appear brownish and white feather bases may be visible. Immature is initially like juvenile, but after one year black of underparts is mixed with white; thereafter, resembles adult non-breeding, but with dark mottling on underparts. Juvenile is very different to juvenile Bridled; has sooty-black head and breast contrasting with whitish lower belly, bold white spotting on mantle, scapulars and upperwing-coverts, pale underwing-coverts. **Voice** Loud, piercing *wide-a-wake*. **HH** Spends much time in aerial manoeuvres. Pelagic.

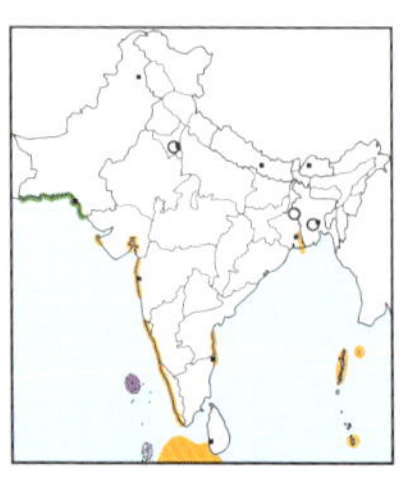

Bridled Tern *Onychoprion anaethetus* 30–32cm

Breeds Vengurla Rocks off S Maharashtra coast and Lakshadweep. In non-breeding season: offshore waters of Pakistan, W India, Andamans, Maldives and Sri Lanka. **ID** Smaller and more elegant than Sooty Tern. In breeding plumage, white forehead patch is narrower and extends over eye as broad white supercilium, and has brownish-grey mantle and wing-coverts which are noticeably paler than black cap. Rump and tail are brownish-grey (strikingly black-and-white in Sooty Tern). Adult non-breeding and immature have less distinct dark loral stripe and crown/nape as these are streaked white, and have pale fringes to upperparts. Juvenile has greyish-white crown, dark mask and white forehead and supercilium (shadow of adult), variable buffish fringes to mantle and wing-coverts, and brownish patch on side of breast. **Voice** Calls include yapping *wep-wep*, like Black-winged Stilt. **HH** Mainly offshore waters.

ad
juv
Indian Skimmer
ad
White Tern
juv
ad
juv
Brown Noddy
ad
juv
ad
juv
Lesser Noddy
ad
juv
Sooty Tern
juv
br
1st-summer
juv
juv
br
non-br
br
Bridled Tern

PLATE 61: SMALL TERNS

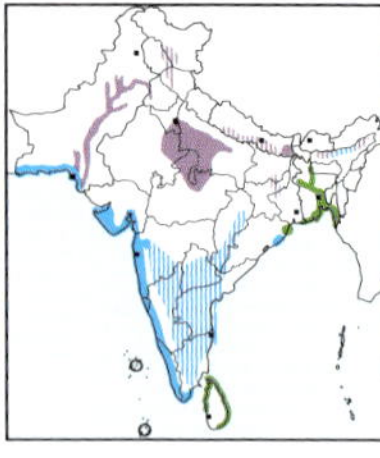

Little Tern *Sternula albifrons* 22–28cm

Resident; breeds locally, widespread in non-breeding season. Visitor: Maldives. **ID** Fast flight with rapid wingbeats and narrow-based wings. Adult breeding has white forehead and black lores, black-tipped yellow bill, orange legs and feet, and black outer primaries. Adult non-breeding and immature have blackish bill, black mask and nape band, dark lesser covert bar, and dark legs. Juvenile has dark subterminal marks to upperpart feathers. Compared with the widespread nominate, *S. a. sinensis,* which breeds on W coast of peninsula and Sri Lanka, has paler grey upperparts, longer tail-streamers, and white (rather than dark) primary shafts. **Voice** Distinctive, rasping *kriet.* **HH** Hovers more frequently and for longer and with faster fluttering wingbeats than other terns except Saunders's. Mainly freshwater lakes and rivers, also, coastal waters.

Saunders's Tern *Sternula saundersi* 20–28cm

Breeds in Pakistan, Gujarat, Sri Lanka and Maldives. In non-breeding season on W and S Indian coasts. **ID** Adult breeding from Little by stouter bill, square-ended white forehead patch (not extending as crescent to eye), paler grey upperparts and greenish-yellow or brownish legs (orange on Little). In flight shows broader black (and more contrasting) outer edge to primaries, broader and more pronounced white trailing edge to wing, and grey rump and centre of tail concolorous with mantle (rump can be grey on some Little, e.g. *S. a. sinensis*). In non-breeding plumage has paler grey upperparts, broad white trailing edge to wing (secondaries and coverts more uniform in Little), and crown is almost entirely white with well-defined dark mask. Juvenile more like Little but shows broad white trailing edge. **Voice** Disyllabic, stronger than Little. **HH** Habits like Little. Coastal waters.

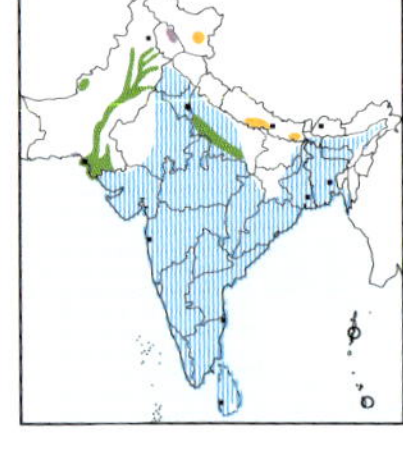

Whiskered Tern *Chlidonias hybrida* 23–29cm

Breeds in Kashmir and erratically in N India; widespread in winter. Vagrant: Maldives. **ID** In breeding plumage, white cheeks contrast with black cap and grey underparts. In non-breeding and juvenile plumage, from White-winged by larger bill, grey rump concolorous with back and tail, and different head pattern (see White-winged). Head markings can be limited to dark mask recalling small Gull-billed. Compared with White-winged Tern, juvenile generally lacks pronounced dark lesser covert and secondary bars and has black-and-buff markings on mantle/scapulars that appear more chequered (more uniformly dark in White-winged Tern). **Voice** Rasping *cherk*; alarm call a more rasping loud *kerch.* **HH** Feeds mainly on insects by hawking or picking from the surface. Inland and coastal waters.

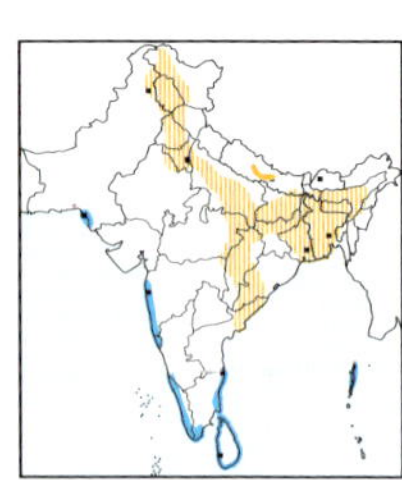

White-winged Tern *Chlidonias leucopterus* 23–27cm

Widespread passage migrant. **ID** In breeding plumage, black head and body contrast with white forewing, and has black underwing-coverts. Latter are last part of plumage to be lost during moult into non-breeding plumage (always white in Whiskered). In non-breeding and juvenile plumage, smaller bill, whitish rump contrasting with grey tail, and different head pattern are distinctions from Whiskered. Black ear-covert patch is bold and reaches below eye, and usually has well-defined black line on nape. First-year shows dark lesser covert and secondary bars, and by late winter these contrast strongly with pale (worn) median and greater coverts, which form pale panel in wing, while mantle also can appear noticeably darker than pale coverts, giving rise to 'saddled' appearance as in juvenile; birds in this plumage are distinct from non-breeding and first-year Whiskered which have more uniform mantle and wings. See Vagrants for differences from Black Tern. **Voice** Loud *krek* when excited. **HH** Flies with great agility to catch insects in the air and swoops to pick them from the water surface. Mainly freshwater wetlands, also, coasts.

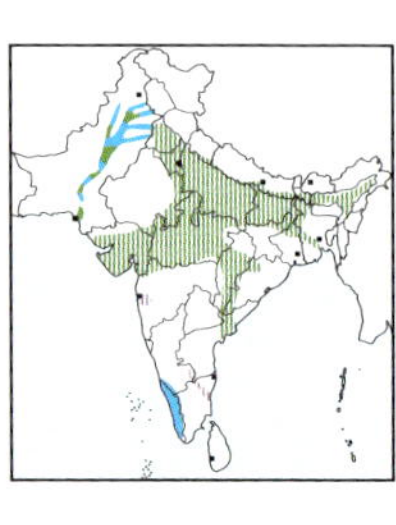

Black-bellied Tern *Sterna acuticauda* 32–35cm

Widespread resident except most of the north-west and S and E India; unrecorded in Sri Lanka. **ID** Smaller than River Tern, with orange to orange-yellow bill (and variable black tip) in all plumages. Adult breeding has grey breast, black belly and vent, and long outer tail feathers. Black cap does not extend to cover lores (compare River Tern). Like River Tern, whitish primaries contrast with grey rest of wing to form striking 'flash' on outer wing in flight. Long orange bill and deeply forked tail are best features from Whiskered Tern. Adult non-breeding and immature have white underparts, shorter tail, and black mask and streaking on crown. Confusingly, can occur with black cap and white underparts, when most like River, but structural differences and orange bill are diagnostic. Juvenile has dark mask and streaking on crown and nape, sandy coloration to head and mantle, and brown fringes to upperparts. **Voice** Short, dog-like barks, *nyap.* **HH** Feeds by plunge-diving, dipping to the surface and picking up prey, and hawking insects. Breeds on large rivers; other inland waters in winter. Globally threatened.

1st-winter
non-br
Little Tern
br
juv
br
br
non-br
br
juv
1st-winter
Saunders's Tern
br
1st-winter
juv
non-br
br
Whiskered Tern
non-br
br
1st-summer
br
non-br
non-br
juv
White-winged Tern
juv
non-br
br
br
Black-bellied Tern

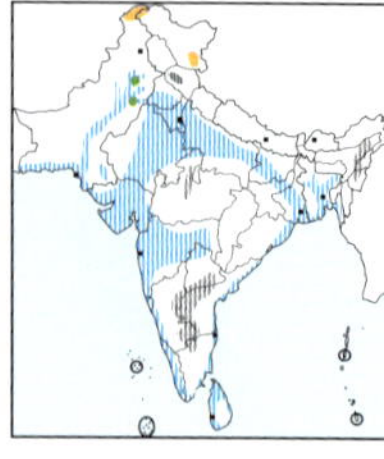

Gull-billed Tern *Gelochelidon nilotica* 33–38cm

Breeds locally in Pakistan and N India; widespread in winter. Very rare passage migrant in Nepal. **ID** From Sandwich Tern by shorter and stouter gull-like bill, broader-based, less pointed wings, and shorter, stockier body. Flight is steady and more gull-like, less graceful, with shallower wingbeats. Does not normally plunge-dive like Sandwich. Rump and tail are grey (white on Sandwich) and concolorous with back in all plumages. Adult breeding has black cap, and darker grey upperparts than in other plumages. Variable black mask in non-breeding and immature plumages (lacking black 'U' across hindcrown of Sandwich). Juvenile less heavily marked on upperparts than juvenile Sandwich, with buffish cast to crown and mantle when fresh. **Voice** Upslurred *kay-wek*, given singly or repeated. **HH** Hawks over sand and mudflats, also, marshes and fields, swooping or dipping to pick up food from surface or in mid-air. Coastal and freshwater wetlands.

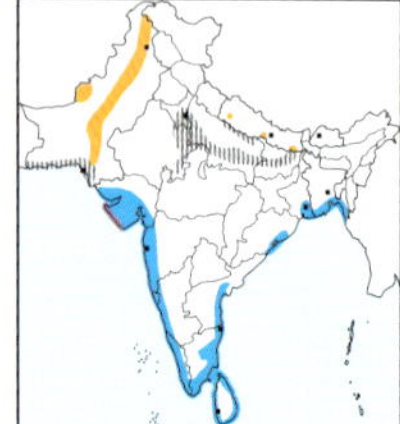

Caspian Tern *Hydroprogne caspia* 47–54cm

Breeds in Pakistan, Gujarat, Sri Lanka; widespread in winter. **ID** Large size and broad-winged/short-tailed appearance. Huge red bill and black underside to primaries. Adult breeding has complete black cap. Adult non-breeding has black-streaked crown and black mask; bill is duller, with more black at tip. First-winter and first-summer are similar to adult non-breeding, but show faint dark lesser covert and secondary bars and dark-tipped tail (but upperwing appears much plainer than in Lesser and Great Crested Terns). Juvenile has narrow dark subterminal bars to scapulars and wing-coverts; forehead and crown are more heavily marked, almost forming dark cap. **Voice** Loud, far-carrying *kretch*. **HH** Fishes by patrolling high above water, hovering occasionally before plunge-diving. Coastal mudflats, saltpans, tidal creeks, brackish lakes and lagoons, large inland lakes and rivers, and marshes.

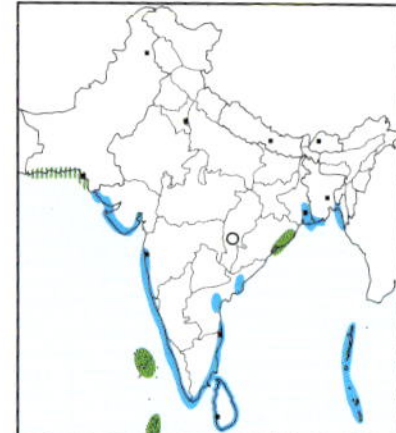

Lesser Crested Tern *Thalasseus bengalensis* 35–43cm

Occurs offshore on all coasts almost all year; breeds in Pakistan, Orissa? Lakshadweep? **ID** From Great Crested by smaller and slimmer orange-yellow to orange bill, smaller size and lighter build (recalling Sandwich Tern), and paler grey coloration to upperparts. From Sandwich by bill colour and grey rump and tail. Adult breeding has black crown and crest including forehead, although black of latter is quickly lost (forehead is never black on Great Crested). Adult non-breeding has black nape band. Juvenile has dark centres to lesser and greater coverts and secondaries, which show as diffuse dark bars across wing, and has dark centres to feathers of mantle, scapulars and tertials. Upperwing pattern is like Great Crested, but dark bars are typically paler and less contrasting. First-winter and first-summer are similar to adult non-breeding, but show darker grey primaries and dark lesser covert and secondary bars. **Voice** Flight call a grating *kerrick*, like Great. **HH** Feeds by plunge-diving from a considerable height. Usually in offshore waters and often far out to sea; also, tidal creeks and harbours.

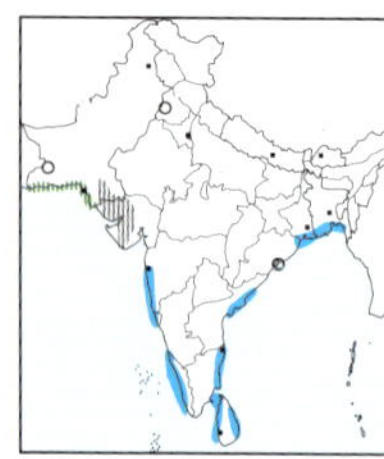

Sandwich Tern *Thalasseus sandvicensis* 34–45cm

Winter visitor: mainly coasts of Pakistan, India, Sri Lanka. Vagrant: Bangladesh, Maldives. **ID** Slim black bill with yellow tip, and more rakish appearance than Gull-billed with narrower, more pointed wings which appear set forward and sharply angled, and longer, tapering body. White rump and tail contrast with greyer back. Adult breeding has black cap with crest. Adult non-breeding has white forehead and crown, and black crest forming U-shaped patch. First-winter and first-summer as adult non-breeding, but with darker lesser-covert and secondary bars, and dark corners to tail. Juvenile more heavily marked than juvenile Gull-billed, with dark subterminal bars to wing-coverts and mantle, and dark pattern to tertials; has black rear crown and nape lacking in juvenile Gull-billed. **Voice** An upward-inflected hoarse *kree-it*. **HH** Habits like Lesser Crested. Coasts, tidal creeks and open sea.

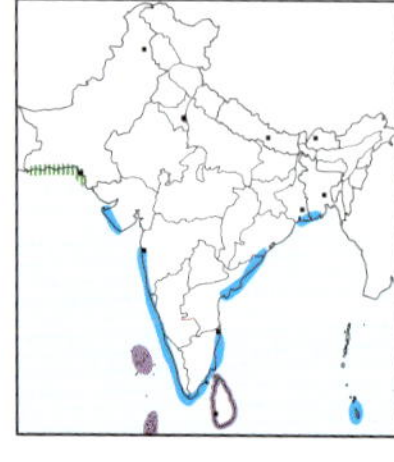

Great Crested Tern *Thalasseus bergii* 43–53cm

Breeding resident: Pakistan, Lakshadweep, Vengurla Rocks, Maldives. Winter visitor to all coasts. **ID** From Lesser Crested by broader, slightly drooping, cold yellow to lime-green bill, and by larger size and stockier build. In adult plumage, shows well-defined whitish fringes to tertials, and has darker grey coloration to upperparts than Lesser Crested. Immature plumages are similar but generally more strongly patterned than in Lesser Crested. *T. b. cristata* with paler grey upperparts, has not been recorded, but may be the subspecies in the Nicobar Islands. **Voice** At nest a loud, raucous, crow-like *kerrak*. **HH** Habits like Lesser. Mainly offshore waters and often at considerable distances out at sea; also, larger tidal creeks and channels.

1st-winter
non-br
br
juv
br
Gull-billed Tern
juv
non-br
br
br
Caspian Tern
juv
1st-winter
non-br
non-br
br
1st-winter
br
Lesser Crested Tern
Sandwich Tern
juv
non-br
br
1st-winter
Greater
Crested Tern
non-br
cristata

PLATE 63: MEDIUM-SIZED TERNS

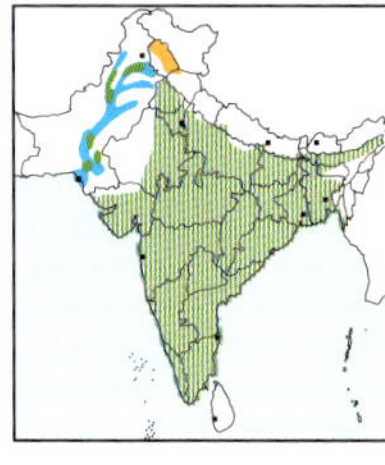

River Tern *Sterna aurantia* 38–46cm

Widespread resident; unrecorded in Sri Lanka. Vagrant: Bhutan. **ID** Adult breeding has stout yellow to pale orange bill, black cap, greyish-white underparts, and long greyish-white outer tail feathers; whitish primaries contrast with otherwise grey wing to form striking 'flash' on outer wing in flight. Black cap is complete (lores white in Black-bellied Tern). In non-breeding plumage lacks elongated outer tail feathers, and has blackish mask and mainly grey crown, and dark tip to bill. Larger size, stocky appearance, and shorter and stouter bill (with distinctly curved culmen) help separate adult non-breeding and immature from Black-bellied. Juvenile has dark fringes to upperparts, black streaking on crown and nape, whitish supercilium, and dark mask extending as dark streaking onto ear-coverts and sides of throat. **Voice** Fairly short, shrill, staccato *kiuk-kiuk* in flight. **HH** Feeds mainly by plunge-diving. Large inland waters. Globally threatened.

Common Tern *Sterna hirundo* 32–39cm

Breeds in Ladakh; has bred Sri Lanka; widespread winter visitor and passage migrant mainly to coasts. Vagrant: Bhutan. **ID** Grey mantle contrasts with white rump and uppertail-coverts (compare Roseate and White-cheeked), although contrast may be less apparent in non-breeders. In breeding plumage, compared with Roseate, has orange-red bill with less black at tip, pale grey wash to underparts, dark trailing edge to underside of primaries and dark outer wedge to upperside, and shorter tail-streamers which do not extend beyond tail at rest. In non-breeding and first-winter has black bill (as in Roseate); has darker grey upperparts, shorter tail with grey outer webs to feathers, shorter and stouter bill, and narrower white trailing edge to wing compared with Roseate. Juvenile has orange legs and bill base (bill becoming black with age). Adult breeding *S. h. tibetana* nesting in north-west subcontinent has darker grey upperparts than the widespread nominate subspecies, with a shorter bill with more extensive black tip. *S. h. longipennis* also occurs. In breeding plumage, it has a mostly black bill, with greyer upperparts and underparts than the nominate and a more distinct white cheek-stripe; legs dark reddish-brown. White rump and uppertail-coverts are best distinctions from White-cheeked. **Voice** Large and varied notes, all with distinctive sharp, irritable quality. **HH** Feeds by plunge-diving. Mainly coastal waters, also large inland waters.

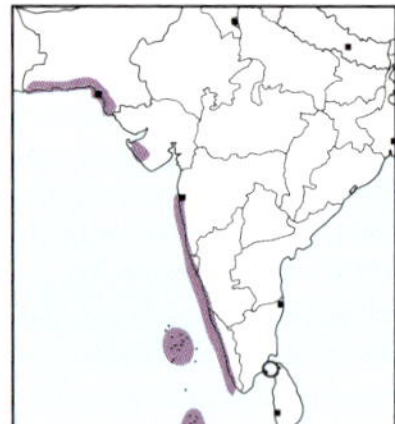

White-cheeked Tern *Sterna repressa* 32–35cm

Breeds Vengurla Rocks. Non-breeding season: offshore waters of Pakistan, W India, Lakshadweep. Vagrant: Maldives. **ID** From very similar Common by darker grey upperparts and uniform grey rump and tail concolorous with back (tail feathers lack white inner webs of Common, and tail therefore appears uniformly grey from above and below); underwing has darker trailing edge and pale central panel. In breeding plumage, darker grey on underparts than Common, and has white cheeks; from adult breeding Whiskered by longer bill, paler grey underparts, and more strongly forked tail. **Voice** Similar to Common but not as harsh; also, has diagnostic hoarse *kee-err* or *kee-ceek*. **HH** Plunges into sea with steep dives when fishing. Offshore waters.

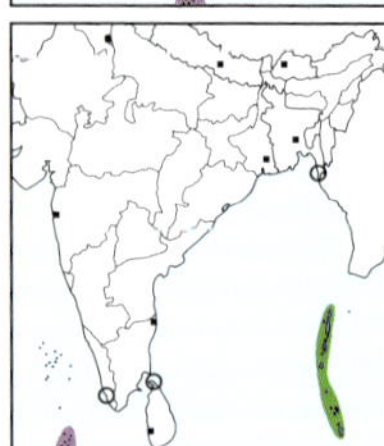

Black-naped Tern *Sterna sumatrana* 33–35cm

Breeding resident: Maldives. Breeding visitor: Andamans, Nicobars. Vagrant: Bangladesh, Sri Lanka. **ID** Adult very pale greyish-white, with black bill and legs, and black mask and nape band. Has whiter mantle and wings than Roseate, with distinct black outer edge to outermost primary, and lacks obvious white trailing edge to upperwing. Nape band is paler and not so well defined in non-breeding plumage. Juvenile has black subterminal marks to upperpart feathers, and black streaking on crown (with less black than juvenile Roseate but otherwise very similar). **Voice** Various short, high-pitched, repeated sharp notes *chit, chip, chrrut, tsip.* **HH** Picks prey from surface while hovering. Inshore waters around islands and lagoons.

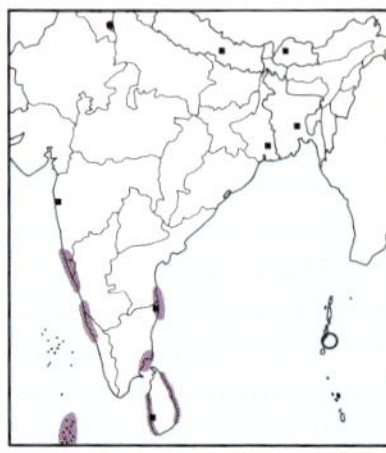

Roseate Tern *Sterna dougallii* 33–38cm

Summer visitor: Vengurla Rocks, islets off South Andaman; islets off W and E Sri Lanka. Breeding resident: Maldives. **ID** Pale grey upperparts and rump concolorous with back, long tail with white outer feathers, broad white trailing edge to wing (visible on inner primaries at rest), lack of prominent dark trailing edge to underside of primaries, and stiff and rapid flight action help separate from Common Tern. In breeding plumage, bill either black, orange or red with extensive black tip or entirely orange, and has variable pink flush to underparts. Juvenile has black bill and legs, black subterminal marks to upperpart feathers, and largely black crown. **Voice** Flight call different from Common and Black-naped, a disyllabic *chu-vee*, recalling Spotted Redshank. **HH** Buoyant, strong, fast flyer, with rapid, shallow beats. Plunge-dives, often submerging completely. Coastal waters and offshore islands.

br
non-br
br
River Tern
juv
1st-winter
br
hirundo
1st-winter
Common Tern
non-br
br hirundo
br
longipennis
juv
juv
non-br
br
br
juv
2nd-winter
White-cheeked Tern
non-br
1st-winter
br
Black-naped Tern
1st-summer
br
br
non-br
juv
Roseate Tern

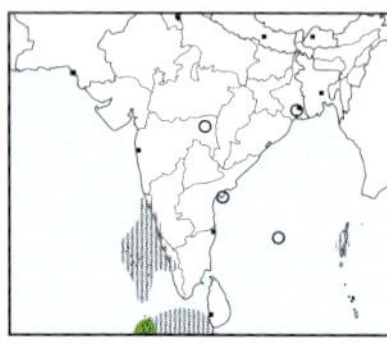

White-tailed Tropicbird *Phaethon lepturus* 60–80cm

Breeding resident: Maldives. Visitor: India and Sri Lanka coasts. **ID** Smaller and more graceful than other tropicbirds. Adult has yellow or orange bill, black diagonal bar across inner upperwing, and white tail-streamers. Juvenile has yellow bill, and lacks black band across nape; shows more black on primaries than juvenile Red-tailed; lacks extensive black on primary coverts of juvenile Red-billed. **Voice** Near colonies staccato, high-pitched notes mixed with squawks. **HH** Habits like Red-billed. Often investigates ships. Pelagic.

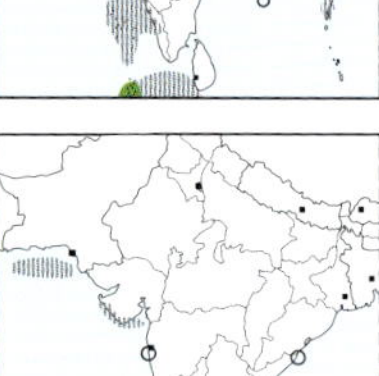

Red-billed Tropicbird *Phaethon aethereus* 90–107cm

Visitor: Pakistan, W India, SW Sri Lanka coasts. Straggler: Maldives. Vagrant: Bangladesh. **ID** Adult has red bill, white tail-streamers, black barring on mantle and scapulars, and much black on primaries. Can have pink flush to body and underwing-coverts. Juvenile has yellow bill with black tip, and black band across nape; shows more black on primaries, with black primary-coverts, compared to juvenile Red-tailed and White-tailed Tropicbirds. **Voice** Loud, monosyllabic, rather finch-like; incessant screams while circling ships. **HH** Aerial seabird. Graceful pigeon-like flight with flapping and circling alternating with long glides. Usually solitary. Feeds by first hovering to locate fish or squid, then plunge-diving on half-closed wings. Pelagic.

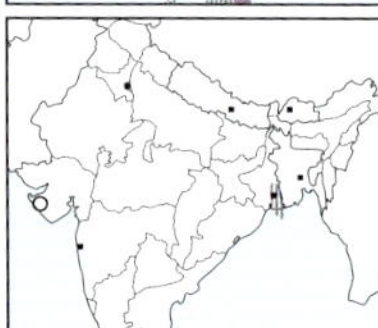

Red-tailed Tropicbird *Phaethon rubricauda* 80–102cm

Breeds (?) Nicobars. Straggler: Maldives. **ID** Adult has red bill and red tail-streamers; lacks black barring on mantle, back and rump; wings largely white (with black primary shafts and markings on tertials). Juvenile has grey or black bill becoming yellower with age, and lacks black nape band; shows less black on primaries and is more heavily barred above than juvenile Red-billed and White-tailed. **Voice** Includes short raspy barks and high nasal yaps. **HH** Habits like Red-billed but rarely visits ships. Pelagic.

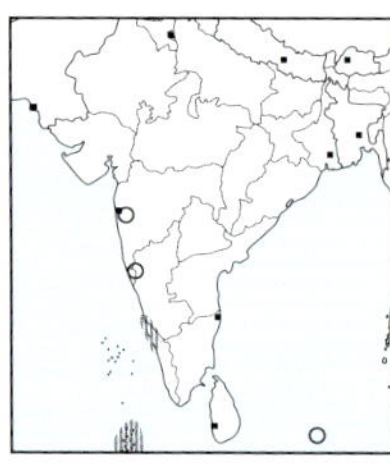

Red-footed Booby *Sula sula* 69–79cm

Non-breeding visitor to coastal waters including Lakshadweep, Maldives, Sri Lanka. **ID** Small and graceful booby. White, brown and intermediate morphs occur; white morph most likely to be encountered in Indian Ocean. Adult white morph from adult Masked by smaller size, variable yellow wash on crown and hindneck, bluish bill, lack of black mask (but does show black on chin), and red legs and feet; in flight, also by black carpal patch on underwing, white tail, and white tertials (black trailing edge does not reach body). Brown morph is similar in plumage to juvenile, but has red legs, blue-grey bill and pinkish facial skin. Intermediate (mainly brown) morphs occur with white head and neck and/or white rump, tail and undertail-coverts. Juvenile is largely brown with greyish legs; from juvenile Brown Booby by dark underwing and dark bill. Immature variable, with pale head, neck and body, variable breast-band, and brown mottling on upperparts and upperwing-coverts. **Voice** Includes a descending series of low cackles. **HH** Flight and feeding habits like Masked. In small groups or flocks at good feeding areas. Attracted to ships. Partly nocturnal. Pelagic.

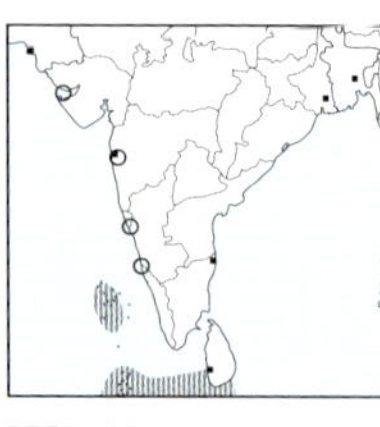

Brown Booby *Sula leucogaster* 64–85cm

Breeds on Lakshadweep? Visitor: Maldives and W coastal waters Pakistan, India, Sri Lanka. **ID** Adult dark brown, with sharply demarcated white underparts and underwing-coverts. Bill typically strikingly greenish or yellowish. Juvenile has pale greyish bill, dusky-brown underparts, with pale panel on underwing-coverts, but overall appearance is like adult. Brown of breast joins brown leading edge of wing (compare juvenile/immature Masked). **Voice** Whistles and nasal barks at colonies. **HH** Flight and feeding habits like Masked. Generally solitary or in small groups. Pelagic, also feeds inshore, where often perches on rocks and buoys.

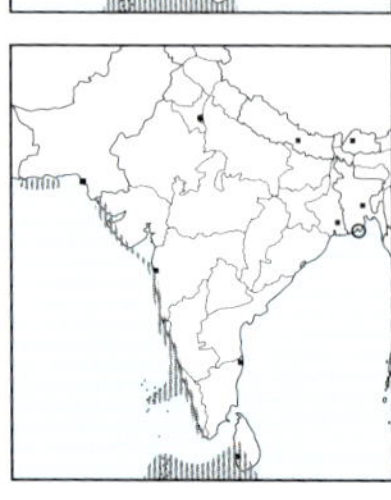

Masked Booby *Sula dactylatra* 74–86cm

Breeds on Lakshadweep? Visitor: Maldives and W coastal waters of Pakistan, India, Sri Lanka. Vagrant: Bangladesh. **ID** Large robust booby. Adult largely white, with black mask and black flight feathers and tail. Yellow bill, black tail and black tertials (which complete black trailing edge of wing) help to separate from adult white-morph Red-footed Booby at distance. Juvenile has brown head, neck and upperparts, with whitish collar and scaling on upperparts; underparts white, and shows much white on underwing-coverts (with white extending onto primary coverts of underwing; compare adult and juvenile Brown). Head, upperparts and upperwing-coverts of immature become increasingly white with age. See Vagrants for differences from Abbott's Booby. **Voice** Honks, yaps, coos and whistles at colonies. **HH** Forages on the wing, scanning the sea, and plunge-dives on sighting fish or squid. Flight direct, with alternating periods of flapping and gliding. Seen in the region singly or in small groups. Pelagic.

ad
Red-billed
Tropicbird
ad
ad
Red-tailed
Tropicbird
White-tailed
Tropicbird
juv
juv
juv
intermediate
morph
juv
imm
Red-footed
Booby
ad
white morph
imm
Brown
Booby
juv
imm
ad
Masked
Booby
ad

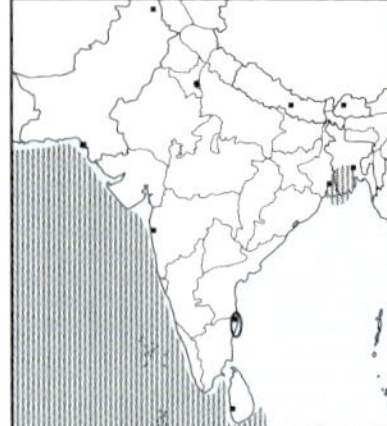

Wilson's Storm-petrel *Oceanites oceanicus* 15–20cm

Visitor: W and S coastal waters of India including Lakshadweep, Sri Lanka. Winter migrant: Maldives. **ID** Square-ended tail, pale band across greater upperwing-coverts, and uniformly dark underwing. White rump extends around to reach thighs. Feet project noticeably beyond tail. Wings are comparatively short and rounded. Frequently seen fluttering over water, with wings held in shallow V, when dangling feet show yellow webs. Direct flight is swallow-like, with fast, shallow wingbeats and occasional gliding. See Vagrants for differences from Band-rumped and Leach's Storm-petrels. **Voice** At sea may give chattering calls. **HH** Occurs singly or is gregarious, and often follows boats. Pelagic.

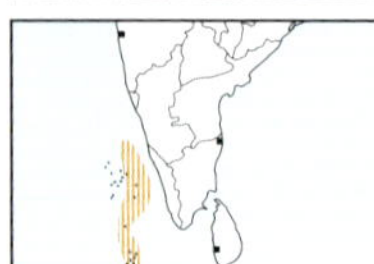

White-faced Storm-petrel *Pelagodroma marina* 18–21cm

Visitor to coastal waters between Nicobars, India and S Sri Lanka; also, Lakshadweep and Maldives. **ID** Adult has white underparts and underwing-coverts, white supercilium contrasting with dark crown and ear-coverts, greyish-brown upperwing-coverts with paler grey greater covert bar and grey rump contrasting with slightly notched black tail. Feet project noticeably beyond tail and wings appear broad and oval-shaped. Has distinctive foraging flight: in light winds, glides slowly with wings held horizontally, legs dangling, and hopping on the surface every few seconds. Also, feeds by dipping and pattering, and frequently flops down on its breast in the water. **Voice** Silent at sea. **HH** Follows boats. Pelagic.

Swinhoe's Storm-petrel *Hydrobates monorhis* 18–20cm

Visitor. Coastal waters of S and SW India, Lakshadweep, Maldives and in summer W coastal waters Sri Lanka. **ID** The only all-dark storm-petrel recorded from the subcontinent. Has pale band across greater upperwing-coverts, angular wings (with pronounced carpal bend), and shallowly forked tail. Fast, swooping flight with some bounding and gliding. Feeds chiefly by dipping; does not patter. See Vagrants for differences from Matsudaira's and Leach's Storm-petrels. **Voice** Silent at sea. **HH** Usually pelagic; also, occurs in coastal waters. **TN** Formerly placed in *Oceanodroma*.

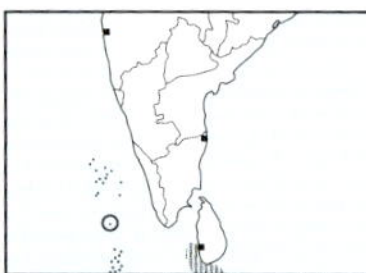

Barau's Petrel *Pterodroma baraui* 38cm

Summer visitor off SW coasts. India and Sri Lanka. **ID** Whitish forehead and dark grey cap, dark rump and tail contrasting with grey lower mantle and back, and grey patches on sides of breast (which do not form complete breast-band). Bill heavy and black. Upperwing varies from being mainly pale with pronounced blackish M-mark to being mainly dark through wear. Largely white underwing with black band on leading and trailing edges; the only *Pterodroma* in the Indian Ocean to show this underwing pattern. Flight relaxed and buoyant, with steep 'shearing' in strong winds. **Voice** Silent at sea. **HH** Often feeds with other seabirds, sometimes near fishing boats. Feeds by seizing prey from the surface or by dipping. Pelagic. Globally threatened.

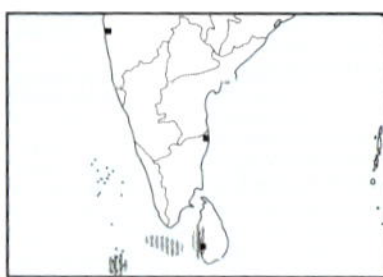

Bulwer's Petrel *Bulweria bulwerii* 26–28cm

Summer visitor off S India, SW Sri Lanka and Maldives. **ID** All-dark, long-winged petrel with long and pointed (or wedge-shaped) tail and pale band on greater upperwing-coverts. From Jouanin's by smaller size, proportionately smaller, squarer head with finer bill, more prominent band on greater coverts (although Jouanin's in worn plumage may show this), and different flight action. Flight springy, erratic and close to the waves, with wings held forward and bowed. In calm conditions, rapid flapping interspersed with short twisting glides. In strong winds, has faster wingbeats and glides in shallow arcs. Compared with Jouanin's sits low on the water with elongated profile. **Voice** Silent away from breeding grounds. **HH** Habits resemble a small gadfly petrel. Tail often held slightly raised. Usually does not follow ships. Pelagic.

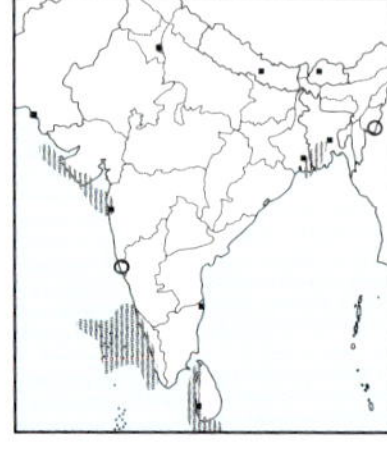

Jouanin's Petrel *Bulweria fallax* 30–32cm

Visitor off W coasts of India and Sri Lanka; also, Maldives. Vagrant: Manipur. **ID** From Bulwer's by larger size and broader wings, larger head and larger, stouter bill, and different flight action; tail is broader and not so pointed and long. Upperwing dark, but can show pale band across greater coverts, as on Bulwer's, through wear. Flight action differs from Bulwer's. In windy conditions, will rise 5m or more above waves in long banking arcs, interspersed with short bouts of leisurely flaps (usually at peak of arc). Otherwise, flies close to surface, with a mix of steady beats and long glides on slightly bowed wings. Compared to Bulwer's sits higher on the water with larger-headed, shorter-bodied profile. Smaller, with less languid flight, than dark-morph Wedge-tailed Shearwater and has stouter bill, held downwards at 45°. **Voice** Unknown. **HH** Habits like Bulwer's. Pelagic.

Wilson's Storm-petrel
ad
ad
White-faced
Storm-petrel
ad
Swinhoe's
Storm-petrel
ad
Barau's Petrel
ad
Bulwer's Petrel
ad
Jouanin's Petrel

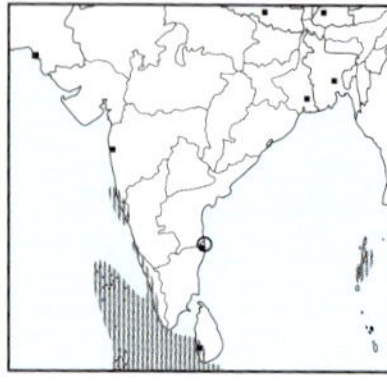

Flesh-footed Shearwater *Ardenna carneipes* 40–48cm

Visitor. India including Lakshadweep, W Sri Lanka and Maldives. **ID** Large, dark, broad-winged shearwater. Pink legs and feet. Underwing dark, although can show pale patch on underside of primaries in strong light. Tail shorter and more rounded than Wedge-tailed. Stout pinkish bill with dark tip. Flight typically relaxed with strong flapping interspersed by long, stiff-winged glides; banks and glides with less flapping in stronger winds. **Voice** May be silent at sea. **HH** Catches food chiefly by plunge-diving and pursuing prey under water; also, by running along the surface between shallow belly-flop dives. Mainly offshore waters; pelagic. **TN** Formerly placed in *Puffinus.*

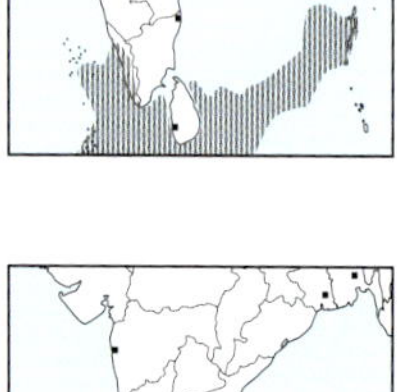

Wedge-tailed Shearwater *Ardenna pacifica* 38–47cm

Visitor. India, Sri Lanka and Maldives. **ID** Large size, long broad wings, long pointed or wedge-shaped tail, and fine dark bill. In calm conditions, lazy flapping and short glides with wings held forward and bowed. Rakish appearance with longer tail and extended neck compared to Flesh-footed. In strong winds flight erratic and bounding, often changing direction and soaring in low arcs between short bursts of flapping. Dimorphic; pale morph has white underparts and underwing-coverts with dark primaries and trailing edge; dark morph all dark including dark underwing (although paler bases to primaries may give impression of pale patch); intermediates occur. **Voice** Silent at sea. **HH** Often follows fishing boats. Feeds mainly on wing, dipping to the surface; also, by plunging head underwater, but seldom completely submerges. Partly pelagic; also, occurs in offshore waters. **TN** Formerly placed in *Puffinus.*

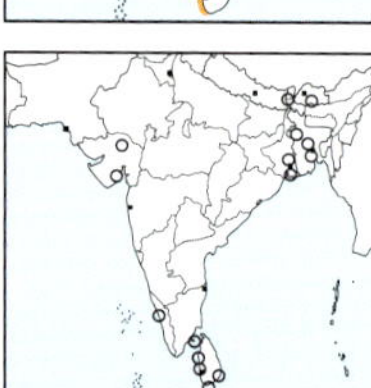

Sooty Shearwater *Ardenna grisea* 40–51cm

S India and Sri Lanka. **ID** Sooty-brown, with whitish flash on underwing-coverts. All-dark bill, and dark legs and feet just extend beyond tail. From very similar Short-tailed Shearwater by longer bill, sloping forehead, longer wings, and more prominent pale panel on underwing contrasting more strongly with dark flight feathers. **HH** Strong deliberate flight action with stiff flaps and long glides. Feeds mainly by plunge-diving, followed by underwater pursuit. Offshore and pelagic waters. **TN** Formerly placed in *Puffinus.*

Short-tailed Shearwater *Ardenna tenuirostris* 40-45cm

India, Pakistan; vagrant: Nepal, Bhutan, Bangladesh and Sri Lanka. **ID** Sooty-brown, with pale grey underwing-coverts. Much like very similar Sooty Shearwater but has shorter bill and steeper forehead, shorter rear body and tail behind wings, and pale panel on underwing tends to be less striking. **HH** Habits similar to Sooty. Coastal waters. **TN** Formerly placed in *Puffinus.*

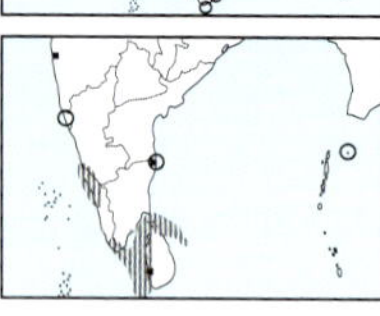

Streaked Shearwater *Calonectris leucomelas* 45–52cm

Visitor. S India and Maldives. Vagrant: Sri Lanka. **ID** White underparts and underwing-coverts and large size. Variable dark streaking on whitish head, and pale bill with dark tip. Flight typically relaxed and gull-like with wings slightly angled at carpal joints, interspersed with gliding on bowed wings. Rises ('shears') high in strong winds, but wings still slightly angled and flapping relaxed. See Vagrants for differences from Cory's Shearwater. **Voice** May be silent at sea. **HH** Frequently with other seabirds and follows fishing boats. Seizes fish and squid from surface; also, makes shallow dives. Pelagic and inshore waters.

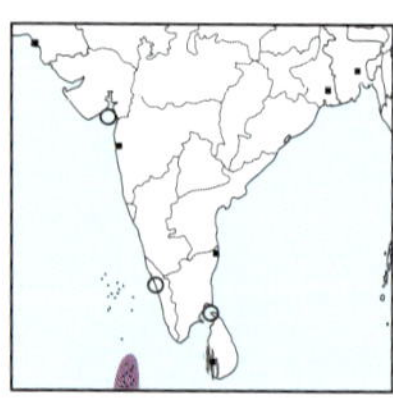

Tropical Shearwater *Puffinus bailloni* 29–31cm

Breeding resident: Maldives. Breeding visitor: Lakshadweep? Vagrant: Sri Lanka? **ID** Small size with comparatively short broad wings. Blackish upperparts, white underparts with dark on breast-sides; white wing-linings, axillaries and flanks, with broad dark margins to underwing. See below for differences from Persian Shearwater. Flies with fairly fast wingbeats interspersed by short glides, although often rises in low arcs in strong winds. Often fans tail when manoeuvring to feed. **Voice** Silent at sea. **HH** Sometimes with other seabirds; occasionally follows fishing boats. Catches prey by plunge-diving and by pattering across surface. Offshore and pelagic waters. **TN** Previously included in Audubon's Shearwater *P. lherminieri* complex.

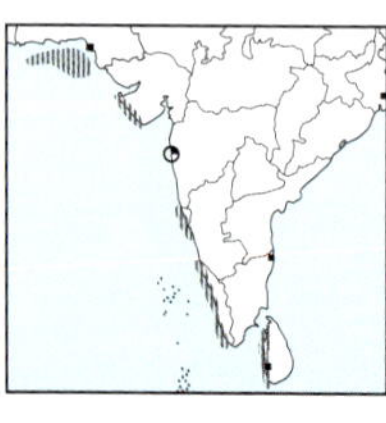

Persian Shearwater *Puffinus persicus* 27–33cm

Summer visitor. Pakistan, W India and Sri Lanka. Vagrant: Maldives. **ID** Slightly larger than Tropical, with longer, broader wings, shorter tail, and longer paler bill. Browner upperparts than Tropical, with less white on underwing-coverts (brownish leading edge), and brownish axillaries and flanks. Often shows diffuse whitish stripe over eye. Flies with fairly fast wingbeats interspersed with short glides low over sea, although often rises in low arcs in strong winds. Often fans tail when manoeuvring to feed. **Voice** Unknown, may be silent at sea. **HH** Habits like Tropical. Mainly offshore waters, also pelagic.

Flesh-footed Shearwater
ad
Wedge-tailed Shearwater
pale morph
dark morph
Sooty Shearwater
ad
Short-tailed Shearwater
ad
Streaked Shearwater
ad
Tropical Shearwater
ad
ad
Persian Shearwater

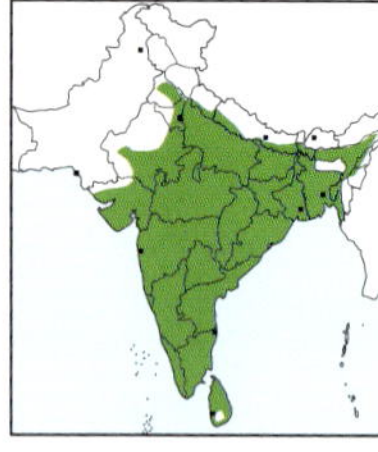

Asian Openbill *Anastomus oscitans* 68–81cm

Resident, moving locally according to water conditions. Widespread in plains; unrecorded in parts of NW subcontinent. **ID** Stout, dull-coloured 'open bill'. Largely white (breeding) or greyish-white (non-breeding), with black flight feathers and tail; legs usually dull pink, brighter in breeding condition. Juvenile has brownish-grey head, neck and breast, and brownish mantle and scapulars slightly paler than the blackish flight feathers. **Voice** Silent except occasional deep moans and bill clattering during greeting ceremony at nest. **HH** Habits like other storks, see Lesser Adjutant. Forages singly or in small to medium-sized flocks. Usually seeks food by submerging its head and open bill into shallow water and probing bottom mud; the bill is quickly closed on any prey. Feeds mainly on molluscs. Freshwater marshes, shallow lakes, reservoirs, jheels, tanks, lagoons and paddyfields; rarely on riverbanks and mudflats.

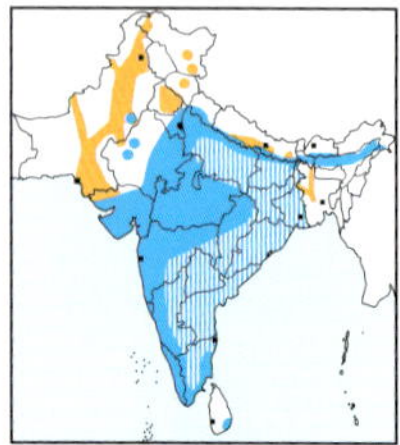

Black Stork *Ciconia nigra* 95–100cm

Winter visitor and passage migrant to much of subcontinent. Vagrant: Sri Lanka. **ID** Adult mainly glossy black, with white lower breast and belly, and red bill and legs; in flight, white underparts and axillaries contrast strongly with black neck and underwing. Juvenile has browner head, neck and upperparts flecked with white; bill and legs greyish-green. **Voice** Silent away from nest. **HH** Similar to other storks, see Lesser Adjutant. Pairs or small parties. Often shy and wary. Forages by walking with measured strides in shallow water. Inland fresh waters including marshes and rivers.

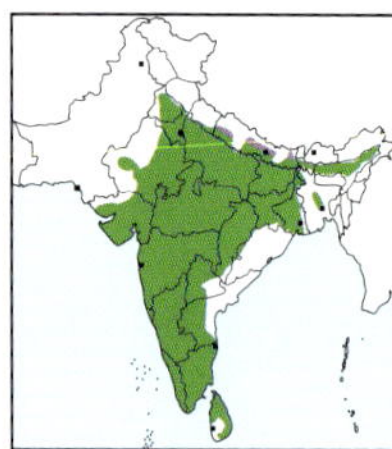

Asian Woolly-necked Stork *Ciconia episcopus* 75–92cm

Widespread sedentary resident; unrecorded in parts of NW or NE subcontinent and E India. Vagrant: Bhutan. **ID** Stocky, largely blackish stork with 'woolly' white neck, black 'skullcap', and white vent and undertail-coverts. Adult has black of body and wings glossed with greenish-blue, purple and copper. Bill black, with variable amounts of red, and legs and feet dull red. Juvenile similarly patterned to adult, but has duller brown body and wings, and feathered forehead. In flight, upperwing and underwing entirely dark. White undertail-coverts extend beyond short, forked black tail. **Voice** Silent except bill clattering at nest. **HH** Similar to other storks, see Lesser Adjutant. Usually singly or in pairs, occasionally in small parties. Hunts on dry or marshy ground and wet grasslands; rarely wades. Flooded grassland, marshes, irrigated fields and riverine areas, usually near open wooded country or in open country. **AN** Woolly-necked Stork.

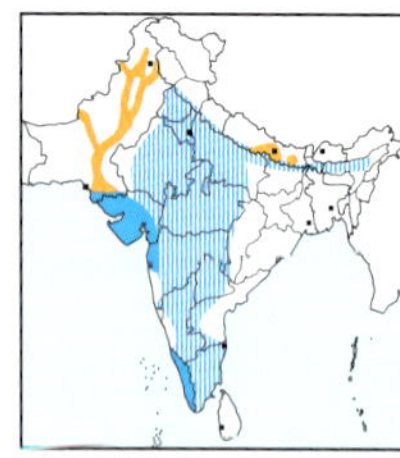

White Stork *Ciconia ciconia* 100–102cm

Widespread winter visitor and passage migrant except parts of NW and NE subcontinent and E India. Vagrant: Nepal, Bangladesh, Sri Lanka. **ID** Mainly white, with black flight feathers and striking red bill and legs. Generally has cleaner black-and-white appearance than Asian Openbill; note tail is white (black in Asian Openbill). Juvenile is like adult but has duller bill with darker tip. **Voice** Silent away from nest. **HH** Habits like other storks, see Lesser Adjutant. Singly or in flocks. Usually shy and difficult to approach. Stalks deliberately on dry or moist ground in search of prey. Grassland and damp ploughed or fallow fields.

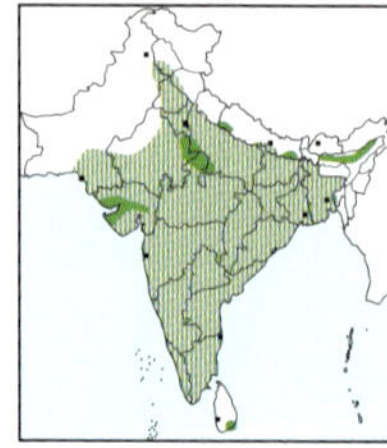

Black-necked Stork *Ephippiorhynchus asiaticus* 110–137cm

Widespread resident except parts of north-west in lowlands but now local and very uncommon. **ID** Large, black-and-white stork with long red legs and huge black bill. In flight, wings white except broad black band across coverts, and tail black. Male has brown iris; yellow in female. Juvenile has fawn-brown head, neck and mantle, mainly brown wing-coverts, and mainly blackish-brown flight feathers; legs dark. **Voice** At nest adults make low-pitched clattering of bill; largely silent away from it. **HH** Forages singly, in well-separated pairs in sight of each other, or in family parties after the breeding season. Usually very wary. Wades slowly and sedately while probing in shallow water and among aquatic vegetation with bill open at the tip. Flies with legs extended beyond tail and neck outstretched like most other storks. Freshwater marshes, lakes, tanks and large rivers; occasionally mangroves, rarely coastal mudflats.

br
non-br
br
Asian
)penbill
imm
Black Stork
ad
ad
ad
ad
ad
Asian
Woolly-necked
Stork
ad
ad
imm
White Stork
♀
♂
imm
ad
imm
ad
imm
Black-necked Stork

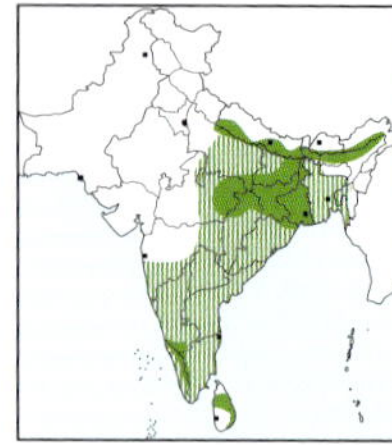

Lesser Adjutant *Leptoptilos javanicus* 110–120cm

Resident and nomadic. Widespread and local in lowlands; unrecorded in Pakistan and NW India. **ID** Flies with neck retracted, as Greater Adjutant, thus has different profile compared to other storks. Smaller than Greater, with slimmer bill that has straighter ridge to culmen (can sometimes appear very slightly upturned towards tip). From adult Greater by smaller size, uniform dark grey to glossy black mantle and wings (lacking paler panel on greater coverts – although this is much less distinct in immature Greater), and white undertail-coverts; neck ruff is largely black (appearing as black patch on sides of breast in flight). Further, has pale frontal Plate, denser hair-like feathering on back of head (forming small crest) and on hindneck, and lacks neck pouch. Adult breeding has red tinge to face and neck, copper spots at tips of median coverts, and narrow white fringes to inner greater coverts and tertials. Juvenile like adult, but upperparts dull black, and head and neck duller and more densely feathered. **Voice** Bill clattering at nest is characteristic of storks, also various moos, squeaks and growls; largely silent away from nest. **HH** Usually found singly. Typical stork behaviour. Forages by walking slowly on dry ground or in shallow water and grabs prey with its bill. Has powerful slow-flapping flight and frequently soars for long periods, often at great heights. In flight the legs are extended behind and neck retracted, unlike other storks except Greater Adjutant. Marshes, forest pools, flooded fields, lakes, drying-up river beds and mangroves.

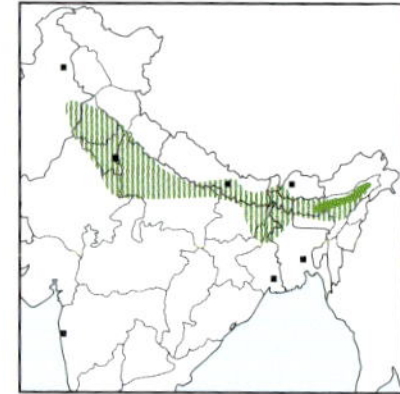

Greater Adjutant *Leptoptilos dubius* 120–152cm

Resident, nomadic and locally migratory. Mainly Assam; rare elsewhere. Vagrant: Pakistan, Bangladesh. **ID** Larger than Lesser Adjutant, with stouter, conical bill with convex ridge to culmen. Adult from adult Lesser by larger size, grey panel on greater coverts and tertials, white neck ruff (lacks or has less pronounced black patch on side of breast in flight), and grey undertail-coverts. Mantle ranges from bluish-grey to slate-grey and prominence of grey wing-panel also varies; can be strikingly silvery-grey. Further, has blackish face and forehead (with appearance of dried blood), more sparsely feathered head and neck (lacking small crest), and larger neck pouch (visible only when inflated). Immature has darker grey wing-covert panel (which contrasts much less with rest of wing) and initially has a brownish (rather than bluish-white) iris. **Voice** Bill clattering and squeals, grunts and moos at nest; largely silent away from it. **HH** Habits like Lesser Adjutant, but less shy and, unlike that species, feeds partly on carrion. Gathers with conspecifics, vultures and kites at refuse dumps. Also hunts small live animals in typical stork fashion, by walking slowly in marshes and shallow waters. Marshes, jheels, lakes and agricultural land.

Painted Stork *Mycteria leucocephala* 93–102cm

Widespread resident except much of the north-west and north-east, moving locally according to water conditions. Widespread in plains; unrecorded in parts of NW and NE subcontinent. **ID** Adult has downcurved yellow bill, bare orange head (redder in breeding season) and pinkish legs; white barring on black upperwing-coverts, pinkish tertials, and black barring on breast. In flight, underwing appears mainly dark, with barring on coverts. Juvenile dirty greyish-white, with grey-brown (feathered) head and neck and brown lesser coverts; bill and legs duller than adult's. Has distinctive appearance in flight, with extended drooping neck and downcurved bill, long wings with deep flapping beats, and long trailing legs. **Voice** Silent except at nest, when clatters bill and gives low moan when greeting mate. **HH** Habits like other storks, see Lesser Adjutant. Found singly, in small parties and sometimes in large flocks. Forages by wading slowly in shallow water with bill open and partly submerged, feeling for prey. Roosts gregariously on trees if available, otherwise on open sandbanks, mud or saltpans. Freshwater marshes, lakes and reservoirs, flooded fields, riverbanks, intertidal mudflats and saltpans.

ad
br
ad
non-br
Lesser Adjutant
br
imm
br
imm
Greater Adjutant
ad
ad
imm
Painted Stork

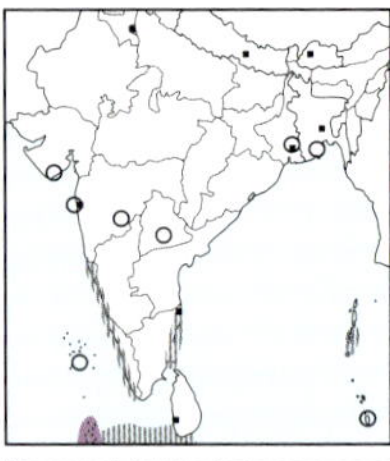

Lesser Frigatebird *Fregata ariel* 66–81cm

Non-breeding visitor to coasts of India, Maldives (has bred) and S and W coasts of Sri Lanka. Vagrant: Bangladesh. **ID** Smaller and more finely built than other two frigatebirds. Adult male all black except white spur extending from breast-sides onto inner underwing. Adult female has black head including throat, white neck-sides, white spur extending from white breast onto inner underwing, and black belly and vent. Juvenile and immature have rufous or white head, blackish breast-band and much white on underparts, which are gradually replaced by adult plumage; always show white spur on underwing (lacking on Great). **Voice** Calls at colonies include hissing, descending roar. **HH** Habits like Great. Pelagic.

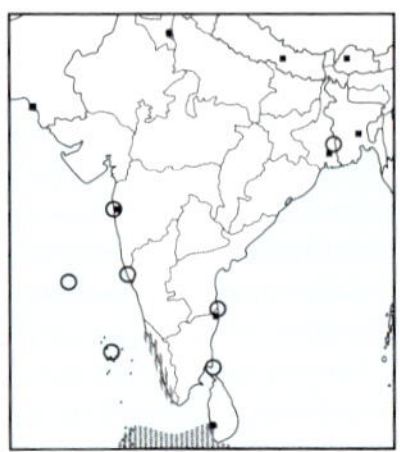

Great Frigatebird *Fregata minor* 85–105cm

Regular summer visitor S and W coasts of Sri Lanka; all coasts of India; Lakshadweep and Maldives. **ID** Adult male is only frigatebird in region with all-black underparts. Adult female has black cap and bluish bill; also grey throat and black neck-sides, and lacks spur of white on underwing. Juvenile and immature have rufous or white head, blackish breast-band and largely white underparts, which are gradually replaced by adult plumage; lack white spur on underwing (shown by all Lesser and some Christmas Island Frigatebirds); inseparable from some juvenile and immature Christmas Island Frigatebirds. **Voice** Normally silent away from nest. **HH** Aerial seabird, rarely landing on water and roosting in trees. In flight can achieve skilful manoeuvres and can soar for long periods with only occasional deep wingbeats. Noted for intercepting boobies, forcing them to disgorge fish and catching the food in mid-air; also, capture their own prey by diving vertically to water surface. Usually solitary at sea, but hundreds may gather around fishing boats to scavenge offal. A storm-driven visitor to coasts of the subcontinent, often occurring in the monsoon. Pelagic.

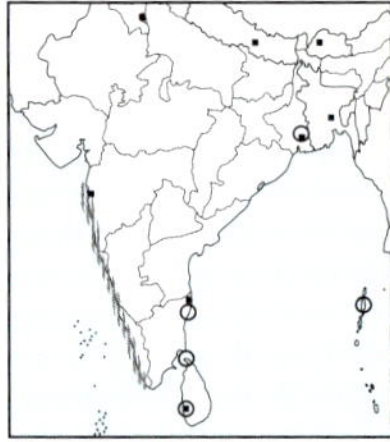

Christmas Island Frigatebird *Fregata andrewsi* 89–100cm

Visitor: Indian coasts. Vagrant: Sri Lanka. **ID** Adult male all black except large white patch on belly. Adult female has black head including throat and pink bill; also white neck-sides, white spur extending from white breast onto inner underwing, black wedge on side of breast, and white belly and vent. Juvenile has buffish to white head, blackish breast-band, and white underparts, with black head of female and black head and breast of male acquired gradually; some show white spur on underwing (always lacking on Great), and lower belly always white (gradually acquires black on both Lesser and Great). **Voice** Normally silent away from nest. **HH** Habits like Great. Pelagic. Globally threatened.

juv
♂ imm
♀
♂
Lesser Frigatebird
imm
♀
♂
juv
Great Frigatebird
Christmas Island
Frigatebird
♂ imm
♀
♂
juv

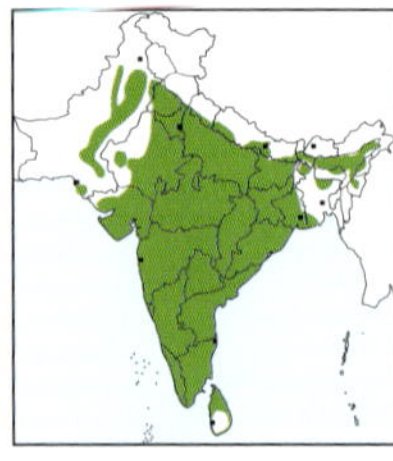

Oriental Darter *Anhinga melanogaster* 85–97cm

Widespread resident; unrecorded in parts of NW and NE subcontinent and Himalayas. **ID** Long, slim head and neck, dagger-like bill, and long tail. In flight, neck is only partly outstretched with kink at base. Adult breeding has dark brown crown and hindneck, white stripe on side of neck, blackish breast and underparts, lanceolate white scapular streaks, and white streaking on wing-coverts. Duller in non-breeding plumage. Immature browner with indistinct neck stripe and buff fringes to coverts forming pale panel on upperwing. Often swims with head and neck above water and body below. **Voice** Harsh rattling and grunting calls near nest. **HH** Spends much time drying its spread wings and tail while on a favoured perch. Unlike cormorants, does not leap up before diving, but slowly submerges. Lakes, ponds, reservoirs, rivers, marshes and other inland waters; also, mangroves and coastal waters. **TN** African and Australasian species sometimes are treated as conspecific, when known simply as Darter.

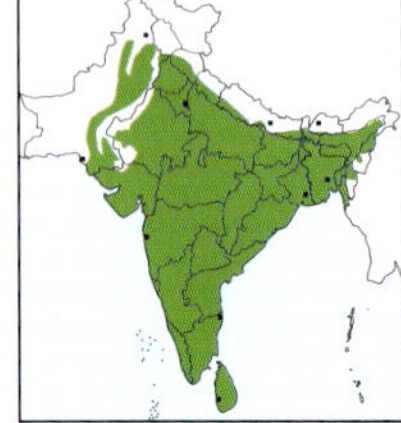

Little Cormorant *Microcarbo niger* 51–56cm

Widespread resident; unrecorded in parts of NW and NE subcontinent. **ID** Smaller than Indian Cormorant, with shorter bill, rectangular-shaped head (with steep forehead), shorter neck and longer-looking tail. Lacks yellow gular pouch. Adult breeding all black, with white plumes on sides of head. Bill, eyes, facial skin and pouch are black. Non-breeding browner (and lacks white head plumes), with whitish chin, and paler bill and pouch. Immature has whitish chin and throat, and foreneck and breast a shade paler than upperparts, with some pale fringes. Like other cormorants, swims with body low in the water, the neck straight and head and bill pointing slightly upwards. In flight the neck is extended and the head held slightly above the horizontal. **Voice** Grunts, croaks, gargles and groans near nest. **HH** On smaller waters occurs singly or in small groups; on large inland waters or estuaries often gathers in great flocks. Frequently hunts in parties, often with Indian, driving the fish towards shallower water. Rivers, lakes, reservoirs, village tanks, marshes, canals, estuaries, saltpans and coastal waters. **TN** Formerly placed in *Phalacrocorax*.

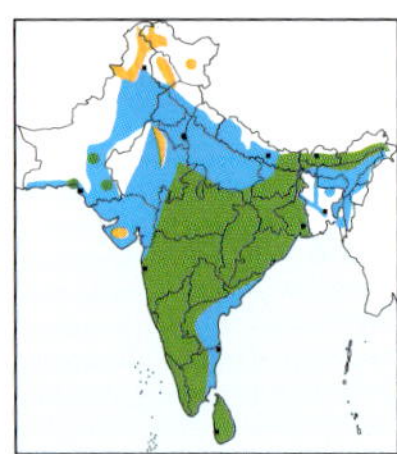

Great Cormorant *Phalacrocorax carbo* 80–100cm

Widespread resident; unrecorded in parts of NW and NE subcontinent. **ID** Larger and bulkier than Indian, with thicker neck, larger and more angular head, and stouter bill. Adult breeding glossy black, with dark gular skin, red spot at base of bill, white cheeks and throat, extensive white plumes covering much of head, and white thigh patch. Non-breeding lacks white head plumes and thigh patch. Base of bill and gular skin are yellow, and white cheeks and throat patch are more extensive than Indian. Immature similar but browner with underparts dark or extensively whitish or pale buff. Flies and swims like a typical cormorant, see Little. **Voice** Deep guttural calls near nest. **HH** Gathers in large numbers to breed, and often roosts communally in winter. Coastal waters, saltpans, reservoirs, lakes, and large inland lakes and rivers.

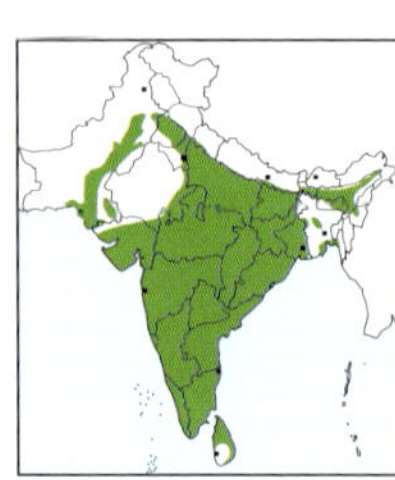

Indian Cormorant *Phalacrocorax fuscicollis* 63cm

Widespread resident; unrecorded in parts of NW and NE subcontinent and Himalayas. Vagrant: Nepal. **ID** Smaller and slimmer than Great Cormorant, with thinner neck, slimmer oval-shaped head, finer-looking bill, and proportionately longer tail. In flight, looks lighter, with thinner neck and quicker wing action. Larger than Little, with longer neck, oval-shaped head and longer bill. Adult breeding glossy black, with blue eyes, dark facial and gular skin, tuft of white behind eye, scattering of white filoplumes on neck. Non-breeding lacks white plumes; has whitish throat, yellowish gular pouch, and browner-looking head, neck and underparts. Immature has brown upperparts and whitish underparts. Flies and swims like a typical cormorant, see Little. **Voice** Includes short, harsh notes near nest. **HH** Frequently fishes with Little. Fresh and salt waters: lakes, rivers, irrigation tanks, estuaries, and saltwater and mangrove creeks.

br
br
Oriental Darter
imm
non-br
imm
imm
br
Little Cormorant
non-br
Great Cormorant
br
non-br
imm
br
Indian Cormorant
br

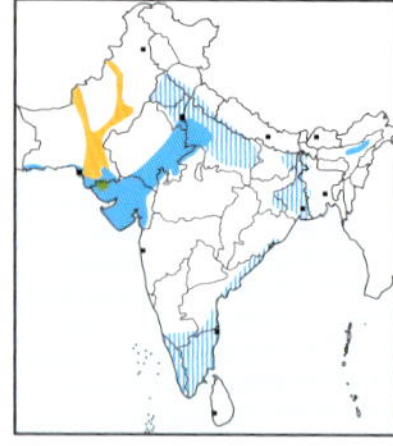

Great White Pelican *Pelecanus onocrotalus* 140–175cm

Mainly a winter visitor to N subcontinent; breeds in Gujarat. Vagrant: Nepal, Bangladesh. **ID** Adult and immature have black underside to primaries and secondaries which contrast strongly with white (or largely white) underwing-coverts. Feathering of forehead narrower than on Dalmatian Pelican, and tapers to a point at bill base. Orbital skin is more extensive and contiguous with bill. Legs and feet pinkish. Pouch yellow or orange-yellow (except when young) and extends further onto neck than other two pelicans. Adult is cleaner and whiter than Dalmatian and Spot-billed Pelicans. Adult breeding has white body and wing-coverts tinged pink, bright orange-yellow pouch and pinkish skin around eye, and short drooping crest. Adult non-breeding has duller bare parts and lacks pink tinge and white crest. Immature has variable amounts of brown on wing-coverts and scapulars. Juvenile has brown head, neck and upperparts, including upperwing-coverts, and brown flight feathers; upperwing appears more uniform brown, and underwing shows pale central panel contrasting with dark inner coverts and flight feathers; greyish pouch becomes yellower with age. **Voice** Adults usually silent, rarely uttering grunts or croaks. **HH** Typical pelican habits. May be found singly, in small flocks or in huge concentrations on larger lakes and lagoons. Often fishes cooperatively by swimming in a semicircular formation, driving fish into shallow waters; each bird then scoops up fish from the water into its pouch, before swallowing the food. Either fly in V-formation or in lines, and often soar for considerable periods in thermals. Roosts in flocks, usually on open sand bars. Large lakes, lagoons and tidal creeks.

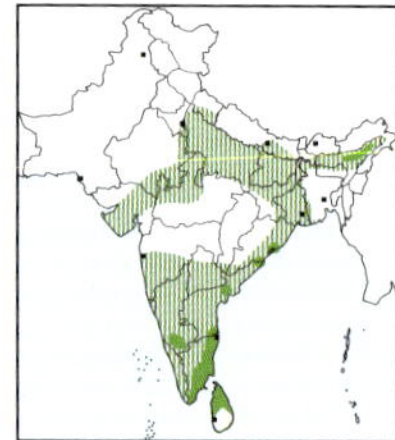

Spot-billed Pelican *Pelecanus philippensis* 127–152cm

Resident and local migrant except parts of NW and NE subcontinent and C India. Breeds in S and NE India and Sri Lanka; widespread in non-breeding season. **ID** Much smaller than Great White and Dalmatian, with dingier appearance, uniform pinkish bill and pouch (except in breeding condition), and black spotting on upper mandible (except juveniles). Pale circumorbital skin looks cut off from bill (appears to be wearing goggles). Tufted crest/hindneck usually apparent even on young birds. Underwing pattern like that of Dalmatian (quite different from Great White), showing little contrast between wing-coverts and flight feathers and paler greater coverts producing distinct central panel. Adult breeding has cinnamon-pink rump, underwing-coverts and undertail-coverts; head and neck appear greyish; has purplish skin in front of eye, and pouch is pink to dull purple, blotched with black. Adult non-breeding dirtier greyish-white, with paler pouch and facial skin. Immature has variable grey-brown markings on upperparts. Juvenile has brownish head and neck, brown mantle and upperwing-coverts (fringed pale buff), and brown flight feathers; spotting on bill initially lacking (and still indistinct at 12 months). **Voice** Adults usually silent, rarely uttering grunts or croaks. **HH** Typical pelican habits, see Great White. Gregarious; fishes alone or cooperatively in a flock. Large lakes, reservoirs and coastal lagoons and estuaries.

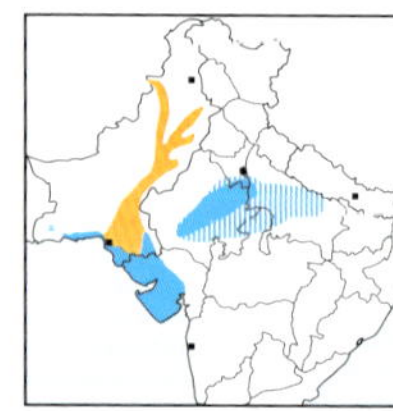

Dalmatian Pelican *Pelecanus crispus* 160–180cm

Winter visitor and passage migrant. Mainly Pakistan and NW India. **ID** In all plumages has greyish underside to secondaries and inner primaries (becoming darker on outer primaries) lacking strong contrast with pale underwing-coverts, and often with whiter central panel. Forehead feathering broader across upper mandible and orbital skin more restricted than on Great White. Legs and feet always dark grey. Tufted crest/hindneck usually apparent even on young birds (as Spot-billed). Larger than Spot-billed, with cleaner and whiter appearance at all ages; lacks 'spotting' on upper mandible, and bill usually darker than pouch. Adult breeding has orange to red pouch and purple skin around eye, and curly or bushy crest. Adult non-breeding more dirty white; pouch and skin around eye pale yellow to pinkish. Immature dingier than adult non-breeding, with some pale grey-brown on upperwing-coverts and scapulars. Juvenile has pale grey-brown mottling on hindneck and upperparts, including upperwing-coverts. **Voice** Adults usually silent, rarely uttering grunts or croaks. **HH** Found singly, in pairs and in flocks, but not in such large congregations as Great White. Fishes individually or cooperatively in a flock like Great White. Large lakes, rivers and coastal lagoons.

Great White Pelican
br
non-br
non-br
imm
juv
br
non-br
imm
br
juv
Spot-billed Pelican
br
non-br
non-br
imm
Dalmatian Pelican

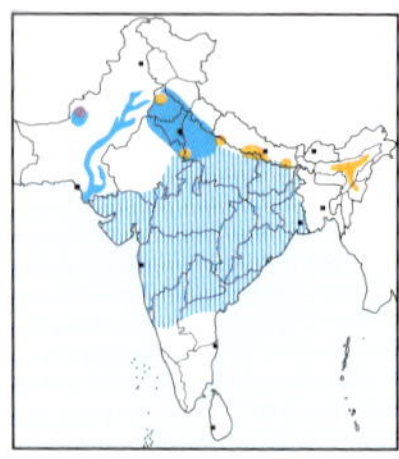

Great Bittern *Botaurus stellaris* 64–80cm

Widespread winter visitor except parts of NW and NE subcontinent and S India. Vagrant: Bangladesh, Sri Lanka. **ID** Comparatively large and stocky, with thick neck, stout body and broad, rounded wings. Large feet extend beyond tail in flight. Golden-brown and cryptically patterned, with black crown and moustachial stripe. Sexes and immature very similar in appearance. **Voice** Typically silent away from breeding areas. Calling has been recorded from Kashmir in summer: a booming *umphh... umphh... umphh.* **HH** Habits are those of a typical bittern. Usually remains hidden in reedbeds and is most often seen flying low over the reed tops. Hunts alone, by walking stealthily through vegetation, often with intervals of standing motionless. Dense tall wet beds of *Phragmites* reeds or *Typha* bulrushes in jheels, freshwater lakes and marshes.

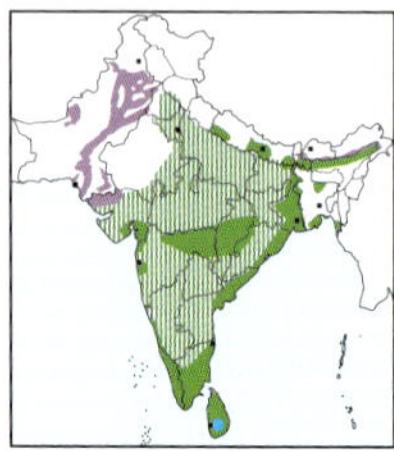

Black Bittern *Ixobrychus flavicollis* 54–66cm

Widespread resident except parts of NW and NE subcontinent, moving locally according to water conditions. **ID** Uniform dark upperparts and wings in all plumages. Male has blackish upperparts, with yellowish malar and sides of neck, and dark streaking on underparts. Female similar but browner upperparts and chestnut-streaked underparts. Juvenile similar but has distinct fringes to upperparts. **Voice** Territorial call a loud booming. **HH** Habits are those of a typical bittern, see Little. Chiefly nocturnal and crepuscular; skulks in dense swamps during the day Most often seen flying at dawn and dusk and in cloudy weather. Reedbeds and submerged bushes mixed with clumps of reeds or sedges. **TN** Often placed in *Dupetor*.

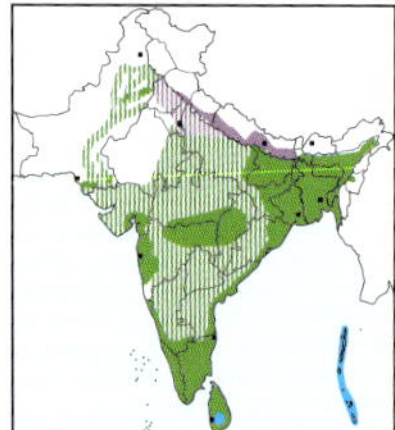

Cinnamon Bittern *Ixobrychus cinnamomeus* 40–41cm

Widespread resident except parts of NW subcontinent, moving locally according to water conditions. **ID** Uniform-looking cinnamon-rufous flight feathers and tail in all plumages. Male has cinnamon-rufous crown, hindneck and mantle/scapulars. Female has browner crown and mantle, and brown streaking on foreneck and breast. Juvenile has buff mottling on dark brown upperparts and is heavily streaked dark brown on underparts. **Voice** Territorial call a loud *kok-kok.* **HH** Habits very similar to Little. Often found in same locality and in same habitat as Yellow. Reedbeds in lakes, jheels and marshes, and flooded paddyfields.

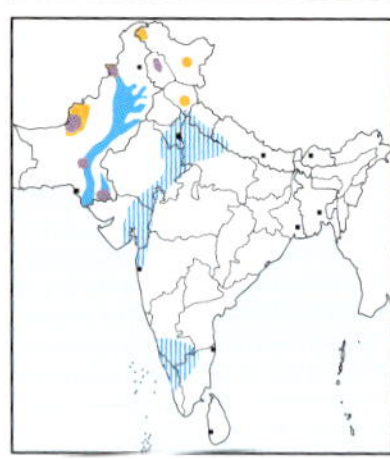

Little Bittern *Ixobrychus minutus* 27–38cm

Resident in Kashmir and Balochistan; recorded more widely in NW and S India and Pakistan. Subject to local movements. **ID** Buffish wing-coverts contrast with dark flight feathers in all plumages. Male has black crown and mantle/scapulars, and buff neck. Female has brown mantle/scapulars with pale edgings, and streaked underparts. Juvenile has streaked upperparts including wing-coverts, and brown streaking on underparts; very similar to juvenile Yellow but streaking on foreneck and breast of Yellow is generally more rufous-orange. Bill is shorter than Yellow's. **Voice** Territorial call a low-pitched, far-carrying and repeated *woof... woof... woof... woof*; flight call an abrupt *quer* or throaty *ker-ack.* **HH** Typical bittern habits. Solitary. Most active at dusk; usually spends day concealed in thick waterside vegetation but may be seen in the daytime in cloudy weather. Forages by creeping through dense vegetation or by standing and waiting at the edges of cover. If disturbed, often freezes with head and bill pointing vertically skywards. Tall reedbeds bordering jheels, lakes, marshes and streams.

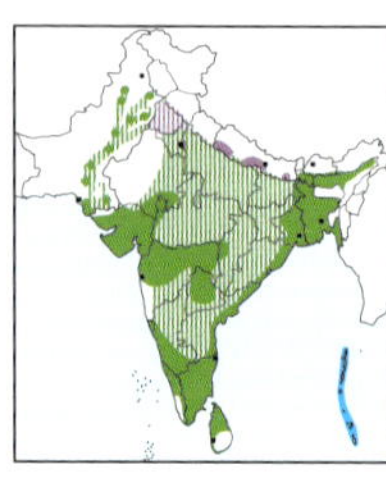

Yellow Bittern *Ixobrychus sinensis* 30–40cm

Widespread resident except parts of NW subcontinent. Moves locally according to water conditions. **ID** Yellowish-buff wing-coverts contrast with dark brown flight feathers. Male has pinkish-brown mantle/scapulars, and face and sides of neck are vinaceous. Female is like male, but has rufous streaking on black crown, variable rufous-orange streaking on foreneck and breast, and buff streaking to rufous-brown mantle and scapulars. Juvenile appears buff with bold dark streaking to upperparts including wing-coverts; foreneck and breast heavily streaked. **Voice** Territorial call a low-pitched *ou-ou.* **HH** Habits very similar to Little. Reedbeds and scrub in swamps, and flooded paddyfields.

Great Bittern
ad
♂
Black Bittern
juv
♂
♀
juv
Cinnamon Bittern
♂
♂
♂
Yellow Bittern
♀
juv
juv
Little Bittern

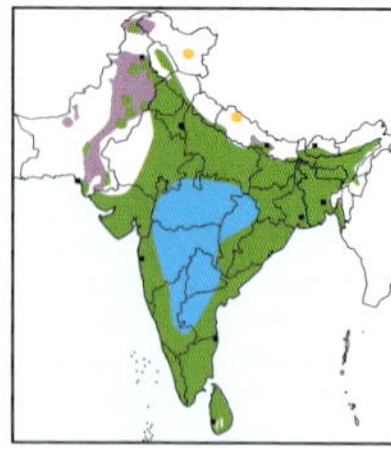

Black-crowned Night Heron *Nycticorax nycticorax* 58–66cm

Widespread resident; unrecorded in parts of NW and NE subcontinent. Moves locally according to water conditions. **ID** Stocky, with thick neck, stout yellowish bill and shortish yellowish legs. Adult has black crown and mantle contrasting with grey wings and whitish underparts. Juvenile has bold buffish spotting on upperparts and is heavily streaked on head and underparts. Immature has unstreaked brown crown and mantle and lightly streaked underparts. **Voice** A distinctive, deep and rather abrupt *wouck* in flight. **HH** Nocturnal and crepuscular except when feeding young. Usually spends day sitting hunched in a densely foliaged tree. Most often seen at dusk, flying singly or in small groups from its roost. Mainly forages singly, sometimes in a loose group. Feeds like a typical heron, see Indian Pond. Ponds, tanks, jheels, lakes, streams, mangroves, estuaries, tidal creeks and coastal lagoons.

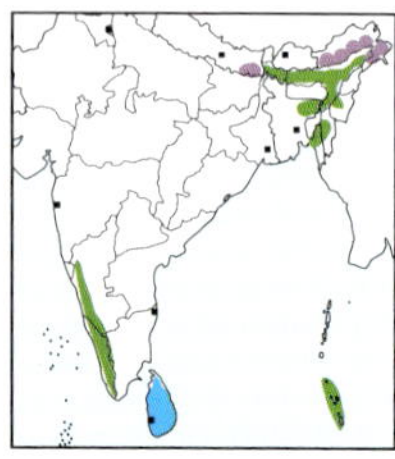

Malayan Night Heron *Gorsachius melanolophus* 45–49cm

Resident and partial migrant in Western Ghats, NE India, Nepal and Nicobars; winter visitor to Sri Lanka. **ID** Stocky, with stout bill and short neck. Adult has black crown and crest, rufous sides to head and neck, rufous-brown upperparts, and black streaking down throat onto breast and belly (more pronounced in female). Facial skin greenish or bluish becoming reddish in breeding condition. Juveniles vary from greyish (NE subcontinent) to rufous (peninsula), finely vermiculated with white, black and rufous-buff, and have bold white spotting on crown and crest. **Voice** A series of about ten deep *oo* notes c.1.5 seconds apart chiefly before dawn and after dusk. **HH** Shy and mainly nocturnal. Skulks in damp places in forest undergrowth during day. If flushed, flies off silently into a nearby densely foliaged tree. Streams and marshes in dense evergreen broadleaved forest.

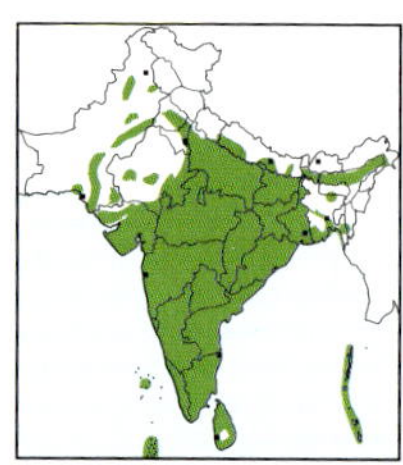

Striated Heron *Butorides striata* 35–48cm

Widespread resident; unrecorded in parts of NW and NE subcontinent. **ID** Small, stocky and short-legged heron. Adult has black crown and crest, black moustachial line, dark greenish upperparts with pale fringes, giving rise to streaked appearance, and greyish underparts. Juvenile has buff streaking and spotting on upperparts and dark-streaked underparts. Immature is like juvenile with uniform brown crown and mantle. **Voice** Usually silent but gives a *k-yow-k-yow* or *k-yek k-yek* call when flushed. **HH** Normally frequents same area day after day. Hunts alone in typical heron fashion, see Indian Pond. Often crepuscular. Activities of coastal birds are dependent on tidal cycle; sometimes active during the day, especially in overcast weather, but they usually keep to thick vegetation on banks of rivers and pools, and are often seen perched on branches overhanging water. Pools, lakes, streams and rivers with dense vegetation on banks; also mangrove swamps and creeks.

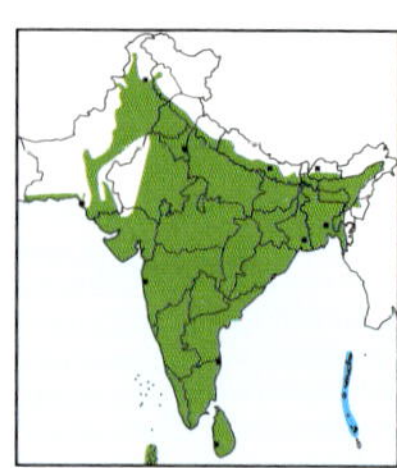

Indian Pond Heron *Ardeola grayii* 39–46cm

Widespread resident; unrecorded in parts of NW subcontinent. **ID** Whitish wings contrast with dark saddle. Adult breeding has yellowish-buff head and neck, with white nape plumes, and maroon-brown mantle/ scapulars. Facial skin and bill bluish and legs reddish in breeding condition. Head, neck and breast streaked/spotted in non-breeding plumage. Facial skin, bill and legs yellowish or greenish. **Voice** A high, harsh squawk when flushed. Birds at nest constantly utter a human-like *wa-koo*. **HH** Usually solitary when hunting, but will gather in large numbers at drying-out pools to feed on stranded fish. Hunts like a typical heron: stands motionless at water's edge, waiting for prey to swim within reach, or by slow stalking in shallow water or on land. Prey normally grasped and killed by battering; less often speared. Roosts communally. Tame and inconspicuous when perched but flies with a startling flash of white wings. Marshes, flooded paddyfields, lakes, village tanks, ditches, lakes, mangrove creeks and tidal mudflats.

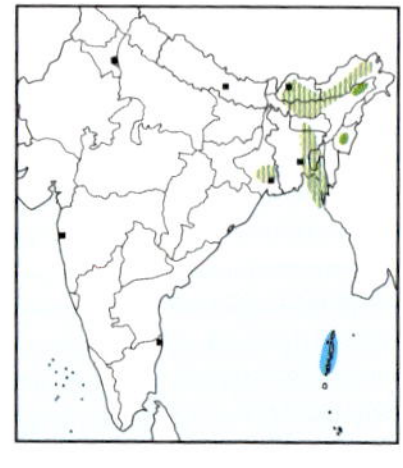

Chinese Pond Heron *Ardeola bacchus* 42–52cm

Resident and winter visitor? Mainly NE India and Andamans. Vagrant: Bhutan, Nepal, Sri Lanka. **ID** As Indian Pond Heron, has whitish wings that contrast with dark saddle. Slightly larger than latter with longer bill. In breeding plumage has maroon-chestnut head, nape plumes and neck, and slaty-black mantle/scapulars. Non-breeding and immature plumages probably not separable from those of Indian Pond. See Vagrants for differences from Javan Pond Heron. **Voice** A series of crooning notes. **HH** Habits very similar to Indian Pond. Marshes and all kinds of freshwater and tidal waters as Indian Pond.

ad
juv
Black-crowned
Night Heron
imm
ad
Malayan Night Heron
ad
imm
Striated Heron
non-br
br
Indian Pond Heron
br
non-br
br
Chinese Pond Heron

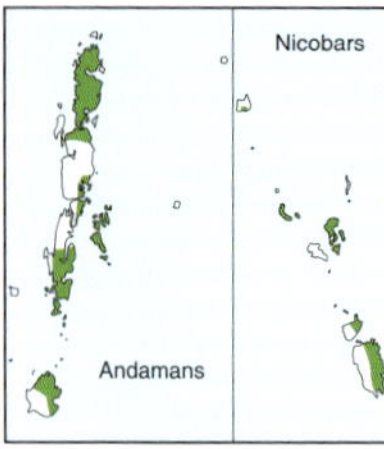

Pacific Reef Heron *Egretta sacra* 58–66cm

Resident. Andamans and Nicobars. Vagrant: Bangladesh. **ID** Legs shorter and stouter than Western Reef (with short leg/feet extension in flight), and is stockier, with shorter and thicker neck. Also, polymorphic; mainly white or slate grey, but can be paler grey or brownish grey in coloration. White throat of dark morph is less conspicuous than in Western Reef. In breeding plumage has short plumes on nape, forming bushy tuft, and plumes on breast and mantle. Juvenile white morph can have grey feathers in plumage. See Vagrants for differences from Chinese Egret. **Voice** Grunted *ork* when feeding and harsh *squak* when disturbed. **HH** Habits very like Western Reef. Rocky coasts, coral beds and sandy shores. **AN** Pacific Reef Egret.

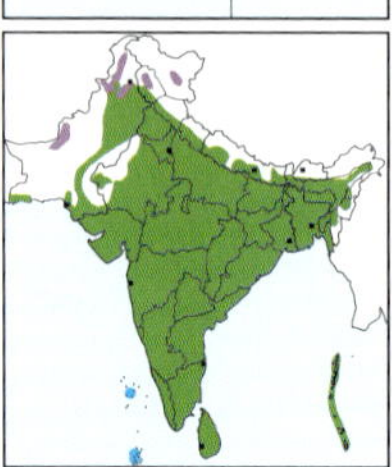

Little Egret *Egretta garzetta* 55–65cm

Widespread resident; unrecorded in parts of NW subcontinent. **ID** Has black bill, black legs with yellow feet, and greyish or yellowish lores. In breeding plumage has two elongated nape plumes, and mantle plumes; lores and feet become reddish during courtship. Bill in non-breeding and immature can be paler and pinkish or greyish at base, or dull yellowish on some. Grey morphs occur; bill shape and coloration best feature from Western Reef Heron. **Voice** Throaty squawk when disturbed and various guttural calls at colonies. **HH** More sociable than the two larger egrets; also found singly. Roosts communally. Lakes, rivers marshes, flooded paddyfields, also estuaries, tidal creeks and mangroves; prefers fresh waters.

Western Reef Heron *Egretta gularis* 55–65cm

Resident and nomadic. Mainly coasts, scattered records inland. **ID** Polymorphic; can be white, pale grey or slate-grey in coloration. Bill longer and stouter than Little Egret and usually appears very slightly downcurved; typically mainly yellowish or brownish-yellow, but may be black when breeding (thus very similar to Little). Legs also slightly shorter and thicker-looking; vary from black with yellow feet to mainly green. Juvenile white morph can have grey feathers in plumage. Juvenile dark morph is paler grey with whiter foreneck and underparts. **Voice** Throaty squawk when disturbed at nest. **HH** Diurnal and partly crepuscular. More active than other egrets when hunting, often running, jumping and turning rapidly. Seashores, estuaries, mangroves, and tidal creeks; occasionally at fresh waters. **AN** Western Reef Egret.

Eastern Cattle Egret *Bubulcus coromandus* 46–56cm

Widespread resident; unrecorded in parts of NW subcontinent. **ID** Small and stocky with short yellow bill and short dark legs. Has orange-buff on head, neck and mantle in breeding plumage; base of bill and legs become reddish in breeding condition. All white in non-breeding plumage. **Voice** A low croak when one bird supplants another, especially at breeding colony. **HH** Gregarious when feeding and roosting. Typically seen in flocks around domestic stock; also feeding on disturbed insects. Forages also in flooded fields. Unlike other egrets feeds mainly on insects. Damp grassland, paddyfields, grass banks of village tanks, canals, lakes and forest clearings; also, rubbish dumps (Sri Lanka). **TN** Formerly treated as conspecific with *B. ibis* as Cattle Egret (see Western Cattle Egret in Vagrants).

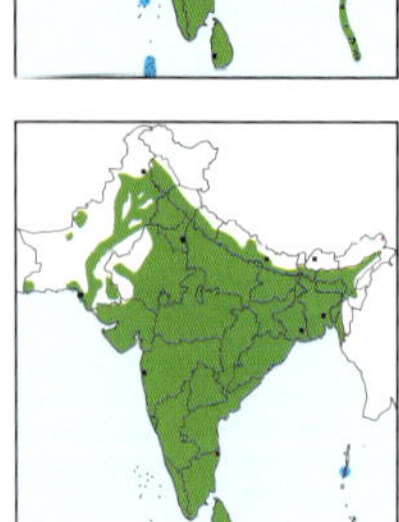

Great Egret *Ardea alba* 80–104cm

Widespread resident; unrecorded in parts of NW subcontinent. Vagrant: Bhutan. **ID** Compared with Medium, is larger and longer-billed, and looks thinner-necked with more angular and pronounced kink to neck. Black line of gape extends behind eye. Bill is black, lores blue and tibia reddish in breeding plumage, and has prominent plumes on mantle. Non-breeding and immature plumages lack plumes; legs are black, bill yellow and lores pale green. **Voice** Low *kraak*, also guttural calls and softer notes during display. **HH** Often solitary when hunting but will feed communally at concentrated food sources. Rivers, lakes, jheels, marshes, estuaries, mangroves and coral reefs. **TN** Formerly placed in *Casmerodius*.

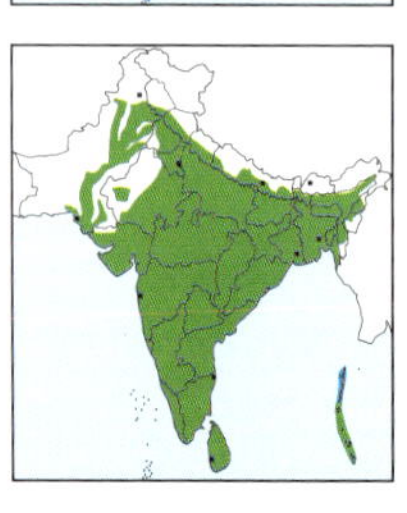

Medium Egret *Ardea intermedia* 65–72cm

Widespread resident; unrecorded in parts of NW subcontinent. **ID** Smaller than Great, with shorter bill and neck. Larger than Eastern Cattle, with longer neck and proportionately smaller head. Black gape-line does not extend beyond eye. Bill is black and lores yellow-green during courtship, and has pronounced plumes on breast and mantle. Lacks plumes and has black-tipped yellow bill (all yellow in Eastern Cattle) and yellow lores outside breeding season. **Voice** Distinctive buzzing calls during display. **HH** Hunts chiefly by slow stalking. Roosts communally. Marshes, flooded grassland, well-vegetated pools; also, open shores of jheels, lakes and reservoirs, mangrove swamps and tidal creeks. **TN** Formerly placed in *Mesophoyx*. **AN** Intermediate Egret.

Pacific Reef Egret
dark morph
non-br
dark morph
juv
white morph
br
non-br
br
non-br
Little Egret
Western Reef Heron
dark morph
non-br
intermediate
morph
white
morph
br
non-br
br
Eastern Cattle Egret
non-br
br
br
Great Egret
non-br
non-br
br
Medium Egret

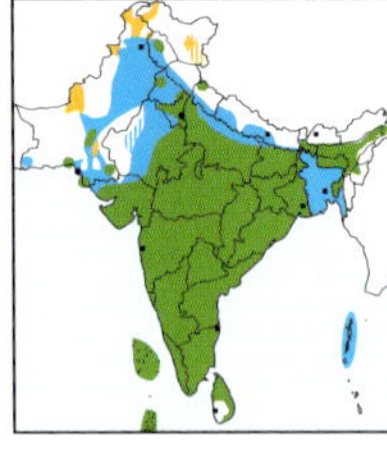

Grey Heron *Ardea cinerea* 90–98cm

Resident, passage migrant and winter visitor. Widespread; unrecorded in parts of the north-west and north-east. **ID** A large, mainly grey heron, lacking any brown or rufous in its plumage. In flight, black flight feathers contrast with grey upperwing- and underwing-coverts, and shows a prominent white leading edge to wing when head-on. Adult has yellow bill, whitish head and neck with black head plumes, and black patches on belly. In breeding season, has whitish scapular plumes and bill and legs become orange or reddish. Immature is duller than adult, with grey crown, reduced black 'crest', greyer neck, less pronounced black patches on sides of belly, and duller bill and legs. Juvenile has dark grey cap with slight crest, dirty grey neck and breast, lacks black patches on belly-sides, lacks plumes, and has dark legs. **Voice** Often calls in flight, a loud *frarnk*. **HH** Forages like a typical heron, see Indian Pond. Usually feeds singly; occasionally gathers in loose parties at good feeding areas. Roosts communally in winter. Prefers to hunt in the open unlike Purple Heron. Perches freely in trees. Inland and coastal waters: lakes, marshes, estuaries, mangroves, tidal creeks, rocky offshore islands and coral reefs.

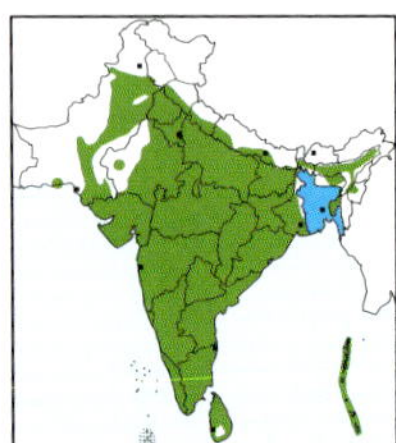

Purple Heron *Ardea purpurea* 78–90cm

Resident and local migrant throughout lowlands in much of subcontinent except parts of north-east and north-west; possibly also a winter visitor. Vagrant: Bhutan? **ID** Rakish, with long, thin neck. In flight, compared to Grey Heron, bulge of recoiled neck is very pronounced, protruding feet large, underwing-coverts purplish (adult) or buff (juvenile) and lacks white leading edge to wing. Adult has chestnut head and neck with black stripes, grey mantle and upperwing-coverts, and dark chestnut belly and underwing-coverts. Juvenile has black crown, buffish neck, and brownish mantle and upperwing-coverts with rufous-buff fringes. **Voice** Flight call like Grey's, but higher-pitched and not so loud *frarnk*. **HH** Active in early mornings and evenings; sometimes also feeds by day. Shyer than Grey, normally feeding out of sight among dense aquatic vegetation. Most often seen in flight. Hunts alone, usually by standing motionless and waiting; less often by slow stalking in shallow water. Inland waters (lakes, jheels, rivers and marshes) with plenty of tall cover, especially *Phragmites* reeds and *Typha* bulrushes.

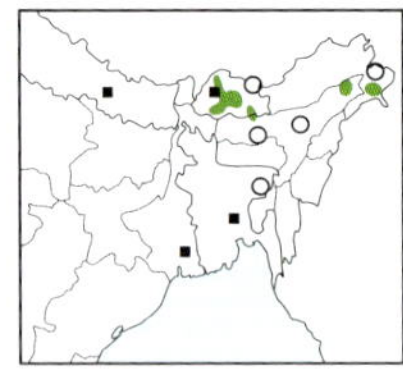

White-bellied Heron *Ardea insignis* 127cm

Sedentary resident. E Himalayan foothills. Vagrant: Bangladesh. **ID** Large size, very long neck (much longer than shown on Plate), huge dark bill, and large dark legs and feet. Grey head with white throat, and white-striped grey foreneck and breast contrasting with white belly. In flight, has uniform dark grey upperwing, and white underwing-coverts contrasting with dark grey flight feathers. In breeding plumage, has greyish-white nape plumes, grey back plumes, and white-striped breast plumes; lores and orbital skin are yellowish-green. Juvenile has browner upperparts and streaked appearance to upperparts. **Voice** A loud, very donkey-like croaking bray, *ock, ock, ock, ock, urrrrr*. **HH** Shy. Singly or in pairs. Hunting methods are like those of other diurnal herons, see Indian Pond. Rivers, marshes and lakes in tropical and subtropical forest. Globally threatened.

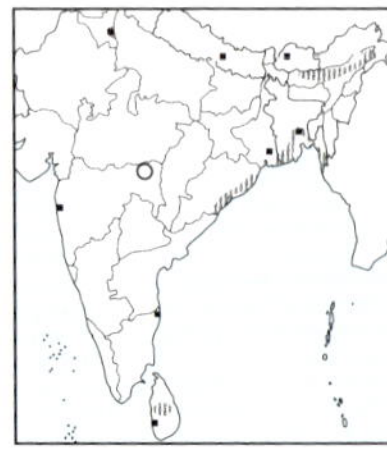

Goliath Heron *Ardea goliath* 135–150cm

Visitor or resident? Mainly NE India. Vagrant: Bangladesh, Sri Lanka. **ID** Recalls giant Purple Heron; in all plumages, distinguished from latter by much larger size, thicker head and neck, huge and heavy bill, and dark legs and feet. Adult has rufous head and neck (lacking black head stripes of Purple), dark bill and lores (lores and much of bill yellow in Purple), grey upperparts, broken blackish stripes on foreneck, and deep purplish-chestnut underparts and underwing-coverts. Juvenile has white foreneck and underparts streaked black, buffish thighs and vent, rufous fringes to feathers of mantle and upperwing-coverts, grey flanks and underwing-coverts. Lores and base to lower mandible yellowish. **Voice** Flight call has been described as a gargling rattle or the bellowing of a calf. **HH** Diurnal, solitary and shy. Forages like a typical heron, see Indian Pond. Usually hunts in shallow water but can wade well away from the shore; sometimes feeds from grass bunds. Rivers, marshes, salt lakes, estuaries and mangroves.

ad
ad
imm
Grey Heron
ad
juv
juv
Purple Heron
ad
juv
White-bellied Heron
ad
Goliath Heron

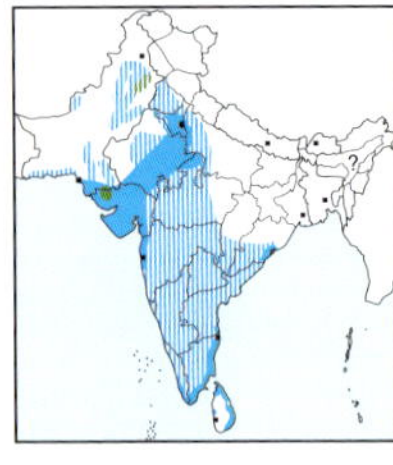

Greater Flamingo *Phoenicopterus roseus* 120–125cm

Resident and winter visitor. Breeds in Gujarat; widespread visitor to plains except parts of NW and NE subcontinent and E India. Vagrant: Nepal, Bangladesh. **ID** Larger than Lesser, with longer, thinner neck and longer legs. Bill larger and less prominently kinked. Adult from adult Lesser by paler pink bill with prominent dark tip, and pink facial skin. Has pinkish-white head, neck and body, although Lesser can be similar. Comparatively uniform crimson-pink upperwing-coverts contrast in flight with paler, whitish body. Immature has greyish-white head, neck and body; brown-streaked coverts, bill grey tipped black, and legs grey (pinker with age). Juvenile has brownish head, neck and body, with heavy brown streaking to upperparts. **Voice** Flocks utter a goose-like *ka-ka* or *a-ha*. **HH** Walks or swims in very shallow water, while sweeping head and neck to and fro, with bill inverted, sieving micro-organisms. Shallow brackish lakes, mudflats, saltpans.

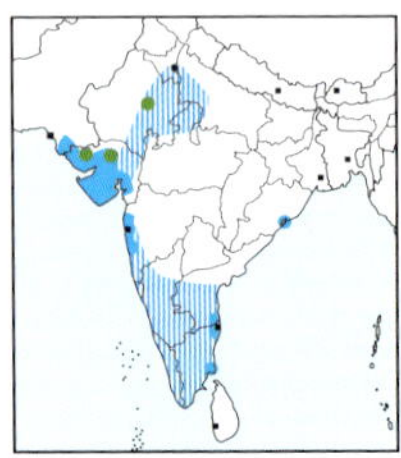

Lesser Flamingo *Phoeniconaias minor* 80–90cm

Breeds in Gujarat; widespread in Indian and Pakistan plains in non-breeding season. **ID** Smaller than Greater; neck and legs appear shorter, and bill is smaller and more prominently kinked. Adult from adult Greater by black-tipped dark red bill (can appear all dark) and dark red facial skin. Coloration of head, neck and body is deeper rose-pink than Greater, although can be as white as Greater. Also shows more restricted area of darker pink on upperwing than Greater, although extent variable in both species. Immature and juvenile like Greater, but bill is darker in Lesser. **Voice** Goose-like honking lower-pitched than Greater Flamingo. **HH** Feeds like Greater. Salt and brackish lagoons, saltpans. **TN** Often placed in *Phoenicopterus*.

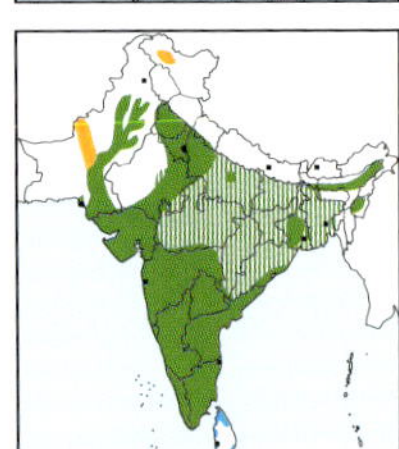

Glossy Ibis *Plegadis falcinellus* 48–66cm

Resident and winter visitor. Mainly W and S subcontinent. Vagrant: Nepal. **ID** Small, dark ibis with fine downcurved bill. Graceful in flight, with extended slender neck, bulbous head, and legs and feet projecting well beyond tail. Adult breeding deep chestnut, glossed purple and green; narrow white surround to bare lores. Adult non-breeding duller, with white streaking on dark brown head and neck, and no white surround to lores. Juvenile like adult non-breeding, but is dark brown with white mottling on head, and only faint greenish gloss to upperparts. **Voice** Normally silent; bleating or croaking noises at nest. **HH** Walks in shallow water or wades belly-deep while probing rapidly into water and mud. Freshwater marshes and large lakes, flooded grassland, paddyfields.

Black-headed Ibis *Threskiornis melanocephalus* 65–76cm

Resident and nomadic; widespread, unrecorded in parts of NE India and NW subcontinent. **ID** Stocky, mainly white ibis with stout downcurved black bill. Adult breeding has naked black head, white lower-neck plumes, patchy and variable faint yellow wash to plumage (e.g. mantle, breast, underwing-coverts and tail), grey scapulars and elongated tertials, with whispery grey plumes. In flight, shows stripe of bare red skin on underside of white forewing and on flanks. Adult non-breeding has all-white body and lacks plumes. Immature has grey feathering on head and neck, and black-tipped wings. **Voice** At nest makes series of grunts; normally silent away it. **HH** Habits like Glossy. Freshwater marshes, tanks, lakes, rivers, flooded grassland, paddyfields, tidal creeks, mudflats, saltmarshes, coastal lagoons.

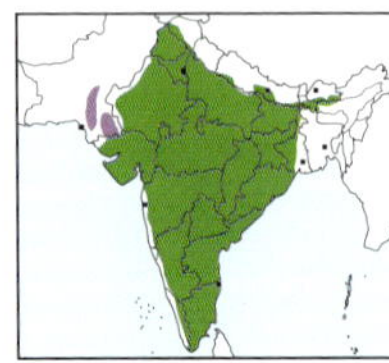

Red-naped Ibis *Pseudibis papillosa* 60–68cm

Widespread resident; absent from parts of NE and NW subcontinent. **ID** Stocky, dark ibis with stout downcurved bill. White shoulder patch and reddish legs. Appears bulky and broad-winged in flight, with only the feet extending beyond tail. Adult has naked black head with red nape, and is dark brown with green-and-purple gloss. Immature dark brown, including feathered head. **HH** Habits like Glossy. Dry grassland, fallow fields, edges of lakes and marshes; near rubbish dumps.

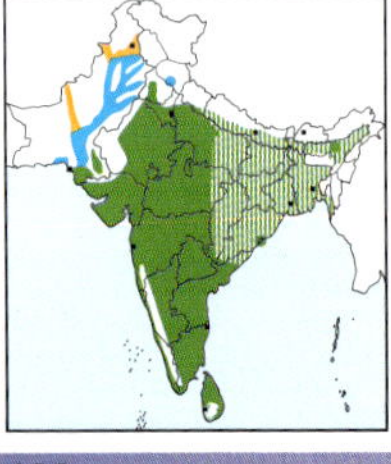

Eurasian Spoonbill *Platalea leucorodia* 70–95cm

Partly resident and nomadic, partly winter visitor. Widespread; unrecorded in parts of India and NW subcontinent. Vagrant: Bhutan. **ID** White, with spatulate-tipped bill. In flight, neck is outstretched, and flapping is stiff and interspersed with gliding. Adult has black bill with yellow tip; has crest and yellow breast-patch when breeding. Juvenile has pink bill; in flight, shows black tips to primaries. **Voice** Usually silent; occasional short grunts and bill clattering at nest. **HH** Wades in shallow water, making side-to-side sweeps of bill, sifting prey. Larger lakes, lagoons, rivers and marshes; also, tidal creeks, mangroves.

imm
ad
juv
ad
ad
Greater Flamingo
juv
ad
imm
Lesser Flamingo
juv
imm
br
non-br
ad
Black-headed Ibis
Glossy Ibis
ad
juv
br
Eurasian Spoonbill
Red-naped Ibis

PLATE 77: OSPREY, BAZAS AND EGYPTIAN VULTURE

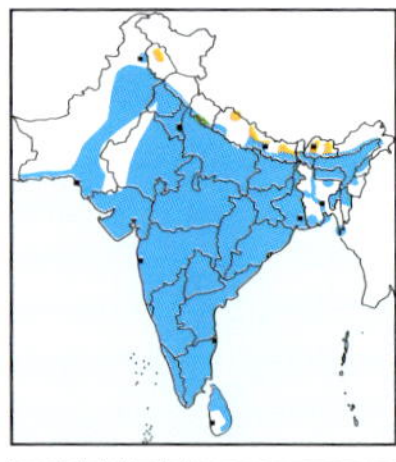

Osprey *Pandion haliaetus* 55–58cm

Widespread in winter except parts of NW and NE subcontinent.. **ID** Long wings, typically angled down at carpals, and short tail. Whitish head with black stripe through eye, white underparts and underwing-coverts, and black carpal patches. Adult has uniform brown upperparts. Juvenile has pale fringes to upperparts, including wing-coverts, with a narrow wing-bar on greater coverts. **Voice** Call is a shrill cheeping whistle, but mostly silent away from nest. **HH** Frequently perches on stakes, dead trees or prominent rocks in or near water. Captures fish in a powerful shallow dive feet first. Major rivers, lakes, jheels, large reservoirs, coastal lagoons and estuaries.

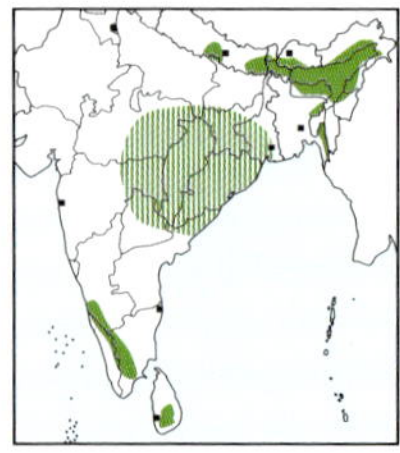

Jerdon's Baza *Aviceda jerdoni* 41–48cm

Resident. E Himalayas, hills of peninsular India, Bangladesh and Sri Lanka. **ID** Long and erect, white-tipped crest. Broad wings (pinched-in at base) and fairly long tail. Indistinct gular stripe, rufous-barred underparts and underwing-coverts, and bold barring on primary tips. At rest, closed wings extend well down tail. Male has greyish head and yellow eye. Female has pale rufous head, dark eye, and less prominent barring on underparts than male. Juvenile has dark streaking on head and breast, and narrower dark barring on tail. **Voice** Display flights accompanied by loud sharp *kip-kip-kip*... or *kikiya, kikiya* calls, rising in pitch and volume before dying away; also, a plaintive mewing *pee-ow*. **HH** Crepuscular and elusive, keeping mostly within cover. Sluggish and slow on the wing. Spends long periods perched on a tree looking for prey which is captured on ground. Tropical and subtropical broadleaved evergreen forest.

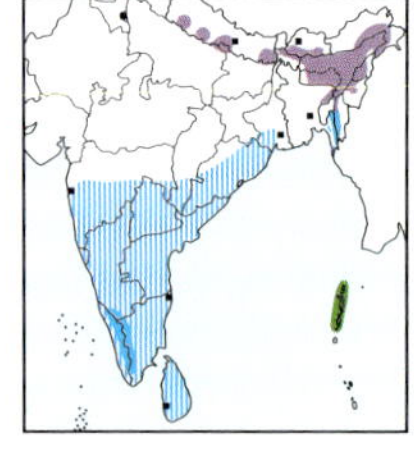

Black Baza *Aviceda leuphotes* 28–35cm

Summer visitor. Himalayan foothills, NE India and Bangladesh. Winter visitor to S and SE India, and Sri Lanka. **ID** Largely black, with long crest, white breast-band, rufous-barred underparts, and greyish underside to primaries contrasting with black underwing-coverts. Wings are broad and rounded, and tail of medium length. Flight corvid-like, interspersed by short glides on flat wings. Male has more extensive patch of white on upperwing (extending to secondaries) compared with female. **Voice** Quavering whistle recalling Black Kite, a shrill gull-like mewing and a weak scream all recorded when perched and in flight. Calls all year not just in breeding season. **HH** Rather crepuscular. Groups of up to five may be seen circling over forest, sometimes larger flocks. Captures prey on ground after short flights; flies to a nearby perch to eat it. Tropical broadleaved evergreen forest with glades or broad streams.

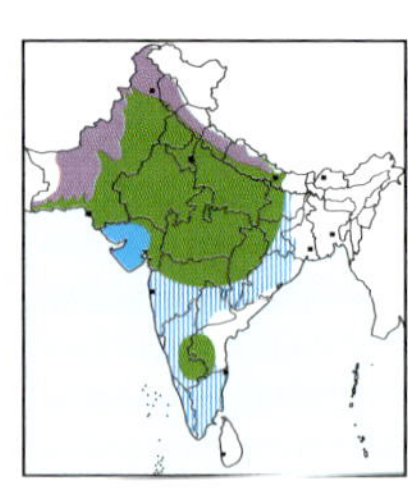

Egyptian Vulture *Neophron percnopterus* 54–70cm

Resident. Widespread in Pakistan, Nepal and India, except the north-east. Vagrant: Bhutan, Bangladesh, Sri Lanka. **ID** Small vulture with long, pointed wings, small pointed head, and wedge-shaped tail. Adult mainly dirty white, with bare yellowish face and black flight feathers. Juvenile blackish-brown with bare grey face; upperparts have variable pale tips to feathers, becoming more uniform with wear. With maturity, tail, body and wing-coverts become whiter and face yellower. **Voice** Rarely heard, but gives various low whistles, groans, grunts, mewing notes, hisses and rattling noises; also, thin whistles in display. **HH** A scavenger closely associated with human habitation. Spends the day soaring and gliding in search of food and perched around villages and rubbish dumps. Gathers at carcasses with other larger vultures. Towns, villages and city outskirts, especially around rubbish dumps and slaughterhouses. Globally threatened.

ad
Osprey
♂
♀
♀
juv
ad
ad
juv
Jerdon’s Baza
ad
Black Baza
juv
ad
imm
Egyptian Vulture
ad
imm

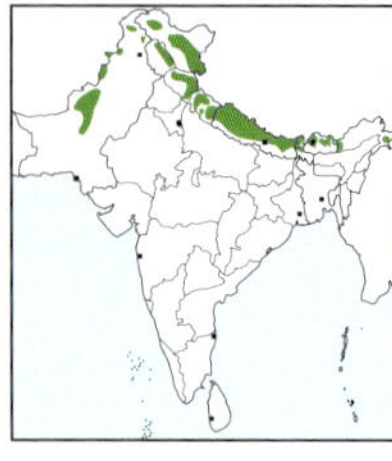

Bearded Vulture *Gypaetus barbatus* 94–125cm

Resident. Pakistan and Himalayas. **ID** Huge size, long and narrow pointed wings, and large wedge-shaped tail. Adult has pale head with black mask and beard, greyish-black upperparts, wings and tail, and cream or rufous-orange underparts contrasting with black underwing-coverts. Juvenile and immature have blackish head and neck and grey-brown underparts; tail is less angular and wings broader resulting in less distinctive profile. Soars and glides on flat wings with slightly bowed primaries. **Voice** Mostly silent. During displays gives shrill whistle and twittering, falcon-like *cheek-echeek-echeek*. **HH** Spends prolonged periods soaring majestically and gracefully over mountainsides. Highly manoeuvrable in flight; rarely flaps wings, and often glides close to the ground, following the curve of mountain slopes. Has unique habit of splitting bones by dropping them onto rock slabs. Mountains. **AN** Lammergeier.

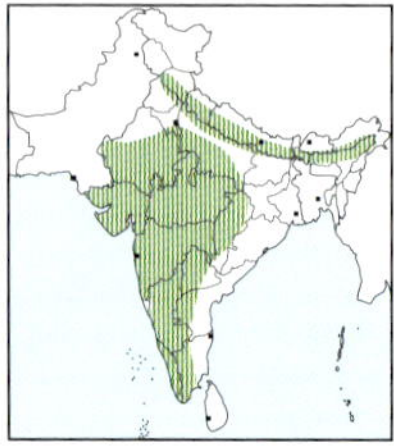

Red-headed Vulture *Sarcogyps calvus* 76–86cm

Resident. Mainly Nepal and India. No recent records from Bhutan. Vagrant: Pakistan. **ID** Comparatively slim and pointed wings. Adult mainly black with bare reddish head and cere, white patches at base of neck and upper thighs, and reddish legs and feet; in flight, greyish-white bases to secondaries show as broad panel (particularly on underwing). Juvenile is browner with white down on head; pinkish coloration to head and feet, white patch on upper thighs, and whitish undertail-coverts are best features. **Voice** Mostly silent, gives hoarse croak, becoming a scream in disputes at carcasses, and a raucous roaring note during courtship and copulation. **HH** Usually singly or in pairs. Frequently feeds on carcasses of small animals that are overlooked by other large vultures; also, feeds timidly with other vultures at carcasses of larger animals. Open country near habitation, and well-wooded hills. Globally threatened.

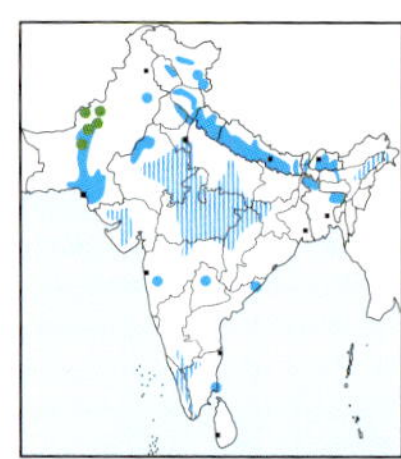

Cinereous Vulture *Aegypius monachus* 102–112cm

Breeds in Pakistan; winters mainly in Pakistan and Himalayas. Vagrant: Bhutan. **ID** Very large vulture with broad, parallel-edged wings. Soars on flat wings (*Gyps* vultures soar with wings held in shallow V). At distance appears typically uniformly dark, except pale areas on head and bill. Adult blackish-brown with paler brown ruff; may show paler band on greater underwing-coverts, but underwing darker and more uniform than *Gyps* species. Juvenile is blacker and more uniform than adult. **Voice** Usually silent. Calls include grunts, croaks and hisses when feeding at carcasses, and during breeding season also querulous mewing and hissing. **HH** Normally solitary by day. Usually roosts communally on ground, often on an open escarpment, close to a steep slope in readiness for suitable thermals. Dominates all other vultures at carcasses. Breeds in mountains; forages in wide range of habitats, including bare mountains, semi-desert, along river courses and savanna grasslands.

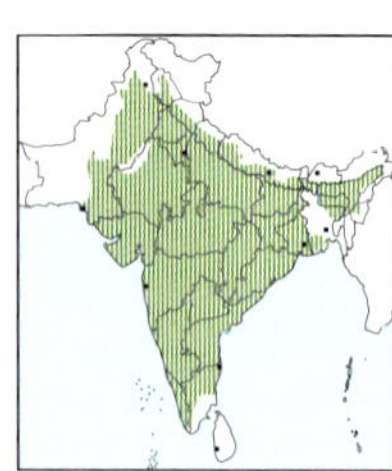

White-rumped Vulture *Gyps bengalensis* 76–93cm

Widespread resident; unrecorded in Sri Lanka. **ID** Smallest of the *Gyps* vultures. Adult mainly blackish, with white neck ruff, white rump and back, greyish panel on secondaries on upperwing, and white underwing-coverts. Juvenile dark brown with streaking on underparts and upperwing-coverts, dark rump and back, whitish down on head and neck, and all-dark bill (grey in adult). In flight, underparts and underwing-coverts of juvenile darker than Indian or Slender-billed, and lacks white on thighs and undertail-coverts of juvenile Red-headed. Juvenile similar in colour to juvenile Himalayan, but smaller and less heavily built, with narrower wings and shorter tail; underparts less heavily streaked, and lacks prominent streaking on mantle and scapulars. **Voice** Croaks, grunts, hisses, squeals at carcasses, nests and roosts. **HH** Cities, towns and villages. Globally threatened.

ad
ad
juv
juv
Bearded Vulture
ad
imm
ad
imm
ad
imm
Red-headed Vulture
juv
ad
ad
Cinereous Vulture
juv
ad
ad
juv
ad
juv
White-rumped Vulture

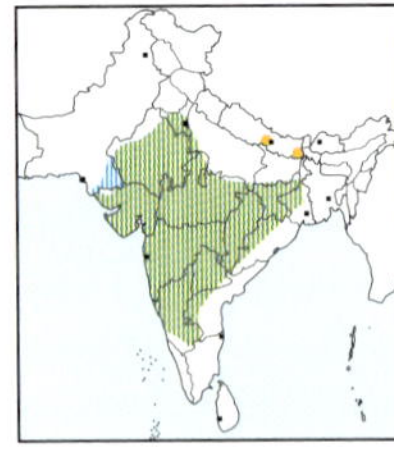

Indian Vulture *Gyps indicus* 83–91cm

Resident. SE Pakistan, through hills of India east to West Bengal and south to Kerala. Uncommon visitor: Nepal. **ID** Key features of adult are sandy-brown body and upperwing-coverts (Eurasian Griffon is more rufescent), blackish head and neck with sparse white down on hindneck (Eurasian Griffon has more extensive covering of white down), white downy ruff, and yellowish bill, and lacks pale streaking on underparts. In flight, lacks broad whitish band on median underwing-coverts of Eurasian Griffon, and has whiter rump and back. See Slender-billed for differences from that species. Much smaller and less heavily built than Himalayan, with darker head and neck, white ruff, and dark legs and feet. Juvenile has feathery buff neck ruff, dark bill and cere with pale culmen, and head and neck have whitish down; distinguished from juvenile Eurasian Griffon by pale culmen, darker brown upperparts with more pronounced pale streaking, and paler and less rufescent coloration to streaked underparts. Best features to distinguish juvenile Indian from juvenile White-rumped are paler and less clearly streaked underparts, paler upper- and underwing-coverts, and whitish rump and back. **Voice** Cackling, grunting and hissing sounds at carcasses. **HH** Cities, towns and villages. Globally threatened.

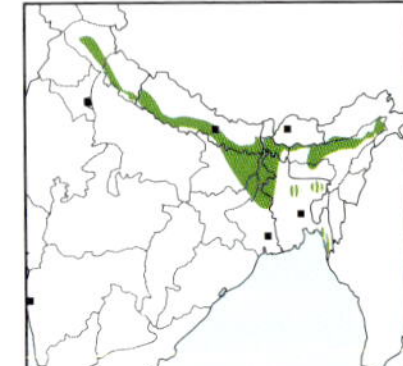

Slender-billed Vulture *Gyps tenuirostris* 77–103cm

Resident. Lower Himalayas from NW India east through Nepal; NE India and Ganges delta. **ID** Bill, head and neck are slenderer than in Indian, with angular crown (and prominent ear canals). Darker and colder brown than Indian, and body appears slenderer, with prominent white thigh patches (especially obvious in flight). In flight, trailing edges to wings appear rounded and pinched-in at the body, and outer primaries appear noticeably longer than the inner primaries. Underside of flight feathers uniformly dark (these have a pale cast and dark tips in Indian). Undertail-coverts appear dark (pale in Indian) and in flight the feet reach the tip of tail (falling short in Indian). Adult has dark bill and cere with pale culmen, lacks any down on head and neck, has dirty white ruff that is small and ragged, and dark claws (yellowish in Indian). Juvenile has mainly dark bill, some white down on head and neck, and pale streaking on underparts. **Voice** Like Indian. **HH** Cities, towns and villages. Globally threatened.

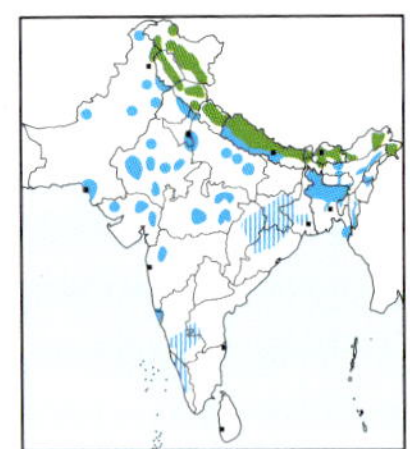

Himalayan Griffon *Gyps himalayensis* 103–110cm

Resident in Himalayas; winters south to N India plains and SW India. **ID** Larger than Eurasian Griffon, with broader body and slightly longer tail. Wing-coverts and body pale buffish, contrasting strongly with dark flight feathers and tail, and ruff is buffish. Underparts lack pronounced streaking. Legs and feet pinkish with dark claws, and has yellowish bill and pale blue cere and facial skin (blackish in Eurasian). Juvenile has brown-feathered ruff, with bill and cere initially black, dark brown body and upperwing-coverts boldly and prominently streaked with buff (wing-coverts almost concolorous with flight feathers), and back and rump also dark brown. Streaked upperparts and underparts and pronounced white bands on underwing-coverts are best distinctions of juvenile from Cinereous Vulture, very similar in plumage to juvenile White-rumped, but much larger and more heavily built, with broader wings and longer tail, underparts more heavily streaked, and streaking on mantle and scapulars. **Voice** Varied grunts and hisses. **HH** Breeds in mountains; winters to the plains. **AN** Himalayan Vulture.

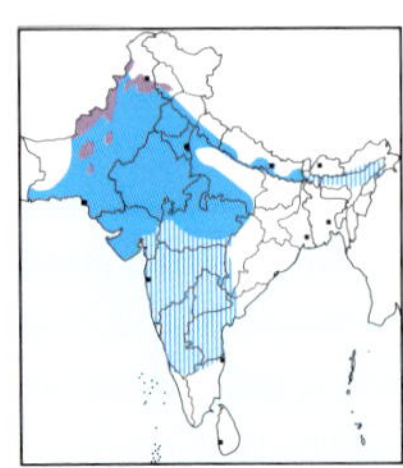

Eurasian Griffon *Gyps fulvus* 106–120cm

Widespread winter visitor and passage migrant, except parts of NE subcontinent and N, S and E India. Vagrant: Bangladesh. **ID** Larger than Indian, with stouter bill. Key features of adult are yellowish bill with blackish cere, whitish head and neck, fluffy white ruff, rufescent-buff upperparts, rufous-brown underparts and thighs with prominent pale streaking, and dark grey legs and feet. Rufous-brown underwing-coverts usually show prominent whitish bands, especially on median coverts (see Indian and Himalayan for comparison). Immature is richer rufous-brown on upperparts and upperwing-coverts (with prominent pale streaking) than adult; has rufous-brown feathered ruff, more whitish down covering grey head and neck, blackish bill, and dark iris (pale yellowish-brown in adult). **Voice** Hisses, grunts and bellowing notes at carcasses. **HH** Semi-desert, dry open plains and hills. **AN** Griffon Vulture.

ad
Indian Vulture
juv
ad
ad
juv
ad
ad
juv
Slender-billed Vulture
ad
juv
juv
ad
Himalayan Griffon
ad
juv
ad
juv
Eurasian Griffon
juv
ad
ad
juv

PLATE 80: SERPENT EAGLES, SHORT-TOED SNAKE AND BLACK EAGLES

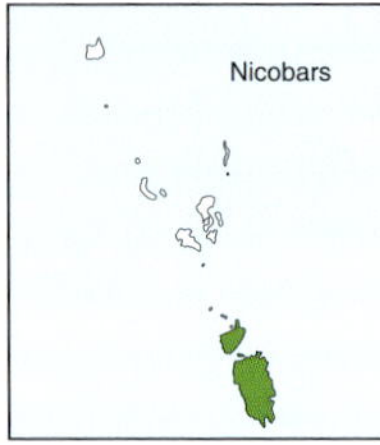

Nicobar Serpent Eagle *Spilornis klossi* 38–42cm

Great Nicobar; reported from Little Nicobar and Menchal. **ID** Very small. Cinnamon scaling to black crown and crest, grey sides of head with dark grey malar, whitish throat with black mesial stripe, and cinnamon collar and underparts (latter without barring or spotting); undertail is more narrowly banded with black than on other serpent eagles. Very small size, dark throat-stripe, and unmarked cinnamon underparts (lacking any spotting on lower underparts) are best distinctions from undescribed subspecies of Crested that is also present on Great Nicobar. Juvenile has buff tips to crown and upperparts; underwing and undertail lack broad black banding. **Voice** Undescribed. **HH** Mixed evergreen forest, mostly in canopy; also in grassland and regenerating habitats. **AN** Great Nicobar Serpent Eagle.

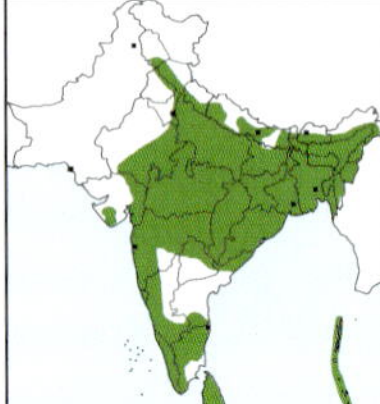

Crested Serpent Eagle *Spilornis cheela* 50–74cm

Widespread resident; unrecorded in most of NW subcontinent and parts of SE India. Vagrant: Pakistan. **ID** Broad, rounded wings. Soars with wings held forward in pronounced V. At rest has black-and-white crest, yellow cere and lores, and unfeathered yellow legs. Adult has broad white bands on wings and tail and white spotting and barring on brown underparts. Juvenile has blackish ear-coverts, whitish head and underparts, narrower barring on tail (than adult), and largely white underwing with fine dark barring and dark trailing edge. Birds of peninsular India *S. c. melanotis*, and especially Sri Lanka *S. c. spilogaster*, are smaller than the northern nominate; adults have unbarred breast and a pale brown band at base of tail. *S. c. davisoni*, of Andamans, and an undescribed subspecies on South Nicobar islands (sympatric with *S. klossi*), have paler underparts and underwing-coverts, narrower banding on underside of wings and two white bands on underside of tail. In the central Nicobars *S. c. minimus* (only *Spilornis* present) is smaller than *davisoni*, with paler underparts and underwing-coverts; has larger spots on lower underparts and almost unmarked underwing-coverts. **Voice** Variety of loud, ringing, musical whistles or screams in flight. **HH** Characteristic habit of soaring over forest in pairs, screaming to each other. Forest and well-wooded country in quite high rainfall areas. **TN** *S. c. minimus* is sometimes recognised as a separate species Central Nicobar Serpent Eagle *S. minimus*.

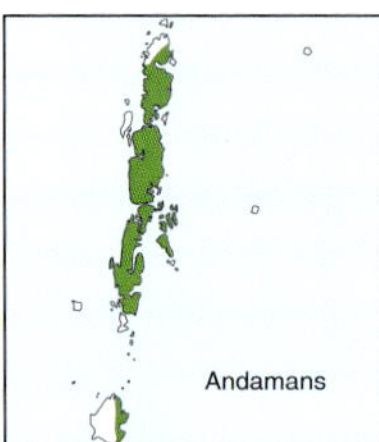

Andaman Serpent Eagle *Spilornis elgini* 51–59cm

Resident. Andaman Islands. **ID** Slightly smaller and much darker than *davisoni* subspecies of Crested which occurs on Andamans. Adult has dark brown underparts and underwing-coverts with white spotting, narrow greyish-white barring on underside of remiges, and two narrow greyish-white bands on undertail. Juvenile paler brown, with white fringes to feathers of crown and nape, dark ear-covert patch, and more prominent banding on underside of wings and tail. **Voice** Clear whistles. **HH** Forest; also open hillsides with scattered trees. Crested and Andaman Serpent Eagles both occur and even display near each other, but Andaman is more common inland. Globally threatened.

Short-toed Snake Eagle *Circaetus gallicus* 62–70cm

Resident and winter visitor. Pakistan, S Nepal and India. Vagrant: Bhutan, Bangladesh. **ID** Long and broad wings, pinched-in at base, and long tail. Head broad and rounded. Soars with wings flat or slightly raised; frequently hovers. When perched, appears big-headed, with wingtips reaching tail end, and shows long unfeathered tarsus. Plumage variable, often with dark head and breast, barred underparts, dark trailing edge to underwing, and broad subterminal tail-band; can be very pale on head, underparts and underwing. In all plumages, pale brown inner wing-coverts contrast with dark greater coverts and flight feathers above. Underwing and undertail are finely barred and lacks dark carpal patch. Juvenile similar in plumage to adult. **Voice** In breeding season gives clear whistled *kyo-kyo-kyo* and plaintive *mee-ok*. **HH** Open country, cultivation, semi-desert and dry, stony scrub-covered hills.

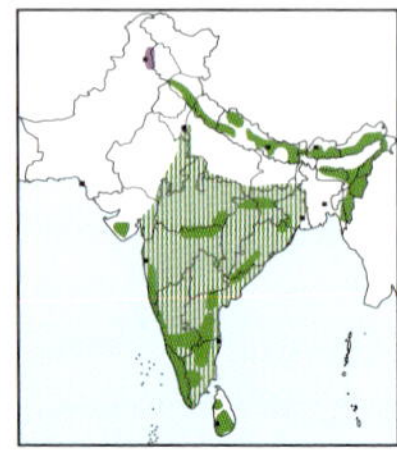

Black Eagle *Ictinaetus malaiensis* 65–80cm

Resident. Himalayas, hills of India, Bangladesh and Sri Lanka. **ID** Distinctive wing shape and long tail. Flies with wings raised in V, with primaries upturned. At rest, long wings extend to tip of tail. Adult brownish-black, with striking yellow cere and feet; in flight, shows whitish barring on uppertail-coverts, and faint greyish barring on tail and underside of remiges (cf. dark morph of Changeable Hawk Eagle, Plate 46). Juvenile as adult; may show indistinct pale streaking to head and underparts. **Voice** Silent, except in breeding season. A repeated, hoarse-sounding, piercing whistle *kheeee kheeee kheeee* during aerial displays; a repeated plaintive *keee-keeeuw*, or *hee-lee-leeuw*, perched or in flight. **HH** Hill and mountain forests; also, mangroves in Bangladesh. **TN** Specific name previously spelt *malayensis*.

ad
Nicobar
Serpent Eagle
juv
minimus
juv
minimus
ad
minimus
Crested
Serpent Eagle
juv
cheela
ad
cheela
juv
cheela
ad
davisoni
soaring
Andaman
Serpent Eagle
juv
ad
ad
juv
ad pale
Short-toed
Snake Eagle
ad dark
ad pale
gliding
soaring
soaring
Black Eagle
ad

PLATE 81: HAWK EAGLES AND RUFOUS-BELLIED EAGLE

Legge's Hawk Eagle *Nisaetus kelaarti* 66–84cm

Resident. SW India and Sri Lanka. **ID** Compared to Mountain Hawk Eagle, has paler crown and streaked ear-coverts, rufous coloration to sides of neck and breast, restricted breast streaking, and barring on underparts is more rufous-brown (but can appear quite similar); underwing-coverts are rufous and lightly marked, and median throat-stripe is finer or almost lacking. Pattern of underparts (largely barred rather than streaked) and comparatively unmarked underwing-coverts help separate from Changeable. Juvenile has variable diffuse rufous-brown bands on underparts (unmarked or with sparse streaking in juvenile Changeable). **Voice** Moderately loud, ringing slightly descending *qui-li-li-lil*; immature call a far-carrying sharp *kik-kik-keeye*, repeated. **HH** Forested areas. **TN** Previously treated as conspecific with Mountain Hawk Eagle.

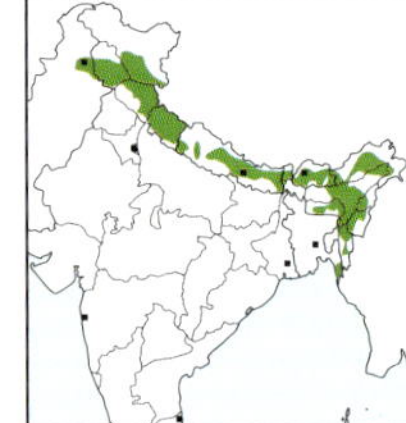

Mountain Hawk Eagle *Nisaetus nipalensis* 66–84cm

Resident. Himalayas, hills of NE India. **ID** Wings broader than Changeable, with squarer wingtips and more pronounced curve to trailing edge, and has proportionately shorter tail. Where ranges overlap in north, from Changeable by prominent crest, blackish crown and ear-coverts (with variable pale supercilium), heavily barred underparts and underwing-coverts, whitish-barred uppertail-coverts, and stronger dark barring on tail. Juvenile has whitish to rufous head and underparts; from juvenile Changeable by more extensive dark streaking on crown and sides of head and neck, white-tipped black crest, and fewer, more prominent tail bars. Immature largely pale on underparts but show bold breast streaking and barring on flanks and vent. **Voice** Generally silent; in breeding season gives high-pitched, shrill piping note followed by one or two softer notes, *kleee-kik kik*. **HH** Habits like Changeable though often seen soaring above forest. Frequents forested hills and mountains.

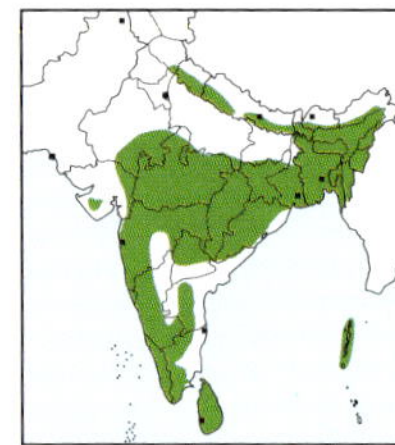

Changeable Hawk Eagle *Nisaetus cirrhatus* 51–82cm

Resident. Base of Himalayas, S Gujarat and E Rajasthan through S Gangetic Plain to S West Bengal, NE India, peninsula, Andamans, Sri Lanka and Bangladesh. **ID** Wings slightly narrower and more parallel-edged, compared to Mountain Hawk Eagle, and has proportionately longer tail. Where ranges overlap in N Subcontinent (*N. c. limnaeetus*), best told from Mountain by lack of prominent crest, paler sides to head, boldly streaked underparts (any barring confined to flanks, thighs and vent), and narrower dark tail barring. Dark morph confusable with Black Eagle; best told by structural differences, greyish underside to tail with diffuse dark terminal band, and extensive greyish bases to underside of flight feathers, which contrast with darker underwing-coverts and wingtips. Juvenile has pale fringes to upperparts (some with largely white forewing), pale buff head, underparts and underwing-coverts, and narrower and more numerous tail-bands than adult. Difficult to separate from juvenile Mountain but has paler head and lacks crest. In peninsular India and Sri Lanka, nominate ('Crested Hawk Eagle') adult has prominent white-tipped crest, heavy brown streaking on breast and rufous-brown belly, thighs and vent (underparts can be largely streaked and similar to *limnaeetus*); there is no dark morph. Juvenile nominate similar to juvenile *limnaeetus* but has white-tipped black crest. *S. c. andamanensis* of Andamans is much smaller, and lacks prominent crest; some have pale, faintly barred thighs and vent. **Voice** Generally silent. In breeding season commonest call a series of piping whistles with emphasis on the last rising note: *kwip-kwip-kwip-kwi-kweee*. **HH** Often perches in forest clearing from where it dashes and pounces on prey. Broadleaved forest, open well-wooded country, and cultivation and villages in or near forest in lowlands and foothills. **TN** Nominate is sometimes split as Crested Hawk Eagle.

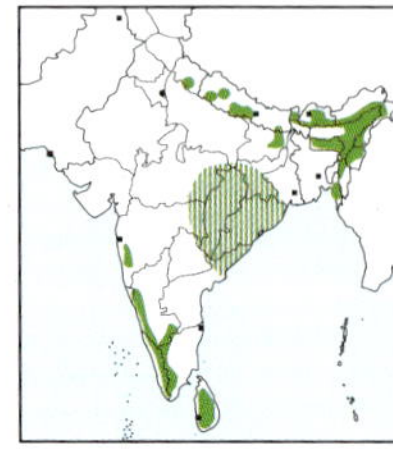

Rufous-bellied Eagle *Lophotriorchis kienerii* 46–61cm

Resident. Himalayas, hills of NE, E and SW India, Bangladesh and Sri Lanka. **ID** Smallish, with buzzard-like wings and tail. At rest, wingtips extend well down tail. Glides and soars on flat wings. Adult has blackish hood and upperparts, white throat and breast, and (black-streaked) rufous rest of underparts. Rufous of underparts and underwing-coverts appear dark at a distance. Greater underwing-coverts tipped with black, forming blackish band, and has dark subterminal band to tail. Upperwing is dark except strikingly pale patches at base of primaries. At rest, shows short crest. Juvenile has white underparts and underwing-coverts, dark mask and white supercilium, dark patch on sides of upper breast, and dark patch on flanks. Undersides of flight feathers and tail are lightly barred (like adult), and secondaries appear darker than rest of underwing; head-on, shows striking white leading edge to wing; upperwing appears dark with strikingly pale patches at base of primaries. Older immatures show a range of intermediate plumages. **Voice** Silent except in breeding season, when gives repeated piercing *keeee*. **HH** Most often seen soaring high over forest. Broadleaved evergreen and moist deciduous broadleaved forest.

ad
juv
Legge's
Hawk Eagle
soaring
juv
ad
ad
Mountain
Hawk Eagle
juv
dark morph
pale morph
ad
cirrhatus
juv
dark
morph
limnaeetus
juv
pale
morph
cirrhatus
ad
Changeable
Hawk Eagle
soaring
ad
juv
ad
Rufous-bellied
Eagle
juv
soaring

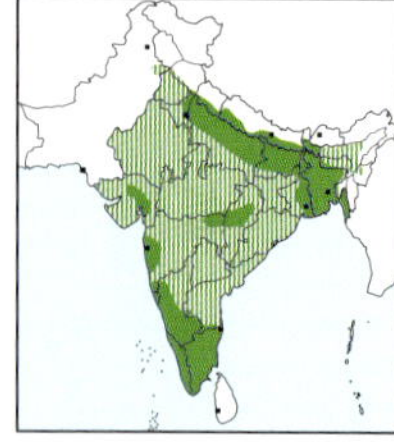

Indian Spotted Eagle *Clanga hastata* 50–60cm

Resident. Mainly N, NE and S subcontinent. Vagrant: Pakistan, Bhutan. **ID** Like Greater Spotted, Indian Spotted is a stocky, medium-sized eagle with short broad wings, a buzzard-like head with comparatively fine bill, long and closely feathered tarsi, and a rather short tail. The wings are angled down at carpals when gliding and soaring. Adult is similar in overall appearance to Greater Spotted Eagle but warmer brown in coloration. Has a wider gape than Greater, with thick 'lips' (gape flanges) visible at a distance, with gape-line extending to back of, or behind, eye (reaching level with centre of eye in Greater). Lacks spiky nape feathers of Greater, and has shorter thigh feathering. Underwing-coverts are paler or same colour as flight feathers (darker in Greater). Juvenile is more distinct from juvenile Greater. Spotting on upperwing-coverts is less prominent, tertials are pale brown with diffuse white tips (dark with bold white tips in Greater), uppertail-coverts are pale brown with white barring (white in Greater), and underparts are paler light yellowish-brown with dark streaking. In some plumages can resemble Steppe Eagle – differences mentioned below for Greater are likely to be helpful for separation (although gape-line is also long in Steppe). **Voice** A very high-pitched cackling laugh and series of sharp, staccato yelps: *kleep kleep kleep*. **HH** Like other eagles, an aggressive and powerful predator which can soar well, often at considerable heights. Hunts by quartering with slow glides over areas within and near forest, usually flying above treetop level; seizes most prey on ground. Wooded areas interspersed with cultivation in lowlands. Globally threatened. **TN** Formerly placed in *Aquila*.

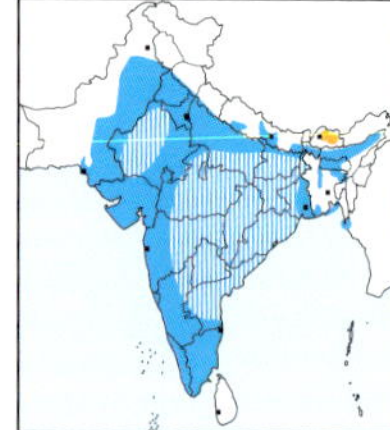

Greater Spotted Eagle *Clanga clanga* 59–71cm

Breeds in NW subcontinent but details not clear; winters mainly in N, NE, W and S subcontinent. Vagrant: Sri Lanka. **ID** Medium-sized eagle with short broad wings, stocky head, and short tail. Wings distinctly angled down at carpals when gliding, almost flat when soaring. See Indian Spotted for differences from that species. Compared to Steppe Eagle has less protruding head in flight, with shorter wings and less deep-fingered wingtips; at rest, trousers less baggy, and bill smaller with rounded (rather than elongated) nostrils and shorter gape; lacks adult Steppe's barring on underside of flight and tail feathers, and dark trailing edge to wing, and has small white crescent at base of primaries and a dark chin. Pale variant '*fulvescens*' from juvenile Imperial Eagle by structural differences, lack of prominent pale wedge on inner primaries on underwing, and unstreaked underparts. Juvenile has bold whitish tips to dark brown coverts. **Voice** Vocalisations like Indian, but lower-pitched, including a thin *kyack, tyuck* or *dyip*, sometimes repeated two or three times, recalling a small dog yapping. **HH** Often perches on a treetop, bush or bank near water. Hunts on wing or on ground. Catches waterbirds by swooping low and scattering flock, isolating an individual. Large lakes, canals, marshes and mangroves. Globally threatened. **TN** Formerly placed in *Aquila*.

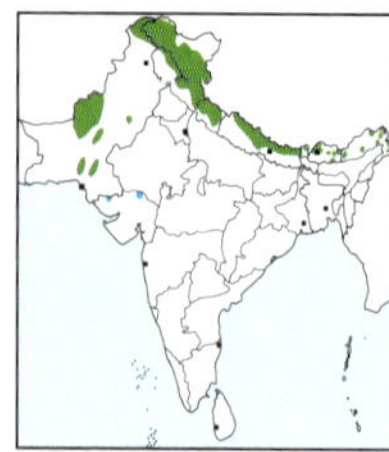

Golden Eagle *Aquila chrysaetos* 70–99cm

Resident. Balochistan and Himalayas. **ID** Large, with long and broad wings (with pronounced curve to trailing edge), long tail, and distinctly protruding head and neck. Wings clearly pressed forward and raised (with upturned fingers) in pronounced V when soaring. Adult has pale panel on upperwing-coverts, gold crown and nape, and two-toned tail. Juvenile has white base to tail and white patch at base of flight feathers on upperwing and underwing. **Voice** Silent except in breeding season. Occasionally gives a loud clear yelping in display *weee-o* and a thin shrill *pleek*. **HH** Soars for hours over mountain ridges. Usually hunts by quartering a slope, flying low, then striking with talons in a swift dash; occasionally pounces from a perch. High rugged mountains, usually well above the treeline.

ad
ad
juv
juv
Indian Spotted Eagle
juv
gliding
gliding
juv
ad
ad
juv
'fulvescens'
juv
Greater Spotted Eagle
juv
sub-ad
gliding
ad
ad
juv
Golden Eagle

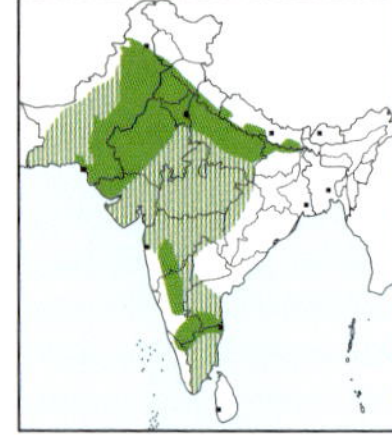

Tawny Eagle *Aquila rapax* 60–75cm

Widespread resident; unrecorded in the north-east and E India. **ID** Compared to Steppe Eagle, hand of wing does not appear so long and broad, tail slightly shorter, and looks smaller and weaker at rest; gape-line ends level with centre of eye (extends to rear of eye in Steppe), and adult has yellowish iris (usually brown in Steppe). Differs from Greater and Indian Spotted in more protruding head and neck in flight, baggy trousers, yellow eyes, and oval nostrils. Adult extremely variable, from dark brown through rufous to pale cream, and unstreaked or streaked with rufous or dark brown. Dark morph very similar to adult Steppe (which shows much less variation); distinctions include less pronounced barring and dark trailing edge on underwing, dark nape, and dark throat. Rufous to pale cream Tawny uniformly pale from uppertail-coverts to back, with undertail-coverts same colour as belly (contrast often apparent on similar species). Pale adults also lack prominent whitish trailing edge to wing, tip to tail and greater covert bar (present on immatures of similar species). Characteristic, if present, is distinct pale inner primary wedge on underwing. Juvenile also variable, with narrow white tips to unbarred secondaries; otherwise as similar-plumaged adult. Immature/subadult can show dark throat and breast contrasting with pale belly, and dark banding on underwing-coverts; whole head and breast may be dark. **Voice** Hollow barking *kau-kau*; also, higher-pitched *ki-ark* given by male in display and mewing *shreep-shreep* by female at nest. **HH** Perches from a vantage point for long periods. Feeds on carrion and refuse; also, small mammals, birds and reptiles, mainly stolen from smaller raptors, and will pounce on small mammals from a perch. Inhabits desert, semi-desert and cultivation in the lowlands. Globally threatened.

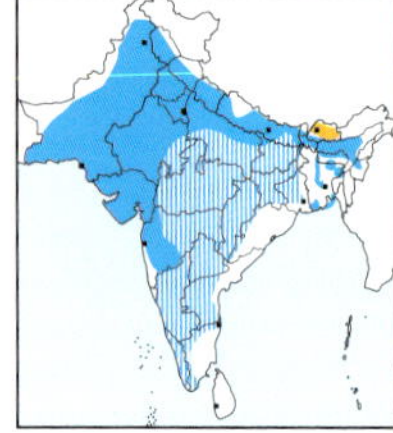

Steppe Eagle *Aquila nipalensis* 60–81cm

Widespread winter visitor mainly to N and C subcontinent. **ID** Broader and longer wings than Greater and Indian Spotted, with more pronounced and spread fingers, and more protruding head and neck; wings flatter when soaring, and less distinctly angled down at carpals when gliding. When perched, clearly bigger and heavier, with heavier bill and baggy trousers. Adult separated from adult spotted eagles by underwing pattern (dark trailing edge, distinct barring on remiges, indistinct/non-existent pale crescents in carpal region), pale rufous nape patch and pale chin. Juvenile has broad white bar on underwing, double white bar on upperwing, and white crescent on uppertail-coverts; prominence of bars on upperwing and underwing much reduced on older immatures (when more similar in appearance to Indian Spotted, which see). **Voice** Generally silent outside breeding season. **HH** Habits like Tawny. Wooded hills, open country and large lakes. Globally threatened.

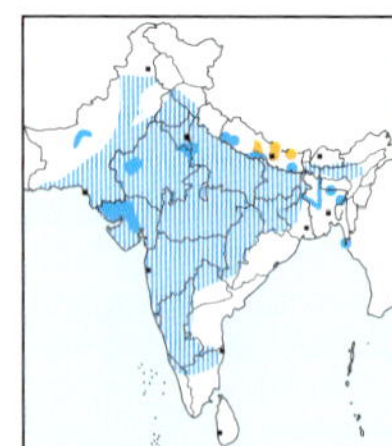

Imperial Eagle *Aquila heliaca* 72–84cm

Winter visitor. Mainly Pakistan and NW India. Vagrant: Bhutan. **ID** Large, stout-bodied eagle with long broad wings, longish tail, and distinctly protruding head and neck. Wings flat when soaring and gliding. Adult has almost uniform upperwing, small white scapular patches, golden-buff crown and nape, and two-toned tail. Juvenile has pronounced curve to trailing edge of wing, pale wedge on inner primaries, streaked buffish body and wing-coverts, uniform pale rump and back (lacking distinct pale crescent shown by other species, except Tawny), and white tips to median and greater upperwing-coverts. **Voice** Mainly silent outside breeding season. **HH** A solitary, majestic eagle. Typically spends most of day perched on a good vantage point, such as a tree, or on the ground. In the region, feeds by robbing other raptors in flight; also takes carrion and small mammals, birds and reptiles taken on the ground. Soars high overhead and can fly at great speeds. Open country in the plains, deserts and around major lakes and wetlands. Globally threatened. **AN** Eastern Imperial Eagle.

sub-ad
ad
ad
juv
ad
Tawny Eagle
gliding
ad
juv
ad
imm
juv
Steppe Eagle
gliding
ad
sub-ad
ad
sub-ad
juv
gliding
juv
Imperial Eagle

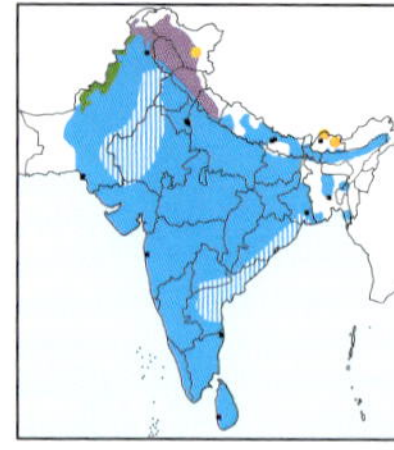

Booted Eagle *Hieraaetus pennatus* 42–51cm

Breeds in Balochistan and Himalayas; widespread in winter, except parts of NW and NE subcontinent. **ID** Smallish eagle which can be kite-like in appearance. Wings are comparatively long and narrow, with ample hand, and tail is long and square-ended. When gliding and soaring, wings are held slightly forward and are flat or slightly angled down at carpal. Twists tail in kite-like fashion. In all plumages, shows small white shoulder patches (at base of leading edge of wing), pale panel on median coverts, pale wedge on inner primaries, pale scapulars, white crescent on uppertail-coverts, and greyish undertail with darker centre and tip. Head, underparts and underwing-coverts are whitish, brown or rufous respectively in pale, dark and rufous morphs. Juvenile much as adult, but shows white trailing edge to wings and tail when fresh. **Voice** Generally silent except in breeding season when gives a shrill, rapidly rising, three-noted whistle, *kli-kli-klee* or *kli-kli-klee-klu*, or a longer series of piping whistles. **HH** A swift and agile hunter, feeding on small mammals, birds and reptiles. Captures prey in trees by swift dive from above into foliage, followed by pursuit through branches. Soars at considerable heights over open country and stoops at great speed on prey on ground. Pairs often hunt cooperatively. Well-wooded country in hills and plains, also, semi-desert with plantations, and groves around cultivation and villages.

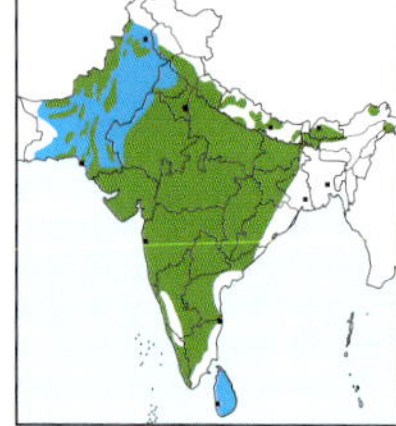

Bonelli's Eagle *Aquila fasciata* 55–67cm

Widespread resident and winter visitor; unrecorded in most of NE and E subcontinent. Vagrant: Bangladesh and Sri Lanka. **ID** Medium-sized eagle with long and broad wings, distinctly protruding head, and long square-ended tail. Soars on flat wings. Adult has pale underparts and forewing, blackish carpals and band along underwing-coverts, greyish underside to flight feathers with diffuse dark trailing edge, whitish patch on mantle, and pale greyish tail with broad dark terminal band. Juvenile has pronounced curve to trailing edge of wing. Best identified by combination of distinctive shape (especially long tail), ginger-buff to reddish-brown underparts and underwing-coverts (with variable dark band along greater coverts), and narrow greyish barring on underside of wings and tail, which both lack dark trailing edge. Also shows pale inner primaries and base to outer primaries on underwing, comparatively uniform upperwing, and small white patch on back. Older immatures show more pronounced dark band on greater underwing-coverts and dark terminal band on wings and tail. **Voice** Generally silent, except in breeding season. In display flight, gives a repeated shrill *iuh* or more drawn-out whistling *eeeuu*, also a fluting, low-pitched *klu-klu-klu*... or *ki-ki-ki*... in alarm. **HH** Usually seen in flight, although soars less than other birds of prey. Normally hunts by perching hidden in a tree and making a quick dash; also quarters slopes, or stoops, and may hunt cooperatively. Well-wooded country in plains and hills; also, desert edges and large lakes in Pakistan.

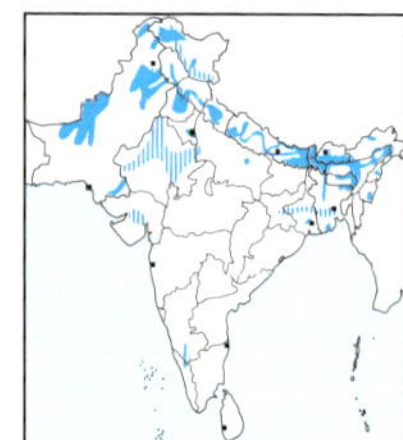

Hen Harrier *Circus cyaneus* 42–50cm

Widespread winter visitor. Mainly Pakistan, Himalayas and N India. **ID** Compared to Pallid and Montagu's, has slower and more laboured flight and is stockier, with broader wings and more rounded hand, normally with five (rather than four) visible primaries at tip. Adult male from male Pallid and Montagu's by combination of dark grey upperparts with extensive black at tips of wings, prominent white uppertail-covert patch, absence of black banding on secondaries (although has variable dark trailing edge to underwing), and dark grey head and breast contrasting with white belly. Adult female has boldly streaked underparts. White band on uppertail-coverts is broader than on Pallid and Montagu's. Has narrow pale neck-collar, but otherwise head pattern is typically plain compared with those species, usually lacking dark ear-covert patch; a distinct dark trailing edge to hand on underwing is a further difference from female Pallid. Juvenile recalls female but has rufous-brown underparts and underwing-coverts, although these are noticeably streaked dark brown (unlike juvenile Pallid and Montagu's). **Voice** Silent outside breeding season. **HH** Like other harriers, has a characteristic hunting method: systematically quarters the ground a few metres above it, gliding slowly on raised wings and occasionally flapping; on locating prey, drops quickly with claws held out to catch it. Roosts gregariously on ground in fields and marshes, often in large numbers and with other harriers. Open country, grassland and cultivation in plains and foothills.

pale
morph
soaring
dark morph
pale morph
Booted Eagle
dark morph
pale morph
ad
juv
soaring
juv
Bonelli's Eagle
ad
ad
Hen Harrier
♂
♂
♂ imm
♀
♀
♂
♀

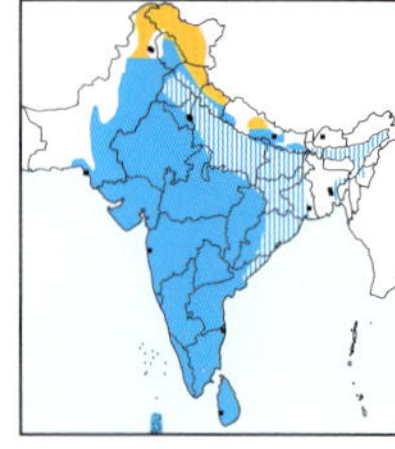

Pallid Harrier *Circus macrourus* 40–48cm

Widespread winter visitor and passage migrant; unrecorded in parts of north-east and W Pakistan. Vagrant: Bangladesh. **ID** Slim-winged and fine-bodied, with buoyant flight, particularly male. Folded wings fall short of tail tip, and legs longer than on Montagu's. Male has pale grey upperparts, dark wedge on primaries, very pale grey head and white underparts, and lacks black secondary bars. Immature male may show rusty breast-band and juvenile facial markings. Female has distinctive underwing pattern: pale primaries, irregularly barred and lacking dark trailing edge, contrast with darker secondaries which have pale bands narrower than on female Montagu's and tapering towards body (although first-summer Montagu's more similar in this respect), and lacks prominent barring on axillaries. Typically, female has stronger head pattern than Montagu's, with more pronounced pale collar, dark ear-coverts and dark eye-stripe, and upperside of flight feathers darker and lacks banding; from female Hen by narrower wings with more pointed hand, stronger head pattern, and absence of dark trailing edge to hand on underwing. Juvenile has unstreaked orange-buff underparts and underwing-coverts; on underwing, primaries evenly barred (lacking pronounced dark fingers), without dark trailing edge, and usually with pale crescent at base; head pattern more pronounced than Montagu's, with narrower white supercilium, more extensive dark ear-covert patch, and broader pale collar contrasting strongly with dark neck-sides. **Voice** Silent outside breeding season. **HH** Habits like Hen, but lighter on the wing, with faster hunting flight. Open country in plains and foothills: semi-desert, grassy slopes, cultivation, scrub-covered plains, and marshes.

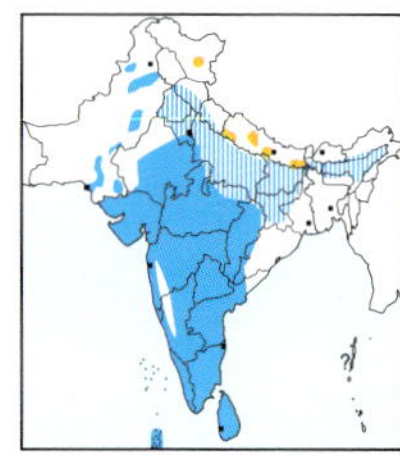

Montagu's Harrier *Circus pygargus* 39–49cm

Widespread winter visitor except parts of NW and NE subcontinent and E India. Vagrant: Bangladesh. **ID** Folded wings reach tail tip, and legs shorter than on Pallid. Male has black band across secondaries, extensive black on underside of primaries, and rufous streaking on belly and underwing-coverts. Female differs from female Pallid in distinctly and evenly barred underside to primaries with dark trailing edge, broader and more pronounced pale bands across secondaries, barring on axillaries, less pronounced head pattern, and distinct dark banding on upperside of secondaries. Juvenile has unstreaked rufous underparts and underwing-coverts, and darker secondaries than female; differs from juvenile Pallid in having broad dark fingers and dark trailing edge to hand on underwing, and paler face with smaller dark ear-covert patch and less distinct collar. Rarely, melanistic morphs occur, which are all blackish except sooty-grey secondaries. Possibly confusable with all-dark juvenile Eurasian Marsh but much more graceful and lightly built. **Voice** Silent outside breeding season. **HH** Habits like Hen, but lighter on the wing. Open country in plains and foothills, including cultivation, scrub-covered plains, grassland and marshes.

♂
♂
♂
♂ imm
♀
♀
Pallid Harrier
♀
Pallid
juv
Montagu's
juv
juv
♂
♂ imm
juv
♂
♀
Montagu's Harrier
♀
♀

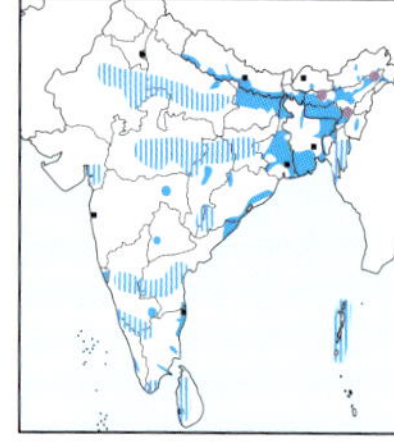

Pied Harrier *Circus melanoleucos* 43–50cm

Breeds in Assam; winter visitor mainly to NE subcontinent and Western Ghats. Vagrant: Pakistan, Bhutan, Sri Lanka. **ID** Usually looks broader in wing and body than Pallid and Montagu's Harriers, and slightly heavier in flight, although male can appear dainty and buoyant. Most likely to be confused with Eastern Marsh Harrier, which see for details. Adult male is distinctive, with black head and breast contrasting with white underparts, black upperparts, median coverts and primaries contrasting with grey of rest of wing, and white leading edge to wing. Yellow cere and iris are especially striking against black of head. Adult female superficially resembles female Pallid and Montagu's, but has paler underwing with narrow dark barring on flight feathers and sparse streaking on underwing-coverts; greyer primary-coverts, primaries and secondaries on upperwing with more pronounced dark banding; pale inner wing-coverts contrasting with brown greater coverts and mantle, and greyer tail with narrower dark barring. Juvenile has dark brown head and upperparts, with short white supercilium and patch below eye (but lacks pronounced white collar of juvenile Pallid), white uppertail-coverts, rufous-brown underparts and underwing-coverts, and pale underside to primaries (with dark fingers) contrasting with dark underside to secondaries. **Voice** Silent outside breeding season when male repeatedly gives *kiiy-veee* (recalling Northern Lapwing) in display and female a rapid *kee-kee-kee*. **HH** Flight and hunting behaviour like Hen, but more graceful on the wing. Open grassland and cultivation in plains and hills.

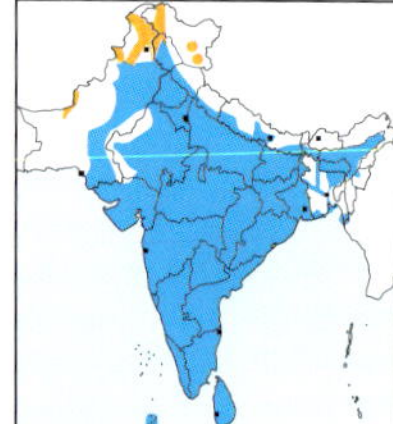

Western Marsh Harrier *Circus aeruginosus* 43–54cm

Widespread winter visitor; unrecorded in parts of W Pakistan and NE India. Vagrant: Bhutan. **ID** A broad-winged, stout-bodied harrier; in common with other harriers, glides and soars with wings held in noticeable V, which helps to separate it from Booted Eagle and Black Kite. Adult male is distinguished from other male harriers by combination of chestnut-brown mantle and upperwing-coverts contrasting with grey secondaries/inner primaries and black outer primaries, pale head (variably streaked brown) and pale leading edge to wing, and brown streaking on breast and belly, becoming uniformly brown on lower belly and vent. Shows variable amount of brown on underwing-coverts, with rest of underwing being white except black tips to primaries. All-dark melanistic morphs are sooty-grey above and blackish below, with grey patch at base of underside of primaries. Adult female is mainly dark brown except creamy crown, nape and throat, creamy leading edge to wing, and paler patch at base of underside of primaries. Juvenile is similar to female, but more uniformly blackish-brown, with pale orange crown and throat, and pale orange tips to greater upperwing-coverts and tail. **Voice** Silent outside breeding season. **HH** Flight and hunting behaviour like Hen, but heavier on the wing. Reedbeds, marshes, lakes, flooded fields; also, coastal lagoons in Bangladesh. **AN** Eurasian Marsh Harrier.

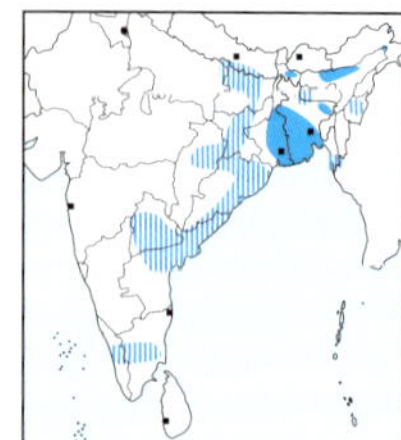

Eastern Marsh Harrier *Circus spilonotus* 47–55cm

Winter visitor, mainly to NE India and Bangladesh. **ID** Differs markedly from Western Marsh, and in some plumages could be confused with Pied and Hen Harriers. Compared with Pied Harrier, it is larger, has broader wings and tail, and is stouter-bodied with more prominent head. Adult male has black streaking on whitish head and breast, and has black mantle and median coverts with feathers boldly edged white. Head and mantle can appear mainly black on some, not unlike adult male Pied Harrier, but has much less black on primaries on underwing, and is never as clean-cut in appearance as that species (i.e. breast is streaked, mantle and back show some white fringes, and lacks clear-cut black bar on median coverts and broad white leading edge to wing). Young males can appear very similar to female Pied; small size, finer build, barring to underside of secondaries and primaries, and prominent barring on tail are useful features for Pied. Adult female has white uppertail-coverts, greyish flight feathers and tail with dark barring, heavily streaked head and breast, and broad diffuse rufous streaking on underparts. Secondaries on underwing appear grey and diffusely barred, with paler patch at base of primaries. Structural differences, more uniform upperwing (darker banding on flight feathers much less distinct), heavily marked underparts and underwing are best features for separation from female Pied. White 'rump' band recalls female Hen or Pallid Harriers, but pattern and coloration of upperwing, underwing and underparts otherwise different. Juvenile rather dark, with cream breast-band and pale patch at base of underside of primaries; head usually mainly cream, with variable dark streaking, and some show pronounced cream streaking on mantle. Can show white band on uppertail-coverts. **Voice** Typically silent in winter, may utter soft *kyu-kyu* or *keeau* at roost. **HH** Flight and hunting behaviour like Hen, but heavier on the wing. Marshes, reedbeds, flooded fields, cultivation and open country in vicinity of water.

Pied Harrier
♂
♂
♂ imm
juv
juv
♀
♀
juv
Western
Marsh Harrier
♂
♂
♀
♀
♀
juv
♂
♂ imm
♀
♂
♂
♂
♀
♀
juv
Eastern
Marsh Harrier

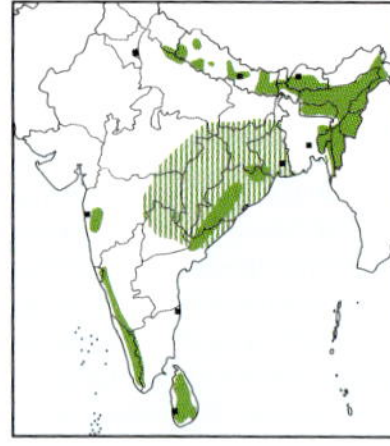

Crested Goshawk *Accipiter trivirgatus* 30–46cm

Resident. Mainly Himalayas, NE and SW India, and Sri Lanka. **ID** Larger size and crest are best distinctions from Besra. Short and broad wings, pinched-in at base. Wingtips barely extend beyond tail base at rest. Yellow (rather than grey) cere and absence of white tips to shorter crest help separate from Jerdon's Baza. Compared with other *Accipiter* species has short stoutish legs and feet. Soars low above canopy in fluttering display flight, with white undertail-coverts prominent. Otherwise, stiff wingbeats are interspersed with glides on level wings. Narrow white line along uppertail-coverts diagnostic if present. Male has dark grey crown and paler grey ear-coverts, well-defined black submoustachial and gular stripes, and rufous-brown streaking on breast and barring on belly and flanks. Female larger with browner crown and ear-coverts, and browner streaking and barring on underparts. Juvenile has paler brown upperparts with pale fringes, rufous or buffish fringes to crown, crest and nape feathers, streaked ear-coverts, and buff or rufous wash to underparts, which are streaked brown (barring restricted to lower flanks and thighs). Birds of SW India, and especially *A. t. layardi* of Sri Lanka, are much smaller than *A. t. indicus* of N subcontinent. *A. t. layardi* has darker brown and sparser barring on underparts; juvenile has unmarked rufous-buff underparts and underwing-coverts (except spotting on flanks and undertail-coverts). **Voice** Often silent. Calls include a scream *he, he, hehehehe* and, when defending nest, loud screams and deep croaks. **HH** Hunting behaviour like Shikra; adept at catching prey in thick forest. Dense deciduous and evergreen broadleaved tropical and subtropical forest; also, wooded gardens in Sri Lanka.

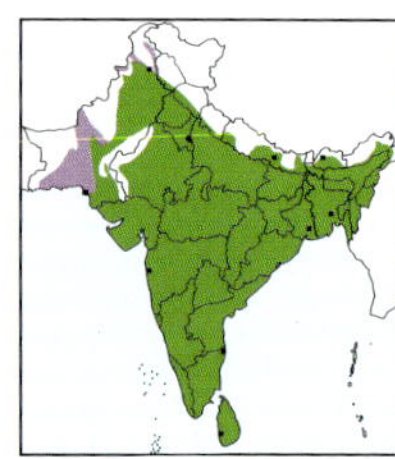

Shikra *Accipiter badius* 30–36cm

Widespread resident, except in parts of north-west. **ID** Adult paler than Besra and Eurasian Sparrowhawk. Underwing pale, with fine barring on remiges, and slightly darker wingtips. Head cuckoo-like compared with other *Accipiter*. Male has pale blue-grey upperparts with contrasting dark grey primaries, indistinct grey gular stripe, fine brownish-orange barring on underparts, unbarred white thighs, and unbarred or lightly barred central tail feathers. Female upperparts more brownish-grey. Juvenile has pale brown upperparts, more prominent gular stripe, and streaked underparts; from juvenile Besra by paler upperparts and narrower tail barring, and from Eurasian Sparrowhawk by streaked underparts. The nominate in S India and Sri Lanka is smaller and darker grey above than other races in the region, with darker tail-bands, and has underparts more closely barred with darker rufous. Birds in NE India also darker and more heavily marked. **Voice** Especially vocal in breeding season, but also at other times. Main call a harsh-sounding *piu-piu-piu*, also, a shrill *kwit-kwit* and loud ringing *kee-kee-kee-kee-kee* (mainly in display). **HH** Perches concealed and captures prey by short swift dash or low flight between trees. Open wooded country and groves around villages and cultivation.

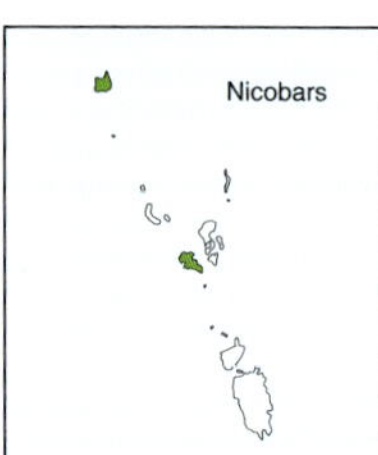

Nicobar Sparrowhawk *Accipiter butleri* 28–34cm

Resident. N and C Nicobars. **ID** Very short primary projection. Male has pale blue-grey upperparts, whitish underparts and underwing-coverts, indistinct gular stripe, and unbarred tail with narrow diffuse terminal band. Female slightly browner on upperparts, with marginally stronger barring on breast. Juvenile has rufous upperparts with dark brown feather centres, rufous-buff underparts with browner streaking, and dark banding on rufous-cinnamon secondaries and tail. **Voice** Gives a shrill double note, *kee-wick* like Shikra. **HH** Mainly eats lizards, hunting behaviour unreported. Upper storey of primary forest. Globally threatened.

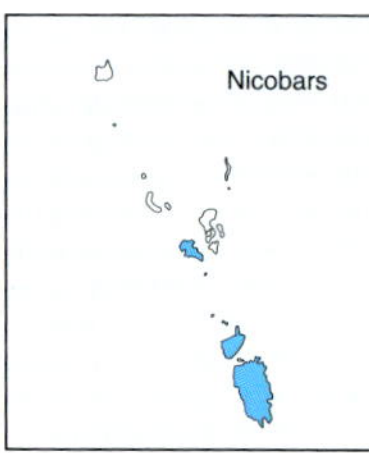

Chinese Sparrowhawk *Accipiter soloensis* 25–35cm

Winter visitor. Nicobars. **ID** Comparatively narrow and pointed wings apparent in flight, with long primary projection at rest (extending nearly halfway down tail). Adult has blue-grey head and upperparts, indistinct grey gular stripe, and unbarred or very lightly barred underparts. Distinctive underwing pattern, with unbarred remiges and coverts, blackish wingtips and dark grey trailing edge. Sexes similar, with little difference in size, although breast coloration of male is pinkish (can be whitish or pale greyish-purple), while breast of female more orange and can show bars of darker grey and upperparts are a shade browner. Has grey orbital ring; iris dark crimson in male and yellow in female and juvenile. Cere orange-yellow. Subadult shows some dark barring on underside of flight feathers. Juvenile has dark brown upperparts and more pronounced gular stripe; compared with juvenile Japanese Sparrowhawk, has distinctive underwing pattern (dark grey wingtips and trailing edge, and largely unmarked underwing-coverts), and bolder rufous-brown spotting and barring on underparts. **Voice** Silent outside breeding season. **HH** Hunts mainly over open ground, taking prey in short stoops from a perch or by gliding or circling low over ground. Forest and wooded country.

♂
♂
juv
Crested Goshawk
juv
juv
Shikra
♂
♀
♀
♂
juv
♂
♂
juv
Nicobar
Sparrowhawk
juv
Chinese
Sparrowhawk

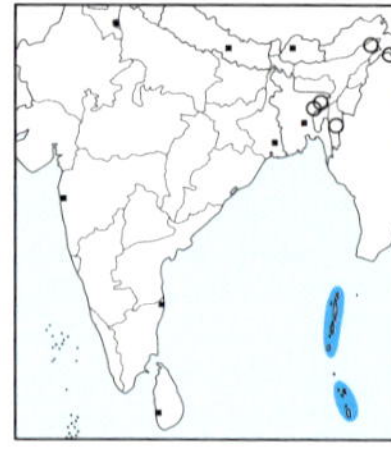

Japanese Sparrowhawk *Accipiter gularis* 23–30cm

Winter visitor. Andaman and Nicobar Islands. Vagrant: Bangladesh. **ID** Very small. Long primary projection (extending nearly halfway down tail). In flight, wings are a shade narrower and more pointed than on Eurasian Sparrowhawk and Besra. Underside of flight feathers and underwing-coverts distinctly barred. In all plumages, pale bars on tail generally broader than dark bars (reverse on Besra). Underpart pattern of adults differs from Besra; juveniles more similar. Male has dark bluish-grey upperparts and pale rufous to pale grey underparts (some with fine grey barring). Very indistinct gular stripe (often not visible in field). Female has browner upperparts, whitish underparts with distinct greyish-brown barring, and indistinct gular stripe. Yellow orbital ring; iris red in male and yellow in female and juvenile. Cere lemon-yellow. Juvenile has dark greyish-brown upperparts with narrow rufous fringes, brown streaking on breast, heart-shaped spots on lower breast and belly, and barring on flanks and underwing-coverts. **Voice** Shrill *kee-bick*, mewing *kew-kew* and chattering *kik-kik-kik*. **HH** Hunting behaviour like Shikra. Different types of forest, including coniferous, deciduous and mixed; also riparian woodland.

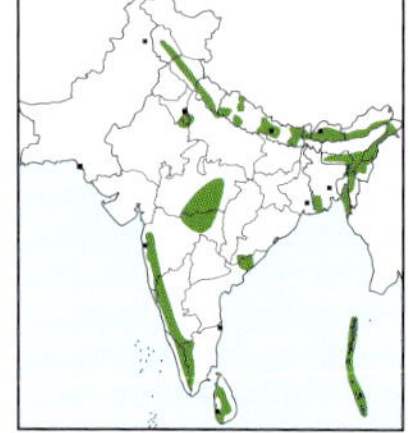

Besra *Accipiter virgatus* 24–36cm

Resident. Himalayas, NE and SW India, Bangladesh and Sri Lanka. Vagrant: Pakistan. **ID** Small, with short primary projection (less than one-third down tail). Upperparts are darker and underwing is strongly barred compared to Shikra, while prominent gular stripe and streaked breast separate it from Eurasian. In all plumages resembles Crested Goshawk, but considerably smaller, lacks crest, and has longer and finer legs. Adult male from Shikra by dark slate-grey upperparts lacking strong contrast with primaries, broad blackish gular stripe, bold rufous streaking on breast and barring on belly, flanks and thighs, and pronounced and broad dark tail barring. Adult female is similar, but upperparts are browner, with blackish crown and nape, and yellow iris (red in male). Juvenile has brown upperparts with rufous fringes, prominent gular stripe, and streaked/spotted breast and belly and barred flanks. From immature Shikra by darker, richer brown upperparts, broader gular stripe, and broader tail barring. From Eurasian Sparrowhawk by streaked underparts. Male *A. v. abdulalii*, on the Andamans and Nicobars has greyish-tawny breast, belly dull tawny and thighs light grey, the entire underparts lacking streaking or barring. Female *abdulalii* is as other subspecies. **Voice** Makes a loud squealing *ki-weeer and* a rapidly repeated *tchew-tchew-tchew* during displays. **HH** Hunting behaviour like Shikra. Expert at dodging and twisting at speed through dense forest undergrowth. Breeds in dense broadleaved forest; also open wooded country in winter.

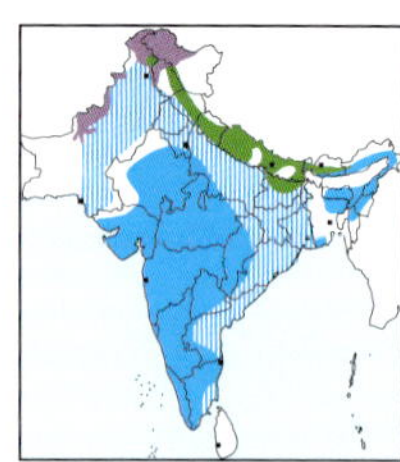

Eurasian Sparrowhawk *Accipiter nisus* 28–40cm

Resident and winter visitor. Breeds in Balochistan and Himalayas; winters in Himalayan foothills and south to S India. Vagrant: Sri Lanka. **ID** Upperparts of adult darker than Shikra, with prominent barring on underparts, underwing and tail. Uniform barring on underparts and absence of prominent gular stripe should separate it from Besra. Male has dark slate-grey upperparts and reddish-orange barring on underparts. Female dark brown on upperparts, with dark brown barring on underparts, and yellow iris (red in some males). Juvenile has dark brown upperparts and barred underparts. Male of resident Himalayan *melaschistos* has darker grey upperparts, with almost black crown and mantle, and stronger rufous barring below. **Voice** Vocal mostly near nest. Main call a series of *kek-kek-kek-kek-kek* cackling notes; calls vary in volume and speed of delivery. **HH** Captures prey in a short swift dash, relying on surprise, or by swift low flight between trees or patches of cover, Well-wooded country, open forest, scrub forest and groves in cultivation.

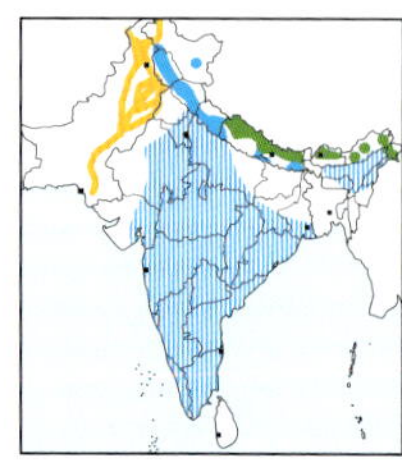

Eurasian Goshawk *Accipiter gentilis* 46–63cm

Winter visitor and resident. Mainly Pakistan and Himalayas. Vagrant: Bangladesh. **ID** Very large, with heavy, deep-chested appearance. Wings comparatively long, with bulging secondaries. Male has grey upperparts (greyer than female Eurasian Sparrowhawk), white supercilium, and finely barred underparts. Female considerably larger with browner upperparts. Juvenile has heavy streaking on buff-coloured underparts. **Voice** Mostly silent, but vocal during courtship and nesting. Like other accipiters, probably depends on vocalisations for communication in forested habitats with limited visibility. Most common call is a shrill chatter and female has a disyllabic *hee-aa*. **HH** Hunting habits like Eurasian Sparrowhawk, but more powerful. Oak and high-altitude coniferous forest, sometimes hunting above the treeline in Himalayas. **AN** Northern Goshawk.

♂
♀
Besra
♀
♂
juv
juv
♀
♀
♂
Japanese
Sparrowhawk
♂
juv
♂
♂
♀
juv
♂
♀
Eurasian
Sparrowhawk
♀
juv
Eurasian
Goshawk
juv
♀

PLATE 89: KITES, ORIENTAL HONEY-BUZZARD AND WHITE-EYED BUZZARD

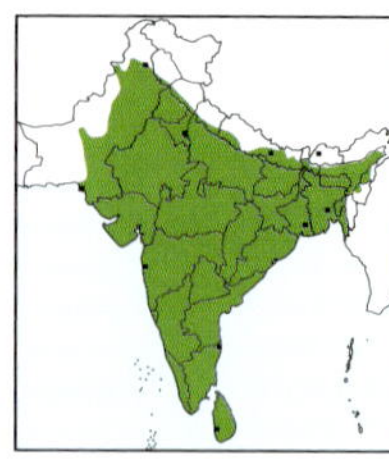

Black-winged Kite *Elanus caeruleus* 30–37cm

Widespread resident; unrecorded in parts of NW and NE subcontinent. Vagrant: Bhutan. **ID** Small size. Grey and white with small black face mask and black 'shoulders'. In flight pointed wings show black forewing and black underside to primaries. Flight buoyant, with much hovering; soars and glides with wings raised. Juvenile has brownish-grey upperparts with pale fringes, and less distinct shoulder patch. **Voice** Mainly high-pitched, weak calls, given most often in breeding season: a piping *pee-oo,* also harsher *kree-uk* in aggression and whistled scream in alarm. **HH** Perches on prominent vantage points. Hunts by quartering and hovering over open ground. Often crepuscular. Grassland interspersed with cultivation or scattered trees, and scrub desert.

Oriental Honey-buzzard *Pernis ptilorhynchus* 52–68cm

Widespread resident; absent in parts of NW and NE subcontinent and SE India. **ID** Tail long and broad, and has narrow neck, small head and bill, and short bare tarsi. Soars on flat wings. Has small crest. Underparts and underwing-coverts range from dark brown through rufous to white, and unmarked, streaked or barred; often shows dark moustachial and gular stripes, and gorget of streaking across lower throat. Lacks dark carpal patch. Male has grey face, two black tail-bands, usually three black underwing bands, and dark iris. Female has browner face and upperparts, three black tail-bands, four narrower black underwing bands, and yellow iris. Juvenile has narrower underwing banding, three or more tail-bands, and extensive dark tips to primaries; cere yellow (grey on adult) and iris dark. Resident *ruficollis* has more pronounced crest than migrant *orientalis*, and in N and C India is noticeably smaller. For differences from European Honey-buzzard see Vagrants. **Voice** Chiefly silent, even in breeding season. Occasionally gives single high-pitched whistle *wheeeeew or whi-whee-uho.* **HH** Spends prolonged periods perched in tree foliage. Usually seen in flight. Mainly eats honey and larvae of bees. Well-wooded country, also, groves in villages, towns and cultivation.

White-eyed Buzzard *Butastur teesa* 36–43cm

Widespread resident; absent in parts of NW, NE and S subcontinent. Vagrant: Bhutan. **ID** Longish, slim wings, long tail, and buzzard-like head. Long, bare legs are yellow. Cere and bill base yellow. Pale median covert panel. Adult has black gular and moustachial stripes, white nape patch, barred underparts, dark wingtips, and rufous tail; iris white. Juvenile has broad whitish supercilium, buffish head and breast streaked dark brown, with throat-stripe indistinct or absent; rufous uppertail more strongly barred; iris initially brown. **Voice** Noisy early in breeding season when gives a plaintive mewing *pit-weer, pit-weer.* **HH** Sluggish, spends long periods perched upright on a vantage point. Hunts mainly by dropping to ground to seize prey. Dry open country: cultivation, scrub, open forest, and scrub desert.

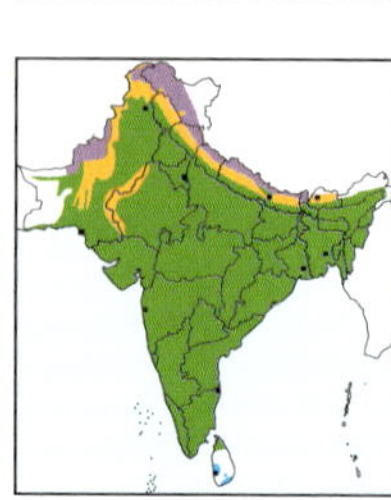

Black Kite *Milvus migrans* 44–66cm

Widespread resident (*M. m. govinda*); common and widespread winter visitor (*M. m. lineatus*). **ID** Shallow tail fork. Much manoeuvring of arched wings and twisting of tail in flight. Dark rufous-brown, with variable whitish crescent at primary bases on underwing, and a pale band across median coverts on upperwing. Juvenile has broad whitish or buffish streaking on head and underparts. *M. m. lineatus* ('Black-eared Kite') is larger than *govinda*, with broader wings, shallower tail fork, and more prominent whitish patch at base of primaries on underwing. Has more pronounced dark mask, with paler crown and throat. Belly and vent are also paler than breast. Juvenile is more heavily and extensively streaked. In older birds, feet and cere are greenish or light blue (deep yellow in *govinda*). **Voice** Often noisy all year. Main call a drawn-out squeal *kleeeeerrrrrr,* sometimes *pee-pee-pee.* **HH** Gregarious all year, often soaring and roosting in large numbers. Strongly associated with human habitation. Bold scavenger, mainly feeding on refuse and offal. Mainly occurs around cities, towns and villages, also, mountains.

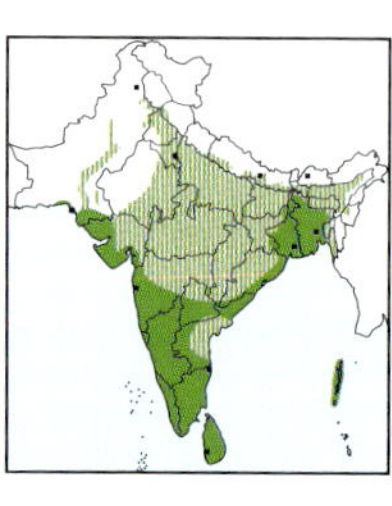

Brahminy Kite *Haliastur indus* 45–51cm

Widespread resident; unrecorded in parts of NW and NE subcontinent. **ID** Small size and kite-like flight. Wings usually angled at carpals. Tail rounded. Adult mainly chestnut, with white head, neck and breast (which are finely streaked black). In flight upperwing, underwing and tail are chestnut, and has black wingtips. Juvenile mainly brown, with pale streaking on head, mantle and breast, large pale patch at base of primaries on underwing, and pale brown and unmarked undertail. **Voice** Mostly silent outside breeding season. Commonest call a plaintive, descending mew or lamb-like bleat. **HH** Frequently perches overlooking water. Gregarious where common. Frequents wide variety of fresh- and saltwater habitats including harbours and around fishing villages.

juv
ad
ad
Black-winged Kite
♀
♂
Oriental Honey-buzzard
ad
soaring
White-eyed Buzzard
ad
♂
juv
juv
♂
soaring
ad
juv
juv
govinda
Black Kite
ad
govinda
ad
lineatus
juv
lineatus
ad
lineatus
juv
lineatus
juv
ad
ad
juv
Brahminy Kite

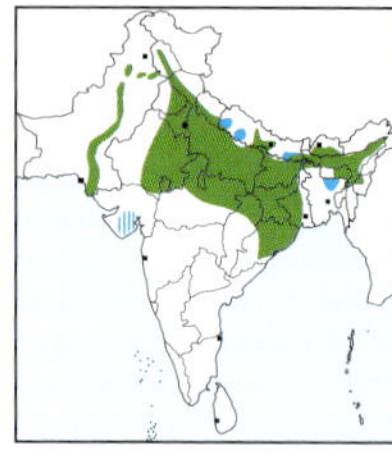

Pallas's Fish Eagle ***Haliaeetus leucoryphus*** 72–84cm

Resident. N subcontinent. **ID** Soars and glides on flat wings. Long, broad wings and protruding (rather small) head and neck. Adult has pale head and neck, dark brown upperwing and underwing, and mainly white tail with broad black terminal band. Juvenile less bulky, looks slimmer-winged, longer-tailed and smaller-billed than juvenile White-tailed; has dark mask, pale band across underwing-coverts, whitish patch on underside of inner primaries, all-dark tail (lacking pale inner webs of White-tailed), and pale crescent on uppertail-coverts. Older immatures have more uniform underwing and whitish tail with mottled dark band. **Voice** Noisy when breeding, usually silent at other times. Loud, guttural and far-carrying *kha-kha-kha-kha* or *gao-gao-gao-gao*; also, a continuous hoarse *ook-kook-kook*. **HH** Perches for long periods close to water. Feeds mainly on fish snatched near the surface, also, on waterbirds by gliding low over the water. Mainly larger rivers and lakes, also, tidal creeks and mangroves. Globally threatened.

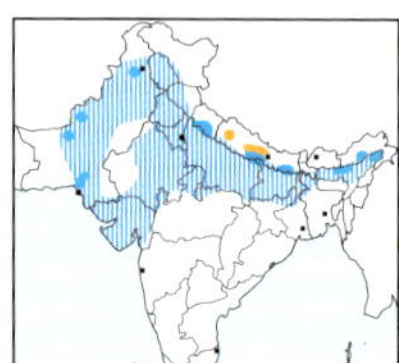

White-tailed Eagle ***Haliaeetus albicilla*** 74–92cm

Widespread winter visitor. Vagrant: Bangladesh. **ID** Huge, with broad parallel-edged wings, short wedge-shaped tail, protruding head and neck, and heavy bill. Soars and glides with wings held level. Adult has yellow bill, pale head, and white tail. Juvenile is mainly blackish-brown with whitish centres to tail feathers, pale patch on axillaries, and variable pale band across underwing-coverts; bill becomes yellow with age. Lacks whitish patch on underside of primaries of Pallas's Fish Eagle. **Voice** Mainly silent in winter. **HH** Catches fish by seizing them near the surface; also, waterbirds and small mammals by flying low along water's edge. Coasts, large lakes and rivers.

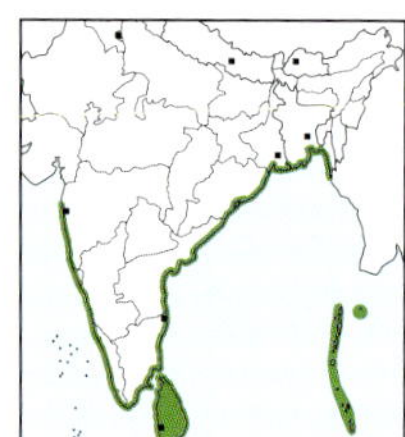

White-bellied Sea Eagle ***Icthyophaga leucogaster*** 75–85cm

Resident. Mainly coasts and offshore islands. **ID** Soars and glides with wings pressed forward and in pronounced V. Distinctive shape, with slim head, bulging secondaries, and short wedge-shaped tail. Adult has white head and underparts, grey upperparts, white underwing-coverts contrasting with black remiges, and mainly white tail. Juvenile has pale head, dark breast-band, whitish tail with dark terminal band and pale wedge on inner primaries. Immatures show mixture of juvenile and adult features. **Voice** Loud, far-carrying and goose-like honking, *ank... ank... ank*, and faster and more duck-like *ka, ka-kaaa*. **HH** Often on a prominent perch, usually near water. Captures prey seized close to water surface after stooping from a perch or from soaring flight. Chiefly coasts and offshore islands. **TN** Sometimes placed in *Haliaeetus*.

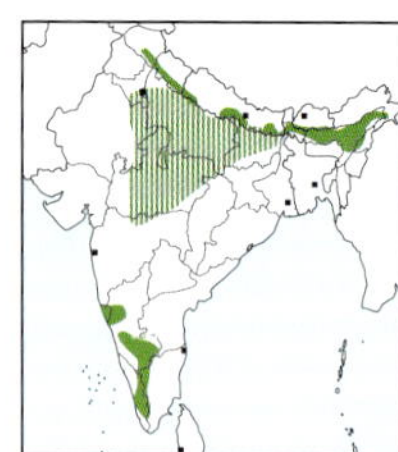

Lesser Fish Eagle ***Icthyophaga humilis*** 51–68cm

Resident. Himalayas and adjacent plains and SW India. **ID** Small, with broad wings and very short tail, and rather small and protruding head and neck. Soars with wings held slightly raised and curved forwards. Smaller than Grey-headed Fish Eagle, with shorter tail. Wingtips almost reach tail tip at rest. In flight, from below, feet reach darker subterminal band. Adult differs from Grey-headed in having dark tail (uppertail is brown becoming darker towards tip; from below shows greyish base with blackish subterminal band which can appear strikingly two-toned). Juvenile has head and underparts uniform grey-brown or with diffuse pale streaking, and upperparts are comparatively uniform compared with juvenile Grey-headed. Has barred tail with narrower dark subterminal band, barred underwing with diffuse dark trailing edge. Subadult more closely resembles adult but has barring on flight feathers of underwing. **Voice** Characteristic penetrating plaintive wail, *pheeow-pheeoow-pheeow* and shorter *pheeo-pheeo*. **HH** Usually seen perched overlooking water. Feeds on fish seized near the surface. Forested streams, rivers and lakes in the lowlands and foothills. **TN** Sometimes placed in *Haliaeetus*.

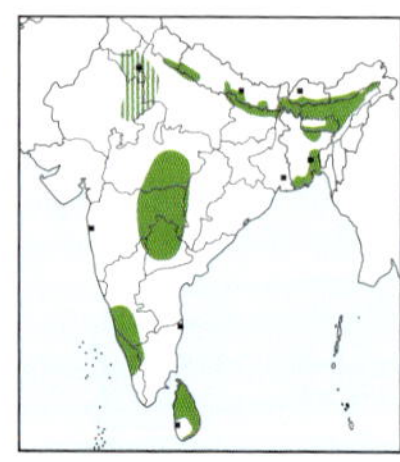

Grey-headed Fish Eagle ***Icthyophaga ichthyaetus*** 61–75cm

Widespread resident; unrecorded in Pakistan. **ID** Larger than Lesser, with longer tail. Wingtips fall noticeably short of tail tip at rest, with white tail base visible beyond closed wings at rest. In flight, from below, feet fall noticeably short of black subterminal band. Adult from Lesser by largely white tail with broad black subterminal band apparent on upper- and underside. Also, darker and browner upperparts and deeper rufous-brown breast resulting in more contrasting grey head and neck. Juvenile has pale head, bold cream streaking on underparts, and bold cream tips to feathers of upperparts creating spotted appearance. Tail has diffuse brown barring, with blackish subterminal band, and pale underwing with dark barring to flight feathers and pronounced dark trailing edg.. **Voice** Most common call a loud far-carrying clanging resembling Indian Grey Hornbill; also, a high-pitched scream, an owl-like *ooo-wok* and loud gurgling calls. **HH** Habits like Lesser. Near slow-running rivers and streams, lakes, reservoirs and tidal lagoons in wooded country. **TN** Sometimes placed in *Haliaeetus*.

Pallas's Fish Eagle
ad
juv
ad
juv
imm
Vhite-tailed Eagle
ad
juv
juv
imm
ad
d
White-bellied
Sea Eagle
juv
ad
juv
imm
Lesser Fish Eagle
ad
juv
Grey-headed Fish Eagle
ad
juv
ad
juv

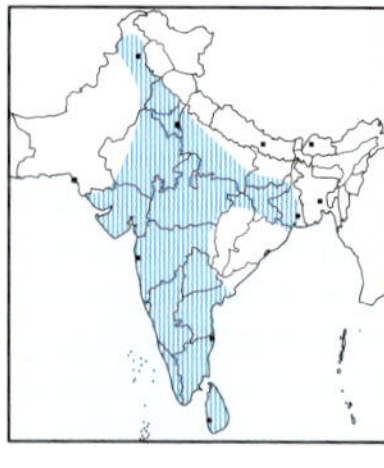

Common Buzzard *Buteo buteo* 40–52cm

Probably widespread winter visitor (*B. b. vulpinus* 'Steppe Buzzard') but status uncertain. Vagrant: Bhutan. **ID** Stocky, with broad rounded wings and moderate-length tail. Plumage very variable and identification can be very challenging. Most numerous rufous morph has rufous on underparts and underwing-coverts, and narrowly-barred rufous tail. Different to Himalayan but can be very similar to typical Long-legged. Intermediate and dark morphs have browner to dark brown underparts and underwing-coverts and lack rufous on tail; can be very similar in plumage to Himalayan and Long-legged (latter best separated by differences in structure; see these species). Juvenile lacks dark trailing edge to wings and tail-band of adult. **Voice** Main call a loud, repeated mew *peee-oo*. **HH** Sluggish; spends much time perched on prominent positions, such as trees, rocks or posts. Soars for prolonged periods. Hunts by pouncing on prey from a vantage point or when soaring and sometimes hovering. Open-country habitats: cultivation, grassland and scrub desert.

Himalayan Buzzard *Buteo refectus* 43–53cm

Resident and winter visitor to Himalayas; also, winter visitor to NW and NE India. **ID** Stocky, with shorter and broader wings with blunter wingtip than Common. Smaller, less eagle-like with weaker bill, and shorter wings, than Long-legged and Upland. Tail is typically grey-brown to greyish-white with diffuse dark barring and dark terminal band. Plumage very variable. A combination of the following, variable, features help separate from some Common Buzzard which can be very similar: pronounced dark moustachial stripe (in some dark chin and forehead); darker belly (can be restricted to sides) than breast, variably separated by pale 'U'-shaped pectoral band, prominent dark carpal patch on underwing, and barred inner primaries. Upland and some Long-legged can be similar in plumage and are best separated by structural differences. Dark morph is probably not safely identified in the field on plumage from dark morphs of other buzzard species. Juvenile lacks dark trailing edge to wings and tail-band of adult. **Voice** Calls like Common, but higher-pitched, thinner in tone and of shorter duration. **HH** Habits like Common. Mountains and cultivated slopes. **TN** Much confusion and further work is needed in relation to Japanese or Eastern Buzzard *B. japonicus*.

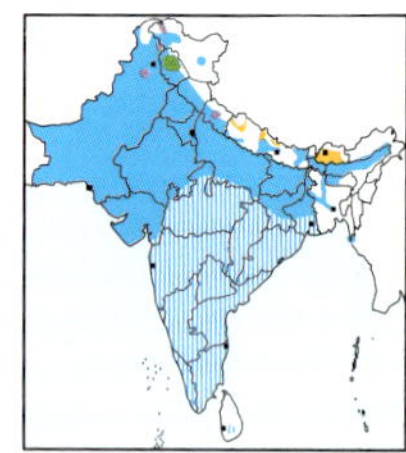

Long-legged Buzzard *Buteo rufinus* 43–62-cm

Breeds in Pakistan Himalayas and Kashmir; mainly winters in Pakistan, Himalayas, Assam and Bangladesh. Vagrant: Sri Lanka. **ID** Larger and longer-necked than Common and Himalayan Buzzards, with bigger bill, more pronounced gape, and longer wings and tail; soars with wings in deeper V. Most differ from Common and Himalayan Buzzards in having combination of paler head and upper breast, rufous-brown lower breast and belly, more uniform rufous underwing-coverts, more extensive black carpal patches, larger pale primary patch on upperwing, pale panel on upperwing-coverts, and unbarred pale orange uppertail. Intermediate and dark morphs much as some plumages of Common and Himalayan Buzzards. Juvenile generally less rufous, with narrower and more diffuse trailing edge to wing, and lightly barred tail, which on many is pale greyish-brown; more prominent dark carpal patches and belly than Common. **Voice** Main call like Common but shorter and less squealing: a loud plaintive mewing scream, *kyaaah*, sometimes lower-pitched. **HH** Habits like Common. Breeds in forested hills and mountains; winters in open-country habitats.

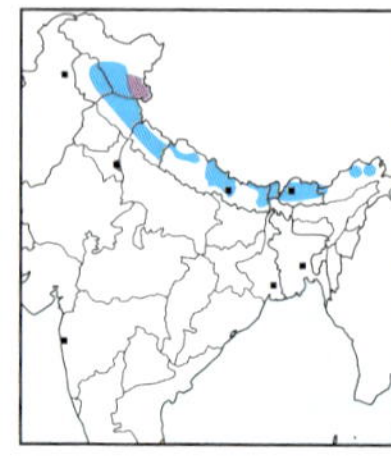

Upland Buzzard *Buteo hemilasius* 66–71cm

Breeds in Ladakh and possibly in Nepal; winters in Himalayas. **ID** Larger, longer-winged and longer-tailed than Himalayan Buzzard; soars with wings in deeper V. Tarsus at least three-quarters feathered (half-feathered or less in other *Buteo* species). 'Classic' pale morph has a combination of large white primary patch on upperwing, greyish-white tail (with fine bars towards tip), whitish head and underparts with dark brown streaking, brown thighs, and extensive black carpal patches (some Himalayan very similar); never has rufous tail or rufous thighs as in many Long-legged. 'Blackish morph' indistinguishable on plumage. Juvenile has less distinct trailing edge to wing than adult, and more prominently barred tail. **Voice** Calls like Common, but more nasal and prolonged. Noisy in breeding season, but otherwise rather silent. **HH** Habits similar to Common. Open country including grassland cultivation in hills and mountains.

ad
dark
morph
ad
rufous
morph
Common Buzzard
ad
Himalayan Buzzard
ad
soaring
ad
intermediate
morph
ad
dark
morph
juv
ad
rufous morph
Long-legged Buzzard
Upland Buzzard
ad
ad
ad
juv
gliding

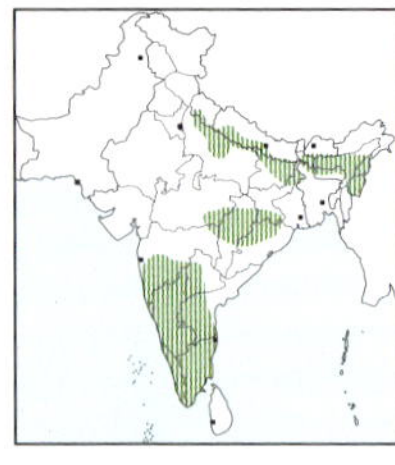

Australasian Grass Owl *Tyto longimembris* 32–38cm

Resident. NE, E and SW India, Uttarakhand, and S Nepal. **ID** Similar to Barn in size and structure, with dark eyes, and pale face and underparts. Upperparts darker and contrast more with underparts than on Barn, being more heavily marked with dark brown (especially on crown and scapulars) and golden-buff (particularly on nape). Further, has dark barring on flight feathers, with dark carpal patch and primary tips, and has dark-barred white or buff tail which usually contrasts with dark uppertail-coverts. Legs longer and feathered only halfway down tarsus (feathered to feet in Barn). Mottled rather than streaked upperparts, lack of prominent streaking on breast, pale bill and black eyes are useful features from Short-eared Owl which may be found in similar habitats. **Voice** Like Barn, though less noisy. **HH** Spends day roosting in a small clearing in tall grass. Hunting behaviour like Barn. Tall grassland. **AN** Eastern Grass Owl.

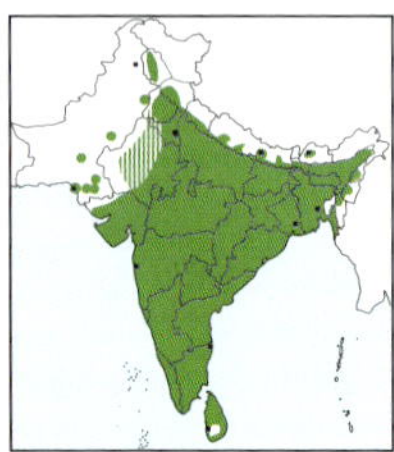

Barn Owl *Tyto alba* 29–44cm

Widespread resident. **ID** Readily identified throughout much of region by combination of unmarked white face and contrasting black eyes, white to golden-buff underparts finely spotted with black, and golden-buff and grey upperparts finely spotted with black and white. Wings and tail appear very uniform in flight, lacking any prominent tail barring or wing patches. **Voice** Varied eerie, screeching and hissing noises. **HH** Mainly crepuscular and nocturnal. Hunts by quartering open country a few metres above vegetation. Habitation and cultivation.

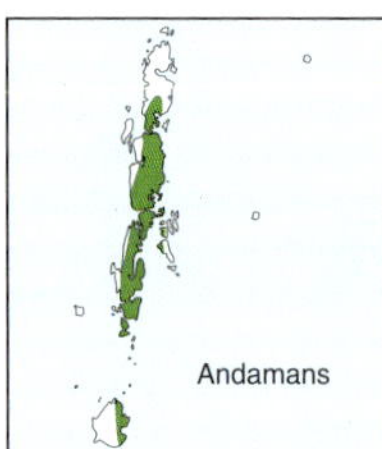

Andaman Masked Owl *Tyto deroepstorffi* 30cm

Resident. Andamans. **ID** Differs from Barn Owl (which does not occur on Andamans) by rufous face and underparts (latter with extensive dark spotting), and darker upperparts heavily marked with rufous and dark brown. Tail is barred. Bill larger, and legs and feet stronger-looking, and in flight, shorter wings and tail, and rufous underwing-coverts. **Voice** A high-pitched, relatively short, slightly down-slurred, raspy screech that breaks off abruptly, *sshreeet*. **HH** Nocturnal. Coastal areas, fields, human settlements, semi-open landscapes with trees. **AN** Andaman Barn Owl.

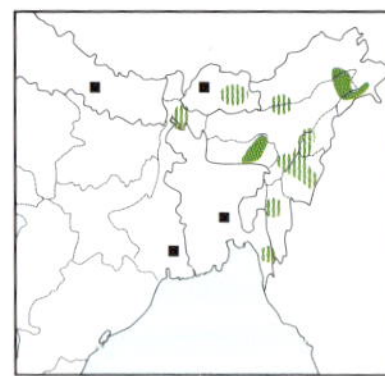

Oriental Bay Owl *Phodilus badius* 23–29cm

Resident. NE India. **ID** Stocky, medium-sized owl with short, rounded wings and short tail. Legs are long and feathered to feet. Bill pale. Eyes very large and dark. Head shape varies with posture but often (e.g. when roosting) very distinctive with wide forehead and oblong-shaped facial discs (can protrude as broad 'ear-tufts'). Has rich chestnut-and-buff upperparts spotted with white and black, vinaceous-pink forehead and facial discs with dark vertical stripe through eye, narrow white-and-blackish necklace and border to facial discs, and vinaceous-pink underparts spotted black. **Voice** Wide variety of calls including a series of eerie, upward-inflected whistles. **HH** Strictly nocturnal. Dense evergreen broadleaved forest.

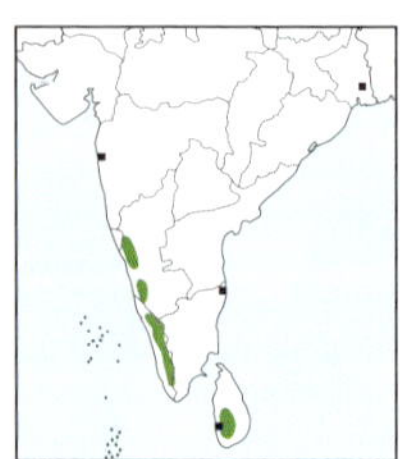

Sri Lanka Bay Owl *Phodilus assimilis* 22–27cm

Resident. SW India and Sri Lanka. **ID** Very similar to Oriental Bay but has darker brown crown and nape (flecked buff and black) and is darker brown on mantle and coverts with more extensive buff and black spots (crown/nape and mantle/coverts of Oriental Bay are brighter and more uniform chestnut with more irregular spotting). Has more pronounced and buffier collar, and more pronounced and complete dark barring on wings and tail. Also, broader dark brown vertical stripe through eyes, joining at bill to form pronounced facial 'V' in some postures. **Voice** Main call a series of 3–4 tremulous whistles, initially rising, then falling: *weeou-wee-youu*. **HH** Wet evergreen and mixed evergreen-deciduous forest, mangroves in lowlands and foothills; dense forests with rich undergrowth in Sri Lanka. Nocturnal. **TN** Previously treated as conspecific with Oriental Bay Owl.

ad
ad
Barn Owl
Australasian Grass Owl
ad
Andaman Masked Owl
ad
ad
at rest
ad
Oriental Bay Owl
Sri Lanka Bay Owl

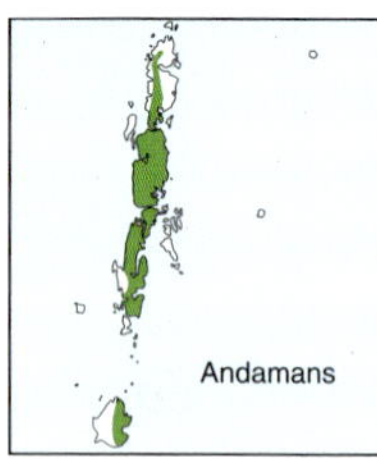

Andaman Scops Owl *Otus balli* 18–19cm

Resident. Andamans. **ID** From Oriental Scops Owl by comparatively uniform upperparts and underparts without bold streaking; white scapular spots are prominent. Facial disc poorly defined, and has small stubby ear-tufts. Crown, nape and mantle have sparse and indistinct buff and dark brown markings. Underparts finely vermiculated with diffuse buffish drop-like spots and irregular well-defined short dark streaks. Weaker legs and feet than Oriental, and tarsus partly bare (feathered to feet in Oriental). Bill and claws are yellow. Occurs in brown and rufous morphs. **Voice** Strong loud *hoot! hoot-curroo*... with characteristically rolled '*r*'. **HH** Habits poorly described. Cultivation and around human habitation.

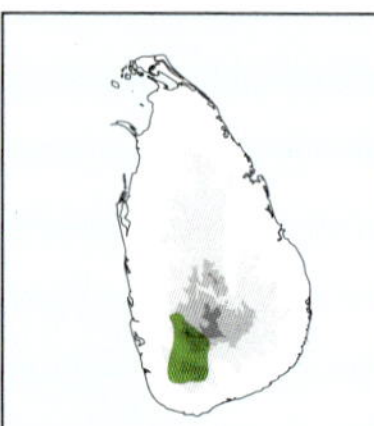

Serendib Scops Owl *Otus thilohoffmanni* 17cm

Resident. Sri Lanka. Endemic, fairly rare and local, in wet lowlands to mid hills. **ID** Small owl with yellow eyes but without true ear-tufts. Uniform rufous upperparts with tiny black spots, facial disc rufous without markings, underparts paler rufous with black spots, bill whitish, legs pinkish-white, and iris orangey in male and yellow in female. When alert, vertical compression of facial disc forms two shorter projections of 'false' ear-tufts. Juvenile like female but has a poorly formed facial disc. **Voice** Song a short, soft but far-carrying musical *whoo-oh*, with first syllable rising and second falling, slightly. **HH** Nocturnal and territorial; in pairs. Larger areas of dense rainforest and submontane forest. Globally threatened.

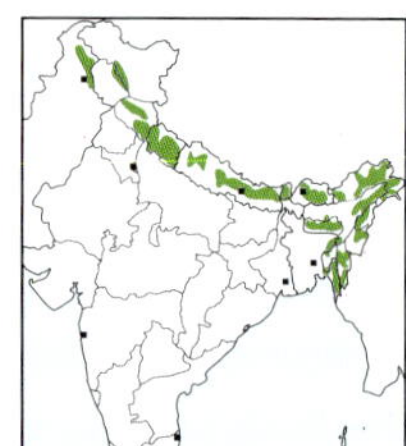

Mountain Scops Owl *Otus spilocephalus* 18–20cm

Resident. Himalayas, NE India and Bangladesh. **ID** From similar species by unstreaked underparts, which are indistinctly spotted with buff and barred brown, and by unstreaked upperparts mottled with buff, brown and white (crown and nape usually the most heavily marked). Has poorly defined facial discs, and stubby ear-tufts (although these can be prominent). Bill, feet and claws typically pale (but can be dark). Often shows a paler band on upper mantle (forming diffuse 'collar'). In W Himalayas (*O. s. huttoni*) are grey or fulvous-brown, while those in E Himalayas (*O. s. spilocephalus*) are rufous. **Voice** Clear, piercing, two-note whistle, *plew-plew*... **HH** Entirely nocturnal and difficult to see like other scops owls. Spends day in a tree hollow. Begins calling about an hour before dark. Chiefly insectivorous. Dense evergreen broadleaved forest.

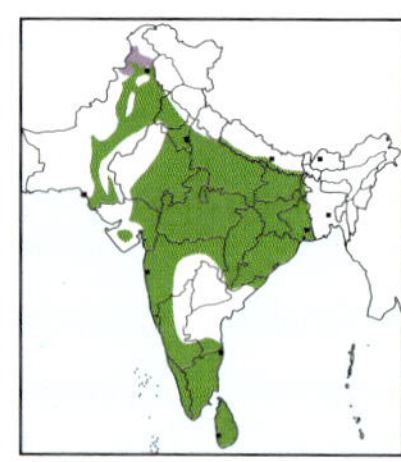

Indian Scops Owl *Otus bakkamoena* 20–22cm

Widespread resident south of Himalayas except most of NW subcontinent and SE India. **ID** From Oriental by larger size, prominent buff nuchal collar edged dark brown, more finely streaked underparts, and buffish (less distinct) scapular spots. Eyes typically dark orange or brown, but can be yellow (yellow in Oriental). Very variable in coloration: can be pale grey-brown (e.g. *O. b. deserticolor* from drier parts of Pakistan) or warm rufous-brown (e.g. in nominate subspecies of Sri Lanka). Very similar to Collared (some probably indistinguishable), and mainly separated by call, which is variable (see below). **Voice** Call is a subdued, frog-like *whuk*, repeated at irregular intervals; also gives a rising series of chattering calls. **HH** Hides by day in a densely foliaged tree, often close against the trunk or in dark tree hollow. Forest and well-wooded areas. **TN** Often considered conspecific with the following species as Collared Scops Owl *O. bakkamoena*.

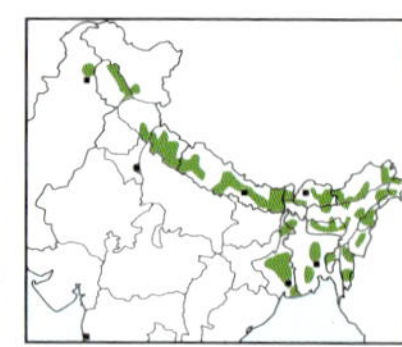

Collared Scops Owl *Otus lettia* 23–25cm

Resident. Himalayas, NE India and Bangladesh. **ID** Separated from Indian mainly by call, although this is not considered to be diagnostic; also, longer ear-tufts are spotted (rather than barred), upperparts more heavily and irregularly marked with short dark streaks and cross-bars (Indian has finer, longer streaks on upperparts), and yellowish bill lacks dark tip. **Voice** Call is softer and less staccato than Indian with a falling inflection, *bwoo*. **HH** Habits like Indian. Forest and well-wooded areas.

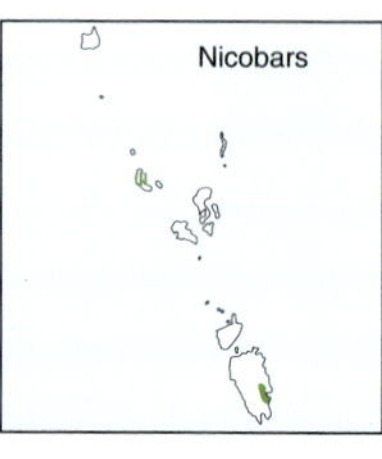

Nicobar Scops Owl *Otus alius* 19–20cm

Resident. Great Nicobar Island. **ID** Quite different from rufous morph of Oriental, which is only other scops owl in the Nicobars. Brownish in coloration and uniform in appearance. Upperparts and underparts diffusely barred brown, buff and white, with the irregular white barring on underparts particularly prominent. Shows prominent white scapular spots. Forehead is streaked and underparts have sparse and irregular dark streaking. Poorly defined facial discs and stubby ear-tufts. Bill, feet and claws are pale. **Voice** Protracted, melancholic, repeated moan on rising scale, *ooo-m*. **HH** Coastal forest.

brown morph
Serendib Scops Owl
ad
ad
huttoni
ad
spilocephalus
Andaman Scops Owl
rufous morph
ediate
rph
thae
brown
morph
marathae
Mountain Scops Owl
ad
Collared Scops Owl
Indian Scops Owl
ad
Nicobar Scops Owl
buff morph
marathae
ad
deserticolor

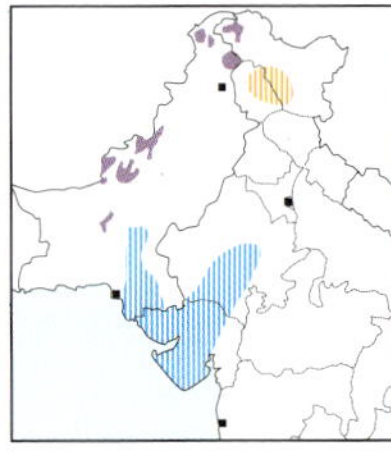

Eurasian Scops Owl *Otus scops* 16–20cm

Summer visitor to N and W Pakistan mountains; winters in S Pakistan and NW India. **ID** Occurs as grey and brown morphs. Not safely distinguishable in the field from Oriental Scops, except by call, but is more finely marked below (finer dark streaks, less marked black cross-bars and smaller white markings) and has longer primary projection (see Oriental). Within range, most likely to be confused with Pallid and best told by prominent white spots on scapulars, pale horizontal bars on underparts, and different call. **Voice** Plaintive bell-like whistle, repeated for many minutes. **HH** Habits like Oriental. Scrub in dry rocky hills and valleys.

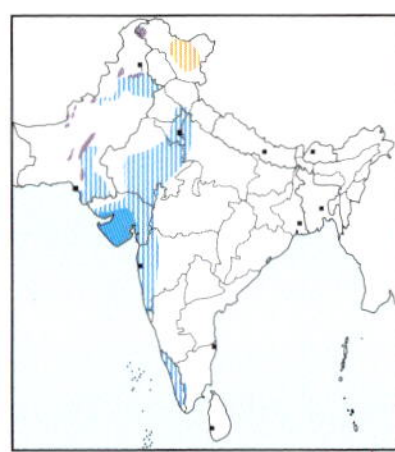

Pallid Scops Owl *Otus brucei* 18–21cm

Resident in Pakistan and winters south to SW India. **ID** Paler and greyer than grey-morph Eurasian Scops, lacking rufous; has less distinct (buff not white) scapular spots, and narrow black streaking on underparts, which lack pale horizontal panels. Facial disc paler and plainer with black border finer but stronger. Primary coverts more strongly patterned, with broad sandy-white bars. Fewer pale bars on tail (2–4 rather than 5–7 on central rectrices) than Eurasian. Primary tips do not project beyond tail (slight projection on Eurasian). Juvenile completely barred below including facial discs, juvenile Eurasian more closely resembles adult. **Voice** Hollow, low-pitched *whoop-whoop-whoop*. **HH** Spends day in crevice, tree hole or thick foliage. Stony foothills in semi-desert.

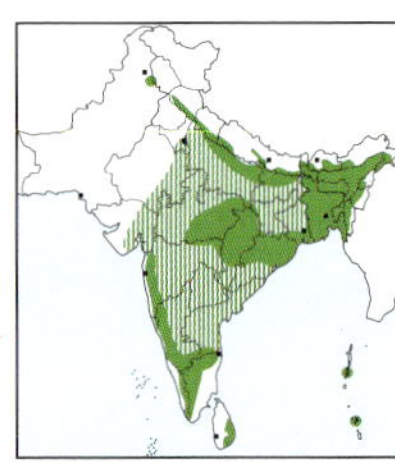

Oriental Scops Owl *Otus sunia* 17–21cm

Resident. Himalayas, India, and Sri Lanka. **ID** Very variable, with grey, brown and rufous morphs. Prominent white scapular spots, streaked underparts and upperparts, lacks prominent nuchal collar. Rufous morph distinct from Eurasian Scops; others appear virtually identical, although Oriental is more heavily marked above and below, and has shorter primary projection (4–5, rather than 6–7, primaries extend beyond tertials). Sri Lankan *O. s. leggei* is smaller and dark, and finely marked below. Nicobar *O. s. nicobaricus* is rufous, and can be uniform bright rufous, including facial discs (without markings except white scapular spots). **Voice** Repeated, rhythmic frog-like *wut chu chraaii*; in Sri Lanka described as a rhythmic clear *wuck kuk-kukurri*. **HH** Hides by day in dense foliage. Forest and around habitation.

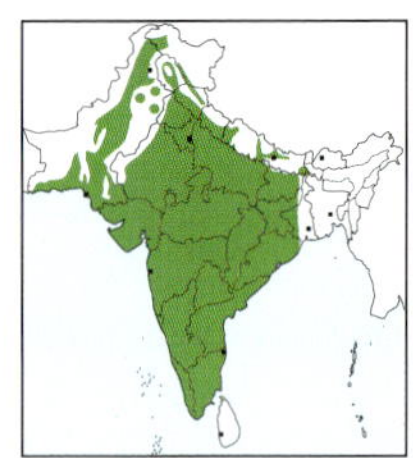

Rock Eagle Owl *Bubo bengalensis* 50–56cm

Resident. Pakistan and Himalayan foothills and south through peninsula; chiefly below 1,500m. **ID** From Eurasian by darker more heavily marked upperparts, pronounced dark border to facial discs, buff scapular spots, and heavily barred wings and tail. From Brown Fish Owl by more upright ear-tufts, pronounced facial discs, broader breast streaking, and entirely feathered legs. **Voice** Deep double hoot on single pitch, *bu-whúoh*, with second note longer and stressed (higher-pitched than Eurasian Eagle). **HH** Rocky hills, scrub, ravines, old mango plantations, groves with aged trees, rocky semi-desert with thorn scrub, and ruins. **TN** Previously treated as conspecific with Eurasian Eagle Owl.

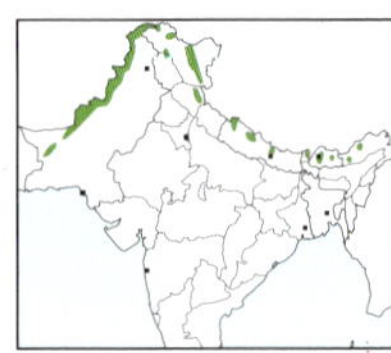

Eurasian Eagle Owl *Bubo bubo* 58–71cm

Resident. Balochistan hills, Himalayas and Arunachal; above 1,800m. **ID** Very large, with pronounced upright ear-tufts. Upperparts mottled dark brown and greyish-buff; underparts heavily streaked on breast with fine cross-barring. Larger, paler and greyer than Indian Eagle Owl, with less heavily marked upperparts, plainer facial discs (lacking pronounced dark border) and less heavily barred wings and tail. **Voice** Call a resonant *whooh-tu*, first note stressed and longer. **HH** Cliffs and open rocky areas.

Pallid
Scops Owl
ad
grey
morph
ad
brown
morph
juv
ad
Eurasian
Scops Owl
ad
nicobaricus
ad
brown/grey
morph
leggei
Oriental
Scops Owl
ad
rufous morph
leggei
ad
grey morph
sunia
ad
rufous morph
sunia
ad
ad
Rock
Eagle Owl
Eurasian
Eagle Owl

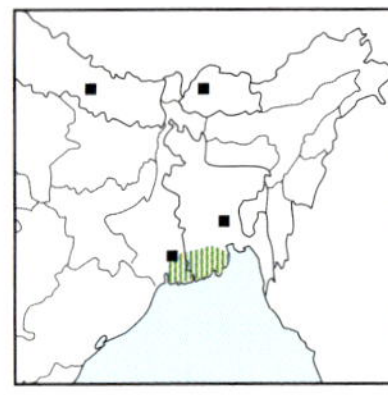

Buffy Fish Owl *Ketupa ketupu* 40–48cm

Resident. Sundarbans in Bangladesh and India; formerly in Assam. **ID** From the much larger Tawny by finer streaking on underparts, with only very fine shaft streaks on belly and flanks, and duller buffish-white to greyish-white barring on flight feathers and tail (more orange-buff on Tawny). From Brown by white forehead (although not always apparent), more rufous-orange upperparts with thicker and more prominent black streaking, orange-buff underparts with more clearly defined black streaking on breast, and no black cross-barring on underparts. **Voice** Loud *kootookookootook...*, ringing *pof pof pof*, and musical *to-whee to-whee*; also, hisses, mews and shrieks. **HH** Forested streams in plains and mangroves.

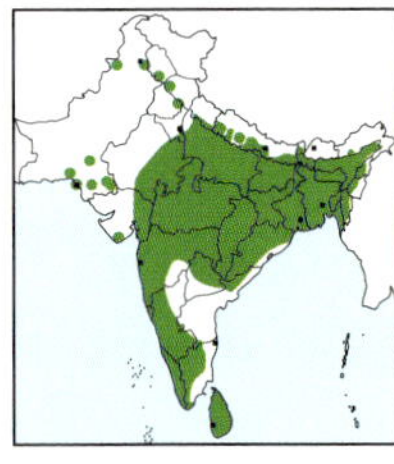

Brown Fish Owl *Ketupa zeylonensis* 48–58cm

Widespread resident except most of NW subcontinent and SE India. **ID** From Tawny and Buffy by combination of duller brown upperparts, finer dark brown streaking on crown, mantle and scapulars, finer streaking on dull buff underparts (with close cross-barring, lacking on other species), and absence of white above the bill. **Voice** Deep, hollow, eerie-sounding, humming *boom boom* or *boo o-boom* repeated at intervals and with ventriloquial quality. **HH** Nocturnal. Forest and well-wooded areas near water in tropical and subtropical zone.

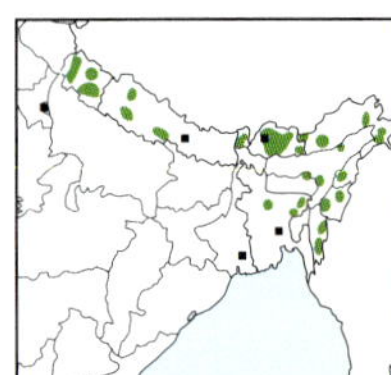

Tawny Fish Owl *Ketupa flavipes* 48–58cm

Resident. Himalayas, NE India and Bangladesh. **ID** From the smaller Brown by pale orange upperparts (much more richly coloured than on Brown) with bolder and more distinct black streaking, bold orange-buff barring on wing-coverts and flight feathers, and broader and more prominent black streaking on pale rufous-orange underparts, which lack black cross-barring; often shows prominent whitish patch on forehead. See Buffy Fish Owl for differences from latter. **Voice** A deep, booming *whoo-huwooh* and a screeching alarm. **HH** Nocturnal. Banks of streams and rivers in dense broadleaved forest in tropical and subtropical zone.

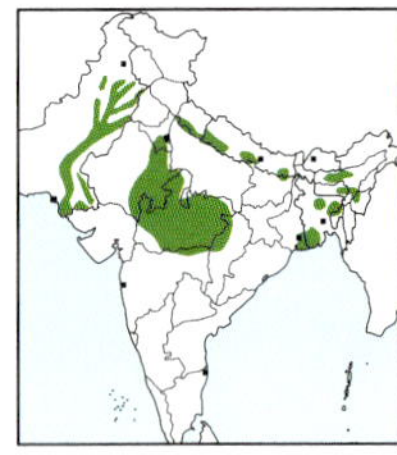

Dusky Eagle Owl *Ketupa coromanda* 48–53cm

Widespread resident; unrecorded in Sri Lanka. **ID** Upperparts greyish-brown, finely vermiculated whitish, with diffuse darker brown streaking; underparts greyish-white, finely vermiculated and more strongly streaked with brown. Has whitish spots on scapulars. Greyer and much less heavily marked than Rock Eagle Owl. From Brown Fish Owl by more upright ear-tufts, more pronounced facial discs, more uniform grey-brown upperparts, less strongly-banded flight feathers, and lack of any rufous tones. Legs feathered to toes (largely unfeathered in Brown Fish Owl). **Voice** Series of deep, accelerating croaking notes, *wo wo wo wo wo-wo-wowowo*, becoming softer with each note; also, a low, deep rumbling *woo-woo-woo*. **HH** Usually nocturnal, emerging an hour before sunset. Well-watered areas with extensive tree cover in tropical zone. **TN** Often placed in *Bubo*.

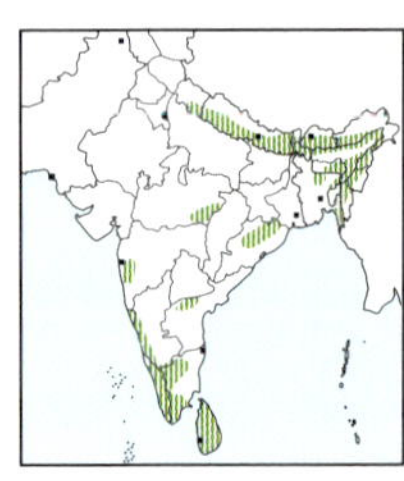

Spot-bellied Eagle Owl *Ketupa nipalensis* 51–63cm

Resident. Himalayas, NE India, Western Ghats, Sri Lanka and Bangladesh. **ID** Very large, with bold chevron-shaped spots on whitish underparts, whitish facial discs, buff-barred dark brown upperparts, large pale bill, and brown eyes. Juvenile very distinctive: crown, mantle, coverts, rump and underparts are white and buff, with brown spotting and barring, and face is off-white. Sri Lankan *K. n. blighi* is smaller, darker and has narrower barring on underparts. **Voice** Deep, low, resounding *hoo hoo*; also, loud, mournful scream with rising and falling rhythm. **HH** Nocturnal. Heavy evergreen and moist deciduous tropical and subtropical broadleaved forest. **TN** Often placed in *Bubo*.

ad
Buffy
Fish Owl
ad
ad
Brown Fish Owl
Tawny Fish
Owl
ad
ad
juv
ad
Dusky Eagle Owl
Spot-bellied
Eagle Owl

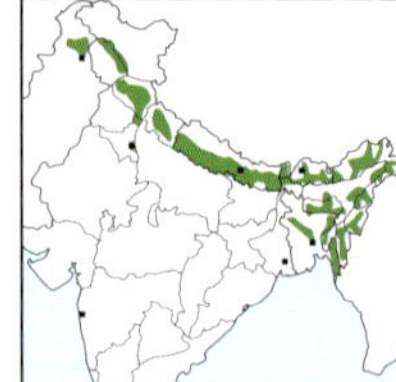

Asian Barred Owlet *Glaucidium cuculoides* 22–25cm

Resident. Himalayas, NE India and Bangladesh. **ID** From Jungle by larger size and longer, fuller-looking tail, buff barring on wing-coverts and flight feathers (wings of Jungle barred rufous and contrast with buff-barred mantle), and less finely barred upperparts, with underparts usually noticeably streaked (barring continues over underparts and onto lower flanks on Jungle). Lower flank pattern varies and may appear barred (but more broadly and diffusely than on Jungle). Juvenile has buff spotting on crown, nape and mantle; breast-barring and flank-streaking more diffuse. In E Himalayas and NE subcontinent (*G. c. austerum* and *G. c. rufescens*) more rufous, with rufous-buff barring and streaking. **Voice** Territorial song: varied series of high barking notes; loud, clear *hooloo hoolo hoolo*, followed by *kok kok*, ending with short, shrill *chiurr*. In breeding season: a bubbling whistle, *wowowowowowowowowo*. **HH** Mainly diurnal, often perching conspicuously on bare branches, from where it scans and listens for prey. Wags tail when alarmed. Broadleaved subtropical and temperate forests.; also, open temperate forest of oak, pine and rhododendron.

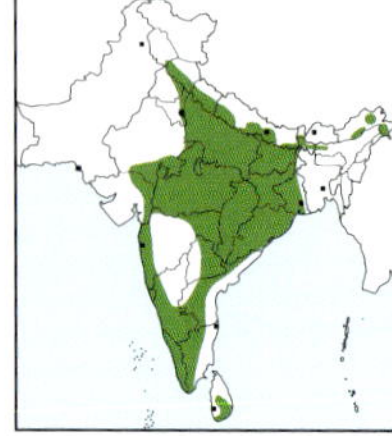

Jungle Owlet *Glaucidium radiatum* 20–22cm

Widespread resident; unrecorded in most of north-west and north-east. **ID** From Asian Barred by smaller size, bright rufous barring on wing-coverts and flight feathers contrasting with buff barring on mantle (wings of Asian Barred are barred with buff and therefore concolorous with mantle), more closely barred upperparts and underparts with bars continuing onto belly and across lower flanks, and more numerous pale bars on tail (with narrower blackish bands). In Malabar coastal strip (*G. r. malabaricum*) more rufous, particularly on breast, crown, mantle and scapulars. **Voice** Series of loud trills, the phrases repeated at intervals of several seconds, starting softly and becoming louder before fading toward end. **HH** Mainly crepuscular, sometimes active in daytime. Spends day in foliage or tree hollow. Open broadleaved forest and second growth in tropical and subtropical zones.

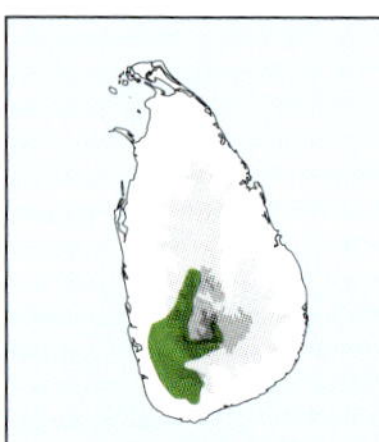

Chestnut-backed Owlet *Glaucidium castanotum* 17–19cm

Resident. Sri Lanka. **ID** Similar to Jungle, which also occurs in Sri Lanka, but back and wing-coverts are bright chestnut (narrowly and diffusely barred with brown and some buff). At a distance, chestnut upperparts contrast markedly with greyish head and blackish tail which is narrowly barred with white. Lower throat and band across breast are barred brown and buff as on Jungle, but belly and flanks are noticeably streaked (rather than barred). Whitish 'eyebrows' are virtually absent. **Voice** Short series of far-carrying *krrraw* notes, begin softly then increase slightly in pitch and volume. Commonly calls during day. **HH** Shy and wary. Diurnal, often calls and hunts in daylight. Generally keeps to tops of tall trees. Dense forests of wet zone.

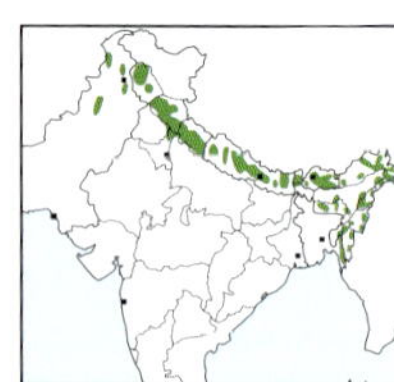

Collared Owlet *Taenioptynx brodiei* 15–17cm

Resident. Himalayas, NE India and Bangladesh. **ID** Most like Jungle Owlet, but much smaller, and has distinct buff (or rufous) 'spectacles' on nape that frame blackish patches (creating pattern resembling an owl's face). Further, crown appears spotted rather than neatly and finely barred, and much of underparts have a streaked or spotted rather than barred appearance (compare Jungle Owlet; barring confined to upper breast and flanks). Occurs as rufous, grey and brown morphs. Rufous birds in E India very striking, with crown, upperparts and tail bright rufous and heavily barred brown, and underparts have bold rufous streaking. **Voice** Call is a pleasant four-noted bell-like whistle *toot... tootoot... toot*, the second and third notes close together and uttered in runs of three or four. **HH** Diurnal and crepuscular. Calls persistently day and night in breeding season. Males turn head while calling to produce ventriloquial effect. Subtropical broadleaved and temperate forest of oak, rhododendron and fir. **TN** Often placed in *Glaucidium*.

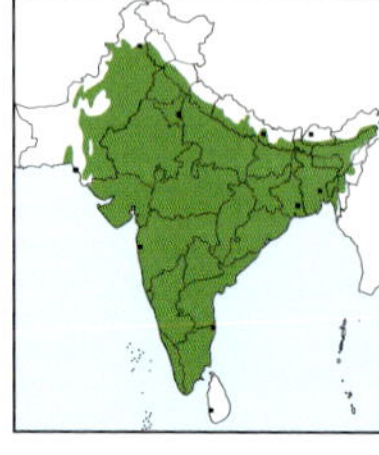

Spotted Owlet *Athene brama* 19–21cm

Widespread resident except SW Pakistan. **ID** From Jungle and Asian Barred by spotted rather than barred appearance (with prominent white spotting on crown, mantle and wing-coverts, and brown spotting rather than close dark barring on underparts). In addition, has whitish surround to facial discs and pale hind collar. In arid regions of W Pakistan, its range overlaps with that of the very similar Little Owl, but has spotted or barred rather than streaked breast and flanks, and irregular white spotting on crown. Birds in N India (*A. b. indica*) are paler, grey-brown in coloration, compared to the nominate subspecies of S India. **Voice** Mixture of screeches, chatters and chuckles. A harsh screechy *chirurr-chirurr-chirurr*, followed by/alternated with *cheevak, cheevak, cheevak*. **HH** Mainly crepuscular and nocturnal, Hides by day in a tree hollow, shady branch of a mature tree, chimney or under roof. Around habitation and cultivation.

Asian Barred Owlet
juv
ad
rufescens
ad
cuculoides
ad
malabaricum
Chestnut-backed
Owlet
ad
Jungle Owlet
ad
radiatum
ad
turning
away
ad
brama
ad
indica
ad
facing
Spotted Owlet
Collared Owlet

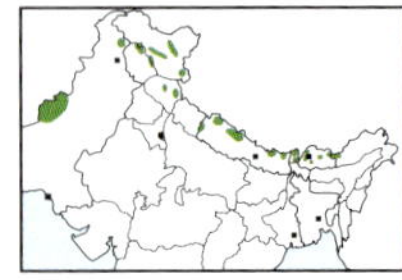

Little Owl *Athene noctua* 21–23cm

Resident. Balochistan and trans-Himalayas. **ID** From smaller Spotted Owlet by streaked rather than spotted breast and flanks, and neatly streaked crown with white streaks arranged in lines (rather than irregularly scattered spots across crown). **Voice** A plaintive *quew* repeated every few seconds and a soft barking *werro-werro*. **HH** Crepuscular and partly diurnal. Most prey captured by pouncing from a vantage point. Cliffs and ruins in semi-desert.

Forest Owlet *Athene blewitti* 20–23cm

Resident. Hills of NC peninsula. **ID** Compared with Spotted has dark grey-brown crown and nape, which is only faintly spotted with white, and lacks prominent white hind collar. Scapulars have some white tips and bars, but are more uniform and not as profusely and irregularly spotted as Spotted. Wings and tail more broadly banded blackish-brown and white, with white-tipped remiges and a broad white tail tip. Breast dark brown and barring on upper flanks broader and more prominent; rest of underparts white, much cleaner than on Spotted. **Voice** Main song a series of quick, plaintive notes; territorial call *kwaak…kwaak, kwaak*, the notes rising in pitch, then falling. **HH** Diurnal and confiding. Fairly open secondary dry deciduous forest. Globally threatened. **TN** Often placed in *Heteroglaux*.

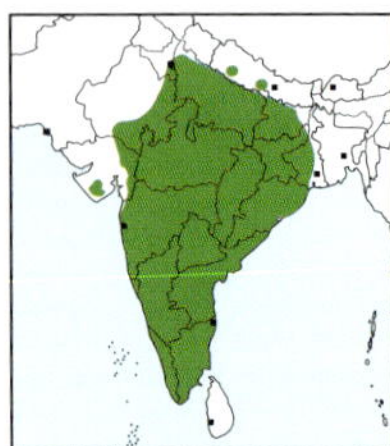

Mottled Wood Owl *Strix ocellata* 41–48cm

Resident. India and S Nepal. **ID** A distinctive owl with dark eyes, black freckling on pale facial discs, white-and-rufous mottling on upperparts, and whitish underparts barred dark brown and mixed with rufous. Shows prominent white 'half-collar' on upper breast. Back and wings barred and mottled dark brown and greyish-white, with some rufous (mainly on coverts and inner edges of remiges). **Voice** Spooky, quavering *whaa-aa-aa-aa-ah* in breeding season; single metallic hoots and a screech at other times. **HH** Chiefly nocturnal. In pairs which roost in shady large tree. Open wooded areas, groves of old, densely foliaged trees around villages and cultivation in the plains.

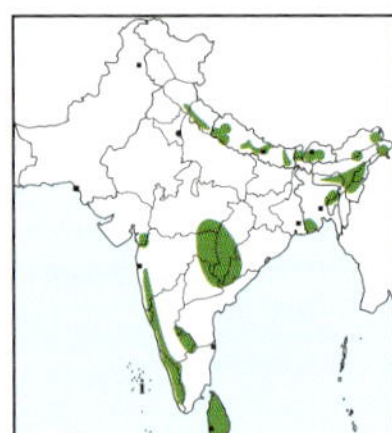

Brown Wood Owl *Strix leptogrammica* 39–55cm

Resident. Himalayas, NE India, Eastern and Western Ghats, Bangladesh and Sri Lanka. **ID** From Mottled by uniform forehead and nape, and mainly brown upperparts (with patch of white barring on scapulars); flight feathers dark brown narrowly barred paler brown. Himalayan *S. l. newarensis* has dark brown face, with prominent white eyebrows, and striking white band on foreneck. Underparts greyish-white heavily barred dark brown. *S. l. indranee* (peninsula) smaller with rufous facial discs. Upperparts more heavily barred, and underparts buffish and barred with brown. **Voice** Calls include a low double hoot *tu-whooo*, and a deep squawk; a musical, *tok….tu-hoo* and a variety of eerie shrieks and chuckles. **HH** Nocturnal. Roosts in large trees in heavy forest. Dense broadleaved subtropical or temperate forest.

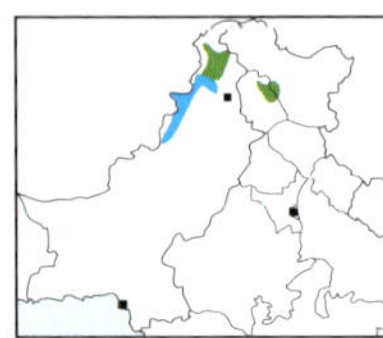

Tawny Owl *Strix aluco* 37–39cm

Resident. N Balochistan, Himalayas of N Pakistan and Kashmir. **ID** Greyer and more uniform in colour than Himalayan. Also, mantle is prominently streaked (rather than mottled/barred), flight feathers are less prominently barred, uppertail more uniform, underparts more heavily streaked (with much less pronounced 'splashes' of white and dark cross-barring). Eyes dark. **Voice** Prolonged, mournful hooting *too-tu-whoo*. **HH** Nocturnal. Roosts in tree, perched close to trunk, partly concealed by leaves. Temperate broadleaved and coniferous forests.

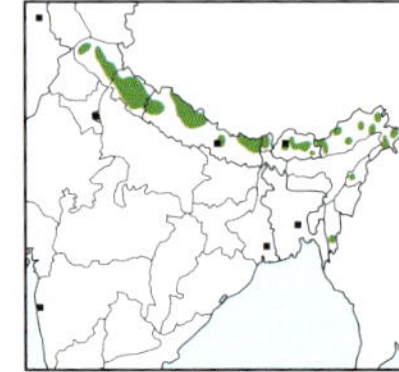

Himalayan Owl *Strix nivicolum* 35–40cm

Resident. Himalayas from W Himachal to Arunachal and NE India. **ID** From Tawny by browner or rufous coloration, mottled/barred mantle, broadly barred flight feathers and tail, and underparts are less prominently streaked and more heavily cross-barred with dark brown and white. Birds in E Himalayas are more rufous below with more pronounced white cross-barring, and facial discs are more rufescent. Eyes dark (as Tawny). **Voice** Song comprises two clear, rapid dove-like hoots, *coo-coo*. **HH** Nocturnal. Subtropical and temperate coniferous forests, oak forest and rocky forested ravines. **AN** Himalayan Wood Owl.

ad
Little Owl
ad
Forest Owlet
ad
indranee
ad
newarensis
ad
Mottled
Wood Owl
Brown
Wood Owl
ad
ad
brown
morph
ad
rufous
morph
Tawny Owl
Himalayan
Owl

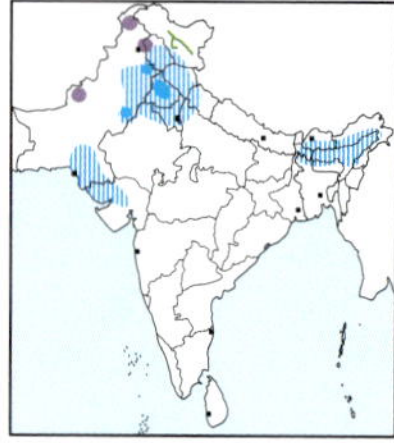

Long-eared Owl *Asio otus* 35–40cm

Mainly a winter visitor to Pakistan and NW India; has bred. Vagrant: Nepal, Bhutan. **ID** From Short-eared at rest by erect ear-tufts, orange-brown coloration to facial discs, orange (rather than yellow) eyes, greyish (rather than buff) background coloration to upperparts, and more heavily streaked belly and flanks. Further differences in flight are finely barred wingtips, lack of white trailing edge to wings, which are more rounded, and more finely barred tail. **Voice** Male's territorial call is a long, drawn, subdued *oo* or *hu*. Mainly silent in non-breeding season. **HH** Nocturnal. Hides in trees and dense thickets in winter, making itself very slim, raises ear-tufts and closes eyes. Hunts by quartering open ground. Stunted trees, dense bushes, light woodland.

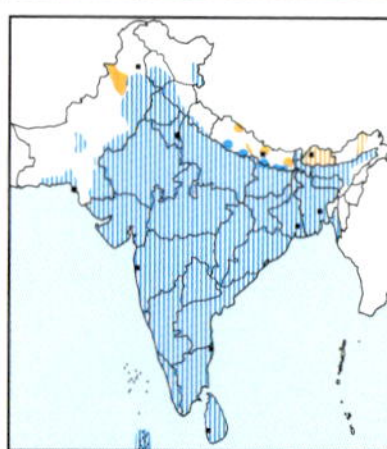

Short-eared Owl *Asio flammeus* 34–42cm

Widespread winter visitor and passage migrant, except parts of NW and NE subcontinent. **ID** From Long-eared at rest by short or apparently no ear-tufts, buffish-white coloration to facial discs, yellow (rather than orange) eyes, buff background coloration to upperparts, and non-existent or indistinct streaking on belly and flanks. Further differences in flight are black wingtips, prominent white trailing edge to upperwing, more boldly barred tail, and narrower wings. **Voice** Generally silent in non-breeding season. **HH** Diurnal and crepuscular. Hunts by quartering low over open country with irregular, rolling flight. Open country with scattered bushes, grassland and semi-desert.

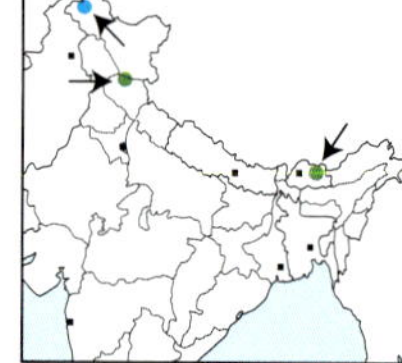

Boreal Owl *Aegolius funereus* 21–28cm

Rare resident? NW India. Vagrant: Pakistan, Bhutan. **ID** Has large, square-shaped head, greyish-white facial discs encircled with black (angular upper edge gives rise to alert expression), and white spotting on forehead and crown. White patches on scapulars and diffusely streaked underparts. Juvenile has uniform brown crown, mantle and underparts, and dark brown facial discs edged white, retaining this plumage for several months. **Voice** Commonest calls a soft, far-carrying, regularly repeated *po-po-po* and a squirrel-like smacking *yiop* or *chiak*. **HH** Nocturnal, retiring to shady tree during day. Scans from a lookout on a tree or boulder and flies down to seize prey. Subalpine juniper scrub and dwarf trees.

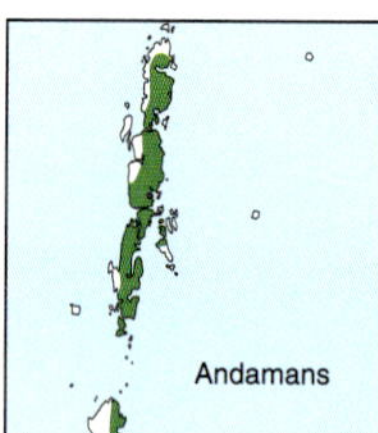

Andaman Hawk Owl *Ninox affinis* 21–28cm

Resident. Andamans. **ID** From sympatric Hume's by smaller size, bold rufous streaking on white underparts, paler greyish-brown upperparts, unmarked undertail-coverts, more broadly barred tail, and different call. Similar to allopatric Brown but is smaller and more compact, has pale bill, less distinct white forehead, which often extends to form narrow whitish 'eyebrows', paler grey-brown upperparts lacking white scapular markings, and more diffuse and extensive rufous streaking on underparts (markings sometimes coalescing so that underparts appear almost entirely rufous). **Voice** Short, hollow, guttural, down-slurred and repeated croak. **HH** Habits like Brown. Forest, secondary woodland and mangroves.

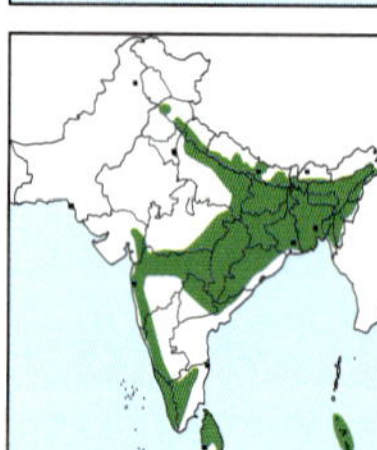

Brown Hawk Owl *Ninox scutulata* 27–33cm

Resident. Himalayan foothills, hills of NE India and Bangladesh; peninsular hills, Sri Lanka and Nicobars. **ID** Hawk-like profile (with slim body, long tail and narrow head). Has uniform brown upperparts showing variable amounts of white spotting on scapulars, all-dark face except variable white patch above bill (but without pale facial discs shown by many owls), and bold rufous-brown streaking and spotting on underparts. Birds in north-east (e.g. *burmanica*), S Western Ghats and Sri Lanka are darker than northern *lugubris*. **Voice** Repeated, mellow rising *whoo-wup, whoo-wup, whoo-wup*. **HH** Crepuscular and nocturnal, roosting in treetops. Tropical and subtropical forest and well-wooded areas.

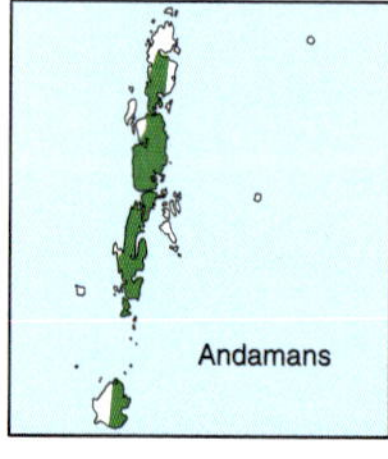

Hume's Hawk Owl *Ninox obscura* 26–30cm

Resident. Andamans. **ID** Almost entirely dark brown, becoming more rufous-brown on underparts, which lack broad well-defined streaking. Has small whitish patch on forehead, indistinct buffish-white spotting on flanks and belly, and strong greyish-white and brown barring on undertail-coverts. **Voice** Like Brown, but slightly higher-pitched: *wooo-oop, wooo-oop, wooo-oop*. **HH** Crepuscular and nocturnal. Lowland forest, forest edge, rubber plantations, near human settlements, often near water. **TN** Formerly treated as conspecific with Brown Hawk Owl.

Long-eared
Owl
ad
Short-eared
Owl
ad
ad
Boreal Owl
Andaman
Hawk Owl
ad
ad
lugubris
ad
burmanica
Brown Hawk Owl
ad
Hume's Hawk Owl

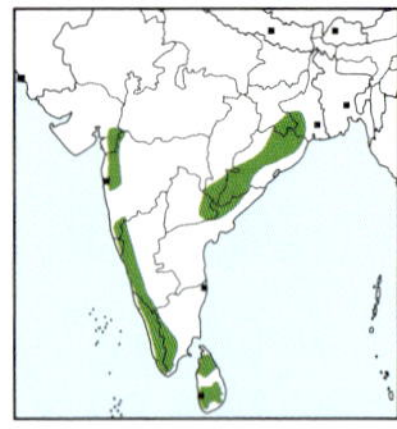

Malabar Trogon *Harpactes fasciatus* 29–30cm

Resident. Western and Eastern Ghats, hills of W Tamil Nadu, Sri Lanka. **ID** Eye-ring and bill can be bright blue. Male has grey to blackish head and breast, white breast-band, pinkish-red underparts, black-and-grey vermiculated wing-coverts. Female: dark cinnamon head and breast, pale cinnamon underparts, and brown-and-buff vermiculated coverts. Immature male resembles female but has grey to brownish-black head and breast, white breast-band, and cinnamon underparts; coverts are vermiculated with buff (grey in older birds). Male of nominate (Sri Lanka) has paler grey head than in peninsular India. **Voice** Throaty *cue-cue-cue* like an oriole; low rolling *krr-r-r-r* in alarm. **HH** Habits and habitat like Red-headed.

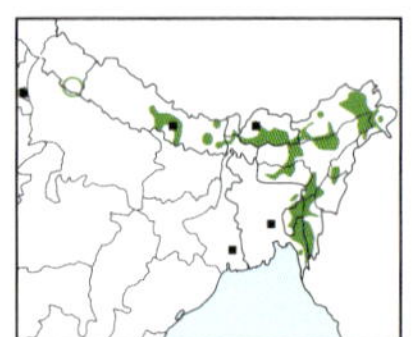

Red-headed Trogon *Harpactes erythrocephalus* 31–35cm

Resident. Himalayas, NE India and Bangladesh. **ID** Eye-ring and bill can be bright blue. Male has crimson head and breast, white breast-band, pinkish-red underparts, and black-and-grey vermiculated wing-coverts. Female is similar but has dark cinnamon head and breast, and brown-and-buff vermiculated coverts. Immature resembles female; older male has grey-vermiculated coverts. **Voice** Descending sequence of mellow notes like an oriole; *tyaup, tyaup, tyaup, tyaup, tyaup*; chattering croak *tewirr* in alarm. **HH** Perches upright almost motionless for long periods. Captures insects on the wing and by swooping to the ground. Midstorey of dense broadleaved evergreen forest with bamboo in tropical and subtropical zones.

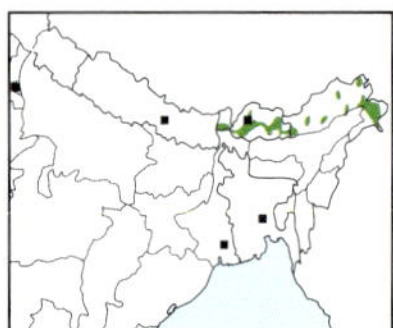

Ward's Trogon *Harpactes wardi* 35–38cm

Resident. E Himalayas in Sikkim, Bhutan, Arunachal Pradesh. **ID** Large trogon. Bill pink (yellow and marked with black in female), eye-ring blue. Male maroon, with deep pink forehead, underparts and outer tail feathers. Has large white patch at base of secondaries. Female browner, with orange-yellow forehead, and yellow underparts and outer tail feathers; coverts and secondaries finely vermiculated buff (pale grey on male). **Voice** Rapid series of mellow *klew* notes; a harsh *whirrur* and chattering notes. **HH** Habits like Red-headed. Lower storey, undergrowth and bamboo in subtropical and temperate broadleaved evergreen forest.

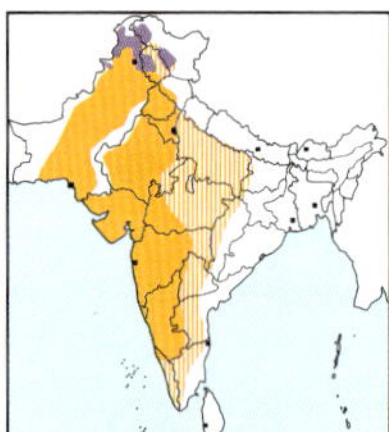

European Roller *Coracias garrulus* 31–32cm

Summer visitor to N Pakistan, Jammu and Kashmir; widespread passage migrant except NE subcontinent and E India. Vagrant: Bhutan, Nepal, Sri Lanka. **ID** From Indian by turquoise-blue head and underparts, and rufous-cinnamon mantle and tertials. Primaries and secondaries black, and has black corners to tail (lacks turquoise band on primaries and dark blue terminal tail-band of Indian). Juvenile is more like juvenile Indian, and best told by turquoise-blue cast to ear-coverts, crown and nape, which contrast with browner mantle, and pattern of wings and tail (as adult). **Voice** Typical call a nasal, grating, crow-like *rak*, single or doubled. **HH** Habits like Indian. Open woodland and cultivation. **AN** Eurasian Roller.

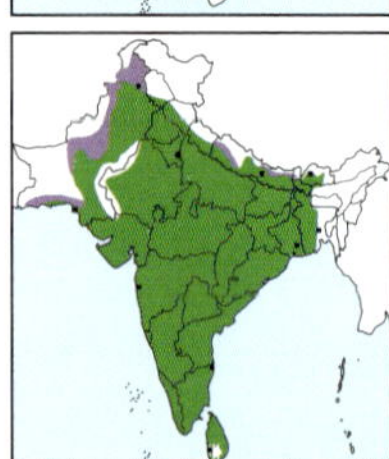

Indian Roller *Coracias benghalensis* 30–34cm

Resident. N Pakistan east to Bangladesh south through subcontinent, and Sri Lanka. **ID** Has rufous-brown on nape and underparts, white streaking on ear-coverts and throat, and greenish mantle. Turquoise band on primaries and dark blue terminal tail-band. Hybrids with Indochinese Roller occur. **Voice** Raucous *check-chack-chack*, with discordant screeches and shrieks. **HH** Spends most of day on prominent perch in open country. Swoops leisurely down to capture prey on ground. Cultivation, open woodland, groves and gardens.

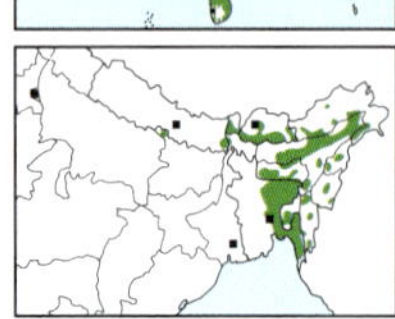

Indochinese Roller *Coracias affinis* 30–34cm

Resident. E Nepal, Bhutan, Bangladesh and NE India. **ID** Darker than Indian Roller. Has brownish-green upperparts, purplish-brown underparts, and blue streaking on throat. In flight, shows turquoise band across primaries, and turquoise on outer tail with dark corners. **Voice** Like Indian. **HH** Habits like Indian. Cultivation, open woodland, tea estates. **TN** Often considered conspecific with Indian Roller.

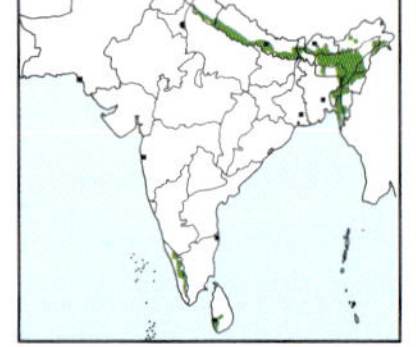

Oriental Dollarbird *Eurystomus orientalis* 27–32cm

Resident and partial migrant. Himalayas, NE and SW India, Bangladesh and Sri Lanka. **ID** Dark greenish to bluish, appearing black at distance, with red bill and eye-ring. In flight, shows turquoise patch on primaries. Flight is buoyant, with broad wings. Juvenile is similar, but duller with dull pinkish bill. **Voice** Typically, rather silent. Commonest call a repeated short, hoarse *chak*. **HH** Small parties often gather and hawk insects on the wing, chiefly in late afternoon and evening. Tropical forest and forest clearings. **AN** Dollarbird.

♀
♂
♂ *fasciatus*
Malabar Trogon
imm
Red-headed Trogon
♂
♀
imm
♀
♂
Ward's Trogon
juv
ad
European Roller
ad
imm
ad
Indian Roller
Indochinese Roller
ad
juv
Oriental Dollarbird

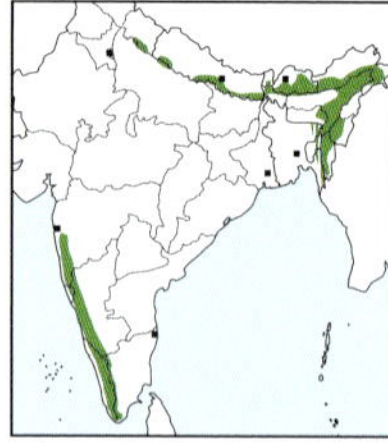

Great Hornbill *Buceros bicornis* 95–105cm

Resident. Himalayas, NE India, Bangladesh and Western Ghats. **ID** Huge, with massive yellow casque and bill, and white tail with black subterminal band. Has black face-band contrasting with yellowish-white nape, neck and upper breast. In flight, shows broad whitish wing-bar and trailing edge to wing. Neck, breast, white wing-bars and base of tail typically stained yellow with preen-gland oils. Male has red iris, black circumorbital skin, and black at each end of casque. Female smaller, with a smaller bill, white iris and red circumorbital skin, and lacks black at ends of casque. Immature lacks casque until at least six months old. **Voice** Loud, deep, retching calls, often in a short series and frequently as a duet. Flight call a loud *ger-onk*. **HH** Has a regular schedule of feeding circuits and roosting flights. Often flies high over the forest for long distances. Mainly eats fruit, especially figs. Mature broadleaved evergreen and moist deciduous forest. Globally threatened.

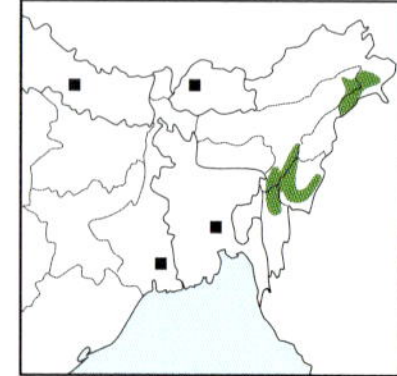

Brown Hornbill *Anorrhinus austeni* 60–65cm

Resident. NE India. **ID** Medium-sized brown hornbill with large and stout pale bill and casque. Male has white cheeks, throat and upper breast, and rufous-brown lower breast and belly. In flight, white tips to tail (except central feathers) and to primaries. Female has entire underparts dusky brown, with pale streaking on crown and sides of head and rufous edging to feathers of throat and breast; lacks white tips to primaries and tail. Both sexes have small buffish-white panel on primaries. Immature is like adult male, but underparts are paler, has pale brown tips to wing-coverts, and orbital skin is pinkish (blue in adult male). **Voice** A high-pitched yelp and piercing screams. **HH** Often with other fruit-eating birds. Usually keeps to canopy of highest forest trees. Broadleaved evergreen forest. **TN** Formerly subsumed in *A. tickelli* as Brown Hornbill.

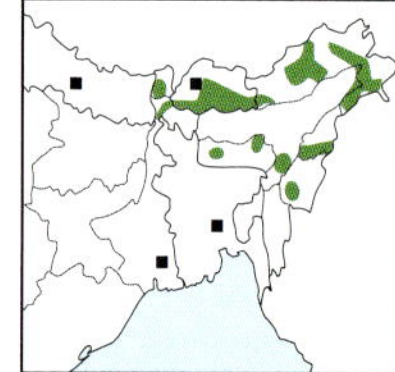

Rufous-necked Hornbill *Aceros nipalensis* 90–100cm

Resident. Himalayas and NE India. **ID** Male from male Wreathed Hornbill by bright rufous head, neck and underparts, black-and-white (rather than all-white) tail, red gular pouch, and blue orbital skin. Female mainly black, and best told from female Wreathed by blue orbital skin, red gular pouch and white terminal band to tail. Both sexes show dark ridges on upper mandible. In flight, both sexes show white wingtips. Immature is similar to adult male, but neck is browner and bill smaller and unmarked. **Voice** Loud croaks, roars and cackling sounds during display; short barking *kuk*. **HH** Feeds on fruits, mainly in canopy. Flies with deep undulations. Tall broadleaved evergreen forest. Globally threatened.

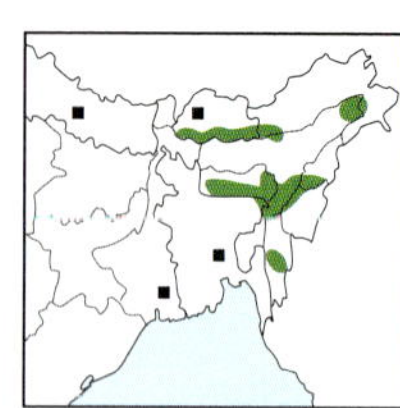

Wreathed Hornbill *Rhyticeros undulatus* 75–85cm

Resident. E Himalayan foothills and NE India, Vagrant: Bangladesh. **ID** Male from slightly larger Rufous-necked by whitish sides of head, foreneck and upper breast (with rufous-brown crown and nape), and all-white tail. Yellow gular pouch (with dark bar) and reddish circumorbital skin. Female has black head and neck and is best told from female Rufous-necked by blue pouch, reddish circumorbital skin, and all-white tail. Both sexes have prominent corrugated casque. In flight, both sexes have all-black wings. Immature is like adult male, but initially lacks casque and corrugations on bill; eyes pale blue rather than red (adult male) or brown (adult female). Corrugations on sides of bill, and casque, begin to develop in first year, with new 'wreaths' added approximately once per year. **Voice** A very loud, gasping *uk-hweerk*, with emphasised second note; less harsh and grating than similar calls of Great. **HH** Maintains regular feeding circuits and roosting flights. Frequently flies high above canopy. Roosts communally in non-breeding season. Broadleaved evergreen forest. Globally threatened.

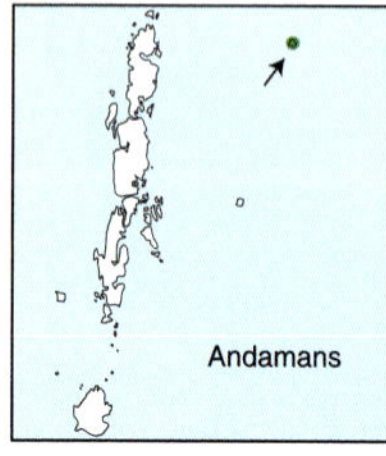

Narcondam Hornbill *Rhyticeros narcondami* 45–50cm

Resident. Narcondam Island, Andamans. **ID** The only hornbill on Narcondam. Like small version of Rufous-necked, but lacks black at base of tail and has bluish-white pouch. Male has rufous head and neck, yellowish-white bill with crimson at base, and blue circumorbital skin. Female has all-black head and neck, and iris is dark olive-brown (rather than reddish as in male). Immature is like adult male, but head and neck are browner and initially lacks casque; has less red at base of bill, and pale grey iris. Casque is grown, but not wreathed, by end of first year. **Voice** Calls include a cackling *ka-ka-ka-ka-ka* and a screech. **HH** Noisy and confiding. Often undertakes leisurely flights in small parties. Mature forest. Globally threatened.

♂
Great Hornbill
♂
♀
♀
♂
Brown Hornbill
♂
imm
Wreathed Hornbill
♀
♂
Rufous-necked Hornbill
♀
♂
Narcondam Hornbill
♀
♂
imm
imm
♂

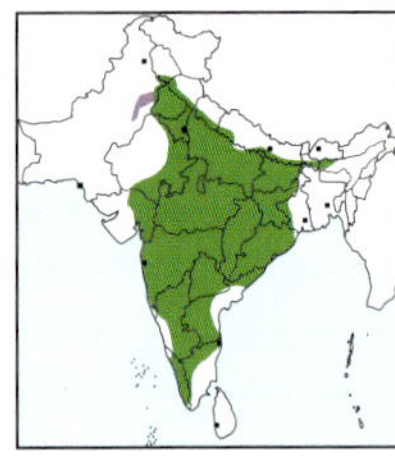

Indian Grey Hornbill *Ocyceros birostris* 50cm

Widespread resident except for parts of NW and NE subcontinent and S India; unrecorded in Sri Lanka. Vagrant: Bangladesh. **ID** Has broad greyish-white supercilium with dark grey ear-coverts, white tips to primaries and secondaries, and white-tipped tail. Prominent blackish casque, and more extensive black at base of bill compared with Malabar Grey Hornbill. Further, lacks pale streaking on head, neck and breast, has paler sandy brownish-grey upperparts, and white trailing edge to secondaries. Tail is also longer than Malabar, and paler brown with dark grey subterminal band and elongated central feathers. Female similar to male, but has smaller casque with less pronounced tip. Immature has bill as female, but smaller, with smaller casque; lacks white wingtips. **Voice** Series of high-pitched penetrating squeals, sometimes given in rapid succession. **HH** Usually in mid-levels in forest. Feeds on fruiting trees, often with other frugivorous species. Occasionally descends to ground to pick up fallen fruit or large insects, or to dust-bathe. Wooded areas with fruiting trees.

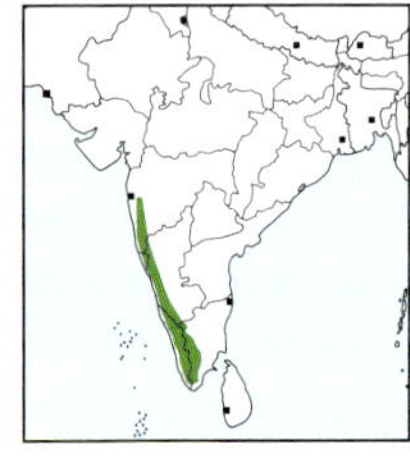

Malabar Grey Hornbill *Ocyceros griseus* 34–37.5cm

Resident. Western Ghats. **ID** Has greyish-white supercilium which broadens behind eye and contrasts with darker ear-coverts. Similar to Indian Grey, but lacks prominent casque and has mainly orange or yellow bill. Further, has greyish-white streaking on head and neck, darker grey upperparts, rufous undertail-coverts, and shorter dark grey tail. In flight, lacks white trailing edge to secondaries. Sexes alike, but female has paler yellow bill with black at base and along culmen. Immature has smaller bill, lacking dark marks at base; also has rufous fringes to mantle and coverts, and less pronounced supercilium. **Voice** Loud, harsh croaks, chuckles, and mock laughter, varied by raucous cackling. **HH** Habits like Indian Grey. Open broadleaved evergreen and moist deciduous forest, especially where figs are common. Globally Threatened.

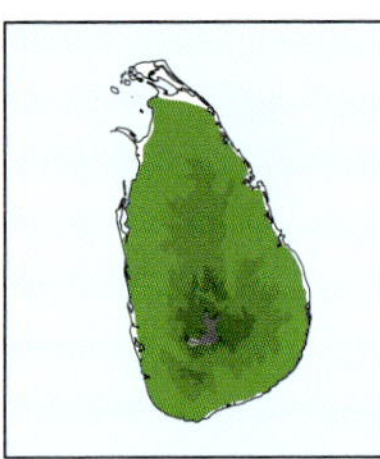

Sri Lanka Grey Hornbill *Ocyceros gingalensis* 45cm

Resident. Sri Lanka. **ID** The only grey hornbill in Sri Lanka. Superficially resembles Malabar Grey but lacks broad greyish-white supercilium and has white underparts. In addition, has steel-grey wing-coverts with distinct black fringes. Outer tail feathers are almost entirely white on older birds (but otherwise dark grey with white tips, as on Malabar). Male has mainly cream-coloured bill with black patches at base. Female has largely black bill with cream stripe along cutting edge of upper mandible. Immature has smaller pale yellowish bill and less pronounced head pattern. **Voice** Loud *kaa... kaa... kakakaka...* or *kuk...kuk-kuk-kuk*. **HH** Habits like Indian Grey. Forest and well-wooded areas in lowlands and lower hills, especially in dry zone.

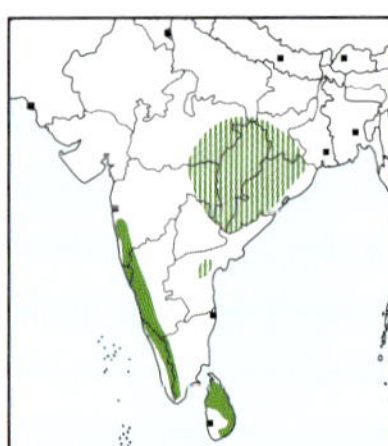

Malabar Pied Hornbill *Anthracoceros coronatus* 65cm

Resident. Western Ghats, E and C India and Sri Lanka. **ID** Very similar to smaller Oriental Pied, but has different casque shape and pattern (axe-shaped in both sexes, with pronounced tip, and large black patch along upper ridge). Also, has white outer tail feathers (can show black at base of these, especially on immatures, but not as extensive as on Oriental), broader white trailing edge to wings (with broad white tips to all but innermost secondaries), and pinkish throat patches. Sexes similar; female has a slightly smaller casque (and lacks black at posterior end), although it is similar in shape, and has pinkish (blue-black on male) circumorbital skin. Bill lacks black at tip (unlike female Oriental Pied). Immature has smaller bill and casque. **Voice** Series of raucous screams *rraah...rrraah...rraah...* and a variety of loud, shrill squeals and cackles. **HH** Habits like Oriental. Open moist broadleaved deciduous and evergreen forest and large fruit trees near villages.

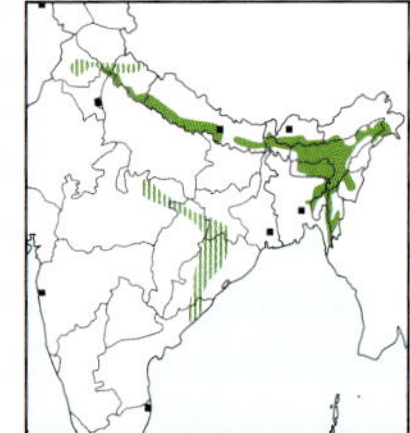

Oriental Pied Hornbill *Anthracoceros albirostris* 55–60cm

Resident. Himalayan foothills, NE, C and E India, and Bangladesh. Vagrant: Pakistan. **ID** Very similar to larger Malabar Pied, and best distinguished by casque pattern and shape (cylindrical, with black patch restricted to tip). Also, has mainly black tail with white tips to all but central feathers, narrower white trailing edge to secondaries, and pale blue (rather than pink) throat patches. Sexes similar, but female smaller with less convex casque lacking projecting tip, and has black at tip of bill and casque. Both sexes have pale blue circumorbital skin. Immature has smaller bill and casque with less black; orbital skin and throat patch whitish. **Voice** Variety of loud, shrill, nasal squeals and raucous chucks, including loud cackling *kleng-kleng, kek-kek-kek-kek-kek*. **HH** Often feeds with Indian Grey and other frugivorous species. Mainly arboreal, but regularly feeds on ground on fallen fruit and insects. Open forest, groves and large fruit trees near villages.

imm
Indian Grey
Hornbill
♂
♂
♀
imm
♂
Malabar Grey
Hornbill
♂
♀
♂
imm
Sri Lanka Grey
Hornbill
♂
imm
Malabar Pied
Hornbill
♂
imm
♀
Oriental Pied
Hornbill
♀

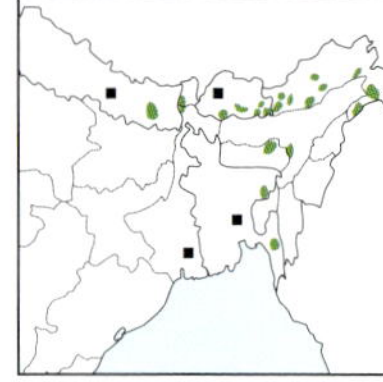

Blyth's Kingfisher ***Alcedo hercules*** 22–23cm

Resident. Mainly NE India. Vagrant: Bangladesh. **ID** From Common and Blue-eared by considerably larger size and larger and longer bill, darker greenish-blue (almost brownish-black) scapulars and wings (with prominent turquoise spotting on lesser and median coverts), almost blackish crown with sharply contrasting turquoise spotting, and less distinct orange loral spot. Has blue ear-coverts like Blue-eared. Female has red on lower mandible. In flight dark mantle and wings contrast with brilliant blue back and rump. **Voice** Similar to Common, but louder and hoarser. **HH** Habits like Common but shy. Shaded streams in dense tropical and subtropical broadleaved evergreen forest.

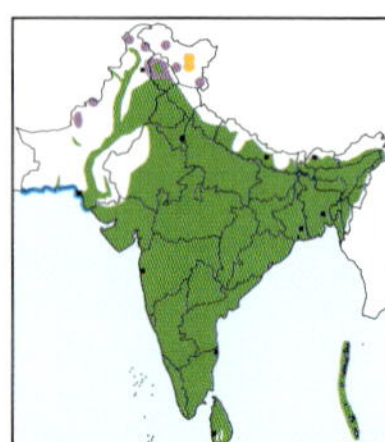

Common Kingfisher ***Alcedo atthis*** 16–18cm

Widespread resident. **ID** From the similar forest-dwelling Blue-eared by orange ear-coverts, paler greenish-blue upperparts, and paler orange underparts. Note, however, that juvenile Blue-eared has rufous ear-coverts. Female has red on lower mandible. Juvenile is like adult, but duller and greener above, with dusky scaling on breast. *A. a. taprobana* (peninsular India and Sri Lanka) is darker blue, less green, although not so blue as Blue-eared. **Voice** Call a high-pitched, shrill *chee*, usually repeated, and *chit-it-it* alarm call. **HH** Uses a post or bank close to water's edge as vantage point. Plunges headlong into water to catch prey. If alarmed flies away swiftly and directly low over water calling. Fresh waters in open country; also, mangroves and seashore in winter.

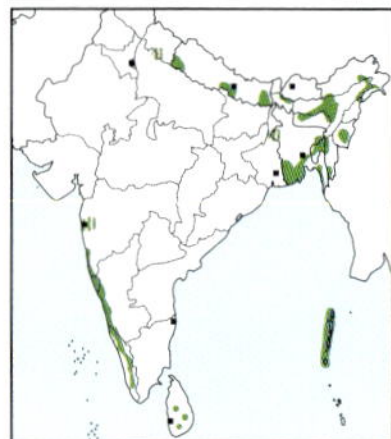

Blue-eared Kingfisher ***Alcedo meninting*** 15.5–17cm

Resident. Himalayan foothills, NE, E and SW India, Bangladesh and Sri Lanka. **ID** From Common by blue ear-coverts (except in juvenile plumage), darker blue upperparts (lacking greenish tones to crown, scapulars and wings), darker brilliant blue back and rump, and deeper orange underparts. Female has red on lower mandible. Juvenile has rufous-orange ear-coverts as on Common but has darker blue upperparts (similar in coloration to adult) and lacks the broad blue moustachial stripe of that species (but can show short black moustachial that does not extend beyond ear-coverts). **Voice** Call a shrill, single *seet* or *tsit*, higher-pitched and less strident than Common. Contact calls are thin, shrill *striiiiit, trrrrrt tit... trrrreu*, etc. **HH** Habits like Common but shy. Mainly streams in dense broadleaved tropical and subtropical forest.

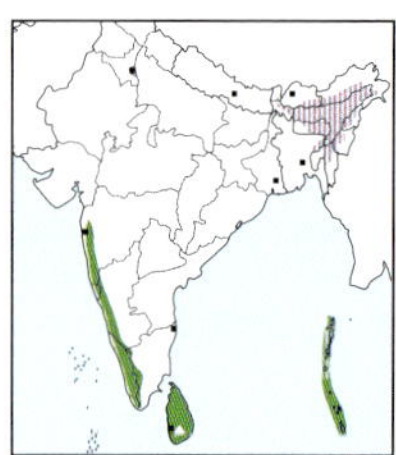

Black-backed Dwarf Kingfisher ***Ceyx erithaca*** 12.5–14cm

Resident. Himalayan foothills, NE and SW India, Bangladesh, Sri Lanka, Andaman and Nicobar Is. **ID** Tiny forest kingfisher with coral-red bill. Has orange head, with variable violet iridescence on crown and nape, blue-black forehead and 'ear patch', black upperparts with the coverts and scapulars boldly marked with blue, pale orange underparts, and orange rump and tail also with violet iridescence. Juvenile is duller; bill initially dark becoming pale yellowish-orange. Underparts whitish with orange breast-band, crown more orange (less violet), and has less blue in upperparts. **Voice** Call a weak, thin *seet*, thinner and higher-pitched than Blue-eared; contact calls include a weak shrill *tit-sreet* and *tit-tit*. **HH** Perches in a shaded position on a rock or low in vegetation. Shady streams in broadleaved evergreen and moist deciduous tropical forest. **AN** Oriental Dwarf Kingfisher.

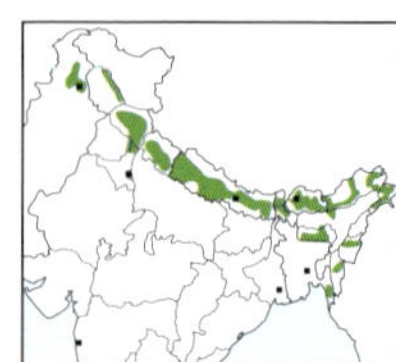

Crested Kingfisher ***Megaceryle lugubris*** 38–43cm

Resident. Himalayas and NE India. Vagrant: Bangladesh. **ID** Very large with prominent crest, often held open. From the much smaller Pied Kingfisher by lack of white supercilium, complete white neck collar, finely spotted breast-band (sometimes mixed with rufous), dark grey back and rump finely spotted paler grey, and dark grey wings and tail finely barred white (lacking Pied's prominent white patches in wing). Female and juvenile similar to male, but have pale rufous underwing-coverts. **Voice** Loud *ket ket* in flight. **HH** Perches on branches overhanging river or on rocks in river. Does not hover. Rocky, fast-flowing mountain rivers and larger rivers in foothills; rarely by lakes.

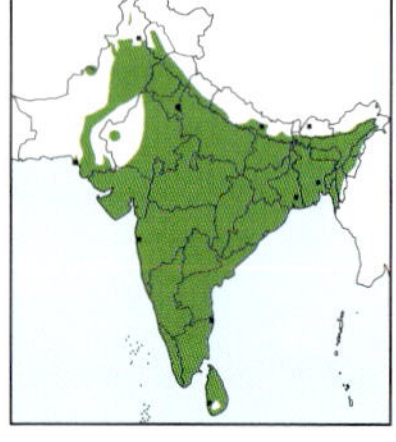

Pied Kingfisher ***Ceryle rudis*** 25–30.5cm

Widespread resident. **ID** Crested black-and-white kingfisher. Has white-streaked black crown and crest, white supercilium contrasting with broad black eye-stripe, white underparts with black breast-band, and black-and-white wings and tail. Male has double breast-band. Female has single, usually broken, breast-band. Upperparts of *C. r. travancoreensis* (SW peninsula) appear black, spotted with white (rather than white, spotted black). **Voice** A sharp *chirruk chirruk* when alert and low-pitched *trrr trrr trrr* in alarm. **HH** Characteristically hunts by hovering over water. Still fresh waters, slow-moving rivers and streams, also, tidal creeks and pools.

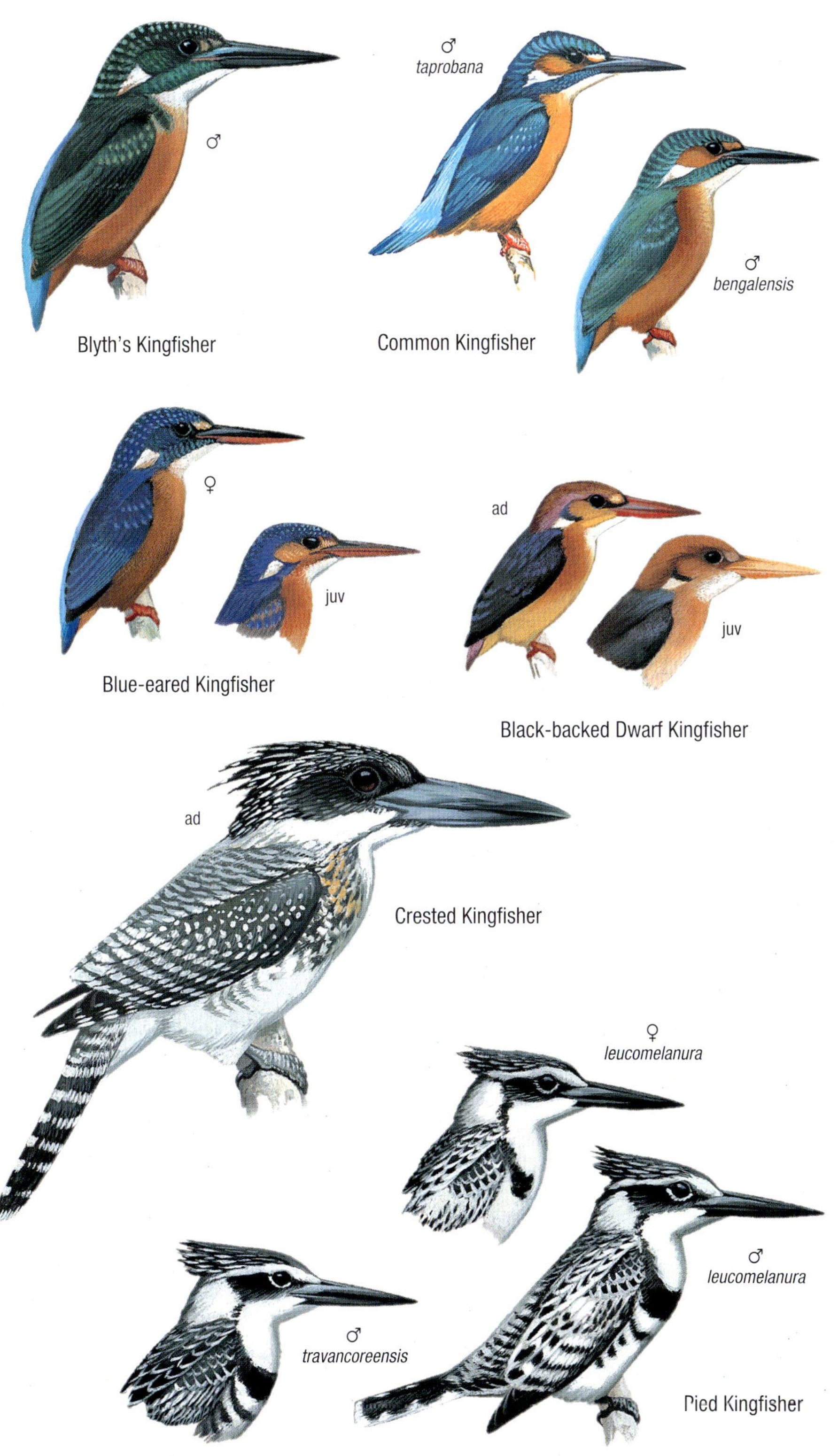

♂
♂
taprobana
♂
bengalensis
Blyth's Kingfisher
Common Kingfisher
♀
juv
ad
juv
Blue-eared Kingfisher
Black-backed Dwarf Kingfisher
ad
Crested Kingfisher
♀
leucomelanura
♂
leucomelanura
♂
travancoreensis
Pied Kingfisher

PLATE 103: KINGFISHERS II

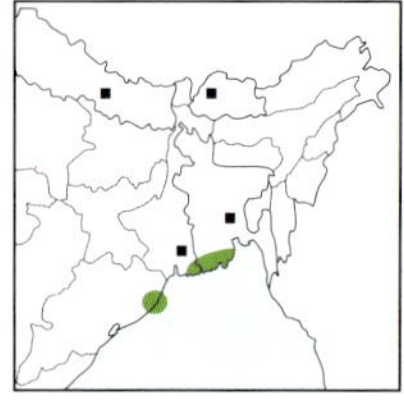

Brown-winged Kingfisher ***Pelargopsis amauroptera*** 35–37cm

Resident. E India and SW Bangladesh. **ID** Very large with huge red bill. From Stork-billed by brown mantle, wings and tail, which contrast strongly with turquoise rump and lower back (especially in flight). Lacks the brown cap of Stork-billed; the entire head and underparts are rich brownish-orange. Juvenile has pale fringes to mantle and wing-coverts, and fine dusky barring on nape and underparts. **Voice** Harsh, cackling, repeated *chak-chak-chak-chak-chak*; also, short, descending sequence of whistles: *tree, treew-treew*. **HH** Watches from a perch fairly high in mangroves. Captures prey by diving into water or by landing on mud and seizing quarry from the surface. Movements slow and deliberate. Coasts, mangrove swamps, tidal rivers and creeks.

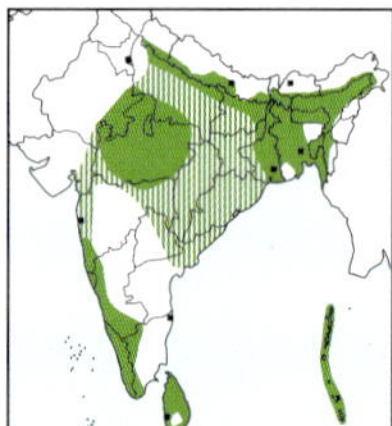

Stork-billed Kingfisher ***Pelargopsis capensis*** 35–41cm

Widespread resident; unrecorded in Pakistan and NW India. **ID** Very large with huge coral-red bill, brownish cap, pale orange-buff collar and underparts, and blue-green upperparts. In flight, shows turquoise rump and lower back. Juvenile has dusky barring on underparts, especially on breast (forming a broad band). *P. c. osmastoni* of the Andamans has paler grey-brown crown which contrasts less with the collar. *P. c. intermedia* of the Nicobars lacks brown cap, has entirely orange-buff head with brown flecks on crown, and much deeper blue upperparts. **Voice** Shrill descending whistle *tree-trew* or *kwee-kwau* and when disturbed loud sharp *wiak-wiak*. **HH** Sluggish and heard more often than seen. Perches, often half-hidden on a branch overhanging water, occasionally diving to catch prey. Shaded lakes, slow-moving waterways in well-wooded country.

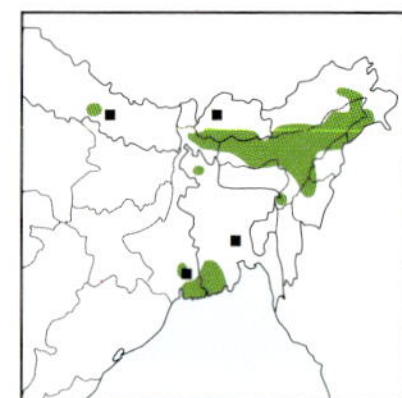

Ruddy Kingfisher ***Halcyon coromanda*** 25–27cm

Resident. E Himalayan foothills, NE India and Bangladesh. **ID** Medium-sized forest-dwelling kingfisher, with large coral-red bill, rufous-orange upperparts with brilliant violet gloss, and paler rufous underparts. In flight, shows striking bluish-white rump. Juvenile is darker and browner on upperparts, and has bluer rump, faint blackish barring on rufous underparts, and blackish bill. *H. c. mizorhina* of the Andamans has a larger bill and is much darker with purplish upperparts and dark chestnut underparts. **Voice** Descending and high-pitched *tititititititi* call, not unlike White-throated. Song a repeated soft, trilling *tyuur-rrrr*. **HH** Secretive and shy. Pools and streams in dense broadleaved tropical and subtropical evergreen forest; also, mangrove swamps.

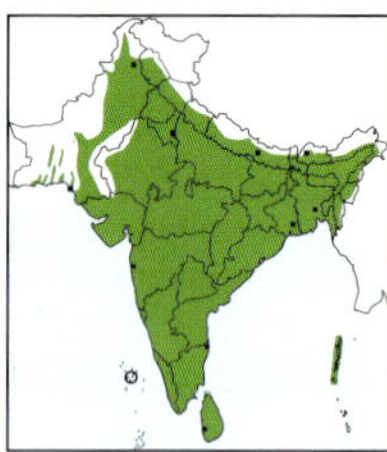

White-throated Kingfisher ***Halcyon smyrnensis*** 26.5–29.5cm

Widespread resident. **ID** Large kingfisher with large red bill, chocolate-brown head and underparts, white throat and centre of breast, and brilliant turquoise-blue upperparts including rump and tail. In flight, shows prominent white patches at base of black primaries. Juvenile duller, with brown bill and dark scalloping on breast. **Voice** Call a loud, rattling laugh. Song a drawn-out musical whistle *kilililí* reeling down the scale. **HH** Spends long periods perched, with head bobbing or tail wagging, before diving after prey. Wide-ranging habitats, often far from water: cultivation, forest edges, gardens, and freshwater and coastal wetlands.

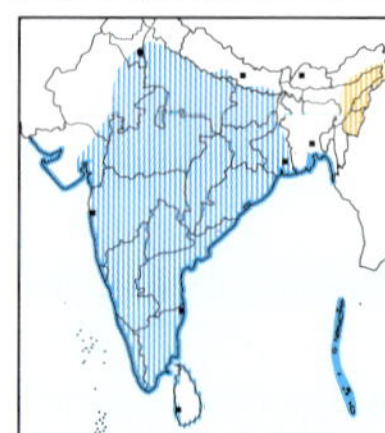

Black-capped Kingfisher ***Halcyon pileata*** 28–31.5cm

Mainly winter visitor to coasts of India and Bangladesh. Vagrant: Pakistan, Bhutan. **ID** Large, mainly coastal kingfisher with coral-red bill. Has black cap, white collar, deep purplish-blue upperparts, black coverts contrasting with blue secondaries, white throat and breast, and pale orange-buff belly and flanks. In flight, bright blue rump and prominent white patches at base of primaries. Juvenile has dusky scalloping on collar and breast. **Voice** A distinctive ringing cackle, *kikikikikiki*, like but higher-pitched than White-breasted. **HH** Perches in open at edges of mangroves, forest or on wires. Dives down obliquely to catch prey. Chiefly coastal wetlands; also, inland along larger rivers. Globally threatened.

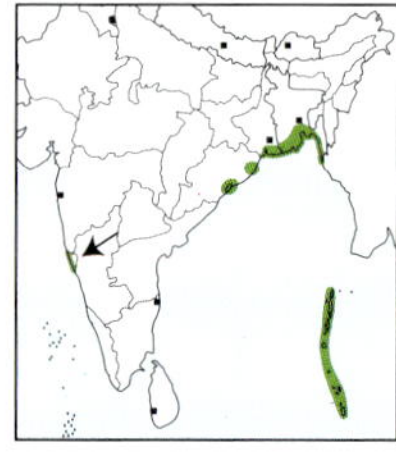

Collared Kingfisher ***Todiramphus chloris*** 23–25cm

Resident. Locally in E and W India, Bangladesh, Andaman and Nicobar Is. **ID** Medium-sized coastal kingfisher with stout mainly blackish bill, blue-green crown and ear-coverts with short white supercilium, white collar, blue-green mantle, blue wings and tail, and white underparts. Female is duller with scaling on sides of breast. Juvenile has scaling on buffish-white underparts and a buff supercilium. Lacks white in wing of Black-capped. In Andamans (*T. c. davisoni*) and Nicobars (*T. c. occipitalis*) has blackish-green ear-coverts and lower border to nape, and buff wash on underparts. *T. c. davisoni* has a short buffish supercilium, while *occipitalis* has broad rufous-buff supercilia which join at nape to form second 'collar'. **Voice** Raucous *krerk-krerk-krerk-krerk*. **HH** Habits like Black-capped. Coastal wetlands; forest edge on Andamans.

ad
Brown-winged Kingfisher
ad
capensis
ad
intermedia
Stork-billed Kingfisher
juv
ad
Ruddy Kingfisher
ad
White-throated Kingfisher
ad
juv
Black-capped Kingfisher
juv
humii
ad
humii
ad
occipitalis
ad
davisoni
Collared Kingfisher

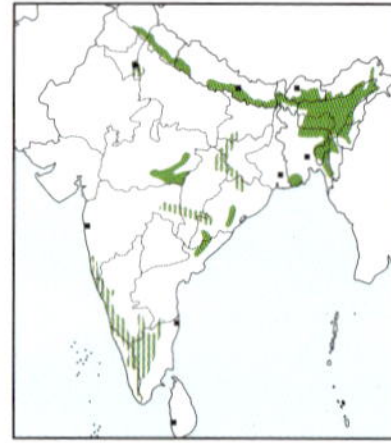

Blue-bearded Bee-eater *Nyctyornis athertoni* 31–35cm

Resident. Himalayan foothills, NE and E India, Western Ghats, hills of W Tamil Nadu and Bangladesh. **ID** Large green bee-eater with a broad square-ended tail. Adult has blue forehead and 'beard', green upperparts, broad greenish streaking on yellowish-buff belly and flanks, and yellowish-buff undertail-coverts and undertail. Yellowish-buff underwing-coverts show in flight. Juvenile is like adult and has blue 'beard' even when very young. **Voice** Gruff *gga gga ggr gr* or *kor-r-r kor-r-r*. **HH** Typically perches in hunched posture with tail hanging vertically. Makes aerial sallies after insects from a vantage point like other bee-eaters. Edges and clearings of dense broadleaved forest.

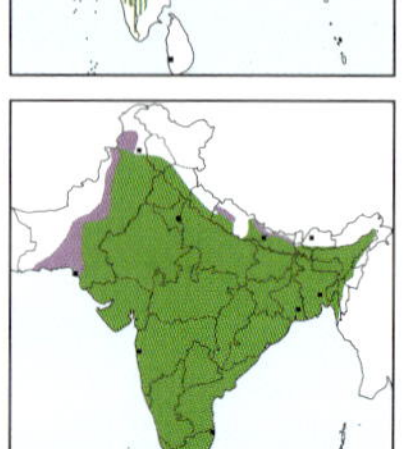

Asian Green Bee-eater *Merops orientalis* 16–18cm (with streamers, up to 7cm more)

Widespread resident and summer visitor. Vagrant: Bhutan. **ID** Small with elongated central tail feathers, blue or green throat with black gorget, variable golden-brown to rufous crown and nape, and green tail. Juvenile has square-ended tail; crown and mantle are green, lacks black gorget, and throat is pale yellowish- or bluish-green. *M. o. beludschicus* of NW subcontinent has blue throat, and green crown and nape with only a faint golden sheen. *M. o. ferrugeiceps* of NE subcontinent has strong rufous cast to crown, nape and upper mantle, green (not blue) throat with blue cheeks, rufous wash to breast-sides, and is darker green overall. **Voice** Pleasant throaty trill, *tree-tree-tree*. **HH** Flies from a perch to snap up a passing insect and circles gracefully back to base. Open country with scattered trees, cultivation, sandy areas on coasts; also, semi-desert and grazing land. **AN** Green Bee-eater.

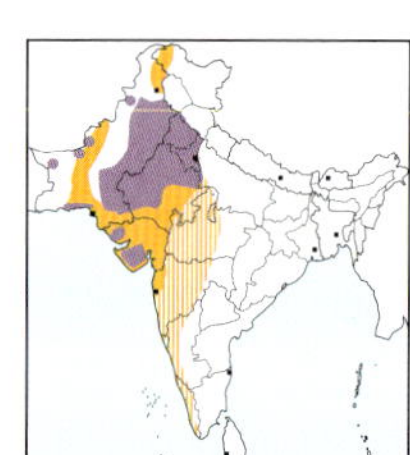

Blue-cheeked Bee-eater *Merops persicus* 31cm (with streamers, up to 7cm more)

Summer visitor and passage migrant. Pakistan and NW India. **ID** From Blue-tailed by bronze-green tail, whitish forehead and turquoise-and-white supercilium, turquoise and green on ear-coverts, and more restricted chestnut on throat. Upperparts and underparts are a purer green (although may show turquoise wash to belly, rump and tail-coverts). Larger size, yellow chin, chestnut throat, and lack of black gorget are best features from Asian Green. Juvenile similar to juvenile Blue-tailed, but rump, uppertail-coverts and tail generally green (some with a touch of turquoise), and has less extensive but more clearly defined rufous throat. **Voice** Rolling *dirririp*, more polysyllabic than European Bee-eater. **HH** Darts out from exposed perch to seize prey; also hawks insects in continuous flight. Near water in arid areas: lakes, irrigation tanks, sandy shores.

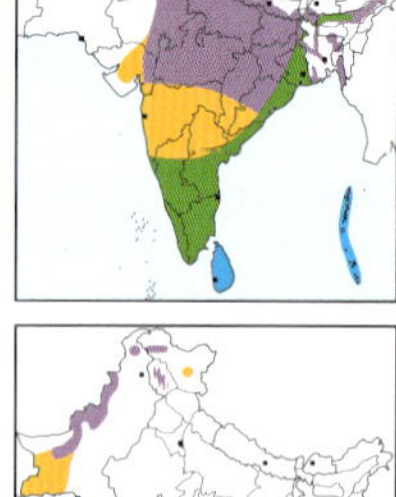

Blue-tailed Bee-eater *Merops philippinus* 28–30cm (with streamers, up to 7cm more)

Breeds in N and NE subcontinent; winters in peninsula, Sri Lanka, Andaman and Nicobar Is. Vagrant: Bhutan. **ID** From Blue-cheeked by blue rump and tail, and green forehead and supercilium concolorous with crown (just a touch of blue on supercilium in front of eye). Chestnut of throat extends onto ear-coverts, and upperparts and underparts are washed rufous and turquoise; turquoise undertail-coverts. Juvenile as juvenile Blue-cheeked, but has strong blue cast to rump, uppertail-coverts and tail, and more extensive but less well-defined rufous throat. **Voice** As Blue-cheeked. **HH** Habits like Blue-cheeked; also hunts from treetops. Near water in more wooded, less dry country than Blue-cheeked.

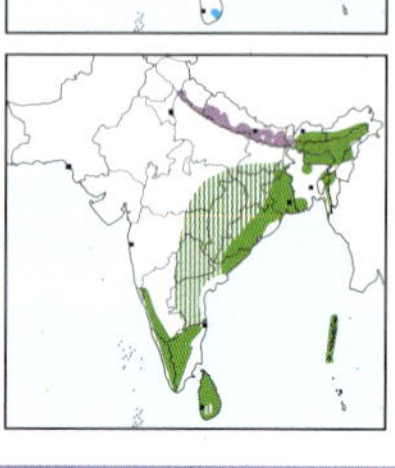

European Bee-eater *Merops apiaster* 25–29cm (with streamers, up to 3.3cm more)

Summer visitor to Vale of Kashmir and N and W Pakistan mountains; passage migrant chiefly in Pakistan. Winters SW India and Sri Lanka. **ID** Adult has combination of yellow throat and black gorget, turquoise underparts, chestnut crown, nape, mantle and patch in wing-coverts, golden-yellow scapulars, and green tail. Female slightly paler, with green in scapulars and less chestnut in wing. Juvenile like washed-out version of adult, with pale fringes to feathers of upperparts and underparts. Lacks elongated central tail feathers and bright chestnut in wing-coverts, and has yellowish-white throat. **Voice** Cheerful, throaty *threep*. **HH** Habits like Blue-cheeked. Open country, cultivation, and vicinity of lakes and watercourses.

Chestnut-headed Bee-eater *Merops leschenaulti* 20–22.5cm

Resident and partial migrant. Himalayas, NE, E, SW and SE India, Bangladesh, Sri Lanka and Andaman Is. **ID** From Asian Green by combination of bright chestnut crown, nape and mantle, yellow throat, turquoise rump, and broad tail with shallow fork. Juvenile duller, with chestnut of upperparts absent or reduced to a wash on crown (crown and nape are uniform dark green in some). **Voice** Very vocal. A *pruik* or *churit*, briefer or less melodious than calls of larger bee-eaters. **HH** Habits like Blue-cheeked, but a forest bird. Vicinity of water in deciduous forest.

Asian Green Bee-eater
Blue-bearded
Bee-eater
ad
beludschicus
ad
juv
beludschicus
ad
orientalis
ad
ferrugeiceps
ad
ad
juv
Blue-cheeked
Bee-eater
Blue-tailed Bee-eater
ad
leschenaulti
ad
juv
juv
Chestnut-headed Bee-eater
European Bee-eater

PLATE 105: EURASIAN HOOPOE AND BARBETS I

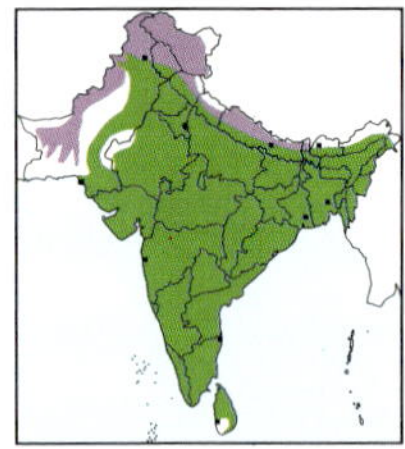

Eurasian Hoopoe *Upupa epops* 19–32cm

Summer visitor to far north; resident and winter visitor to much of rest of subcontinent. **ID** Mainly rufous-orange to orange-buff, with striking black-and-white wings and tail, black-tipped fan-like crest usually held flat, and downcurved bill. Broad, rounded wings; like a giant butterfly in flight. **Voice** A repetitive *poop, poop, poop, poop*; like call of Himalayan Cuckoo, which usually has four notes instead of two or three. **HH** Searches for insects and their larvae on ground, running and walking about, probing and pecking. Flight is undulating, slow and butterfly-like. Open country, cultivation and villages. **AN** Common Hoopoe.

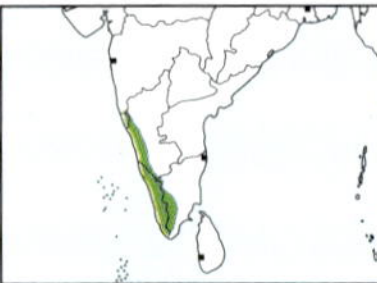

Malabar Barbet *Psilopogon malabaricus* 11–13cm

Resident. Western Ghats. **ID** From Coppersmith by crimson cheeks, throat and breast, black streaking on breast, unstreaked green belly and flanks, and diffuse blue band on sides of head and breast. Juvenile mainly green with traces of red on forehead and throat; unstreaked underparts best feature from juvenile Coppersmith. **Voice** Like Coppersmith, although generally softer and faster-paced. **HH** Habits like Coppersmith. Moist evergreen biotope. **TN** Formerly placed in *Megalaima*.

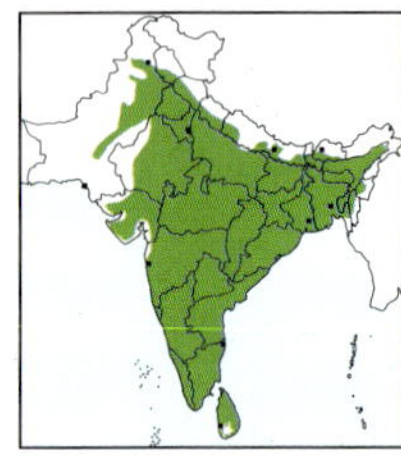

Coppersmith Barbet *Psilopogon haemacephalus* 17cm

Resident. Widespread east of Indus River. **ID** A small, brightly coloured barbet, with crimson forehead and patch on breast, yellow patches above and below eye contrasting with blackish hindcrown and sides of head, yellow throat, dark streaking on belly and flanks, and bright red legs and feet. Juvenile lacks red on forehead and breast; prominent pale yellow patches above and below eye (surrounded by dark olive sides of head and moustachial stripe), whitish throat, olive-green breast-band, and broad olive-green streaking on belly and flanks. **Voice** Call a loud, metallic, monotonous, repetitive *tuk, tuk, tuk* etc. **HH** Particularly vocal in the heat of the day. In early morning often suns itself on a bare treetop. Sometimes congregates in flocks of up to 100 or more with other frugivores at fruiting trees. Can cling to and climb tree trunks like a woodpecker, using its tail as support. Open wooded country, groves near villages and wooded urban gardens. **TN** Formerly placed in *Megalaima*.

Crimson-fronted Barbet *Psilopogon rubricapillus* 16–17cm

Resident. Sri Lanka. **ID** Small size. From Coppersmith by orange (rather than yellow) supercilium, cheeks, throat and upper breast, smaller and less distinct red patch on breast, unstreaked green belly and flanks, and diffuse blue patch on sides of head and neck. Juvenile duller than adult, and lacks striking 'face' pattern and streaked underparts of juvenile Coppersmith; predominantly green with traces of adult head pattern (e.g. yellow on throat, blue wash on neck-sides and moustachial stripe, and orange-yellow on cheeks and supercilium). **Voice** Call is like a slow Coppersmith, although mellower. **HH** Habits like Coppersmith. Evergreen forest, forest edges, plantations of fruiting trees, remnant forest patches, farmland with trees, and urban gardens. **TN** Formerly placed in *Megalaima*.

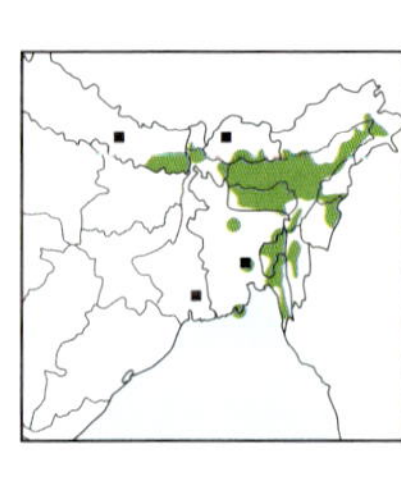

Blue-eared Barbet *Psilopogon cyanotis* 17cm

Resident. E Himalayan foothills, NE India and Bangladesh. **ID** A small barbet with black forehead, blue throat and a complex black, blue, red and yellow pattern on sides of head. Easily told from larger Blue-throated by blackish forehead and blue crown, multicoloured face, and smaller all-dark bill. Juvenile is mainly green, with blue wash to face and throat, and lacks black and red head markings. **Voice** Call a disyllabic, repetitive *tk-trrt* repeated about 120 times a minute, and a throaty whistle. **HH** Habits like Coppersmith. Usually found singly, perched atop a tall forest tree. Dense, broadleaved evergreen forest. **TN** Formerly placed in *Megalaima* and listed as *M. australis*.

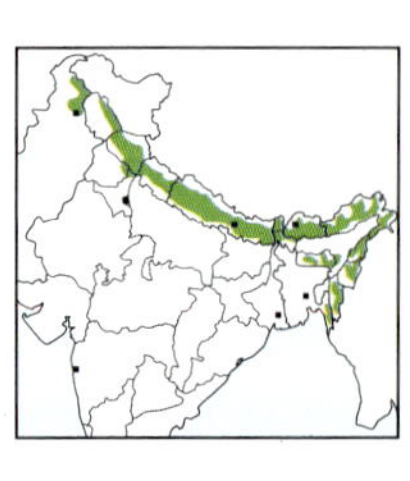

Great Barbet *Psilopogon virens* 33cm

Resident. Himalayas, NE India and Bangladesh. **ID** Largest of the barbets and unmistakable, with large pale yellow bill, violet-blue head, brown breast and mantle, olive-streaked yellowish underparts, and red undertail-coverts. Duller and paler in W Himalayan *P. v. marshallorum*, with more extensive yellowish-green streaking on hindneck. Juvenile duller with greener head. **Voice** Call a monotonous, incessant and far-reaching *piho piho* uttered throughout the day. A second call, a repetitious *tuk, tuk, tuk*, often given in a duet, presumably with a female. **HH** Usually singly or in groups of up to five or six but congregates in larger numbers at fruit-laden trees. Mainly moist, subtropical and temperate forest; also, well-wooded country. **TN** Formerly placed in *Megalaima*.

ad
Eurasian Hoopoe
ad
Malabar Barbet
ad
juv
Coppersmith Barbet
ad
juv
Crimson-fronted Barbet
ad
juv
Blue-eared Barbet
ad
Great Barbet

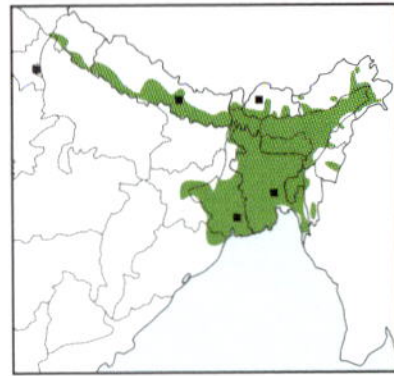

Lineated Barbet *Psilopogon lineatus* 28cm

Resident. Himalayan foothills, NE and E India, and Bangladesh. **ID** From similar Brown-headed by bold white streaking on head, upper mantle and breast (extending onto centre of belly), with usually whitish chin and throat (can be dusky brown on some). Underparts can look white, streaked with brown. In addition, has less extensive naked yellowish patch around eye which (unlike Brown-headed) is usually separated from the pinkish bill (giving rise to spectacled appearance). Uniform unspotted wing-coverts. Juvenile has less prominent streaking and is more like Brown-headed, but orbital skin as adult and has unspotted wing-coverts. Note differences in range. **Voice** Monotonous *kotur, kotur, kotur*, slightly mellower and softer than Brown-headed. **HH** Habits very similar to Brown-headed. Open deciduous forest, well-wooded areas and roadside avenues with fruiting trees. **TN** Formerly placed in *Megalaima*.

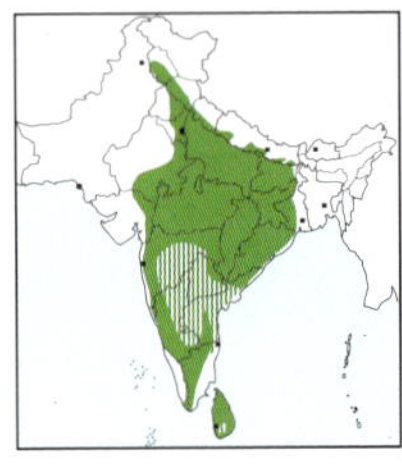

Brown-headed Barbet *Psilopogon zeylanicus* 27cm

Widespread resident; unrecorded in Pakistan. **ID** From similar Lineated by much finer whitish streaking on head and breast (which look more uniformly brown), brown chin and throat concolorous with breast, and virtual absence of streaking on belly and flanks. In addition, has whitish-tipped wing-coverts (albeit rather indistinct in *inornatus*), more extensive bare orange patch around eye which invariably extends to bill (eye patch becomes yellow in non-breeding season), and deeper reddish-orange bill (orange-brown in non-breeding season). *P. z. inornatus* of W India has more uniform brown head and breast with less prominent streaking than northern *P. z. caniceps*, while *P. z. zeylanicus* of SW India and Sri Lanka has darker brown head and breast and more prominent streaking on nape and breast than *inornatus*. **Voice** Monotonous *kutroo, kutroo, kutroo* or *kutruk, kutruk, kutruk* uttered throughout the day. **HH** Singly or in groups up to 20 or more with other frugivores in favoured fruiting trees, especially figs. Very noisy in hot weather, often calling in chorus. Broadleaved forest, wooded areas and trees near habitation. **TN** Formerly placed in *Megalaima*.

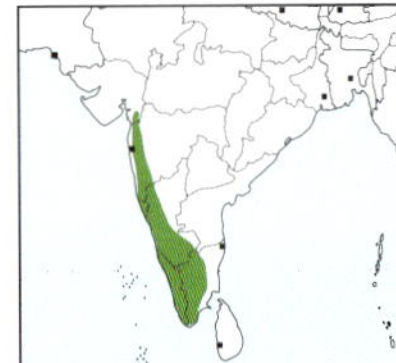

White-cheeked Barbet *Psilopogon viridis* 23cm

Resident. Western Ghats and hills of Tamil Nadu. **ID** From Brown-headed by smaller size, shorter bill, bold white cheek-stripe and white supercilium (contrasting with naked black skin around eye and dark brown crown and nape), whitish chin and throat, and diffuse but broad white spotting/streaking on breast. Juvenile similar, but brown of head paler, and throat and breast whiter (with indistinct brown streaking). **Voice** Call very similar to Brown-headed: *pucock, pucock, pucock*. **HH** Habits like Brown-headed. Broadleaved evergreen and moist deciduous wooded areas, gardens, groves. **TN** Formerly placed in *Megalaima*.

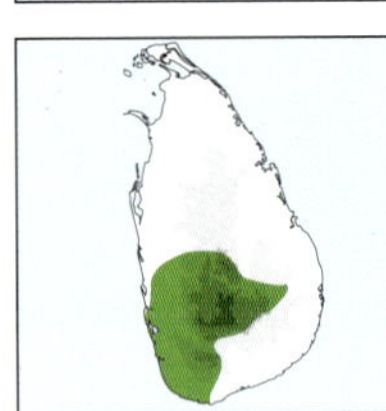

Yellow-fronted Barbet *Psilopogon flavifrons* 21–22cm

Resident. Sri Lanka. **ID** A medium-sized, mainly green barbet. Has yellow forehead, forecrown and malar stripe, and pale turquoise-blue supercilium, cheeks and throat. Circumorbital skin blackish. Also has paler centres to green breast feathers, resulting in scaled appearance, and dark legs and feet. **Voice** Rolling, ascending *kowowowowowo* that changes into a repetitive *kuiar kuiar, kuiar*. **HH** Habits like Brown-headed. Usually singly or in pairs. Broadleaved forest and well-wooded gardens. **TN** Formerly placed in *Megalaima*.

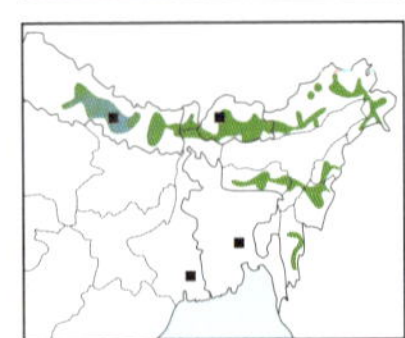

Golden-throated Barbet *Psilopogon franklinii* 23cm

Resident. Himalayas, NE India. **ID** A medium-sized barbet, From Blue-throated by broad black stripe behind eye, greyish-white (not blue) cheeks, and yellow crown centre, chin and upper throat. Has turquoise shoulder and panel in primaries. From below, from smaller Coppersmith by uniform green breast and dark legs and feet. Juvenile is duller and yellow is less prominent. **Voice** Wailing, repetitive *peeyu, peeyu*, recalling Great but higher-pitched; also, a monotonous *pukwowk, pukwowk, pukwowk*. **HH** Habits very similar to Brown-headed. Moist, broadleaved subtropical and temperate forest. **TN** Formerly placed in *Megalaima*.

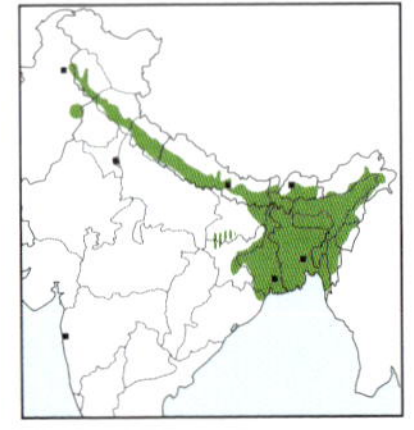

Blue-throated Barbet *Psilopogon asiaticus* 23cm

Resident. Himalayas, NE India and Bangladesh. **ID** A medium-sized barbet, with red forehead, black band across centre of crown, red hindcrown, orange orbital ring, and blue face, throat and upper breast. In NE, possibly confusable with Blue-eared Barbet, but is larger, has red on crown, uniform blue sides of head, and larger pale bill (with variable dark culmen and tip). Juvenile like adult, but head pattern duller and poorly defined (with red of crown intermixed with green and black). **Voice** Loud, harsh *took-a-rook, took-a-rook* uttered very rapidly. **HH** Habits like Brown-headed. Evergreen and deciduous trees, especially figs; open forest, groves and gardens. **TN** Formerly placed in *Megalaima*.

ad
ad
inornatus
Brown-headed Barbet
paler variant
Lineated Barbet
ad
caniceps
ad
juv
ad
Yellow-fronted Barbet
White-cheeked Barbet
ad
juv
ad
Golden-throated Barbet
Blue-throated Barbet

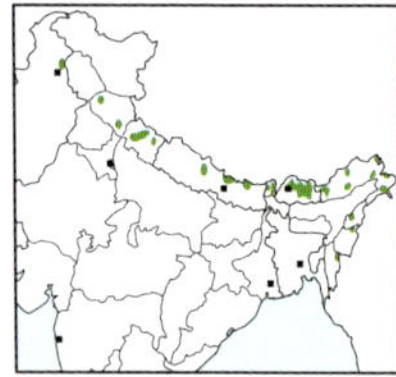

Yellow-rumped Honeyguide *Indicator xanthonotus* 15–16cm

Resident. Himalayas and NE India. Vagrant: Pakistan. **ID** Finch-like with stout bicoloured bill. Male has a bright orange-yellow forehead, malar region and throat. Dark olive upperparts, with narrow olive-yellow edges to feathers of mantle and wings, golden-yellow lower back and rump, and dark, square-ended tail. Inner edges of tertials are white, forming parallel lines down 'back'. Female similar, but smaller and duller, with less yellow on head. Juvenile has all-pinkish bill and lacks yellow on head. **Voice** Song of displaying male a very high-pitched, thin, simple, quickly repeated, upslurred note, sometimes followed by a similar downslurred one. Commonest call a single *weet*. **HH** Feeds on bees' wax, also on bees and other insects caught in clumsy aerial sallies returning to a favourite perch. Male defends nests of Giant Rock Bee and mates with females that visit the nests to feed. Sluggish. Near Giant Rock Bee nests on cliffs, and adjacent forest.

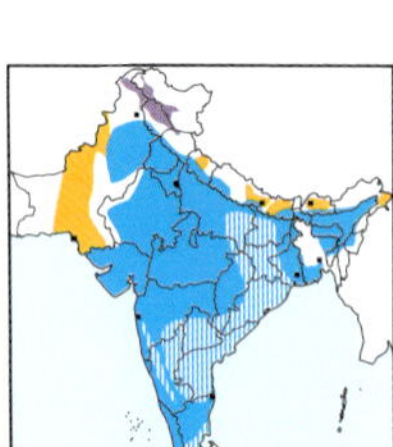

Eurasian Wryneck *Jynx torquilla* 16–18cm

Breeds in NW Himalayas; widespread in winter. Vagrant: Sri Lanka, Andaman Is. **ID** Cryptically patterned in grey, buff and dark brown. Has dark stripe through eye, irregular dark stripe on nape and mantle, buff to pale rufous throat and breast finely barred with black, and long, barred tail. **Voice** Series of *kwia* notes, slightly ascending, like call of small falcon. **HH** Unobtrusive. Feeds mainly on ground, picking up ants and other insects. Breeds in edges of forests and orchards; winters in scrub, thickets and bushes at cultivation edges.

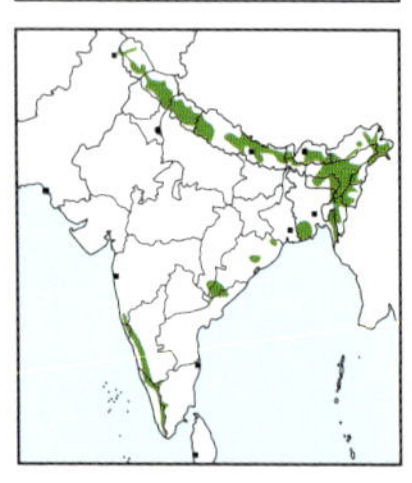

Speckled Piculet *Picumnus innominatus* 9–10.5cm

Resident. Himalayas, hills of SW, E and NE India, and Bangladesh. **ID** Tiny size. Has broad whitish supercilium and moustachial stripe, contrasting with blackish ear-covert patch and malar stripe. Underparts white to yellowish-white heavily spotted black. Also, greyish crown, yellowish-green upperparts, and short, square-ended blackish tail with white on central and outer feathers. Male has dull orange forehead and forecrown, marked with black. Female has uniform forehead and crown. **Voice** High *ti-ti-ti-ti-ti* by territorial male; frequently a high-pitched squeaky *sik-sik-sik*. **HH** Often with mixed species feeding parties of insectivores. Drums loudly. Forages on slender twigs, often on small bushes close to ground. Creeps along branches in typical woodpecker fashion, also, upside-down like a tit. Bushes and bamboo in broadleaved forest and second growth.

White-browed Piculet *Sasia ochracea* 9–10cm

Resident. Himalayas, NE India and Bangladesh. **ID** Tiny size and tailless appearance. Has greenish-olive upperparts (variably washed rufous) and rufous underparts, very short black tail, fine white supercilium behind eye, and red iris and orbital skin. Male has golden-yellow on forehead; rufous on female. **Voice** Short, sharp *chi* call; fast high-pitched trill starting with call, *chi-rrrrrrra*, by territorial male **HH** Habits like Speckled. Rapid, tinny drumming often on bamboo; also, loud tapping. Dense bushes and bamboo in broadleaved forest and dense second growth.

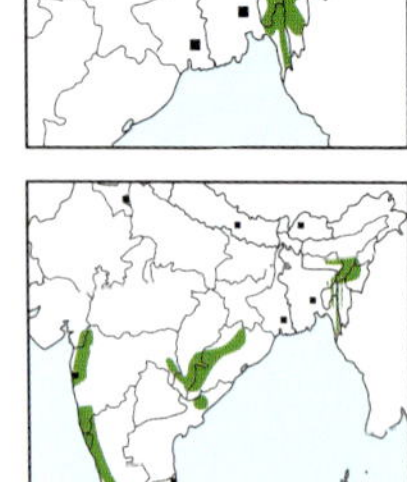

Heart-spotted Woodpecker *Hemicircus canente* 15–17cm

Resident. Mainly hills of NE, W and E India. Vagrant: Bangladesh. **ID** Looks top-heavy both at rest and in flight, with large crested head and very short tail (the latter obscured by wings at rest). Easily identified by prominent black crest, black heart-shaped spotting on white tertials and some coverts and scapulars, and white throat, becoming dusky olive or grey on rest of underparts. White rump in flight. Male has white speckling on forehead. Female has white forehead and forecrown. Juvenile is like female, but forehead and forecrown are spotted black, and feathers of upperparts have narrow whitish fringes. **Voice** Very vocal. Calls include a squeaky, nasal *ki-yew*, a high-pitched *kee...kee* and a quarrelsome *kirrick*. **HH** Drums weakly and infrequently. Often with mixed feeding parties of insectivores. Forages by creeping actively along outermost twigs and branches high in trees. Broadleaved evergreen and moist deciduous forests and coffee plantations.

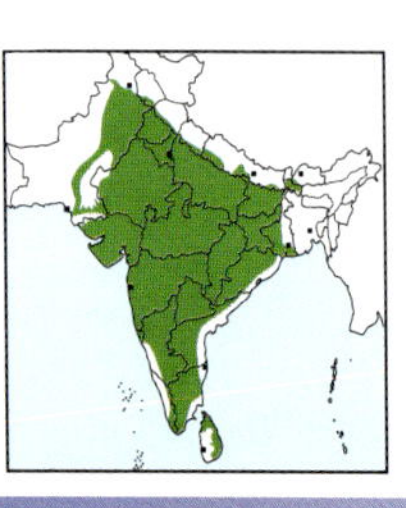

Yellow-crowned Woodpecker *Leiopicus mahrattensis* 17–18cm

Resident. Widespread east of Indus River. Vagrant: Bangladesh. **ID** From Brown-fronted by yellowish forehead and forecrown, white-spotted mantle and wing-coverts, bold white barring on central tail feathers, whitish rump, and diffuse brown moustachial stripe and patch on sides of neck. Underparts dirty grey, with fairly heavy brown streaking, and has small red patch on lower belly. Male has red hindcrown and nape. Female has yellowish to brownish hindcrown and nape. *L. m. pallescens* (north and north-west) has more heavily spotted and paler upperparts, and less noticeably streaked underparts. **Voice** Sharp *click, click*, and *kik-kik-kik-r-r-r-r-h*. **HH** Open wooded areas. **TN** Formerly placed in *Dendrocopos*.

♀
ad
♂
Yellow-rumped Honeyguide
Eurasian Wryneck
♀
♂
♀
Speckled Piculet
♂
White-browed Piculet
♀
juv
♂
♂
Heart-spotted Woodpecker
♀
Yellow-crowned Woodpecker

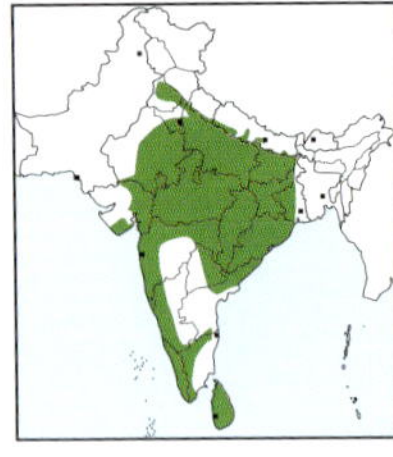

Brown-capped Pygmy Woodpecker *Yungipicus nanus* 13cm

Resident. Widespread; unrecorded in Pakistan. Vagrant: Bangladesh. **ID** Very small with small bill. From Grey-capped by brown crown (warmer than mantle), browner upperparts, and dusky underparts which are streaked (sometimes faintly) with brown. Further, throat is evenly mottled and streaked brown, and stripe behind eye is brown and concolorous with crown. White spotting on central tail feathers is a further feature (although see Grey-capped). At close range shows bare reddish orbital ring. Eyes often appear strikingly pale. Male has small crimson patch on sides of hindcrown. *Y. n. gymnopthalmos* (Sri Lanka) has darker brown crown concolorous with upperparts compared to the widespread nominate, and underparts are whiter and unstreaked (or only faintly so). *Y. n. cinereigula* (SW peninsula) is intermediate. **Voice** Rapid rattle on rising scale, increasing in volume before ending. **HH** Habits like Grey-capped. Light deciduous forest, trees in cultivation, bamboo and second growth. **TN** Formerly placed in *Dendrocopos*.

Grey-capped Pygmy Woodpecker *Yungipicus canicapillus* 14–16cm

Resident. Himalayas, NE India and Bangladesh. **ID** Very small with small bill. From Brown-capped by grey crown (blackish on sides and towards nape), blackish stripe behind eye, and clearer dark streaking on whitish to fulvous underparts. Also, tends to show diffuse blackish malar stripe and whiter throat. Upperparts blacker in background coloration. Lacks white spotting on central tail feathers, except forms in north-east (south of Brahmaputra) and Bangladesh. Male has crimson on nape. Male *Y. c. semicoronatus* (E Himalayas) has more extensive red on sides of crown, meeting in narrow band on nape, than *Y. c. mitchellii* (W Himalayas). **Voice** Short, soft *tzit*; doubled *chip-chip*; high quickly repeated *tit-tit-erh-r-r-r-r-h*, and irregular squeaking, *kweek-kweek-kweek*. Unobtrusive drumming. **HH** Creeps along branchlets and woody stems, often in canopy. Broadleaved forest, secondary forest and trees in cultivation. **TN** Formerly placed in *Dendrocopos*.

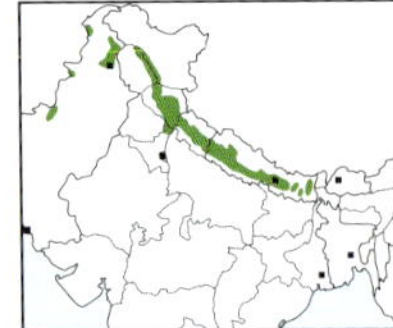

Brown-fronted Woodpecker *Dendrocoptes auriceps* 19–20cm

Resident. Hills of Balochistan and Himalayas. **ID** From Yellow-crowned by white-barred mantle, brownish forehead and forecrown, and prominent black moustachial stripe and patch on sides of breast. Also has smaller bill, well-defined black streaking on underparts, pinkish undertail-coverts, and all-black central tail feathers. Male has red nape and yellow hindcrown. Female has dull yellow hindcrown and nape. **Voice** Rapidly repeated, *chitter-chitter-chitter-r-rh*. **HH** Subtropical and temperate forest. **TN** Formerly placed in *Dendrocopos*.

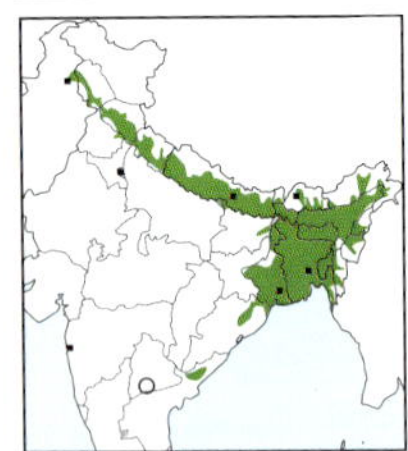

Fulvous-breasted Woodpecker *Dendrocopos macei* 18–20cm

Resident. Himalayas, NE and E India, and Bangladesh. **ID** A medium-sized woodpecker with white-barred black mantle and wings, and lightly streaked dirty buff underparts. Male has red on crown, which is black on female. Much larger than Pygmy Woodpeckers with red or black crown, lacking dark stripe behind eye, and with pronounced moustachial stripe and red undertail-coverts. Very similar to Stripe-breasted of north-east (see that species). **Voice** Call an abrupt *skik*, sharper than Grey-capped and higher than Stripe-breasted, given singly or in series; rattle comprising call note and a series of slightly lower *pil* notes. **HH** Often with mixed-species feeding flocks. Forages mainly on tree trunks and larger branches. Forest edges, open broadleaf forest and broadleaf/conifer forest and trees in cultivation.

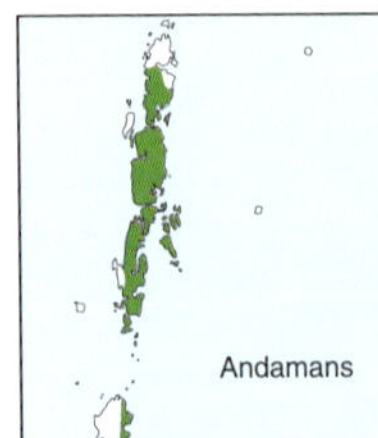

Freckle-breasted Woodpecker *Dendrocopos analis* 16–18cm

Resident. Andamans. **ID** Smaller than Fulvous-breasted with prominent black spotting on breast, streaking on ear-coverts, bolder white barring on central tail feathers, and a pale bill. Male has duller red crown and nape, and female has brown tone to crown (with blacker nape and sides to crown). **Voice** Calls include *tsik* notes slowly repeated; softer *tsip* call sometimes repeated in a short trill; a loud chatter *kut-kut-kut-*... on rising scale and a harsh fast rattle. Drums in quiet, weak rolls. **HH** Sometimes in mixed feeding parties. Prefers middle and upper levels of tall trees; also, in bushes and on ground. Open forest, secondary forest, open country with scattered trees, plantations and gardens. **AN** Spot-breasted Woodpecker.

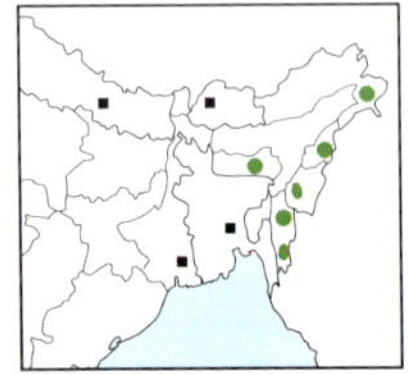

Stripe-breasted Woodpecker *Dendrocopos atratus* 21–22cm

Resident. NE Indian hills. **ID** From similar Fulvous-breasted by more boldly streaked underparts (especially on breast and, on some, streaking extends to lower throat). Further subtle differences include narrower white barring to black mantle (white bars narrower than black ones, and lacking on upper mantle), white (rather than buff) sides of head and neck, dull olive-yellow (rather than buff) underparts, and slightly longer bill. Also, red on head of male is brighter and extends onto nape. **Voice** An explosive *tchick* and a whinnying rattle. **HH** Forages mostly at middle to upper levels. Open pine and oak forest.

♀
nanus
♂
nanus
♂
gymnopthalmus
Brown-capped
Pygmy Woodpecker
♂
♀
Grey-capped
Pygmy Woodpecker
♂
♀
Brown-fronted
Woodpecker
♂
♀
Fulvous-breasted
Woodpecker
♂
Freckle-breasted
Woodpecker
♂
♀
Stripe-breasted
Woodpecker

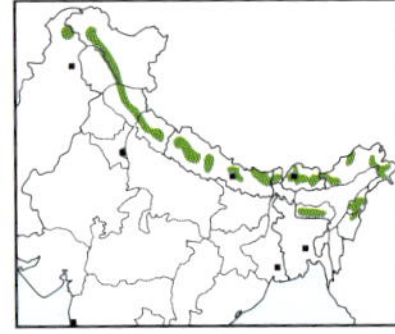

Rufous-bellied Woodpecker *Dendrocopos hyperythrus* 20–25cm

Resident. Himalayas, NE India and Bangladesh. **ID** Distinctive with white-barred mantle and wings, whitish face, and uniform rufous-orange sides of neck and underparts. Male has red crown and nape (more extensive in west of range). Female has white-spotted black crown and nape. Juvenile has blackish streaking on buff throat and blackish barring on rufous-buff underparts, and both sexes show scarlet feather tips on blackish crown. **Voice** In alarm *ptíkitititititit*. **HH** Subtropical and temperate forest.

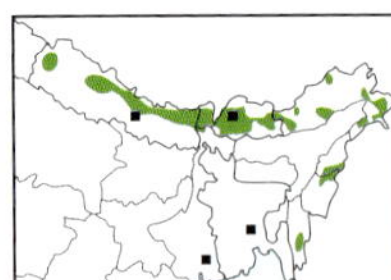

Darjeeling Woodpecker *Dendrocopos darjellensis* 23–25cm

Resident. Himalayas, NE India. **ID** From Himalayan by black streaking on yellowish-buff underparts, yellowish-buff to pale orange sides of neck, absence of black rear border to ear-coverts, and male has black crown and red nape. Best told from Crimson-breasted by larger size and bill, and yellowish-buff patch on neck. **Voice** Single *tsik* calls, as fast series in alarm; trill-like rattle. **HH** Feeds at all levels. Forest.

Great Spotted Woodpecker *Dendrocopos major* 20–24cm

Resident. NE Indian hills. **ID** Most closely resembles Himalayan, but underparts are darker, dirty buffish-brown, has black bar extending on sides of breast (almost joining to form breast-band on some), and crown of male is all black (red on Himalayan, though see below). Also, undertail-coverts are a deeper red (extending to lower belly), dark border to ear-coverts joins nape rather than crown, and has smaller whitish/buffish patch on sides of neck. Juvenile has red on crown, and therefore more closely resembles male Himalayan. **Voice** Single *kix* and a *krrarraarr*. **HH** Usually in upper storey. Oak and pine forest.

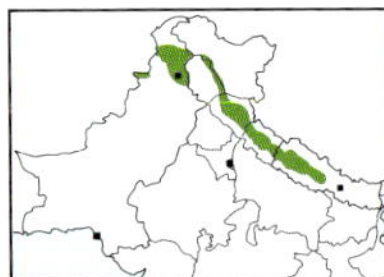

Himalayan Woodpecker *Dendrocopos himalayensis* 23–25cm

Resident. W Himalayas. **ID** From Darjeeling by unstreaked underparts, black rear edge to ear-coverts, and red crown of male (although juvenile male Darjeeling has reddish crown). W Himalayan *D. h. albescens* is whitish or greyish-white on the underparts; C and E Himalayan nominate is buff or yellowish on underparts. **Voice** A single *kit*, a rapid *tri-tri-tri-tri* and high-pitched *chisik-chisik*. **HH** Favours coniferous forest.

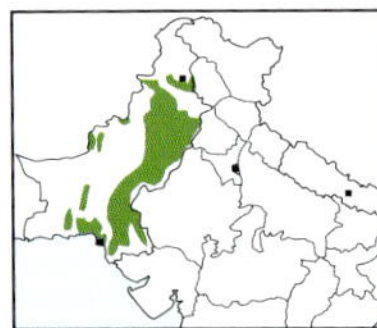

Sind Woodpecker *Dendrocopos assimilis* 20–22cm

Resident. Widespread in Pakistan just extending into NW India. **ID** Very closely resembles Himalayan, although has different range and habitat. Subtle differences include slightly smaller size, absence of black border to ear-coverts, large white patch on forehead, larger white 'shoulder' patch (with white extending to scapulars), broader white barring on wings, and whiter underparts. **Voice** High-pitched *chir-rur-rirh-rirh* and *wicka toi-whit, to-whit, toi-whit*. **HH** Forages restlessly on slender branches of scrub and small trees. Dry forest and plantations.

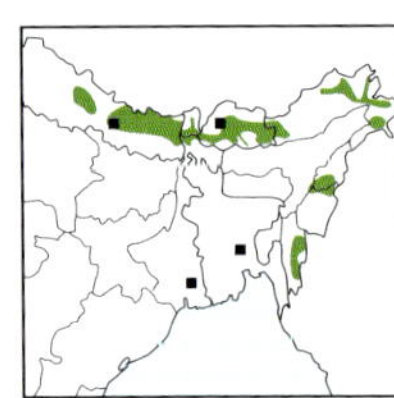

Crimson-naped Woodpecker *Dryobates cathpharius* 17–19cm

Resident. Himalayas, NE India. **ID** Smaller than Darjeeling Woodpecker with smaller bill; also male has red of nape extending to rear and sides of neck, while female has a diffuse, but fairly distinct, orange-red patch at rear of ear-coverts. In addition, compared to Darjeeling, both sexes have a diffuse red patch on breast, lack heavy barring on flanks and thighs, and have indistinct red streaking on undertail-coverts (wholly pale red on Darjeeling). Male *D. c. pyrrhothorax* (NE India south of Brahmaputra) has a larger red patch on upper breast, all-red undertail-coverts. **Voice** Loud, monotonous *tchick*, higher-pitched than Darjeeling; shrill *kee-kee*. **HH** Broadleaved forest. **TN** Formerly placed in *Dendrocopos*. **AN** Crimson-breasted Woodpecker.

Darjeeling
Woodpecker
♂
♂
♀
Rufous-bellied
Woodpecker
♀
♂
♂
himalayensis
♀
himalayensis
Great Spotted
Woodpecker
♀
Himalayan
Woodpecker
♂
albescens
♂
♂
cathpharius
♀
cathpharius
♂
pyrrhothorax
♀
Sind Woodpecker
Crimson-naped
Woodpecker

PLATE 110: WOODPECKERS AND FLAMEBACKS I

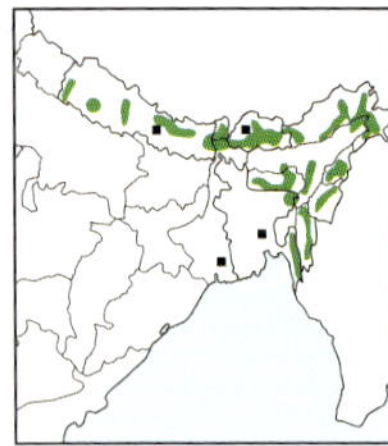

Bay Woodpecker *Blythipicus pyrrhotis* 26.5–30cm

Resident. Himalayas, NE India and Bangladesh. **ID** From Rufous by long yellowish bill. It is also larger with more angular head shape, and has more broadly barred and brighter rufous upperparts, diffuse streaking on forehead and crown, darker brown underparts, and largely unbarred tail. Male has prominent scarlet patch on sides of neck, extending onto nape. Female lacks scarlet patch. Juvenile has more prominent barring on mantle, diffuse rufous and dark brown barring on underparts, and more prominent pale streaking on head. **Voice** Loud descending laughter *keek, keek-keek-keek-keek-kerere-kerere*. **HH** Shy and elusive. Sometimes with mixed-species flocks. Mainly forages within a few metres of ground on moss-covered trunks, dead stumps and fallen logs, also on ground. Dense broadleaved evergreen forest and dense second growth.

Rufous Woodpecker *Micropternus brachyurus* 25cm

Resident. Himalayas, NE, E and W India, Bangladesh and Sri Lanka. **ID** A medium-sized, rufous-brown woodpecker with short black bill and shaggy crest (latter sometimes not apparent). Heavily barred black on mantle, wings, flanks and tail. Male has diffuse scarlet flash on ear-coverts, lacking in female. **Voice** A high-pitched, nasal *keenk keenk kenk*. **HH** Diagnostic drumming, like stalling engine *bdddd-d-d-d-d-d-d-dt*. Forages in trees at all heights; often seen digging into tree-ant nests. Also, feeds on ground on fallen rotten logs, termite nests and cow dung. Broadleaved forest and second growth, often with bamboo.

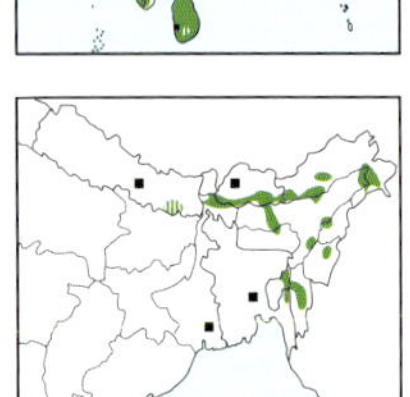

Pale-headed Woodpecker *Gecinulus grantia* 25–27cm

Resident in Himalayas from far E Nepal (where no recent records) east to Arunachal Pradesh, NE India and Bangladesh. **ID** A smallish, mainly unbarred woodpecker with small, pale grey bill. Head appears domed or with shaggy nape. Easily distinguished by golden-olive head and neck (with beady black eye), dull crimson to crimson-brown upperparts, brown primaries barred buffish-pink, and dark olive underparts. Male has crimson-pink on crown. **Voice** Vocalisations like Bay Woodpecker. Nasal *chaik-chaik-chaik-chaik*, repeated 4–5 times, accelerating and becoming lower towards end; loud rattles, *kereki kereki kereki kereki*, when agitated. **HH** Drumming loud and even-pitched. Forages noisily, often low down on large bamboos and tree trunks, sometimes on fallen logs. Chiefly in bamboo jungle; also, moist broadleaved secondary forest.

Greater Flameback *Chrysocolaptes guttacristatus* 30–34cm

Resident. Himalayas, hills of India and Bangladesh. **ID** From Himalayan and Common by larger size and longer S-shaped neck, longer bill, white or black-and-white spotted hindneck, pale eyes, and four (not three) toes. In addition, has clearly divided moustachial stripe (with obvious white oval centre), clean single black line on centre of throat, and white spotting on black breast. Male has red crest. Female has black crown and crest with white spotting (white streaking in Himalayan and Common). **Voice** Fast series of insect-like notes, monotonous or varying in speed and pitch, e.g. *di-di-di-di-di-di-di* or *tibittitititit*. **HH** Broadleaved forest and groves; also, mangroves in Bangladesh. **TN** Previously subsumed in *C. lucidus*. **AN** Greater Goldenback.

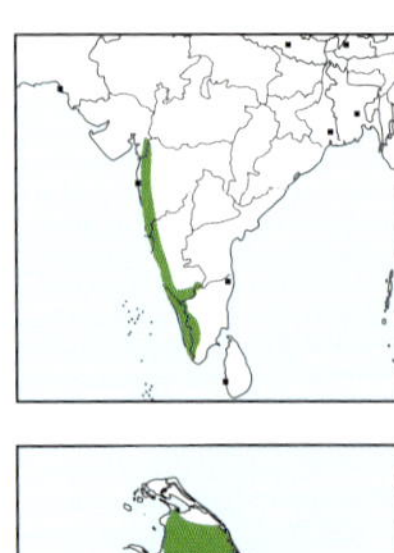

Malabar Flameback *Chrysocolaptes socialis* 30–34cm

Resident. Western Ghats, south from Gujarat. **ID** Much as allopatric Greater Flameback but is more compact, with stronger olive coloration to upperparts and more extensive red on rump. Similar to sympatric Common Flameback but has larger bill, divided moustachial stripe and white hindneck. **Voice** Rather high-pitched thin fast rattle repeated at irregular intervals; in flight a nasal, plaintive series of 3–5 loud notes, repeated a few times. **HH** Very little published information. Habits probably similar to Greater Flameback. Forests, requires large trees. **TN** Recently split from Greater Flameback.

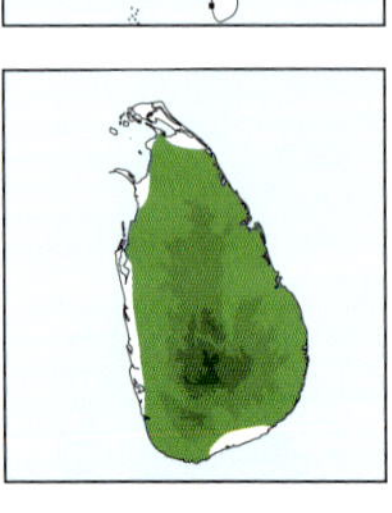

Crimson-backed Flameback *Chrysocolaptes stricklandi* 29–30cm

Resident. Sri Lanka. **ID** Strikingly different from Greater, with crimson upperparts, pale bill, and broader black stripe through eye (with indistinct or no white supercilium). Larger than Red-backed Flameback which can also have crimson upperparts, with large pale bill, whitish eye, white-spotted hindneck, and divided moustachial stripe. Male has red crest. Female has black crown and crest with white spotting. **Voice** Sharp, metallic, monotone *kiriri... kirirriri* like a giant cicada. **HH** Forest and well-wooded areas. **TN** Previously *C.* (*lucidus*) *stricklandi*. **AN** Crimson-backed Goldenback.

♂
♀
Bay Woodpecker
♂ juv
♂
♀
Rufous
Woodpecker
♂
Greater
Flameback
♀
♂ juv
♂
♀
Pale-headed
Woodpecker
♂
Malabar
Flameback
♂
Crimson-backed
Flameback
♀

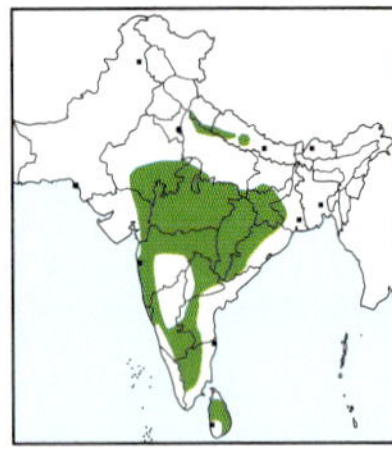

White-naped Woodpecker *Chrysocolaptes festivus* 29cm

Resident. Widespread in India, also, W Nepal and Sri Lanka. **ID** Large, with large bill and divided moustachial stripe. Best told by white hindneck and mantle contrasting with black scapulars and back (which form black V). Rump also black. Male has red crest. Female has yellow hindcrown and crest. **Voice** Tinnier, higher-pitched rattle than flamebacks; all phrases drop noticeably in pitch, reminiscent of Crested Kingfisher. **HH** Light deciduous forest, scrub and scattered trees.

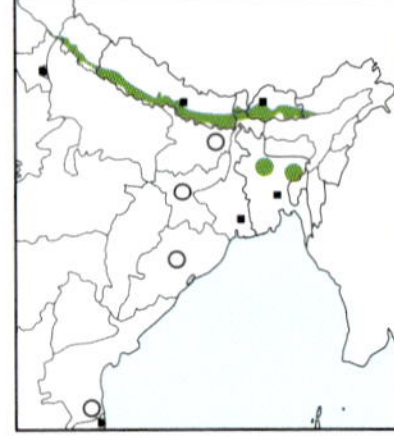

Himalayan Flameback *Dinopium shorii* 30–32cm

Resident. Himalayas, NE India, and locally in hills of peninsula and Bangladesh. **ID** Smaller size and bill than Greater Flameback, with black hindneck, and brownish-buff centre of throat (plus breast on some) with black spotting forming irregular border. Has indistinctly divided moustachial stripe (centre is brownish-buff, with touch of red on male). Also, has reddish or brown eyes, and three toes. Breast irregularly streaked and scaled with black, and on some almost unmarked. Male has red crest. Female has white streaking to black crown and crest (white spotting in female Greater). See Common Flameback. **Voice** Rapid repeated *klak-klak-klak-klak-klak*, slower and not as loud as Greater. **HH** Tall broadleaved mature forest. **AN** Himalayan Goldenback.

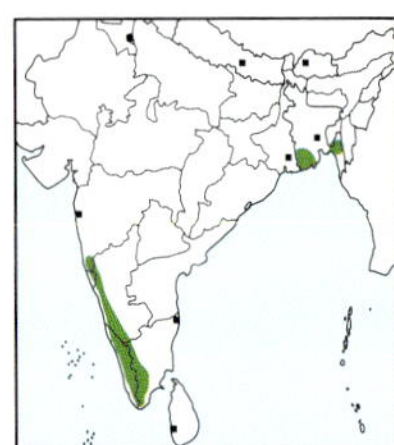

Common Flameback *Dinopium javanense* 28–30cm

Resident. Hills of SW India and Bangladesh. **ID** Smaller size and bill than Greater, lacking cleanly divided moustachial, and has black hindneck. Reddish or brown eyes, and three toes. Smaller size and bill compared to Himalayan. Moustachial stripe lacks clear dividing line (usually solid black, but can appear divided on some, like Himalayan). Also, Common has an irregular line of black spotting on centre of throat (brownish-buff line in Himalayan), and breast of Common is more heavily marked with black. Rump red (black in Black-rumped). **Voice** Variable. Calls include: *kowp-owp-owp-owp* in flight; single or double *kow* when perched; nasal *wicka*-like calls in display. **HH** Broadleaved evergreen and semi-evergreen forest in peninsula; moist deciduous forest and wooded areas in NE India; mangroves in Bangladesh. **AN** Common Goldenback.

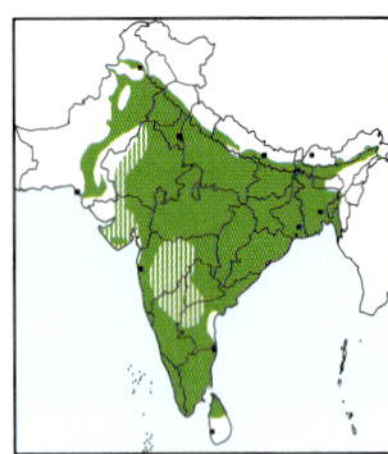

Black-rumped Flameback *Dinopium benghalense* 26–29cm

Widespread resident. **ID** Best identified by combination of black lower back and rump, different head pattern (white-spotted black throat and black stripe through eye, but no moustachial stripe), barred primaries, and (variable) white or buff spotting on blackish lesser wing-coverts. Further, female has red hindcrown and crest. **Voice** Single strident *klerk* and a sharp whinnying rattle starting low and slowly, rising and accelerating, before ending very fast. **HH** Forages at all levels in trees and on ground. Light forest, plantations, groves, trees around villages and cultivation. **AN** Lesser Goldenback.

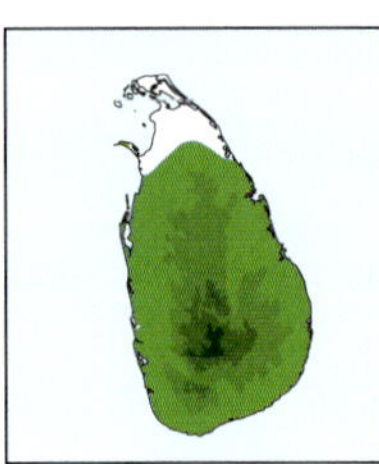

Red-backed Flameback *Dinopium psarodes* 28cm

Resident: Sri Lanka. Northern race (*D. p. jaffnense*) has upperparts varying from golden-yellow to orangey or crimson-red, and areas of white on head are comparatively extensive. The nominate southern race has crimson upperparts and areas of white on head are reduced to a narrow supercilium and moustachial stripe. Spotting on wing-coverts when present aids identification from Crimson-backed Flameback – see latter for other differences. Both sexes have red crest, with crown red-spotted in male and white-spotted in female. **Voice** Song an accelerating rattling scream *ki-ki-ki...kikiki...krrr*; also, a rasping *ke-ke-ke*. **HH** Habits like Black-rumped. Lowland forest, wooded gardens and plantations. **TN** Formerly treated as conspecific with Black-rumped Flameback.

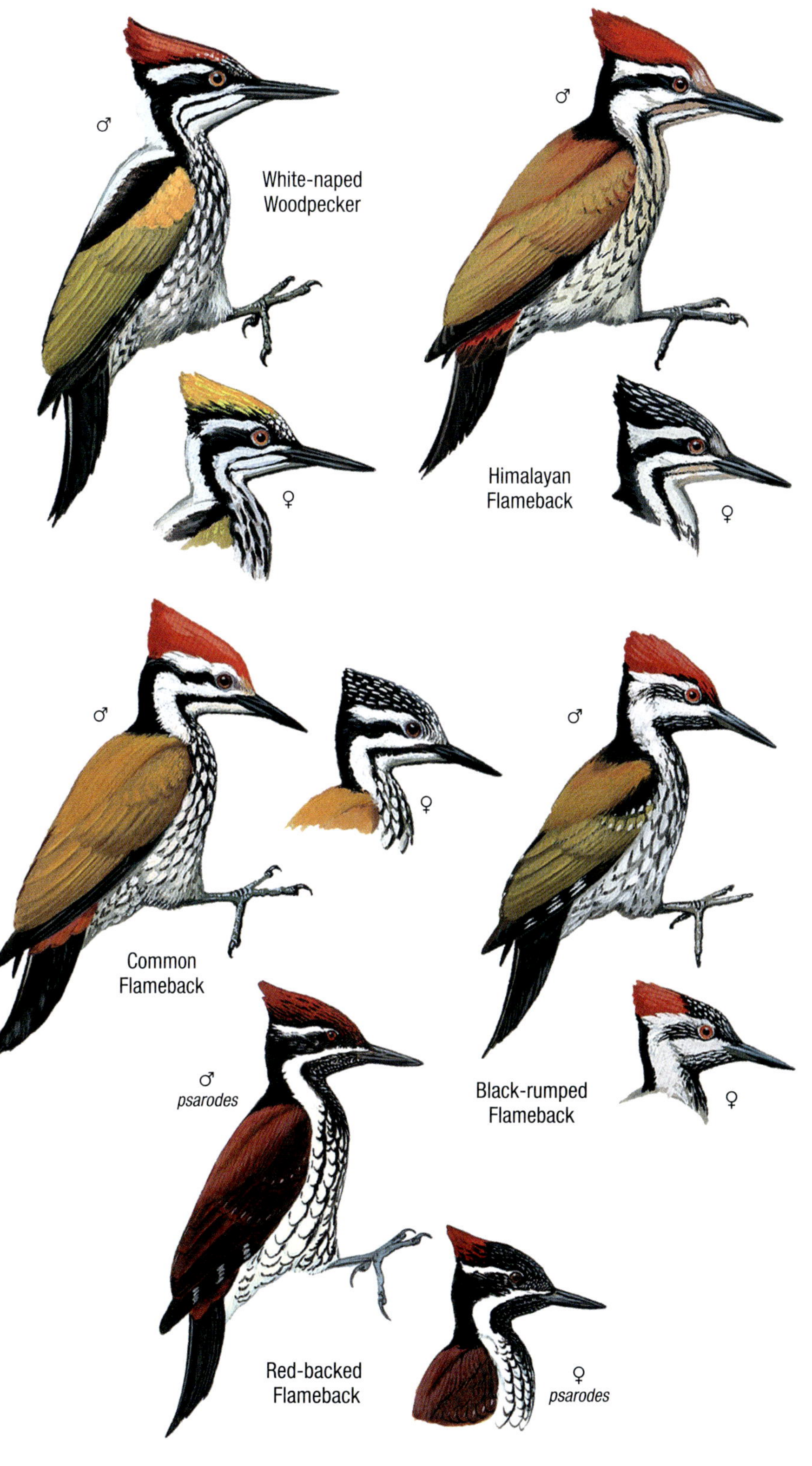
♂
White-naped
Woodpecker
♀
♂
Himalayan
Flameback
♀
♂
♀
Common
Flameback
♂
Black-rumped
Flameback
♀
♂
psarodes
Red-backed
Flameback
♀
psarodes

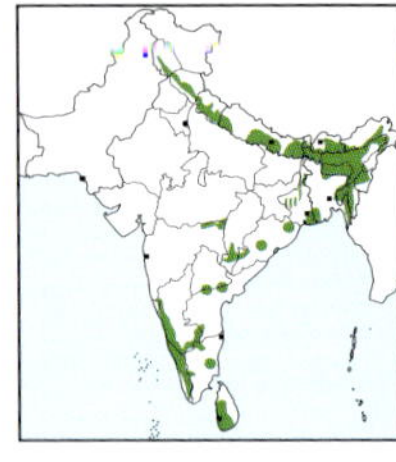

Lesser Yellownape *Picus chlorolophus* 25–28cm

Resident. Himalayas, hills of India, Bangladesh and Sri Lanka. Vagrant: Pakistan. **ID** From Greater Yellownape by smaller size and smaller mainly dark bill, red and white head markings, rufous panel in wing, indistinct whitish barring on primaries, and white barring on underparts. Male has red moustachial and line above eye. In peninsular India and Sri Lanka *P. c. chlorigaster* and *P. c. wellsi* are smaller and darker green on upperparts, with variable white spotting on underparts, and lack (or have indistinct) white stripes on sides of head (head is more uniform dark greyish-olive); males have red crown and less yellow on nape and females have red on rear crown. **Voice** Buzzard-like, drawn-out *pee-oow* and a descending series of shrill *kwee* notes. **HH** Often with mixed-species parties. Feeds chiefly in smaller trees; also, understorey shrubs. Deciduous and broadleaved evergreen forest, second growth, open woodland and rubber and coffee plantations in S India.

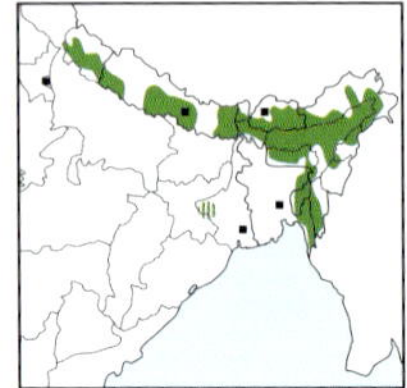

Greater Yellownape *Chrysophlegma flavinucha* 32–35cm

Resident. Himalayas, NE and E India, and Bangladesh. **ID** Striking orange-yellow crest and nape. From Lesser by larger size and pale bill, brown on crown, and lack of red and white markings on head. Further differences include dark olive sides of neck adjoining dark-spotted white foreneck, uniform underparts, black barring on rufous primaries, and pale yellow (male) or rufous-brown (female) throat. **Voice** Plaintive, descending *pee-u... pee-u* and a single metallic *chenk*. **HH** Often with itinerant, mixed-species foraging flocks. Feeds at all levels of trees. Deciduous and broadleaved evergreen forest and forest edges. **TN** Formerly placed in *Picus*.

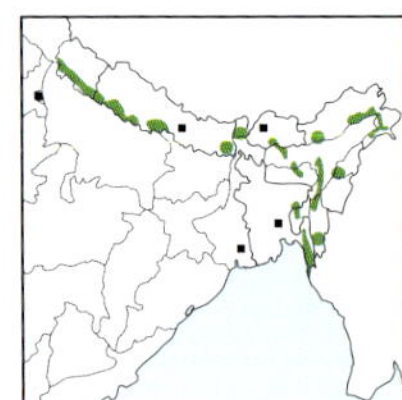

Great Slaty Woodpecker *Mulleripicus pulverulentus* 45–50cm

Resident. Himalayas, NE India and Bangladesh. **ID** Giant slate-grey woodpecker with huge pale bill, long serpentine neck and long tail. Fine whitish speckling on head and neck. Male has pinkish-red moustachial patch and pink on lower throat. Throat is pale yellow in both sexes. Juvenile is much as adult with browner cast to body. **Voice** Loud whinnying cackle of 2–5 notes, *woikwoikwoikwoik*, initial note often slightly higher-pitched, final one distinctly lower, usually given in flight. Single *dwot* calls, perched or in flight, and low soft mewing notes by partners at close range. **HH** Usually in pairs, regularly in noisy family parties of 3–6 or more birds. Forages chiefly on trunks and major branches in large trees. Hops slowly and jerkily in spirals up trunks and large branches with apparent difficulty. Birds follow each other in flight, which is less undulating than other woodpeckers, with slow deliberate wingbeats. Drumming not reported. Tall mature trees in tropical sal and broadleaved evergreen forest and forest clearings with scattered mature trees. Globally threatened.

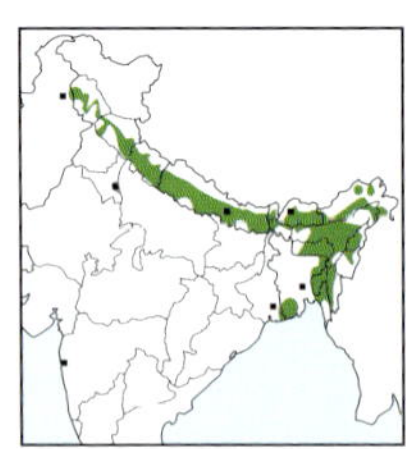

Grey-headed Woodpecker *Picus canus* 28–33cm

Resident. Himalayas, NE and E India, and Bangladesh. **ID** Has plain grey face, black nape and moustachial, dark bill, and uniform greyish-green underparts. Male has red forehead and forecrown (black in female). Juvenile duller, with greyer upperparts, less pronounced moustachial, and whitish barring on underparts. W Himalayan *P. c. sanguiniceps* is darker and greener on upperparts and underparts than E Himalayan *P. c. hessei*, which has bronze sheen to upperparts and yellower underparts. **Voice** High-pitched *-tac, -tac, -tac, -tac*, fading at end; staccato, musical rattle in alarm. **HH** Often feeds on ground on ants and termites, moving about with heavy hops. Broadleaved and mixed conifer forest.

♀
chlorolophus
♂
chlorolophus
♂
chlorigaster
Lesser Yellownape
♂
Greater Yellownape
♀
♂
♀
Great Slaty
Woodpecker
♂
♀
Grey-headed Woodpecker

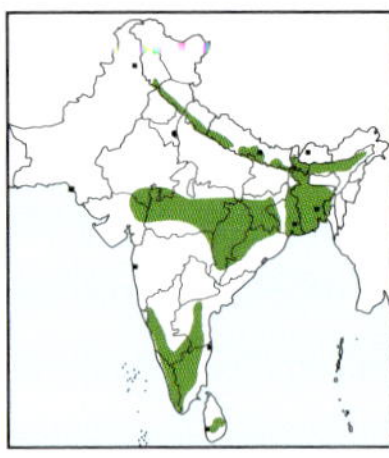

Streak-throated Woodpecker *Picus xanthopygaeus* 30cm

Widespread resident; unrecorded in Pakistan. **ID** From similar Scaly-bellied Woodpecker by olive streaking on throat and upper breast. Also smaller, with smaller bill and usually darker upper mandible, indistinct moustachial stripe (often obscured by pale streaking), and comparatively uniform tail. Male has red crown, which is black (streaked grey) on female. Juvenile has grey bases to feathers of mantle and scapulars, creating mottled appearance to upperparts. **Voice** Rather silent; a sharp single *queemp*. **HH** Frequently joins mixed parties of insectivores. Open broadleaved forest, second growth and forest plantations.

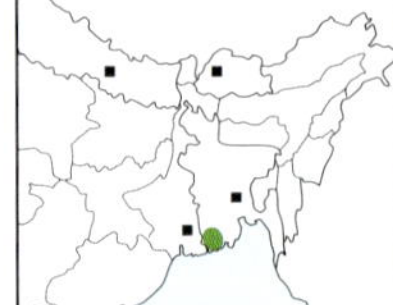

Streak-breasted Woodpecker *Picus viridanus* 30–33cm

Resident. Bangladesh Sundarbans. **ID** From Streak-throated Woodpecker by unmarked or indistinctly marked olive foreneck and upper breast. Other features mentioned in the literature (plainer grey ear-coverts, red eye, more pronounced blackish moustachial, blacker tail) appear to be variable in both Streak-breasted and Streak-throated, and may be unreliable in the field. **Voice** Calls include explosive *kirrr*; a short, strident series *cheu-tcheu-tcheu-tcheu* and a squirrel-like *kyup*. **HH** Commonly feeds on ground on ants. Mangroves.

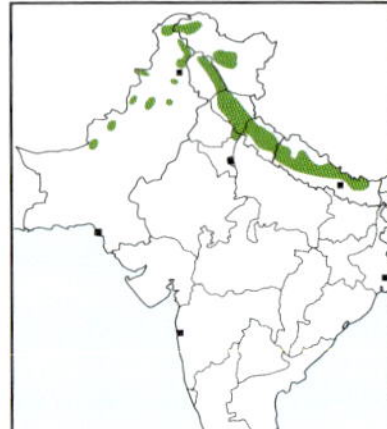

Scaly-bellied Woodpecker *Picus squamatus* 35cm

Resident. Hills of Balochistan and Himalayas. **ID** From similar Streak-throated by larger size, larger yellowish bill, more prominent dark moustachial stripe, unstreaked throat and upper breast, more boldly scaled underparts, and prominent whitish barring on tail. Male has red crown; black (streaked grey) on female. Juvenile has mottled upperparts, and dark spotting and scaling on throat and breast which could cause confusion with Streak-throated (although is larger and has white-barred tail). **Voice** Flight call a repeated *kuik-kui-kuik*; advertising call a quavering, rapidly repeated *klee-gu-kleeguh*. **HH** Hunts on tree trunks and often also on ground. Coniferous and mixed oak/coniferous forests; in Pakistan also juniper scrub and bushes on streambeds in desert.

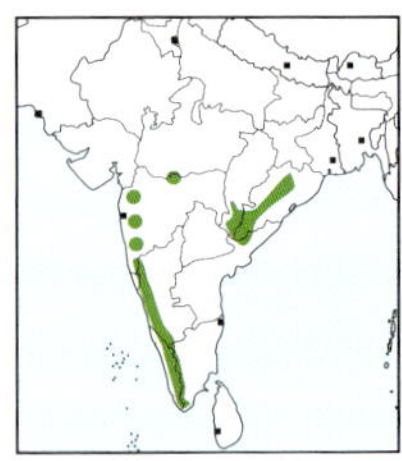

White-bellied Woodpecker *Dryocopus javensis* 40–48cm

Resident. Western and Eastern Ghats. **ID** A large black woodpecker with a white to cream belly and strikingly pale eyes. Has long black bill, slender neck and long tail. Male has a red crown and moustachial stripe; red only apparent on the hindcrown in female. In flight, shows a white rump and underwing-coverts. Juvenile much as adult. **Voice** Loud *kiyow* or *keer* call note; long calls *kek-ek-ek-ek-ek*, 3–4 notes per second, both in flight and when perched. Both sexes drum, loud accelerating rolls. **HH** Noisy woodpecker, excavating and frequently hammering loudly. Forages on live and dead trees, large fallen logs and dead stumps. Has slow, deliberate wingbeats like a crow's. Prefers primary forest and forest edges, also, secondary forest with large trees. Moist deciduous evergreen and semi-evergreen broadleaved forest and plantations; in SW India favours bamboo and teak plantations and tall shade trees in coffee and cardamom plantations.

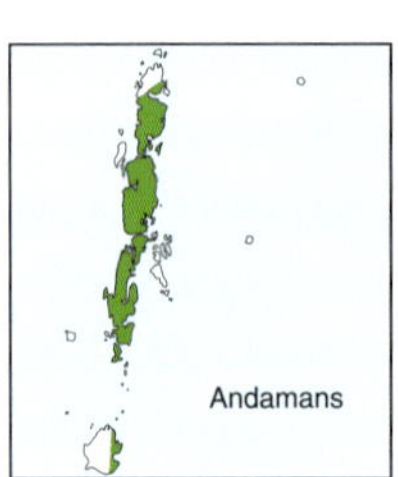

Andaman Woodpecker *Dryocopus hodgei* 38cm

Resident. Andamans. **ID** A large black woodpecker, with strikingly pale eyes. Has black bill, slender neck and long tail. Rump and underwing coverts also black. Male has a red crown and moustachial stripe; red is restricted to the hindcrown on the female. **Voice** Loud, chattering *kuk-kuk-kuk* ending in a whistling *kui*; also, loud sharp *kik, kik, kik*. **HH** Habits very like White-bellied. Large trees in evergreen forest. Globally threatened.

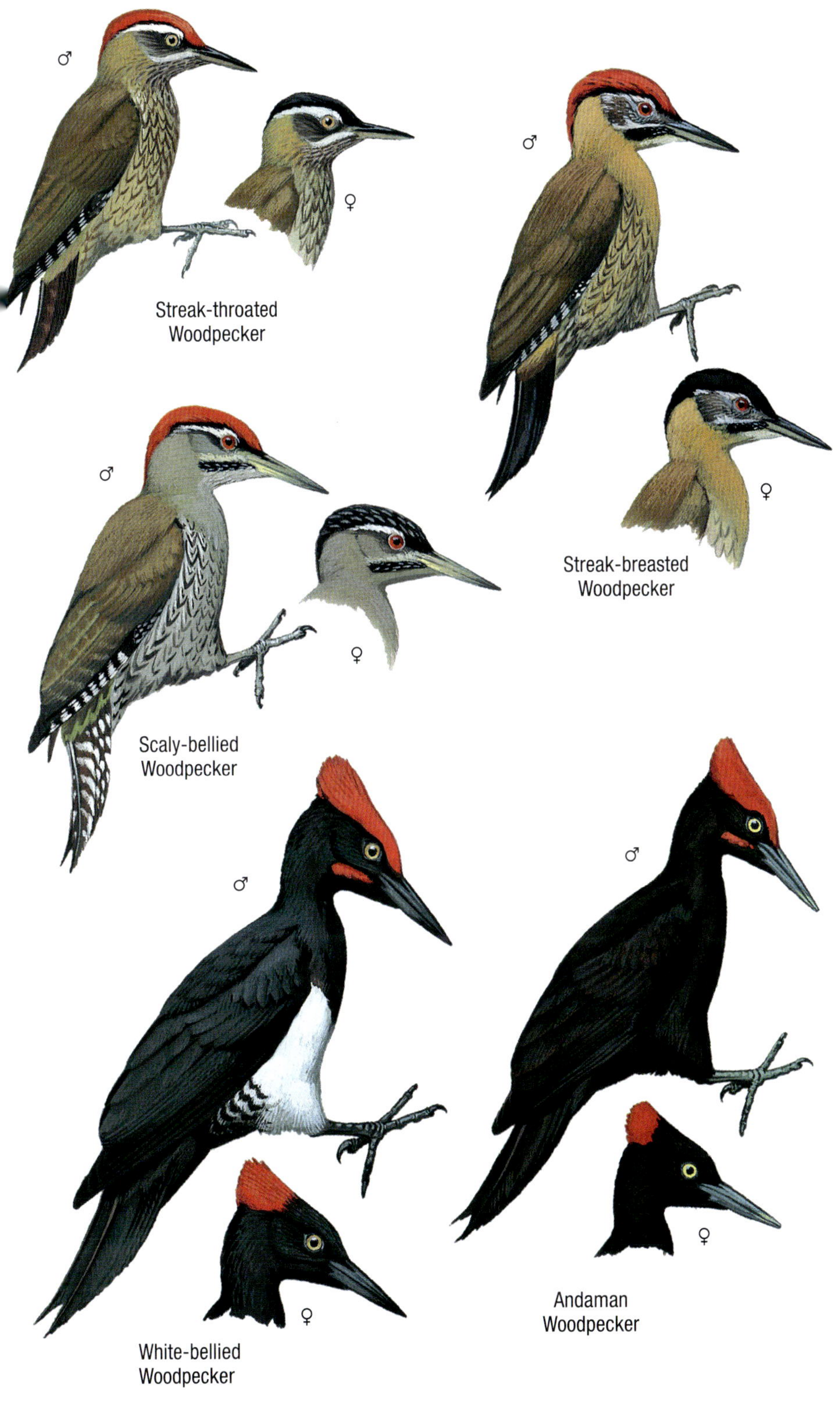
♂
♀
Streak-throated Woodpecker
♂
♀
Streak-breasted Woodpecker
♂
♀
Scaly-bellied Woodpecker
♂
♀
White-bellied Woodpecker
♂
♀
Andaman Woodpecker

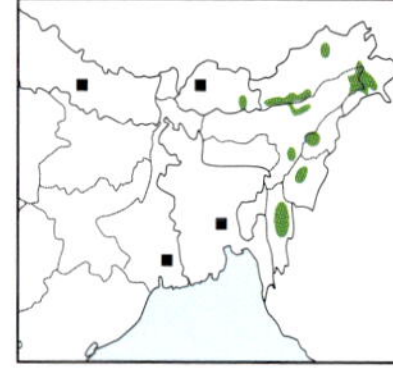

Pied Falconet *Microhierax melanoleucos* 15–19cm

Resident. E Himalayas and NE India. **ID** Larger than Collared. Adult has white underparts, and lacks white hind collar. Mask appears broader, and supercilium narrower, than Collared. Juvenile similar but has yellowish bill and orbital skin (black in adult). **Voice** A low chattering series of shrill peeping whistles, which rise and fall in pitch and volume *kip-kip-kip...* and a low chattering call. **HH** Habits like Collared but is a more powerful predator. Mainly eats insects and birds, some much larger than itself by stooping on them like a *Falco* falcon. Forest clearings, tea plantations and wooded foothills.

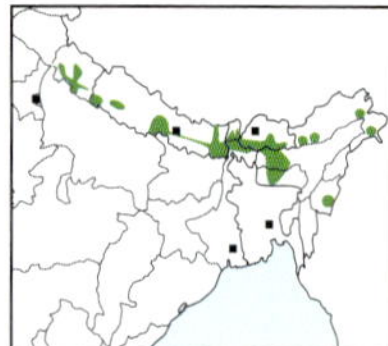

Collared Falconet *Microhierax caerulescens* 14–18cm

Resident. Himalayas, Manipur and NE Odisha. **ID** Very small, with rather broad wings and long, square-ended tail. Flies with rapid beats interspersed with long glides. Rather shrike-like when perched. Adult has white collar, black crown and eye-stripe, and rufous-orange underparts. Juvenile has rufous-orange on forehead and supercilium, white throat and yellowish bill. **Voice** High-pitched *kli-kli-kli* or *killi-killi-killi*. **HH** Found singly, in pairs or small parties, which sometimes huddle together on a branch. Rather crepuscular. Perches on dead branches of a forest tree and makes short, swift darting sorties to seize prey. Often slowly pumps tail and bobs head when perched. Edges and clearings of broadleaved tropical forest.

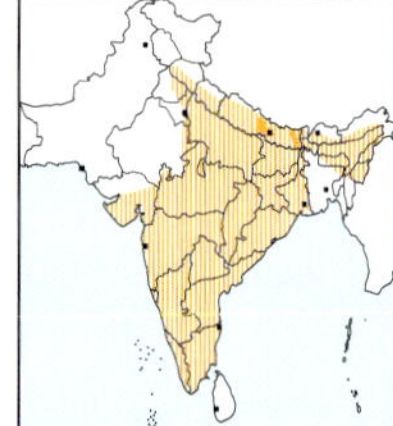

Lesser Kestrel *Falco naumanni* 29–32cm

Widespread passage migrant. Vagrant: Bhutan, Bangladesh, Sri Lanka. **ID** Slightly smaller and slimmer than Eurasian Kestrel. Flapping shallower and stiffer. Claws whitish (black on Eurasian). When perched wingtips reach or nearly reach tip of tail (falling short in Eurasian). Male has uniform blue-grey head (without dark moustachial stripe), unmarked rufous upperparts, blue-grey greater coverts, and almost plain orange-buff underparts. In flight, underwing whiter with more clearly pronounced darker trailing edge and wingtips; tail often looks more wedge-shaped. First-year male more like Eurasian; best distinguished by structural differences and unmarked rufous mantle and scapulars. Female and juvenile have less distinct moustachial stripe than Eurasian and lack any suggestion of dark eye-stripe; underwing tends to be cleaner and whiter, with primary bases unbarred (or only lightly barred), coverts less heavily spotted, and dark primary tips more pronounced. **Voice** Mainly silent. **HH** Hunts in similar manner to Eurasian but is more agile in flight. Generally hovers less than Eurasian and for shorter periods. Mainly insectivorous. Roosts communally. Open grassland and cultivation.

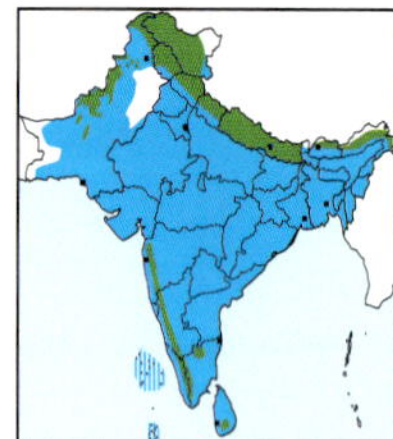

Eurasian Kestrel *Falco tinnunculus* 27–35cm

Resident in mountains of Pakistan, Himalayas and Western Ghats and Sri Lanka; widespread winter visitor. **ID** Long, rather broad tail; wingtips more rounded than on most falcons. Frequently hovers. Male has greyish head with diffuse dark moustachial stripe, rufous upperparts heavily marked with black, and grey tail with black subterminal band. Female and juvenile have rufous crown and nape streaked black, diffuse and narrow dark moustachial stripe, rufous upperparts heavily barred and spotted black, and dark barring on rufous tail; underwing more heavily barred than male's. **Voice** Rather silent when not breeding. Commonest call a fast, shrill, yelping *kik-kik-kik-kik...* or a more drawn-out, piercing *kee-kee-kee-kee....* **HH** Usually found singly or in pairs. Characteristically hovers over open country with rapidly beating wings and fanned tail, while scanning the ground for prey. Cultivation, grassland and semi-desert in hills and plains, and open subalpine and alpine slopes. **AN** Common Kestrel.

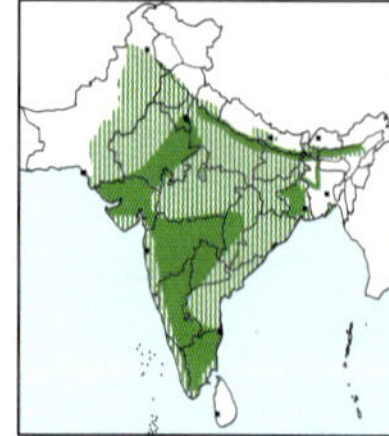

Red-necked Falcon *Falco chicquera* 28–34cm

Widespread resident; unrecorded in most of the north-east and W Pakistan. Vagrant: Bhutan, Sri Lanka. **ID** Powerful falcon with pointed wings and longish tail. Flight usually fast and dashing. Adult has rufous crown, nape and narrow moustachial stripe, pale blue-grey upperparts with fine dark barring, white underparts finely barred with black, and grey tail with broad black subterminal band. In flight, blackish primaries contrast with rest of upperwing. Sexes alike, but female larger. Juvenile similar but darker, with fine dark shaft streaking on crown, fine rufous fringes to upperparts, and underparts with fine rufous-brown barring. **Voice** Rather silent except when nesting; calls include shrill, querulous screams *ki-ki-ki-ki-ki* and rasping *yak, yak, yak*. **HH** A dashing falcon. Usually hunts cooperatively in pairs, one bird pursuing prey and the other cutting off its escape. Feeds mainly on small birds taken on the wing. Cultivation with groves, open country with trees and groves at desert edges.

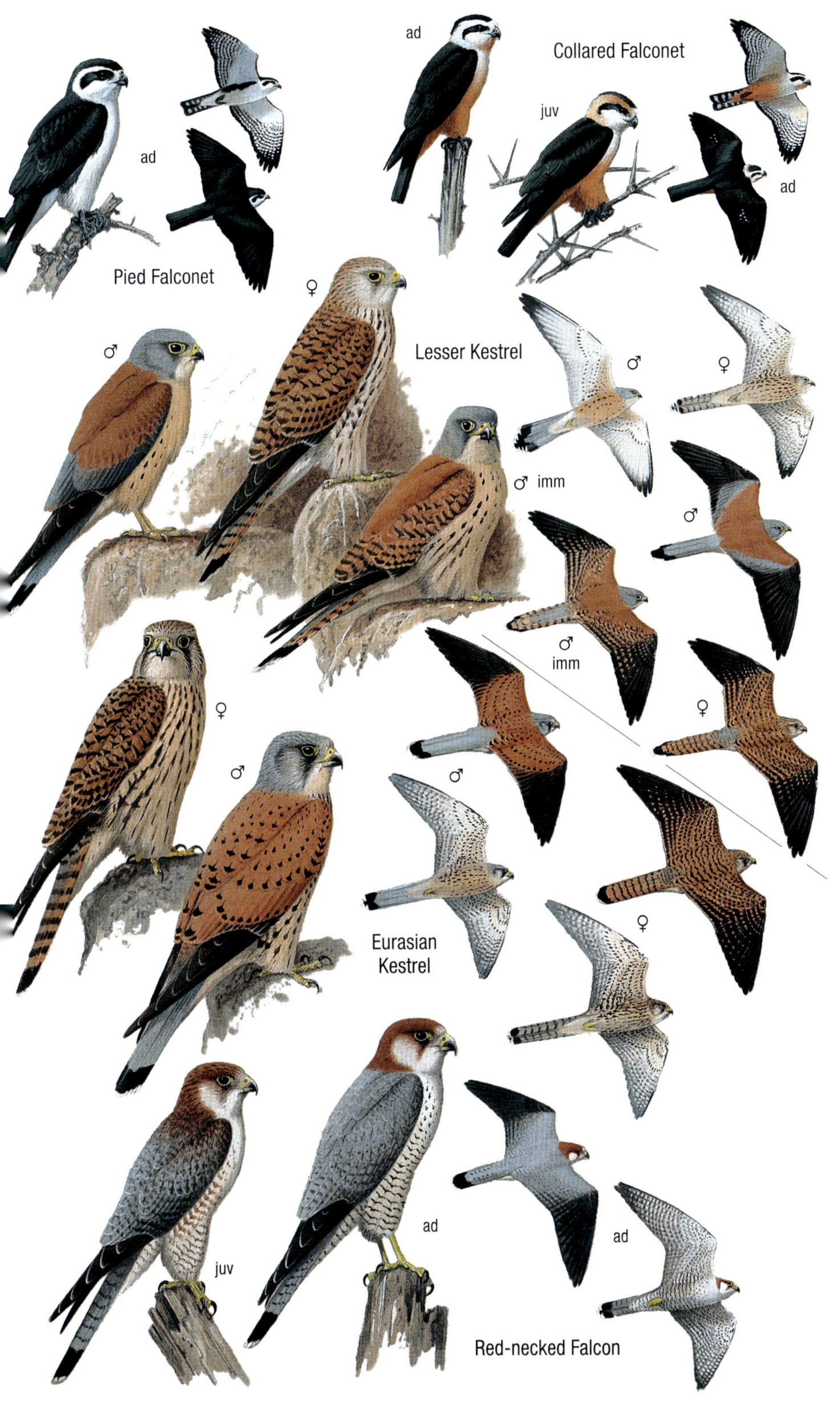
ad
Collared Falconet
juv
ad
ad
Pied Falconet
♀
Lesser Kestrel
♂
♂
♀
♂ imm
♂
♂
imm
♀
♀
♂
♂
Eurasian
Kestrel
♀
juv
ad
ad
Red-necked Falcon

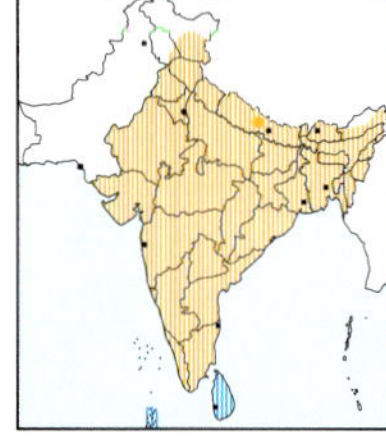

Amur Falcon ***Falco amurensis*** **28–30cm**

Widespread passage migrant. **ID** In all plumages, has red to pale orange cere, eye-ring, legs and feet. Frequently hovers. Similar in shape to Eurasian Hobby but has slightly more rounded wingtips and slightly longer tail. Male dark grey, with rufous thighs and undertail-coverts and white underwing-coverts. First-year male has mixture of adult male and juvenile characters. Female has dark grey upperparts, short moustachial stripe, whitish underparts with some dark barring and spotting, and orange-buff thighs and undertail-coverts; uppertail barred; underwing white with strong dark barring and dark trailing edge. Juvenile like female but has rufous-buff fringes to upperparts, rufous-buff streaking on crown, and boldly streaked underparts. See Vagrants for differences from Red-footed Falcon. **Voice** Fast-repeated, nasal *kew-kew-kew* at communal roost. **HH** Highly gregarious and crepuscular falcon. Forms communal roosts, often with Lesser Kestrels. Hunts by hawking insects and by hovering like Eurasian Kestrel, albeit less persistently. Open country.

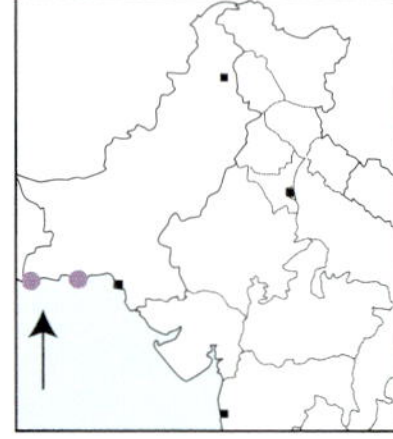

Sooty Falcon ***Falco concolor*** **32–36cm**

Summer visitor. Makran coast, Pakistan. **ID** Slim, with very long wings and tail (latter wedge-shaped at tip). Flight swift with strong deep wingbeats, interspersed with gliding and soaring. Adult entirely pale to dark slate-grey with blackish flight feathers. Eye-ring, cere and feet are strikingly yellow. Juvenile has dark mask and moustachial, buffish cheeks, narrow buff fringes to upperparts, and yellowish-brown underparts and underwing-coverts which are diffusely streaked. Uppertail is unbarred in both adult and juvenile. **Voice** Generally silent, except around nest. Most frequent calls are a fast-repeated *kee-kee-kee...* or series of more drawn-out nasal notes *keeeah-keeeah-keeeah-keeeah*. **HH** Most often seen hunting flying prey at dusk. Very swift and agile in pursuit resembling Eurasian Hobby; usually catches prey on the wing by gliding just above the victim; also, stoops on prey on ground. Feeds chiefly on migrant birds, also, insects and bats. Desert and arid coastal areas and islands. Globally threatened.

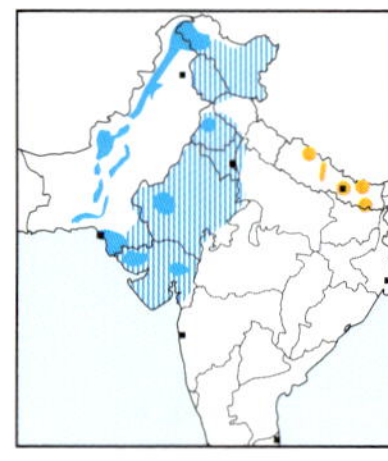

Merlin ***Falco columbarius*** **24–32cm**

Winter visitor. N subcontinent. Vagrant: Bhutan, Bangladesh. **ID** Small and compact, with short, pointed wings. Flight typically swift, with rapid beats interspersed by short dashing glides with wings closed into body. Wingtips fall noticeably short of tail when perched. Fine supercilium and weak moustachial in all plumages. Male has blue-grey upperparts, broad black subterminal tail-band, diffuse patch of rufous-orange on nape, and rufous-orange streaking on underparts. Female and juvenile have brown upperparts with variable buffish markings, heavily streaked underparts, and strongly barred uppertail. **Voice** Mainly silent away from nest. **HH** Normally found singly. Bold dashing falcon. Usually hunts in low flight with fast wingbeats and short glides, catching prey in a surprise attack; will also pursue birds in a long chase. Various open-country habitats, including cultivation, scrub and scrub desert.

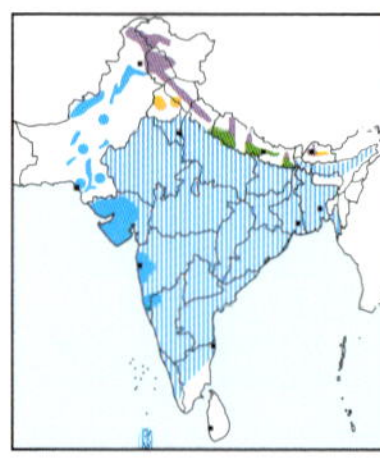

Eurasian Hobby ***Falco subbuteo*** **28–36cm**

Breeds in Himalayas; widespread winter visitor. Vagrant: Sri Lanka. **ID** Slim, with long pointed wings and mid-length tail. Hunting flight swift and powerful, with stiff beats interspersed by short glides. Adult has broad black moustachial stripe, cream underparts with bold blackish streaking, and rufous thighs and undertail-coverts. Juvenile has dark brown upperparts with buffish fringes, pale buffish underparts which are more heavily streaked, and lacks rufous thighs and undertail-coverts. **Voice** Usually silent except when breeding, when gives plaintive, excited *tew-tew-tew-tew...* and shriller *kree-kree-kree-kree-kree....* **HH** Markedly crepuscular. Graceful falcon, with fast acrobatic flight in pursuit of flying prey, usually birds and insects. Often perches on isolated trees. Well-wooded areas; also, open country and cultivation in winter.

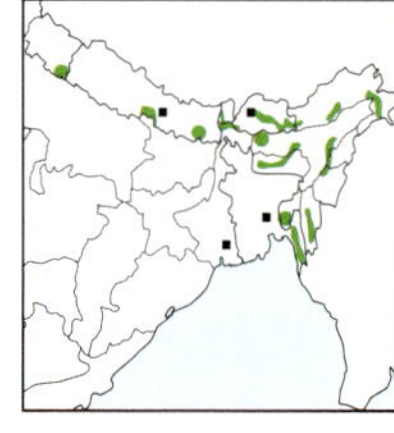

Oriental Hobby ***Falco severus*** **24–30cm**

Resident. Mainly Himalayas and NE India. **ID** Similar to Eurasian, albeit slightly stockier, with shorter tail. Slimmer in wings and body than Peregrine. Adult has complete blackish hood (lacking white cheeks of Eurasian Hobby), bluish-black upperparts and sides of breast (suggesting half-collar), and unmarked rufous underparts and underwing-coverts. Straight cut to black cheeks and absence of any barring on underparts help to distinguish from *peregrinator* subspecies of Peregrine but some *peregrinator* in S India and Sri Lanka can be more similar with all-dark hood and largely unmarked underparts, when finer build of Oriental is best feature. Juvenile has browner upperparts and heavily streaked rufous-buff underparts. **Voice** Generally silent, except around nest. Fast-repeated *kee-kee-kee* is most frequent call. **HH** Habits very similar to Eurasian Hobby. Mainly feeds on large insects. Open or lightly wooded hills.

Amur Falcon
♂
♂
♀
♂
imm
ad
juv
♂
imm
♀
Sooty
Falcon
ad
juv
♂
♀
Merlin
ad
imm
Oriental
Hobby
ad
juv
ad
ad
juv
Eurasian
Hobby

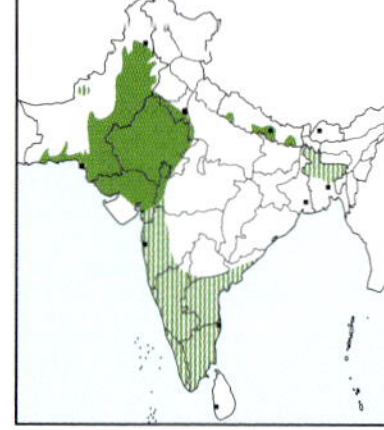

Laggar Falcon *Falco jugger* 39–46cm

Widespread resident; unrecorded in parts of NE and E subcontinent and Sri Lanka. **ID** Large falcon, although smaller, slimmer-winged and less powerful than Saker. At rest and in flight wings and tail appear longer than Peregrine. Adult has rufous crown, whitish supercilium, dark stripe through eye extending to nape, narrow but long and prominent dark moustachial stripe, brownish-grey to dark brown upperparts (can be greyer than illustrated), and rather uniform uppertail. Underparts and underwing-coverts vary, can be largely white or heavily streaked, but lower flanks and thighs usually wholly dark brown; typically has dark panel on underwing-coverts. Juvenile like adult, but crown duller, moustachial broader, underparts very heavily streaked (almost all dark on belly, flanks and underwing-coverts), and has greyish bare parts; from juvenile Peregrine by paler crown, finer moustachial, more heavily marked underparts, and unbarred uppertail. **Voice** Drawn-out, shrill *whi-ee-ee* or more prolonged *whi-eee-eee* given in excitement or alarm. **HH** Often in pairs. Usually seen perched on a regular vantage point; also circles high overhead. Hunts mainly by flying rapidly and low, seizing prey on the ground. Open arid country, cultivation, thorn scrub, scrub desert, rocky escarpments and sand dunes in plains and low hills.

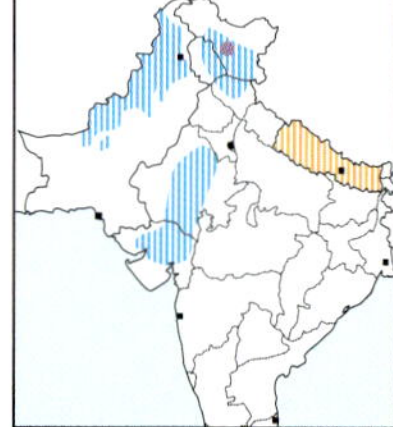

Saker Falcon *Falco cherrug* 45–57cm

Winter visitor. Mainly Pakistan and Gujarat. Vagrant: Bangladesh. **ID** Large falcon with long wings and long tail. Wingbeats slow in level flight, with lazier flight action than Peregrine. At rest, tail extends noticeably beyond closed wings (wings fall just short of tail tip on Laggar and are equal to tail on Peregrine). Adult has paler crown, less clearly defined moustachial stripe and paler rufous-brown upperparts than Laggar; underparts generally not so heavily marked as on latter, with flanks and thighs usually clearly streaked and not appearing all brown (although some overlap exists); outer tail-feathers more prominently barred. Juvenile (not illustrated) has greyish cere, and greyish legs and feet; otherwise similar to adult, but crown more heavily marked, moustachial stripe stronger, underparts more heavily streaked, and upperparts darker brown; some probably indistinguishable from juvenile Laggar. *F. c. milvipes*, a rare winter visitor, has broad orange-buff barring on upperparts, and mainly barred rather than streaked flanks and underwing-coverts. **Voice** Generally silent, except around nest. **HH** Usually seen singly, sometimes in pairs. Spends long periods perched on rocks. When hunting, flies fast and low, swiftly strikes prey on the ground from behind; also stoops on aerial prey like Peregrine. Desert and semi-desert, mainly in foothills and mountains; also Indus plains. Globally threatened.

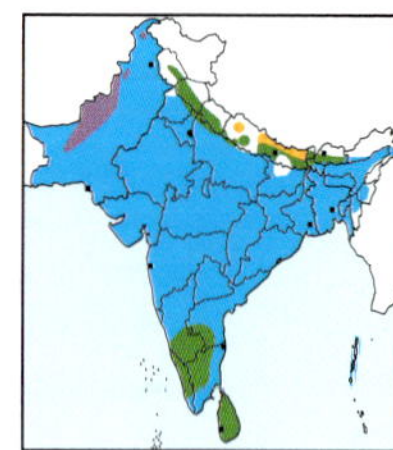

Peregrine Falcon *Falco peregrinus* 36–58cm

Widespread resident and winter visitor. **ID** Heavy-looking falcon with broad-based but pointed wings and short, broad-based tail. Flight strong, with stiff, shallow beats and occasional short glides. *F. p. calidus*, a winter visitor throughout the subcontinent, has slate-grey upperparts, broad and clean-cut black moustachial stripe, and whitish underparts with narrow blackish barring; juvenile *calidus* (not illustrated) has browner upperparts, heavily streaked underparts, broad moustachial, pale supercilium and nape patches, and barred uppertail. May show pale supercilium. *F. p. peregrinator* ('Shaheen'), resident throughout subcontinent, has dark grey upperparts with more extensive black hood (and less pronounced moustachial), and rufous underparts with dark barring on belly and thighs; juvenile *peregrinator* has darker brownish-black upperparts than adult, and paler underparts with heavy streaking. In S India and Sri Lanka, *peregrinator* can show almost complete black hood, lacking distinct moustachial, and almost uniform underparts. *F. p. pelegrinoides* ('Barbary Falcon'), which breeds N and W Pakistan and winters east to NW India, has pale blue-grey upperparts, buffish underparts with only sparse streaking and barring, rufous on crown and nape, a fine pale supercilium, and a narrow dark moustachial. In flight, underwing appears pale with dark wingtips and crescent-shaped carpal patch. Possibly confusable with Red-necked Falcon, but larger and stockier, lacks barring on underparts, has more evenly barred tail, and at rest wingtips reach tail tip (fall short of tail in Red-necked). Juvenile *pelegrinoides* has darker brown upperparts than adult with narrow rufous-buff fringes, heavily streaked underparts and underwing-coverts, and only a trace of rufous on forehead and supercilium. **Voice** Calls include a loud, harsh, chattering *kak kak kak kak*... oft-repeated; shrill, whining or wailing calls and a chitter *chi chi chi chi*.... **HH** Generally seen singly or in pairs. Bold, aggressive and powerful falcon, highly skilful in flight. Usually takes prey on the wing, over open country or water. Scans for prey by circling high overhead, usually higher than other falcons. Breeds in rugged hills and mountains; winters around large lakes, rivers, marshes, sea cliffs, coastal lagoons and mangroves; *pelegrinoides* also resident in dry rocky hills and stony semi-desert in Pakistan.

Laggar Falcon
ad
juv
ad
ad
juv
Saker Falcon
cherrug
cherrug
ad
cherrug
ad
milvipes
ad
peregrinator
Peregrine Falcon
ad
peregrinator
juv
peregrinator
ad
calidus
ad
calidus
juv
peregrinator
ad
pelegrinoides
juv
pelegrinoides
ad
pelegrinoides
juv
pelegrinoides

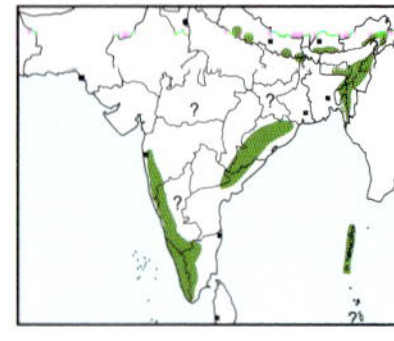

Vernal Hanging Parrot *Loriculus vernalis* 13–15cm

Resident. Mainly NE and E India, Western Ghats and Bangladesh. **ID** Small (sparrow-sized), stocky green parrot with red rump and uppertail-coverts, and red bill. Adult has yellowish-white iris. Male has turquoise throat patch, which is lacking or much reduced in female. Immature similar to female, but red rump and uppertail-coverts are mixed with green, and has brown iris. **Voice** High-pitched buzzy *tzeet...tzeet* and a fast *tzee-zee-zeet*. **HH** Extremely rapid flight with slight undulations. Broadleaved evergreen and moist deciduous forest.

Sri Lanka Hanging Parrot *Loriculus beryllinus* 13–14cm

Resident. Sri Lanka. **ID** Similar to Vernal Hanging Parrot, but has larger bill, crimson forehead and crown, and golden-orange cast to nape and mantle. Has turquoise wash on throat (as Vernal). Immature has greyish-green forehead, orange cast to green crown (with a few patches of red), and a faint turquoise wash to throat. **Voice** As Vernal. **HH** Habits like Vernal. Wooded country, groves, plantations, coconut groves and gardens.

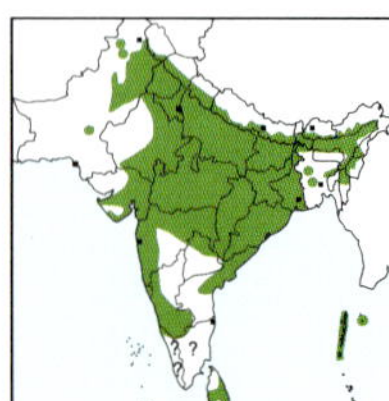

Alexandrine Parakeet *Psittacula eupatria* 50–62cm

Widespread resident; unrecorded in W Pakistan. **ID** From Rose-ringed by combination of larger size, maroon shoulder patch, and massive bill. Deeper, more raucous call and slower and more laboured flight are additional pointers. Male has black chin stripe joining pink and turquoise hind collar, both of which are lacking on female and immature. Male lacks black loral stripe of male Rose-ringed. Immature has less distinct maroon shoulder patch and shorter tail. **Voice** Includes a loud guttural *keeak* or *kee-ah*, deeper and more raucous than Rose-ringed. **HH** Flies with deliberate wingbeats, accompanied by harsh scream. Deciduous forest and well-wooded areas.

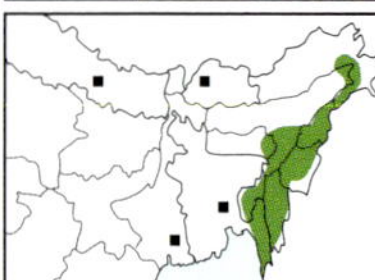

Grey-headed Parakeet *Psittacula finschii* 36–40cm

Resident. NE India and Bangladesh. **ID** Compared to Slaty-headed, has paler ashy-grey head, yellowish-green wash to upperparts (pronounced on nape), paler green underparts, and lilac-blue tail (greener on Slaty-headed) with paler yellowish-cream tip. Female like male but has darker green mantle and lacks maroon shoulder patch. Larger than female and immature Blossom-headed; has longer tail with larger yellowish-white tip, darker grey head with black chin stripe, marked blue-green collar, and larger bill. Immature has brownish-green head, later becoming dull slate-grey, lacks black chin stripe and half-collar of adult; not separable from immature Slaty-headed. **Voice** Includes a strident upslurred pleasant-sounding whistle, *pweEEh*. **HH** Habits like Slaty-headed. Hill forest and cultivation.

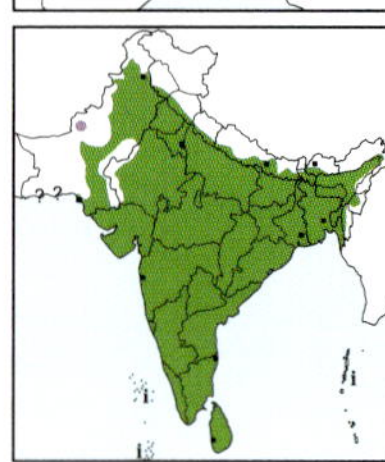

Rose-ringed Parakeet *Psittacula krameri* 37–43cm

Widespread resident. **ID** From Alexandrine by smaller size, lack of maroon shoulder patch, and smaller bill. Dark blue-green (rather than pale yellowish) uppertail is a further feature. Male has black chin stripe joining pink hind collar. Female lacks the chin stripe and collar and is all green (with indistinct paler green collar). **Voice** Includes screeches, higher-pitched than Alexandrine's, *kreeh-kreeh-kreeh-kreeh....* **HH** Deciduous forest, wooded areas and cultivation.

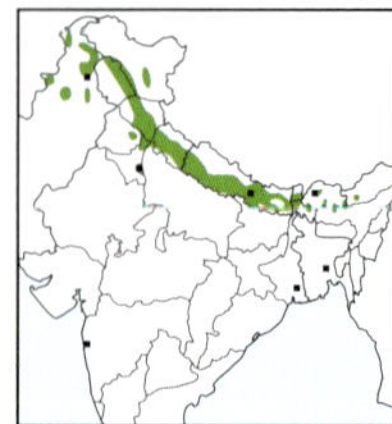

Slaty-headed Parakeet *Psittacula himalayana* 39–41cm

Resident. Himalayas. **ID** Adult has grey head, stout red bill, and yellow-tipped tail. From below, undertail is strikingly yellow. Male has maroon shoulder patch, lacking in female. Larger than female Plum-headed; head is a darker slate-grey with black chin stripe and half-collar, has a stouter red bill with pale yellow lower mandible, lacks yellowish collar, and has yellow (rather than white) tip to tail. Immature is like female and immature Rose-ringed but has darker, dull green head, yellow tip to tail (may not be apparent on younger birds). See Grey-headed Parakeet for differences. **Voice** Includes a strident whistle shriller than Grey-headed. **HH** Very agile in flight, keeping in compact flocks. Hill forest and well-wooded areas, especially near orchards and cultivation.

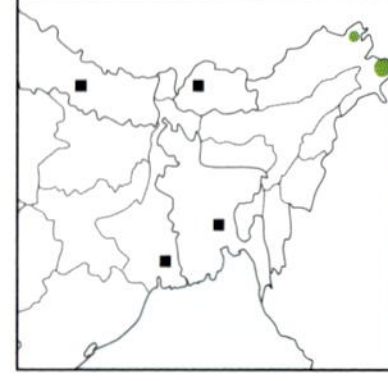

Derbyan Parakeet *Psittacula derbiana* 46–50cm

Arunachal Pradesh: local resident, probably migrates altitudinally, usually above 2,500m. **ID** Male has violet-grey crown and ear-coverts (brighter on forecrown, blue-green around eyes), black forehead and chin stripe, striking greenish-yellow patch in wing-coverts, violet-grey breast and belly, and blue central tail-feathers. Adult female very similar, but has pinkish wash to violet-grey underparts and all-black bill (upper mandible red on male). Larger size and coloration of underparts are best distinctions from female Red-breasted Parakeet, which occurs at much lower altitudes. Immature has greener head, and is generally duller than adult; very young birds have orange-red bill. **Voice** Includes a short nasal note, *nyaah*, in flight. **HH** Conifer forest, and cultivation during harvest.

♂
Vernal Hanging Parrot
imm
♂
imm
Sri Lanka Hanging Parrot
♂
Alexandrine Parakeet
♀
♂
♀
imm
Grey-headed Parakeet
♂
♀
Rose-ringed Parakeet
♂
♀
imm
Slaty-headed Parakeet
♂
♀
Derbyan Parakeet

Plum-headed Parakeet *Psittacula cyanocephala* 33–37cm

Widespread resident; unrecorded in NW and parts of NE subcontinent. **ID** Male has plum-red and purplish-blue head, yellow upper mandible, and white-tipped blue-green tail. Female has greyish head; smaller-bodied with daintier head and bill than Slaty-headed, with lilac cast to paler grey head (lacking black chin stripe and half-collar), yellow upper mandible, yellowish collar and upper breast, and white tip to tail. Juvenile has green head with buffish forehead, lores and cheeks. **Voice** Commonest call a steeply upslurred nasal whistle, *huEET*. **HH** Flies between forest trees with great agility. Like other parakeets roosts communally in large numbers. Moist deciduous forest, well-wooded areas, cultivation in forest.

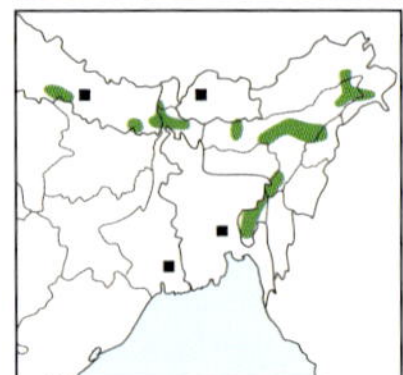

Blossom-headed Parakeet *Psittacula roseata* 30–36cm

Resident. Mainly NE Indian hills and Bangladesh. **ID** Male from male Plum-headed by paler pink and lilac-blue on head. Also, lacks turquoise collar and has pale yellow tip to tail. Female like female Plum-headed, but has paler greyish-blue head, less distinct collar, maroon shoulder patch, pale yellow tail-tip; from Grey-headed by smaller size, shorter tail with smaller yellow tip, paler greyish-blue head, indistinct collar, lack of black chin stripe. **Voice** Commonest call a short strident upslurred whistle, *krreE*. **HH** Habits like Plum-headed. Open forest, well-wooded areas, cultivation in forest clearings.

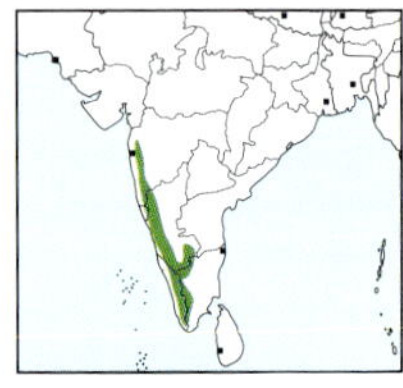

Malabar Parakeet *Psittacula columboides* 36–38cm

Resident. Western Ghats. **ID** Male has blue-grey head with green lores and cheeks, blue-green collar, pale blue-grey breast and mantle with variable pinkish tinge, blue primaries and yellow-tipped blue tail. Female similar, but has blackish bill, lacks blue-green collar, and has greener upperparts and underparts. Immature greener, with indistinct dark collar; head variably washed dull turquoise and blue-grey; blue in wings and yellow-tipped blue tail help separate from Rose-ringed. **Voice** Commonest call a high-pitched, grating, repeated screech, *krreeeh*. **HH** Habits like Plum-headed. Mainly tropical and subtropical, broadleaved evergreen forest.

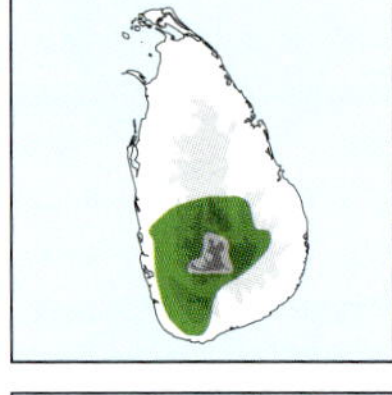

Layard's Parakeet *Psittacula calthrapae* 29–31cm

Resident. Sri Lanka. **ID** Male has bluish-grey head and mantle, with green lores and cheeks, broad green collar, green wings (brighter lime-green lesser coverts), green underparts, violet-grey lower back and rump, and violet-blue tail with yellowish tip. Female similar, but upper mandible blackish. Immature mainly green, with slightly darker head; violet-blue cast to lower back and rump, and yellow-tipped blue-green tail help separate from Rose-ringed. **Voice** Includes a fast series of short nasal screeches, e.g. *keh-kyeh-kyeh-kyeh-kyeh*. **HH** Habits like Plum-headed, but more arboreal. Forest edges and clearings, plantations, gardens with large trees.

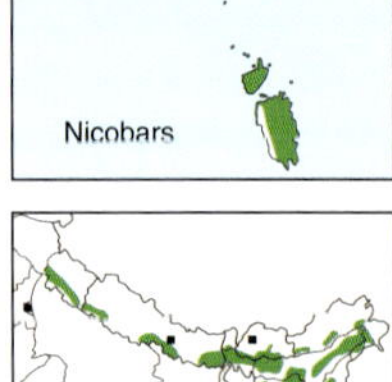

Nicobar Parakeet *Psittacula caniceps* 56–61cm

Resident. Great and Little Nicobar. **ID** Male is mainly yellowish-green, with buffish-grey head, black forehead, broad black chin stripe, and blackish flight feathers with bluish edges. Female has bluish-grey tinge to crown and nape, and black (rather than red) upper mandible. **Voice** Not well documented. Includes a loud and raucous, crow-like, drawn-out *krraah*. **HH** Arboreal, usually in upper branches of tall trees. Tall forest.

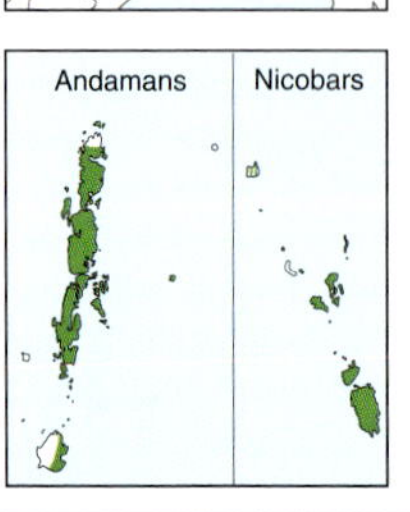

Red-breasted Parakeet *Psittacula alexandri* 33–38cm

Resident. Himalayan foothills, NE India and Bangladesh. **ID** Male has lilac grey crown and ear-coverts (with variable pinkish wash), broad black chin stripe, deep lilac-pink breast and belly, greenish-yellow lesser wing-coverts, and yellowish-tipped blue-green tail. Female similar, but has blue-green tinge to head, purer peach-pink breast, and black upper mandible. Immature duller, with green underparts and orange-red bill. **Voice** Commonest call a short, very nasal squawk, oft-repeated, e.g. *kyah...kyah...* or *keh-keh-keh-keh-keh*. **HH** Usually quiet while feeding in treetops. Open forest, second growth, shifting cultivation in hills.

Long-tailed Parakeet *Psittacula longicauda* 40–48cm

Resident. Andamans and Nicobars. **ID** Male has green cap, pinkish-red cheeks, broad black chin stripe, variable pale turquoise and lilac wash to green of mantle, and blue central tail and edges of primaries. Female similar, but has black upper mandible; also, uniformly green above, and has paler, peach-coloured cheeks. Immature uniform green, with less distinct cheek stripe; has touch of pinkish to ear-coverts, and yellowish edges to primaries. *P. l. nicobarica* (Nicobars) differs from *P. l. tytleri* (Andamans) in being larger and more yellow-green on the upperparts. **Voice** Flight call a short, nasal, repeated *kyeh*. **HH** Dashes from one tree to another; twists and turns between forest trees. Cultivation, gardens, nearby forest, mangroves. Globally threatened.

Plum-headed
Parakeet
♀
♂
imm
♂
♀
♀
♂
imm
imm
Blossom-headed
Parakeet
Malabar
Parakeet
imm
♂
Layard's
Parakeet
♀
♂
♀
imm
Nicobar
Parakeet
♂
♂
tytleri
imm
♀
Red-breasted
Parakeet
imm
tytleri
Long-tailed
Parakeet
♂
nicobarica
♀
nicobarica

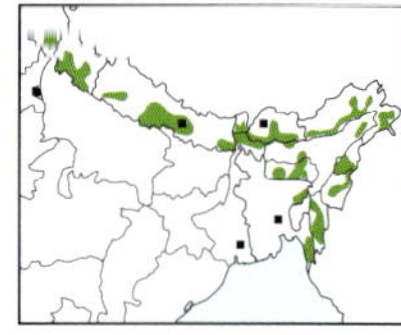

Long-tailed Broadbill *Psarisomus dalhousiae* [illegible]cm

Resident. Himalayan foothills, NE India and Bangladesh. **ID** 'Dopey-looking' with big head, large eye, stout lime-green bill, long thin blue tail, and upright stance. Mainly green with black cap, blue crown, and yellow 'ear' spot, throat and collar. Shows white patch at base of primaries in flight. Juvenile has green cap and lacks blue crown spot. **Voice** A loud, piercing *pieu-wieuw-wieuw-wieuw*. **HH** Similar to Grey-lored. Arboreal, keeps in forest canopy or midstorey in flocks of up to 20 birds. Broadleaved evergreen and semi-evergreen forest.

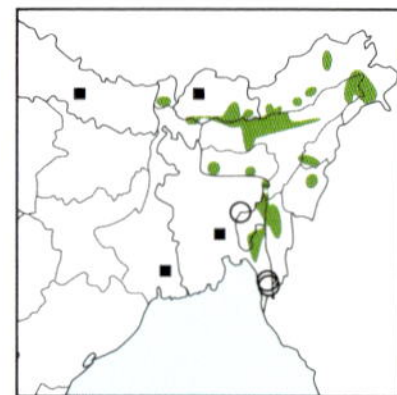

Grey-lored Broadbill *Serilophus lunatus* 16–17cm

Resident. Himalayan foothills, NE India and Bangladesh. **ID** Big head, crested appearance, large eye, stout bluish bill, upright stance, and sluggish movements give rise to distinctive jizz. Has blackish supercilium, yellow eye-ring, pale chestnut tertials and rump, complex white-and-blue pattern to black wings, and black tail. White patch at base of primaries in flight. Female has a broken white necklace. Juvenile like adult but has dark bill. **Voice** A melancholy *ki-uu*, like a rusty hinge, a thin high-pitched *kitikitikit* trill in flight, and peculiar insect-like clicks and chirps. **HH** In pairs or small groups in lower canopy. Very upright when perched. Active in early morning and evening, when it forages; at other times often unobtrusive and lethargic. Broadleaved evergreen and semi-evergreen forest. **AN** Silver-breasted Broadbill.

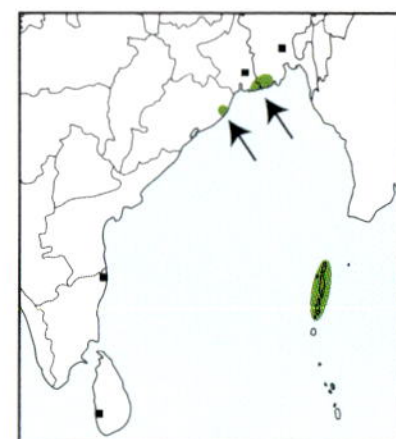

Mangrove Whistler *Pachycephala cinerea* 15.5–17cm

Resident. Sundarbans in India and Bangladesh, and Andamans. **ID** Rather drab, with thick black bill, grey-brown upperparts, greyish-white throat and breast merging into silvery-white of rest of underparts (some with whiter throat). **Voice** Variable phrase with 2–4 introductory notes and last note louder, shriller and more explosive. **HH** Solitary outside breeding season, in pairs when breeding. Forages unobtrusively in trees, from the roots to canopy. Gleans insects from branches, trunk and foliage. Mangroves.

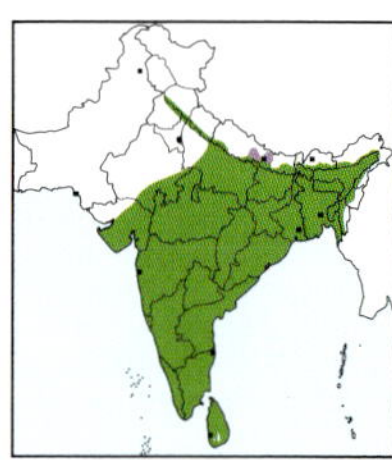

Common Iora *Aegithina tiphia* 12.5–13.5cm

Widespread resident; unrecorded in north-west. **ID** In all plumages has plain face with pale eye, yellow underparts, and bold white wing-bars. From Marshall's Iora in all plumages by uniform black tail (male) or greenish tail (female). Very variable. Crown and mantle of breeding males vary from uniform black (*multicolor* of S India and Sri Lanka), to black mixed with much yellow on mantle (e.g. *humei* of C peninsula), to mainly yellowish-green (e.g. *tiphia* of Himalayas and north-east). Females very similar to non-breeding males. **Voice** Long, drawn-out two-toned whistling song; piping *tu-tu-tu-tu* call. **HH** Singly or in pairs, each bird calling to the other frequently. Arboreal. Searches methodically among foliage for insects and caterpillars; hops on branches and sometimes hangs upside-down. Open broadleaved forest, well-wooded areas, second growth and large trees in open country.

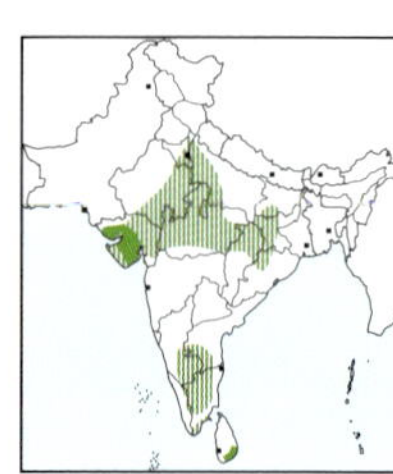

White-tailed Iora *Aegithina nigrolutea* 13.5cm

Resident. N, C and S peninsular India. Sri Lanka. **ID** From Common Iora in all plumages by extensive white in tail, with central feathers varying from black with a white tip to largely white or greyish-white with irregular black bases. Tertials have broader white fringes. Male breeding has black crown and nape, yellow hind collar (not usually shown by any subspecies of Common), and black mantle with variable yellowish-green mottling. Male non-breeding has yellowish-green upperparts and is like female. Female has yellower head compared to Common. **Voice** Very vocal, has wide repertoire like Common Iora, including sweet, whistled songs; separated from Common by ascending nasal wheeze, often followed by a scolding *dzwee-chrrrt*. **HH** Habits much like Common. Sparse scrub, thorn jungle and groves. **AN** Marshall's Iora.

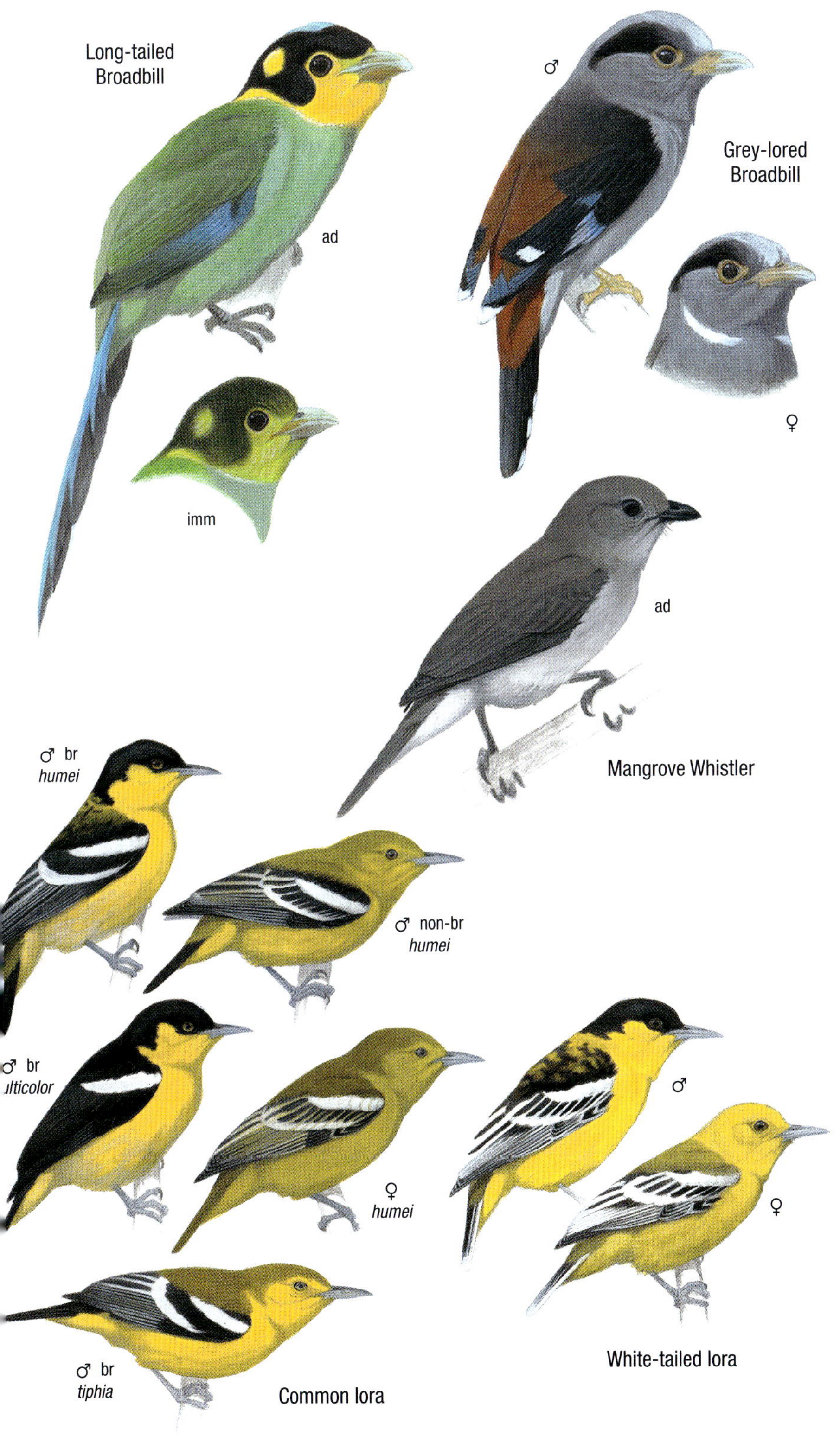
Long-tailed
Broadbill
ad
imm
♂
Grey-lored
Broadbill
♀
ad
Mangrove Whistler
♂ br
humei
♂ non-br
humei
♂ br
ulticolor
♀
humei
♂
♀
♂ br
tiphia
Common Iora
White-tailed Iora

PLATE 120: PITTAS

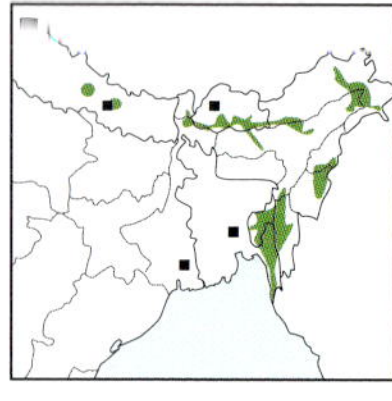

Blue-naped Pitta *Hydrornis nipalensis* 22–25cm

Resident. Himalayas, NE India and Bangladesh. **ID** Large pitta with fulvous sides of head and underparts, and uniform green to blue-green upperparts including rump and tail. Often shows black eye-stripe and/or patch at rear of ear-coverts, and sometimes a suggestion of a dark necklace. Male has glistening blue hindcrown and nape. Female has rufous-brown crown and smaller, greenish-blue patch on nape. Juvenile mainly brown, streaked and spotted buff, with brownish-white supercilium; wings and tail brownish-green. **Voice** Powerful double whistle. **HH** Broadleaved evergreen forest, moist ravines, dense second growth. **TN** Formerly placed in *Pitta.*

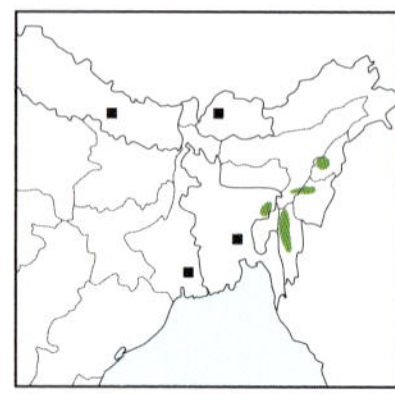

Blue Pitta *Hydrornis cyaneus* 22–24cm

Resident. NE India and Bangladesh. **ID** Large pitta with flame-red on hindcrown, black stripe through eye and black malar stripe, bold black spotting and barring on underparts, and blue rump and tail. In flight, small white patch in wing. Male has blue upperparts and pale blue wash to underparts. Female has dark olive upperparts with variable blue tinge, and breast is washed with buff; occasionally lacks red on hindcrown. Juvenile mainly dark brown, streaked and spotted rufous-buff, with prominent buff supercilium and dark eye-stripe. **Voice** Liquid *pleoow-whit* song, the first part falling, the second sharp and short; *skyeew* call. **HH** Typical pitta, see Indian. Broadleaved evergreen forest, moist ravines. **TN** Formerly placed in *Pitta.*

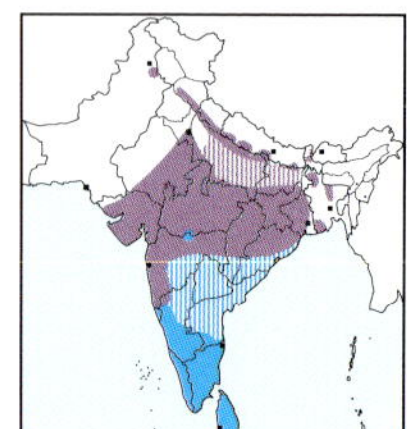

Indian Pitta *Pitta brachyura* 18cm

Resident. Breeds in Himalayan foothills and NE India; winters in S India and Sri Lanka. **ID** Has bold black stripe through eye contrasting with white throat and supercilium, and buff lateral crown-stripes separated by black centre to crown. Underparts buff, with reddish-pink lower belly and vent. Upperparts green, with shining blue uppertail-coverts and forewing. In flight, small white patch on wing. Juvenile much duller with lateral crown-stripes scaled with black. See Vagrants for differences from Blue-winged Pitta. **Voice** Sharp two-note whistle, second note descending, *pree-treer.* **HH** Usually seen singly or in pairs. Keeps mainly to forest floor. Forages by flicking leaves and other vegetation and probing into leaf litter and damp earth. Usually progresses on ground by long hopping bounds. Skulking and often most easily located by its call. Sings and roosts in trees or bushes, sometimes high up. Mainly broadleaved forest with dense undergrowth.

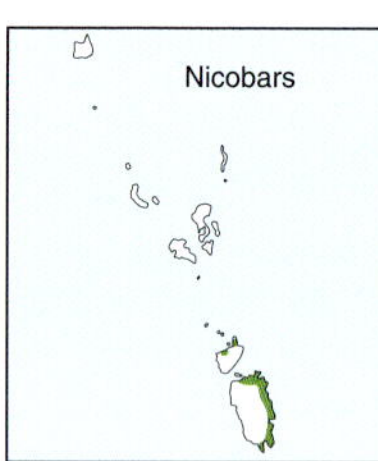

Nicobar Hooded Pitta *Pitta abbotti* 12–14cm

Resident. Great and Little Nicobar. **ID** Very similar in appearance to larger Western Hooded Pitta but darker, with browner forehead and crown (often with darker centre to crown), and is more olive above and bluer below, with smaller white wing patch. **Voice** Sharp monotone series of 3–4 whistles, like a small puppy's yelp, regularly repeated (compared to a double whistle, delivered at a slower pace, in Western Hooded). **HH** Typical pitta, see Indian. Lowland and hill rainforest; tall second growth with dense understorey. **TN** Formerly conspecific with Hooded Pitta *P. sordida.*

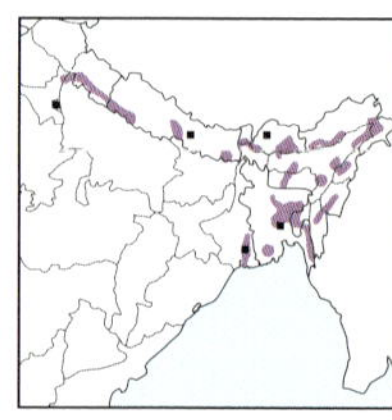

Western Hooded Pitta *Pitta sordida* 16–19cm

Summer visitor (or resident?) Himalayas, NE India and Bangladesh. **ID** Has largely black head with chestnut crown and nape, glistening blue forewing and uppertail-coverts, green breast and flanks, and scarlet belly and vent with black abdomen patch. Larger white wing patch in flight than Indian. Juvenile duller with black scaling on crown, white patch on median coverts, brownish chin, dirty white throat, and brownish underparts with dull pink belly and vent. **Voice** Loud, explosive double whistled song, *wieuw-wieuw*; calls include *skyeew* for contact and a bleating, whining note in distress. **HH** Typical pitta, see Indian. Broadleaved evergreen and moist deciduous forest, often near water. **AN** Hooded Pitta.

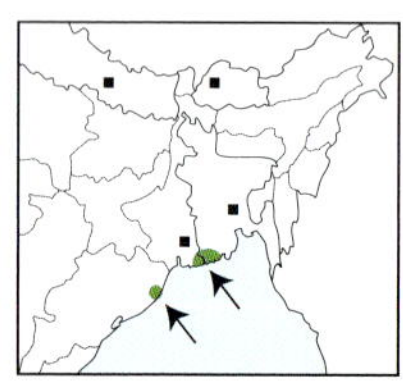

Mangrove Pitta *Pitta megarhyncha* 18–21cm

Resident. Sundarbans, Odisha, Bangladesh. **ID** Similar to Indian Pitta, but larger and has larger and longer bill. Crown uniform brownish-buff, lacking black centre, and has paler sides which may show as indistinct supercilium. Lacks white patch below eye of Indian. Upperparts darker green with deeper blue wing-coverts and rump/uppertail-coverts, and larger white wing patch than Indian. Juvenile duller than adult with black scaling on crown. **Voice** Loud, slurred *tae-laew* repeated regularly; *skyeew* alarm call. **HH** Typical pitta, see Indian. Mangroves.

♂
♀
Blue-naped
Pitta
imm
♂
Blue Pitta
♀
imm
imm
ad
Nicobar
Hooded Pitta
ad
imm
imm
ad
ad
Indian Pitta
Western
Hooded Pitta
Mangrove Pitta

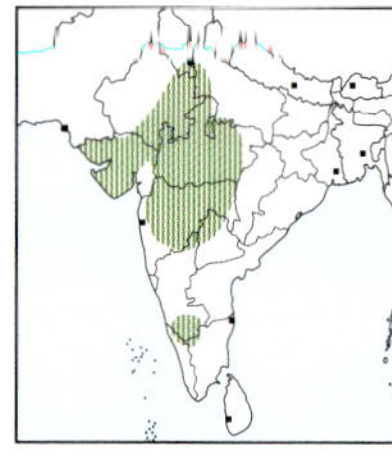

White-bellied Minivet *Pericrocotus erythropygius* 15–15.5cm

Resident. Mainly N and C India. **ID** Small minivet; both sexes with extensive white wing patch, orange and white on rump, and white sides to tail. Male has black upperparts and white underparts with pale orange or pink breast-patch (can be faint); superficially recalls Siberian Stonechat but has much longer tail. Female has whitish forehead and supercilium, grey-brown upperparts and white underparts. Rump coloration and more extensive white wing patch are best features from female Ashy and Brown-rumped Minivets. **Voice** Song a medley of disjointed *chup* and *tsip* notes, plus higher thin wheezes and whistles; *tsip-i-tsip* flight call. **HH** Habits like Small, but less arboreal, often feeds on small bushes. Dry open scrub and forest, thorn bushes in semi-desert.

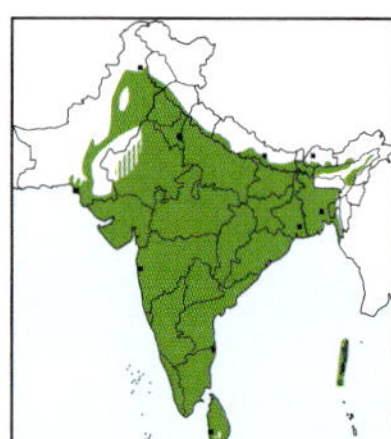

Small Minivet *Pericrocotus cinnamomeus* 16cm

Widespread resident. **ID** Small size. Considerable subspecies variation in subcontinent. Palest is *pallidus* of north-west; brightest is *malabaricus* of SW peninsula. Wing-panel varies from bright orange to buffish. Male has dark grey to pale grey upperparts, black to dark grey throat, and underparts vary from deep orange to mainly white with narrow orange breast-band. Female has pale sandy-grey to slate-grey upperparts, and underparts vary from mainly orange-yellow to mainly white. In *pallidus* flame-orange uppertail-coverts is only bright patch in plumage. Juvenile has upperparts scaled with buff. **Voice** Continuous high-pitched *swee-swee* etc. **HH** Typical minivet. Forages actively in tree canopy. Feeds on insects by flitting about in foliage to glean prey from leaves, buds and bark, sometimes hovers or makes short aerial sallies. In pairs when breeding; small parties at other times. Continually utters contact calls. Light forest, groves, plantations, orchards, trees at cultivation edges.

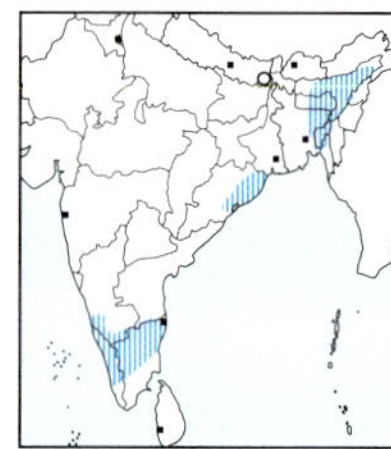

Ashy Minivet *Pericrocotus divaricatus* 18–21cm

Winter visitor. Mainly C and S India. Vagrant: Nepal. **ID** Grey and white, lacking any yellow or red in plumage. In flight, shows whitish wing-bar, especially prominent on underwing. Male has black cap and hindcrown with white forehead (white does not extend prominently behind eye as in Brown-rumped and has narrow band of black over top of bill which is usually not apparent in Brown-rumped). Upperparts cleaner grey with rump same shade as mantle (paler and browner in Brown-rumped) and underparts strikingly white. Female has grey 'cap', with black lores and narrow white forehead and supercilium. Head pattern cleaner than in Brown-rumped with black band across top of bill usually apparent; also, underparts whiter and upperparts including rump uniform grey. Immature has little or no white on head, and has brownish-grey upperparts, white tips to tertials and greater coverts, and faint brownish scaling on neck-sides and breast. **Voice** Flight call more rasping than other minivets, an unmelodious *tchue-de... tchue-dee-dee... tchue-dee-dee*. **HH** Typical minivet, see Small. Very active and restless; usually seen on topmost branches of trees. Evergreen forest.

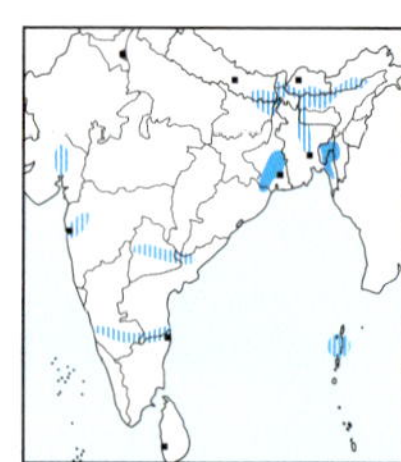

Brown-rumped Minivet *Pericrocotus cantonensis* 18–19cm

Bangladesh, India. Scarce winter visitor to Bangladesh (north-east, Madhupur NP and rarely south-east). Vagrant: Nepal. **ID** Grey, dull brown and white, lacking any yellow or red in plumage. In flight, shows striking wing-bar, especially prominent on underwing. Male from Ashy by grey (rather than black) hindcrown and nape and more extensive white on forehead (reaching noticeably behind eye and lacking dark band over top of bill). Also, upperparts tinged brown, breast and belly washed vinous-brownish, rump paler and brownish, and wing patch (if present) pale buff. Upperparts can appear greyish and underparts whitish, more like Ashy, but rump appears paler. Compared to male, female has less distinct head pattern, and is paler above with rump less sharply contrasting. Female from Ashy by paler rump, browner upperparts, more diffuse white forehead lacking dark band over top of bill, and underparts less clean. **Voice** Whirring trill. **HH** Typical minivet, see Small. Evergreen and deciduous forest. **AN** Swinhoe's Minivet.

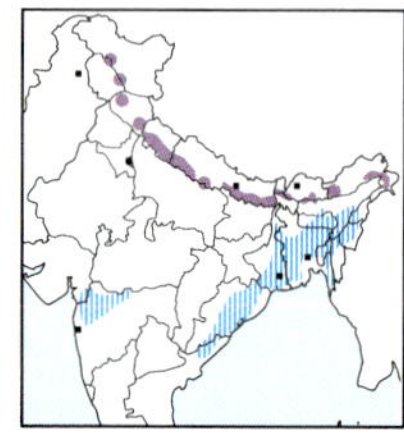

Rosy Minivet *Pericrocotus roseus* 18–20cm

Resident. Breeds in Himalayas and NE India; winters mainly NE and E India and Bangladesh. **ID** Male has grey-brown upperparts, white throat, pinkish-red edges to tertials, and pinkish underparts and rump. Female from other female minivets by combination of grey to grey-brown upperparts, with indistinct greyish-white forehead and supercilium, dull and indistinct olive-yellow rump, whitish throat, and pale yellow underparts. Male has red wing-panel and sides to tail (yellow in female) as similar species. Juvenile has upperparts scaled with yellow. **Voice** Whirring trill. **HH** Habits like Small, but rather less active. Forages high up and in middle branches of trees and in bushes. Broadleaved deciduous and evergreen forest, open woodland and gardens.

White-bellied Minivet
♀
♂
♀
pallidus
Small Minivet
♂
malabaricus
♂
pallidus
♀
malabaricus
♂
♀
♂
cinnamomeus
♀
cinnamomeus
Ashy Minivet
♂
♀
♀
♂
Brown-rumped Minivet
Rosy Minivet

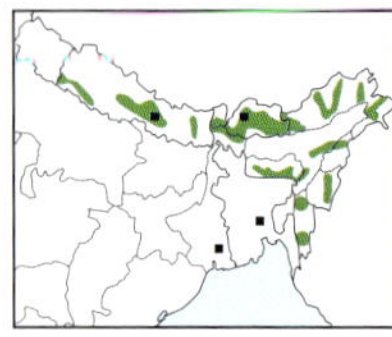

Grey-chinned Minivet *Pericrocotus solaris* 15–19cm

Resident. Himalayas and NE India. **ID** Male has grey chin and pale orange throat, grey ear-coverts, slate-grey upperparts, orange-red underparts and rump, and orange-red wing patch and outer tail feathers. Female has grey forehead and supercilium, grey ear-coverts, and whitish chin and sides to yellow throat. Juvenile has pale yellow fringes to feathers of upperparts. **Voice** Distinctive rasping *tsee-sip*. **HH** Typical minivet habits, see Small. Forages in canopy and midstorey of forest. Moist deciduous and evergreen broadleaved forests.

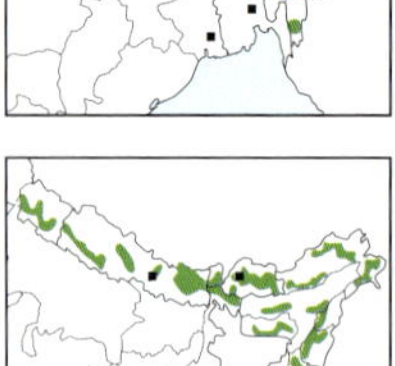

Short-billed Minivet *Pericrocotus brevirostris* 19–20cm

Resident. Himalayas and NE India. **ID** Male lacks extension of red wing patch on the secondaries of Long-tailed Minivet. Additional subtle differences are deeper crimson-red underparts and rump, and more extensive and glossier black throat (extending to upper breast), Female has yellow forehead and yellow cast to ear-coverts (more yellow in these areas than Long-tailed), and deep yellow throat concolorous with the rest of the underparts. Immature male is like female but has orange-yellow underparts and orange on wings and tail. Juvenile as female but has slightly browner upperparts with white tips to feathers, resulting in scaly effect. **Voice** Distinctive loud, high-pitched, monotone whistle, often coupled with dry *tup* contact notes. **HH** Typical minivet habits, see Small. Open broadleaved forest and forest edges.

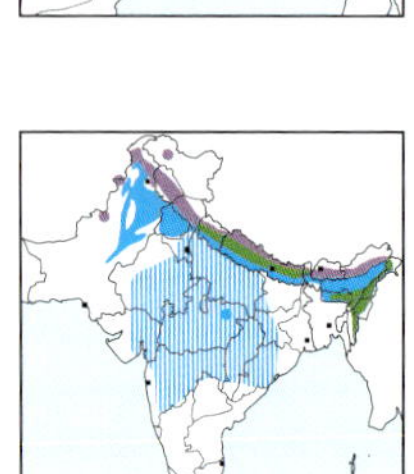

Long-tailed Minivet *Pericrocotus ethologus* 17.5–20.5cm

Resident. Breeds in N Balochistan, Himalayas, NE India and Bangladesh; winters south to C India. **ID** From very similar Short-billed by different shape of red wing patch (with red extending as narrow panel on tertials and secondaries). Also, underparts a more scarlet-red, and black throat is less extensive and duller. Female best told by narrow area of yellow on forehead and supercilium. Ear-coverts more uniformly grey than on female Short-billed and has distinctly paler yellow throat (than breast); where ranges overlap has brighter rump and uppertail-coverts than that species. Juvenile like female, but browner above, with whitish tips to feathers of upperparts, coverts and tertials giving scaly effect, and paler below, with brown barring on throat and breast. **Voice** Distinctive, sweet double whistle *pi-ru*, the second note lower than the first. **HH** Typical minivet habits, see Small. Highly gregarious throughout the year, except when nesting; sometimes in flocks of 30+. Forages chiefly in treetops. Open broadleaved and coniferous forests; also, well-wooded areas in winter.

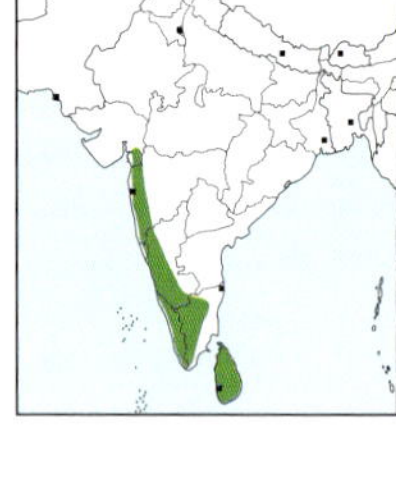

Orange Minivet *Pericrocotus flammeus* 17–22cm

Resident. SE Gujarat and N Maharashtra through Western Ghats and SW Eastern Ghats; Sri Lanka. **ID** Much larger than Small Minivet, which is the only other minivet in the region, with isolated orange (male) or yellow (female) patch on tertials. Male has flame-orange underparts and blacker upperparts compared to male Small. Female has cold grey upperparts, pure yellow underparts with yellow on forehead compared to female Small. By comparison with Scarlet Minivet, Orange is smaller and shorter-tailed; male has flame-orange (versus scarlet) coloration to underparts and pattern to wing; female has less yellow on forehead and darker grey ear-coverts. **Voice** Loud, piercing whistles *sweep-sweep-sweep-sweep* and *weep-weep-weep-wit-wip*. **HH** Very similar to Scarlet. Broadleaved evergreen, semi-evergreen and deciduous forests. **TN** 'Lumped' species *P. flammeus* referred to as Scarlet Minivet.

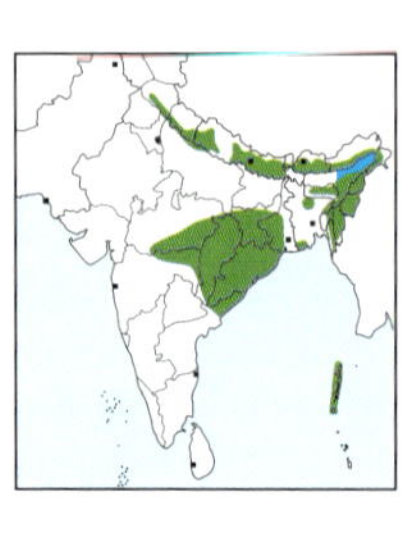

Scarlet Minivet *Pericrocotus speciosus* 17–22cm

Resident. Himalayas, hills of C and E India, Eastern Ghats of N Andhra, Andamans, Bangladesh and Sri Lanka. **ID** From Long-tailed and Short-billed Minivets by larger size, stockier build with larger head, orange-red underparts, and circular red (male) or yellow patch at tips of tertials and inner secondaries. Yellowish forehead and forecrown and yellow ear-coverts are further differences from female Long-tailed. Immature male like female, but underparts, rump and wing patches orange-yellow. **Voice** Piercing, loud *twee-twee-tweetywee-tweetyweetywee*. **HH** Typical minivet habits, see Small. Highly gregarious in non-breeding season; often in flocks of up to 30 birds. Open broadleaved forest, also conifers. **TN** Formerly treated as *P. (flammeus) speciosus*.

Short-billed Minivet
♂
♂
Grey-chinned Minivet
♀
♀
♀
♂
Long-tailed Minivet
♂
♀
♂
Orange Minivet
♀
Scarlet Minivet

PLATE 123: CUCKOOSHRIKES AND BAR-WINGED FLYCATCHER-SHRIKE

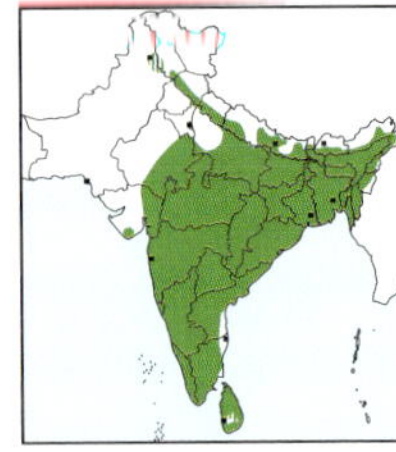

Indian Cuckooshrike *Coracina macei* 28–30.5cm

Widespread resident; unrecorded in north-west. **ID** Male nominate (peninsula) and *C. m. layardi* (Sri Lanka) have grey throat and breast and barred underparts; females have barred underparts. *C. m. nipalensis* (Himalayan foothills and north-east) has broader whitish fringes to wing feathers; male has uniform grey underparts; female has barring on belly and flanks (like nominate male). *C. m. andamanensis* (Andamans) is like *nipalensis* but paler with bigger bill. In all subspecies male has blacker mask than female. Juvenile heavily scaled with brown and white. **Voice** Rich fluty *pi-io-io* song; loud wheezy *jee-eet* call. **HH** Noisy. Usually in topmost tree branches, but sometimes descends to ground to feed. Open woodland, groves and trees in cultivation. **AN** Large Cuckooshrike.

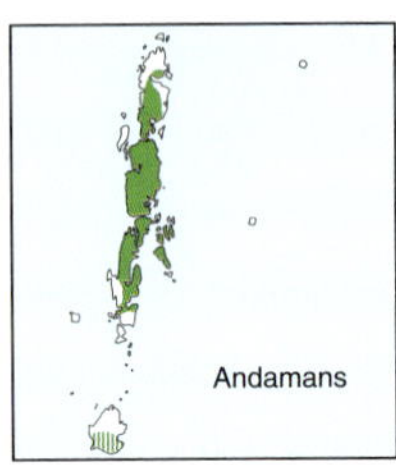

Andaman Cuckooshrike *Coracina dobsoni* 23.5–25cm

Resident. Andamans. **ID** Smaller and darker grey than Indian with crimson iris. Male has dark grey throat and breast, and broad blackish barring on rest of underparts including vent (white in Indian Cuckooshrike). Female is entirely barred below including vent. Juvenile is very scaly above; has pale rufous tips and fringes to greater coverts and tertials, barred underparts, rufous cast to throat and breast, and pale bill with dark tip. Immature has adult-like upperparts, some retained juvenile pale tips to wing feathers, with underparts and bill as juvenile. **Voice** Clear whinnying whistles *kliu-kliu-kliu-kliu*; also grating *gree-ew gree-ew*. **HH** Regularly joins mixed-species flocks. Forested habitats, especially evergreen, often in tall trees. **TN** Formerly subsumed in Bar-bellied Cuckooshrike *C. striata*.

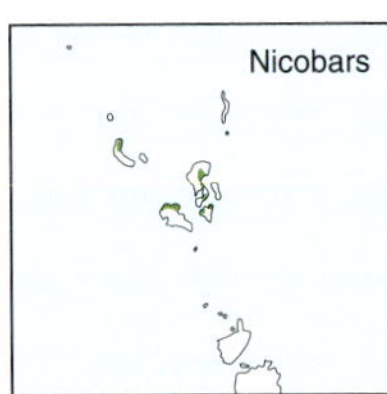

Pied Triller *Lalage nigra* 16.5–18cm

Resident. Nicobars. **ID** Male has white supercilium and black eye-stripe, black upperparts, broad white fringes to wing feathers, grey rump, white-tipped black tail, and white underparts with grey wash to breast. Female has slate-grey upperparts, slight buffish wash to faintly barred underparts, and narrower white fringes to wing-coverts. Juvenile has browner upperparts with faint buff barring and streaked underparts. **Voice** Nasal chuckles and rattling notes; also *kew kew* followed by 2–8 *kyhek* or *chack* notes on descending scale; whining *whier* contact call. **HH** Forages at all levels in trees, occasionally on ground. Forest edges and second growth.

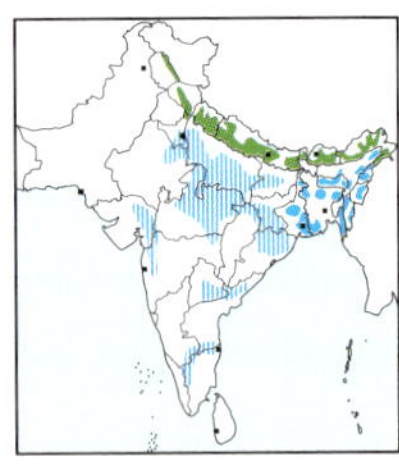

Black-winged Cuckooshrike *Lalage melaschistos* 19.5–24cm

Resident. Breeds in Himalayas and NE Indian hills; winters mainly in Himalayan foothills, E and NE India and Bangladesh. **ID** Male has dark slate-grey head and body, black wings, fine white tips to undertail-coverts, and bold white tips to underside of long tail. Female is similar but paler grey, with wings not so contrastingly black, and has faint barring on belly and vent. Juvenile has head and body boldly scaled white, with white tips to wing-coverts and tertials. Immature like adult but has pale tips to tertials, greater coverts and primary coverts. **Voice** Descending monotonous *pity-to-be*. **HH** Often with other insectivores. Forages in foliage, usually high in trees, sometimes in undergrowth. Undulating flight. Open forest, forest edges and groves. **TN** Formerly placed in *Coracina*.

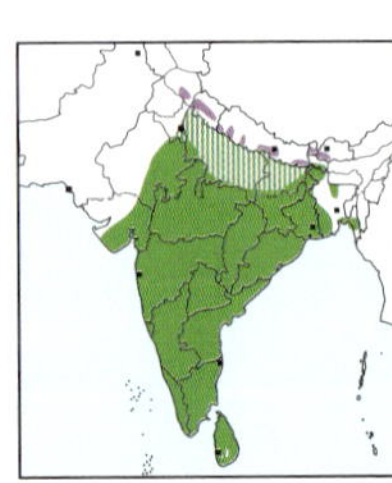

Black-headed Cuckooshrike *Lalage melanoptera* 19–20cm

Widespread resident; unrecorded in Pakistan. **ID** Male has dark slate-grey head, neck and upperparts, with pale grey mantle and underparts; wings darker grey than mantle and have broad pale fringes to coverts and tertials. Female from female Black-winged by prominent supercilium, stronger dark grey-and-white barring on underparts, pale grey back and rump contrasting noticeably with shorter and squarer blackish tail (with bold white tips on underside), and broader white fringes to coverts and tertials. Juvenile upperparts barred white. Widespread *C. m. sykesi* has white breast and belly and paler grey mantle, and is thus more clearly 'black-headed' than Himalayan nominate in NW. **Voice** Clear, mellow whistling notes, followed by quick repeated *pit-pit-pit*. **HH** Habits like Black-winged. Open broadleaved forest, groves and second growth. **TN** Formerly placed in *Coracina*.

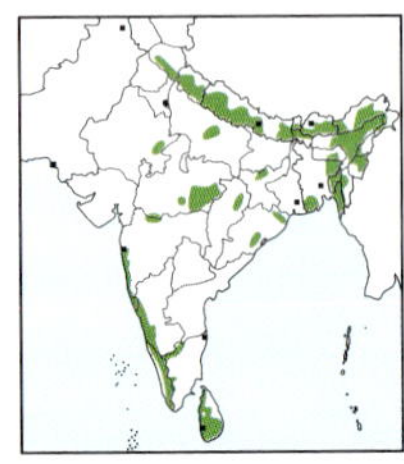

Bar-winged Flycatcher-Shrike *Hemipus picatus* 14–15cm

Resident. Himalayas, hills of India, Bangladesh and Sri Lanka. **ID** Dark cap contrasts with white sides of throat; has white wing patch and white rump. Female has brown cap. Males of northern populations are brown-backed, but in peninsular India and Sri Lanka are black-backed. Juvenile has buffish tips to feathers of upperparts. **Voice** Continuous *tsit-ti-ti-ti-ti* or *whiriri-whriri-whiriri*; high-pitched trilling *sisisisisisi* and insistent tit-like *chip*. **HH** Mainly in canopy; often with mixed insectivorous species flocks. Hunts in foliage and by frequent sallies. Open broadleaved forest and forest edges.

♂
nipalensis
♀
macei
♂
macei
Indian Cuckooshrike
♂
♀
imm
Andaman
Cuckooshrike
♂
♀
Pied Triller
♂
♀
Black-winged
Cuckooshrike
♂
sykesi
♂
melanoptera
♀
Black-headed
Cuckooshrike
♀
picatus
♂
picatus
♂
capitalis
Bar-winged
Flycatcher-Shrike

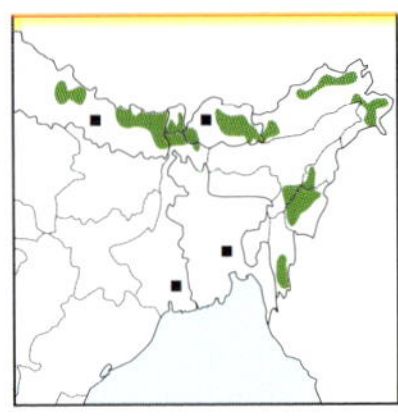

Black-headed Shrike-babbler *Pteruthius rufiventer* 18.5–20cm

Resident. Himalayas and NE Indian hills. **ID** Male has black hood, grey throat and breast, rufous-brown mantle, olive-yellow patch on sides of breast, pinkish-buff underparts, and rufous tips to black tertials and tail. Female duller with grey face and black patch on ear-coverts, black hindcrown and nape, olive-green mantle (variably marked with black), and olive wings and tail. Rufous uppertail-coverts, grey throat and breast, brownish-pink underparts, and rufous tip to tail help separate female from female White-browed Shrike-babbler. **Voice** Bright, repeated *pew-pew-peee-tu* song; also mellow, plaintive repeated *wip-wiyu* with pause after first note; calls include harsh, scolding *rrrrt-rrrrt-rrrr-rrrrt-rrrrt...* in alarm. **HH** Lethargic. Dense moist broadleaved forest.

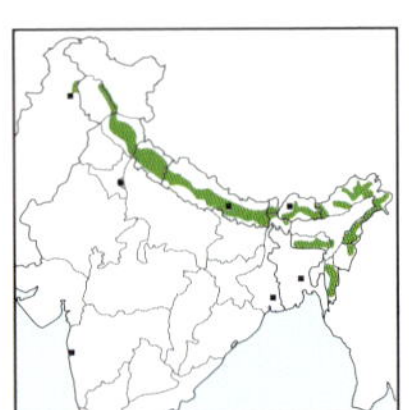

White-browed Shrike-babbler *Pteruthius aeralatus* 11.5–15cm

Resident. Himalayas and NE Indian hills. **ID** Male has black cap with white supercilium behind eye, grey upperparts, white tips to black wings, rufous tertials, and whitish underparts with pinkish flanks. Female has grey cap (sometimes with suggestion of paler grey supercilium), olive mantle, and largely yellowish-olive wings and tail. Larger size and rufous tertials help separate female from Green. Unmarked mantle, rufous tertial patch, uniform buffish-white underparts, white primary tips, and yellowish tip to tail help separate female from female Black-headed. **Voice** Song a rhythmic three- or six-noted *yip-yip-yip* or *yip-dip-dip* with stress on first or last note; short *pink* and grating churr in alarm. **HH** Feeds chiefly in canopy. Rather slow-moving. Mainly broadleaved forest, also conifers. **TN** Formerly subsumed in *P. flaviscapis*.

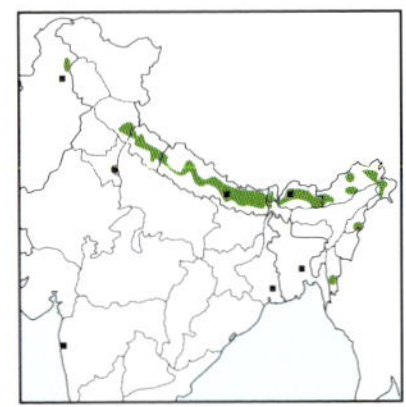

Green Shrike-babbler *Pteruthius xanthochlorus* 12–13cm

Resident. Himalayas and NE Indian hills. **ID** Small and stocky with big-headed appearance. Grey cap, stubby blackish bill, olive-green upperparts, white or yellowish-white greater covert wing-bar, blackish primary coverts, greyish-white throat and breast, and pale yellow belly. Sexes similar, but female has paler olive-grey crown. Juvenile has olive-brown crown and mantle, paler underparts, and yellowish wing-bar. *P. x. occidentalis* (W Himalayas) has blue-grey crown, which is dark grey on male *P. x. xanthochlorus* (E Himalayas) (although female is much as male *xanthochlorus*). *P. x. hybrida* (hills south of the Brahmaputra River) has a prominent white eye-ring. **Voice** Rapid, tit-like *whee-tee whee-tee whee-tee* song; grating *chaa* call. **HH** Forages unobtrusively. Rather sluggish. Broadleaved, coniferous and mixed forests.

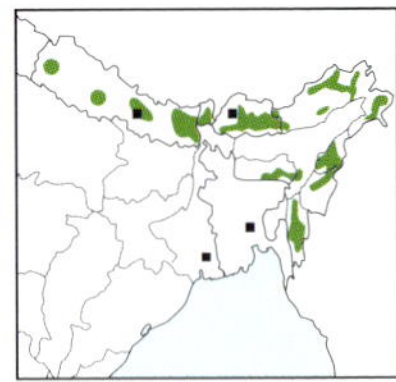

Black-eared Shrike-babbler *Pteruthius melanotis* 11.5–12cm

Resident. Himalayas and NE Indian hills. **ID** A small, stocky shrike-babbler. Black crescent on ear-coverts is best feature from Clicking Shrike-babbler. Male has chestnut throat and breast and white wing-bars. Female has chestnut reduced to malar region and has buff wing-bars. Juvenile is like female but has olive-brown upperparts (lacking grey patch on nape), and underparts are paler lacking any chestnut. **Voice** Bright *tew wee, tew we tew-wee* song; *dz-wee-tik* call and rasping alarm call. **HH** Arboreal and rather lethargic. Moist broadleaved evergreen forest.

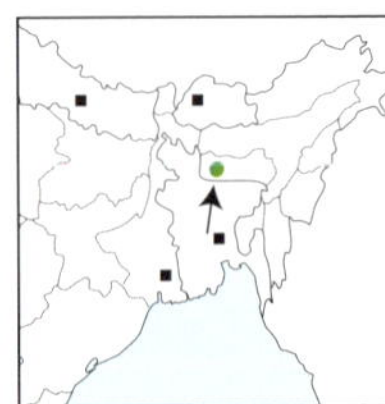

Clicking Shrike-babbler *Pteruthius intermedius* 11.5–12cm

Resident. Meghalaya. **ID** A small, stocky shrike-babbler. From Black-eared by lack of black border to ear-coverts in both sexes. Also, male has dark chestnut forehead and bright yellow forecrown, more restricted darker chestnut throat and upper breast, no grey on nape, and silvery-white (not blue-grey) wing-panel. Female unknown, but presumably like female nominate (Myanmar), which differs from female Black-eared in having dull chestnut forehead and upper throat, no grey hind collar, and whitish (not yellow) underparts. **Voice** Song a series of well-separated clicks; calls include variable buzzy, slightly nasal *jer-jer-jer* or sharply rising *tew-chi-chi* notes. **HH** Singly or in pairs, often joining mixed-species flocks in midstorey and canopy. Sluggish. Broadleaved evergreen forest and forest edge. **TN** Formerly subsumed in Chestnut-fronted Shrike-babbler *P. aenobarbus*.

White-bellied Erpornis *Erpornis zantholeuca* 11–13cm

Resident. Himalayas, NE India and Bangladesh. **ID** Crested and yuhina-like, with black beady eye. Olive-yellow upperparts, white underparts, and bright yellow undertail-coverts, pinkish bill and legs. Juvenile duller, with brownish cast to upperparts, and shorter crest. **Voice** Song a short, high-pitched, descending trill *si-i-i-i-i*. Calls include subdued, metallic *chi* and *cheaan* alarm. **HH** Although lively, it is quiet and unobtrusive. Forages chiefly at mid-levels, also in undergrowth and canopy. Broadleaved forest and second growth, especially edges and clearings. **TN** Formerly placed in *Yuhina* but not related to babblers.

♂
Black-headed
Shrike-babbler
♀
♂
White-browed
Shrike-babbler
♀
♂
hybrida
♂
occidentalis
♂
xanthochlorus
Green
Shrike-babbler
♂
♀
Black-eared
Shrike-babbler
♂
aenobarbus
Clicking
Shrike-babbler
♀
intermedius
ad
White-bellied
Erpornis

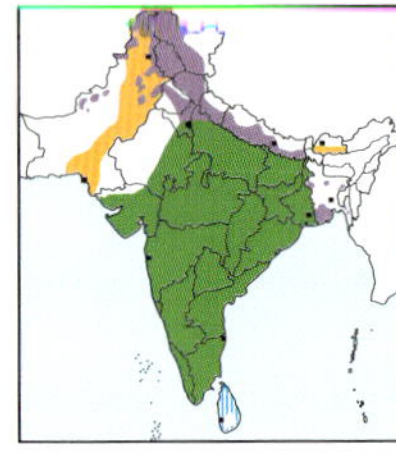

Indian Golden Oriole *Oriolus kundoo* 24–25cm

Summer visitor to W Pakistan, Himalayas and N plains; resident N and C India; winters further south. **ID** Adult male has small black eye patch, golden-yellow head and body, largely black wings with yellow carpal patch and prominent tips to tertials/secondaries, and yellow-and-black tail. Adult female has yellowish-green upperparts, blackish streaking on whitish underparts (with variable yellow on sides of breast), brownish-olive wings, yellow rump, brownish-olive tail with yellow corners. Some (older?) females have unstreaked (or faintly streaked) yellow underparts and brighter yellow upperparts. Immature like adult female, but bill and eyes dark; initially duller on upperparts and more heavily streaked on underparts; suggestion of dark stripe behind eye recalls Slender-billed. See Vagrants for differences from Eurasian Golden Oriole. **Voice** Loud, fluty *weela-whee-oh* song; harsh, nasal *kaach* call. **HH** Typical oriole. Arboreal and usually keeps hidden in leafy canopy. Usually seen singly, in pairs or family parties. Flight powerful and undulating, with fast wingbeats. Feeds mainly on insects and fruit. Open deciduous woodland. **TN** Has been considered race of Eurasian Golden Oriole *O. oriolus*.

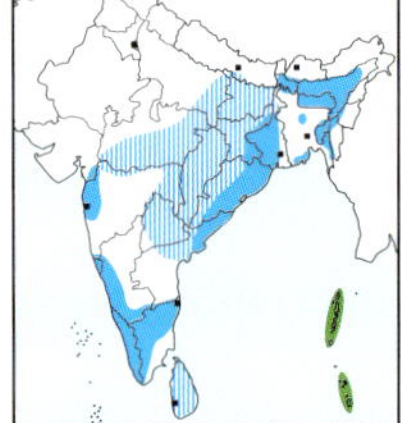

Black-naped Oriole *Oriolus chinensis* 23–28cm

Winter visitor to Kerala, Sri Lanka and Bangladesh; resident on Andamans and Nicobars; status elsewhere uncertain. **ID** Larger, stouter bill than Slender-billed. Black mask typically broader across nape than Slender-billed (similar width in some; poorly defined in immature). Male has yellow mantle and wing-coverts concolorous with underparts (brighter than in Slender-billed). Mantle and wing-coverts olive in female (as Slender-billed). Female and immature not separable from Slender-billed by plumage. Heavier bill and diffuse nape band if present are best features from immature Indian Golden. In Andamans (*O. c. andamanensis*) and Nicobars (*O. c. macrourus*) has largely black wings; *O. c. macrourus* also has larger bill and broader nape band. **Voice** Cat- or jay-like squeal; song like Indian Golden. **HH** Typical oriole, see Indian. Broadleaved forest and well-wooded areas.

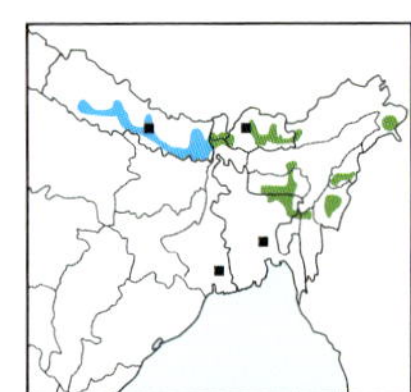

Slender-billed Oriole *Oriolus tenuirostris* 21–25cm

Breeds in E Himalayas and NE India; winters west to C Nepal and Bihar. **ID** Long, slender, slightly downcurved bill, and narrower nape band, compared to Black-naped Oriole. Male similar in coloration to female Black-naped, with olive-yellow mantle, but broad yellow tips to tertials and edges to flight feathers. Female like male, but has dull black nape band, duller yellow head and underparts, and duller olive-yellow upperparts. Immature initially has dark bill and eye, more uniformly olive wings, and whitish underparts with black streaking; nape band and eye-stripe can be very diffuse. Diffuse nape band if apparent, and longer bill, are best features from immature Indian Golden. **Voice** Mellow, fluty notes *wheeow* or *chuck, tarry-you*; diagnostic high-pitched woodpecker-like *kick* call. **HH** Typical oriole, see Indian. Well-wooded areas and large trees in open country.

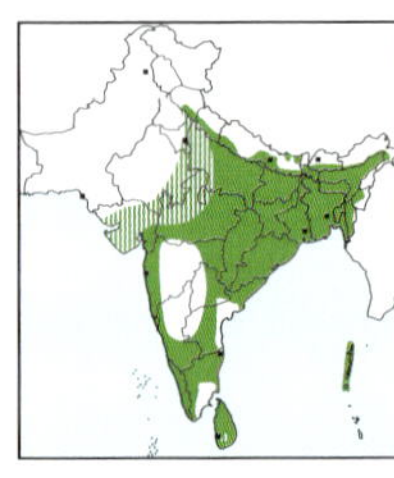

Black-hooded Oriole *Oriolus xanthornus* 23–25cm

Widespread resident; unrecorded in Pakistan. **ID** Adult male has glossy black head contrasting with golden-yellow body, bold yellow edges to black tertials and secondaries, and black-centred yellow tail. Eye red and bill pink. Adult female similar but has olive-yellow mantle. Immature has dark bill and eye, yellow forehead, yellow streaking on crown and sides of head, black streaking on white throat, yellow underparts with diffuse black streaking on breast, and duller wings with narrow yellowish edges to flight feathers. **Voice** Song a mix of mellow, fluty notes and harsh notes; harsh nasal *kwaak* call. **HH** Typical oriole, see Indian, but not shy. Frequently seen flying from tree to tree. Sometimes with itinerant bands of insectivores. Open broadleaved forest and well-wooded areas.

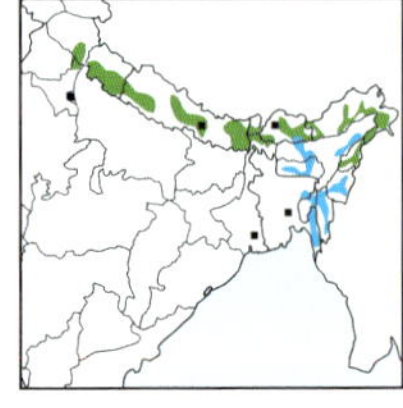

Maroon Oriole *Oriolus traillii* 25.5–28cm

Resident. Himalayas and Nagaland. Winters elsewhere in NE India and Bangladesh. **ID** Maroon rump, vent and tail in all plumages. Adult has blue-grey bill and pale yellow iris. Male has black head, breast and wings contrasting with glossy maroon body. Female similar but duller maroon mantle, whitish belly and flanks with diffuse maroon-grey streaking. Immature has uniform brown upperparts, including wings, whitish underparts streaked dark brown, brown iris. Juvenile has orange-buff fringes to upperparts and tips to coverts. **Voice** Rich fluty *pi-io-io* song; nasal squawking call. **HH** Typical oriole, see Indian. Rather shy and usually keeps among foliage of tall trees. Dense, moist broadleaved deciduous and evergreen forest.

♂
♀
Black-naped
Oriole
♂
macrourus
Indian
Golden Oriole
imm
♀
♂
chinensis
♂
♀
imm
imm
Slender-billed
Oriole
♂
♀
imm
Black-hooded
Oriole
imm
♂
♀
Maroon Oriole

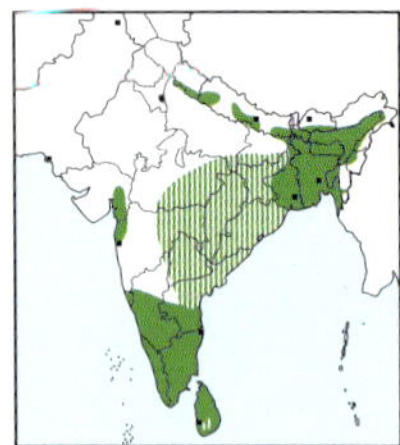

Ashy Woodswallow *Artamus fuscus* 16–19cm

Resident. Mainly E, SE and S subcontinent. **ID** Adult has stout blue-grey bill, uniform slate-grey head, greyish-maroon mantle, and pinkish-grey underparts. In flight, shows white-tipped tail and greyish-white band on uppertail-coverts. Juvenile has browner upperparts with buff fringes, paler grey throat (with indistinct brownish barring). **Voice** Song is drawn-out pleasant twittering, starting and ending with harsh *chack* notes; harsh *chek-chek-chek* call. **HH** In flocks of up to 30 birds. Perches on dead branches, near treetops, telegraph wires or other vantage points, and makes frequent aerial sallies. Flies in a wide circle with rapid wingbeats alternating with glides. Distinctive habit of wagging stumpy tail when perched. Open wooded country.

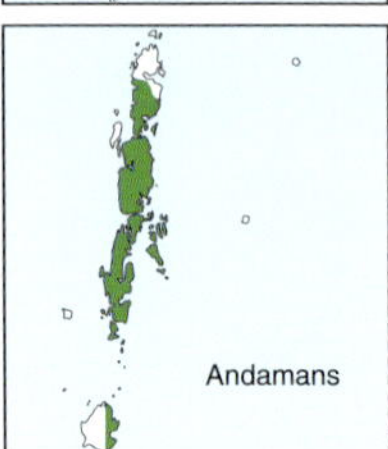

White-breasted Woodswallow *Artamus leucorynchus* 17.5–19.5cm

Resident. Andamans. **ID** The only woodswallow occurring on the Andamans. Similar in appearance to Ashy but has broader white band on lower rump and uppertail-coverts, and white lower breast, belly and vent (contrasting with dark grey head). Lacks white terminal band to tail. Juvenile has uniform brown upperparts with buff fringes, and greyish-white throat. **Voice** As Ashy. **HH** Habits like Ashy. Forest clearings, also open woodland.

Malabar Woodshrike *Tephrodornis sylvicola* 16.5–18.5cm

Resident. SE Gujarat (historically) and S Western Ghats. **ID** Male from male Large by more uniform grey crown, nape and mantle, greyer wings and tail, and darker pinkish-grey throat and breast with well-defined whitish submoustachial stripe. Female like male but a shade browner on upperparts with less clear-cut mask, and paler base to bill. **Voice** Song which often begins with grating note, is a loud, ringing, slow-paced series of *ker-wíck-er-wíck* or *wíckywíckywícky-wíck-er-wíck* notes; also, harsh shrike-like calls. **HH** Usually in pairs or small groups; often with mixed-species foraging flocks. Hunts in tree crowns, also in understorey, often makes sallies. Edges and clearings of broadleaved evergreen forest and well-wooded areas; favours moister forest than Large.

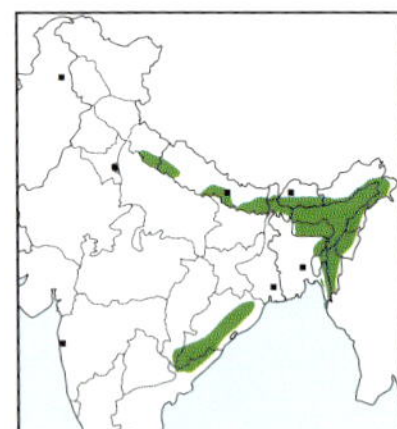

Large Woodshrike *Tephrodornis virgatus* 18.5–23cm

Resident. Himalayan foothills, NE and E India, and Bangladesh. **ID** From Common Woodshrike by larger size and bill, lack of pale supercilium, striking white lower back and rump, and uniform grey-brown tail. Female has poorly defined brown mask compared to male, with paler bill, darker eye, and brown crown and nape concolorous with mantle. Juvenile scaled with buff and brown on upperparts, and tertials, and tail feathers are diffusely barred and have buff fringes and dark subterminal crescents. **Voice** Musical *kew-kew-kew-kew*; also, harsh shrike-like calls. **HH** Quiet and unobtrusive. Seeks insects in foliage, on trunks and branches, usually high in trees. Often joins other insectivores. Broadleaved forest and well-wooded areas.

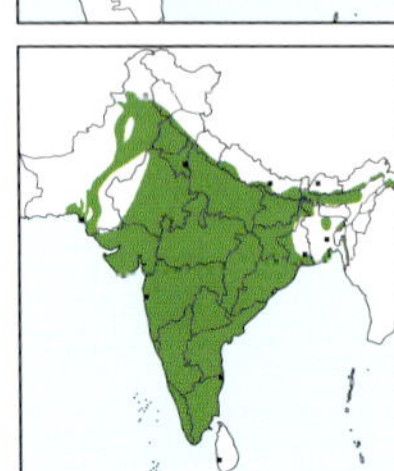

Common Woodshrike *Tephrodornis pondicerianus* 13–18cm

Widespread resident. **ID** From Large and Malabar by smaller size, white supercilium above dark mask, lack of white rump, and dark brown tail with white sides. Iris brown. Sexes similar. Juvenile has buffish-white supercilium, whitish spotting on crown and mantle, pale and dark fringes to tertials and tail feathers, and indistinct brown streaking on breast. Immature like adult but retains some juvenile feathers on upperparts, wings and tail. **Voice** Plaintive whistling *weet-weet*, followed by an interrogative *whi-whi-whi-wheee* and accelerating trill *pi-pi-i-i-i-i*. **HH** Dry country. Habits like Large Woodshrike. Open broadleaved forest, second growth and well-wooded areas.

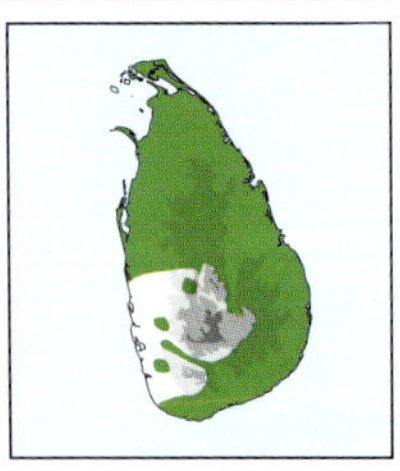

Sri Lanka Woodshrike *Tephrodornis affinis* 12.8–14.2cm

Resident. Sri Lanka. **ID** Only woodshrike in Sri Lanka. Male has narrow whitish supercilium contrasting with dark mask, whitish submoustachial stripe, white rump and white sides to dark tail. Female is browner with more prominent supercilium, browner bill and iris, and faintly streaked underparts. Juvenile has white spotting on crown and mantle. **Voice** Sweet whistles *twee-twee-twee-twee* in slightly varying pattern. **HH** Habits presumably like Common. Open forest, well-wooded areas and scrub with scattered trees.

ad
Ashy
Woodswallow
ad
White-breasted
Woodswallow
♂
Malabar
Woodshrike
♀
♂
Large
Woodshrike
imm
Common
Woodshrike
ad
♂
Sri Lanka
Woodshrike

PLATE 127: FANTAILS, MONARCH AND PARADISE-FLYCATCHERS

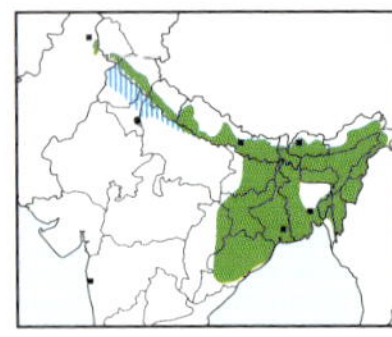

White-throated Fantail *Rhipidura albicollis* 17.5–20.5cm

Resident. Himalayas, NE India, Bangladesh and Indian peninsula. **ID** From White-browed Fantail by narrow white supercilium and white throat, lack of spotting on wing-coverts, slate-grey underparts, and smaller white tips to tail. Juvenile browner, with body feathers, wing-coverts and tertials tipped rufous; throat dark. **Voice** Song a descending series of weak whistles *tri... riri... riri... riri... riri*; squeaky *cheek* call. **HH** Breeds in broadleaved forest, also second growth and groves in winter.

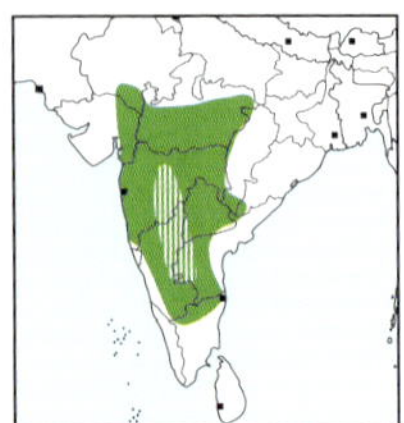

Spot-breasted Fantail *Rhipidura albogularis* 14.5–17cm

Resident in peninsula north to Rajasthan. **ID** From White-browed by narrow white supercilium and white throat, lack of white spotting on wing-coverts, white-spotted grey breast, buff belly, and much less white in tail. Underparts quite different from White-throated and has longer white supercilium and much less white in tail. Juvenile like adult, with rufous spots on wing-coverts. Hybridises with White-throated in NE peninsula, where it has a dark grey crown contrasting with olive-brown mantle and unspotted grey breast and flanks. **Voice** Song like White-browed but slower; calls include scratchy *check*. **HH** Wooded areas and second growth, prefers moister habitat. **TN** Formerly treated as White-spotted Fantail *R.* (*albicollis*) *albogularis*.

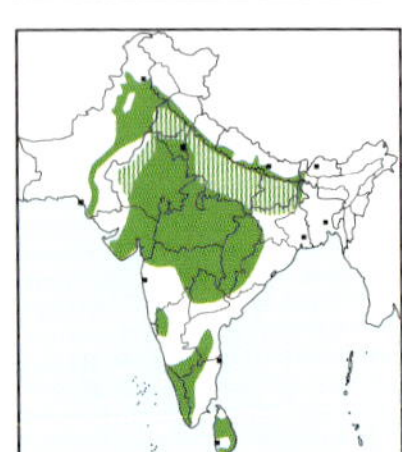

White-browed Fantail *Rhipidura aureola* 17–18.5cm

Widespread resident. **ID** From White-throated and White-spotted by broader white supercilia, which meet on forehead and extend back to nape, by variable blackish throat and white submoustachial stripe, and white spotting on wing-coverts. Throat is spotted with variable amounts of white or grey (and can sometimes appear almost white, as in White-throated). Underparts white. Juvenile like adult, but has browner upperparts, with rufous tips to body feathers, tertials and coverts. **Voice** Song an ascending, then descending, series of clear whistles; harsh *chuck* call. **HH** Forest and wooded areas, more open and drier than White-throated.

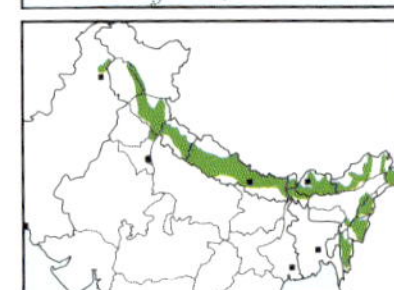

Yellow-bellied Fairy-Fantail *Chelidorhynx hypoxanthus* 11.5–12.5cm

Resident. Himalayas and NE India. **ID** From other fantails by yellow forehead and supercilium, dark mask, yellow underparts, greyish-olive upperparts, and blackish tail boldly tipped with white. Long, fanned tail is best feature from Black-faced Warbler. Male has black mask, which is dark olive-brown on female. Juvenile resembles female but lacks yellow on forehead and has duller and paler supercilium and underparts, and greyer upperparts. **Voice** Constant *sip sip* notes strung together to form trilling song. **HH** Forest. **AN** Yellow-bellied Fantail.

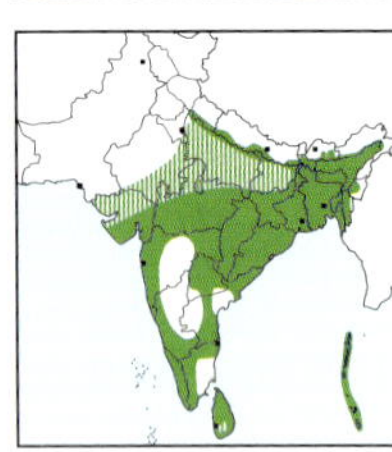

Black-naped Monarch *Hypothymis azurea* 15–17cm

Widespread resident; unrecorded in Pakistan. **ID** Male almost entirely azure-blue, with black nape patch, black gorget on upper breast (except in Sri Lanka), beady black eye, black feathering at bill base. Female duller blue head, lacks black nape patch or gorget, and has blue-grey breast and grey-brown mantle, wings and tail. Male *H. a. tytleri* of Andamans has blue or mainly blue (not white) belly. Male *H. a. ceylonensis* of Sri Lanka lacks gorget, has a smaller nape patch, and is generally more purplish-blue than in peninsula; female brighter blue on head, neck and breast, and has blue wash to browner mantle. **Voice** Rasping, high-pitched *sweech-which* and ringing *pwee-pwee-pwee-pwee*. **HH** Broadleaved forest and well-wooded areas.

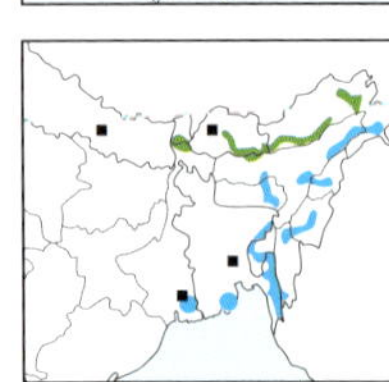

Blyth's Paradise-flycatcher *Terpsiphone affinis* 19–23cm

Summer visitor; E Nepal, Bhutan, Arunachal Pradesh. Winters NE India, Bangladesh, Andaman and Nicobar Islands.. **ID** Differs from Indian by its smaller bill and much shorter and more rounded crest; tail of male usually shorter. White male has more pronounced black shaft streaks on upperparts. Rufous male lacks clear-cut divide between black throat and white or pale grey breast in Indian). Rufous male and female have rufous rather than white vent. See Vagrants for account of Amur Paradise-flycatcher. **Voice** Song different from Indian, a less varied series of repeated upslurred notes. **HH** As Indian Paradise-flycatcher. **TN** Previously treated as conspecific with Indian and Amur as Asian Paradise-flycatcher.

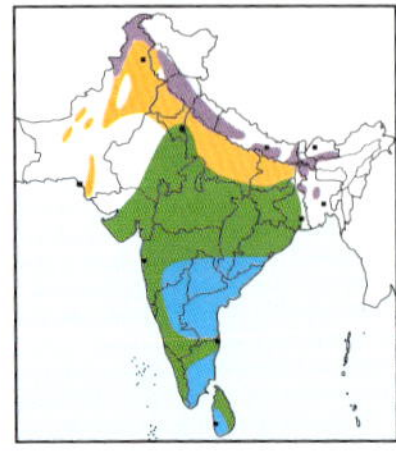

Indian Paradise-flycatcher *Terpsiphone paradisi* 20cm

Widespread resident. **ID** Male has black head and crest, with white or rufous upperparts and long tail-streamers. Intermediates, showing rufous and white in plumage, occur. Female and immature are like rufous male but have shorter crest and short square-ended tail; throat and lower ear-coverts greyer. Juvenile like female but has indistinct pale centres and dark fringes to breast feathers. See Vagrants for Amur Paradise-flycatcher. **Voice** Song a slow warble, *peety-to-whit*, repeated quickly; calls include nasal *chechwe* and a harsh *wee poor willie weep-poor willie*. **HH** Forest and well-wooded areas. **AN** Asian Paradise-flycatcher.

White-throated
Fantail
ad
Spot-breasted
Fantail
ad
White-browed
Fantail
juv
ad
ad
Yellow-bellied
Fairy-Fantail
Black-naped
Monarch
♀
styani
♂
styani
♂
ceylonensis
♀
ceylonensis
♂
white
morph
♂
rufous
morph
Blyth's
Paradise-flycatcher
♀
♂
white
morph
♂
rufous
morph
Indian
Paradise-flycatcher
♀

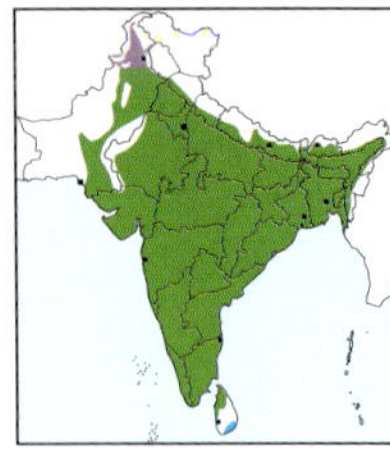

Black Drongo *Dicrurus macrocercus* 30–31cm

Widespread resident. **ID** Glossy blue-black, with deeply forked tail (although tail fork usually lost during moult). From Ashy Drongo, which can also appear dark and glossy, by blacker upperparts and shiny blue-black throat and breast, merging into black of rest of underparts; also, usually shows white rictal spot and eye is duller. First-winter has black underparts with bold whitish fringes that sometimes form white patches; upperparts and breast have glossy sheen. Juvenile has uniform dark brown upperparts and underparts. Tail short, with only a slight fork, when young. **Voice** Harsh *ti-tiu*, and *cheece-cheece-chichuk*; pairs duet during breeding season. **HH** Crepuscular. Makes frequent sallies to seize insects in mid-air or on ground from vantage point. More open country than other drongos; open cultivation, around villages and suburbs of towns and cities.

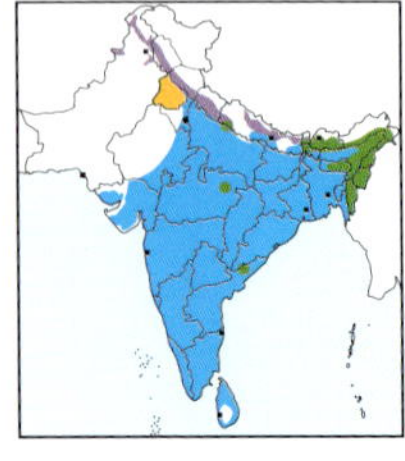

Ashy Drongo *Dicrurus leucophaeus* 25.5–29cm

Breeds in Himalayas and NE Indian hills; winters in plains in peninsula and Sri Lanka. **ID** Adult from Black by dark grey (rather than black) underparts; this difference in coloration is especially apparent on throat, breast and flanks. Upperparts slate-grey with strong blue-grey gloss, but can appear black and much like Black Drongo. Often appears slimmer, with longer, more deeply forked tail, has more striking bright red iris, and lacks white rictal spot which is often apparent at close range on Black. First-winter has brownish-grey underparts with indistinct pale fringes (underparts blacker and whitish fringes more distinct in Black). Juvenile as juvenile Black. E and NE subcontinent *hopwoodi* paler grey without gloss. Vagrant *salangensis* even paler with white lores and ear-coverts; pale grey coverts and secondaries contrast with blackish primaries. **Voice** Like Black but more varied and a good mimic, includes whistling *kil-ki-kil*. **HH** Usually uses bare branches near treetop as vantage point. Very agile in pursuit of insects like other drongos. Breeds in open broadleaved forest and coniferous forest; winters in well-wooded areas.

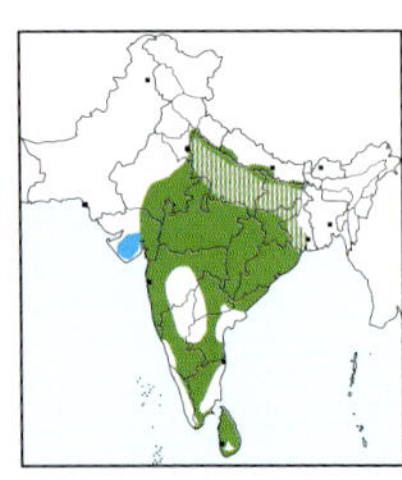

White-bellied Drongo *Dicrurus caerulescens* 24cm

Widespread resident; unrecorded in Pakistan and the north-east. **ID** Whitish from belly downwards, although white less extensive in Sri Lanka, where wet zone subspecies (*leucopygialis*) has white restricted to vent and undertail-coverts. Smaller than Black and Ashy, and tail is shorter and fork is typically shallower. Upperparts glossy slate-grey, much as Ashy (and therefore less black than Black). Throat and breast browner in first-winter compared with adult, and border between breast and white belly less clearly defined. Juvenile has dark brown upperparts lacking slate-grey gloss. **Voice** Similar to Black, but more continuous, richer and with fewer harsh notes, frequent changes of tempo and much mimicry. **HH** Hawks insects from exposed perches. Swift, strong undulating flight. Bold and pugnacious. Highly crepuscular. Open forest, well-wooded areas and plantations.

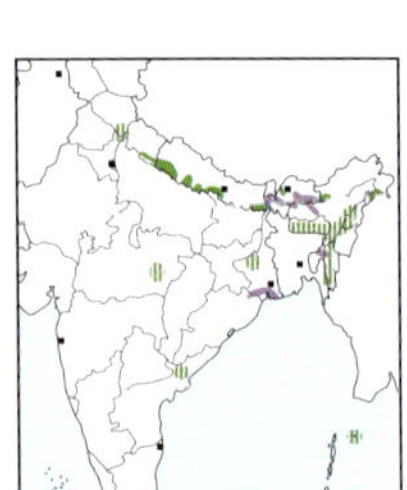

Crow-billed Drongo *Dicrurus annectens* 27–32cm

Summer visitor/resident (?) in Himalayan foothills and NE India; winters in NE India and Bangladesh. **ID** From Black by much stouter bill, more extensive area of rictal bristles (resulting in tufted forehead not unlike Lesser Racket-tailed), and shorter, broader tail that is widely splayed at tip but not deeply forked (outer feathers more noticeably curving outwards). Also note habitat differences from Black. First-winter has white spotting from breast to undertail-coverts (recalling first-winter Greater Racket-tailed). Juvenile has uniform brownish-black upperparts and underparts without gloss. **Voice** Loud, musical whistles and churrs; has characteristic descending series of harp-like notes. **HH** Usually hunts from midstorey of forest or lower canopy. Associates in loose flocks on migration. Dense broadleaved evergreen and moist deciduous forest.

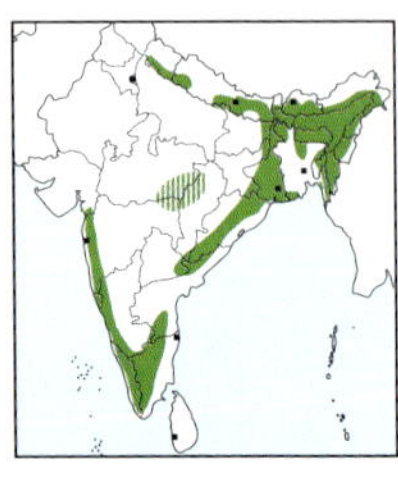

Bronzed Drongo *Dicrurus aeneus* 22–24cm

Resident. Himalayan foothills, NE India, Bangladesh and Eastern and Western Ghats. **ID** Small size, with flatter bill compared to Black and less deeply forked tail (which can be almost square-ended on moulting or juvenile birds). Also note habitat differences. Adult strongly glossed metallic blue-green. Juvenile has brown underparts, and duller and less heavily spangled upperparts. **Voice** Loud, varied musical whistles and churrs. **HH** Usually singly or in pairs. A regular member of mixed feeding parties of insectivores. Hunts in shady areas of forest, in overgrown forest clearings, along forest paths and by forested rivers. Broadleaved evergreen and moist broadleaved forest and plantations.

Black Drongo
ad
imm
juv
ad
longicaudatus
imm
longicaudatus
ad
salangensis
ad
hopwoodi
Ashy Drongo
imm
caerulescens
ad
caerulescens
ad
leucopygialis
White-bellied
Drongo
imm
ad
Crow-billed Drongo
ad
juv
Bronzed Drongo

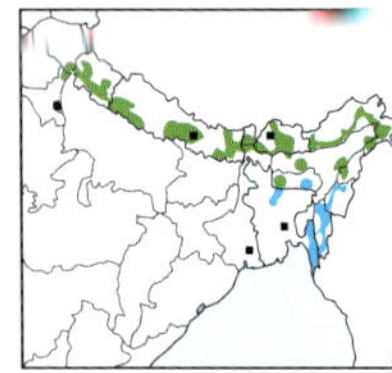

Lesser Racket-tailed Drongo *Dicrurus remifer* 25–27.5cm

Resident. Himalayan foothills and Nagaland. Winters elsewhere in NE India and Bangladesh. **ID** Tufted forehead without crest (giving rise to rectangular head shape), square-ended tail, and smaller size and bill than Greater Racket-tailed; has smaller flattened rackets. As Greater, tail-streamers and rackets can be missing or broken in adult, and are missing in juvenile and first-winter. Adult very glossy. Juvenile lacks gloss and is black on underparts; lacks white markings on underparts in first-winter (shown by Greater). **Voice** Loud, varied, musical whistling, screeching and churring, with much mimicry. **HH** Singly or in pairs, often associated with roving mixed flocks of other forest species. Normally keeps to leafy canopy in dense forest, in forest clearings, or forest edges and along streams. Dense broadleaved evergreen and moist deciduous forest.

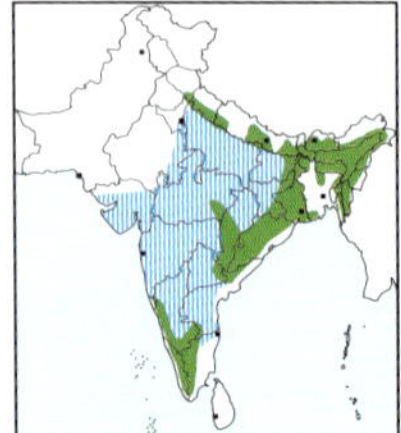

Hair-crested Drongo *Dicrurus hottentottus* 32cm

Resident. Himalayan foothills, NE India, Bangladesh and Eastern and Western Ghats. **ID** Broad tail with upward-twisted corners, and long downcurved bill. Adult has extensive spangling, and hair-like crest. Juvenile browner and lacks spangling; also lacks crest and has square-ended tail with less pronounced upward twist to outer feathers. **Voice** Loud *chi-wiii*, the first note stressed and second rising or sometimes the *wiii* note given singly. **HH** Singly or in small parties. Frequently joins flocks of insectivores. Feeds mainly on flower nectar, also insects. Broadleaved evergreen and moist deciduous forest. **AN** Spangled Drongo.

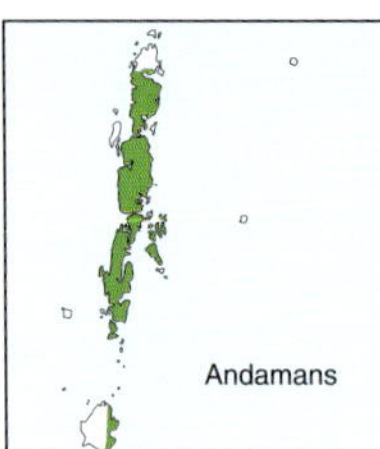

Andaman Drongo *Dicrurus andamanensis* 28–29cm

Resident. Andamans. **ID** Larger and longer bill than Black Drongo. Tail long and broad with pronounced fork and outer feathers twisting inwards at tip. Has several hair-like filaments on forehead (less distinct than Hair-crested Drongo). Juvenile browner and less glossed, and initially has square-ended tail. **Voice** Song a uniform series of repeated loud, jangling groups of notes, last metallic and bell-like. Calls include loud, liquid *tseep* repeated monotonously for several minutes, and very short, hard, squeaky jangles. **HH** Insect prey caught mostly by aerial hawking. Frequently perches on vertical trunk like a woodpecker, pressing tail against bark, ascends in flitting hops to take ants. Gregarious, in flocks of 12–20; often forages with other species. Evergreen and broadleaved moist lowland forests and edges; open forest and scrub-jungle.

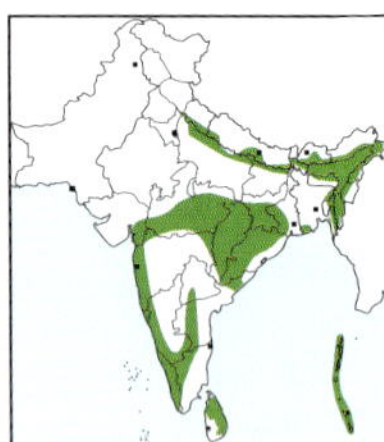

Greater Racket-tailed Drongo *Dicrurus paradiseus* 32cm

Widespread resident; unrecorded in Pakistan. **ID** Adult from Lesser Racket-tailed Drongo (where ranges overlap) by larger size and less tidy appearance, larger bill, crested head, forked tail, and longer, twisted tail-rackets. Tail-streamers and rackets can be missing or broken, and tail can appear almost square-ended when in moult (or juvenile plumage). Juvenile initially lacks rackets; is less heavily glossed than adult and has much-reduced crest. Has white fringes to belly and vent in first-winter plumage. Considerable subspecies variation in size, length of tail-streamers and size of crest. Subspecies in S India, Sri Lanka, Andamans and Nicobars have much-reduced or almost non-existent crest and can look very like Lesser Racket-tailed (but latter does not occur in these areas). **Voice** Loud, varied musical whistling, screeching and churring, with much mimicry. **HH** Habits like other drongos, but more sociable, often in small groups and joins mixed parties of other species. Often crepuscular. Forages in lower to middle forest storeys. Broadleaved forest and bamboo jungle.

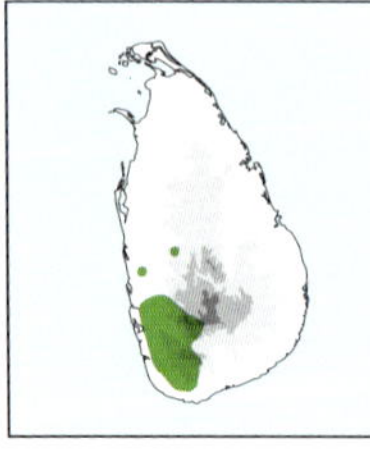

Sri Lanka Drongo *Dicrurus lophorinus* 31–34cm

Resident. Sri Lanka wet zone. **ID** Similar to Greater Racket-tailed, but has a long and deeply forked tail, slightly twisted at the tips, and lacks terminal rackets. Crest is a shorter, rounded tuft. Some intermediates with Greater Racket-tailed reported. **Voice** As Greater. Very noisy with wide range of metallic calls and rich melodious notes and whistles; often mimics other birds. **HH** Hawks insects in air, swooping down to catch them. Very sociable; several pairs often forage together and with other forest birds. Tall, dense moist forests with plenty of undergrowth in lowlands and lower hills.

ad
imm
Lesser Racket-tailed Drongo
ad
juv
Hair-crested Drongo
ad
grandis
imm
ceylonicus
ad
ad
ad
ceylonicus
imm
Andaman Drongo
Greater Racket-tailed Drongo
Sri Lanka Drongo

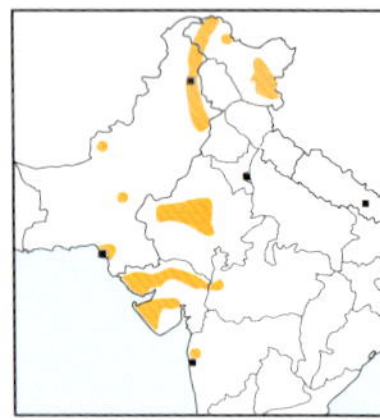

Red-backed Shrike *Lanius collurio* 17–19cm

Southbound passage migrant. Pakistan and NW India. **ID** Male has rufous mantle, pink underparts, and white sides to tail. Absence of black forehead and white in wing help separate from Bay-backed. Female from female Red-tailed and Brown by grey cast to head and especially nape, contrasting slightly with rufous-brown mantle, and dark brown tail with white outer edge. Juvenile and first-winter have scaled upperparts (mantle more uniform in first-winter Brown); tail more rufous-brown and can approach Red-tailed in coloration. Finer bill, squarer tail, blacker mask, grey cast to nape/rump and dark subterminal borders to paler-centred tertials help separate juvenile from juvenile Brown (tertials of latter are dark with clean pale fringes). See Vagrants for differences from Woodchat Shrike. **Voice** Typical shrike-like grating call. **HH** Habits like Brown. Conspicuous when feeding, more secretive at other times. Bushes and cultivation in dry country, and scrub desert.

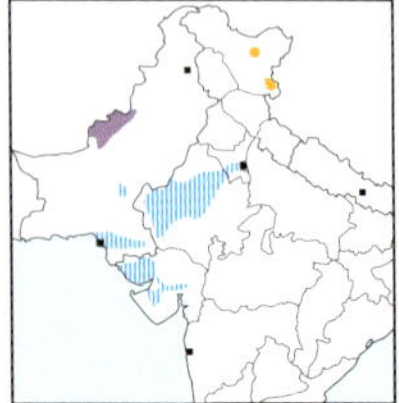

Red-tailed Shrike *Lanius phoenicuroides* 16.5–18cm

Breeds in Balochistan, small numbers winter in NW subcontinent. **ID** Compared to Isabelline, male has rufous cast to crown and nape, contrasting with darker grey-brown mantle, whiter forehead and supercilium, whiter underparts, and deeper rufous-brown tail. These features are often apparent in female and first-winter, but identification from Isabelline is less reliable and some probably not distinguishable. Contrast between crown/nape and mantle and brighter tail, as well as white patch in wing when present, are helpful features from Brown Shrike (which see for further differences). Male has complete black mask. Lores whitish in female and has faint scaling on breast and flanks; white patch at base of primaries usually apparent. Juvenile has dark scaling to upperparts and underparts (mantle uniform by first-winter but retains juvenile coverts and tertials which have dark subterminal borders). Hybridises with Red-backed Shrike, which can result in some confusing variations. **Voice** Grating call. **HH** Habits like Red-backed. Open dry scrub; generally prefers drier and more thorny vegetation than used by Red-backed.

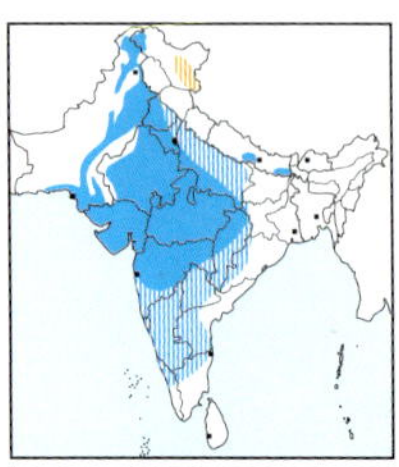

Isabelline Shrike *Lanius isabellinus* 16.5–18cm

Winter visitor mainly to NW subcontinent. **ID** Has pale sandy-brown crown and mantle, contrasting with rufous rump and tail. Underparts buffish (whiter in Red-tailed). Supercilium buffish. Female has paler ear-coverts than male, with pale lores, and usually has faint dark scaling on breast and flanks. Both sexes have small white patch at base of primaries, less distinct in female. Juvenile has dark scaling to upperparts and underparts (mantle uniform by first-winter but retains juvenile coverts and tertials which have dark subterminal borders). **Voice** Grating call. **HH** Habits like Red-backed. Open dry scrub; generally prefers drier and more thorny vegetation than used by Red-backed.

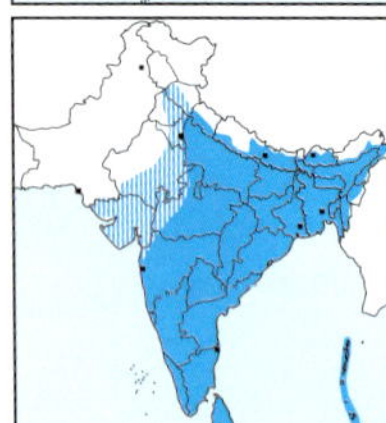

Brown Shrike *Lanius cristatus* 17–20cm

Widespread winter visitor; unrecorded in Pakistan. **ID** Compared to Red-tailed Shrike typically has darker and more uniform rufous-brown upperparts (lacking noticeable contrast between crown and mantle and mantle and tail – although see *L. c. lucionensis* below) and warmer rufous flanks. Also, thicker bill, more graduated tail (with narrower feathers) and lacks white patch at base of primaries (apparent in male and some female Red-tailed). Female is like male but has paler lores and faint dark scaling on breast and flanks. Juvenile has dark scaling to upperparts and underparts (mantle uniform by first-winter). *L. c. lucionensis* (winter visitor to Sri Lanka and Andamans/Nicobars) has greyish-white supercilium, grey cast to crown and nape, and more noticeable rufous rump and tail. **Voice** Rich varied chattering song; typical shrike grating call. **HH** Watches from top of bush, tree, post or telegraph wire; swoops down to catch prey. Typically undulating flight over long distances. Forest edges, open secondary scrub and hillsides with scattered bushes.

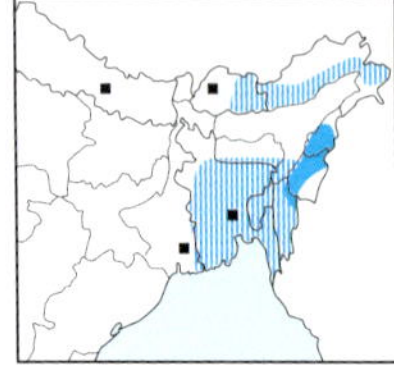

Burmese Shrike *Lanius collurioides* 19–21cm

Passage migrant. Mainly NE India. **ID** Male has dark grey crown and nape with variable contrast with black ear-coverts (often appears to have uniform dark hood). Deep chestnut upperparts including rump, and white sides to long slim black tail. Female like male with whitish lores. Both sexes with white patch at base of primaries. Chestnut (versus white) rump helps separate from Bay-backed Shrike, and prominent white sides and tips to tail from Long-tailed. Juvenile has dark-barred, two-toned upperparts, with grey-brown crown and nape (variably spotted and barred buff), and rufous coloration to rest of upperparts. Underparts barred. First-winter like adult with paler upperparts and some barring on underparts. **Voice** Loud, rapid, harsh chattering alarm call. **HH** Habits like Brown. Second growth and bushes in cultivation.

Red-backed Shrike
1st-winter
♀
♂
♀
♂
Red-tailed Shrike
♂
♀
1st-winter
Isabelline Shrike
1st-winter
1st-winter cristatus
♀ cristatus
♂ cristatus
juv cristatus
♀
♂
Burmese Shrike
juv
♂ lucionensis
Brown Shrike

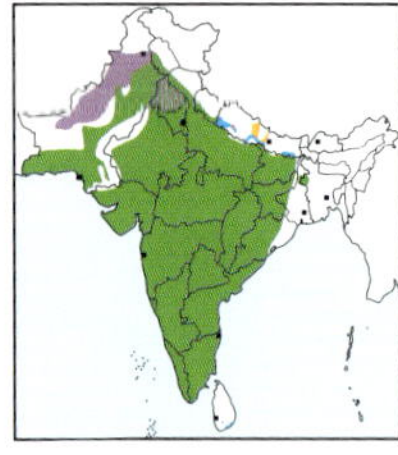

Bay-backed Shrike *Lanius vittatus* 17–19cm

Widespread resident; unrecorded in the north-east and Sri Lanka. **ID** Male has black forehead and mask, pale grey crown and nape, deep maroon mantle, whitish rump, white patch at base of primaries, and black tail with white sides. Female very similar but often duller with narrower or less distinct dark forehead. Juvenile from juvenile Long-tailed Shrike by smaller size and shorter tail, and more intricately patterned wing-coverts and tertials (with buff fringes and dark subterminal crescents). First-winter like washed-out version of adult, lacking black forehead; variably retains juvenile wing and tail feathers. **Voice** Pleasant, rambling warbling song with much mimicry; harsh churring call. **HH** Habits like Brown. Quite tame and fairly conspicuous. Open dry scrub, and bushes in cultivation.

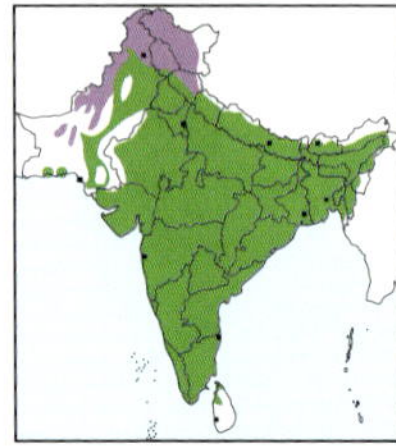

Long-tailed Shrike *Lanius schach* 20–25cm

Widespread resident. **ID** Large, long-tailed shrike. Adult has grey mantle, rufous scapulars and upper back (except *caniceps* of peninsular India and Sri Lanka which has little or no rufous above), narrow black forehead, rufous-buff sides to black tail, and small white patch on primaries. Juvenile has (dark-barred) rufous-brown upperparts and barring on underparts; dark greater coverts and tertials neatly fringed with rufous. First-winter is like adult but retains juvenile tertials, coverts and tail feathers. Himalayan *tricolor* has black hood (black crown, ear-coverts and nape) and is deeper rufous on mantle. Juvenile *tricolor* has mottled crown which becomes blackish hood with age; barred both above and below. **Voice** Pleasant subdued rambling warbling song with much mimicry; harsh grating call. **HH** Habits like Brown. Noisy and conspicuous. Bushes in cultivation, open forest, gardens.

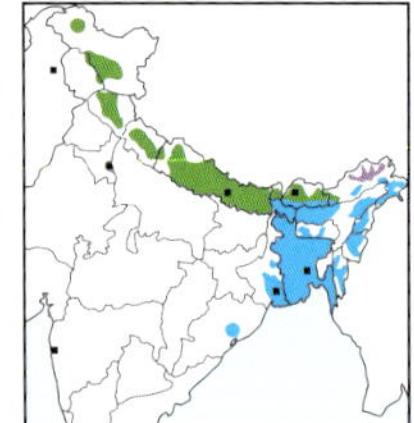

Grey-backed Shrike *Lanius tephronotus* 21–23cm

Breeds in Himalayas; winters in Himalayas and on adjacent plains in N and NE India and in Bangladesh. **ID** Adult from Long-tailed by stouter bill, uniform (darker) grey upperparts, with rufous on uppertail-coverts (but no rufous on scapulars and upper back) and browner tail. Also lacks (or has only very indistinct) white patch at base of primaries, and lacks or has a narrow black forehead band (can be very similar). Juvenile has brown ear-coverts; cold grey upperparts (except rufous-brown uppertail-coverts), with indistinct black subterminal crescents and buff fringes to feathers; rufous fringes to black-centred coverts and tertials; and dark scaling on breast and flanks. Uniform cold grey base coloration to upperparts is best distinction from juvenile Long-tailed. Hybridises in NW Himalayas with Long-tailed ('*lahulensis*') when has rufous on scapulars and upper back, a white patch at base of primaries, and finer bill. **Voice** Subdued and musical song, with mimicry of other birds. Harsh grating call. **HH** Habits like Brown. Noisy and conspicuous. Territorial all year. Breeds in montane forest clearings and meadows with scattered small trees or large bushes. Winters in bushes on hillsides, open scrub and second growth.

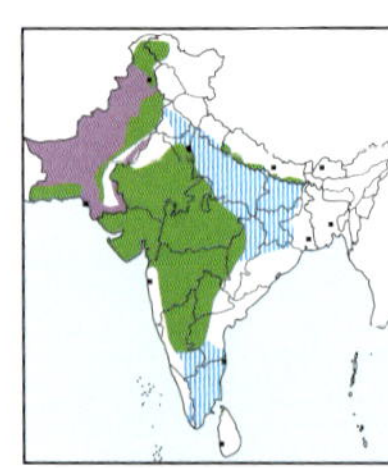

Great Grey Shrike *Lanius excubitor* 24–25cm

Resident. Mainly N, NW and W subcontinent. **ID** Most likely to be confused with Grey-backed and Long-tailed. Adult from those species by paler grey mantle and white scapulars, bold white markings on black wings and tail, greyish rump, and white breast and flanks. Black of mask extends over forehead and on sides of neck. Has extensive white patch at base of primaries and, with inner webs of secondaries and tips of outer webs also largely white, shows much white in wing at rest and in flight. Juvenile has sandy cast to grey crown and mantle, with very indistinct barring on crown, buff tips to tertials and median and greater coverts, and faint buffish wash to underparts; mask is grey and does not extend over forehead as on adult. *L. e. pallidirostris* ('Steppe Grey Shrike') breeds in extreme W Pakistan; winters east to Rajasthan. Lacks black on forehead and has more restricted dark mask (including dusky to whitish lores in female, lores typically strikingly pale in first-winter plumage); also has paler grey mantle, and often shows a pink wash on breast; white on secondaries is confined to tips and basal half of inner webs, and therefore shows less white on wing at all times. Bill has striking horn-coloured base outside breeding season and in first-winter plumage. See Vagrants for differences from Lesser Grey Shrike. **Voice** Chattering subdued song with harsh notes; mimics other birds. **HH** Habits like Brown, but wary. Dry country, open thorn scrub, dry deciduous forest, cultivation edges. **TN** Includes Southern Grey Shrike *L. meridionalis*, formerly treated as a separate species.

1st-winter
♀
♂
juv
Bay-backed Shrike
juv
tricolor
ad
tricolor
juv
erythronotus
Long-tailed
Shrike
1st-winter
tephronotus
ad
tephronotus
Grey-backed
Shrike
ad
erythronotus
ad
caniceps
ad
'lahulensis'
juv
pallidirostris
♂
pallidirostris
1st-winter
pallidirostris
Great Grey Shrike
juv
lahtora
♂
lahtora

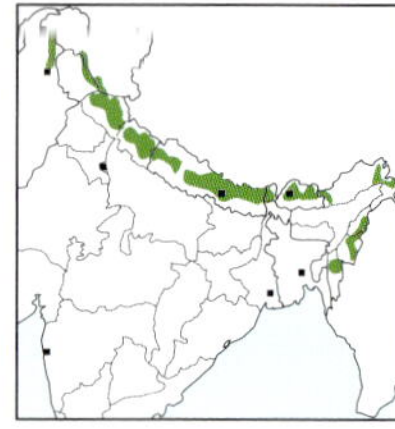

Eurasian Jay ***Garrulus glandarius*** **34–35cm**

Resident. Himalayas and NE India. **ID** Pinkish- to reddish-brown, with beady eye, stout black bill and black moustachial stripe. Wings and tail mainly black, with patches of cobalt-blue barring. In flight, shows prominent white rump that contrasts with black tail. Flight action slow and laboured, with rather jerky beats of its rounded wings. In W Himalayas *G. g. bispecularis* has vinaceous-fawn body; *G. g. interstinctus* of E Himalayas is darker reddish-brown. **Voice** Loud, rasping *skaaaak-skaaaak* alarm call, also crow-like *kraah*. **HH** Singly, in pairs or family parties in breeding season; in autumn and winter often in flocks with blue magpies and Black-headed Jays. Dense, moist mainly broadleaved forest, chiefly oaks.

Black-headed Jay ***Garrulus lanceolatus*** **28–33cm**

Resident. NW mountains of Pakistan and Himalayas. **ID** Has black (slightly crested) head, white-streaked black throat, stout grey bill, and pinkish-fawn upperparts and underparts variably washed blue-grey. Wings have patches of blue barring, like Eurasian Jay, but also white carpal patch and tips to tertials and flight feathers. In flight, pinkish-fawn rump (rather than white in Eurasian), and has longer mainly blue tail with black cross-bars and white tip. Juvenile similar, but duller and browner. **Voice** Alarm call like Eurasian, but usually single, flatter *skaaaak*. **HH** Habits like Eurasian. In autumn and winter often forages in parties with Eurasian Jay or Yellow-billed Blue Magpie. Mixed temperate forest, mainly of oaks, often in more open forest than Eurasian.

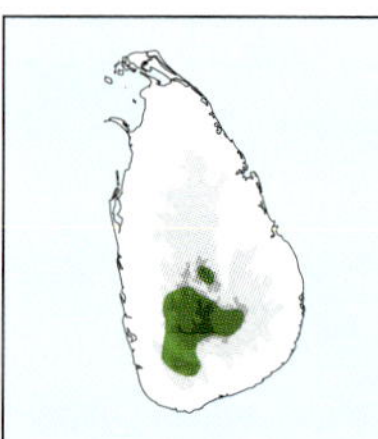

Sri Lanka Blue Magpie ***Urocissa ornata*** **40–47cm**

Resident. Sri Lanka. **ID** Very distinctive, with red bill, eye-ring and legs/feet, chestnut head, breast and flight feathers, blue body, and long white-tipped blue tail. Juvenile duller, with brown eye-ring, and grey wash to blue body (especially underparts). **Voice** Often very noisy. Very varied loud calls, including far-carrying ringing *ching-ching*, rasping *crakrakrakrak* and whistling *whee-whee*. **HH** In pairs or small groups, often joins mixed-species feeding parties in non-breeding season. Rather shy. Forages at all levels in forest, sometimes swings upside-down on branch. Evergreen broadleaved forest in wet zone and mountains. Globally threatened.

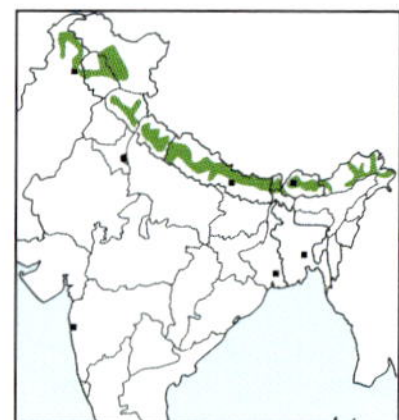

Yellow-billed Blue Magpie ***Urocissa flavirostris*** **55–61cm**

Resident. Himalayas and NE India. **ID** From Red-billed Blue by yellow or orange-yellow bill, small white crescent on nape, duller blue-grey mantle and wings. Can show faint yellowish wash on underparts in fresh plumage. Juvenile like adult, but has duller head and upperparts, more extensive white on nape, and dull olive-yellow bill. **Voice** Wheezy *bu-zeep-peck-peck-peck, pop-upclea, pu-pu-weer* and a high-pitched *clear-clear*. **HH** Usually in pairs or flocks of up to ten. Parties cross clearings in single file. Forages with agility, hopping from branch to branch, also feeds on ground, progressing in long hops with tail held high. Moist broadleaved, coniferous and mixed forest.

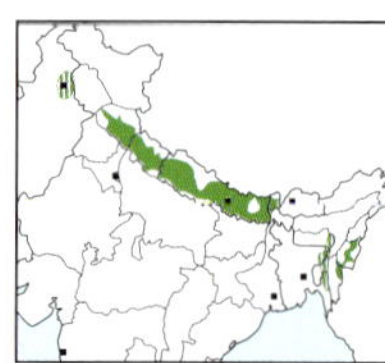

Red-billed Blue Magpie ***Urocissa erythrorhyncha*** **60–68cm**

Resident. Himalayas and NE India. Vagrant Bangladesh. **ID** From Yellow-billed by red or orange-red bill, more extensive white nape (with white speckling on hindcrown), and brighter turquoise-blue mantle and wings. Juvenile has duller blue-grey upperparts, dull brownish-red bill, and a more extensive white crown. Darker purplish-blue mantle in eastern *U. e. magnirostris*. **Voice** Piercing *quiv-pig-pig*, softer *beeee-trik*, subdued *kluk* and sharp *chwenk-chwenk*. **HH** Habits like Yellow-billed. Broadleaved and mixed forests and trees in cultivation and near villages.

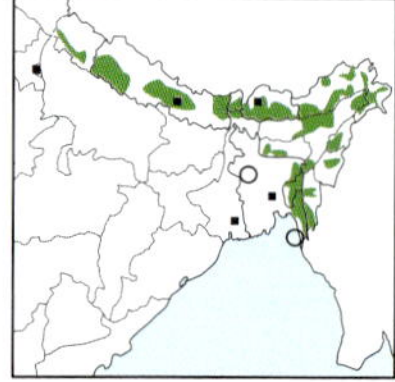

Common Green Magpie ***Cissa chinensis*** **37–39cm**

Resident. Himalayas, NE India and Bangladesh. **ID** Mainly lurid green, with red bill and legs, black mask, rufous-chestnut wings, black-and-white-tipped tertials and secondaries, and long, graduated black-and-white-tipped green tail. In captivity green coloration can bleach to pale blue and chestnut wings can fade to olive-brown. Juvenile like adult, but has dull yellow bill and legs, shorter crest, and paler underparts. **Voice** Very variable: harsh *chakakakakakakak* or *chkakak-wi*; high-pitched *wi-chi-chi, jao... wichitchit... wi-chi-chi, jao* with shriller *jao* notes and complex high shrill whistles combined with mimicry. **HH** In pairs or small parties, often with roaming mixed-species flocks. Usually remains within foliage. Forages in forest understorey and on ground under thick vegetation. Broadleaved evergreen and moist deciduous forest.

ad
bispecularis
Eurasian Jay
ad
Black-headed Jay
ad
Yellow-billed
Blue Magpie
juv
Sri Lanka
Blue Magpie
ad
ad
Red-billed
Blue Magpie
juv
ad
Common
Green Magpie

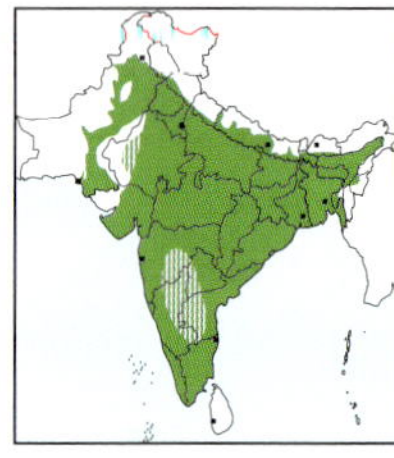

Rufous Treepie *Dendrocitta vagabunda* 46–50cm

Widespread resident; unrecorded in Sri Lanka. **ID** Adult from Grey by combination of uniform slate-grey hood (extending to breast), rufous-brown mantle and scapulars, pale grey wing-coverts and tertials contrasting with black of rest of wing, fulvous-buff underparts, and black-tipped silver-grey tail. In flight, pale grey wing-panel, whitish subterminal tail-band, and rufous rump are useful features from Grey. Juvenile like adult but has browner hood (less well demarcated from mantle), buffish wash to wing-coverts, and tail feathers have pale buffish tips. Five races in subcontinent; vary mainly in length of tail and richness of mantle and underpart colour. **Voice** Varied harsh metallic and mewing notes. **HH** Frequent member of mixed parties of insectivores. Chiefly arboreal, keeping high in trees. Open wooded country.

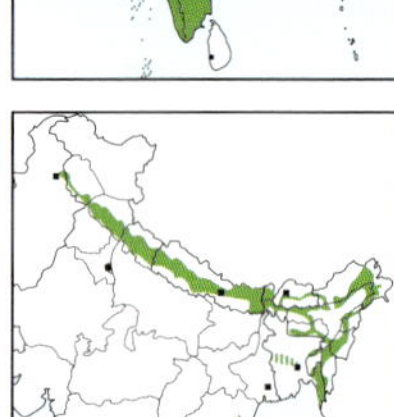

Grey Treepie *Dendrocitta formosae* 36–40cm

Resident. Himalayas, NE India, Eastern Ghats and Bangladesh. **ID** Dull-coloured treepie with blackish face contrasting with grey crown, nape and underparts, dull brown mantle, black wings with white patch at base of primaries, grey rump, and rufous undertail-coverts. Juvenile is like adult, but has narrower black forehead, dusky throat concolorous with upper breast, browner crown and nape, whitish belly, and rufous tips to wing-coverts. **Voice** Wide variety of calls, often a loud, metallic, undulating *klok-kli-klok-kli-kli*. **HH** Usually in flocks of up to 20, often with other forest species. Broadleaved forest, second growth and well-wooded country.

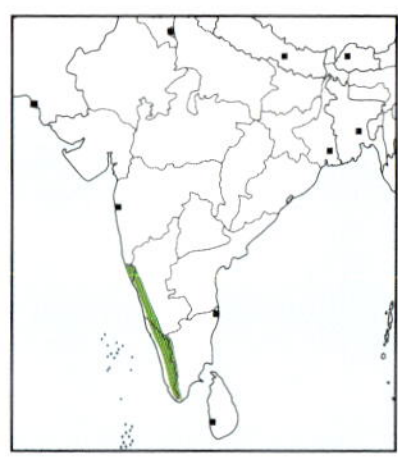

White-bellied Treepie *Dendrocitta leucogastra* 45cm

Resident. Western Ghats and SE India. **ID** A striking white, black and rufous treepie with very long grey tail with extensive black at tip. Adult has black face and throat contrasting with white nape and underparts, rufous-brown mantle, black wings with white patch at base of primaries, white rump, and bright rufous undertail-coverts. Juvenile is like adult, but has narrower and shorter central tail feathers, buff fringes to white body feathers, and diffuse demarcation between black throat and white underparts. **Voice** Calls like Rufous, but harsher and more metallic, frequently mimics Greater Racket-tailed Drongo. **HH** Mainly keeps to middle and lower storeys, also in shrubs and on ground. Often follows roving bands of insectivores. Humid broadleaved evergreen hill forest and second growth.

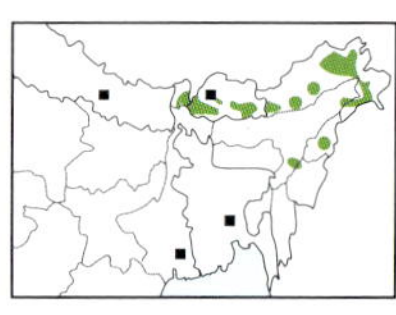

Collared Treepie *Dendrocitta frontalis* 38cm

Resident. Himalayas and NE India. **ID** From Rufous by black face and throat contrasting with pale grey nape and breast, and all-black tail. Additional features are smaller size, black tertials, and rufous lower belly and vent. Juvenile like adult but duller, with brownish fringes to grey of head and breast. **Voice** Wide variety of loud calls, some musical, others scratchy. **HH** Habits like Grey. Dense, humid broadleaved evergreen forest with bamboo thickets.

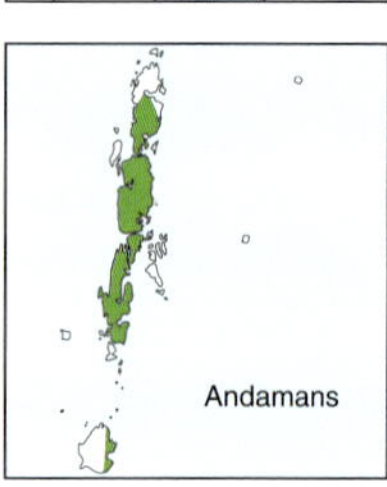

Andaman Treepie *Dendrocitta bayleii* 32cm

Resident. Andamans, where the only treepie. **ID** A small treepie, with blue-grey head and neck (but blacker face) merging into dull rufous-brown mantle and bright rufous underparts; also, blackish wings with white patch at base of secondaries, and blackish tail. Iris strikingly yellow. Juvenile has browner hood, brownish fringes to wing-coverts, duller iris, and shorter and greyer tail. **Voice** Calls include fluty, oriole-like whistle, *kiu-duu*, regularly repeated, and harsh rasping *kyow* or *kiayow*. **HH** Habits like Grey. Dense broadleaved evergreen forest. Globally threatened.

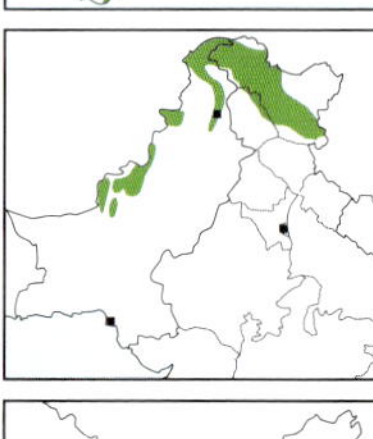

Eurasian Magpie *Pica pica* 46–50cm

Resident. Mountains of N and W Pakistan, and Ladakh. **ID** Body mainly black (with weak purple-and-green sheen), with white scapulars, flanks and belly. Metallic blue-black wings, with white inner webs to primaries showing as a white flash in flight. Tail is long, graduated, and metallic bronze-green and purple. Juvenile resembles adult but has greyish-black head and breast. *P. p. bactriana* of W Himalayas has white rump. **Voice** Staccato *chack-chack-chack-chack*... etc., uttered in bursts of eight or more notes; also enquiring *ch'chack* and squealing *keee-uck*. **HH** Bold and conspicuous, often in open, resting on walls and rooftops or feeding on ground. Open cultivated upland valleys.

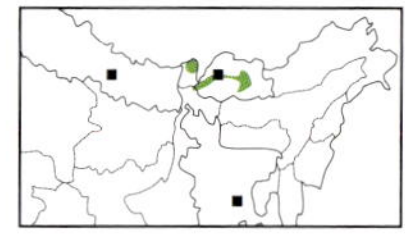

Black-rumped Magpie *Pica bottanensis* 46–50cm

Resident. N Bhutan and doubtfully Sikkim. **ID** Compared to Eurasian Magpie, has black rump, shorter tail, stout bill and very little gloss in plumage. **Voice** Any possible differences from Eurasian Magpie not described. **HH** As Eurasian. **TN** Formerly treated as conspecific with *P. pica*.

Rufous Treepie
imm
vagabunda
ad
vagabunda
ad
pallida
ad
Grey Treepie
imm
ad
Collared Treepie
ad
White-bellied
Treepie
ad
Eurasian
Magpie
ad
Andaman Treepie
imm
ad
Black-rumped
Magpie

PLATE 134: NUTCRACKERS, CHOUGHS AND CROWS I

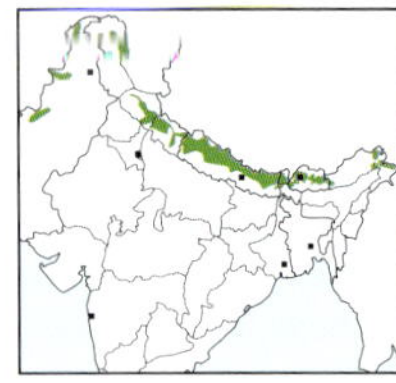

Eurasian Nutcracker *Nucifraga caryocatactes* 27.2–32cm

Resident. Mountains of NW Pakistan and Himalayas. **ID** Largely brown, with bold white spotting on head and body, white vent, and white sides and tip to tail. Juvenile duller and less cleanly spotted. Spotting sparser than on Kashmir Nutcracker, looks much browner, and flanks and lower belly are almost unspotted and contrast strongly with white vent. **Voice** Far-carrying dry and harsh *kraaaak*; quiet song of various piping, squeaking, whistling and whining notes. **HH** Sedentary and mainly territorial all year. Typically, perches on tops of tall trees. Often flicks tail, revealing white sides. Easily located by its distinctive calls. Coniferous forest. **AN** Spotted Nutcracker.

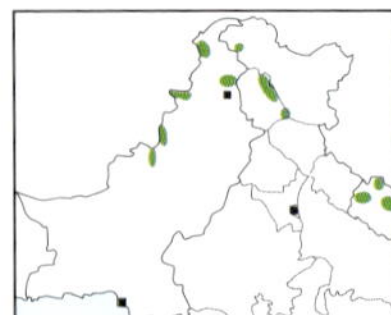

Kashmir Nutcracker *Nucifraga multipunctata* 32–35cm

Resident. Mountains of NW Pakistan and NW India. **ID** Compared to Eurasian Nutcracker has larger white spots on body, wing-coverts and tertials, and thus looks much whiter. Bill is also finer (on some, strikingly long and thin). **Voice** Possibly indistinguishable from Eurasian in field. **HH** Habits like Eurasian. Coniferous forests and mixed conifer-oak forests where conifers are dominant, around villages and encampments. **AN** Large-spotted Nutcracker. **TN** Formerly treated as conspecific with Eurasian Nutcracker.

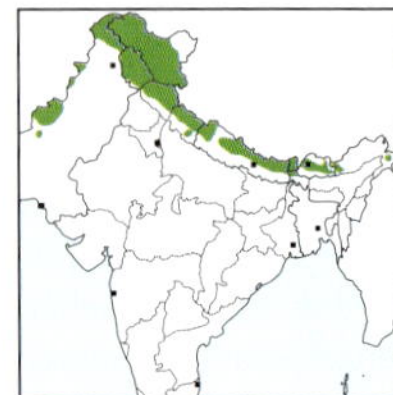

Red-billed Chough *Pyrrhocorax pyrrhocorax* 38–41cm

Resident. Mountains of W Pakistan and Himalayas. **ID** Longer, more downcurved red bill is best feature from Yellow-billed Chough. Call also distinctive. In flight, has broader wingtips with more pronounced fingered primaries, and square-ended tail that equals width of wing base. Vigorous digging with downcurved bill can aid identification. Juvenile lacks metallic gloss of adult, has dark legs, and shorter browner bill (slimmer and more noticeably downcurved than in Yellow-billed). **Voice** Distinctive far-carrying, nasal *chaow... chaow*. **HH** Gregarious all year, often several hundred together in winter. Forages by probing and digging in ground and turning over stones and dung. High mountains with cliffs and adjacent short turf alpine pasture, also cultivation in winter.

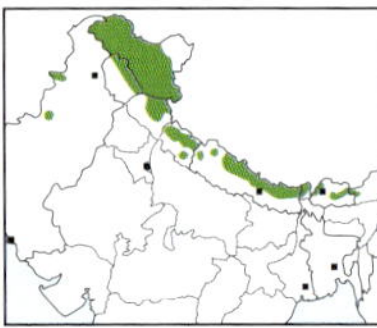

Yellow-billed Chough *Pyrrhocorax graculus* 34–38cm

Resident. Mountains of W Pakistan and Himalayas. **ID** Shorter and straighter yellow bill is best feature from Red-billed. In flight, has narrower wingtips with less pronounced fingered primaries, more pronounced curve to trailing edge of wing, and longer rounded tail. Juvenile lacks gloss of adult and has dark legs and duller bill. **Voice** Far-carrying rippling *preeep* and descending whistled *sweeeoo*. **HH** Habits like Red-billed, but more confiding. Scavenges around settlements. High mountains with cliffs, alpine pastures and cultivation. **AN** Alpine Chough.

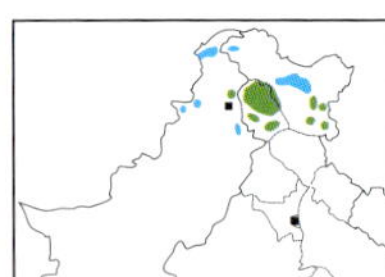

Eurasian Jackdaw *Corvus monedula* 34–39cm

Resident. Mountains of W and N Pakistan, and NW Himalayas. **ID** Adult has silky-grey nape and hindneck, whitish half-collar, slate-grey underparts, and pale grey iris. Juvenile has darker grey nape and hindneck, and darker grey iris. Flight fast; looks blunt-headed in flight with oval-shaped wings. **Voice** Abrupt repeated *chjack... chjack* call; a low drawn-out *chaairurr* and high slurred *kyow*. **HH** Sociable, bold and inquisitive. Open cultivated valleys and damp pastures.

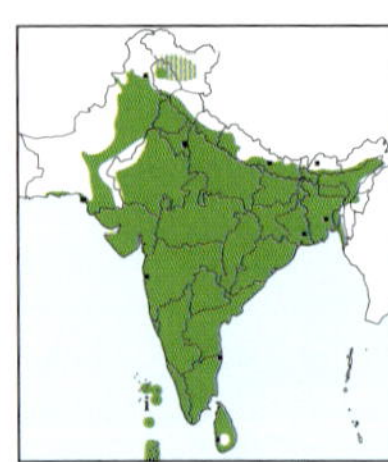

House Crow *Corvus splendens* 40–43cm

Widespread resident. **ID** Two-toned appearance, with paler nape, neck and breast. Adult has gloss to black of plumage, and 'collar' is well defined and becomes paler with wear. Juvenile lacks gloss, and 'collar' is duskier and less well defined. Four subspecies are recognised in the subcontinent. The north-westernmost *zugmayeri* has a paler smoky-white 'collar', strongly contrasting with black of plumage. 'Collar' is darker and greyer in the widely distributed nominate but is less well defined in the two subspecies in S India/Sri Lanka and the Maldives. **Voice** Main call a flat, dry *kaaa-kaaa*, weaker than Large-billed. **HH** Gregarious when feeding and roosting. Adapted to exploit human activity. Scavenges at rubbish dumps, in streets and on riverbanks. Around human habitation and nearby cultivation.

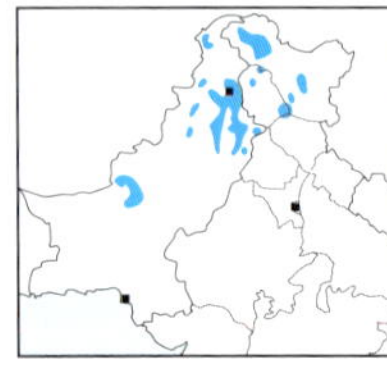

Rook *Corvus frugilegus* 44–46cm

Winter visitor. Pakistan, Ladakh and Jammu. **ID** Adult has whitish skin around base of bill and throat. Juvenile has black feathering on face and throat, and lacks gloss to black plumage. Juvenile more closely resembles Carrion and Large-billed, and best told by thinner and more pointed bill (with straighter ridge to culmen), steeply rising forehead and peaked crown, and shaggy 'trousered' thighs. In flight, tail more rounded or wedge-shaped. **Voice** Drier and flatter *kaah* call compared to Carrion Crow; also high-pitched *kraa-a*. **HH** Highly gregarious, often with other corvids. Struts about on ground, stopping to dig and probe in search of food. Cultivation and short pastures near habitation.

ad
Eurasian Nutcracker
ad
Kashmir Nutcracker
ad
juv
Red-billed Chough
ad
Yellow-billed Chough
ad
Eurasian Jackdaw
ad
zugmayeri
ad
splendens
House Crow
juv
ad
Rook

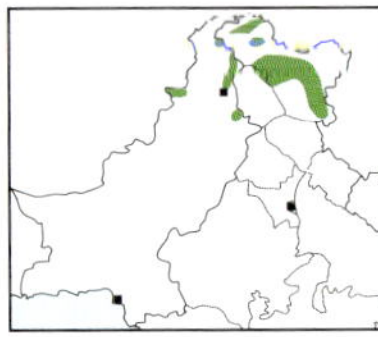

Carrion Crow *Corvus corone* 48–56cm

Resident. Mountains of N Pakistan and NW India. **ID** From Large-billed Crow by smaller bill with straighter culmen, and flatter forehead and crown. Wingtips almost reach tail tip at rest (noticeably shorter than tail in Large-billed). **Voice** Call a stronger and more resonant *kraa* than Large-billed. **HH** Usually singly or in pairs, often with Rooks or House Crows. Forages in cultivation and pastures, scavenges at refuse tips and readily takes carrion. Open country with cultivation, often near upland villages.

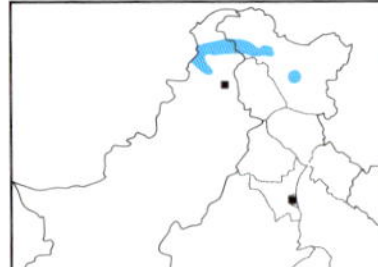

Hooded Crow *Corvus cornix* 48–54cm

Winter visitor to N Pakistan. Vagrant Ladakh. Superficially like House Crow, but whole head and most of breast is black, mantle is grey not black, and underparts are uniformly grey to vent. **Voice** Most frequently heard call slightly softer, more rolling *aaarrr*, less hoarse than Carrion. **HH** Habits like Carrion. Wide range of habitats including towns, refuse dumps, cultivation, scrub, forest clearings, coasts. **TN** Formerly treated as conspecific with *C. corone*.

Large-billed Crow *Corvus macrorhynchos* 46–59cm

Resident. Mountains of N Balochistan and Himalayas from N Pakistan east to Arunachal, and south through the peninsula, also Sri Lanka. **ID** Lacks any contrast between head and neck/breast as in House Crow, and bill is stouter with more pronounced curve to culmen. Birds in Himalayas (e.g. *intermedius*) larger, with heavier bill, wedge-shaped tail, and harsher calls, compared with birds in N India and peninsula ('Indian' Jungle Crow' *C. m. culminatus* and 'Eastern Jungle Crow' *C. m. levaillantii*). 'Jungle Crows' are more similar in size and shape to House Crow although bill is still heavier with more pronounced curve to culmen. Note that House Crow in the peninsula is darker and more uniform than in north, but still shows contrast between head and neck/breast. **Voice** Call of *intermedius* (W Himalayas) a very guttural *graak, graak*; of E Himalayan *tibetosinensis* a fairly hoarse *kyarrh, kyarrh*; of *culminatus* a loud, throaty *kyearh, kyearh*; of *levaillantii* a nasal *nyark, nyark*, first rising then falling. **HH** Usually singly, in pairs or small groups, but roosts communally in large numbers. Inquisitive, bold and omnivorous. Frequently scavenges and eats carrion. Follows goats and sheep in mountain pastures. Himalayan birds indulge in aerial gambolling. Wide habitat range. **TN** Eastern Jungle Crow *C.* (*m.*) *levaillantii* and Indian Jungle Crow *C.* (*m.*) *culminatus* now treated as subspecies of *C. macrorhynchos*.

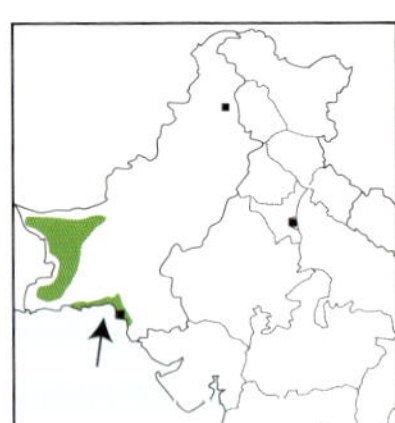

Brown-necked Raven *Corvus ruficollis* 52–56cm

Resident. Pakistan. **ID** From Large-billed Crow by brown cast to head, neck and breast. In bright light, or when worn, brown of neck is often not apparent. Compared to Large-billed, has raven-like appearance, with longer and more angled wings showing more pronounced fingered primaries, and more markedly wedge-shaped tail. Very similar to 'Punjab' Raven, which also has brownish cast to head and neck, and best told by thinner bill, less shaggy throat owing to shorter hackles, and slimmer build; at rest folded wings reach tail tip (falling slightly short of tail on 'Punjab' Raven). **Voice** Distinctive call – dry, rising *aarg-aarg-aarg*. **HH** Habits like Common Raven. Generally shy and wary, but quite bold if not persecuted. Desert.

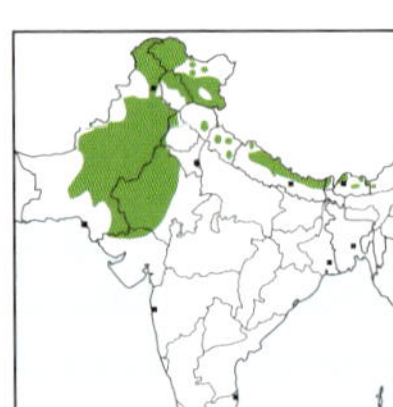

Common Raven *Corvus corax* 58–69cm

Resident. High Himalayas. **ID** From Large-billed, which can appear raven like, by longer neck, longer and more angled wings with more pronounced fingered primaries, and more markedly wedge-shaped tail. On the ground, further differences are larger appearance, with more rugged and shaggy look, stouter bill with straighter culmen, prominent throat hackles and flatter crown, more extensive nasal bristles (reaching centre of bill), and wingtips fall just short of tail (noticeably short on Large-billed). In Pakistan and NW India 'Punjab Raven' *C. c. laurencei* is smaller, with less pronounced throat hackles. Has brownish cast to head and neck, and thus easily confused with Brown-necked. Best told by stouter bill with straighter culmen, shaggy throat owing to pronounced throat hackles, stockier build, and deeper, more guttural and raucous call. At rest, folded wings fall slightly short of tail. **Voice** Typical call a deep, resonant croaking *wock... wock*. **HH** Agile in flight, can soar and glide well; performs impressive aerobatics, often tumbling, diving with closed wings and rolling on to back in mid-air. Solitary, in pairs or family parties in breeding season, in flocks at communal roosts. Dry rocky areas above treeline. **AN** Northern Raven.

Hooded Crow
ad
ad
Carrion Crow
ad
intermedius
Large-billed
Crow
ad
levaillantii
ad
culminatus
ad
Brown-necked
Raven
ad
corax
ad
laurencei
Common Raven

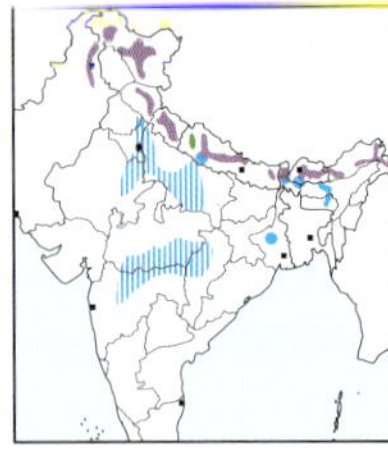

Fire-capped Tit *Cephalopyrus flammiceps* 8.5–9.5cm

Breeds in Himalayas; resident in NE India; winters in Nepal and C India. **ID** Flowerpecker-like, with greenish upperparts and yellowish to whitish underparts. Lacks crest, has sharply pointed bill. Male breeding has bright orange forecrown, chin and throat, and golden-yellow breast. Female breeding has yellowish forecrown and olive-yellow throat and breast. Adult non-breeding similar but throat whitish. Juvenile duller with pale grey underparts (no trace of yellow). In north-east (*olivaceus*) upperparts darker olive-green than nominate of W and C Himalayas; orange restricted to forehead and centre of throat; breast greener on breeding male. **Voice** Calls include high-pitched *tsit, tsit* or soft *whitoo-whitoo*, song a series of high-pitched notes. **HH** Forages mainly in treetops. Unobtrusive. Temperate deciduous broadleaved or mixed deciduous/coniferous forest.

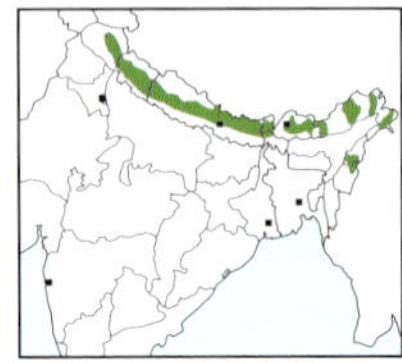

Yellow-browed Tit *Sylviparus modestus* 9–10cm

Resident. Himalayas and NE India. **ID** Very small, with slight crest and rather stubby bill. Olive-green upperparts, yellowish eye-ring, fine yellow supercilium, and yellowish-buff underparts. From Fire-capped by stouter bill, crested appearance, rather uniform wings with less distinct (olive-buff) greater covert bar, and lack of pale rump or distinct pale tertial fringes. In W Himalayas (*simlaensis*) has brighter yellowish-olive upperparts and yellowish underparts compared to nominate of C and E Himalayas. **Voice** Sharp, very high-pitched, well-spaced *tis* or *tis-tis-tis*, also very high-pitched thin *tis-tis-tis-sisisisisi*. **HH** Quiet and unobtrusive. Frequently hangs upside-down, constantly flicks wings. Mainly mixed broadleaved forests.

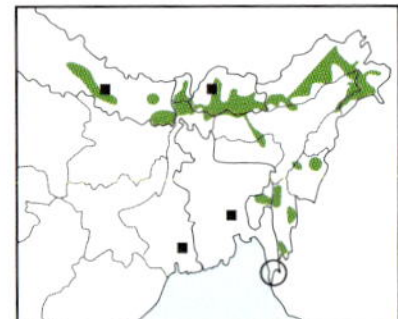

Sultan Tit *Melanochlora sultanea* 20–21cm

Resident. C and E Himalayas and NE Indian hills. Vagrant Bangladesh. **ID** A huge, bulbul-like tit. Male largely glossy blue-black, with bright yellow crest and yellow underparts below black breast. Female similar, but black of plumage is duller blackish-olive (especially on throat and breast). Juvenile has shorter crest and fine yellowish-white tips to greater coverts. **Voice** Song a series of five ringing *chew* notes; loud, squeaky whistling call, *tcheery-tcheery-tcheery*. **HH** Slow and deliberate movements. Usually keeps to treetops. Broadleaved evergreen forest.

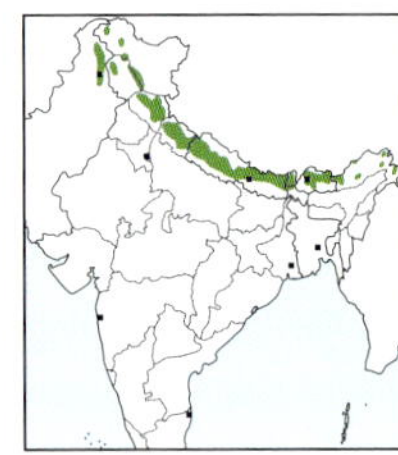

Coal Tit *Periparus ater* 10–12cm

Resident. Himalayas. **ID** Black crest, white nape and cheeks, and black throat and breast. Whitish tips to median and greater coverts. Small size and whitish wing spots separate it from other black-crested tits. Juvenile lacks crest, and cap and bib are brownish, with bib very poorly defined; stronger olive cast to mantle, and yellowish wash to cheeks and breast. 'Spot-winged' Tit *P. a. melanolophus* from WC Nepal westwards differs from *aemodius* by having rufous breast-sides and flanks, dark grey belly and darker blue-grey mantle. Hybridises with nominate in WC Nepal and intergrades occur. **Voice** Song a low-pitched, slow *wee-tsee... wee-tsee... wee-tsee*; calls include thin *tsi tsi, pip, pip-sziu* and plaintive *tsi-tsu-whichooh*. **HH** Typical tit but chiefly in upper half of trees. Mainly coniferous forest, also coniferous/broadleaved forest. **TN** Rufous-naped and Rufous-vented Tits formerly placed in *Parus*.

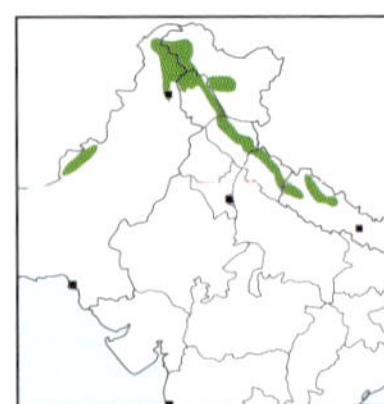

Rufous-naped Tit *Periparus rufonuchalis* 13cm

Resident. Balochistan and W Himalayas. **ID** From Rufous-vented by larger size, more extensive black bib (extending to upper belly), grey (rather than rufous) lower belly. Also has variable rufous wash to white nape and rufous patch on sides of breast. Note that eastern subspecies of Rufous-vented has grey belly, but otherwise above-mentioned features still hold. From 'Spot-winged' Tit (see Coal Tit) by larger size, uniform wings, and more extensive black bib. Juvenile has shorter crest; mantle and belly are suffused brown, undertail-coverts are buff, and black bib is duller and less extensive. **Voice** Monotonous, repeated two-note whistling song. Three-noted call, first two are metallic squeaks, third is downward-inflected whistle. **HH** Typical tit. Forages in canopy, in bushes and on ground. Coniferous forest.

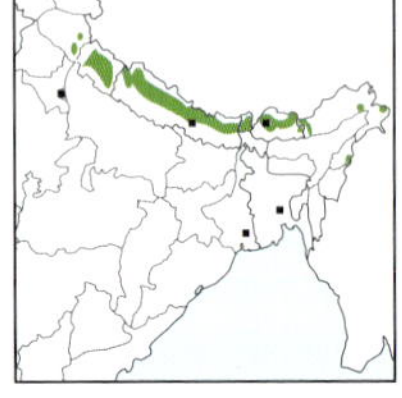

Rufous-vented Tit *Periparus rubidiventris* 12–13cm

Resident. Himalayas and Nagaland. **ID** Where ranges overlap in W Himalayas, best told from Rufous-naped Tit by smaller size, rufous belly concolorous with vent, and less extensive black bib (not reaching belly). From 'Spot-winged' Tit (see Coal Tit) by absence of broad white tips to median and greater coverts. In E Himalayas (*beavani*) has greyish belly (variably washed buff), buffish cheeks and purer blue-grey mantle. Juvenile has shorter crest and duller cap, yellowish cheeks, and bib is less clearly defined. **Voice** Very varied calls including *seet, piu* and *chit*; variable rattling song. **HH** Typical tit, see Green-backed, but forages in treetops. Coniferous, coniferous/broadleaved and broadleaved forests.

♂ br
flammiceps
♂
non-br
ad
Yellow-browed Tit
juv
♀
Fire-capped Tit
♂
Sultan Tit
(not to scale)
♀
juv
melanolophus
juv
emodius
ad
melanolophus
juv
ad
aemodius
ad
Coal Tit
Rufous-naped Tit
juv
rubidiventris
ad
beavani
Rufous-vented Tit
ad
rubidiventris

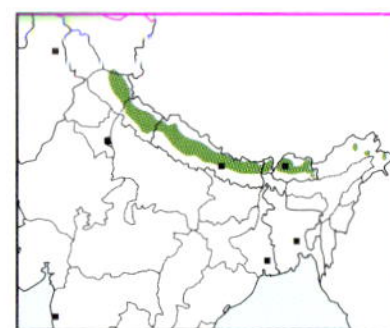

Grey-crested Tit *Lophophanes dichrous* 11.5–12.5cm

Resident. Himalayas. **ID** Very different in coloration from other crested tits. Adult has greyish crest and upperparts, buffish-white half-collar and submoustachial stripe, greyish-buff throat, and orange-buff underparts. Juvenile has shorter crest, and paler and less uniform underparts. **Voice** Song a *whee-whee-tz-tz-tz*; rapid *cheea, cheea* and *ti-ti-ti-ti-ti* alarm calls. **HH** Typical tit, see Green-backed. Chiefly in middle and lower storeys. Mainly broadleaved forest, also coniferous and mixed forests. **TN** Formerly placed in *Parus*.

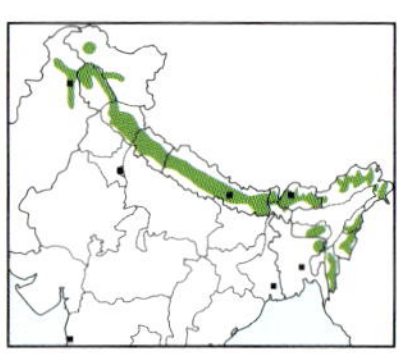

Green-backed Tit *Parus monticolus* 12.5–13cm

Resident. Himalayas and NE Indian hills. Vagrant Bangladesh. **ID** From Cinereous Tit by bright green mantle and back, yellow on breast-sides and flanks, and double white wing-bars. Wings look bluish owing to blue edges to remiges. Female has duller black throat and narrower stripe on centre of belly. Juvenile duller than adult, and white cheeks and wing-bars are washed with yellow. **Voice** Song includes loud, pleasant, ringing *whitee... whitee*. **HH** Highly acrobatic, often hanging upside-down. Gregarious in non-breeding season, joining roving flocks of other insectivores. Forages chiefly in lower and middle storeys. Broadleaved forests, moister forests than Cinereous.

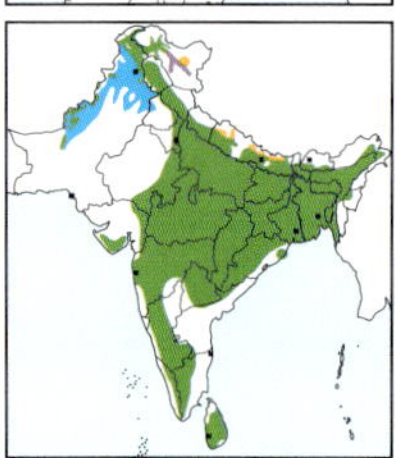

Cinereous Tit *Parus cinereus* 14cm

Resident. Widespread in hills of subcontinent. **ID** Black breast centre and line down belly, greyish mantle, greyish-white breast-sides and flanks, and white wing-bar. Lacks bright green-and-yellow colours of Green-backed Tit. Juvenile has yellowish-white cheeks and underparts, and yellowish-olive wash to mantle. Larger and paler in north-west; smaller and darker to east and south. **Voice** Extremely variable. Song includes loud, clear whistling *weeter-weeter-weeter, wreet-chee-chee*; calls include *tsee tsee tsee* and harsh churring. **HH** Typical tit. Forests and well-wooded country. **TN** Formerly treated as conspecific with Great Tit *P. major*.

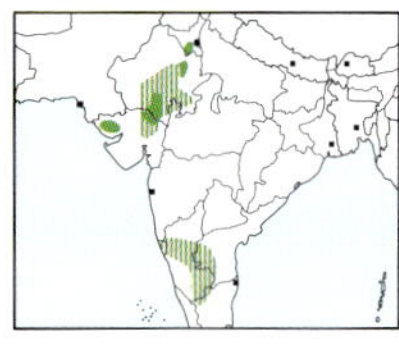

White-naped Tit *Machlolophus nuchalis* 12–13cm

Resident. NW and S India. **ID** Black mantle and wing-coverts (grey on Cinereous Tit) and extensive patches of white on wing. Striking white nuchal patch, lacks black lower border to white cheeks, and has white breast-sides and flanks (washed yellow in some). Male has glossy black (versus dull black) mantle and whiter tertials and base of secondaries than female. **Voice** Very like Cinereous. **HH** Similar to Cinereous. Shy. Thorn scrub-forest in north-west, moist deciduous forest in Kerala. Globally threatened. **TN** Formerly placed in *Parus*.

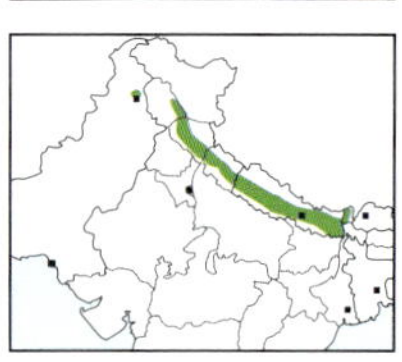

Himalayan Black-lored Tit *Machlolophus xanthogenys* 13–14cm

Resident. Himalayas. **ID** Where ranges overlap in E Himalayas, best told from Yellow-cheeked by black forehead and lores (yellow in Yellow-cheeked), black border to yellow cheeks, uniform greenish upperparts with black streaking confined to scapulars, and yellowish wing-bars. Sexes similar and juvenile only slightly duller with shorter crest. **Voice** Song includes *pui-pui-tee, pui-pui-tee*; calls include *tzee-tzee-wheep-wheep-wheep*. **HH** Habits like Green-backed, but mainly in upper storey. Open forests and second growth, mainly broadleaved. **TN** Formerly placed in *Parus*. **AN** Black-lored Tit.

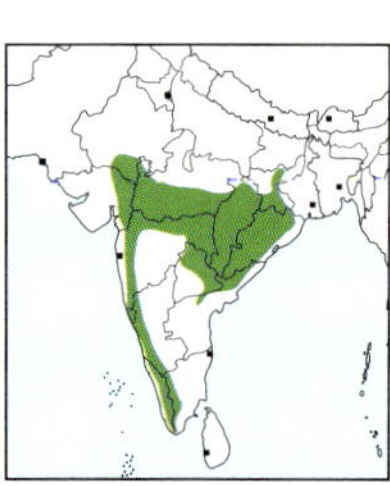

Indian Yellow Tit *Machlolophus aplonotus* 13–14cm

Resident. Peninsular hills. **ID** Male nominate in N and E peninsula is like Himalayan Black-lored but duller and has white (rather than yellow) wing-bars; often a short yellow supercilium in front of eye. Female has greyish-olive rather than black bib and ventral stripe, and paler yellow cheeks and underparts. In S India (*travancoreensis*) is duller, particularly in female, with less yellow on underparts and flanks mainly grey; juvenile has dark-streaked olive crown. **Voice** Song like Himalayan Black-lored, but starts with double or triple high clear notes, then falls to lower wheezy or hard notes. Calls include single, repeated high notes. **HH** Well-wooded areas. **TN** Formerly placed in *Parus* and considered conspecific with Himalayan Black-lored Tit.

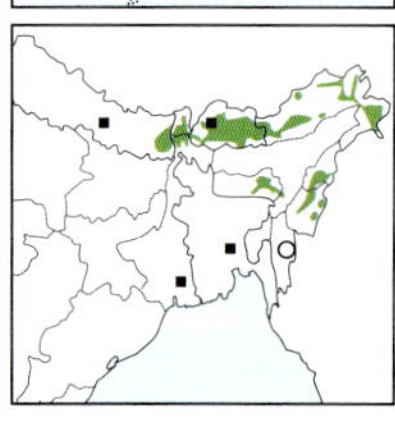

Yellow-cheeked Tit *Machlolophus spilonotus* 13.5–15.5cm

Resident. E Himalayas and NE Indian hills. **ID** Where ranges overlap in E Himalayas, best told from Himalayan Black-lored by yellow forehead and lores, absence of black border to yellow cheeks, black streaking on greenish mantle, and white wing-bars. Juvenile like adult, but duller, with shorter sooty-black crest, and has yellowish-white wing-bars. Sexes similar in nominate E Himalayan subspecies. Female *M. s. subviridis* of north-east, south of the Brahmaputra River, has olive (rather than black) bib and ventral line, and mantle is less heavily marked with black. **Voice** Song comprises three ringing notes rapidly repeated up to six times, *chee-chee-pui*; calls resemble Cinereous Tit. **HH** Typical tit, see Green-backed. Chiefly in lower forest canopy. Open broadleaved forest. **TN** Formerly placed in *Parus*.

ad
Grey-crested Tit
juv
ad
Green-backed Tit
ad
juv
Cinereous Tit
ad
White-naped Tit
ad
juv
Himalayan
Black-lored Tit
♀
aplonotus
ad
♂
aplonotus
juv
travancoreensis
Indian Yellow Tit
ad
juv
Yellow-cheeked Tit

PLATE 138: TITS III

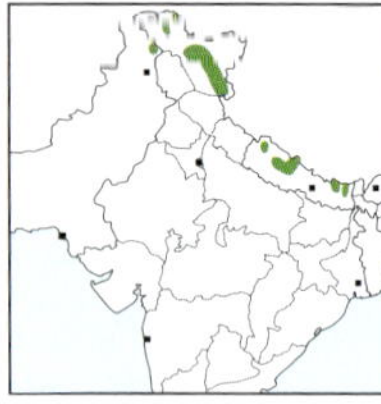

Ground Tit *Pseudopodoces humilis* 19–20cm

Resident. Himalayas in extreme N India and N Nepal. **ID** Upright and ground-dwelling with downcurved black bill. Bounces along on ground and has weak, fluttering flight. Sandy-brown and buffish-white. Largely buffish-white tail with brown central feathers, black lores, whitish nape, broad white tips to alula. Juvenile has shorter bill and lacks black lores. **Voice** Munia-like *cheep* and whistling *chip* followed by quick-repeated *cheep-cheep-cheep-cheep*. **HH** Terrestrial. Very active, pecks ground vigorously seeking invertebrates. Makes long bounding hops and flicks wings; often rests on walls and rocks, bobbing up and down and flicking tail. Tibetan steppe. **AN** Groundpecker.

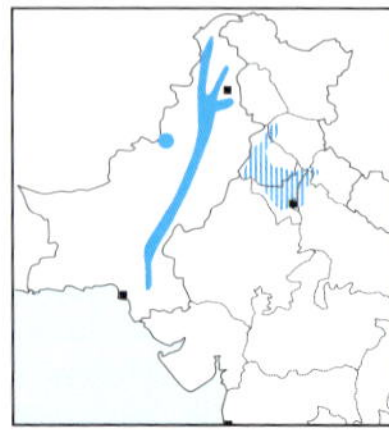

White-crowned Penduline Tit *Remiz coronatus* 10–11cm

Winter visitor to Pakistan and NW India. **ID** Male has blackish mask and variable nape band, whitish crown and collar, and chestnut band on mantle. Nape band absent in fresh plumage; crown largely black in worn plumage. Female and first-year male are duller and paler with pale grey crown and collar, and mask is browner and barely extends across nape Juvenile has brownish-buff upperparts and buffish underparts, and lacks adult's dark mask and chestnut band on mantle; distinctive features are dark cinnamon panel on greater coverts, with buffish-white tips forming wing-bar. **Voice** Thin high-pitched *tsee, tseeuh* or repeated *tee-tsee-tsee*. **HH** Reedbeds, acacia trees in riverine forest and irrigated forest plantations.

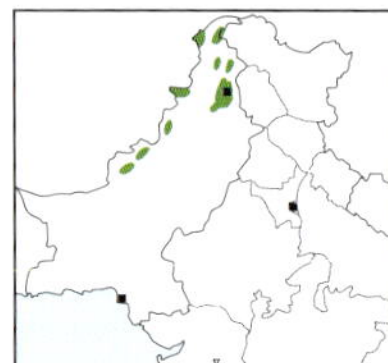

White-cheeked Tit *Aegithalos leucogenys* 11cm

Resident. Balochistan and extreme W Himalayas. **ID** Adult best told by a combination of black bib and throat, narrow dark mask, pronounced white cheeks, cinnamon crown, yellowish iris, and grey-brown mantle. Juvenile has buffish-white throat and streaking on breast; from adult and juvenile White-throated Tit by narrower dark mask and uniform cinnamon-buff forehead and crown (White-throated has white forehead). **Voice** Quiet, high-pitched contact calls; song includes bubbling *ti-ti-tsup*, sunbird-like *sip-sip* and seesawing *we-ti... we-ti*. **HH** Prefers open scrub forest, also tamarisk bushes along rivers.

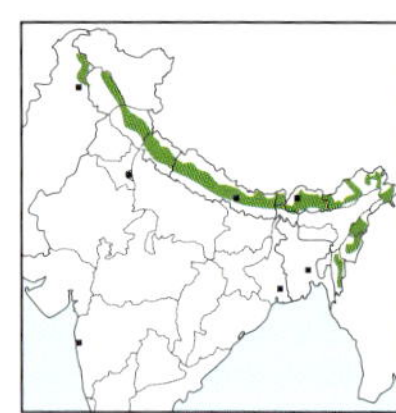

Black-throated Tit *Aegithalos concinnus* 10.5cm

Resident. Himalayas and NE Indian hills. **ID** Adult best told by combination of rufous crown, white chin and black throat, and grey mantle. Juvenile has white throat and indistinct black-spotted breast-band. Juvenile is possibly confusable with White-throated, but lacks white forehead and has narrower and clearly defined black mask, yellow iris, and paler buff breast and belly. In north-east, south of the Brahmaputra River (*manipurensis*), has paler rufous-cinnamon crown, indistinct white supercilium (mixed with black), and white breast-band that separates black throat from chestnut breast and flanks. **Voice** Includes a churring *trrrt trrrt* and a rapid, low-pitched twittering *tir-ir-ir-ir-ir*; alarm is a drier *tzit-tzit-tzit*. **HH** Typical tit. Usually in flocks of same species, often in company with mixed parties of small insectivores. Mainly in middle and lower storeys. Broadleaved or moist mixed broadleaved-coniferous forest, second growth and bushes in open forest.

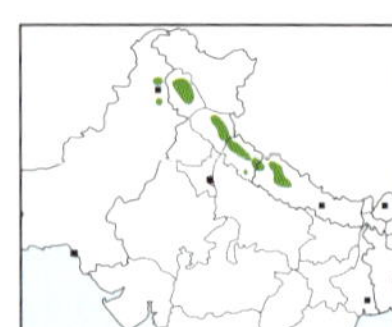

White-throated Tit *Aegithalos niveogularis* 11.5cm

Resident. W Himalayas. **ID** Adult best told by combination of white forehead and forecrown, whitish throat, and dark iris. Diffuse blackish mask and cinnamon underparts, with darker breast-band. Juvenile has dusky throat, more prominent breast-band, and paler lower breast and belly. **Voice** Song a rapid, chattering *tweet-tweet* interspersed with high-pitched *tsi-tsi* notes and short warbles; calls include frequently uttered *t-r-r-r-r-t*. **HH** Bushes in birch/coniferous forest and in deciduous forest, also high-altitude scrub.

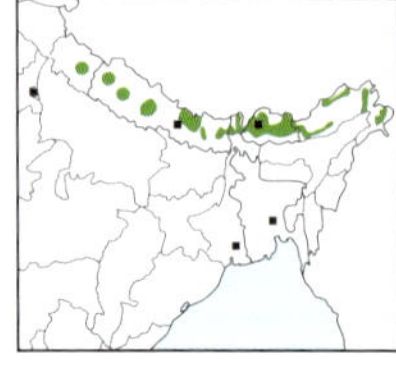

Black-browed Tit *Aegithalos iouschistos* 11cm

Resident. C and E Himalayas. **ID** Adult from other *Aegithalos* by combination of broad black mask, rufous-buff forehead and centre of crown, rufous-buff cheeks and deeper cinnamon-rufous underparts, and silvery-white bib bordered by blackish chin and sides to throat. Iris yellow (brown in White-throated). Juvenile like adult, but crown-stripe, cheeks and underparts paler buff. In Arunachal Pradesh, *A. i. bonvaloti* is paler, with white centre of crown, throat, breast, collar and vent. Dark malar stripe prominent against white of throat. **Voice** Varied feeble purrs, mellow *tup* notes and squeaky notes like Black-throated calls. **HH** Broadleaved, coniferous and broadleaved/coniferous forest. **AN** Rufous-fronted Tit.

ad
Ground Tit
♂
fresh
White-crowned
Penduline Tit
♂
worn
♀
juv
juv
ad
White-cheeked Tit
ad
manipurensis
ad
iredalei
juv
iredalei
Black-throated Tit
juv
ad
White-throated Tit
ad
juv
Black-browed Tit

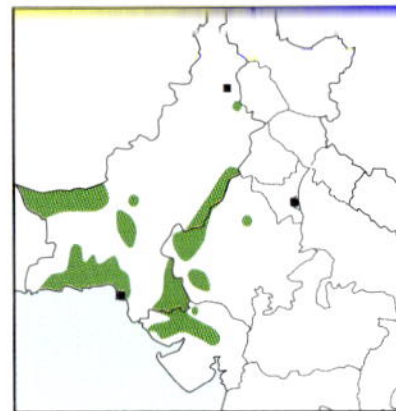

Greater Hoopoe Lark *Alaemon alaudipes* 19–23cm

Resident. Pakistan, W Rajasthan and Kachchh. **ID** Very distinctive, with long slightly downcurved bill and long legs. Prominent white supercilium, black eye-stripe and moustachial, indistinct black malar, black-spotted breast, and sandy grey-brown upperparts. In flight, shows very striking prominent white-and-black pattern to wings, and has black tail with grey centre and white sides. Female smaller than male, with shorter bill and poorly defined head pattern and breast spotting. Juvenile has shorter, straighter bill, with whitish fringes and dark grey subterminal crescents to feathers of upperparts. **Voice** Song a series of flute-like whistles. **HH** Singly or in pairs. Usually escapes by running very quickly, often for several hundred metres; walks slowly when foraging. Extensive areas of desert, especially low sand dunes and barren clay flats.

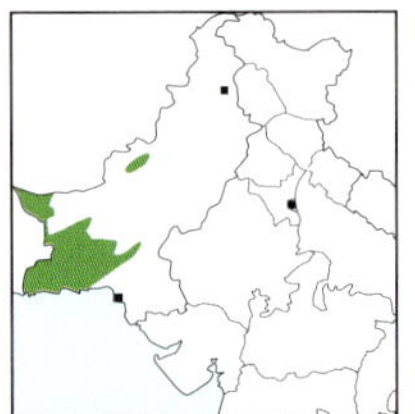

Bar-tailed Lark *Ammomanes cinctura* 14cm

Resident. Balochistan. **ID** Similar to Desert Lark and best told by distinct blackish terminal bar to rufous tail. Also, tertials are orangey-buff (colder grey-brown on Desert) and contrast more markedly with blackish primaries. Further, is smaller and stockier than Desert, with more upright stance, and has shorter and finer bill (mainly pinkish-horn; dark culmen and tip, with pale yellow lower mandible in Desert). Juvenile like adult, although looks scruffier, and paler, more creamy-coloured, with a less distinct tail bar. **Voice** Song comprises quiet fluty notes, with louder, mournful *see-oo-lee* like a creaking door; *twer* call. **HH** Habits like Rufous-tailed. Low stony hills and barren gravelly plains.

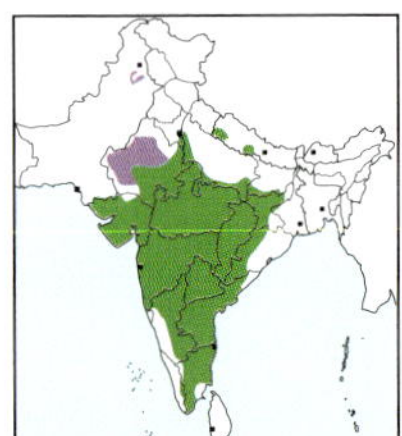

Rufous-tailed Lark *Ammomanes phoenicura* 16cm

Resident. Plains in N Pakistan, S Nepal and India. **ID** From Desert by much darker grey-brown upperparts, rufous-orange underparts and underwing-coverts, and more prominent dark spotting/streaking on throat and breast. Has rufous-orange uppertail-coverts, and rufous-orange tail has broad and well-defined dark terminal bar. Juvenile like adult but less prominently streaked on breast and paler rufous on underparts. **Voice** Song comprises sweet *tee-hoo* phrases with low-pitched husky whistles and chirrups. **HH** In pairs or scattered flocks. Often escapes by running away quickly. Frequently adopts an upright posture on the ground. Cultivation, fallow and ploughed fields, stubbles and open country with scattered bushes and stony outcrops.

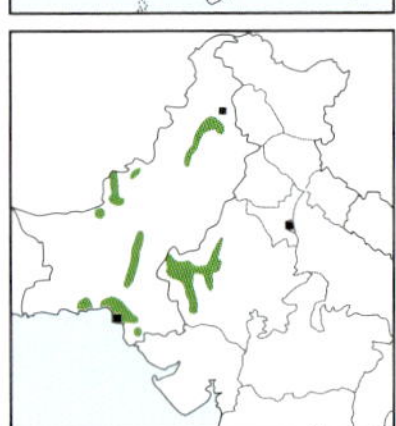

Desert Lark *Ammomanes deserti* 15–17cm

Resident. Pakistan and NW India. **ID** From Rufous-tailed by much paler upperparts, buffish to greyish-white underparts (with weak breast streaking), and grey-brown tail with rufous restricted to sides and without distinct dark tail bar. Bill size and coloration and absence of distinct dark tail bar are best features from similar Bar-tailed (which see for further differences). Juvenile has buff-brown upperparts with faint buff fringes, and tail lacks blackish centre. **Voice** Song comprises well-spaced, rising and falling, flute-like whistles, *pee-pyooh, peef-poof,* interspersed with warbling phrases; *cuu* or *puu* call. **HH** Usually progresses on ground with a fast walk; runs occasionally. Searches busily for food among stones. Well camouflaged on ground, often perches on rocks and walls. Low, very arid rocky foothills, also fallow land in desert-canal cultivation.

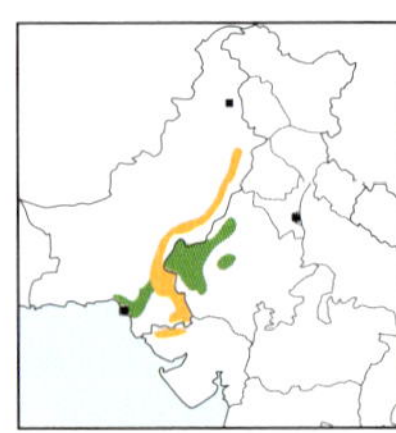

Black-crowned Sparrow Lark *Eremopterix nigriceps* 10–11cm

Resident. Pakistan and NW India. **ID** From Ashy-crowned by brownish-black crown and nape, with whitish forehead; nape white on some, forming collar, with brownish-black patch on upper mantle. Upperparts sandier than Ashy-crowned. Female has more sandy-brown upperparts than female Ashy-crowned, with buffier breast and unstreaked belly. Both sexes show dark underwing-coverts in flight (as Ashy-crowned). **Voice** Song a short, repeated, warbled *dwee-di-ul-twee-e-h* followed by a lower-pitched *d-e-e-e-e-h, de-e-e-e-h* as it parachutes down. **HH** In non-breeding season keeps in flocks. Walks and runs quickly and erratically, and crouches close to ground to feed. Sandy deserts.

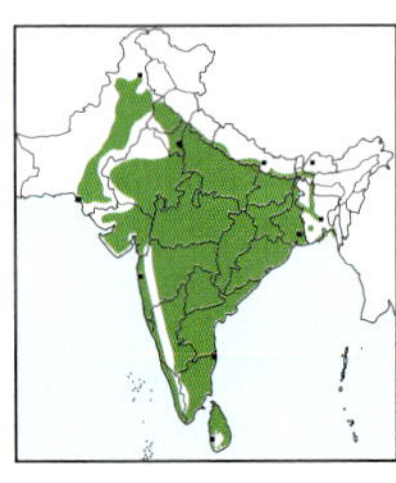

Ashy-crowned Sparrow Lark *Eremopterix griseus* 11–12cm

Widespread resident. **ID** From Black-crowned by grey crown and nape, contrasting with brownish-black lores and supercilium. Female has stout greyish bill, uniform head (lacking dark eye-stripe), rather uniform upperparts (with almost unstreaked mantle and scapulars), indistinct and diffuse breast streaking, and blackish underwing-coverts (latter can be difficult to see in field); underparts lightly washed rufous in S peninsula. From female Black-crowned by darker ear-coverts, browner upperparts and streaked belly. Juvenile has rufous-buff fringes to upperparts. **Voice** Song less varied than Black-crowned, a short flute-like *tweedle-deedle-deedle,* followed by drawn-out whistle *wheeh* in descent. **HH** Habits like Black-crowned, but less gregarious. Cultivation, open dry scrub and dry tidal mudflats.

ad
Greater Hoopoe Lark
ad
Bar-tailed Lark
ad
Rufous-tailed Lark
ad
Desert Lark
♀
Ashy-crowned
Sparrow Lark
Black-crowned
Sparrow Lark
♂
♂

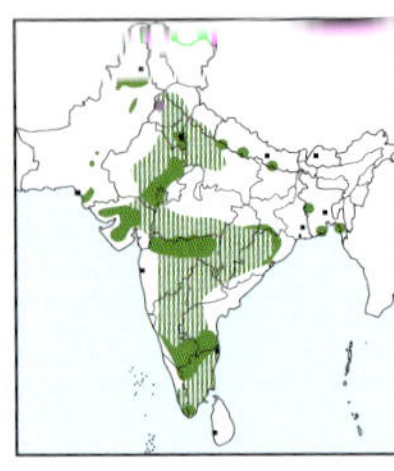

Singing Bushlark *Mirafra cantillans* 13–15cm

Resident. Plains and foothills in Pakistan, India and Bangladesh. **ID** Stocky, stout-billed, broad-winged lark with slight crest. Like other *Mirafra* shows rufous in wing, although this is less prominent than on other species. From Indian and Jerdon's Bushlarks by comparatively uniform brownish-buff ear-coverts, weaker and less extensive spotting on breast, and longer tail with whitish outer tail feathers; upperparts generally more diffusely streaked, and colder grey-brown; throat whiter than rest of underparts, and often shows diffuse brownish- to rufous-buff breast-band. Bill distinctly shorter and stouter than Oriental Skylark and has shorter crest. **Voice** Sweet and full song with much mimicry, more varied than other *Mirafra*. **HH** Distinctive display flight, towering high on flickering wings. Other habits like Indian. Open dry scrub, fallow cultivation and grassland.

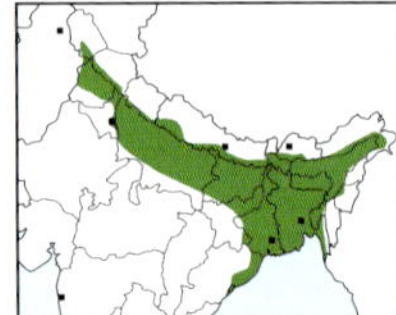

Bengal Bushlark *Mirafra assamica* 16cm

Resident. Mainly plains and Plateaux of N subcontinent. **ID** From Indian and Jerdon's by diffusely streaked brownish-grey upperparts, buffish supercilium, and dirty rufous underparts (with paler throat and greyish flanks). Rufous wing-panel is brighter and more prominent than in other *Mirafra*. **Voice** Song a repeated series of thin, high-pitched disyllabic notes, usually in prolonged song flight; call a series of thin, high-pitched short notes. **HH** Habits like Indian. Open grassy areas, often slightly wet ground.

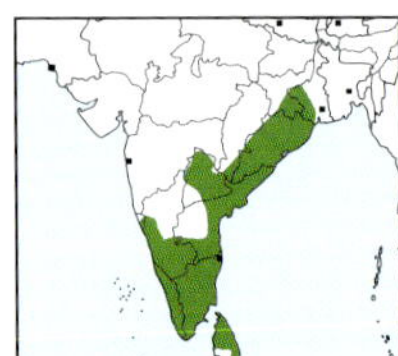

Jerdon's Bushlark *Mirafra affinis* 13.5–15cm

Resident. Peninsular India and Sri Lanka. **ID** Similar to Singing and Indian, but larger and stockier, with larger and longer bill and shorter tail (especially compared to Singing). Has heavily spotted breast, buffish wash to underparts, buffish lores, prominent rufous on wing, rufous-buff outer webs to outer tail feathers, rufous-buff upperparts with prominent dark streaks, and dark-centred coverts and tertials. **Voice** Song a dry metallic rattle from a perch or during short song flight; calls a thin drawn-out whistle and short thin rattle. **HH** Habits like Indian. Dry open areas with bushes and trees.

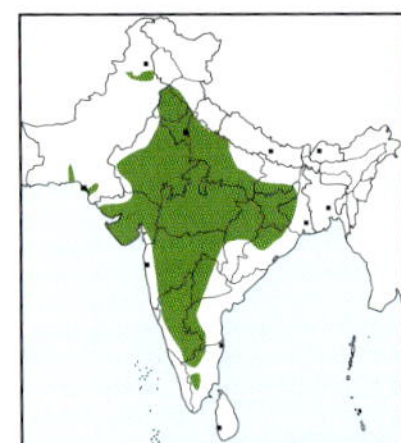

Indian Bushlark *Mirafra erythroptera* 13.5–15cm

Resident. Plains and Plateaux in Pakistan and India; unrecorded in NE subcontinent. **ID** From Singing by more prominent spotting on ear-coverts and malar region (with more pronounced dark border to ear-coverts), more pronounced dark spotting on breast, more extensive rufous on wing (very prominent in flight), and rufous-buff outer webs to outer tail feathers. Upperparts generally more heavily streaked, and warmer sandy-buff to rufous-buff, with rufous cast to crown often apparent; underparts tend to be more uniform whitish to buffish-white than on Singing. From Jerdon's by smaller and shorter bill, smaller size, slightly longer tail, more prominent white supercilium (especially in front of eye), whiter underparts, more rufous on wing, paler centres to tertials and coverts, and shorter hindclaw. *M. e. sindiana* of NW subcontinent has sandy-buff upperparts, whereas the more southerly and easterly *M. e. erythroptera* is more rufous-buff above. **Voice** Song a *tit-tit-tit*, followed by long, drawn-out upward inflected whistles *tsweeeih-tsweeeih-tsweeeih*. **HH** Feeds by running about on ground. Often perches on bushes if disturbed. Stony scrub and fallow cultivation in open plains and Plateaux.

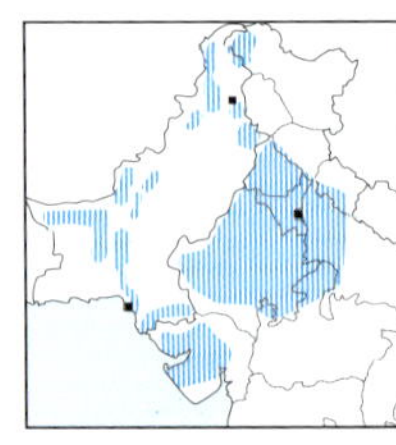

Bimaculated Lark *Melanocorypha bimaculata* 17–18cm

Winter visitor. Pakistan and N and NW India. **ID** Large, stout-billed and stocky lark with long, broad-based wings and comparatively short tail. Prominent white supercilium and eye-ring, black patch on side of breast, dark grey underwing lacking white trailing edge, and whitish tip to tail. **Voice** Guttural *prrp* or *chirp*. **HH** Runs when feeding, picking up insects from ground. Fairly upright stance; hides by squatting and freezing. Semi-desert, paddy stubbles, fallow fields, edges of lakes and dry coastal mudflats.

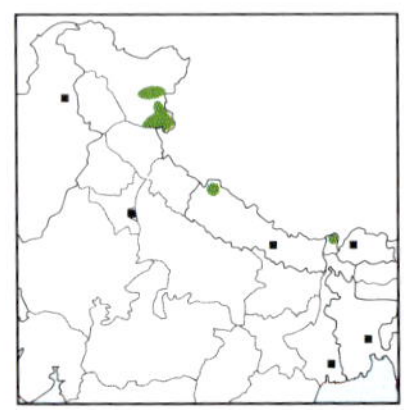

Tibetan Lark *Melanocorypha maxima* 21–22cm

Resident. Ladakh and Sikkim, India, Humla in NW Nepal. **ID** Black patch on side of breast recalls Bimaculated, but is much larger than that species, with rather small-headed, long-necked appearance, and has much longer and thinner bill. Rather uniform head, lacking prominent supercilium or eye-stripe (crown and nape diffusely streaked), and crown, ear-coverts and rump can be distinctly rufous. Breast diffusely spotted and/or washed with grey. White trailing edge to secondaries, and white sides and broad white tip to outer tail feathers. Juvenile has dark blackish-brown upperparts with whitish fringes, and yellowish underparts with diffuse dark spotting on breast. **Voice** Song a disjointed, staccato, hiccupping stutter, with some warbled phrases, rich in mimicry. Call a coarse, rippled *tchui-lip*. **HH** Male sings from top of grassy hump, twitching open his wings excitedly. Marshes around high-altitude lakes and bogs.

ad
Singing Bushlark
ad
Bengal Bushlark
ad
Jerdon's Bushlark
ad
Indian Bushlark
ad
Bimaculated Lark
ad
ad
Tibetan Lark

Horned Lark ***Eremophila alpestris*** **18cm**

Resident. High Himalayas. **ID** Male has black-and-white head pattern, with black mask, 'horns' and band across crown. Also, black breast-band and sandy upperparts with vinous cast to nape. Female similar but mask duller, crown and mantle heavily streaked, and lacks vinous cast to nape. Juvenile has suggestion of dark mask, spotted (with yellowish-buff) upperparts, and underparts have pale yellowish wash. Black mask joins black of breast in *E. a. albigula* of NW subcontinent. **Voice** Song *tsit-tsit-tsit* notes; followed by short warbling phrases and longer whistles; quiet *tsit-tsit* call. **HH** Breeds on stony ground and alpine pastures, winters in fallow cultivation, and on stony and sandy ground.

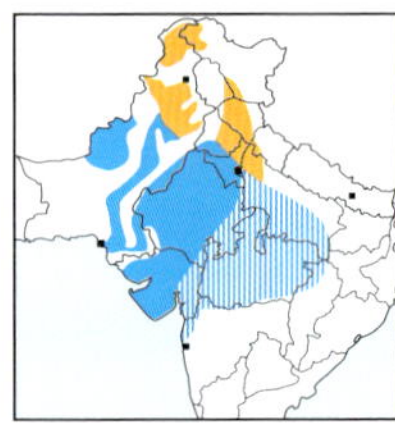

Greater Short-toed Lark ***Calandrella brachydactyla*** **14–15cm**

Widespread winter visitor; unrecorded in Sri Lanka and parts of India. **ID** Stouter bill than Sand Lark, with more prominent supercilium and eye-stripe, and more prominent streaking on upperparts including prominent dark centres to median coverts. Dark breast-side patches often apparent, although breast can be streaked and more like Sand Lark. Tertials reach primary tips on closed wing (falling short of primaries in Sand). See Hume's and Mongolian Short-toed Larks for differences from those species. **Voice** Dry *tchirrup* or *chichirrup* flight call. **HH** Gregarious in winter and passage, running and flying about restlessly. Open stony grassland, fallow cultivation, and semi-desert.

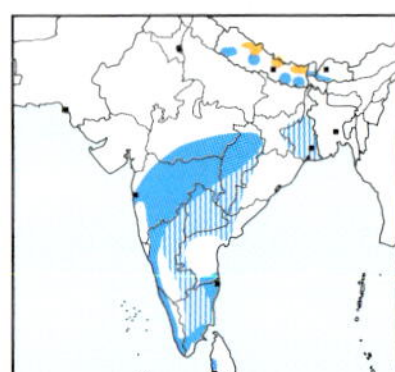

Mongolian Short-toed Lark ***Calandrella dukhunensis*** **14–15cm**

Scarce. Winters mainly in S and E India. **ID** Extremely like Greater Short-toed with variable dark patch on sides of breast, but has warmer upperparts, variable rufous-buff breast-band, and rufous-buff ear-coverts and wash on flanks. Warmer coloration than Sand Lark (and other differences noted above between Greater Short-toed and Sand also apply). See account for Hume's Lark for differences from latter. **Voice** Different from Greater, a fast series of *heu-du-du-du* or single or repeated harsh *cherp*, *chep*, *trup* or *chup*, and repeated *trup*. **HH** As Greater. Open short grass and fallow cultivation. **TN** Until recently treated as conspecific with *C. brachydactyla*.

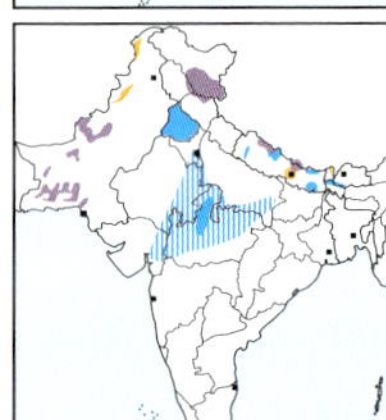

Hume's Lark ***Calandrella acutirostris*** **13–14cm**

Summer visitor to Balochistan and Himalayas; winters mainly in S Nepal and N India. **ID** Greyer and less heavily streaked upperparts than Greater and Mongolian, with pinkish uppertail-coverts. Head pattern usually less pronounced, with rather uniform ear-coverts, dark lores (pale in Greater and Mongolian), and less pronounced supercilium and eye-stripe. Bill yellowish with pronounced dark culmen and tip. As Greater and Mongolian, dark breast-side patch usually apparent, but has greyish-buff breast-band. Flight call also different. **Voice** Full, rolling *tiurr* or *tiyrr* flight call; aerial display song a mellow, variable *tee-leu-ee-lew*. **HH** Breeds in high-altitude semi-desert and in Pakistan in lower rocky hills; winters in fallow cultivation.

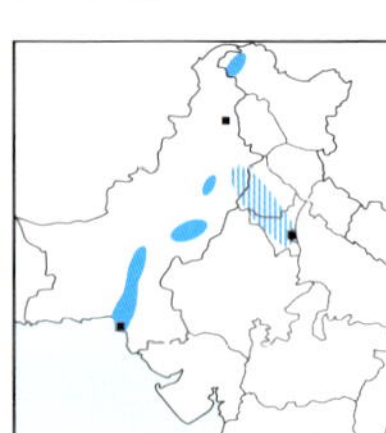

Turkestan Short-toed Lark ***Alaudala heinei*** **13cm**

Winter visitor. Pakistan and India. **ID** From *Calandrella* larks by noticeable extension of primaries beyond tertials on closed wing. Bill shorter and stouter. Has gorget of well-defined streaking on breast (but no dark patches on sides), with streaking on lower throat and flanks, more finely streaked upperparts (pale, sandy-buff in coloration), less striking head pattern with less prominent supercilia (which appear to join over bill) and streaked forehead and ear-coverts. Confusingly very similar to Sand Lark but has stouter/deeper-based bill, is larger and more elongated with longer tail, and upperparts are more warmly coloured and distinctly streaked. **Voice** Calls distinct from Greater; include rattling *prt*, *prrtt*, *prrirrick* or *chirrit*. **HH** Habits like Greater, but less gregarious. Stony foothills. **TN** Formerly treated as conspecific with Lesser Short-toed Lark *A. rufescens* and *Alaudala* was previously subsumed in *Calandrella*. Asian Short-toed Lark *Calandrella cheleensis* no longer accepted as occurring in the region.

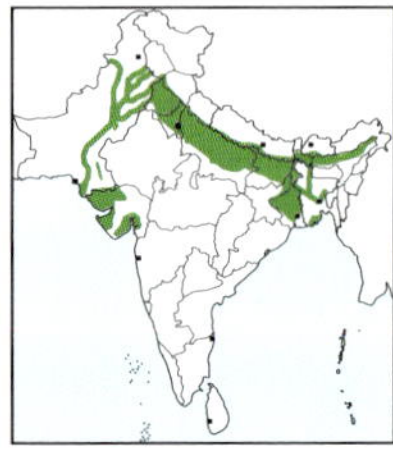

Sand Lark ***Alaudala raytal*** **12cm**

Resident. Widespread in N subcontinent. **ID** Small lark with short tail, rounded wings and distinctive, jerky and fluttering flight. Also has comparatively slender bill, lightly streaked sandy-grey upperparts (streaking most prominent on crown), whitish underparts with fine sparse streaking on breast (but no dark patches on breast-sides). Primaries extend beyond tertials on closed wing which is an additional feature from *Calandrella* larks. Bill shorter and thicker in *A. r. adamsi* in NW of range. See Turkestan Short-toed Lark for differences from latter. **Voice** Rolling, deep and guttural *prr... prr* call; aerial display song a series of short, rapidly delivered and repeated undulating warbling notes. **HH** Runs about in zigzagging spurts. Banks of lakes, rivers and tidal creeks, coastal dunes. **TN** Formerly in *Calandrella*.

♂
albigula
♀
longirostris
♂
longirostris
Horned Lark
ad
with breast
patches
ad
with streaked
breast
Greater
Short-toed Lark
ad
ad
Mongolian
Short-toed Lark
Hume's Lark
ad
ad
Turkestan
Short-toed Lark
Sand Lark

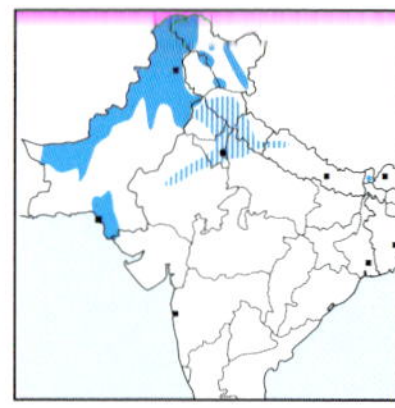

Eurasian Skylark *Alauda arvensis* 17.5–19cm

Winter visitor. Pakistan and N India, Nepal vagrant. **ID** Larger than Oriental Skylark, but very similar to some in plumage, and has slight crest. From that species by longer tail, noticeable extension of primaries beyond tertials on closed wing (tertials almost reach primary tips on Oriental), white outer tail feathers (more buffish on Oriental), pronounced whitish trailing edge to secondaries, and proportionately shorter and stouter bill. Upperparts paler sandy-brown (than most subspecies of Oriental) and underparts whiter. Lacks rufous cast to ear-coverts and the (indistinct) rufous panel on wing of Oriental. **Voice** Calls include a grating *chirriup* and liquid *trruwee*. **HH** Habits as Oriental. Cultivation and grassland.

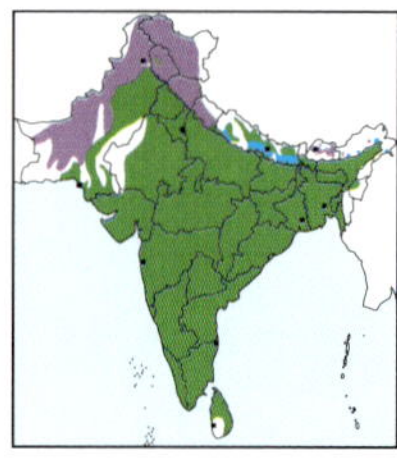

Oriental Skylark *Alauda gulgula* 15.5–18cm

Widespread resident and winter visitor. **ID** Very variable in colour and prominence of streaking on upperparts and underparts. See Eurasian for differences from that species. Bill much finer than in bushlarks. Six races in region, varying from *A. g. inconspicua* of NW and N subcontinent, which has sandy-buff base colour to upperparts, and whitish underparts with rufous-buff wash on breast, to *A. g. australis* of W peninsula and Sri Lanka, which has warmer rufous-buff base colour to more heavily streaked upperparts, and base colour of underparts is a uniform rufous-buff. **Voice** Aerial flight song comprises bubbling warbles and shorter whistles with much variation; call a grating, throaty *bazz, bazz*. **HH** In pairs in breeding season, often in flocks in winter. Walks about methodically seeking insects and seeds from ground and on plants. Crouches and freezes to escape notice. Perches on stone walls, low stumps, and stones. During song flight male sings for several minutes while circling, then nearly closes his wings and descends to the ground in a steep dive. Grassland, cultivation and coastal mudflats.

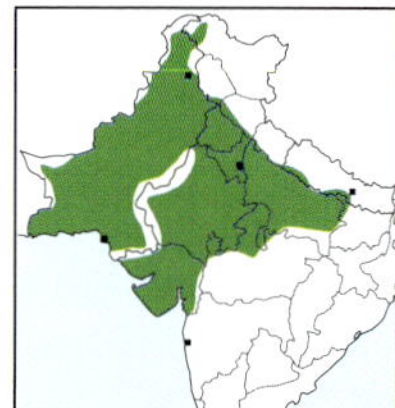

Crested Lark *Galerida cristata* 17–19cm

Resident. Widespread in N subcontinent. **ID** From Oriental Skylark by larger size and erect crest, broader rounded wings, rufous-buff outer tail feathers and underwing, and different calls and song. Larger and paler than more southerly Malabar Lark, and much less heavily streaked on upperparts and breast. *G. c. magna* of NW Pakistan is warmer, more sandy-coloured above than greyer eastern subspecies. **Voice** Song a long, varied combination of whistles, tremolos, twitters and double notes, rather soft and melancholic, with much mimicry, slower and clearer than Oriental Skylark; calls include a fluty *du-ee* and similar *tuee-tuu-teeooo*. **HH** Habits as Oriental. Desert, semi-desert, dry cultivation and coastal mudflats.

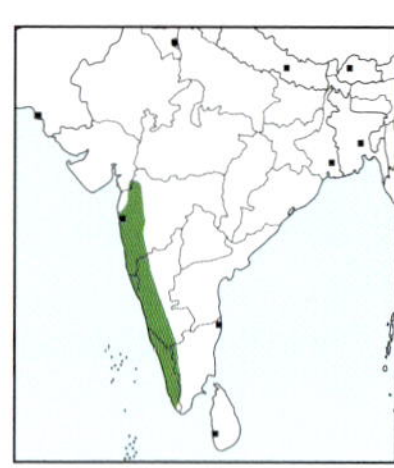

Malabar Lark *Galerida malabarica* 16cm

Resident. Plains and hills in W peninsular India. **ID** Smaller than Crested, with stouter bill, darker and more rufescent upperparts with much stronger blackish streaking, heavily spotted breast (washed buff or rufous-buff) and pale rufous outer tail feathers and underwing-coverts. From Tawny Lark by larger size, much longer bill, dark rear border to ear-coverts (not shown), paler but more heavily streaked breast, streaked rump, and buffish-white belly and flanks. From *australis* subspecies of Oriental Skylark by stouter bill, longer crest, larger breast streaking, pale rufous (rather than buffish-white) outer tail feathers, and different call. **Voice** Song comprises melancholy and fluty notes, very similar to Crested; call a pleasant undulating *chew-chew-you*. **HH** Habits as Oriental. Cultivation, grass-covered hills, and open scrub.

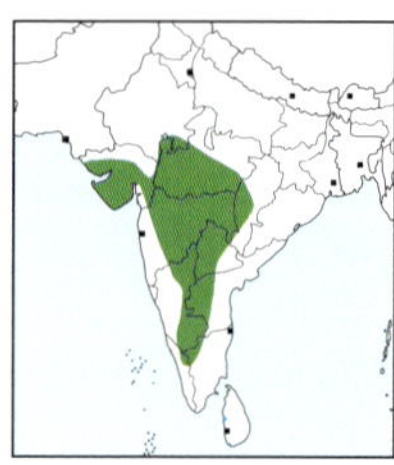

Tawny Lark *Galerida deva* 14cm

Resident. Mainly C India. Small lark with prominent upstanding crest. **ID** From Malabar by smaller size, stouter bill, pale rufous underparts (lacking whitish belly), finer and less extensive streaking on breast (confined to narrow band across upper breast, and almost lacking on some), and rather uniform pale rufous rump. Possibly confusable with *australis* subspecies of Oriental Skylark, but has stouter bill, longer crest, less extensive breast streaking, and pale rufous (rather than buffish-white) outer tail feathers. **Voice** Song is like Singing Bushlark, a spirited melodious, stumbling song very rich in mimicry; calls like Crested. **HH** Habits like Crested, except song flight, which is very similar to Singing Bushlark. Stony, scrubby areas and dry cultivation. **AN** Sykes's Lark.

ad
Eurasian Skylark
ad
australis
Oriental Skylark
ad
inconspicua
ad
Crested Lark
ad
Malabar Lark
ad
Tawny Lark

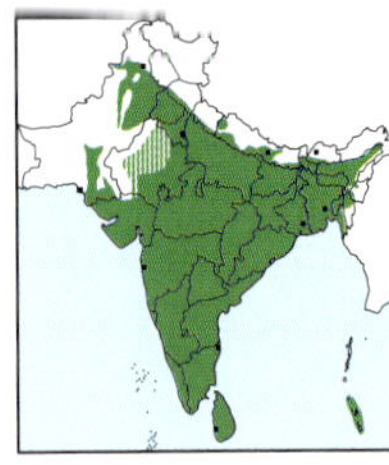

Zitting Cisticola *Cisticola juncidis* 10cm

Widespread resident. **ID** Adult breeding has diffusely streaked grey brown crown, and often rather distinct buff or rufous rump. Adult non-breeding has longer tail (except peninsular *C. j. salimalii*), more heavily streaked upperparts and often less distinct rump; some have brighter rufous-buff upperparts but lack the more clearly defined rufous nape of Golden-headed Cisticola. First-winter has sulphur-yellow wash to underparts and less heavily streaked upperparts. In Sri Lanka wet zone, *C. j. omalurus* is larger, with heavier bill, and has more faintly streaked and dusky upperparts. See Golden-headed for differences from that species. **Voice** Repeated *pip* in display flight; call a single or repeated *plit*. **HH** Distinctive display: circles widely over its territory, with bouncing flight, beats wings rapidly as it rises, drops a little, then rises again, while repeating a short monotonous call. Fields and grassland.

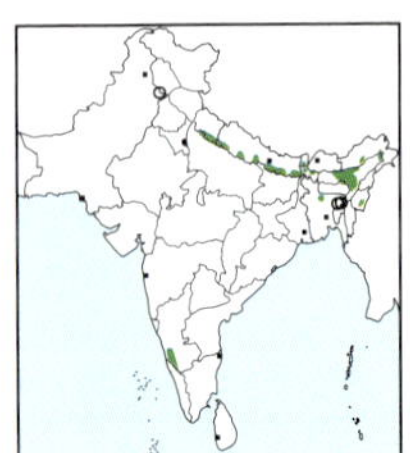

Golden-headed Cisticola *Cisticola exilis* 10cm

Resident. Terai, NE and S Indian hills, and Bangladesh. **ID** In all plumages from Zitting by blacker tail with narrow buffish or greyish tips (broader white tips in Zitting), unstreaked rufous nape and sides of neck, and rufous (rather than whitish) supercilium. Breeding male *C. e. erythrocephala* (Western Ghats) has unstreaked rufous crown and nape, and rufous-buff underparts (often forming breast-band). Breeding male *C. e. tytleri* (north and north-east) has unstreaked creamy-white crown and underparts, rufous-brown wash to nape and sides of neck, and unstreaked olive-grey rump. Female and non-breeding male of both subspecies have heavily streaked crown and mantle, and more closely resemble Zitting. Tail much longer in non-breeding plumage. First-winter has yellow wash to underparts. **Voice** Song 1–2 jolly doubled notes introduced by buzzy wheeze: *bzzeeee... joo-ee*; the wheeze often repeated separately. **HH** Habits like Zitting but display flight is faster, less jerky and ends in a nose-dive. Tall grassland; scrubby hillsides in S India. **AN** Bright-capped Cisticola.

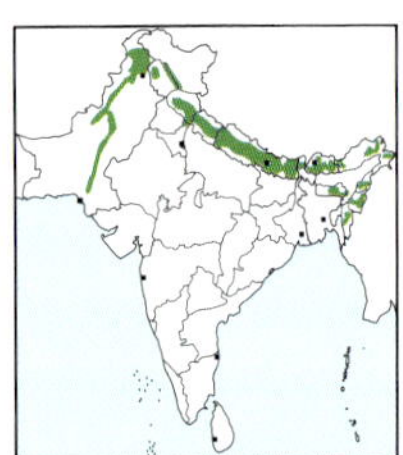

Himalayan Prinia *Prinia crinigera* 16cm

Resident. Himalayas, hills of Pakistan and NE India. **ID** Large, long-tailed, hill-dwelling prinia with stout bill. Adult breeding has dark grey-brown (and very worn) upperparts with ill-defined blackish streaking, dark lores, buffish-white underparts with variable dark grey mottling, narrow rufous-brown edges to remiges, and black bill. Adult non-breeding has rufous-brown (and fresh) upperparts with prominent dark brown streaking, buff lores and eye-ring, warm buff underparts, especially flanks, broad rufous-brown fringes to remiges, and orange-tinged lower mandible; undertail has rufous-buff tips and dark subterminal bands. Female smaller with less marked seasonal variation than male. Juvenile has olive-brown upperparts, with indistinct streaking (mainly on crown), and warm buff or pale yellowish underparts. **Voice** Monotonous wheezy *chitzereet-chitzereet-chitzereet* song; *tchak-tchak* call. **HH** Skulking. In breeding season, males sing frequently from exposed perch. Scrubby hillsides, and long grass in open forest. **AN** Striated Prinia.

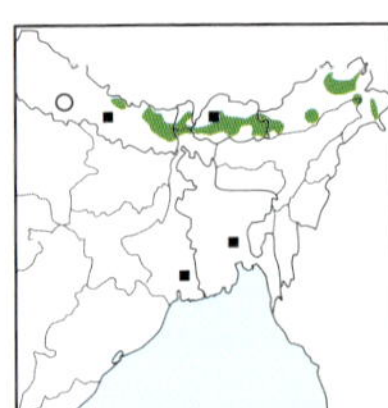

Black-throated Prinia *Prinia atrogularis* 17cm

Resident. E Himalayas. **ID** Large, long- and narrow-tailed, hill-dwelling prinia. Adult breeding has black throat and breast, white moustachial stripe and breast spotting, greyish head (lacking or with indistinct white supercilium) and breast-sides, greyish olive-brown upperparts and tail, olive-buff panel on wing and olive-buff flanks. Adult non-breeding has white supercilium, buff underparts with variable dark mottling/streaking on sides of throat and breast (sometimes covering whole throat and breast), and rufous-brown edges to remiges. From Himalayan by white supercilium contrasting with dark lores, unstreaked upperparts (can appear diffusely streaked, especially on lower back), and longer and finer bill. Juvenile is like non-breeding adult, but has yellowish wash on underparts and darker olive breast-band. **Voice** Song a series of a repeated complex note, almost mechanical and vehemently delivered *szelik...szelik...szelik...*; calls include soft *pit*. **HH** Scrub and grass hillsides, long grass in open pine forests, bushes at cultivation edges.

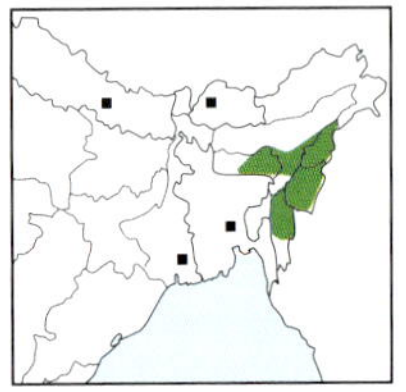

Rufous-crowned Prinia *Prinia khasiana* 16–18cm

Resident. NE Indian hills. **ID** Large, long-tailed, hill-dwelling prinia. Adult breeding is superficially like Black-throated, but has rufous crown, less extensive black on breast, rufous-brown upperparts, and warmer buff flanks. Lacks black throat in non-breeding plumage. White supercilium, unstreaked rufous-brown upperparts, and buff underparts with variable dark mottling/ streaking on sides of throat and breast help separate non-breeding plumage from Himalayan. **Voice** Song like Black-throated. Calls poorly described. **HH** Open grassy hillsides with scattered bushes, open pine forest, bushes in cultivation. **TN** Formerly treated as conspecific with *P. atrogularis*.

br
non-br
Zitting
Cisticola
♂ br
tytleri
non-br
tytleri
Golden-headed
Cisticola
♂ br
erythrocephala
non-br
erythrocephala
non-br
br
non-br
non-br
Himalayan
Prinia
br
br
Black-throated
Prinia
Rufous-crowned
Prinia

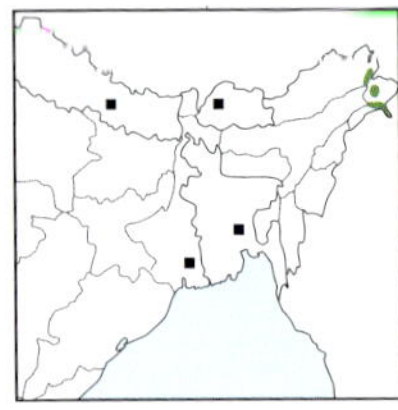

Hill Prinia *Prinia superciliaris* 18cm

Resident. NE Arunachal. Formerly E Naga hills. **ID** Adult has grey crown and nape merging into browner upperparts, prominent white supercilium contrasting with grey ear-coverts, variable (often bold) black streaking on breast, and cinnamon flanks. Most likely to be confused with non-breeding Black-throated but has more prominent white supercilium, clean white throat, and streaking on breast is broader and more clearly defined. **Voice** Song a sharp, clear and strident disyllabic *schlee-ulp* or *cho-ee*, or slower, up- and then downslurred *schleeu, schleeu*..., clearer and more musical than Black-throated; upturned *chissip* call. **HH** Habits like Himalayan. Scrubby clearings, cultivated and grassy areas, undergrowth in open, dry woodland.

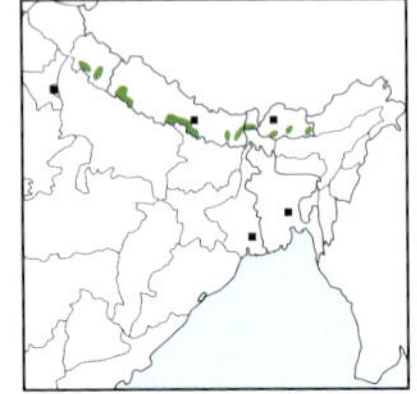

Grey-crowned Prinia *Prinia cinereocapilla* 11cm

Resident. Himalayan foothiils from E Himachal to Bhutan. **ID** Superficially resembles a small, short-tailed Ashy Prinia. Bill fine and black in all plumages. In non-breeding plumage, forehead and supercilium orange-buff, latter extends noticeably (and becomes whiter) beyond eye. Shows noticeable contrast between purer blue-grey crown and more rufescent-brown nape and mantle compared with Ashy. Supercilium absent in breeding plumage and crown and ear-coverts are uniform slate-grey. Juvenile undescribed. **Voice** Song a squeezed-out *cheeeeeeeesum-zip-zip-zip*; rapid repeated *tzit* call. **HH** Forages low in bushes. Very active. Favours *Themeda* grassland close to forest, also bushes in grassland, second growth. Globally threatened.

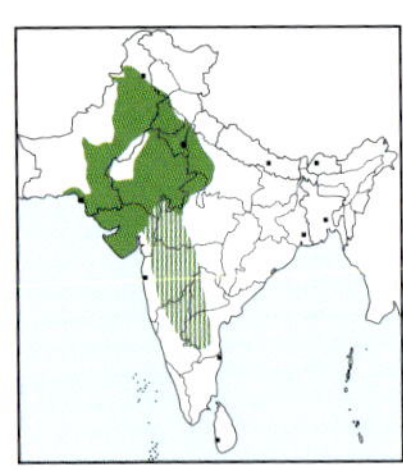

Rufous-fronted Prinia *Prinia buchanani* 12cm

Resident. Pakistan and N and C India. **ID** Adult has rufous-brown forehead and crown, and broad white tips to all but central tail feathers (very prominent in flight). Underparts lack buff wash, which is often apparent on Plain, and has pale yellowish lower mandible (all black in breeding Plain). In worn plumage, crown becomes greyer-brown and almost concolorous with mantle. Juvenile has uniform pale rufous-brown upperparts (lacking distinct rufous crown) and buffier underparts; bold white tail tips best feature. **Voice** Song begins with stuttering series of short notes (diagnostic for this species), followed by strongly ascending *chid-le-weeest* and repeated *chid-le-ee*. Calls include *chirrup* and high-pitched descending trill. **HH** Mainly terrestrial. Mainly dry open stony slopes with thorn scrub, also dry juniper and *Pinus gerardiana* forest and *Acacia* scrub.

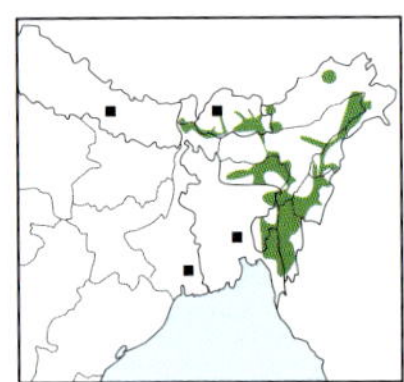

Rufescent Prinia *Prinia rufescens* 11–12cm

Resident. E Himalayas, hills of NE and E India and Bangladesh. **ID** Adult breeding has grey crown and ear-coverts, white supercilium and black bill. Adult non-breeding from Grey-breasted by larger and stouter bill (with pale base to lower mandible), more rufescent upperparts and tail (with buffish or grey, rather than white, tips), stronger rufous wash on flanks, and nasal buzzing call. Juvenile has greyish-olive cast to crown, yellowish on underparts. **Voice** Song a rhythmic *chewp-chewp-chewp-chewp*; calls include buzzy *peez-eez-eez-eez*. **HH** Tall grassland, grass under deciduous forest, bushes around terraced cultivation, open wooded areas, second growth and forest edges.

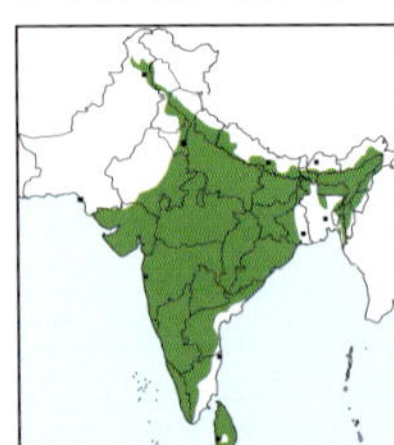

Grey-breasted Prinia *Prinia hodgsonii* 10–12cm

Widespread resident. **ID** Adult breeding has grey 'cap' and upperparts, and variable greyish breast-band (poorly defined in north and north-east). Adult non-breeding (except Sri Lanka) has white supercilium and dark lores, olive-brown upperparts with rufescent cast, and white to greyish underparts. *P. h. pectoralis* (Sri Lanka) has grey upperparts and breast all year. See Rufescent Prinia for differences from that species. **Voice** Song a rhythmic undulating *tirr-irr-irr-irr*; laughing, high-pitched *hee-hee-hee-hee* call. **HH** Gregarious in winter. Bushes at forest edges, in clearings, around cultivation and in villages and second growth.

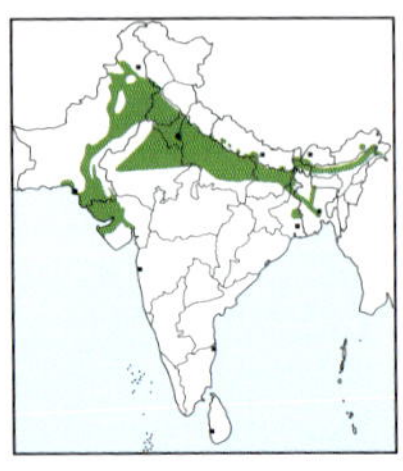

Delicate Prinia *Prinia lepida* 10–12cm

Resident. Lowlands in N subcontinent. **ID** Small prinia with streaked sandy grey-brown upperparts, white underparts, and cross-barred tail. Much smaller, with finer bill than Himalayan, with paler sandy upperparts and whiter underparts. *P. l. stevensi* (Brahmaputra and lower Ganges) has darker and greyer upperparts and duller greyish-white underparts. *P. l. stevensi* is very similar in coloration to Swamp Babbler, and occurs in similar habitat, but is much smaller with finer bill, has prominent pale fringes to wing-coverts and remiges, and has slimmer tail (with white tips and dark subterminal spots). **Voice** Fast, rhythmic wheezy warbling song *ze-r witze-r wit*; nasal buzzing *bzreep* call. **HH** Often perches in open on tops of bushes or reeds. Medium to short *Saccharum* grassland and bushes, especially by wetlands. **TN** Formerly treated as conspecific with Graceful Prinia *P. gracilis*.

br
br
Grey-crowned Prinia
non-br
Hill Prinia
ad
juv
br
Rufous-fronted Prinia
br
rufula
non-br
rufula
non-br
Grey-breasted Prinia
non-br
hodgsonii
Rufescent Prinia
♂
pectoralis
ad
lepida
♀
pectoralis
Delicate Prinia

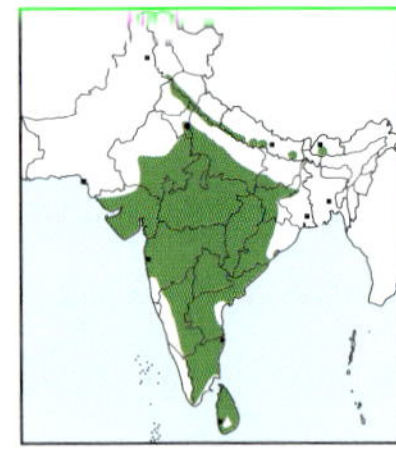

Jungle Prinia *Prinia sylvatica* 14–16cm

Widespread in lowlands and foothills; unrecorded in Pakistan. **ID** Larger-bodied and stouter-billed than Plain Prinia, with sturdier-looking tail; supercilium usually less distinct than Plain (diagnostic when absent). Adult breeding has grey upperparts, largely white outer rectrices and black bill. Adult non-breeding has longer tail with buffish outer tips, orange-brown lower bill, and is more rufescent-brown above. Female smaller with less seasonal variation than male. Juvenile has more olive-brown upperparts, with more rufescent wings, and can have yellowish wash on underparts. *P. s. valida* (Sri Lanka) has darker and greyer upperparts, longer and stouter all-black bill, lacks (or has only very indistinct supercilium), and shows no seasonal variation (e.g. lacking any white in tail). Larger size and bill, lack of supercilium above and behind eye, and more unform wings are best distinctions from Sri Lankan race of Plain Prinia. **Voice** Loud, pulsing song *zee-chu* repeated metronomically. **HH** Rather less active than small prinias. Flits about bushes and grass; occasionally pops to top of vegetation and then dives down again. Sings from exposed perch. Scrub and tall grass in open dry areas.

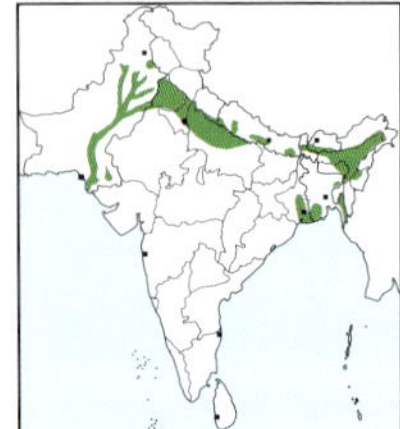

Yellow-bellied Prinia *Prinia flaviventris* 12–14cm

Resident. Widespread in N subcontinent. **ID** Adult breeding has slate-grey crown and ear-coverts, white throat and breast, dark olive-green upperparts, and yellowish belly and vent. Whitish supercilium in non-breeding plumage. Juvenile has yellowish olive-brown upperparts (no blue-grey on head) and uniform pale yellow underparts. *P. f. sindiana* (north-west) paler on belly and flanks than *P. f. flaviventris* (north-east). **Voice** Song a sharp *chirp* followed by a five-note trill. **HH** Very active; forages in tall grass, occasionally clambering to the top; sometimes feeds on ground. Tall grass by wetlands.

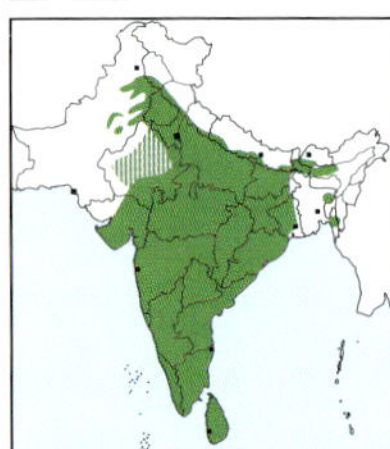

Ashy Prinia *Prinia socialis* 12–13cm

Widespread resident. **ID** Slate-grey crown and ear-coverts, red eye, slate-grey (breeding) or rufous-brown (non-breeding) mantle, orange-buff wash on underparts, and prominent black subterminal marks (and whitish tips) to tail feathers. White supercilium in non-breeding plumage. Juvenile has greenish upperparts and buffish-yellow underparts. *P. s. inglisi* (north-east) and *P. s. brevicauda* (Sri Lanka) have grey upperparts all year. *P. s. brevicauda* has short tail, and often whiter underparts; birds with white underparts can be confused with Grey-breasted but have blue-grey cast to upperparts and never show greyish breast-band. **Voice** Song a wheezy *jimmy-jimmy-jimmy*. **HH** In pairs in breeding season, otherwise solitary. Very lively. Forages low down in grass and bushes and on ground. Tall grass and scrub at cultivation edges, rivers and forest, and open second growth.

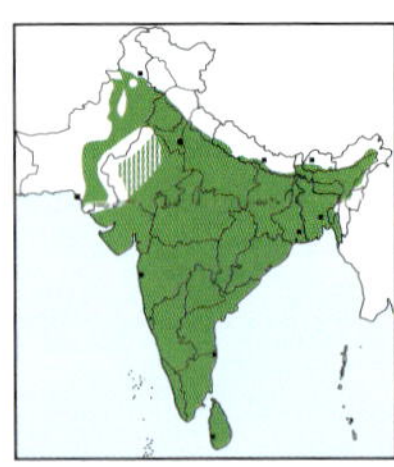

Plain Prinia *Prinia inornata* 11cm

Widespread resident. **ID** Adult breeding has black bill, grey-brown upperparts and whitish underparts, with largely white outermost rectrices. Adult non-breeding has longer tail, pale base to lower mandible, warm brown upperparts, more rufescent wings and tail, buff tips and dark subterminal marks to rectrices, and warm buff wash to underparts. Juvenile more rufescent. *P. i. insularis* (Sri Lanka) is larger-billed, has darker and greyer upperparts (with little seasonal variation), and tail lacks any white. See Jungle Prinia for differences from that species. **Voice** Song a rapid, wheezy trill, *tlick tlick tlick*. **HH** In pairs or small parties, depending on season. Feeds actively in low vegetation. Tall crops, reeds, grassland, scrub and tall grass, and mangroves.

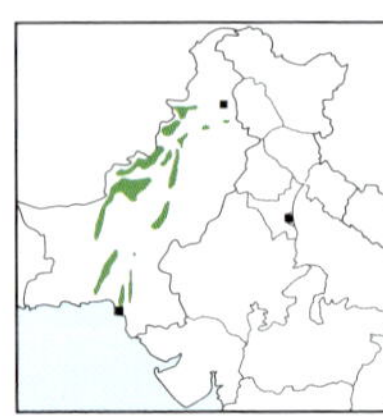

Scrub Warbler *Scotocerca inquieta* 10cm

Resident. Pakistan hills. **ID** Superficially resembles Delicate Prinia, but stockier, with bigger head, and blunter, broader and darker tail. Main differences are broad vinous-buff supercilium, blackish lores and eye-stripe, fine dark streaking on white throat, vinous-buff ear-coverts, breast-sides and flanks, greyish cast to upperparts, with boldly streaked crown (and ill-defined streaking on mantle), and dark undertail (except white tips). **Voice** Song a series of trilled and musical notes and phrases like a tit's, *tsi-tsi-tsi-tsi-tsi-hue*, often interspersed with call notes; calls include clear *che-wee* or *te-hee*. **HH** In pairs or small parties. Rather wren-like and very active. Mainly terrestrial. Rummages in plant debris under bushes, often in open among stones, also in tops of bushes and small trees. Arid scrub and grassland, dry stony and scrubby slopes. Confined to natural vegetation; avoids cultivated areas. **AN** Streaked Scrub Warbler.

non-br
gangetica
br
gangetica
br
flaviventris
Yellow-bellied
Prinia
Jungle Prinia
non-br
flaviventris
br
brevicauda
juv
flaviventris
br
stewarti
non-br
stewarti
br
franklinii
non-br
inornata
Ashy Prinia
ad
br
inornata
Plain Prinia
Scrub Warbler

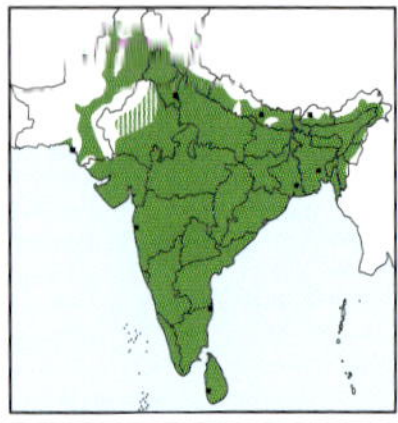

Common Tailorbird *Orthotomus sutorius* 10–14cm

Widespread resident. **ID** Has long (slightly downcurved) pale bill, rufous forehead and forecrown, greenish upperparts, and dull whitish or buffish underparts. Breeding male has elongated central tail feathers. Juvenile lacks rufous on forecrown. Subspecies *sutorius* in Sri Lanka has darker and greener upperparts and more extensive rufous cap (lacking whitish supercilium). **Voice** Song a loud *pitchik-pitchik-pitchik*; calls include loud, quick-repeated *pit-pit-pit* and quick *cheep-cheep*. **HH** Bushes in gardens, cultivation edges and forest edges.

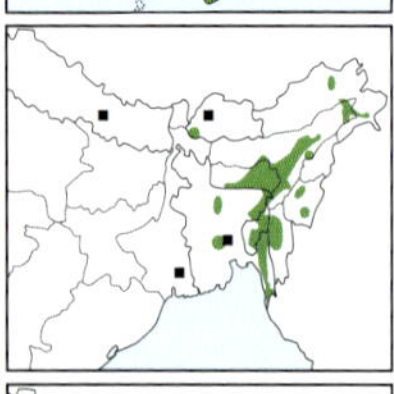

Dark-necked Tailorbird *Orthotomus atrogularis* 11–12cm

Resident. E Himalayas, NE India and Bangladesh. **ID** From Common by rufous hindcrown, lack of whitish supercilium, yellow bend of wing, yellow flanks and undertail-coverts, brighter green upperparts, and different call. Never has elongated central tail feathers. Male has blackish lower throat and sides of breast (note Common, when calling or singing, reveals dark bases to neck feathers and can look similar). Juvenile lacks rufous on forecrown. **Voice** Song a rather high, agitated, repeated *pirrah*; calls consist of nasal, staccato, high-pitched *kri-i-i-l*, a short *tew* and dry *prrp-prrp*. **HH** Dense scrub, bamboo thickets and evergreen forest edges.

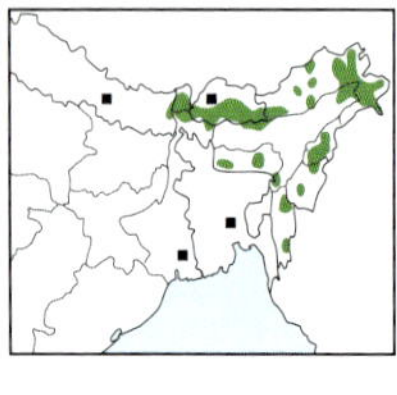

Mountain Tailorbird *Phyllergates cucullatus* 10–12cm

Resident. E Himalayas and NE India. Vagrant Bangladesh. **ID** From other tailorbirds by brighter orange-rufous forecrown, yellowish supercilium contrasting with dark grey eye-stripe, grey ear-coverts, grey nape and sides of breast, and bright yellow belly and undertail-coverts. Confusable with Broad-billed Warbler, but has long (slender) bill, less extensive rufous on crown, grey nape, yellowish supercilium, and whiter throat. Juvenile has olive-green crown and nape (concolorous with mantle), and diffuse eye-stripe. **Voice** Song a thin, high-pitched and melodious whistle of 4–6 notes, up and down the scale; dry *trrit* call. **HH** Evergreen forest and second growth. **TN** Formerly placed in *Orthotomus*.

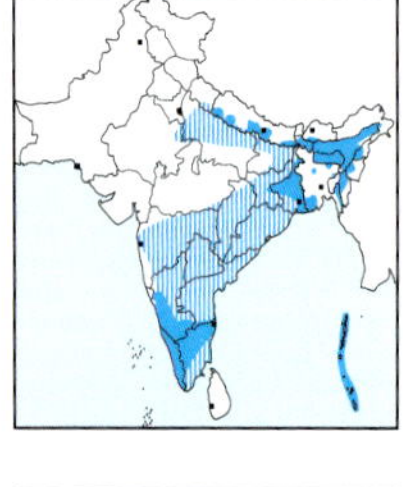

Thick-billed Warbler *Arundinax aedon* 18–21cm

Widespread winter visitor; unrecorded in Pakistan and Sri Lanka. **ID** From large *Acrocephalus* by short, stout bill (with striking pale lower mandible but no dark tip), rounded head (with crown feathers often raised), and 'plain-faced' appearance (pale lores and lacks prominent supercilium and any suggestion of a darker eye-stripe). Tail appears long and graduated, and wings short. Upperparts have rufous suffusion, especially to fringes of remiges, rump and uppertail-coverts (never apparent on Clamorous Reed Warbler) and is warmer buff on breast and flanks. Plumage varies however, and some are more olive-brown above and whiter below. **Voice** Hard *shak*, tongue-clicking *tuc* and loud chattering calls. **HH** Tall grass and scrub, reeds and bushes at forest edges. **TN** Formerly placed in *Phragamaticola*.

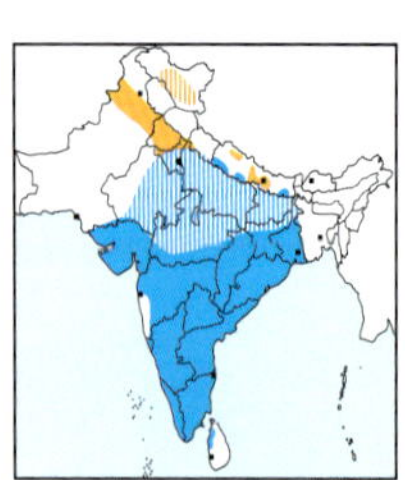

Booted Warbler *Iduna caligata* 11–12.5cm

Widespread in winter; unrecorded in parts of north-east. **ID** Small, with sandy-brown to grey-brown upperparts and off-white underparts. Has square-ended tail and short undertail-coverts. Often shows faint whitish edges and tip to tail and fringes to tertials. Supercilium usually reasonably distinct and square-ended behind eye, and can be bordered above by a diffuse dark line. Typically, shorter-tailed, and shorter- and finer-billed, than Sykes's, with more prominent dark tip to lower mandible. Usually has more prominent supercilium, extending noticeably behind eye, and upperparts are warmer brown. Typically appears more *Phylloscopus*-like, owing to shorter bill, and more frequently feeds on ground. Some can be longer-billed and -tailed making field identification very problematic. Possibly confusable with Common Chiffchaff, but lacks any greenish or olive tones, and has pale base to lower mandible and pale legs. **Voice** Hard *chur chur* call. **HH** Scrub and bushes in dry habitats, favours acacias.

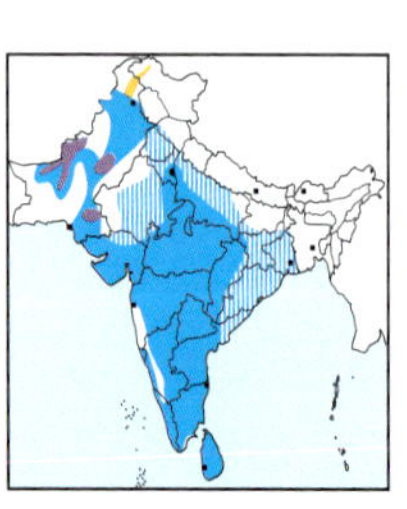

Sykes's Warbler *Iduna rama* 11.5–13cm

Breeds locally in Pakistan; winters widely in the subcontinent. **ID** Typically longer-tailed and longer-billed than Booted, lacking dark tip to lower mandible. Greyer and whiter than Booted (which is more rufescent above and buffier below in fresh plumage) but can be very similar. Supercilium is less prominent particularly behind eye, and lores pale. Tertials more uniform with less distinct darker centres and paler fringes. More arboreal in habits. Confusable with larger and more robust Blyth's Reed, but has paler greyish-brown upperparts, pale sides to tail and edges to remiges, longer-looking, square-ended tail, and shorter undertail- and uppertail-coverts. **Voice** Song a fast mixture of scratchy and clearer notes; calls include a dry clicking *chek* and fuller *tslek*. **HH** Breeds in desert and semi-desert with scattered vegetation, especially tamarisks. Winters in open semi-desert with acacia.

♀
guzuratus
♂
guzuratus
♂
sutorius
Common
Tailorbird
♂
Dark-necked
Tailorbird
♀
Mountain Tailorbird
ad
juv
Thick-billed
Warbler
ad
ad worn
ad fresh
1st winter
Booted
Warbler
ad worn
ad fresh
Sykes's
Warbler
1st winter

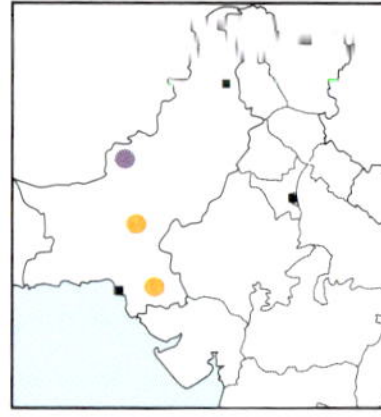

Upcher's Warbler *Hippolais languida* 14–15cm

Summer visitor to Balochistan. **ID** From Sykes's by larger size and heavier appearance, with broader and fuller tail and longer primary projection beyond tertials. Bill stronger looking. Upperparts greyer, and wings and tail often look noticeably darker than rest of upperparts. Supercilium short and barely extends beyond eye. On breeding grounds has distinctive habit of bobbing (often fanned) tail, on passage flicks tail downwards. From Blyth's Reed by paler and greyer upperparts, shorter extension of undertail-coverts, squarer-ended and darker tail, white edges and tips to outer rectrices, blacker remiges and wing-coverts with prominent pale fringes in fresh plumage (especially apparent on tertials, often forming pale panel on secondaries), and browner legs and feet. **Voice** Song a mix of nasal, hard notes and clear, more melodious ones, very variable, with much mimicry; loud deep *chuk* call. **HH** Much less skulking than Blyth's Reed; frequently perches in open. Open bushy hillsides.

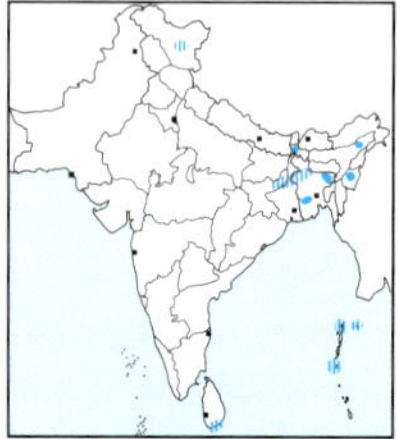

Black-browed Reed Warbler *Acrocephalus bistrigiceps* 13.5–14cm

Winter visitor. Mainly NE India and Bangladesh. Vagrant: Nepal. **ID** Unstreaked upperparts. From Paddyfield by broader and more clear-cut supercilium and more pronounced blackish lateral crown-stripes; also has shorter tail and longer primary projection beyond tertials, is more neatly proportioned, and has dark grey (rather than pale brown) legs and feet. Rufescent above, with warm buff sides of breast and flanks, in fresh plumage (upperparts olive-brown in worn plumage). **Voice** Call a soft repeated *chuk*, harsh *chur* in alarm. **HH** Typical small *Acrocephalus*. Lively and adept at climbing up and down plant stems. Usually flies only for short distances, low over vegetation. Tall grass, reedbeds and paddyfields.

Moustached Warbler *Acrocephalus melanopogon* 12–13cm

Mainly winter visitor. Pakistan and N and NW Indian plains. Vagrant: Nepal. **ID** From other *Acrocephalus* regular in the subcontinent by combination of broad white square-ended supercilium (which broadens behind eye, and contrasts with blackish sides of crown and blackish eye-stripe), greyish ear-coverts and fine dark moustachial line, and streaked rufous-brown mantle (streaking can be faint and indistinct). Throat and breast can be strikingly white and can show cinnamon-buff flanks and vent. Has distinctive habit of cocking tail in chat-like fashion. Bill, legs and feet dark. **Voice** Calls include a harsh *trr-trr* and hard *tcht*; song varied and scratchy, although contains clear notes and trills including a subdued *lu-lu-lu-lu*. **HH** Unobtrusive, less skulking than other *Acrocephalus*. Moves low down in partly submerged reeds, often clinging to vertical stems and stretches down to water surface to pick up insects. Tall reedbeds and tamarisks.

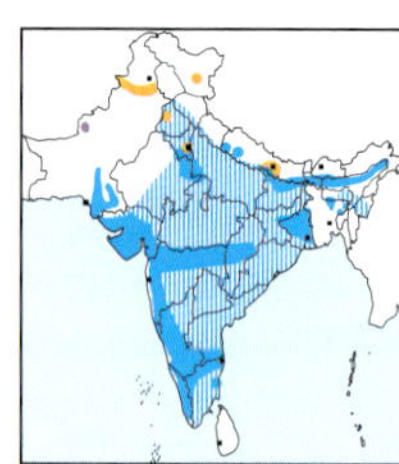

Paddyfield Warbler *Acrocephalus agricola* 12–14cm

Widespread winter visitor; unrecorded in Sri Lanka; has bred Balochistan. **ID** Compared to Blyth's Reed has more prominent white supercilium behind eye (often with diffuse dark upper edge), more pronounced dark eye-stripe, shorter bill with well-defined dark tip, and typically has dark centres and contrastingly paler edges to tertials (uniform on Blyth's). Often shows pale half-collar and a greyer and darker crown than nape/mantle. Has rufous cast to mantle and rump in fresh plumage, when Blyth's is more olive on upperparts, and flanks are more strongly washed with buff. Worn upperparts greyer or sandier but retain rufous cast to rump (absent on Blyth's). Legs and feet yellowish-brown to pinkish-brown (dark grey in Blyth's). See Blunt-winged and Black-browed for differences from those species. **Voice** Soft *dzak* call. **HH** Reedbeds and paddyfields.

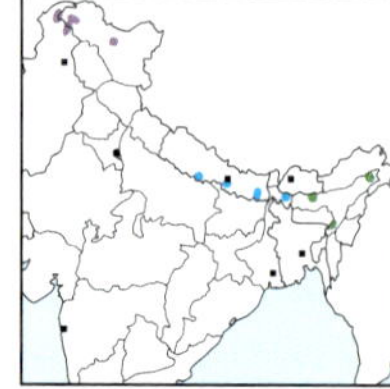

Blunt-winged Warbler *Acrocephalus concinens* 13–14cm

Breeds in far W Himalayas; resident in Assam, winters in Nepal and West Bengal. **ID** Subtle differences from Paddyfield: shorter and less distinct supercilium (typically barely extends beyond eye); absence of dark border above supercilium (sometimes not apparent on Paddyfield); lack of dark stripe behind eye (with uniform ear-coverts); longer and stouter bill (with pale lower mandible lacking well-defined dark tip of most Paddyfield), and longer tail (accentuated by even shorter primary projection). Confusable with Blyth's Reed; when fresh, has more rufous tones, with warm buff breast and flanks, when worn retains rufous on rump. Also appears shorter-billed than Blyth's Reed, has longer and more rounded tail, more prominent fringes to tertials, and a shorter and more rounded primary projection. *A. c. stevensi* (north-east) differs from *A. c. haringtoni* (north-west) in being darker brown on upperparts and duskier on underparts with indistinctly paler throat. **Voice** Song varied; short, repeated phrases, mainly whistles, clear notes and some buzzing ones. Calls include a quiet *tcheck* and soft drawn-out *churr*. **HH** Breeds in dense vegetation around wetlands; winters mainly in reedbeds beside wetlands, also tall grass and bushes.

Upcher's Warbler
ad worn
ad fresh
ad fresh
ad fresh
Black-browed
Reed Warbler
Moustached
Warbler
ad worn
juv
ad spring
Paddyfield Warbler
ad fresh
ad worn
ad fresh
haringtoni
ad
stevensi
Blunt-winged Warbler

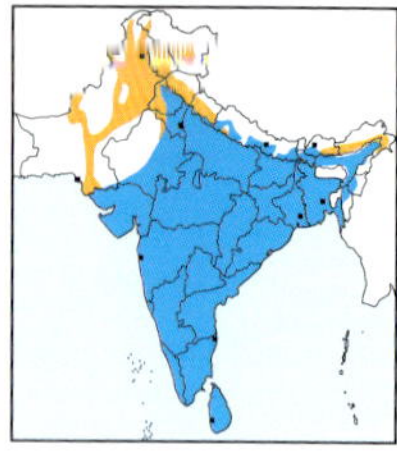

Blyth's Reed Warbler ***Acrocephalus dumetorum*** 12–14cm
Widespread winter visitor and passage migrant. **ID** Compared with Paddyfield has longer bill (usually lacking well-defined dark tip), olive-brown to olive-grey upperparts, and uniform wings. Supercilium is comparatively indistinct and barely apparent behind eye. Has noticeable olive cast to upperparts and edges of remiges in fresh plumage, but first-winter can have slight rufous cast to upperparts (and is closer in coloration to Paddyfield). Larger and more robust than Sykes's Warbler, with shorter-looking, more round-ended tail, and longer undertail- and uppertail-coverts. Lacks pale sides to tail and edges to wing feathers, and sandy tones to upperparts of Sykes's. **Voice** Call a soft *chek* or grating *chek-tchr*. **HH** Typically hops and creeps about in bushes, sometimes also in trees and ground cover. Frequently flicks, raises and fans tail. Bushes and trees at forest edges, wooded areas and cultivation.

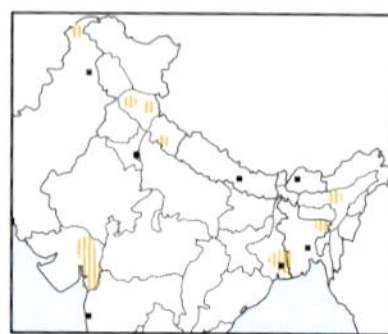

Large-billed Reed Warbler ***Acrocephalus orinus*** 13–14cm
Probably a passage migrant. Scattered records in India. Vagrant: Pakistan. **ID** Extremely similar in appearance to Blyth's Reed. In fresh plumage is less olive, more rufous-tinged. Structurally has a longer and slightly broader bill, a longer and more sloping forehead, more rounded wings, and longer and more graduated tail with more pointed feathers. Much smaller with weaker bill and feet than Clamorous Reed. **Voice** Undescribed in subcontinent; song like Blyth's Reed. **HH** Undescribed in subcontinent.

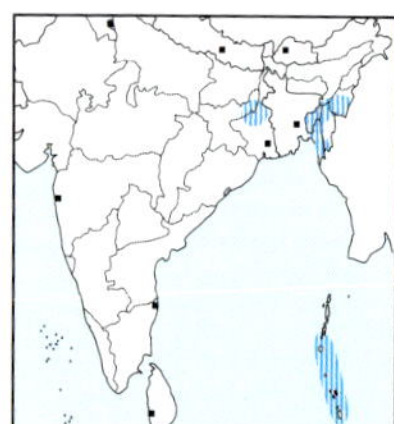

Oriental Reed Warbler ***Acrocephalus orientalis*** 17–19cm
Winter visitor. Mainly NE India. Vagrant: Nepal. **ID** A large *Acrocephalus*. Smaller, with shorter and squarer tail, than Clamorous, with a longer primary projection beyond tertials. Bill looks shorter and stouter. Usually has faint streaking on sides of throat and across breast, and well-defined whitish tips to outer rectrices. Streaking on underparts can, however, be occasionally lacking or not visible in the field, while a few Clamorous can also show faint streaking. Upperparts vary from olive-brown to rufous-brown and usually has rich buff breast and flanks. See Vagrants for differences from Great Reed Warbler. **Voice** Calls like Clamorous. **HH** Reedbeds and bushes.

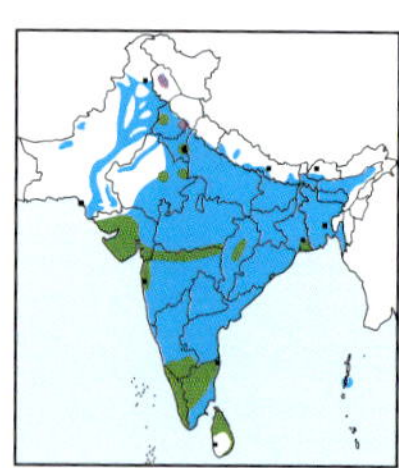

Clamorous Reed Warbler ***Acrocephalus stentoreus*** 18–20cm
Breeds locally in Pakistan, India and Sri Lanka; widespread in winter. **ID** Large size, long bill, short primary projection, whitish supercilium, and lack of white at tip of tail help to distinguish from other *Acrocephalus*. In fresh plumage, greyish-olive upperparts and whitish underparts (with variable buff wash to breast and flanks). Worn birds have colder and greyer upperparts and whiter underparts. *A. s. amyae* (north-east) is richer brown above and more strongly washed buff below, with a less distinct supercilium, compared to the widely distributed largely migrant race *A. s. brunnescens*. *A. s. meridionalis* (Sri Lanka) is also darker and richer brown with browner flanks, and often smaller. **Voice** Song a loud repeated *karra-karra-karet-karet*; call a loud and deep, hard *tak* or soft *karrk*. **HH** Reedbeds and bushes around wetlands.

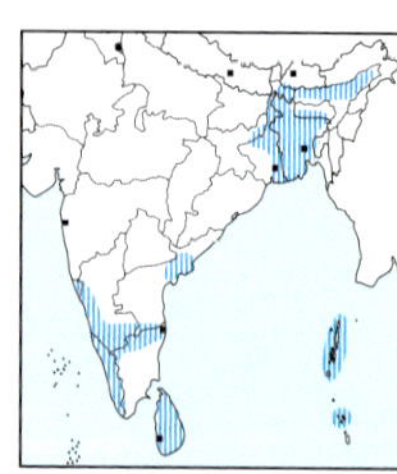

Pallas's Grasshopper Warbler ***Helopsaltes certhiola*** 13–14cm
Winters locally in subcontinent. Vagrant: Nepal. **ID** Larger and more robust than Common Grasshopper Warbler; more prominent supercilium contrasting with greyer crown, more heavily streaked mantle with rufous tinge, rufous rump and uppertail-coverts, cleaner and narrower fringes to tertials (often whiter tips), rufous olive-brown breast-sides and flanks (contrasting with white of rest of underparts), and unstreaked undertail-coverts. In flight has dark, white-tipped tail, which contrasts with rufous uppertail-coverts. Juvenile has yellowish wash to underparts, light breast spotting, less distinct supercilium, and more olive-brown and less heavily streaked crown and mantle. **Voice** Includes hard, drawn-out, descending rattle *trrrrrrrrr*; quiet, varied high-pitched twittering song, leads into ringing whistled *che-che-che-che-che*. **HH** Habits like Common Grasshopper. Reedbeds, paddyfields. **AN** Rusty-rumped Warbler. **TN** Formerly placed in *Locustella*.

ad worn
ad fresh
Blyth's Reed Warbler
1st winter
ad
Large-billed
Reed Warbler
ad fresh
brunnescens
ad fresh
ad
amyae
Oriental
Reed Warbler
ad worn
Clamorous
Reed Warbler
ad
meridionalis
ad
juv
Pallas's
Grasshopper Warbler

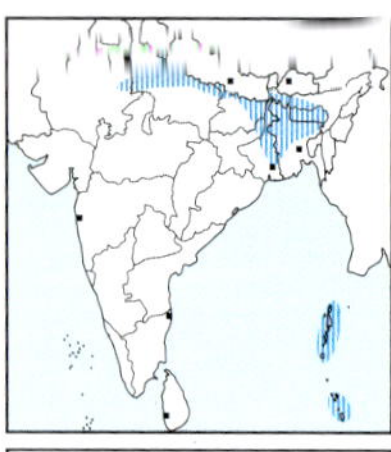

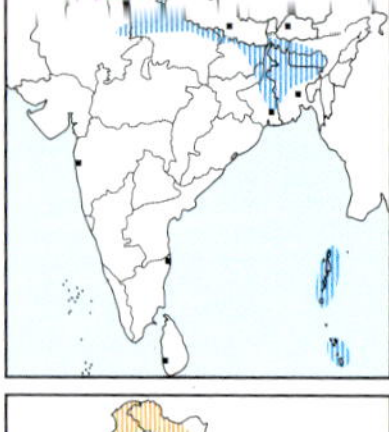

Lanceolated Warbler *Locustella lanceolata* 12–13.5cm

Winter visitor. Lowlands, mainly N subcontinent; unrecorded in Pakistan. Vagrant: Nepal. **ID** From Common Grasshopper Warbler by bold, fine streaking (almost spotting) on throat, breast and flanks, and stronger streaking on upperparts. In addition, is smaller, has shorter tail and stouter bill, and in fresh plumage warmer brown upperparts and warmer buff flanks, lacking yellow on underparts. Some very similar to Common: streaking on undertail-coverts is less extensive but blacker and more clear-cut, and tertials are darker with clear-cut pale edges. **Voice** Includes shrill *cheek-cheek-cheek-cheek*; song an even, sustained, high-pitched, insect-like reeling. **HH** Habits like Common Grasshopper. Tall grassland, bushes around marshes, ditches, paddyfields.

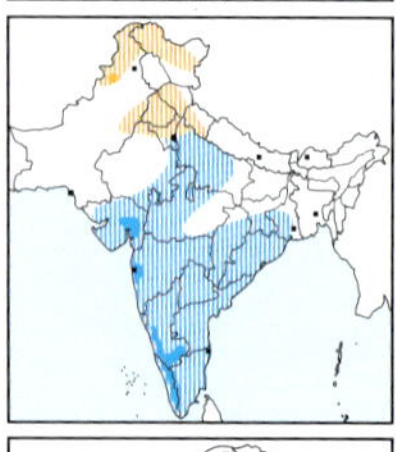

Common Grasshopper Warbler *Locustella naevia* 12–12.5cm

Widespread winter visitor. Vagrant: Nepal. **ID** From Pallas's Grasshopper Warbler by olive-brown coloration to upperparts including rump and tail, and less prominent supercilium. From Lanceolated Warbler by (usually) unmarked or only lightly streaked throat and breast, and less heavily streaked upperparts (especially rump and uppertail-coverts). Some Common Grasshopper Warblers are as heavily streaked as a lightly streaked Lanceolated. First-winter can have yellowish wash on underparts. **Voice** Song an insect-like reeling; hard *sit* call. **HH** Creeps and hops about low down among grass and reeds. Grassland, reedbeds, paddyfields. **AN** Grasshopper Warbler.

Long-billed Bush Warbler *Locustella major* 14cm

Resident. W Himalayas. Vagrant: Nepal. **ID** From other bush warblers by combination of longer and finer bill, prominent white supercilium, whiter underparts, with whiter lower throat and breast, and olive-buff or buff flanks, longer tail, and unmarked undertail-coverts. Extent of spotting varies (from covering entire throat and upper breast, to being almost absent except on ear-coverts and malar region). Upperparts warm olive-brown when fresh; cold greyish-olive when worn. Has warmer chestnut-brown fringes to remiges which show as wing-panel. Juvenile has cloudy spotting and yellowish wash to underparts. **Voice** Song a monotonous, sustained, mechanical clicking *pikha-pikha-pikha*. **HH** Very secretive. Breeds on bushy hillsides, upland terraced cultivation, edges of alpine meadows and forest clearings. **TN** Formerly placed in *Bradypterus*.

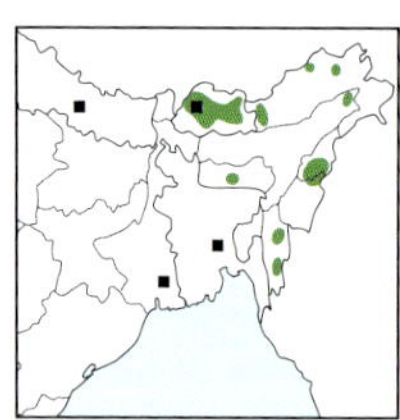

Brown Bush Warbler *Locustella luteoventris* 13–14.5cm

Resident. E Himalayas and NE Indian hills. Vagrant: Nepal. **ID** Very similar to Chinese Bush Warbler but has warmer brown upperparts (with slight rufescent cast), and warm rufous-buff ear-coverts, sides of neck and breast, and flanks, contrasting with silky-white of rest of underparts. Also has indistinct rufous-buff supercilium to eye (and concolorous with lores) and lacks prominent pale tips to undertail-coverts. No spotting on throat and breast. Juvenile has yellowish wash to underparts and has band of diffuse brown mottling on breast. **Voice** Sings from a hidden low perch: monotonous insect-like, staccato reeling, *tk-tk-tk-tk-tk-tk-tk-tk-tk-tk*; hard *tak* call. **HH** Skulking and reluctant to fly. Grassy hills; in pine forest undergrowth in Khasi hills. **TN** Formerly placed in *Bradypterus*.

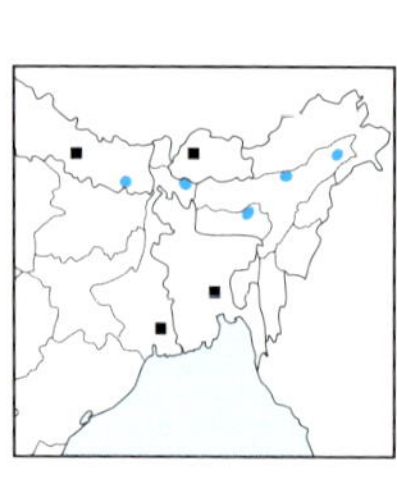

Chinese Bush Warbler *Locustella tacsanowskia* 13cm

Winter visitor. Nepal and India. **ID** Very similar to Brown Bush Warbler, but has greyer-brown upperparts with olive cast, olive grey-brown ear-coverts and breast (latter often with yellowish wash), olive-buff flanks, and pale tips to undertail-coverts (lacking or only just apparent on Brown). Shows variable (sometimes indistinct) whitish supercilium to eye (and concolorous with lores). Some have fine spotting on lower throat. Longer tailed than West Himalayan and Spotted Bush Warblers with less prominent pale tips to undertail-coverts. Juvenile has yellowish lores, strong yellowish wash to breast and flanks, a diffuse band of brown mottling on breast, yellowish-buff undertail-coverts, and stronger olive wash to upperparts. **Voice** Song a rasping insect-like *dzzzeep-dzzeeep-dzzeep* etc.; low *chir-chirr* call. **HH** Usually keeps under cover. Reedbeds, grass and bushes, paddyfields. **TN** Formerly placed in *Bradypterus*.

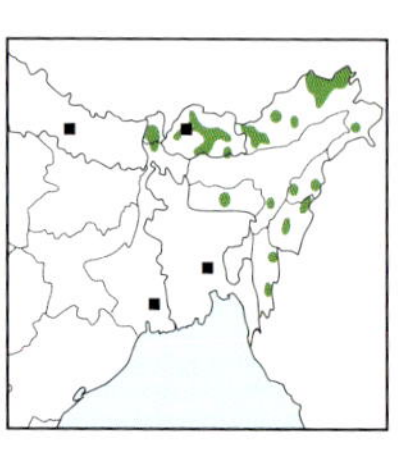

Russet Bush Warbler *Locustella mandelli* 13.5cm

Resident. E Himalayas and NE India. **ID** From Spotted and West Himalayan Bush Warblers by longer and broader tail, less boldly marked undertail-coverts (with diffuse pale tips), indistinct and off-white supercilium (not extending behind eye), and brown ear-coverts, sides of breast and flanks concolorous with upperparts. Some have brown spotting on lower throat and upper breast, but less prominent than most Spotted. Darker rufous-brown upperparts and flanks, pale tips to undertail-coverts, and lack of striking white belly, help separate from Brown Bush Warbler. **Voice** Song a monotonous, metallic and buzzing *zree-ut zree-ut*. **HH** Forest edges, second growth. **TN** Formerly placed in *Bradypterus*.

ad fresh
juv
Lanceolated Warbler
ad fresh
ad fresh
bright
individual
juv
Common
Grasshopper Warbler
juv
ad fresh
Long-billed
Bush Warbler
juv
ad worn
Brown
Bush Warbler
ad
juv
Chinese
Bush Warbler
ad worn
ad fresh
ad
Russet
Bush Warbler
juv

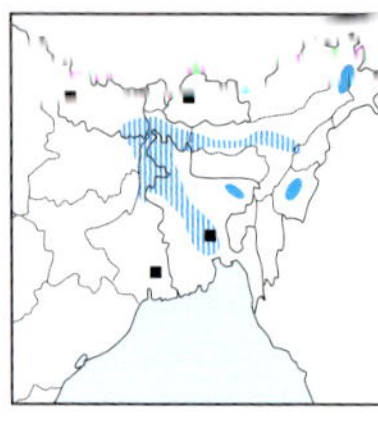

Baikal Bush Warbler *Locustella davidi* **12cm**

Uncommon and local winter visitor to NE India and Bangladesh. Vagrant: Nepal. **ID** From Spotted Bush Warbler by broader white edges to undertail-coverts, relatively short tail compared to undertail-coverts, paler brown upperparts, brownish wash on sides of neck and across breast concolorous with upperparts (lacking grey breast-band of Spotted), typically weaker and browner spotting on throat and breast, and buffish supercilium. **Voice** Song a dry, rasping, monotonous, drawn-out *brzzzzzz* . . . . . . *brzzzzzz* . . . . . . *brzzzzzz* . . . . . . each note increasing in loudness towards the end, and separated from the next one by a distinct, variably long pause; calls include a hard, raspy, irregularly spaced *tshuk*. **HH** Dense reed-swamp vegetation, reedbeds and tall grass. **TN** Formerly placed in *Bradypterus*.

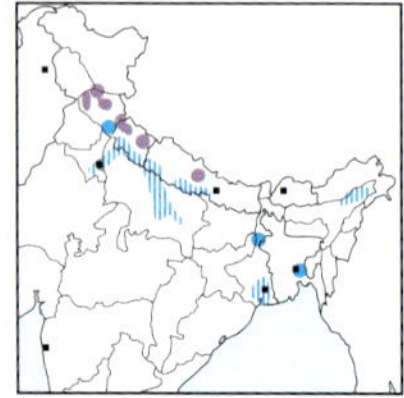

West Himalayan Bush Warbler *Locustella kashmirensis* **13cm**

Resident. W Himalayas. Winters in nearby plains and east to West Bengal, Assam and Bangladesh. **ID** Two morphs occur. One is much like Spotted Bush Warbler, but has whiter supercilium, is slightly paler and less richly coloured on the upperparts, with paler grey sides of neck and breast, has paler brown flanks and undertail-coverts (latter with broader white tips), and shorter tail. The so called 'buff-breasted morph' is more distinctive and is thought to be unique, with buffy supercilium and ear-coverts, buffy wash on sides of neck and across breast, and usually lacks spotting (occasionally with fine gorget of speckling). Juvenile as juvenile Spotted. **Voice** Song a rhythmic, mechanical series of clicks and buzzes, the first 1–5 click notes start at a lower pitch: *tre-tre-tre-triptreez-triptreeez, tre-tre-tre-trip-treez-trip-treeez, tre-tre-tre-trip-treez-trip-treeez*... clicks with a buzz at end; call a very short hard *tshak*. **HH** Habitat as Spotted. **TN** Formerly placed in *Bradypterus*.

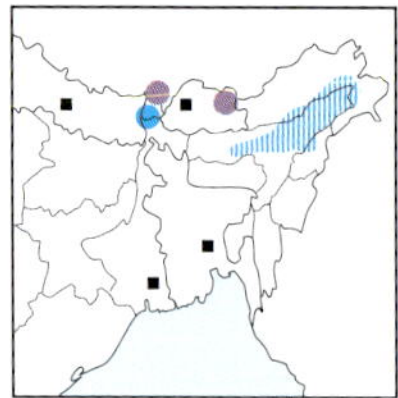

Spotted Bush Warbler *Locustella thoracica* **13cm**

Breeds in E Himalayas; winters in foothills and NE Indian plains. Nepal status uncertain. **ID** From other bush warblers except West Himalayan by combination of spotting on throat and breast (can be indistinct), fine greyish supercilium, dark olive-brown upperparts with rufescent cast, grey ear-coverts and breast, olive-brown flanks, and boldly patterned undertail-coverts with dark brown centres and sharply defined white tips. Juvenile lacks grey on underparts and has cloudy olive-brown spotting and faint olive-yellow wash to underparts. **Voice** Song a sequence of mechanical clicks and buzzes, beginning with a medium-pitched click, followed by five very high-pitched clicks (higher pitched than West Himalayan) and a single buzz, much shorter than West Himalayan: *trick-he-dee, trick-he-dee* ... or *tri-tri-tri-tree, tri-tri-tri-treez*; harsh, emphatic *shtak* call. **HH** Summers in high-altitude shrubbery and tall herbaceous vegetation above treeline; winters in reedbeds and tall grass. **TN** Formerly placed in *Bradypterus*.

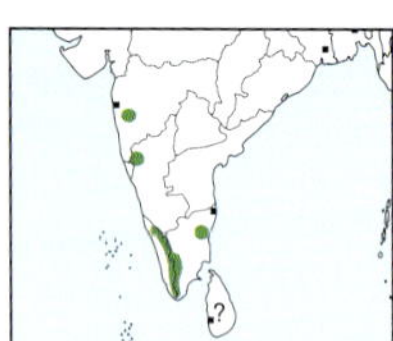

Broad-tailed Grassbird *Schoenicola platyurus* **18cm**

Resident. Western Ghats and Sri Lanka. **ID** Readily identified by stout bill, long and broad dark tail, unstreaked upperparts, and whitish underparts. Has buffish supercilium. In south of range has rufous-brown upperparts and rufous-buff wash to breast and flanks. In north has paler, sandy greyish-brown upperparts and whiter underparts. **Voice** Song a shrill and sweet trill ending with a few warbling and *chack* notes. **HH** Tall grass, sedges, bamboo and bushes on open hillsides. Globally threatened.

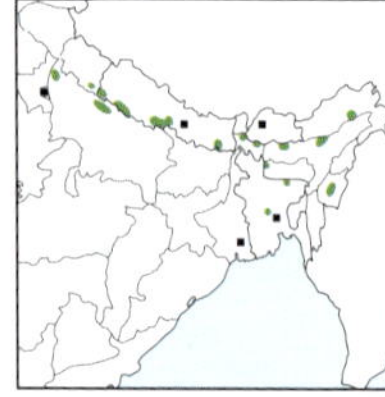

Indian Grassbird *Graminicola bengalensis* **16cm**

Resident. Terai and NE plains. **ID** Dark upperparts with rufous streaking on crown and lower mantle, and white or buff streaking on nape and upper mantle. Face rather plain with short whitish eyebrow, pale lores, and rufous wash to ear-coverts. Largely rufous rump and wings. Tail blackish broadly tipped white. Underparts white with rufous-buff breast-sides and flanks. **Voice** Song a subdued high *er-wi-wi-wi-, you-wuoo, yu-wuoo*, followed by a series of harsh notes and ending with wheezy sounds; usual calls are subdued, harsh scolding. **HH** In Nepal in grassland of *Phragmites* and *Saccharum*; in NE India in short dry grassland <1m tall. **AN** Rufous-rumped Grassbird.

Baikal
Bush Warbler
ad non-br
ad br
juv
juv
ad
buff morph
ad
juv
West Himalayan
Bush Warbler
ad
Spotted
Bush Warbler
ad 'southern''
Broad-tailed
Grassbird
ad 'northern''
ad
Indian Grassbird

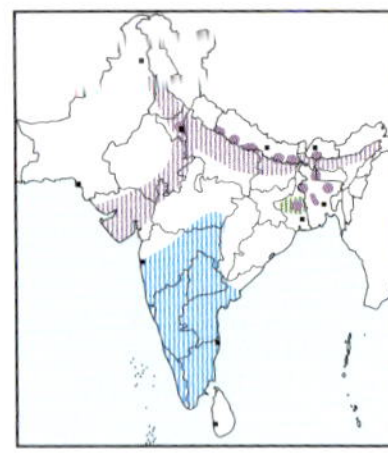

Bristled Grassbird *Schoenicola striata* 14.5–17cm

Local resident. Mainly lowlands in India and Nepal. **ID** From Striated by smaller size, stout bill, less distinct supercilium (barely apparent behind eye), and shorter (broader) tail with pale shafts, buffish-white tips and more prominent dark cross-barring (undertail appears blackish with broad whitish tips, although these can be lost through wear). In addition, breast and flanks lack the streaking apparent on worn Striated. In fresh plumage, underparts washed with buff and feathers of upperparts and wings have broad buff fringes. Upperparts become greyer-brown and underparts whiter when worn. Male much larger than female and has dark (versus pale) bill. **Voice** Song a disyllabic *trew-treuw* repeated at 2–3-second intervals; strong, harsh *cha* and softer *zip* calls. **HH** Tall grassland with bushes, and paddyfields. Song flight very different to Striated, circling airborne for many minutes. Globally threatened. **TN** Formerly placed in *Chaetornis*.

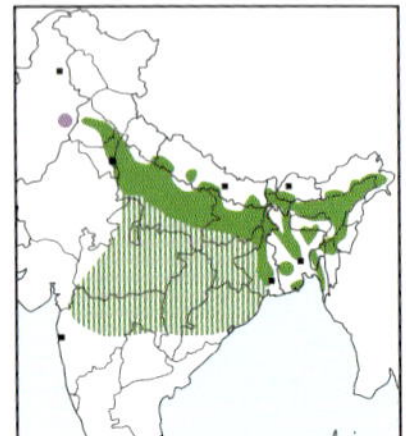

Striated Grassbird *Cincloramphus palustris* 22–28cm

Resident. Lowlands in N and C subcontinent. **ID** A large, babbler-like 'warbler' with brownish-buff upperparts prominently streaked black, whitish supercilium, rufous crown, whitish underparts with fine brown streaking on breast and flanks, and long, graduated tail. In fresh (non-breeding) plumage, supercilium and underparts strongly washed with pale yellow, streaking on underparts partially obscured, and has pale lower mandible (bill all dark in breeding plumage). Male distinctly larger than female. **Voice** Song a strong rich warbling, *chot-chot-chot-chot which-u-quieee-chot-trrrrt-kwit-kwit-kwit-cheee-chwot*; also subdued whistle followed by loud explosive *wheeechoo*. Song flight a short steep climb, then parachutes down. **HH** Tall damp grassland, reedbeds and tamarisks. **TN** Formerly placed in *Megalurus*.

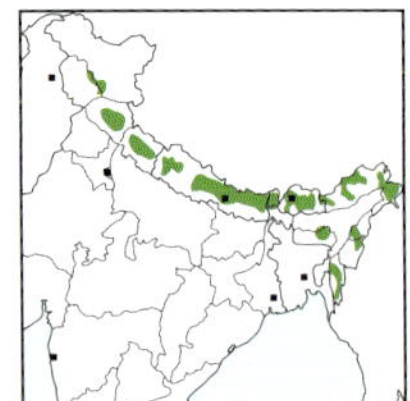

Scaly-breasted Cupwing *Pnoepyga albiventer* 8.5–10cm

Resident. Himalayas and NE Indian hills. **ID** Rotund and tailless with boldly scaled underparts, occurring in white and fulvous colour morphs. From Pygmy Cupwing by larger size (appears noticeably larger than Eurasian Wren or Grey-bellied Tesia), more rounded appearance, and more ponderous movements. Usually shows well-defined buff spotting on sides of crown and neck (occasionally on entire crown and mantle), which is lacking on Pygmy, but spotting on head and upperparts can be much reduced. Juvenile considerably smaller and has uniform dark chestnut-brown upperparts, while underparts are sooty-grey to brown and lack bold scaling. *P. a. pallidior* (W and C Himalayas) has paler olive-brown upperparts than nominate (E Himalayas). **Voice** Strong warbling song, *tzee-tze-zit-tzu-stu-tzit*, rising then ending abruptly. **HH** Very skulking, often flicks wings. Hops about among mossy boulders and roots. In breeding season, males sometimes sing in open. Dense undergrowth in moist forests, often near streams. **AN** Scaly-breasted Wren Babbler.

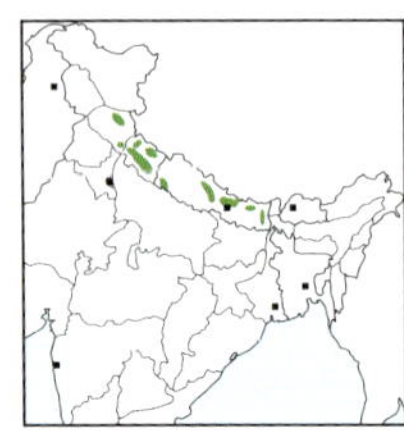

Immaculate Cupwing *Pnoepyga immaculata* 8.5–10cm

Resident. Himalayas from Himachal to E Nepal. **ID** Similar in size and appearance to Scaly-breasted Cupwing, with longer and heavier bill; best separated by song. Feathers of underparts more elongated, resulting in narrower arrowhead-shaped black centres and pale fringes (and streaked appearance). Upperparts more uniform, lacking buff spotting on crown, mantle and wing-coverts, which is usually apparent on Scaly-breasted (particularly characteristic are the unmarked areas above and behind the eye and on neck-sides). White morph tinged ochre, appearing distinctly dirty compared to most Scaly-breasted; fulvous morph deep rusty-yellow on underparts (less saturated than the deep rusty colour of Scaly-bellied). Upperparts paler olive-brown than nominate Scaly-breasted; coloration similar to that of *P. a. pallidior*. **Voice** Eight high-pitched piercing notes, repeated, *si-su-si-si-swi-si-si-si*. **HH** Habits, see Scaly-breasted. Boulders and herbaceous vegetation near running water at forest edge. **AN** Nepal Wren Babbler.

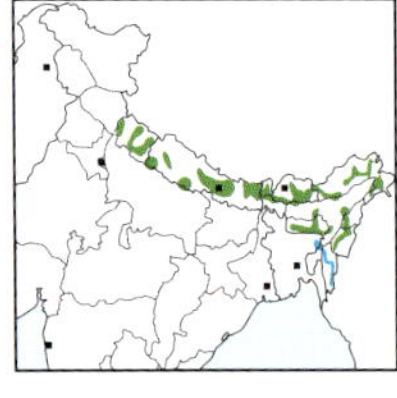

Pygmy Cupwing *Pnoepyga pusilla* 7.5–9cm

Resident. Himalayas and NE India. Vagrant: Bangladesh. **ID** From Scaly-breasted by smaller size (appears similar in size to Eurasian Wren or Grey-bellied Tesia) and by distinctive song. Spotting on upperparts confined to lower back and wing-coverts (lacking well-defined buff spots on crown and neck which are usually present on Scaly-breasted). Juvenile has uniform dark brown upperparts, and underparts are sooty-grey and lack bold scaling. **Voice** Song a loud, slowly drawn-out *see-saw*, repeated monotonously. **HH** See Scaly-breasted. **AN** Pygmy Wren Babbler.

♂
Bristled Grassbird
Striated Grassbird
ad
worn
ad
fresh
ad
fulvous morph
albiventer
ad
white morph
albiventer
Scaly-breasted Cupwing
ad
pallidior
Immaculate Cupwing
ad
fulvous morph
ad
white morph
ad
fulvous morph
ad
white morph
Pygmy Cupwing

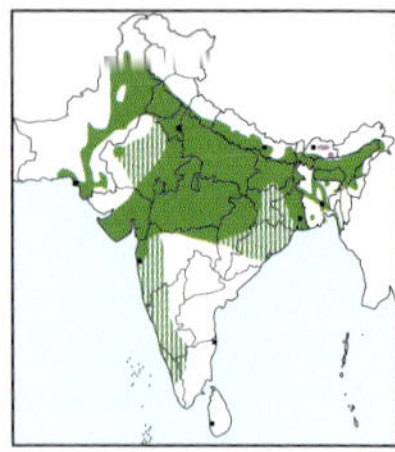

Grey-throated Martin *Riparia chinensis* 10–11cm

Resident. Mainly N and C subcontinent, also Western Ghats. **ID** Has brownish-grey throat and breast, and dingy white rest of underparts. On some, throat is a little paler than breast. Underwing darker than on Sand Martin and Pale Martin, flight weaker and more fluttering, and has shallower indent to tail; darker brown upperparts than nominate Pale, with paler rump (although note subspecific variation in Pale). Juvenile has rufous fringes to upperparts (especially tertials and rump/uppertail-coverts), and throat and breast are paler and washed pinkish-buff. **Voice** Harsh twittering song; calls include short, twangy *chyip, chyip.* **HH** Around rivers, streams and lakes and over terrestrial habitats like grassland and paddyfields. **TN** Formerly treated as Plain Martin *R. paludicola.*

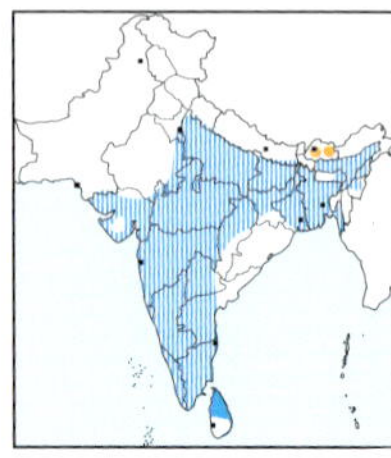

Sand Martin *Riparia riparia* 12cm

Status in region uncertain as range confused with that of Pale Martin. **ID** Adult from Grey-throated Martin by white throat and half-collar, and by brown breast-band which is generally well defined against whitish underparts. In addition, appears stockier and more purposeful in flight, and has a more prominently forked tail. Compared to nominate Pale Martin, upperparts slightly darker brown including rump, breast-band is dark and clearly defined, throat is white and clearly demarcated from dark brown ear-coverts, and tail fork is deeper. See Pale Martin for further details. Juvenile has buff fringes to upperparts and buff tinge to throat, and breast-band can be less clearly defined. **Voice** Characteristic call a dry rasp, less rolling than similar call of Western House Martin; song a pleasant twittering mixed with rasping call. **HH** Around large waterbodies; in summer, around rivers and streams.

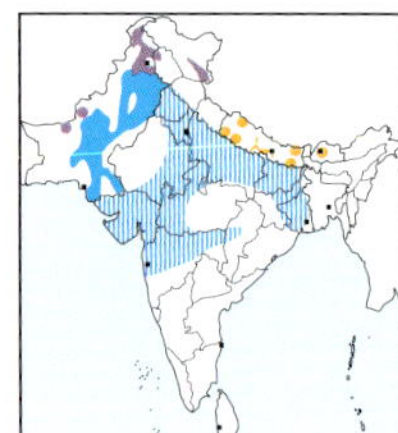

Pale Martin *Riparia diluta* 12cm

Breeds Pakistan and Ladakh. Winters mainly N and C India. **ID** Very similar to Sand Martin, with confusing subspecific variation. Nominate (wintering in north-west and north) has paler and greyer upperparts, the breast-band is pale and weakly defined, throat is greyish-white and grades into the pale greyish-brown ear-coverts, and tail fork is shallower. Breeding *indica* (north-west) is smaller with very shallow tail fork, and is similar in size to and easily confusable with Grey-throated, but is a shade paler, has whiter throat, and shows less contrast between rump and back. Wintering *tibetana* comparatively large and as dark as Sand Martin (and easily confusable) although breast-band is paler and less distinct. Juvenile *indica* has dusky throat recalling Grey-throated, but stronger contrast between breast and belly (lacking pinkish buff wash on breast of juvenile Grey-throated) and upperparts are paler with paler fringes buff (less rufous). **Voice** Song a short, grating twittering. **HH** Mainly open country, often near water.

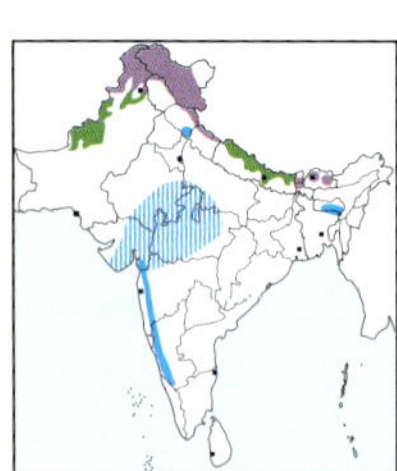

Eurasian Crag Martin *Ptyonoprogne rupestris* 14–15cm

Resident. Breeds in Pakistan hills and Himalayas; winters mainly in Western Ghats and C India. **ID** Larger and darker than Rock Martin. Upperparts and underwing-coverts darker brown, with dusky throat, dusky-brown flanks and vent, and more distinct pale fringes to undertail-coverts; blackish underwing-coverts contrast more with rest of underwing. From Dusky Crag by larger size, paler brown upperparts, and paler underparts with throat and breast noticeably paler than belly and vent. Juvenile has buff to rufous fringes to upperparts; underparts washed with buff, and chin/throat less distinctly marked. **Voice** Song a series of soft twittering notes; calls include *prrrt* and *zirr* alarm. **HH** Rocky cliffs and gorges, ancient hill forts.

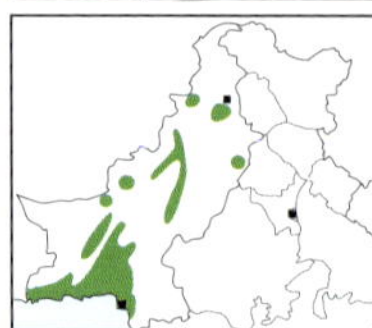

Rock Martin *Ptyonoprogne fuligula* 13cm

Resident. Mainly S Pakistan. **ID** Very similar to Eurasian Crag Martin but is smaller and paler. Specifically, has dark lores and patch around eye, unmarked buffish-white throat, paler sandy-grey vent and undertail-coverts, and paler underwing-coverts which contrast less with rest of underwing. Upperparts paler sandy-grey, and rump can appear especially pale. Juvenile has pale fringes to upperparts. **Voice** Song a series of short phrases, including squeaky whistles, throaty rattles, buzzy chitters and gargling notes. **HH** Rocky gorges and cliffs in arid hills.

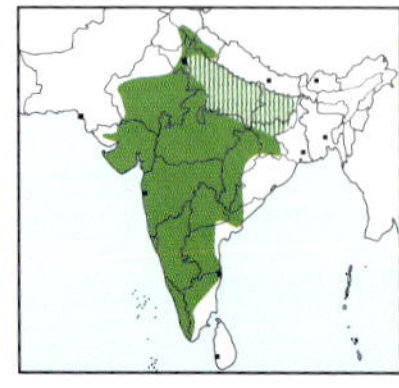

Dusky Crag Martin *Ptyonoprogne concolor* 13–14cm

Resident. Mainly N and peninsular India. Vagrant: Sri Lanka. **ID** Similar to Eurasian but is smaller and more slightly built, and much darker and more uniformly coloured. Upperparts and underparts are darker brown, with breast and belly not noticeably paler than vent. Throat a slightly warmer and paler buff-brown, with indistinct darker brown streaking. Underwing also appears more uniform. Juvenile has rufous fringes to upperparts and paler throat. **Voice** Soft twittering song; calls include soft *chit-chit.* **HH** Hilly and mountain areas with cliffs, gorges and caves; in lowland areas around ancient forts and old buildings in towns and cities.

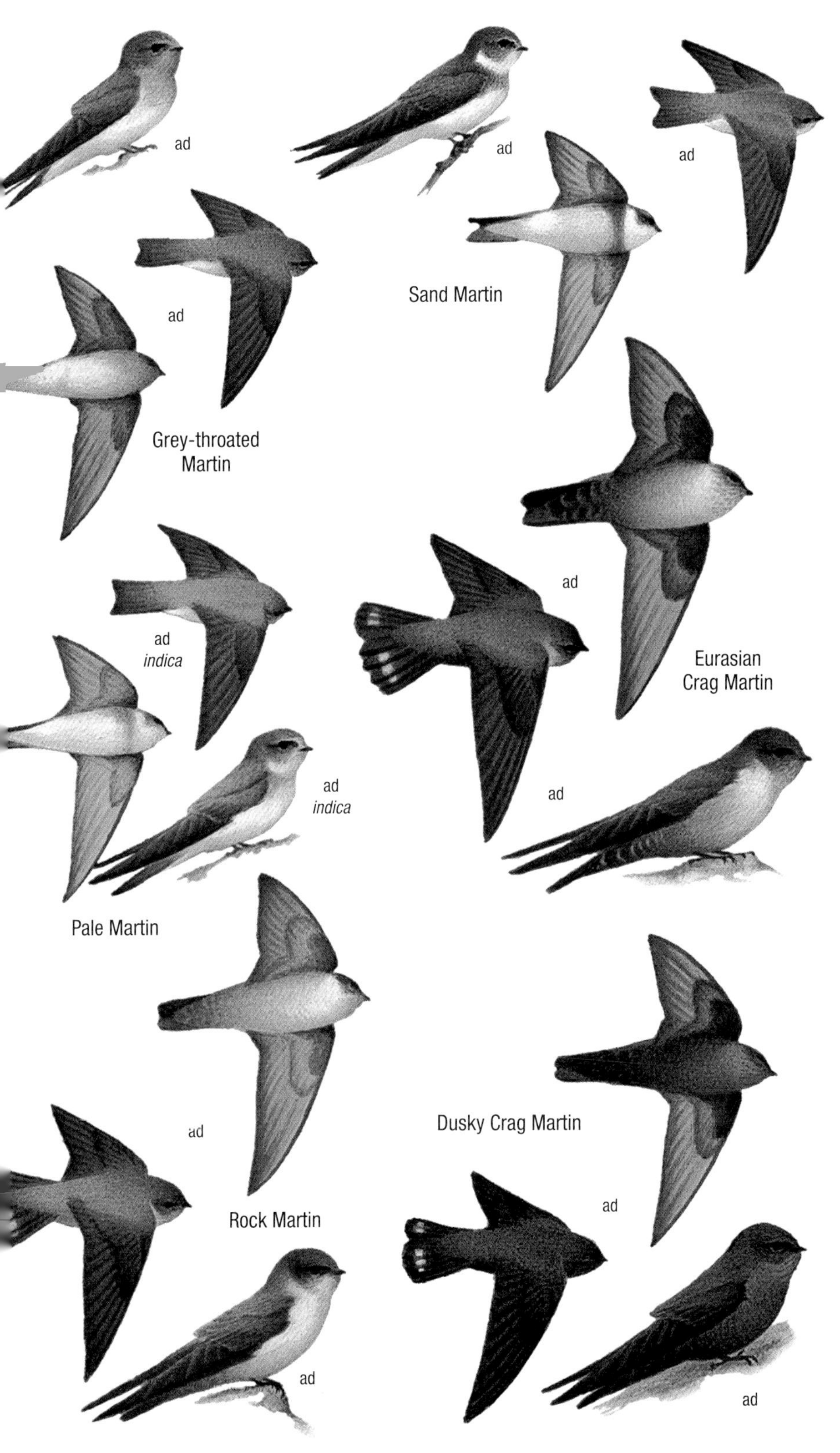
ad
ad
ad
Sand Martin
ad
Grey-throated
Martin
ad
ad
indica
Eurasian
Crag Martin
ad
indica
ad
Pale Martin
ad
Dusky Crag Martin
ad
Rock Martin
ad
ad

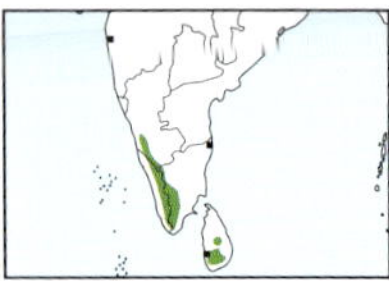

Hill Swallow ***Hirundo domicola*** 12.5cm

Resident in S Western Ghats and Sri Lanka hill zone, wandering to foothills. **ID** As Pacific but smaller with longer-looking tail, and metallic green gloss to upperparts (more purplish-blue in Pacific). **Voice** Songs includes pleasant twittering; calls include an abrupt, high-pitched *chit.* **HH** Much less gregarious than Barn. Often perches on telegraph wires. Grassy hills around tea and coffee plantations; around bungalows and factory sheds.

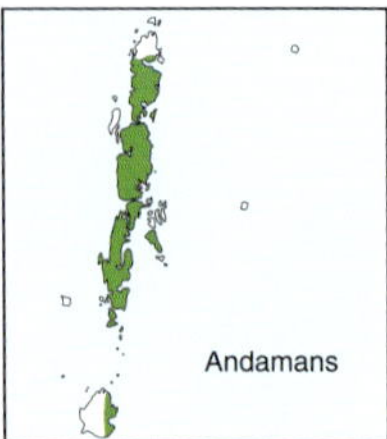

Pacific Swallow ***Hirundo tahitica*** 13cm

Resident. Andamans. **ID** From Barn by more extensive rufous on throat, lack of breast-band, dingy underparts and underwing-coverts, and blackish undertail-coverts with whitish fringes; lacks tail-streamers. Upperparts have purplish gloss, and many have fine dark streaking on underparts. Juvenile has browner (less glossy) upperparts, with very little rufous on forehead and has paler rufous throat. **Voice** Song a rambling mix of musical and harsh notes resembling Barn; calls include a harsh staccato note. **HH** Habits like Barn, less dashing in flight. Open country along coasts and rivers.

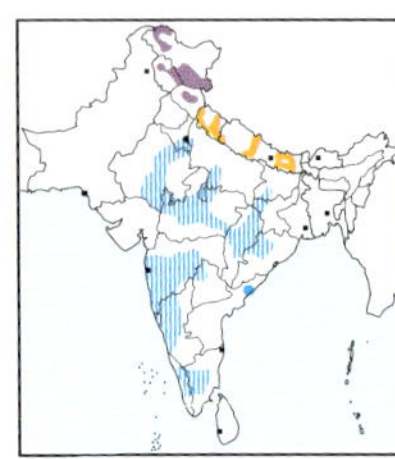

Western House Martin ***Delichon urbicum*** 13–14cm

Summer visitor to W Himalayas; winter visitor and passage migrant elsewhere. **ID** Adult from Asian House Martin by combination of whiter underparts, longer and more deeply forked tail, paler underwing-coverts, and more extensive and cleaner white rump. Juvenile has browner (less glossy) upperparts, is rather dingy below with brownish centres to some feathers of vent and undertail-coverts, whitish tips to tertials, and has shallower tail fork (and is very similar to Asian). **Voice** Soft twittering song; flight call a rolling scratchy *prrit-prrit* and *jeet-jeet* in alarm. **HH** Gregarious all year, hunts in scattered parties, often with other hirundines. Flight is much less swift, with less swooping and twisting than Barn Swallow, and it usually flies higher than that species. Mountain valleys with suitable cliffs and gorges, also close to terraced cultivation and villages. **AN** Common House Martin.

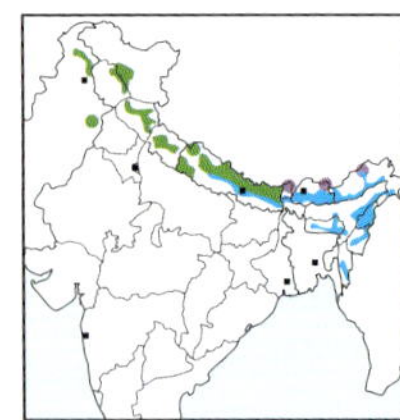

Asian House Martin ***Delichon dasypus*** 12–13cm

Resident. Himalayas to Arunachal; winters NE India. **ID** Adult is very similar to Western House Martin and best distinguished by uniform pale dusky grey-brown wash to underparts, shallower fork to shorter tail (appearing almost square-ended when spread), and darker underwing with dark grey coverts, concolorous with underside of flight feathers. Most adult Asian have variable dusky-brown centres to undertail-coverts, which are lacking on adult Common House Martin but present on juvenile of latter. Rump patch often looks smaller, and dirty white compared to Western. Juvenile has browner upperparts, stronger dusky wash to underparts, broad white tips to tertials, and squarer-shaped tail. **Voice** Like Common. **HH** Habits Like Western. High alpine slopes, grassy hill slopes with cliffs, around mountain villages and over forest.

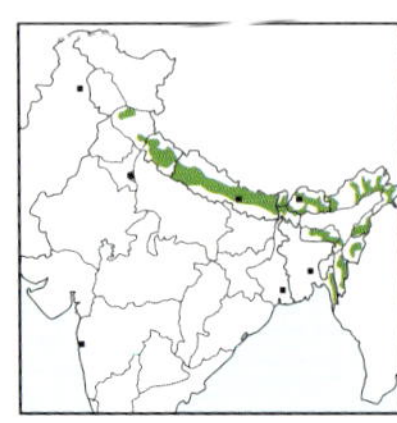

Nepal House Martin ***Delichon nipalense*** 11.5–12.5cm

Resident. Himalayas and NE Indian hills. **ID** Smaller and more compact than Western and Asian, with almost square-cut tail. Underwing-coverts and undertail-coverts are black contrasting sharply with white underparts. Extent of black on throat varies, with only chin black in W Himalayas and south-east of range; in C and E Himalayas has variably mottled blackish throat, giving rise to dark-headed appearance. Juvenile duller and browner on upperparts with buffish wash to underparts. **Voice** Not very vocal; flight call a high-pitched *chi-i.* **HH** Habits like Western. Over forest, river valleys, mountain ridges with cliffs, forest and around villages.

ad
Hill Swallow
juv
ad
ad
Pacific Swallow
Western
House Martin
ad
ad
ad
Asian
House Martin
ad
Nepal
House Martin
ad
ad

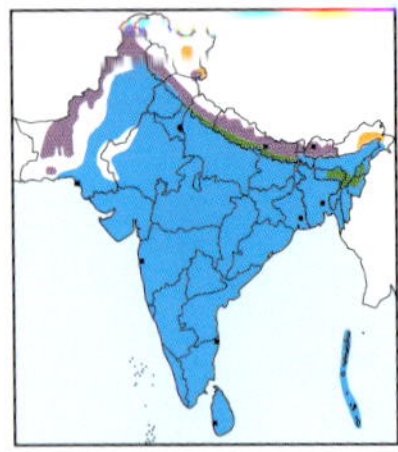

Barn Swallow *Hirundo rustica* — 17–19cm

Breeds in Pakistan hills, Himalayas and NE India; widespread further south in winter. **ID** Adult has bright red forehead and throat, blue-black breast-band and upperparts, and long tail-streamers. Underparts vary from white to rufous. Immature has duller orange forehead and throat, breast-band is browner and less well defined, upperparts are duller, and has shorter tail-streamers. *H. r. tytleri,* a winter visitor to NE subcontinent, has rufous underparts and narrower breast-band. **Voice** Song a varied twittering; clear *vit vit* and in alarm a sharp *vheet vheet.* **HH** Swift and agile flight with frequent banks and turns. Gregarious in non-breeding season. Cultivation, lakes and rivers in open country; often near water in winter.

Wire-tailed Swallow *Hirundo smithii* — 14–21cm

Widespread resident; unrecorded in parts of NW, NE and SE subcontinent. Vagrant: Sri Lanka. **ID** From Barn Swallow by chestnut crown, brighter blue upperparts, glistening white underparts, and fine. filamentous projections to outer tail feathers. White underwing-coverts contrast more strongly with dark underside of flight feathers. Can have pinkish or buffish wash to breast. Wire-like tail-streamers are frequently broken, entirely lost, or difficult to see, tail then appears square-ended. Juvenile has brownish cast to blue upperparts and dull brownish crown and lacks tail-streamers. Possibly confusable with Streak-throated but larger and proportionately longer-winged/shorter-tailed, and has whiter, unstreaked underparts and underwing-coverts. **Voice** Twittering song; calls include a double *chirrik-weet, chit-chit* and *chichip chichip.* **HH** Habits like Barn. Open country and cultivation near lakes, rivers and canals.

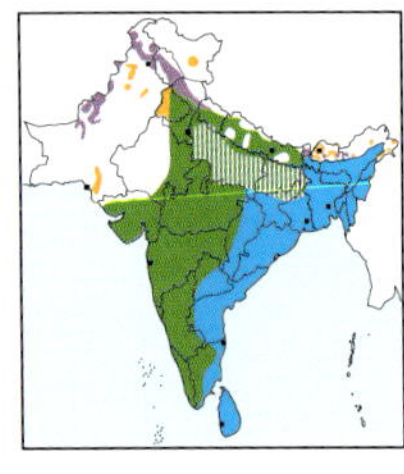

Red-rumped Swallow *Cecropis daurica* — 16–17cm

Widespread resident; unrecorded in parts of NW and NE subcontinent. **ID** From Barn Swallow in having rufous-orange sides of neck (creating collar in some subspecies), rufous-orange rump, finely streaked buffish-white underparts, and black undertail-coverts. Compared to Barn, is bulkier and has slower and more buoyant flight, gliding strongly for prolonged periods. Juvenile has duller upperparts, paler neck-sides (and collar) and rump, buff tips to tertials, and shorter tail-streamers. Considerable racial variation, differing mainly in strength of streaking on and colour of underparts and rump, and prominence of collar. In north-west *C. d. rufula* has whitish underparts and rump, and is unstreaked. In peninsula, *C. d. erythropygia* is lightly streaked with chestnut rump. In Himalayas, *C. d. nipalensis* is heavily streaked. **Voice** Distinctive *treep* call; twittering song. **HH** Habits like Barn. Summers in upland cultivation and over open grassy hill slopes; rocky gorges and cliffs in Balochistan. Winters in open scrub, cultivation and forest clearings.

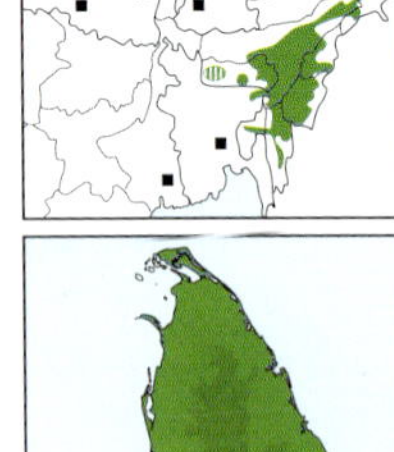

Striated Swallow *Cecropis striolata* — 19cm

NE India, Bangladesh. **ID** From Red-rumped by larger size, stronger (broader and blacker) streaking on underparts and sides of neck, darker rufous face, non-existent or sometimes poorly defined rufous collar, and broader and blacker shaft streaking on rump. Collar can, however, be incomplete in Red-rumped. Juvenile duller on upperparts, and has paler rump, shorter tail-streamers, broader and browner (and more diffuse) streaking below, and buff fringes to coverts and tertials. **Voice** Song a soft twittering. **HH** Habits similar to Red-rumped. Steep cliffs in open hilly areas and forest clearings.

Sri Lanka Swallow *Cecropis hyperythra* — 13–14cm

Resident in lowlands and lower hills of Sri Lanka. **ID** From Red-rumped, by deep chestnut underparts, non-existent or poorly defined chestnut collar, and dark chestnut rump. **Voice** Calls include a slow rising nasal *chueet* and a distinctive musical, whistled drawn-out *pfweeouu*; song a musical twitter. **HH** Paddyfields, open fields and hillsides and lightly wooded areas.

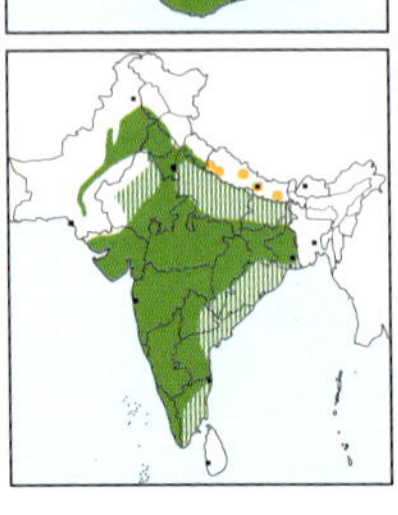

Streak-throated Swallow *Petrochelidon fluvicola* — 11–12cm

Resident. Indus plains; widespread in N and C India; mainly winter visitor to Nepal. Vagrant: Sri Lanka. **ID** A small, compact swallow with slight fork to long broad tail and a weak fluttering flight. Adult from other swallows by combination of lightly streaked chestnut crown and nape, dirty off-white underparts (with brown streaking on chin, throat and breast), narrow white streaks on mantle, and brownish rump. Juvenile has duller, browner crown, and brown-toned mantle and wings, with buff fringes (most obvious on scapulars and tertials). From juvenile Grey-throated Martin by larger size, chestnut cast to crown, blue gloss to mantle, and heavily streaked throat. Streaked throat is best distinction from juvenile Wire-tailed Swallow. **Voice** Song a twittering *chirp*; sharp *trr trr* call in flight. **HH** Habits like Barn. Cultivation and open country near water: rivers, canals, reservoirs and lakes.

juv
rustica
ad
rustica
ad
tytleri
ad
rustica
Barn Swallow
ad
rustica
ad
juv
Wire-tailed
Swallow
ad
ad
ad
juv
ad
ad
nipalensis
ad
nipalensis
Striated
Swallow
juv
Red-rumped
Swallow
ad
ad
ad
juv
Streak-throated
Swallow
ad
Sri Lanka
Swallow

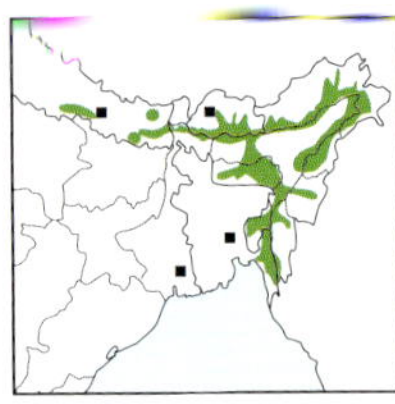

White-throated Bulbul *Alophoixus flaveolus* 21.5–22cm

Resident. Himalayas, NE India and Bangladesh. **ID** Adult striking with prominent brownish crest and puffed-out white throat. Also , whitish lores and grey ear-coverts (streaked white), yellow breast and belly, and olive-green upperparts with rufous-brown cast to wings and tail. Bill stout and pale. Juvenile has browner upperparts, more rufescent wings and tail, and brownish wash to underparts. **Voice** Repeated chacking *chi-chack* and nasal *cheer.* **HH** Creeps and clambers about bushes and low forest storey in flocks. Bushes and undergrowth in dense broadleaved evergreen forest and second growth.

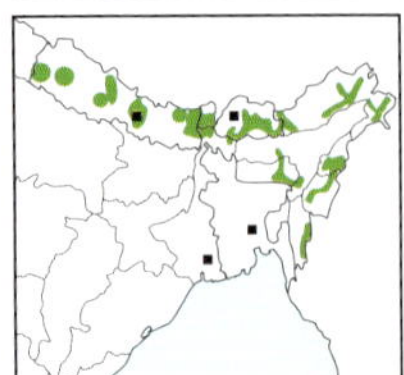

Striated Bulbul *Pycnonotus striatus* 21–23cm

Resident. Himalayas and NE Indian hills. **ID** A crested, green bulbul with bold yellowish-white streaking on underparts, and fine white streaking on crest, ear-coverts and upperparts. Bright yellow lores, eye-ring and throat, and yellow undertail-coverts. In flight, the olive-green tail has pale yellow tips to outer feathers. Juvenile duller and less heavily streaked, with shorter crest. **Voice** Distinctive, repeated disyllabic *chi-chirp.* **HH** In small flocks outside breeding season. Less noisy than most other bulbuls. Forages mostly in treetops. Feeds on berries. Mainly broadleaved evergreen forest, also, moist oak-rhododendron forest and in NE India in deciduous forest.

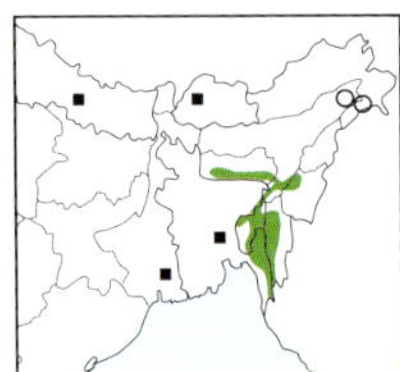

Cachar Bulbul *Iole cacharensis* 17.5–18cm

Resident. NE India and Bangladesh. **ID** A rather nondescript, olive bulbul, with slight crest. Has slight rufous coloration to crown which is furrowed (and appears streaked), and contrasts with pale yellow lores and supercilium giving rise to capped appearance. Underparts unstreaked pale yellow with cinnamon vent, and has rufescent coloration to uppertail-coverts and tail. Bill pale greyish-horn. Legs and feet brownish-pink. Iris greyish. See Grey-eyed Bulbul for differences from that species. **Voice** Disyllabic musical *whe-ic.* **HH** Rather secretive and quiet. Feeds in tops of higher bushes and treetops. Dense, moist, broadleaved evergreen forest and second growth. **TN** Formerly treated as conspecific with Olive Bulbul *I. viridescens.*

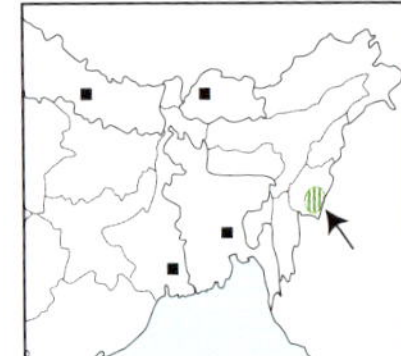

Grey-eyed Bulbul *Iole propinqua* 17–19cm

Resident. Manipur. **ID** Rather nondescript, olive bulbul with cinnamon vent and slight crest. Crown has rufescent cast and is furrowed (appearing streaked). Very similar to Cachar Bulbul. Lores and supercilium greyer, has paler throat, upperparts are olive-brown (less olive) and underparts are duller (less yellow and more olive). Bill pale greyish-horn and iris greyish, similar to Cachar. Calls distinctive. **Voice** Distinctive loud, very nasal *uuu-wit* or *beret*, second note stressed. **HH** Forages in canopy and midstorey. Shy and unobtrusive. Broadleaved evergreen and mixed deciduous forest; also, secondary forest.

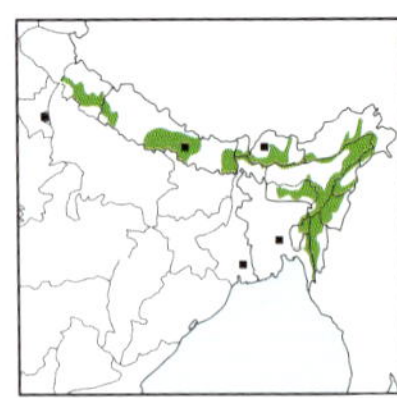

Ashy Bulbul *Hemixos flavala* 20–21cm

Resident. Himalayan foothills, NE India and Bangladesh. **ID** A distinctive, crested bulbul, with black mask, tawny ear-coverts, grey upperparts and greyish-brown tail, olive-yellow wing-panel, white throat, and pale grey breast merging into whitish belly. Juvenile like adult, but has shorter crest, browner upperparts, and duller wing-panel. **Voice** Loud ringing call of 4–5 notes, the second or third highest and the last two descending. **HH** In pairs in breeding season, otherwise in noisy parties. Arboreal, forages in middle and upper storeys. Broadleaved forest, also forest edges in winter.

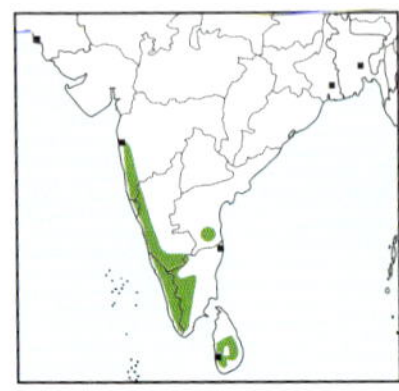

Yellow-browed Bulbul *Acritillas indica* 20cm

Resident. Western Ghats and Sri Lanka. **ID** From other olive bulbuls by bright yellow supercilium and prominent eye-ring, yellow throat and underparts, and uniform olive-green upperparts. Black bill and dark eye are striking. Olive-green upperparts and ear-coverts (latter with some yellow streaking) and yellow underparts give distinctive two-tone appearance. Juvenile duller and browner than adult, with paler bill. Three subspecies are recognised in the subcontinent, varying in tone of greenish upperparts and brightness of yellow of underparts. **Voice** Noisy, often heard before it is seen. Song a slow repetition of pleasant inflected, nasal *pru-eep* or *pru-eehp-eehp.* **HH** In pairs or noisy small flocks in lower and middle storeys. Moist broadleaved forest and second growth.

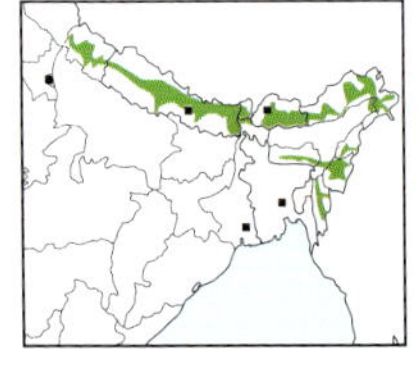

Mountain Bulbul *Ixos mcclellandii* 21–24cm

Resident. Himalayas and NE India. **ID** A distinctive bulbul, with white streaking on shaggy brown crest, white-streaked greyish throat, and cinnamon-brown breast with buff streaking. Greenish mantle, wings and tail, and yellowish vent. Juvenile has shorter crest, uniform grey throat, and browner upperparts. **Voice** Metallic ringing or squawking *tsiuc tsiuc.* **HH** In pairs or small parties. Often puffs out throat. Usually in forest canopy, also second growth and bushes.

White-throated
Bulbul
juv
ad
ad
Striated Bulbul
ad
Cachar Bulbul
Grey-eyed
Bulbul
ad
juv
ad
Yellow-browed
Bulbul
ad
Ashy Bulbul
ad
Mountain Bulbul

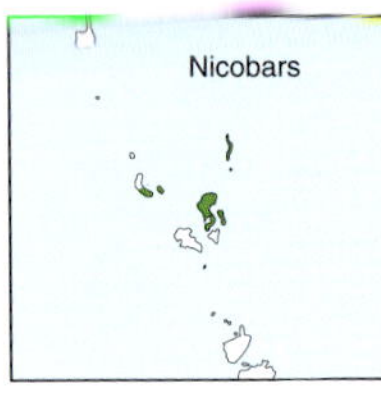

Nicobar Bulbul *Ixos nicobariensis* 20cm

Resident. Nicobars. **ID** A rather drab olive bulbul, with large, mainly yellow bill. Dark brown crown and nape, grey face, and olive upperparts with browner wings and tail. Underparts whitish, faintly washed yellow, with variable brown on breast-sides sometimes forming diffuse breast-band. Juvenile duller with browner upperparts. **Voice** Song is variable, consisting of melodic thrush-like whistles, including harsh chattering notes like Black. Calls include a loud harsh chatter. **HH** Feeding behaviour appears to be opportunistic. Mainly forest, also gardens and second growth. **TN** Sometimes placed in *Hypsipetes*.

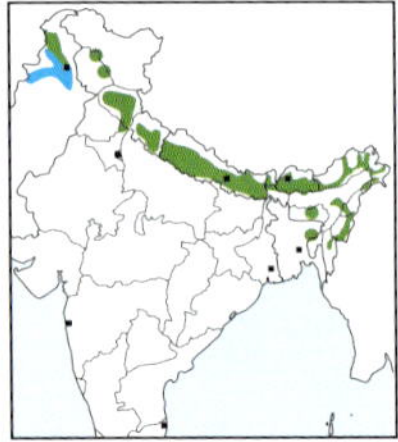

Black Bulbul *Hypsipetes leucocephalus* 23.5–26.5cm

Resident. Himalayas and NE India. **ID** A slate-grey to blackish bulbul, with slight crest. Crest is black and has variable black surround to grey ear-coverts. Also, bright red bill, legs and feet, pale fringes to undertail-coverts, and shallow fork to tail (at times recalling a drongo). Juvenile lacks crest; has whitish throat, grey breast-band, brownish cast to upperparts, and brownish bill, legs and feet. In north-east *H. l. nigrescens* is dull black compared with the paler slate-grey of *H. l. psaroides*, which occupies most of Himalayan range. **Voice** Song a monotonously repeated series of three or four rising and falling notes, also screeching and mewing notes. Large flocks give a continuous, shrill, nasal, chattering babble. **HH** Tall forest, mainly of broadleaf trees.

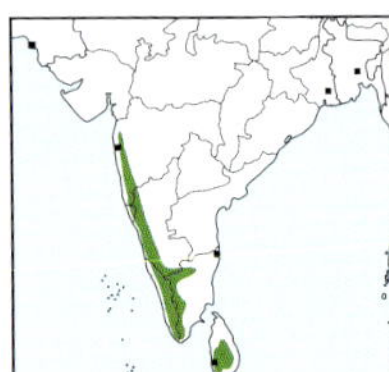

Square-tailed Bulbul *Hypsipetes ganeesa* 21–24cm

Resident. Western Ghats and Sri Lanka. **ID** Darker grey than Black Bulbul, with squarer tail. Crown black but otherwise head is more uniform (lacking black surround to grey ear-coverts). Like Black has bright red bill, legs and feet. **Voice** Much harsher and less nasal than Black. Calls of Indian and Sri Lankan subspecies differ: Indian has higher-pitched, harder, shriller vocalisations, Sri Lankan *humii* noticeably lower and more guttural. **HH** In India in wide variety of forest types, including heavily degraded forests mixed with plantations; in Sri Lanka in wet lowland forests. **TN** Formerly conspecific with Black Bulbul.

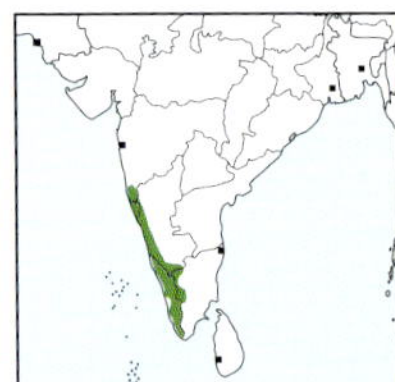

Grey-headed Bulbul *Microtarsus priocephalus* 17–19cm

Resident. SW India. **ID** A grey-and-green bulbul with peaked crown. Has greyish head, greenish-yellow forehead and black chin, striking yellowish bill and bluish-white iris, olive-green upperparts, and uneven black barring on grey-green rump. At rest tail appears grey, but in flight has blackish outer feathers with grey tips. Juvenile has olive-green head, rather than grey, and greener rump, uppertail-coverts and tail. **Voice** Calls incessantly; an explosive, metallic, wheezy repeated *jzhwink*, also a chiming *chraink*. **HH** Feeds on berries and fruits; often with other frugivores. Usually in evergreen forest; also, bamboo, canebrakes, and *Lantana* scrub in deserted clearings. **TN** Formerly placed in *Pycnonotus*.

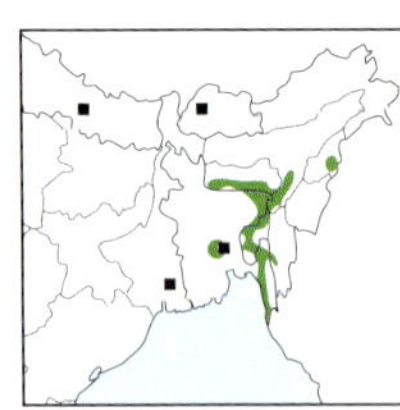

Black-headed Bulbul *Microtarsus melanocephalus* 16–18cm

Resident. NE India and Bangladesh. **ID** A crestless, olive-green and yellow bulbul with black head (with metallic blue sheen in certain lights). From Black-crested by lack of crest, striking yellow panel on wing, and broad black subterminal band and yellow terminal band to tail. Iris is a striking pale blue. Male brighter olive above and yellower below than female. Rare grey morph has greyish nape and underparts (except yellow vent and undertail-coverts). Juvenile darker and duller; chin and throat more olive-green, forehead dark olive; upperparts darker olive, primaries browner, contrasting less with yellow wing-panel. **Voice** Song a hesitant series of short, tuneless whistles; call a ringing metallic *chewp*. **HH** Arboreal, from treetops to undergrowth. Broadleaved evergreen, semi-evergreen and mixed deciduous forests; also, second growth. **TN** Formerly *Pycnonotus atriceps*.

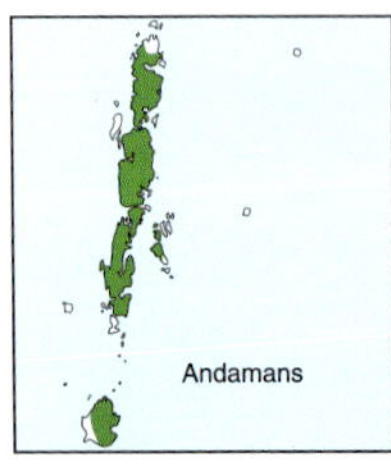

Andaman Bulbul *Microtarsus fuscoflavescens* 14–17cm

Resident. Andamans. **ID** Differs from Black-headed by dusky olive-green head, with darker glossy forehead and blackish throat. Wing-panel duller olive and much less striking than in Black-headed. Tail pattern as Black-headed, with narrower black subterminal band. Bill blue-grey with variable darker tip (all black in Black-headed). Like Black-headed has striking pale blue iris. Male brighter olive above and yellower below than female. Juvenile like female. **Voice** Song a jolting series of unmelodious short piping whistles; call a penetrating *cherk*. **HH** Usually in pairs, sometimes with mixed feeding parties. Evergreen and light deciduous forests, and second growth. **TN** Formerly placed in *Pycnonotus* and considered conspecific with Black-headed.

ad
Nicobar Bulbul
juv
ad
Black Bulbul
ad
Square-tailed Bulbul
ad
Grey-headed Bulbul
ad
juv
ad grey morph
Black-headed Bulbul
ad
Andaman Bulbul

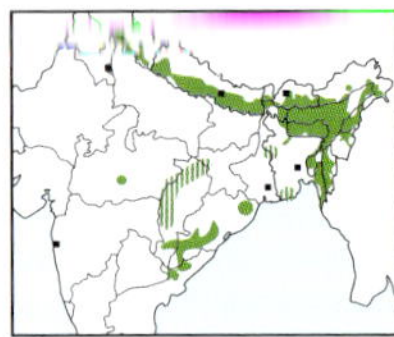

Black-crested Bulbul *Rubigula flaviventris* 18.5–19.5cm

Resident. Himalayas, NE India and Bangladesh. **ID** A black-headed bulbul with olive-green upperparts and yellow underparts. From Black-headed by erect black crest, uniform olive-green wings, olive-brown tail, and striking yellow iris. Juvenile has dull black head and shorter crest, and paler yellow underparts. **Voice** Song sweet and musical, lacking harsh notes: *weet-tre-trippy-weet*. **HH** Moist broadleaved forest with dense undergrowth, thick secondary forest and thickets in abandoned forest clearings. **TN** Formerly placed in *Pycnonotus*.

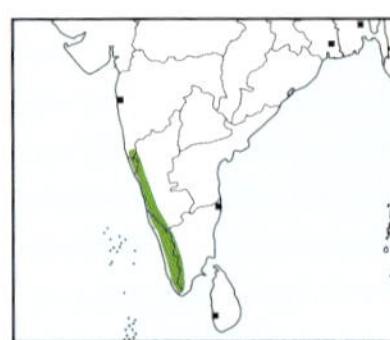

Flame-throated Bulbul *Rubigula gularis* 19.5cm

Resident. Western Ghats. **ID** A black-capped bulbul with olive-green upperparts and yellow underparts. Shows slight crest, and has ruby-red throat, bright yellow breast and belly, striking yellow iris, and indistinct pale tips to outer tail feathers. Juvenile similar but cap browner and has yellow throat. **Voice** Song sweet, hurried and rather high-pitched; calls include subdued churring *prririt*. **HH** Evergreen forest, *Lantana* thickets and bushes along rivers. **TN** Formerly placed in *Pycnonotus*.

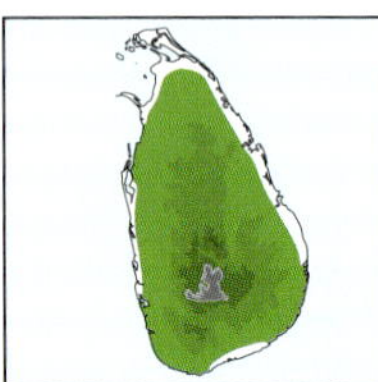

Black-capped Bulbul *Rubigula melanictera* 18–19cm

Resident. Sri Lanka. **ID** A black-capped bulbul with olive-green upperparts and yellow underparts. Lacks crest and has yellow throat concolorous with rest of underparts, dull red or brown iris, and bold white tips to outer tail feathers. Juvenile similar but cap browner. **Voice** Several short, soft whistling songs, some with a 'mournful' quality; call a quick *pit... pipit....* **HH** Open woodland, second growth, forest edges and gardens. **TN** Formerly placed in *Pycnonotus*.

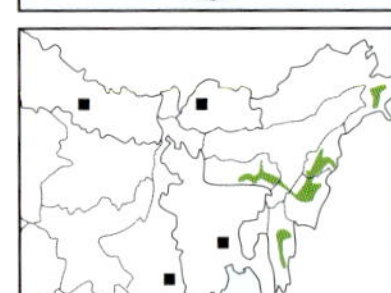

Crested Finchbill *Spizixos canifrons* 19–22cm

Resident. NE Indian hills. **ID** Largely olive-green and yellow. Stout, pale bill, upright crest, and dark tip to tail. Adult has blackish crest and throat, and grey forehead and ear-coverts. Juvenile has short greenish crest, diffuse head pattern and brownish breast-band. **Voice** Song a long bubbling trill *purr-purr-prruit-prruit-prruit*, also a loud series of sputtering notes; gentle scolding, bubbling trills or rattles in alarm. **HH** Broadleaved forest both evergreen and deciduous, second growth and semi-cultivation.

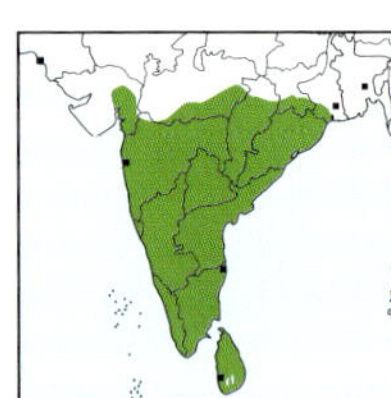

White-browed Bulbul *Pycnonotus luteolus* 20cm

Resident. Peninsular India and Sri Lanka. **ID** A rather nondescript, olive bulbul. Adult has prominent white supercilium, narrow dark eye-stripe, white crescent below eye and dark moustachial stripe, white-streaked ear-coverts, and yellowish chin and malar patch. Pale greyish-olive breast merges into yellowish-white belly; yellowish undertail-coverts. Juvenile has browner upperparts and breast, less distinct supercilium, and uniform olive-brown ear-coverts. **Voice** Simple distinctive song: a cacophonous explosion of loud discordant babbles, usually lasting 1–3 seconds; calls include a rasping *churr*. **HH** Shy, heard more often than seen. Open and dry scrub habitat, arid forest with dense understorey.

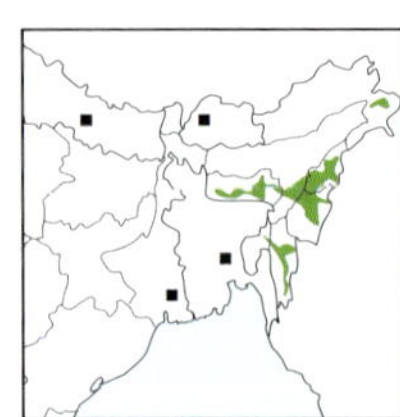

Flavescent Bulbul *Pycnonotus flavescens* 21.5–22cm

Resident. NE Indian hills. Vagrant: Bangladesh. **ID** Has short white supercilium contrasting with black lores, black bill, slight crest, olive-brown upperparts with greenish cast, brownish-grey underparts (mixed with yellow), yellow undertail-coverts, and olive-yellow wings and tail. Juvenile has less prominent supercilium, browner upperparts, rufous edges to flight feathers and paler bill. **Voice** Song a jolly phrase of usually 3–6 notes; harsh alarm call. **HH** Arboreal. In flocks of 6–30 birds. Rather quiet. Forages in bushes and trees, rather than perching conspicuously on top. Favours forest edges and clearings in montane and submontane broadleaved evergreen forest with much undergrowth; also, second growth, scrub, grasslands and deserted cultivation.

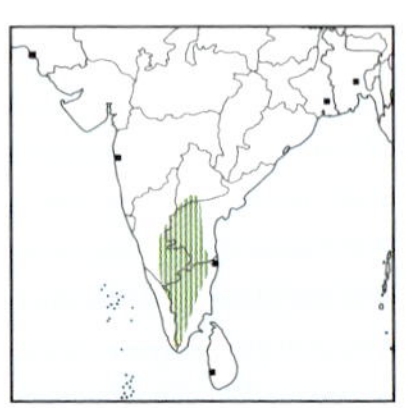

Yellow-throated Bulbul *Pycnonotus xantholaemus* 18.5–19.5cm

Resident. S Indian hills. **ID** A crestless bulbul with plain yellow-green head and bright yellow throat. Grey mantle and breast, yellow vent and undertail-coverts, and broad whitish tip to tail. Wings and tail yellowish-green. **Voice** A rich, low warbling song, individual notes very quick, at first rising, then falling in pitch, then more constant in pitch; like White-browed Bulbul song, but many more sweet notes; pleasant nasal call, a mellow *rhid-tu-tu*. **HH** In pairs or small groups of up to six birds. Shy, but often sits on large boulders in the open. Stony slopes with tall shrubs and boulders, thorn scrub, and moist deciduous woodland, often with dense *Lantana* and *Ziziphus*. Globally threatened.

Black-crested
Bulbul
ad
juv
ad
Black-capped
Bulbul
ad
Flame-throated
Bulbul
juv
Crested Finchbill
ad
ad
White-browed Bulbul
ad
ad
Flavescent
Bulbul
ad
Yellow-throated
Bulbul

Yellow-eared Bulbul *Pycnonotus penicillatus* 20cm

Resident. Sri Lanka. **ID** A striking bulbul, with yellow tuft behind eye and yellow patch on ear-coverts, white eyebrow and tuft extending from lores, and black crown, eye-stripe and moustachial stripe. Juvenile duller with less clear-cut pattern to head. **Voice** A loud sweet-toned whistle *wheet wit wit*, usually in flight; alarm note a low *crr crr*. **HH** Fairly shy. Gathers in large numbers when trees are fruiting. Prefers middle canopy and low bushes. Forest, well-wooded areas and gardens.

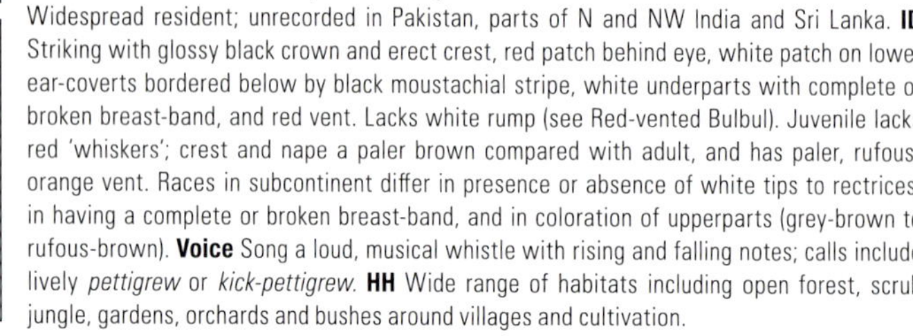

Red-whiskered Bulbul *Pycnonotus jocosus* 20cm

Widespread resident; unrecorded in Pakistan, parts of N and NW India and Sri Lanka. **ID** Striking with glossy black crown and erect crest, red patch behind eye, white patch on lower ear-coverts bordered below by black moustachial stripe, white underparts with complete or broken breast-band, and red vent. Lacks white rump (see Red-vented Bulbul). Juvenile lacks red 'whiskers'; crest and nape a paler brown compared with adult, and has paler, rufous-orange vent. Races in subcontinent differ in presence or absence of white tips to rectrices, in having a complete or broken breast-band, and in coloration of upperparts (grey-brown to rufous-brown). **Voice** Song a loud, musical whistle with rising and falling notes; calls include lively *pettigrew* or *kick-pettigrew*. **HH** Wide range of habitats including open forest, scrub jungle, gardens, orchards and bushes around villages and cultivation.

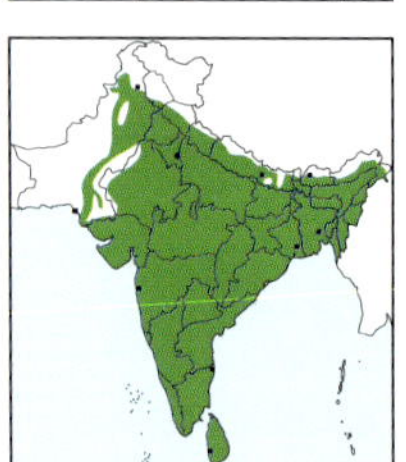

Red-vented Bulbul *Pycnonotus cafer* 20–23cm

Widespread resident. **ID** Mainly brown bulbul. Has short-crested black head, white rump, white-tipped black tail, and red vent. White rump helps separate from other bulbuls in flight. Juvenile has browner head, rufous edges to flight feathers, buffish cast to white rump, and lacks white tips to tail. Considerable subspecies variation, mainly in extent to which black of head reaches onto mantle and breast, and in prominence of pale fringes to feathers of mantle and breast. In north-west, frequently hybridises with White-eared and Himalayan. **Voice** Two songs: at dawn a melodious song with flute-like whistles; other is a short, rapidly repeated *wheet-wheet-ear*; in alarm a loud, sharp *peep* or rapidly repeated series of *peep-peep-peep* notes. **HH** Bold, tame and quarrelsome. In pairs or small loose flocks. Open deciduous forest, second growth, gardens and light scrub.

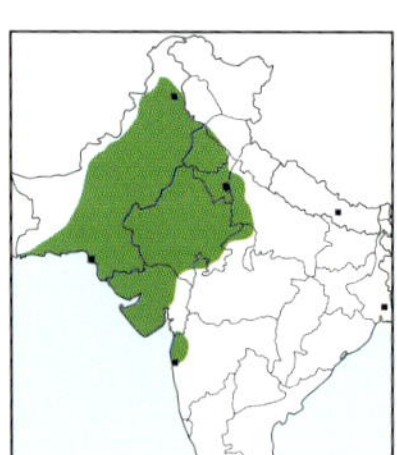

White-eared Bulbul *Pycnonotus leucotis* 17.5–19cm

Resident. Pakistan and NW India. **ID** A white-cheeked bulbul with brown upperparts, whitish underparts (with variable brownish-grey flanks), yellow vent, and white tip to tail. From Himalayan by black crown and nape, more extensive white cheek patch, short or non-existent crest and stouter bill. In north-west, hybridises with Himalayan ('*humii*'), where it has short crest. Also hybridises with Red-vented (which see). **Voice** Short, fast, burbling melodies, repeated with small variations, *ghe-did, ghe-did* etc., very similar to Himalayan. Calls include a mellow *pip* or *pip-pip*. **HH** Bold, cheerful and confiding. Very lively and conspicuous, often on tops of perches, posturing and flicking wings. Dry habitats of semi-desert type, thorn scrub, dry cultivation with thickets, gardens and orchards.

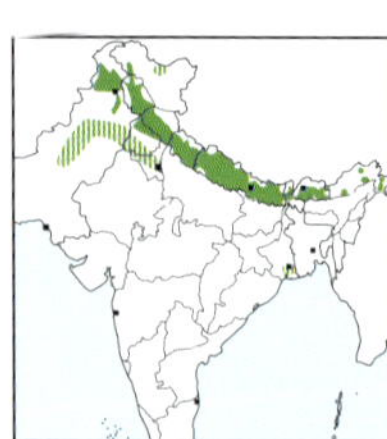

Himalayan Bulbul *Pycnonotus leucogenys* 19–20cm

Resident. N Pakistan hills and Himalayas. **ID** A crested bulbul with white cheeks, black mask and throat, brownish-grey upperparts, yellow vent, and white tip to tail. From White-eared by prominent forward-pointing brown crest, brown nape, smaller white cheek patch with black crescent at rear, and variable narrow white supercilium. Hybridises with White-eared and Red-vented (which see for details). **Voice** Song a variable combination of melodious phrases, *we-did-de-dear-up, whet-what*, and *who-lik-lik-leer*; *plee-plee-plee* flight call, and *wik-wik-wik-wiker* in alarm. **HH** Habits like White-eared. Dry habitats: open dry scrub, hillsides with scattered raspberry and *Berberis* bushes, bushes around towns and villages, second growth.

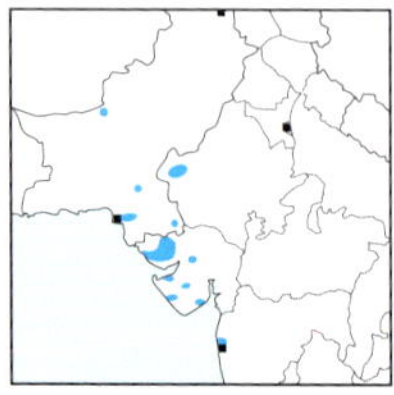

Hypocolius *Hypocolius ampelinus* 23cm

Winter visitor. S Pakistan, Rajasthan and Gujarat. **ID** Long-tailed but rather short-winged. Often raises crown feathers, giving rise to crested appearance. Male mainly grey, with black mask extending to nape, buffish forehead and throat, and black tip to tail. In flight, black primaries with prominent white tips. Female and immature browner and lack black mask; have well-defined creamy-white throat, less white in primaries and diffuse dark tip to tail. **Voice** A mellow liquid *tre-tur-tur*, and a descending *whee-oo*. **HH** Gregarious in winter, in flocks of up to 20. Forages chiefly by hopping and clambering about in trees and bushes; sometimes descends to ground to pick up insects. Semi-desert with scattered thorn scrub of berried bushes, around oases and date-palm groves. **AN** Grey Hypocolius.

Yellow-eared
Bulbul
ad
Red-whiskered
Bulbul
ad
fuscicaudatus
ad
emeria
juv
emeria
ad
humayuni
White-eared
Bulbul
ad
humii
Red-vented
Bulbul
ad
bengalensis
ad
ad
leucotis
Himalayan
Bulbul
juv
bengalensis
♀
♂
Hypocolius

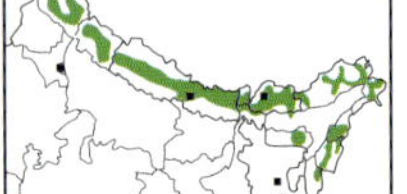
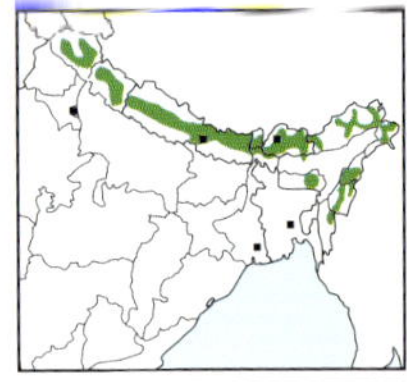

Ashy-throated Warbler *Phylloscopus maculipennis* 9–10cm

Resident. Himalayas and NE Indian hills. **ID** Yellow rump and double yellowish wing-bars. From Lemon-rumped by greyish-white supercilium and crown-stripe contrasting with dark grey lateral crown-stripes and eye-stripe, greyish ear-coverts, throat and breast, yellow belly, and white in tail (apparent as it is flicked open; from below appears largely white with dark border). Possibly confusable with Buff-barred, but smaller and more compact, with smaller bill, yellowish wing-bars, greyish-white supercilium and crown-stripe, two-toned grey-and-yellow underparts, and more clearly defined yellow rump. **Voice** Song a whistled series of sweet phrases all the same tone, *ti-wee-ty wee-ty wee-ty*, also *whee-tew-whee-tew*; call a short *swit*. **HH** Summers mainly in broadleaved forest; also, second growth in winter.

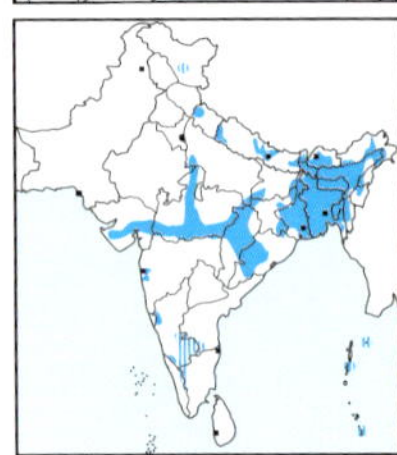

Yellow-browed Warbler *Phylloscopus inornatus* 10–11cm

Winter visitor. E Himalayas, NE, C and S India, and Bangladesh. **ID** In fresh plumage, has brighter greenish-olive upperparts compared to Hume's, and has yellowish-white supercilium, ear-coverts and wing-bars; median covert wing-bar is well defined, and underparts white with variable amounts of yellow. In worn plumage, close in coloration to Hume's, but has pale base to lower mandible, and legs are paler pinkish- or greyish-brown (bill and legs darker on Hume's). **Voice** Loud rising *chewiest* call, different from Hume's. **HH** Groves and open forest.

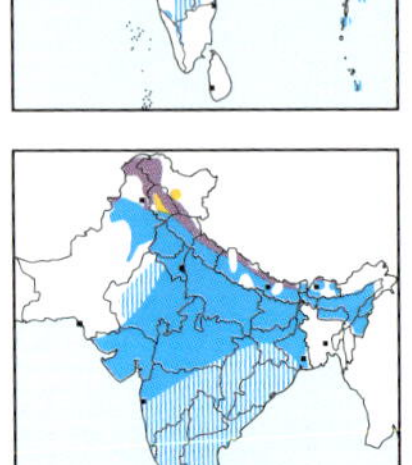

Hume's Warbler *Phylloscopus humei* 10–11cm

Breeds in Himalayas; winters in plains. Vagrant: Bangladesh. **ID** Compared to Yellow-browed has greyish-olive upperparts, with variable yellowish-green on mantle and back, and browner crown, while supercilium, ear-coverts and greater covert wing-bar buffish-white. Median covert bar poorly defined. Bill all dark, legs blackish-brown. Supercilium, wing-bars and underparts white when worn, upperparts much greyer. *P. h. mandellii* (winter visitor to north-east) has darker olive-green upperparts, with dirty yellowish-white supercilium and underparts, more pronounced paler crown-stripe and different call. **Voice** Song a repeated *wesoo*, often followed by descending high-pitched *zweeeeeeeoooo*; disyllabic *whit-hoot* or *visu-visu* and sparrow-like *chwee* calls; strikingly disyllabic, repeated *tjis-ip* in *mandellii*. **HH** Breeds in subalpine forest and shrubbery; winters in open broadleaved forest and well-wooded areas. **TN** *P. h. mandellii* sometimes treated as separate species ('Mandellii's Leaf Warbler'). **AN** Hume's Leaf Warbler.

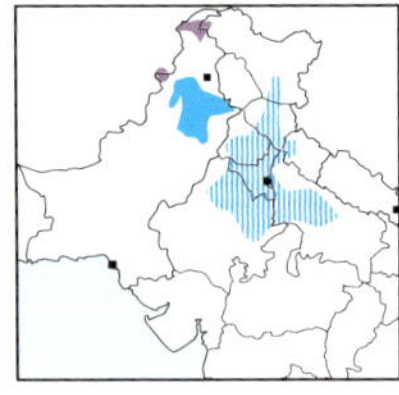

Brooks's Leaf Warbler *Phylloscopus subviridis* 9–10cm

Breeds in Pakistan Himalayas; winters in plains and hills in Pakistan and N India. **ID** From Hume's Warbler by indistinct greenish-yellow crown-stripe, yellow supercilium (often brighter in front of eye and joining across forehead), yellow wash to cheeks and throat, brighter yellowish-olive upperparts, and (poorly defined) yellowish rump. In worn plumage, general coloration approaches worn Hume's, but always has yellowish supercilium and usually some yellow on throat. Bill has yellowish base to lower mandible (all dark in Hume's). Lacks dark sides to crown and dark bases to wing-coverts and secondaries of Lemon-rumped. **Voice** Song of distinctive sibilant trills; call different from Hume's, a loud piercing *chwee*. **HH** Summers in coniferous and mixed forest; winters in bushes and well-wooded areas.

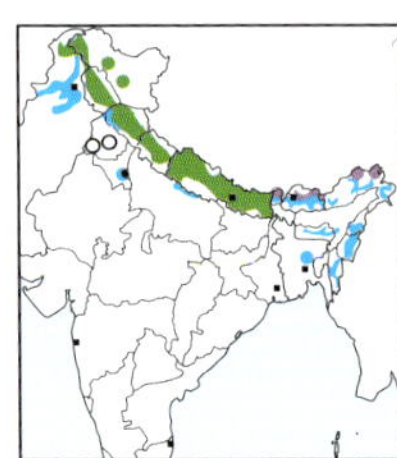

Lemon-rumped Warbler *Phylloscopus chloronotus* 9–10cm

Resident. Breeds in Himalayas; winters lower down and in NE Indian hills. Vagrant: Bangladesh. **ID** Has broad yellowish-white supercilium and crown-stripe (contrasting with dark olive sides of crown), double yellowish-white wing-bars, well-defined yellowish (sometimes almost whitish) rump, and whitish underparts. Lacks white on tail. *P. c. simlaensis* (W Himalayas) has brighter yellowish-green upperparts, and brighter yellow supercilium and crown-stripe, compared with nominate (C and E Himalayas). See Vagrants for differences from Pallas's Leaf Warbler. **Voice** Two songs: one a drawn-out thin rattle followed by a series of stammering notes on same pitch; the other a stuttering series of notes with alternating pitch; high-pitched *uist* call. **HH** Breeds in coniferous, mixed and broadleaved forests; winters in forest and second growth.

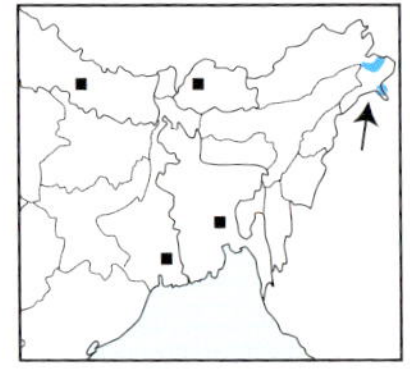

Sichuan Leaf Warbler *Phylloscopus forresti* 9–10cm

Winter visitor to NE India. **ID** Not safely distinguished in the field from Lemon-rumped Warbler (due to possible hybridisation or introgression) except by call and song. Upperparts darker greyish green, has brighter sulphur yellow rump and bill is all dark (pale at base of lower mandible in Lemon-rumped). **Voice** Call *tsuist*, longer than calls of Lemon-rumped. Two distinct songs, one a thin buzzing rattle that ends in slower series of *ti* notes; the other a prolonged series of several different notes given singly or in a series. **HH** Feeds in canopy and understorey. Montane mixed coniferous-broadleaved forests, also pine forest.

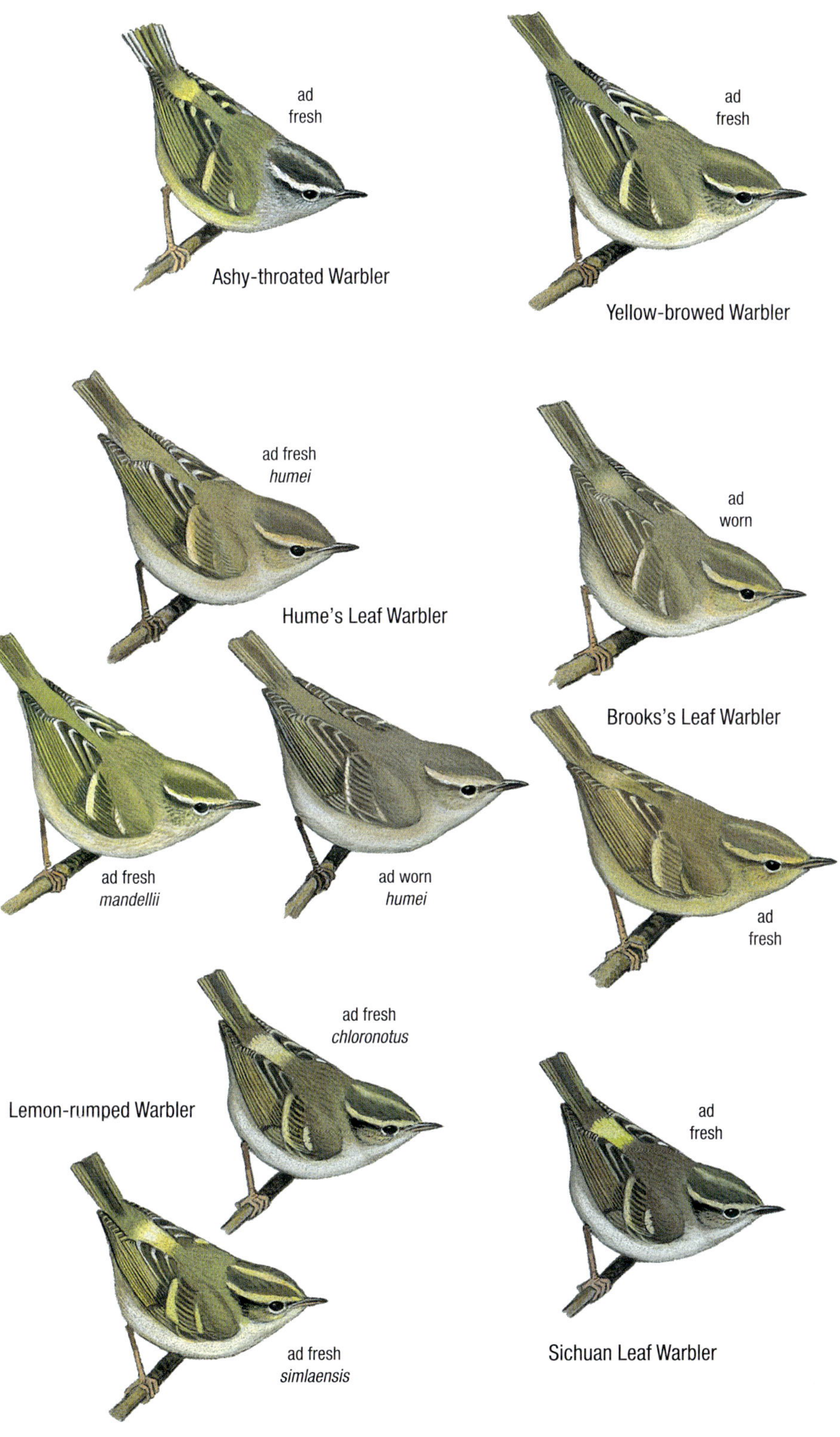
ad
fresh
Ashy-throated Warbler
ad
fresh
Yellow-browed Warbler
ad fresh
humei
Hume's Leaf Warbler
ad
worn
ad fresh
mandellii
ad worn
humei
Brooks's Leaf Warbler
ad
fresh
ad fresh
chloronotus
Lemon-rumped Warbler
ad fresh
simlaensis
ad
fresh
Sichuan Leaf Warbler

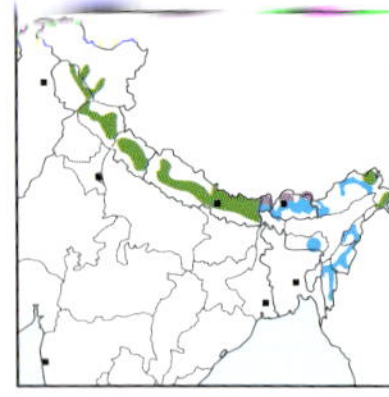

Buff-barred Warbler *Phylloscopus pulcher* 10–11cm

Resident. Himalayas and NE Indian hills. **ID** Buffish-orange wing-bars, white on tail (apparent when flicked open), yellowish supercilium, and small yellowish rump patch. Poorly defined dull yellowish centre to rear crown. Otherwise, upperparts dark olive-green, with greyer sides to crown, and underparts are dull, sullied with grey and can be washed with yellow. From below, tail appears largely white with dark border. *P. p. kangrae* (NW Himalayas) brighter than nominate (C and E Himalayas), with more yellowish-olive upperparts and cleaner yellow underparts **Voice** Song a high-pitched twitter, preceded by, or ending in, a drawn-out trill; call a short, sharp *swit*. **HH** Breeds in subalpine shrubbery and forest; winters in broadleaved forest.

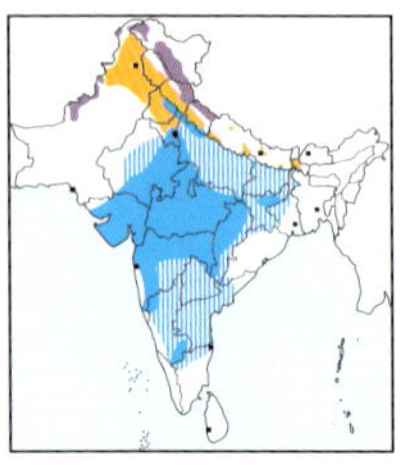

Sulphur-bellied Warbler *Phylloscopus griseolus* 10–11.5cm

Breeds in hills of W Pakistan and W Himalayas; winters mainly in N and C India. **ID** From Tickell's by colder brownish-grey upperparts lacking any greenish tones, greyish-white edges to remiges, and duller buffish underparts (yellow purest on belly). Supercilium bright sulphur-yellow, brighter than throat, and has grey-brown ear-coverts and sides of breast (yellow on Tickell's and contrast with more prominent dark eye-stripe). **Voice** Soft *quip* call, distinct from Tickell's; song a very short, high-pitched trill of several notes on same pitch, beginning with high thin whistle: *tseeep-tyi-tyi-tyi-tyi-tyi*. **HH** Distinctive habit of climbing trees and walls/rock faces. Breeds on stony slopes with scattered trees and bushes; winters in rocky areas and around old buildings.

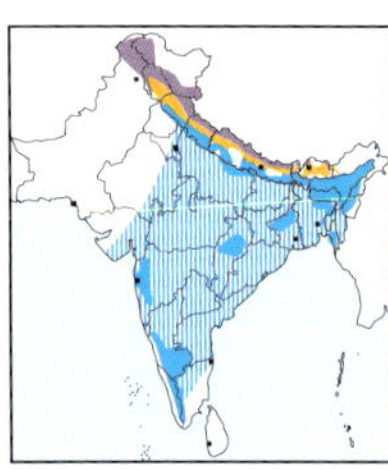

Tickell's Leaf Warbler *Phylloscopus affinis* 10–11cm

Breeds in Himalayas; widespread in winter; unrecorded in Sri Lanka. **ID** From Sulphur-bellied by greenish-brown upperparts, greenish edges to wing feathers, and brighter lemon-yellow underparts. Supercilium similar in coloration to throat, and eye-stripe more clearly defined than on Sulphur-bellied, contrasting with yellowish ear-coverts. Bill longer, with brighter base to lower mandible and distinct dark tip. Worn birds may lack greenish cast to upperparts, have paler yellow supercilium and underparts, and coloration can be like Sulphur-bellied. Confusable, due to coloration, with Aberrant Bush Warbler, but has shorter and squarer tail, longer extension of primaries beyond secondaries, and different call. **Voice** Song a short *chip... whi-whi-whi-whi*, like Sulphur-bellied but hard introductory note is different; call a *chit*, not as hard as Dusky. **HH** Breeds in open country with bushes; winters in bushes at edges of forest and cultivation.

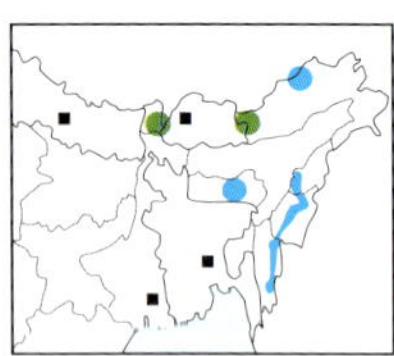

Buff-throated Warbler *Phylloscopus subaffinis* 10.5–11cm

NE India. **ID** Very similar in appearance to Tickell's and best told by less prominent buffish-yellow supercilium and yellowish-buff underparts. Duskier on ear-coverts, has less distinct eye-stripe, and extensive dark tip to lower mandible. **Voice** Song a series of soft notes, *tuee-tuee-tuee-tuee-tuee*, similar to Tickell's but generally slower and weaker, and sometimes starts with soft *trr* or *trr trr*. Call a soft, almost insect-like *chirrup*. **HH** Dense undergrowth of grassland and bushes.

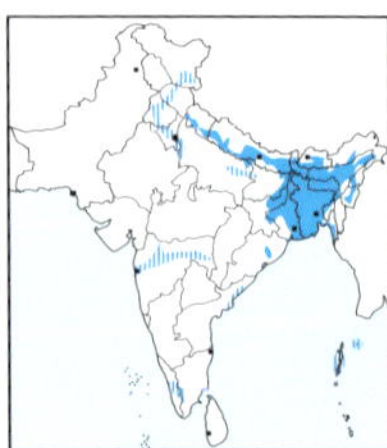

Dusky Warbler *Phylloscopus fuscatus* 11–12cm

Winter visitor. Mainly Himalayan foothills, NE India and Bangladesh also locally in N India and peninsula. Vagrant Sri Lanka. **ID** Whitish underparts, often with buff on sides of breast and flanks, and dark brown to paler greyish-brown upperparts. Hard chacking call diagnostic. Appears stockier than Common Chiffchaff, with more prominent supercilium and stronger dark eye-stripe, lacks olive-green edges to wing feathers and yellow at bend of wing, has paler legs, and pale base to lower mandible. North-east wintering *P. f. weigoldi* darker above, and duskier below, with touch of yellow on underparts in fresh plumage. **Voice** Hard *chack chack* call. **HH** Bushes and long grass.

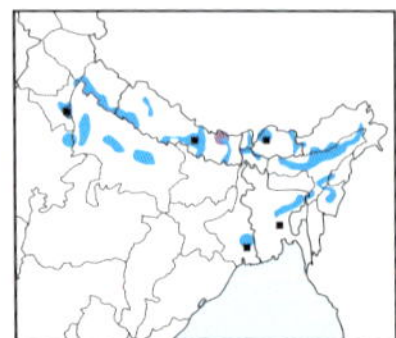

Smoky Warbler *Phylloscopus fuligiventer* 10–11cm

Breeds in C and E Himalayas; winters in adjacent foothills and plains. Vagrant: Bangladesh **ID** From Dusky and Sulphur-bellied by smaller size, short-looking tail, darker sooty-olive upperparts (with greenish tinge in fresh plumage), short, indistinct supercilium (with bold white crescent below eye), and mainly dusky-olive underparts (with oily yellow centre). **Voice** Song a monotonous *tsli-tsli-tsli-tsli-tsli*; throaty *thrup thrup* call. **HH** Breeds in subalpine shrubbery and alpine meadows; winters in dense vegetation near water.

ad fresh
pulcher
Buff-barred Warbler
Sulphur-bellied Warbler
ad
fresh
ad
fresh
Tickell's Leaf Warbler
ad
fresh
Buff-throated Warbler
ad
fresh
Dusky Warbler
ad
fresh
Smoky Warbler

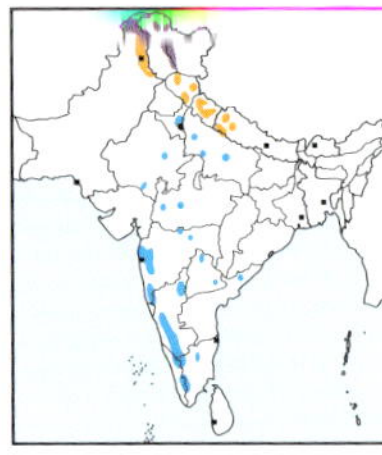

Tytler's Leaf Warbler *Phylloscopus tytleri* 10–12cm

Breeds in W Himalayas; winters mainly in Western Ghats. **ID** From Greenish by long, slender, mainly dark bill, shorter tail, lack of wing-bar (can be lacking on worn-plumaged Greenish), and different call. Supercilium tends to look finer and is offset by rather broad and well-defined dark olive lores and eye-stripe. In fresh plumage, has dark greenish cast to upperparts, supercilium is yellowish-white, and has variable yellowish wash to ear-coverts and underparts. In worn plumage, supercilium and underparts whitish, and upperparts greyer. **Voice** Song a distinctive, even-paced, high-pitched, rising and falling *pi-tsi-pi-tsu*; call a disyllabic *chiwee chiwee*, second note higher and has upward inflection. **HH** Very active, often found in thickets, also conifer trees. Breeds in coniferous forest and subalpine shrubbery; winters in broadleaved forest.

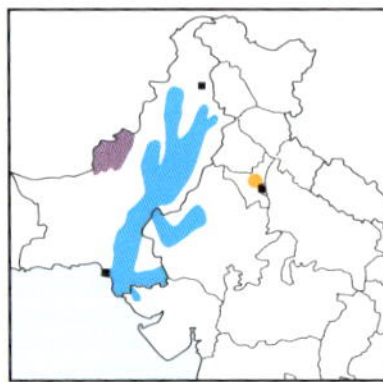

Plain Leaf Warbler *Phylloscopus neglectus* 9–10cm

Breeds in hills of Balochistan; winters mainly in Pakistan lowlands. **ID** Smaller than Common Chiffchaff with proportionately larger head and shorter tail; distinctive calls. Flicks wings, but does not seem to bob tail, and hovers frequently. Lacks yellowish or greenish tones on upperparts (including wings), which are paler and greyer. **Voice** Song a frequently repeated, soft twittering warble, including *zilitzwit, twissa twissa, chit-chuwich-chissa*; calls include hard *tak-tak*, low-pitched *churr* and finch-like nasal *nap* or *chap*. **HH** Breeds in juniper and pine forests; winters in open wooded areas.

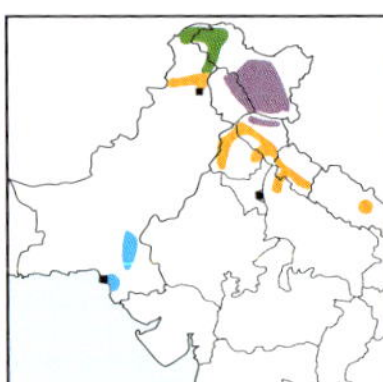

Mountain Chiffchaff *Phylloscopus sindianus* 10.5–12cm

Pakistan and NW India; breeds in Himalayas, winters in plains and foothills. Vagrant: Nepal. **ID** Much as Common Chiffchaff but lacks olive-green tinge to rump and has buffish edges to wing and tail feathers. In fresh plumage, shows warm buff coloration to ear-coverts, breast-sides and flanks (although Common can be similar) and upperparts are warmer sandy brown. Bend of wing often whitish (usually brighter yellow on Common). Worn birds not safely identifiable on plumage but call is different. **Voice** Song a frequently repeated tinny-sounding *chit-chiss-chyi-chiss-chit-chiss-chyi-chip-chit-chyi*; distinctive disyllabic *swe-eet* call. **HH** Breeds in subalpine shrubbery; winters in trees and bushes near water.

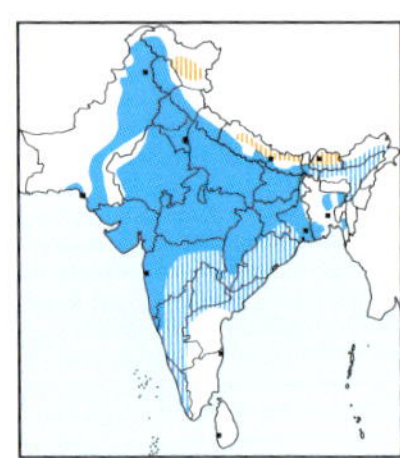

Common Chiffchaff *Phylloscopus collybita* 11–12cm

Winter visitor. Subcontinent except W Pakistan and parts of NW, NE and SE India. **ID** Whitish or buffish supercilium, and greyish to brownish upperparts with olive-green cast to rump, wings and tail. Underparts whitish, with buffish or greyish on sides of breast and flanks. Blackish bill and legs, less prominent supercilium (with prominent whitish crescent below eye) and absence of wing-bar help separate from Greenish Warbler. **Voice** Calls include a plaintive *peu* or *hweet*. **HH** Forest bushes, crops and reedbeds.

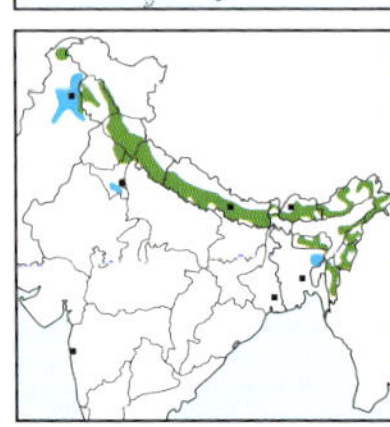

Grey-hooded Warbler *Phylloscopus xanthoschistos* 10–11cm

Resident. Himalayas and NE Indian hills. **ID** From other *Phylloscopus* by combination of greyish-white supercilium, grey crown and mantle, bright yellow underparts, and white in outer tail. Has diffuse pale grey central crown-stripe and darker lateral crown-stripes. *P. x. albosuperciliaris* (W Himalayas) has paler grey lateral crown-stripes and mantle (with brownish cast) compared to races in E Himalayas and north-east (e.g. nominate), which are purer and darker grey in these areas, with noticeable contrast between grey of mantle and green of back. **Voice** Song a brief, incessantly repeated high-pitched warble, *ti-tsi-ti-wee-tee*; high-pitched *psit-psit* and plaintive *tyee-tyee* calls. **HH** Arboreal, hunts restlessly, mainly in midstorey. Broadleaved and broadleaved/coniferous forest and second growth. **TN** Formerly placed in *Seicercus*.

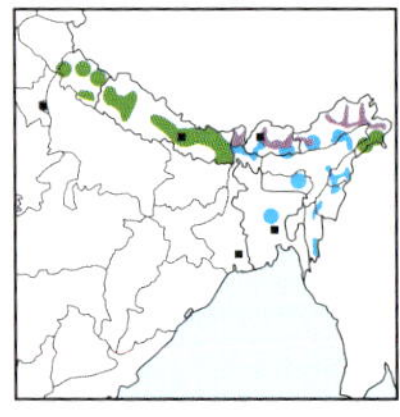

Chestnut-crowned Warbler *Phylloscopus castaniceps* 9–10.5cm

Resident. Himalayas and NE Indian hills. **ID** Easily told from other *Phylloscopus* by combination of small size, chestnut crown with diffuse dark brown lateral crown-stripes, bright lemon-yellow rump, grey sides of head with white eye-ring, grey throat and upper breast contrasting with white lower breast and belly, and bright yellow flanks. Grey on sides of head, double yellow wing-bar, prominent yellow rump, prominent white eye-ring are best features for separation from larger and longer-billed Broad-billed Warbler. **Voice** A 5–7-note song, extremely high-pitched, sibilant and slightly undulating. **HH** Often with mixed foraging flocks of warblers and tits. Flits restlessly about middle and upper storeys. Frequently hovers, flutters and makes aerial sallies. Broadleaved forest, mainly oak. **TN** Formerly placed in *Seicercus*.

ad
fresh
ad
fresh
ad
worn
Tytler's Leaf Warbler
ad
worn
Plain Leaf Warbler
ad
fresh
ad worn
tristis
Mountain
Chiffchaff
ad fresh
tristis
ad
xanthoschistos
Common Chiffchaff
Grey-hooded
Warbler
ad
ad
albosuperciliaris
Chestnut-crowned
Warbler

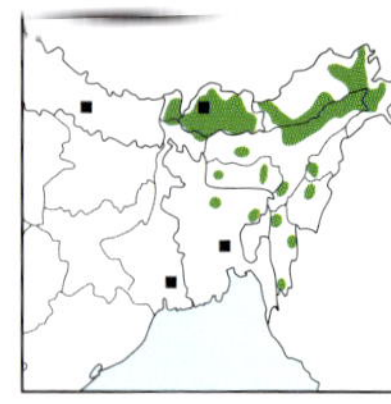

White-spectacled Warbler *Phylloscopus intermedius* 11–12cm

Resident. Mainly E Himalayas and NE Indian hills. Vagrant: Bangladesh. **ID** Has white eye-ring and grey crown. From Grey-cheeked Warbler by yellow chin and upper throat, clearer grey supercilium and crown-stripe contrasting with well-defined dark grey lateral crown-stripes, greenish (rather than grey) lower ear-coverts, yellowish lores, and lower mandible entirely pale orange (mainly dark in Grey-cheeked). Can show touch of yellow on anterior edge of white eye-ring, which is not apparent on Grey-cheeked. **Voice** Song a combination of sweet variable phrases each consisting of 5–8 rapidly delivered notes including *tuitittuitittuitit*; sharp *che-wheet* call. **HH** Often joins mixed parties of insectivores in non-breeding season. Flits actively about undergrowth and bushes. Frequently makes aerial sallies, and flutters and hovers among foliage and twigs. Dense, moist broadleaved evergreen and pine forest. **TN** Formerly *Seicercus affinis*.

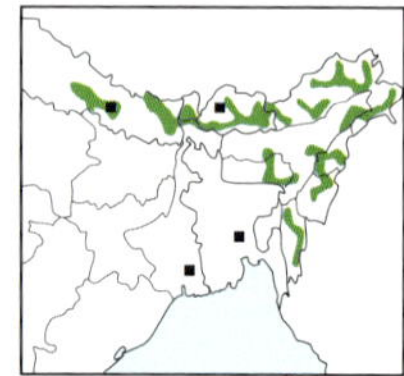

Grey-cheeked Warbler *Phylloscopus poliogenys* 10–11cm

Resident. E Himalayas and NE Indian hills. **ID** Grey crown and prominent white eye-ring like White-spectacled, but has whitish chin and upper throat, darker grey ear-coverts, and more uniform dark grey head, with poorly defined crown-stripe and diffuse dark sides to crown. Also, bill smaller with darker lower mandible, and yellow wing-bar more pronounced. **Voice** Song like White-spectacled but less melodic, and notes more slurred together, phrases include *titsi-titsi-chi*; calls include an explosive *twit...twit*. **HH** Habits like White-spectacled. Evergreen broadleaved forest and bamboo. **TN** Formerly placed in *Seicercus*.

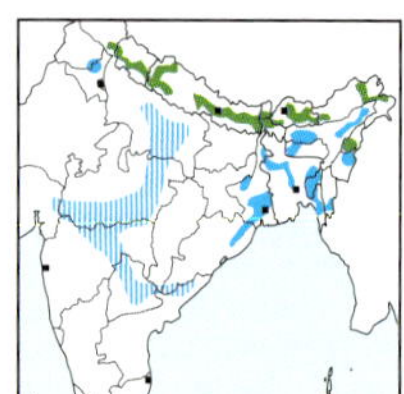

Green-crowned Warbler *Phylloscopus burkii* 11–12cm

Breeds in Himalayas and NE Indian hills; winters lower down in same hills, also Bangladesh and N, C and E India. **ID** Yellow eye-ring, yellowish-green face and green crown. Compared with Whistler's, sides to crown blacker and more clearly defined on forehead, has narrower eye-ring (broken at rear), and usually lacks wing-bar. See Whistler's for further information. From Grey-crowned by green crown. **Voice** Song a variety of quite rich phrases, e.g. *weet-weeta-weeta-weet* interspersed with short trills; call a soft, whipping *huit*. **HH** Feeding behaviour like White-spectacled. Understorey in broadleaved, coniferous and mixed forests and second growth. **TN** Formerly placed in *Seicercus*.

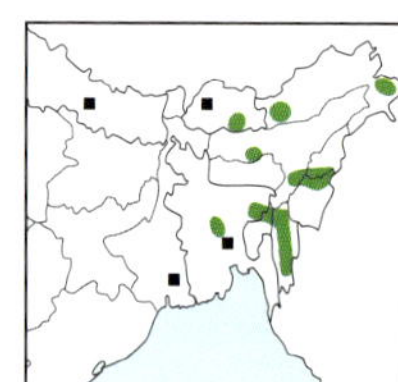

Grey-crowned Warbler *Phylloscopus tephrocephalus* 10–11cm

Resident or summer visitor. NE Indian hills and E Bhutan. **ID** Much like Green-crowned, with yellow eye-ring and dark sides to crown, but crown and supercilium greyer (less olive). Sides of crown blacker than in Whistler's (which also has green crown), but lacks prominent wing-bar, has narrower eye-ring (broken at rear) and longer bill. **Voice** Song easily told from similar species by presence of tremolos and trills; alarm call a short metallic *chilip*. **HH** Feeding behaviour like White-spectacled. Understorey in broadleaved evergreen forest, second growth and bamboo. **TN** Formerly placed in *Seicercus*.

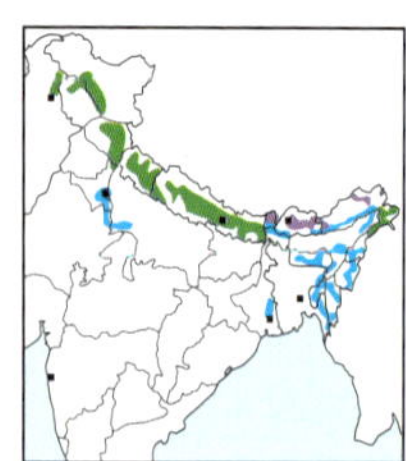

Whistler's Warbler *Phylloscopus whistleri* 11–12cm

Resident. Himalayas and locally in N and E India, and Bangladesh. **ID** Very similar to Green-crowned; dark sides of crown are not as black and are diffuse on forehead, and yellow eye-ring is broader at rear. Generally, upperparts are duller greyish-green, underparts duller yellow, wing-bar usually more distinct, and bill smaller/shorter. Shows more white in outer-tail feathers; there is much white on basal half of outer web of outermost tail rectrix (generally lacks white in this area in Green-crowned). **Voice** Song a simple *witchu-witchu* is best means of separation from Green-crowned. **HH** Feeding behaviour like White-spectacled. Breeds in understorey in broadleaved, coniferous and mixed forest, and high-altitude shrubbery and second growth in winter. **TN** Formerly placed in *Seicercus*.

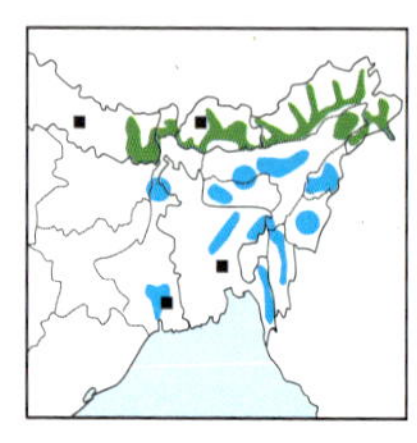

Yellow-vented Warbler *Phylloscopus cantator* 10–11cm

Resident. E Himalayas; winters to NE Indian hills and Bangladesh. **ID** From Blyth's Leaf by yellow throat, upper breast and undertail-coverts contrasting with white lower breast and belly. In addition, smaller in size, has brighter yellow supercilium and crown-stripe contrasting with darker lateral crown-stripes, and has brighter yellowish-green upperparts. **Voice** Song is several single notes on same pitch, ending in two slurred notes: *seep, seep, seep to-you* with the accent on *you;* double call note softer than other *Phylloscopus* with accent on second note. **HH** Often in mixed-species itinerant flocks in winter. Forages actively in lower storey, bushes and lower branches of large trees. Breeds in dense, moist broadleaved evergreen forest; also winters in deciduous forest.

White-spectacled Warbler

Grey-cheeked Warbler

Green-crowned Warbler

Grey-crowned Warbler

Whistler's Warbler

Yellow-vented Warbler

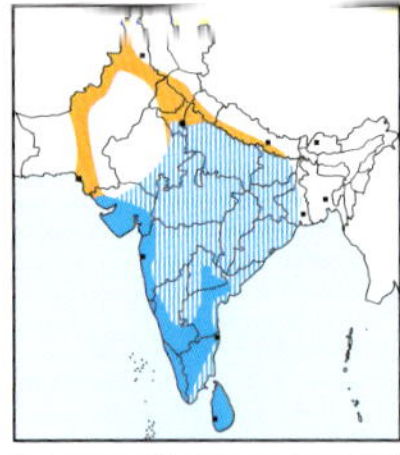

Green Warbler *Phylloscopus nitidus* 10–11cm

Winters mainly in W Ghats and Sri Lanka. **ID** In fresh plumage, upperparts are brighter and purer green than *viridanus* Greenish, and has one, sometimes two, slightly broader and yellower wing-bars, while supercilium and cheeks are noticeably yellow, and underparts have a much stronger yellow suffusion. When worn, upperparts duller, although still brighter than on Greenish, and supercilium and underparts retain yellowish wash, although some are probably indistinguishable. **Voice** Trisyllabic *chis-ru-weet* call (disyllabic in Greenish). **HH** Forages at all levels but prefers upper canopy. Dense forest, wooded gardens and orchards.

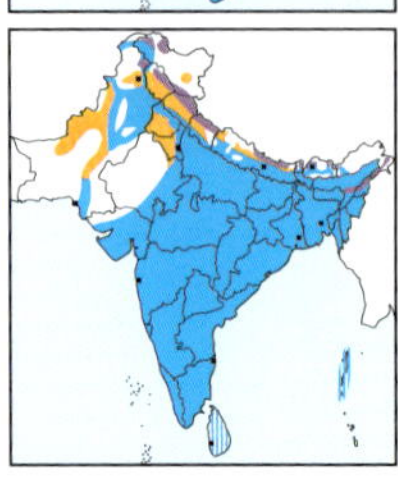

Greenish Warbler *Phylloscopus trochiloides* 10–11cm

Breeds in Himalayas and NE Indian hills; widespread in winter. **ID** Variable *Phylloscopus* with uniform crown, fine wing-bars, and distinctive call. In fresh plumage *P. t. ludlowi* and *P. t. viridanus* (W Himalayas; more widespread in winter) have olive-green upperparts, a single white wing-bar, yellowish-white supercilium, and whitish underparts with faint yellowish suffusion. When worn, upperparts duller and greyer and underparts whiter, and wing-bar can be absent. Nominate (C and E Himalayas and north-east) has darker oily green upperparts (with darker crown), mottled ear-coverts, dusky underparts with diffuse oily yellow wash, and darker bill (with orange at base of lower mandible); often shows trace of second (median covert) wing-bar. Nominate can appear very similar to Large-billed Leaf; best told by call. See Vagrants for differences from Two-barred and Arctic Warblers. **Voice** *P. t. viridanus* has loud, slurred and abrupt disyllabic *chi-weee* call; loud, repeated *chi-chi-chi-chiwee-chiweee* song. *P. t. trochiloides* has *chis-weet* call; *chis-weet, chis-weet* song. **HH** Forages from canopy down to ground. Breeds in broadleaved and coniferous forest and subalpine shrubbery; winters in well-wooded areas.

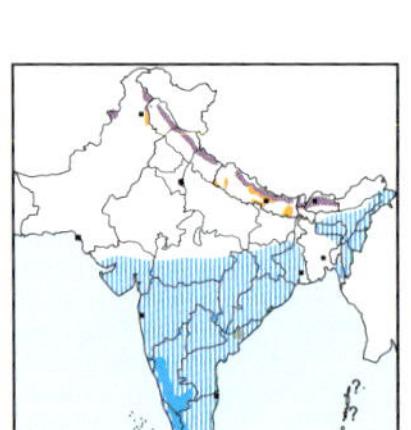

Large-billed Leaf Warbler *Phylloscopus magnirostris* 12.5–13cm

Breeds in Himalayas; winters mainly in NE and S India, and Sri Lanka. **ID** From *viridanus* Greenish (where ranges overlap in W Himalayas and peninsula) by larger size and stockier appearance; larger mainly dark bill; darker oily green upperparts (with darker crown); more striking yellowish-white supercilium, and broader dark eye-stripe with greyish mottling on ear-coverts. Underparts tend to look rather dirty, often with diffuse streaking and oily yellow wash (but can be whiter and much as Greenish). Yellowish-white greater covert wing-bar, often with a trace of second (median covert) bar. Much more like nominate Greenish and best told by distinctive call and song. Also larger, has larger bill with more pronounced hooked tip, and more prominent supercilium and broader dark eye-stripe. Some very similar in appearance to nominate Greenish. **Voice** Song a series of loud flute-like whistles, *tee-ti-tii-tu-tu*, running down the scale, last two notes drawn out, and repeated quickly; clear, whistled, rising *der-tee* call. **HH** Forages mainly in canopy and on tree branches, rather than in foliage. Breeds in forest along mountain streams; winters lower down in evergreen forest.

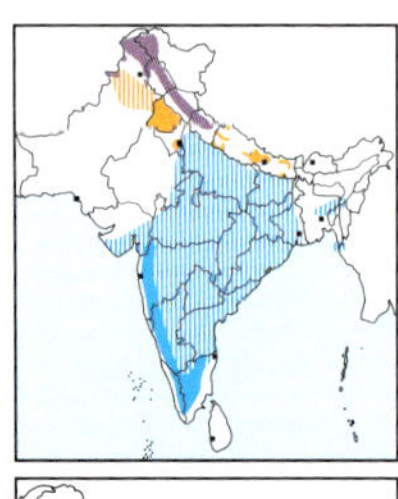

Western Crowned Warbler *Phylloscopus occipitalis* 11–13cm

Breeds in N Pakistan hills and W Himalayas; winters in India, Nepal and Bangladesh. Vagrant: Sri Lanka. **ID** Very similar to Blyth's Leaf but appears larger and more elongated, with larger and longer-looking bill. Upperparts generally duller greyish-green, and whitish underparts are strongly suffused with grey. Median and greater covert wing-bars are less prominent and head pattern tends to be less striking (supercilium and crown stripe duller and contrast less with dusky-olive sides to crown, which may be darker towards nape). **Voice** Song is several calls run together; frequently repeated *chit-weei* call. **HH** Diagnostic habit of flicking alternately one wing then the other. Breeds in coniferous and mixed forest; winters in evergreen broadleaved forest.

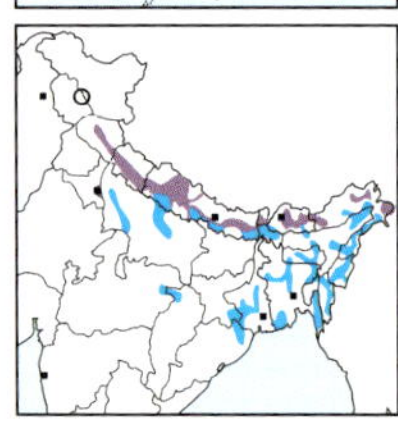

Blyth's Leaf Warbler *Phylloscopus reguloides* 10.5–12cm

Breeds in Himalayas; winters in foothills and adjacent plains. **ID** Very similar to Western Crowned. Head pattern tends to be more striking, with yellower supercilium and crown-stripe, and darker lateral crown-stripes (can be almost black). Underparts generally have distinct yellowish wash, and upperparts are a darker purer green. Wing-bars more prominent (broader, and often divided by dark panel on greater coverts). *P. r. kashmiriensis* (W Himalayas) tends to have brighter yellowish-green upperparts than nominate (C Himalayas), and lateral crown-stripes tend to be less dark; *P. r. assamensis* (north-east) tends to be darker green on the upperparts with stronger yellow wash below. **Voice** Trilling song: *ch-ti-ch-ti-chi-ti-ch-ti-chee*; constantly repeated disyllabic *pit-chee*, or trisyllabic *pit-chew-a* call. **HH** Characteristic habit of clinging upside-down to trunks like a nuthatch. Breeds in broadleaved, coniferous and mixed forest; winters in open forest and forest edges.

ad
worn
ad
fresh
Green Warbler
ad fresh
viridanus
ad fresh
trochiloides
Greenish Warbler
ad worn
viridanus
ad
fresh
ad
fresh
Large-billed Leaf Warbler
Western Crowned Warbler
ad fresh
kashmiriensis
Blyth's Leaf Warbler
ad fresh
reguloides

PLATE 164: TESIAS AND BUSH WARBLERS I

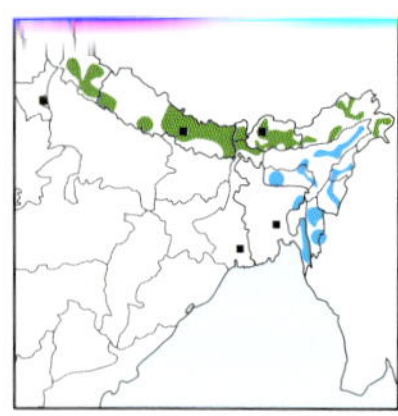

Grey-bellied Tesia *Tesia cyaniventer* — 9–10cm

Resident. Himalayas; winters to hills of NE India and Bangladesh. **ID** From Slaty-bellied by paler grey underparts, becoming almost whitish on throat and centre of belly, and by concolorous olive-green crown and mantle, with brighter lime-green supercilium. Also, more prominent black stripe behind eye, and stouter bill with dark tip and yellow basal two-thirds to lower mandible. Juvenile has dark olive-brown upperparts and olive cast to grey of underparts; like adult, has brighter green supercilium and dark eye-stripe. **Voice** Song is much slower than Slaty-bellied and lacks its explosive jumble of notes; loud and rattling *trrrrrk* call. **HH** Habits like Chestnut-headed. Breeds in thick undergrowth in dense broadleaved forest, often near streams, shady broadleaved forest in winter.

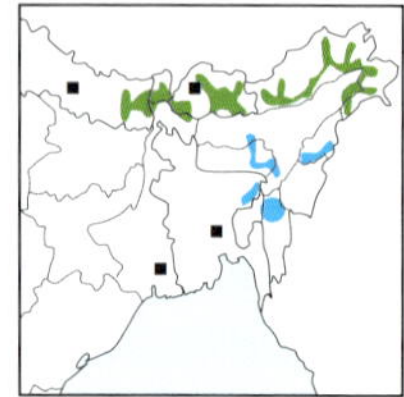

Slaty-bellied Tesia *Tesia olivea* — 9–10cm

Resident E Himalayas; winters to NE Indian hills. Vagrant: Bangladesh. **ID** Best told from Grey-bellied by uniform dark slate-grey underparts, and yellowish-green crown which is distinctly brighter than mantle (although some have duller and less contrasting crown and may show suggestion of brighter supercilium). Additional features are less prominent black stripe behind eye, and finer bill with brighter orange or orange-red lower mandible without dark tip. Juvenile is said to be like juvenile Grey-bellied, but with darker olive-green underparts. **Voice** Song comprises 4–11 measured whistles followed by explosive tuneless jumble of notes; calls include sharp *tchirik*. **HH** Habits like Chestnut-headed. Thick undergrowth in moist evergreen forest, often near streams.

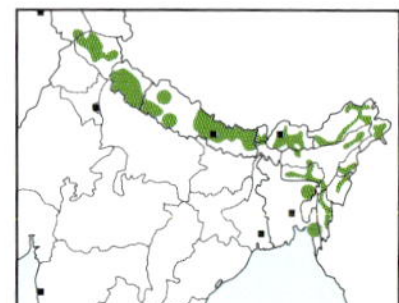

Chestnut-headed Tesia *Cettia castaneocoronata* — 8–9.5cm

Resident. Himalayas and NE Indian hills. Vagrant: Bangladesh. **ID** Adult has bright chestnut 'hood', prominent white crescent behind eye, dark olive-green mantle and wings, and bright yellow underparts with olive-green sides of breast and flanks. Juvenile has dark olive upperparts with brownish cast (lacking chestnut head of adult), and dark rufous underparts. **Voice** Song an explosive *cheep-cheeu-chewit*; sharp, explosive *whit* call. **HH** Skulks amongst forest undergrowth close to ground. Thick undergrowth in moist forest. **TN** Formerly in *Tesia*.

Pale-footed Bush Warbler *Hemitesia pallidipes* — 11–12.5cm

Resident. Himalayas, NE and E India and S Andamans. **ID** From Brownish-flanked by whiter underparts (contrasting with brownish-olive breast-sides and flanks), more rufescent upperparts, shorter (square-ended) tail, strikingly pale pinkish legs and feet, and different song and call. Possibly confusable with Dusky Warbler; best told by very pale legs and feet, shorter tail, more rounded wings with very short primary projection beyond tertials, and different call. In Andamans (*H. p. osmastoni*) has larger bill, darker and richer brown upperparts, and warmer buff breast-sides and flanks. **Voice** Song a loud, explosive *zip... zip-tschuk-o-tschuk*; call a quiet *chip-chip* or *chick-chick*. **HH** Typical bush warbler habits, see Chestnut-crowned. Tall grass and bushes at forest edges and secondary scrub. **TN** Formerly placed in *Cettia*.

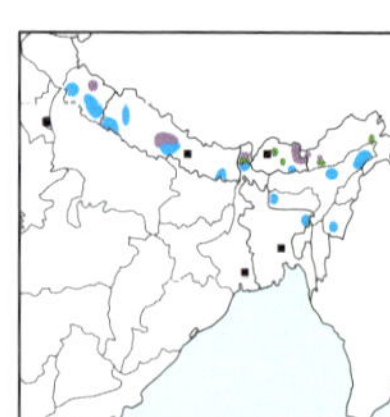

Chestnut-crowned Bush Warbler *Cettia major* — 13cm

Resident. Himalayas; winters in NE Indian hills. Vagrant: Bangladesh. **ID** Large *Cettia* with chestnut crown. From Grey-sided by larger size and more robust appearance, shorter-looking tail, larger bill, longer supercilium (indistinct and rufous-buff in front of eye), and whiter underparts (particularly throat and centre of breast) with brown rather than grey flanks. Juvenile lacks chestnut on crown, and is more olive above and below, with greyish-buff supercilium behind eye; whiter throat and belly separate it from juvenile Grey-sided. **Voice** Song a short whistle followed by explosive shrill warble of 3–4 notes, *i i-wi-wi-wirri-wi*; call very similar to Grey-sided. **HH** Typical bush warbler habits. Very skulking in non-breeding season, but less so when nesting. Calls frequently. Typically seeks insects and spiders by flitting and hopping about in vegetation close to ground. Breeds in rhododendron shrubbery and bushes in forest; winters in lowland reedbeds.

Grey-sided Bush Warbler *Cettia brunnifrons* — 10–11cm

Resident. Himalayas; winters to NE India. Vagrant: Bangladesh. **ID** Small *Cettia* with chestnut crown, whitish underparts, grey sides to breast and brownish-olive flanks. From Chestnut-crowned by smaller size, smaller bill, longer-looking tail, shorter supercilium (whitish-buff and well defined in front of eye) and greyer underparts. Juvenile lacks chestnut crown, with rufous-brown upperparts and brownish-olive underparts. **Voice** Song a loud wheezing *sip ti ti sip*, repeated continually often with nasal notes before and after song; call a bunting-like *pseek*. **HH** Similar to other bush warblers, see Chestnut-crowned. Less skulking in breeding season; males emerge from cover to sing on top of bush or rock. Feeds chiefly in bushes and low vegetation, also on ground. Breeds in high-altitude shrubbery and bushes at forest edges; winters in scrub and forest undergrowth.

ad
juv
Grey-bellied Tesia
ad
Slaty-bellied Tesia
juv
Chestnut-headed Tesia
ad
ad
osmastoni
ad
pallidipes
Pale-footed Bush Warbler
ad
ad
juv
juv
Chestnut-crowned Bush Warbler
Grey-sided Bush Warbler

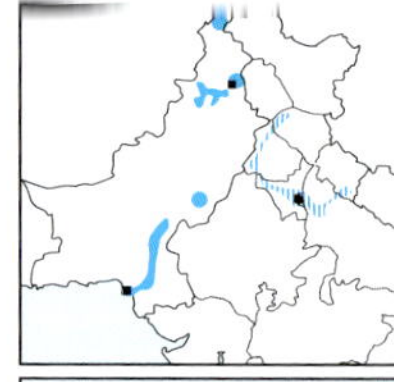

Cetti's Warbler *Cettia cetti* 13.5–14.5cm

Winter visitor and passage migrant. Pakistan and NW India. **ID** Large, mainly brown bush warbler. Very white on breast, with indistinct greyish-white supercilium. From Pale-footed by larger size, more robust appearance and larger tail, shorter and less prominent supercilium, greyish (rather than olive) breast-sides and flanks, dull white tips to long greyish-brown undertail-coverts. **Voice** Song comprises explosive liquid notes *chit... chit... chitity chit... chitity chit*; call an explosive *chit*. **HH** Skulking. Reedbeds and tamarisks.

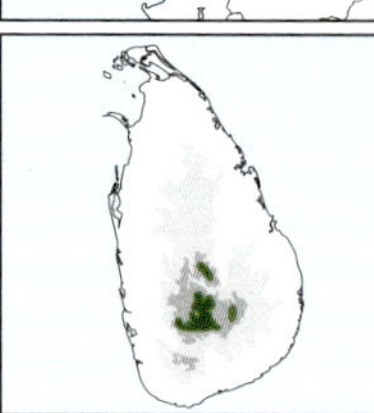

Sri Lanka Bush Warbler *Elaphrornis palliseri* 15–16cm

Resident. Sri Lanka. **ID** Large, stocky warbler. Dark olive-brown upperparts with rufescent cast to wings and tail, greyer ear-coverts and indistinct paler grey supercilium, orange-buff throat, and olive-grey underparts with olive-yellow wash especially to belly. Iris bright red in male, white in female. Juvenile similar but lacks orange-buff on throat, which is washed olive-yellow and mottled dark olive. **Voice** Song a brief, sharp, sometimes squeaky jingle; sharp metallic *tchik* and repeated, tailorbird like *tchwit* calls. **HH** Dense forest undergrowth.

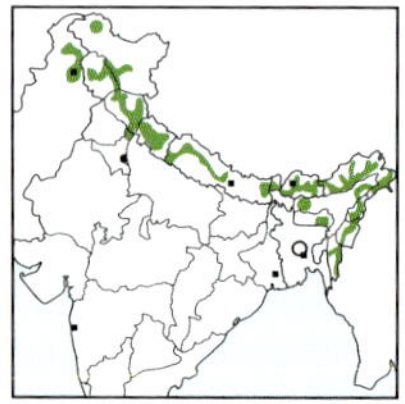

Brownish-flanked Bush Warbler *Horornis fortipes* 11–12.5cm

Resident. Himalayas and NE India. Vagrant: Bangladesh. **ID** From Pale-footed by duskier underparts, which are mainly pale buffish-grey with brownish-olive flanks. Also, longer (rounded) tail, brownish legs and feet, more olive upperparts, less prominent supercilium and eye-stripe, and different song and call. Nominate (E Himalayas and north-east) has warmer, rufous-brown upperparts compared to *H. f. pallidus* (W Himalayas), brownish-buff (rather than buffish-grey) coloration to throat and breast, and buffish (rather than greyish-white) supercilium. Juvenile (June–August) has yellow underparts; confusable with Aberrant Bush Warbler, but upperparts browner, shorter tail and different call. **Voice** Song a loud whistle, *weeee*, followed by explosive *chiwiyou*; *chuk* call; hard, regularly repeated *tak* or *chak*. **HH** Skulking. Breeds in dense undergrowth in forest, thickets on hillsides and cultivation edges. **TN** Formerly placed in *Cettia*.

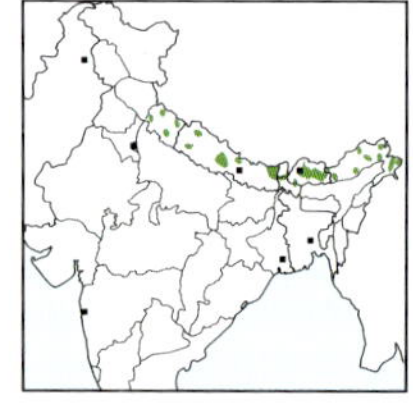

Hume's Bush Warbler *Horornis brunnescens* 11cm

Resident. Himalayas. **ID** From Brownish-flanked by smaller and finer bill, paler rufous-brown upperparts with strong olive cast (especially to lower back and rump), noticeable rufous fringes to tertials, paler underparts with yellowish belly and flanks (yellow sometimes barely apparent), paler legs and feet, and shorter, square-ended tail. Possibly confusable with dull Aberrant Bush Warbler but is smaller, with shorter tail, whiter underparts, and paler rufous-brown upperparts lacking any greenish coloration. **Voice** Song a thin, high-pitched *see-saw see-saw see-saw*; call a rapidly repeated *trrrt, trrt*. **HH** Secretive and skulking. Forages low down in bamboo clumps. Bamboo stands. **TN** Formerly placed in *Cettia*.

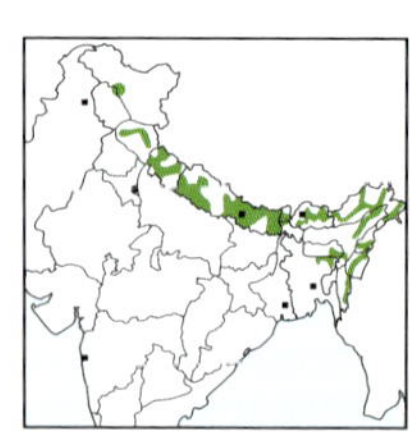

Aberrant Bush Warbler *Horornis flavolivaceus* 12–14cm

Resident. Himalayas and NE Indian hills. Vagrant: Bangladesh. **ID** From other bush warblers by yellowish-green cast to olive upperparts, yellowish supercilium, and buffish-yellow to olive-yellow underparts. Confusable with Tickell's Leaf Warbler, but has longer, 'loosely attached' and rounded tail, usually held slightly cocked, shorter and more rounded wings, and grating call accompanied by much wing-flicking. In worn plumage, supercilium and underparts show less yellow. Juvenile has more uniform buffish-yellow underparts. In NE India (*weberi*) is browner above, and more buffish below (yellowish only on belly). **Voice** Song a short warble, followed by long inflected whistle *dir dir-tee teee-weee*. Call a soft *brrrt-brrrt*, different from Tickell's. **HH** Secretive. Forages in thick undergrowth or on ground. Breeds in bushes at forest edges and shrubbery; winters in dense bushes and undergrowth. **TN** Formerly placed in *Cettia*.

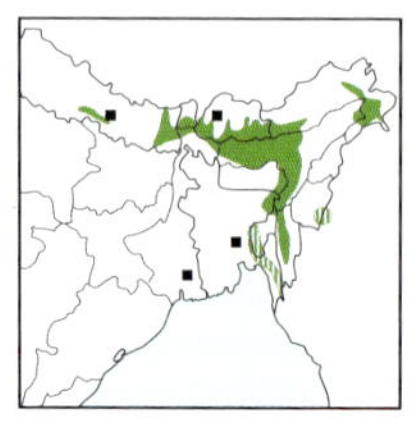

Yellow-bellied Warbler *Abroscopus superciliaris* 9cm

Resident. Himalayas, hills of NE India and Bangladesh. **ID** A small brightly coloured warbler with a long bill and longish narrow tail. White supercilium, dark crown and eyestripe, yellowish-olive upperparts, white throat and yellow rest of underparts. Confusable only with Grey-hooded Warbler, and best distinguished by white throat, yellowish-olive (rather than grey) mantle, and lack of white on tail. Separated from *Phylloscopus* warblers by combination of rather long bill, brownish-grey crown, white throat, yellow rest of underparts, and by fairly narrow tail, lacking prominent undertail-coverts, giving distinctive profile. Tail appears pale brownish-buff from below. **Voice** Song a halting cheery ditty of six notes, ascending at end, *tue-do-du-do-di-dee*. **HH** Very active, feeds in bamboo, bushes and lower branches. Bamboo jungle and bamboo in forest, often near streams.

ad
juv
Sri Lanka
Bush Warbler
Cetti's Warbler
♂
ad
pallidus
Brownish-flanked
Bush Warbler
juv
fortipes
ad
fortipes
ad
Hume's
Bush Warbler
ad
fresh
Aberrant Bush
Warbler
ad
ad
worn
Yellow-bellied
Warbler

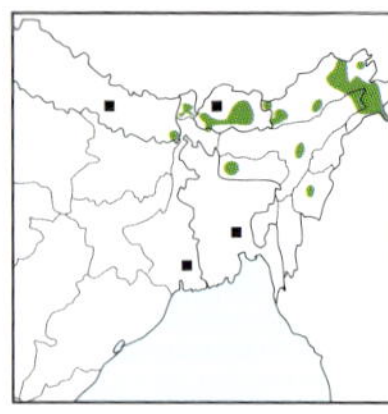

Rufous-faced Warbler *Abroscopus albogularis* 8–9cm

Resident. E Himalayas and NE Indian hills. **ID** Readily told by pale rufous face (lacking prominent eye-ring), buff crown (with blackish lateral crown-stripes), blackish mottling on throat, yellow band on breast, whitish rump, uniform wings (lacking wing-bars), and lack of white on tail. **Voice** Song a repeated very high-pitched, drawn-out plaintive whistle *titiriiiii... titiriiiii... titiriiiii...titriiii* etc.; shrill twittering call. **HH** Very active, restlessly flicks wings and flares tail. Outside breeding season often in small parties with other small insectivores. Usually keeps to undergrowth and lower branches of trees. Bamboo clumps at edges and in more open areas of moist deciduous and evergreen broadleaved forest; also, bamboo and scrub jungle.

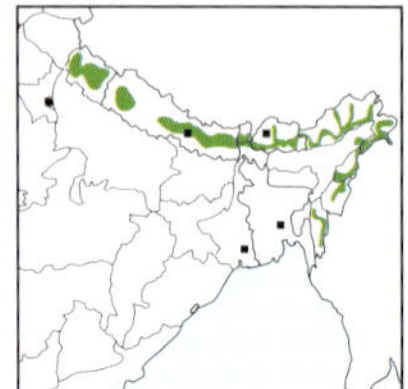

Black-faced Warbler *Abroscopus schisticeps* 10cm

Resident. Himalayas and NE Indian hills. **ID** Striking with yellow supercilium and throat and black mask. Bill and legs/feet pinkish. Grey crown and nape, and uniform olive-green upperparts lacking any wing-bar. Superficially resembles Yellow-bellied Fairy-Fantail but has much shorter tail. Nominate (C Himalayas) has yellow extending to breast and flanks. *A. s. flavimentalis* (north-east) has yellow of underparts restricted to throat and white breast and flanks. **Voice** Song a high-pitched, excited, sweet trill *tirririr-tsii tirririr-tsii tirririr-tsii* or *tit sirriri-sirriri sirriri tit-sirriri*. **HH** Usually in fast-moving parties of 10–15 birds, often with other warblers and small babblers. Forages in the midstorey and in tall bushes in forest. Moist oak and mixed broadleaved forest, especially in moss-covered trees, creepers, bamboo and thick undergrowth.

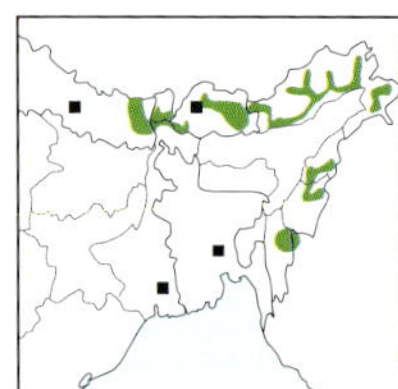

Broad-billed Warbler *Tickellia hodgsoni* 10cm

Resident. E Himalayas and NE Indian hills. **ID** A distinctive warbler with chestnut forehead and crown, greyish-white supercilium and dark grey eye-stripe, greyish ear-coverts, throat and breast, and yellow belly, flanks and vent. Slightly yellower rump. Chestnut crown, grey throat and breast, and white on tail are best features from Yellow-bellied Warbler. Very similar in plumage to Mountain Tailorbird; best distinguished by shorter (and broader) bill, darker and more extensive chestnut on crown, uniform olive-green mantle and nape (nape grey in Mountain Tailorbird), and greyish-white supercilium. **Voice** Song a series of very thin, high-pitched whistles, repeated at intervals *si-seeee-ee-eee...si-seeee-ee-eee......siiiiiiiiii...... siiiiiiiiii*, rising in pitch; also rapid, rather metallic jumbled notes. **HH** Often with itinerant mixed-species parties of small birds. Hovers and flycatches from twigs and lower branches of trees close to or in forest understorey. Bamboo and other undergrowth in dense montane, evergreen broadleaved forest.

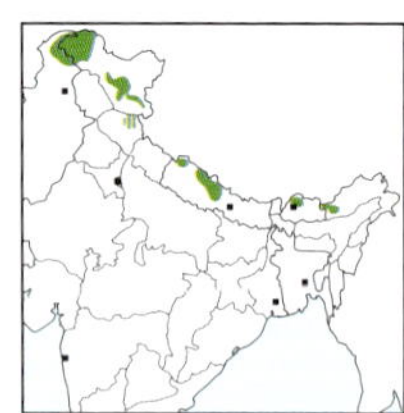

White-browed Tit Warbler *Leptopoecile sophiae* 8.5–10cm

Resident. N Himalayas from Pakistan to W Arunachal. **ID** All plumages have buffish or white supercilium, rufous crown, greyish upperparts, white outer tail feathers, lilac flanks and vent and bluish rump and tail. Male has lilac wash to crown, and violet-blue sides to head, throat and breast. Female has pale grey-brown head-sides and buffish-white underparts (except lilac wash to flanks, which can be obscured). Male *L. s. obscura* (C Himalayas) has darker upperparts and deeper purple underparts, lacking clearly defined buff belly, compared to male nominate (W Himalayas). Female *obscura* has darker, deeper rufous crown, and greyer underparts. **Voice** No territorial song, but at times male gives quiet murmuring and melodious whispering; calls include a trilling *sirrrrr* or *tszirr-tszirrpétszirrp* for contact by both sexes all year, also a thin, plaintive *psee* or more drawn-out *pseee*. **HH** Forages very actively in bushes and undergrowth; flits and hops among branches and foliage, can hang upside-down like a tit, and sometimes flutters into air to capture flying insects. Frequently cocks its tail. Often in small parties, sometimes with other insectivores. Mainly in trans-Himalayas. Dwarf juniper, *Caragana* scrub, or dwarf rhododendron above treeline in trans-Himalayan semi-desert; also winters in *Hippophae* thickets or willows along streams.

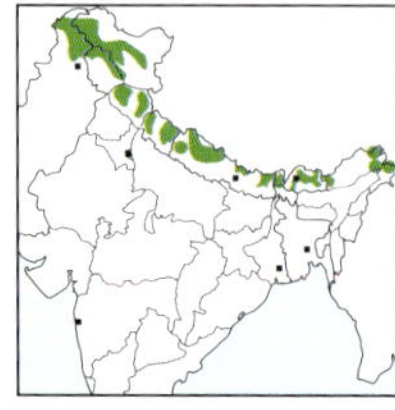

Goldcrest *Regulus regulus* 8.5–9.5cm

Resident. Himalayas. **ID** Small and plump, with greenish upperparts, recalling *Phylloscopus* warbler. Best distinguished by very plain face, which lacks supercilium and eye-stripe, by pale ring around large dark eye, and by brilliant yellow to orange crown bordered by black. Juvenile lacks striking crown pattern of adult. **Voice** Trisyllabic, high-pitched *see-see-see* call; song a similarly high-pitched *see-seesisyu-seesisyu-seesisyu-sweet*. **HH** Arboreal; often in mixed flocks with tits, treecreepers and leaf warblers. Forages actively among foliage, usually in forest canopy. Constantly flits from twig to twig in search of insects; frequently hovers, flutters and flicks wings; also clings upside-down to twigs. Mainly coniferous forest.

ad
Rufous-faced Warbler
ad
schisticeps
Black-faced Warbler
ad
Broad-billed Warbler
ad
flavimentalis
♂
sophiae
♂
obscura
White-browed Tit Warbler
♀
sophiae
♀
obscura
juv
Goldcrest
♂

PLATE 167: *CURRUCA* WARBLERS

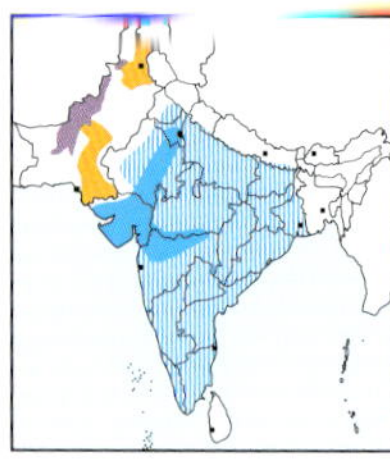

Eastern Orphean Warbler *Curruca crassirostris* 15cm

Summer visitor to Pakistan; winters mainly in India. Vagrant: Bangladesh and Nepal. **ID** Larger and bigger-billed than Lesser Whitethroat; more ponderous movements, and heavier appearance in flight. Adult has blackish hood, pale grey mantle, blackish tail and pale iris, white in male (always dark in Lesser). First-year has crown concolorous with mantle, darker grey ear-coverts and dark iris, and can appear like Lesser Whitethroat. Eastern Orphean often shows darker-looking uppertail, eye-ring is absent or indistinct, and has greyish centres and pale fringes to undertail-coverts; features variable and difficult to see in the field. **Voice** Strong, varied thrush-like warbling song; call a *tack* or *tchak*, deeper and harder than Lesser Whitethroat, also loud *trrr* rattle. **HH** Breeds on bush-covered hillsides; winters in dense scrub, riverine forest, groves and bushes in semi-desert. **TN** Formerly placed in *Sylvia* and treated as conspecific with Western Orphean Warbler *S. hortensis*.

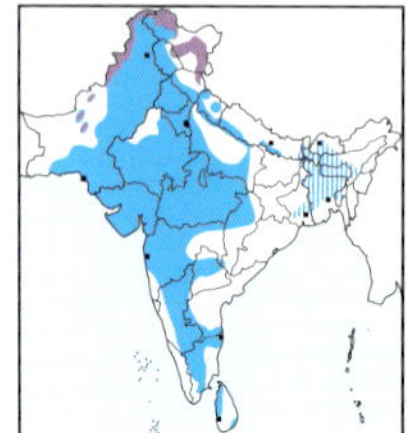

Lesser Whitethroat *Curruca curruca* 12.5–14cm

Breeds in W Himalayas; widespread winter visitor. Vagrant: Bangladesh. **ID** Brownish-grey upperparts, dull whitish underparts (can have pinkish flush to breast in fresh plumage), slate-grey crown (greyer and slightly darker than mantle), and darker lores and ear-coverts (forming diffuse mask). Bill blackish and legs and feet grey. *C. c. minula* ('Desert Whitethroat'), a passage migrant and winter visitor to NW subcontinent, is slightly smaller than widespread wintering *C. c. halimodendri*, with finer bill. Has paler, sandy grey-brown upperparts with sandy fringes to coverts and edges to secondaries forming sandy panel on wing. Forehead and crown paler grey, and usually lacks darker 'mask', giving 'plain-faced' appearance. Underparts often washed warm buff. *C. c. althaea* ('Hume's Whitethroat') breeds in W Himalayas and is a widespread winter visitor. It is slightly larger than *halimodendri*, with larger and stouter bill, darker, purer grey mantle, and darker grey crown with blackish ear-coverts resulting in dark-hooded appearance and can show strong greyish wash to sides of breast. **Voice** Calls include short, hard *tek*. *C. c. althaea* song a loud, continuous bubbling warble, usually starting with rapidly bubbling *wrichoo-wrichoo-wrichoo-wrichoo -richoo-tiee-diee-dee-dee*. **HH** Breeds in scattered juniper and holly oak scrub in Pakistan, scattered cotoneaster and *Berberis* bushes in Kashmir, and *Lonicera*, willows and fruit trees in Ladakh. Winters in scrub, acacias and deciduous woodland. **TN** Formerly placed in *Sylvia*.

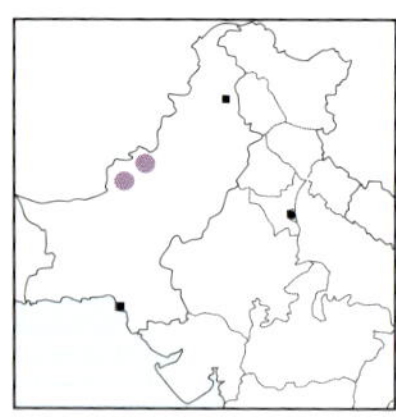

Ménétries's Warbler *Curruca mystacea* 13cm

Summer visitor. Balochistan. **ID** Small size, with long tail. Male has blackish hood, blue-grey upperparts, and pinkish wash to throat and breast, with white submoustachial line. Some males have whitish underparts and paler grey head (showing less contrast with mantle). Orange-buff eye-ring, reddish orbital ring and orange-brown iris. Female/first-winter has rather uniform sandy grey-brown upperparts and whitish underparts; eye-ring whiter and orbital ring and iris duller. Lacks any suggestion of darker mask, has strikingly dark tail, and has orange-brown to reddish (rather than grey) legs and feet, which help separate from Lesser Whitethroat. Tail frequently half-cocked and swung side to side. **Voice** Song a melodic and rich warble often with some harsh notes; calls include rattling *tzerrr*. **HH** Scrub in semi-desert. **TN** Formerly placed in *Sylvia*.

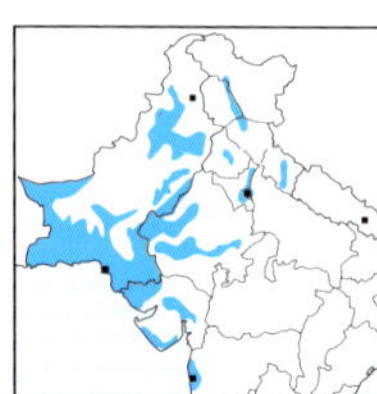

Asian Desert Warbler *Curruca nana* 11.5cm

Winter visitor. Pakistan and NW India. Vagrant: NW Bengal. **ID** Small and very distinctive. In all plumages has sandy-brown upperparts, rufous rump and uppertail-coverts, and rufous central tail feathers. Underparts whitish with buffish wash becoming greyish on sides of breast. Iris, bill base, and legs and feet yellowish. Eye-ring whitish. Sexes and first-winter very similar. **Voice** Pleasant *tiri-tityu-tyu-ty-tyuyu* song, often starting with rattle followed by fluting warble and ending with whistle; call a nasal rattle. **HH** Scattered scrub in sandy or stony desert, rocky hills, and low vegetation on coastal mudflats. **TN** Formerly placed in *Sylvia*.

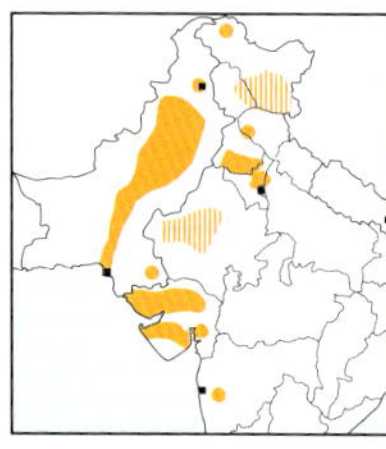

Greater Whitethroat *Curruca communis* 14cm

Passage migrant in Pakistan and NW India. **ID** Larger and longer-tailed than Lesser Whitethroat, with broad, well-defined, sandy-brown to pale rufous-brown fringes to greater coverts and tertials, pale base to lower bill, and orange-brown to pale brown (not grey) legs and feet. Adult male has grey crown and ear-coverts merging into greyish mantle; breast and flanks can show pinkish wash and has reddish-brown iris. Adult female and first-winter have pale grey-brown crown, ear-coverts and mantle, and iris is dull brown or olive. **Voice** Scratchy warbling song, *cheeechiwee-cheechiweechoo-chiwichoo*; calls include sharp *tack-tack*, harsh *tcharr* and in alarm lower-pitched *chur*. **HH** Scattered bushes in semi-desert, crops and bushes, and herbaceous plants around cultivation. **TN** Formerly placed in *Sylvia*.

♂
1st-winter
Eastern Orphean Warbler
♀
ad
halimodendri
Lesser Whitethroat
ad
althaea
ad
minula
♂
Ménétriés's
Warbler
ad
♀
Asian Desert Warbler
♀
Greater Whitethroat
♂

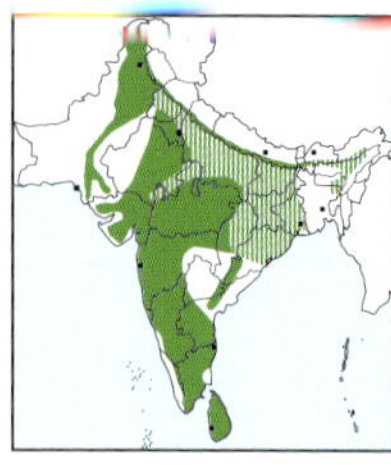

Yellow-eyed Babbler *Chrysomma sinense* 18–23cm

Widespread resident; unrecorded in parts of the north-west, south-east and north-east. **ID** Long-tailed babbler with rounded head and stout, dark bill (recalling a giant prinia in shape). Most distinctive features are yellow iris and thick orange orbital ring, white lores and supercilium, striking white throat and breast merging into buffish underparts, and yellow legs and feet. Juvenile has browner bill, dark eye and duller eye-ring. *C. s. hypoleucum* (widespread) is duller brown to grey-brown above with more striking rufous-brown wings than nominate (NE India, north of Brahmaputra), which has richer, more chestnut-brown upperparts. *C. s. nasale* (Sri Lanka) is more uniformly greyish-brown above with wings only a shade more rufous compared to *hypoleucum*. **Voice** Song variable, rapid twittering trill *tri-rit-ri-ri-ri-ri* ending in a two-noted *toway-twoh*. **HH** Skulking; often foraging close to ground. Calls briefly from a conspicuous perch before diving back into undergrowth. Tall grassland, also thickets, bamboos and reeds.

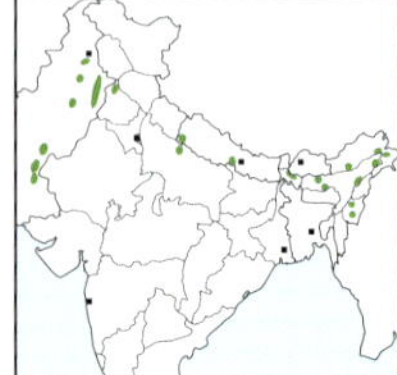

Jerdon's Babbler *Chrysomma altirostre* 17cm

Resident. Plains of Pakistan, Nepalese terai and NE India. **ID** From Yellow-eyed by paler yellowish-brown bill, greyish lores and supercilium, brown iris and yellow orbital ring, and fleshy-brown legs and feet. *C. a. scindicum* (Indus plains) has olive-brown upperparts and greyish-white throat and breast (not brilliant white as on Yellow-eyed, and lacks bright rufous-brown on the wing). *C. a. griseigulare* (NE subcontinent) has greyer throat and breast, richer chestnut-brown upperparts, and richer buff belly, flanks and vent. **Voice** Both subspecies have descending song: a loud, piercing, series *tew-tew-tew-tewwww-tewwwwww*, each subsequent note somewhat longer and lower in frequency than the previous. **HH** Habits similar to Yellow-eyed. Male sings from top of tall stem. Reedbeds and tracts of tall grassland. Globally threatened.

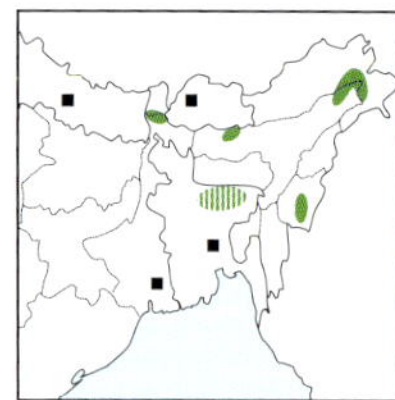

Black-breasted Parrotbill *Paradoxornis flavirostris* 19cm

Resident. NE Indian plains and (formerly) Bangladesh and Nepal. **ID** Medium-sized parrotbill with rufous-brown head and olive-brown upperparts, black patch on ear-coverts, and huge yellow bill. From Spot-breasted Parrotbill (note different distribution) by black breast-patch and solid black chin (with white-'flecked' throat and malar area), rufous-buff (rather than pale buff) underparts, darker rufous-brown crown and nape, even stouter bill, and different call. **Voice** Songs comprise nasal *whit-whit-whit-whit* or *we-we-we-we* ascending in pitch and a harsher, crowing *woi-woi-woi-woi*. **HH** Skulking; usually keeps low in vegetation. If disturbed, normally flutters a few metres into thicker cover. Reedbeds and tall grass. Globally threatened.

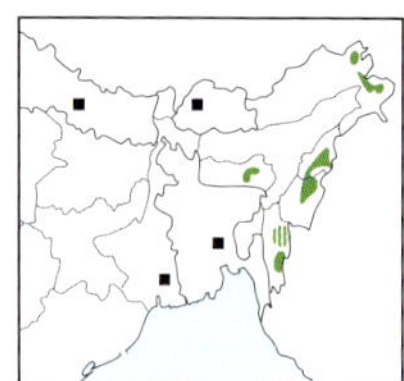

Spot-breasted Parrotbill *Paradoxornis guttaticollis* 18–22cm

Resident. NE Indian hills and (formerly) Bangladesh. **ID** Medium-sized parrotbill with rufous head and upperparts, black patch on ear-coverts, and large yellow bill. From Black-breasted (note distribution) by black arrowhead-shaped spotting on buffish-white throat and breast (lacking bold black patch on breast), pale buff (rather than rufous-buff) underparts, brighter rufous crown and nape, less stout bill, and different call. **Voice** Typical territorial call consists of 3–7 loud, even-pitched staccato notes, *whit-whit-whit-whit-whit-whit-whit* or a more plaintive series. **HH** Habits similar to Black-breasted. Grass and scrub, bushes and bamboo.

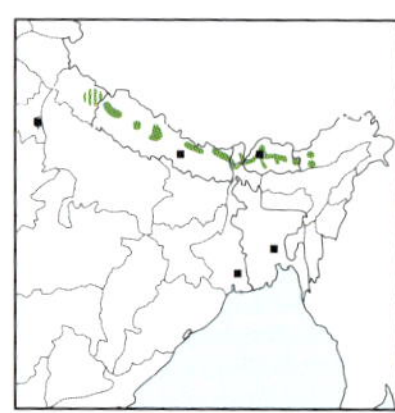

Great Parrotbill *Conostoma aemodium* 27.5–28.5cm

Resident. Himalayas. **ID** Large parrotbill rather laughingthrush-like in shape and behaviour, with striking orange bill. From Brown by larger size and paler grey-brown coloration, larger cone-shaped bill, buffish-white forehead contrasting with brown lores, paler and more uniform grey-brown sides of head, throat and breast, and grey sides to tail. Lacks dark lateral crown-stripes of Brown. Has rufous-brown panel on wings, as Brown. **Voice** Halting, loud, song of 2–4 clear whistles *truu-dree-dreeu*; also, more plaintive nasal wheezes, squeals, cackles and chirrs. **HH** Keeps mainly to undergrowth, occasionally ascending tall trees. Slow-moving; hops and clambers about. Bamboo stands in forest, usually oak-rhododendron or fir-rhododendron.

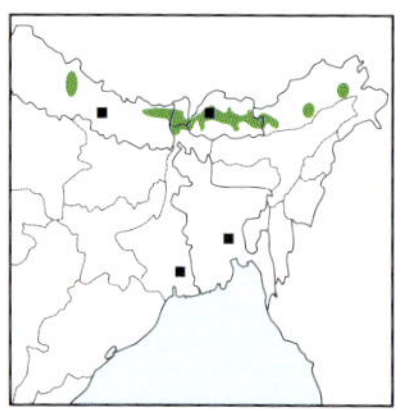

Brown Parrotbill *Cholornis unicolor* 21cm

Resident. Himalayas. **ID** From Great Parrotbill by smaller size and stocky shape, smaller and much stouter (duller yellow) bill, diffuse blackish lateral crown-stripes broadening on nape, grey 'spectacles', diffuse grey mottling on dull brown ear-coverts, dusky grey and rather untidy-looking throat and breast merging into olive-brown of flanks and belly, and browner tail. Has rufous-brown panel on wings, as Great. **Voice** Song a repeated clear, loud *ii-wuu-iiew* (last note clear, louder and rising slightly) or a quickly repeated *whiiiu*. **HH** Usually in small parties that skulk in undergrowth and call frequently to each other. Weak fluttering flight. Mainly dense bamboo stands, also rhododendron and other bushes in temperate and subalpine zones.

ad
hypoleucum
ad
sinense
Yellow-eyed Babbler
ad
scindicum
ad
griseigulare
Jerdon's Babbler
ad
Black-breasted Parrotbill
ad
Spot-breasted Parrotbill
ad
Great Parrotbill
ad
Brown Parrotbill

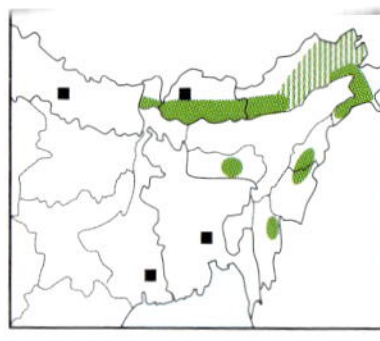

Grey-headed Parrotbill *Psittiparus gularis* 18.5cm

Resident. E Himalayas and NE Indian hills. **ID** Medium-sized parrotbill with stout orange bill. From other parrotbills by combination of grey head, with black lateral crown-stripe broadening towards nape, black throat, whitish surround to eye and malar stripe, rufous-brown mantle and wings, and white or buffish-white underparts. **Voice** Usual calls include short, quite harsh, rather slurred *jieu* or *jiow* notes; soft *chip* notes and soft short, rattle *chrrrat*. **HH** Less skulking than other parrotbills. Frequents middle and lower storeys. Broadleaved forest, bushes and bamboo stands.

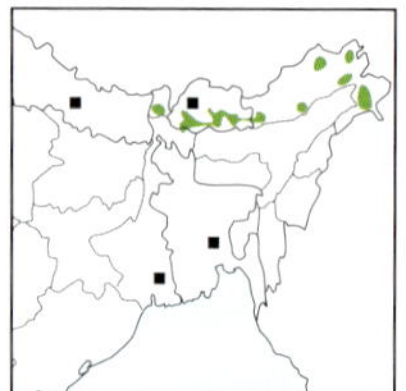

White-breasted Parrotbill *Psittiparus ruficeps* 19–19.5cm

Resident. NE India (Sikkim and N West Bengal east to E Arunachal Pradesh in Mishmi Hills), Bhutan. **ID** Rufous head, with variably prominent blue lores and orbital skin. Very similar to Rufous-headed Parrotbill with whiter underparts and buff restricted to flanks (note different range). From Pale-billed Parrotbill by larger size, more rounded crown, longer and less stubby bill (with darker base and upper mandible), deep rufous-orange ear-coverts (well demarcated from throat), and blue lores/orbital skin. Lacks dark eyebrow, although note *C. a. oatesi* (Darjeeling and Sikkim) also lacks this. From juvenile White-hooded Babbler by much stouter bill. **Voice** Song a loud, very high, thin, slightly descending, repeated series of 4–6 whistled notes, *he-he-he-hew-hew*; calls include clear, rising *which*, followed by hard rasping *dzip dzip*. **HH** Typically skulks in undergrowth and lower levels. Weak flight. Bamboo in or near moist broadleaved evergreen tropical and subtropical forests. **AN** Formerly known as Greater Rufous-headed Parrotbill.

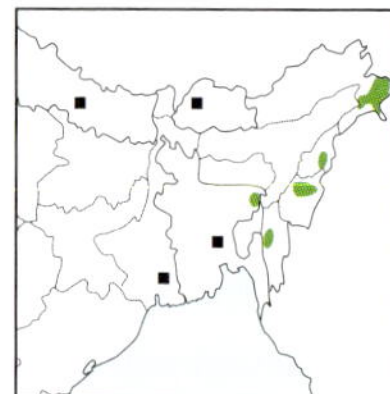

Rufous-headed Parrotbill *Psittiparus bakeri* 19–19.5cm

Resident. SE Arunachal Pradesh, NE Indian states south of Brahmaputra River. Vagrant: Bangladesh. **ID** Rufous head, with variably prominent blue lores and orbital skin. Very similar to White-breasted Parrotbill but with buff wash to throat and breast (note different range). From Pale-billed Parrotbill by larger size, more rounded crown, longer and less stubby bill (with darker base and upper mandible), lack of black eyebrow, deep rufous-orange ear-coverts (well demarcated from throat) and blue lores/orbital skin. **Voice** A *chipi-wííí yúú* with third note lower-pitched than second. Calls include short, sharp *wic-wic-wic, wic-it*, loud metallic rattles and distinctive twanging *jhaowh*. **HH** Habits like White-breasted. Bamboo in or near moist broadleaved evergreen tropical and subtropical forests. **TN** Formerly treated as conspecific with *P. ruficeps*.

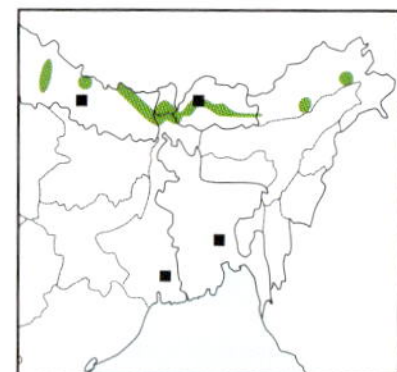

Fulvous Parrotbill *Suthora fulvifrons* 12–12.5cm

Resident. Himalayas. **ID** Small, comparatively long-tailed parrotbill, lacking black, white and grey pattern of Black-throated. Main differences from latter are fulvous (rather than grey or rufous) crown and supercilium, olive-brown (rather than black) lateral crown-stripes, lack of striking white malar patch, and fulvous face and underparts. **Voice** Thin, high-pitched *si-si ssuuu-juuu* with *suuu* part rising and harsher final note; also, *si-si-sissu-suu-u* and *si-si-sissu-suue*. **HH** Flocks move rapidly through bamboo, continually twittering. Climbs with agility about stems. Bamboo stands in temperate and subalpine zones.

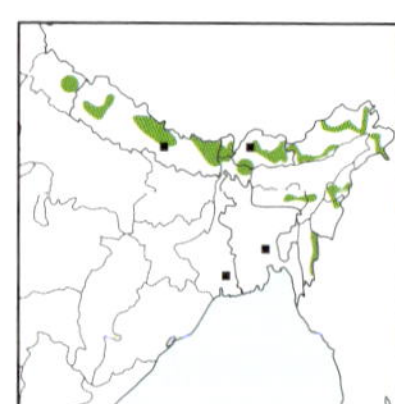

Black-throated Parrotbill *Suthora nipalensis* 11.5cm

Resident. Himalayas and NE Indian hills. **ID** Small parrotbill. All races show broad blackish lateral crown-stripes and black throat, striking white malar patch, and black primary-covert patch. *S. n. nipalensis* and *S. n. garhwalensis* (C Himalayas) have grey crown and ear-coverts; *S. n. humii* to the east has brownish-orange crown and ear-coverts and brighter orange-brown mantle; *S. n. crocotia* (E Bhutan) similar to *humii*, but has cinnamon-orange crown and duller ear-coverts and mantle; *S. n. poliotis* (E Himalayas south to Manipur) has rufous crown, slate-grey ear-coverts, extensive black throat and grey underparts; *S. n. patriciae* (Mizoram hills) similar to *poliotis*, but has deep fulvous (rather than grey) breast. **Voice** Flocks give general hubbub of dry, chattering trills. **HH** Habits similar to Fulvous, but faster-moving. Bamboo and dense undergrowth in forests.

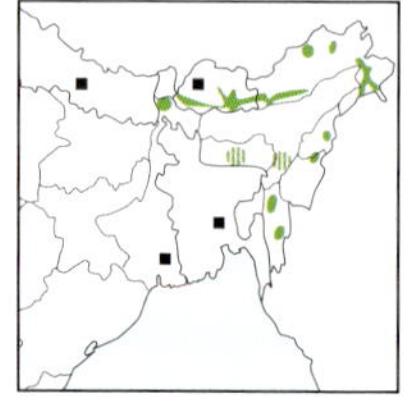

Pale-billed Parrotbill *Chleuasicus atrosuperciliaris* 15cm

Resident. E Himalayas and NE Indian hills. **ID** Rufous head, with whitish 'spectacles'. From White-breasted and Rufous-headed Parrotbills by smaller size, tufted nape, smaller and stouter mainly pinkish bill, feathered whitish-grey to blue-grey eye-ring and lores, and paler buffish-orange ear-coverts. *C. a. oatesi* (Darjeeling and Sikkim) lacks black eyebrow and has whitish underparts. Black eyebrow prominent (and is a further difference from White-breasted and Rufous-headed where ranges overlap) and underparts buff in nominate (south and east of Brahmaputra River). **Voice** Flocks call with subdued, rapid, jumbled, chattering, interspersed with harsher, more metallic notes. **HH** Habits similar to White-breasted. Bamboo in or near broadleaved evergreen forest. **AN** Formerly known as Lesser Rufous-headed Parrotbill.

ad
Grey-headed
Parrotbill
ad
White-breasted
Parrotbill
ad
Rufous-headed
Parrotbill
ad
ruficeps
Fulvous Parrotbill
ad
atrosuperciliaris
ad
nipalensis
Pale-billed
Parrotbill
ad
humii
ad
crocotius
ad
poliotis
Black-throated
Parrotbill
ad
oatesi

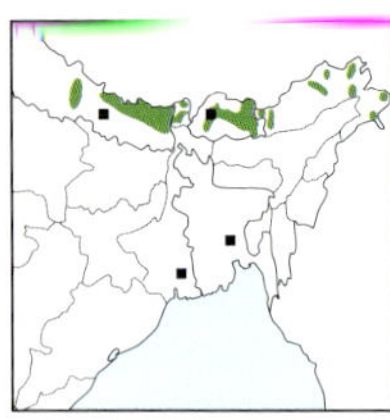

Fire-tailed Myzornis *Myzornis pyrrhoura* 11–13cm

Resident. Himalayas. **ID** Mainly brilliant emerald-green, with fine black bill, black mask and scaling on crown, and red-and-orange panels on black wings. Sexes similar but female has orange-buff throat (throat/upper breast red in male), greyish belly and flanks (more orange in male), less extensive white tips to flight feathers, and duller red sides to tail. **Voice** A *trrrr-trrrr-trrr* preceded by a high-pitched squeak; repeated *tzip* in alarm. **HH** Forages chiefly in bushes. Probes blossoms for nectar; also hunts invertebrates by searching foliage, hovering, making short sallies, and creeping up mossy trunks. Rhododendron and juniper shrubbery; mossy oak-rhododendron forest and bamboo stands.

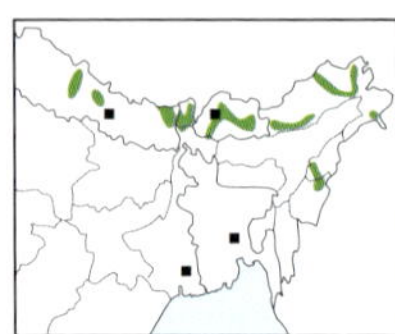

Golden-breasted Fulvetta *Lioparus chrysotis* 10–11.5cm

Himalayas and NE Indian hills. **ID** Dark grey head with silver-grey ear-coverts, grey upperparts, golden-yellow underparts, and orange-yellow wing-panel and sides to tail. *L. c. albilineatus* (hills south of the Brahmaputra River) has a white crown-stripe. **Voice** A thin high-pitched series of five notes, slightly descending. High-pitched buzz in alarm. **HH** In non-breeding season, flocks often with parrotbills and White-browed Fulvettas. Hangs upside-down like tit while foraging. Low and medium levels in bamboo forest.

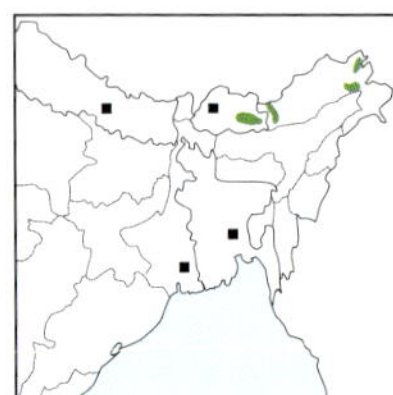

Ludlow's Fulvetta *Fulvetta ludlowi* 11.5cm

Resident. E Himalayas. **ID** Lacks broad white supercilium of White-browed and has dark eyes. Also has uniform brown head, lacking obvious dark lateral crown-stripes, and has prominent rufous-brown streaking on throat. In some head is chestnut-brown and contrasts with grey mantle (e.g. Mishmi Hills); in others head is more greyish-brown and concolorous with mantle (e.g. W Arunachal). From Manipur Fulvetta by browner crown and ear-coverts, and more prominent throat streaking. **Voice** Songs include two thin, high-pitched notes followed by short, lower-pitched trill, repeated every few seconds. Rattling *trri, tchrr* and *trrrrrt* in alarm. **HH** Habits similar to Streak-throated. Bushes and bamboo in broadleaved and coniferous forests. **AN** Brown-throated Fulvetta.

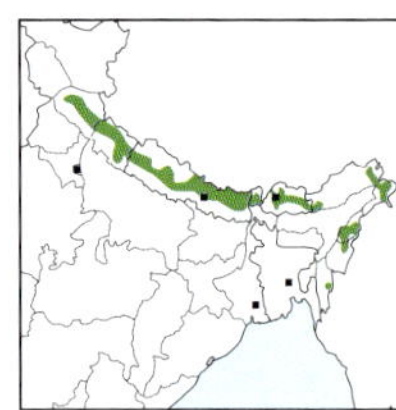

White-browed Fulvetta *Fulvetta vinipectus* 11cm

Resident. Himalayas and NE Indian hills. **ID** Variable with broad white supercilium, contrasting with dark crown and ear-coverts, strikingly pale eye, and black-and-grey panels in wing. Two W and C Himalayan races have unstreaked white throat: *F. v. kangrae* (W Himalayas) has chestnut-brown crown and darker ear-coverts than nominate (C Himalayas), which has duller crown concolorous with ear-coverts. Three eastern races have streaked throat: *F. v. chumbiensis* (E Himalayas) has grey-brown crown and mantle, dark-brown lateral crown-stripes and brown streaking on throat; *F. v. perstriata* (E Arunachal) has blacker ear-coverts and lateral crown stripes, broad reddish-brown streaks on throat, white crescent below eye, and (unlike other races) white supercilium extends to bill; *F. v. austeni* (hills south of Brahmaputra) has brown crown and mantle, reddish-brown lateral crown-stripes and streaking on throat. **Voice** Song a rapid *chit-it-it-it-or-key* and *tew-tu-tu-wheeee*. Faint *czzzzz* and *vek vek* in alarm. **HH** When not breeding, keeps in flocks, sometimes with other babblers and tits. Forages restlessly low down in bushes and undergrowth. Tit-like actions, but slower-moving. Subalpine shrub and bamboo in forest.

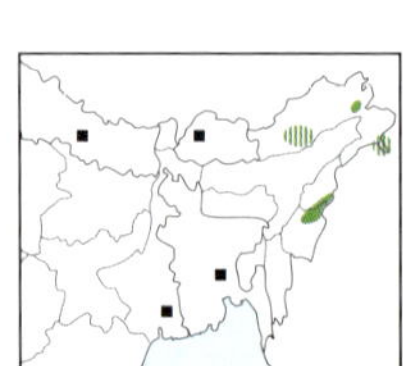

Manipur Fulvetta *Fulvetta manipurensis* 11–13cm

Resident. Arunachal and NE Indian hills. **ID** Grey-brown fulvetta with prominent brown lateral crown-stripes and diffuse pinkish-brown streaking on throat. Lacks white supercilium of White-browed. From Brown-throated by greyish ear-coverts and buffish to greyish crown, mantle and breast, and less prominent throat streaking. Eyes pale to dark. **Voice** Songs include repeated high-pitched *si-swu* or *see si-wu*. **HH** In non-breeding season keeps in small flocks of 6–8, often with other small babblers or warblers. Creeps about in undergrowth and bushes, rarely showing. Broadleaved evergreen forest, bamboo and bushes.

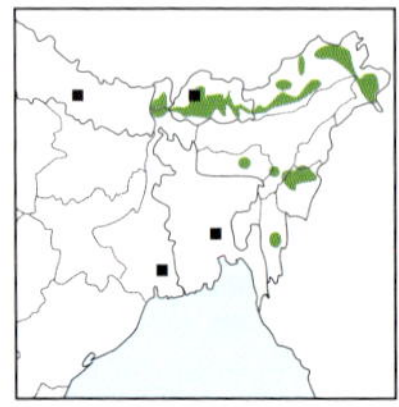

Yellow-throated Fulvetta *Schoeniparus cinereus* 10–11cm

Resident. E Himalayas and NE Indian hills. **ID** Striking head pattern with prominent yellow supercilium contrasting with black eye-stripe and sides to crown. Yellowish forehead and greyish crown mottled with black, and yellowish ear-coverts heavily mottled with grey. Upperparts dark olive-green. Throat yellow becoming more olive on breast and belly, and greyish-olive on breast-sides and flanks. **Voice** High-pitched, pulsed trill often descending and trailing off; also, a coarse rattle *chrt-trrt*. **HH** Usually in mixed species feeding parties. Forages low in undergrowth; constantly darts about vegetation. Undergrowth in dense broadleaved subtropical forest. **TN** Formerly placed in *Pseudominla*.

♂
♀
Fire-tailed Myzornis
ad
chrysotis
Golden-breasted
Fulvetta
ad
albilineatus
White-browed
Fulvetta
ad
Ludlow's Fulvetta
ad
kangrae
ad
austeni
ad
chumbiensis
ad
Manipur Fulvetta
ad
Yellow-throated
Fulvetta

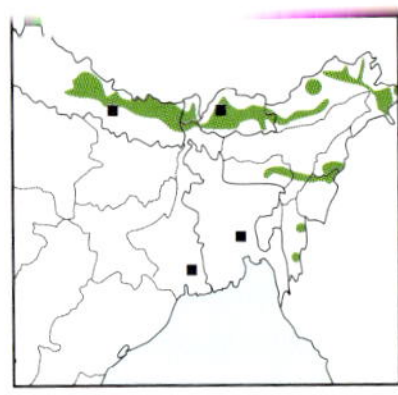
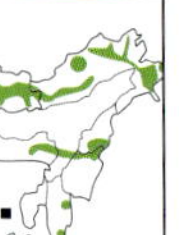

Rufous-winged Fulvetta *Schoeniparus castaneceps* 10–13cm

Resident. Himalayas and NE Indian hills. **ID** From other fulvettas by combination of dark chestnut crown and nape (streaked buffish-white), white supercilium contrasting with black eye-stripe, short black moustachial stripe, black band on wing-coverts, and rufous wing panel. Also has unmarked whitish throat and underparts, with buff flanks. **Voice** Song a rich undulating and descending warble. Usual call a wheezy, descending trill *tsi-tsi-tsi-tsi-tsirr.* **HH** Hunts busily at low and medium levels; sometimes climbs up mossy trunks. In mixed foraging parties. Moist broadleaved forest and clearings. **TN** Formerly placed in *Pseudominla*.

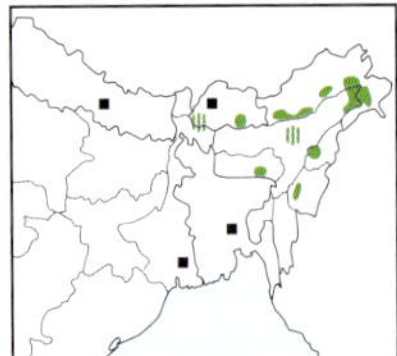

Rufous-throated Fulvetta *Schoeniparus rufogularis* 14–15cm

Resident. E Himalayas and NE Indian hills. **ID** Strikingly patterned with rufous crown and collar, blackish lateral crown-stripes, white eye-ring, lores and supercilium contrasting with grey ear-coverts, white throat and breast, and uniform brown wings. **Voice** Song a fairly loud, shrill, quickly delivered *wich-wichu-wichoi*; *wi-chuw-i-chewi-cheeu.* Constant low chattering in alarm or loud, shrill explosive *whit. . . .whit-whit.* **HH** In small flocks, often with other babblers in non-breeding season. Skulking; hunts close to and sometimes on ground in dense vegetation. Bamboo stands and undergrowth in moist, tropical evergreen forest.

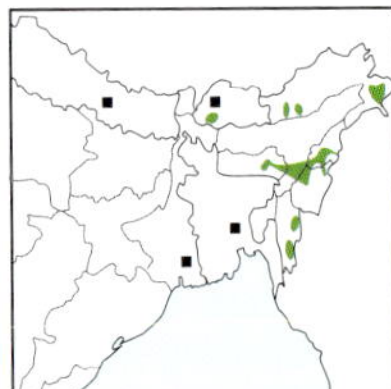

Rusty-capped Fulvetta *Schoeniparus dubius* 14–15cm

NE Indian hills. **ID** Large, long-tailed fulvetta. Bright rufous forehead, rufous crown and nape with dark brown scaling, broad white supercilium contrasting with black lateral crown-stripes, and dark brown ear-coverts and neck-sides, the latter prominently buff-streaked. Wings uniform olive-brown (lacking rufous panel of Rufous-winged). **Voice** Song similar to Rufous-throated but less shrill, less variation and has fewer notes per phrase. In alarm, a low grumbling rattle, sometimes with squeaky note at end. **HH** In pairs or small parties with other babblers, depending on season. Usually forages on ground in dense undergrowth or low bushes; sometimes on lower part of a trunk, like a nuthatch. Bushes and dense undergrowth in forest.

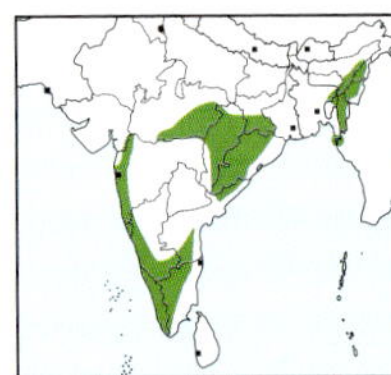

Brown-cheeked Fulvetta *Alcippe poioicephala* 16.5cm

Resident. Hills of India and Bangladesh. **ID** Large, rather nondescript fulvetta, with beady dark eye and stout blackish bill, lacking any pattern to head. Greyish crown and nape, grey-brown to olive-brown mantle, brown to rufous-brown wings and tail, and greyish-white to buff-coloured underparts, with paler throat and centre of breast. *A. p. fusca* in north-east has suggestion of darker lateral crown-stripes and has pale lower mandible. **Voice** Bustling, whistled song *tiew-teuw-tu-tee-tiu-tiu-wheet* repeated; *churr* call. **HH** Undergrowth in moist forest, bamboo stands and second growth.

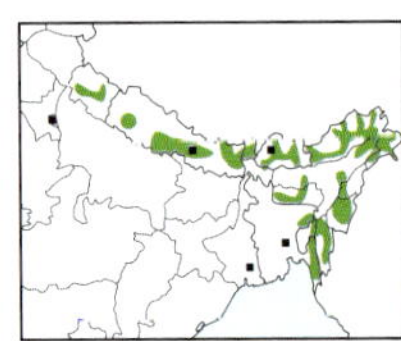

Nepal Fulvetta *Alcippe nipalensis* 12.5–13cm

Resident. Himalayas, hills of NE India and Bangladesh. **ID** A distinctive fulvetta with grey head and blackish lateral crown-stripes, prominent white eye-ring, olive-brown upperparts, and whitish underparts with buff flanks. **Voice** Short buzzes and metallic *chit* notes; also, a short fast trill of varying speed. **HH** Dense undergrowth in moist forest, bamboo stands and second growth.

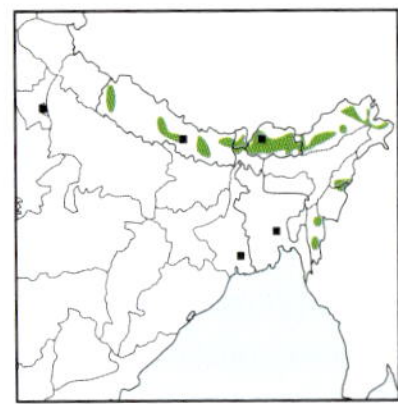

Himalayan Cutia *Cutia nipalensis* 17–19cm

Resident. Himalayas and NE Indian hills. **ID** A stocky, slow-moving nuthatch-like babbler. Male has blue-grey crown and blue-black mask, rufous mantle, white underparts with bold blackish barring on buffier flanks, and blue-grey wing panel. Female has duller grey crown, brown mask, and black-streaked olive-brown mantle. Both sexes have black tail just showing as dark tip beyond long rufous uppertail-coverts, and bright orange legs and feet. Juvenile is duller than respective adult, and black barring is much reduced (restricted to lower flanks). **Voice** Loud ringing series of 10–15 sharp *toot* notes, falling off towards end; pairs converse with short buzzy squawk calls and single or double *toots*; other calls include an upturned *hwee* and scolding *trt.* **HH** Usually in canopy. Forages among foliage and mossy branches and trunks. Mossy broadleaved evergreen and oak forests.

ad
Rufous-winged
Fulvetta
ad
Rufous-throated
Fulvetta
ad
Rusty-capped
Fulvetta
ad
Brown-cheeked
Fulvetta
ad
Nepal Fulvetta
♂
♀
Himalayan Cutia

PLATE 172: MISCELLANEOUS BABBLERS AND WHITE-EYES

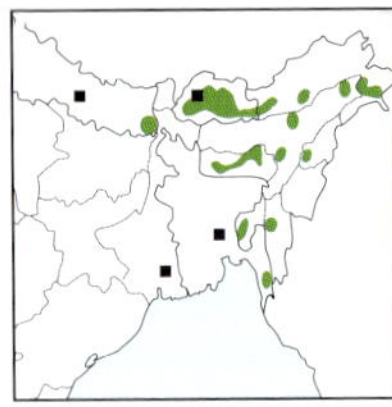

White-hooded Babbler *Gampsorhynchus rufulus* 23–24cm

Resident. E Himalayas and NE Indian hills. **ID** Bull-headed, long-tailed babbler. Adult has white head and underparts (with buff wash on flanks), contrasting with rufous-brown upperparts and tail; latter tipped pale buff. Iris strikingly yellow and has pinkish base to bill. Variable white on wing-coverts, but often obscured by feathers of mantle. Juvenile has rufous-orange crown and ear-coverts, rufous-brown upperparts, and whitish throat, becoming buff below; may be confusable with one of the rufous-headed parrotbills but has thinner bill, whitish eye-ring and ear-coverts do not contrast so strongly with white throat. **Voice** Usual call a harsh, stuttering rattle or cackle; contact calls soft and quiet. **HH** Bamboo and undergrowth in moist forest and second growth.

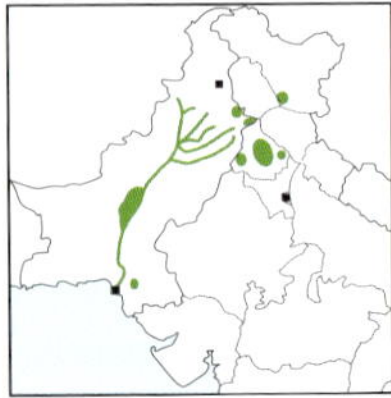

Rufous-vented Grass Babbler *Laticilla burnesii* 17cm

Resident. Indus plains in Pakistan and NW India. **ID** Prinia-like with long, loosely attached tail (shorter in female). Dark streaking on upperparts, whitish throat and breast, conspicuous whitish eye-ring, and rufous-chestnut undertail-coverts. Streaked upperparts have greyish cast to crown and warm rufous-brown cast to nape and upper mantle. Lacks well-defined pale tips and dark subterminal bands visible on undertail of Striated Prinia. Juvenile has more uniform sandy grey-brown upperparts (with indistinct streaking), and buffish wash to underparts; uniform wings, rufous (albeit paler than adult) undertail-coverts, and broad tail are best features. From Swamp Grass Babbler by distinct light rufous undertail-coverts, slightly richer body coloration and longer wings. **Voice** Song a clear, high-pitched warbling, rising in pitch, very different from similar species except Swamp; nasal rattle in alarm. **HH** Low-lying grassy riverine plains with scattered trees and shrubs; particularly stands of *Saccharum* grass. **TN** and **AN** Formerly treated as Rufous-vented Prinia *Prinia burnesii*.

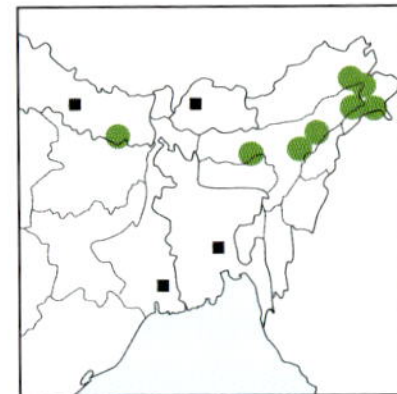

Swamp Grass Babbler *Laticilla cinerascens* 12.5–14cm

Resident. Brahmaputra plains in NE India, W Bihar and Nepal, and Bangladesh where probably extirpated. **ID** Cold olive-grey coloration to streaked upperparts (with greyer forecrown), white throat and greyish-white underparts, with grey flanks, and grey (rather than rufous) undertail-coverts. Has prominent white eye-ring and pale lores. Tail broad (but shorter than Rufous-vented Grass Babbler). Female smaller and shorter-tailed than male. Considerably larger than similarly coloured Delicate Prinia, with broader tail (lacking white tips and dark subterminal spots). The recently described subspecies *nepalicola* is known only from Koshi Tappu Wildlife Reserve, Nepal and is more similar in appearance to Rufous-vented but has paler rufous undertail-coverts, thinner and fainter streaking on upperparts and sides of breast; it lacks cinnamon coloration on hind collar, and is greyer above with shorter tail. **Voice** Song an elaborate warble, resembling Rufous-vented, but longer, more mellow, more varied, rising and falling in pitch, and faster. **HH** Tall grassland by rivers or in marshes, particularly stands of *Saccharum* or *Vetiveria*. Globally threatened. **TN** and **AN** Formerly treated as Swamp Prinia *Prinia cinerascens*.

Sri Lanka White-eye *Zosterops ceylonensis* 11cm

Resident. Sri Lanka. **ID** From Indian by slightly larger size and longer bill, duller green upperparts (lacking bright yellow forehead), poorly defined greyish lores with grey extending diffusely onto ear-coverts and sides of throat, and duller olive-yellow throat and breast. **Voice** Song a rapid, lively jingle, *tchrinchi-tchrinchi*.... Calls almost constantly given, soft, high chirps, quicker and more metallic than Indian. **HH** Habits like Indian. Forest, wooded areas, garden trees and shrubs.

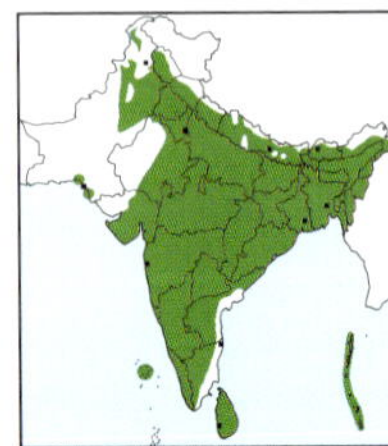

Indian White-eye *Zosterops palpebrosus* 10cm

Widespread resident, including Sri Lanka; unrecorded in parts of the north-west. **ID** The only white-eye except in Sri Lanka. Distinctive, with prominent white eye-ring, black bill and lores, green to yellowish-green upperparts, bright yellow throat and vent, and whitish rest of underparts with variable greyish wash. In Andamans and Nicobars it is larger and darker, with larger bill. In SW peninsula (*nilgiriensis*) can interestingly look more like Sri Lanka White-eye, with larger bill, darker green upperparts and duller underparts. **Voice** Plaintive *cheer* or *prree-u* call, given almost continuously; tinkling jingle song. **HH** Outside breeding season in flocks of up to 50 birds. Arboreal; favours flowering shrubs and trees. Forages actively amongst foliage and flowers, often clinging upside-down. Open broadleaved forest, groves, gardens orchards and mangroves; also, cardamom plantations in S India. **AN** Oriental White-eye.

White-hooded
Babbler
ad
juv
ad
ad
cinerascens
Rufous-vented Grass Babbler
ad
nepalicola
Swamp Grass Babbler
ad
ad
Sri Lanka
White-eye
Indian
White-eye

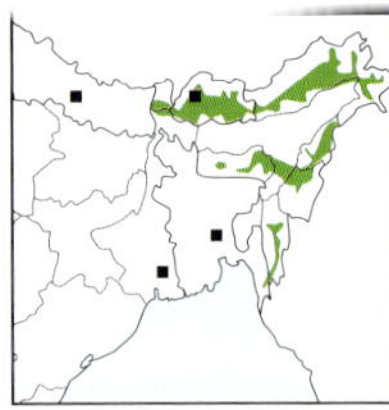

Striated Yuhina *Staphida castaniceps* 13–14cm

Resident. E Himalayas and NE Indian hills. **ID** Not as crested as other yuhinas, and the only one to show white on tail. Main features are pale grey eye-ring and short supercilium behind eye, rufous ear-coverts with fine white streaking, white streaking on greyish-olive mantle, uniform greyish-white underparts, and white tips to graduated tail. Two predominantly Himalayan subspecies, *Y. c. rufigenis* and *Y. c. plumbeiceps*, have a grey crown finely scaled greyish-white; *Y. c. castaniceps* (hills east and south of the Brahmaputra) has rufous crown and nape scaled pale grey on forecrown, with nape concolorous with ear-coverts. **Voice** Loud cheeping or twittering *chir-chit... chir-chit*; also, a short, nasal descending *chrrr*. **HH** In parties, sometimes with other insectivores. Fast-moving; works rapidly through the midstorey. Actions more tit-like than other yuhinas. Broadleaved forest with a thick, bushy understorey and second growth in tropical and subtropical zones.

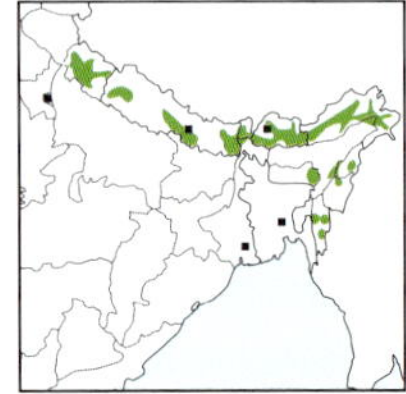

Black-chinned Yuhina *Yuhina nigrimenta* 9–10cm

Resident. Himalayas and NE Indian hills. **ID** Small, short-tailed, mainly olive-brown yuhina with grey-streaked black crest to greyish head, black chin and lores, and white to pale grey throat and upper breast contrasting with buffish of rest of underparts. Bill fine and downcurved, with red lower mandible and dark tip, and legs and feet are orange-yellow. **Voice** Flocks give a constant twittering and buzzing; calls include high *de-de-de-de* and *zee-zoe-zen*; soft *whee-to-whee-de-der-n-whee-yer* song. **HH** Forages busily, mainly in low bushes, sometimes moving into canopy; hangs upside-down on twigs in tit-like fashion. Moist subtropical broadleaved evergreen forest, second growth and overgrown clearings.

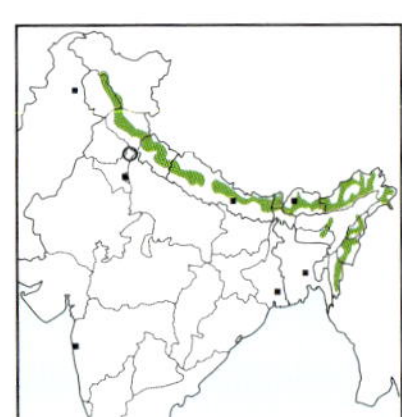

Whiskered Yuhina *Yuhina flavicollis* 12–13.5cm

Resident. Himalayas and NE Indian hills. **ID** Separable from other yuhinas by combination of grey-brown crest, prominent black moustachial stripe, yellowish to rufous hind collar, and a prominent white eye-ring. Sides of breast and flanks olive-brown, streaked white. *Y. f. albicollis* of W Himalayas has a mainly whitish hind collar with narrow rufous band below nape. Nominate of C and E Himalayas and the similar *Y. f. rouxi* of the hills east and south of the Brahmaputra have a more rufous hind collar. **Voice** Thin, rather squeaky *swii swii-swii*; clear, metallic ringing note and loud ringing notes issued in chorus from flocks. **HH** Outside breeding season, in mixed feeding parties with other small insectivores. Not shy. Hunts energetically in bushes and middle level of forest; flits from branch to branch and sometimes makes aerial sallies after insects. Bushes and broadleaved subtropical and temperate forests, wooded areas and second growth.

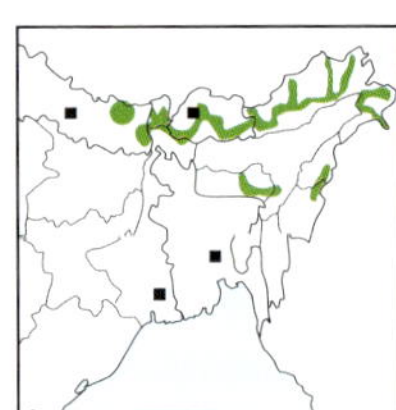

White-naped Yuhina *Yuhina bakeri* 12–13.5cm

Resident. E Himalayas and NE Indian hills. **ID** From other yuhinas by combination of stout bill, rufous crest, white nape (especially prominent when crest raised), blackish lores, bold white 'feathery' streaking on rufous ear-coverts, fine white shaft streaking on mantle, and fine brown streaking on pinkish-buff breast. **Voice** Hurried series of high thin notes repeated every 1–3 seconds, *tsu'tsu'tsu* or *du'du'du*, etc. Calls include very thin, piercing, high-pitched, short, metallic notes, **HH** In pairs or small parties, depending on season; often with other small babblers, tits and warblers. Forages actively, mainly in middle level of forest and bushes. Broadleaved, evergreen subtropical forest.

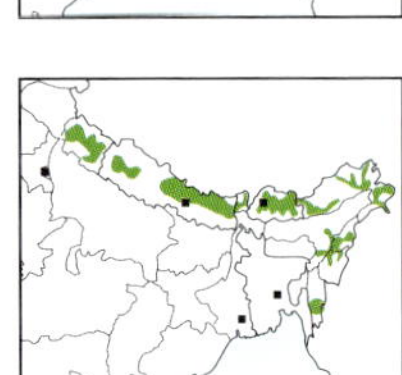

Stripe-throated Yuhina *Yuhina gularis* 14cm

Resident. Himalayas and NE Indian hills. **ID** Largest yuhina, with erect, forward-pointing crest. Best distinguished by combination of olive-brown crest, black streaking on pale vinaceous throat, rufous-orange wing panel contrasting with black primaries, and brownish-orange belly and vent. **Voice** Nasal, descending *queee* call, often in long series. **HH** Outside breeding season, typically in parties, often with other small babblers, tits and warblers. Usually frequents higher bushes and lower branches in forest. Often feeds on nectar of flowering rhododendrons. Temperate broadleaved and broadleaved-coniferous forest.

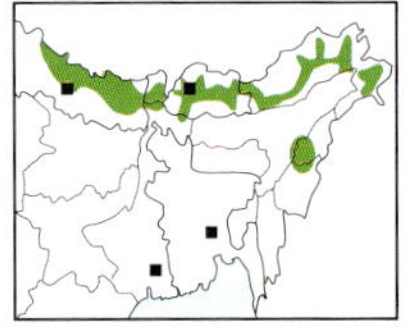

Rufous-vented Yuhina *Yuhina occipitalis* 12–14cm

Resident. Himalayas. **ID** Has rufous nape and vent; grey crest and ear-coverts finely streaked with white, and grey hindneck; white eye-ring and black moustachial stripe, and vinaceous underparts. Fine and slightly downcurved reddish bill, and reddish legs. **Voice** Constant chittering; song a high-pitched strong *zee-zu-drrrrr, tsip-ch-e-e-e-e*; also, *z-e-e... zit* in alarm. **HH** Habits similar to Stripe-throated, but forages more in treetops. Temperate and subalpine broadleaved forest, especially oak and rhododendrons.

ad
rufigenis
ad
castaniceps
Striated Yuhina
ad
Black-chinned
Yuhina
ad
flavicollis
ad
Whiskered
Yuhina
ad
albicollis
White-naped
Yuhina
ad
ad
Stripe-throated
Yuhina
Rufous-vented
Yuhina

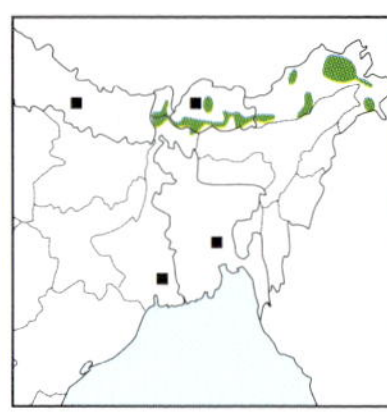

Black-crowned Scimitar Babbler *Pomatorhinus ferruginosus* 24cm

Resident. E Nepal east to E Arunachal Pradesh. **ID** Downcurved red bill and striking white supercilium. From Red-billed by stouter, shorter and brighter red bill, blackish crown and nape, deep rufous breast and belly, larger and broader white supercilium, and bright rufous feathering on forehead. See Brown-crowned for differences from that species. **Voice** Soft querulous whistles, *whu, whiu...whiu* and *whoiee*; oriole-like mewing *weeeaaa*, shrill, short *yep-yep-yep...*; and short squeaks combined with harsh scolding *tchrrrt-tchrrrrt, whitchitit...*; harsh alarm *krrrrrt, kru-ruruttt, krrrrirrrutut .....*, less scratchy and piercing than Red-billed. **HH** Habits similar to Red-billed. Bamboo thickets and dense undergrowth in broadleaved evergreen forest and second growth. **AN** Coral-billed Scimitar Babbler.

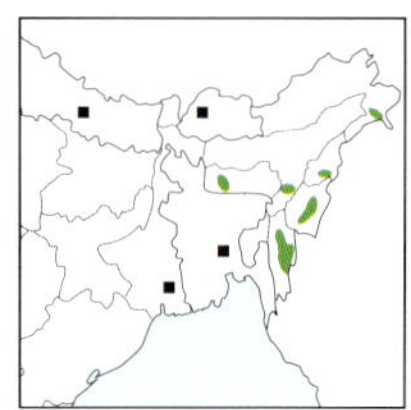

Brown-crowned Scimitar Babbler *Pomatorhinus phayrei* 24cm

Resident. NE India (S Assam and Manipur) and SE Arunachal Pradesh. **ID** Downcurved red bill and striking white supercilium. From Red-billed by stouter, shorter and brighter red bill, deeper buff lower throat and breast contrasting with white upper throat and malar stripe, broader black mask, darker olive-brown upperparts, and slate-grey sides of crown; supercilium has a touch of buff in front of eye (white on Red-billed). From Black-crowned by brown centre of crown with black lateral crown stripes, less rufescent upperparts, paler rufous-buff underparts, and lacks bright rufous feathering on forehead. **Voice** Several birds may produce wide variety of sounds together, including soft, questioning *whu, whiu*, miaowing *whheeeei*, shrill yelping *yep-yep-yep...*, short squeaky notes and harsh scolding *whit whit-tchrrrrt...*; harsh *krrrrrt, krururuttt* in alarm, less scratchy and piercing than Red-billed. **HH** Habits similar to Red-billed. Dense undergrowth in broadleaved evergreen forest, bamboo and second growth. **TN** Formerly treated as conspecific with Black-crowned as Coral-billed Scimitar Babbler.

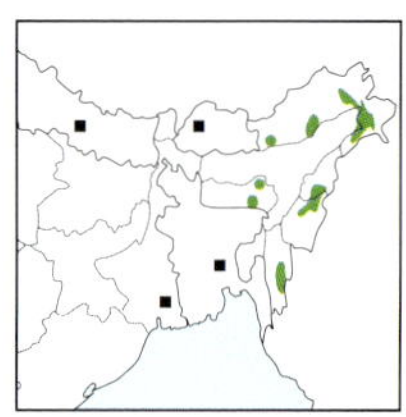

Red-billed Scimitar Babbler *Pomatorhinus ochraceiceps* 22–24cm

Resident. Arunachal and NE Indian hills. Vagrant: Bangladesh. **ID** Downcurved reddish bill and striking white supercilium. From Black-crowned and Brown-capped Scimitar Babblers by longer, finer and orange-red bill, narrower blackish mask (browner at rear), white or paler buff breast and belly, and paler olive-brown upperparts with brighter ginger-buff cast to crown (lacking dark lateral crown-stripes). Racial variation *P. o. stenorhynchus* (Mishmi Hills, Arunachal Pradesh) has pale buff rather than white breast and belly, and gingery-buff cast to sides of neck, compared with *P. o. austeni* (hills south of the Brahmaputra in Meghalaya, Nagaland, Manipur and Mizoram). **Voice** Hurried, hollow piping *wu-wu-wu* or *wu-wu-whip* or *pu-pu*, sometimes combined with antiphonal nasal *wyee*; also, very rapid *wi-wuwu* and human-like whistle *u-wip*; harsh scratchy alarm *whi-chutututut*. **HH** Typical scimitar babbler habits. Usually singly, in pairs or small parties. Very skulking. Searches for insects on ground, in bushes or on lower tree branches; also probes flowers of trees and bushes for nectar. Dense undergrowth in broadleaved evergreen forest and bamboo thickets.

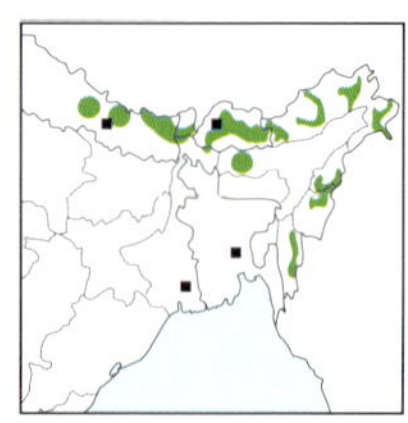

Slender-billed Scimitar Babbler *Pomatorhinus superciliaris* 20cm

Resident. C and E Himalayas and NE India. **ID** Long, slender, downcurved black bill, fine and feathery white supercilium contrasting with slate-grey crown and ear-coverts, grey-streaked white throat, and deep rufous underparts. **Voice** A repeated powerful tremulous *pwoorr* or slower *toop-toop-toop-toop*; both types used in duets, with female interjecting a 2–4-note whistle, *bu-tu-wheip-wheip*. Excited staccato chittering interspersed with piercing, rapid *pee-pee-pee* in alarm. **HH** Skulking and shy; usually keeps out of sight among thick undergrowth. Forages in similar fashion to Red-billed. Bamboo thickets and dense undergrowth in moist broadleaved forest. **TN** Formerly placed in *Xiphirhynchus*.

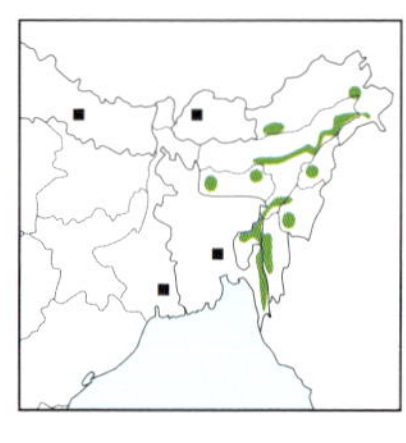

Large Scimitar Babbler *Erythrogenys hypoleucos* 26–28cm

Resident. Hills of NE India and Bangladesh. **ID** From other scimitar babblers by combination of larger size, lack of white supercilium, stouter, straighter and pale-coloured bill, dark eye, grey ear-coverts, rufous on sides of neck, white streaking on grey sides of breast, dark olive-brown upperparts with slight rufous tinge, and stout grey legs and feet. **Voice** Loud, hollow, variable piping notes, usually three per phrase with pairs often calling antiphonally *wiu-pu-pu-wup-up-piu* etc.; loud harsh grating alarm *whit-tchtchtchtch* etc. **HH** Very secretive and most easily located by its call. Mainly terrestrial, progressing in ungainly hops. Cane brakes, bamboo thickets, reeds, tall grass and dense undergrowth in broadleaved evergreen forest. **TN** Formerly placed in *Pomatorhinus*.

ad
Black-crowned
Scimitar Babbler
ad
Brown-crowned
Scimitar Babbler
ad
Red-billed
Scimitar Babbler
ad
Slender-billed
Scimitar Babbler
ad
Large
Scimitar Babbler

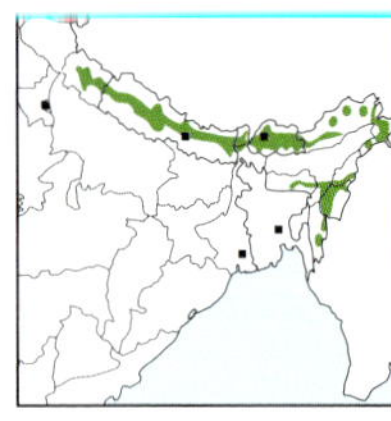

Streak-breasted Scimitar Babbler *Pomatorhinus ruficollis* 16–19cm

Resident. Himalayas and NE India. **ID** Striking white supercilium contrasting with black ear-coverts and downcurved yellow bill. From similar White-browed by diffuse olive-brown streaking on breast and belly, merging into olive-brown on flanks, brighter rufous patch on sides of neck which extends across nape as a diffuse band, smaller size, and smaller and less downcurved bill. Eye dark in Himalayan range (yellow in White-browed). Juvenile has brighter rufous upperparts, rufous breast with some white streaking, and smaller, almost straight bill. **Voice** Soft, musical *of-an-on* call; varied song, typically a rising *pouki-wurki pouki-wurki*, or falling *prrurti-witeu-witeu*; harsh, scolding rattles in alarm, *whi-whi-whi whi-whi-whi-whichiti….* **HH** Thick forest undergrowth and dense scrub.

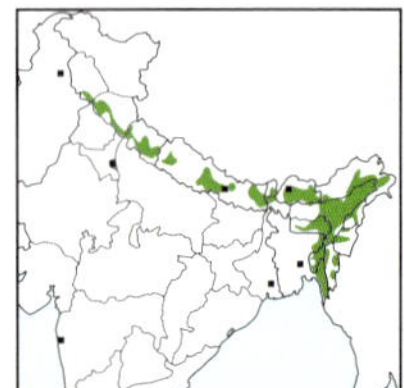

White-browed Scimitar Babbler *Pomatorhinus schisticeps* 19–23cm

Resident. Himalayan foothills, hills of NE India and Bangladesh. **ID** Striking white supercilium contrasting with black ear-coverts, and downcurved yellow bill. From similar Streak-breasted by clean white centre to breast and belly, chestnut sides to neck and breast (latter with variable white streaking), larger size, and larger, more downcurved bill. Juvenile smaller, with smaller bill and olive-brown crown; more closely resembles Streak-breasted, but centre of breast white and sides of breast chestnut. **Voice** Single note followed by trilled *hoo*t or evenly spaced three-noted hoot or whistle; harsh mocking *whihihihihi* and *whichitit* in alarm. **HH** Dense bushes, bamboo thickets, thick forest understorey and well-vegetated ravines.

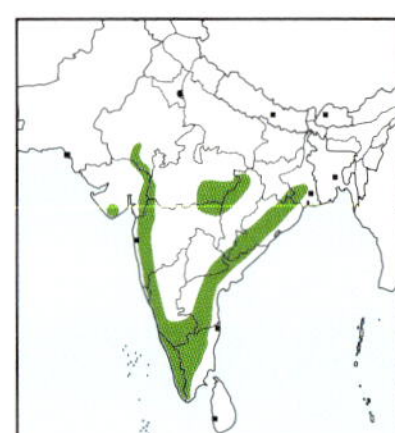

Indian Scimitar Babbler *Pomatorhinus horsfieldii* 22cm

Resident. Hills of peninsular India, Sri Lanka. **ID** Grey sides of breast and flanks and lacks pale eye of White-browed, but is the only scimitar babbler in peninsular India. Striking white supercilium contrasting with dark ear-coverts, and downcurved yellow bill. Four races are described from the peninsula. Compared to the nominate, the palest is *P. h. obscurus* (Rajasthan, Gujarat and Madhya Pradesh), which has grey upperparts with slightly darker grey crown, ear-coverts, breast-sides and flanks. Darkest is *P. h. travancoreensis* (Western Ghats), which has brownish-black crown, darker olive upperparts, and black ear-coverts, sides of breast and flanks; juvenile *travancoreensis*, however, may show rufous on sides of neck and breast. **Voice** Male gives musical flute-like *wot-ho-ho-ho* followed by quiet *krukru* or *krokant* from the female; sharp *kir-r-r-r* in alarm. **HH** Dense scrub, bamboo and thick forest understorey.

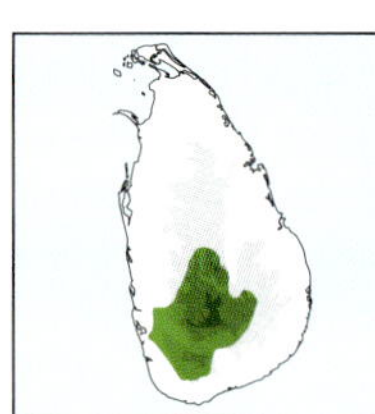

Sri Lanka Scimitar Babbler *Pomatorhinus melanurus* 19–21cm

Resident. **ID** Browner upperparts and coloration to flanks compared with Indian, but is the only scimitar babbler in Sri Lanka. Striking white supercilium contrasting with dark ear-coverts, and downcurved yellow bill. Wet zone nominate has chestnut-brown upperparts and sides of breast and flanks (olive-brown in dry zone *holdsworthi*). **Voice** Male gives variety of loud, bubbling and low whistling notes; duetting *woop-oop-oop, yok-ko-ko* and similar sounds, answered by short trill by female; chirps and rattles in alarm. **HH** Forest, well-wooded areas.

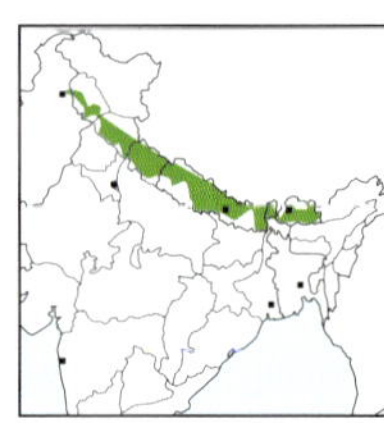

Rusty-cheeked Scimitar Babbler *Erythrogenys erythrogenys* 26cm

Resident. Himalayas. **ID** Rufous lores and ear-coverts. Unmistakable throughout W and C Himalayan range: lacks white supercilium, and has pale bill, rufous forehead, ear-coverts, sides of breast, flanks and vent. *E. e. haringtoni* (E Himalayas) has greyer or noticeably grey-streaked/spotted throat and upper breast; grey spotting on breast can be well defined, but pattern is continuous with that of throat (throat is always white on Spot-breasted, see latter for further differences). **Voice** Loud, far-carrying three-noted calls *quoit* or *khowi* followed by staccato *quit* from female; also ringing *khwir jot-khwir-jot*, often followed by *khuwiyiu* and quickly answered by female. **HH** Thick forest undergrowth, dense bushes, second growth, bamboo thickets and well-vegetated ravines. **TN** Formerly placed in *Pomatorhinus*.

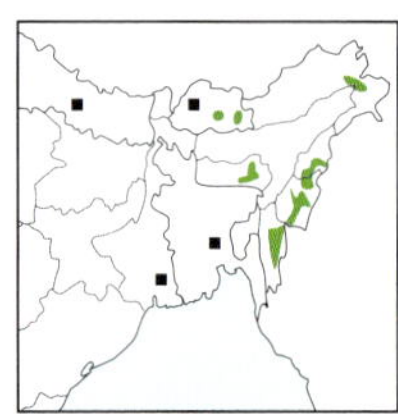

Spot-breasted Scimitar Babbler *Erythrogenys mcclellandi* 22–23cm

Resident. Hills of NE India. Vagrant: Bangladesh. **ID** From Large Scimitar Babbler by smaller size, finer bill, yellow eye, rufous forehead and ear-coverts, bold brown spotting on white breast, uniform olive-brown breast-sides and flanks, paler olive-brown upperparts, and brownish rather than lead-grey legs and feet. Unmarked white throat, more pronounced black malar, clearly-defined black spotting on breast, and olive-brown sides of neck and flanks, are differences from Rusty-cheeked. **Voice** Quite low-pitched, persistent, fluty *tiuu-tuu*, first note stressed, followed by a higher-pitched *tiuuk*; apparently a duet with mate; harsh rattle preceded by quick high notes, *wi-wi-chitit* in alarm. **HH** Forest undergrowth and second growth. **TN** Formerly conspecific with *Pomatorhinus erythrocnemis* (now split as Black-necklaced Scimitar Babbler *Erythrogenys erythrocnemis*).

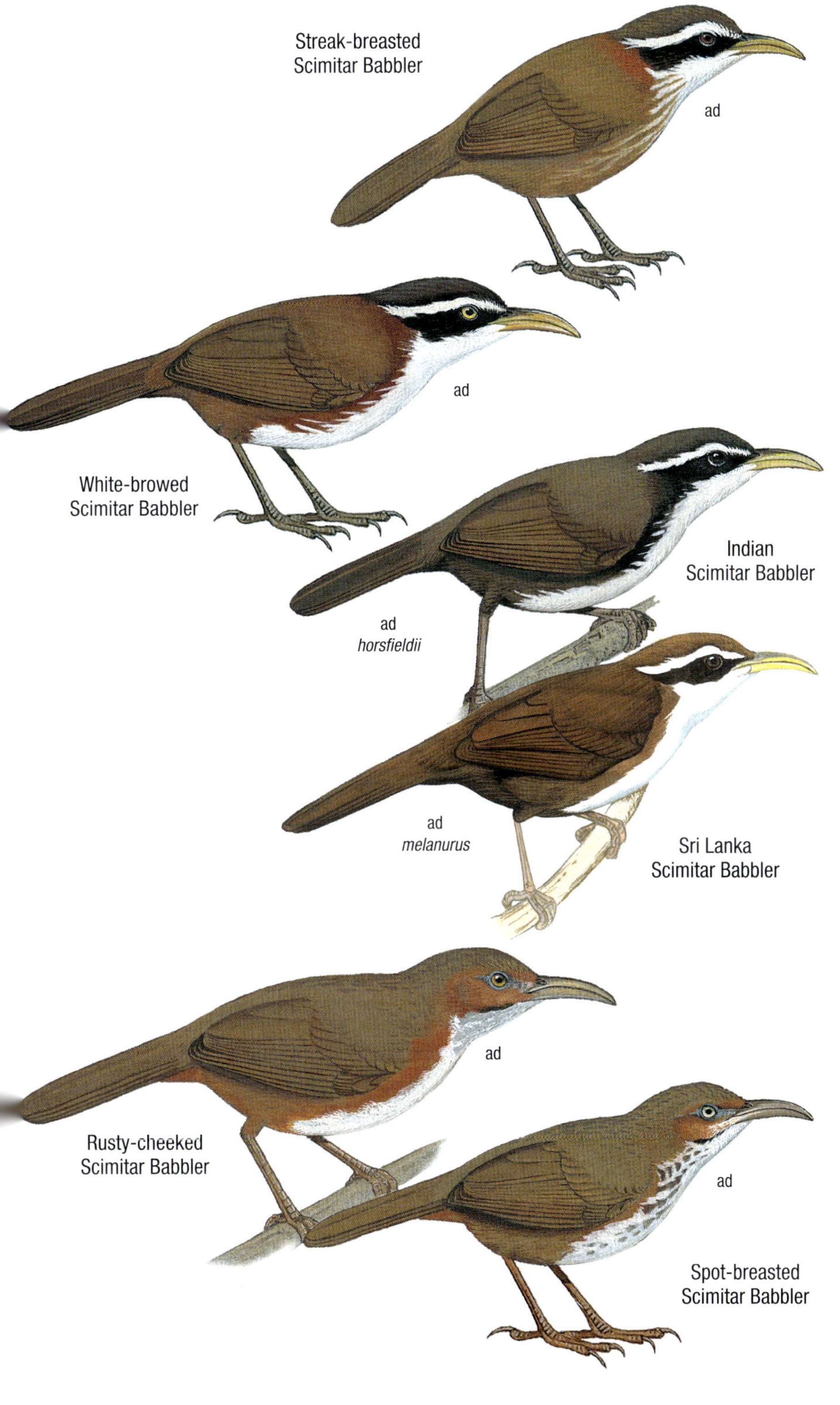
Streak-breasted
Scimitar Babbler
ad
ad
White-browed
Scimitar Babbler
Indian
Scimitar Babbler
ad
horsfieldii
ad
melanurus
Sri Lanka
Scimitar Babbler
ad
Rusty-cheeked
Scimitar Babbler
ad
Spot-breasted
Scimitar Babbler

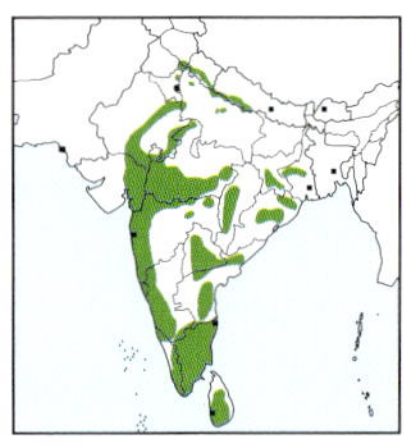

Tawny-bellied Babbler *Dumetia hyperythra* 13cm

Resident. Peninsular India, S Nepal and Sri Lanka. **ID** Fairly long-tailed, rufous-coloured babbler. Forehead and forecrown rufous-buff, sides of head and underparts orange-buff, mantle olive-brown, and wings and tail brown, the tail with faint barring. Eye pale, with bare bluish orbital skin, and bill pale pinkish. Legs and feet pinkish. Four subspecies described from the subcontinent. Widespread nominate (N, C and E India) has throat concolorous with rest of the underparts. The other three to south and west have white throat and centre to belly, including *D. h. phillipsi* (Sri Lanka) which has variable white eyebrow and crescent below eye. **Voice** Whistling seven-note song; flocks give cheeping *sweech-sweech.* **HH** Tall grass and scrub, avoids evergreen biotope.

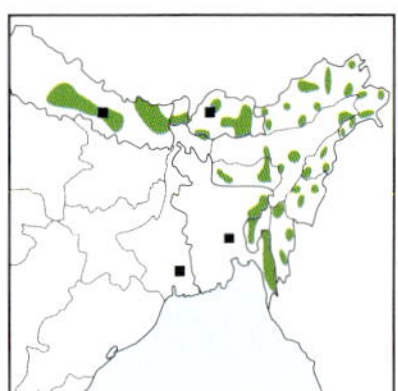

Dark-fronted Babbler *Dumetia atriceps* 13cm

Resident. Western Ghats and Sri Lanka. **ID** Stocky, shortish-tailed and bull-headed babbler, with pale grey bill and striking yellow eyes. The only babbler in region which has a combination of black on head, rufous-brown to olive-brown upperparts, and whitish underparts (with olive-brown to buffish flanks and vent). Two subspecies in the Western Ghats have dark crown and ear-coverts (crown black in *D. a. atriceps* and sooty-brown in *D. a. bourdilloni*), while the two subspecies in Sri Lanka have black of head restricted to forehead and ear-coverts (with *D. a. nigrifrons* having more rufous upperparts than *D. a. siccata*). **Voice** Unobtrusive *tup*, scolding *churr* and nasal mewing, also a loud, throaty grating call. **HH** Dense undergrowth, thickets near streams, reedbeds and bamboo in evergreen biotope. **TN** Formerly placed in *Rhopocichla.*

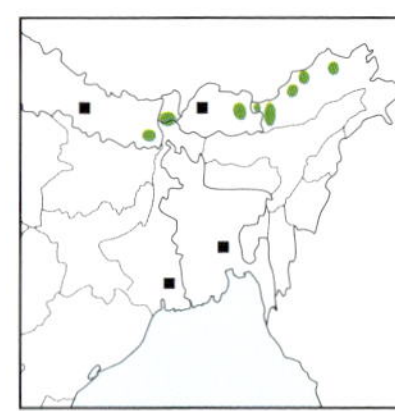

Grey-throated Babbler *Stachyris nigriceps* 12–15cm

Resident. Himalayas, hills of NE India and Bangladesh. **ID** From other *Stachyris* babblers by combination of blackish crown with white streaking, white eye-crescents, black lateral crown-stripe and greyish supercilium, and black-and-white or mainly grey chin and throat. Subspecies variation mainly in pattern of throat and colour of ear-coverts and underparts: e.g. *S. n. nigriceps* (C and E Himalayas) has chin and throat mainly grey with diffuse white malar, buff-brown ear-coverts and buff underparts, whereas *S. n. coltarti* (Nagaland) has chin and throat mainly black, with prominent white malar stripe, and brighter orange-buff ear-coverts and underparts. **Voice** High-pitched, tinkling trill, prefaced by single note; scolding *chrrrt* in alarm. **HH** Undergrowth and bamboo thickets in dense moist forest and second growth.

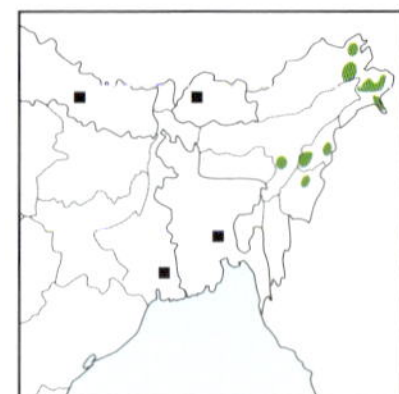

Sikkim Wedge-billed Babbler *Stachyris humei* 18cm

Resident. E Himalayas to NE Arunachal. **ID** Striking, with wedge-shaped bill, broad but diffuse grey supercilium and spotting on sides of neck, boldly marked upperparts, diffuse brown barring on wings and tail, and sturdy blackish legs and feet. From Cachar Wedge-billed by black face and underparts (becoming greyish-white on belly) with fine white shaft streaking, more pronounced greyish supercilium, and fine shaft streaking on olive-buff-centred feathers of crown and mantle (lacking pale tips to nape and mantle feathers). **Voice** Songs include loud, melodious whistles, often given in duet; alarm a subdued low *hrrrh hrrrh hrrrh hrrr'it hrrrh hrrrh....* **HH** Understorey of broadleaved evergreen forest with bamboo. **AN** and **TN** Formerly treated as Himalayan Wedge-billed Babbler *Sphenocichla humei.*

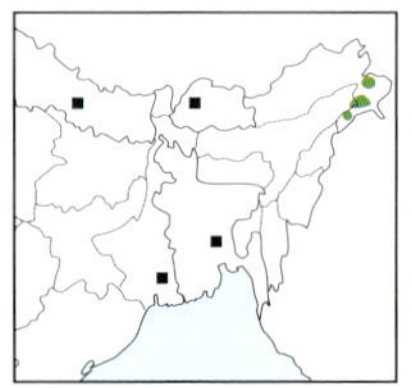

Cachar Wedge-billed Babbler *Stachyris roberti* 18cm

Resident. SE Arunachal Pradesh, N Cachar, Nagaland and Manipur. **ID** Like Sikkim Wedge-billed has wedge-shaped bill, boldly marked upperparts, diffuse brown barring on wings and tail, and sturdy blackish legs and feet. From Sikkim by heavily scaled underparts, with browner throat, sides of neck and breast heavily marked by greyish-white arrowhead-shaped fringes. Also has rufous-brown forehead, and more olive-brown upperparts, with diffuse pale tips to feathers of nape and mantle. Greyish supercilium much less well-defined. **Voice** Song a clear, loud, fluty, melodious, repeated *uu-wii-wu-yu* (*wii* highest, *yu* lowest), very different from Sikkim. They have same calls. **HH** Understorey of broadleaved evergreen forest with bamboo. **AN** and **TN** Formerly treated as Manipur Wedge-billed Babbler *Sphenocichla roberti.*

Snowy-throated Babbler *Stachyris oglei* 15cm

Resident. Arunachal Pradesh hills and extreme E Assam. **ID** Large, distinctive *Stachyris* babbler, with stout bill and short tail. Has striking pattern to head and neck, with white supercilium connected to white-splashed crescent on side of neck, broad black eye-stripe which connects with black patch at rear of ear-coverts, chestnut crown and nape with black sides, and striking white throat. Also has grey breast and belly, olive-brown flanks, and fine black barring on wings and tail. **Voice** Calls include bursts of rapid, thin, high-pitched rattling *kd'd'd-kd'd'd'd'd, kd'd'd...* in alarm. Song undescribed. **HH** Understorey of dense, moist forest, bamboo and scrub in ravines.

Tawny-bellied
Babbler
ad
hyperythra
ad
albogularis
ad
atriceps
ad
nigriceps
ad
nigrifrons
Dark-fronted
Babbler
ad
coltarti
Grey-throated
Babbler
ad
Sikkim
Wedge-billed Babbler
ad
Cachar
Wedge-billed Babbler
ad
Snowy-throated
Babbler

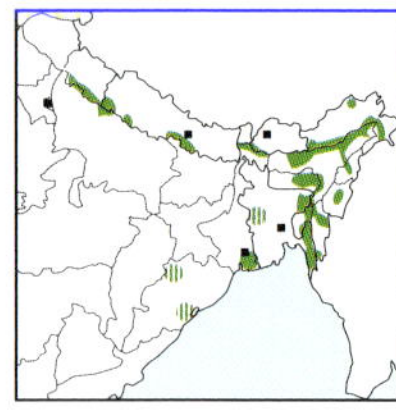

Chestnut-capped Babbler *Timalia pileata* 15.5–17cm

Resident. Himalayan terai and foothills, N and NE Indian plains and Bangladesh. **ID** A stocky, thick-necked babbler with bright chestnut cap, white forehead and supercilium connected to white throat and breast, and thick black bill and black lores (resulting in masked appearance). Fine black streaking on white breast, slate-grey sides of neck, buffish-olive flanks and vent, and buff belly. Tail faintly barred. **Voice** Fast, high-pitched, descending trill, varying in length, not as high-pitched as Grey-throated; *tzt* contact note and a *pic-pic-pic* alarm call. **HH** In small parties in non-breeding season. Keeps out of sight in thick cover. Clambers up and down stems systematically searching for insects. Tall grass, reedbeds and scrub in low-lying wet areas; also grass-covered plateaux in Khasi Hills.

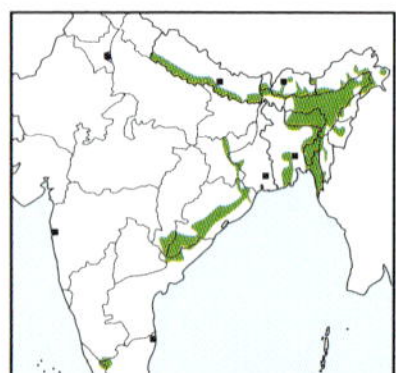

Pin-striped Tit Babbler *Mixornis gularis* 11–14cm

Resident. Himalayan foothills, hills of NE, E and S India, and Bangladesh. **ID** Rather scruffy-looking babbler with rufous-brown cap, yellow eyes, pale yellow supercilium, olive mantle, rufous-brown wings and tail, and pale yellow underparts with fine dark streaking on throat and breast. **Voice** Especially noisy, readily located by distinctive call; loud monotonous repeated *chuk-chuk-chuk*; *bizz-chir-chur* in alarm. **HH** Depending on season, in pairs or small parties, often with other species. Creeps and clambers about unobtrusively. Undergrowth in broadleaved forest and thin bamboo jungle. **TN** Formerly placed in *Macronus*.

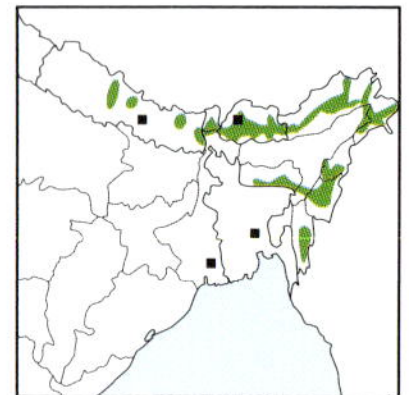

Golden Babbler *Cyanoderma chrysaeum* 10–12cm

Resident. Himalayas, hills of NE India and Bangladesh. **ID** Distinctive babbler with yellow forehead and black-streaked yellow crown, black lores and moustachial stripe, olive-green upperparts and yellow underparts. *C. c. chrysaeum* (E Himalayas and south to Manipur) has yellowish-olive upperparts and bright chrome-yellow underparts. *C. c. binghami* (Mizoram and south to Bangladesh hills) has duller olive-green upperparts and duller yellow underparts. **Voice** Like some of the slower variations of Rufous-capped, but Golden almost always has a single introductory note, and hesitates before it strings together 5–8 *toots* on same pitch. Dry, scolding chitter that is quiet compared to other babblers. **HH** Usually in mixed parties in non-breeding season. Continually on the move. Bamboo thickets, overgrown deserted cultivation clearings and dense undergrowth in moist forest. **TN** Formerly placed in *Stachyridopsis*.

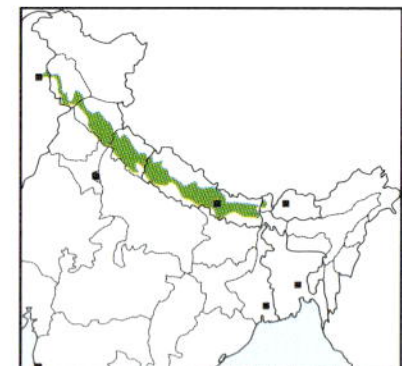

Black-chinned Babbler *Cyanoderma pyrrhops* 10cm

Resident. Himalayas. **ID** Small, rather bull-headed babbler, with black lores, chin and centre of throat. Also has olive-buff crown with dark streaking, buffish ear-coverts, orange-buff underparts, and olive-brown upperparts (lacking any rufous in plumage). Iris red. **Voice** Pleasant bell-like piping, *whit-whit-whit-whit*, which is very short and repeated at irregular intervals. Calls include soft *chir* and harsh scolding *tchirrirrrr*. **HH** In pairs or small parties, often with other species, depending on season. Active and restless. Undergrowth in open forest, forest edges and second growth. **TN** Formerly placed in *Stachyridopsis*.

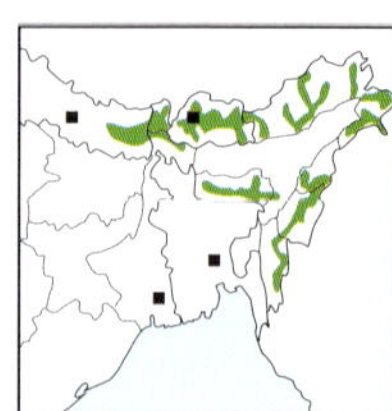

Rufous-capped Babbler *Cyanoderma ruficeps* 12cm

Resident. E Himalayas and NE Indian hills. **ID** Very similar to Buff-chested, but rufous cap is more sharply defined and extends further onto rear crown. In addition, has brighter olive upperparts, pale yellow throat (faintly streaked black), and yellowish-buff face and underparts (which contrast more with mantle). Lacks greyish supercilium and/or surround to eye. Juvenile as adult, but duller, with paler underparts and a paler crown; more closely resembles Buff-chested. **Voice** Series of 7–8 notes, *pee-pi-pi-pi-pi-pi pi*; call a four-noted whistle *whi-whi-whi-whi*; flocks give conversational chittering. **HH** In pairs in breeding season, otherwise in actively moving parties with other species. Feeding actions sometimes tit-like. Bamboo thickets and dense undergrowth in moist forest. **TN** Formerly placed in *Stachyridopsis*.

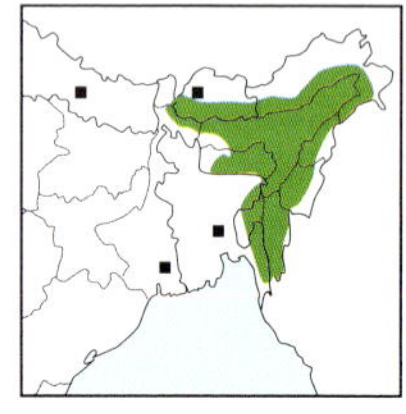

Buff-chested Babbler *Cyanoderma ambiguum* 12cm

Resident. E Himalayan foothills, NE and E Indian hills, and Bangladesh. **ID** Very similar to Rufous-capped Babbler, but rufous cap is less sharply defined and does not extend onto rear crown. In addition, has white throat (faintly streaked black), greyish supercilium and/or surround to eye, olive-brown (rather than buff) ear-coverts concolorous with mantle, and buffish breast and flanks, becoming paler on belly. Juvenile as adult, but has more rufous fringes to wings and tail, paler underparts, and rufous cap is paler. **Voice** Indistinguishable from Rufous-capped. **HH** Habits like Rufous-capped. Bushes and bamboo thickets in deserted clearings, thick undergrowth in open forest and densely vegetated ravines. **TN** Formerly treated as conspecific with Rufous-fronted Babbler *Stachyridopsis rufifrons*.

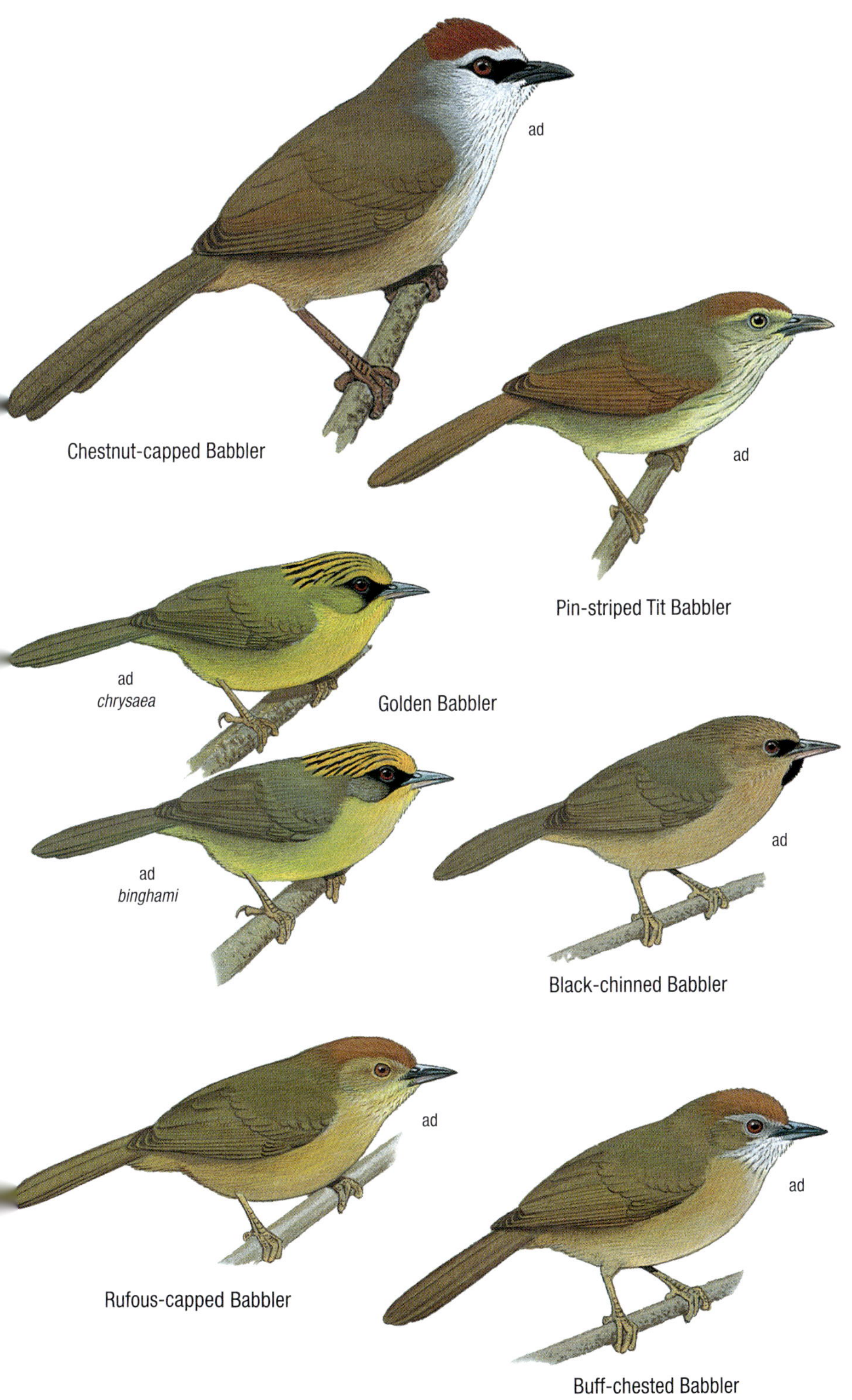

Chestnut-capped Babbler

Pin-striped Tit Babbler

Golden Babbler

Black-chinned Babbler

Rufous-capped Babbler

Buff-chested Babbler

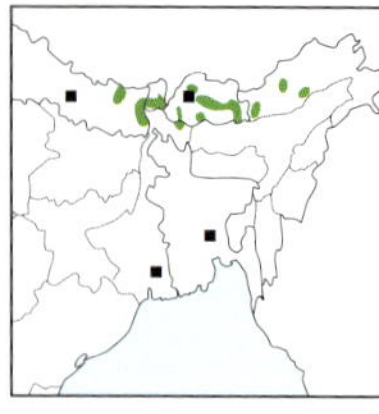

Rufous-throated Wren Babbler *Spelaeornis caudatus* 9cm

Resident. E Himalayas. **ID** From Pygmy Cupwing by grey face, rufous-orange throat and breast (latter with some dark streaking and barring), with paler rufous-orange coloration extending onto dark-scaled flanks, white-barred or -spotted rather than scaled appearance to belly, no buff spotting on wing-coverts, and short, square-ended tail. Can show touch of white on chin and malar region. Some birds paler orange-buff on throat and breast. Juvenile resembles adult, but is smaller, lacks dark scaling on upperparts, and lacks white spotting and black barring on underparts. **Voice** Sudden outburst of 3–5 rapidly repeated *swediddy* notes; intense warble of 2–4 notes, *swichu-wichu-wichu*. Call *dzik*. **HH** Terrestrial and very secretive, usually keeping out sight, but male often sings in the open. Mossy rocks and undergrowth in moist forest.

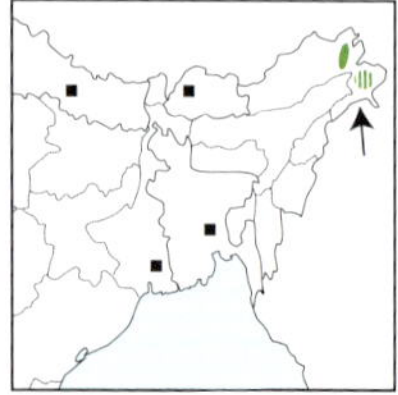

Mishmi Wren Babbler *Spelaeornis badeigularis* 9cm

Resident. Mishmi Hills, E Arunachal Pradesh. **ID** From Pygmy Cupwing by white chin, rusty-orange throat, white-barred or -spotted rather than scaled appearance to breast and belly, lack of buff spotting on wing-coverts, and presence of short, stubby tail. Compared to Rufous-throated, has more white on chin, darker brown upperparts, and deeper (and more clearly defined) rusty-orange throat with dark streaks (rusty colour does not extend to breast and flanks, which are barred/spotted with white on black on breast, and washed dark brown on flanks). **Voice** Similar to Rufous-throated, but more variable, often ascending and including short trills. **HH** Shy and skulking; mostly keeps within 1m of ground. Undergrowth of moist forest. **AN** Rusty-throated Wren Babbler.

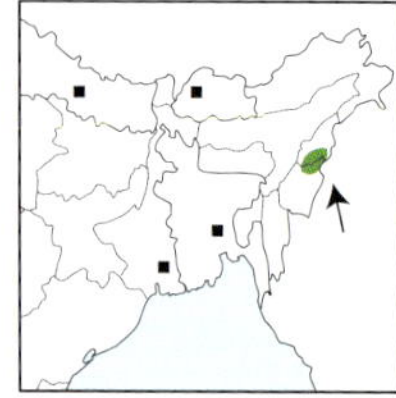

Naga Wren Babbler *Spelaeornis chocolatinus* 10cm

Resident. NE Indian hills. **ID** Slim and long-tailed with grey face and scaly appearance to brown upperparts. From Tawny-breasted Wren Babbler (note different range) by smaller size, darker upperparts, black-tipped white spotting on sides of breast and flanks, and black speckling on white belly. Male has white throat and centre of breast, and olive-brown sides of breast and flanks. Female has rufous-brown sides of breast and flanks, less grey on face, and rufous wash to throat and centre of breast. See also Chin Hills and 'Lisu' Wren Babblers, although note range differences. **Voice** Loud, melodic, explosive whistle, *wheeuw*; soft *chir* in alarm. **HH** Usually seen foraging among undergrowth within 0.5m of ground. Dense undergrowth and mossy rocks in moist forest and on hillsides. Globally threatened. **AN** Long-tailed Wren Babbler.

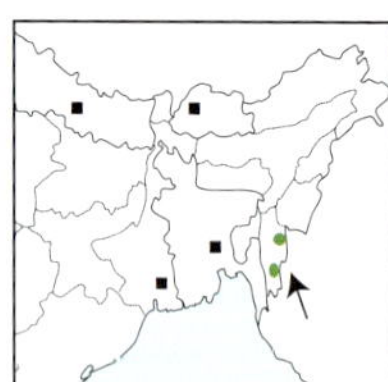

Chin Hills Wren Babbler *Spelaeornis oatesi* 11–12cm

Resident. Lushai Hills, Mizoram. **ID** Slim and long-tailed with scaly appearance to brown upperparts. Very similar to Naga Wren Babbler, having (less pronounced) grey face, and black-tipped white spotting on sides of breast and flanks, but has pronounced and extensive black flecking and spotting to white throat and centre of breast. Sexes similar. **Voice** Repeated loud, short, abrupt, undulating warbling phrases, e.g. *chiwi-chiwi-chiwi-chewo*, first note highest, last short. Calls include soft *tuc tuc tuc*.... **HH** Habits like Naga Wren Babbler. Understorey of moist forest.

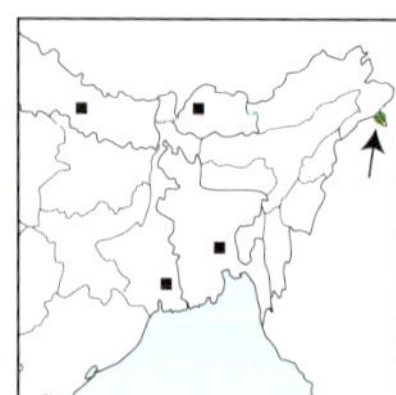

'Lisu' Wren Babbler *Spelaeornis* sp.

Presumably resident. Mugaphi slopes, upper reaches of Noa-Dihing valley, far E Arunachal Pradesh. **ID** Both sexes similar to extralimital Grey-bellied *S. reptatus* (with grey face) but has white belly without any prominent black markings. As Grey-bellied, background coloration to breast and flanks in male is brown and fulvous brown in female. From Naga Wren Babbler (note different range) by more extensive grey on face and darker underparts and only narrow white belly lacking prominent black markings. **Voice** Primary song sweet, 4–7 notes, variable in syntax but consistent in frequency and similar in basic notes, resembling Naga, but lacking trills of Grey-bellied. **HH** Temperate forest with dense undergrowth. **TN** Previously identified as Grey-bellied Wren Babbler but now believed to be a new taxon, with Grey-bellied no longer regarded as occurring in India.

ad
Rufous-throated
Wren Babbler
ad
Mishmi
Wren Babbler
♂
Naga
Wren Babbler
♀
♂
Chin Hills
Wren Babbler
♀
♂
'Lisu'
Wren Babbler
♀

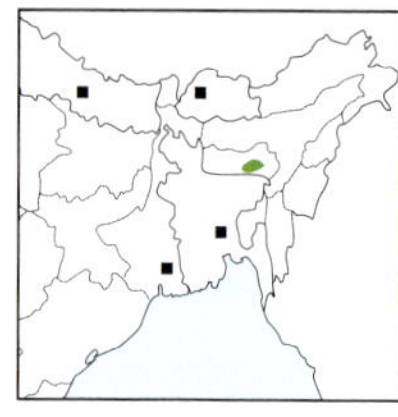

Tawny-breasted Wren Babbler *Spelaeornis longicaudatus* 11–12cm

Resident. Meghalaya. **ID** Slim and long-tailed with scaly appearance to brown upperparts. From similar species by orange-buff underparts that are either unmarked or have only very light blackish speckling and paler shaft streaking on sides of breast. Has whitish chin and centre of belly and greyish face. Possibly confusable with Buff-breasted Babbler but is considerably smaller, has diffuse dark scaling and pale centres to feathers of upperparts, and a grey face. Juvenile has rufous-brown upperparts, lacking dark scaling. **Voice** Song a loud, rather shrill, fairly short warble, e.g. *chídiweet-chídiweet-chídiweet*, with minor variants; very like song of Chin Hills Wren Babbler, but a bit slower, more slurred, and more complex. Soft churring alarm call. **HH** Dense low vegetation and boulders by streams in ravines in moist forest.

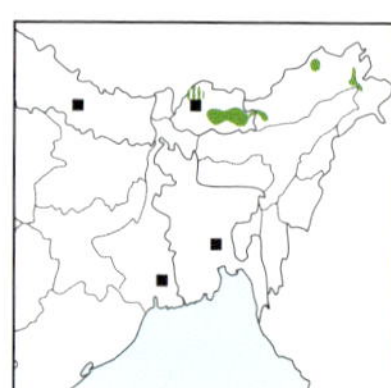

Bar-winged Wren Babbler *Spelaeornis troglodytoides* 10cm

Resident. Bhutan, W and SE Arunachal. **ID** Long-tailed with dark-barred wings and tail. Blackish crown merging into chestnut nape and mantle boldly spotted white and buff. *S. t. sherriffi* (Bhutan and W Arunachal) has white throat and centre of breast, and rest of underparts rufous with variable splashes of white on flanks. *S. t. souliei* (WC Arunachal) has throat and breast variably marked with rufous. Juvenile entirely rufous below, lacking white spotting on crown and nape. *S. t. indiraji* (SE Arunachal) has mainly rufous underparts with more contrasting grey-and-black barred wings and tail. **Voice** Powerful, mellow, rapid warble of five repeated notes, regularly reiterated, *tu-lulu-lulu-lulu-lulu*. Call a faint *churr*. **HH** Forages in bushes, bamboo and undergrowth rather than on ground. Moist forest.

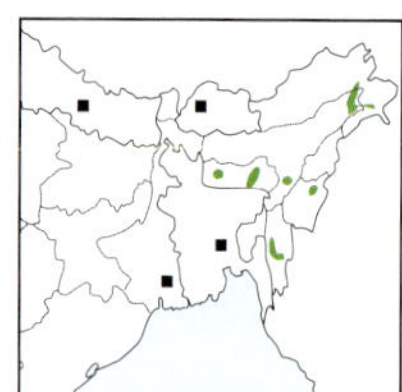

Streaked Wren Babbler *Gypsophila brevicaudata* 12cm

Resident. NE Indian hills. Vagrant: Bangladesh. **ID** Large and rather untidy-looking, with prominent tail and less rotund appearance compared to cupwings. Grey lores, supercilium and ear-coverts (resulting in grey-faced appearance), whitish throat diffusely streaked grey, olive-brown breast, becoming brighter rufous-brown on flanks and vent, olive-brown upperparts with dark brown fringes (resulting in an untidy streaked or scaled appearance), and prominent buff tips to wing-coverts and tertials. Greyish edges to primaries form panel on wing. **Voice** Song og very variable, repeated loud, clear, melancholy ringing whistles, *chi-oo, peee-oo, pu-ee, chiu-ree, chewee-chui* and *pee-wi*; sometimes a single *pweeee*. Harsh, prolonged, scolding rattles in alarm. **HH** Hops quickly around moss-covered boulders on forest floor. Moist, thick forest on steep, rocky ground and in ravines. **TN** Formerly placed in *Napothera*.

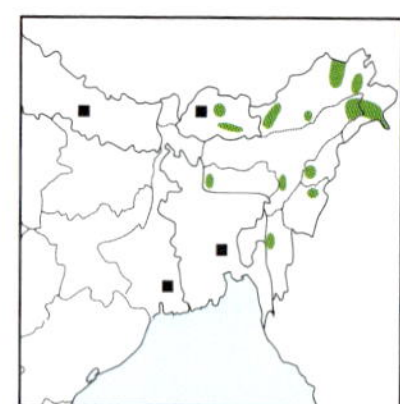

Eyebrowed Wren Babbler *Napothera epilepidota* 10–11cm

Resident.NE India and Bhutan. **ID** A small, long-billed but short-tailed wren babbler. The only wren babbler in subcontinent with a prominent supercilium and dark eye-stripe. Additional features include dark brown upperparts, indistinctly scaled with black, very prominent white spotting on wing-coverts, bold dark spotting on throat and breast, and broad diffuse streaking on flanks and belly. *N. e. roberti* (south of Brahmaputra River) has buff supercilium, sides of throat and breast; these are white in *N. e. guttaticollis* (NE Himalayas). **Voice** Song a thin, plaintive, falling whistle *cheeeeeeu*, repeated at 2–5-second intervals; rather subdued, prolonged rattles in alarm. **HH** Very skulking. Hops about among leaf litter, boulders and logs. Moist forest.

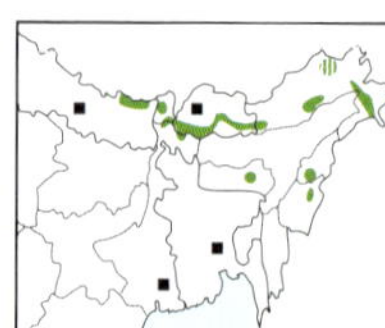

Long-billed Wren Babbler *Napothera malacoptila* 11–12cm

Resident. E Himalayas and NE Indian hills. **ID** Large, short-tailed wren babbler with long, downcurved bill. Buffish-white throat and buff belly, broad buff streaking to brown breast and flanks, and brown upperparts with fine buff shaft. Also narrow dark moustachial stripe, less distinct malar stripe, and rufous-brown vent and undertail-coverts. **Voice** Series of short, clear bell-like whistles; churring repeated *prurr purr prrit* alarm. **HH** Forest undergrowth on rocky ground, steep ravines and overgrown, abandoned clearings. **TN** Formerly placed in *Rimator*.

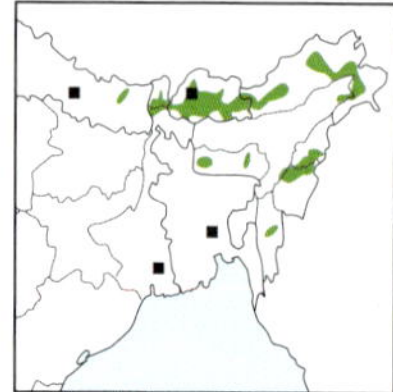

Spotted Elachura *Elachura formosa* 10cm

Resident. E Himalayas, hills of NE India and Nepal. **ID** Dark brown with a noticeable tail. From similar species by broad dark brown barring on rufous-brown wings and tail, irregular white flecking on grey-brown sides of head and upperparts (especially prominent on nape, sometimes forming collar, and wing-coverts), and white and dark brown mottling and dark brown vermiculations on buffish underparts. Underparts can appear dark, with pattern difficult to see in the field. Lacks intense barring on mantle, back, wing-coverts and underparts of Eurasian Wren. **Voice** High-pitched, repeated, faltering whistling song, *did-did-did-dit, did-di-di-did*; sputtering *put-put-put*….trill call. **HH** Habits like Pygmy Cupwing. Dense undergrowth in moist broadleaved forest; long grass and scrub in winter. **AN** Spotted Wren Babbler.

♂
Tawny-breasted
Wren Babbler
♀
ad
Bar-winged
Wren Babbler
ad
roberti
ad
ad
guttaticollis
Streaked Wren Babbler
Eyebrowed
Wren Babbler
ad
ad
Long-billed
Wren Babbler
Spotted Elachura

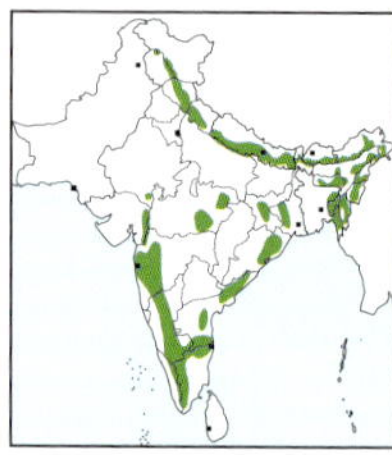

Puff-throated Babbler *Pellorneum ruficeps* 15–17cm

Resident. Himalayan foothills, hills of peninsular and NE India, and Bangladesh. **ID** Comparatively long-tailed. Has rufous or chestnut crown, prominent buff supercilium, white throat (often puffed out), and heavily streaked whitish underparts. Considerable subspecies variation in colour of crown (rufous-brown to chestnut), ear-coverts (buff and concolorous with supercilium to chestnut and concolorous with crown), darkness and size of brown spotting, colour of mantle (olive-brown to rufous-brown), and whether the mantle and sides of neck are unstreaked or streaked. **Voice** Halting song *swee ti-ti-hwee hwee hwee tis wee-u* rambles up and down the scale, often for minutes; calls include a plaintive whistled *ne-menue*. **HH** In pairs or family parties. Very skulking, staying on or near ground. Runs or makes long hops when foraging. Dense thickets, bamboo and undergrowth in broadleaved forest undergrowth and second growth.

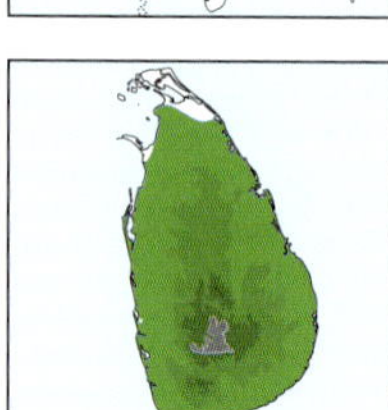

Brown-capped Babbler *Pellorneum fuscocapillus* 16cm

Resident. Sri Lanka. **ID** Brownish-black crown and nape with faint buff shaft streaking, dark olive-brown upperparts, and deep cinnamon sides of head and underparts. *P. f. babaulti* (dry zone lowlands) has paler cinnamon-buff sides of head and underparts, and paler greyish-brown upperparts compared to subspecies in hills (nominate) and wet zone lowlands (*P. f. scortillum*). **Voice** Like Puff-throated. **HH** Heard more often than seen. Feeds on or near ground. Scrub, other thick ground cover and forest undergrowth.

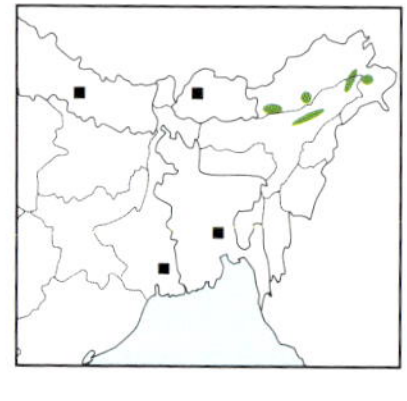

Marsh Babbler *Pellorneum palustre* 15cm

Assam, Arunachal Pradesh and NE Bangladesh, where possibly extirpated. **ID** Dark, longish-tailed babbler (compared to other *Pellorneum*) with white throat, indistinct greyish supercilium, prominent white eye-crescents and bold brown streaking on breast and flanks. Superficially resembles Puff-throated Babbler, but smaller, lacks rufous crown and buff supercilium, and has rufous-buff wash to sides of throat, breast and flanks. **Voice** Song includes a rich variety of churring and rattling notes mixed with clear whistles and trills; rattling notes often resemble a crackling sound. **HH** Very skulking but calls frequently. Reedbeds and tall grassland. Globally threatened.

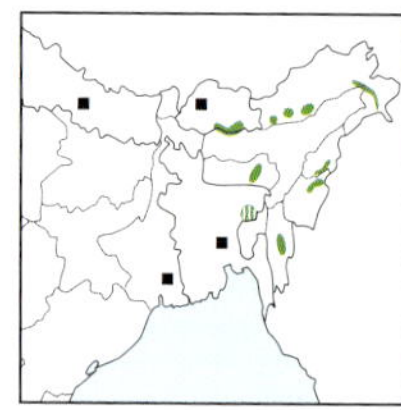

Spot-throated Babbler *Pellorneum albiventre* 14–15cm

Resident. E Himalayan foothills, hills of NE India and Bangladesh. **ID** From Buff-breasted Babbler by white throat with faint arrowhead-shaped grey spotting (can be lacking). *P. a. ignotum* (E Himalayas) has grey lores and supercilium, greyish breast-band, well-defined white belly, lacks rufescent cast to upperparts, and has short and rounded tail, which further help separate from Buff-breasted. Nominate (south and east of Brahmaputra) has browner face, more uniform and warmer brown underparts (with diffuse white belly), and has a longer tail, compared with *ignotum*, and is closer in coloration to Buff-breasted. **Voice** Rich thrush-like song, quickly delivered and complex including much repetition; calls include a harsh *chrr-chrr-chrr-chrrrit* and slightly explosive *tip-tip-tip*. **HH** Habits like Puff-throated. Scrub and thickets of second growth or bamboo; avoids dense forest.

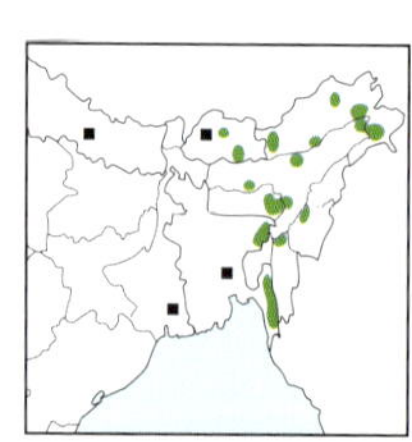

Buff-breasted Babbler *Pellorneum tickelli* 13–15cm

Resident. NE Indian hills and Bangladesh. **ID** More neatly proportioned, with smaller head and proportionately longer tail than Abbott's, plus smaller bill, buff lores, throat and breast (some with quite noticeable brown streaking), and has duller buff to olive-brown flanks and darker olive-brown upperparts. Also lacks rufous coloration to uppertail-coverts and sides of tail. Confusable with the more similarly sized Spot-throated, but has buff lores, faint whitish shaft streaks on more rufescent crown, buff-coloured throat and breast, and square-ended tail (longer than Himalayan *P. a. ignotum*). **Voice** Song a loud sharp *wi-twee* or *witweewitweewitwee*; also a loud *tchew-tchew...tchew* sometimes interspersed with jolly high-pitched or rattling notes; calls include a rattling *trrrit-trrrit-trrrit*. **HH** Habits similar to Abbott's. Dense scrub and thick undergrowth in moist forest and bamboo thickets along streams. **TN** Formerly placed in *Trichastoma*.

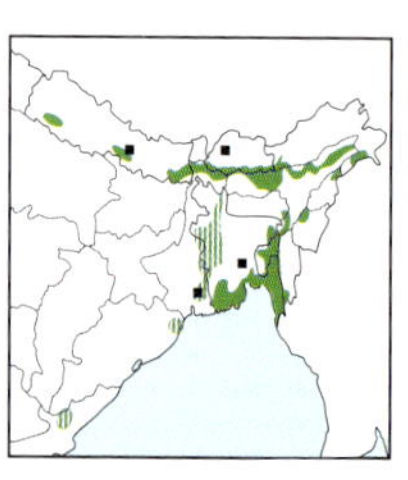

Abbott's Babbler *Malacocincla abbotti* 15–17cm

Resident. Himalayan foothills, NE Ghats, NE India and Bangladesh. **ID** From Spot-throated and Buff-breasted by larger size, with bigger head and larger bill, and rufous cast to uppertail-coverts and tail. Further from Buff-breasted by greyish (rather than buff) lores, more pronounced grey supercilium, white throat and upper breast, and proportionately shorter tail. Further from Spot-throated by unspotted throat, and rufous-buff breast-sides, flanks and undertail-coverts. **Voice** Song 3–4 whistles, rendered *three cheers for me*, with last note highest; sometimes duets with mate giving one or two *peep* notes. **HH** Singly or in pairs. Skulking and mainly terrestrial. Dense thickets in moist forest; favours stream banks.

Puff-throated Babbler
ad
mandellii
ad
ruficeps
ad
Brown-capped
Babbler
ad
Marsh Babbler
ad
ignotum
Spot-throated
Babbler
ad
ad
Buff-breasted Babbler
Abbott's Babbler

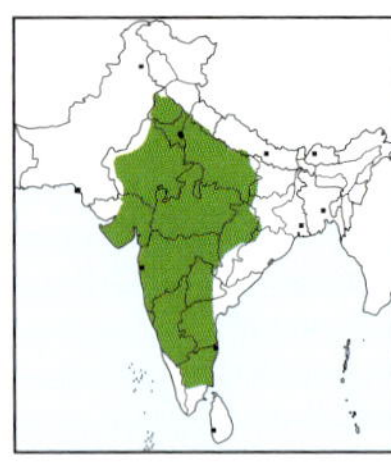

Large Grey Babbler ***Argya malcolmi*** 27–28cm

Resident. Pakistan, W Nepal and Indian peninsula. **ID** Large, pale grey babbler with darker grey mottling on upperparts and prominent white sides to long graduated tail. Additional features include greyish-pink throat and breast (lacking dark mottling), pale grey forehead (created by ashy shaft streaks), dark grey lores, pale yellow iris, dull-coloured bill, and brownish-grey legs and feet. Juvenile smaller and has paler grey upperparts which lack dark mottling. **Voice** Monotonous, plaintive, drawling *kay-kay-kay-kay* (flatter and less squeaky than Jungle) and a noisy chattering in alarm. **HH** Habits like Jungle. Open dry scrub, cultivation, gardens and around villages; usually avoids wooded areas favoured by Jungle, prefers less dry habitats than Common, though locally shares same habitats as both species. **TN** Formerly placed in *Turdoides*.

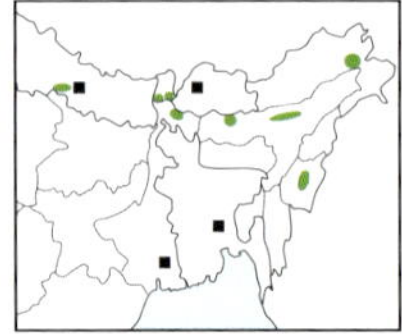

Slender-billed Babbler ***Argya longirostris*** 23cm

Resident. Lowlands of C Nepal and NE subcontinent. **ID** From other babblers by downcurved blackish bill, whitish to buffish lores and buff ear-coverts, unstreaked dark rufous-brown upperparts, whitish throat, and unstreaked deep buff underparts. **Voice** Includes shrill, rather high-pitched series of notes with short introduction; a clear, rather high-pitched *wii-wii-jiu-di* and a discordant high-pitched, repeated *tiu-tiu-tiu*. **HH** Skulks in tall, thick grass. Tall grassland, especially near water. Globally threatened. **TN** Formerly placed in *Turdoides*.

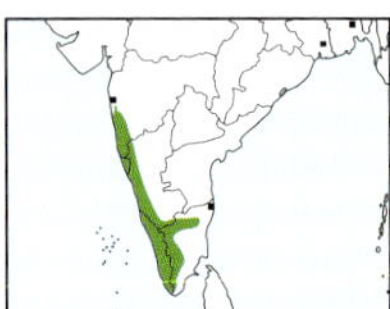

Rufous Babbler ***Argya subrufa*** 24–25cm

Resident. SW Indian hills. **ID** Has grey forehead and forecrown, blackish lores, striking white iris, black upper mandible contrasting with yellow lower mandible, chestnut-brown upperparts, and unstreaked rufous underparts. Juvenile has dark grey iris. **Voice** High-pitched, shrill, sometimes frenzied squabbling or scolding squeaks. **HH** In small parties. Very secretive; usually creeps about out of sight in undergrowth. Thick cover and edges of clearings in moist forests; favours habitats intermixed with tall grass and bamboo. **TN** Formerly placed in *Turdoides*.

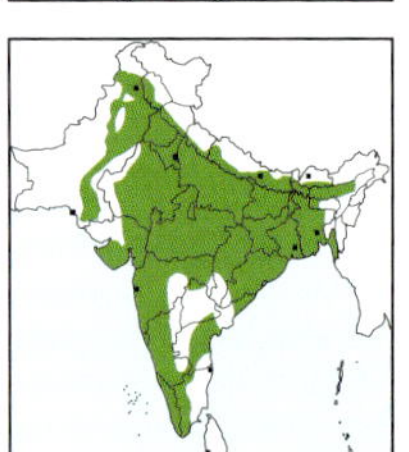

Jungle Babbler ***Argya striata*** 25cm

Widespread resident. **ID** From Large Grey by smaller and stockier appearance, shorter, broader-looking tail lacking prominent white sides, pale lores, mottling on throat and breast, yellowish bill (can be horn-brown in winter), and orange legs and feet. From Yellow-billed Babbler of peninsula by uniform crown and less heavily mottled throat and breast. Races in subcontinent vary in colour and prominence of streaking on underparts. *A. s. sindiana* in north-west is paler and greyer, with *A. s. malabarica* in SW India brownest. *A. s. somervillei* (NW Ghats) distinctive, with prominent diffuse brown streaking on throat and breast, orange-buff lower underparts, orange-brown tail, dark brown primaries contrasting with paler grey-brown wing-coverts, and more uniform mantle. **Voice** Harsh *ke-ke-ke* given frequently. often becoming a chorus of excited, discordant squeaking and chattering. **HH** Gregarious, noisy and excitable. Feeds chiefly on ground, hopping about and busily turning over leaves. Deciduous forest, cultivation and gardens; also, plantations along roads and canals. **TN** Formerly placed *Turdoides*.

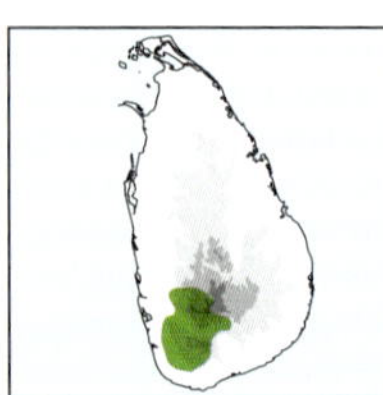

Orange-billed Babbler ***Argya rufescens*** 25cm

Resident. Sri Lanka. **ID** Distinctive babbler with orange bill and legs, chestnut-brown upperparts, cinnamon-rufous face and underparts (becoming browner on belly and flanks), and greyish crown and nape. Leg and bill colour are useful from Ashy-headed Laughingthrush (which see). Juvenile has greyish chin and browner underparts. **Voice** Flock gives continual flow of loud squeaking and chirping sounds, sometimes loud laughing calls. **HH** In troops of 10–15 or more birds. Forage c.2m above ground to around lower canopy level. Often in mixed-species feeding flocks. Undisturbed wet-zone forest. **TN** Formerly placed in *Turdoides*.

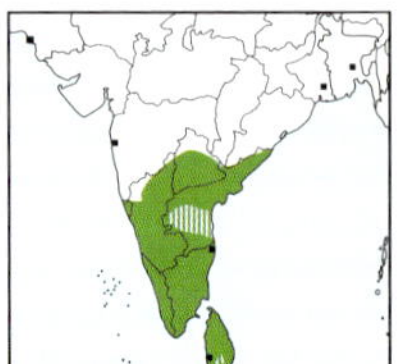

Yellow-billed Babbler ***Argya affinis*** 21–23.5cm

Resident. Peninsular India and Sri Lanka. **ID** From Jungle by creamy-white lores, forehead and crown, dark mottling on throat and breast (diffusely streaked on most similar Jungle races), and pale grey panel on wings. In flight pale buff rump and base to tail contrasts with darker rest of tail. Paleness of head and extent of mottling on throat and breast vary. Juvenile has darker brownish-buff crown and lacks darker mottling; best told from Jungle by combination of paler crown and nape showing slight contrast with mantle, buff wing-panel, and paler rump and base to tail. *A. a. taprobanus* (Sri Lanka) has more uniform grey-brown upperparts and underparts, lacking whitish crown and nape and dark mottling on throat and breast. Similar to allopatric Jungle but with more striking pale wing panel. **Voice** Very high-pitched, intense, piercing piping calls. **HH** Habits similar to Jungle and often with that species. In noisy excitable parties. Low scrub in drier, more open areas than Jungle. **TN** Formerly placed in *Turdoides*.

ad
Large Grey
Babbler
ad
Slender-billed
Babbler
ad
Rufous
Babbler
ad
striata
ad
orientalis
Jungle Babbler
ad
somervillei
ad
Orange-billed
Babbler
ad
affinis
Yellow-billed Babbler
ad
taprobanus

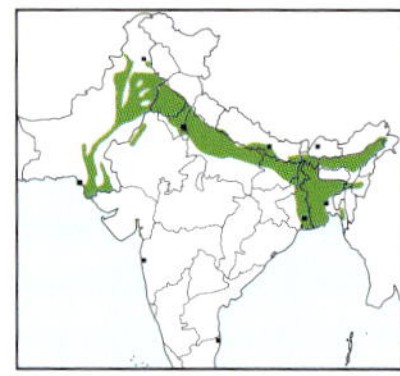

Striated Babbler *Argya earlei* — 25cm

Resident. Plains of N subcontinent. **ID** From Common by diffuse white moustachial, streaked or mottled appearance to fulvous throat and breast (unstreaked and white on Common). Also slightly larger size and proportionately shorter tail, deeper buff breast and belly, blue-grey legs and feet (varying to olive-brown), and greyer face with golden-yellow iris. **Voice** Song a loud repeated series of *tiew-tiew-tiew-tiew* calls, interspersed with *quip-quip-quip* calls from other group members. **HH** Habits like Common. Reedbeds and tall grass along rivers, irrigation canals and marshes; usually wet habitats where it replaces Common. **TN** Formerly placed in *Turdoides*.

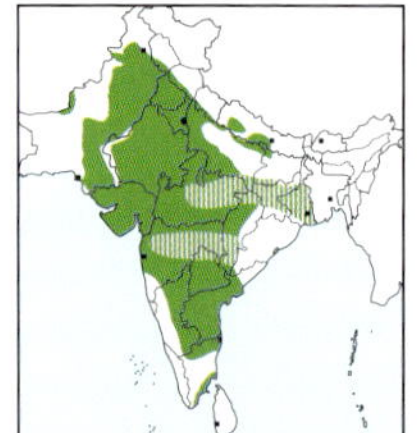

Common Babbler *Argya caudata* — 20–26cm

Widespread resident; unrecorded in most of NE and E India, W Pakistan and Sri Lanka. **ID** From Striated by unstreaked whitish throat and unstreaked centre to breast (streaking on underparts restricted to breast-sides). Also slightly smaller, colder whitish or greyish-buff underparts, generally darker bill, yellowish legs and feet, and darker, more orange-brown iris. In Balochistan, *A. c. huttoni* ('Afghan Babbler') larger with larger bill than widespread nominate, plus paler and greyer upperparts and fine dark streaks on breast and flanks. **Voice** A series of pleasant, rapid fluty whistles, and a louder, more drawn-out *pieuu-u-u pie-u-u pi-e-u-u*; also, a higher-pitched *qwee qwe-e-e qwe-e-e* alarm. *A. c. huttoni* (Quetta region, Pakistan) has distinctive two-noted whistle, *qwee-yur-qwee-yur*. **HH** In small flocks, each flock maintaining its own territory all year. Thorn scrub and open country with scattered low bushes and grass clumps. **TN** *A. c. huttoni* sometimes treated as separate species 'Afghan Babbler'. Formerly placed in *Turdoides*.

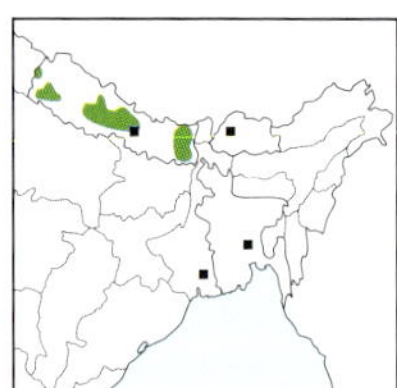

Spiny Babbler *Turdoides nipalensis* — 25cm

Resident. Nepal Himalayas. **ID** Has downcurved blackish bill (with grey base to lower mandible), white on face, dark brown upperparts without prominent streaking, white to pale blue iris, and strong, fine black streaking on throat and breast. Variable, some with largely white face and underparts, and restricted streaking, others with just white lores and malar, buffer underparts and more heavily streaked. **Voice** Song complex, varied, rich, and full of mimicry, comprising a series of alternating quickly repeated notes. Call a clear *el-el-el-el-el*, alarm a low churr. **HH** Very skulking except early in breeding season when males often sing in open. Dense scrub on hillsides with scattered trees; favours thicker areas away from cultivation.

Ashy-headed Laughingthrush *Argya cinereifrons* — 24–25cm

Resident. Sri Lanka. **ID** Plain-coloured with greyish head, rufous-brown upperparts and tail, tawny underparts with paler throat, and striking whitish eye. From Orange-billed Babbler (can occur together) by dark bill and legs and greyish head. Juvenile has brighter rufous underparts and duller eye. **Voice** Hoarse, comical, short squeaks, guffaws, short titters, chuckles, whinnies, sharp metallic notes, and harsh nasal or wheezy mews. **HH** Shy, though noisy. Often joins mixed feeding flocks with other species, generally keeps close to ground. Dense wet forest and bamboo thickets. Globally threatened. **TN** Formerly placed in *Garrulax*.

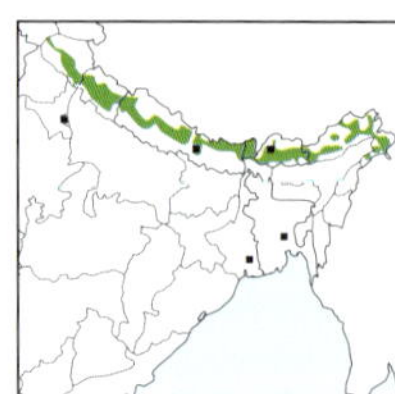

Striated Laughingthrush *Grammatoptila striata* — 29.5–34cm

Resident. Himalayas and Nagaland. **ID** Large with stout black bill and floppy crest, giving rise to dome-headed appearance. Chestnut crown, russet upperparts and brownish underparts are profusely covered with white to buffish-white streaking. Wings more rufous-brown, with greyish-white panel. Lack of dark barring on wings and tail helps to distinguish from barwings. *G. s. cranbrooki* (north-east) has broad black stripe behind eye, not shown by other subspecies in subcontinent, and white streaking on crown is indistinct or absent and white streaking on mantle and underparts is much finer. **Voice** A whistled *hoo-wee...chew-chew*, gurgling *which-we-we-heet-chuuu* and soft *poor-poor*. **HH** Habits similar to other laughingthrushes but more arboreal, forages at all forest levels. Dense broadleaved forest. **TN** Formerly placed in *Garrulax*.

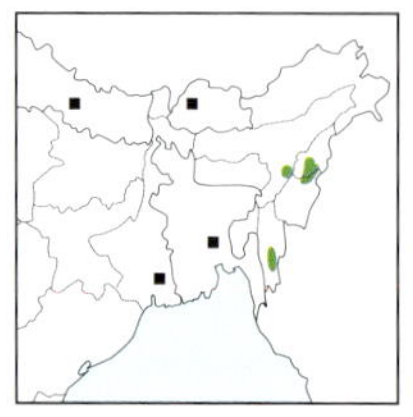

Brown-capped Laughingthrush *Trochalopteron austeni* — 24cm

Resident. NE Indian hills. **ID** A rufous-brown laughingthrush, with a plain brownish face and throat, rufous-brown crown and nape with irregular buff shaft streaking, barred/scaled rufous-brown and white underparts, rufous olive-brown mantle (lacking black spots), and rufous-brown wings with white tips to greater coverts, tertials and secondaries. In flight, tail shows narrow white tips to blackish outer feathers, with rufous-brown central feathers. **Voice** Song of loud, plaintive, jolly phrases *whit-wee-wi-weeoo*, *whit-wi-chooee* etc.; subdued harsh *grrrret-grrrret-grrrret...* in alarm. **HH** Undergrowth in oak and rhododendron forest; bushes and bamboo thickets at forest edges and clearings; also, in ravines. **TN** Formerly placed in *Garrulax*.

ad
Striated Babbler
ad
Common Babbler
ad
huttoni
ad
ad
Spiny Babbler
ad
Ashy-headed Laughingthrush
ad
vibex
ad
cranbrooki
Striated Laughingthrush
ad
Brown-capped Laughingthrush

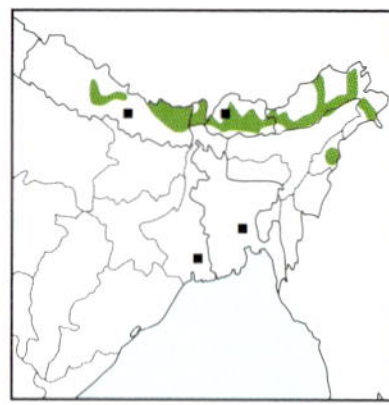

Scaly Laughingthrush *Trochalopteron subunicolor* 23–25.5cm
Himalayas, E Arunachal and Nagaland. **ID** A black-scaled olive-brown and rather plain laughing-thrush with greyer head. From Blue-winged by more uniform head (lacking black supercilium), yellowish-olive wing patch, less extensive and paler blue-grey panel on primaries, olive belly and vent, olive uppertail-coverts and central tail feathers which are concolorous with rest of upperparts, and white tips to outer tail feathers. Eye can be strikingly whitish or yellowish, or dark. **Voice** Usual song is two- or three-part wolf-whistle (descends on last note); buzzy and more slurred than several similar laughingthrush songs. **HH** Thick undergrowth in moist broadleaved and broadleaved-coniferous forest and rhododendron shrubberies. **TN** Formerly placed in *Garrulax*.

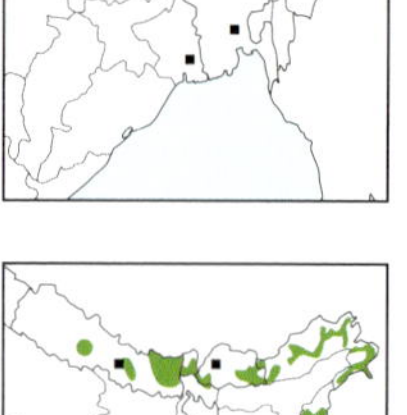

Blue-winged Laughingthrush *Trochalopteron squamatum* 22–25cm
Resident. Himalayas and NE India. **ID** A black-scaled olive-brown and grey laughingthrush bearing a superficial resemblance to Scaly Laughingthrush. From Scaly by black supercilium, silvery-blue outer webs to primaries forming prominent wing panel (brighter and more extensive than on Scaly), largely rufous wings with darker outer edge, chestnut-brown flanks and vent, rufous uppertail-coverts, and rufous-tipped dark tail. Striking white eye (brown in juvenile). Male has grey cast to crown, and blacker tail. Female has browner crown and dark olive tail. **Voice** Includes striking, rich wolf-whistle, *whééóóówhééet* upslurred and then downslurred at beginning, rest strongly upslurred. **HH** Dense undergrowth in moist broadleaved evergreen forest and bamboo thickets, especially near water. **TN** Formerly placed in *Garrulax*.

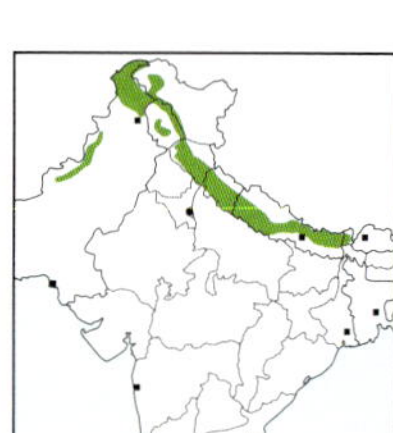

Streaked Laughingthrush *Trochalopteron lineatum* 18–20cm
Resident. Pakistan hills and Himalayas east to Sikkim. **ID** Small, finely streaked laughingthrush. Fine dark streaking on crown and nape, fine white streaking on mantle and underparts, and grey tips to tail with diffuse black subterminal band on outer feathers. Four subspecies recognised: nominate (Kashmir to E Uttarakhand) has greyish cast to crown and nape, rufous ear-coverts, grey underparts with white shaft streaking bordered by rufous-brown, largely rufous-brown wings, and rufous sides to tail. Races to the west paler and greyer, with duller ear-coverts. *T. l. setafer* (Nepal) darker and more rufous overall, with rufous ear-coverts thus less prominent. **Voice** Song a short rapid trill followed by a loud ringing whistle, *trit-ititit chu-wheeeah*, higher in pitch than Variegated. **HH** Bushes at cultivation edges and along roadsides, scrub-covered hillsides and second growth. **TN** Formerly placed in *Garrulax*.

Bhutan Laughingthrush *Trochalopteron imbricatum* 19–20cm
Resident. Bhutan to W Arunachal Pradesh. **ID** Similar to Streaked but more uniformly brown, with more uniform brown crown and nape (only indistinct darker shaft streaking), grey-brown (rather than rufous) ear-coverts with white streaking, brown underparts finely streaked white, more olive-brown wings, and much narrower white tail tips. **Voice** Similar to Streaked but shorter. **HH** Similar to Streaked: scrub in open forest, forest edges and second growth. **TN** Formerly placed in *Garrulax*.

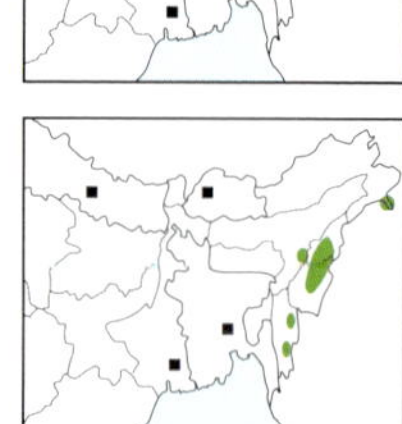

Striped Laughingthrush *Trochalopteron virgatum* 23cm
Resident. NE Indian hills. **ID** Medium-sized laughingthrush with very prominent white streaking on upperparts and underparts. Broad whitish to buffish supercilium and moustachial patch, dark chestnut throat merging into rufous-buff breast and belly, largely chestnut wings with white-tipped greater coverts, and uniform brown tail. **Voice** Two territorial calls given antiphonally by pair-members: (1) a plaintive, hurried *chwi-pieu*, (2) a loud staccato, rattling trill, usually with shorter introductory note, *cho-prrrrrrt*. Calls include harsh *chit* and *chrrrrrr*. **HH** Dense undergrowth in moist, broadleaved evergreen forest and thick second growth. **TN** Formerly placed in *Garrulax*.

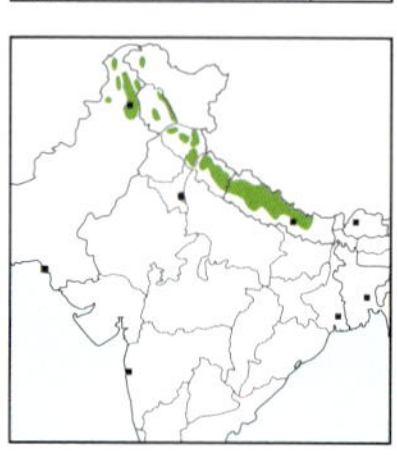

Variegated Laughingthrush *Trochalopteron variegatum* 24–26cm
Resident. W and C Himalayas. **ID** A complex-patterned, mainly grey-and-olive laughingthrush without spotting or scaling. Has rufous-buff forehead and broad whitish or buffish malar 'wedge', black mask and centre of throat, rufous greater coverts (sometimes obscured), black inner webs to tertials, black primary coverts and patch on secondaries, rufous vent, and black base, grey subterminal band and narrow white tip to tail. *T. v. simile* (W Himalayas) has grey wing-panel and outer-tail feathers. Nominate (C and E Himalayas) has olive-tinged upperparts, golden-olive wing-panel and outer tail feathers, and variable golden-olive wash to grey subterminal tail-band. **Voice** Loud, penetrating whistle *pit-we-weer* that may be preceded by a softer *whi-chu-whi-wheear*, lower-pitched than Streaked; alarms calls include rapid squeaking. **HH** Thick undergrowth in open coniferous, broadleaved and broadleaf-coniferous forests, bushes at forest edges, and rhododendron shrubbery and bushes around cultivation. **TN** Formerly placed in *Garrulax*.

ad
Scaly
Laughingthrush
ad
Blue-winged
Laughingthrush
ad
lineatus
Streaked
Laughingthrush
ad
Bhutan
Laughingthrush
ad
Striped
Laughingthrush
ad
variegatus
ad
similis
Variegated
Laughingthrush

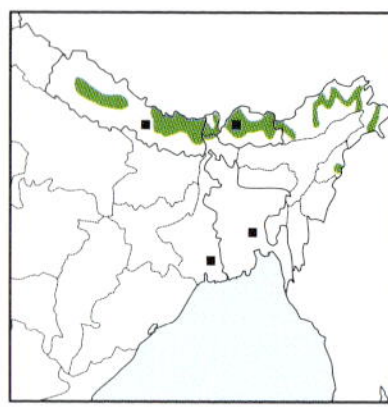

Black-faced Laughingthrush *Trochalopteron affine* 24–26cm

Resident. Himalayas, SE Arunachal and Nagaland. **ID** A distinctive, mainly rufous-brown laughingthrush with black supercilium and ear-coverts, and white malar stripe and patches on sides of neck. Has black chin and centre of throat, greyish-white scaling on breast, variable grey mottling on upperparts, olive-yellow panel on blue-grey wings, black primary coverts patch, and olive-yellow tail with broad grey tip. *T. a. bethelae* (E Himalayas) has deeper rufous-brown underparts with indistinct greyish fringes to breast compared to the nominate (W and C Nepal). **Voice** Song a loud *tew-wee-to-whee-to-whee-you-whee*; repeated, rapid *dze* in alarm. **HH** Broadleaved, coniferous and broadleaf-coniferous forests, and shrubberies above the treeline. **TN** Formerly placed in *Garrulax*.

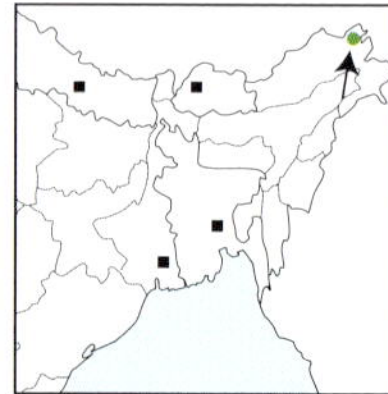

Elliot's Laughingthrush *Trochalopteron ellioti* 23–25cm

Arunachal Pradesh; probably a rare, local resident. **ID** Mainly grey-brown laughingthrush, lacking prominent markings on head and body. Faint whitish fringes to ear-coverts, throat and breast (difficult to see in field), yellowish-olive outer webs to secondaries and inner primaries forming prominent patch on otherwise mainly grey wing, cinnamon rear flanks and undertail-coverts, and yellowish-olive sides to white-tipped grey tail. **Voice** Haunting, interrogative, whistled song, *tu weir...tee-u* repeated, often for long periods. **HH** Singly, in pairs or small parties; sometimes in larger groups of up to 20 birds in winter. Forages on, or close to, ground. Mixed temperate forest and adjacent scrub. **TN** Formerly placed in *Garrulax*.

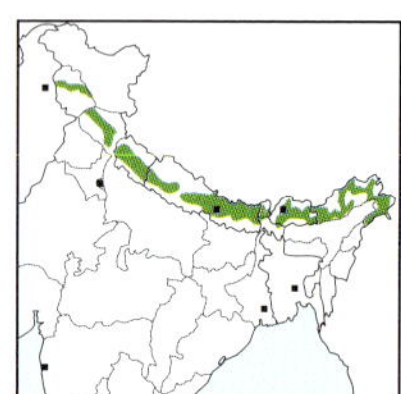

Chestnut-crowned Laughingthrush *Trochalopteron erythrocephalum* 24–26cm

Resident. Himalayas. **ID** Common features across range are chestnut on head, dark throat, dark spotting/scaling on mantle and breast, mainly olive-yellow wings with maroon greater coverts (often obscured), and olive-yellow sides to tail. There is considerable subspecies variation in region. For example, nominate (W Himalayas) has chestnut crown and nape, chestnut ear-coverts with white fringes and variable black spotting, greyish-olive mantle and buffish-olive breast and belly. *T. e. nigrimentum* (E Himalayas) has chestnut forehead and nape but black-streaked grey crown, blackish ear-coverts with white fringes, and chestnut mantle, foreneck and breast. **Voice** Song of nominate: quick, clear, emphatic, 1–2 strongly upslurred then downslurred notes; *nigrimentum:* loud, high, rising *wi-eeoo*. **HH** Dense undergrowth in broadleaved forest; thick bushes at cultivation edges. **TN** Formerly placed in *Garrulax*.

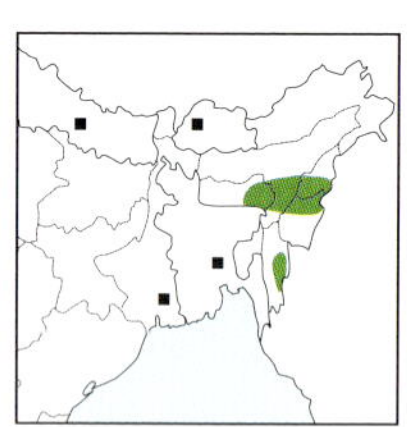

Assam Laughingthrush *Trochalopteron chrysopterum* 23–25cm

Resident. NE Indian hills. **ID** Compared to Chestnut-crowned, nominate (Meghalaya) has brighter crown, grey supercilium and ear-covert streaking, chestnut throat merging into rufous breast, and diffuse brown spotting on mantle and breast. *T. c. godwini* (S Assam and Manipur) darker with bold markings on mantle and breast. *T. c. erythrolaemum* (E Manipur and Mizoram) has chestnut crown and ear-coverts and greyer mantle. **Voice** Songs differ from Chestnut-crowned in their lower pitch, mellower quality, and greater complexity and length. **HH** Understorey and bamboo in broadleaved evergreen, pine and mixed forests; stunted oaks and dwarf rhododendron scrub. **TN** Formerly placed in *Garrulax*.

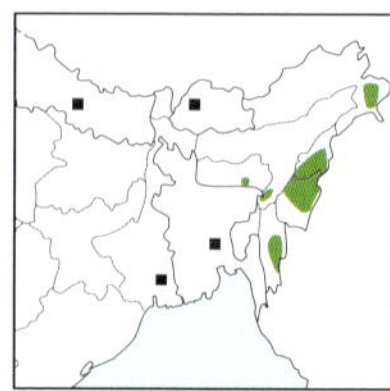

Spot-breasted Laughingthrush *Garrulax merulinus* 25–26cm

Resident. NE Indian hills. **ID** Dark-coloured, long-billed and short-tailed laughingthrush. From other laughingthrushes by bold brown spotting on buff or rufous-buff throat and breast, with narrow whitish or buff supercilium behind eye, uniform rufescent olive-brown upperparts, wings and tail, and olive-brown flanks. **Voice** Song loud, rich and melodious, a prolonged, rambling series of rich musical phrases, with much mimicry. **HH** Habits like other laughingthrushes. Very secretive, in parties of 10–20 birds, feeds on ground. Dense undergrowth in heavy moist forest, bamboo thickets, overgrown forest clearings and dense second growth.

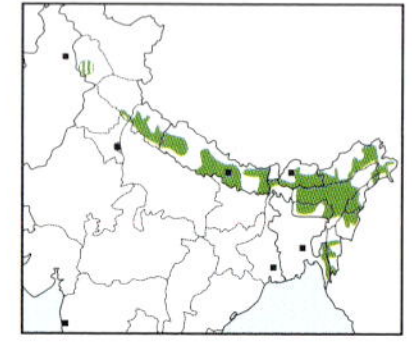

White-crested Laughingthrush *Garrulax leucolophus* 26–31cm

Resident. Himalayas, NE India and Bangladesh. **ID** Large, with white crest and black mask. Also, contrasting white throat and upper breast, grey nape, chestnut mantle and band on lower breast, and dark olive-brown wings and tail. **Voice** Very noisy, flocks uttering sudden bursts of cackling laughter-like sounds, *pick-wo, pick-wo*, etc. reaching a crescendo. **HH** Similar to other laughingthrushes. Quite wary. Forages chiefly on the ground. Broadleaved forest with dense undergrowth, second growth and bamboo thickets.

ad
affinis
Black-faced Laughingthrush
ad
Elliot's Laughingthrush
ad
nigrimentum
Chestnut-crowned Laughingthrush
ad
erythrocephalum
ad
chrysopterum
Assam Laughingthrush
ad
Spot-breasted Laughingthrush
ad
White-crested Laughingthrush

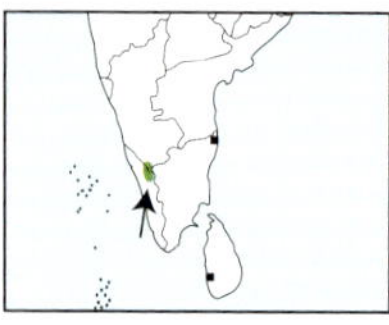

Banasura Laughingthrush ***Montecincla jerdoni*** 20.5–23cm

Resident. Western Ghats from Brahmagiri Hills in SE Karnataka and adjacent Ambalappara in Kerala. Disjunct populations on Banasura Peak, Wayanad and south of Thamarassery Ghat Pass in Chembra, Vellarimala, and Vavulmala in SW Wayanad and NW Malappuram. **ID** From Nilgiri by grey ear-coverts, and lower throat and (dark-streaked) breast. Black chin separates from Palani. **Voice** Song a variable series of 3–6 nasal whistles, usually with a second bird in duet, giving a hoarse, Rufous Treepie-like laughing. **HH** Dense forest undergrowth, thickets along stream, favours wild raspberry; tea and cardamom plantations. Globally threatened. **TN** Formerly treated as conspecific with Nilgiri Laughingthrush as Black-chinned Laughingthrush *Garrulax cachinnans*.

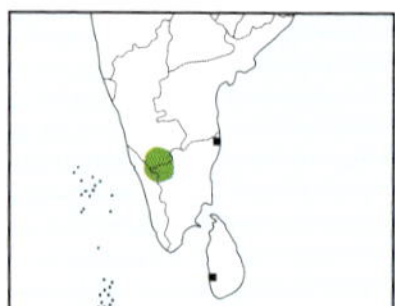

Nilgiri Laughingthrush ***Montecincla cachinnans*** 22.5–23.5cm

Resident. Mainly Nilgiri Hills in NW Tamil Nadu and western cliff faces in adjacent Kerala in S Western Ghats. Recently found in Silent Valley National Park and Bhavani Range in Palakkad district, Kerala, also south of Attappady Plateau in montane regions of Muthikulam-Elival Hills. **ID** Rufous underparts, white supercilium contrasting with dark grey-brown crown, and black eye-stripe and chin. From Banasura by rufous ear-coverts, lower throat and breast. **Voice** Rich vocabulary of songs and calls: characteristic song a loud, nasal *pee-ko-ko* or *pe-keko-keko-k*, often followed by a hoarse Rufous Treepie-like laughing. **HH** Dense undergrowth in forest, also gardens, scrub and hill guava trees. Globally threatened. **TN** Formerly treated as conspecific with Banasura Laughingthrush as Black-chinned Laughingthrush *Garrulax cachinnans*.

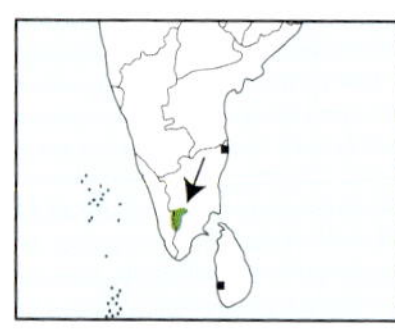

Palani Laughingthrush ***Montecincla fairbanki*** 20.5cm

Resident. Western Ghats in C and S Kerala and neighbouring Tamil Nadu. **ID** From Ashambu Laughingthrush by more prominent white supercilium and black stripe behind eye, darker slate-grey crown, darker and more uniform grey throat and breast (with diffuse darker streaking), and rufous underparts lacking white belly. Lacks black chin of Banasura. **Voice** Song of short, mellow, clear notes, starting with 1–2 steeply ascending, hesitant querulous notes, joined in duet by slightly descending series of more abrupt notes, *kweer-kweer*. **HH** Forest edges, thickets along streams and secondary forest. **TN** Formerly treated as conspecific with Ashambu Laughingthrush as Kerala Laughingthrush *Garrulax fairbanki*.

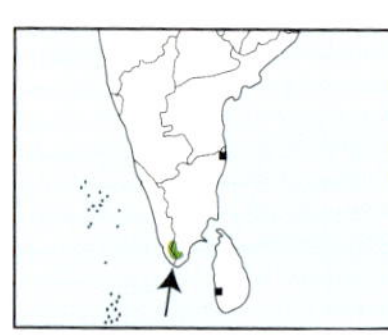

Ashambu Laughingthrush ***Montecincla meridionalis*** 20.5cm

Resident. Extreme S Kerala and extreme S Tamil Nadu, south of 9°N, extreme S India. **ID** From Palani Laughingthrush by shorter white supercilium (barely extends behind eye), brownish-grey centre to crown with black sides, grey-streaked whitish breast and belly with rufous restricted to flanks. Lacks black chin and rufous belly of Banasura. **Voice** Not documented; probably similar to Palani. **HH** Forest edges, secondary forest, scrub, also, plantations with thicket-lined streams. Globally threatened. **TN** Formerly treated as conspecific with Palani Laughingthrush as Kerala Laughingthrush *Garrulax fairbanki*.

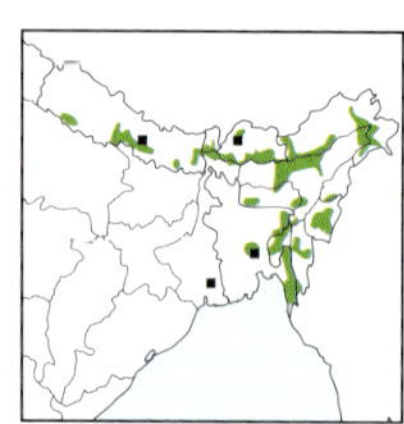

Lesser Necklaced Laughingthrush ***Garrulax monileger*** 24–31.5cm

Resident. Himalayas, NE India and Bangladesh. **ID** Smaller than Greater Necklaced with finer, dark bill, yellow eye with dark eye-ring, dark lores, and brownish (rather than slate-grey) legs and feet. Lower black border of ear coverts does not extend to bill, and white throat is bordered with rufous-orange adjacent to necklace. Has narrower necklace thinner and often almost obscured by rufous at centre (although can be uniformly broad), and white of breast-sides extends as crescent below black necklace. Also has olive-brown (not dark grey) primary coverts concolorous with rest of coverts. Juvenile similar, but with dusky necklace. **Voice** Tuneful sequences of very short, mellow whistles, *tu'tu'tu'tu-tuwa...*, and mellow, sweet, gently downslurred, whistled *tieew, ti-tiew*. **HH** Dense moist broadleaved forest with thick undergrowth; second growth.

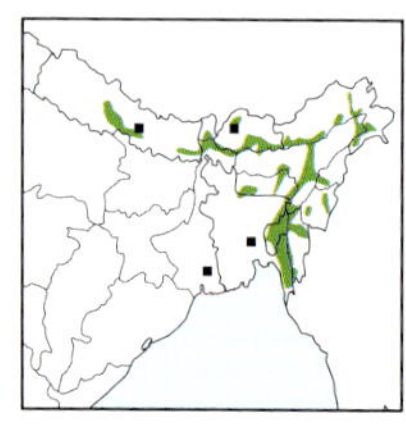

Greater Necklaced Laughingthrush ***Pterorhinus pectoralis*** 26.5–34.5cm

Resident. Himalayas, NE India and Bangladesh. **ID** Larger than Lesser Necklaced, with stouter (paler-based) bill, dark eye and yellow eye-ring, complete black moustachial stripe (bordering either black or white, or streaked black-and-white ear-coverts), uniform buff or white throat without two-toned appearance, blackish primary coverts which contrast with mantle and wings, broader necklace clearly defined in centre, and slate-grey (rather than brownish) legs and feet. As Lesser Necklaced, shows broad white tip to blackish outer tail in flight. **Voice** Songs include repeated, clear, ringing, slightly descending *kléér-éér-éér-éér-eer ....* or *kléér-éér*, and sequence of alternating upslurred mellow whistles, *tu-twéétu-twéétu-twéé....* **HH** Habitat like Lesser Necklaced, often with that species. **TN** Formerly placed in *Garrulax*.

ad
Banasura
Laughingthrush
ad
Nilgiri
Laughingthrush
ad
Palani
Laughingthrush
ad
Ashambu
Laughingthrush
ad
Lesser Necklaced
Laughingthrush
ad
Greater Necklaced
Laughingthrush

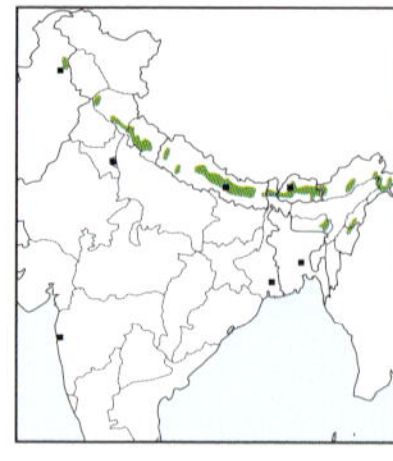

Rufous-chinned Laughingthrush *Ianthocincla rufogularis* 23–25.5cm

Resident. Himalayas and NE India. **ID** Irregular black spots and bars on upperparts and underparts. Rufous chin and upper throat, blackish cap, black-mottled moustachial stripe extending to patch on sides of neck, whitish to rufous lores, banding on wings, and black subterminal band and rufous tip to tail. In W and C Himalayas *I. r. occidentalis* has olive-brown upperparts and tail, and distinct rufous ear-coverts. In E Himalayas nominate has rufous-brown upperparts and tail, and grey face (without rufous patch on ear-coverts); rufous chin can be almost absent. *I. r. rufitinctus* (Meghalaya) has entire throat rufous, buff rather than grey bands on wing, and buff (rather than greyish-olive) wash to breast and belly. **Voice** Squeals, chuckles and chatters; pleasant whistling song *swee-tu...tu-tu-wee-u*. **HH** Similar to other laughingthrushes but less gregarious and noisy. Secretive. Dense undergrowth in subtropical broadleaved forest and bushes at forest edges. **TN** Formerly placed in *Garrulax*.

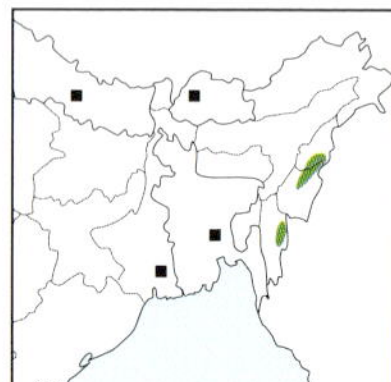

Moustached Laughingthrush *Ianthocincla cineracea* 21–24cm

Resident. NE Indian hills. **ID** Small, mainly greyish olive-brown laughingthrush, distinguished by greyish supercilium and ear-coverts, strikingly pale bill and eye, black eye-stripe, crown and broad moustachial stripe, the latter breaking up into black streaking on sides of throat, black subterminal bands and white tips to tertials and secondaries, grey panel on wing with black primary coverts patch, and white-tipped black subterminal tail-band. **Voice** Calls include rather high-pitched, quickly repeated short churrs, sometimes interspersed with hard chuckling staccato notes. **HH** Habits like other laughingthrushes. Dense undergrowth and bushes in moist forest and second growth. **TN** Formerly placed in *Garrulax*.

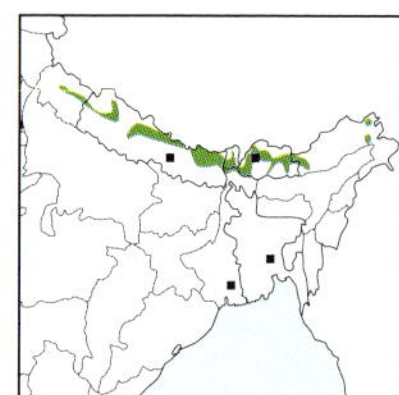

Spotted Laughingthrush *Ianthocincla ocellata* 30–33cm

Resident. Himalayas. **ID** Large, chestnut laughingthrush, with profuse black-based white spotting on chestnut upperparts. Also, blackish cap, rufous supercilium, lores and chin, deep chestnut ear-coverts, blackish throat becoming black barring on breast, buff lower breast and belly, chestnut-and-black wings with grey panel and white tips to primaries, and white tips to chestnut, grey and black tail. **Voice** Song repeated rich mellow fluty phrases, e.g. *wu-it, wu-u, wu-u*, often joined by more jarring, rising *fu'u'uwheen*. Calls include repeated screeching, strident, guttural *schuwee*. **HH** Similar to other laughingthrushes. Often with Black-faced. Inquisitive. Undergrowth and bamboo in broadleaved and coniferous forest and rhododendron shrubbery. **TN** Formerly placed in *Garrulax*.

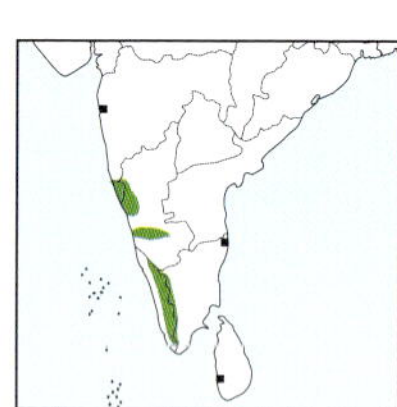

Wayanad Laughingthrush *Pterorhinus delesserti* 23–26cm

Resident. Western Ghats. **ID** Distinctive with yellowish or pink lower mandible (bill can look entirely pale), black mask with slightly paler slate-grey crown and nape, chestnut-brown back and wing-coverts, white throat and greyish breast and belly, rufous vent, and blackish-brown tail. Has reddish eye, bare dull blue or grey patch behind eye, and greyish to pink legs and feet. **Voice** Frenzied, discordant series of screeches, squeals and cracked rattles; penetrating nasal whistling song of 2–4 descending notes, *tree-tree-true*. **HH** Moist broadleaved evergreen forest and cardamom sholas. **TN** Formerly placed in *Garrulax*.

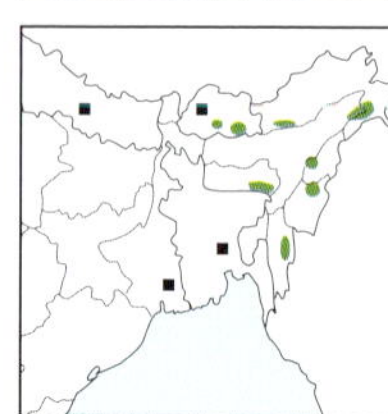

Rufous-vented Laughingthrush *Pterorhinus gularis* 23–25.5cm

Resident. E Himalayan foothills, hills of NE India and Bangladesh. **ID** From smaller Yellow-throated Laughingthrush by longer bill, rufous flanks and vent, rufous-brown upperparts (especially rump and uppertail-coverts), rufous outer tail feathers (lacking white at tip) contrasting with brown central feathers (darker blackish-brown towards the tip), grey sides to breast, darker grey crown and nape, yellow chin (with a tiny amount of black at base of bill), and orange legs and feet. Juvenile similar to adult, but has blackish crown and rufous markings on grey breast. **Voice** Includes clear, very sweet, chiming, slightly upslurred then strongly downslurred whistles; harsh rattling churrs interspersed with nasal, discordant, high-pitched whistled phrases. **HH** Dense evergreen undergrowth, dense scrub and second growth. **TN** Formerly placed in *Garrulax*.

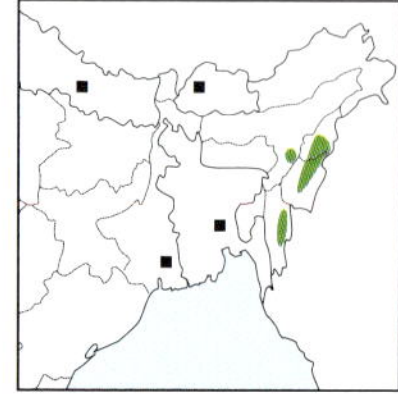

Yellow-throated Laughingthrush *Pterorhinus galbanus* 23–24.5cm

Resident. Hills of NE India. Vagrant: Bangladesh. **ID** From larger Rufous-vented by small and stout bill, greyish-olive flanks and yellowish (rather than rufous) lower belly and vent, cinnamon-brown (rather than rufous-brown) upperparts, paler crown and nape, greyish tail becoming blacker towards the tip (with broad white tips), noticeable black chin, greyish wing-panel, and greyish legs and feet. Undertail-coverts and most of undertail white (with dark base to tail). Has red eye and bare bright blue patch behind eye. **Voice** Song loud and melodious, comprising five equally spaced whistles. **HH** Tall grass with trees and bushes and edges of dense evergreen broadleaved forest. **TN** Formerly placed in *Garrulax*.

ad
occidentalis
Rufous-chinned
Laughingthrush
ad
rufogularis
ad
Moustached
Laughingthrush
Spotted
Laughingthrush
ad
ad
Wynaad
Laughingthrush
ad
Rufous-vented
Laughingthrush
ad
Yellow-throated
Laughingthrush

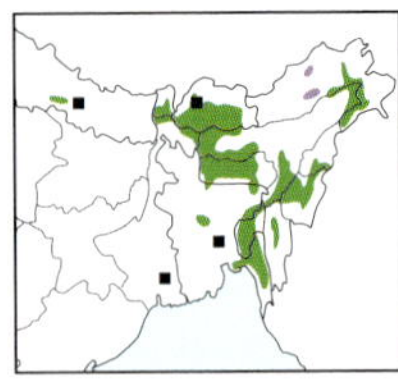

Rufous-necked Laughingthrush *Pterorhinus ruficollis* 27cm

Resident. Himalayas, NE India and Bangladesh. **ID** Small, mainly olive-brown laughingthrush, with prominent rufous patch on sides of neck, and black face, throat and centre of breast. Also has grey crown and nape, and rufous vent and centre of lower belly. Tail uniform brownish-black. Juvenile duller, with browner crown. **Voice** Vocalisations include shrill whistles that run up the scale then end with several downslurred double notes, scolding whistles, descending trills, chittering babbles and hoarse squawks. **HH** Forest edges, second growth, bamboo thickets and bushes in cultivation. **TN** Formerly placed in *Garrulax*.

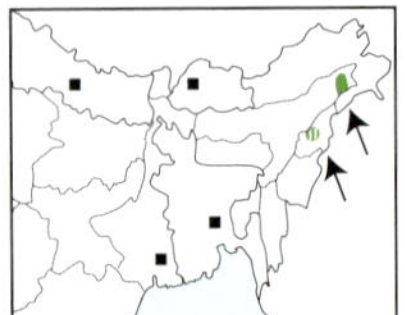

Chestnut-backed Laughingthrush *Pterorhinus nuchalis* 23–26cm

Resident. E Assam, SE Arunachal and Nagaland. **ID** Small laughingthrush with white ear-coverts and sides of throat, white spot on forecrown, black forehead, lores, chin and centre of throat, blue-grey crown, bright rufous mantle, and grey underparts. Diffuse blackish terminal band to tail. **Voice** Includes variety of mellow whistles, alternating between higher and lower short, slurred notes; may include mimicry. **HH** Chiefly dense bushes on stony, scrub-covered ravines and hills. **TN** Formerly placed in *Garrulax*.

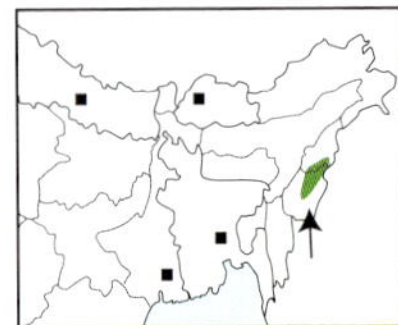

White-browed Laughingthrush *Pterorhinus sannio* 22–24cm

Resident. Nagaland and Manipur. **ID** Small, mainly brown laughingthrush with broad buffish-white supercilium, lores and 'feathery' patch on cheeks, chestnut-brown crown (often raised as crest) and throat, cinnamon-brown ear-coverts and sides of neck, dirty buff underparts, uniform olive-brown upperparts and tail, and rufous undertail-coverts. **Voice** Harsh, shrill, explosive *tcheu* or *tchow*; harsh *tcheurrrr* or *chrrrrik* in alarm. **HH** Undergrowth in dense forest, second growth, scrub-covered hillsides, bamboo thickets. **TN** Formerly placed in *Garrulax*.

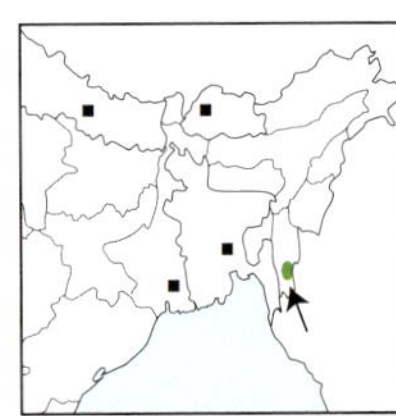

Mount Victoria Babax *Pterorhinus woodi* 25–26cm

Resident. Mizoram. **ID** Dark-streaked rufous-brown crown, pale ear-coverts with dark streaking, striking yellow eye, dark chestnut submoustachial stripe, bold chestnut-brown streaking on greyish upperparts, and broad chestnut streaking on breast-sides and flanks, with buffish-white underparts. Bill downcurved. Juvenile similar to adult, but less heavily streaked, with shorter tail and straighter bill. **Voice** Songs include jolly *wee-wer-choh, whí* or *phi-phu-chu, whí (*first three notes clearly spaced and descending, fourth higher or omitted); calls include harsh thin grating buzzing. **HH** Open broadleaved forest, forest edge, second growth; scrub and grass on hillsides. **TN** and **AN** Formerly treated as conspecific with Chinese Babax *Babax lanceolatus*.

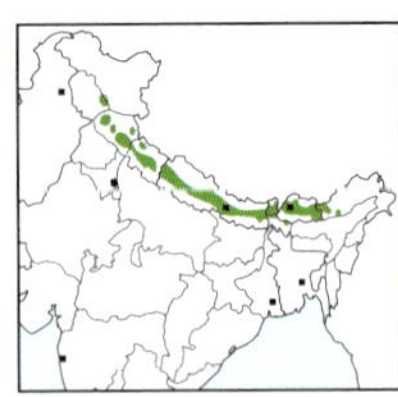

White-throated Laughingthrush *Pterorhinus albogularis* 28–30.5cm

Resident. Himalayas. **ID** Large, with striking white throat and upper breast, brownish-olive breast-band, and pale rufous-orange underparts. Additional features include black lores, pale blue eyes, rufous-orange forehead, and indistinct grey panel on wing. In flight, shows broad white tips to tail feathers. Juvenile similar to adult but has less distinct breast-band and paler rufous-buff belly and flanks. **Voice** Shrill wheezy whistles, e.g. *hiuuuu*, gentle *chrrrr*, soft *teh* and subdued chattering; harsh *chrrr-chrrr-chrrr…* in alarm. **HH** Broadleaved and mixed forest; second growth. **TN** Formerly placed in *Garrulax*.

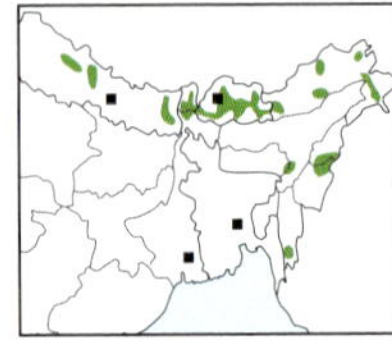

Grey-sided Laughingthrush *Pterorhinus caerulatus* 27–29cm

Resident. Himalayas and NE India. **ID** Rufous-brown and white, with grey breast-sides and flanks, bare bluish-slate eye-patch, black face and variable white cheek patch, black scaling on crown, and more rufescent edges to flight feathers and tail. *P. c. subcaerulatus* (Meghalaya) has extensive white cheek patch and white tips to outer tail feathers. **Voice** Squealing *klee-loo*, jovial *ovik-chor-r-r*, loud *joy-to-weep*, *poo-ka-ree*, *new-jeriko*; *chik-chi-chik* alarm call **HH** Undergrowth in dense, moist forest; bamboo thickets. **TN** Formerly placed in *Garrulax*.

ad
Chestnut-backed
Laughingthrush
Rufous-necked
Laughingthrush
ad
ad
White-browed
Laughingthrush
ad
Mount Victoria
Babax
ad
White-throated
Laughingthrush
ad
Grey-sided
Laughingthrush

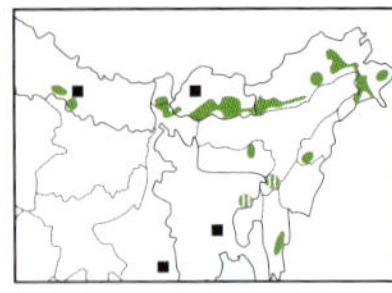

Long-tailed Sibia *Heterophasia picaoides* 28–34.5cm

Resident. E Himalayas and NE Indian hills. Vagrant: Bangladesh. **ID** From other sibias by very long tail with whitish tips, grey head and upperparts, paler grey underparts, and dark grey wings with white patch on secondaries. Whitish tail tips are especially prominent on underside. **Voice** Calls include thin, metallic, high-pitched *tsittsit* and *tsic* notes, interspersed with dry, even-pitched rattling. **HH** Broadleaved evergreen forest.

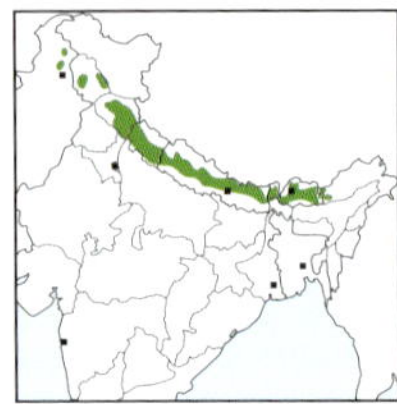

Rufous Sibia *Heterophasia capistrata* 21–24cm

Resident. Himalayas. **ID** Black cap, rufous to orange nape, rump/uppertail-coverts and underparts, grey tip and black subterminal band to tail, and grey panels on mainly black wings. Nominate (W Himalayas) has paler orange nape and underparts (especially on throat), and grey-brown mantle. *H. c. nigriceps* (W and C Nepal) and *H. c. bayleyi* (E Himalayas) have deeper rufous nape and underparts; *nigriceps* has a brighter rufous-brown mantle almost concolorous with nape; *bayleyi* has colder, darker brown mantle contrasting with nape. **Voice** Song a clear, flute-like *tee-dee-dee-dee-dee-o-lu*, the first five notes on the same pitch, the sixth lowest and the last in between; call a rapid *chi-chi*, alarm a harsh *chrai-chrai-chrai*. **HH** Mainly broadleaved forest, favours oaks. **TN** Formerly placed in *Malacias*.

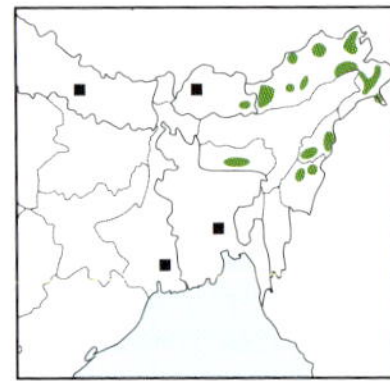

Beautiful Sibia *Heterophasia pulchella* 23cm

Resident. E Himalayas and NE Indian hills. **ID** Bluish-slate crown, slate-grey upperparts and slightly paler underparts. Wings patterned black, chestnut-brown and grey. Tail has broad grey tip and black subterminal band. Ear-coverts can be solidly black, forming contrasting patch (*H. p. nigroaurita*), or black can be restricted to lores. **Voice** Song a loud, strident *ti-ti-titi-tu-ti*, descending slightly towards end. Generally, less descending, higher-pitched and shriller than Grey Sibia. Calls include continuous low, rattling *chrrrrrrrrr*. **HH** Moist broadleaved forest. **TN** Formerly placed in *Malacias*.

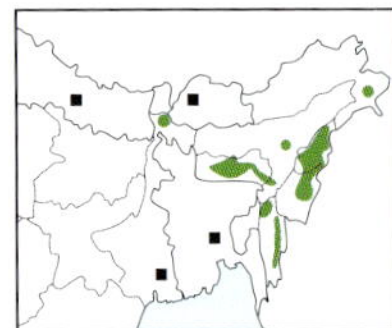

Grey Sibia *Heterophasia gracilis* 22.5–24.5cm

Resident. N Bengal and NE Indian hills. **ID** Lacks rufous. Has black cap, grey upperparts, black wings (with largely grey tertials), and mainly grey tail with broad black subterminal band. Underparts whitish with buff rear flanks and undertail-coverts. **Voice** Song a loud, strident, far-carrying series of well-spaced high-pitched, shrill whistles, usually descending towards end or from start; harsh, grating calls. **HH** Broadleaved forest, but mainly pine forest in Khasi Hills. **TN** Formerly placed in *Malacias*.

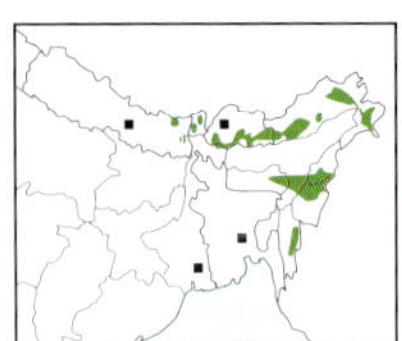

Rufous-backed Sibia *Leioptila annectens* 18.5–20cm

Resident. E Himalayas and NE Indian hills. **ID** Small, short-tailed sibia. Black cap, black-and-white-streaked upper mantle merging into rufous back and rump, and white underparts with deep buff flanks and vent. Black wings have white fringes to tertials and grey edges to primaries and secondaries. Black tail is tipped white (from below, showing as large white spots at tip of undertail). Also has yellow base to lower mandible and yellow legs and feet. **Voice** Song repeated loud, strident jolly phrases. **HH** Dense, moist broadleaved forest.

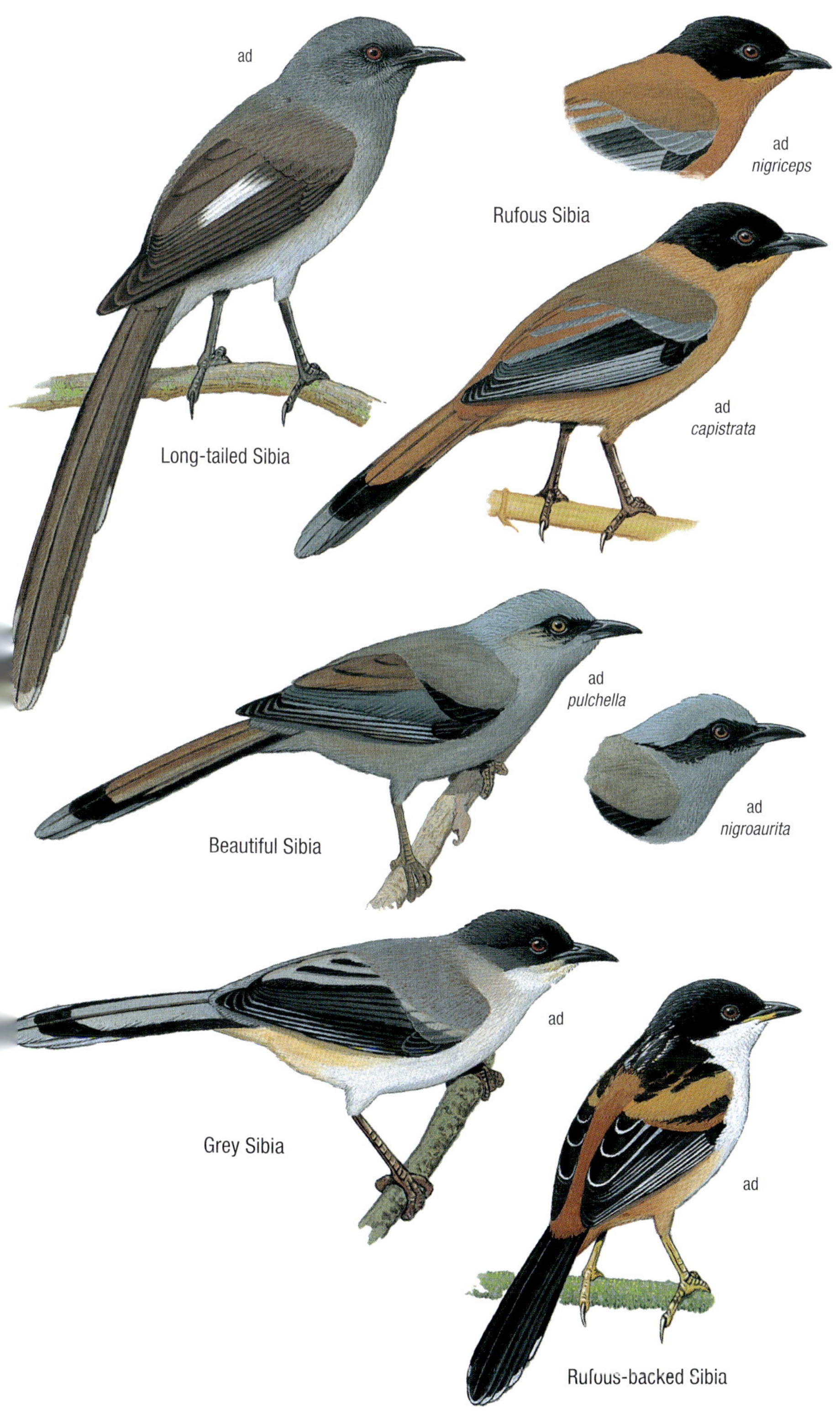
ad
ad
nigriceps
Rufous Sibia
Long-tailed Sibia
ad
capistrata
ad
pulchella
ad
nigroaurita
Beautiful Sibia
ad
Grey Sibia
ad
Rufous-backed Sibia

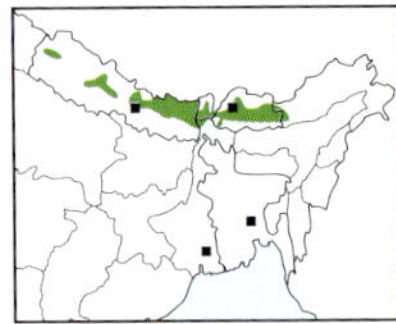

Hoary-throated Barwing *Actinodura nipalensis* 21cm

Resident. Himalayas. **ID** From other barwings by uniform (or very faintly-streaked) greyish throat and breast, prominent buffish-white shaft streaking on dark brown crest, grey ear-coverts contrasting with dark moustachial stripe, and diffuse buff streaking on mantle and scapulars. Also has shorter, more strongly barred tail with pronounced dark tail-band, and lacks rufous 'front' of Rusty-fronted. **Voice** Some 1–2 whistling notes followed by a soft trill; a series of long, whistling notes; jay-like alarm. **HH** Mossy oak-rhododendron forest.

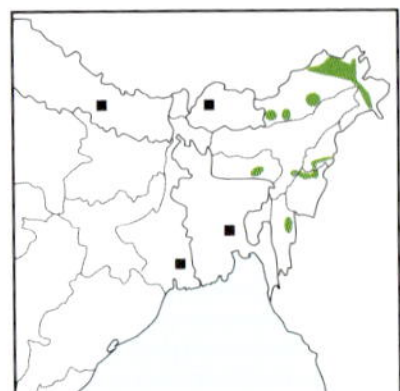

Streak-throated Barwing *Actinodura waldeni* 20–22cm

Resident. E Himalayas and NE Indian hills. **ID** Two races; *A. w. daflaensis* (E Himalayas) has greyish-white underparts diffusely streaked brownish-grey, and is similar in appearance to Hoary-throated (no known overlap in range, but apparently hybridises in W Arunachal): best told by prominent streaking on underparts, lack of bold shaft streaks on crown and nape (crown feathers have narrow pale fringes), poorly defined moustachial stripe, and uniform rufous-brown mantle. *A. w. waldeni* (hills south of Brahmaputra River) has tawny-brown underparts with fulvous streaks. Lacks rusty 'front' to head of Rusty-fronted, and further differences are brown crown and nape faintly streaked buff, streaked underparts, and blackish terminal band to shorter tail. **Voice** Song loud, rich, throaty whistles with strongly slurred first notes. **HH** Mossy forest.

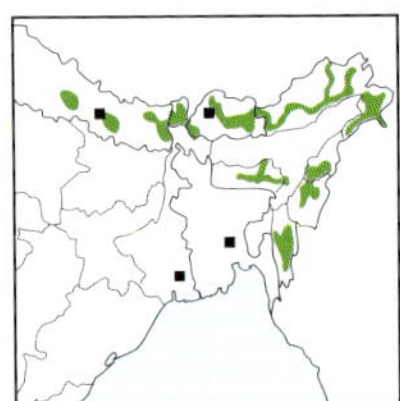

Rusty-fronted Barwing *Actinodura egertoni* 21.5–23.5cm

Resident. Himalayas and NE Indian hills; formerly in NE Bangladesh. **ID** Slimmer and longer-tailed than other barwings, and best told by combination of rufous 'front' to head, stout yellowish bill (or base to bill), uniform grey crown and nape contrasting with mantle (without prominent streaking), rufous underparts, greyish-buff (rather than rufous-brown) barring on wings, and rufous-brown and more diffusely barred tail (lacking blackish terminal band). Juvenile has crown and nape rufous-brown and concolorous with mantle, making rufous forehead less prominent. Four subspecies in subcontinent, differing slightly in coloration of mantle (olive-brown to rufous-brown) and in greyness of crown and ear-coverts. **Voice** Three-note whistle *ti-ti-ta*, the first accentuated, the last lower. **HH** Dense understorey in moist forest.

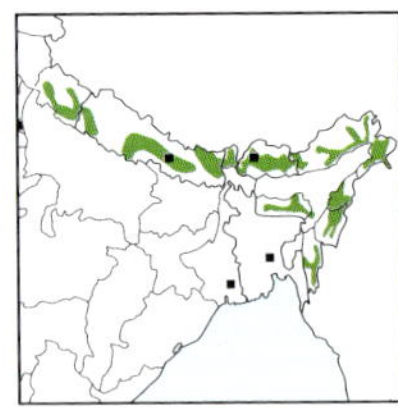

Blue-winged Minla *Actinodura cyanouroptera* 14–15.5cm

Resident. Himalayas and NE Indian hills. **ID** Slim babbler with long square-ended tail. Although colourful, can look drab at long range, with dark-capped, pale-faced appearance, yellowish bill, fulvous-brown mantle, vinous-grey underparts, and blue panels in wings and tail. At close range has pale violet-grey crown and nape, with violet-blue streaking on forehead and sides of crown. White underside to dark-bordered tail striking when viewed from below. Juvenile has brownish-grey crown and nape, and buffish underparts. **Voice** A clear, whistled *pi-piu* with emphasis on first note, and loud *swit*. **HH** Bushes in broadleaved or mixed forest; well-wooded country. **AN** Blue-winged Siva. **TN** Formerly placed in *Siva*.

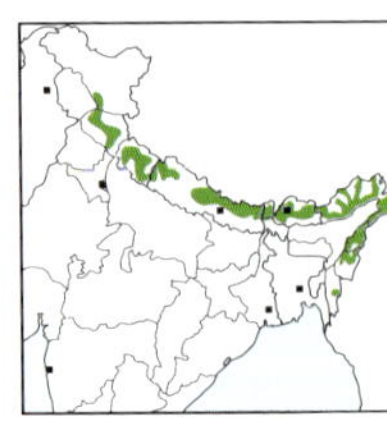

Chestnut-tailed Minla *Actinodura strigula* 16–18.5cm

Resident. Himalayas and NE Indian hills. **ID** Orange crown and nape, grey ear-coverts with prominent whitish eye-ring and black moustachial stripe, yellow chin, and black-and-white barring on throat. Upperparts olive-brown and underparts yellowish. Has black primary coverts patch, grey fringes to black-centred tertials, and orange-yellow wing panel. Shows orange-yellow at sides and tip of tail, also visible when viewed from below. Juvenile has less distinct throat barring and duller crown and nape. **Voice** Slurred whistle *jo-ey, joey dii*, the last note highest; ringing metallic *chew*. **HH** Broadleaved oak-rhododendron and mixed forest. **AN** Bar-throated Siva. **TN** Formerly placed in *Siva*.

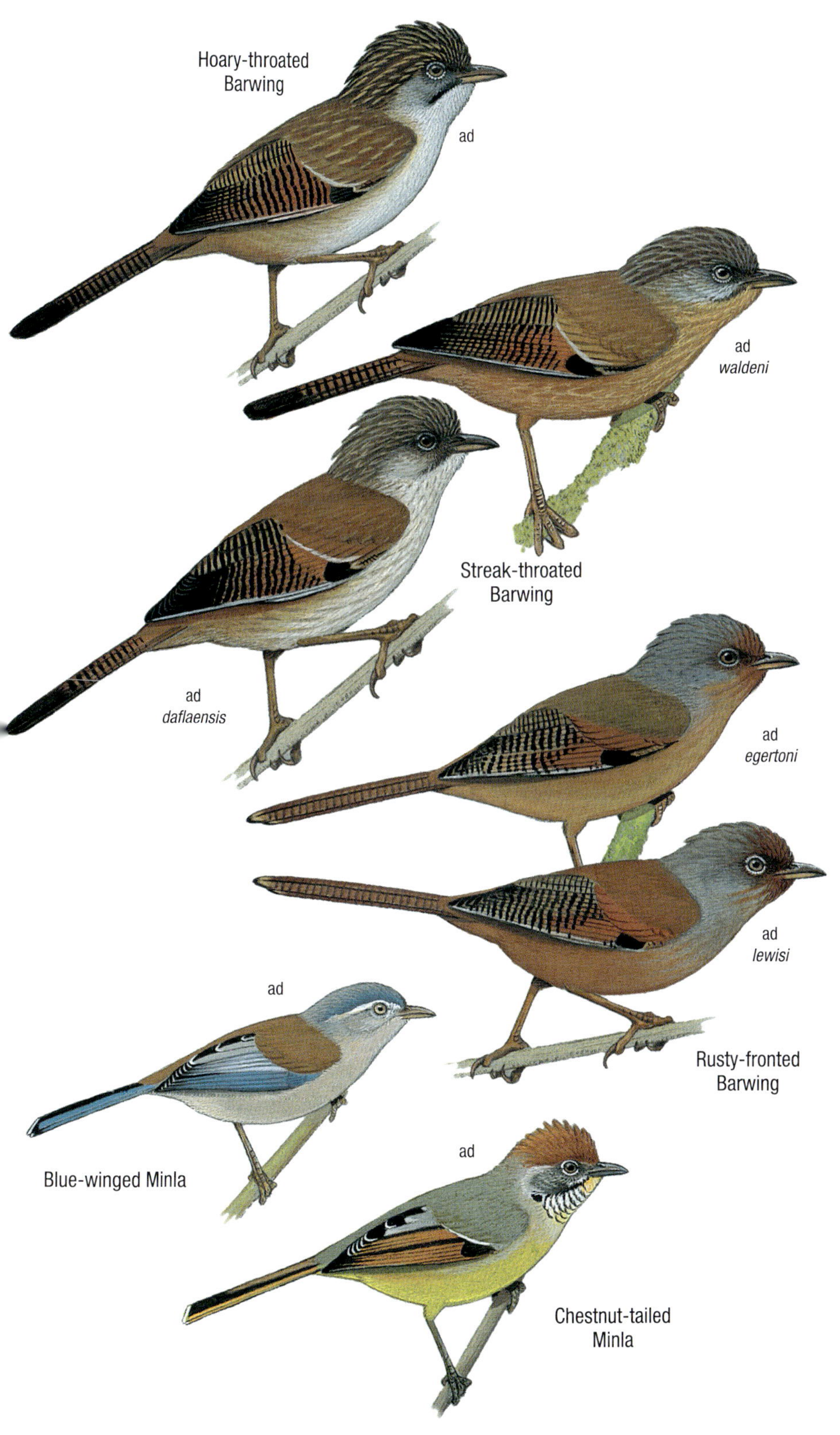
Hoary-throated
Barwing
ad
ad
waldeni
Streak-throated
Barwing
ad
daflaensis
ad
egertoni
ad
lewisi
ad
Rusty-fronted
Barwing
Blue-winged Minla
ad
Chestnut-tailed
Minla

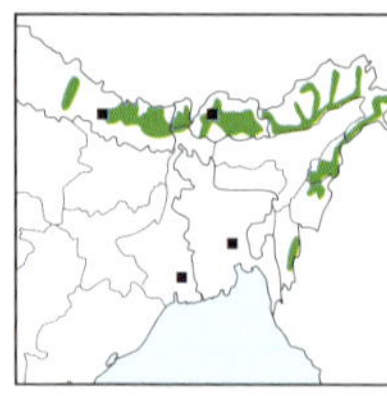

Red-tailed Minla *Minla ignotincta* 13–14.5cm

Resident. Himalayas and NE Indian hills. **ID** A slim, long-tailed babbler. Black crown and ear-coverts, broad white supercilium and striking pale eye. Also, prominent white tips to black tertials and yellowish underparts. Male differs from female in having deep maroon-brown (rather than olive-brown) upperparts, red (rather than orange-yellow) wing panel, and red (rather than pinkish) sides and tip of tail. **Voice** Varied calls including a high-pitched *wi-wi-wi*, a loud repeated *chik*, high-pitched *tsi* and tit-like *whi-whi-te-sik-sik*. **HH** Moist, dense broadleaved or mixed forest.

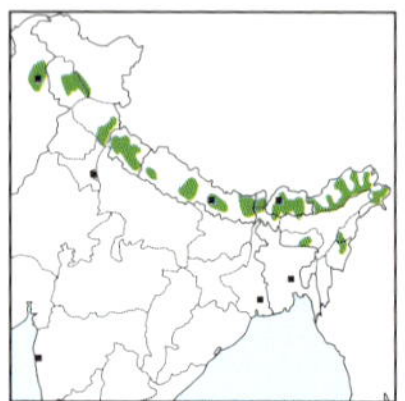

Red-billed Leiothrix *Leiothrix lutea* 12–13cm

Resident. Himalayas and NE Indian hills. **ID** Stocky with domed head and forked tail. Largely red bill, pale mask and greyish ear-coverts, dark moustachial stripe, and yellow throat merging into orange breast. The forked black tail is partly overlaid by long, white-tipped uppertail-coverts. Crimson, orange and yellow edges to wing feathers (crimson edges lacking in female). Female duller than male, including paler throat and breast. Juvenile has buff throat and grey breast and flanks (lacking yellow below of adult) and has paler bill. *L. l. kumaiensis* (W Himalayas) has greyer (less olive) upperparts and flanks than *L. l. calipyga* (C and E Himalayas). **Voice** Rapid, thrush-like song of up to 15 notes; rattled calls. **HH** Thick undergrowth in broadleaved forest.

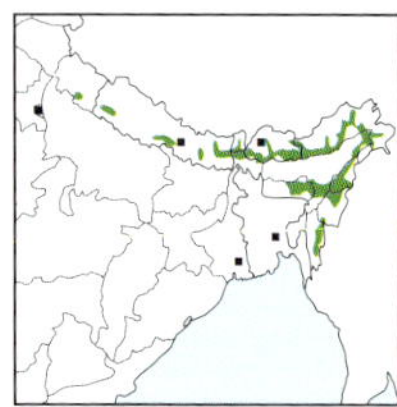

Silver-eared Mesia *Leiothrix argentauris* 15.5–17cm

Resident. Himalayas and NE Indian hills. **ID** Striking, with orange-yellow bill, black cap and moustachial stripe, silver-grey ear patch, and orange forehead, nape, throat and breast. Has grey mantle, crimson-and-yellow wing panels, and yellow sides to black tail. Male has crimson uppertail- and undertail-coverts. Female paler yellow on throat and breast, nape is olive-yellow, and has olive-yellow uppertail-coverts and orange-buff undertail-coverts. Juvenile has brown crown. **Voice** Cheerful descending whistled song *che tchu-tchu che-rit*; calls include a flat piping *pe-pe-pe-pe-pe*. **HH** Bushes and forest undergrowth in evergreen biotope. **TN** Formerly placed in *Mesia*.

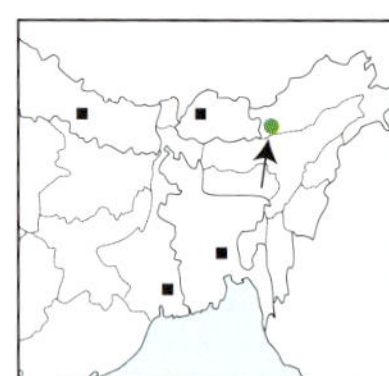

Bugun Liocichla *Liocichla bugunorum* 22cm

Resident. Eaglenest Wildlife Sanctuary, Arunachal Pradesh. **ID** Olive with a black cap, prominent orange-yellow lores, and yellow post-ocular spot. Yellow, red and white patches in wings; black tail with red tip, and crimson undertail-coverts. Pinkish feet. Bill darker on basal half and pale horn towards tip. **Voice** Fluty calls on descending scale, slightly slurred and inflected at end: *weee–keew, yu–weee–keew, wieuu–weei–tuui–tuuuw–tuoow.* **HH** Disturbed hillsides and ravines with dense shrubs and small to medium-sized trees. Globally threatened.

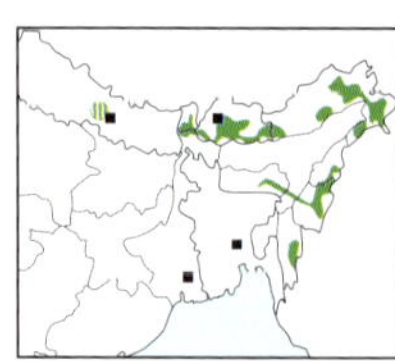

Red-faced Liocichla *Liocichla phoenicea* 21–23cm

Resident. E Himalayas and NE India. **ID** A striking, mainly olive-brown liocichla with crimson ear-coverts and sides to neck, black supercilium, crimson panel in wings, crimson undertail-coverts, and rufous-orange tip to black tail (undertail appears entirely rufous-orange). **Voice** Loud, plaintive, cheerful song of 3–8 notes: *chewi-ter-twi-twitoo*; *chi-cho-choee-wi-chu-chooee* etc.; mewing *jji-uuuu*, harsh, grating *chrrrt-chrrrt* in alarm. **HH** Undergrowth in moist forest and thickets.

♂
Red-tailed Minla
♀
♀
juv
♂
Red-billed Leiothrix
♂
Silver-eared Mesia
♀
juv
ad
Bugun Liocichla
ad
Red-faced Liocichla

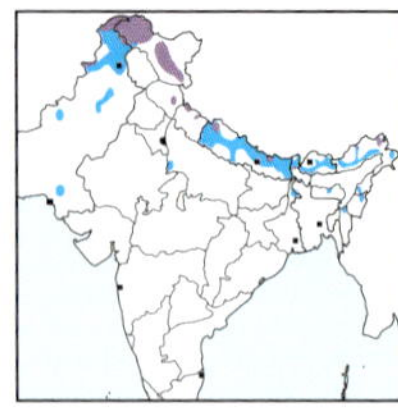

Wallcreeper *Tichodroma muraria* 16cm

Resident. Himalayas; winters down to foothills and plains. **ID** Long, downcurved, black bill. In flight, wings rounded and reveal largely crimson wing-coverts and bases to black flight feathers, with two rows of white spots on primaries. Also has white corners to tail. Adult male breeding has black throat and upper breast. Adult female breeding has whitish chin and variable blackish patch on lower throat and upper breast. Adult non-breeding has white throat and upper breast, and brown cast to crown. Juvenile has straighter bill, and underparts are paler and more uniform grey. **Voice** Song a variable repeated sequence of high whistles, increasing in strength and speed, *ti-tiu-treeh*; thin piping call and high whistles. **HH** Clings to cliffs and walls, foraging actively. Progresses in short, jerky hops, constantly flicking wings and tail. Rock cliffs and gorges; also ruins and stony riverbeds in winter.

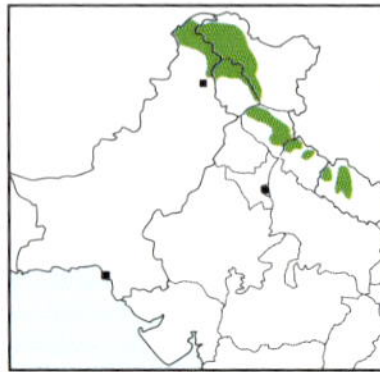

White-cheeked Nuthatch *Sitta leucopsis* 13cm

Resident. W Himalayas. **ID** Very distinctive nuthatch, with black crown and nape, white face and throat with beady eye, and whitish underparts with buffish wash becoming rufous on rear flanks and undertail-coverts. **Voice** Call likened to a young goat bleating: a continuous rapid series of low-pitched squeaks, *quww-queeh-quee-queeeh*; call similar, but slower. **HH** Typical nuthatch, see White-tailed. Feeds in upper canopy; most easily located by its distinctive call. In breeding season, males sometimes perch conspicuously on tall treetops, calling and flicking wings. Coniferous and broadleaved-coniferous forests.

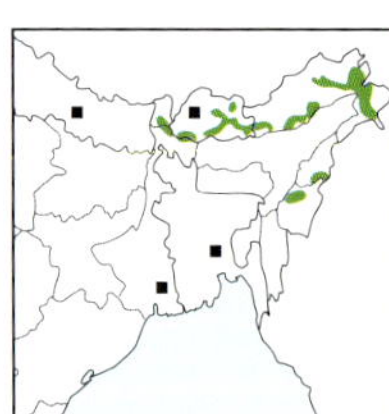

Beautiful Nuthatch *Sitta formosa* 16.5cm

Resident. E Himalayas and NE Indian hills. **ID** Large nuthatch with black upperparts, streaked blue, and rufous-orange underparts. Black crown and mantle with white and blue streaking, blue 'scapular lines', and broad bluish-white fringes to coverts and tertials. From below, outer tail feathers show broad white tips and, in flight, white patch at base of primaries contrasts with blackish underwing-coverts. **Voice** Calls include soft, sweet, liquid *plit* and explosive *chit*, latter also protracted into *chit-it chit-it chit-it...* or *chit'it-it chirririt*. **HH** Similar to other nuthatches, see White-tailed, but on larger branches and trunks; rather slow and deliberate, reminiscent of Himalayan Cutia. Mature broadleaved forest with large, spreading epiphyte-laden trees. Globally threatened.

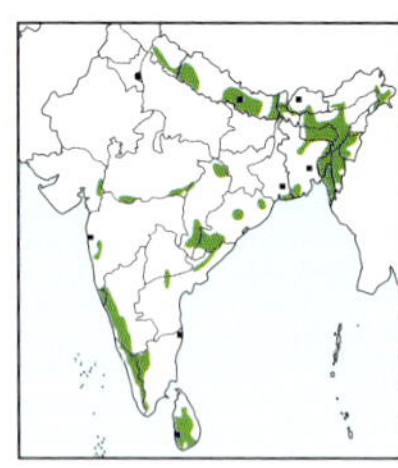

Velvet-fronted Nuthatch *Sitta frontalis* 12–13.5cm

Resident. Himalayas, Indian hills, Bangladesh and Sri Lanka. **ID** Striking, with violet-blue upperparts, black forehead, black-tipped red bill, startling yellow iris and eye-ring, and lilac suffusion to ear-coverts and underparts. Male has black eye-stripe extending behind eye (lacking in female) with stronger lilac suffusion on underparts (more cinnamon, less lilac in female). Juvenile has blackish bill and duller and greyer upperparts; underparts lack lilac suffusion and are washed orange-buff. **Voice** Song a series of *sit* notes, sometimes becoming a fast, hard rattle; calls include hard *chat* and thinner *sip*. **HH** Like other nuthatches, see White-tailed, but more active. Forages from canopy down to undergrowth, but not on ground. Open broadleaved forest and well-wooded areas.

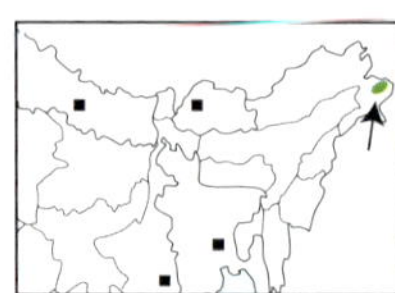

Yunnan Nuthatch *Sitta yunnanensis* 12cm

Resident, Helmet Top 2,250m and Tilam Top in Arunachal Pradesh. **ID** A small nuthatch with fine white supercilium. Upperparts grey and underparts warm buff (becoming greyer when worn). **Voice** Calls include nasal *nit*, sometimes repeated, a shorter, more abrupt and higher-pitched *tit*, low nasal *toik* and a harsh scolding *schri-schri-schri....* **HH** Typical nuthatch, see White-tailed. Tall mature pine forest, with dense understorey of bushes.

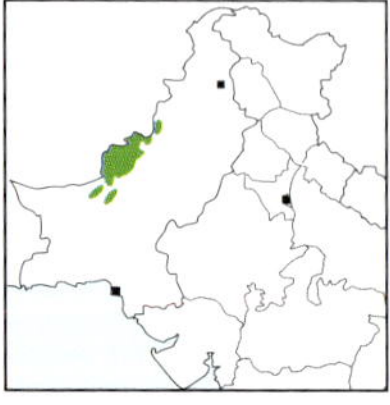

Eastern Rock Nuthatch *Sitta tephronota* 15–16cm

Resident. Balochistan. **ID** Large, with very large, slightly upturned-looking bill. Long black eye-stripe, extending to side of mantle, pale blue-grey upperparts, and whitish underparts with orange-buff rear flanks and undertail-coverts. **Voice** Song a loud, far-carrying trill, with duetting by pair members; short single or double call, *tsik*. **HH** Often keeps to same locality all year. Feeding behaviour like other nuthatches, but chiefly on rock faces, cliffs and boulders. Rocky mountains with scattered scrub and rock outcrops, rocky gorges and ridges.

♂ br
non-br
Wallcreeper
ad
White-cheeked
Nuthatch
ad
Beautiful Nuthatch
♂
♀
Velvet-fronted
Nuthatch
ad
Yunnan Nuthatch
Eastern Rock
Nuthatch

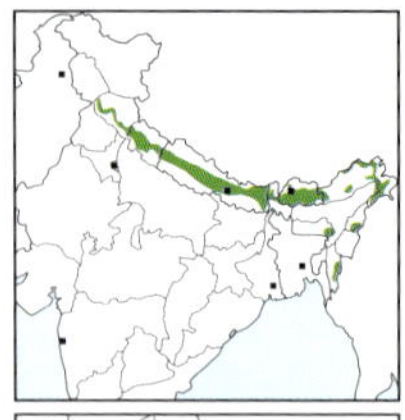

White-tailed Nuthatch *Sitta himalayensis* 12cm

Resident. Himalayas and NE Indian hills. **ID** From Kashmir by white at base of central tail feathers (although this can be very difficult to see in the field). Also smaller, with relatively shorter bill. Sexes similar. White-tailed has less distinct cheek patch compared to Kashmir (cheeks off-white or buff, and ear-coverts more cinnamon-orange). From female Chestnut-bellied by uniform undertail-coverts, and underparts are paler and less uniform. **Voice** Song variable series of clear whistles, e.g. *dwi-dwi-dwi-dwi*. **HH** Typical nuthatch. Can move with ease upwards, downwards, sideways and upside-down on trunks and branches. In winter associates with other insectivores in foraging flocks. Frequents the upper half of trees, occasionally low bushes. Broadleaved and mixed broadleaved-coniferous forest.

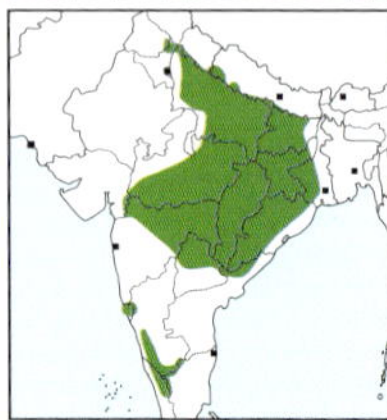

Indian Nuthatch *Sitta castanea* 12.5cm

Resident. Indian hills. Vagrant: Bangladesh. **ID** Compared to Chestnut-bellied is smaller, with shorter, slender bill. Scalloping on undertail-coverts grey (same colour as mantle) and crown/nape are distinctly paler than mantle, while underparts of male are a darker reddish-chestnut. Female has paler orange-buff underparts than male. **Voice** Song a loud, mellow, rapid trill, level or slightly falling in pitch towards end, *chi-li-li-li-li-li-li-li*. **HH** Typical nuthatch, see White-tailed. Deciduous forest, village groves, roadside trees, sometimes gardens.

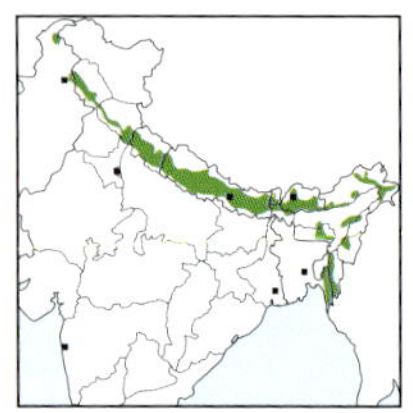

Chestnut-bellied Nuthatch *Sitta cinnamoventris* 13–14cm

Resident. Himalayan foothills, hills of NE India and SE Bangladesh. **ID** From Kashmir and White-tailed Nuthatches by whitish scalloping on undertail-coverts. Male always shows striking white cheek patch. Female similar, but underparts paler, and more similar to Kashmir Nuthatch, but underparts richer, darker and more uniform cinnamon-brown, and clearly defined white chin and cheeks. Lacks white at tail base of White-tailed; also, underparts are darker, and cheek patch is more prominent. From Indian Nuthatch by larger bill, crown concolorous with mantle and much more prominent white scalloping on undertail-coverts. **Voice** Songs include a low-pitched, shrill, fast, slurred trill that rises slightly (or rises and falls), repeated every few seconds, *treeeee*. **HH** Open deciduous forest, especially sal, scattered trees, mango groves and bamboo clumps; in pine In W Himalayas and hill evergreen forest in NE India.

Chestnut-vented Nuthatch *Sitta nagaensis* 12.5–14cm

Resident. NE Indian hills. **ID** Maroon-chestnut rear flanks and undertail-coverts, latter with bold white spotting. Upperparts pale blue-grey and black eye-stripe extends as broad stripe to sides of neck. In NE India, underparts of nominate are dull buffish-grey to whitish (more buffish in female). In NE Arunachal, what is assumed to be *S. n. montium* has underparts orange-buff and similar to White-tailed but this species has uniform undertail-coverts. **Voice** Song a level bubbling, trill *duiduiduiduiduidui*; call a distinctive nasal *chuueep*. **HH** Typical nuthatch, see White-tailed. Feeds in the middle and lower forest storeys; frequently also on the ground. Open forest.

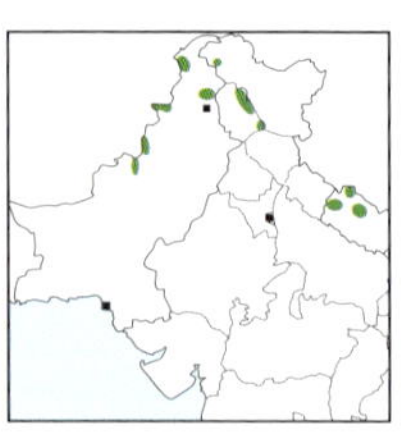

Kashmir Nuthatch *Sitta cashmirensis* 14cm

Resident. W Himalayas and Indian hills. **ID** Compared with Chestnut-bellied, has uniform undertail-coverts and less prominent white cheeks. Larger and longer-billed than White-tailed, with more pronounced white cheeks, and no white at base of tail. Female similar to male, but underparts paler, with flanks and undertail-coverts more deep cinnamon, and whitish cheek patch less clearly defined. Female therefore very similar to White-tailed, but ear-coverts whiter and underparts more pinkish-cinnamon. **Voice** Song a series of rapidly repeated high-pitched whistles *pee-pee-pee-pee-pee*; loud rasping jay-like call is diagnostic and separates it from White-tailed. **HH** Forages at lower levels than White-cheeked, often in understorey, sometimes on ground. Deciduous and broadleaved-coniferous forest and well-wooded country.

Eurasian Wren *Troglodytes troglodytes* 9–10cm

Resident. Balochistan and Himalayas. **ID** Small, with stubby tail. Barred wings and tail, and variably barred underparts. *T. t. magrathi* (extreme NW) has grey-brown upperparts with fine, dense (and indistinct) dark barring, and greyish underparts with paler throat. *T. t. neglectus* (W Himalayas) has darker brown upperparts with heavy blackish barring, and smoky-brown underparts including throat. *T. t. nipalensis* (C and E Himalayas) is the darkest and sooty-brown all over. **Voice** Song a powerful, rapidly delivered warbling and trilling; calls include a hard *check* and rattling *churr*. **HH** Sprightly, always on move, creeping and flitting among rocks and low vegetation. Breeds amongst rocks on or above treeline; winters on stone walls around villages and fields, stony riverbeds and coniferous forest undergrowth. **AN** Winter Wren.

ad
White-tailed Nuthatch
♂
Indian Nuthatch
♀
♂
♀
Chestnut-bellied
Nuthatch
ad
nagaensis
ad
montium
Chestnut-vented
Nuthatch
ad
neglectus
♂
ad
nipalensis
♀
Kashmir
Nuthatch
Eurasian Wren

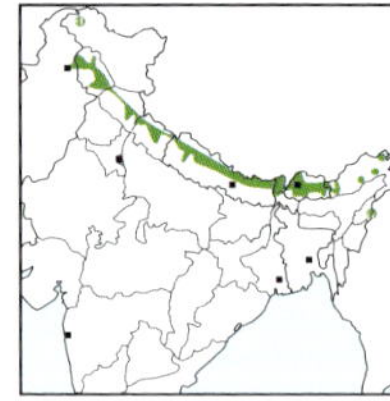

Hodgson's Treecreeper *Certhia hodgsoni* 11–12cm

Resident. Himalayas. **ID** From Bar-tailed Treecreeper by combination of (generally) shorter, less downcurved bill, uniform (unbarred) tail, and more prominent buff banding on wing. From Sikkim by whitish throat and breast, dull brown tail and more pronounced white supercilium. From Rusty-flanked by lack of prominent white border to rear of ear-coverts, and duller buffish flanks. Nominate (W Himalayas) comparatively pale and grey above, with pronounced whitish streaking. In C and E Himalayas (*mandellii* and *khamensis*) darker and browner above: former has indistinct rufescent streaking on upperparts, more rufescent rump and buffish flanks; latter has paler, more buffish streaking on upperparts and greyish flanks. **Voice** Song a high-pitched, rising then descending *tzee-tzee-tzizizi*; call a thin, piercing *tsee-tsee-tsee*. **HH** Typical treecreeper habits, see Rusty-flanked. Mainly coniferous forest mixed with birch, rhododendron or oak, also pure oak or birch.

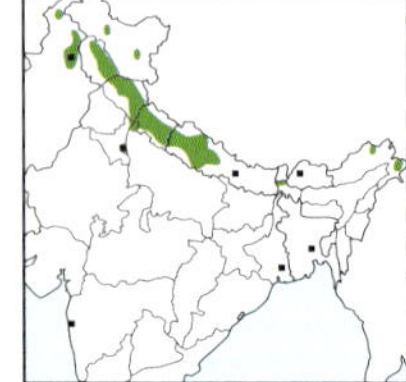

Bar-tailed Treecreeper *Certhia himalayana* 14cm

Resident. Pakistan mountains, W Himalayas and SE Arunachal Pradesh. Vagrant: Bangladesh. **ID** From other treecreepers by combination of (generally) longer, more downcurved bill and dark cross-barring on tail. Supercilium and pale banding on wings less distinct than on Hodgson's. White throat and dull whitish or dirty greyish-buff underparts are further differences from Sikkim and Rusty-flanked. Birds in W Himalayas paler and greyer above, becoming darker with more pronounced whitish streaking in E Himalayas. **Voice** Song a high-pitched trill of 7–9 notes *chi-chi-chi-chiu-chiu-chiu-chu*, rising slightly in tone and increasing in speed at start. Call a weak, high-pitched thin *tsi-tsi*. **HH** Typical treecreeper habits, see Rusty-flanked. Breeds mainly in coniferous forest, also rhododendron and birch, and well-wooded areas in winter.

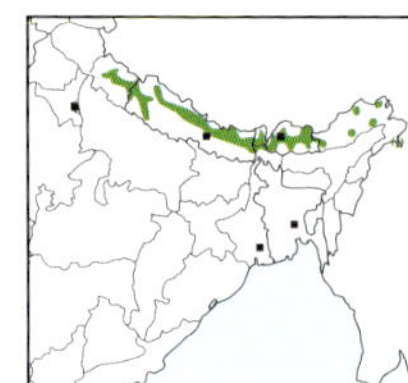

Rusty-flanked Treecreeper *Certhia nipalensis* 14cm

Resident. Himalayas. **ID** From other treecreepers by combination of shorter, straighter bill, well-defined buffish supercilium, which continues around (and contrasts with) dark ear-coverts, and creamy-buff breast and belly with warm rufous flanks. Crown and nape blackish with fine buff streaks. Supercilium of Hodgson's may extend, rather indistinctly, behind ear-coverts, but ear-covert patch is paler and smaller. Also has unbarred tail (compare Bar-tailed), and white throat (compare Sikkim). **Voice** Distinctive song: two slow notes followed by rapid, penetrating, accelerating trill ending abruptly *si-si-sss-rt-rt-t*; calls include high thin *sit* call and penetrating *zip*. **HH** Small, quiet and arboreal, with a stiff tail used as a prop when climbing. Forages by creeping up vertical trunks and underside of branches, spiralling upwards in a series of jerks. Breeds in oak, oak-rhododendron-fir and hemlock forest; winters in broadleaved forest.

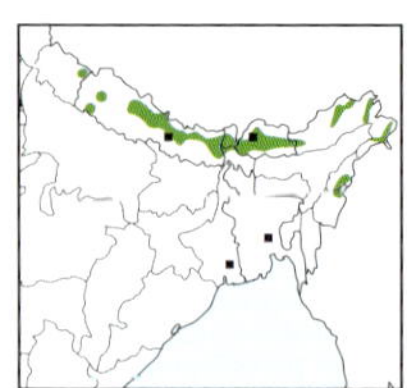

Sikkim Treecreeper *Certhia discolor* 14cm

Resident. Himalayas. **ID** From other treecreepers, where ranges overlap, by brownish-buff throat and breast, becoming paler on belly and flanks. Unbarred rufescent tail is additional feature from Bar-tailed, and less distinct brown-buff supercilium, which does not enclose ear-coverts is an additional feature from Rusty-flanked. **Voice** Song a long monotonous rattle; calls an explosive *chit* or *tchip* and higher, thinner *tsit* or *seep*. **HH** Typical treecreeper habits, see Rusty-flanked. Mainly broadleaved forest, especially mossy oak forest, also mixed forest. **AN** Brown-throated Treecreeper.

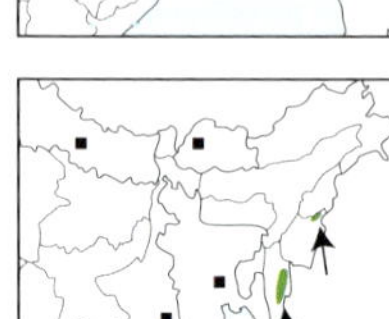

Hume's Treecreeper *Certhia manipurensis* 14cm

Resident. Manipur and Mizoram. **ID** Similar to Sikkim but has cinnamon-orange throat and breast, and warmer brown upperparts. Whitish to buffish supercilium and eye-ring quite prominent. **Voice** Song distinctive: a monotonous hesitant rattle, slower than Sikkim's, *tchi-tchi tchi-tchi tchi-tchi tchichip*, etc. A loud, explosive *chit* or *tchip* call sometimes becoming a rattle. **HH** Typical treecreeper. Broadleaved and mixed broadleaved and pine forest.

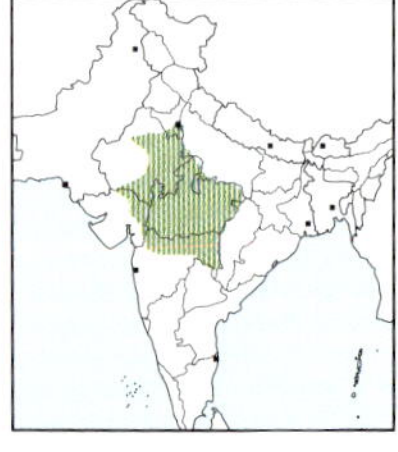

Indian Spotted Creeper *Salpornis spilonota* 13–15cm

Resident. N and C India. **ID** Larger and stockier than treecreepers, with shorter and broader, slightly rounded tail (which is not pressed against tree for support). Brown upperparts, including wings, boldly spotted and barred with white, greyish-white tail banded with dark brown, and underparts washed with orange-buff and spotted with brown. Prominent whitish supercilium and dark eye-stripe. **Voice** Song a series of plaintive descending whistles, *tchiu-tchuwu-tchuwu*; call a faint *see-ee*, and almost croaking *kek-kek-kek-kek-kek-kek*. **HH** Forages by fluttering and clambering rapidly from tree base to upper branches; does not spiral trunks like treecreepers. Clings upside-down to branches. Typically moves to new trunk or branch by 'tumbling' with open wings. Open deciduous forest and mango groves. **AN** Spotted Creeper.

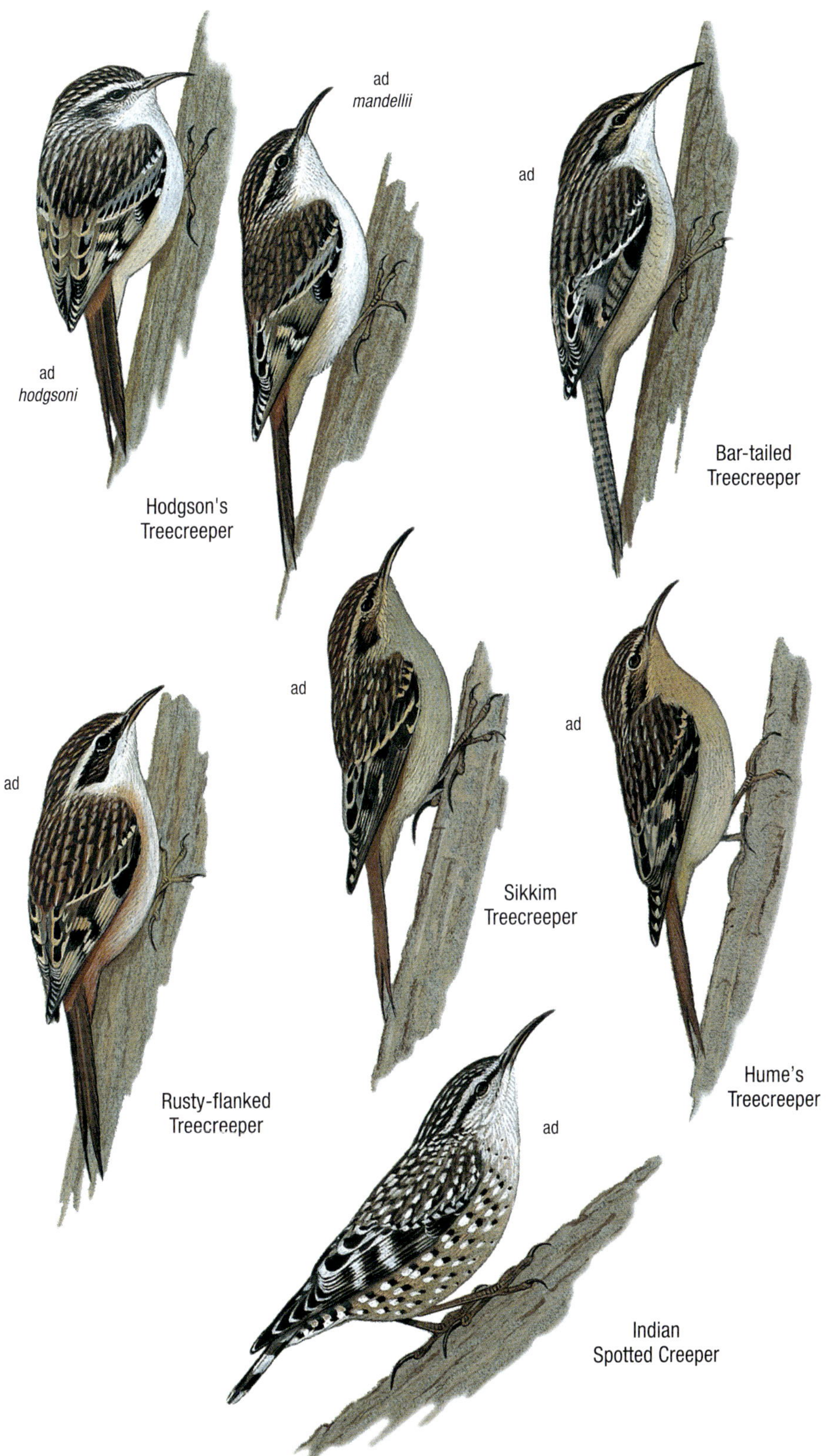
ad
hodgsoni
ad
mandellii
Hodgson's
Treecreeper
ad
Bar-tailed
Treecreeper
ad
Rusty-flanked
Treecreeper
ad
Sikkim
Treecreeper
ad
Hume's
Treecreeper
ad
Indian
Spotted Creeper

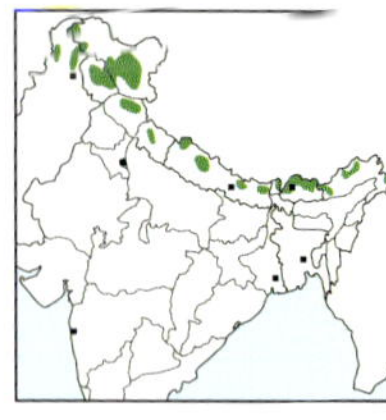

White-throated Dipper *Cinclus cinclus* 17–20cm

Resident. Himalayas. **ID** From Brown by white throat and breast contrasting with brown belly; also has brown head and nape merging into blackish-slate mantle, wings and tail. A rare colour morph, with brown throat and breast, has been recorded in Ladakh. Juvenile from juvenile Brown by greyer upperparts, without prominent spotting, and by whiter underparts which are finely scaled. *C. c. leucogaster*, which has an all-white belly, has been recorded in N Pakistan. **Voice** Call an abrupt, rasping *jeet*; song a quiet mix of grating and twittering notes. **HH** Aquatic; usually seen perched on a mid-stream rock, bobbing up and down. Highly territorial in winter and summer. Regularly submerges to swim underwater or walk on streambed in search of invertebrates. Fast-flowing mountain streams.

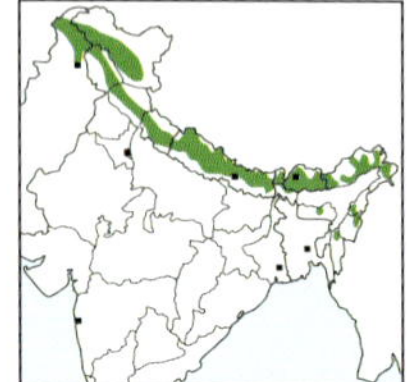

Brown Dipper *Cinclus pallasii* 21–23cm

Resident. Himalayas and NE India. **ID** Adult is all brown, lacking white throat and breast of White-throated. Juvenile from juvenile White-throated by browner coloration with conspicuous buff spotting on upperparts and underparts (lacking paler throat and breast), and more prominent pale fringes to wing feathers. Adult *C. p. dorje* (E Himalayas) is slightly darker than *C. p. tenuirostris* (NW); juvenile has pale rufous spotting on darker blackish-brown upperparts and underparts, and less prominent pale fringes to wings, compared with juvenile *tenuirostris*. **Voice** Call an abrupt *dzit-dzit*, less harsh than White-throated; song stronger and richer. **HH** Like White-throated. Fast-flowing mountain streams and small mountain lakes.

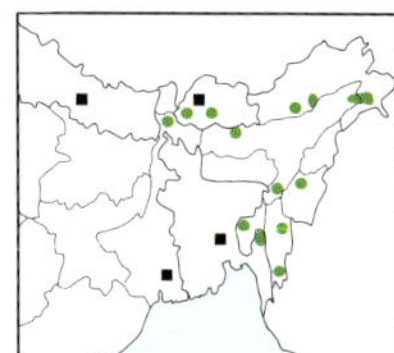

Golden-crested Myna *Ampeliceps coronatus* 19–21cm

Resident. N Bengal, Assam, Arunachal and NE India. **ID** Small, stout-billed myna. Male largely glossy black, with bushy, golden-yellow forehead and crown, yellow throat, naked orange-yellow orbital patch, and yellow patch at base of primaries. Female similar but has less extensive yellow crown and smaller yellow throat patch. Juvenile dark brown, slightly paler below, with pale yellow throat and pale yellow patch on wing. **Voice** Higher-pitched, more metallic whistle than Common Hill and a bell-like note. **HH** Habits very similar to Common Hill. Moist forest, open woodland, and tall trees in forest clearings.

Sri Lanka Myna *Gracula ptilogenys* 25cm

Resident. Sri Lanka. **ID** Compared with Southern Hill Myna (which also occurs in Sri Lanka), has stouter orange-red bill with dark blue base, and different shape and positioning of wattles (lacks bare patch on side of head, but has two oval-shaped wattles that extend from nape). Male is glossed purplish-blue on mantle; more greenish on female. Juvenile has duller bill, much smaller and paler yellow wattles, and less gloss to plumage, with unglossed brownish-black underparts. **Voice** Various very loud whistles, lower in pitch than Common Hill, also creaking and guttural 'conversational' notes. **HH** In the canopy. In non-breeding season, often in small groups. Gathers in large numbers at fruiting trees. Forest, well-wooded country, plantations and gardens. **AN** Sri Lanka Hill Myna.

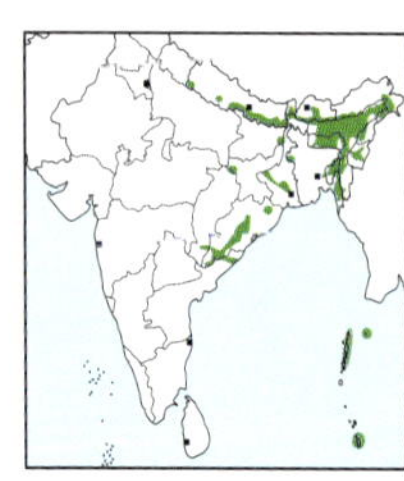

Common Hill Myna *Gracula religiosa* 25–29cm

Resident. Himalayan foothills, NE Indian hills, E. Ghats, Bangladesh, Andamans and Nicobars. **ID** Large myna with yellow wattles and large orange to yellow bill. Plumage all black except prominent white wing patches. Adult has purple-and-green gloss to plumage and bright orange bill. Juvenile has duller yellowish-orange bill, paler yellow wattles, and less gloss to plumage, with unglossed brownish-black underparts. **Voice** Extremely varied, loud piercing whistles, screeches, croaks and wheezes; noticeably lower, fuller, clearer and mellower than Southern, with much mimicry. **HH** Active and noisy. Strictly arboreal; mainly forages in trees, sometimes in fruiting bushes, hopping on branches. Usually seen in small flocks in treetops; will gather in large flocks at fruiting trees, along with other frugivores. Moist forest, wooded areas, forest edges and clearings and plantations.

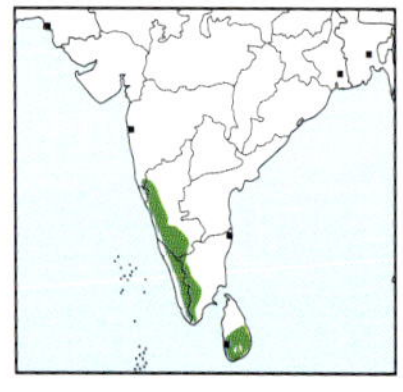

Southern Hill Myna *Gracula indica* 23–25cm

Resident. W Ghats and Sri Lanka. **ID** Smaller with a finer bill than Common (although no overlap in range) and has eye wattles distinctly separated from those on nape, with the latter extending up sides of crown. Bill finer than Sri Lanka Myna, lacking blue at base, and has wattles on sides of head. Eye dark (often white in Sri Lanka Myna). **Voice** Loud, piercing musical whistles, and harsh guttural notes; alarm a loud squeaky wheeze; calls generally higher-pitched and less variable than Common Hill. **HH** Habits like Common Hill. Wooded country, moist forest and well-wooded cultivated areas. **AN** Lesser Hill Myna.

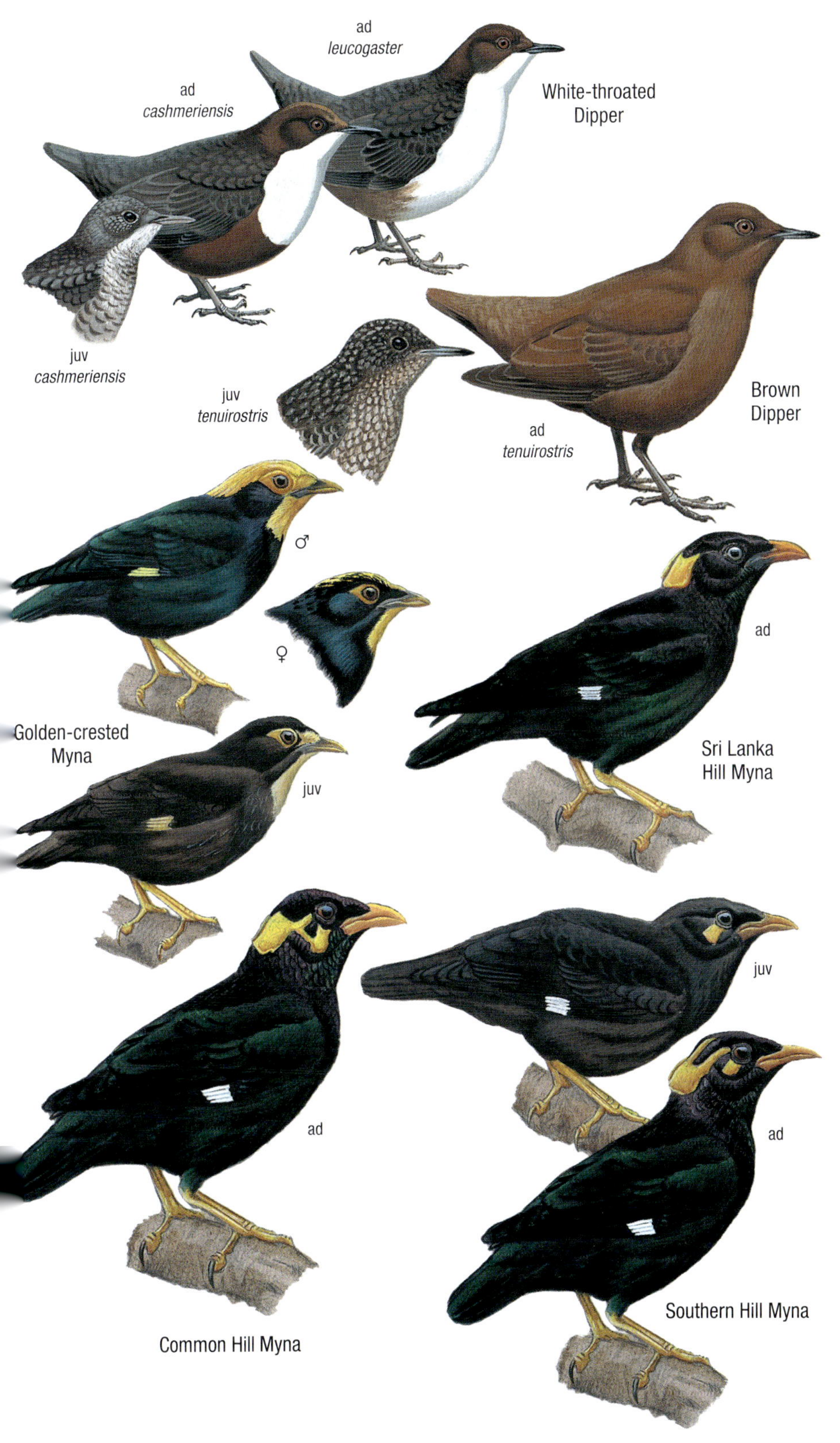
ad
leucogaster
ad
cashmeriensis
White-throated
Dipper
juv
cashmeriensis
juv
tenuirostris
ad
tenuirostris
Brown
Dipper
♂
♀
ad
Golden-crested
Myna
juv
Sri Lanka
Hill Myna
juv
ad
ad
Common Hill Myna
Southern Hill Myna

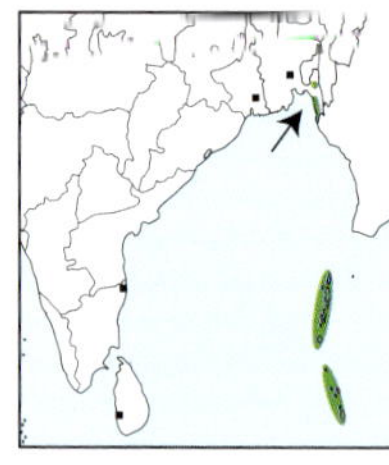

Asian Glossy Starling ***Aplonis panayensis*** 17–20cm

Resident on Andamans and Nicobars; formerly in Assam and NE India. Vagrant: Nepal. **ID** Adult glossy greenish-black, with bright red eye and stout black bill. Juvenile has blackish-brown upperparts with variable greenish gloss, and buffy-white underparts heavily streaked blackish-brown (streaking also with variable greenish gloss); eye yellowish-white. Adult bluer with dark eye in *A. p. tytleri* (Andamans) and eye whitish in *A. p. albiris* (Nicobars). **Voice** Calls have a metallic quality, a repeated *tsuu tsuu*, also shrill whistles, and descending *tseeeer*; high-pitched trill at roost. **HH** Chiefly arboreal. Feeds on insects, nectar and small figs with other starlings in flowering and fruiting trees. Coconut groves, forest edges and clearings with tall fig trees.

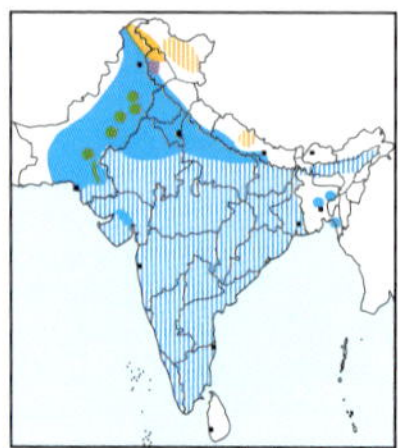

European Starling ***Sturnus vulgaris*** 25cm

Mainly winter visitor to N subcontinent; also partly resident in Pakistan, and summer visitor to Kashmir. **ID** Adult breeding is metallic green and purple with yellowish bill. Adult non-breeding has dark bill; upperparts heavily spangled with buff, wing feathers have broad buff fringes, and underparts boldly spotted with white. Juvenile entirely dusky brown, with whiter throat, and buff fringes to wing-coverts and flight feathers. **Voice** Song a varied combination of chirps, twitters, clicks and whistles with much mimicry. **HH** Typical starling, see Indian Pied. Forms large feeding flocks and huge, noisy roosts. Cultivation, damp grassland and irrigated lawns. **AN** Common Starling.

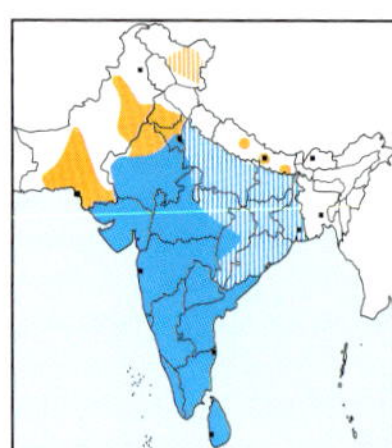

Rosy Starling ***Pastor roseus*** 19–24cm

Passage migrant in Pakistan and N India; winter visitor mainly to W and S India and Sri Lanka also Andamans. Vagrant: Bangladesh. **ID** Adult has blackish head with shaggy crest, pinkish mantle and underparts, blue-green gloss to wings, and dark-based reddish bill. In non-breeding and first-winter plumage much duller; pink of plumage partly obscured by buff fringes; black by greyish fringes, and bill is yellowish. Juvenile mainly sandy-brown, with stout yellowish bill, and broad pale fringes to wing feathers. **Voice** Song a long series of bubbling, warbling, whistled and grating phrases without mimicry. **HH** Typical starling, see Indian Pied, but often forms huge flocks at rich feeding sources; also feeds on nectar in flowering trees, cultivation and damp grassland.

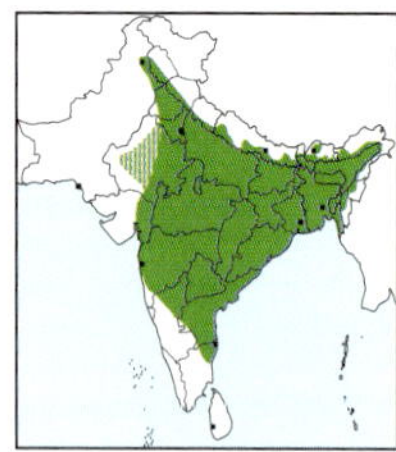

Indian Pied Starling ***Gracupica contra*** 22–25cm

Resident. Widespread in N, C and E subcontinent. **ID** Black and white, with white cheek patch and scapular line. Orange orbital skin and base to large, pointed yellowish bill. In flight, white uppertail-coverts contrast with black tail. Juvenile has black of plumage replaced by brown; white cheeks are washed with brown and less distinct, and breast-band is not clearly defined. *G. c. superciliaris* (Manipur) has white streaking on forehead and forecrown. **Voice** Song a prolonged series of melodic phrases interspersed by whistling, croaking, buzzing and chuckling notes, with much mimicry. **HH** Typical starling. Mainly terrestrial, has confident, waddling walk. Congregates in noisy roosts. Restless and garrulous. Flight direct, strong and fast. Cultivation, damp grassland, habitation, refuse dumps and sewage works. **AN** Asian Pied Starling.

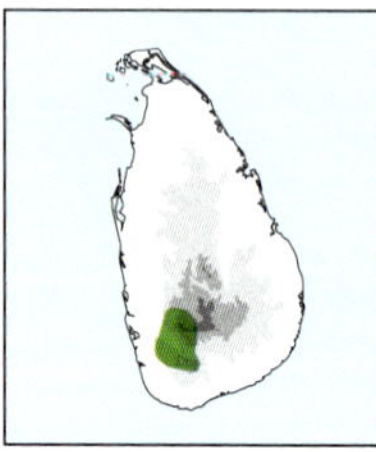

White-faced Starling ***Sturnornis albofrontatus*** 20cm

Resident. Sri Lanka. **ID** Adult has dirty white forehead and face, dark lavender-grey upperparts with slight green gloss, pale lavender-grey underparts with white streaking (underparts look brown-streaked from a distance). Bill and eye-ring pale bluish. Juvenile has dull brown upperparts and dark grey underparts, with whitish supercilium, dark eye-stripe, and white ear-coverts and throat. **Voice** Sharp, far-carrying *chyeck* with a ringing quality or at a slightly lower pitch without this quality. **HH** Arboreal, feeds chiefly in treetops on fruits, also nectar and insects. In pairs, small groups, or large mixed-species flocks. Undisturbed rainforest; also fruiting trees nearby. Globally threatened.

juv
ad
ad non-br
Asian Glossy
Starling
ad br
ad
juv
European
Starling
juv
Rosy Starling
ad
ad
supercilliaris
juv
contra
ad
contra
White-faced
Starling
juv
Indian Pied Starling

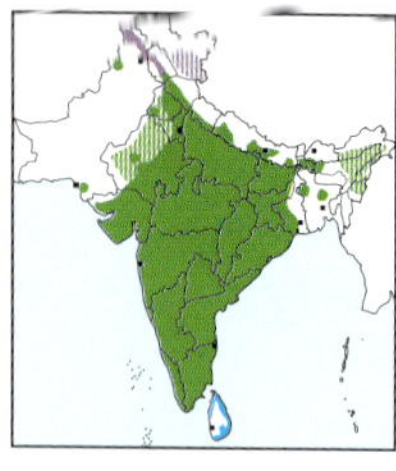

Brahminy Starling ***Sturnia pagodarum*** 20cm

Widespread resident; unrecorded in parts of north-west and north-east. **ID** Myna-like profile. In flight, shows white sides and tip to dark tail, and uniform wings without white wing patch. Adult has black crest, and rufous-orange sides of head and underparts (with paler shaft streaking). Yellowish bill with blue base, and blue or yellow skin behind eye. Juvenile lacks crest, but has grey-brown cap, paler orange-buff underparts, duller bill and eye patch. **Voice** Song a short, gurgling, drawn-out cry followed by a bubbling yodel. **HH** Cultivation with groves, open, dry forest, thorn scrub.

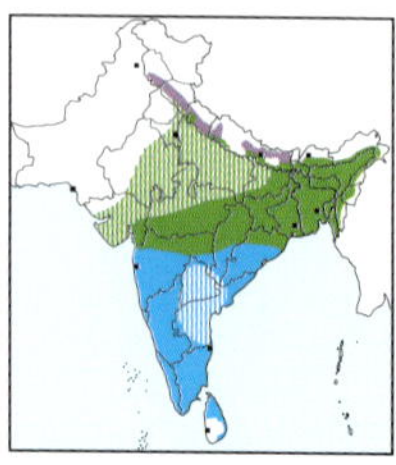

Chestnut-tailed Starling ***Sturnia malabarica*** 18.5–20.5cm

Resident in NE subcontinent and summer visitor to W and C Himalayas; winter visitor south to S India and Sri Lanka. **ID** Adult has grey head and upperparts, with whitish forehead and throat, and whitish lanceolate feathers on crown and nape and sides of neck and breast. Underparts rufous (variable in extent) and tail mainly chestnut with grey central feathers. Bill yellow with bluish base, eye whitish. Female more uniformly pale grey, and underparts are paler rufous-buff. Juvenile has pale sandy-grey upperparts and greyish-white underparts. **Voice** Rambling series of short, gravelly notes; low squeaky churrs with sudden outbursts of warbling and wheezing. **HH** Open wooded areas.

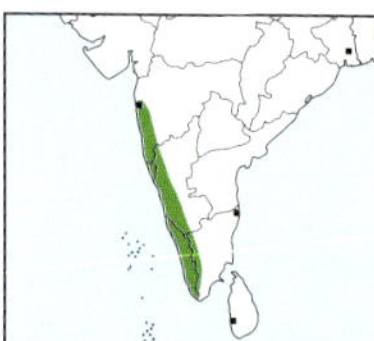

Malabar Starling ***Sturnia blythii*** 18.5–20.5cm

Resident in SW Peninsula. Differs from Chestnut-tailed in having white head and breast, which contrast strongly with grey of mantle and rufous of belly and flanks. Female has white of head confined to forehead and forecrown, and underparts are paler rufous. **Voice** Song more nasal and less harsh than Chestnut-tailed. **HH** Like Chestnut-tailed and often in flocks with that species. **AN** Blyth's Starling.

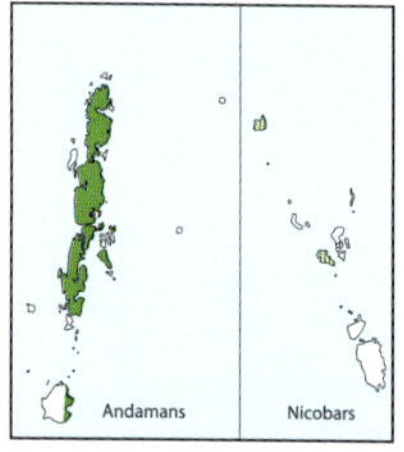

White-headed Starling ***Sturnia erythropygia*** 20cm

Resident. Andamans and Nicobars. **ID** Cream-white head and underparts, grey upperparts, glossy greenish-black wings and tail. Yellow bill with blue base, yellowish legs, and pale blue eyes. Juvenile has brownish-grey shaft streaks on crown, and rufous fringes to wing feathers. Nominate (Car Nicobar) has rufous rump and undertail-coverts and sides/tip of tail. *S. e. andamanensis* (Andamans) has pale grey rump, white sides/tip of tail, cream to buff undertail-coverts. **Voice** Song a loud series of musical notes and mimicry, mixed with snarling, snorting, squawks and rattles. **HH** Forest clearings and edges, secondary woodland, grassland, cultivation.

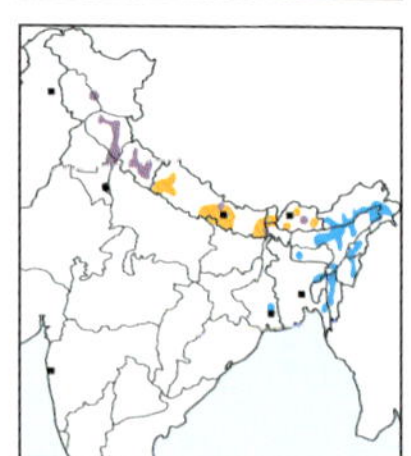

Spot-winged Starling ***Saroglossa spilopterus*** 19cm

Summers in Himalayan foothills east to Bhutan. Winters in Assam, Arunachal and NE India. Vagrant: Bangladesh. **ID** White wing patch and yellow eye. Male has blackish mask, reddish-chestnut throat, pale rusty-orange breast, dark-scalloped greyish upperparts and rufous tail. Female has browner upperparts and whitish underparts with greyish-brown markings on throat and breast. Juvenile similar to female, but has buff wing-bar, more uniform upperparts and dark eye. **Voice** Song a continuous harsh, unmusical jumble of discordant notes; calls include an explosive scolding *kwerrh* and a grating nasal *schaik*. **HH** Prefers to feed on flower nectar. In noisy flocks, often with mynas and drongos on flowering and fruiting trees, rarely on ground. Has bullying manner when feeding. Open broadleaved forest and well-wooded areas.

Chestnut-tailed
Starling
juv
Brahminy
Starling
juv
♂
ad
♂
Malabar Starling
ad
andamanensis
♀
♂
White-headed Starling
Spot winged Starling

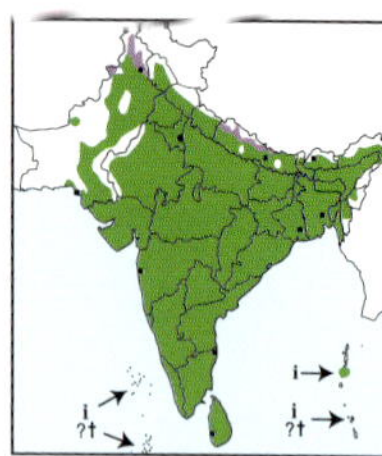

Common Myna *Acridotheres tristis* 25cm

Widespread resident; unrecorded in parts of NW and NE subcontinent. **ID** Brownish myna with yellow orbital skin, white wing patch and white tail tip. Adult has glossy black head and breast merging into maroon-brown of rest of body. Bill and legs yellow and eye black. Juvenile duller, with brownish-black head and paler brown throat and breast. In Sri Lanka (*A. t. melanosternus*) is darker with more extensive yellow orbital skin. **Voice** Song disjointed, noisy and tuneless, with gurgling and whistling; alarm call a distinctive, harsh *chake-chake*. **HH** Habitation and cultivation.

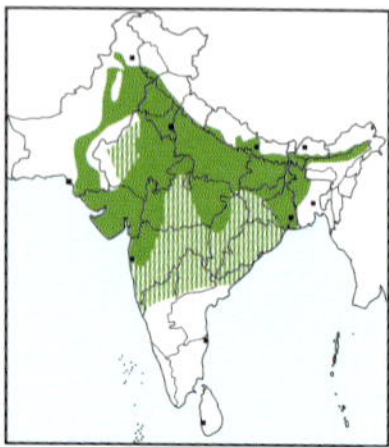

Bank Myna *Acridotheres ginginianus* 22cm

Resident. Widespread in N and C subcontinent. **ID** From Common by smaller size, bluish-grey coloration, small frontal crest, orange-red orbital patch, orange-yellow bill, red eye, orange-buff patch at base of primaries and on underwing-coverts, and orange-buff sides and tip to tail. Juvenile duller and browner than adult, with buffish-white wing patch and rufous-buff tips to tail. **Voice** Similar to Common, but not so loud and strident. **HH** Cultivation, damp grassland and habitation.

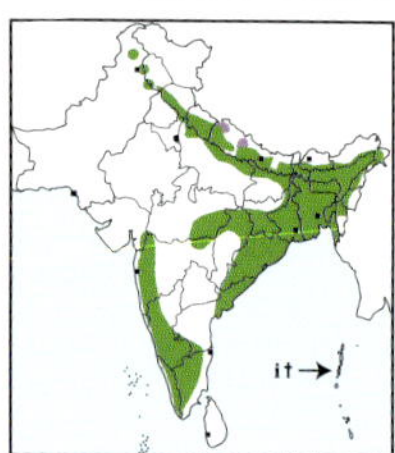

Jungle Myna *Acridotheres fuscus* 24cm

Resident. Himalayas south to Bangladesh and Andhra Pradesh, and W India. **ID** Adult resembles Bank Myna, but has more prominent frontal crest, white patch at base of primaries and white tip to tail, and lacks bare orbital skin. Eye pale. Black of crown and ear-coverts merges into grey or grey-brown upperparts (with less distinct 'cap' than Bank). Bill orange, with dark blue base to lower mandible. Juvenile browner, with darker brown head; has pale shafts on ear-coverts, pale mottling on throat, all-yellow bill, and frontal crest is much reduced. *A. f. mahrattensis* (peninsular India) browner (less slate-grey) above compared to nominate (north and north-east) and has grey or bluish-white (rather than lemon-yellow) iris. In extreme north-east (*A. f. fumidus*) is darker, sootier, above and below. **Voice** Song similar to Common. **HH** Cultivation near well-wooded areas, and edges of habitation.

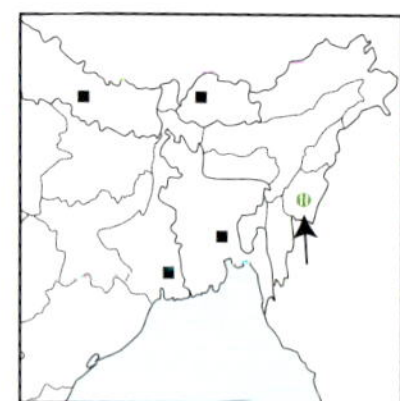

Collared Myna *Acridotheres albocinctus* 25cm

Resident. Manipur but few recent records. **ID** Adult mainly dark grey, with large whitish patches on sides of neck that join as white streaking on hindneck, and has white tips to dark grey undertail-coverts. Neck patch strongly washed buff in fresh plumage. Eye pale blue, bill orange. Variable frontal crest and shaggy hind crest. White patch on wing smaller than in Great. Juvenile dark brown, with paler throat and belly; diffuse brownish white patch on side of neck (smaller than adult's), which is best feature from juvenile Great. **Voice** Undocumented, presumably similar to others in genus. **HH** Often feeds and roosts with Great. Open country with elephant grass, moist areas including marshes and cultivation, and villages.

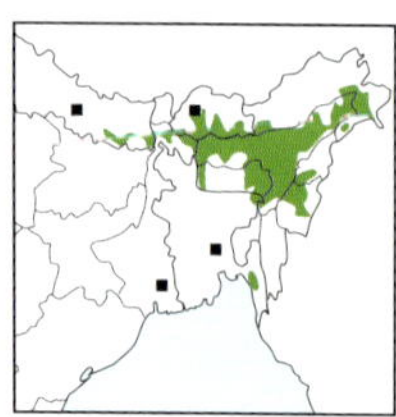

Great Myna *Acridotheres grandis* 24.5–27.5cm

Resident. NE India, Nepal and Bangladesh. **ID** Similar to Jungle Myna, but has uniform blackish-grey upperparts (little contrast between crown and mantle and rump and tail), and uniform dark grey underparts (including belly and flanks), strongly contrasting with white undertail-coverts. Further, has more prominent frontal crest, all-yellow bill, and reddish to orange-brown iris. Juvenile browner and lacks prominent frontal crest; throat diffusely mottled with white on some birds. Brown belly with diffuse brownish-white fringes and broad whitish tips to brown undertail-coverts are best distinctions from juvenile Jungle. **Voice** Song very similar to Common Myna. **HH** Open country with elephant grass, cultivation and villages.

ad
tristis
Common Myna
ad
ad
juv
Bank Myna
ad
fuscus
ad
Jungle Myna
juv
fuscus
juv
ad
mahrattensis
ad
juv
Collared Myna
Great Myna

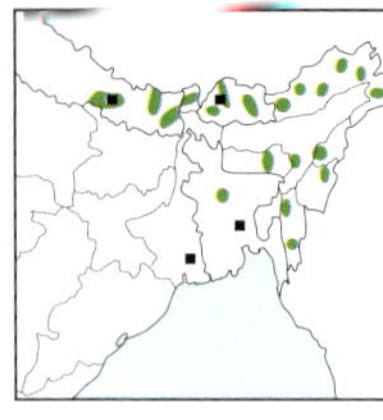

Purple Cochoa *Cochoa purpurea* 25–28cm

Summer visitor. Himalayas, mainly east from Nepal, and NE Indian hills. Vagrant: Bangladesh. **ID** Adult male is dull purplish-grey with lilac-blue crown, black mask, lilac panels on wing, and lilac-blue tail with black tip. Adult female recalls male (with similar pattern to wings and tail) but has rusty-brown upperparts and brownish-orange underparts. Both sexes have lilac-blue eye-ring and small bare patch behind eye (pinkish in Green Cochoa). Juvenile has black scaling to crown, indistinct buff streaking and spotting on upperparts, orange-buff underparts with bold black barring, and buff tips to wing-coverts; wings and tail as adult. **Voice** Song a flute-like *peeeee*; also, *peeee-you-peeee*; low chuckling call. **HH** Quiet and unobtrusive. Rather lethargic, perching still for long periods in canopy and midstorey. Seen most often in spring when males sing from treetops. Mainly dense, moist broadleaved evergreen forest; pine forest in Khasi Hills.

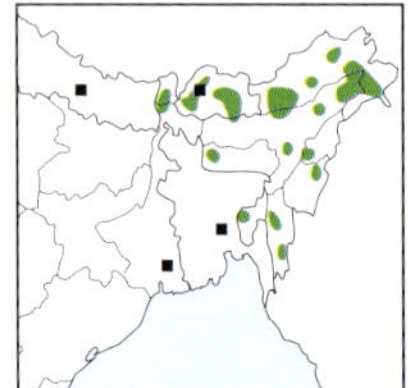

Green Cochoa *Cochoa viridis* 25–28cm

Resident. Himalayas and NE India. Vagrant: Nepal. **ID** Adult mainly green, with shining blue crown and nape (plus black lores and supercilium), faint black scaling on mantle, silvery-blue panels on wing, and silvery-blue tail with black tip. As Purple Cochoa, tail is all black from below. Sexes similar, but female has a bronze panel at base of secondaries. Both sexes have pinkish eye-ring and small bare patch behind eye (lilac in Purple). Juvenile has wing and tail patterns as adult, but has white crown with black scaling, orange-buff spotting and dark scaling on upperparts and underparts, and buff tips to wing-coverts. Adult-like wings and tail, and heavily spotted upperparts, are best features from juvenile Purple. First-winter male darker brownish-green above than adult male (closer in coloration to Purple), and first-winter female has white cheek patch and yellowish-green underparts. **Voice** Pure, drawn-out monotone whistle, thinner and weaker than Purple. **HH** Similar habits to Purple. Dense moist, broadleaved evergreen forest, usually on steep ground.

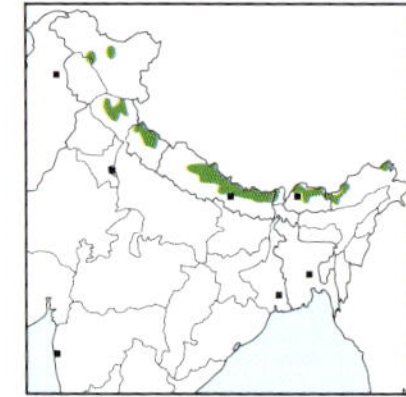

Grandala *Grandala coelicolor* 19–23cm

Resident. Himalayas. **ID** A slim, long-winged, starling-like chat. A strong, streamlined flier, often in large flocks; on the ground, flicks open wings and tail. Adult male almost entirely purple-blue with glistening sheen, black lores, wings and tail. Adult female and immature male dark brown, streaked white, with blue wash to rump and uppertail-coverts, and white patches on wing. Juvenile similar to female but darker brown and more boldly streaked; lacks blue on rump and uppertail-coverts. **Voice** No territorial song as highly sociable. Sounds include a short, sweet, downslurred *chyuuu*; calls include ringing finch-like *tji-u* and shrill *dee dee dee*. **HH** Chiefly in flocks, comprising up to several hundred birds in non-breeding season; in summer 50 or more may congregate. Flocks circle buoyantly for long periods high over valleys and ridges, catching insects on the wing; also seeks insects on ground. Often perches upright on rocks, recalling a rock thrush. Rocky slopes and ridges, and stony meadows; alpine zone in summer, lower altitudes in winter.

Purple Cochoa
♀
♂
♀ juv
♂ juv
Green Cochoa
♂
♀
♂ first-year
♀ first-year
juv
Grandala
♂
♀

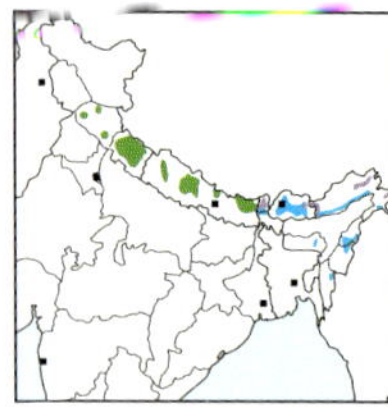

Long-tailed Thrush *Zoothera dixoni* 25–27cm

Resident. Himalayas. Winters in NE India. **ID** Best told from Alpine and Himalayan Thrush by comparatively broad and prominent wing-bars (buff tips to median coverts form distinct spotting), with blackish centres to coverts, which are darker than mantle. Bill and face pattern closer to Alpine than Himalayan: has pale base to lower mandible, and boldly marked face (with pale lores and extensive paleness on ear-coverts, typically with more clearly defined dark malar and ear-covert spot than Alpine). Upperparts colder and greyer than Alpine and especially Himalayan (valid only in C and E Himalayas). **Voice** Song comprises long-sustained, rambling series of mainly harsh notes. **HH** Habits similar to Alpine. Breeds in forest understorey; in winter, also second growth and open country with bushes.

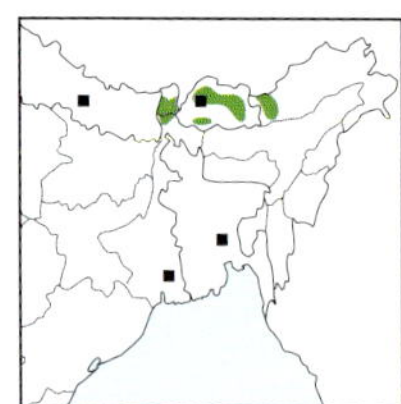

Alpine Thrush *Zoothera mollissima* 25–27cm

Resident. Himalayas. Winters in Meghalaya and Manipur. **ID** From Himalayan Thrush by colder, grey-brown upperparts, shorter bill with pinkish or yellowish base to lower mandible, yellowish or orangish legs and feet, and subtly different face pattern. Lores more extensively pale, as are ear-coverts and typically shows more pronounced dark patch at rear. See Long-tailed Thrush for differences from that species. **Voice** Song consists of short, hurried strophes of highly variable complex notes. Mainly rasping, grating, scratchy, cracked voice and a few squeaky, clearer notes. Rather even tempo, begins and ends rather abruptly. **HH** Secretive and shy. Male often sings from treetops, but keeps hidden. Feeds mainly on ground and flies into cover when disturbed. Summers on mossy rock-and-grass slopes with bushes and above treeline; winters in pastures bordering forest and forest glades. **AN** Plain-backed Thrush.

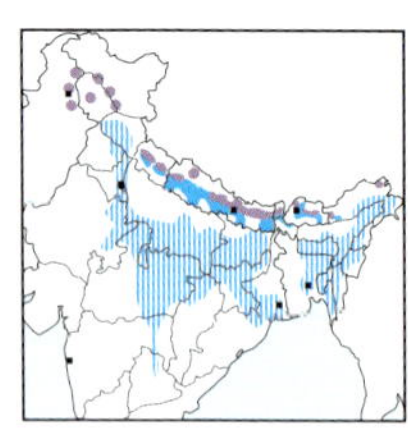

Himalayan Thrush *Zoothera salimalii* 25–27cm

Resident. E Himalayas. **ID** From Alpine by warmer, rufous-brown upperparts, longer all-dark bill, pinkish legs and feet, and subtly different face pattern. Area of paleness on lores is more restricted and has dark bar between bill and eye which can extend below eye; ear-coverts are less extensively pale and usually does not show dark patch at rear. See Long-tailed Thrush for differences from that species. **Voice** Much more musical and 'thrush-like' than Alpine. A mix of rich, drawn-out clear notes and shorter, thinner ones, with hardly any harsh scratchy notes. Slower speed, with variation in pitch among notes more pronounced than Alpine; song seems to trail off at end. **HH** Very secretive, shuns open areas. Breeds in old coniferous forest with rhododendrons, other broadleaved trees, and lush undergrowth of scrub and herbs; winters in dense broadleaved forest.

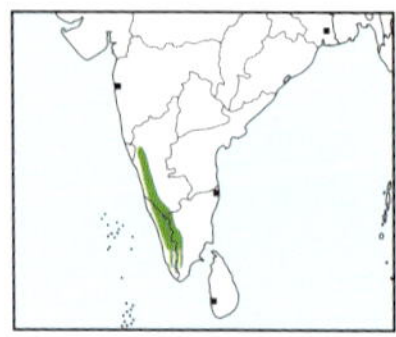

Scaly Thrush *Zoothera dauma* 28–30cm

Breeds in Himalayas and Nagaland. Winters south to Maharashtra, Odisha, Bangladesh and Mizoram. **ID** Boldly scaled with pale face, large black eye, and dark patch on ear-coverts. In Himalayas from Alpine and Long-tailed by bold black scaling on golden olive upperparts, and golden-olive panels on wing, with dark bar at tip of primary coverts. See Vagrants for comparison with White's Thrush. **Voice** Song a rather rapid, broken series of abrupt, simple, rich notes mixed with squawks. Often sings very early and very late in day. **HH** Shy, retiring and quiet. Forages on forest floor by searching among leaf litter; progresses on ground by walking and running. Flies up into thick foliage at least disturbance. Breeds in mature forest with thick bushy understorey; winters in dense forest, grassy clearings and well-wooded areas.

Nilgiri Thrush *Zoothera neilgherriensis* 28cm

Resident. Western Ghats. **ID** Has darker, browner and more uniform upperparts than Scaly (mantle and scapulars lack the golden-olive subterminal spots which give Scaly its spangled appearance). Also bill is larger, and face plainer and more regularly marked with black (lacking dark patches). **Voice** Song a highly complex series of strophes, similar to Scaly. **HH** Wags tail and rear body, flicks wings and tail. Shy and skulking in dark wet ravines in dense evergreen forest and sholas.

Sri Lanka Thrush *Zoothera imbricata* 24cm

Resident. Sri Lanka. **ID** Smaller than Scaly with shorter tail, and bill is proportionately longer; upperparts darker olive-brown (lacking spangling), has rufous-buff ground colour to underparts, with narrower black scaling, and head is more uniformly marked. **Voice** Song a series of eight or more rich single whistles, *tiyeuur*, each mellower and more slurred than Scaly, only given at dawn and dusk; calls include repeated high, long-drawn whistle and brief scolding in alarm. **HH** Habits like Scaly. Feeds mainly on ground, scratching amongst dead leaves. Dense, moist forest and adjoining well-wooded areas.

Long-tailed Thrush
ad
juv
ad
Alpine Thrush
ad
Himalayan Thrush
juv
ad
Scaly Thrush
ad
ad
Nilgiri Thrush
Sri Lanka Thrush

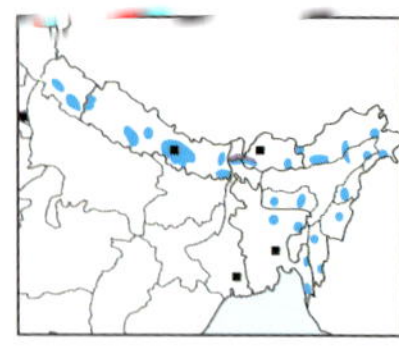

Dark-sided Thrush *Zoothera marginata* 24–25cm

Resident. Himalayas and NE India. Vagrant: Bangladesh. **ID** From Long-billed by smaller size, smaller bill, rufous-brown upperparts and wing panel, and paler underparts with prominent scaling on breast and flanks; also more strongly patterned sides of head (variable, but usually with paler lores, more distinct dark and pale patches on ear-coverts, pale crescent behind). **Voice** Song a thin whistle like Scaly, but softer and shorter; soft deep guttural *tchuck* call. **HH** Habits like Long-billed. Dense moist forest near streams.

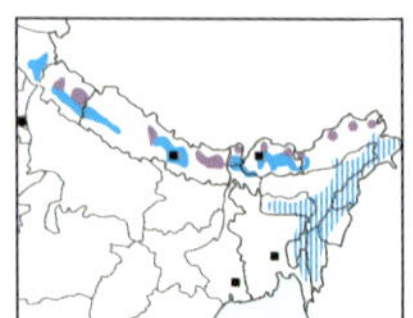

Long-billed Thrush *Zoothera monticola* 26–28cm

Resident. Himalayas and NE India. Vagrant: Bangladesh. **ID** From Dark-sided by larger size and bill, more uniform head-sides (dark lores, diffuse dark malar stripe and narrow white throat patch), dark slaty-olive upperparts, darker and more uniform breast and flanks (both with diffuse dark spotting), and dark spotting on whitish belly. **Voice** Song a loud, slow plaintive whistle of 2–3 notes; alarm a loud *zaaaaaaaa*. **HH** Solitary, shy and crepuscular; skulks on ground. Dense moist forest with thick undergrowth.

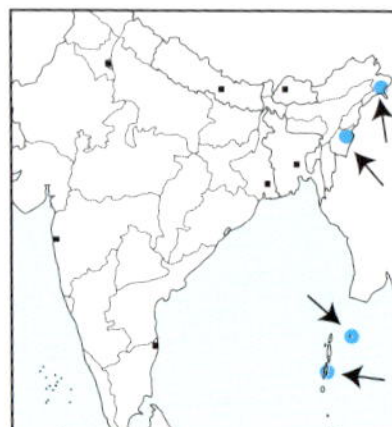

Siberian Thrush *Geokichla sibirica* 20.5–23cm

Winter visitor. Andaman and Nicobar Islands, Gujarat, Maharashtra, SW Bengal and Manipur **ID** Male dark slate-grey, with striking white supercilium and broad white fringes to undertail-coverts. First-winter male resembles adult male, but is paler grey, has buff supercilium, buff markings on throat, browner wings, buff tips to greater coverts and pale mottling on underparts. Female has buff supercilium, dark malar stripe, and dark spotting and scaling on underparts. Compared to female Pied, supercilium typically extends around ear-coverts, tips to median and greater coverts are much less prominent or non-existent, lacks pale tips to tertials, and flanks are washed with olive-brown. **Voice** Soft *stit* contact call; soft *chrssss* in alarm. **HH** Usually terrestrial, also visits fruiting trees. Thick undergrowth in forest. **TN** Formerly placed in *Zoothera*.

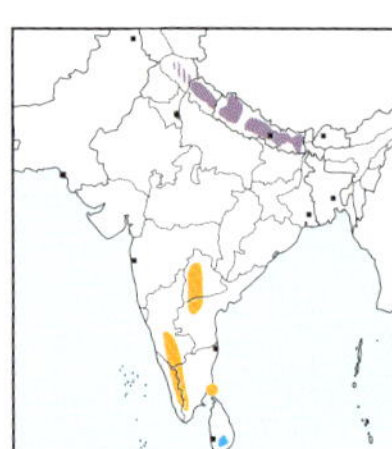

Pied Thrush *Geokichla wardii* 18–20cm

Breeds in Himalayas; winters in S India and Sri Lanka. **ID** Adult male has white supercilium, prominent white tips to wing feathers (median and greater coverts, tertials and secondaries), white barring on rump, white-and-black barred flanks, and yellowish bill and legs. Female has buff supercilium, olive-brown upperparts, prominent buff tips to wing-coverts and tertials, buff spotting on olive-brown breast, and white belly and flanks (with prominent dark scaling). First-winter male similar to adult male, but black of head/body duller, throat mainly white with dark malar, black breast spotted white, and supercilium and tips to wing-coverts buffish. Juvenile has buff streaking on mantle and breast. **Voice** Song 2–4 sweet high-pitched notes, the last often a short rattle; spitting *ptz ptz-ptz-ptz* in alarm. **HH** Usually keeps to ground or undergrowth. Forages mainly by hopping on ground, rummaging amongst leaf litter. Open broadleaved forest, forest edges, second growth with scattered trees; thickly vegetated ravines. **TN** Formerly placed in *Zoothera*.

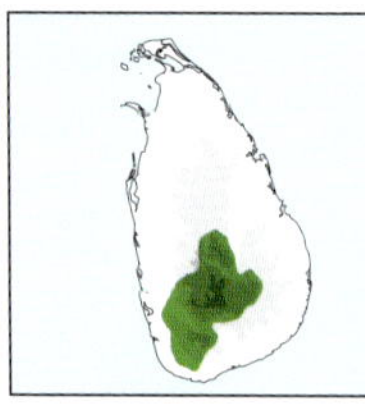

Spot-winged Thrush *Geokichla spiloptera* 21–23cm

Resident. Sri Lanka. **ID** Adult has diffuse black crescent behind ear-coverts and patch through eye, bold (but sparse) black spotting on white breast and flanks, and prominent white tips to median and greater coverts. Juvenile has diffuse head pattern, buff streaking on mantle, scaled breast, and less distinct buff tips to wing-coverts. **Voice** Varied songs, rich whistled melodies, given from cover; call a plain, very high-pitched sibilant whistle. **HH** Crepuscular and rather shy. Dense, moist forest and well-wooded areas. **TN** Formerly placed in *Zoothera*.

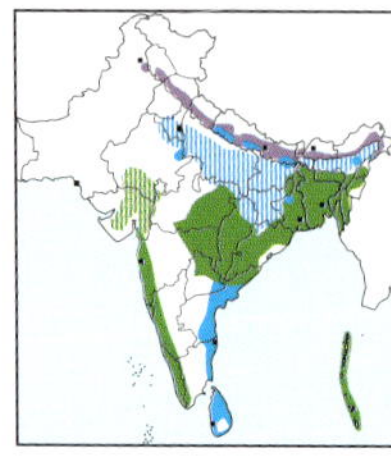

Orange-headed Thrush *Geokichla citrina* 20–23cm

Summer visitor to Himalayas; resident in NE, C and W India, Bangladesh and Andaman and Nicobar Islands; winter visitor to E India and Sri Lanka. **ID** Adult has orange head and underparts; male with blue-grey mantle, female with olive wash to mantle. Juvenile has buffish-orange streaking on upperparts and mottled breast. Shows white bands on underwing in flight. Nominate (Himalayas and north-east, winters south to peninsula and Sri Lanka) has head entirely orange (although may show very indistinct dark vertical bar below eye and at rear of ear-coverts). *G. c. cyanotus* (peninsula) has vertical blackish or chestnut stripes across white ear-coverts, and white throat. *G. c. andamanensis* and *G. c. albogularis* (Andamans and Nicobars) lack the white shoulder patch of the two continental races, have pale throat and face and diffuse vertical orange stripe below eye. **Voice** Rich, sweet, variable song of short, frequently repeated phrases; thin *tzeet* in flight. **HH** Crepuscular; shy, quiet and terrestrial. Damp, shady places in forests, often near water; ravines, plantations and well-wooded areas. **TN** Formerly placed in *Zoothera*.

ad
Dark-sided Thrush
ad
Siberian Thrush
♂
Long-billed Thrush
♀
juv
♂
♂
1st winter
♀
Pied Thrush
ad
juv
♂
cyanotus
♂
citrina
juv
citrina
Spot-winged Thrush
Orange-headed
Thrush
♀
citrina

Sri Lanka Whistling Thrush *Myophonus blighi* 19–21.5cm

Resident. Sri Lanka. **ID** Small with short tail and stout black bill. Male dark blue with blacker head, with some glistening blue on body, especially pronounced on inner wing-coverts. Female brown, with blue shoulder patch; has rufescent cast to lores, throat and breast. Juvenile similar to female, but has more rusty-brown underparts, with ochre shaft streaks on head, neck and breast. **Voice** Very high-pitched whistling *reee* or *reee-reee* call; song comprises high-pitched whistles on varying pitch. **HH** Like Blue Whistling, but shy. Mountain streams in moist, dense montane forest. Globally threatened.

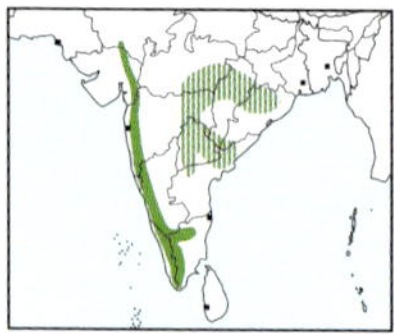

Malabar Whistling Thrush *Myophonus horsfieldii* 25–30cm

Resident. Hills of C and W India. **ID** Adult blackish, with blue forehead and shoulders. Bill black. Wings and tail edged with glistening blue. Juvenile more sooty-brown and lacks blue forehead. **Voice** Song comprises slow, clear whistles up and down the scale, slower and mellower than Blue Whistling; intense penetrating *schree* call, less harsh than Blue Whistling. **HH** Habits like Blue Whistling but shy. Rocky, fast-flowing hill streams in forest, second growth, well-wooded areas and cardamom plantations.

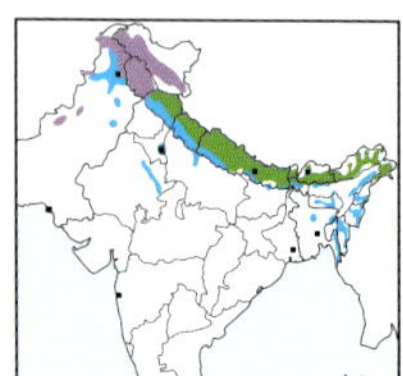

Blue Whistling Thrush *Myophonus caeruleus* 29–35cm

Resident. N Balochistan, Himalayas and NE India. **ID** Adult is dark blue-black, with head and body spangled with glistening silvery-blue. Forehead, shoulders and fringes to wings and tail are brighter blue. Silvery-blue spots on median coverts particularly striking. Has stout yellow bill. Juvenile browner and lacks blue spangling. Wings and tail duller blue than adult. **Voice** Melodic song, with clear whistles up and down scale; calls include a shrill *kree*. **HH** Crepuscular, starts singing before dawn. Forages on ground, moving by long hops and short rapid runs, turns over leaves and digs in soft ground. Forest and wooded areas, usually close to streams or rivers.

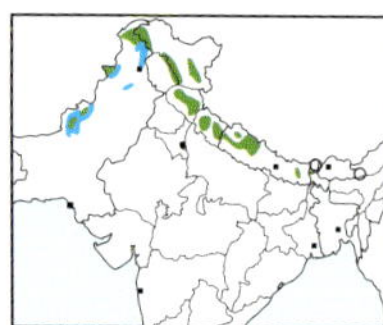

Mistle Thrush *Turdus viscivorus* 27–28cm

Resident. Balochistan and W Himalayas. **ID** Large size, pale grey-brown upperparts, whitish edges to wing feathers, and spotted breast. Juvenile has buffish-white spotting to upperparts; lacks golden-buff bands on wing of Scaly Thrush. **Voice** Song loud, ringing and rather melancholy, with short repeated phrases and long pauses; calls include characteristic rattle. **HH** Summers in open coniferous forest and juniper shrubbery, also in open rocky areas with stunted junipers; winters on grassy slopes and at forest edges.

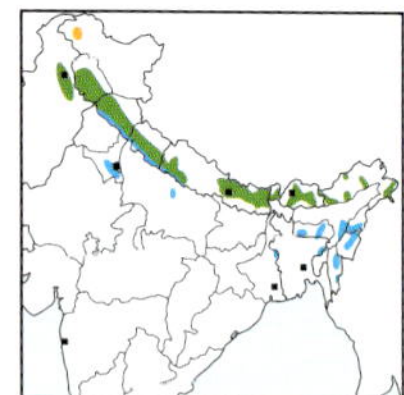

Grey-winged Blackbird *Turdus boulboul* 27–29cm

Resident in Himalayas and winters south to NE India. **ID** Adult male is black, with pale grey panel on wing (created by largely grey greater coverts and tertials), and diffuse grey scaling on belly and flanks (whiter and more prominent on vent and undertail-coverts). Bill orange and legs yellowish. Female is olive-brown; has paler rufous-brown panel on wing (with greater coverts becoming paler buffish or greyish towards tips, contrasting with dark brown primary coverts). Juvenile has orange-buff streaking above, orange-buff tips to median coverts, and brown barring on orange-buff underparts; wing panel similar to adult. **Voice** Rich melodious song, with repeated two-note whistles; *chook-chook-chook* call. **HH** Solitary or in pairs in breeding season; in small flocks, sometimes with other thrushes, in winter. Feeding behaviour similar to other *Turdus*, see Tickell's. Summers in moist broadleaved and mixed forests; winters in open forest, and forest edges.

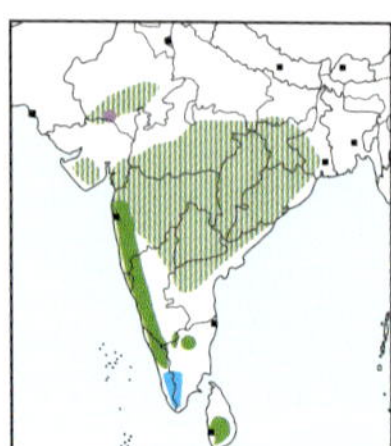

Indian Blackbird *Turdus simillimus* 19–22cm

Resident. Hills of peninsula and Sri Lanka. **ID** Variable. *T. m. nigropileus/spencei/simillimus* males have brownish slate-grey upperparts, with darker brown to blackish crown and ear-coverts, resulting in capped effect (especially *nigropileus*) and underparts are paler brownish-grey, with whitish lower belly and undertail-coverts in *spencei*. All have distinct eye-ring, patch of orange post-orbital skin, and orange legs and feet. Females are more uniform brown, with paler underparts; lack distinct dark malar of female Tickell's Thrush. Juveniles have buffish underparts with broad dark barring and spotting, and indistinct buff shaft streaks on upperparts. Male *T. m. bourdilloni* (SW peninsula) and smaller *T. m. kinnisii* (Sri Lanka) are uniform slate-grey (purer bluish-grey in *kinnisii*). Bare parts of *kinnisii* can be bright red. Female *bourdilloni* fairly uniform olive-brown, with warmer buffish olive-brown on breast and a slightly paler (and diffusely streaked) throat. Female *kinnisii* similar to male. **Voice** Song a rapid series of rich, varied, short, and usually paired notes with much mimicry; in Sri Lanka a distinctive, sharp series of warbling whistles. Calls include a rapid hard rattle; in Sri Lanka a high ascending trill. **HH** Breeds in moist forest and well-wooded areas; winters lower down in similar habitat.

♂
♀
Sri Lanka
Whistling Thrush
Malabar
Whistling Thrush
ad
juv
juv
ad
Blue
Whistling Thrush
juv
ad
Mistle Thrush
juv ♂
♂
♀
Grey-winged Blackbird
♂
kinnisii
♀
nigropileus
Indian Blackbird
♂
nigropileus

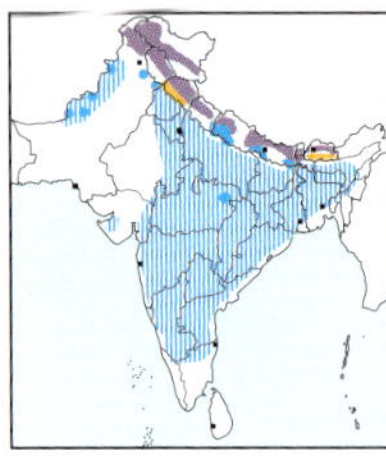

Tickell's Thrush *Turdus unicolor* 20–25cm

Resident. Summers Himalayas; winters mainly further east and south in India and W Pakistan. **ID** Small, compact thrush with rather plain face, yellowish or pale brown bill, and pale legs. Male pale bluish-grey with whitish belly and vent. Yellow bill and fine yellow eye-ring. First-winter male similar but has pale throat and submoustachial stripe and dark malar stripe, pale tips to greater coverts, and often has spotting on breast. Female from female Indian Blackbird by combination of smaller size, white throat, dark (streaked) malar stripe, spotting on breast (if present), and orange-buff wash to breast and flanks. Female Black-breasted Thrush has much brighter orange sides to breast. **Voice** Song a series of phrases with slurred and staccato notes, regionally variable; in Murree Hills (Pakistan) a three-note whistled warble; calls include soft *juk-juk*. **HH** Feeds on ground. If disturbed flies up into nearby canopy. Summers in open forest and well-wooded areas, heavy forest in Kashmir; winters in well-wooded areas.

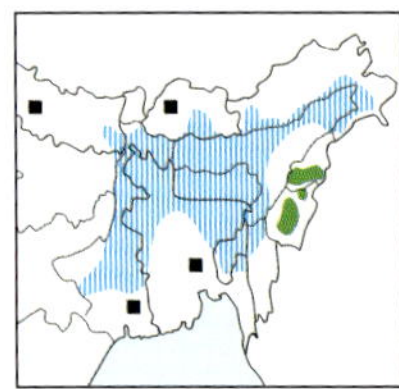

Black-breasted Thrush *Turdus dissimilis* 22–23.5cm

Resident in NE India; winters south to Bangladesh. Vagrant: Nepal. **ID** Male has black head and breast, grey upperparts, orange lower breast and flanks, and white belly and vent. Female has dark olive-grey upperparts, plain face, prominent dark (streaked) malar stripe and dark spotting on olive-grey upper breast, whitish throat (variably streaked dark) and submoustachial stripe, and orange lower breast and flanks. Lack of supercilium and boldly spotted breast separate it from Eyebrowed Thrush. **Voice** Song sweet and mellow, 3–8 notes per phrase; calls include a resounding *tup-tup... tup-tup-tup-tup-tup* etc. **HH** Very shy. Breeds in moist, broadleaved forest; also scrub and mangroves in winter.

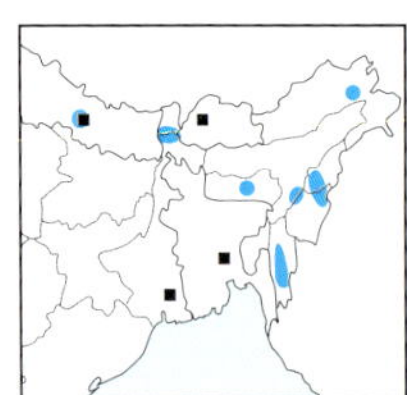

Grey-sided Thrush *Turdus feae* 22–23.5cm

Winter visitor. Mainly NE India. Vagrant: Nepal. **ID** Superficially resembles Eyebrowed, with white supercilium, dark lores and white crescent below eye. Adult male has rufescent-olive upperparts, including crown and ear-coverts, and grey underparts, becoming paler on belly and vent. Female similar to male, but is whiter on throat, breast and belly, and has brown-streaked malar stripe. In first-winter, grey of breast and flanks variably washed rufous-brown, and coloration of underparts can approach that of dullest Eyebrowed. Best told by rufescent crown, ear-coverts and sides of neck (these areas have distinct greyish cast on Eyebrowed). First-winter similar to female, but has pale tips to greater coverts. **Voice** Calls include thin *zeeee*, thinner than Eyebrowed, and a crisp rattle. **HH** Wary. Winters in forest, often with Eyebrowed. Globally threatened.

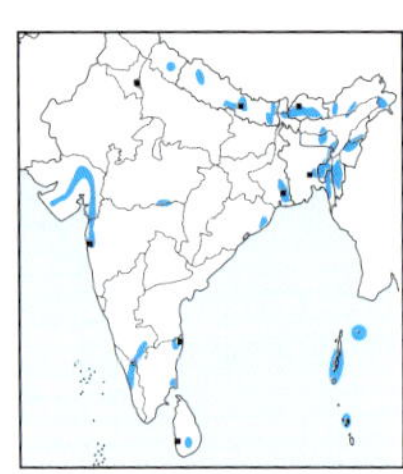

Eyebrowed Thrush *Turdus obscurus* 21–23cm

Winter visitor. E Himalayas and NE India. **ID** Striking features are white supercilium and white crescent below eye, contrasting with dark lores. From Grey-sided by peachy-orange flanks contrasting with white belly. Adult male has blue-grey head, including throat, with just a small area of white on chin. Female has olive-brown crown and nape, browner ear-coverts, white throat and submoustachial stripe, dark malar stripe, narrow grey gorget across upper breast, and duller orange breast and flanks. First-winter similar to female but has fine greater covert wing-bar; first-winter males brighter, with more grey on ear-coverts and upper breast. **Voice** Call a thin drawn-out *tseep*. **HH** Escapes into canopy if alarmed; sometimes with other thrushes. Habits similar to other *Turdus*, see Tickell's. Open forest.

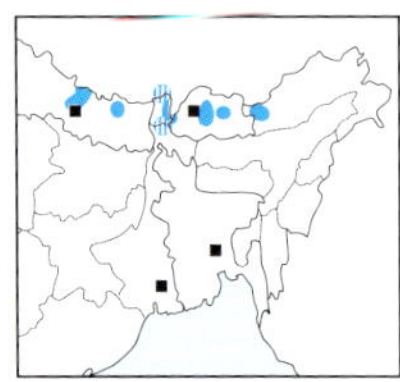

White-backed Thrush *Turdus kessleri* 28cm

Winter visitor. E Himalayas. **ID** Male from Chestnut by black head, neck and upper breast, and creamy-white mantle and lower breast. Female mirrors pattern of male: head, neck and breast are greyish-brown, mantle variably pale grey-brown to greyish-cream but always shows contrast with hindneck, and has variable, diffuse buffish division between brown of upper breast and ginger-brown of rest of underparts; rump and uppertail-coverts have distinct ginger cast. **Voice** Calls include nasal rattle, soft *dug dug*. **HH** Shrubberies and stands of juniper, *Berberis* bushes and potato fields. **AN** Kessler's Thrush.

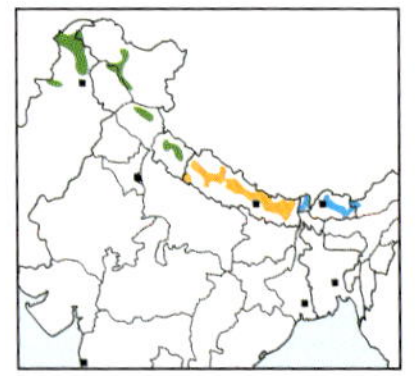

Tibetan Blackbird *Turdus maximus* 23–28cm

Resident in NW Himalayas. Winters from Uttarakhand to Arunachal Pradesh. **ID** Larger with longer wings and tail than Common Blackbird (see Vagrants). Male black with yellow bill, and lacks or has indistinct yellow orbital ring. Female uniform dark sooty-brown, lacking paler throat, with duller yellow bill. **Voice** Song a series of rapid metallic notes, squeaks, wheezes and guttural caws, with pure whistles, very repetitious; calls include rattling *chak-chak-chak*. **HH** Summers on rocky and grassy slopes with dwarf juniper; winters in juniper stands or shrubberies.

♂
1st-winter
♂
♀
Tickell's Thrush
♂
♀
Black-breasted Thrush
♂
♀
Grey-sided Thrush
♂
♀
1st-winter
Eyebrowed Thrush
♂
♀
White-backed Thrush
♂
♀
Tibetan Blackbird

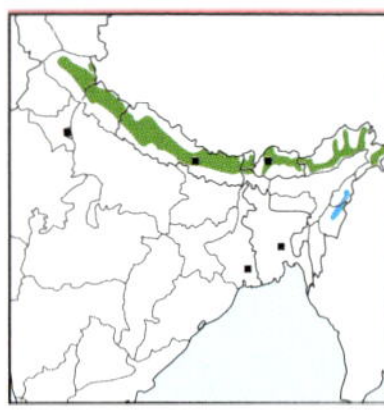

White-collared Blackbird *Turdus albocinctus* 26–28cm

Resident. Himalayas and NE India. **ID** Adult male is mainly black, with white throat and broad white collar; bill and legs yellow. Female has variable pale greyish-white to buffish collar, greyish head, while rest of plumage is rufous-brown with pale feather fringes on underparts. Juvenile lacks collar; has orange-buff streaking on upperparts, orange-buff tips to coverts (forming double wing-bar), and orange-buff underparts with dark brown spotting and barring. **Voice** Song a melancholy series of repeated, soft, descending whistles, *hoo-ee, hoo-ou, hoo-uu*; calls include a coarse chuckling chatter. **HH** Broadleaved, coniferous and mixed forests; forest clearings and edges.

Chestnut Thrush *Turdus rubrocanus* 25–28cm

Resident in far W Himalayas, winters from Nepal east to NE India. **ID** Male has grey head with buffish-grey collar; rest of body mainly chestnut and has blackish wings and tail. Female very similar but duller; head and hindneck pale brownish-grey (lacking distinct collar) and wings and tail are brown. Juvenile has buff shaft streaking on upperparts and dark spotting and barring on underparts; back, rump and uppertail-coverts have a distinct chestnut cast. Compared to nominate race, male *T. r. gouldii* (rare E Himalayas and north-east in winter) has a darker slate-grey head and neck (lacking collared effect); female has darker brownish-grey head. **Voice** Song a series of repeated, loud rich musical phrases, with much mimicry; *kwik* in alarm. **HH** Summers in coniferous and mixed forest; winters in open wooded areas.

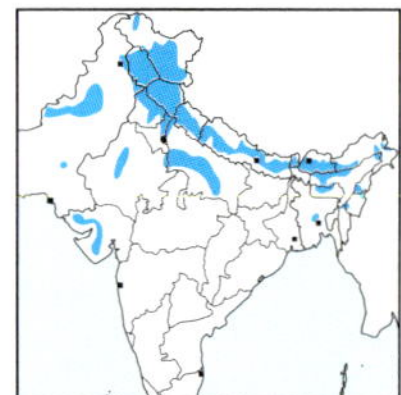

Black-throated Thrush *Turdus atrogularis* 24–27cm

Winter visitor. N subcontinent. **ID** Adult male has black supercilium, throat and breast (with narrow white fringes in fresh plumage), grey upperparts and whitish underparts. Female similar to male, but typically has white or buffish throat, black-streaked malar stripe and black gorget of spotting across breast. First-winter has fine white supercilium, white tips to greater coverts and pale-fringed tertials. First-winter male resembles adult female. First-winter female is less heavily marked and has finely streaked breast and flanks. **Voice** Calls include thin *seet* and throaty chuckling in alarm. **HH** Winters on grassy scrubby hillsides, in forest edge, well-wooded areas and cultivation.

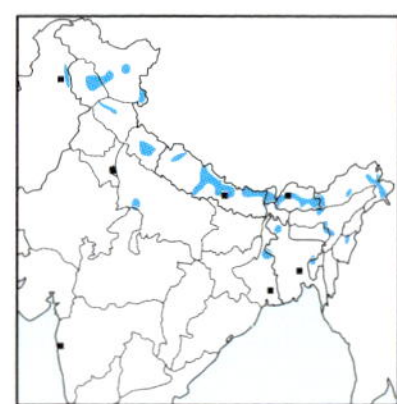

Red-throated Thrush *Turdus ruficollis* 24–27cm

Winter visitor. Himalayas and NE India. **ID** Uniform grey upperparts and wings. Always shows reddish-orange at sides of tail, which can be very prominent in flight (from below undertail can appear entirely orange). Adult male has red supercilium, throat and breast (with narrow white fringes in fresh plumage), grey upperparts and whitish underparts. Female similar to male, but typically has white or buffish throat, black-streaked malar stripe, and red of breast is a gorget of spotting. First-winter has white tips to greater coverts and pale-fringed tertials. First-winter male resembles adult female. First-winter female is less heavily marked and has finely streaked breast and flanks; usually shows rufous wash to supercilium, throat and/or breast. **Voice** Calls include hoarse high *kwee-kweek*, and a thin *tseep* in flight. **HH** Winters in open juniper woodland, scrub and orchards.

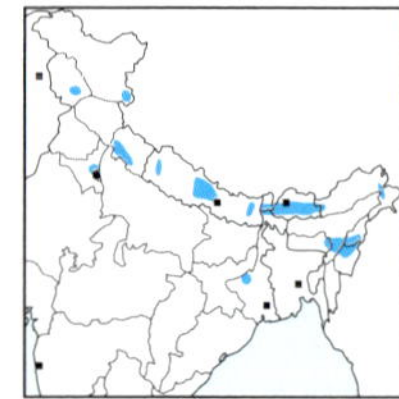

Dusky Thrush *Turdus eunomus* 23–25cm

Winter visitor. Himalayas and NE India. **ID** Adult male has a broad white supercilium and throat contrasting with dark crown and ear-coverts, a chestnut wing-panel, rufous-brown mantle with dark feather centres, double gorget of blackish spots across breast, and bold spotting on the flanks contrasting with the white underparts. Female similar but is usually duller and less strikingly patterned, and usually has a more distinct black-streaked malar stripe. First-winter variable, but duller than the adult: crown and ear-coverts greyer and supercilium less pronounced, the double gorget of spotting less distinct, upperparts greyer, and has browner (and less distinct) wing panel. See Vagrants for comparison with Naumann's Thrush (hybrids occur). **Voice** Includes staccato *chuck* in mild alarm; shrill strident rhythmic *chek-chek-chek-chek* when going to roost, and a shrill rasping *spirr* when flushed. **HH** Open cultivated areas and pastures with scattered trees.

juv
♂
♀
White-collared Blackbird
♂ gouldii
♂ rubrocanus
♀ 1st-winter
Black-throated Thrush
Chestnut Thrush
♀ rubrocanus
♂
♀
♂
♀
♀ 1st-winter
Red-throated Thrush
♂
1st-winter
Dusky Thrush

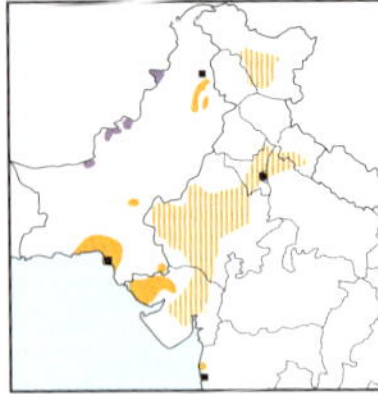

Rufous-tailed Scrub Robin *Cercotrichas galactotes* 15cm

Southbound passage migrant through Pakistan and NW India; also breeds in W Pakistan. **ID** Bright rufous rump and long, fan-shaped tail, the latter frequently held acutely cocked. Outer rectrices tipped with white and subterminally marked with black. Adult has creamy-white supercilium with black eye-stripe, blackish moustachial line, sandy-grey upperparts with pale fringes to wing feathers, and creamy-white underparts. Juvenile has faint mottling on throat and breast. **Voice** A sustained sweet, repetitive warbling and variable fluty twittering; calls include hard *tek tek*, *si-sip* for contact, and *zi-zi-zi* in alarm. **HH** Feeds on ground in open, hopping in short spurts, also feeds in low bushes. Distinctive habit of cocking tail right over back, also bobs head and turns body, drops and flicks wings, and fans and jerks tail. Breeds in scattered clumps of *Saccharum* cane grass, *Tamarix* and thorn bushes; on migration habitat includes dry scrub-jungle.

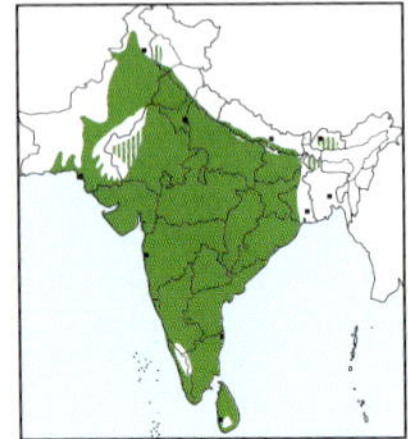

Indian Robin *Copsychus fulicatus* 16cm

Widespread resident except for the north-east, N Himalayas and parts of the north-west. **ID** Reddish vent and black tail (frequently held cocked) in all plumages. Male has white shoulders and black underparts. Female mainly brown with greyer underparts, some showing suggestion of paler supercilium. Juvenile darker brown than female; lacks spotting and scaling typical of juvenile chats, but throat is lightly mottled. In Sri Lanka and S India (e.g. nominate) upperparts of male glossy blue-black and concolorous with underparts; female has brown underparts concolorous with underparts. In northern subspecies upperparts of male brownish contrasting with underparts; female has greyer underparts, contrasting slightly with brown upperparts. **Voice** Very short, high-pitched warbling song; clear two-toned whistling *pi-pear* warning call. **HH** Bold, sprightly and terrestrial. Hops and runs about over open stony ground, sometimes perching low down in bushes or on stones. Frequently flips tail and sometimes holds it vertically over back. Dry stony areas with scrub and cultivation edges. **TN** Formerly placed in *Saxicoloides*.

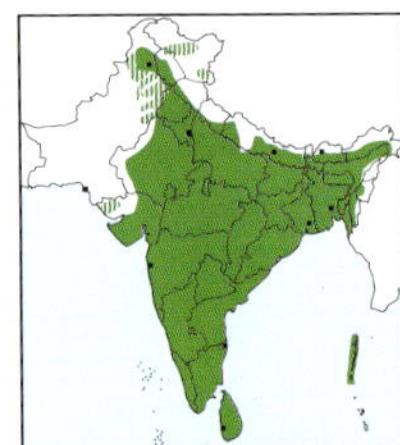

Oriental Magpie Robin *Copsychus saularis* 19–21cm

Widespread resident; unrecorded in most of north-west. **ID** In all plumages has white wing patch and white at sides to long, frequently cocked tail. Male has glossy blue-black head, upperparts and breast, and striking white belly. Female has bluish-grey head, upperparts and breast. Juvenile has indistinct orange-buff spotting on upperparts, rufous fringes to wing feathers, and orange-buff wash and diffuse dark scaling on throat and breast. Female *C. s. ceylonensis* (Sri Lanka) has darker, glossy blue upperparts and is more similar to male. Female *C. s. andamanensis* (Andamans) also has slight gloss to upperparts and rufous wash below. **Voice** Spirited, clear and varied whistling song; calls include plaintive *swee-ee* or *swee-swee*, harsh *chr-r* in alarm. **HH** Confiding and conspicuous, partly crepuscular. Forages chiefly by hopping on ground in the open. Tail usually held cocked and frequently lowered and fanned, then closed and jerked up, while wings are often drooped and flicked. Gardens, groves and open dry broadleaved forest.

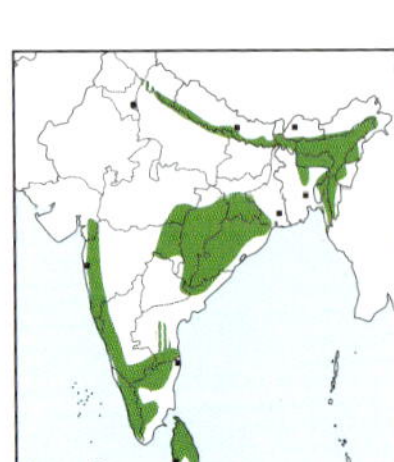

White-rumped Shama *Copsychus malabaricus* 22–27cm

Resident. Himalayan foothills, NE, E and W India, Bangladesh and Sri Lanka. **ID** Long, graduated dark tail with white sides and rump. Male has glossy blue-black upperparts and breast, rufous-orange underparts. Female duller, with brownish-grey upperparts; tail shorter and squarer. Juvenile has orange-buff spotting on upperparts, and orange-buff throat and breast with fine scaling. Female *C. m. leggei* (Sri Lanka) similar to male. **Voice** Song comprises rich melodious phrases, *oi-o-lee-nou*; call a musical *chir-chur* and *chur-chi-churr*, harsh scolding in alarm. **HH** More often heard than seen. Keeps close to ground in undergrowth and low trees in broadleaved forest; favours bamboo.

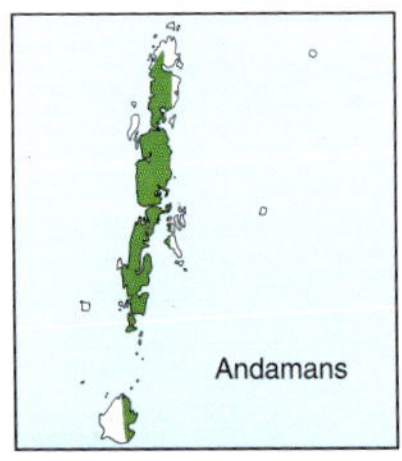

Andaman Shama *Copsychus albiventris* 25cm

Resident. Andamans. **ID** Male similar to White-rumped but has white belly (with rufous flanks and on vent); tail shorter, with central tail feathers less protruding from rest of tail. Female similar to male, but has shorter tail and less gloss on throat and upperparts. **Voice** Song like White-rumped but shorter, lower-pitched, and with rich guttural tone. Calls may be given continually in late afternoon when preparing to roost, reported to include *chee-ee*. **HH** Usually keeps low above ground or is terrestrial. Dense forest, scrub and gardens; favours densely vegetated ravines near water.

Rufous-tailed
Scrub Robin
♂
fulicatus
♀
cambaiensis
♂
cambaiensis
Indian Robin
♂
juv
Oriental
Magpie Robin
♀
♂
White-rumped
Shama
♀
juv
♂
Andaman
Shama
♀

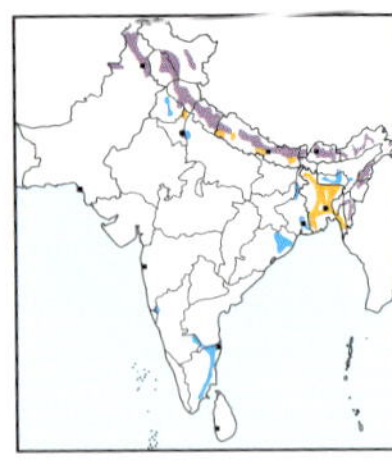

Dark-sided Flycatcher *Muscicapa sibirica* 13–14cm

Breeds in Himalayas and NE India; winter quarters poorly known. **ID** From Asian Brown Flycatcher by small dark bill, and longer primary projection (exposed primaries equal to or distinctly longer than tertials). Appearance at times not unlike a perched hirundine. Very prominent white eye-ring (broader behind eye), darker sooty-brown upperparts, and breast and flanks more heavily marked, with narrow whitish throat patch and line down centre of belly. Juvenile has finely streaked and sparsely spotted upperparts, heavy dark mottling on breast and flanks, and orange-buff wing-bar. **Voice** Very soft and weak, a complex pattern of thin, high-pitched, repetitive phrases, including sibilant *tsee-tsee-tsee-tsee*, followed by melodious trills and whistles. Calls include a series of short, metallic tinkling notes, *chi-up, chi-up, chi-up*. **HH** Characteristically perches upright on favoured prominent vantage point, such as dead branch or telegraph wire, flying out to catch prey and returning to same perch. Clearings and edges of broadleaved or coniferous temperate and subalpine forest.

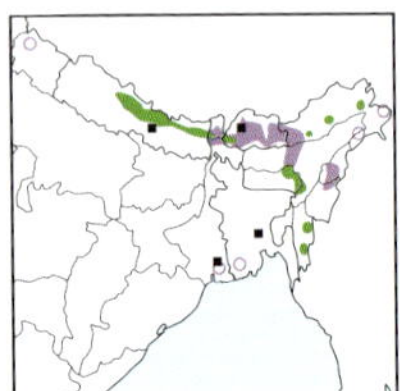

Ferruginous Flycatcher *Muscicapa ferruginea* 12–13cm

Probably summer visitor. Breeds in E Himalayas and NE India. **ID** Compact, with large head, large eye, prominent white eye-ring and short dark bill. Adult has blue-grey cast to head (with darker malar stripe), rufous-brown mantle, rufous-orange rump and tail sides, rufous-orange underparts, and prominent rufous fringes to greater coverts and tertials. Juvenile has orange-buff spotting on upperparts, rufous-orange median and greater covert wing-bars, and dark scaling on breast. **Voice** Song includes several harsh or shrill notes, *tsit-tittu-tittu*, first note shorter than others, and followed by a series of high-pitched whistles; call a quiet accentor-like trill. **HH** Normally solitary. Partly crepuscular, unobtrusive and very quiet, usually keeping to middle or lower forest storey. Hawks insects from branch in similar fashion to other brown flycatchers, see Dark-sided. Humid broadleaved forest, especially of oaks, also firs (Himalayas); dense mixed jungle (Assam).

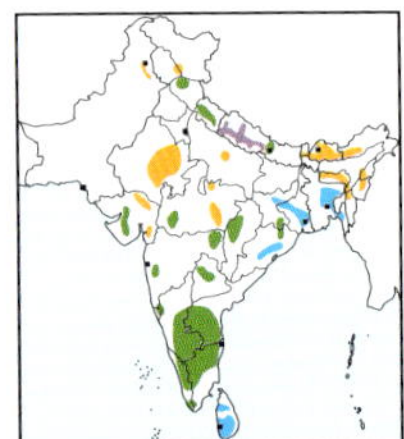

Asian Brown Flycatcher *Muscicapa dauurica* 12–14cm

Breeds in Himalayan foothills and hills of C and W India; winters in S, C and E India and Sri Lanka. **ID** Grey-brown with short tail, large head, and huge-looking eye with prominent eye-ring. From Dark-sided by larger bill with more extensive orange base to lower mandible, less prominent white eye-ring, shorter primary projection, and paler underparts (with light grey-brown wash or streaking to breast and flanks). Juvenile has prominent buffish spotting on upperparts, whitish underparts with fine dark scaling on breast, and creamy-white wing-bar. **Voice** Song comprises short trills interspersed with two- or three-note whistling phrases, louder than Dark-sided; call a weak trilling *sit-it-it-it*. **HH** Usually solitary, partly crepuscular, rather quiet flycatcher. Perches in lower tree branches and makes hunting sallies. Open subtropical broadleaved forest, plantations, groves and wooded areas; in Pakistan, damp ravines in mixed chir pine-deciduous forest.

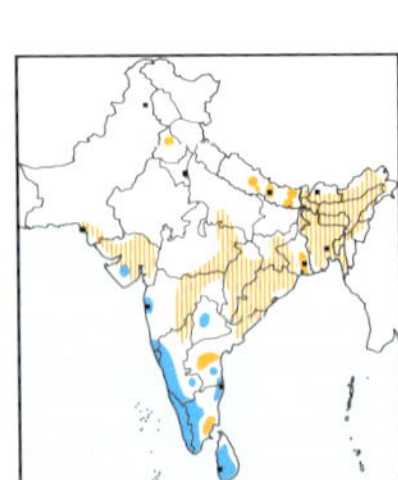

Brown-breasted Flycatcher *Muscicapa muttui* 13-14cm

Breeds in NE India; winters in SW India and Sri Lanka. Vagrant: Nepal. **ID** Compared with Asian Brown has larger bill with entirely pale lower mandible, pale legs and feet, more pronounced pale submoustachial stripe and darker malar, rufous-buff edges to greater coverts and tertials, rufescent tone to rump and tail, more pronounced brown or grey-brown breast-band, and warmer brownish-buff to orange-buff flanks. Juvenile streaked rufous-buff on upperparts and breast. **Voice** Song a pleasant, feeble series of short even-pitched whistles; calls include a thin *sit* and a very rapid *chi-chi-chi-chi-chi* with last two notes lower. **HH** Usually solitary. Quiet, retiring, partly crepuscular. Hawks insects in typical manner of brown flycatchers, see Dark-sided. Perches on lowest branches. Territorial in winter and breeding season. Dense thickets in broadleaved evergreen forest, often near streams in Sri Lanka.

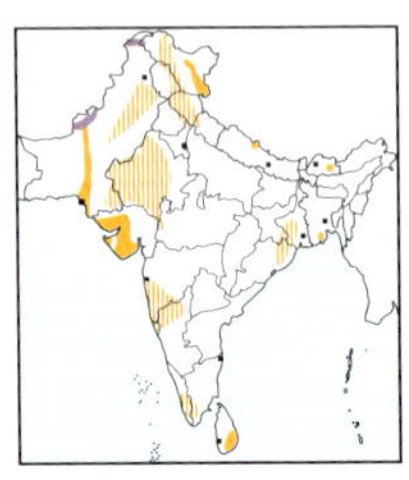

Spotted Flycatcher *Muscicapa striata* 13.5–14.5cm

Summer visitor to Balochistan and Himalayas in Pakistan; passage migrant in Pakistan and India. Vagrant: Nepal and Bhutan. **ID** From Dark-sided Flycatcher by larger size, longer bill, paler grey-brown upperparts, faint dark streaking on forehead and crown, indistinct eye-ring, and diffuse grey-brown streaking on throat and breast. Juvenile has buffish-white spotting on upperparts and dark scaling on underparts. **Voice** Unobtrusive sequence of short, squeaky, very high-pitched single or disyllabic notes interspersed with trills; thin, scratchy calls. **HH** Mainly solitary. Perches upright, characteristically with the head partly sunk between the shoulders. Often flicks wings and tail. Hunts in similar way to other brown flycatchers, see Dark-sided. Breeds in juniper forest, scrub forest, ravines with scattered trees and open pine forest.

ad
juv
Dark-sided
Flycatcher
ad
juv
Ferruginous
Flycatcher
ad
worn
ad
fresh
juv
Asian Brown
Flycatcher
Brown-breasted
Flycatcher
ad
ad
Spotted Flycatcher

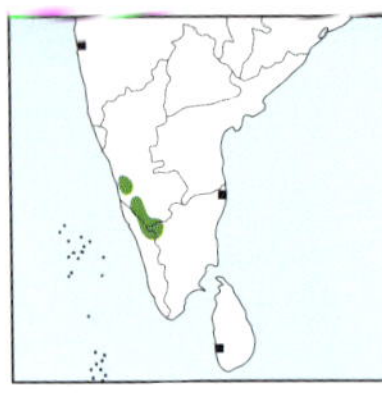

Nilgiri Sholakili ***Sholicola major*** 14cm

Resident. Hills of Kerala and Tamil Nadu north of Palghat Gap, and S Karnataka. **ID** Stocky, big-headed chat-like bird with long legs and reddish eye. Adult has variable bright blue forehead and supercilium to eye, dark lores, slaty-blue head, breast and upperparts, and white belly. Flanks and undertail-coverts rufous. **Voice** Song a jumble of shrill whistles, harsh notes and buzzes, sometimes with mimicry; calls include harsh rattle. **HH** Secretive; creeps through vegetation and around fallen timber. Dense undergrowth in evergreen forest. Globally threatened. **TN** Formerly treated as Nilgiri Blue Robin *Myiomela major*.

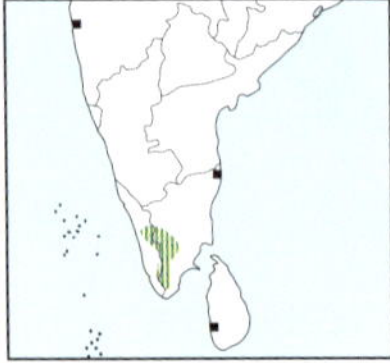

White-bellied Sholakili ***Sholicola albiventris*** 14cm

Resident. Hills of Kerala and Tamil Nadu south of Palghat Gap. **ID** As Nilgiri, but has slaty-blue flanks concolorous with breast, and more striking (but variable) whitish or bluish-white forehead and supercilium to eye, which contrast with blackish lores. Vent and undertail-coverts white and connect with white belly. Possibly confusable with White-bellied Blue Flycatcher but more chat-like in appearance (often on ground) with longer legs, shorter tail and prominent white supercilium and slaty-blue flanks. *S. a. ashambuensis* of Ashambu Hills (southernmost Western Ghats) ('Ashambu Sholakili') smaller with shorter legs and longer bill, and is paler blue with considerably larger white belly patch. **Voice** Loud, bright, thrush-like series of short phrases, each comprising rich whistles and buzzy notes, rising and falling several times; more musical and warbling than Nilgiri Sholakili. **HH** Forages in low vegetation or on ground. Wet undergrowth in forest patches and densely wooded ravines, vegetation by streams. Globally threatened. **TN** Formerly treated as White-bellied Blue Robin *Myiomela albiventris*.

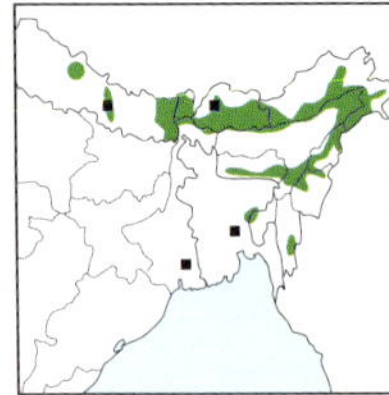

Large Niltava ***Niltava grandis*** 20–22cm

Resident. Himalayas and NE India. **ID** A very large, stocky niltava. Male is dark blue (often appearing entirely black in poor light), with blackish face and tufted forehead. Brilliant blue crown, neck patch, shoulder patch and rump. Female has bright blue patch on side of neck (which can be obscured), blue-grey cast to hindcrown, dark olive-brown upperparts with rufescent wings and tail, clearly defined (narrow) buff throat, and rufous-buff forecrown and lores. Lacks white patch at base of throat of female Rufous-bellied. **Voice** Melancholy song of 3–4 ascending whistles. **HH** Often perches still for long periods. Usually in midstorey. Dense, moist broadleaved forest, especially near streams.

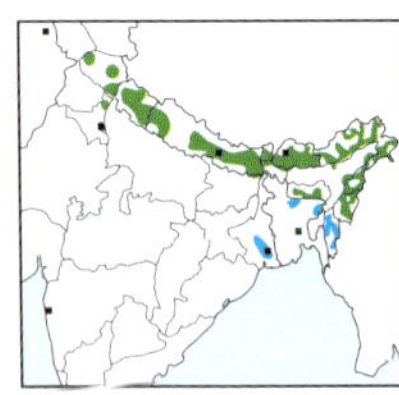

Small Niltava ***Niltava macgrigoriae*** 11–14cm

Resident. Himalayas and NE India. **ID** Small size. Male dark blue (greyer below), with brilliant blue forehead, neck patch and rump. Female dusky brown with indistinct blue neck patch and rufescent wings and tail; lacks oval patch at base of throat of female Rufous-bellied. **Voice** Thin, high-pitched song, *twee-twee-twee-twee*, which rises then falls. **HH** Rather shy and elusive. Keeps to shady undergrowth and bushes, flying out occasionally to catch insects. Bushes at track edges, along streams, in forest clearings; also reed and grass jungle in plains in winter.

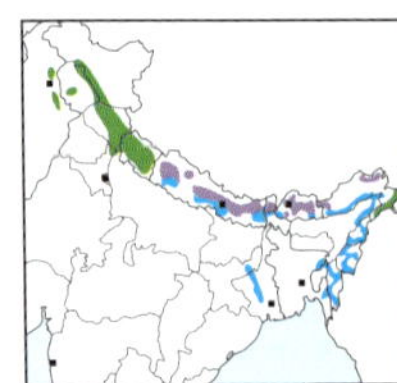

Rufous-bellied Niltava ***Niltava sundara*** 15–18cm

Resident. Himalayas and NE India. **ID** Male has dark blue upperparts and orange underparts, with brilliant blue crown, neck patch, shoulder patch and rump. Female is dull olive brown, with well-defined oval-shaped whitish patch on lower throat/upper breast (can be obscured), and rufous forehead, wings and (particularly) tail. Also has small blue patch on side of neck (often difficult to see). **Voice** Song *sweeee-eh tri-tri-tr-tih*; rasping *z-i-i-i-f-cha-chuk* in alarm. **HH** Usually perches quietly low down in forest, occasionally darting out or dropping to ground to catch insects. Bushes and undergrowth in broadleaved or mixed forest and second growth.

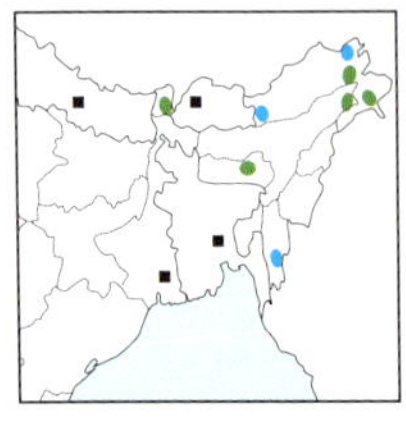

Chinese Vivid Niltava ***Niltava oatesi*** 19cm

Resident. E Himalayas and NE Indian hills . **ID** Superficially resembles Rufous-bellied, but larger and slimmer in appearance, and is typically more arboreal and found away from dense cover. Compared to male Rufous-bellied, male has duller blue crown and nape, and blue shoulder patch and rump are less striking. Also, orange of breast extends as a variable wedge onto lower throat. Female lacks white oval-shaped patch at base of throat shown by female Rufous-bellied. Resembles female Large in coloration, with narrow buffish throat, but is smaller, lacks blue neck patch, and has less rufescent wings and tail. **Voice** Slow song of mellow whistles interspersed with scratchier notes. **HH** Usually keeps to midstorey and canopy. Broadleaved evergreen and mixed forest. **TN** Formerly treated as conspecific with Vivid Niltava *N. vivida*.

Nilgiri Sholakili
ad
White-bellied Sholakili
ad
♂
♀
♂ juv
Large Niltava
♂
Small Niltava
♀
♂ juv
♂
♀
♀ juv
♂
♀
Rufous-bellied Niltava
Chinese Vivid Niltava

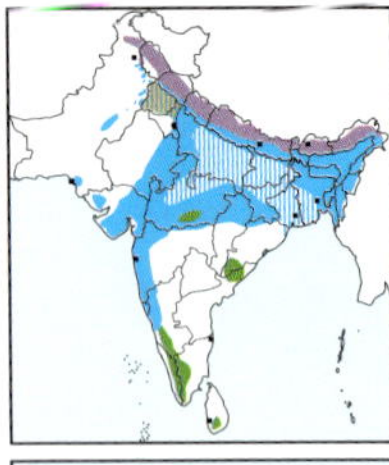

Grey-headed Canary-flycatcher *Culicicapa ceylonensis* 12–13cm

Resident. Breeds in Himalayas, hills of India, Bangladesh; winters in Himalayan foothills, and plains in Pakistan and N, NE, W and parts of E India. Resident in SW and locally in E India, and Sri Lanka. **ID** Distinctive with upright stance, crested appearance and flycatcher-like behaviour. Has grey head and breast, greenish mantle, yellow belly, flanks and vent, and orange legs and feet. **Voice** Song loud and squeaky, high-pitched five-note sequence, *tit-titu-wheeee*, the first two notes descending, the rest rising. **HH** Conspicuous and noisy all year. Forest and open wooded country; in S India in broadleaved evergreen forest, sholas and other wooded areas. **TN** Not related to typical flycatchers. Placed in Stenostiridae with Yellow-bellied Fairy-Fantail.

Dull-blue Flycatcher *Eumyias sordidus* 14–15cm

Resident. Sri Lanka. **ID** Stocky, bull-headed flycatcher; the only all-'blue' flycatcher in Sri Lanka. Adult is dull ashy-blue, with greyish-white belly, flanks and vent. Black lores and chin, bordered by cobalt-blue (especially on forehead). Sexes similar, although female is slightly duller. Juvenile has buff spotting on brown upperparts, and black scaling on buffish throat and breast; wings and tail as adult, with buff tips to coverts. **Voice** Sweet, soft mournful song of 6–8 notes, rising and falling in pitch. **HH** Quiet; frequently uses low perch. Forest edges and well-wooded areas.

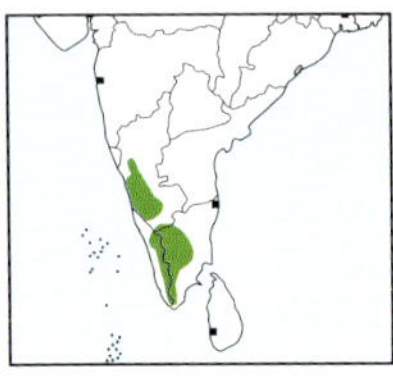

Nilgiri Flycatcher *Eumyias albicaudatus* 15cm

Resident. Western Ghats. **ID** Male is almost entirely dark indigo-blue, with brighter blue forehead and supercilium and black lores. From male White-bellied by blue-grey belly and flanks, diffuse whitish fringes to blue-grey undertail-coverts, and white at base of tail (can be difficult to see). Darker and bluer coloration and white in tail are best features from Verditer Flycatcher. Female distinctive, with dusky blue-grey upperparts and paler underparts, white fringes to undertail-coverts, and white at base of tail. Coloration of upperparts and underparts and white in tail help separate from female Verditer. Juvenile has buff spotting on brown upperparts, and white underparts with black scaling; wings and tail as adult, with buff tips to coverts. **Voice** Song a hesitant melancholy warble of 8–12 notes, *dwe te-te dtwe de-twe he-te-te-dwe*; slower and less intense than Verditer. **HH** Evergreen biotope in hills, thick vegetation near streams, forest edges and clearings.

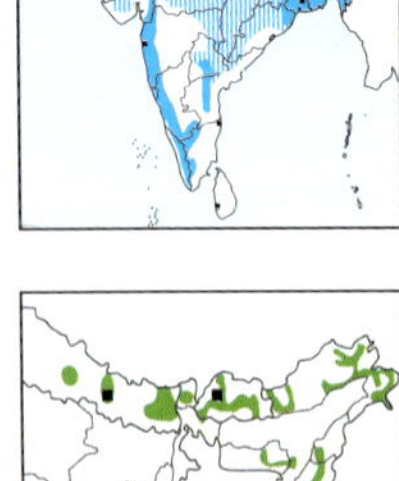

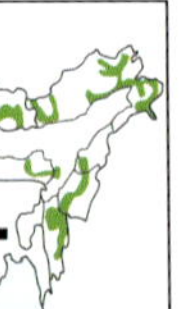

Verditer Flycatcher *Eumyias thalassinus* 15–17cm

Summer visitor to Himalayas and NE India; widespread in winter except for the north-west and Sri Lanka. **ID** Male is entirely greenish-blue, with brighter forehead and throat, and black lores. Female similar, but duller and greyer, and has dusky lores. Female confusable with male (but not female) Pale Blue Flycatcher, but has shorter bill, turquoise-blue upperparts, and uniform greyish turquoise-blue underparts (lacking contrast between breast and belly). See Nilgiri Flycatcher. Juvenile has turquoise cast to grey-brown upperparts, with fine orange-buff spotting, and bold orange-buff spotting on brown underparts; wings and tail as adult, with buff tips to coverts. **Voice** Song a series of rapid, undulating, strident notes, gradually descending the scale. **HH** Sallies forth from exposed perch in treetops. Open forest, forest clearings and edges, groves and gardens.

White-gorgeted Flycatcher *Anthipes monileger* 11.5–13cm

Resident. Himalayas and NE India. **ID** Compact with large domed head; typically found close to the ground. Adult is mainly olive-brown but has large white throat patch enclosed by black gorget. Juvenile lacks black-bordered white throat of adult; has dark brown upperparts streaked warm buff, buff tips to greater coverts, and buffish underparts diffusely streaked dark brown. Black bill and pinkish legs and feet. Nominate (E Himalayas) has orange-buff supercilium, which is white in *A. m. leucops* (east and south of Brahmaputra). **Voice** A thin high-pitched whistling song. **HH** Secretive. Undergrowth in moist broadleaved forest, thick bushes and bamboo.

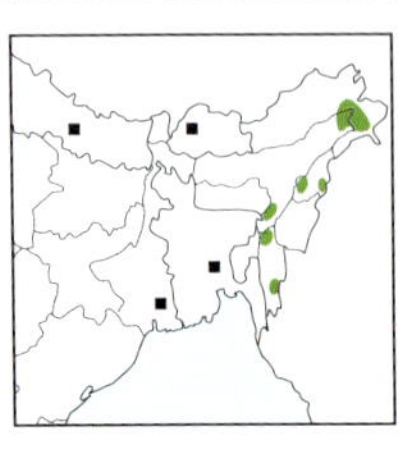

White-tailed Flycatcher *Leucoptilon concretum* 18–19cm

Resident. Breeds in E Arunachal Pradesh, E Meghalaya and Mizoram. **ID** Flycatcher shape, shorter tail, and short pale legs help separate from White-tailed Blue Robin. Large size, with prominent white in tail (exposed when quickly flicked open). Male mainly slaty-blue (with brighter blue forehead), with white belly and undertail-coverts. Female has white patch on lower throat; blue cast to crown and white in tail are best features from female Rufous-bellied Niltava. **Voice** Song comprises variable, piercing, sibilant whistles *tii-tuu-tii-tuu-tii, huiiee*; harsh *scree* in alarm. **HH** Slower moving and less active than most flycatchers; often spreads its tail. Gleans insects from foliage and branches; also captures insects in flight. Inhabits lower forest storey. Dense forest, often close to streams. **TN** Formerly placed in *Cyornis*.

ad
Grey-headed Canary
Flycatcher
ad
juv
Dull-blue
Flycatcher
♂
♀
♀
♂
♂
juv
♂
juv
Nilgiri Flycatcher
Verditer Flycatcher
ad
leucops
juv
monileger
♂
ad
monileger
♀
White-tailed
Flycatcher
White-gorgeted Flycatcher

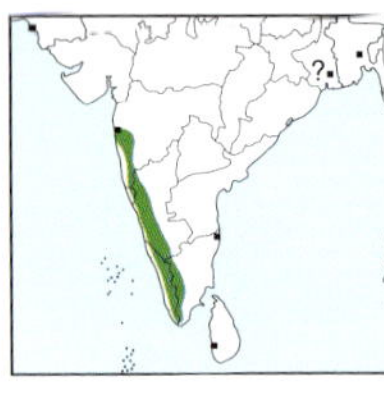

White-bellied Blue Flycatcher *Cyornis pallidipes* 15cm

Resident. Western Ghats and W Tamil Nadu hills. **ID** Male from male Nilgiri by larger and longer bill, dark indigo-blue coloration, white belly and undertail-coverts (latter lacking blue-grey feather centres), and absence of white at base of tail. Female similar to female Blue-throated Blue Flycatcher but has striking orange-red throat and breast (with cream chin), strong grey cast to head, more extensive cream on lores and forehead, brighter chestnut tail, and is larger with longer bill. Juvenile has unmarked buff throat and white belly (juvenile female with chestnut tail). **Voice** Song is a series of lengthy, faltering, unmelodious high-pitched, squeaky notes, often only audible at close range. Call a low *tsk-tsk*. **HH** Rather lethargic and inconspicuous. Has striking habit of lifting and fanning tail. Frequents undergrowth and lower forest storey. Hunts among foliage, also pursues insects in flight and sometimes descends to ground. Dense broadleaved evergreen forest, sholas and thick hillside vegetation.

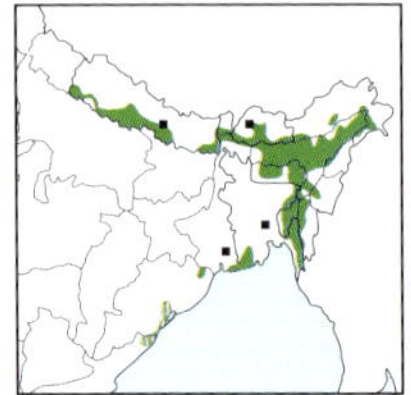

Pale-chinned Blue Flycatcher *Cyornis poliogenys* 15.5–18cm

Resident. Himalayan foothills, NE and E India, and Bangladesh. **ID** Similar to females of other *Cyornis* flycatchers; best told by greyish crown and ear-coverts, prominent eye-ring, well-defined cream throat, and creamy-orange breast and flanks which merge with belly. In Eastern Ghats, '*vernayi*' (now thought to be a hybrid with Tickell's) has blue-grey wash to upperparts. **Voice** Song a high-pitched series of 4–11 notes, slightly rising and falling, sometimes interspersed with harsh *tchut-tchut* call-notes. **HH** Forages in bushes and undergrowth in forest, also higher in trees, and sometimes on ground where it resembles a chat. Bushes and undergrowth in open broadleaved forest; more open areas in winter. **AN** Pale-chinned Flycatcher.

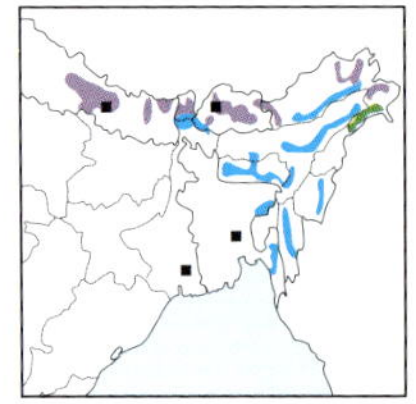

Pale Blue Flycatcher *Cyornis unicolor* 16.5–18cm

Mainly summer visitor to Himalayas; mainly winter visitor to E Himalayan foothills, NE India and E Bangladesh. **ID** Male from Verditer by longer bill and pale blue coloration (lacking greenish cast), with distinctly greyer belly. Shining blue forecrown and dusky lores. Female very different from Verditer. Best told by a combination of large size, brownish-grey upperparts, uniform greyish underparts (lacking paler throat, with greyish-white centre of belly and dark buff undertail-coverts) and rufous-brown uppertail-coverts and tail. Juvenile has bold orange-buff spotting on scapulars and heavily scaled underparts; wings and tail as adult, with buff tips to coverts. **Voice** Rich, melodious thrush-like song with descending sequences, usually ending in harsh *chizz*, unlike other *Cyornis*. **HH** Generally frequents middle and upper storeys in forest, sometimes near ground. Pursues insects like a typical flycatcher, but usually moves from one perch to another, instead of returning to same one. Moist, dense broadleaved forest, second growth and bamboo.

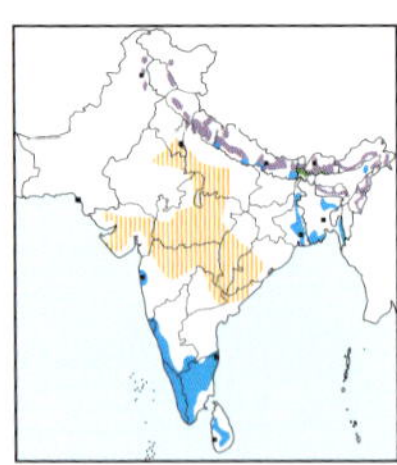

Blue-throated Blue Flycatcher *Cyornis rubeculoides* 14–15cm

Summer visitor to Himalayas; winters in C and E Himalayan foothills and south to Bangladesh, S and SW India and Sri Lanka. **ID** Male has blue throat (some with orange wedge) and well-defined white belly and flanks. Female has narrow and poorly defined creamy-orange throat, and orange breast well demarcated from white belly (except in NE India) (compare Pale-chinned Blue and female Hill). Olive-brown head and upperparts and rufescent tail are best features from female Tickell's. **Voice** Short, sweet song, recalls Tickell's but faster and higher-pitched. **HH** Frequents bushes and branches close to the ground. Sallies after insects but does not use a regular perch. Open forest, groves and well-wooded areas.

White-bellied
Blue Flycatcher
♂
♀
♀
juv
ad
poliogenys
ad
'vernayi'
juv
poliogenys
Pale-chinned
Blue Flycatcher
♂
juv
Pale
Blue Flycatcher
♂
♀
♂
♀
♂
juv
Blue-throated
Blue Flycatcher

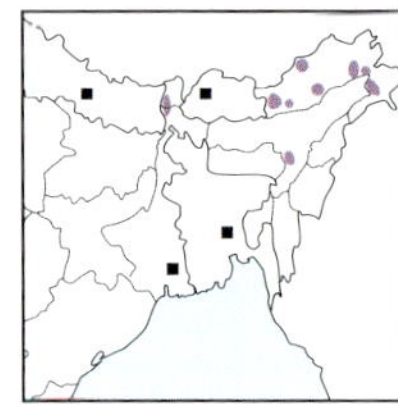

Large Blue Flycatcher *Cyornis magnirostris* 15cm

Summer visitor to E Himalayas. **ID** From Tickell's and Hill by larger size, longer bill (with prominent hooked tip) and longer primary projection. Upperparts of male deeper blue than Tickell's. Throat shows paler contrast with breast, and undertail-coverts creamy (throat concolorous with breast, and undertail-coverts white, in Hill). Female from female Blue-throated Blue and Hill by combination of larger size and bill, sharper demarcation between ear-coverts and creamy throat, with throat paler than breast, and creamy undertail-coverts. Note, however, that plumage and structural differences from Hill have recently been found to be unreliable in the field and that Hill and Large Blue are best differentiated by song. **Voice** Variable musical song is slower, with longer and fewer notes per phrase, and lacks descending tone, compared with Hill. **HH** Remains still on perch for long periods. Forages in undergrowth and shaded lower levels of forest, occasionally darting to seize passing insects. Chiefly evergreen hill and moist broadleaved forests.

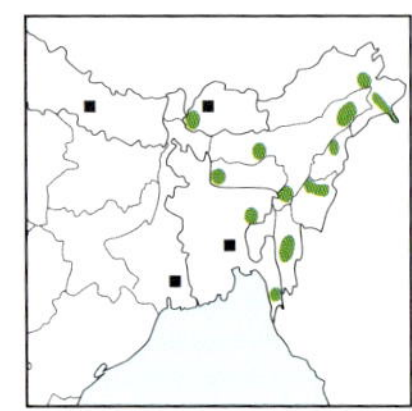

Hill Blue Flycatcher *Cyornis whitei* 14–15.5cm

Resident in NE India. **ID** Similar in size and structure to Tickell's Blue Flycatcher. Male from male Tickell's by deeper blue upperparts but otherwise very similar. From Blue-throated Blue by orange throat and orange breast grading into orange belly. Female from female Tickell's by brownish head and upperparts (including wings and tail). From female Blue-throated Blue by orange of breast extending onto flanks. See Large Blue for differences from that species. **Voice** Song comprises sweet, variable melodious warbling sequences, usually starting with thin *si*; calls include a hard *tac* and scolding *trrt-trrt-trrt*. **HH** Usually sallies after flying insects from low perch, especially in shady forest areas. Often descends to ground to catch prey. Dense, moist broadleaved forest. **TN** Formerly treated as conspecific with *C. banyumas* as Hill Blue Flycatcher.

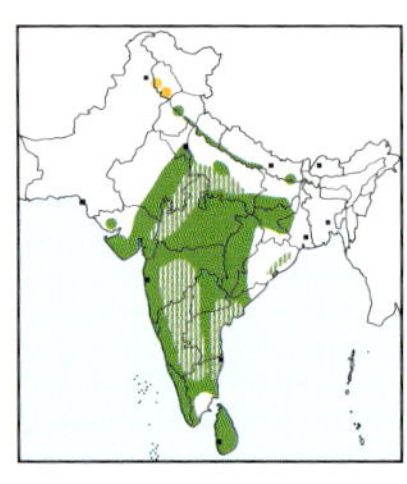

Tickell's Blue Flycatcher *Cyornis tickelliae* 14–15cm

Resident. S Jammu and Kashmir east to S Nepal, peninsular India and Sri Lanka. **ID** Male from Blue-throated Blue by orange throat. Very similar to male Large and Hill Blue Flycatchers but upperparts a purer blue, and note additional structural difference from Large (which see). Female has blue-grey cast to upperparts (brighter on supercilium, shoulder, rump and tail), orange breast, and white to pale orange belly and flanks. See Pale-chinned Blue Flycatcher for account of '*vernayi*'. **Voice** Song a short metallic trill of 6–10 fast, tinkling notes, the first half descending and second half ascending; both sexes sing in alarm. Calls include a hard *tac* and *trrt-trrt*; in Sri Lanka more varied, including short trills and clacking notes. **HH** Flits actively about bushes, undergrowth and low branches, hawking insects in mid-air. Drier habitats than Blue-throated; open dry forest, bushes in forest and along streams, groves, wooded gardens, scrub and bamboo.

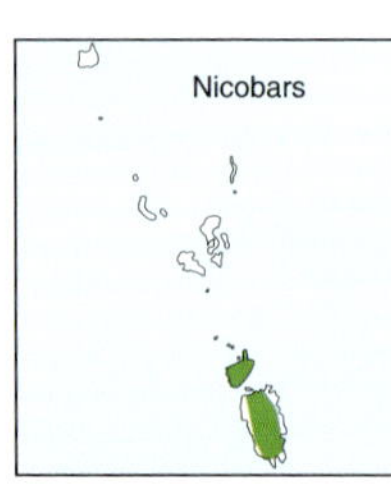

Nicobar Jungle Flycatcher *Cyornis nicobaricus* 14–15cm

Resident. S Nicobars (Great and Little Nicobar). **ID** Large, mainly brown flycatcher with long rufescent-brown tail. Has long bill (with yellowish lower mandible and hooked tip), large eye with orange-buff eye-ring, whitish throat, mottled brownish breast, and pale pinkish legs. Sexes similar. **Voice** Song a loud, rich and rapid series of descending whistles, ending with low, soft *trrrr.* On Great Nicobar a wider variety of songs, most more evenly descending ending with a few staccato notes or soft *trrr.* **HH** Forages in lower canopy, undergrowth, also on ground. Forest, forest edges and bushes. **TN** Formerly placed in *Rhinomyias.*

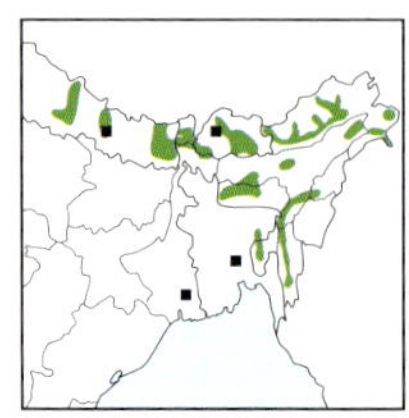

Pygmy Flycatcher *Ficedula hodgsoni* 9–10cm

Resident. Himalayas and NE India. **ID** A very small flycatcher with short tail and tiny bill, giving rise to flowerpecker-like appearance. Has curious habit of stretching head forward, dropping and spreading wings and fanning tail. Male has blue upperparts (with bright blue forecrown), and underparts almost entirely orange. Female and first-year male have olive-brown upperparts and orange-buff underparts. **Voice** Song a short, weak *tzzit-che-che-che-heeeee*; call a low *churr.* **HH** Keeps to canopy, also dense bushes in lower forest storey. Very active. Hunts insects by making short sallies, searching leaves, hovering before flowers like a warbler, and also by dropping to the ground. Breeds in dense, moist montane broadleaved forest, winters in tall deciduous forest, secondary scrub at forest edges, clearings and along streams. **TN** and **AN** Formerly treated as Pygmy Blue Flycatcher *Muscicapella hodgsoni.*

♀
♂
Large
Blue Flycatcher
♂
♀
Hill
Blue Flycatcher
♀
tickelliae
♂
tickelliae
juv
tickelliae
ad
Tickell's
Blue Flycatcher
Nicobar Jungle
Flycatcher
♂
♀
Pygmy Flycatcher

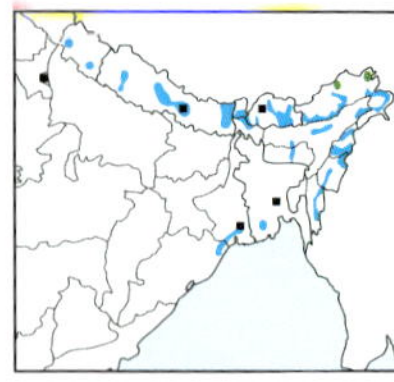

Slaty-backed Flycatcher *Ficedula erithacus* 13–13.5cm

Winter visitor. Himalayas and NE India. **ID** Small, long-tailed flycatcher with very short bill. Male has deep blue upperparts (blacker on face), bright orange underparts (becoming whiter on belly) and black tail with white patches at base. Lacks any glistening blue in plumage. Female rather nondescript, with olive-brown upperparts and greyish-olive underparts, poorly defined whitish throat, lores and eye-ring. First-year male resembles female. **Voice** Short and abrupt flute-like song of descending whistles. **HH** Breeds in oak-rhododendron and fir-pine forests. Winters in moist broadleaved forest, shrubberies and bamboo. **TN** Formerly treated as *F. hodgsonii*.

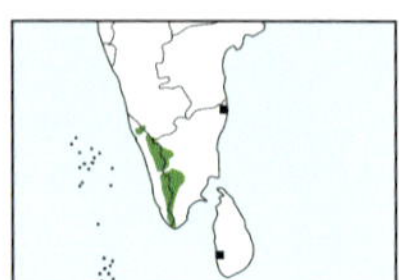

Black-and-orange Flycatcher *Ficedula nigrorufa* 11–13cm

Resident. Western Ghats. **ID** Small, compact flycatcher. Male is almost entirely rufous-orange, with black hood and wings. Female similar, but has dark olive-brown hood, orange-buff lores and brownish-black wings. **Voice** Song an insect-like, high-pitched and metallic *chiki-riki-chiki* or *cheee-ri-ri-ri*, repeated frequently. Contact call, a low-pitched *pee*, and *zit-zit* in alarm. **HH** Evergreen sholas with dense undergrowth, cardamom and coffee plantations, often near streams.

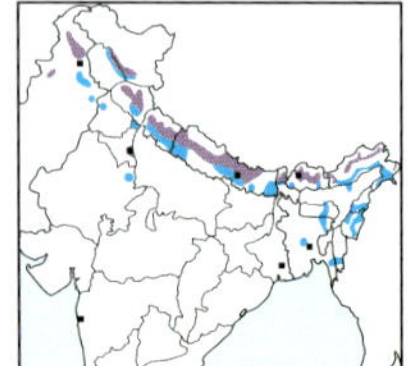

Slaty-blue Flycatcher *Ficedula tricolor* 12.5–13cm

Summer visitor Himalayas; winter visitor Himalayan foothills and NE India. **ID** Male has dark blue upperparts with brighter blue forehead, blue-black sides of head and breast contrasting with white (or orange-buff) throat, and blue-black tail with white patches at base. Female has warm brown upperparts and rufous uppertail-coverts and tail. First-year male as female. Male *F. t. tricolor* (W and C Himalayas) has greyish-white belly and flanks; female has well-defined whitish throat, Male *F. t. cerviniventris* (NE hill states) has orange-buff throat and wash to underparts; underparts of female *cerviniventris*, including throat, entirely warm orange-buff. Birds in E Himalayas intermediate. **Voice** Song 3–4 high-pitched whistles, the first drawn out, second short and emphasised and third a lower, rapid trill. **HH** Breeds in subalpine shrubbery, forest edges and undergrowth; winters in forest undergrowth, dense bush-covered ravines, reedbeds, and tall grass.

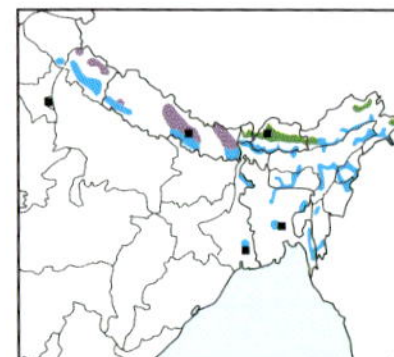

Snowy-browed Flycatcher *Ficedula hyperythra* 11–13cm

Summer visitor Himalayas; winters Himalayan foothills and NE India. **ID** Small, compact, short-tailed flycatcher, with large head, typically found close to the ground. Male has short, broad white supercilium, dark slaty-blue upperparts with rufous-brown wings, rufous-orange throat and breast, and white patches at base of tail. Female by combination of small size and compact shape, dark olive-brown upperparts, orange-buff supercilium and eye-ring, and faint rufous panel on wing. Some females have white supercilium. Pinkish legs and feet. **Voice** Quiet, high-pitched wheezy song. **HH** Humid broadleaved forest with dense undergrowth, favours bamboo and ravines.

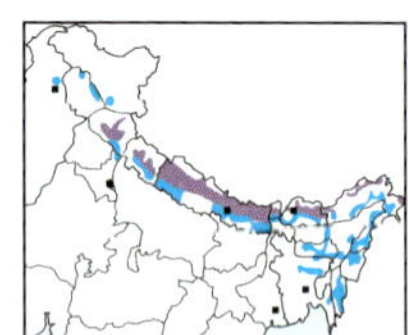

Rufous-gorgeted Flycatcher *Ficedula strophiata* 13–14.5cm

Breeds Himalayas; winters Himalayan foothills and NE India. **ID** Male has dark olive-brown upperparts, blackish face and throat, prominent white forehead and eyebrow, small rufous patch in centre of grey breast (can be difficult to see), and large white patches at sides of tail. Female similar, but has less distinct eyebrow, duller and less distinct rufous 'gorget', and paler grey face and throat. **Voice** Song a thin, evenly spaced *zreet-creet-creet-chirt-chirt*. **HH** Broadleaved or conifer-broadleaved forest, thick secondary scrub.

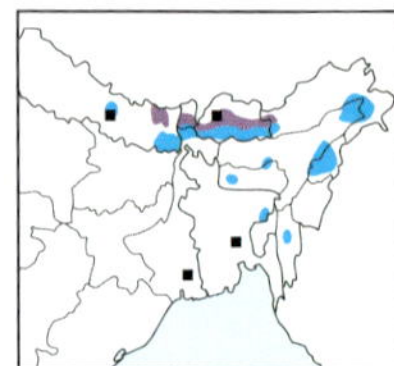

Sapphire Flycatcher *Ficedula sapphira* 10–12cm

Breeds Himalayas; winters Himalayan foothills, NE India and Bangladesh. **ID** Breeding male has bright blue upperparts and sides of breast (with glistening blue crown and rump), orange throat and centre to breast, and white belly and undertail-coverts. Non-breeding and immature male have brown head and mantle, and brownish sides of breast. Female has olive-brown upperparts, orange throat and breast, and rufous rump and tail. Small size and tiny bill help separate from female *Cyornis* flycatchers. **Voice** Song a series of short rattles introduced by several thin or high-pitched notes, *tssyi tchrrrt, tschrrrt, tschrrrt, tschrrrt*.... **HH** Moist evergreen broadleaved forest.

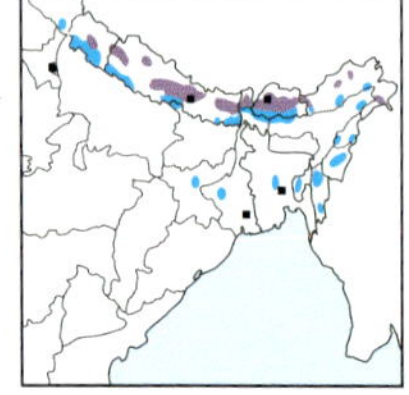

Little Pied Flycatcher *Ficedula westermanni* 10–11cm

Breeds Himalayas; winters Himalayan foothills, NE India and Bangladesh. **ID** Small, compact, bull-headed flycatcher, with small dark bill. Arboreal habits. Male is striking, with mainly black upperparts and white underparts, long broad white supercilium, white patch on wing, and white sides to base of tail. Female has brownish-grey upperparts (tinged warm brown on forehead, lores and around eye) and whitish underparts with brownish-grey wash to breast and flanks. **Voice** Song a series of thin, high-pitched notes followed by a rattle *pi-pi-pi-pi-pi-pi-churrr-r-r-r-r-r*; calls include single low *chur* and mellow *tweet*. **HH** Breeds in broadleaved deciduous and evergreen forest; winters also in open wooded country, orchards, trees around cultivation, and reedbeds.

♂
♀
Slaty-backed Flycatcher
♂
♀
Black-and-orange Flycatcher
♂ cerviniventris
♀ cerviniventris
♂ tricolor
Slaty-blue Flycatcher
♀ tricolor
juv tricolor
♂
♀
juv
Snowy-browed Flycatcher
♀
♂
Rufous-gorgeted Flycatcher
juv
♂ br
♂ juv
♀
♂ non-br
Sapphire Flycatcher
♂
♀
Little Pied Flycatcher
♂ juv
♀ juv

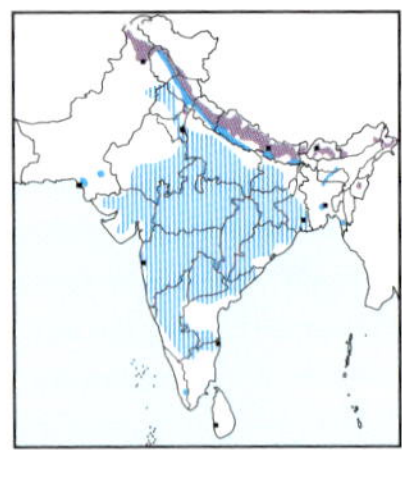

Ultramarine Flycatcher *Ficedula superciliaris* 11.5–12cm

Summer visitor to Himalayas and resident in NE India; winters in Himalayan foothills and south to S India. **ID** Small, compact, arboreal flycatcher with small bill. Male has deep blue upperparts and sides of neck/breast, and white underparts. Female has greyish-brown upperparts and whitish underparts, with greyish patches on sides of breast (mirroring pattern of male); some have blue cast to uppertail-coverts and tail. Well-defined grey patches on breast-sides help separate from female Little Pied. First-year male resembles female, but has blue cast to mantle, wings and tail. Male nominate (W Himalayas) has white supercilium and white patches at base of tail, which are typically lacking in E populations (*F. s. aestigma*). **Voice** Feeble, disjointed, high-pitched song with trills and chirps. **HH** Breeds in broadleaved or pine forest; winters in open deciduous woodland and well-wooded areas.

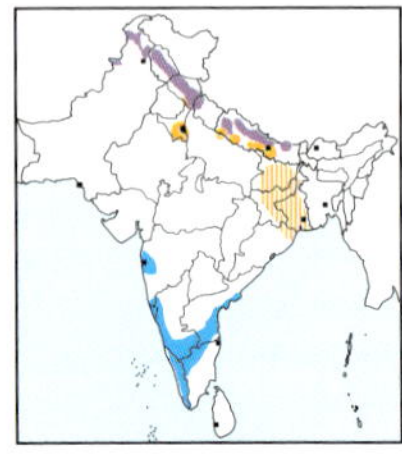

Rusty-tailed Flycatcher *Ficedula ruficauda* 14cm

Breeds in Himalayas; winters mainly in SW India. **ID** Rufous uppertail-coverts and tail, resulting in (female) redstart-like appearance. Larger than Asian Brown, with flatter forehead, and crown feathers are often slightly raised, giving crested appearance to nape. Further, has rather plain face, with only faint supercilium (back to eye) and indistinct eye-ring, and entirely orange lower mandible and cutting edges to upper mandible. **Voice** Song loud and melodious compared to closely related species: a drawn-out, rising and falling mournful whistle followed by a rapid warbling. Calls include a bullfinch-like *peu-peu* and short, deep churring. **HH** Favours forest clearings and edges. Breeds in open mixed coniferous-broadleaved forest; winters in edges and clearings of lowland evergreen broadleaved forest. **TN** Formerly placed in *Muscicapa*.

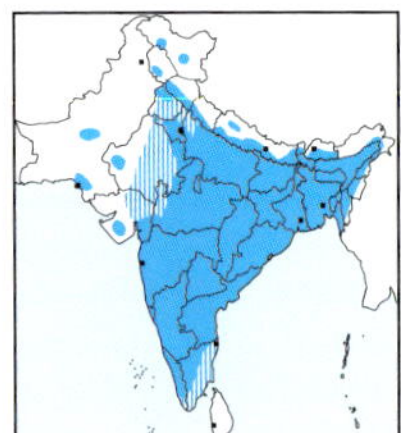

Taiga Flycatcher *Ficedula albicilla* 11.5cm

Widespread winter visitor except the north-west. **ID** Very similar to Red-breasted. Male has orange restricted to throat, bordered below by grey breast-band; female and first-winter have colder grey-brown upperparts than Red-breasted, with pronounced black uppertail-coverts (browner in Red-breasted), and underparts are whiter with grey on breast. Bill mainly dark. **Voice** Calls include a buzzing *drrrrrrt*, drier than Red-breasted. **HH** Open forest, plantations, and scrub at cultivation edges.

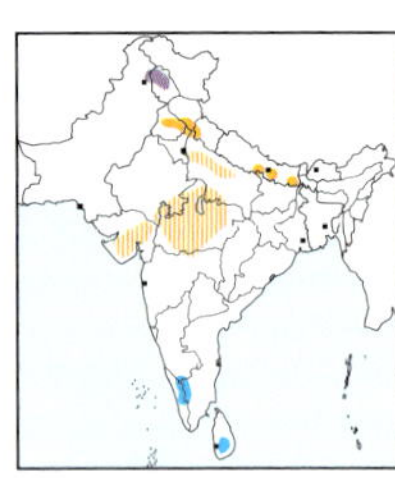

Kashmir Flycatcher *Ficedula subrubra* 13cm

Resident. Breeds in NW Himalayas; winters in Sri Lanka and Western Ghats. **ID** Very similar to Red-breasted and Taiga Flycatchers, with white-sided black tail that is frequently cocked. Male has deep rufous underparts (extending to lower breast and flanks), diffuse black border to throat and breast, and darker grey-brown upperparts. Bill can be mainly orange and quite striking. Female and first-winter male variable, but usually with some mottled rufous-orange on throat and breast, and pronounced grey sides to neck and breast. Can resemble male Red-breasted, but rufous is often more pronounced on breast than on throat, and often continues as a wash onto belly and/or flanks; upperparts slightly darker grey-brown. First-winter female lacks 'orange' on underparts. Darker grey-brown upperparts and grey wash to sides of neck and on breast are best distinctions from female Red-breasted; pale base to bill helps separate it from Taiga. **Voice** Song a short, sweet phrase, *sweet-eat, sweet-eat-did-he*; calls include a staccato rolled twitter, also, a sharp *chack* and a rattling *purr*. **HH** Breeds in deciduous forest; winters in forest edges, tea estates and gardens. Globally threatened.

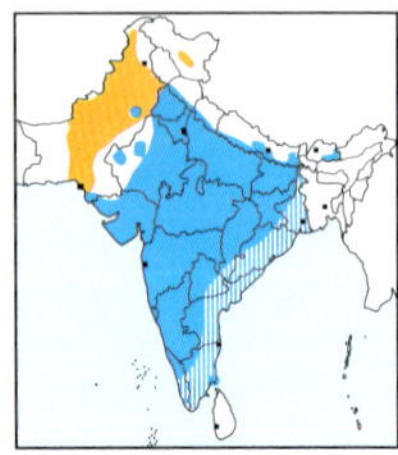

Red-breasted Flycatcher *Ficedula parva* 11.5cm

Widespread winter visitor and passage migrant except for the north-east and parts of the north-west. **ID** Has white sides to long blackish tail, which is frequently cocked; bill has distinctly paler base to lower mandible. Male has red throat and upper breast, and creamy-white rest of underparts. Many males lack red throat until second or third year and resemble females. Female lacks grey cast to crown and face of male, and underparts are creamy-white, suffused buff on breast. First-winter has orange-buff greater covert wing-bar. **Voice** Calls include a *tic* unlike usual call of Taiga, also a quiet, dry *trrt, trrt*. **HH** Open forest, scrub at cultivation edges, orchards and roadside trees.

♂
superciliaris
♂
aestigma
Ultramarine
Flycatcher
♀
superciliaris
♂ 1st-year
superciliaris
juv
superciliaris
ad
ad
Rusty-tailed
Flycatcher
♂
♀
juv
♀
Taiga Flycatcher
juv
♂
Kashmir
Flycatcher
♂
♀
Red-breasted Flycatcher

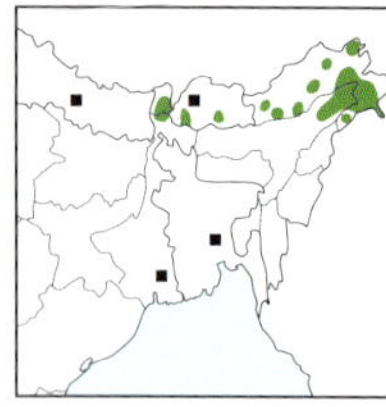

Rusty-bellied Shortwing *Brachypteryx hyperythra* 12–13cm

Resident. E Himalayas. **ID** Male has a short white supercilium (sometimes obscured), dark blue upperparts including wings and tail, and rufous-orange underparts. Much shorter supercilium and rufous-orange vent and undertail-coverts help separate from Indian Blue Robin. Orange chin and undertail-coverts, dark blue wings, shorter tail and longer legs help separate from Snowy-browed Flycatcher. Female has olive-brown upperparts, rufous-orange underparts with whitish centre to belly, and lacks white supercilium. **Voice** Song similar to Lesser, but faster, longer and more musical, a high-speed warble; calls include *chack*. **HH** Skulking and largely terrestrial. Breeds in dense bamboo, undergrowth in broadleaved evergreen forest, also steep, damp and densely vegetated gulleys. Winters in thick secondary scrub, forest undergrowth, overgrown gulleys, bamboo, reeds and grassland.

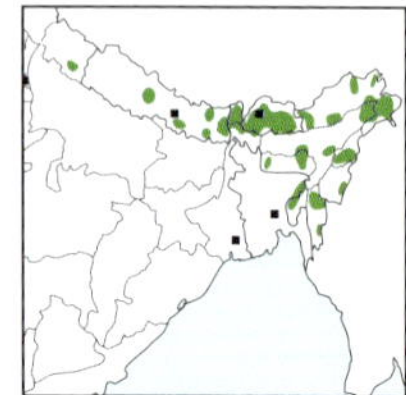

Lesser Shortwing *Brachypteryx leucophris* 11–13cm

Resident. Himalayas, NE India and Bangladesh. **ID** Smaller and shorter-tailed than Himalayan, with long pinkish legs. Male slaty-blue with white throat and belly. Female has rufous-brown upperparts, white throat and belly, and rufous-brown wash and diffuse scaling on breast and flanks. Both sexes have short white supercilium which can be obscured. First-year male similar to female but greyer above and on breast. Male *B. l. carolinae* (NE Indian hills) does not occur in grey form and has rufous upperparts and whitish underparts with variable scaling on breast. **Voice** Song a brief melodious warble of 10–12 notes, the first notes alternating up and down, then accelerating into a rapid jumble; calls include hard *tock-tock* and plaintive whistle. **HH** Very skulking. Keeps mostly to forest floor among thick undergrowth. Seeks insects by hopping on the ground among leaf litter, or by working through low stems and branches. Thick undergrowth in damp broadleaved forest and second growth.

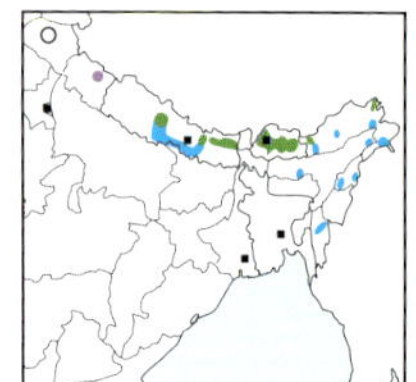

Himalayan Shortwing *Brachypteryx cruralis* 13cm

Resident. Himalayas and NE India. **ID** Larger than Lesser with longer tail and dark legs. Male dark slaty-blue, with black lores and fine white supercilium. Female has brown upperparts with more rufescent wings, and brownish underparts with paler belly. Rufous-orange forehead and over eye, and more uniform brownish underparts (lacking striking white throat and belly) help separate from female Lesser. Immature male similar to female but has fine white supercilium. Juvenile has orange-buff spotting on underparts. **Voice** Song consists of high-pitched penetrating whistles, often introduced by slower disyllabic notes; calls include a scolding rattle and penetrating whistled *hweeep*. **HH** Very secretive. Skulks on ground under dense low cover in forest. Progresses on ground like a chat; alternately hops rapidly in short spurts, then pauses briefly. Undergrowth in moist, dense evergreen forest and thickets in damp ravines; also winters in tall grassland. **TN** Previously treated as conspecific with White-browed Shortwing *B. montana*.

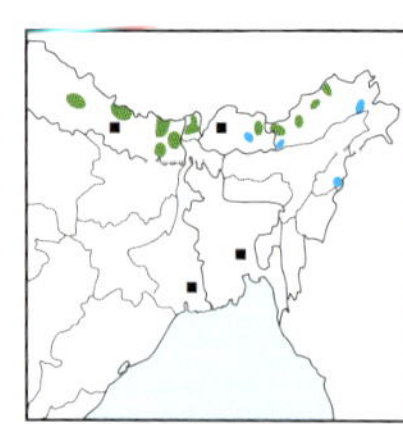

Gould's Shortwing *Heteroxenicus stellatus* 12–13cm

Resident or summer visitor. Himalayas. **ID** Adult has chestnut upperparts, slate-grey underparts (blacker around face) with white arrowhead-shaped spotting on belly and flanks. Juvenile has rufous streaking on head, mantle and breast, and greyish-black belly and flanks with broad whitish V-shaped spots. **Voice** Song a series of very high-pitched notes gradually becoming louder and accelerating: *tsitsitssiutssiutssiutsitsi*; *tik tik* in alarm. **HH** Often very confiding and comes out more in the open than other shortwings. Hops about on ground among fallen branches and roots. Breeds in dense rhododendron and bamboo growth, juniper shrubbery and thick undergrowth in fir and rhododendron forest; winters in boulder-strewn gullies, ravines with dense dwarf rhododendron, bamboo, fir and juniper forest, and with moss and fern undergrowth.

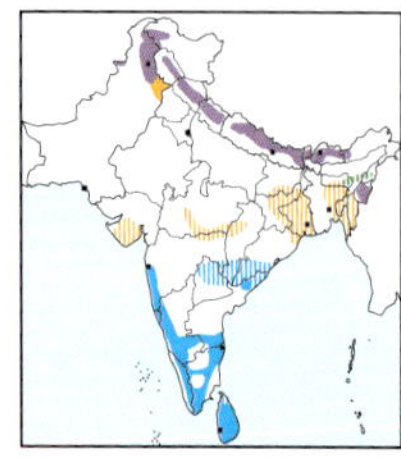

Indian Blue Robin *Larvivora brunnea* 13–15cm

Resident. Breeds in Himalayas and NE India; Winters in hills of SW, S and E India and Sri Lanka. **ID** From White-browed Bush Robin by horizontal stance, short tail (frequently bobbed and fanned), and long pale legs and large feet. Male has blue upperparts, white supercilium and rufous-orange underparts; chin paler, and vent and undertail-coverts are white; further differences from White-browed are shorter and broader white supercilium, (usually) black ear-coverts, and whitish centre to belly and vent. Female has olive-brown upperparts, orange-buff eye-ring (and sometimes supercilium to above eye), and orange-buff underparts diffusely mottled with brown, with whiter belly and vent. First-year male variable; some with buffish supercilium, dull blue upperparts, and dull orange breast and flanks. **Voice** Song comprises 3–4 piercing whistles followed by rapid, tumbling notes: *tit-tit-titwit-tichu-tichu-chuchu-cheeeh*; hard *tek-tek-tek* call. **HH** Breeds in dense undergrowth in moist forest or forest clearings; winters in evergreen forest and tea and coffee plantations. **TN** Formerly placed in *Luscinia*.

♂
Rusty-bellied Shortwing
♂
♂
Lesser Shortwing
♀
♀
♂ 1st-year
♂
♀
♂ 1st-year
Himalayan Shortwing
♀
juv
ad
Indian Blue Robin
♂
Gould's Shortwing

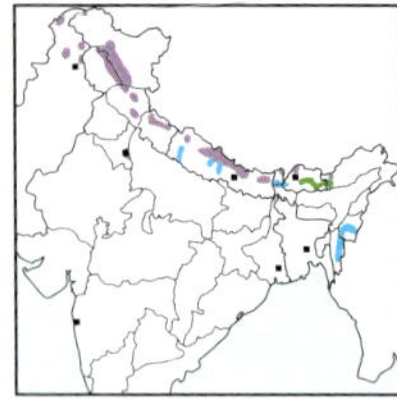

White-bellied Redstart *Luscinia phaenicuroides* 18–19cm

Resident. Breeds in Himalayas; winters in foothills and NE Indian hills. **ID** Long, graduated tail often held cocked and fanned. Male almost entirely dark slaty-blue with white belly, rufous tail sides, and white spots on alula. Female has olive-brown upperparts, white throat and belly, and chestnut on tail. First-year male resembles female, but is darker brown; head, mantle and breast have some blue, and tail has blue cast. **Voice** Song 3–4 whistling notes, the second drawn out, rising then falling, followed by a lower-pitched note. **HH** Breeds in subalpine shrubbery, in Pakistan in *Viburnum* thickets and dense herbage; winters in thick undergrowth and forest edges. **TN** Formerly placed in *Hodgsonius*.

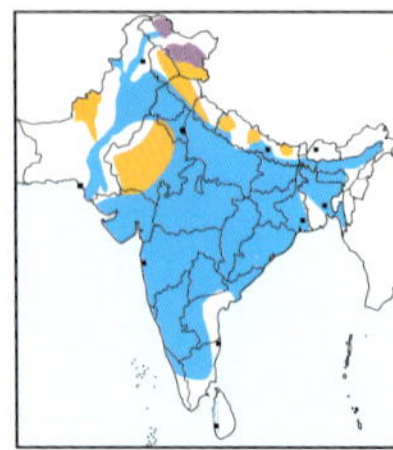

Bluethroat *Luscinia svecica* 15cm

Summer visitor to NW Himalayas; widespread in winter. **ID** Prominent white supercilium and rufous tail sides in all plumages. Male has variable blue, black and rufous pattern to throat and breast (obscured by whitish fringes in fresh plumage). Female has black submoustachial stripe and band of black spots across breast; older females can have breast-bands of blue and rufous. *L. s. abbotti* breeds in north-west and nominate is one of at least two races wintering in the region. **Voice** Long and varied song, with characteristic accelerating bell-like notes, e.g. *tree tree tree tree*; deep *chack* or *chack-chack* call. **HH** Summers in scrub along streams and lakes; winters in scrub and tall grass, often near water.

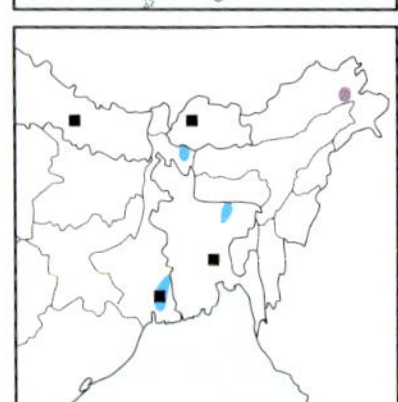

Firethroat *Calliope pectardens* 14cm

Rare winter visitor to north-east and Bangladesh. Vagrant: Nepal. **ID** Male has flame-orange throat and breast bordered at sides with black, white patch on sides of neck, and white sides to base of blackish tail. Male non-breeding has blue upperparts, and tail as breeding male, but underparts are similar to female. First-winter male has olive-brown upperparts, with slaty-blue back and wing-coverts; tail as adult male and underparts as adult female. Female has olive-brown upperparts, with rufous cast to uppertail-coverts, and buffish underparts; tail brown. Very similar to female Indian Blue Robin, but has orange-buff vent and undertail-coverts and dark legs and feet. **Voice** Song lengthy and varied, with sweet, repeated musical notes interspersed by harsher discordant notes. **HH** Dense wetland thickets and swamp forest, usually near water . **TN** Formerly placed in *Luscinia*.

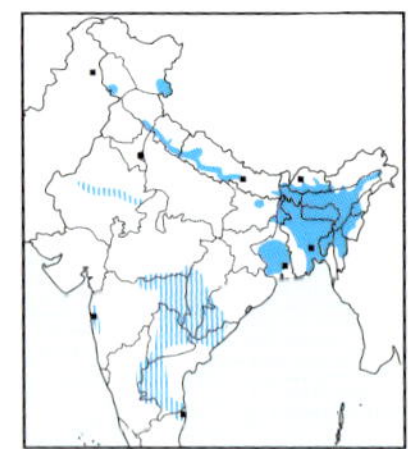

Siberian Rubythroat *Calliope calliope* 14–16cm

Winter visitor. Himalayan foothills, peninsula and NE India and Bangladesh. **ID** Male lacks black breast-band and white sides and tip to tail of Himalayan and Chinese Rubythroats, and has olive-brown upperparts. Female from female Himalayan and Chinese by olive-brown upperparts, olive-buff wash to breast and flanks, lack of white tip to tail, and has pale brown or pinkish legs. First-winter as adult (i.e. male has red throat), with retained juvenile buff tips to greater coverts and tertials. **Voice** Loud, clear double whistle *ee-uh* and hard *schak* calls, song a long, pleasant scratchy warble. **HH** Bushes and thick undergrowth, often near water. **TN** Formerly placed in *Luscinia*.

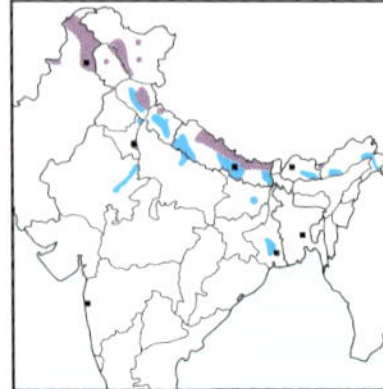

Himalayan Rubythroat *Calliope pectoralis* 14–16cm

Resident. Breeds in Himalayas; winters mainly foothills and NE India. **ID** Male from Siberian by lack of white submoustachial stripe, black breast (fringed white and partly obscured when fresh), greyer upperparts, and blackish tail with white sides and tip. Female from Siberian by grey-brown upperparts, grey breast and flanks contrasting with belly, white tail tip and black legs. First-winter male like adult (i.e. male has red throat), but buff tips to greater coverts and tertials, and tail browner with less white. **Voice** Song a loud, shrill series of variable undulating warbling phrases. Call a repeated *trrrr*. **HH** Breeds in subalpine bushes and *Caragana* scrub interspersed with scree and grassy slopes above treeline. **AN** White-tailed Rubythroat. **TN** Formerly placed in *Luscinia*.

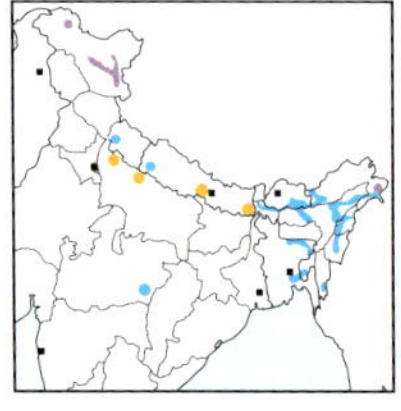

Chinese Rubythroat *Calliope tschebaiewi* 14–16cm

Breeds in E Ladakh. Winters from Uttarakhand east to Arunachal and NE India. **ID** Male as Himalayan but has white submoustachial stripe, slightly larger red throat patch, narrower black breast-band, and dark markings on belly and flanks. From male Siberian by greyer upperparts, black breast-band and blackish tail with white sides and tip. Female as Himalayan but has pale submoustachial stripe (mirroring pattern of male). **Voice** Very similar to Himalayan but generally has shorter phrases. **HH** Breeds in subalpine and alpine areas with bushes, boulders and scree, often near water; winters in lowland dense scrub. **AN** and **TN** Formerly placed in *Luscinia* and treated as conspecific with Himalayan Rubythroat as White-tailed Rubythroat.

♂
♀
White-bellied
Redstart
♀ 1st-win
svecica
♂ br
abbotti
♂ non-br
svecica
Bluethroat
♂
♀
Firothroat
♂
♀
Siberian
Rubythroat
♀
♂
♀
juv
Himalayan Rubythroat
♀
♂
Chinese Rubythroat

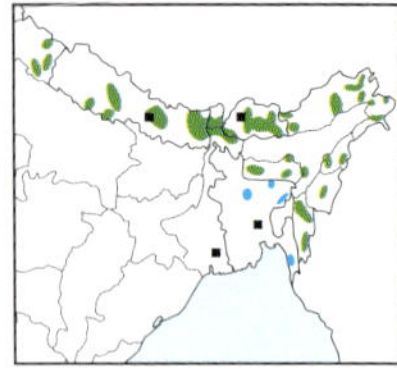

White-tailed Blue Robin *Myiomela leucura* 17–19cm

Resident. Himalayas and NE Indian hills also winter records from Bangladesh. **ID** White patches on tail in all plumages (visible as tail is slowly dipped and spread). Male blue-black, with glistening blue forehead and shoulders; concealed white patch on side of neck. Female olive-brown with whitish lower throat. First-year male similar to female but with blue on uppertail-coverts. **Voice** Loud, clear, jangling whistling song of 7–8 notes; calls include one- or two-note whistle. **HH** Undergrowth in moist broadleaved forest, often near streams, favours bamboo. **AN** White-tailed Robin.

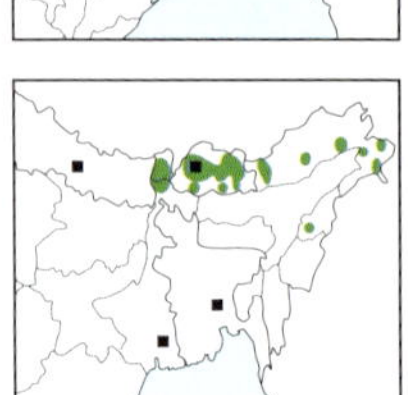

Blue-fronted Robin *Cinclidium frontale* 18–20cm

Resident. E Himalayas. **ID** Long, graduated all-dark tail lacking any white or rufous, which is frequently fanned. Male deep blue, with glistening blue forehead, supercilium and bend of wing. Female almost entirely dark brown with slightly paler underparts. From female White-bellied Redstart by dark brown tail and more uniform brown underparts. More terrestrial with longer legs and horizontal carriage compared with White-tailed Blue Robin. First-year male similar to female but has blue on forehead, and dark throat, lores and shoulders. **Voice** Song a series of melodic phrases, e.g. *tuuee-be-tue*; harsh, buzzy *zshwick* in alarm. **HH** Dense undergrowth in moist forest and dense vegetation at forest edges and in gullies.

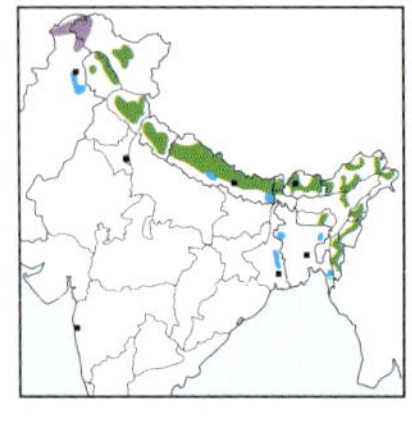

Himalayan Bluetail *Tarsiger rufilatus* 15cm

Resident. Breeds in Himalayas; winters south to NE Indian hills and NE Bangladesh. **ID** Well-defined white throat, orange flanks and blue uppertail-coverts and tail. Male has blue upperparts and breast-sides and white centre of breast and belly. Supercilium and shoulder patch brighter turquoise blue. Female has olive-brown upperparts and breast-sides, prominent whitish eye-ring and suggestion of greyish supercilium. First-winter as female, and male can breed in this plumage. See Vagrants for comparison with Red-flanked Bluetail. **Voice** Song a series of short, pleasant and rolling *tree trr-tretritt*, rising then falling; calls include a deep croaking *tock-tock*. **HH** Breeds in conifer and conifer-oak forests; winters in broadleaved evergreen forest, thickets, clearings and open woodland. **TN** Formerly treated as conspecific with Red-flanked Bluetail.

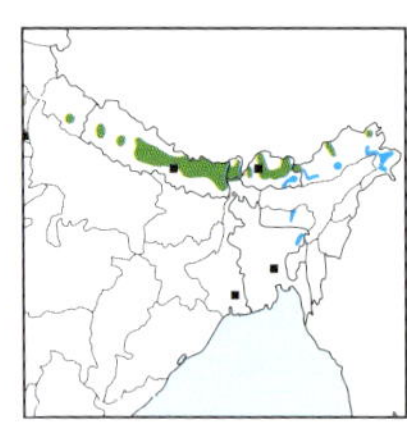

Rufous-breasted Bush Robin *Tarsiger hyperythrus* 12–13cm

Resident. Breeds in Himalayas; winters south to NE Indian hills and NE Bangladesh. **ID** Carriage and profile as Himalayan Bluetail. Long legs help separate from blue flycatchers. Male has blue upperparts, blacker ear-coverts, glistening blue supercilium and shoulders, narrow rufous-orange throat, and rufous-orange underparts with white belly and vent. Female has blue uppertail-coverts and tail; compared with female Himalayan Bluetail has orange-buff throat, and browner breast and flanks (lacking white throat and orange flank patch of Himalayan). **Voice** Song a lisping warble *zeew..zee..zee..zee*; call a *duk-duk-duk-squeak*. **HH** Mainly in lower forest storey. Summers in bushes in edges and clearings of dwarf rhododendron-birch forest and fir-rhododendron forest; winters in moist undergrowth of oak-rhododendron forest, favouring stream edges.

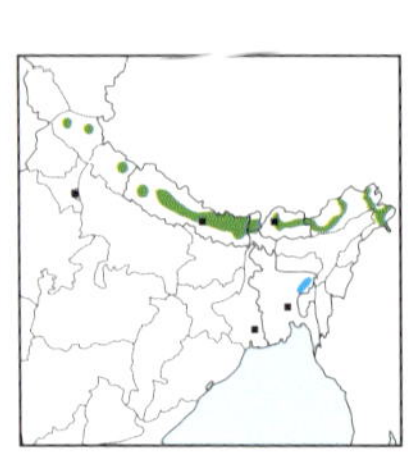

White-browed Bush Robin *Tarsiger indicus* 13–15cm

Resident. Himalayas and NE Indian hills and NE Bangladesh. **ID** Upright stance, rounded head, long tail (frequently cocked) and dark legs are good features from Indian Blue Robin. Male also has longer and finer supercilium (reaching nape), darker slaty-blue upperparts, and entirely rufous-orange belly and vent. Some males show fine white moustachial stripe. Female has long (sometimes part-concealed) buffish-white supercilium and orange-buff throat concolorous with underparts. First-summer male as female; can breed in this plumage. **Voice** Song a bubbling double-phrased *shri-de-de-dew....shri-de-de-dew*; call a repeated *trrrr*. **HH** Mainly terrestrial. Summers mainly in subalpine forest with dense undergrowth and bamboo; winters in dense forest understorey.

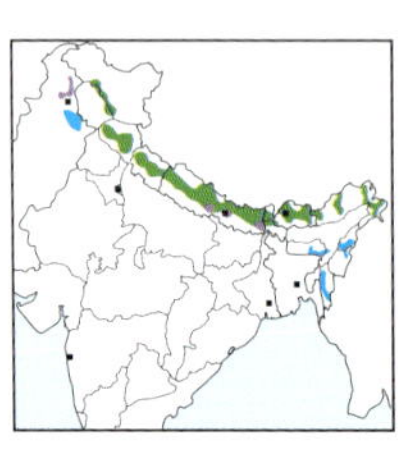

Golden Bush Robin *Tarsiger chrysaeus* 14–15cm

Resident. Himalayas and NE Indian hills. **ID** Male has blackish mask, orange supercilium, orange scapular line, orange underparts, and orange rump and sides to black tail. Female has prominent orange-buff eye-ring, duller (and less distinct) buffish-orange supercilium and underparts, uniform golden-olive upperparts, pale orange uppertail-coverts and sides to olive-brown tail. First-summer male as female but has more contrasting tail pattern. Both sexes with long pale legs and pale lower mandible. **Voice** Song a high wispy *tze-du-tee-tse* ending in a lower *chur-r-r-r-r*; purring croak, *trr-trr* call, also a harder *tcheck-tcheck*. **HH** In bushes or on ground. Summers in subalpine shrubbery near treeline and bushes in coniferous forest clearings and edges; winters in forest undergrowth and dense secondary scrub.

♂
♀
♀
juv
Blue-fronted
Robin
White-tailed
Blue Robin
♂
♀
♂
juv
♂
♀
Himalayan
Bluetail
juv
♀
Rufous-breasted
Bush Robin
♂
♂
♀
♀
White-browed
Bush Robin
juv
juv
Golden Bush Robin

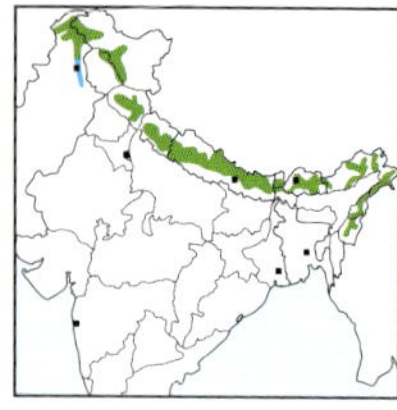

Little Forktail *Enicurus scouleri* 12–14cm

Resident. Himalayas and NE Indian hills. **ID** Small with short black tail with prominent white sides, black band on white rump, and prominent white forehead. Juvenile lacks white forehead, has brownish-black upperparts, and white underparts with dark scaling on throat and breast. **Voice** Generally silent. **HH** Always close to water; unlike other forktails is not dependent on tree cover. Continually fans and closes tail. Feeds by standing on or running over partly submerged rocks, picking up invertebrates from the water. Less active and restless than other forktails. Rushing mountain streams, often near waterfalls; also, slower-moving streams and rivers in winter.

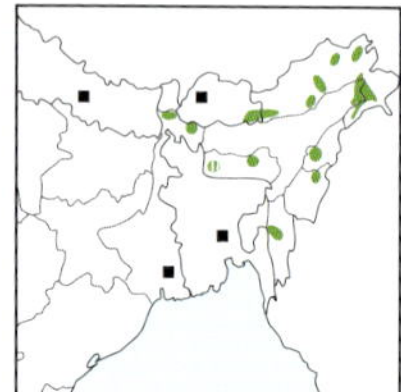

White-crowned Forktail *Enicurus leschenaulti* 25–28cm

Resident. E Himalayan foothills and NE Indian hills. **ID** Resembles Black-backed, but is larger, with longer tail, has prominent white forehead and forecrown, and black of throat extends to breast. White does not extend behind eye as in Black-backed, and forehead feathers often held erect creating a small crest. Narrower white band on wing compared with Black-backed. Lacks white patch at base of primaries which is usually (but not always) visible as a small white wedge in Black-backed. Unspotted black mantle separates it from Spotted. Juvenile lacks white forehead, has brownish-black upperparts, brownish-black throat and breast with white streaking, brown mottling on upper belly, and brown flanks. **Voice** Call a harsh *scree* or *scree chit chit*; also, an elaborate, high-pitched whistling song. **HH** Habits similar to Spotted. Very shy and flies off immediately if disturbed. Fast-flowing rivers and streams in dense tropical evergreen forest.

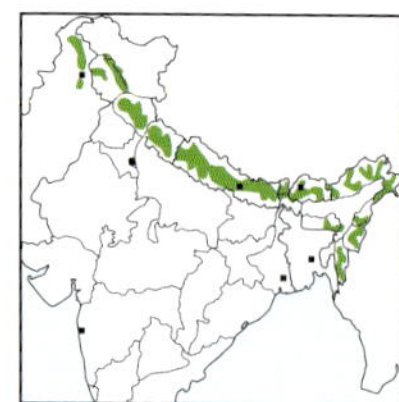

Spotted Forktail *Enicurus maculatus* 25–26cm

Resident. Himalayas and NE Indian hills. **ID** From other forktails by combination of large size and very long tail, white spotting on black mantle (forming white collar towards nape), prominent white forehead and black of throat extending to breast. White-spotted mantle separates it from White-crowned. Juvenile lacks white forehead, has brownish-black upperparts, paler brownish-black throat and breast with white streaking, brown mottling on upper belly and brown flanks. *E. m. guttatus* (E Himalayas and north-east) differs from nominate (W and C Himalayas) in being smaller, lacking white scaling on black breast, and having fewer and smaller white spots on mantle. **Voice** Calls include a shrill, rasping *kreee* or *tseek* or more disyllabic *tsueee* closely resembling Blue Whistling Thrush, but lower and less shrill; also, a creaky *cheek-chik-chi-chi-chik-chik* and repeated high penetrating *tjeet* in flight. **HH** Singly or in pairs, always close to water. Like other forktails has characteristic habit of constantly swaying its tail slowly up and down and usually holds it above the horizontal. Very restless, frequently turns from side to side. Walks daintily over stones at water's edge or hops from stone to stone in mid-stream, picking up invertebrates. Has graceful, undulating flight low over water. Rocky streams in forest and shaded wooded ravines; avoids larger rivers, lakes and open country.

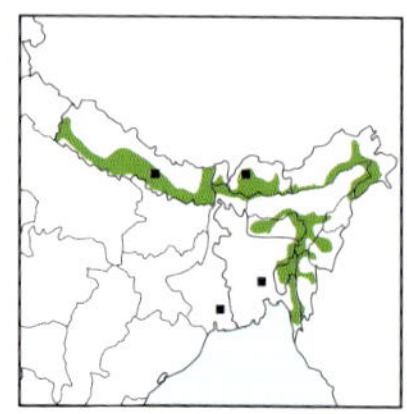

Black-backed Forktail *Enicurus immaculatus* 20–25cm

Resident. Himalayan foothills, NE India and Bangladesh. **ID** From Slaty-backed by black (rather than slate-grey) crown and mantle, and typically shows more extensive white on forehead and only a narrow white wedge at base of primaries at rest. Crown and mantle can appear a shade paler/greyer than wing-coverts and throat, causing potential confusion, but not the contrast of Slaty-backed. Smaller, with white restricted to forehead, and white breast, compared to White-crowned. Juvenile has shorter tail, lacks white forehead and supercilium, has brownish-black upperparts, and dark scaling on white breast. **Voice** Call a hollow *huu*, like Grey Bushchat call, often followed by a shrill *zeee*. **HH** Habits similar to Spotted. Fast-flowing streams in moist tropical and subtropical broadleaved forest.

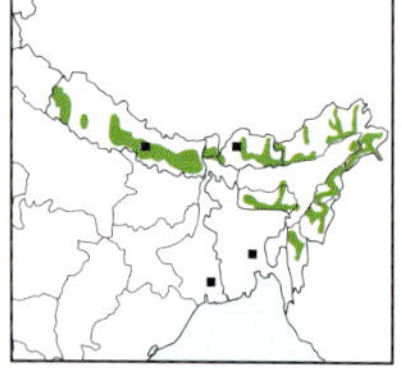

Slaty-backed Forktail *Enicurus schistaceus* 20–25cm

Resident. Himalayas and NE India. **ID** From Black-backed by slate-grey (rather than black) crown and mantle, contrasting with black throat and wing-coverts. Typically, has less white on forehead and a more extensive white crescent at base of primaries at rest than Black-backed. Juvenile has shorter tail, lacks white forehead and supercilium, has brown upperparts and dark scaling on white breast. **Voice** Calls include a high, thin, sharp, metallic screech, *teenk* and short, shrill, high, thin *seet*. **HH** Habits similar to Spotted. Large fast-flowing rocky streams in forest and wooded lake margins in tropical and subtropical zones.

ad
Little Forktail
ad
White-crowned
Forktail
juv
Spotted Forktail
ad
ad
Black-backed
Forktail
ad
Slaty-backed
Forktail

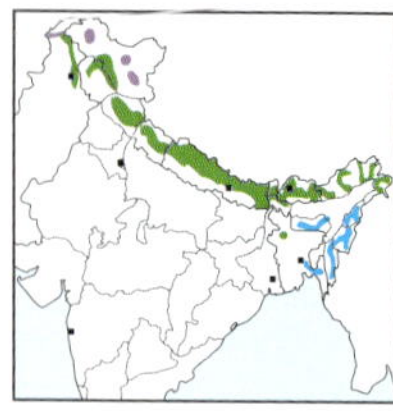

Blue-fronted Redstart *Phoenicurus frontalis* 15–16cm

Resident. Breeds in Himalayas; winters in foothills, NE Indian hills and Bangladesh. **ID** Orange rump and tail sides, with black centre and tip to tail in all plumages. Male has blue head and upperparts, with brighter blue forehead and supercilium, and chestnut-orange underparts; heavily obscured by rufous-brown fringes in non-breeding and first-winter plumages. Female has dark brown upperparts and underparts, orange wash to belly, and prominent buffish eye-ring; tail pattern best feature from other female redstarts. **Voice** Song 1–2 harsh trilling warbles, then short whistling phrases; calls include *ee-tit*. **HH** Breeds in subalpine shrubbery and on stony slopes with scattered bushes above treeline; winters in bushes and open forest.

Plumbeous Redstart *Phoenicurus fuliginosus* 12–13cm

Resident. Breeds in Himalayas and NE Indian hills; winters south to Bangladesh. **ID** Stocky and short-tailed; constantly flicks tail open while moving it up and down. Male slaty-blue with rufous-chestnut tail. Female and first-year male have black-and-white tail and white spotting on grey underparts. Juvenile resembles female (with same tail pattern) but has buff spotting on browner upperparts and black scaling on buffish underparts. **Voice** Song a rapidly repeated, insect like *streee-treeee-treee-treeeh*; strident *peet-peet* in alarm. **HH** Fast-flowing mountain streams and rivers. **AN** Plumbeous Water Redstart. **TN** Formerly placed in *Rhyacornis*.

Rufous-backed Redstart *Phoenicurus erythronotus* 15cm

Winter visitor. Hills of Pakistan and W Himalayas. **ID** Large size. Can appear rather shrike-like, tail can be held slightly cocked, and flicks tail and drops wings in a flycatcher-like manner. Male has black mask contrasting with grey crown and nape, rufous-orange mantle with blackish scapulars, blackish wings with white patch on inner wing-coverts and white primary coverts, and rufous-orange throat and breast; duller with colours heavily obscured by pale fringes in non-breeding and first-winter plumages. Female has buffish eye-ring, double buffish wing-bars, broad buff fringes to tertials and dark brown centre to tail. **Voice** Calls include a soft croaking *gre-er*. **HH** Dry hills, ravines and valleys with scattered bushes, and scrub forest. **AN** Eversmann's Redstart.

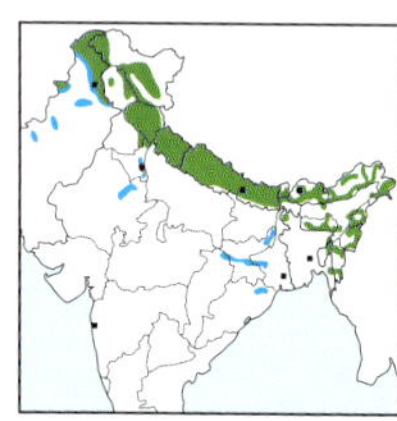

White-capped Redstart *Phoenicurus leucocephalus* 18–19cm

Resident. Breeds in Himalayas and NE Indian hills; winters south to Balochistan and NW and E India. **ID** Adult has white cap contrasting with blue-black rest of head, mantle and breast. Tail rufous with broad black terminal band. Lacks white patch in wing of White-winged Redstart. Sexes similar. Juvenile has black fringes to white crown and blackish underparts with rufous fringes. **Voice** Song a weak, drawn-out undulating whistle; main call a far-carrying, upward-inflected *tseeit tseeit*. **HH** Chiefly mountain streams and rivers; in summer also alpine meadows and rocky areas far from water. **AN** White-capped Water Redstart. **TN** Formerly placed in *Chaimarrornis*.

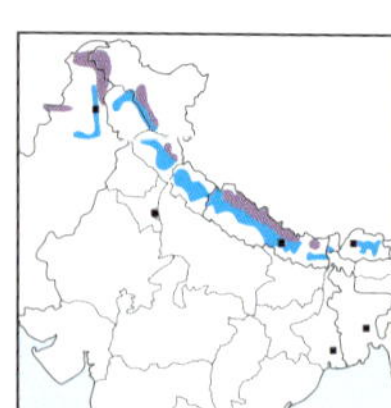

Blue-capped Redstart *Phoenicurus coeruleocephala* 15cm

Resident. Himalayas. **ID** Male differs from other redstarts in lacking any rufous in plumage. Has blue-grey crown and nape, black upperparts and tail, blackish wings and white patch on coverts and fringes to tertials, black throat and breast, and white rest of underparts; coloration heavily obscured by brown fringes in non-breeding and first-winter plumages (when crown appears browner). Female superficially resembles other female redstarts, but has duskier underparts, whitish belly and undertail-coverts, prominent double wing-bar, blackish tail and chestnut rump. Juvenile has dark brown barring on upperparts and underparts; juvenile male has broad white edges to tertials. **Voice** Pleasant repetitive warbling song *trrri-trrru-trrri-trrru-trrri-trrru*; call a rapid *tit-tit-tit*. **HH** Breeds on rocky slopes with juniper and open forest; winters in open forest and second growth.

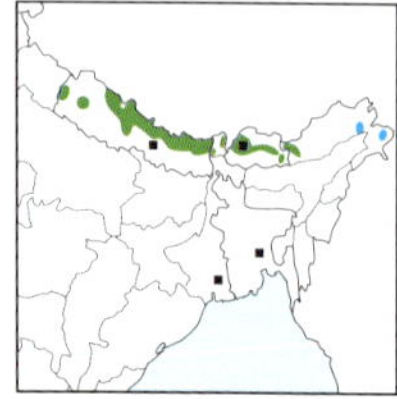

White-throated Redstart *Phoenicurus schisticeps* 15cm

Resident and winter visitor. Himalayas; unrecorded in Pakistan. **ID** In all plumages has white throat, white wing patch, rufous rump/uppertail-coverts and sides to tail base contrasting with otherwise blackish tail. Adult male has blue crown and nape (with brighter blue forehead), black ear-coverts and mantle, and rufous on scapulars and underparts. In fresh plumage, has rufous fringes to head and upperparts and buff fringes to underparts, less distinct than in some other redstarts. Adult female has grey-brown head and mantle, and paler grey-brown breast, becoming more buffish on belly. **Voice** Song a quiet series of short, trilled phrases, each comprising 2–3 consecutive note types, each starting hesitantly and usually accelerating towards end. Calls include a drawn-out *zieh*, followed by a rattle. **HH** Breeds in open shrubbery on rocky slopes and ridges, also bushes in open forest; winters in meadows, fallow cultivation and rocky, bushy slopes.

Blue-fronted Redstart
♂
♀
juv
Plumbeous Redstart
♂
♀
juv
♂ br
♂ 1st-win
White-capped Redstart
ad
juv
♀
Rufous-backed Redstart
♂ br
♂ 1st-win
♂
♀
♂ juv
Blue-capped Redstart
White-throated Redstart
♂ juv

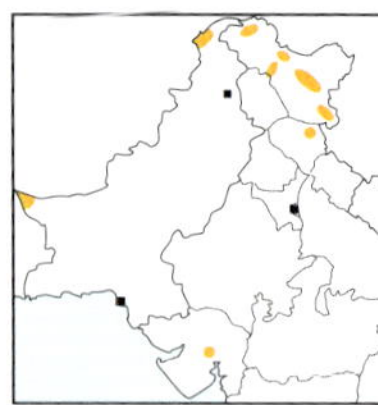

Common Redstart ***Phoenicurus phoenicurus*** 13–14.5cm

Spring passage migrant. Mainly Pakistan. **ID** Male from male Black by paler grey crown, nape and mantle, generally more prominent white band on forehead and line to above eye, black of throat does not extend onto breast, and has white centre to belly. Lacks white wing flash of Hodgson's Redstart (except *samamisicus*) and black of throat does not extend onto breast. Plumage duller and heavily obscured by pale fringes in non-breeding and first-winter plumages. Hodgson's does not have a distinct fresh plumage, and first-winter male of that species is as female. Female similar to female Black and Hodgson's, but has warmer brown upperparts and buffish underparts, with whiter throat and belly, and variable orange wash to breast and flanks. Male *P. p. samamisicus* (vagrant) has white wing flash. **Voice** Calls include distinctive *hweet*. **HH** Arid scrubby areas.

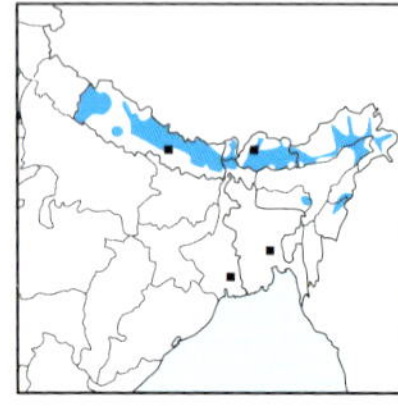

Hodgson's Redstart ***Phoenicurus hodgsoni*** 15cm

Winter visitor. Himalayas and NE Indian hills. **ID** Male has grey upperparts, white wing patch, and black throat and upper breast. Black extends further onto breast than in Common Redstart, which lacks prominent white wing patch (except for vagrant. *P. p. samamisicus*). Does not have distinct fringes in fresh plumage, obscuring bright coloration, unlike in Common. White wing patch is narrower and more elongated than in Daurian Redstart, and has more uniform grey mantle with black of throat extending to breast. Female has grey-brown upperparts and grey underparts with variable whitish area on belly and orange-buff vent; very similar to Black but lacks rufous-orange wash to flanks and belly of latter. First-winter male as female. **Voice** Calls include rattling *tschrr* in alarm. **HH** Stony river beds, bushes, open forest and forest edges.

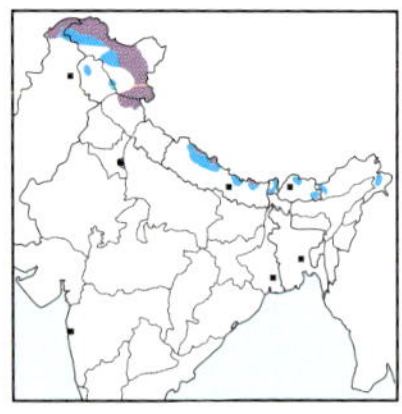

White-winged Redstart ***Phoenicurus erythrogastrus*** 18cm

Resident and winter visitor. Himalayas. **ID** Large size and stocky appearance. Male has white cap, black upperparts and large white patch on wing. Slightly duller in fresh plumage due to indistinct grey feather fringes. Female has buff-brown upperparts and buffish underparts. Resembles large female Black Redstart but has warmer brown upperparts, buffish underparts and more uniform rufous-orange tail. First-winter as respective adult. Juvenile has diffuse buff spotting and brown scaling; male has blacker wings with white wing patch. **Voice** Song a short whistling phrase *teet-teet-teet* followed by a wheezy burst; calls include weak *lik*. **HH** Breeds in dry rocky alpine meadows and glacial moraine; winters in stony pastures, scrub patches and along river beds. **AN** Güldenstädt's Redstart.

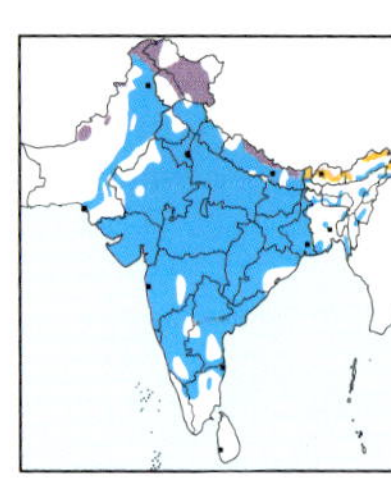

Black Redstart ***Phoenicurus ochruros*** 14–15cm

Resident. Breeds in Pakistan mountains and N Himalayas; widespread in winter except for most of Pakistan. **ID** Male has black or dark grey upperparts, black breast and rufous underparts; in fresh plumage has black duller owing to extensive brownish-grey fringes to body feathers. Female and first-year male are almost entirely dusky brown with rufous-orange wash on lower flanks and belly. From female Hodgson's by rufous-orange wash to lower flanks and belly; from female Blue-capped by rufous-orange tail concolorous with rump/uppertail-coverts and lack of prominent wing-bars. Lack of black terminal band to tail separates it from female Blue-fronted. Juvenile has diffuse dark scaling on upperparts and underparts, and fine buff greater covert bar. Male *P. o. phoenicuroides* (W Himalayas) has grey crown, nape and lower back; these areas are much blacker in *P. o. rufiventris* (C and E Himalayas). Female *phoenicuroides* can approach female Common Redstart in coloration of upperparts and underparts, and identification tricky, but Common is whiter on throat, belly and undertail-coverts. **Voice** Song a scratchy trill, followed by a short wheezy jingle; calls include short *tsip* and rapid rattle. **HH** Breeds in Tibetan steppe habitat above treeline; winters in cultivation, plantations by roadsides and canals, and riverine forest.

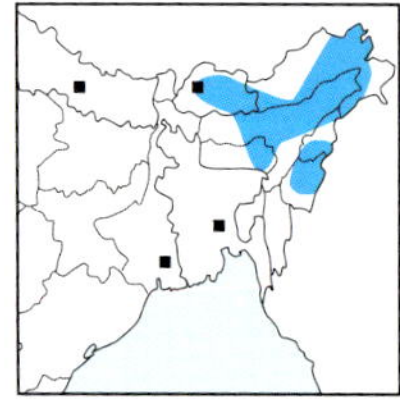

Daurian Redstart ***Phoenicurus auroreus*** 14–15cm

Winter visitor to E Himalayas and NE Indian hills. Vagrant: Nepal. **ID** Adult male has prominent white wing patch, blackish mantle, and black of throat does not extend to breast. Adult male in fresh plumage and first-winter male have black of mantle and coverts partly obscured by brown fringes (mantle appears brown, diffusely streaked black), and grey of crown and black of throat are duller owing to dark grey fringes. Adult female similar to female Black but has prominent white wing patch and darker centre to rufous tail. **Voice** Song a variable series of short, sweet, mostly descending phrases: 1–2 short clear notes followed by scratchy trill and wheezy jingling flourish. Calls include short, penetrating whistle. **HH** Breeds in open forest, around villages and trees in cultivation at high altitude; winters in bushes and second growth.

♂
1st-win
♂ br
♀
Common Redstart
♂
♀
Hodgson's Redstart
♂
♀
♂
juv
White-winged Redstart
♂
rufiventris
♂
phoenicuroides
♀
phoenicuroides
juv
phoenicuroides
Black Redstart
♂ non-br
♀
Daurian Redstart

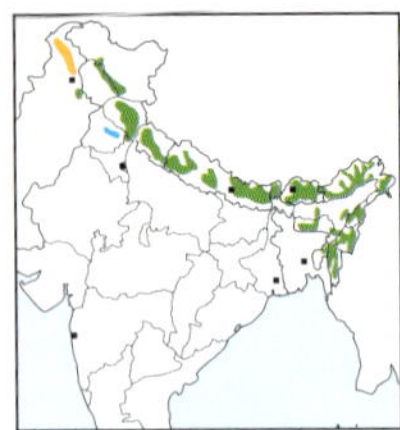

Chestnut-bellied Rock Thrush *Monticola rufiventris* 21–23cm

Resident. Himalayas and NE India. **ID** Male lacks white on wing; has chestnut-red underparts and blue upperparts including rump, uppertail-coverts and tail; crown brighter blue than blackish ear-coverts. Female has orange-buff lores and neck patch, dark malar stripe, dark barring on slaty olive-brown upperparts, and heavy scaling on underparts. Non-breeding and first-winter male similar to breeding male but have fine buff fringes to mantle, scapulars and throat. Juvenile resembles female (with buff neck patch) but has pale spotting on upperparts, and more boldly spotted underparts; male with blue on wing. **Voice** Undulating, fluty song, more subdued and softer than Blue-capped. **HH** Open forest on rocky slopes.

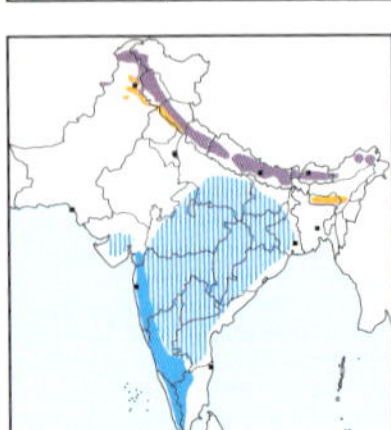

Blue-capped Rock Thrush *Monticola cinclorhyncha* 16–19cm

Summer visitor to Himalayas; winters mainly in Western Ghats. **ID** Male has white wing patch and blue-black tail, which contrast with rufous-orange rump/uppertail-coverts; also, blue crown and throat, contrasting with blackish ear-coverts and mantle, and rufous-orange underparts; pattern and coloration obscured by pale fringes in non-breeding and first-winter plumages. Female has olive-brown upperparts, with barred rump and whitish underparts boldly scaled with brown; lacks buff neck patch of Chestnut-bellied, blue cast to upperparts of Blue, and orange-red tail of Rufous-tailed. Juvenile resembles female but has buff spotting on crown and mantle, and buff fringes to coverts and tertials. **Voice** Short, fluty undulating song. **HH** Summers in open dry forest; dry rocky slopes with scattered trees; winters in moist deciduous forest and well-wooded areas.

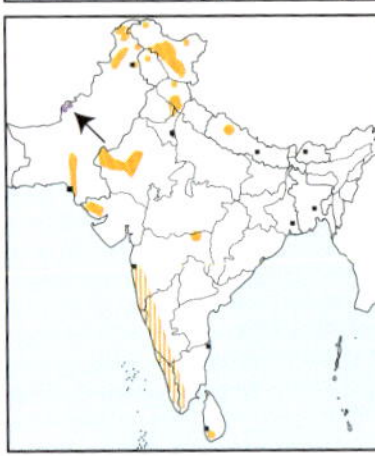

Rufous-tailed Rock Thrush *Monticola saxatilis* 16–19cm

Breeds Balochistan; passage migrant Pakistan and Ladakh. Vagrant: Nepal. **ID** The only rock thrush with orange-red uppertail-coverts and tail. Male has bluish head/mantle, white back and orange-red underparts; pattern and coloration much obscured by pale fringes in non-breeding and first-winter plumages. Female has grey-brown upperparts, finely spotted white and barred black (more uniform in worn plumage); underparts orange-washed and boldly scaled brown. **Voice** Song softer, more flowing than Blue Rock, with much mimicry and variety. **HH** Open rocky hillsides.

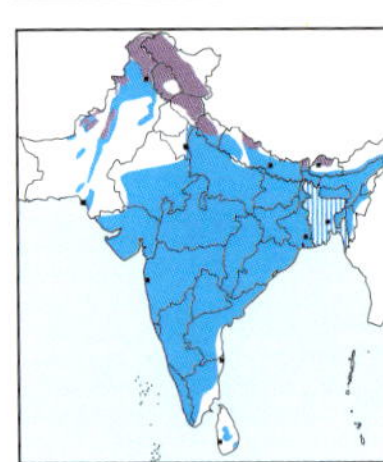

Blue Rock Thrush *Monticola solitarius* 20–23cm

Resident and winter visitor. Breeds in Balochistan and W Himalayas; widespread in winter. **ID** Male is almost entirely indigo-blue, with darker wings and tail; blue coloration obscured by pale fringes in non-breeding and especially first-winter plumages. Female has bluish cast to slaty-brown upperparts and buff scaling on underparts. Smaller than, and lacks buff neck patch of, female Chestnut-bellied. Juvenile resembles female but lacks any blue, has buff spotting and brown fringes to crown and mantle, and buff fringes to wing-coverts and tertials. Vagrant *philippensis* has rufous breast and belly; birds in north-east show variable amount of red on vent and are presumably intergrades. **Voice** Short and repetitive song with fluty phrases often with long pauses. **HH** Breeds on open rocky slopes; winters in dry rocky areas, rocky streambeds and ruins.

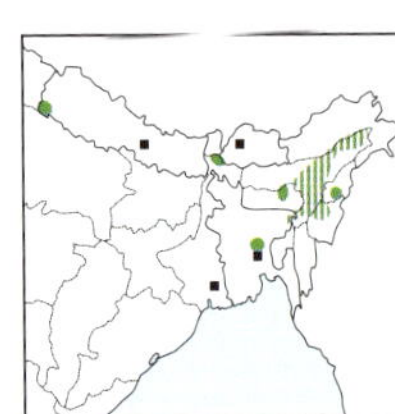

Jerdon's Bushchat *Saxicola jerdoni* 15cm

Resident. Mainly NE Indian plains and Himalayan foothills. **ID** Male has blackish upperparts, including rump and tail, and white underparts, with white throat clearly demarcated from black ear-coverts. Female and first-winter male similar to female Grey Bushchat, with rufous-brown upperparts, rufous rump and uppertail-coverts, and pale brownish-buff underparts with white throat. Lacks prominent supercilium and darker mask of Grey Bushchat (although some show slight suggestion of supercilium, and head pattern of Grey can be more uniform); has longer, more graduated tail lacking rufous at sides. **Voice** Song a a series of sweet, clear, thin, mellow, warbled phrases, often ending with rapidly trilled flourish; calls include a plaintive whistle, higher-pitched than other chats. **HH** Tall grassland; grass and reeds along rivers.

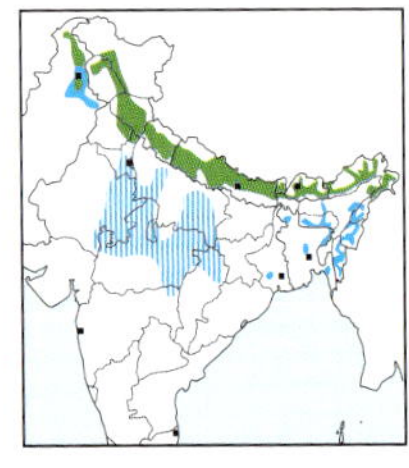

Grey Bushchat *Saxicola ferreus* 14–15cm

Resident. Breeds in Himalayas and NE Indian hills; winters south to N Indian plains. **ID** Male has white supercilium and dark mask; upperparts mainly grey with diffuse streaking and brownish cast in fresh plumage to almost black in worn (breeding) plumage; whitish underparts with grey breast and flanks. Has white patch on inner wing (often obscured) and brownish-black tail with white outer feathers. Female has buff supercilium contrasting with dark brown ear-coverts, and rufous rump and tail sides. First-winter as fresh-plumaged adult. Juvenile has buff spotting on upperparts and buffish underparts with distinct dark scaling. **Voice** Song brief and repeated: starts with 2–3 emphatic notes and ends with a trill. **HH** Bushes at forest edges and clearings, scrub-covered hillsides, second growth.

Chestnut-bellied Rock Thrush
♂
♀
♂ juv
♀ juv
♂ br
Blue-capped Rock Thrush
♂ 1st-win
♀
♂ br
♂ 1st-win
Rufous-tailed Rock Thrush
♀
♂ *philippensis*
♂ br *pandoo*
♂ 1st-win *pandoo*
♀ *pandoo*
Blue Rock Thrush
♂
♀
erdon's
ushchat
♂ fresh
♂ worn
♀
Grey Bushchat

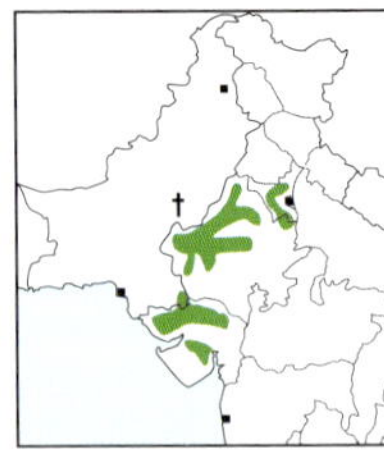

White-browed Bushchat *Saxicola macrorhynchus* 15cm

Resident. Mainly Rajasthan, India. **ID** Slimmer than other bushchats with longer tail and wings and longer and slimmer bill. Male has broad white supercilium, white patch on inner wing-coverts, white primary coverts, whitish underparts with buff wash to breast and much white in tail (all but central pair of rectrices have mainly white inner webs). Crown, mantle and ear-coverts blackish, and uppertail-coverts whitish, when worn (breeding). Crown, mantle and ear-coverts appear streaked when fresh (non-breeding) due to buffish fringes, and uppertail-coverts are buffish. Female similar to male in fresh plumage but lacks darker ear-coverts, lacks white on tail and primary coverts, and white on inner wing-coverts is reduced or lacking. First-winter male is similar to fresh adult male but white in tail less extensive and strongly tinged with buff and has dark primary coverts. **Voice** Low musical song, *twitch-chhe chee chee*; sharp *chip-chip* call. **HH** Frequently perches atop bushes. On ground has characteristic habit of puffing up its breast and swaying sideways making its whitish breast and belly conspicuous. Dry sandy desert plains with low herbs and very scattered bushes. Globally threatened. **AN** Stoliczka's Bushchat.

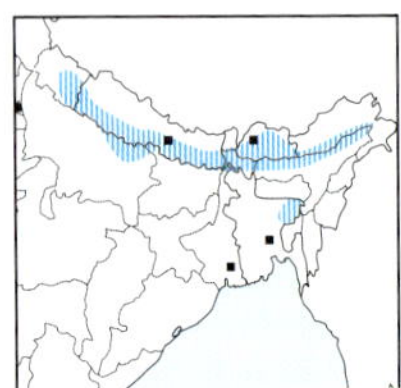

White-throated Bushchat *Saxicola insignis* 17cm

Winter visitor. N Indian plains and Nepal terai. **ID** Larger than Siberian Stonechat, with larger and longer-looking body, smaller-looking head and large bill. Male has white throat extending to form almost complete white collar, and has more white on wing than Siberian (including white patch at base of primaries). As Siberian, male in worn (breeding) plumage has blacker crown, ear-coverts and mantle, which appear streaked in fresh (non-breeding plumage) due to rufous-brown fringes. Rump whitish when worn and tinged rufous when fresh. Female similar to female Siberian; best told by size and structure, has broad buffish-white wing-bars and small whitish patch at base of primaries. **Voice** Metallic *teck-teck* call. **HH** Habits similar to Siberian Stonechat. Tall grasslands, reedbeds, tamarisks along watercourses and cane fields. Globally threatened. **AN** Hodgson's Bushchat.

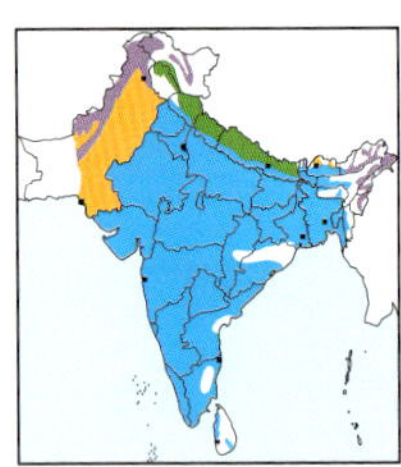

Siberian Stonechat *Saxicola maurus* 12.5cm

Breeds W and N Pakistan, Himalayas and NE India; widespread winter visitor. **ID** Breeding male has black head, white patches on neck and wing, orange breast and whitish rump. In fresh (non-breeding plumage) male has warm buff fringes to feathers of crown, mantle and wings, black of throat partly obscured by pale fringes, and has buff rump and wash to underparts. Female and first-winter lack black throat; pale supercilium, warm buff to brownish upperparts with dark streaking, and buff rump and wash to underparts. Three rather similar subspecies occur. *S. m. przevalskii* (not illustrated), a winter visitor to north and north-east, is perhaps the most distinctive, being larger and darker, with underparts almost entirely deep rufous-orange on both sexes. **Voice** Short jingling warble combining sweet thin whistles and dry trills; *whit trac-trac* in alarm. **HH** Usually in pairs. Perches prominently. Frequently flicks wings and jerks tail up and down. Summers in open country with bushes, high-altitude semi-desert; winters in scrub, reedbeds and cultivation. **TN** Formerly treated as conspecific with *S. torquatus* as Common Stonechat.

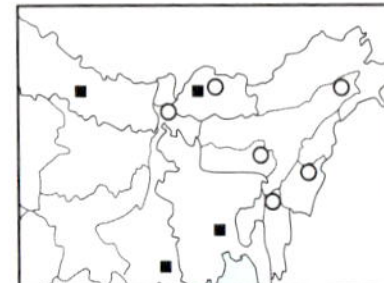

Amur Stonechat *Saxicola stejnegeri* 12.5cm

Winter visitor to north-east. **ID** Extremely like Siberian Stonechat with heavier bill and longer tail. Non-breeding male and first-winter more rufous above with rufous to rufous-buff rump, which is variably streaked (although unstreaked in some, as in Siberian). **Voice** Very similar to Siberian. **HH** Found in a wide variety of open landscapes, often on exposed perches. **TN** Formerly treated as conspecific with *S. torquatus* as Common Stonechat.

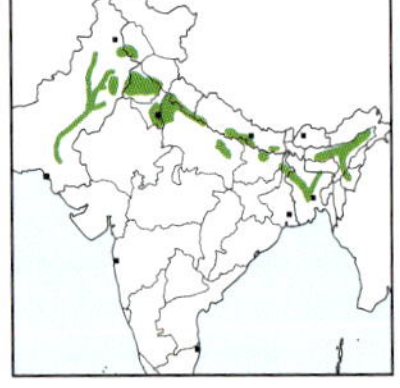

White-tailed Stonechat *Saxicola leucurus* 12–14cm

Resident. N subcontinent, mainly in plains. **ID** Male very similar to Siberian, but inner webs of all but central tail feathers largely white; showing much white in tail in flight but barely apparent at rest. Tends to show more restricted area of rusty-orange on breast, although some Siberian are very similar, and black throat extends beyond black hood forming 'bib'. Female has greyer upperparts, with diffuse and less distinct streaking, compared to Siberian. Tail paler grey-brown (blacker on Siberian), with diffuse pale tips and edges to feathers, and rump generally paler dirty buff. In NE India, male has darker orange on underparts, less white in tail; female darker and browner above (and more heavily streaked), although tail has pale edges. **Voice** Differences in song from Siberian poorly described; *peep-chaaa* alarm. **HH** Habits very similar to Siberian. Reeds and tall grassland, often in wet areas and near large rivers.

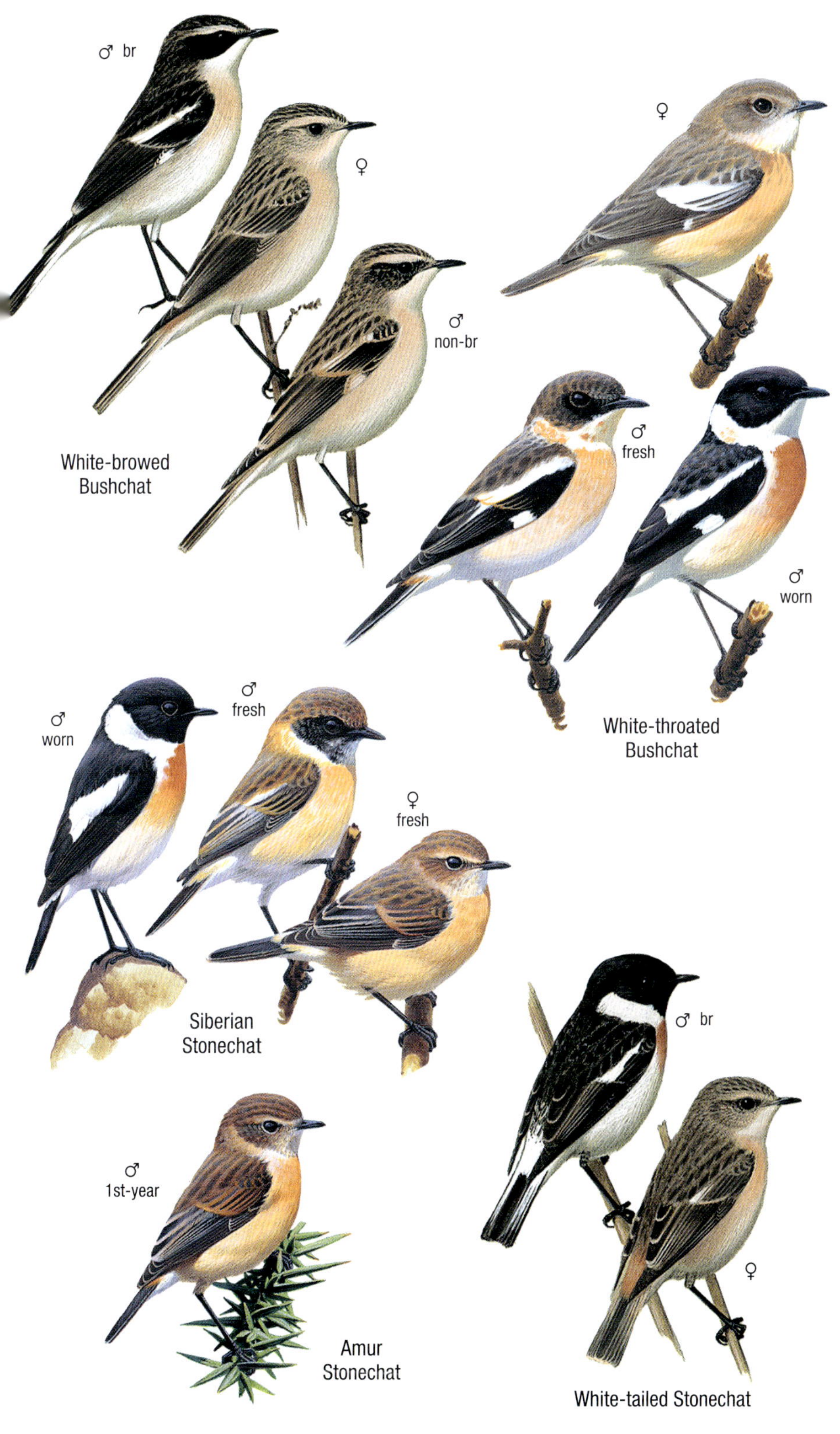
♂ br
♀
♂
non-br
White-browed
Bushchat
♀
♂
fresh
♂
worn
White-throated
Bushchat
♂
worn
♂
fresh
♀
fresh
Siberian
Stonechat
♂ br
♂
1st-year
♀
Amur
Stonechat
White-tailed Stonechat

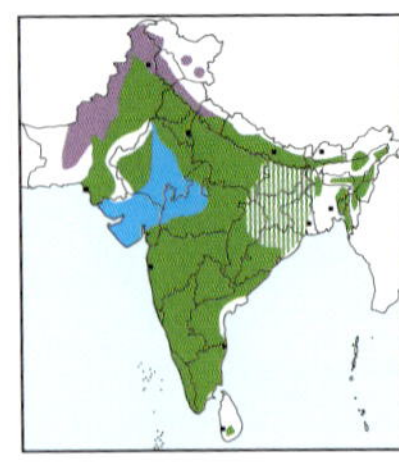

Pied Bushchat *Saxicola caprata* 13–14cm

Widespread resident. **ID** Male black except white rump and patch on wing; rufous fringes to body and wings in non-breeding and first-winter. Extent of white belly variable, most extensive in *S. c. bicolor* (north) and lacking in *S. c. atratus* (Sri Lanka). Female has dark brown upperparts and rufous-brown underparts, with slightly paler throat. Rump rufous-orange, contrasting with black tail. Head uniform but may show vague supercilium. **Voice** Song a brisk and whistling *chip-chepee-chewee chu*; calls include plaintive *chep chep-hee*. **HH** Habits similar to Siberian Stonechat. Territorial all year. Mainly cultivated and open country with scattered bushes or tall grass clumps; reeds and tall grass around canals and tanks; in Pakistan also juniper or pine forest and saline flats.

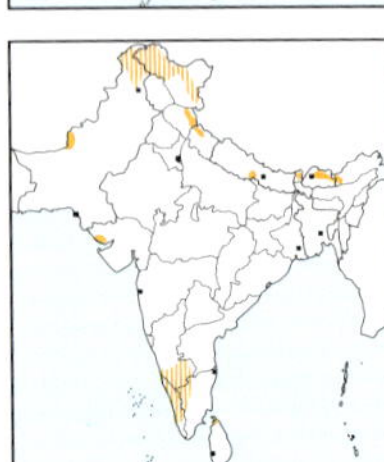

Northern Wheatear *Oenanthe oenanthe* 15cm

Passage migrant. Mainly Pakistan. **ID** Breeding male has blue-grey upperparts, white supercilium and black mask, pale orange breast and blackish wings. Breeding female greyish to olive-brown above with dull black wings; lacks black mask of male. Very similar to female Finsch's but has more prominent supercilium, lacks rufous patch on ear-coverts, and never shows dark grey/black on throat. Adult winter and first-winter have brownish-buff upperparts and buff wash below. Easily confusable with Isabelline but note structural differences (see that species) and slightly darker and browner upperparts and blackish centres to wing-coverts and tertials (with brighter and more rufous fringes); shows more white at sides of tail. Supercilium buffish in front of eye and whiter behind. **Voice** Hard *chack* call. **HH** Open stony ground and cultivation.

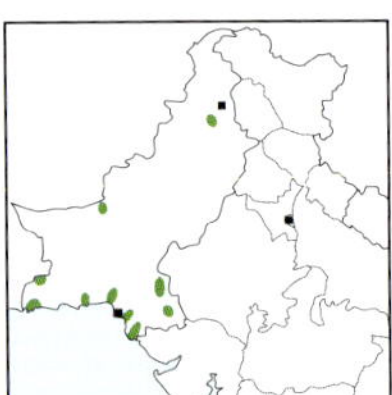

Hooded Wheatear *Oenanthe monacha* 17.5cm

Resident. Balochistan and SW Pakistan. **ID** Appears elongated, with long bill and tail, but relatively short legs (less upright stance than most wheatears). Flight rather buoyant. Male has white crown, black throat extending to breast, and largely white outer tail feathers (tips may be blackish). In fresh non-breeding plumage, has buffish or greyish wash to crown and pale fringes to upperparts and wings. Female grey-brown above and buffish below; sandy to rufous-buff rump and tail, with brown central tail feathers and rather plain-faced appearance. First-winter male as non-breeding male but tail as female. **Voice** Song short, melodious phrases, mixed with 'stone-clicking notes'; also, a brief thrush-like whistle; *wit-wit* in alarm. **HH** Barren desert.

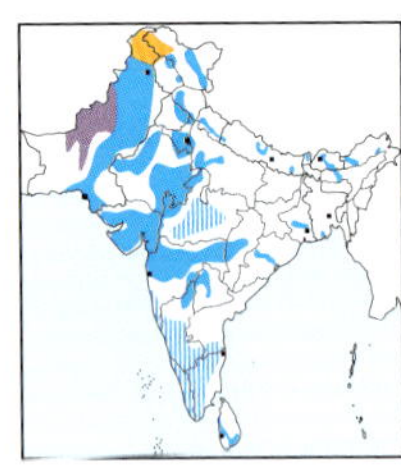

Isabelline Wheatear *Oenanthe isabellina* 16–17cm

Breeds in Pakistan; mainly winters in Pakistan, NW and C India. Vagrant: Nepal. **ID** Plain sandy-brown and buff. Stance upright and head and bill look rather large, legs long and tail short. From female Desert by structural features, more white at base and sides of tail, sandy-brown wings with contrastingly dark alula, and underwing-coverts whitish (rather than black) giving rise to pale underwing. Structural differences, sandier coloration including wings (with dark alula) and shorter tail with less white at sides are best features from female and first-winter Northern. Supercilium whitish in front of eye and buffish behind. Sexes similar but lores black in male. **Voice** Variable song, with changes of speed, a mix of hard and harsh notes and clear whistles; hard *chack* call. **HH** Breeds on stony plateaux and valleys; winters in sandy semi-desert.

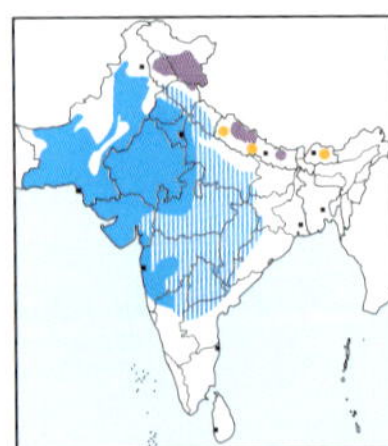

Desert Wheatear *Oenanthe deserti* 14–15cm

Breeds in NW Himalayas; winter visitor mainly to Pakistan and NW India. **ID** Comparatively small and well-proportioned wheatear, with largely black tail and contrasting white rump. Male has sandy-brown upperparts and black throat, with black on neck reaching black of wings (black partly obscured in fresh non-breeding and first-winter plumages). Female lacks black throat and has colder grey-brown crown and mantle; blackish centres to wing-coverts and tertials in fresh plumage, largely black wings when worn, and black underwing-coverts are useful differences from Isabelline. **Voice** Song: 2–4 mournful, descending whistles, often with grating notes ending with trill or whistles; *swii-tuk-tuk* in alarm. **HH** Breeds on rocky or sandy plateaux; winters in barren semi-desert, on gravel slopes or sand dunes.

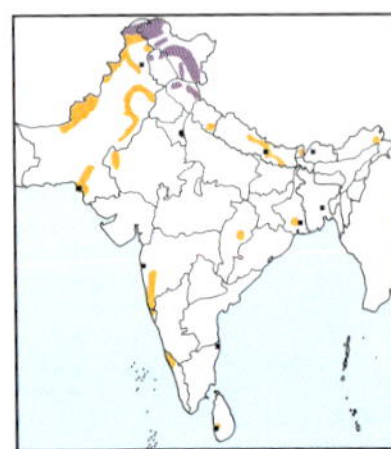

Pied Wheatear *Oenanthe pleschanka* 14.5–16cm

Breeds in NW; passage migrant more widely. Vagrant: Nepal. **ID** Has narrow black edge to outer tail and often only a narrow/broken terminal black band (broad inverted 'T' on Variable). On breeding male, white of nape extends to mantle, black of throat does not reach upper breast, and breast is washed buff (differences from *capistrata* race of Variable). Non-breeding and first-winter have pale fringes to upperparts and wings; males have grey-brown crown and mantle, and black of face and throat is partly obscured (distinct from Variable, which lacks prominent pale fringes). Breeding female not separable from female Variable, except by tail pattern. **Voice** Song lark-like fluting and whistling, with much mimicry. **HH** Open stony ground

♂ br
♀
♂
1st-win
Pied Bushchat
♂ br
♀ br
Northern
Wheatear
1st-win
br
♂
♀
Isabelline
Wheatear
non-br
Hooded
Wheatear
♂
1st-win
♂
♀
♀
non-br
♂ br
♀ br
♂
non-br
Desert Wheatear
♂
1st-win
♀
1st-win
Pied Wheatear

PLATE 221: BROWN ROCK CHAT AND WHEATEARS II

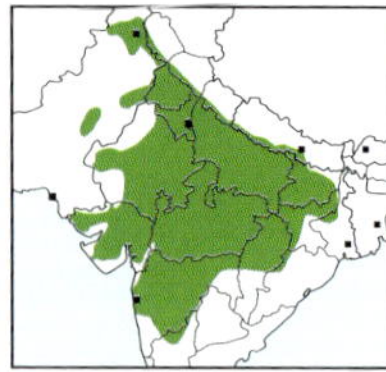

Brown Rock Chat *Oenanthe fusca* 17cm

Resident. Mainly Pakistan, lowland Nepal and N India. **ID** Smaller and longer-tailed than Blue Rock Thrush. Both sexes brown, with more rufescent underparts and blackish tail. Tail frequently (slowly) cocked and spread, and body frequently bobbed. Lacks chestnut vent of female Indian Robin. Juvenile darker brown, without rufous. **Voice** Song sweet, warbling and thrush-like, with mimicry; short harsh *tchk-tchk-tchk* in alarm. **HH** Territorial, often in same locality all year. Rocky hills, quarries, cliffs and buildings in towns and cities. **TN** Formerly placed in *Cercomela*.

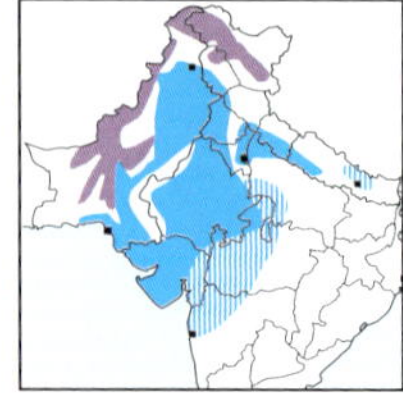

Variable Wheatear *Oenanthe picata* 15cm

Breeds in Balochistan and N Pakistan; winter visitor mainly to Pakistan and NW India. **ID** Very variable. Black terminal band to tail broader and more even than Pied Wheatear. Males can be mainly black (*O. p. opistholeuca*), have black head with white underparts (nominate; very similar to Hume's), or white crown and white underparts (*O. p. capistrata*; very similar to Pied). Nominate male from Hume's by smaller bill and slimmer appearance, black of throat extending to breast and white of rump reaching onto lower back. Breeding male *O. p. capistrata* differs from breeding male Pied by white of nape not extending to mantle, black of throat reaching upper breast, and lack of buff wash to breast. Non-breeding and first-winter male *capistrata* do not lose clear-cut white crown and lack Pied's prominent pale fringes to mantle/scapulars and wing feathers. Females can be mainly sooty-brown or have greyish upperparts with variable greyish-white underparts. In worn (spring/summer) plumage, many females are inseparable from female Pied except by tail pattern, but in fresh plumage Variable does not show Pied's prominent pale fringes to mantle/scapulars and wing feathers. **Voice** Song a long and complex mix of low-pitched whistles, chirrups and trills, with much mimicry; calls include *chek-check*. **HH** Frequently bobs head and forebody, and flicks wings and tail. Usually has upright stance. Forages chiefly by running or hopping on ground a short distance, or drops onto prey from a low perch. Breeds in barren valleys and low hills around villages and old buildings; winters in plains; stony desert foothills, cultivation and village edges.

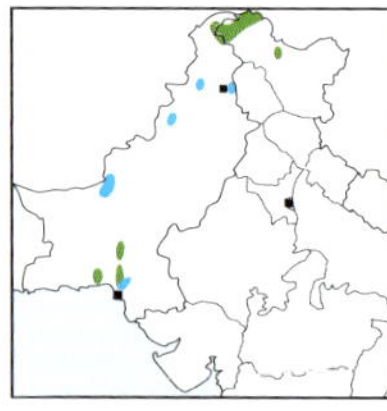

Hume's Wheatear *Oenanthe albonigra* 17cm

Resident. Mainly Pakistan; vagrant to India. **ID** All-black head and largely white underparts differ from other wheatears in subcontinent except *picata* race of Variable. Best told by stockier appearance and domed head, larger bill, longer primary projection, glossy sheen to black of plumage (except when worn); black of throat does not extend so far down breast and white of rump reaches further up back. Sexes alike. First-winter similar to adult, but duller and browner (lacking any sheen) and has buff tips/fringes to wing-coverts. **Voice** Song a loud and cheerful *chew-de-dew-twit*, lacking discordant notes of most wheatears; quiet *chit-it-it* in alarm. **HH** Habits typical of wheatears, see Variable. Very barren stony slopes often with huge boulders.

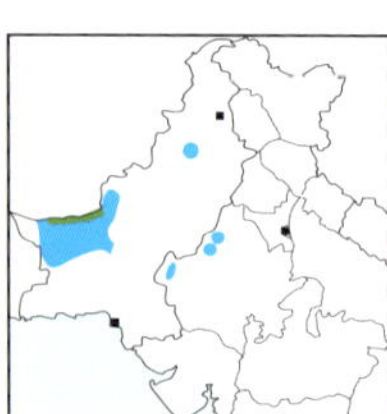

Finsch's Wheatear *Oenanthe finschii* 14cm

Winter visitor. Balochistan and far NW India. **ID** Male has creamy-buff to white mantle and upper back (black in Variable and Pied), and appearance changes little with wear. Has a broader black terminal tail-band than most Pied. Adult female and first-winter have warmer rufous ear-coverts and paler grey-brown upperparts than female Variable and Pied, with contrast between mantle and coverts. In fresh plumage in autumn, throat and breast of female paler than Variable and Pied; when worn in spring/summer, can be blackish on lower throat. **Voice** Song a very varied mix of clear whistles, rich warbling and scratchy, grating sounds; descending *seep* in alarm. **HH** Habits typical of wheatears, see Variable. Desolate dry stony hills and valleys.

Persian Wheatear *Oenanthe chrysopygia* 14.5cm

Breeds in Balochistan; winter visitor to Pakistan and NW India. Vagrant: Nepal. **ID** In all plumages from other wheatears in region by rufous-orange lower back and rump and rufous sides to tail. Male has grey-brown crown and mantle, indistinct pale supercilium and black lores, and warm brown ear-coverts. Broad buff fringes to wing feathers when fresh (autumn), with wings appearing uniform grey-brown when worn (spring). Female similar to male but lacks black lores and has more sandy-brown upperparts. First-winter similar to fresh plumage adult female. **Voice** Song a series of short, slow sweet phrases separated by pauses; calls include a loud grating *chek-chek* in agitation. **HH** Habits typical of wheatears, see Variable. Summers on dry rocky slopes; winters in semi-desert, on stony or sandy ground with scattered bushes, and on low rocky hills and ravines. **AN** Red-tailed Wheatear.

ad
Brown Rock Chat
♀ opistholeuca
♂ picata
♀ picata
♂ opistholeuca
♂ capistrata
♀ capistrata
Variable Wheatear
Hume's Wheatear
ad
♂
♀
Finsch's Wheatear
♀ 1st-win
♂ br
♂ non-br
Persian Wheatear

PLATE 222: FLOWERPECKERS I

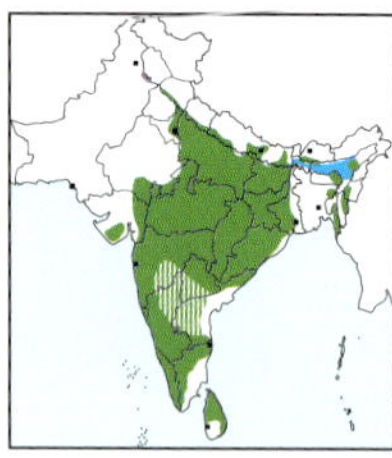

Thick-billed Flowerpecker ***Dicaeum agile*** 9–10.5cm

Widespread resident; unrecorded in parts of NE, NW and E subcontinent. **ID** From other flowerpeckers by combination of stout bluish-grey bill, indistinct dark malar stripe, lightly streaked breast, comparatively long and broad, fairly dark tail with white tip (can be rather indistinct) and orange-red iris. Juvenile has pinkish bill. *D. a. pallescens* (north-east) has finer bill, is more olive-green above and more prominently streaked below with yellowish vent. **Voice** The *tchup-tchup* call is not as hard as *chick* call of Pale-billed. **HH** Distinctive habit of jerking its tail side to side. Frequently flies from one tree to the next and has a regular feeding circuit. Eats mainly figs of peepul and banyan, also mistletoe berries. Forest and well-wooded country.

Yellow-vented Flowerpecker ***Dicaeum chrysorrheum*** 9–10cm

Resident. Himalayas, hills of NE India and Bangladesh. **ID** From other flowerpeckers by blackish streaking on white or yellowish-white underparts and orange-yellow vent. Also has blackish malar stripe, curved black bill, white loral stripe, red eye, bright olive-green upperparts with contrasting blackish primaries, and blackish tail. Juvenile has duller upperparts and greyish-white underparts with paler yellow vent and less prominent streaking. **Voice** Short distinctive *dzeep*; flight call a repeated *zit-zit-zit*, and soft squeaks. **HH** Especially fond of mistletoe berries. Forages at all levels. Forest, forest edges and well-wooded areas; mainly broadleaved; distribution linked to mistletoe.

Yellow-bellied Flowerpecker ***Dicaeum melanozanthum*** 11.5–13cm

Resident. Himalayas and NE Indian hills and NE Bangladesh. **ID** A large, stout-billed flowerpecker. White spots at tip of undertail. Male has bluish-black upperparts and breast-sides, white centre of throat and breast, and yellow rest of underparts. Bright red eye. Female a dull version of male, with olive-brown upperparts, olive-grey sides of breast, and dull olive-yellow belly and vent. Juvenile male similar to female but has brighter yellow underparts and blue-black cast to mantle and back. **Voice** Agitated *zit-zit-zit-zit call.* **HH** Habits similar to other flowerpeckers, but slower-moving. Broadleaved forest including open forest and clearings and edges of dense forest.

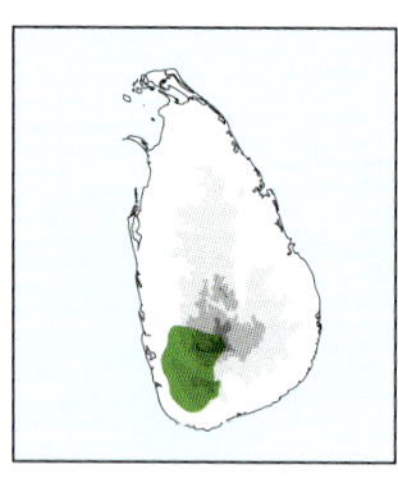

White-throated Flowerpecker ***Dicaeum vincens*** 9–10cm

Resident. Sri Lanka. **ID** Stout-billed flowerpecker. Male has bluish-black upperparts, white throat and breast, yellow belly, white undertail-coverts, and white tips to outer tail feathers. Female like a dull version of male, with blue-grey cap and dark olive mantle and back. Juvenile resembles female, but has uniform dirty yellow underparts, upperparts are more uniform olive-brown and has orange base to lower mandible. **Voice** Calls and song higher-pitched than Thick-billed and Pale-billed. Songs include *treeti, treeti, treetitit*; calls include rapid high-pitched *tchik-tchik-tchik-tchik*. **HH** Singly, in pairs or small family parties. Forages mostly at high levels in trees. Often joins mixed feeding flocks. Eats fruits, probably including mistletoes, also nectar, spiders and small insects. Forest and adjoining wooded areas. **AN** Legge's Flowerpecker.

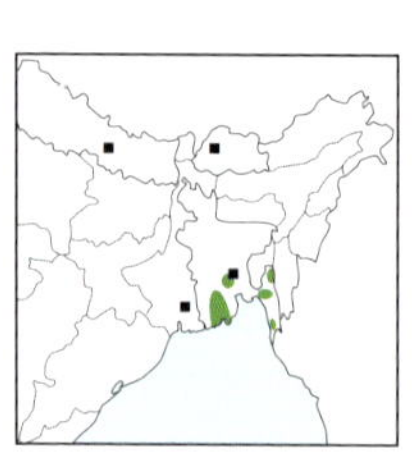

Orange-bellied Flowerpecker ***Dicaeum trigonostigma*** 8–9cm

Resident. SW and SE Bangladesh. **ID** Male blue-grey and orange. Female from other female flowerpeckers by combination of olive-grey throat and upper breast, yellowish-orange underparts, greenish upperparts (with variable blue-grey cast to crown and mantle), blue-grey wing-panel and dull orange rump contrasting with dark tail. Juvenile similar to female but duller, with olive-brown upperparts, olive-yellow rump, and olive-yellow centre to belly and undertail-coverts; bill orange with dark tip. Juvenile male has blue edges to rectrices. **Voice** Song sharp, high-pitched, metallic *ptit-ptit.ptit-ptit-ptit-tsi*; also high, thin, rapid *psee-psee-psee-psee-psee-psee*, each note upwardly inflected; call a harsh *dzit*. **HH** Spends much time in treetops. Food includes soft fruits, mistletoes, nectar, pollen, insects and spiders. Mainly mangroves, also clearings and edges of evergreen forest.

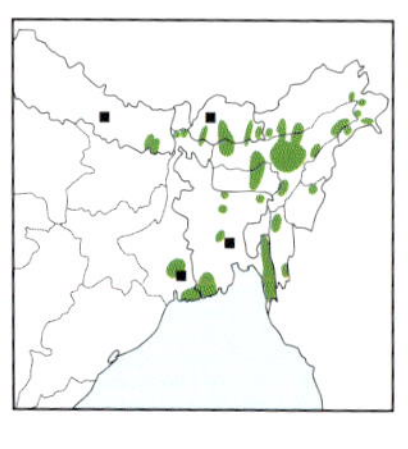

Scarlet-backed Flowerpecker ***Dicaeum cruentatum*** 7–9cm

Resident. E Himalayan foothills, NE India and Bangladesh. **ID** Male has largely scarlet crown and upperparts contrasting with black sides to head, wings and tail. Underparts whitish with black patch on sides of breast. Female has scarlet rump contrasting with blackish tail, olive-brown upperparts and faint buffish wash to whitish underparts. Juvenile as female but lacks scarlet rump (usually a touch of orange); bright orange-red bill with variable blackish tip. **Voice** Song a thin, repeated *tissit, tissit*...; call a hard, metallic *tip..tip..tip* etc. **HH** Solitary or in pairs in breeding season, occasionally small parties at other times. Very active. Broadleaved forest, second growth and orchards; distribution linked to presence of mistletoe.

Thick-billed
Flowerpecker
ad
ad
Yellow-vented
Flowerpecker
♂
♂
Yellow-bellied
Flowerpecker
♀
White-throated
Flowerpecker
♀
♂
♂
♀
♀
Orange-bellied
Flowerpecker
Scarlet-backed
Flowerpecker

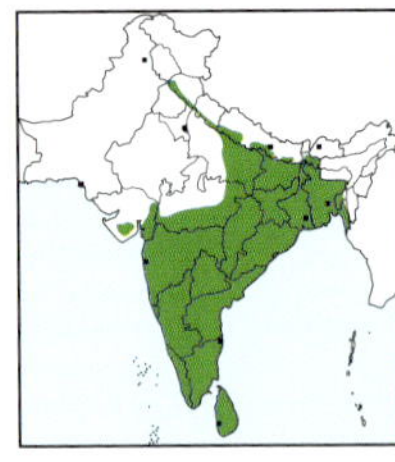

Pale-billed Flowerpecker *Dicaeum erythrorhynchos* 8cm

Widespread resident; unrecorded in parts of NE and NW subcontinent. **ID** From Nilgiri and Plain Flowerpeckers by stout and downcurved pinkish bill. Very plain, including face (with beady dark eye); greyish-olive upperparts with slight greenish cast, and pale greyish underparts with variable yellowish-buff wash. Bill can have dark tip and culmen ridge. *D. e. ceylonense* (Sri Lanka) has darker, more olive upperparts, and shows stronger contrast between crown and face; bill has brown culmen and tip but can be all pinkish or appear greyish. **Voice** Hurried chittering song lower-pitched than Thick-billed; calls include sharp *chik chik chik*. **HH** In pairs in breeding season, otherwise parties of up to ten birds. Constantly on the move, all the while giving its sharp call. Flits about actively, usually in the canopy. Strong, bounding and dipper flight, covering large distances in the day. Feeds chiefly on mistletoe berries. Open broadleaved forest and well-wooded areas; distribution linked to mistletoe.

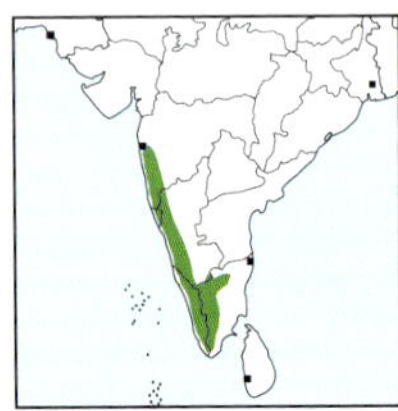

Nilgiri Flowerpecker *Dicaeum concolor* 7.5–8cm

Resident. Western Ghats. **ID** Compared to Plain Flowerpecker of Himalayas and north-east, has darker olive-brown upperparts and paler greyish-white underparts, with faint yellowish-buff wash on breast and belly. From Pale-billed by silvery-grey bill (with variable darker culmen ridge and tip), darker and browner upperparts which contrast more strongly with underparts, and more pronounced pale lores and supercilium (contrasting with darker crown). Juvenile more similar to Pale-billed with orangey bill with obvious dark tip and culmen. **Voice** Songs include very high, thin, short, trilled and repeated *tseep-tsip-tsip* and very short, more rapid, descending trilled *tse e e ep*. Calls include hard, very short staccato ticking. **HH** Extremely active and restless, usually in pairs or small parties. Very fond of mistletoe berries; also eats nectar, insects and spiders. Edges and clearings of broadleaved forest, groves, orchards and tea and coffee plantation; distribution linked to mistletoe.

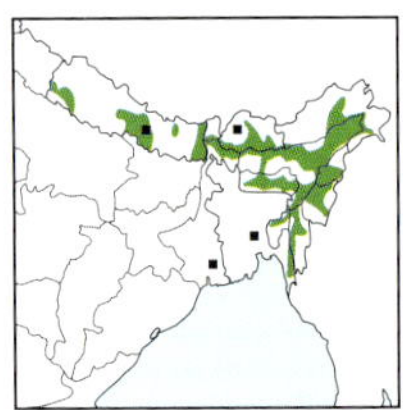

Plain Flowerpecker *Dicaeum minullum* 7.5–9cm

Resident. C and E Himalayan foothills, hills of NE India and Bangladesh. **ID** From Pale-billed by finer greyish bill (with variable darker culmen ridge and tip) and shorter tail. Olive-green upperparts and edges to flight feathers and dusky greyish-olive underparts with yellow on throat and belly are further differences from Pale-billed. Juvenile has paler base to bill and is brighter and greener above and yellower below. **Voice** Song very high, thin and repeated *tsit tsit tsit-si-si-si-si*. Calls include short hard repeated *chik*. **HH** Habits very similar to Nilgiri. Edges and clearings of broadleaved forest, also groves and plantations; distribution linked to mistletoe.

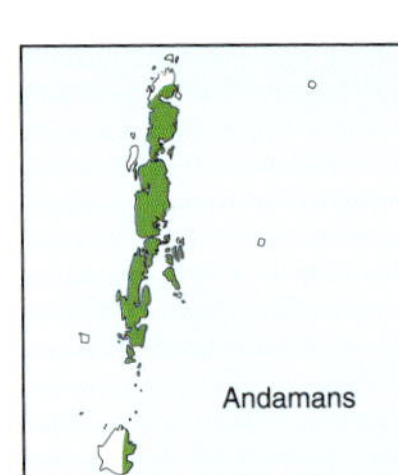

Andaman Flowerpecker *Dicaeum virescens* 8cm

Resident. Andamans. **ID** Has brighter green upperparts than Plain, with grey throat and breast contrasting with yellow lower belly, flanks and vent. Crown faintly speckled. Tail glossy black. **Voice** Song a high-pitched note ascending in pitch, followed by a fast series of higher-pitched, sibilant notes, *sweee-see-see-see-see-see-see*. **HH** Frequently seen in canopy of mistletoe-laden trees. Forests, second growth, plantations and groves.

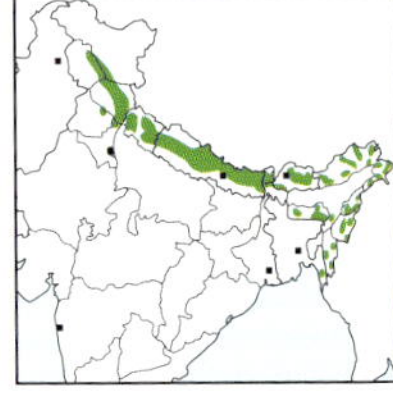

Fire-breasted Flowerpecker *Dicaeum ignipectus* 7–9cm

Resident. Himalayas and NE Indian hills. **ID** Male has dark metallic blue or green upperparts, buff-coloured underparts, scarlet breast-patch and black centre of belly. Female has olive-green upperparts and orange-buff underparts with olive breast-sides and flanks. Sides of head darker than throat and can show pale submoustachial stripe. Juvenile has whiter throat merging into pale greyish-olive of underparts, and duller olive upperparts than female (more similar to Plain but stronger contrast between ear-coverts and throat, and usually at higher elevation). **Voice** Songs include a high-pitched alternation of 2–3 notes at a different pitch: *see-bit-see-bit-see-bit-see-bit* and a high-pitched series of typically 5–8 staccato notes delivered at an increasing pace while rising in pitch; call a clicking *chip*. **HH** Strictly arboreal, usually frequenting the canopy. Continually flies about restlessly, twisting and turning in different directions when perched and calling frequently. Broadleaved forest, second growth and orchards; distribution linked to mistletoe.

ad
Pale-billed Flowerpecker
ad
Nilgiri Flowerpecker
ad
Plain Flowerpecker
ad
Andaman Flowerpecker
♀
♂
Fire-breasted Flowerpecker

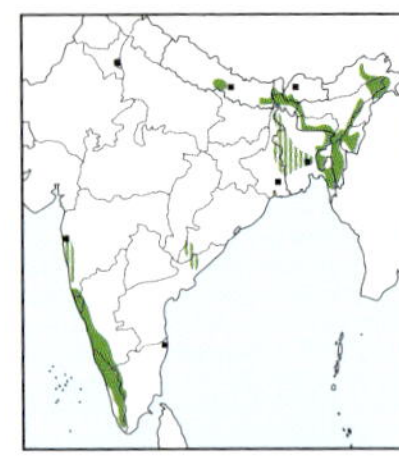

Little Spiderhunter *Arachnothera longirostra* 13.5–16cm

Resident. E Himalayan foothills, hills of NE, E and SW India and Bangladesh and adjacent plains. **ID** From Streaked Spiderhunter by smaller size and proportionately longer bill, unstreaked olive-green upperparts, whitish throat and breast merging into pale yellow of rest of underparts, whitish crescents above and below eye, and dark moustachial stripe. Juvenile has orangey lower mandible and legs/feet (dark in adult). **Voice** Song a rapidly repeated *wit-wit-wit-wit...*; call an abrasive *itch*. **HH** Keeps to lower forest storey. Restless and noisy. Frequently clings upside-down while probing blossoms for nectar. Wild bananas and bamboos in broadleaved evergreen and moist deciduous forest, second growth and sholas; often along streams.

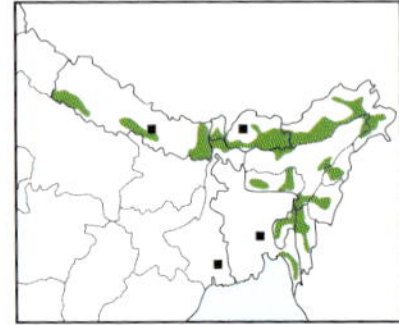

Streaked Spiderhunter *Arachnothera magna* 17–20.5cm

Resident. Himalayas, NE India and Bangladesh. **ID** From Little by larger size, bold streaking on dark olive-green upperparts and bold streaking on yellowish-white underparts. Orange legs and feet. **Voice** Song a strident chatter; call a sharp *chirirrik* or *chirik chirik*. **HH** Usually singly or in pairs, often with mixed itinerant hunting parties. Forages in upper forest storey. Fast-moving, flight strong and undulating, almost woodpecker-like. Chiefly feeds on nectar. Broadleaved evergreen and moist deciduous forest with dense undergrowth.

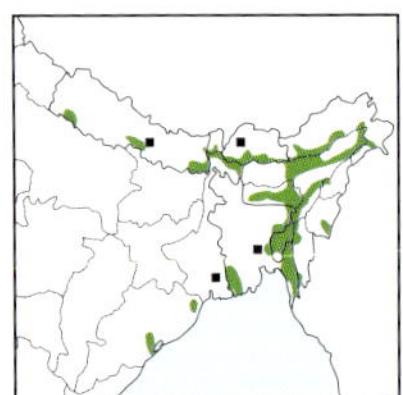

Ruby-cheeked Sunbird *Chalcoparia singalensis* 10–11cm

Resident. C and E Himalayan foothills, NE and E India and Bangladesh. **ID** Shorter, straighter bill than other sunbirds, with rufous-orange throat and yellow underparts. Male has metallic green upperparts and 'ruby' cheeks. Female lacks 'ruby' cheeks and has dull olive-green upperparts. Juvenile entirely yellow below. **Voice** Song a rapid, high-pitched *switi-ti-chi-chu... tusi-tit...swit-swit...switi-ti-chi-chu...switi-ti-chi-chu...*; call a disyllabic *wee-eest* with rising inflection. **HH** Active, continually flitting about on low branches and bushes. Forages in upper storey occasionally lower. Probes flowers for nectar, gleans insects from leaves and often feeds at spiders' webs. Open forest, forest clearings and edges, scrub jungle and mangroves; favours evergreen biotope.

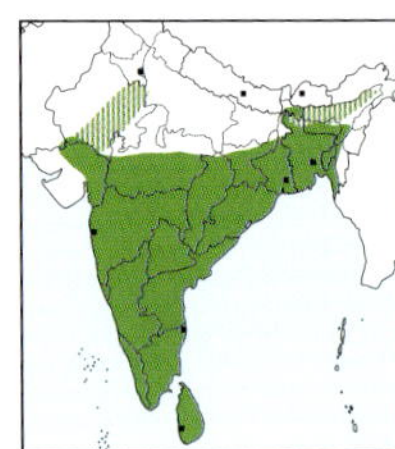

Purple-rumped Sunbird *Leptocoma zeylonica* 10cm

Resident. Widespread in C, NE and S India, Bangladesh and Sri Lanka. Vagrant: Nepal. **ID** Male has narrow maroon breast-band, maroon head-sides and mantle, metallic blue/green crown and shoulder patch, and yellow lower breast and belly with distinctive greyish-white flanks. No eclipse plumage in male (unlike Purple). Female has greyish-white throat, yellow breast, whitish flanks, olive rump and rufous-brown wing-panel. Juvenile uniform yellow below; rump colour separates it from Crimson-backed, and rufous-brown on wings from Purple. **Voice** Calls include a high-pitched *ptsee...ptsee*, and a metallic *chit*, different from Crimson-backed and Purple calls. High, broken twittering song comprises calls strung together. **HH** Arboreal, constantly on the move, flitting and darting actively from flower to flower, often hovering momentarily in front of them, and calling incessantly. Cultivation, gardens, second growth and open deciduous woodland.

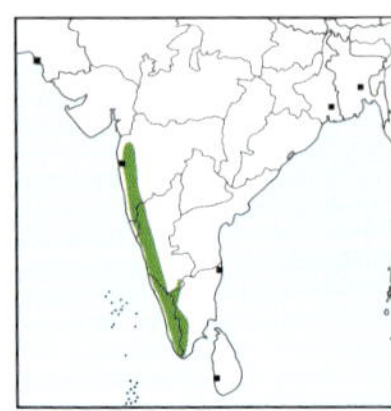

Crimson-backed Sunbird *Leptocoma minima* 8cm

Resident. Hills of W India. **ID** Smaller and finer-billed than Purple-rumped. Male has metallic green crown, broad crimson breast-band (bordered below with black) and crimson mantle, and whitish belly (with variable light yellowish wash). Depending on light, shows iridescent purple on throat. Lacks metallic green shoulder patch and bright-yellow breast contrasting with white flanks of Purple-rumped. Eclipse male as female but has metallic purple rump and crimson scapulars and back. Female has crimson rump, olive-green upperparts and edges to wings, and uniform yellowish underparts. Lacks rufous-brown wing-panel and bright yellow breast contrasting with white flanks of Purple-rumped. **Voice** Calls include a flowerpecker-like *thlick-thlick*, not as hard as Nilgiri, and a nasal *spziew*. Fast song lacks power and variety of larger species; introduction often *tsee-sit-see-su....tse-sit-swee...* then breaks into erratic twitters and trills. **HH** Active and acrobatic; clings upside-down to plants, also hovers. Defends flowering trees against other sunbirds, also against flowerpeckers. Favours flowers of *Erythrina* and Loranthaceae species. Singly, in pairs or in small groups. Evergreen biotope, chiefly in foothills: forest, sholas, gardens and flowering shade trees in plantations.

ad
Little Spiderhunter
ad
Streaked Spiderhunter
Ruby-cheeked
Sunbird
♂
♀
♂
Purple-rumped
Sunbird
♀
juv
♂ br
♀
♂
eclipse
Crimson-backed
Sunbird

PLATE 225: SUNBIRDS II

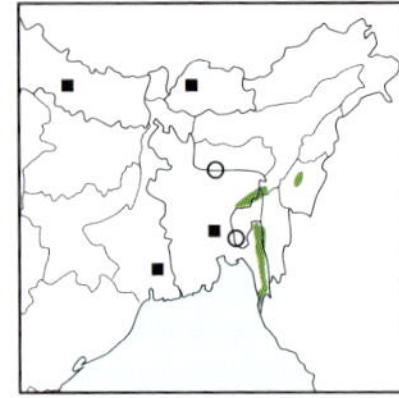

Van Hasselt's Sunbird *Leptocoma brasiliana* 9–10cm

Resident. Plains of NE India and Bangladesh. **ID** Small, short-billed sunbird. Male has metallic green crown, purple throat, black mask and mantle, maroon breast and belly, and blue scapular line and rump. No eclipse plumage. Female has plain face, dull yellowish underparts with more olive-coloured throat and olive-green upperparts. **Voice** Songs include *psweet, psweet, psweet, psweet, psweet, psweet...psit-it, psitit, psweet, psweet...* repeated irregularly; calls include piercing, thin, strongly upslurred *pswééét*, more subdued, staccato, quick, disyllabic *fut-chít*, and short, high trills. **HH** Usually forages high up; hovers to take insects or water from leaves and nectar from flowers; also hangs from flowers. Evergreen and semi-evergreen forest, open forest and gardens. **TN** and **AN** Formerly treated as conspecific with Purple-throated Sunbird *L. sperata*.

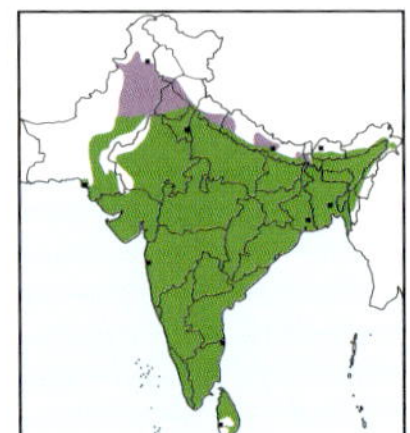

Purple Sunbird *Cinnyris asiaticus* 10–11cm

Widespread resident; unrecorded in parts of NE and NW subcontinent and Sri Lanka. **ID** Shorter and less downcurved bill than Loten's. Male is metallic blue-green and purple becoming blacker on belly and vent. Variable narrow maroon crescent on breast, which can be lacking or not apparent. Bright yellow or orange pectoral tufts usually hidden beneath wing. Female has uniform yellowish underparts, with faint supercilium and darker mask (whiter below in worn plumage). Eclipse male as female but has a broad blackish stripe on centre of throat and breast, metallic blue wing-coverts and glossy black wings and tail. Juvenile brighter yellow on entire underparts than female with pale orange at base of lower mandible. **Voice** Song a pleasant, descending *swee-swee-swee swit zizi-zizi*; call a buzzing *zit* and high-pitched, upward-inflected *swee* or *che-wee*. **HH** More insectivorous than other sunbirds. Male sings from top of a bare tree or telegraph wire, while jerking from side to side. Open deciduous forest and gardens.

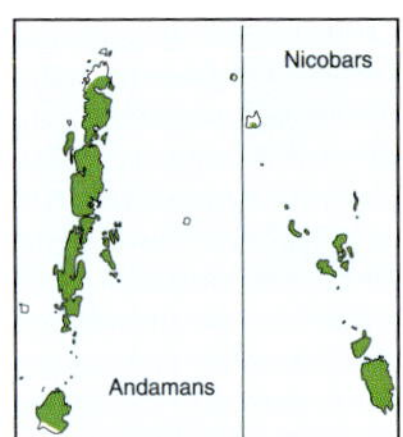

Ornate Sunbird *Cinnyris ornatus* 11cm

Resident. Andamans and Nicobars. **ID** *C. o. andamanicus* (Andamans) has olive-green upperparts, metallic purple-and-green throat and yellow belly and vent. Female similar to female Purple but greener above and brighter yellow below. Eclipse male as female but has broad blackish stripe on centre of throat and breast. *C. o. klossi* (Nicobars) has brighter yellow underparts in both sexes; male has metallic purple or blue feathers on forehead. Male *C. o. proselius* (Car Nicobar) similar to *klossi* but smaller with shorter bill. **Voice** Loud, sharp *tsip, tsip...*, irregular or in long series (Great Nicobar), and wheezy, insistent *jha-zyéw, jha-zyéw...* (Katchal, in C Nicobars). **HH** Usually at low levels. Hovers and gleans for insects and spiders, also nectar. Forests, mangroves, scrub, coastal vegetation, farmland, plantations, gardens. **TN** Recent 'split'. Previously included as Olive-backed Sunbird *C. jugularis*.

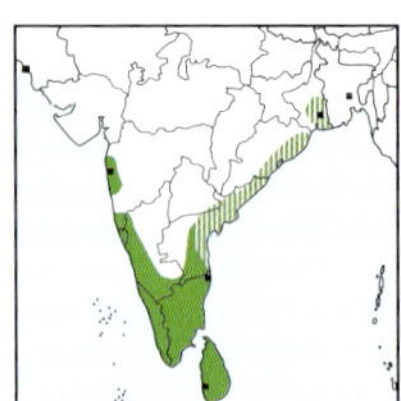

Loten's Sunbird *Cinnyris lotenius* 13cm

Resident. W and S Indian peninsula and Sri Lanka. **ID** Larger, with longer, sharply downcurved bill, compared to Purple, and longer more graduated tail. Male from Purple by broad maroon band on breast and dusky-brown wings, belly and flanks. Immature male as female but has broad blackish stripe on centre of throat and breast and metallic blue-green wing-coverts. Existence of eclipse plumage in male uncertain. Female has dark olive-green upperparts and pale yellow underparts (greyer-brown above and whiter below in worn plumage). Upperparts generally darker than on Purple, and ear-coverts and sides of neck contrast with throat and breast, creating hooded appearance (lacking supercilium). Juvenile similar to female with pale orange base to lower mandible. **Voice** Song a slow *tichit-wut...tichit-wu-eet...wue-wue-wue-wue*, last notes accelerating; also, a repeated *cheewit-cheewit cheewit*. Call a harsh *chit chit*, similar to Little Spiderhunter, lacking buzzing quality of Purple call. **HH** Continually jerks its head to and fro. Forages at different levels. Takes invertebrates by gleaning from foliage and hovering, also nectar. Well-wooded country and gardens in moist deciduous biotope.

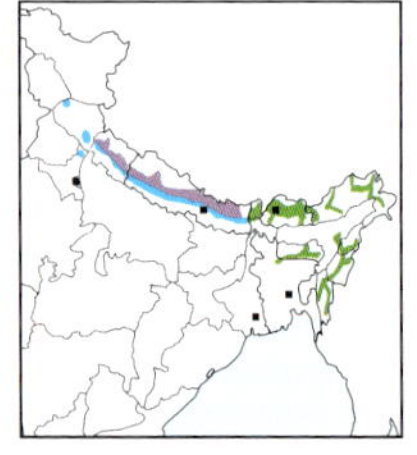

Fire-tailed Sunbird *Aethopyga ignicauda* 8.5–20cm

Resident. Himalayas and NE Indian hills. **ID** Male has scarlet nape and mantle, and very long scarlet tail. Crown and throat metallic purple and underparts yellow (washed orange on breast). Female similar to female Green-tailed, but has straighter bill, squarer tail (lacking white tips) with trace of brownish-orange at sides, more pronounced yellow belly and more noticeable olive-yellow on rump (but not forming prominent band of female Black-throated and Mrs Gould's). Eclipse/immature male similar to female, but has brighter yellow belly, and scarlet uppertail-coverts and tail-sides. **Voice** Song high-pitched, monotonous *dzidzi-dzidziddzidzidzidzi*. **HH** Particularly vivacious sunbird. In breeding plumage, the male's long red tail swirls in flight. Breeds in rhododendron shrubbery and conifer-rhododendron forest; winters in broadleaved and mixed forest.

♀
Van Hasselt's
Sunbird
♂
♂
eclipse
♀
juv
♂ br
Purple
Sunbird
♂
klossi
♂
andamanicus
♂ br
Ornate Sunbird
Loten's
Sunbird
♀
♂ br
♀
Fire-tailed
Sunbird
♂
imm
♀
♂
non-br

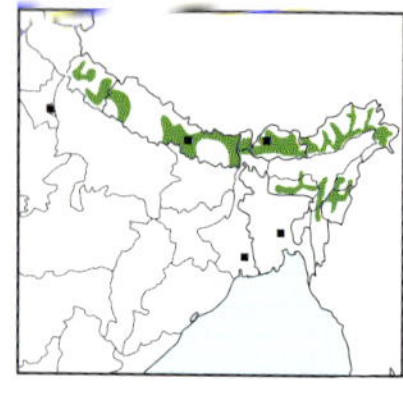

Black-throated Sunbird *Aethopyga saturata* 10–15cm

Resident. Himalayas and NE India. **ID** Male has black throat and breast, greyish-olive underparts and crimson mantle. Metallic purple crown, nape and malar stripe, and dark metallic purple tail. Female has pale yellow rump band; from Mrs Gould's by greyish-olive underparts (without any yellow); longer, dark and noticeably downcurved bill, and narrow or indistinct pale tips to outer tail feathers. **Voice** Song a twittering comprising sharp, high-pitched *swi*, *tis* and *tsi* notes and rapid metallic trills. **HH** Mainly feeds on nectar, also arthropods in bushes and lower branches in forest and second growth.

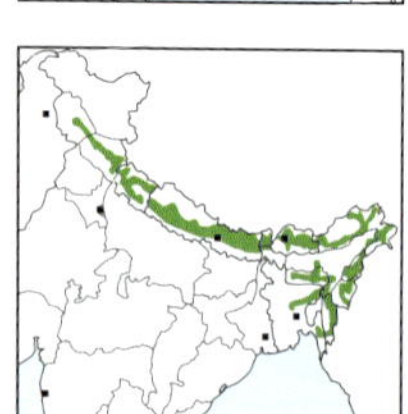

Mrs Gould's Sunbird *Aethopyga gouldiae* 10–15cm

Resident. Himalayas, NE Indian hills and Bangladesh. **ID** Male from male Green-tailed by metallic purplish-blue crown, ear-coverts and throat; crimson sides of neck, mantle and back (reaching yellow rump); yellow belly, and blue to purplish blue uppertail-coverts and tail. Female from other female sunbirds except Black-throated by pale yellow rump band (similar to Lemon-rumped Warbler). From female Black-throated by yellowish underparts, especially lower breast and belly (some have greyish throat and breast), broad and well-defined white tips to outer-tail feathers, and shorter and straighter bill with noticeably pale lower mandible. Short bill, yellow rump, yellower underparts, and shorter, squarer tail are best features from female Green-tailed. Juvenile male similar to female but has bright yellow breast and belly. *A. g. dabryii*, with scarlet breast, has been recorded in north-east. **Voice** Fast repeated *tzip* call, *tshi-stshi-ti-ti-ti* and lisping *squeeeeee*. **HH** Very lively. Forages at all levels, from bushes to the canopy. Montane oak-rhododendron and conifer forests.

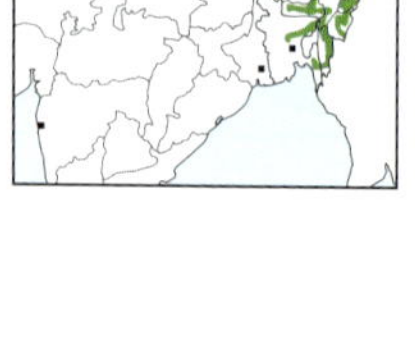

Green-tailed Sunbird *Aethopyga nipalensis* 10–15cm

Resident. Himalayas, NE India and NE Bangladesh. **ID** Male from Mrs Gould's by maroon mantle and olive-green back (although note racial variation), dark metallic blue-green crown and throat, and blackish sides of head. Has blue-green uppertail-coverts and tail (can appear blue, but not purplish-blue as on Mrs Gould's). Female has greyish-olive throat and breast (very grey on some), becoming yellowish-olive on belly and flanks. Best separated from female Mrs Gould's and Black-throated by lack of well-defined yellow rump band (although rump and uppertail-coverts are yellowish-green) and longer, noticeably graduated tail with prominent white tips to outer tail feathers and slim central tail feathers extending noticeably beyond rest. *A. n. horsfieldi* (W Himalayas) has only narrow maroon band on mantle compared to nominate of C and E Himalayas; male *A. n. victoriae* (Mizoram) has all-green mantle. **Voice** Song *tchiss tchiss-iss-iss-iss*, beginning high, then a low note followed by a rising one, and finally high notes; loud *chit chit* call. **HH** Often with mixed-species foraging flocks in non-breeding season. Feeds on small arthropods and nectar. Oak-rhododendron and mixed forest, second growth and gardens.

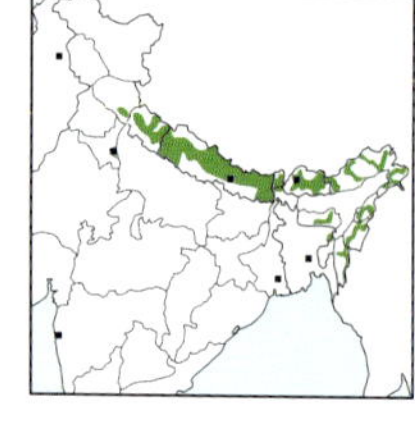

Vigors's Sunbird *Aethopyga vigorsii* 10–15cm

Resident. Western Ghats. **ID** Larger than Crimson, with no overlap in range. In male, central tail feathers extend only just beyond rest of tail, and has scarlet throat and breast finely streaked yellow, uniform grey rest of underparts, and uniform grey-brown wings lacking yellowish-olive edges. Female has dark olive upperparts and grey underparts. Immature male similar to female, but has dull scarlet throat and breast. **Voice** Sharp, harsh *chi-wee* richer and more strident than similar call of Crimson. **HH** Forages mainly in small groups, generally in upper levels but often lower. Takes nectar and probably small insects and spiders. Evergreen and moist deciduous forest and forest edges, especially around flowering trees and shrubs.

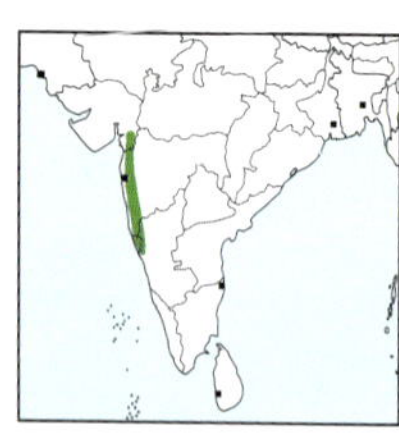

Crimson Sunbird *Aethopyga siparaja* 10–11cm

Resident. Himalayas, hills of NE and E India and Bangladesh; also N and NE plains. **ID** Male has crimson mantle, scarlet throat and breast, and yellowish-olive belly. Female has yellowish-olive underparts; lacks yellow rump or prominent white on tail. Immature male as female but has red throat and breast. Male *A. s. nicobarica* (Nicobars) smaller, has violet-purple (rather than green) crown, rump and tail, grey belly and vent, and lacks elongated central tail feathers. **Voice** Rapid, tripping song of 3–6 sharp notes, *tsip-it-sip-it-sit*, lacking the intense chittering of Black-throated and Green-tailed songs and very different from Mrs Gould's. **HH** Especially fond of red flowers. Forages mainly low down in bushes, also flowers in coconut trees and occasionally in other flowering trees. Bushes in open broadleaved forest, groves and gardens; also, mangroves in Bangladesh.

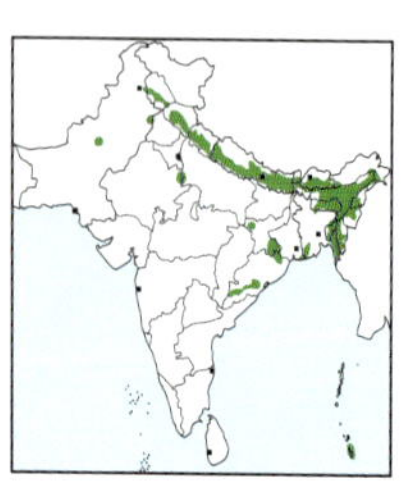

Black-throated Sunbird
♀
♂
♀
♂
nipalensis
Mrs Gould's Sunbird
♂
♀
nipalensis
♀
Green-tailed Sunbird
♀
♂
Vigors's Sunbird
♂
Crimson Sunbird

PLATE 227: ASIAN FAIRY-BLUEBIRD AND LEAFBIRDS

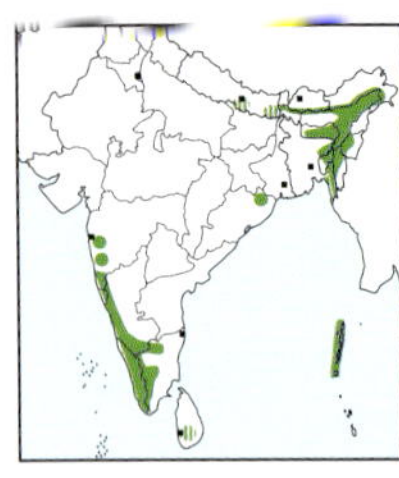

Asian Fairy-bluebird *Irena puella* 21–26cm

Resident. E Himalayan foothills, hills of NE, E and S India, Bangladesh and Sri Lanka. **ID** Male has glistening violet-blue upperparts and black underparts. Female and first-year male entirely dull blue-green, with dusky lores and blackish flight feathers. Both sexes have striking red eye. Juvenile entirely dull brown. **Voice** A liquid *tulip wae-waet-oo* and various shorter liquid notes. **HH** Usually in small flocks when not breeding. Forages actively for fruit and nectar, usually in canopy but will descend to bushes. Broadleaved evergreen and dense, moist deciduous forest.

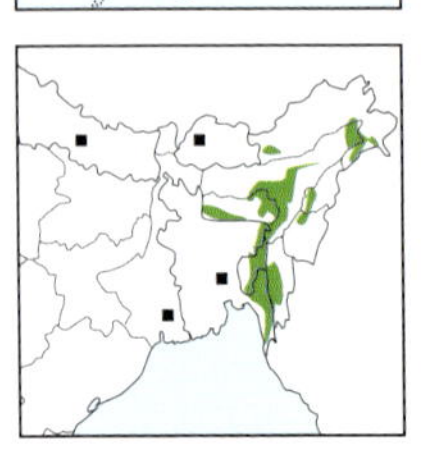

Blue-winged Leafbird *Chloropsis cochinchinensis* 16–20cm

Resident. Hills of NE India and Bangladesh. **ID** In all plumages, from other leafbirds by blue panel in wing and blue sides to tail. Lacks well-defined golden-orange forehead of Golden-fronted Leafbird. Male has small violet-blue moustachial stripe, black mask with diffuse yellow border, golden cast to crown and nape, and bright blue shoulder patch. Female is almost entirely green, with golden cast to crown and nape; throat pale bluish-green, with brighter turquoise moustachial. Juvenile has green head, with slight suggestion of turquoise moustachial. **Voice** Varied whistles, chuckles and rattles, with much mimicry, difficult to separate from other leafbirds. **HH** Typical leafbird. Singly, in pairs or family parties. Arboreal, often in thick foliage in canopy. Searches leaves for invertebrates, also feeds on berries and nectar. Pugnacious, and will drive other birds away from flowering trees. Flight swift, usually over a short distance. Open forest, forest edges, well-wooded areas and isolated large trees near villages or in cultivation.

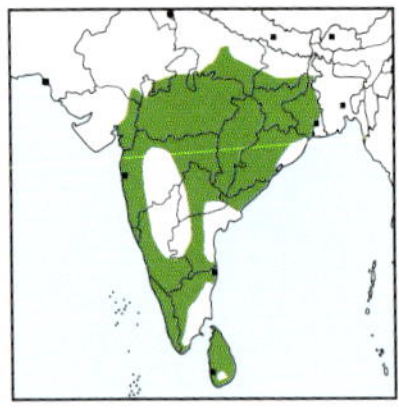

Jerdon's Leafbird *Chloropsis jerdoni* 17–18.5cm

Resident. Peninsular India and Sri Lanka. **ID** Greenish wings and tail (lacking blue panels) differ from Blue-winged, as do lack of golden cast to nape and less distinct yellow border to dark mask. Male lacks golden forehead of Golden-fronted and has smaller dark mask. Female has broad diffuse yellow border to turquoise throat (female Golden-fronted has black throat). Juvenile has turquoise throat, brighter in moustachial region. **Voice** Song: random, varied combinations of loud, clear whistles, buzzing notes and rich, sharp notes, similar to Golden-fronted, but richer and slower; calls include a jarring rattle. **HH** Habits similar to Blue-winged. Open forest, second growth and well-wooded areas; favours relatively dry conditions.

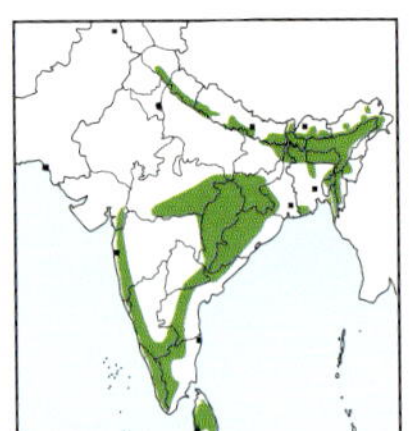

Golden-fronted Leafbird *Chloropsis aurifrons* 17–19cm

Resident. Himalayas, NE, E, S and SW India, Bangladesh and Sri Lanka. **ID** Adult best told from other leafbirds by golden-orange forehead (dull on some birds, especially females). Also lacks blue panels in wings and tail of Blue-winged and has more extensive black throat compared to Blue-winged and Jerdon's. Juvenile all green, with diffuse yellowish patch on forecrown and a touch of blue in moustachial region. Nominate (north-east, south to Odisha) has purplish-blue throat and broad golden-yellow collar (especially pronounced on breast). *C. a. frontalis* (S India) and *C. a. insularis* (Sri Lanka) have purplish-blue restricted to moustachial, and yellow collar less prominent or absent. **Voice** Wide variety of harsh and whistling notes. A very good mimic of other birds. Song a cheery series of rising and falling liquid chirps, bulbul-like in tone: *chur-chee-dip-chur-chirpy-chirpy*. **HH** Habits similar to Blue-winged. Usually in pairs in breeding season and in small parties at other times. Broadleaved evergreen and deciduous forest and second growth, in more wooded habitats than Blue-winged.

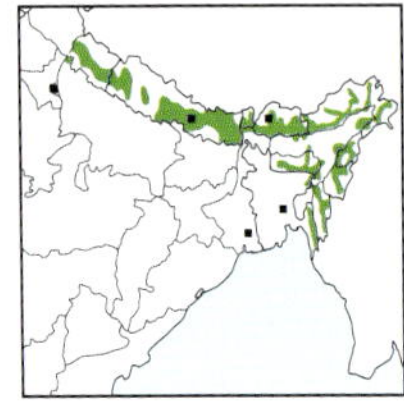

Orange-bellied Leafbird *Chloropsis hardwickii* 18–19cm

Resident. Himalayas, NE India and Bangladesh. **ID** Male from other leafbirds by black of throat extending to breast, orange belly and vent, large blue moustachial stripe, and purplish-blue flight feathers and tail. Female largely green; orange centre of belly and vent and large blue moustachial stripe are best distinctions from other leafbirds. Juvenile all green with blue moustachial and some have touch of orange on underparts. **Voice** Song a variable series of far-carrying, melodious, varied rippling and chuckling phrases including much mimicry. **HH** Habits similar to Blue-winged. Singly or in pairs; often with other species in flowering trees. Montane broadleaved evergreen and deciduous forest, forest edge, second growth and well-wooded areas.

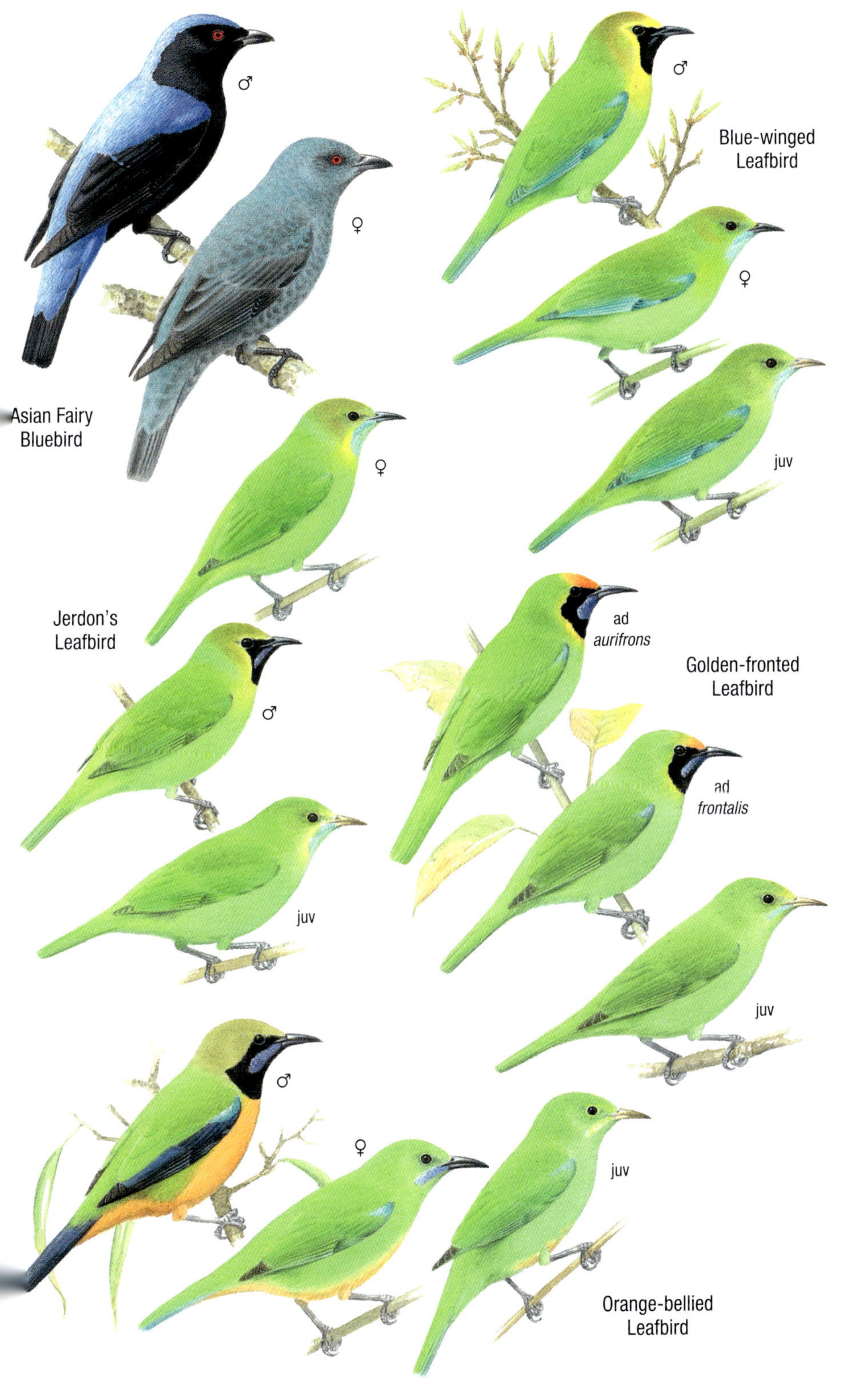
Asian Fairy
Bluebird
♂
♀
Blue-winged
Leafbird
♂
♀
juv
Jerdon's
Leafbird
♀
♂
juv
ad
aurifrons
Golden-fronted
Leafbird
ad
frontalis
juv
♂
♀
juv
Orange-bellied
Leafbird

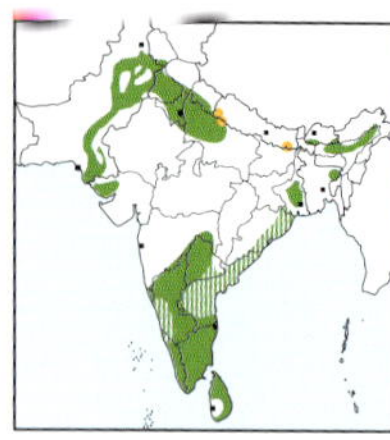

Streaked Weaver *Ploceus manyar* 15cm

Mainly resident. Pakistan, N, S and E India and the north-east. **ID** Breeding male has yellow crown, dark brown head-sides and throat, and heavily streaked breast and flanks. Other plumages typically show strongly streaked underparts. However, can be only lightly streaked on underparts, when best told from Baya Weaver by combination of yellow supercilium and neck patch, heavily streaked crown, dark or heavily streaked ear-coverts, and pronounced dark malar and moustachial stripes. When streaking absent on underparts, streaked crown, nape and rump are best features from Black-breasted. Juvenile browner and buffier with unmarked underparts and head pattern shadows that of adult. **Voice** Song soft, continuous trill. **HH** Reedbeds, seasonally flooded areas.

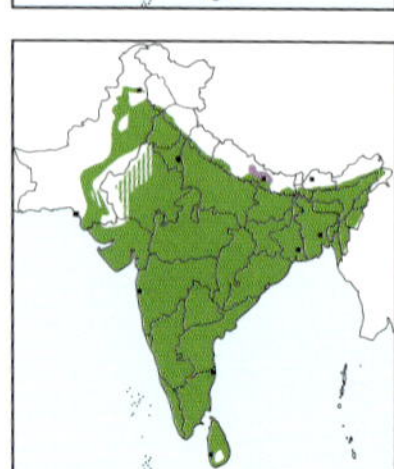

Baya Weaver *Ploceus philippinus* 15cm

Widespread resident; unrecorded in parts of NE and NW subcontinent. **ID** Breeding male of nominate has yellow crown, dark brown ear-coverts and throat, unstreaked yellow breast, and yellow streaking on mantle and scapulars. Breeding male *burmanicus* (north-east) has greyer face, buff or pale grey throat, and buff breast. Non-breeding male, female and juvenile usually have unstreaked buffish underparts; streaking can be as prominent as a poorly marked Streaked, but has less distinct and buffish supercilium, lacks yellow neck patch, and lacks pronounced dark moustachial and malar stripes. Non-breeding male, female and juvenile *burmanicus* more rufous-buff on supercilium and underparts. **Voice** Song a series of chittering notes, followed by a wheezy whistle, then a buzz, ending with chirps, **HH** Grassland and scrub with scattered trees, mangroves.

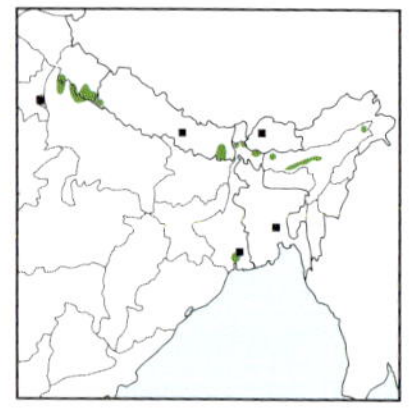

Finn's Weaver *Ploceus megarhynchus* 17cm

Resident. N and NE India and S Nepal. **ID** Large weaver with heavy bill and long tail. Male breeding from other weavers by bright yellow head with variable dark brown ear-coverts (sometimes just a dark spot or lacking), golden-yellow underparts, and yellow rump and uppertail-coverts. Mantle and back boldly streaked dark brown. Dark patches on breast. Female breeding and first-year male have pale yellow to yellowish-brown head, and pale yellow to buffish-white underparts; mantle rich brown with dark streaking. Adult non-breeding lacks yellow and is similar to Baya; upperparts darker grey-brown with head and neck more uniform. Breeding male *P. m. salimalii* (NE subcontinent) differs from nominate in browner rump and white undertail-coverts (sometimes also white belly). **Voice** Song a loud, harsh chatter ending with a wheeze, harsher than Baya. **HH** Mainly grassland with scattered trees, also rice and sugarcane cultivation. Globally threatened.

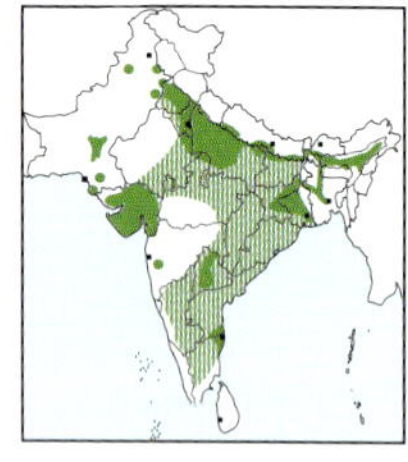

Black-breasted Weaver *Ploceus benghalensis* 15cm

Resident. Mainly Indus and Gangetic plains. **ID** Breeding male has yellow crown and black breast. Throat may be black or white, and some variants have white ear-coverts and throat. In non-breeding male and female, breast-band is blotchy or restricted to small patches at sides, and may show indistinct, diffuse streaking on lower breast and flanks. In these plumages has yellow supercilium (often white behind eye), distinct yellow patch on side of neck, and yellow submoustachial stripe (with black malar); more similar to Streaked Weaver, except crown, nape and ear-coverts more uniform; rump also indistinctly streaked and, like nape, contrasts with heavily streaked mantle. Juvenile browner and buffier with unmarked underparts and head pattern shadows that of adult. **Voice** Soft, quiet *tsi-tsi-tsisik-tsisik-tsik-tsik* song. **HH** Seasonally flooded grassland, reedy marshes; irrigated cultivation in winter.

Green Avadavat *Amandava formosa* 10cm

Resident. Widespread in C India. **ID** Male breeding has red bill, lime-green upperparts, bold black-and-white barring on flanks, and yellowish underparts. Female similar but has duller greyish-green upperparts, less prominent grey-and-white barring on flanks, greyish throat and breast, and duller yellow vent and undertail-coverts. Juvenile lacks bright green in plumage; has black bill (becoming red later), olive-green cast to upperparts, yellow undertail-coverts, and pink legs and feet. **Voice** Song similar to Red Avadavat, but louder, ending in prolonged trill. **HH** Grass and low bushes, tall grassland, sugarcane fields and open forest with bushes, often near water. Globally threatened.

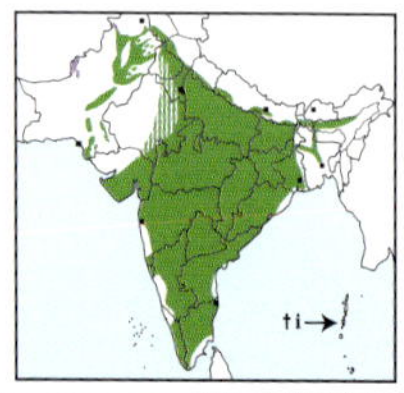

Red Avadavat *Amandava amandava* 9.5–10cm

Widespread resident, except in parts of NE and NW subcontinent and Sri Lanka. **ID** Breeding male mainly red (blacker on wings) with irregular white spotting. Non-breeding male and female have grey-brown upperparts and buffish-white underparts; best told by black mask, red bill, red rump, and white tips to wing-coverts and tertials. Juvenile lacks red in plumage and has black bill; buff wing-bars and tertial fringes, any red in bill (if present), and pink legs and feet help separate from juvenile munias. **Voice** Song a weak, high-pitched warble. **HH** Tall wet grassland, reedy marshes, sugarcane fields and tamarisk scrub near cultivation; in Assam also villages and gardens.

♂ br
♀
♂ br
philippinus
Streaked
Weaver
♂
non-br
♂ br
burmanicus
♀
philippinus
♂ non-br
philippinus
♀ br
Baya Weaver
♀
burmanicus
Finn's Weaver
♂ br
non-br
♂ br
♂ br
non-br
non-br
Black-breasted
Weaver
♂ br
juv
♂
Green Avadavat
♀
♀
Red Avadavat

PLATE 229: SILVERBILL AND MUNIAS

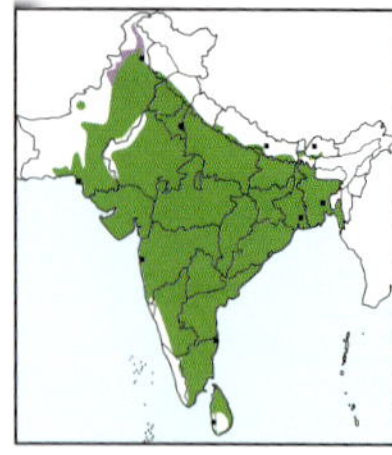

Indian Silverbill *Euodice malabarica* 11cm

Widespread resident, except in NW and NE subcontinent and Himalayas. **ID** Male has greyish bill, fawn-brown upperparts, whitish face and underparts with faintly barred flanks, long and pointed black tail, and white rump and uppertail-coverts. Female duller with plainer face and flanks are uniform buff. Juvenile has dark mottling on rump and tail is shorter and more rounded. **Voice** Contact call *tchrip*; flight call a repeated *chir-rup*; song a series of short, abrupt trills. **HH** Typical estrildid. Feeds chiefly on small seeds taken on ground or by clinging to stems. Gregarious outside breeding season and roosts communally. If disturbed, flock takes off in a close-knit pack and flies into nearby cover. Dry cultivation, grassland and thorn scrub.

Scaly-breasted Munia *Lonchura punctulata* 10–12.5cm

Widespread resident; unrecorded in parts of the north-west. **ID** Adult has chestnut-brown face, throat and upper breast, whitish underparts boldly scaled with black, and olive-yellow to rufous-orange on uppertail-coverts and edges of tail. Juvenile has uniform brown upperparts and buff to rufous-buff underparts, with whitish belly (probably indistinguishable from juvenile Tricoloured). **Voice** Typical song a series of *klik-klik-klik* or *tit-tit-tit* notes followed by a short series of whistles and churrs, ending with longer *weeee*; contact calls include a repeated *tit-ti tit-ti* and a loud *kit-teee kit-teee*. **HH** Typical estrildid, see Indian Silverbill. Often roosts in nests, sometimes built for that purpose. Open secondary forest with grassland patches and bushes, bush-covered hillsides and cultivation.

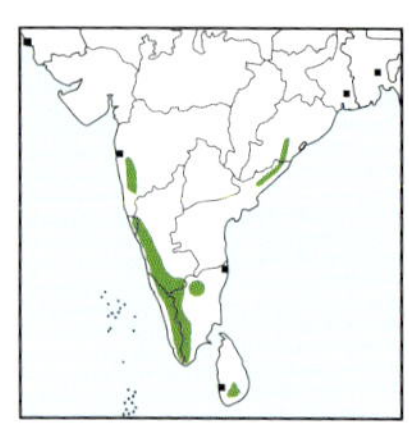

Black-throated Munia *Lonchura kelaarti* 12cm

Resident. Hills of SW and E India, and Sri Lanka. **ID** Blackish face and bib, and pinkish-cinnamon sides of neck and breast. Adult nominate (Sri Lanka) has white underparts marked with brownish-black, and white-spotted blackish uppertail-coverts; juvenile has white throat with blackish barring, and diffuse brown and rufous-buff barring below. Populations in peninsula (e.g. *jerdoni*) have unmarked cinnamon underparts contiguous with sides of breast, and pale-spotted brownish uppertail-coverts; juvenile has warm buffish-brown underparts with diffuse buff streaking and mottling (lacks whitish rump of juvenile White-rumped). **Voice** Song barely audible series of five notes; high-pitched, nasal *tay* and *chirp* calls. **HH** Habits very like other estrildids, see Indian Silverbill, but travels more than other species, often high up. Usually at higher altitudes and in wetter habitats than White-rumped. Forest clearings, scrub, tea estates and grassland.

White-rumped Munia *Lonchura striata* 11–12cm

Resident. Widespread in subcontinent except north and north-west. **ID** Dark breast, streaked upperparts and white rump. *L. s. striata* (peninsula and Sri Lanka) has unstreaked whitish belly, blackish face, throat and breast; juvenile similar but lacks streaking on upperparts, has buff fringes to breast. *L. s. acuticauda* (Himalayan foothills and north-east) rufous-brown on side of head/neck, rufous-brown to whitish fringes on dark brown breast, and faint brownish streaking to greyish-buff belly; juvenile barred brown-buff on throat and breast. *L. s. fumigata* (Andamans) and *L. s. semistriata* (Nicobars) similar to *striata*: *fumigata* lacks upperpart streaks and has warm buff underparts; *semistriata* has pale fringes to breast, pale buff underparts. **Voice** Song a rising and falling series of twittering notes; calls include a twittering *tr-tr-tr* and *brrt*. **HH** Typical estrildid, see Indian Silverbill. Open wooded areas and scrub near cultivation.

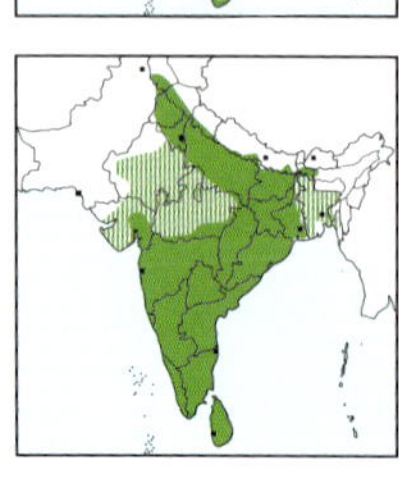

Tricoloured Munia *Lonchura malacca* 11–12cm

Resident. Widespread except parts of the north-west and north-east. **ID** Adult has black head and upper breast, rufous-brown upperparts, and black belly centre and undertail-coverts. Lower breast and flanks white. Juvenile has uniform brown upperparts and buff to whitish underparts. **Voice** Song a series of hardly audible soft squeaks followed by long thin, whining and descending nasal whistle, *weeeeee*; calls include a nasal downturned *nyek, nyek*. **HH** Typical estrildid, see Indian Silverbill. Marshy areas with tall grass or reeds and grassland. **AN** Black-headed Munia.

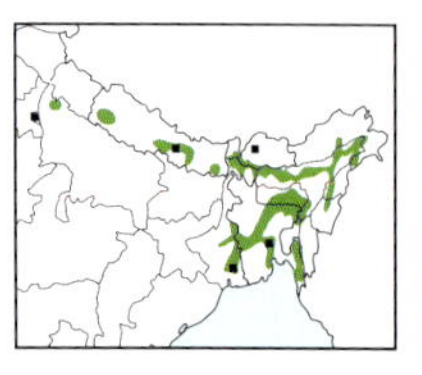

Chestnut Munia *Lonchura atricapilla* 11–12cm

Resident. N, NE and E subcontinent. Hybridises with Tricoloured in E peninsula. **ID** Similar to Tricoloured but has chestnut lower breast and flanks. Juvenile is warmer buff on underparts than Tricoloured. **Voice** Song a series of hardly audible soft clicks, followed by extended *weee...*, ending with slurred notes; contact calls include loud *pink pink*. **HH** Typical estrildid, see Indian Silverbill. Grassland, wetlands including freshwater marshes and brackish margins of coastal mangroves and nearby cultivation and gardens.

juv
♂
Indian Silverbill
ad
juv
Scaly-breasted
Munia
ad
jerdoni
ad
kelaarti
Black-throated
Munia
imm
kelaarti
White-rumped
Munia
ad
striata
ad
acuticauda
ad
juv
Tricoloured Munia
ad
Chestnut Munia

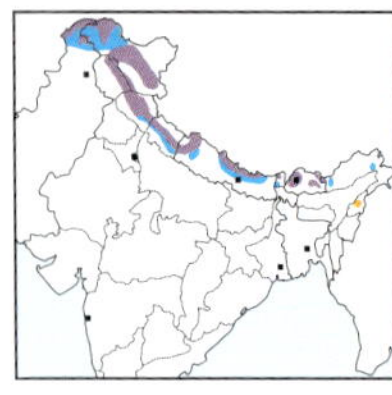

Alpine Accentor *Prunella collaris* 15.5–17cm

Resident. Himalayas. **ID** From smaller Altai by comparatively uniform grey head and breast, diffusely streaked mantle, and (white-tipped) blackish coverts that form dark panel on wing. Has chestnut streaking on flanks but, unlike on Altai, streaks usually merge so flanks appear wholly chestnut. Both species show white or buffish tips to tail feathers in flight. Juvenile has adult wing pattern, but dark mottling on crown and nape, and dark brown streaking on buffish underparts. **Voice** Song melodious with ringing, whistling and squeaking notes; calls include rolling *churrupp*. **HH** Breeds in alpine zone on open stony slopes, rocky pastures; near upland villages in winter.

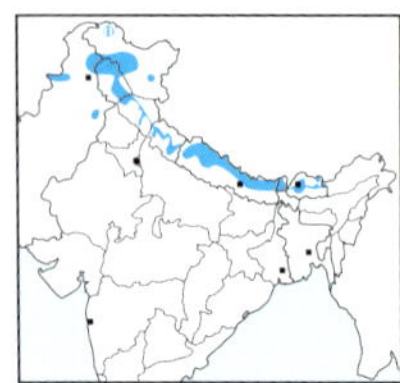

Altai Accentor *Prunella himalayana* 15cm

Winter visitor. Himalayas. **ID** From larger Alpine by more extensive white throat and diffuse rufous spotting/streaking on breast (extending onto flanks). Typically, has diffuse malar stripe of black spotting, and black gorget on lower throat, which can be well defined in some birds. Although variable, also often shows brownish ear-coverts and greyish supercilium. Like Alpine, has white tips to wing-coverts, but usually lacks striking black panel on wing. Mantle is more heavily streaked and can show prominent pale 'braces'. **Voice** Song a trilling warble; double *tee-tee* flight call. **HH** Grassy and stony slopes and plateaux.

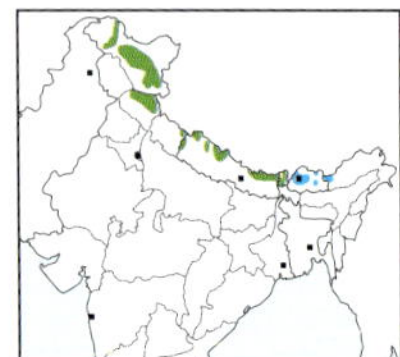

Robin Accentor *Prunella rubeculoides* 16–17cm

Resident. Himalayas. **ID** Adult has rusty-orange band on breast. From Rufous-breasted Accentor by uniform brownish-grey head including throat, diffusely streaked upperparts, and unstreaked white belly (with limited streaking on flanks). Juvenile very similar to juvenile Rufous-breasted but has more diffusely streaked underparts (with streaking hardly evident on belly and flanks) and poorly defined supercilium. **Voice** Song high-pitched *tzwe-e-you, tzwe-e-you*; ringing *pi-pi-pi-pi* in alarm. **HH** Breeds in dwarf scrub and sedge clumps around streams and lakes; winters on stony ground and around upland villages.

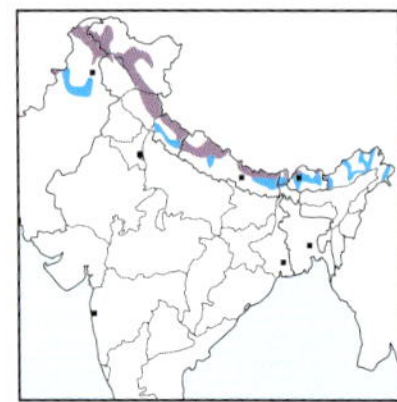

Rufous-breasted Accentor *Prunella strophiata* 15cm

Resident. Himalayas. **ID** Adult has rusty-orange band on breast. Best told from Robin Accentor by striking head pattern. Prominent supercilium (whitish in front of eye, becoming broader and rufous behind), blackish ear-coverts and sides to crown, and whitish throat (with variable black streaking, typically forming diffuse malar stripe and band on lower throat). Also has black streaking on grey neck-sides and dark streaking on belly and flanks. Some variation exists, some have duller (streaked) and less extensive rufous on breast, and less well-marked head pattern. More heavily streaked underparts and more prominent supercilium (offset by brown ear-coverts and crown-sides) help separate juvenile from juvenile Robin Accentor. **Voice** Melodious trilling and warbling song; penetrating *trr-r-rit trrr-r-it* call. **HH** Breeds in dwarf shrubbery in alpine and subalpine zones; winters in bushes in cultivation, upland pastures and scrub.

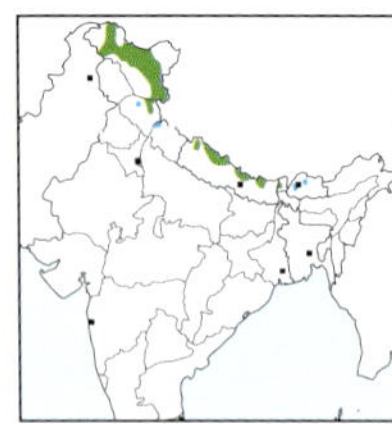

Brown Accentor *Prunella fulvescens* 15cm

Resident. N Himalayas. **ID** Adult has broad whitish supercilium (contrasting with blackish ear-coverts), grey-brown upperparts with only very faint streaking, and pale orange-buff underparts with whiter throat (see Vagrants for differences from Radde's Accentor). Juvenile has more heavily streaked upperparts with rufous-buff cast, brown mottling on supercilium and crown, browner ear-coverts (with less striking head pattern) and brown streaking on breast. Tibetan *sushkini* (north-east) has more prominent brown streaking on upperparts and deeper buff underparts. **Voice** Song a variable warbling *tuk-tileep-tilee-tileep-tileep*; weak, ringing trill call. **HH** Dry scrubby and rocky slopes; also, around upland villages in winter.

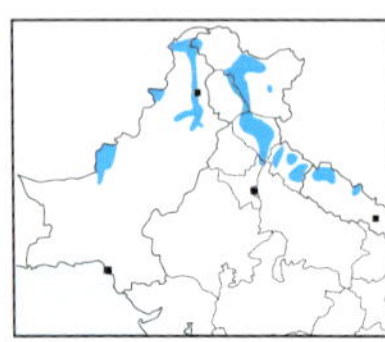

Black-throated Accentor *Prunella atrogularis* 15cm

Winter visitor. W Himalayas and Balochistan. **ID** Broad white to orange-buff supercilium and submoustachial stripe, black chin and upper throat, blackish crown-sides and ear-coverts, dark brown streaking on mantle, and orange-buff breast and flanks. In first-winter black throat can be partly obscured by pale fringes or, rarely, is completely absent. Heavy dark streaking on mantle and flanks, and mottled ear-coverts, help separate such birds from Brown. **Voice** Weak, ringing trill *si-si-si-si* call. **HH** Bushes near cultivation, dry scrub-covered hills.

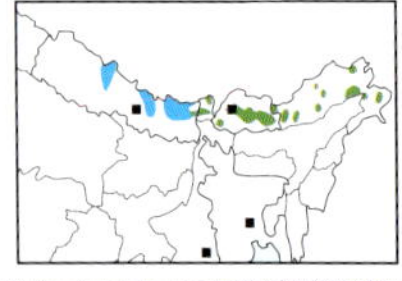

Maroon-backed Accentor *Prunella immaculata* 14.5cm

Resident in E Himalayas; winters in C Himalayas. **ID** Adult has grey head and breast, white scaling on forehead, yellow iris, maroon-brown mantle and grey panel on wing. Juvenile has similar wing pattern to adult but has streaked upperparts and underparts. **Voice** Song poorly documented; very high and feeble *tzip* call. **HH** Moist rhododendron and mixed coniferous-rhododendron forest.

Altai Accentor
Alpine Accentor
ad
ad
juv
juv
Robin Accentor
ad
ad
1st-winter?
Rufous-breasted
Accentor
ad
juv
Brown Accentor
juv
Maroon-backed
Accentor
ad
ad
juv
Black-throated Accentor
♀
1st-win

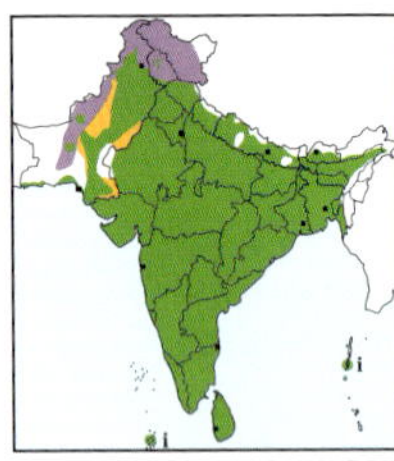

House Sparrow *Passer domesticus* 15cm

Widespread resident, except in parts of NE and NW subcontinent. **ID** Breeding male has grey crown with chestnut sides and nape, and black throat and upper breast; duller in non-breeding plumage when head pattern and black throat/breast partly obscured by pale fringes. Female has pale buff supercilium, dark brown streaking on buffish mantle and unstreaked greyish-white underparts (faintly washed buff on flanks). Juvenile as female, with broader buff-brown fringes to upperparts; juvenile male with greyish chin. **Voice** Song a long series of *chirrup*, *cheep* and *churp* notes; monotonous *chirrup* call. **HH** Breeds in habitation; also winters in cultivation.

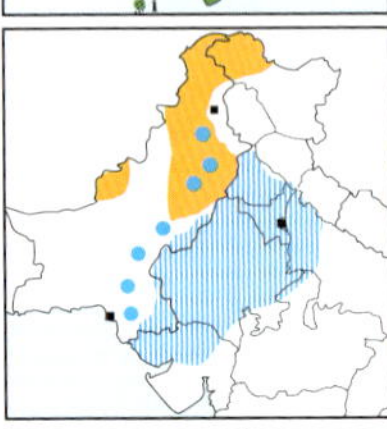

Spanish Sparrow *Passer hispaniolensis* 15–16cm

Winter visitor. Pakistan and N India. Vagrant: Nepal. **ID** Breeding male from male House by chestnut crown, fine white supercilium, extensive black on breast becoming black streaking on flanks and belly, and largely black mantle with distinct buffish-white 'braces'. In non-breeding plumage duller, with head and body pattern partially obscured by pale fringes (although features distinct from House, especially dark flank markings, still apparent). Female very similar to female House, but generally has longer whitish supercilium, fine grey streaking on breast and flanks, and buffish-white 'braces' on mantle. **Voice** Call more metallic *chweeng* or squeaky *cheela* notes than House. **HH** Cultivation, especially cereal crops, semi-desert.

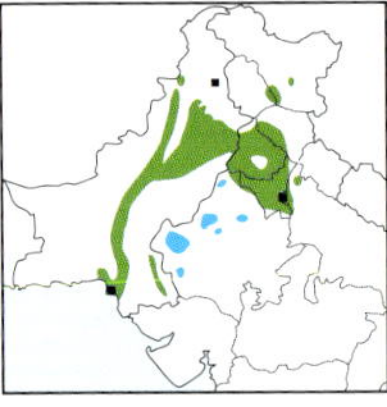

Sind Sparrow *Passer pyrrhonotus* 12.5–13cm

Mainly resident. Pakistan and NW India. **ID** Smaller and slimmer than House with finer bill. Male has grey (rather than chestnut) nape, with chestnut of head brighter and reduced to broad crescent surrounding ear-coverts; also, grey cheeks contrasting with white sides to neck, small black throat and chestnut (rather than grey) lower back (extending to rump in some birds). Pattern only slightly obscured by buff fringes in non-breeding plumage. Female best told from House by smaller size and slimmer structure; also, more prominent buffish-white supercilium, warmer buffish-brown (not brownish-grey) lower back and rump, and greyer cast to ear-coverts contrasting with white sides to neck. Juvenile as female. **Voice** Call similar to House but a higher-pitched *chu-wit*. Song high-pitched chirrups and interspersed with rapid grating, short twitters and whistles. **HH** Trees by waterways, riverine forest.

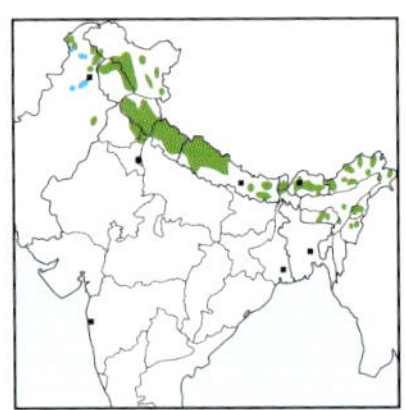

Russet Sparrow *Passer cinnamomeus* 14–15cm

Resident. Himalayas and NE Indian hills. **ID** Slimmer than Eurasian Tree Sparrow, with finer bill. Breeding male has bright chestnut crown, nape and mantle (latter with variable dark and buff streaking) and lacks black cheek patch of Tree. Underparts variable, greyish to washed with yellow. Brightness of head and mantle coloration obscured in non-breeding plumage. Female has more prominent supercilium and eye-stripe than female House; also has unstreaked buff or rufous-brown scapulars, rufous-brown lower back and rump, and sometimes a faint yellowish wash to underparts. **Voice** Call like House, but more musical and softer *cheep* or *chilp*; *swee... swee* and rapid *chit-chit-chit* in alarm; song *cheep-chirrup-cheweep* frequently repeated. **HH** Open forest, forest edges and cultivation near upland villages.

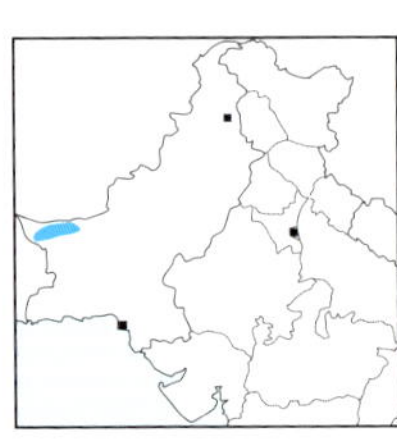

Dead Sea Sparrow *Passer moabiticus* 12cm

Winter visitor. Balochistan. **ID** Breeding male has grey head with buff supercilium and black stripe through eye, small black throat patch, white line below eye, broad white submoustachial stripe and yellow patch on side of neck. Further, has narrow streaking on upperparts, variable yellow wash on underparts and chestnut coverts forming panel on wing. Non-breeding male has grey of head suffused sandy-olive, and black of chin and throat are tipped whitish. Female smaller and slimmer than House and has more prominent buffish-white supercilium, indistinct yellow spot on side of neck, sandy-buff upperparts and yellowish underparts. **Voice** Calls include *chet-chet-chet*, and a liquid *chrelp*. **HH** Bushes, especially tamarisks near streams.

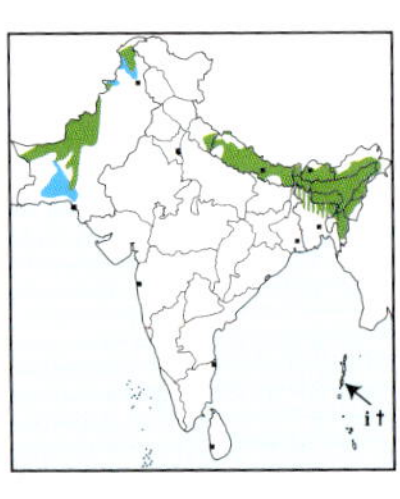

Eurasian Tree Sparrow *Passer montanus* 14cm

Mainly resident. Balochistan, Himalayas, NE India, Eastern Ghats and Bangladesh. **ID** Adult has dull chestnut crown, black spot on whitish ear-coverts, small black throat patch not extending to breast, and white collar separating chestnut nape from brown-streaked mantle. Sexes alike. Juvenile similar to adult but has paler chestnut crown and diffuse black patches on ear-coverts and throat. Paler in north-west (*dilutus*), becoming darker brown or rufous-brown on upperparts in north and north-east (e.g. *malaccensis*). **Voice** Call a monotonous *chip chip*, harder than similar call of House; song a running-together of this note, interspersed with *tsweep* or similar calls. **HH** Habitation and cultivation.

♂
♂ br
House Sparrow
♀
♀
Spanish Sparrow
♂
non-br
♂
♂
Sind Sparrow
Russet Sparrow
♀
♀
♂
ad
malaccensis
ad
dilutus
Eurasian Tree
Sparrow
Dead Sea
Sparrow
♀

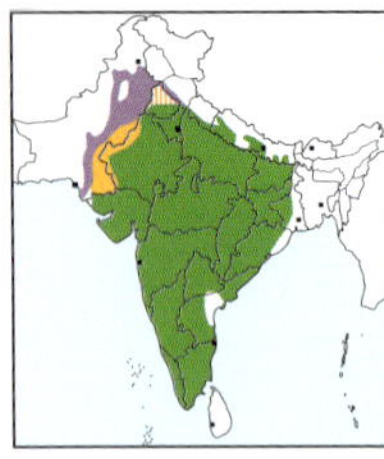

Yellow-throated Sparrow *Gymnoris xanthocollis* 12.5–14cm

Resident. Pakistan, Nepal and Indian peninsula. **ID** Male from other sparrows by finer bill, uniform (unstreaked) brownish-grey head and upperparts, and yellow patch on lower throat. Has chestnut lesser coverts and prominent double white wing-bar. Female similar, but has brown lesser coverts, buff-tinged tips to median coverts and yellow on throat is faint or absent. Juvenile similar to female, but upperparts more sandy-brown, with pale buffish supercilium and lacks any yellow on throat. **Voice** Calls like House; song a repetitive series of *chip*, *chillup* and *chalp* notes, more liquid than House. **HH** Open dry forest, thorn trees at edges of cultivation; in Pakistan also irrigated plantations. **AN** Chestnut-shouldered Petronia.

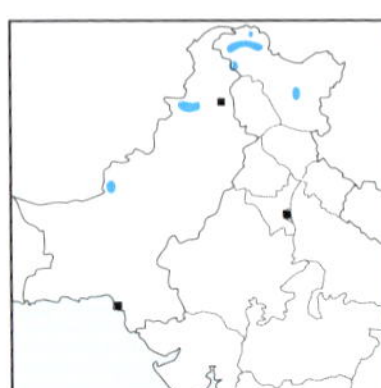

Rock Sparrow *Petronia petronia* 14–15.5cm

Winter visitor. Pakistan. **ID** Stocky and short-tailed with large bill and striking head pattern. In flight shows white tips to tail and pale patch at base of primaries. Has broad whitish supercilium, dark brown lateral crown-stripe and eye-stripe, and pale central crown-stripe. Also, buffish-white stripes or 'braces' on mantle, diffuse grey-brown streaking on breast and flanks, whitish fringes to grey-brown undertail-coverts, and yellow patch on lower throat (can be difficult to see). Juvenile similar to adult but has warmer brown upperparts and lacks yellow throat patch. See Vagrants for comparison with Pale Rockfinch. **Voice** Calls include nasal *waip*, *kriep* and metallic *zveeh-vu*. **HH** Dry, stony ground in mountains.

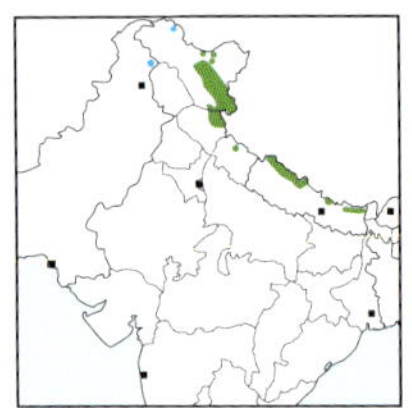

Black-winged Snowfinch *Montifringilla adamsi* 17cm

Resident. N Himalayas. **ID** Adult from other snowfinches in region by largely white greater and median coverts and white fringes to inner secondaries and outermost tertial (forming broad white wing-panel). Additional features are combination of indistinct blackish throat with plain grey-brown lores and forehead, and dull grey-brown head and upperparts. In flight tail largely white with blackish centre and tip. Adult non-breeding has orange (rather than blackish) bill with dark culmen and tip. Juvenile lacks black throat, is more buffish in coloration, with buffish (rather than white) sides to tail. From other juvenile snowfinches by buffish-white wing-panel. **Voice** Rapid sparrow-like, staccato chattering song. **HH** Rocky high-altitude semi-desert, often near villages and upland cultivation. **AN** Tibetan Snowfinch.

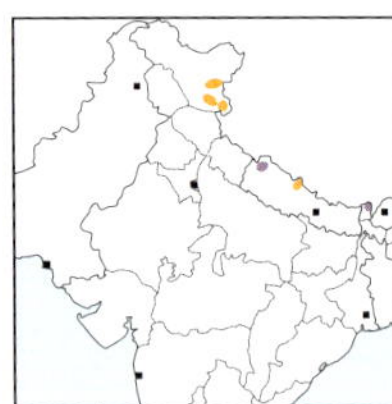

White-rumped Snowfinch *Onychostruthus taczanowskii* 15–17cm

Passage migrant, possibly resident. N Himalayas. **ID** Adult from other snowfinches by white rump (very conspicuous in flight) and pale greyish upperparts (with prominently streaked mantle and scapulars). Additional features are black lores, white throat, white forehead and supercilium, white sides to tail (lacking dark terminal bar) and white panel at base of secondaries and inner primaries (secondaries otherwise black broadly tipped whitish). Bill pale silvery-grey with dark tip. Juvenile has warmer brown mantle and wings, buffish breast and flanks, buff sides to tail and orange bill. **Voice** Simple weak song of clipped wheezes and whistles. **HH** High-altitude stony plateaux and among pika colonies. **TN** Formerly placed in *Montifringilla*.

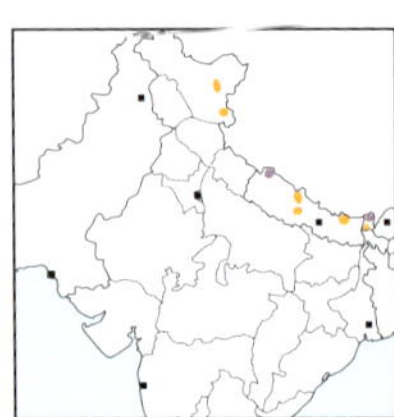

Rufous-necked Snowfinch *Pyrgilauda ruficollis* 13–15cm

Passage migrant, possibly resident. N Himalayas. **ID** Adult has rufous nape and sides of neck and breast, white cheeks, and largely white underparts. From Blanford's by greyish-white forehead, fine black malar stripe, white throat, and conspicuous streaking on mantle and scapulars. White patch in median coverts (visible in flight), and broad buffish greater covert wing-bar. In flight shows pale tail with darker centre and tip. Female has duller rufous 'neck' and less white in wing. Juvenile lacks adult head pattern and initially has orange bill. Also duller, with buffish tinge to breast and flanks, warm cinnamon tinge to ear-coverts and neck-sides, and buffish median and greater covert wing-bars. From juvenile Blanford's by dark malar stripe and streaked mantle and scapulars. **Voice** Song an erratic repetition of simple sparrow-like notes. **HH** Stony high-altitude steppe grassy plateaux. **TN** Formerly placed in *Montifringilla*.

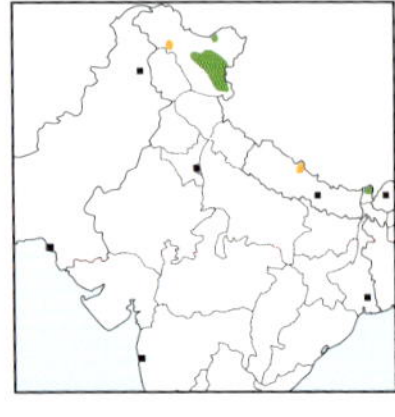

Blanford's Snowfinch *Pyrgilauda blanfordi* 15cm

Resident and passage migrant. N Himalayas. **ID** Adult has rufous nape and sides of neck and breast and white cheeks. From Rufous-necked by black centre to white forehead, black 'spur' in front of eye dividing white supercilium, and black chin and centre of throat. Rather uniform wing-coverts (lacking prominent wing-bars), white panel in secondaries, and mantle and scapulars are unstreaked (or, rarely, very faintly streaked). Also has stouter bill. In flight shows pale wing panel, and whitish sides to tail with darker centre and tip. Juvenile lacks adult head pattern and initially has orange bill; from juvenile Rufous-necked by unstreaked mantle and scapulars. **Voice** Rapid twittering song. **HH** High-altitude steppe country.

♂
♀
Yellow-throated Sparrow
ad
juv
Rock Sparrow
juv
ad
Black-winged Snowfinch
ad
White-rumped Snowfinch
ad
Rufous-necked Snowfinch
ad
Blanford's Snowfinch

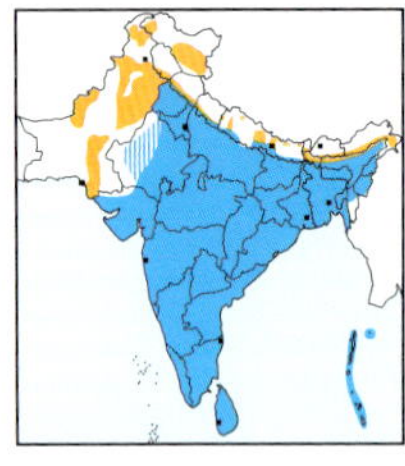

Western Yellow Wagtail *Motacilla flava* 16.5cm

Widespread in winter; mainly passage migrant to the north-west and Himalayas. **ID** Male breeding has olive-green upperparts and yellow underparts, with considerable subspecies variation in head coloration and pattern. In non-breeding plumage head pattern is similar but less clearly defined. Female breeding usually shows some features of breeding male. First-winter typically has brownish-olive upperparts, whitish underparts with variable yellowish wash, and buff or whitish wing-bars and fringes to tertials. Some first-winters, however, have greyish upperparts, whitish underparts (lacking yellow) and broader white wing-bars, and closely resemble first-winter Citrine Wagtail as well as Eastern Yellow Wagtail. Compared to Citrine, grey-and-white first-winter Yellow typically show the following features: narrower white supercilium that does not extend around ear-coverts to join white of throat; grey forehead concolorous with crown; dark lores resulting in complete dark eye-stripe; pale base to lower mandible; and narrower white wing-bars. Juvenile has dark malar stripe and band on breast. Five subspecies occur and breeding males are distinctive. *M. f. beema* ('Sykes's Blue-headed') has bluish-grey head, complete and distinct white supercilium, white chin, and usually a white submoustachial stripe contrasting with yellow throat; ear-coverts often extensively white with grey lower border. *M. f. leucocephala* ('White-headed') has whole head to nape white, with a variable blue-grey cast on ear-coverts and rear crown; chin white, and throat yellow as rest of underparts. *M. f. feldegg* ('Black-headed') has black head, lacking any supercilium, and usually a white chin and poorly defined submoustachial stripe contrasting with yellow throat. *M. f. thunbergi* ('Grey-headed') has dark slate-grey crown with darker ear-coverts, typically lacking supercilium (but may show narrow white line behind eye). *M. f. lutea* ('Yellow-headed') has mainly yellow head, with variable amounts of yellowish-green on crown, nape and ear-coverts (concolorous with mantle). Intergrades occur resulting in variations, e.g. *M. f. 'superciliaris'* is probably an intergrade between *beema* and *feldegg*, and looks like the latter but with a white supercilium. **Voice** A shrill, drawn-out monosyllabic *tsweep* or *tseer*, occasionally disyllabic *tsi-weep* or *sree-sreeh* generally without any rasping quality, and quite distinct from Citrine, although *feldegg* has a harsher *tsreep* call. **HH** Grassy margins of lakes and marshes, irrigated fodder crops and damp pastures, especially near grazing livestock. **AN** Yellow Wagtail.

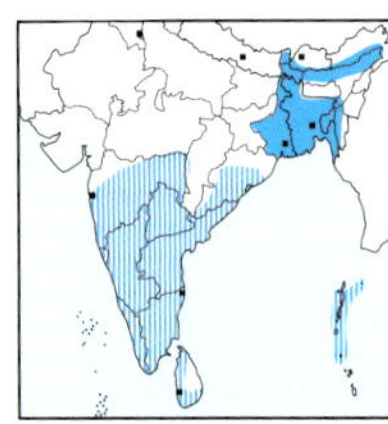

Eastern Yellow Wagtail *Motacilla tschutschensis* 18cm

Winter visitor and passage migrant although range unclear due to challenge of identification from Western Yellow Wagtail. **ID** Races occurring unclear and several possible. Male breeding *M. t. plexa* ('Siberian') and *M. t. macronyx* ('Manchurian') are not safely distinguishable from *M. flava thunbergi*. Male breeding *M. t. tschutschensis* ('Alaskan') has white supercilium, grey crown and grey to blackish ear-coverts, but some are very similar to *M. flava beema*, although ear-coverts are typically uniform lacking white centre (usually just a broken white eye-ring). Male breeding *M. t. taivana* ('Green-headed') is more distinctive with olive crown and back, yellow supercilium and dark ear-coverts. Female, non-breeder and immature are not safely identifiable in the field at present. Grey-and-white first-winters are common and strikingly clean grey and white (differences from Citrine as for Western Yellow). Best distinguished from Western by call (supported by use of sonograms), biometrics (hindclaw – longer in Eastern but some overlap) and genetic analysis. **Voice** Flight call often harsher and more rasping than Western Yellow and closer to Citrine. **HH** As Western Yellow. **TN** *M. t. plexa* is recognised here as distinct from *M. f. thunbergi*, whereas *M. t. simillima* and *M. t. angarensis* are included in *M. t. tschutschensis*.

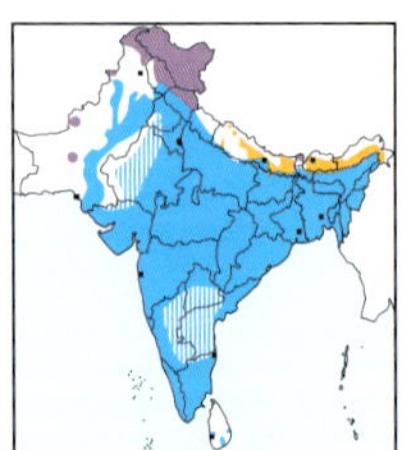

Citrine Wagtail *Motacilla citreola* 16.5–20cm

Breeds in Balochistan and N Himalayas; widespread in winter. **ID** Adult male breeding is readily distinguished by yellow head and underparts, black or grey mantle, and broader white tips to median and greater coverts. Female breeding and adult non-breeding have broad yellow supercilium that surrounds ear-coverts to join yellow of throat, greyish crown, nape, ear-coverts and mantle, and mainly yellow underparts. Non-breeding female can be very pale buffish-yellow on underparts. Yellow surround to ear-coverts, pale lores, broad white wing-bars (albeit narrower when worn), greyish upperparts, white undertail-coverts, and greyish breast-sides and flanks help separate female from Western and Eastern Yellow. Juvenile lacks any yellow, has brownish crown, ear-coverts and mantle, buffish supercilium (with dark upper edge) and surround to ear-coverts, and buffish-white underparts with gorget of black spots on breast. First-winter has grey upperparts and is similar to some first-winter Western and Eastern Yellow, but has broader white supercilium, which usually surrounds ear-coverts; pale brown forehead; pale lores; all-dark bill; pale centre to ear-coverts; slightly darker lateral crown-stripe; broader white wing-bars; and white undertail-coverts. Grey-and-white first-winter confusable with some plumages of White, but lacks black breast-band, has more prominent supercilium, shows less white on wing-coverts (two distinct wing-bars) and has different call. By early November, first-winter Citrine has yellowish supercilium, ear-covert surround and throat. Two races in region with distinctive male plumages: *M. c. calcarata* (which breeds) has black upperparts and deeper yellow underparts; nominate has grey mantle and back with variable black collar. **Voice** Call a sharp rasping *tzreep*, similar to Eastern Yellow although harsher and more buzzing; song a repetition of similar sounds. **HH** Breeds in high-altitude wet grassland and marshy patches on alpine slopes below glaciers and melting snow; winters on marshes, around lakes, tanks, jheels and on wet fields.

Western Yellow Wagtail
juv
beema
♀
beema
♂ br
beema
grey-and-white
1st-winter
beema
♂
leucocephala
1st-winter
lutea
♂
lutea
1st-winter
thunbergi
♂
ldegg
♂
'superciliaris'
♂
thunbergi
♂
taivana
♂
chutschensis
♂
macronyx
Eastern Yellow Wagtail
Citrine Wagtail
♂ br
calcarata
1st-winter
(late)
calcarata
juv
calcarata
♀
calcarata
vinter
rly)
arata
♂ br
citreola

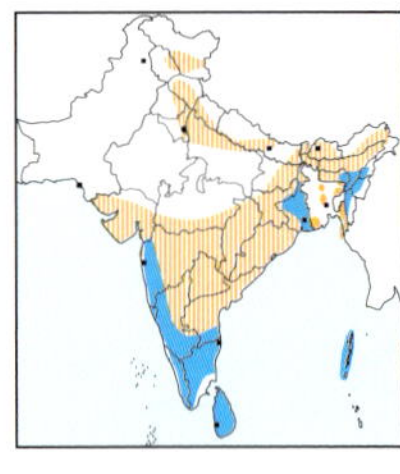

Forest Wagtail *Dendronanthus indicus* 16–18cm

Mainly a winter visitor to NE and SW India and Sri Lanka. **ID** A forest-dwelling wagtail; from other wagtails by combination of broad yellowish-white median and greater covert wing-bars and white patch on secondaries, double black breast-band (lower one broken in centre of breast), olive-brown to greyish upperparts, white supercilium and whitish underparts. Legs and feet, and lower mandible, are strikingly pink. Sexes and first-winter alike. **Voice** Call a strident metallic *pink* or *dzink-dzzt*; song a repetitive intense Great Tit-like see-sawing. **HH** Sways body and tail from side-to-side when feeding on the ground and when flushed into nearby vegetation and walks effortlessly along branches. Does not nod tail up and down like other wagtails. Forages chiefly on ground on paths and in clearings in tropical evergreen forest; also, in shade-coffee and cardamom plantations, deciduous forest and mangroves in winter.

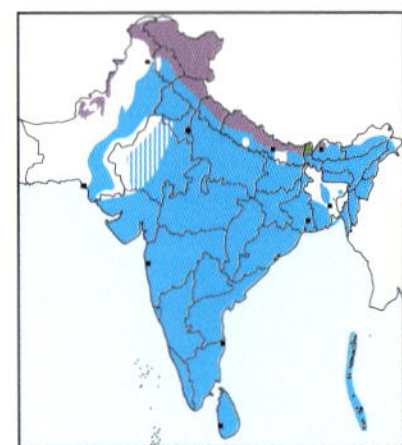

Grey Wagtail *Motacilla cinerea* 17–20cm

Breeds in Balochistan and Himalayas; widespread in winter. **ID** Much longer-tailed than other wagtails (most noticeable in flight). In all plumages, has white supercilium, grey upperparts and yellow vent and undertail-coverts. In flight, shows narrow white wing-bar and yellow rump. At rest, shows whitish fringes to tertials but otherwise wings are blackish, lacking broad fringes to coverts of Western and Eastern Yellow and Citrine Wagtails. Breeding male has black throat, with rest of underparts yellow. Female breeding lacks well-defined black bib but may show black mottling on chin/throat. Adult non-breeding and first-winter have white throat and pale yellowish to buffish-white underparts, with yellow vent. Juvenile much as non-breeding, but has brownish cast to upperparts, and buffish supercilium and sides to breast. **Voice** Call a sharp *stit* or *zee-fit*; song a series of call-like notes. **HH** Forages by delicately tripping among stones of riverbeds, wading in the shallows and fly-catching from a perch or on the ground. Nods tail incessantly. Breeds by fast-flowing rocky mountain streams; winters by slower streams in lowlands and foothills.

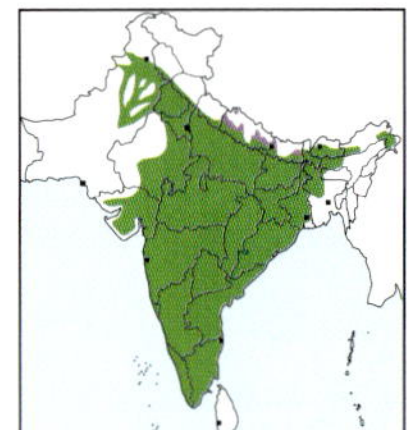

White-browed Wagtail *Motacilla maderaspatensis* 21–24cm

Widespread resident except parts of the north-west and north-east. **ID** Very large wagtail. Combination of black mantle and black head with white supercilium separates it from all subspecies of White Wagtail. Sexes similar (although most females are dark grey on upperparts) and shows no variation in non-breeding plumage. First-winter similar, but has greyer crown and mantle. Juvenile has brownish-grey head, mantle and breast, with indistinct whitish supercilium. **Voice** Call a distinctive, loud *chiz-zat*; song a clear, high-pitched jumble of loud, pleasant whistling notes. **HH** Typical wagtail, walking with a deliberate gait, running rapidly and nodding tail up and down. Usually in pairs all year. Banks of rivers, pools, lakes, canals and around irrigation barrages.

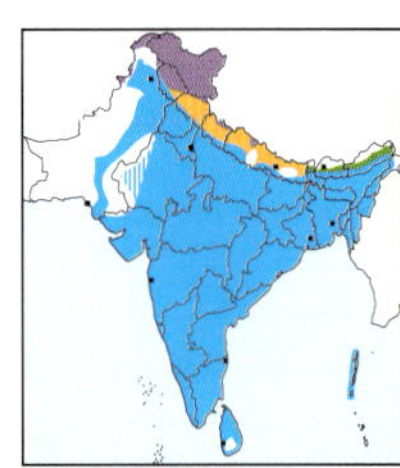

White Wagtail *Motacilla alba* 16.5–18cm

Breeds in Himalayas; widespread in winter. **ID** Extremely variable, with black-and-white head pattern, grey or black mantle, and largely white to mainly black wing-coverts. Black-backed birds perhaps confusable with White-browed, but latter is much larger and has a largely black head with a broad white supercilium. Subspecies variation among breeding adults (sexes are similar) is covered below. There is considerable variation in pattern of black on head and breast of non-breeding and first-winter birds, although in some subspecies non-breeders retain characteristics of breeding plumage. Juveniles of the two subspecies that breed have grey head, mantle and breast with whitish supercilium. *M. a. alba* (including '*dukhunensis*') (widespread winter visitor) has grey mantle, white forehead and face, and black hindcrown/nape, throat and breast. *M. a. personata* (breeds north-west, widespread winter visitor) has grey mantle and black head and breast, with white forehead and face patch, giving rise to white-masked appearance. *M. a. alboides* (breeds north, winters more widely in north and east) is much as *personata*, but has black mantle and back, although upperparts of female are variably mixed with grey. *M. a. leucopsis* (winter visitor to north, north-east and Andamans) has black mantle and back, otherwise has head pattern as breeding male *alba* but with white throat. *M. a. ocularis* (uncommon visitor to north and north-east) has grey mantle and back, and is much as *alba* but has black eye-stripe in all plumages. *M. a. baicalensis* (widespread winter visitor) has grey mantle and back and is much as *alba* but has white chin and upper throat contrasting with black breast. **Voice** Call a loud *tslee-vit*; song a lively twittering and chattering with call-like notes. **HH** Typical wagtail. Readily perches on telegraph wires, roofs of buildings and, less commonly, in trees. Breeds by streams and rivers in open country in hills and mountains; winters in open country near water, e.g. marshes, running waters, lakes, wet fields, also lawns and fallow cultivation.

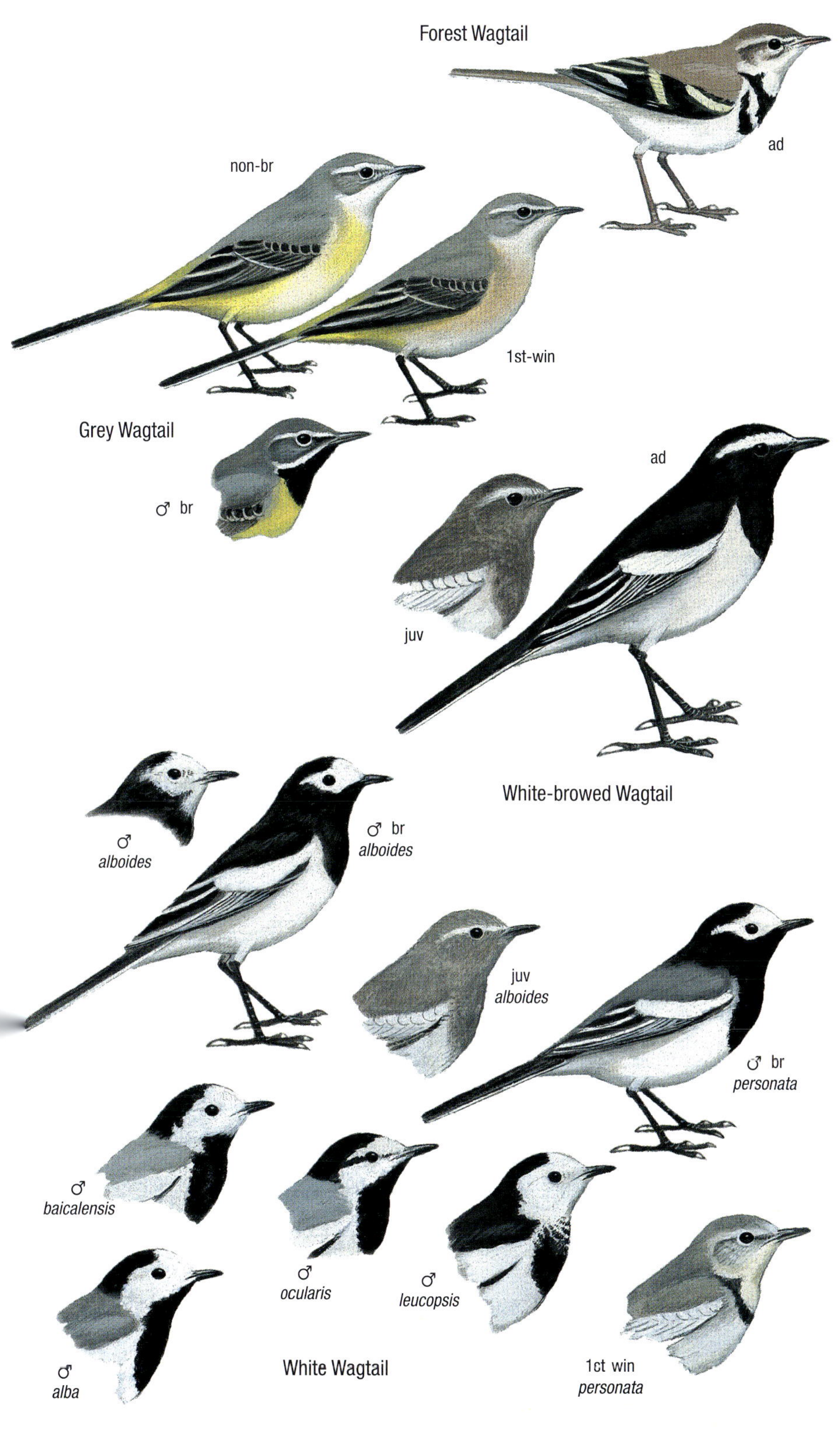

Forest Wagtail
ad
non-br
1st-win
Grey Wagtail
♂ br
ad
juv
White-browed Wagtail
♂
alboides
♂ br
alboides
juv
alboides
♂ br
personata
♂
baicalensis
♂
ocularis
♂
leucopsis
♂
alba
White Wagtail
1ct win
personata

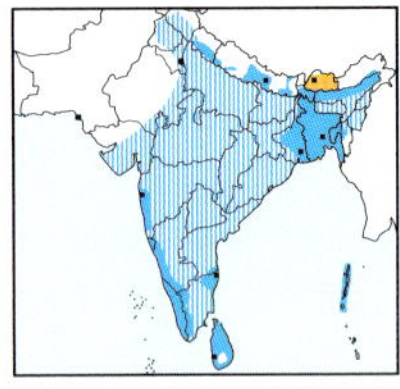

Richard's Pipit ***Anthus richardi*** 17–18cm

Widespread winter visitor except the north-west. **ID** Large size, upright stance, larger bill, longer legs and hind claw, and call are best features from otherwise similar Paddyfield Pipit; when flushed, typically gains height and distance with deep undulations. **Voice** Distinctive, loud, explosive *schreep* call. **HH** Moist grassland and cultivation.

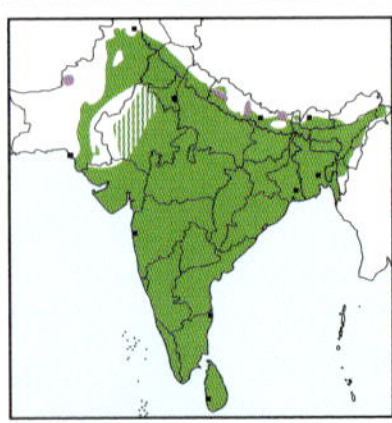

Paddyfield Pipit ***Anthus rufulus*** 15–16cm

Widespread resident, except in parts of NE and NW subcontinent. **ID** Smaller and stockier than Richard's, with shorter tail and different call; when flushed, has comparatively weak flight. Juvenile/first-winter Tawny can be very similar, but lores of Paddyfield often pale (can be dark) and shows warm ginger-buff wash across breast and on flanks (underparts more uniform cream-white on Tawny); flight call differs. *A. r. waitei* (north-west) paler sandy-grey above than widespread nominate, and less heavily streaked above and below (very similar to Tawny). *A. r. malayensis* (S peninsula and Sri Lanka) darker and more heavily streaked. **Voice** Song repetitive *chip-chip-chip*; weak *chup-chup-chup*; weak *chip-chip-chip* or *chilt* call with almost chattering quality. **HH** Short grassland, stubbles, fallow fields.

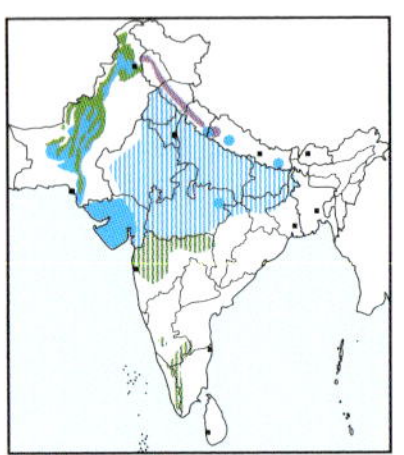

Long-billed Pipit ***Anthus similis*** 20cm

Resident. Hills of Pakistan and India, and W Himalayan foothills; also N plains in winter. **ID** Considerably larger than Tawny, with large bill and shorter-looking legs. Like Tawny has dark lores. *A. s. decaptus* (north-west) most similar to Tawny, but bill darker, upperparts darker and greyer, lacks distinct dark malar and moustachial, and has more unform and deeper buff to greyish-buff underparts. *A. s. jerdoni* (N subcontinent) more distinctive, with deeper orange-buff underparts, rufous fringes to tertials and coverts, and rufous-buff outer edge to tail. *A. s. similis* and *A. s. travancoriensis* of the peninsula have darker grey-brown upperparts and warm rufous-buff underparts; breast more heavily streaked. **Voice** Song a slow, measured *chirrit-chirrit-chirrit-teeweeh-pr-chirrit-chirrit-tweeweeh*; calls a sharp *wheet* and loud ringing *che-vlee*. **HH** Breeds on dry grassy, rocky or scrub-covered slopes; winters in dry cultivation and scattered scrub.

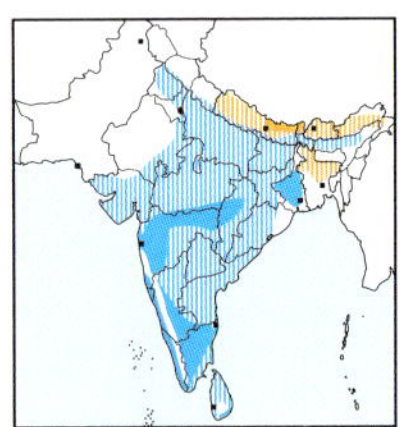

Blyth's Pipit ***Anthus godlewskii*** 15–17cm

Widespread winter visitor except in parts of NW, NE and E India. **ID** Compared to Richard's, very subtle differences are slightly smaller size and more compact appearance, shorter tail, shorter hindclaw, shorter and more pointed bill, shorter legs, and call. Shape of centres to adult buff-fringed median coverts distinctive (square-shaped black centres with broad pale buff tips; centres diffuse and more triangular in Richard's; no differences in juvenile feathers which are retained into first-winter). Best distinctions from Paddyfield Pipit are call, larger size and pattern of adult median coverts (Paddyfield is as Richard's Pipit). **Voice** Wheezy *spzeeu* call, softer and more nasal than Richard's, and different from Paddyfield. Also a short *chep* or *chip* more similar to Paddyfield. **HH** Grassland, cultivation and marshes.

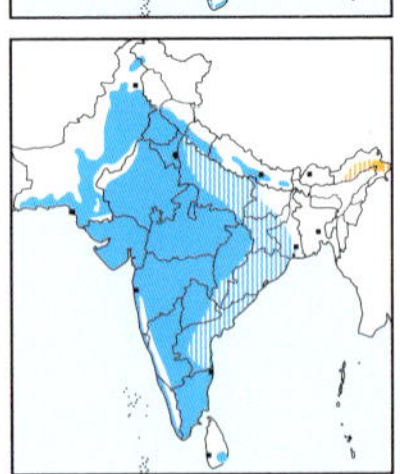

Tawny Pipit ***Anthus campestris*** 16.5–17cm

Widespread winter visitor except parts of the north-west and north-east. **ID** Adult and first-winter have plain or only very faintly streaked upperparts and unstreaked or only very lightly streaked breast. Juvenile plumage (upperparts and breast noticeably streaked) can be retained until midwinter. Subtle differences from Paddyfield are dark lores and eye-stripe contrasting with supercilium, which tends to be broader and square-ended, and more uniform buffish-white underparts. **Voice** Loud *tchilip* call distinctive, but softer *chep* similar to calls of Paddyfield and Blyth's. **HH** Stony semi-desert, uncultivated bare ground and fallow cultivation.

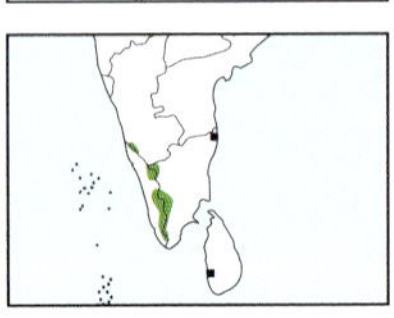

Nilgiri Pipit ***Anthus nilghiriensis*** 17–17.5cm

Resident. SW Indian hills. **ID** Large, heavily streaked pipit. Compared to Paddyfield, has shorter tail, more heavily streaked upperparts, boldly streaked flanks and dark lores, lacks malar stripe and patch, and has darker and stouter bill. **Voice** Feeble song: initially quiet and hesitant, accelerating into a trill *tsip-tsip-tsip-sip-sip-sip* and ending abruptly; weak *see-see* call, unlike Paddyfield. **HH** Grassy upland slopes interspersed with bushes and trees. Globally threatened.

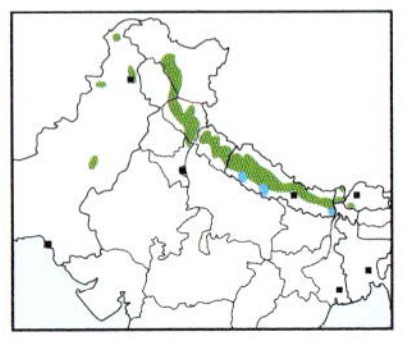

Upland Pipit ***Anthus sylvanus*** 17cm

Resident. Pakistan hills and Himalayas. **ID** Large, heavily streaked pipit with short broad bill and rather narrow, pointed tail feathers. Fine black streaking on underparts (especially flanks) whitish supercilium; ground colour of underparts varies from warm buff (fresh plumage) to rather cold and grey (worn plumage). Lacks prominent wing-bars. **Voice** Distinctive song: high pitched penetrating two-note whistle, *whit-tsee, whit-tsee* repeated monotonously; sparrow-like *chirp* call. **HH** Rocky and grassy slopes, abandoned terrace cultivation.

Richard's Pipit
ad
juv
ad
waitei
Paddyfield
Pipit
juv
rufulus
ad
rufulus
Long-billed Pipit
ad
jerdoni
Blyth's Pipit
1st-win
ad
travancoriensis
ad
ad
Nilgiri Pipit
ad
juv
ad worn
Tawny Pipit
1st-win
ad fresh
Upland Pipit

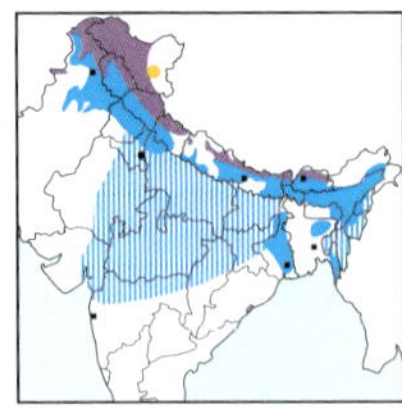

Rosy Pipit ***Anthus roseatus*** 15–16.5cm

Breeds in high Himalayas; winters in plains and foothills in N subcontinent. **ID** Always has boldly streaked mantle with olive cast and olive to olive-green edges to wing feathers. Adult breeding has mauve-pink wash to underparts with irregular black spotting on breast and flanks; pinkish to buff supercilium very prominent (extending down behind ear-coverts), with broad dark eye-stripe and moustachial stripe, and whitish eye-ring. Female is less pink below with heavier breast streaking than male. In non-breeding plumage, olive cast to heavily streaked mantle, more prominent supercilium and dark lores help separate from Water and Buff-bellied Pipits. Legs pale and longish bill all dark. **Voice** Song *tit-tit-tit-tit-tit teedle-teedle*; weak *seep-seep* call. **HH** Breeds on slopes above treeline. Winters in marshes, damp grassland, cultivation.

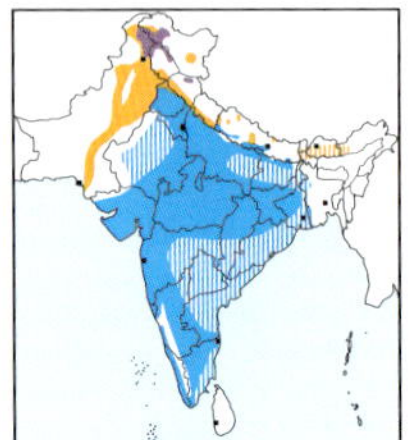

Tree Pipit ***Anthus trivialis*** 14–15cm

Resident and winter visitor. Breeds in NW Himalayas; widespread in winter except the north-east; unrecorded in Sri Lanka. **ID** Buffish-brown to greyish ground colour to upperparts (lacking greenish-olive cast of Olive-backed Pipit) and buffish edges to wing feathers (greenish-olive in Olive-backed). Head pattern typically less prominent, but can appear similar. *A. t. haringtoni*, which breeds in north-west, generally colder and greyer than widespread wintering nominate, and more boldly streaked, with larger, darker bill. **Voice** Call a harsher *teez* than Olive-backed, but much overlap; song louder and far-carrying, ending in finch-like trill *chik-chik...chia-chia-wich-wich-tsee-a-tsee-a tsse-a*. **HH** Breeds on grassy slopes at treeline. Winters in fallow cultivation; open country with scattered trees.

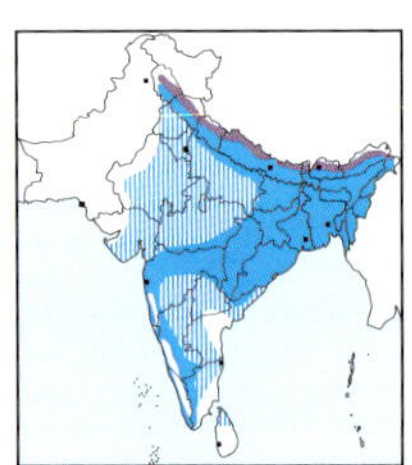

Olive-backed Pipit ***Anthus hodgsoni*** 15–17cm

Breeds in Himalayas; widespread in winter, except north-west and south-east. **ID** Greenish-olive cast to upperparts and edges to wing feathers. Has more striking head pattern than Tree, with more prominent supercilium (buffish in front of eye and white behind), stronger dark eye-stripe and line above supercilium, and shows more distinct whitish spot and blackish patch on rear ear-coverts. Worn upperparts become greyish-olive, and breast loses warm buff wash; separation from Tree thus more difficult. *A. h. yunnanensis*, a widespread winter visitor, is much less heavily streaked above than nominate (and Tree Pipit). **Voice** Weak *see* flight call, fainter than Tree; faster, drier and higher-pitched song. **HH** Breeds in open forest and shrubbery above treeline. Winters in forest clearings, plantations, cultivation with scattered trees.

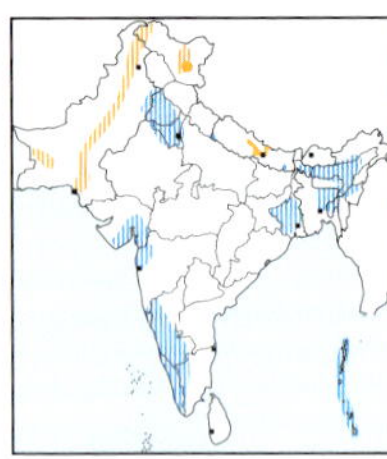

Red-throated Pipit ***Anthus cervinus*** 14–15cm

Winter visitor. Mainly N subcontinent. **ID** Adult has reddish throat and upper breast, paler and more restricted on female and autumn/winter birds. First-winter lacks reddish throat (is buffy-white) and is similar in coloration to nominate Tree Pipit, but typically has more heavily streaked upperparts, often with pale 'braces', heavily streaked rump, well-defined and broad white wing-bars, strongly contrasting blackish centres and whitish fringes to tertials, more pronounced dark malar patch, and more boldly streaked breast and (especially) flanks. Very different call, browner upperparts, heavily streaked rump/uppertail-coverts, and absence of olive in wing help separate from non-breeding Rosy; also has less prominent supercilium, pale lores and pale base to lower mandible. **Voice** Drawn-out *seeeeee* call. **HH** Marshes, wet grassland, stubble.

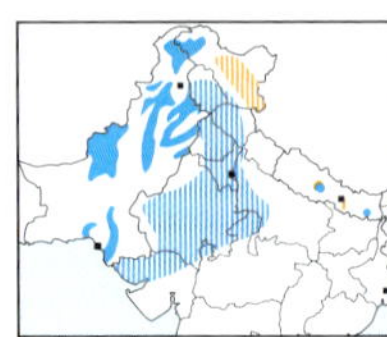

Water Pipit ***Anthus spinoletta*** 15–17cm

Winter visitor. Pakistan, N India, Nepal. Vagrant: Bhutan. **ID** Has lightly streaked upperparts, usually has dark legs and pale lores; underparts less heavily marked than Rosy and Buff-bellied Pipits. In breeding plumage has orange-buff wash to supercilium and underparts, with greyish cast to upperparts; usually lacks any suggestion of dark malar stripe and patch, and underparts are typically unstreaked or with a few fine streaks. In non-breeding plumage, has poorly defined malar stripe and weak streaking on breast. **Voice** Call like Buff-bellied. **HH** Marshes, wet grassland, cultivation.

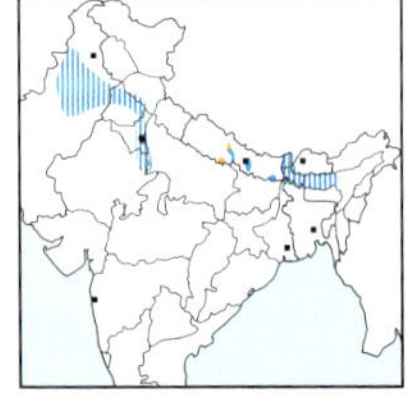

Buff-bellied Pipit ***Anthus rubescens*** 16cm

Winter visitor. Pakistan, N India, Nepal and Bhutan. **ID** Lightly streaked upperparts, lack of olive-green on wing and pale lores help separate it from Rosy in all plumages. In breeding plumage has deeper orange-buff wash to underparts than Water and lacks grey cast to upperparts; breast and flanks more heavily (but irregularly) spotted with black and has more pronounced malar stripe and patch, although there is some overlap (some Buff-bellied being more lightly streaked). In non-breeding plumage, compared to Water, has darker greyish-brown upperparts which are slightly less prominently streaked; black malar stripe and patch, and bold black spotting/streaking on breast and flanks, are much more pronounced. Legs usually pale (but can be dark). **Voice** Call like Rosy, but thinner and sharper. **HH** Like Water.

♂ br
Rosy Pipit
non-br
♂ br
ad
trivialis
Olive-backed
Pipit
ad fresh
hodgsoni
ad
haringtoni
Tree Pipit
ad worn
hodgsoni
ad
yunnanensis
♂ br
br
Red-throated
Pipit
Water Pipit
1st-win
non-br
br
non-br
Buff-bellied Pipit

Common Chaffinch *Fringilla coelebs* 16cm

Winter visitor. Pakistan hills and N Himalayas. **ID** Double whitish wing-bars in all plumages. Lacks white rump of Brambling but has prominent white sides to tail. Male has blue-grey crown and nape, dusky-pink face and underparts, and maroon-brown mantle; brighter in breeding plumage. Female duller than female Brambling, with greyish-brown upperparts and dull greyish-buff underparts. **Voice** Metallic *chink* call. **HH** Often in small flocks with other finches or buntings. Hops and walks with distinctive short, quick steps accompanied by slightly nodding head movements while foraging on ground. Undulating flight. Upland fields with nearby bushes and coniferous forest, also orchards.

Brambling *Fringilla montifringilla* 16cm

Winter visitor. Pakistan hills and N Himalayas. **ID** Male non-breeding and female from Common Chaffinch by orange breast and flanks (contrasting with white belly), orange greater covert wing-bar, lacks prominent white at sides to tail, and has white rump. Bill pale orange with dark tip. Head and mantle of male become blacker towards breeding season as feather fringes are lost with wear, and bill becomes black. **Voice** Deep nasal *zweee* call. **HH** Habits similar to Common Chaffinch. Upland fields bordered by bushes and coniferous forest, also orchards.

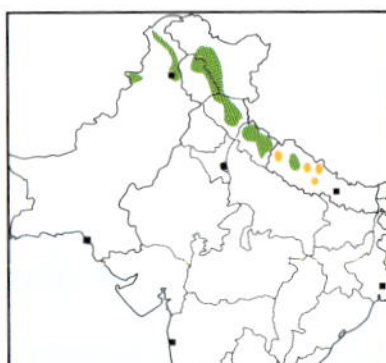

Black-and-yellow Grosbeak *Mycerobas icterioides* 22cm

Resident. W Himalayas. **ID** Male is very similar to male Collared. Black of plumage duller (less glossy) and has black thighs. Nape, upperparts and underparts are generally a purer, paler lemon-yellow. Female very different from female Collared: mantle and breast pale grey and concolorous with head, and belly, flanks and rump pale peachy-orange. Immature male similar to adult female, but has yellow rump and blackish wings and tail, with patches of black on scapulars and throat. **Voice** A throaty whistle, *pi-riu, pir-riu, pir-riu*; song a rich *prr-trweeet-a-troweeet* or *tookiyu, tookiyu*. **HH** Habits like Collared. Fir-spruce and pine forest.

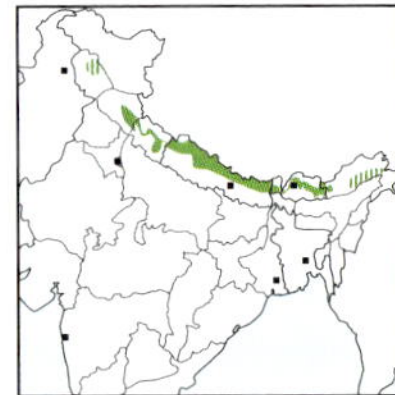

Collared Grosbeak *Mycerobas affinis* 22cm

Resident. Himalayas. **ID** Male is very similar to male Black-and-yellow, although black of plumage is strongly glossed, has yellow thighs, yellow of plumage more golden-yellow, and nape has strong orange cast. Female very different from female Black-and-yellow: grey head is well demarcated from olive-yellow of underparts, and has greyish-olive mantle, largely yellowish-olive wings, and olive-yellow rump contrasting with black tail. Immature male resembles adult male, but duller and mantle is mottled with black. **Voice** Mellow, rapid *pip-pip-pip-pip-pip-pip-ugh* call; a sharp *kurr* in alarm; song a loud, rising whistle, *ti-di-li-ti-di-li-um*. **HH** In pairs in breeding season, otherwise in small flocks. Usually seen in flight or in treetops. Often first located by its calls. Flight strong, swift and undulating. Coniferous and mixed broadleaved-coniferous forest.

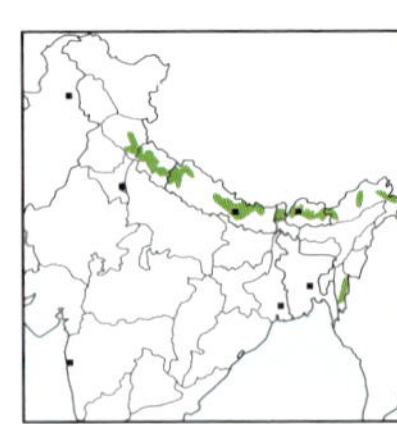

Spot-winged Grosbeak *Mycerobas melanozanthos* 22cm

Resident. Himalayas and NE India. **ID** Stocky, short-tailed and stout-billed grosbeak. Both sexes have broad white tips to greater coverts, tertials and secondaries. Male has black head and upperparts (including rump) and lemon-yellow underparts. Female has bold blackish streaking on yellow head and body, and striking head pattern with yellow supercilium, broad black stripe through ear-coverts and black malar stripe. Juvenile as female, but underparts whiter. Immature male similar to female but head mainly black. **Voice** Rattling *krrrr* or *charrarauk* call; song a loud, melodious whistle *tew-tew-teeeu*, also an oriole-like *tyop-tiu* or *tyu-tio*. **HH** Habits similar to Collared. Breeds in coniferous-broadleaved forest; winters in broadleaved forest.

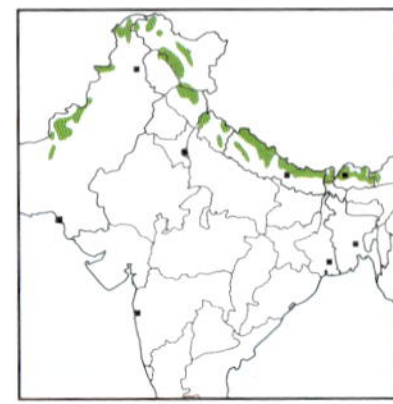

White-winged Grosbeak *Mycerobas carnipes* 22cm

Resident. Pakistan mountains and Himalayas. **ID** A long-tailed grosbeak. Male has black head, mantle and breast, olive-yellow rump and rest of underparts, yellow tips to greater coverts and tertials, and large white patch at base of primaries (very prominent in flight). Female resembles male, with distinctive white patch at base of primaries, but black is replaced by sooty-grey, grey underparts become dull yellowish-olive on lower belly and vent, and has dull olive-yellow rump. Juvenile similar to adult female but browner, with paler fringes to upperparts and olive-yellow tips to median (as well as greater) coverts. First-year as female; first-summer male has yellower rump, vent and belly, and more olive mantle. **Voice** Call a soft, nasal *schwenk* or squawking *wit*; song a *wet-et-et-un-di-di-di-dit*. **HH** Habits similar to Collared. Woodpecker-like flight, strong and undulating, interspersed with glides, with fast, whirring wingbeats. Closely associated with junipers: dwarf juniper shrubbery near the treeline, juniper-fir-rhododendron forest, and pine-juniper forest.

♂ non-br
♀
Common Chaffinch
♂ non-br
Brambling
♂ br
♀
♂
Black-and-yellow Grosbeak
♀
♂ juv
♂
Collared Grosbeak
♀
♂ juv
♂
♀
Spot winged Grosbeak
♂
White-winged Grosbeak
♀

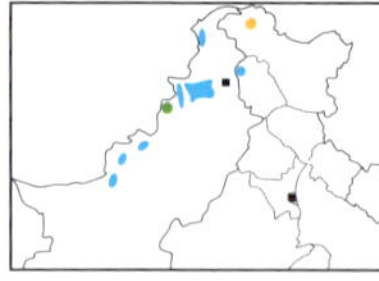

Hawfinch *Coccothraustes coccothraustes* 16–18cm

Winter visitor. Mainly Pakistan, also Jammu. **ID** Stocky, short-tailed finch with huge bill. Mainly fawn-brown, with pale wing-covert panel, and black chin and lores. In flight, white band across primaries and white tip to tail. Female duller than male, with pale brown head and secondaries are broadly edged pale grey. **Voice** Distinctive *see-tic* or *tic* call, also, hoarse whistle, *tzeep*. **HH** Unobtrusive and shy. Flight rapid and bounding. Wild olive forest and orchards.

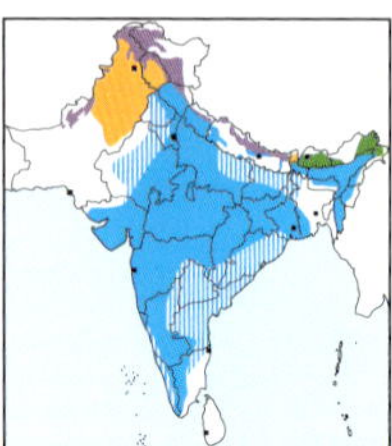

Common Rosefinch *Carpodacus erythrinus* 14.5–15cm

Breeds in Balochistan and Himalayas; widespread in winter; unrecorded in Sri Lanka. **ID** Compact, with short, stout bill. Male has red head, breast and rump. Female and first-year male have streaked upperparts and underparts, rather plain face with beady black eye, and double wing-bar. Juvenile more heavily streaked than female. Migrant nominate subspecies has less red in male, and female is less heavily streaked, compared to resident subspecies. **Voice** Distinctive, rising *ooeet* call; sharp *chay-eeee* in alarm; monotonous whistling *weeeja-wu-weeeja* song. **HH** Breeds in high-altitude shrubbery, bush-covered slopes with scattered trees, and open coniferous forest. Winters in cultivation with bushes; open wooded country.

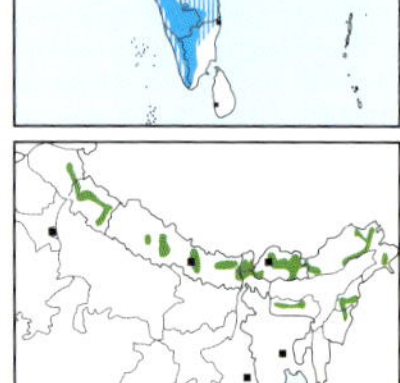

Scarlet Finch *Carpodacus sipahi* 18–19cm

Resident. Himalayas and NE India. **ID** A stocky, short-tailed finch, with stout pale bill. Male mainly bright scarlet, with darker wings and tail. Female has bright yellow rump; upperparts olive-green with diffuse dark feather centres and may show white mottling on crown and mantle; underparts similar but greyer, and become paler towards vent. Some female-plumaged birds have orange rump and orange-brown tinge to crown, nape and mantle. **Voice** Loud, pleasant *too-eee* and *kwee-i-ur* calls; liquid *par-ree-reeeeee* song. **HH** Edges, clearings and ravines in broadleaved forest. **TN** Formerly placed in *Haematospiza*.

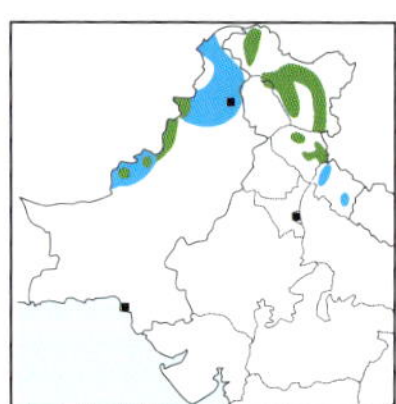

Blyth's Rosefinch *Carpodacus grandis* 18–20cm

Resident. Pakistan mountains and W Himalayas. **ID** Stockier than White-browed, with much larger bill. Male's crown and mantle are paler and greyer, with pinkish wash, and streaking on upperparts is less prominent. Pink-streaked supercilium is broad and contrasts with dark eye-stripe but barely extends across forehead and lacks prominent wing-bars of White-browed. Female best told by combination of large size and huge bill, pale grey coloration to (heavily streaked) upperparts including rump, broad and diffuse supercilium weakly offset against greyish eye-stripe, and heavily streaked underparts. Both sexes similar to Himalayan Beautiful Rosefinch but latter much smaller, with smaller bill and is proportionately longer-tailed. **Voice** Rather metallic twittering flight call; song a series of wheezy notes and squeaky whistles. **HH** Breeds in dry high-altitude forest and shrubbery. Winters in wild olives, thorn scrub and orchards. **AN** Red-mantled Rosefinch. **TN** Formerly treated as *Carpodacus rhodochlamys*.

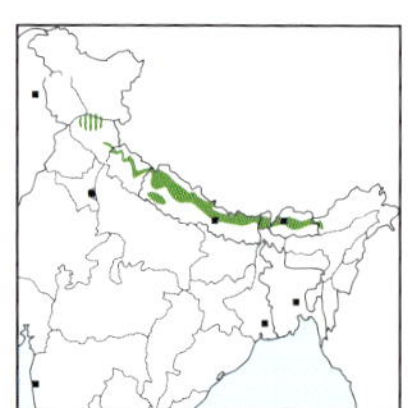

Himalayan Beautiful Rosefinch *Carpodacus pulcherrimus* 13–15cm

Resident. Himalayas. **ID** Small, compact rosefinch. Male has lilac-pink supercilium, rump and underparts, cold pinkish-grey coloration to heavily streaked crown and mantle, and pronounced streaking on underparts. Female has heavily streaked upperparts and underparts, poorly defined pale supercilium which is finely streaked, and rather pale and well-streaked ear-coverts. Similar to female Pink-browed but supercilium less distinct (unstreaked and offset against dark ear-coverts in Pink-browed), has whiter background colour to underparts, and rump and uppertail-coverts concolorous with back. **Voice** Calls include harsh *chaaannn* in flight, also soft *trip*; song undescribed. **HH** Breeds in high-altitude shrubbery and stony slopes above treeline. Winters on bush-covered slopes; cultivation with bushes. **AN** Beautiful Rosefinch.

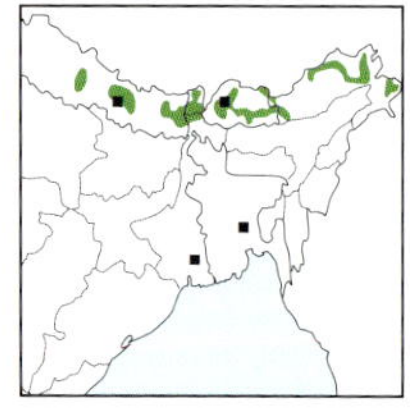

Dark-rumped Rosefinch *Carpodacus edwardsii* 16–17cm

Resident. C and E Himalayas. **ID** Male confusable with Spot-winged, but pink tips to coverts and tertials much less prominent, lacks obvious pink on rump, and has dark breast and flanks. Female from Pink-browed by larger size, stockier appearance, stouter bill, darker brown upperparts and deeper brownish underparts (breast tends to be shade darker than belly), whilst pale fringes to tertials have distinctly paler tip to outer edge (more even on Pink-browed). Pale tips to coverts and tertials less prominent than on Spot-winged, and has darker (browner) underparts, less distinct supercilium, paler ear-coverts and more finely and sparsely streaked throat and breast. First-summer male has pink wash to supercilium, ear-coverts and breast. **Voice** Calls include an abrupt, high-pitched, metallic *tswii*, and rasping *che-wee* in alarm; song undescribed. **HH** Breeds in high-altitude shrubbery and rhododendron-fir forest. Winters in open rhododendron or birch forest; slopes with bamboo and scrub.

ad
Hawfinch
♂ erythrinus
♀ erythrinus
♂ roseatus
Common Rosefinch
♀ roseatus
♀ variant
♂
Scarlet Finch
♀
♂
Blyth's Rosefinch
♀
♂
♀
Himalayan Bcautiful Rosetinch
♂
♀
Dark-rumped Rosefinch

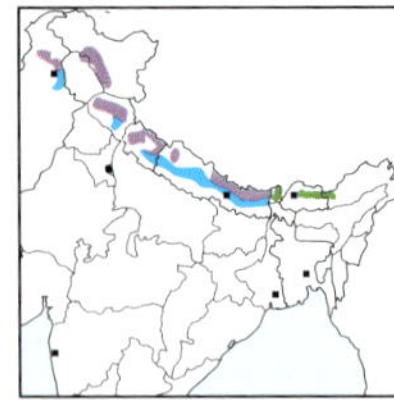

Pink-browed Rosefinch *Carpodacus rodochroa* 14–15cm

Resident. Himalayas. **ID** Small, compact rosefinch. Male has pink supercilium, rump and underparts, maroon-pink crown and ear-coverts, and pinkish-brown mantle. Female and first-year male are heavily-streaked and have prominent buff supercilium contrasting with dark ear-coverts, brownish-buff mantle, tawny rump, and strong tawny wash from breast to undertail-coverts. Supercilium and contrasting dark ear-coverts more pronounced than in female Himalayan Beautiful and Dark-rumped, and lacks pale tips to greater coverts and tertials of female Spot-winged. **Voice** Song sweet, lilting, upward-inflected whistles; calls include *per-lee*. **HH** Breeds in high-altitude open forest and shrubbery; winters in oak forest and bush-covered slopes.

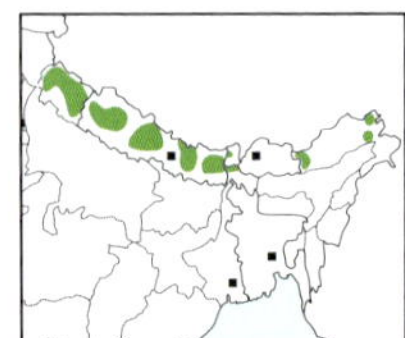

Spot-winged Rosefinch *Carpodacus rodopeplus* 16–17cm

Resident. Himalayas. **ID** Male is confusable with Dark-rumped but has more prominent pinkish tips to wing-coverts and tertials, darker and more uniform maroon upperparts (splashed with pink), more uniform pink underparts (with some dark mottling on breast but never a broad dark band) and splashes of pink on rump. Female has prominent buff supercilium, buff tips to greater coverts and tertials, and fulvous underparts with bold streaking on throat and breast. Head pattern more striking than in female Dark-rumped; also has paler and more heavily streaked throat, and more prominent spots on coverts and tips to tertials. From female Pink-browed by larger size and bill, darker ear-coverts (appearing as a dark mask), more heavily streaked throat and breast, and well-defined pale tips to coverts and tertials (pale tertial fringes evenly narrower in Pink-browed). **Voice** Song undescribed; nasal *churr-weeee* call. **HH** Breeds in rhododendron shrubbery and alpine meadows; winters in bushes and bamboo in forest.

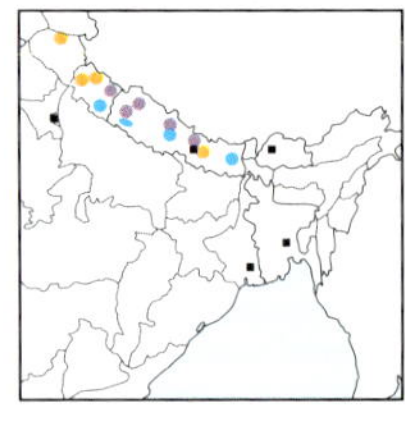

Vinaceous Rosefinch *Carpodacus vinaceus* 13cm

Resident. Himalayas. **ID** Male is mainly crimson, with bright pink supercilium and pinkish-white tips to tertials (lacking when worn). Smaller than Spot-winged, lacking pink spots on coverts, and has more uniform crimson upperparts and underparts. Female rather uniform warm brown; from other female rosefinches by absence of supercilium (plain-faced appearance), whitish tips to tertials (lacking when worn), and warm brownish-buff coloration to lightly streaked underparts (almost concolorous with upperparts). Lightly streaked underparts (if apparent) and lack of wing-bars are best features from female Dark-breasted. **Voice** Song *pee-dee, be do-do*; calls include hard *pwit* with whiplash quality. **HH** Dense moist mixed forest with bamboo; bushes on hillsides.

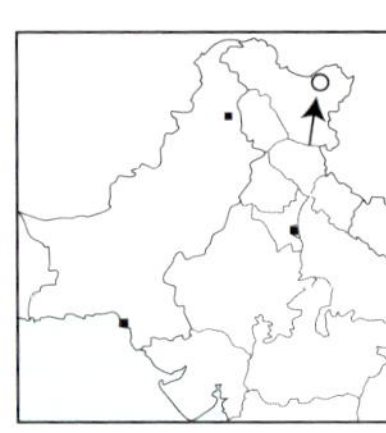

Sillem's Rosefinch *Carpodacus sillemi* 15cm

Status uncertain. NW trans-Himalayas. **ID** Small, conical bill, with stout bristles at its base, and extremely long wings. Male is unlike any other rosefinch with tawny head, unstreaked sandy-brown mantle, and whitish underparts and rump. Bill black and bristles buff. Superficially confusable with Black-headed Mountain Finch, but lacks any black on head and has much longer wings. Female has pale orange bill, bristles are white, and has rather uniform face with small black eye. Upperparts sandy-grey and lightly streaked, underparts white with fine streaking, and has whitish rump. **Voice** Undescribed. **HH** Specimens collected at 5,125m and photographed at 5,000m on barren plateaux. **AN** Sillem's Mountain Finch. **TN** Formerly placed in *Leucosticte*.

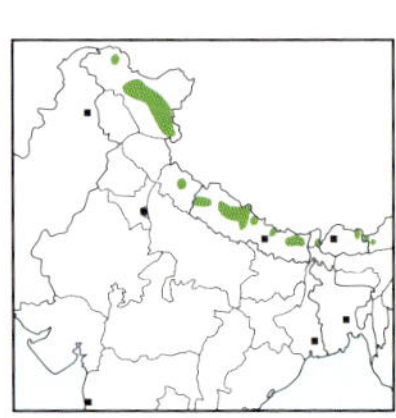

Streaked Rosefinch *Carpodacus rubicilloides* 19–20cm

Resident. N Himalayas. **ID** Large with long tail. Male from Great by deeper crimson-pink head and underparts (with smaller white spots), prominently streaked upperparts, and dark centres to wing feathers. Female nondescript, lacking supercilium. From Great by darker grey upperparts with heavier streaking, more heavily streaked ear-coverts and underparts, and darker centres to wing-coverts and tertials. Lacks pale supercilium and dark eye-stripe of female Blyth's. **Voice** Song slowly descending *tsee-tsee-soo-soo-soo*; calls include bullfinch-like *dooid dooid*. **HH** High-altitude semi-desert.

Great Rosefinch *Carpodacus rubicilla* 19–21cm

Resident. N Himalayas. **ID** Large with long tail. Male from Streaked by paler rose-pink head and underparts, and paler sandy-grey upperparts which are only faintly streaked. Female and first-year male similar to female Streaked and Blyth's, but have paler, sandy-brown upperparts (only faintly streaked), less heavily streaked ear-coverts and underparts, paler, more uniform wing-coverts and tertials, and unstreaked rump. Lacks pale supercilium and dark eye-stripe of female Blyth's. In flight, both sexes show white edge to outer tail feathers (barely apparent on Streaked). **Voice** Intermittent whistling song, often descending at end; calls include loud *tooey tooey*. **HH** Arid, rocky, sparsely vegetated ground in alpine zone.

♂
♀
Spot-winged Rosefinch
♂
♀
Pink-browed Rosefinch
♂
♀
♂
Vinaceous Rosefinch
♀
♀
♂
Sillem's Rosefinch
♀
♂
Streaked Rosefinch
Great Rosefinch

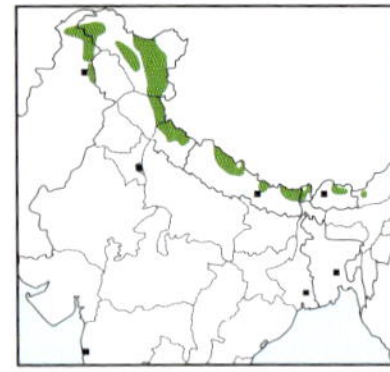

Red-fronted Rosefinch *Carpodacus puniceus* 20cm

Resident. N Himalayas. **ID** Large size, conical bill and short tail. On male, red of plumage contrasts with brown crown, eye-stripe and upperparts. Belly, flanks and vent are grey-brown and heavily streaked. Female and first-year male lack supercilium, and have dark and heavily streaked upperparts, with heavy streaking on underparts. Breast variably washed pale yellow, and rump and uppertail-coverts more olive than back or are yellow. **Voice** Song a short *twiddle-le-de* and a varied series of louder, more melodious and plaintive downslurred whistles; calls include bulbul-like cheery whistle. **HH** High-altitude rocky slopes with dwarf juniper.

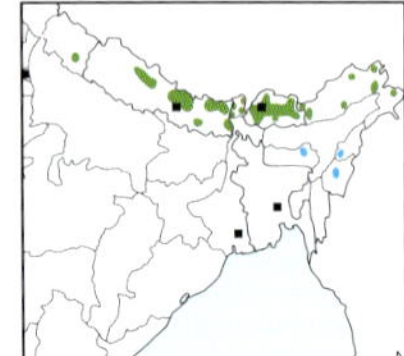

Crimson-browed Finch *Carpodacus subhimachalus* 19–20cm

Resident in Himalayas and winters in NE India. **ID** Short, stubby bill. Male has red forehead, throat and upper breast, greenish cast to orange-red upperparts, and greyish underparts. Female has olive-yellow forehead and supercilium, and greyish nape, ear-coverts and throat. Breast olive-yellow and belly greyish. Upperparts greenish-olive with brighter olive-yellow rump. Forehead, supercilium and breast orange in immature male. **Voice** Song a loud, melodious and varied warbling; call a melodic sparrow-like *chirp*. **HH** Breeds in high-altitude shrubbery, especially junipers; winters in forest and thick undergrowth. **TN** Formerly placed in *Propyrrhula*.

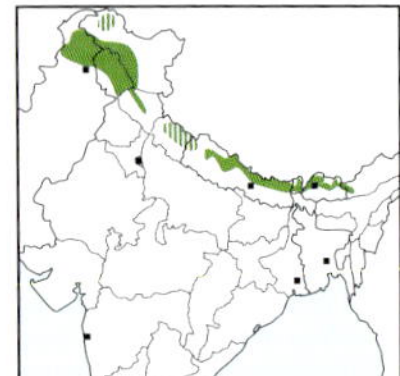

Himalayan White-browed Rosefinch *Carpodacus thura* 17–18cm

Resident. Himalayas. **ID** Male has pink rump and underparts. Most similar to Pink-browed but larger and longer-tailed, with iridescent white streaking to pink supercilium and throat, dark-streaked brown upperparts (lacking pinkish coloration) and prominent pinkish tips to wing-coverts. Female and first-year male have prominent supercilium and dark eye-stripe, buff tips to coverts, heavily streaked underparts and (heavily streaked) olive-yellow (female) or reddish-brown (first-year male) rump. Female nominate (C Himalayas) has ginger-brown throat and breast, with whitish cheeks and belly. Female *C. t. blythi* (W Himalayas) has colder grey-brown upperparts, less striking head pattern and orange-buff wash to throat and breast; streaking on underparts stronger than Pink-browed with contrast between buff breast and whiter belly. See Vagrants for comparison with Chinese White-browed Rosefinch. **Voice** Song of short whistles followed by 3–4 short warbled notes, then several longer whistles. Calls include piping *pupupipipi*. **HH** Breeds in high-altitude dwarf rhododendron and juniper shrubbery and open fir-juniper-rhododendron forest; winters on bushy hillsides. **AN** White-browed Rosefinch.

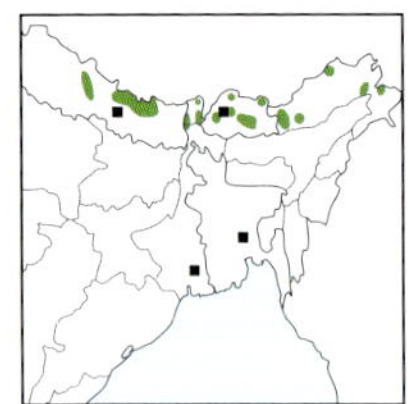

Blanford's Rosefinch *Agraphospiza rubescens* 13–15cm

Resident. C and E Himalayas. **ID** Slimmer bill than Common Rosefinch. Male largely dull crimson, with distinct greyish cast to breast and belly. Duller than male Common, which is brighter geranium-red on head and throat/breast. First-summer male browner, especially on mantle, wings and underparts. Female rather plain and dark and lacks supercilium. From female Dark-breasted Rosefinch by slightly stouter bill, more uniform wings (lacking prominent pale wing-bars and tips to tertials), more uniform upperparts, reddish or bright olive cast to rump and paler underparts. **Voice** Loud musical warbling song; calls include hard, metallic *ti-tip, tu-tip* and faster *tu-tiptiptip*. **HH** Glades in coniferous and conifer-birch forest. **TN** Formerly placed in *Carpodacus*.

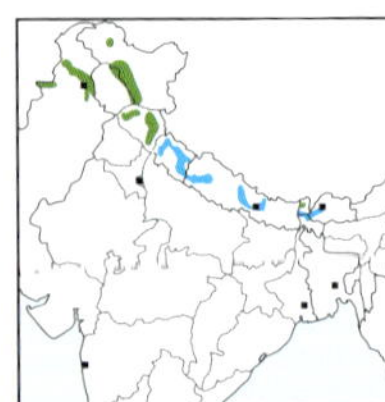

Spectacled Finch *Callacanthis burtoni* 17–18cm

Resident. Himalayas. **ID** A large, stocky finch with conical yellowish bill. Wings black with bold whitish tips to greater coverts and flight feathers, and has white tip to black tail. Male has blackish hood, pinkish-red forehead and 'spectacles', maroon-brown mantle and pinkish-red wash to underparts. 'Spots' on wing-coverts pinkish-white. Female has paler head with orange-yellow forehead and 'spectacles', olive-brown mantle and buffish-brown underparts with yellowish wash to breast. Juvenile has buff eye patch. **Voice** Song long sequence of mainly downward-inflected whistles; loud *pwee* and softer *tew-tew* calls. **HH** Breeds in conifer and rhododendron forests; winters in coniferous and mixed coniferous-broadleaved forests.

Dark-breasted Rosefinch *Procarduelis nipalensis* 15–16cm

Resident. Himalayas. **ID** Slim, with slender bill. Male has maroon-brown upperparts, breast-band and eye-stripe. Forehead, supercilium, throat and belly are bright pink. Female lacks supercilium, and has unstreaked underparts, diffusely streaked mantle, buffish wing-bars and tips to tertials, and olive-brown rump. From female Blanford's by more prominent wing-bars and tips to tertials, streaking on mantle and lack of reddish or bright olive cast to rump. First-summer male similar to female but has maroon-brown upperparts. **Voice** Monotonous chipping song; calls include a plaintive, wailing double whistle. **HH** Breeds in high-altitude forest and shrubbery; winters in forest clearings and cultivation. **TN** Formerly placed in *Carpodacus*.

♀
♀
Red-fronted
Rosefinch
Crimson-browed
Finch
♂
♂
♂
thura
♀
thura
Himalayan
White-browed
Rosefinch
♂
♂
♀
Blanford's
Rosefinch
Spectacled Finch
♀
♀
♂
Dark-breasted
Rosefinch

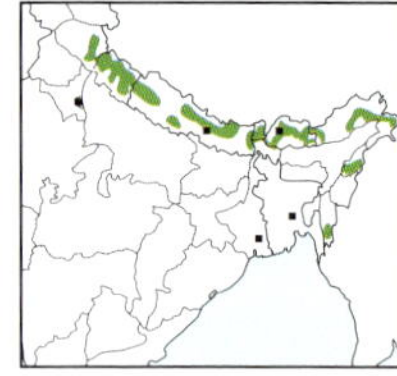

Brown Bullfinch *Pyrrhula nipalensis* 16–17cm

Resident. Himalayas and NE India. **ID** Adult has grey-brown mantle, grey underparts, narrow white rump band and long tail. Additional features include narrow black surround to bill, black lores and scaling on forehead and crown, white patch below eye. Lacks any extensive red, yellow or orange in plumage. Sexes similar, but male has crimson-pink outer edge to inner tertial (yellow in female), which is visible only at close range. Juvenile has brownish-buff upperparts and warm buff underparts and lacks adult head pattern. **Voice** Song repeated mellow *her-dee-a-duuee*; calls include mellow *per-lee*. **HH** Dense moist forest.

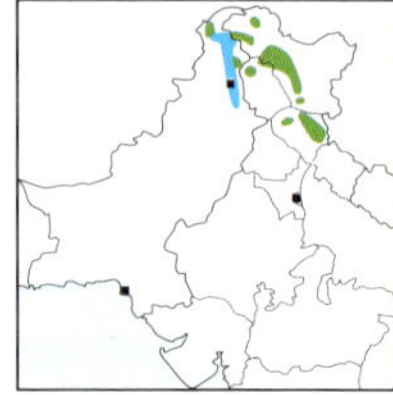

Orange Bullfinch *Pyrrhula aurantiaca* 14cm

Resident. W Himalayas. **ID** Male from Red-headed by brownish-orange upperparts, orange-buff wing-bars, lack of white surround to black face, and deep orange underparts. Some (first-year?) males are paler orange above and below. Female from Red-headed by grey crown and nape, lack of white surround to black face, buff-brown upperparts, brownish-orange underparts and buffish wing-bars. Female very similar to E Himalayan Grey-headed. Juvenile similar to female, but head and body almost uniform pale orange, and black on face much reduced. **Voice** Song *tew-tew*, followed by rising and falling metallic warbling phrases; call upward-inflected *twetya*. **HH** Open coniferous and birch-coniferous forests.

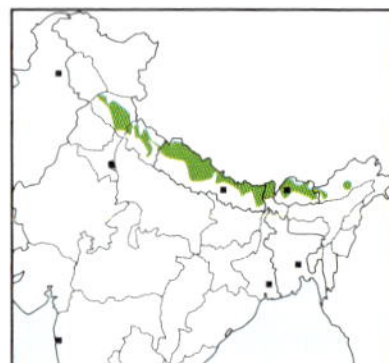

Red-headed Bullfinch *Pyrrhula erythrocephala* 17cm

Resident. Himalayas. **ID** Male has orange crown, nape and breast, and grey mantle. Female has yellow crown and nape. Wing-bars of both sexes are greyish-white. White surround to black face (may be lacking) and paler orange underparts with whiter belly are additional features that help separate from Orange Bullfinch. First-year male similar to female but has olive-yellow breast and upper flanks. Juvenile similar to female but browner, and head and upperparts are warm brown. **Voice** Song low, mellow *terp-terp-tee*; calls include soft, mellow *pew-pew*. **HH** Breeds mainly in birch forest; winters in mixed forest, favours rhododendron.

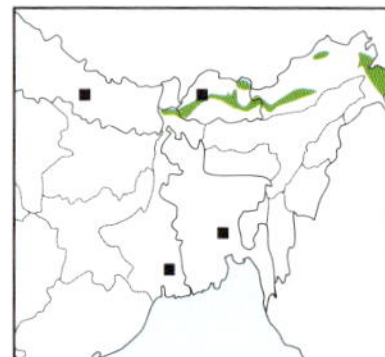

Grey-headed Bullfinch *Pyrrhula erythaca* 15–17cm

Resident. E Himalayas. Vagrant: Nepal. **ID** Male from Red-headed by grey crown and nape, deeper orange-red underparts, black band on upper rump and longer tail. Female from female Red-headed by grey crown and nape, fawn-brown mantle, pinkish-brown underparts and blackish band on upper rump. Juvenile very similar to female, but crown and nape more greyish-olive, mantle dull grey-brown and underparts dull brown, and has broad buffish-brown tips to greater coverts. **Voice** Song soft, mellow, whistled warble; calls include piping *soo-ee*. **HH** Conifer-rhododendron forest; willow thickets.

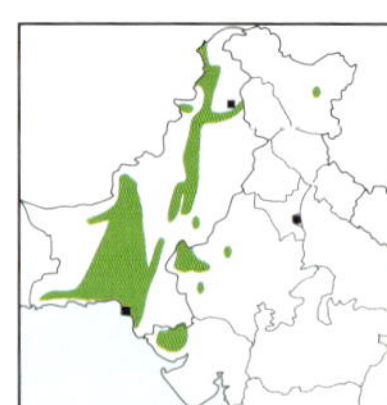

Trumpeter Finch *Bucanetes githagineus* 12.5–15cm

Resident in Pakistan and NW India. **ID** Stocky, with very stout bill From Mongolian by comparatively uniform wings and tail, stouter bill and distinctive nasal calls. Some can show indistinct pale panels in wing due to pale fringes to secondaries but these are not well-defined patches as in Mongolian. Breeding male has reddish bill, pinkish face and wash to underparts, grey cast to crown and nape, pink edges to wing and tail feathers, and pink rump. Non-breeding male duller with yellow bill. Female more uniform sandy-brown, with only traces of pink in plumage (e.g. on greater coverts, and edges to wing and tail feathers) and bill is also yellow. Juvenile as female but lacks any pink; has buff fringes to tertials and greater coverts. **Voice** Song drawn-out, buzzing, rising *cheeeee*; calls include soft *weechp* in flight. **HH** Dry rocky hills; stony semi-desert.

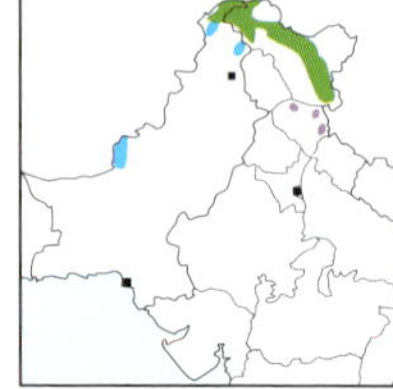

Mongolian Finch *Bucanetes mongolicus* 14–15cm

Resident in Pakistan and Ladakh; winter visitor to Balochistan. Vagrant: Nepal. **ID** Similar to Trumpeter Finch but usually shows pronounced whitish or buffish edges to bases of greater coverts and tertials/secondaries forming well-defined pale panels on wing, as well as more pronounced pale edges to tail (prominent in flight). Crown and mantle usually more obviously streaked. Looks slimmer and larger-tailed and has smaller and less stout bill. Breeding male has pinkish-red head and breast, pink edges to greater coverts and primaries, prominent white panels on wing, and pink rump. Non-breeding male and female have less pink in plumage (e.g. uniform buffish underparts, and just traces of pink to tips of greater coverts and edges of primaries). Pale wing-panels can be buffish and less distinct in female. Juvenile lacks pink in plumage and has buff fringes to tertials and greater coverts. **Voice** Song a pleasant, repeated *doe-mi-sol-mi*; quiet four-noted rattle in flight. **HH** Dry stony slopes.

ad
Brown
Bullfinch
juv
♂
Orange
Bullfinch
♀
juv
♂
Red-headed
Bullfinch
♀
Grey-headed
Bullfinch
♀
♂
1st-sum
♂
♂
juv
♀
♂
Mongolian Finch
Trumpeter Finch

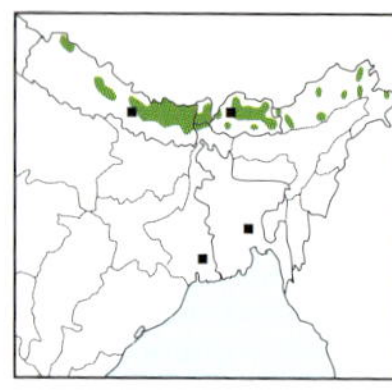

Gold-naped Finch *Pyrrhoplectes epauletta* 13–15cm

Resident. Himalayas. **ID** Small, stocky finch with fine bill. Has white 'stripe' on tertials in both sexes. Male black, with orange crown and nape, and orange flash at sides of breast (exposed axillaries). Female has olive-green head, grey nape and mantle, and rufous-brown wing-coverts and underparts. Juvenile as female but duller. First-winter male can show scattered orange feathers on nape and black feathers on underparts. **Voice** Thin, high-pitched *teeu*, *purl-lee* and squeaky *plee-e-e* calls; song a rapid *pi-pi-pi-pi* and soft bullfinch-like piping. **HH** Undergrowth in oak-rhododendron forest, rhododendron shrubbery and bamboo thickets.

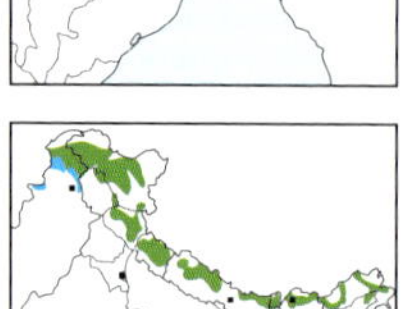

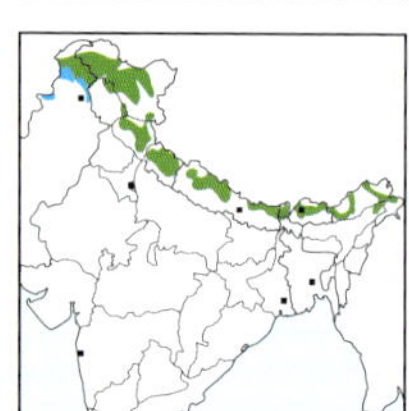

Plain Mountain Finch *Leucosticte nemoricola* 14–15cm

Resident. Himalayas. **ID** Mantle boldly streaked with pale 'braces'. Median coverts dark-centred, with bold white fringes, and greater coverts tipped white (forming well-defined wing-bar) with variable dark central panel. Unstreaked grey rump contrasts with mantle/back, and has prominent white tips to uppertail-coverts. Tertials and inner secondaries edged white, forming narrow panel on closed wing, but this is less obvious than on Black-headed Mountain Finch. Juvenile is warmer rufous-buff on head, mantle and underparts than adult, and mantle is less heavily streaked; has rufous-buff fringes to tertials and tips to coverts. First-winter retains rufous on head. In W Himalayas (*L. m. altaica*) has more unform head (and is more easily confused with Black-headed) compared to nominate in C and E Himalayas which has more pronounced darker (streaked) crown and more prominent pale supercilium. **Voice** Song a sharp twitter *dui-dip-dip-dip*; call a soft twittering *chi-chi-chi-chi*. **HH** Breeds in alpine meadows and grassy and stony slopes; winters in open forest and upland cultivation.

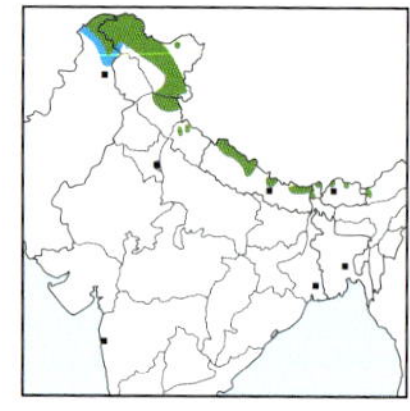

Black-headed Mountain Finch *Leucosticte brandti* 16.5–19cm

Resident. Himalayas. **ID** From Plain in all plumages by unstreaked to lightly streaked mantle, and rather pale and comparatively uniform wing-coverts. Broad white edges to primary coverts and to tertials/secondaries form more striking white panel on wing than Plain, and has more prominent white edges to outer rectrices. Adult breeding has sooty-black head and nape; male has pink on rump (indistinct on female). Shows less black on head in non-breeding plumage. Juvenile and first-summer have buffish head and mantle, and tertials and wing-coverts have warm buff edges. **Voice** Song a short weak trill; calls include loud *twitt-twitt*, harsh *churr* in alarm. **HH** Alpine meadows and open stony slopes. **AN** Brandt's Mountain Finch.

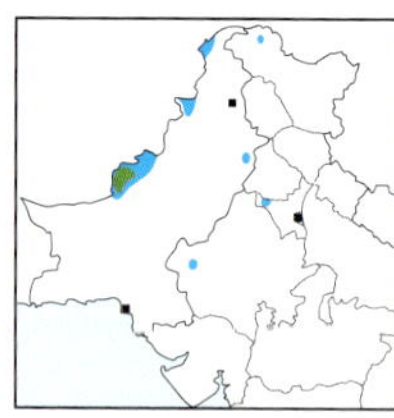

Desert Finch *Rhodospiza obsoleta* 14.5–15cm

Resident. Balochistan. Winter visitor to NW India. **ID** In all plumages is sandy-coloured and unstreaked, with pink edges to wing-coverts and secondaries, white edges to remiges and outer edges to tail, and black centres to tertials. Adult breeding has black bill (yellowish in non-breeder). Male has black lores. Female has duller wing pattern than male. Juvenile has duller wings with buffish edges to coverts and tertials. **Voice** Distinctive purring *r-r-r-r-r-ee* or *prrrt-prrrt*; harsh *turr* and sharp *shreep* calls; song a rambling mixture of call notes and harsh trills. **HH** Lowland and submontane dry open plains; semi-desert and wadis with sparse vegetation; irrigated areas and cultivation edges.

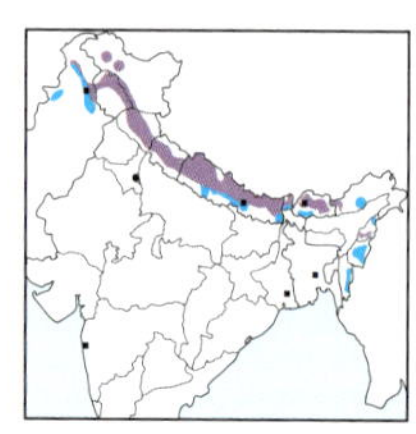

Yellow-breasted Greenfinch *Chloris spinoides* 12–14cm

Resident. Himalayas and NE India. **ID** Male has blackish-olive upperparts, yellow supercilium and crescent behind ear-coverts, yellow underparts and rump, and broad yellow panels on wing. Adult female has paler olive upperparts with faint dark streaking, less distinct head pattern and duller yellow underparts. Juvenile has heavy streaking on buffish-olive upperparts and buffish-yellow underparts; faint yellowish supercilium and submoustachial stripe. *C. s. heinrichi* (Nagaland and Manipur) has darker upperparts and lacks yellow submoustachial stripe and crescent below eye of nominate. **Voice** Call light twittering followed by a harsh *tsswee*; song an extended, more varied version of call. **HH** Breeds in open oak-rhododendron and deciduous-coniferous forests, grassy slopes and upland cultivation; winters in similar habitat lower down. **TN** Formerly placed in *Carduelis*.

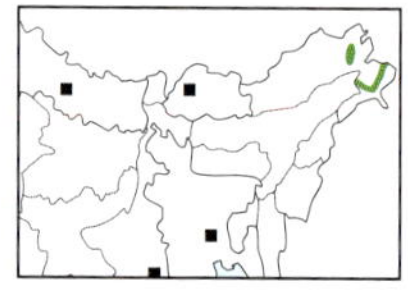

Black-headed Greenfinch *Chloris ambigua* 12–15cm

Resident. NE India. **ID** Both sexes have large patches of yellow in wing and sides to tail, greenish mantle, greyish-white greater covert wing-bar, and greyish underparts. Male has dull black head. **Voice** Calls include a high-pitched metallic twitter, often given in flight. **HH** Habits very like Yellow-breasted Greenfinch. Open mountain woodland, forest edge, scrub on hillsides and cultivation edges.

♀
Golden-naped Finch
♂
br
juv
Plain Mountain Finch
1st-sum
Black-headed
Mountain Finch
♂ br
♂ br
♀
Desert Finch
juv
♀
♀
♂
♂
Yellow-breasted
Greenfinch
Black-headed
Greenfinch

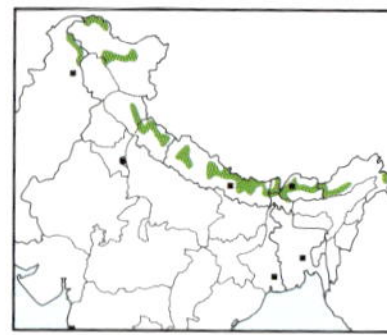

Red Crossbill *Loxia curvirostra* 14–20cm

Resident. Himalayas. **ID** Has dark bill with crossed mandibles and deeply forked tail. Male is rusty-red, with darker wings and tail. First-winter/summer male duller orangey-red, albeit with much variation (some being greenish-yellow). Female olive-green, with brighter greenish-yellow rump and dark wings and tail. Juvenile buffish and boldly streaked above and below; mandibles are not initially crossed. **Voice** Hard *chip chip* call; song a loud series of call notes developing into *cheeree-cheeree-choop-chip-chip-cheeree*. **HH** Coniferous forest, favours hemlocks.

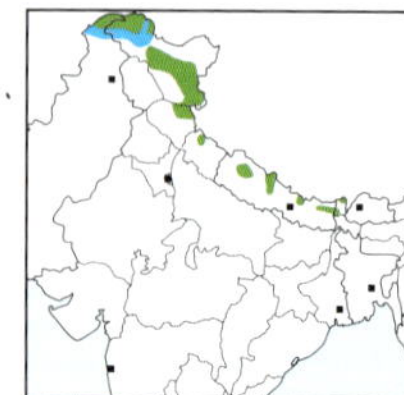

Twite *Linaria flavirostris* 12–14cm

Resident. N Himalayas. **ID** Rather plain and heavily streaked, with buff wing-bars and white edges to wings and tail. Small bill is yellowish (black in breeding male). Male has pinkish rump (obscured in non-breeding plumage). *L. f. montanella* (westernmost Himalayas) is sandy-buff and only lightly streaked on breast and flanks. *L. f. rufostrigata* (Ladakh eastwards) is much darker and more heavily streaked, and throat and breast are rich buff. **Voice** Characteristic call: *ditoo*, *didoo* or *didoowit* together with twanging *twayeee*. Song an extension of calls and includes some chattering notes. **HH** Gregarious in non-breeding season. Flight light, rapid and undulating. Dry Tibetan plateaux semi-desert and stony slopes. **TN** Formerly placed in *Carduelis*.

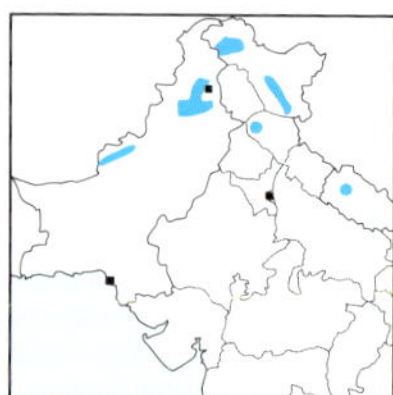

Eurasian Linnet *Linaria cannabina* 13–14cm

Winter visitor. Mainly Pakistan Himalayas. Vagrant: Nepal. **ID** From Twite by greyish crown, ear-coverts and nape, browner mantle, whitish rump and larger greyish bill. Male has chestnut-brown mantle and wing-coverts, with variable dark streaking on mantle. In breeding plumage, crown, nape and ear-coverts purer grey, and crimson forehead and breast. Female and first-winter have duller brown mantle, with dark brown streaking, and dark streaking on breast and flanks. **Voice** Rapid *chi-chi-chi-chi* call. **HH** In flocks, often with other finches and buntings. Feeds chiefly on ground, but perches readily in bushes. Flight undulating and fast. Open stony slopes, upland meadows and fallow fields. **AN** Common Linnet. **TN** Formerly placed in *Carduelis*.

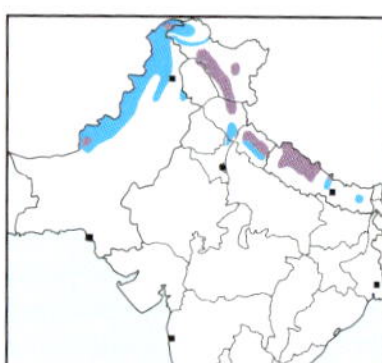

European Goldfinch *Carduelis carduelis* 13–14.5cm

Resident and winter visitor. Pakistan hills and W and C Himalayas. **ID** Adult largely grey-brown with red face, yellow panel on black wings with white on tertials, and white rump. First-winter lacks red face. Juvenile also lacks red face; upperparts and breast faintly streaked, and has buffish tips to coverts and tertial markings. **Voice** Liquid twittering call; song a varied mix of twittering, interspersed with repeated *tew-tew-tew* and *tuwee-it* phrases. **HH** In small parties all year, often larger flocks in winter, but rarely with other finches. Upland cultivation and orchards, shrubbery above treeline and open coniferous forest.

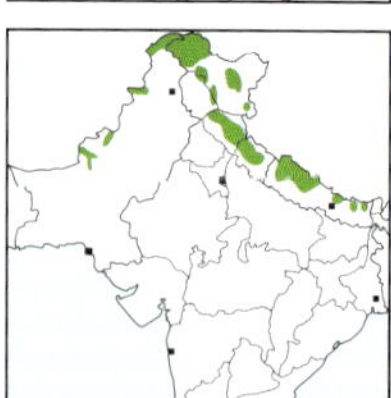

Fire-fronted Serin *Serinus pusillus* 10.5–13cm

Resident. Balochistan mountains and W and C Himalayas. **ID** Male has scarlet forehead and largely black head and breast. Mantle and belly/flanks are boldly streaked with black and washed olive-yellow. Buffish-orange wing-bars, yellowish edges to wing and tail feathers, and olive-yellow rump/uppertail-coverts. Female generally duller, with less red on forehead, and black of head and breast is browner. In fresh plumage (autumn/winter), black of head on both sexes is partly obscured by buff fringes and forehead is duller. Juvenile has cinnamon-brown crown, ear-coverts and throat, with lightly streaked crown and buffish wing-bars. **Voice** A rapid, ringing *trillit-drillt* and soft *dueet*; song a melodious, rippling trill interspersed with twittering. **HH** Gregarious all year, forming large flocks in winter. Breeds near treeline in dwarf juniper and birch scrub and Tibetan steppe habitat; winters on stony and bushy slopes and stubbles of upland cultivation. **AN** Red-fronted Serin.

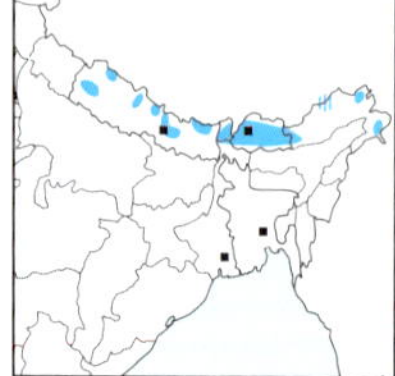

Tibetan Siskin *Spinus thibetanus* 10–12cm

Winters in C and E Himalayas (and may breed). **ID** Lacks yellow panels on wing in all plumages. Adult male has olive-green upperparts, yellow supercilium and border behind ear-coverts, yellowish-green rump and yellow underparts. Wing and tail feathers broadly edged yellowish-green. Female has blackish streaking on darker greyish-green upperparts, more clearly defined wing-bars, paler yellow throat and breast, and whitish belly (with black flank and breast streaking). Juvenile duller green, tinged brownish-buff on upperparts, with duller rump, buff fringes to greater coverts, paler (more heavily streaked) underparts. See Vagrants for comparison with Eurasian Siskin. **Voice** Soft chattering call interspersed with a wheezy *twang*; song a nasal buzzing *zeezle-wwzle-eeze*, interspersed with trills. **HH** In flocks in winter, sometimes several hundred birds; pairs in breeding season. Feeds mainly in treetops, often on alder or birch. Breeds in hemlock, birch and mixed fir-birch forests; winters chiefly in alders. **AN** Tibetan Serin. **TN** Formerly placed in *Serinus*.

juv
♀
Red Crossbill
♂
Twite
♂
montanella
♂
rufostrigata
♀
rufostrigata
♂
non-br
♂ br
♀
Eurasian Linnet
ad
juv
♀
♂
juv
Fire-fronted Serin
European Goldfinch
♂
♀
Tibetan Siskin

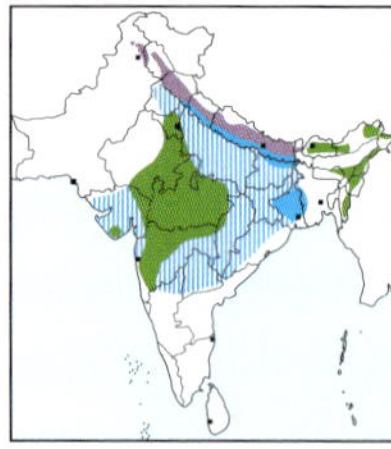

Crested Bunting *Emberiza lathami* 16cm

Resident. Himalayan foothills and hills of N, NE and C India. **ID** Always has crest and chestnut on wing and tail (chestnut may be indistinct in worn plumage). Tail lacks white. Male has glossy bluish-black head and body (with paler fringes when fresh) and pink bill. Female and first-winter male streaked on upperparts and breast; face rather plain with prominent eye-ring and pale submoustachial stripe; first-winter male darker and more heavily streaked than female, with olive-grey underparts. Juvenile as female but has buffier and more heavily streaked underparts, and shorter crest. **Voice** Call *tip* or *pink*; song *tsri-tsri-tsi-tsu-tsu-tsu*, last three notes descending. **HH** Dry rocky and grassy hillsides; terraced cultivation. **TN** Formerly placed in *Melophus*.

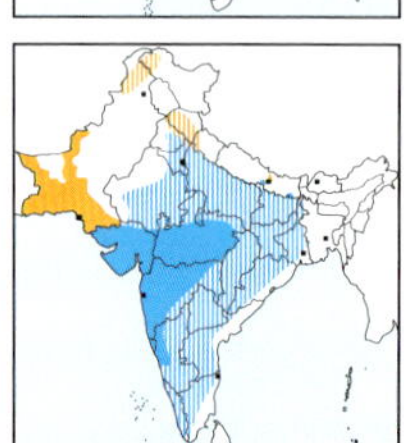

Black-headed Bunting *Emberiza melanocephala* 15.5–17.5cm

Winter visitor to N, W and WC India and SE Nepal; passage migrant in Pakistan. **ID** Large bunting with long, full tail without any white. Larger than Red-headed Bunting with longer bill. Male has black on head and chestnut on mantle (coloration largely obscured in fresh, non-breeding plumage). Female when worn may show ghost pattern of male with greyish-olive head and rufous tinge to mantle and back; fresh female almost identical to Red-headed, but indicative features (not always apparent) include rufous fringes to mantle and/or back, slight contrast between throat and greyish ear-coverts, and more uniform yellowish underparts. Immature has buff underparts, usually with some streaking and spotting on breast, and yellow undertail-coverts. **Voice** Flight call *plut*. **HH** Cereal crops.

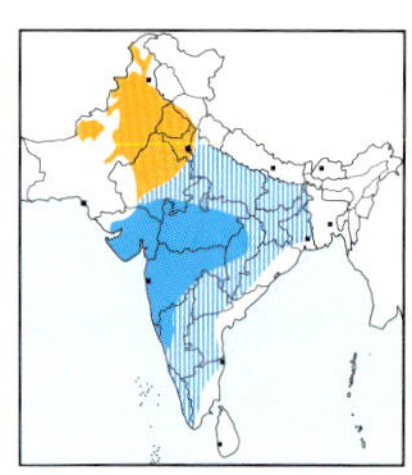

Red-headed Bunting *Emberiza bruniceps* 15–16.5cm

Winter visitor, mainly to NW and WC India; passage migrant in Pakistan. Vagrant: Nepal. **ID** Smaller than Black-headed, with shorter, more conical bill; like that species has long, full tail lacking any white. Male has mainly rufous head, yellowish-green mantle and scapulars with dark streaking, and yellow rump and uppertail-coverts. In fresh (non-breeding) plumage, rufous of head partly obscured by pale fringes. Female when worn may show rufous on head and breast, and yellowish to crown and mantle, and are distinguishable from female Black-headed. Fresh female almost identical to Black-headed, but indicative features include paler throat than breast, suggestion of buffish breast-band, and forehead and crown often virtually unstreaked. Immature often inseparable from Black-headed but may exhibit some of the features mentioned above. **Voice** Calls include rather harsh *prrit*. **HH** Cultivation.

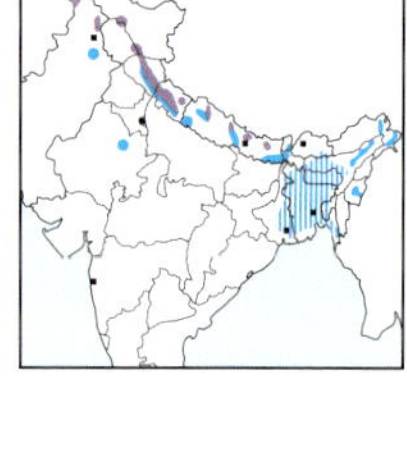

Chestnut-eared Bunting *Emberiza fucata* 16cm

Resident and winter visitor. Breeds in W Himalayas; winters east to NE India and Bangladesh. **ID** Adult has chestnut ear-coverts, finely streaked grey crown and nape, black streaking on white breast, and chestnut on breast-sides and flanks. These features are striking on males in worn (breeding) plumage, duller and less distinct in non-breeding male and female. Some first-winter birds rather nondescript, but plain head with warm brown ear-coverts, lacking darker lateral crown stripes, and prominent eye-ring distinctive, rufous rump and pinkish lower mandible. Juvenile has prominent supercilium and dark sides to crown and edges to ear-coverts, which have a pale centre (plumage lost quickly after fledging). **Voice** Rapid twittering song; calls include explosive *pzick*. **HH** Dry rocky and bushy hills; also winters in marshes, wet stubbles, grassland with bushes.

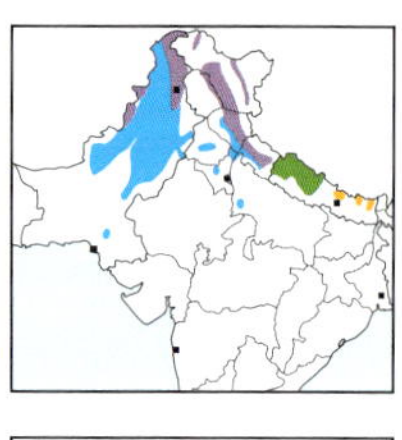

Rock Bunting *Emberiza cia* 15–16.5cm

Resident. Breeds in Pakistan mountains and W Himalayas; winters down to adjacent plains. **ID** Male has grey head and breast, with black head markings. Rump and rest of underparts deep rufous. Female is dull version of male, with less pronounced head pattern. Juvenile warm buff, heavily streaked brown, with dark border to ear-coverts; has rufous tinge to rump and belly. *E. c. par* (north-west) has pale rufous-orange underparts and mantle compared to W Himalayan *stracheyi*. **Voice** Song fast, ringing *ziterit zit zit ziterit zit*; sharp *tsee* and soft *yip* calls. **HH** Breeds on dry grassy and rocky slopes; also winters in lowland fallow cultivation and stubbles.

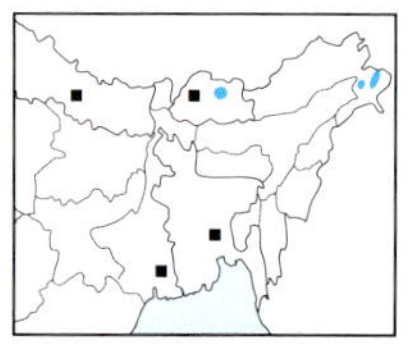

Godlewski's Bunting *Emberiza godlewskii* 17cm

Arunachal Pradesh: altitudinal migrant, breeds 1,225m. Bhutan: vagrant. **ID** Superficially similar to Rock Bunting but note easterly distribution. Male has dark chestnut lateral crown-stripes, stripe behind eye and rear border to ear-coverts. Lores and moustachial stripe black. Median covert wing-bar white. Male non-breeding and first-winter similar to breeding male, but paler, with less striking head pattern. Female very similar to respective male. **Voice** Song variable; begins with high-pitched *tsitt* notes; calls like Rock. **HH** Dry slopes with bushes and rocks.

♂
1st-win
♂
♀
Crested
Bunting
Black-headed
Bunting
♂ br
♂
non-br
♀
worn
imm
♀
fresh
Red-headed
Bunting
♂
non-br
imm
♂ br
Chestnut-eared
Bunting
♀
♂
1st-win
♂
stracheyi
♂ br
juv
♀
stracheyi
Rock
Bunting
♂
par
♂
non-br
Godlewski's
Bunting

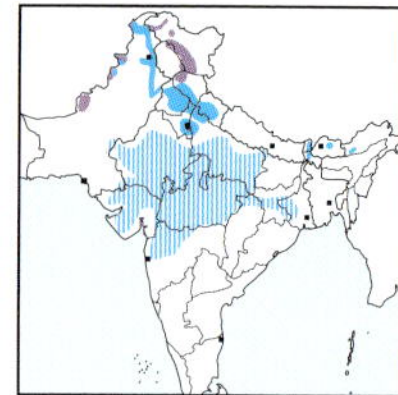

White-capped Bunting *Emberiza stewarti* 15cm

Breeds in Pakistan mountains and W Himalayas; winters in foothills and valleys of Pakistan and NC India. Vagrant: Nepal. **ID** Male has grey head and upper breast, black supercilium and throat, and chestnut breast-band. Mantle chestnut, unstreaked or lightly streaked dark brown. In fresh (non-breeding) and first-winter plumage, head and body patterns partly obscured by pale fringes. Female has rather plain head with pale supercilium; crown and mantle are diffusely streaked, underparts finely streaked and washed buff, and has chestnut rump. Most similar to female Pine Bunting but smaller, with plainer head (indistinct dark border to ear-coverts, less pronounced supercilium, but more striking white eye-ring), lacking striking white belly, and different call. Juvenile similar to female, but head rather pale with indistinct streaking. **Voice** Song a monotonous *jing jing jing*; distinctive twittering *chus-chua-chua* call. **HH** Typical bunting, see Grey-necked. Gathers in small flocks in winter, often with other buntings and finches. Dry grassy and rocky low hills, dry scrub forest; also fallow fields and waste ground with scattered bushes in winter.

Yellowhammer *Emberiza citrinella* 16–16.5cm

Winter visitor. Indian, Nepal and Pakistan Himalayas. **ID** Most show yellow on supercilium, throat and belly, olive-yellow tinge to crown and olive tinge to mantle, which help separate from Pine Bunting. Compared with female and first-winter Yellow-breasted Bunting, head pattern less striking (with less distinct supercilium, lateral crown-stripe and dark border to ear-coverts), has less prominent wing-bars and is longer-tailed. Some first-winter females lack yellow and are very difficult to separate from female Pine, but belly never pure white, has yellowish (rather than whitish) edges to primaries and base of tail, and crown is more evenly streaked (Pine shows more pronounced pale supercilium and crown-stripe). Hybrids with Pine can show variety of intermediate characters. **Voice** As Pine. **HH** Like Pine. Upland cultivation.

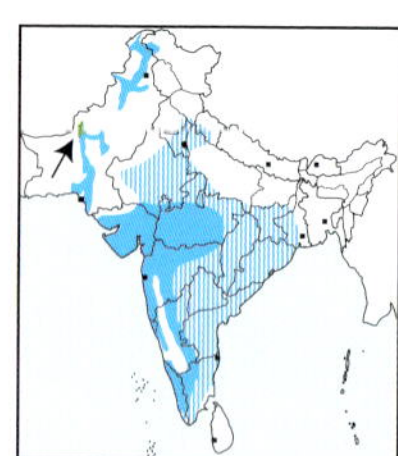

Pine Bunting *Emberiza leucocephalos* 16–17.5cm

Winter visitor. Pakistan hills and Himalayas. **ID** A long-tailed, chestnut-rumped bunting. Male has chestnut supercilium and throat, whitish crown and ear-covert spot, whitish gorget below chestnut throat, and chestnut streaking on breast and flanks, although pattern can be very obscured in winter. Female has greyish supercilium and nape/neck-sides, dark border to ear-coverts, usually some chestnut streaking on breast/flanks, and white belly. Head pattern more striking than smaller female White-capped Bunting, which lacks white belly. Chestnut rump and streaking on breast/flanks, and different call, are best distinctions from female Reed Bunting. **Voice** Calls include a short *dzik*, rasping *dzuh* and rolling *prul-lullu*. **HH** Quite shy, often flying some distance if disturbed. Has very upright stance when perched, but horizontal when foraging on ground. Flocks often roost with other buntings and finches. Stubble and fallow fields in dry hills.

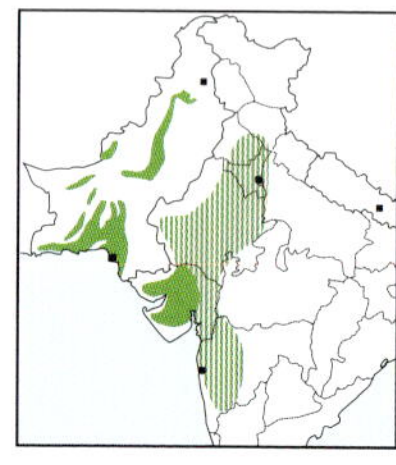

Grey-necked Bunting *Emberiza buchanani* 15–17cm

Breeds in Balochistan; winters mainly in Pakistan and C and W India. Vagrant: Nepal. **ID** In all plumages has pinkish-orange bill and rather plain head with whitish eye-ring and yellowish, buffish or white submoustachial stripe and throat. Male has blue-grey head, variably mottled deep rusty-pink breast and belly, and diffusely streaked sandy-brown mantle with pronounced rufous scapulars. Rump sandy-grey. Female very similar to male but generally paler, with buffish cast to grey head and nape (often with some streaking). First-winter/juvenile often have only slight greyish cast to head and underparts are warm buff (with variable rufous cast); crown and underparts faintly streaked. See Vagrants for comparison with Ortolan Bunting. **Voice** Four rising notes followed by lower-pitched terminal flourish, *tsee-tsee-tsee-tsee-dew-dedew*; soft click call. **HH** Typical bunting; in small flocks in winter, pairs when breeding. Hops and creeps inconspicuously on ground when foraging. Dry rocky hills with sparse bushes and stony ground with scattered bushes.

Striolated Bunting *Emberiza striolata* 12–13cm

Resident. Pakistan and NW India. **ID** Smaller and shorter-tailed than Rock Bunting. Lacks obvious white on tail (Rock has much white on outer tail feathers) and has orange lower mandible (bill all grey on Rock). Male has black eye-stripe and moustachial stripe, and white supercilium and submoustachial stripe; throat and breast streaked, underparts brownish-buff with variable rufous tinge, and wings appear mainly rufous with sandy-brown mantle. Female duller with sandy-brown head and browner head markings. Juvenile browner than female, with less distinct head pattern. **Voice** Song a short *trip trip te-tree-cha, tre-tree-cha*; flight call *chielp* like a sparrow. **HH** Typical bunting, see Grey-necked. Makes regular journeys to drink. Rocky areas with arid scrub, usually near water; may occur around cultivation in winter.

♂ non-br
♂ br
♀
White-capped Bunting
♂ br
♀
♂ non-br
Yellowhammer
♂ br
♀
♂ non-br
Pine Bunting
♂
1st-win
♀
Grey-necked Bunting
♂
♀
Striolated Bunting

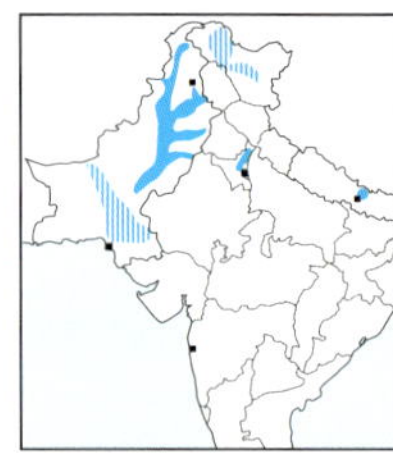

Reed Bunting *Emberiza schoeniclus* 14–15cm

Winter visitor. Pakistan and NW India. Vagrant: Nepal. **ID** Male in breeding plumage has black head and breast and white submoustachial stripe; pattern obscured by fringes in fresh (non-breeding) plumage, when has dark lateral crown-stripes and buffish supercilium and submoustachial stripe. First-winter male similar to male non-breeding, with both usually having black on throat and breast. Female superficially resembles Little Bunting but lacks warm chestnut lores, ear-coverts and supercilium, dark moustachial and malar stripes reach bill, has more boldly streaked mantle, often showing pale 'braces', less prominent rufous-brown wing bars, bolder but more diffuse streaking on breast and flanks, and stouter bill with convex culmen. **Voice** Call a distinctive *tseeu* and harsh *chirp*. **HH** Typical bunting, see Grey-necked. Hops and creeps when foraging, with body horizontal and tail held up. Very upright stance when perched. Frequently flicks and spreads tail, showing white outer feathers. Flight jerky and undulating. Reedbeds and irrigated crops. **AN** Common Reed Bunting.

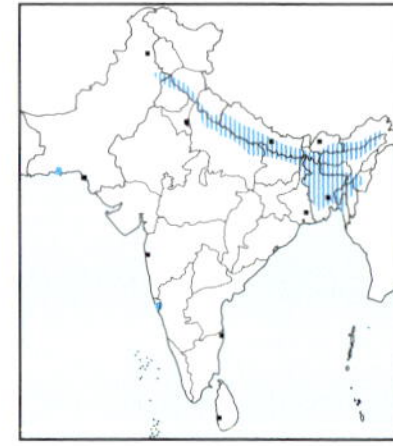

Yellow-breasted Bunting *Emberiza aureola* 14–15.5cm

Winter visitor. Mainly Nepal, NE India and Bangladesh. **ID** A stocky, comparatively short-tailed bunting. More direct, less undulating flight compared with other buntings, when appears more weaver- or sparrow-like. Male has yellow underparts with chestnut streaking, black face and chestnut breast-band (obscured by pale fringes when fresh) and white inner wing-coverts. Female and first-winter have striking head pattern with broad yellowish supercilium and pale crown stripe, dark lateral crown-stripes and dark border to ear-coverts. Underparts pale yellow to yellowish-white, boldly streaked mantle (with pale 'braces' often apparent) and prominent white median covert bar. Juvenile as female but underparts paler yellowish-buff, with fine, dense streaking on breast and flanks. Head pattern and upperparts more strikingly marked than in Chestnut Bunting, has white median covert bar, much white in tail, and lacks chestnut rump, compared with that species. **Voice** Calls include a soft *chup* and metallic *tick* very like Little. **HH** Typical bunting, see Grey-necked. Gregarious in winter. Not shy. Hops and creeps inconspicuously on ground and flies up into bushes or trees if disturbed. Cultivation and grassland. Globally threatened.

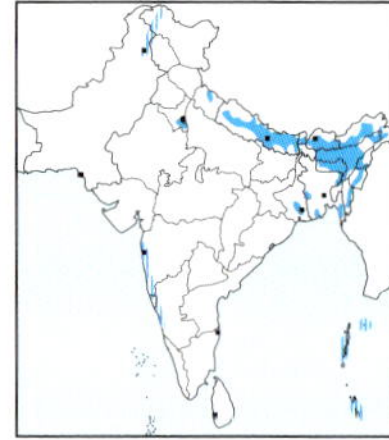

Little Bunting *Emberiza pusilla* 12–13.5cm

Winter visitor. Himalayas, NE India and Bangladesh. **ID** Small size. From Reed by chestnut ear-coverts (and often supercilium and crown-stripe), and absence of dark moustachial stripe. Has more pointed bill (with almost straight culmen) and more prominent eye-ring than Reed, and more uniform grey-brown mantle lightly streaked dark brown (lacking pale 'braces'), more finely streaked breast and flanks, and more prominent pale median and greater covert wing-bars. **Voice** Call a sharp *tzic*. **HH** Typical bunting, see Grey-necked. Usually in small flocks. Unobtrusive. Flocks hop about on ground with a horizontal posture. Stubbles and ploughed or grass fields.

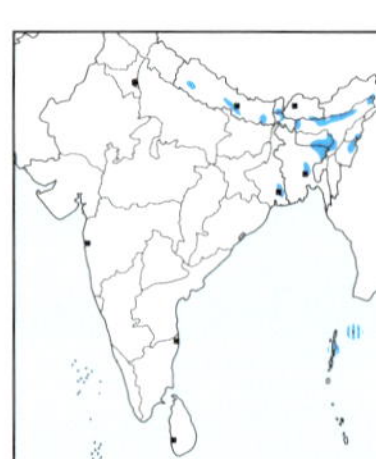

Black-faced Bunting *Emberiza spodocephala* 13.5–16cm

Winter visitor. Mainly NE India. **ID** A small bunting with rather fine bill. Male has greenish-grey head with blackish lores and chin forming distinct mask, greenish-grey breast and yellow underparts. Non-breeding male duller and may show yellow submoustachial stripe and throat and indistinct supercilium. Female has yellowish supercilium and submoustachial stripe, and pale oily yellow underparts. Upperparts grey-brown and strongly streaked. From Chestnut Bunting by greyish-olive rump, prominent white in tail, pale yellow throat concolorous with yellow below, olive-grey wash to breast and strong streaking on flanks. **Voice** Call a soft *tsip* or sharper *tzit*. **HH** Typical bunting, see Grey-necked. Singly, in pairs or small flocks. Usually forages in or near cover. Long grass, paddy stubbles and standing paddy and marsh edges; often near water.

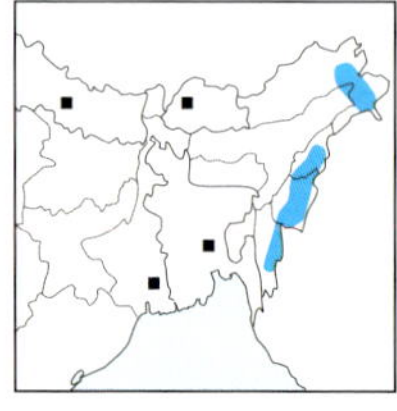

Chestnut Bunting *Emberiza rutila* 14–15cm

Winter visitor. Mainly NE India. Vagrant: Nepal. **ID** Small size and small, fine bill. Male has chestnut head and breast, with coloration obscured in fresh plumage (especially in first-winter). Female has buff throat and yellow underparts; head pattern less striking than Yellow-breasted. Has chestnut rump and little or no white on tail, which are further differences from Yellow-breasted and also help separate from Black-faced. **Voice** Usual call a sharp *tzic* like Little, also a high *teseep*. **HH** Behaviour very like other buntings, see Grey-necked. Unobtrusive. Forages mainly on ground, flying up to branches of nearby trees when disturbed. Paddy stubbles, forest clearings and open forest and scrub.

♂ br
Common
Reed Bunting
♀
♂
non-br
♂ br
♀
juv
Yellow-breasted Bunting
♂
1st-win
Little Bunting
♂
non-br
♂ br
Black-faced
Bunting
♀
♂
1st-win
♀
♂
non-br
Chestnut Bunting

APPENDIX – VAGRANTS

Vagrant species are those occurring irregularly in the subcontinent, mostly with fewer than ten records for the entire region. The following species have previously been considered to have valid records for the area concerned but this is no longer the case: Buff-throated Monal Partridge *Tetraophasis szechenyii*, Tibetan Eared Pheasant *Crossoptilon harmani*, Snow Goose *Anser caerulescens*, Velvet Scoter *Melanitta fusca*, Stock Dove *Columba oenas*, Black-fronted Dotterel *Charadrius melanops*, Oriental Stork *Ciconia boyciana*, Great-billed Heron *Ardea sumatrana*, Soft-plumaged Petrel *Pterodroma mollis*, White-bellied Storm-petrel *Fregetta grallaria*, Omani Owl *Strix butleri*, Eastern Buzzard *Buteo japonicus*, Plain-pouched Hornbill *Rhyticeros subruficollis*, Laced Woodpecker *Picus vittatus*, 'Intermediate Parakeet *Psittacula intermedia*', Asian Short-toed Lark *Alaudala cheleensis*, Radde's Warbler *Phylloscopus schwarzi*, Eastern Crowned Warbler *Phylloscopus coronatus*, Giant Laughingthrush *Ianthocincla maxima*, Prince Henry's Laughingthrush *Trochalopteron henrici* (previously known as Brown-cheeked Laughingthrush *Garrulax henrici*), Giant Babax *Pterorhinus waddelli*, Pere David's Snowfinch *Pyrgilauda davidiana*, Siberian Accentor *Prunella montanella*, Java Sparrow *Padda oryzivora*.

ANATIDAE

Mute Swan *Cygnus olor* 127–152cm

Pakistan and India. **ID** Adult white with orange bill with black base and knob. Juvenile mottled sooty-brown and has grey bill with black base. **HH** Mainly lowland fresh waters, favours medium to large-sized waterbodies, especially large slow-moving rivers and lakes.

Tundra Swan *Cygnus columbianus* 115–140cm

Pakistan, Nepal and India. **ID** Adult white with black-and-yellow bill; yellow of bill typically forms oval-shaped patch. Juvenile smoky-grey with pinkish bill. Smaller in size, with shorter neck and more rounded head, compared to Whooper. **HH** Winters on marshes, grasslands and farmland, often on estuaries.

Whooper Swan *Cygnus cygnus* 140–165cm

Pakistan, Nepal and India. **ID** Adult white with black-and-yellow bill; yellow of bill extends as wedge towards tip. Juvenile smoky-grey, with pinkish bill. Longer neck and more angular head shape than Tundra. **HH** Winters on freshwater lakes and marshes, coastal bays and brackish lagoons, also agricultural land with large waterbodies nearby for roosting.

Tundra Bean Goose *Anser serrirostris* 66–80cm

Nepal, India and Bangladesh. **ID** Black bill with orange band, and orange legs. Compared to Greylag Goose, head, neck and upperparts are darker and browner. In flight lacks pale grey forewing of Greylag and has uniformly dark underwing. From Taiga Bean by shorter and stouter neck, stockier head, and stouter bill with smaller band of orange. **HH** Open country including marshes and agricultural land. **TN** Previously treated as conspecific with Taiga Bean Goose as Bean Goose *A. fabalis*.

Taiga Bean Goose *Anser fabalis* 76–89cm

India. **ID** Very similar to Tundra Bean Goose but has longer neck, slimmer head and longer bill which is more extensively orange (although extent of orange is variable and can be similar to Tundra). **HH** Open country including marshes and agricultural land.

Red-breasted Goose *Branta ruficollis* 53–56cm

India. **ID** Unmistakable, with reddish-chestnut cheek patch, foreneck and breast, and white surround to cheek patch and line on neck. Black crown, hindneck and upperparts, and white band dividing chestnut breast from black belly. Juvenile similar but duller and less clearly marked: chestnut duller and upperparts browner. Wing-coverts more extensively fringed with white (forming at least three complete white lines on closed wing). **HH** Winters in lowland farmland with lakes and reservoirs nearby for roosting. Globally threatened.

Long-tailed Duck *Clangula hyemalis* 38–47cm

Pakistan, Nepal and India. **ID** Small, stocky duck with stubby bill and pointed tail. Swims low in water and partly opens wings before diving. Both sexes show dark upperwing and underwing in flight. Winter male mainly white; has dark cheek patch and breast, and long tail. Female and immature male variable; usually with dark crown and pale face with dark cheek patch. **HH** Winters mainly at sea, also inland in large, deep freshwater lakes or brackish lagoons. Globally threatened.

COLUMBIDAE

European Turtle Dove *Streptopelia turtur* 27–29cm

Pakistan, India and Maldives. **ID** White sides and tip to tail. From *meena* race of Oriental Turtle by smaller size and slimmer build; broader, paler rufous-buff fringes to scapulars and wing-coverts; more buffish- or brownish-grey rump and uppertail-coverts; and greyish-pink breast, becoming whitish on belly and undertail-coverts. Juvenile lacks neck-barring. **HH** Cultivation in drier mountains and valleys. Habits similar to Oriental Turtle. A ground-feeder, gleaning grain from cultivation, also forages on dusty tracks. Globally threatened.

Namaqua Dove *Oena capensis* 20–28cm

India. **ID** A small dove, with long, graduated tail. Flight fast, with rapid, occasionally interrupted, wingbeats. In flight, shows rufous on primaries and underwing and black tips to outer-tail feathers. Mainly sandy-grey above and white below, with black bars on wing. Male has black face and throat (lacking in female) and red bill with yellow tip (mainly dark grey in female). Juvenile similar to female with black-and-white markings on upperparts. **HH** Feeds on ground, meandering slowly along paths and tracks. Open areas mainly in agricultural land.

PTEROCLIDAE

Pallas's Sandgrouse *Syrrhaptes paradoxus* 27–41cm

India. **ID** A large pin-tailed sandgrouse with elongated outer primaries. Both sexes have pale orange throat and patch on sides of head, pale grey breast, sandy upperparts with bold black spotting and barring, prominent black patch on belly and largely white underwing in flight. Male has narrow gorget of black barring on breast and unbarred sandy wing-coverts. Female lacks black gorget and has extensive black barring on mantle and wing-coverts, and narrow black bar on lower throat. **HH** Typical sandgrouse. Wary, rising with a clatter of wings when disturbed, flying off rapidly and directly. Mainly arid steppe and semi-desert with sparse vegetation, also dry fallow fields and abandoned cultivation.

CUCULIDAE

Horsfield's Bronze Cuckoo *Chalcites basalis* 17cm

India. **ID** Small cuckoo, with bronze-green upperparts, paler feather fringes on mantle, coverts and tertials. Underparts whitish with finely streaked throat and diffuse dark barring on flanks. Has whitish supercilium and broad dark eye-stripe curving down behind whitish cheeks. A touch of rufous at base of outer tail. Bill black. Juvenile has grey-brown upperparts with less distinct supercilium and greyish-white underparts. **HH** Forages in foliage and on ground for insects, mainly caterpillars; flight swift and direct. Open woodland and scrub in arid and semi-arid areas.

RALLIDAE

Red-legged Crake *Rallina fasciata* 23–25cm

India. **ID** Adult from adult Slaty-legged Crake by red legs, white or buff barring on wings, rufous-brown upperparts similar in coloration to head and breast, and indistinct whitish to rufous-buff throat. Juvenile from juvenile Slaty-legged by red legs, and barring on wings. Barring on wings and more extensive black-and-white barring on underparts help separate from Ruddy-breasted Crake (which also has red legs). **HH** Typical rail; very skulking. Reedy swamps and marshes, paddyfields, watercourses, and wet areas in forests and second growth.

Corn Crake *Crex crex* 27–30cm

Pakistan, India and Sri Lanka. **ID** A stocky crake with stout pinkish bill and legs. Rufous-chestnut on wings (especially obvious in flight), buff-brown upperparts boldly streaked dark brown, greyish foreneck and breast, and rufous-brown and white barring on flanks. Juvenile has buffish rather than grey neck, neck and breast. **HH** Habits similar to other crakes, crepuscular. Grassland and crops, also fallow cultivation and rough grass near rivers and pools.

White-browed Crake *Poliolimnas cinereus* 15–20cm

India. **ID** A small crake, similar in size to Ruddy-breasted. Striking head pattern with short white supercilium, longer white cheek stripe and black mask. Rest of head, neck and breast mainly grey, with warm buff flanks and vent. Upperparts brown, streaked black. Bill orangish yellow at tip becoming red at base. Legs greenish-yellow. Juvenile has less distinct head pattern (crown and mask brown, and white supercilium and cheek stripe less prominent) and lacks red at base of bill. **HH** Less shy than most crakes; forages on mud patches, watercourse margins and on floating vegetation. Freshwater and brackish wetlands, especially those with abundant floating vegetation.

GRUIDAE

Hooded Crane *Grus monacha* 91–100cm

Pakistan. **ID** Small crane. Adult uniform dark grey, with white head and upper neck and black forehead; red patch on forecrown visible at close range. Immature has strong cinnamon wash to greyish-white head and neck. In flight, almost uniform slate-grey upperwing and underwing. **HH** Habits similar to other cranes. Feeds by digging and by picking food off surface. In non-breeding season: open wetlands, grassland, fields, banks of rivers and lakes, and marshes. Globally threatened.

OTIDIDAE

Great Bustard *Otis tarda* 75–105cm

Pakistan. **ID** Very large, stocky bustard. In all plumages has greyish head and upper neck, cinnamon lower neck, cinnamon upperparts with bold black barring, and white underparts. Pattern of white on wing differs from other bustards (secondaries are black, and white is most prominent on greater coverts). Male larger than female, with thicker neck and more extensive white on wing (tertials and wing-coverts show more white). **HH** Similar to Great Indian Bustard. Feeds chiefly in early mornings and late afternoons. Flight steady, quite close to ground, and can be sustained for long distances. Open grassland and crops, without trees. Globally threatened.

GAVIIDAE

Red-throated Loon *Gavia stellata* 53–69cm

Pakistan, India and Nepal. **ID** Upturned-looking bill and rounded head. In non-breeding plumage, paler grey and whiter than similar Arctic. Grey of crown and hindneck paler and less extensive compared to Arctic and does not contrast so strongly with white of ear-coverts and foreneck. Red throat and uniform grey-brown upperparts in breeding plumage. **HH** Typical loon. Catches prey by underwater pursuit. Frequently swims with body almost completely submerged. Coastal waters, large lakes and rivers. **AN** Red-throated Diver.

Arctic Loon *Gavia arctica* 58–73cm

India and Bhutan. **ID** Straight bill and square-shaped head help distinguish it from Red-throated in all plumages. Blackish upperparts and white underparts in non-breeding plumage (more grey and white in Red-throated) and typically shows white flank patch (more striking than Red-throated). Unmistakable in breeding plumage, with black throat and black-and-white chequered upperparts. **HH** Typical loon habits, see Red-throated. Flooded land, lakes and coastal waters. **AN** Black-throated Diver.

DIOMEDEIDAE

Light-mantled Albatross *Phoebetria palpebrata* 78–93cm

India. **ID** A finely built, largely dark albatross with slender wings and long, pointed tail. Only really confusable with Sooty Albatross *P. fusca* (not recorded in region). Adult from Sooty by silver-grey mantle contrasting with brown head; also prominent white crescents behind eye, and blue (rather than yellow) line along lower mandible. Immature shows paler grey mantle than immature Sooty but some Sooty can appear similar and caution is needed. **HH** Sometimes feeds in association with whales, occasionally follows ships. Food usually taken on or close to the ocean surface. Pelagic.

OCEANITIDAE

Black-bellied Storm-petrel *Fregetta tropica* 19.5–21cm

Sri Lanka and India. **ID** Upperside resembles Wilson's Storm-petrel with prominent white rump and feet extending beyond tail. Upperwing-coverts blacker and upperwing can appear wholly dark. Differs from Wilson's in largely white underwing-coverts and white flanks. **HH** Flight erratic, zigzagging from side to side. Pelagic.

HYDROBATIDAE

Band-rumped Storm-petrel *Hydrobates castro* 17.6–20cm

Maldives. **ID** A medium-sized storm-petrel, all dark except for conspicuous white oval rump-patch and pale upperwing bands. From smaller Wilson's by slightly forked, not square, tail (although Wilson's tail can appear forked at times) and by the legs/feet not projecting beyond the tail. At close range, bill is noticeably heavy. **HH** Typical flight is buoyant, with tight twists and short glides. Pelagic. **TN** *Oceanodroma castro.*

Matsudaira's Storm-petrel ***Hydrobates matsudairae*** 24–25cm

Maldives. **ID** Very similar to Swinhoe's Storm-petrel but larger, has longer and broader wings, and more pronounced tail fork, slower flight action with lazy flapping interspersed by prolonged glides, and has distinct white patch at base of primaries (vaguely apparent in Swinhoe's). **HH** Feeds mainly on wing, by dipping and snatching from surface. Pelagic, often far from coast. Globally threatened.

Leach's Storm-petrel ***Hydrobates leucorhous*** 18–22cm

Maldives. **ID** Similar to Swinhoe's but has white rump which is usually divided by a narrow dark central line. Flight buoyant and tern like interspersed with short glides. From Wilson's by larger size, forked tail, longer and more angular wings, less prominent white rump. Flight action more relaxed and feet do not extend beyond tail. **HH** Feeds by pecking at prey while hovering over surface, occasionally pattering on surface, or sitting on water. Pelagic. Globally threatened.

Cape Petrel ***Daption capense*** 38–40cm

Sri Lanka. **ID** A stocky, broad-winged, black-and-white petrel. Has black head, white upperparts untidily marked with black, black tail-band, black upperwings with bold white patches, mainly white underwings with broad black border, and white underparts. **HH** Typically feeds on surface by picking up small food items while sitting on water, also patters on surface. Pelagic.

Cory's Shearwater ***Calonectris borealis*** 44–49cm

India. **ID** Similar to slightly smaller Streaked Shearwater, with lazy gull-like flight action. Main difference from Streaked is rather uniform grey-brown head and hindneck (concolorous with upperparts), lacking any white streaking, and stouter yellowish bill with dark at tip. **HH** In calm seas, three or four slow, even shallow, downbeats between glides on bowed wings. More active flight in wind and in gales high, towering climbs. Pelagic.

ARDEIDAE

Schrenck's Bittern ***Ixobrychus eurhythmus*** 33–42cm

Sri Lanka. **ID** Slightly larger than Yellow Bittern. Male has maroon head (with darker cap), hindneck and mantle. Mantle contrasts strongly with greyish buff wing-coverts patch that in turn contrasts strongly with dark flight feathers. Underparts yellowish buff with dark central stripe from throat to breast. Bill dark and facial skin pink in breeding condition. Female and immature superficially similar but mantle blackish mottled with white, wing-coverts similarly coloured but still show as paler panel in flight due to heavier white/buff markings, and underparts extensively streaked with chestnut to dark brown. Dark brownish (rather than rufous) flight feathers and tail are helpful features from female/juvenile Cinnamon Bittern. Darker upperparts with profuse white mottling are helpful versus female/juvenile Yellow Bittern. **HH** Mainly crepuscular. Marshes with reedbeds and wet grassland.

White-eared Night Heron ***Oroanassa magnifica*** 54–56cm

India and Bangladesh. **ID** Larger than Malayan Night Heron. Adult and immature very distinctive with striking black-and-white pattern to head and neck, and yellowish patch on sides of neck. Underparts dark, boldly splashed with white. Upperparts of adult uniform dark brown; heavily splashed white in immature. **HH** Presumably nocturnal. Wet areas in dense forest in hills or mountains. Globally threatened.

Javan Pond Heron ***Ardeola speciosa*** 46cm

India. **ID** Adult breeding is similar to Chinese Pond Heron, with blackish mantle, but head and neck are paler creamy to orange buff (darker chestnut in Chinese. Not safely separable in non-breeding and immature plumages. **HH** Often feeds at dusk, habits similar to Indian Pond Heron. Mainly freshwater marshes, ponds, lakes, paddyfields and other flooded areas.

Chinese Egret ***Egretta eulophotes*** 65–68cm

India. **ID** Structurally similar to Litte Egret, although bill is longer and broader-based, and appears slightly downcurved, with slightly shorter legs and stouter neck. Longer-necked and -legged than Pacific Reef Heron. Distinctive in breeding plumage, with yellow bill, blue lores and bushy crest. Legs black and feet yellow like Little. In non-breeding plumage, bill becomes darker (yellow at base), lores yellow, and legs and feet more greenish-yellow, when rather similar to Pacific Reef Heron. **HH** Very active feeder in shallow water, chasing prey with wings

open or half-spread and repeatedly stabbing into water. Mainly coastal, in estuaries and bays. Globally threatened.

Western Cattle Egret *Bubulcus ibis* 42–52cm
Pakistan. **ID** Very similar to Eastern Cattle Egret. Structurally, has a shorter bill and legs, and longer tail. In breeding plumage, the orange-buff coloration is less extensive and confined to the crown, nape and plumes on the back and breast. The plumes are longer and wispier. **HH** Grassland, and often around cattle. May forage in fields where crops are being planted and harvested.

SULIDAE

Abbott's Booby *Papasula abbotti* 79cm
India. **ID** Superficially similar to Masked Booby, but more rakish, with longer wings and tail, thin neck and large head and bill. Upperwing mainly black with irregular narrow white leading edge, and white blotching on coverts (showing more black on upperwing than Masked). Underwing largely white except narrow black outer edge to primaries (less black on underwing than Masked). Mantle, back and rump blotched with black (all white in Masked). Sexes and immatures similar in plumage. Adult male and immature have greyish bill and black tip; female has pink bill and black tip. **HH** Feeds on fish, probably by plunge-diving like other boobies. Pelagic. Globally threatened.

PHALACROCORACIDAE

Pygmy Cormorant *Microcarbo pygmaeus* 45–55cm
Pakistan. **ID** On average, larger and bulkier than Little Cormorant. Adult breeding has chestnut head and upper neck (becoming nearly black prior to breeding), with more profuse white plumes than breeding Little. Non-breeding and immature very similar to Little, although tend to be browner on body and have more extensive whitish mottling on breast and belly; in adult non-breeding chin and throat whitish, gradually merging into brown of foreneck (on Little, chin more clearly demarcated). **HH** Habits similar to Little Cormorant. Lowland fresh waters, including lakes and slow-flowing rivers, also sometimes brackish or salt waters. **TN** Previously placed in *Phalacrocorax*.

CHARADRIIDAE

European Golden Plover *Pluvialis apricaria* 26–29cm
Pakistan and India. **ID** Very similar in plumage to Pacific Golden Plover. Stockier with shorter and stouter bill and shorter legs. Underwing-coverts and axillaries largely white. At rest, primaries do not extend beyond tail as in Pacific. In flight, toes do not project beyond tail (noticeable projection in Pacific). Breeding plumage similar to Pacific, but shows more white on sides of breast and flanks. In non-breeding plumage, supercilium usually less distinct and is rather plain-faced, compared to Pacific. **Voice** A mellow, drawn-out, pure whistle, *puuuu*. **HH** Habits similar to Pacific. Grassland and mud on lakeshores and in estuaries.

American Golden Plover *Pluvialis dominica* 24–28cm
India. **ID** Very similar in structure and appearance to Pacific Golden Plover. A subtle structural difference at rest is that the primaries extend well beyond the tail but the tertials fall short of it, and has finer bill. In breeding plumage, black extends from belly to cover flanks and vent (although some Pacific can show extensive black on underparts, and in moult they can be very similar). Juvenile and non-breeding plumage greyer (less golden) than Pacific, typically with more prominent white supercilium. **Voice** Most frequent flight call outside breeding season a whistled *que* or *que-del*. **HH** Habits similar to Pacific. Variety of inland and coastal habitats: pastures, agricultural land including burnt fields, mudflats, shores and estuaries.

Eurasian Dotterel *Eudromias morinellus* 20–22cm
Pakistan. **ID** A stocky plover with comparatively short, yellow legs. Very distinctive in breeding plumage, with prominent white supercilium, narrow white breast-band and chestnut-and-blackish belly. In juvenile and non-breeding plumage, belly buffish, but retains distinctive supercilium and suggestion of narrow breast-band. **Voice** Mostly silent in winter. **HH** Often rather tame but inconspicuous. Dry open country including stony steppe, ploughed farmland, marginal cultivation and semi-desert. **TN** Previously placed in *Charadrius*.

Oriental Plover *Anarhynchus veredus* 22–25.5cm

India, Bangladesh and Sri Lanka. **ID** From Caspian Plover by larger size, longer neck and legs, brown underwing-coverts and axillaries (uniformly dark underwing) and uniformly dark upperwing typically lacking any sign of white wing-bar. Yellowish or pinkish legs. **Voice** Calls include a sharp whistled *chip-chip-chip* in flight. **HH** Gait and feeding behaviour typical of plovers. Dry open grassland, including playing fields; sparsely vegetated ground with dry, bare areas, mudflats and sandbanks. **TN** Previously placed in *Charadrius*.

Eastern Curlew *Numenius madagascariensis* 60–66cm

Bangladesh. **ID** Large size and very long, curved bill. Dark back and rump and heavily barred underwing-coverts and axillaries. Underparts washed buff in adult breeding and juvenile (ground colour of Eurasian Curlew's breast and belly is whiter), although underparts in non-breeding adult paler and more like Eurasian. **Voice** Calls include a powerful *coour-leee*, overall deeper than Eurasian. **HH** Habits similar to Eurasian. Mainly muddy coastal areas including bays and estuaries; also muddy banks of inland lakes and rivers. Globally threatened.

SCOLOPACIDAE

Sharp-tailed Sandpiper *Calidris acuminata* 17–22cm

India, Pakistan and Sri Lanka. **ID** Recalls Wood Sandpiper in shape, or a very large Long-toed Stint in both shape and plumage. Rufous crown (indistinct in winter) and prominent supercilium. Adult non-breeding greyish with breast-band of fine streaking with streaking extending to flanks. Adult breeding has dark markings over entire underparts, with arrowhead markings on flanks and bright rufous fringes to feathers of mantle and scapulars. Juvenile similar to adult breeding but has buff wash to lightly streaked breast. **Voice** Call when flushed a *wheep*, usually given in a short twittering sequence. **HH** Feeds by picking and probing and is frequently hidden among vegetation. Wide range of freshwater and coastal wetlands, including mudflats, shallow brackish lagoons, flooded grassland, and vegetation on drier wetland edges. Globally threatened.

Buff-breasted Sandpiper *Calidris subruficollis* 18–20cm

India and Sri Lanka. **ID** Recalls a tiny Ruff, with shorter and straighter bill, large eyes and bright yellow legs. Upperwing lacks wing-bar and has no white on rump or tail. White underwing has dark crescent on primary coverts (underwing entirely white in Ruff). In all plumages face and underparts are buff, and dark upperparts are neatly fringed with buff. **Voice** Usually silent. **HH** Feeds by picking prey from ground and vegetation; walks quickly and often changes direction. Short grass, mud and seashore. **TN** Previously placed in *Tryngites*.

Pectoral Sandpiper *Calidris melanotos* 19–23cm

India and Sri Lanka. **ID** In all plumages has sharply demarcated gorget of streaks coming to a point in centre of breast, unmarked belly and pale legs tinged yellowish. Clearly defined breast-band and unmarked flanks are best feature from Sharp-tailed Sandpiper in all plumages. In flight has narrow white bar on upperwing and clear white sides to lower rump and uppertail-coverts. When alert has erect stance with neck stretched. **Voice** Flight call a reedy *trrit*. **HH** Creeps or squats in wet vegetation, mud, edges of reedbeds. Wide range of freshwater and coastal wetlands, but rare on mudflats.

Long-billed Dowitcher *Limnodromus scolopaceus* 27–30cm

India and Bangladesh. **ID** Rather snipe-like in shape and feeding action. Superficially resembles Bar-tailed Godwit or Asian Dowitcher but smaller and has shorter legs (greyish, yellowish or greenish rather than black). In flight, a clear white trailing edge to the wing, barred rump and tail, and a striking white back. In all plumages has pronounced white supercilium. In breeding plumage has rufous underparts, with some barring and spotting, and dark upperparts have narrow rufous fringes. In non-breeding plumage, grey upperparts and breast, and white belly. Juvenile recalls non-breeding adult, but has rufous fringes to mantle and scapulars, and buff wash to underparts. **Voice** Call a high, thin *keek*. **HH** Forages by probing, using a distinctive 'sewing-machine' motion, also by jabbing. Shallow water in freshwater wetlands, coastal mudflats and wet meadows.

Great Snipe *Gallinago media* 27–29cm

India and Sri Lanka. **ID** Medium-sized, bulky snipe, with broader wings than Common and Pin-tailed, and slower and more direct flight. Additional features include heavily barred underwing, narrow but distinct white wing-bars and prominent white at sides of tail (latter two features less pronounced in juvenile). White wing-bars and white belly help to distinguish from Wood Snipe. **Voice** When flushed, usually rises silently, or occasionally utters a hoarse croak. **HH** Soon settles again after being flushed; flight slower, straighter, without zigzagging [illegible] paddyfields, and short grass at lake edges.

Red Phalarope *Phalaropus fulicarius* 20–22cm

India, Bangladesh and Pakistan. **ID** Typically seen swimming. Stockier than Red-necked Phalarope, with stouter bill that is often pale or yellowish at base. Adult breeding has red neck and underparts and white face patch. Adult non-breeding has more uniform and paler grey mantle, scapulars and rump than Red-necked. Juvenile has dark upperparts evenly fringed buff (lacking mantle and scapular stripes of Red-necked). **Voice** Call a short *pit*. **HH** Habits similar to Red-necked. Pelagic, also inland waters after storms.

LARIDAE

Black Noddy *Anous minutus* 35–40cm

India. **ID** Extremely similar to Brown and Lesser Noddies. Adult from adult Brown by smaller and slimmer appearance, faster more fluttering flight, brownish-black plumage, and slimmer and straighter bill, longer than head. In flight, all-dark upperwing and underwing, lacking paler bar on upperwing-coverts and any pale on underwing-coverts; centre of uppertail paler and greyer and often contrasts strongly with blackish rest of upperparts. Distinguished from Lesser Noddy by black lores with well-defined white forehead and crown. **HH** Habits of a typical noddy. Pelagic.

Sabine's Gull *Xema sabini* 27–33cm

India. **ID** Slightly smaller than Black-headed Gull with pointed wings and forked tail. Distinctive wing pattern in all plumages, with white inner primaries and secondaries contrasting with black outer primaries and brown (immature) or grey (adult) wing-coverts. Adult has black bill with yellow tip; grey hood in breeding plumage, and white head and grey nape in non-breeding plumage. Juvenile has brownish-grey nape and shoulder patch, and scaled pattern to grey-brown mantle and wing-coverts; mantle grey in first-winter. **HH** Quick and agile in flight, shearing in gales. Picks food items from surface. Pelagic, also coastal waters.

Black-legged Kittiwake *Rissa tridactyla* 38–41cm

India, Bangladesh and Pakistan. **ID** Adult has solid black tips to upper-and underwing. Head white in summer and has grey hindneck in winter. Yellow bill and short black legs. First-year has dark 'W' pattern across wings and black tail-band; juvenile and some first-winters have white head with black ear-spot and black half-collar; 'W' much faded in first-summer. **HH** Very manoeuvrable in flight, shears in gales. Pelagic. Globally threatened.

Franklin's Gull *Leucophaeus pipixcan* 32–36cm

India. **ID** Slightly smaller than Black-headed Gull with shorter and stouter bill. Adult has darker grey mantle and wings, with pronounced white trailing edge and white band separating grey from black of wingtips (which have large white mirrors). In breeding plumage has black hood with bold white eye-crescents. First-winter has extensive black mask and rear crown (white eye-crescents still prominent), brownish wing-coverts and black wingtips, and well-defined black tail-band. **HH** Swims gracefully and buoyantly. Coasts including bays and estuaries.

White-eyed Gull *Ichthyaetus leucophthalmus* 39–43cm

India and Maldives. **ID** Superficially similar to Sooty Gull, with dark grey mantle and wings with striking white trailing edge and dark underwing. In breeding plumage, black head and foreneck, striking white eye-crescents, white neck patch and long and slender, mainly red bill, becoming duller and less clean-cut in non-breeding plumage. Immature similar to adult non-breeding although bill is dark. Juvenile has scaled appearance to upperparts. Sooty Gull has much stouter, mainly greenish bill with pronounced dark tip in all plumages. **HH** Coasts, roosts on rocks, reefs and piers.

Black Tern *Chlidonias niger* 23–28cm

India and Sri Lanka. **ID** Superficially similar to White-winged Tern. In breeding plumage, told from White-winged by grey rather than black mantle, uniform grey underwing, and grey (rather than white) rump and tail. Non-breeding and juvenile have dark patch on side of breast (lacking in White-winged) and grey rump and tail. Juvenile shows less contrast between mantle and upperwing-coverts (juvenile White-winged shows distinctly darker saddle). **HH** Habits similar to White-winged. Flies with great agility, turning this way and that, to catch insects in the air, and swooping to pick them delicately from the water's surface. Coasts and inland in marshes, pools and lakes.

Arctic Tern *Sterna paradisaea* 28–39cm

India. **ID** Very similar to Common Tern. Uniform translucent primaries with well-defined dark trailing edge, lack of dark secondary bar, shorter bill and shorter legs are good features that separate it from Common in all plumages. In breeding plumage has dark red bill normally lacking black tip and longer tail streamers than Common. Juvenile shows white trailing edge to wing. **HH** Takes prey from the surface by plunge-diving, diving to the surface or dipping; occasionally takes insects. Recorded inland in region, but usually on coasts.

STERCORARIIDAE

South Polar Skua *Stercorarius maccormicki* 50–55cm

India, Sri Lanka and Maldives. **ID** Slightly smaller and slighter than Brown Skua, with finer bill. Pale morph distinctive: pale sandy-brown head and underparts contrasting with dark brown mantle and upperwing- and underwing-coverts. Dark morph lacks heavy pale streaking/mottling of Brown, and usually has pale forehead, dark cap/head and paler hindneck; uniform (unbarred) underwing-coverts, axillaries and uppertail- and undertail-coverts are best distinctions from dark juvenile Pomarine Jaeger. Intermediates occur. Juvenile has pale to mid-grey head and underparts, and dark grey upperparts. **HH** Habits similar to Brown Skua. Normal flight direct, with steady shallow wingbeats, but swift, dashing and hawk-like in pursuit of gulls and terns. Coastal waters and pelagic.

STRIGIDAE

Snowy Owl *Bubo scandiacus* 53–66cm

Pakistan. **ID** A huge owl, mainly white, with variable dark markings and striking yellow eyes. **HH** A powerful, terrestrial owl, frequently active in daylight. Usually scans from an exposed perch and also seeks prey by flying low and sometimes even hovering. Open country. Globally threatened.

ACCIPITRIDAE

European Honey Buzzard *Pernis apivorus* 52–60cm

India. **ID** Very similar to Oriental Honey Buzzard with similar wide variation in plumages, but does not show gorget on throat and has dark carpal patch on underwing in most plumages. Slightly smaller with narrower wings. Adult male has grey head like Oriental but has yellow eye (dark in male Oriental) and three narrower dark bands on tail (two much broader bands in male Oriental). Female and juvenile more similar to Oriental in tail-bands. **HH** Glides on drooped wings; soars on flat or slightly raised wings. Feeds mainly on wasps and hornets, also bumblebees and some other insects. Forests and woods, mainly deciduous, also mixed forests.

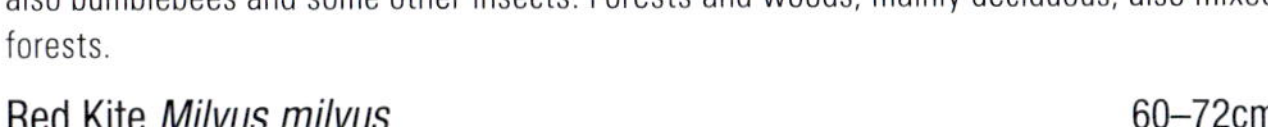

Red Kite *Milvus milvus* 60–72cm

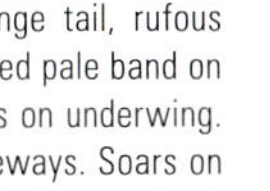

India. **ID** Similar to Black Kite, but has more deeply forked rufous-orange tail, rufous underparts and underwing-coverts, and whitish head. Also, more pronounced pale band on upperwing-coverts and more obvious whitish patches at base of primaries on underwing. **HH** Elegant, active flight with deep wingbeats and forked tail twisted sideways. Soars on flat or bowed wings. Lightly wooded semi-desert, also more open areas including farmland, scrub and wetlands.

Rufous-winged Buzzard *Butastur liventer* 35–41cm

India. **ID** Similar structurally to White-eyed Buzzard. Adult has greyish head and underparts, rufous-brown upperparts and rufous flight feathers and tail. Underwing-coverts white and underside to flight feathers pale and only lightly barred. Lacks dark gular stripe. Juvenile similar but head and underparts browner. **HH** Flight like an *Accipiter*, with fast wingbeats interspersed with short glides. Open country, dry woodland and scrub; also near rivers, agricultural land and marshes in plains and foothills.

Grey-faced Buzzard *Butastur indicus* 41–48cm

India. **ID** Similar structurally to White-eyed Buzzard. Adult and immature have white throat and broad dark gular stripe. Adult has grey face, rufous-brown or grey-brown upperparts, breast and barring on flanks. In flight, broad, dark tail-bands and pale crescent on uppertail-coverts. Juvenile has white supercilium and nape patch and bold dark streaking on white underparts. **HH** Often hunts from a perch, waiting to spot prey and dive down on it. Wooded areas and open country in hills and valleys.

Rough-legged Buzzard *Buteo lagopus* 50–60cm

India. **ID** Structurally recalls Upland Buzzard. Adult readily distinguished from Upland and other buzzards by broad black subterminal band to white tail (visible from above and below). Typically also has all-dark (or black-barred) belly and whitish underwing-coverts with large black carpal patches. In juvenile tail is white at base but has less distinct dark subterminal band and pattern more closely resembles Upland, but has extensive black belly and whiter head, combined with largely white underwing-coverts and black carpal patches; resulting appearance quite different to Upland. **HH** Hovers frequently or hangs motionless in air when hunting. Open country: grasslands, agricultural land and marshes.

MEROPIDAE

Blue-throated Bee-eater *Merops viridis* 21–32.5cm

India. **ID** Striking bee-eater with chestnut crown and nape, blue throat merging into green underparts (without black gorget), and blue rump and tail with elongated central tail feathers. Juvenile duller with green crown and nape and lacks elongated central tail feathers. **Voice** Most common call a repeated rolling *prrrp*. **HH** Watches for passing bees from a high perch, dashes to capture prey in flight, taking it back to perch. In forest canopy and clearings and along channels in mangrove forest.

FALCONIDAE

Red-footed Falcon *Falco vespertinus* 27–33cm

Pakistan. **ID** Like Amur Falcon has red to pale orange cere, legs and feet (yellow in juvenile). Male as Amur but has grey (rather than white) underwing-coverts. Female from female Amur by orange-buff underparts and pale buff crown. Juvenile from juvenile Amur by buffish underparts. Juvenile similar to juvenile Hobby, but has paler cap, paler grey-brown upperparts, prominent dark trailing edge to underwing and prominently barred uppertail. **HH** Graceful and agile in flight, sometimes hovers with fast-beating wings. Open habitats with some trees for perching and roosting. Globally threatened.

PITTIDAE

Blue-winged Pitta *Pitta moluccensis* 18–20cm

India. **ID** Very similar to Indian Pitta, but buffish sides to crown lack white lower edge, lacks white crescent below eye, has black chin, wing-coverts and rump are deeper blue, and has much more extensive white patch in primaries. From Mangrove Pitta by smaller bill, black chin, stronger contrast between buffish sides to crown and black (rather than rufous-brown) centre to crown. **HH** Forages on ground like other pittas, hopping like a thrush. Wide range of wooded habitats including dry and moist forests, secondary forests, mangroves, scrub.

ORIOLIDAE

Eurasian Golden Oriole *Oriolus oriolus* 24–25cm

India, Pakistan and Sri Lanka. **ID** Male from male Indian Golden by mainly black wings (with smaller yellow carpal patch and only indistinct whitish tips to tertials/secondaries), two-thirds black on outer tail feathers, and black mask does not extend behind eye. Female and immature variable, and much like 'Indian', but with less yellow on outer tail feathers; also, often greyer or more olive and less heavily streaked below. Bill shorter, less downcurved than 'Indian', and darker red in adult. **Voice** and **HH** As Indian.

MONARCHIDAE

Amur Paradise-flycatcher *Terpsiphone incei* 17.5–22cm

India and Bangladesh. **ID** Has smaller bill and smaller crest than Indian Paradise-flycatcher with darker chestnut upperparts; rufous male has grey (rather than white or greyish-white) breast; female has clearly defined dark hood. Bill shorter and shallower than Blyth's Paradise-flycatcher; rufous male and female have darker chestnut upperparts and white vent; female has clearly defined dark hood. **Voice** and **HH** As Indian Paradise-flycatcher. **TN** Previously treated as conspecific with Indian and Blyth's Paradise-flycatchers as Asian Paradise-flycatcher.

LANIIDAE

Tiger Shrike *Lanius tigrinus* 17–18.5cm

India and Bhutan. **ID** Superficially similar to Burmese Shrike but stockier, with heavier bill and shorter tail. Has heavily barred and scaled upperparts in all plumages (upperparts unbarred in adult Burmese). Adult has grey crown and nape; male has solid black forehead and mask, and white underparts; female lacks black forehead and has dark scaling on underparts. Juvenile has rufous crown and nape and is very heavily scaled above and on white underparts. **Voice** Alarm a loud, scolding chatter. **HH** Keeps in cover more than other shrikes. Mainly hunts by gleaning insects from branches and leaves unlike other shrikes, but also hunts insects from exposed perches. Edges and clearings of lowland, broadleaved forests, also cultivation and gardens.

Lesser Grey Shrike *Lanius minor* 19–23cm

India and Nepal. **ID** Smaller than Great Grey Shrike, with long extension of primaries beyond tertials. Adult has more extensive black forehead compared to Great Grey, different pattern of white in wing (broad white patch at base of primaries and all-black secondaries except white at tips) and shorter and squarer tail with less white at sides. First-winter similar to adult but lacks black forehead. **Voice** Call a harsh grating. **HH** Typical shrike habits, but more upright posture with tail often held down, and flight less undulating than other shrikes. Open dry country with plenty of scattered or grouped trees.

Woodchat Shrike *Lanius senator* 18–19cm

Pakistan and India. **ID** Adult is striking with chestnut hindcrown and nape, black upperparts with white scapulars and rump, and white underparts. Sexes similar though female is duller. Prominent white patch in primaries in flight. Juvenile heavily scaled; from juvenile Red-backed Shrike by paler, more prominently scaled crown and nape, whitish centres to scapulars, pale rump and whitish patch at base of primaries. **Voice** In alarm a harsh *kreck*, usually in series. **HH** Typical shrike habits. Partly open country with bushes and open woodland.

Masked Shrike *Lanius nubicus* 17–18.5cm

India. **ID** Small-bodied shrike with long tail. Male has black upperparts, white forehead and supercilium, white shoulder and primary patches, and white underparts with peach-coloured flanks. Female similarly patterned but upperparts greyish-brown. First-winter similar to female with barring on crown, mantle and flanks. **Voice** In alarm a *krrr.* **HH** Hunts by sitting and waiting for prey but uses less exposed perches than other shrikes. Dry areas with woodland or scrub.

CORVIDAE

Pied Crow *Corvus albus* 46cm

India. **ID** Similar in size to Large-billed Crow, with white collar and underparts contrasting strongly with black of head, upper breast, and rest of upperparts and underparts. White underparts contrast strongly with black underwing in flight. **Voice** Typical call a deep, guttural *kraaak*. **HH** Wide range of open-country habitats including forest clearings, open woodland, grassland, also villages and urban areas including rubbish dumps.

PARIDAE

Azure Tit *Cyanistes cyanus* 13–14cm

Pakistan. **ID** Small short-billed tit with longish tail. Mainly whitish head, with dark stripe through eye and band on nape, grey mantle, white underparts and broad white wing-bar and tips to tertials. **Voice** Calls include a hard, scolding *chr-r-r-r-r-rit.* **HH** Typical tit. Often remains in cover. Quite a strong, bounding, undulating flight. Seasonally dry riverbed bushes and a range of wooded habitats.

PANURIDAE

Bearded Reedling *Panurus biarmicus* 14.5–17cm

Pakistan. **ID** A round-bodied, long-tailed babbler-like bird with a small yellow bill. White edges to primaries form a wing-panel. Male has grey head with black moustache, rufous mantle, tail and flanks, and black undertail-coverts. Female and juvenile have plain buff head and lack black undertail-coverts. Distinctive ringing *ping-ping* flight call. **HH** Acrobatic on reed stems; feeds on ground below. Reedbeds.

ACROCEPHALIDAE

Sedge Warbler *Acrocephalus schoenobaenus* 13cm

India. **ID** Similar in appearance to Moustached Warbler, with broad white supercilium and streaked mantle. Head pattern less striking than Moustached; also has buffish olive-brown upperparts, well-defined buffy fringes to tertials and greater coverts, and longer primary projection. **Voice** Song energetic, varied and scratchy. Less repetitive and rhythmic than Reed Warbler. Hard *tuk* and short *trrrr* calls. **HH** Mainly forages low down in dense vegetation, picking invertebrates from twigs and leaves or catching prey in flight. Dense vegetation at wetland edges.

Common Reed Warbler *Acrocephalus scirpaceus* 13cm

Pakistan. **ID** Very similar in appearance to Blyth's Reed Warbler, but has longer primary projection. In worn (breeding) plumage, rather pale brown above and white below (Blyth's Reed is more grey-toned), whilst in fresh (non-breeding) plumage it is more rufescent (Blyth's Reed more olive-toned). Supercilium less prominent, bill longer and primary projection also longer, compared with Paddyfield and Blunt-winged Warblers. **Voice** Calls include a *che* and in alarm a hoarse *chreeh*. Song a varied series of scratchy notes that is less musical (lacking clear, rising notes of Blyth's Reed). **HH** On migration and in winter uses a variety of habitats including reeds, thickets and tall grasses. Often along watercourses, but also away from water in scrub and at forest edges.

Great Reed Warbler *Acrocephalus arundinaceus* 19–20cm

Pakistan and India. **ID** Differs from Clamorous Reed in having a shorter, stouter bill, longer primary projection and shorter-looking tail. Primary projection is roughly equal to length of tertials, with 8–9 exposed primary tips visible beyond tertials (primary projection in Clamorous two-thirds of tertial length, with 6–7 exposed tips visible). **Voice** Call a hard *crek*. Song a rhythmic series of frog-like *karra-karra-karra* notes. **HH** On migration and in winter uses a range of habitats including reeds and marshy vegetation; also away from water in thickets, tall grass, fields and forest clearings.

HIRUNDINIDAE

Siberian House Martin *Delichon lagopodum* 13–14cm

India. **ID** Like Western House Martin but more extensively white on rump and uppertail-coverts, and has less pronounced tail fork. From Asian House by more white on rump/uppertail-coverts, cleaner white underparts and more pronounced tail fork. Note, in non-breeding and juvenile plumages white areas are more dusky and field identification is probably unreliable. **Voice** Song twittering phrases lasting several seconds; call a buzzy or grating *prrrrt* (lower pitched and more uniform than Western). **HH** Foraging habits little known; presumably similar to Western House. Open areas, valleys, rocky hillsides, towns and villages. **TN** Formerly placed with *Delichon urbicum* as Common House Martin.

PHYLLOSCOPIDAE

Willow Warbler *Phylloscopus trochilus* 11–12.5cm

India. **ID** Similar to Common Chiffchaff but has pale brown to orangey legs and feet, larger-looking bill with orange basal two-thirds of lower mandible, more prominent supercilium (and less prominent pale crescent below eye) and longer primary projection. Does not frequently bob tail like Common Chiffchaff. Lacks wing-bar, and supercilium is less prominent than Greenish Warbler. There is considerable variation in plumage: upperparts vary from olive-brown with yellowish-green tinge to brownish-grey virtually without greenish tinge; and throat, breast and supercilium from being strongly washed yellow to being entirely whitish. **Voice** Call a distinctly disyllabic *who-eet*, different from Common Chiffchaff. May sing in non-breeding areas: short, sweet, whistling song, descending overall. **HH** Mainly feeds by taking insects from leaves in tree canopy, also hovers and sallies for insects. Trees, bushes and scrub.

Wood Warbler *Phylloscopus sibilatrix* 11–13cm

India. **ID** Striking *Phylloscopus* with uniform yellowish-green crown and upperparts, yellow supercilium and throat/upper breast, and brilliant white underparts. Has dark centres to tertials and greater coverts, and yellow edges to wing feathers. Very long wings and short tail give rise to distinctive profile from below. **Voice** Call a single *pew*. Song rhythmic repetition of call note between more frequent trills – metallic, ticking firming up into short, fast trill. **HH** Forages for insects in canopy and undergrowth, also hovers and makes flycatching sallies. Many forest and woodland habitats including moist evergreen forest, moist thickets, forest edge, dry woodland, wooded savanna and scattered trees in forest clearings, fig trees and mangroves.

Chinese Leaf Warbler *Phylloscopus yunnanensis* 9–10cm

India. **ID** Very similar to Lemon-rumped Warbler and very difficult to separate in the field. Pale coronal stripe poorly defined and only obvious towards nape, sides to crown not as dark, lacks black rear border to ear-coverts and lacks black panel at base of secondaries. Otherwise, paler green upperparts and duskier underparts with yellowish cast, but these differences are very subtle. **Voice** Call in non-breeding season usually a single *tueet*. Very distinctive song: a hard, metallic, mechanical, monotonous *tsiridi-tsiridi-tsiridi-tsiridi-...*, often lasting a minute or more, resembling that of Himalayan Prinia. **HH** Forages in canopy and understorey, sometimes hovering and making short flights. Broadleaved deciduous forest.

Pallas's Leaf Warbler *Phylloscopus proregulus* 9–10cm

India. **ID** Similar to Lemon-rumped but has brighter yellow supercilium, especially in front of eye, yellow coronal stripe, and darker sides to crown resulting in bolder head pattern. Also has greener upperparts, yellower wing-bars and whiter underparts. **Voice** Call a soft, nasal, upturned *dweet*. Song a loud and lengthy, melodious series of trills and whistles. **HH** Forages in canopy and bushes; often catches prey by hovering in front of foliage or in short flights. Coniferous, mixed and broadleaved deciduous forests.

Two-barred Warbler *Phylloscopus plumbeitarsus* 10–11cm

India. **ID** Similar to Greenish Warbler but when fresh shows two broader yellowish-white wing-bars. Often worn in winter, with narrower wing-bars and may lack the shorter upper wing-bar. **Voice** Song similar to Greenish but a slightly faster series of whistles, warbles and chatters, with more slurred and jumbled notes. Usual call a trisyllabic, rather sparrow-like *chireewee*. **HH** Actively forages in middle levels of trees. Deciduous and secondary forest, scrub and bamboo.

Arctic Warbler *Phylloscopus borealis* 11–13cm

India. **ID** Extremely similar to *viridanus* race of Greenish Warbler. Prominent supercilium is generally longer and finer but in front of eye it falls short of forehead; also has a darker broader eye-stripe, which usually reaches unbroken to base of bill. **Voice** Best identified by very distinctive buzzing *dziit* call. Song a loud and vigorous, rattling trill, usually preceded by one or two buzzy or quiet *tzick* notes. **HH** Constant wing-flicking. Forages mainly in canopy, also in understorey and undergrowth. Open woodland, mangroves and groves.

Claudia's Leaf Warbler *Phylloscopus claudiae* 11.5–12cm

India. **ID** On current knowledge only separable from Blyth's Leaf Warbler by song. Has similar or slightly less white on outer tail feathers. **Voice** Song usually consists of one or two introductory notes followed by medium to rapid trills of a single note. However, one population (S Shaanxi) sings verses of repeated syllables instead of trill songs. **HH** Forages in canopy, slowly flicking wings alternately. Forests, secondary forest, scrub and bushes in foothills.

Pale-legged Leaf Warbler *Phylloscopus tenellipes* 10–11cm

India and Bangladesh. **ID** Superficially resembles Greenish Warbler. Always distinguished by very pale grey-pink legs and feet, whitish tip to dark bill and distinctive, high-pitched call. Often has buff wash to ear-coverts and olive-brown cast to upperparts, especially rump. Crown distinctly greyer and usually contrasts with mantle. Underparts whitish (never showing any yellow). **Voice** Call a weak, high-pitched *tsip* or *tsick*; song a weak, insect-like trill. See Sakhalin Leaf Warbler as not safely separable from latter except by voice. **HH** Forages low down in vegetation or on ground. Collected on a boat, elsewhere in mangroves and scrub in winter.

Sakhalin Leaf Warbler *Phylloscopus borealoides* 11.5cm

India. **ID** Not safely distinguished in the field from Pale-legged Leaf Warbler except by voice, although indicative features include stronger contrast between crown/nape and greener mantle, more rufescent rump and longer primary projection beyond tertials (7–8, versus 5–6 primaries in Pale-legged). **Voice** Call a clear, high-pitched *teep*, fuller and stronger (and not as high-pitched) as Pale-legged. Song very different; a short, undulating series of weak high-pitched whistles. **HH** Lowland woods, parks and gardens.

SCOTOCERCIDAE

Asian Stubtail *Urosphena squameiceps* 9.5–10.5cm

India, Nepal and Bangladesh. **ID** Very short tail. Otherwise, similar to Pale-footed Bush Warbler but has more rufescent upperparts, longer and more prominent buffish supercilium, and brownish-black eye-stripe that almost reaches hindcrown. White underparts, long pale pinkish

legs and large feet. **Voice** Song a high-pitched cicada-like *see-see-see-see-see-see-see-see-see-see*, increasing in speed and volume towards end. Call a short *stit*. **HH** Feeds on ground or among low vegetation in forest. Hops jerkily about on long flexed legs. Broadleaved forest.

Korean Bush Warbler *Horornis canturians* 15–18cm

India. **ID** Large plain rufous bush warbler lacking wing-bar and coronal stripes. Dark brown eye-stripe and well-marked buff eyebrow. From Thick-billed Warbler by pale supercilium, rufescent crown, less buffy underparts, slender bill and smaller size. **Voice** Call a short dry rattle *trrr*, frequently repeated. **HH** Forages on ground or low in vegetation. Secondary scrub, thickets and edges of cultivation. **AN** Manchurian Bush Warbler. **TN** Previously placed in *Cettia*.

AEGITHALIDAE

Crested Tit Warbler *Leptopoecile elegans* 10cm

India. **ID** Small and tit-like. White crest, blue wings and tail, lavender flanks and white outer tail. Male has blue mantle, chestnut head and pale rufous breast. Female has white face, throat and upper breast, blackish nape, and chestnut mantle, wing-coverts and flanks. **Voice** Calls include very thin descending *pseeee*. **HH** Forages high in trees, often along branches like a nuthatch. Coniferous forest.

SYLVIIDAE

Eurasian Blackcap *Sylvia atricapilla* 14cm

India. **ID** A grey-and-whitish *Sylvia*, slimmer than Garden Warbler. Male has distinctive black cap; brown in female. **Voice** Song is rich, throaty, vigorous and musical; typically low at start, increasing in speed and volume, and generally more forceful than Garden. Call a hard *tack*. **HH** Feeds at medium and high levels, with rather slow movements. Bushes and woodland rich in berries.

Garden Warbler *Sylvia borin* 14cm

India and Maldives. **ID** Stout-billed, stocky appearance. Olive-brown to grey-brown upperparts and buffish-white underparts, with white throat. Rather featureless, but has dark eye, a whitish eye-ring and just a faint suggestion of a greyish supercilium. Plain-faced appearance aids separation from *Iduna* and *Acrocephalus* warblers. **Voice** Song sometimes resembles Blackcap but generally longer phrases, simpler and more even delivery with a fast, bubbling tempo. Call *chek* or *tsak*, a little softer than Blackcap. **HH** Quite skulking, slow and sedate movements, sits still for lengthy spells. Woods, forest edges and bushes.

Barred Warbler *Curruca nisoria* 15.5cm

Pakistan and India. **ID** Large size, stout bill and pale edges and tips to tertials and wing-coverts in all plumages. Plain-faced appearance recalls Garden Warbler. Adult has greyish upperparts, yellow iris and variable dark barring on whitish underparts. First-winter has greyish olive-brown upperparts and buffish underparts, with barring on undertail-coverts and occasionally on flanks. **Voice** Song a musical and vigorous warble of variable short phrases combined with rattling. Call a long, loud fading rattle *trr-rr-rr-t-t-t*. **HH** Moves slowly or stays still for long spells. Dry open woodland and bushes. **TN** Previously placed in *Sylvia*.

ZOSTEROPIDAE

Chestnut-flanked White-eye *Zosterops erythropleurus* 10.5–11.5cm

India. **ID** Similar in appearance to Indian White-eye, but has chestnut flanks (flanks paler in female and coloration can be very weak). Also, upperparts including crown greener (lacking yellower forehead). **Voice** Loud piercing *tsee*. **HH** Deciduous or broadleaved evergreen forest and second growth.

STURNIDAE

Purple-backed Starling *Agropsar sturninus* 16–19cm

Pakistan, Nepal, India, Bangladesh and Sri Lanka. **ID** A small stocky starling with short tail and stout bill. Adult male has pale grey head, nape and underparts, purplish-black hindcrown patch and mantle, white tips to median coverts and rear scapulars forming prominent white V from behind, and glossy greenish-black wings with greyish-white tips to inner greater coverts and tertials. Female and juvenile duller; wing-bars and tips to scapulars less prominent in juvenile. **Voice** Call when flushed a slow, soft, drawn-out *chirrup*. **HH** Typical starling. Has jaunty walk and short bounding run. Woodland edge, second growth, cultivation, gardens and parks. **AN** Daurian Starling.

Chestnut-cheeked Starling *Agropsar philippensis* 16.5–17cm

India and Bangladesh. **ID** Male resembles Purple-backed Starling, but head pale tinged yellowish-buff to brown, with diagnostic chestnut patch on ear-coverts and side of neck; darker grey breast and flanks, whitish fringes on secondaries but lacks whitish tips to scapulars, greater coverts and tertials. Female and juvenile similar to Purple-backed but have whitish fringes on secondaries and lack whitish tips to scapulars, greater coverts and tertials. **Voice** Flight call a melodious *chrueruchu*. **HH** Forages mainly in treetops. Open country including cultivation and second growth; also, urban areas.

White-shouldered Starling *Sturnia sinensis* 17–20cm

Nepal and India. **ID** Adult male has silky-grey head and body and white forehead and throat; white scapulars and wing-coverts form large white patch that contrasts with black of rest of wing. Body may have rusty-orange wash. Female and juvenile browner, with less or no white on wing. Pale grey uppertail-coverts and black tail with greyish-white sides and tip help separate birds lacking white on wing from Chestnut-tailed. **Voice** Alarm a harsh *kaar*. **HH** Typical starling habits. Scrub, cultivation and villages.

White-cheeked Starling *Spodiopsar cineraceus* 22–24cm

Nepal and India. **ID** Mainly grey starling with blacker head; bill and legs orange. White on forehead and patch on ear-coverts. In flight has uniform grey upperwing and white underwing-coverts, and whitish rump and tips to tail. Juvenile similar to adult but duller. **Voice** Call a creaking, monotonous *chir-chir-chay-cheet-cheet*. **HH** Mainly feeds on ground, using open bill to probe just below ground and capture prey. Open country, including cultivation, pastures, open woodland, parks and urban areas.

Red-billed Starling *Spodiopsar sericeus* 21–24cm

India. **ID** Male very distinctive with red bill, whitish head and breast, grey mantle and underparts, and black wings and tail with white patch at base of primaries. Female duller with brownish wash to head and browner mantle and underparts (pale head is much less striking). **HH** Forages on ground and in trees. Cultivation, gardens, scrub in lowlands and open areas with scattered trees in hills.

TURDIDAE

White's Thrush *Zoothera aurea* 24–30cm

India. **ID** Extremely similar to smaller Scaly Thrush with longer bill, primary projection and tail. Probably not safely identifiable in the field except by different song, although features described for Indian records include stronger white eye-ring, heavily mottled cheeks, less prominent dark ear-spot, strongly spotted malar region, and two-toned tertials (inner webs darker than outer webs) with pale tips. **Voice** Song is very different however, a long, flat mournful whistle. Call includes a thin, plaintive *srreeeet*. **HH** Forages on ground or in low vegetation, with bobbing walk, often rapidly fanning and raising tail; turns over leaf litter with bill. Broadleaved forest, gardens, parks and other grassy areas with trees nearby.

Chinese Thrush *Turdus mupinensis* 23cm

India. **ID** Superficially resembles Long-tailed Thrush, with olive-brown upperparts, white tips to median and greater coverts, dark border to ear-coverts and stripe below eye, and bold dark markings on white underparts. Smaller with shorter tail than Long-tailed, with black spotting (rather than barring or scaling) on white underparts. Uniform orange underwing-coverts (lacking white bands on underwing of Long-tailed). **Voice** Song a measured series of pleasant well-spaced phrases, each of 3–5 fairly evenly pitched notes. Calls very poorly known, possibly mostly silent. **HH** On ground has rather sturdy, upright gait, emphasised by its long legs and bill held slightly uptilted. Walks or runs in usual thrush manner. In India observed foraging among leaves on ground in tropical broadleaved evergreen forest, sometimes perched on fallen logs.

Japanese Thrush *Turdus cardis* 21–22cm

India. **ID** Male is distinctive with black head and upperparts and white underparts with bold black spotting; lacks white supercilium and white in wing. First-summer male similar but has grey upperparts. First-winter male has brownish cast to grey upperparts and underparts are heavily spotted, with orange-buff wash to breast and flanks. Female has brown upperparts and bold black spotting in malar region and on underparts, with orange-buff wash on breast and flanks. **Voice** Calls include thin *tsweee* and hollow *chuk*. **HH** Scratches in leaf litter. Woodlands, especially near cultivation.

Song Thrush *Turdus philomelos* 20–23cm

Pakistan and India. **ID** Small and rather compact thrush. Adult superficially resembles Mistle Thrush, with bold black spotting on underparts. Best told by much smaller size and more compact shape, darker olive-brown upperparts, uniform wings and tail, and orange-buff underwing-coverts. Head rather plain, lacking supercilium. First-winter as adult but has buff tips to greater coverts. **Voice** Call a thin, sharp *tik*. **HH** Seeks snails on ground or berries in bushes and trees. Light woodland, parks and gardens.

Redwing *Turdus iliacus* 20–24cm

Pakistan. **ID** Small, rather short-tailed and compact thrush with spotted/streaked underparts. Best told from Song Thrush by prominent whitish supercilium and red patch on flanks when perched and red underwing-coverts in flight. **Voice** Distinctive high, thin *seeeeh*. **HH** Winters in open woodland, orchards and scrubby thickets, wherever there are berry-bearing trees or bushes and grassy areas for foraging.

Chinese Blackbird *Turdus mandarinus* 28–29cm

India. **ID** Male as Eurasian Blackbird. Female dark sooty-black to sooty-brown with paler throat usually lacking spotting on throat and breast of Eurasian. **Voice** Calls include short *sri* in flight and perched, and longer *s'r'r'r'r* in flight. **HH** Forages mostly on ground; also in trees and bushes when feeding on berries and fruit. Open woodland, especially deciduous, also edge habitats including parks, gardens, plantations and orchards, and grassland areas with shrubs nearby.

Eurasian Blackbird *Turdus merula* 25–28cm

Pakistan. **ID** Adult male is brownish-black, with yellow orbital ring and bill. Female dark brown, with brown bill; has whitish throat, streaked dark brown, and diffuse brown spotting on breast. Shorter-tailed than Tibetan Blackbird; male Tibetan lacks prominent yellow orbital ring of Eurasian; female Tibetan is more uniform dark brown without paler throat. **Voice** Calls include loud *chak* and repeated loud *pink pwink pwink* especially at dusk. **HH** Feeds on ground and on fruit and berries in trees and bushes. Winters in forest and woodland edges, orchards and gardens. **AN** Common Blackbird.

Fieldfare *Turdus pilaris* 24–28cm

India. **ID** Adult has blue-grey head, chestnut-brown mantle and much of wing, blue-grey rump and uppertail-coverts contrast with black tail, black streaking on throat, crescent-shaped spotting on breast and flanks, and orange-buff wash to spotted breast. Shows white on underwing in flight. First-winter very similar to adult but duller especially on upperparts. **Voice** In alarm a loud deep *tjetjetjetje*. **HH** Winters in fields, especially rough pasture and arable land within easy reach of tall trees and thick hedgerows with berries, also woodland edges and orchards.

Naumann's Thrush *Turdus naumanni* 23–25cm

Nepal and Bhutan. **ID** Adult male very distinctive, with rufous supercilium and underparts and white scaling on belly and flanks. In other plumages, confusable with Red-throated Thrush, but has more pronounced buff supercilium, broadening behind eye, and belly, flanks and undertail-coverts are prominently marked with rufous. Rufous in tail in all plumages, as in Red-throated Thrush. Hybridises with Dusky Thrush; hybrids have head pattern more similar to Dusky. **Voice** Calls include an insistent *swer-swer-swer* in alarm, thin rasping *zeep* when taking off, and conversational *que-que-que*. **HH** Rhododendron forest and adjacent open hillsides.

MUSCICAPIDAE

Zappey's Flycatcher *Cyanoptila cumatilis* 16–17cm

India. **ID** A large flycatcher. Male has turquoise upperparts with shining crown and bend of wing, dark greenish-blue face and throat, and white underparts. Very similar to Blue-and-white Flycatcher. Female has rufous-brown upperparts with rufous rump and tail; rather plain face lacking prominent eye-ring. Throat and breast brownish-buff with clear demarcation from white of rest of underparts. First-winter male similar to female but has blue wings. See Blue-and-white Flycatcher for differences from that species. **Voice** Song similar to Blue-and-white Flycatcher, but lower in frequency and less variable in pitch; call a harsh *tchuk tchuk tchuk*. **HH** Watches for insect prey from prominent perch. Habitat Not described in non-breeding season.

Blue-and-white Flycatcher *Cyanoptila cyanomelana* 16–17cm

India and Sri Lanka. **ID** Similar to Zappey's Flycatcher. Male differs in having deeper blue upperparts, black face and throat, pale grey flanks, and white centre to tail base (rather than white sides). Female darker than female Zappey's. Like Zappey's, first-winter male is similar to female but has blue wings. **Voice** Song a rich, melodious and erratic *hi-hwi-pipipi, tsi tsi tsi*; calls include a harsh *tchk tchk*. **HH** Perches in open, often on wire or dead tree. Forest, scrub, parks and gardens.

European Robin *Erithacus rubecula* 14cm

Pakistan. **ID** Rotund and well-proportioned robin, often looks big-headed. Adult has olive-brown upperparts, including tail, and rusty-red throat, breast and face. **Voice** Sings all year. A series of phrases with high-pitched notes mixed with melodious warbles. Calls include a staccato *tic*. **HH** Seeks food by hopping on ground and by watching for prey on ground from a low perch. Woodland, farmland, gardens, orchards and plantations.

Siberian Blue Robin *Larvivora cyane* 13–14cm

Nepal, Bangladesh and India. **ID** Male has dark blue upperparts, black sides to throat and breast, and white underparts. Female has olive-brown upperparts, pale buff throat and breast, the latter faintly scaled dark brown, and usually has blue on uppertail-coverts and tail. Female similar to female Indian Blue Robin but lacks orange-buff on breast and flanks of latter. First-winter male similar to female, but has blue on mantle. **Voice** Calls include a *tak* or rapid low *tek-tek-tek*. **HH** Seeks prey by running and hopping about on ground and in low undergrowth. Bushes and undergrowth.

Common Nightingale *Luscinia megarhynchos* 16–17cm

Pakistan. **ID** Much as Bluethroat in shape and behaviour, but longer-tailed. Rather nondescript, with greyish olive-brown upperparts, greyish-white underparts and whitish throat. Rufous uppertail-coverts and long rufous tail, indistinct head markings and pale fringes to wing-coverts and remiges. **Voice** Song is loud, rich and varied comprising a series of full mellow phrases, with some clear and fluty notes, others bubbling, rattling and churring. Territorial in winter quarters, often singing from cover (usually in morning). **HH** Keeps in thick cover, difficult to see, even when singing. Dense forest edge and second growth and thickets, usually feeding on ground.

Red-flanked Bluetail *Tarsiger cyanurus* 13–14cm

India. **ID** Similar to Himalayan Bluetail, but has pale turquoise-blue (versus dark blue) upperparts, whitish (versus than bluish) supercilium in front of eye, and buffier (versus pure white) underparts. Female like Himalayan Bluetail, but breast is paler contrasting less with white on throat and has whiter belly. First-winter is like female. **Voice** Calls include low throaty frog-like *tok-tok-tok*. **HH** Forages on ground and in low bushes; also sallies for insects. Broadleaved forest, dense undergrowth and thickets, clearings, and open woodland; often seen along tracks.

Yellow-rumped Flycatcher *Ficedula zanthopygia* 13–13.5cm

India and Sri Lanka. **ID** All plumages show yellow rump that separates it from all other flycatchers in subcontinent. Male has yellow underparts, black upperparts except white wing flash and supercilium, and white undertail-coverts. Female/first-winter have greyish-olive upperparts and a pale yellow wash below. **Voice** Call a slow, dry, rattled *tr-r-r-t*. Song a series of low, melodious whistles like a thrush. **HH** Mainly arboreal, keeping just below canopy. Lowland forest, parks, large gardens, undergrowth along rivers and streams, coastal scrub and mangroves.

Mugimaki Flycatcher *Ficedula mugimaki* 12.5–13.5cm

India. **ID** Small flycatcher with short bill and very long wings. Male is the only flycatcher recorded in subcontinent with combination of black upperparts, orange throat and breast, short white supercilium, and prominent white patches in wing. White at sides of tail in flight. First-winter male has greyer upperparts, less prominent supercilium behind eye and white in wing reduced to narrow whitish tips to median and greater coverts forming double wing-bar. Female has pale orange throat and breast, brown upperparts, narrow double wing-bar and lacks white in tail. **Voice** Song a loud trill. Calls include a metallic rattling *turrr.* **HH** Hunts insects in sallies from exposed perch; also hovers in front of foliage and picks prey from ground. Forests, second growth, parks and gardens.

Whinchat *Saxicola rubetra* 12–14cm

India and Sri Lanka. **ID** Similar in shape to Siberian Stonechat but supercilium more prominent and in flight shows white patches at base of tail. Breeding male is striking with black ear-

coverts, white chin and malar stripe, orange throat and breast, and white patch on primary coverts. Breeding female is similar but lacks white patch on primary coverts and has browner ear-coverts. Non-breeding and first-winter much less striking, with brown ear-coverts and buff underparts; additional features from Siberian Stonechat are heavily streaked rump, more boldly streaked mantle and often spotting/streaking on breast. **Voice** Calls include *siu-tek tek*. **HH** Perches upright atop bush or isolated tall stem. Wide range of open habitats with low perches, including grassland, forest edges and clearings.

BOMBYCILLIDAE

Bohemian Waxwing *Bombycilla garrulus* 19–23cm

Pakistan, Nepal, India. **ID** Mainly fawn-brown, with prominent crest. Has black mask and throat, grey rump and uppertail-coverts contrasting with blackish tail that has broad yellow tip, and waxy red-and-yellow markings on coverts. Starling-like appearance in flight. **Voice** Distinctive soft ringing trill in flight. **HH** Feeds on berries in non-breeding season. Acrobatic when feeding; frequently visits water to drink. Open country, forest edges and gardens with fruiting trees and bushes.

PRUNELLIDAE

Radde's Accentor *Prunella ocularis* 15–16cm

Pakistan. **ID** Very similar to Brown Accentor but has dark brown crown (paler than ear-coverts in Brown), heavily streaked mantle, spotted malar stripe, buffish breast-band and streaked flanks. Some show no dark markings on malar and flanks. Confusion also possible with first-winter Black-throated Accentor, which may not show dark throat, but has white supercilium and darker crown and ear-coverts. **Voice** Call a weak ringing trill. **HH** Typical accentor habits. Creeps and hops about on ground unobtrusively. Shrubs, often bordering streams in mountainous areas.

ESTRILDIDAE

Pin-tailed Parrotfinch *Erythrura prasina* 11.5–15cm

Bhutan. **ID** Munia-like. Male has red rump and 'pin-tail'. Otherwise has green upperparts, blue face, and buff underparts with red on belly. Female like dull version of male, lacking blue face and red on belly, and has shorter, wedge-shaped red tail. **Voice** Calls include a loud, high-pitched *tseet-tseet*. **HH** Forest edges, secondary scrub and paddyfields in lowlands and low hills.

PASSERIDAE

Pale Rockfinch *Carpospiza brachydactyla* 13.5–14.5cm

India and Pakistan. **ID** Very nondescript with plain grey-brown upperparts and paler underparts, and indistinct pale supercilium and wing-bars. Lacks prominent streaking on upperparts and underparts, and striking head pattern, of Rock Sparrow. Most similar to female Yellow-throated Sparrow but has stouter bill with downcurved culmen, lacks white median covert wing-bar, and has white tips to tail. **Voice** Call a high-pitched nasal *twee*. **HH** Forages on ground and among low vegetation. Cultivation.

MOTACILLIDAE

Meadow Pipit *Anthus pratensis* 14.5–15cm

India and Pakistan. **ID** Subtle differences from Tree Pipit include slimmer build, slimmer and weaker bill, and less boldly streaked breast but more boldly streaked flanks. Lacks prominent white supercilium, broad white wing-bars and distinct greenish edges to tertials and secondaries of Rosy Pipit. **Voice** Call a soft *sip-sip-sip*, most similar to Rosy Pipit. **HH** Grassy lake margins and fields.

FRINGILLIDAE

Pink-rumped Rosefinch *Carpodacus waltoni* 12.5cm

India. **ID** Male is brighter and deeper pink on underparts than male Himalayan Beautiful Rosefinch with more prominent supercilium, paler sandier upperparts, and lightly streaked flanks. Female very similar to female Himalayan Beautiful, but also has sandier upperparts and lightly streaked flanks. **Voice** Calls include a sharp *pink*. **HH** Forages on ground, usually around edges of trees or bushes. Hillsides with sparse vegetation, forest edges, scrub and edges of cultivation.

Pale Rosefinch *Carpodacus stoliczkae* 14.5–16cm

India. **ID** Distinctive medium-sized rosefinch with unstreaked (or very lightly streaked) sandy-grey upperparts; lacks supercilium in all plumages. Bill small and conical. Male has crimson forehead, face and throat, becoming paler pink below, and has pink rump. Female lacks pink and is plain sandy-grey on face and underparts. **Voice** Calls include a sharp *trizp* in flight. **HH** Forages mainly on ground, also in bushes. Arid habitats: scrub on sides of mountains and hills, in valleys and desert edge, also edges of cultivation.

Three-banded Rosefinch *Carpodacus trifasciatus* 17–19.5cm

India and Bhutan. **ID** Both sexes have broad double wing-bars and white band on scapulars. Upperparts and underparts of male mainly pinkish-crimson, with variable greyish edges to feathers of mantle. Belly and lower flanks white contrasting with pinkish-crimson breast. Crimson of male plumage replaced by orange-yellow on female. **Voice** Generally silent. **HH** Lethargic, spending long periods perched motionless in bushes or trees. Upland village fields.

Chinese White-browed Rosefinch *Carpodacus dubius* 17cm

India. **ID** Very similar to Himalayan White-browed Rosefinch. Male has whiter supercilium, uniform pink ear-coverts and darker pink underparts lacking white streaking on breast. Female as female Himalayan White-browed but lacks ginger-brown on throat and breast. **Voice** Calls include a fast, chattering series of nasal notes. **HH** Forages on ground and in low bushes. Hillside scrub.

Eurasian Crimson-winged Finch *Rhodopechys sanguineus* 15–18cm

Pakistan. **ID** A large finch with stout yellowish bill, pink on wing, blackish crown giving capped appearance, dark streaking on brown mantle, dark-streaked ear-coverts, brown breast-band and streaking on flanks; belly and crescent below brown breast strikingly white. Superficially resembles Mongolian or Desert Finches. **Voice** Calls include a chat-like *wee-tll-ee*. **HH** Forages almost entirely on ground. Edges of coniferous forest, low scrub in foothills and edges of cultivation. **AN** Crimson-winged Finch.

European Greenfinch *Chloris chloris* 14.5–16cm

Pakistan and India. **ID** In all plumages has yellow patches in wing and sides to tail, and stout pinkish bill. Breeding male has greyish head, greenish upperparts and yellowish-green underparts. Female and non-breeding male duller with brownish-green upperparts and greyer underparts. Juvenile similar to female but has streaked upperparts and dark streaking on whitish underparts. **Voice** In alarm a sharp, plaintive and rising *diuweee*. **HH** Wide range of habitats including, in winter, open fields, bushes and weedy areas.

Eurasian Siskin *Spinus spinus* 11–12cm

Pakistan, Nepal and India. **ID** Most likely to be confused with female Tibetan Siskin. Male distinguished by black crown and chin, and black-and-yellow wings. Female differs from female Tibetan in wing pattern (yellowish patches at base of secondaries and primaries) and brighter yellow rump; bill marginally longer and slimmer. **Voice** Call a distinctive, high-pitched, ringing *toolee*. **HH** Forages mainly in trees, moving restlessly about branches and hanging upside-down tit-like from cones. Conifers. **TN** Previously placed in *Carduelis*.

CALCARIIDAE

Lapland Longspur *Calcarius lapponicus* 14–15.5cm

Bhutan and India. **ID** A stocky, long-winged small bird, with stout yellowish bill. In most plumages has chestnut face with narrow dark border to ear-coverts, chestnut edges to greater coverts, double white wing-bar, and striking white belly. Non-breeding male has chestnut on nape and suggestion of black breast-band. Breeding male has black face, throat and breast. **Voice** In flight and when flushed a rattling call and a short whistled *chu*; also, a slightly hoarse *chup*, often from high-flying birds. **HH** Rather wary, creeps away on ground or 'freezes', then rises quite high when flushed. Powerful flight. Winters in stubbles, pastures, shores and any open ground with access to seeds.

EMBERIZIDAE

Corn Bunting *Emberiza calandra* 17–19cm

Pakistan and India. **ID** A large, buff-brown, stocky bunting with a stout pale bill, comparatively short tail and heavily streaked upperparts and underparts. Lacks white in tail. **Voice** Call a very hard *tik* and rolling *dchrrut*. **HH** Perches readily on telegraph wires and bushes; occasionally flicks wings and tail. Cultivation and grasslands.

Meadow Bunting *Emberiza cioides* 17cm

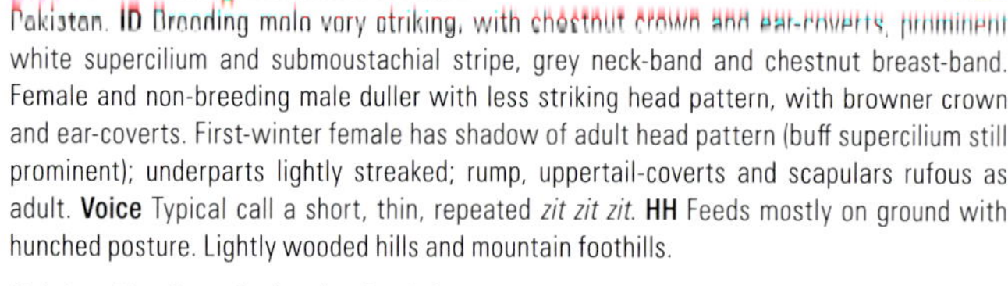

Pakistan. **ID** Breeding male very striking, with chestnut crown and ear-coverts, prominent white supercilium and submoustachial stripe, grey neck-band and chestnut breast-band. Female and non-breeding male duller with less striking head pattern, with browner crown and ear-coverts. First-winter female has shadow of adult head pattern (buff supercilium still prominent); underparts lightly streaked; rump, uppertail-coverts and scapulars rufous as adult. **Voice** Typical call a short, thin, repeated *zit zit zit*. **HH** Feeds mostly on ground with hunched posture. Lightly wooded hills and mountain foothills.

Ortolan Bunting *Emberiza hortulana* 16–17cm

Pakistan and India. **ID** Similar to Grey-necked Bunting, with pinkish-orange bill, plain head and prominent eye-ring. Adult has olive-grey head and breast, and yellow submoustachial stripe and throat. Female similar, with streaking on crown and breast. First-winter and juvenile more heavily streaked on mantle, malar region and breast than Grey-necked; submoustachial stripe and throat are buffish, but often with touch of yellow which helps separate from Grey-necked. **Voice** Chief flight call a ringing disyllabic *tsleeu*. **HH** Hops and creeps inconspicuously on ground. Generally in dry habitats: orchards, open woodland, cultivation and rocky habitats.

Rustic Bunting *Emberiza rustica* 14–15cm

India, Nepal and Bhutan. **ID** Striking head pattern (broad supercilium, dark sides to crown and border to ear-coverts), rufous streaking on breast and flanks, white belly, rufous on nape, and prominent white median covert bar. Crown feathers frequently raised. **Voice** Call a sharp *tzic* similar to Little Bunting. **HH** Restless and active, feeding quickly. Fairly horizontal stance on ground and often holds tail up. Wide range of habitats in winter including lowland woodland, riverine scrub, moist grassland and thick vegetation at cultivation edges. Globally threatened.

Yellow-browed Bunting *Emberiza chrysophrys* 13–15cm

India. **ID** In all plumages has white crown-stripe, dark sides to crown, yellow supercilium becoming white towards nape, dark ear-coverts with white spot at rear, and whitish underparts that are boldly streaked. Dark head pattern of male is blacker than in female and first-winter. **Voice** Calls include a sharp *zick*, similar to Little Bunting. **HH** Forages mostly on ground. Winters in scrub and weedy areas, often near forest edges.

Tristram's Bunting *Emberiza tristrami* 14–15cm

India and Bangladesh. **ID** In all plumages has striking head pattern with whitish crown-stripe and supercilium contrasting with dark sides to crown and ear-coverts. Mantle grey-brown, streaked black, and has chestnut rump. Male in breeding plumage has black throat. **Voice** Call an explosive *tzick*, usually repeated irregularly. **HH** Forages on ground. Evergreen forest.

REFERENCES

Acharya, B. K. & Chettri, B. (2012) Effect of climate change on birds, herpetofauna and butterflies in Sikkim Himalaya: a preliminary investigation. Pp. 141–160 in Arrwatia, M. L. & Tambe, S. (eds) *Climate change in Sikkim - patterns, impacts and initiatives.* Information & Public Relations Department, Government of Sikkim, Gangtok, Sikkim.

Badola, S. (2021) *Who's Hoo? How to identify owls in illegal wildlife trade this International Owl Awareness Day.* TRAFFIC India, New Delhi. www.traffic.org/news/whos-hoo-how-to-identify-owls-in-illegal-wildlife-trade-this-international-owl-awareness-day/

BCN, DNPWC & DOFSC (2023) *Nepal's Important Bird and Biodiversity Areas: Key Sites for Conservation.* Bird Conservation Nepal, Department of National Parks & Wildlife Conservation and Department of Forests and Soil Conservation, Kathmandu.

BirdLife International (2003) *Saving Asia's Threatened Birds: a Guide for Government and Civil Society.* BirdLife International, Cambridge, UK.

CBD (2022) Kunming-Montreal Global Biodiversity Framework. www.cbd.int/doc/decisions/cop-15/cop-15-dec-04-en.pdf

Deccan Herald (2023) www.deccanherald.com/india/danger-looms-as-pesticides-reign-supreme-on-india-s-farms-2776637

Dunn, P. O. & Moller, A. P. (2014) Changes in breeding phenology and population size of birds. *J. Anim. Ecol.* 83: 729–739.

FAO (2020) Global Forest Resources Assessment 2020: Main report. FAO, Rome. https://doi.org/10.4060/ca9825en

Grimmett, R., Inskipp, C. & Inskipp, T. (1998) *Birds of the Indian Subcontinent.* Christopher Helm, London.

Grimmett, R. Inskipp, C. & Inskipp, T. (2011) *Field Guide to Birds of the Indian Subcontinent.* Helm, London.

Grimmett, R., Thompson, P. & Inskipp, T. (2021) *Field Guide to Birds of Bangladesh.* Helm, London.

Grimmett, R., Inskipp, C., Inskipp, P. & Sherub (2019) *Field Guide to Birds of Bhutan and the Eastern Himalayas.* Helm, London.

Hussain, A. & Khan A. A. (2021) Wild birds trade in Dera Ismael Khan and Bannu divisions of Khyber PakhtunKhwa (KPK) Province, Pakistan. *Braz. J. Biol.* September 2021. doi: 10.1590/1519-6984.247915.

Ilyhas, F. (2018) Illegal trade in wildlife rife across Pakistan, says study. *Dawn.* 12 March 2018. www.dawn.com/news/1394654

Inskipp, C. & Baral, H. S. (2011) Potential impacts of agriculture on Nepal birds. *Our Nature* (2010) 8: 270–312. www.nepjol.info/index.php/ON/article/view/4339/3655

Inskipp, C. & Baral, H. S. (2019) *Nepal's forest birds: their status and conservation.* Fully revised edition. Himalayan Nature, Kathmandu.

IPCC (2023) Summary for Policymakers. In: Climate Change 2023: Synthesis Report. Contribution of Working Groups I, II and III to the Sixth Assessment Report of the Intergovernmental Panel on Climate Change [Core Writing Team, H. Lee and J. Romero (eds.)]. IPCC, Geneva, Switzerland, pp. 1-34, doi: 10.59327/IPCC/AR6-9789291691647.001

Katuwal, H. B. (2016) Sarus Crane in lowlands of Nepal: is it declining really? *J. Asia-Pacific Biodiversity* 9(3): 259–262. www.doi.org/10.1016/j.japb.2016.06.003

Mozaffer, F., Menon, G. I. & Ishtiaq, F. (2022) Exploring the thermal limits of malaria transmission in the western Himalaya. *Ecol. & Evol.* 12(9): e9278.

Mundial, B. (2006) *Unlocking Opportunities for Forest-Dependent People in India.* P. 107. Grant Milne, WB Report, 34481-IN.

Prakash, V., Galligan, T. H., Chakraborty, S. S., *et al.* (2019) Recent changes in populations of Critically Endangered *Gyps* vultures in India. *Bird Conservation International* 29: 55–70.

Prakash, V., Green, R. E., Rahmani, A. R., *et al.* (2005) Evidence to support that diclofenac caused catastrophic vulture population decline. *Curr. Sci.* 88: 1533–1534.

Praveen J. (2025) *Birds of India: The new synopsis.* Nature Conservation Foundation, Mysuru.

Praveen J., Karuthedatu, D., Sankar, S., Duraiswami, H., Yobin, Y. & Baruah, R. (2022) What is the identity of the *Spelaeornis* wren-babbler that occurs on the slopes of Mugaphi Peak in south-eastern Arunachal Pradesh? *Indian BIRDS* 18: 107–113.

Rahmani, A., Zafar-ul Islam, M. & Kasambe, R. M. (2016) *Important Bird Areas in India. Priority Sites for Conservation.* Revised and updated. Bombay Natural History Society, Indian Birds Conservation Network, Royal Society for the Protection of Birds & BirdLife International, Delhi.

Rajeshkumar, S., Ragunathan, C. & Rasmussen, P. C. (2012) An apparently new species of *Rallina* crake from Great Nicobar Island, India. *BirdingASIA* 17: 44–46.

Rigal, S., Dakos, V., Alonso, H., *et al.* (2023) Farmland practices are driving bird population decline across Europe. *Proc. Natl. Acad. Sci. USA* 120(21), e2216573120.

SoIB (2023) State of India's Birds, 2023: Range, trends, and conservation status. The SoIB Partnership. www.stateofindiasbirds.in/wp-content/uploads/SoIB-2023_report.pdf

Srinivasan, U., Velho, N., Lee, J. S. H., *et al.* (2021) Oil palm cultivation can be expanded while sparing biodiversity in India. *Nature Food* 2: 442–447.

Stattersfield, A. J., Crosby, M. J., Long, A. J. & Wege, D. C. (1998) *Endemic Bird Areas of the World: Priorities for Biodiversity Conservation.* BirdLife International, Cambridge, UK.

Uddin, M., Dutta, S., Kolipakam, V., *et al.* (2021) High bird mortality due to power lines invokes urgent environmental mitigation in a tropical desert. *Biol. Conserv.* 261: 109262.

UN (2023) UN DESA Policy Brief No. 153: India overtakes China as the world's most populous country. UN DESA Publications.

ILLUSTRATION CREDITS

Below is a comprehensive list of the artists who have contributed illustrations for this book. Please note that this list shows plate references, not page numbers.

Richard Allen: 27–30, 31 (part), 222 (part), 223–226, vagrants

Adam Bowley: 22 (part), 23 (part), 119–120, 121 (part), 123 (part), 126

Clive Byers: 139–143, 144 (part), 145, 146 (part), 150 (part), 151 (part), 159–167, 172 (part), 228–238, 239 (part), 240–246

Daniel Cole: 7–16, 31 (part), 32–33, 194 (part), 195–197

John Cox: 18–21, 22 (part), 23 (part), 24–25

Carl d'Silva: 71–74, 75 (part), 76, 99–109, 110 (part), 111 (part), 112, 113 (part), 117–118, 121 (part), 122 (part), 123 (part), 125 (part), 127 (part), 128, 129 (part), 132–134, 138 (part), 194 (part), vagrants

Gerald Driessens: 26, 34–36, 152–154

Martin Elliott: 55 (part), 56, 57 (part), 58–60, 61 (part), 62–63

Kim Franklin: 77 (part), 78, 79 (part)

John Gale: 57 (part), vagrants

Alan Harris: 37 (part), 38–40, 54 (part), 67–68, 77 (part), 79 (part), 84 (part), 85–87, 88 (part), 89 (part), 91 (part), 92–98, 114–116, 135, 198 (part), 199 (part), 200 (part), 201–211, 213–217, 218 (part), 219 (part), 220–221, 222 (part), 227, vagrants

Ren Hathway: 199 (part), 200 (part), vagrants

Peter Hayman: 41–53, 54 (part), 55 (part)

Dave Nurney: 110 (part), 111 (part), 113 (part), 122 (part), 125 (part), 127 (part), 129 (part), 144 (part), vagrants

Derek Onley: vagrants

Chris Orgill: vagrants

Craig Robson: 124, 136–137, 138 (part), 151 (part), 168–171, 172 (part), 173–177, 178 (part), 179 (part), 180–193

Chris Rose: 198 (part), 212, 218 (part), 219 (part)

Brian Small: 146 (part), 147–149, 150 (part), vagrants

Jan Wilczur: 1–6, 17, 64–66, 69, vagrants

Martin Woodcock: 155 (part), 156 (part), 157–158

Tim Worfolk: 37 (part), 61 (part), 70, 75 (part), 77 (part), 80–83, 84 (part), 88 (part), 89 (part), 90, 91 (part), 130–131, 155 (part), 156 (part), 178 (part), 179 (part), 239 (part), vagrants

INDEX

C

D

E

G

H

I

J

K

N

U

V

W

X

Y

Z